Year	GDP*	Consumption	Investment	Government Purchases	Net Exports**	Real GDP in billions of chained 2000 dollars	Percentage Change from Previous Year		
							Real GDP	Consumer Price Index	Unemployment Rate
1970	1039	649	152	234	4	3772	0.2	5.6	4.9
1971	1127	702	178	247	1	3899	3.4	3.3	5.9
1972	1238	771	208	264	−3	4105	5.3	3.4	5.6
1973	1383	852	244	282	4	4342	5.8	8.7	4.9
1974	1500	933	249	318	−1	4320	−0.5	12.3	5.6
1975	1638	1034	230	358	16	4311	−0.2	6.9	8.5
1976	1825	1152	292	383	−2	4541	5.3	4.9	7.7
1977	2031	1279	361	414	−23	4751	4.6	6.7	7.1
1978	2295	1429	438	454	−25	5015	5.6	9.0	6.1
1979	2563	1592	493	501	−23	5173	3.2	13.3	5.8
1980	2790	1757	479	566	−13	5162	−0.2	12.5	7.1
1981	3128	1941	572	628	−13	5292	2.5	8.9	7.6
1982	3255	2077	517	681	−20	5189	−1.9	3.8	9.7
1983	3537	2291	564	734	−52	5424	4.5	3.8	9.6
1984	3933	2503	736	797	−103	5814	7.2	3.9	7.5
1985	4220	2720	736	879	−115	6054	4.1	3.8	7.2
1986	4463	2900	747	949	−133	6264	3.5	1.1	7.0
1987	4740	3100	785	1000	−145	6475	3.4	4.4	6.2
1988	5104	3354	822	1039	−110	6743	4.1	4.6	5.5
1989	5484	3599	875	1099	−88	6981	3.5	4.6	5.3
1990	5803	3840	861	1180	−78	7113	1.9	6.1	5.6
1991	5996	3986	803	1234	−28	7101	−0.2	3.1	6.8
1992	6338	4235	865	1271	−33	7337	3.3	2.9	7.5
1993	6657	4478	953	1291	−65	7533	2.7	2.7	6.9
1994	7072	4743	1097	1326	−94	7836	4.0	2.7	6.1
1995	7398	4976	1144	1369	−91	8032	2.5	2.5	5.6
1996	7817	5257	1240	1416	−96	8329	3.7	3.3	5.4
1997	8304	5547	1390	1469	−102	8704	4.5	1.7	4.9
1998	8747	5880	1509	1518	−160	9067	4.2	1.6	4.5
1999	9268	6283	1626	1621	−261	9470	4.5	2.7	4.2
2000	9817	6739	1736	1722	−380	9817	3.7	3.4	4.0
2001	10128	7055	1614	1826	−367	9891	0.8	1.6	4.7
2002	10470	7351	1582	1961	−424	10,049	1.6	2.4	5.8
2003	10971	7710	1670	2092	−501	10,321	2.7	1.9	6.0
2004	11,734	8,214	1928	2216	−624	10,756	4.2	3.3	5.5
2005	12,486	8,746	2103	2363	−727	11,135	3.5	3.4	5.1

* Numbers may not add up because of rounding.
** From 1929–1937, 1942, 1954, and 1959 net exports was less than ± $0.5 billion.
Source: www.bea.gov

Economics

EIGHTH EDITION

Stephen L. Slavin

Union County College
Cranford, New Jersey

The New School University
New York City

Boston   Burr Ridge, IL   Dubuque, IA   Madison, WI   New York   San Francisco   St. Louis
Bangkok   Bogotá   Caracas   Kuala Lumpur   Lisbon   London   Madrid   Mexico City
Milan   Montreal   New Delhi   Santiago   Seoul   Singapore   Sydney   Taipei   Toronto

McGraw-Hill
Irwin

ECONOMICS

Published by McGraw-Hill/Irwin, a business unit of The McGraw-Hill Companies, Inc., 1221 Avenue of the Americas, New York, NY, 10020. Copyright © 2008 by The McGraw-Hill Companies, Inc. All rights reserved. No part of this publication may be reproduced or distributed in any form or by any means, or stored in a database or retrieval system, without the prior written consent of The McGraw-Hill Companies, Inc., including, but not limited to, in any network or other electronic storage or transmission, or broadcast for distance learning.

Some ancillaries, including electronic and print components, may not be available to customers outside the United States.

This book is printed on acid-free paper.

1 2 3 4 5 6 7 8 9 0 DOW/DOW 0 9 8 7 6

ISBN   978-0-07-351127-6
MHID 0-07-351127-7

Editorial director: *Brent Gordon*
Publisher: *Gary Burke*
Executive sponsoring editor: *Paul Shensa*
Senior developmental editor: *Tom Thompson*
Editorial assistant: *Robin Pille*
Senior marketing manager: *Douglas Reiner*
Media producer: *Jennifer Fisher*
Senior project manager: *Laura Griffin*
Production supervisor: *Debra R. Sylvester*
Senior designer: *Adam Rooke*
Photo research coordinator: *Lori Kramer*
Photo researcher: *Keri Johnson*
Lead media project manager: *Becky Szura*
Cover image: *© 2006 Maria Rendon*
Typeface: *10/12 Times New Roman*
Compositor: *Techbooks*
Printer: *R. R. Donnelley*

Library of Congress Cataloging-in-Publication Data

Slavin, Stephen L.
    Economics / Stephen L. Slavin.—8th ed.
        p. cm.
    Includes index.
    ISBN-13: 978-0-07-351127-6 (alk. paper)
    ISBN-10: 0-07-351127-7 (alk. paper)
    1. Economics. I. Title.
HB171.5.S6276 2008
    330—dc22   2006044435

www.mhhe.com

Preface to the Instructor

As an undergraduate economics student, I never imagined writing a textbook—let alone one going into its eighth edition. Back in those good old days, economics texts were all stand-alone books without any supplements, and seldom cost students more than five dollars. While we certainly need to keep up with the times, not all change is for the good. Surely not when our students are paying $140 for textbooks they barely read.

Why not write a book that students would actually enjoy reading and sell it at a price they can afford? Rather than serving up the same old dull fare, why not just have a conversation with the reader, illustrating various economic concepts anecdotally?

Occasionally a reviewer has complained that I've made economics too easy. If only my writing were *that* good! But if making economics more accessible to today's college students is a crime, then I hereby plead guilty.

More than 30 years ago, while still a graduate student, I got a part-time job helping to ghostwrite an introductory text for a major publisher. I asked my editor why so many economics texts were ghostwritten. She smiled and said, "Economists can't write."

Economics can be a rather intimidating subject, with its extensive vocabulary, complicated graphs, and quantitative tendencies. Is it possible to write a principles text that lowers the student's anxiety level without watering down the subject matter? To do this, one would need to be an extremely good writer, have extensive teaching experience, and have solid academic training in economics. In this case, two out of three is just not good enough.

Why did I write this book? Probably my moment of decision arrived more than 20 years ago when I mentioned to my macro class that Kemp-Roth cut the top personal income tax bracket from 70 percent to 50 percent. Then I asked, "If you were rich, by what percentage were your taxes cut?"

The class sat there in complete silence. Most of the students stared at the blackboard, waiting for me to work out the answer. I told them to work it out themselves. I waited. And I waited. Finally, someone said, "Twenty percent?"

"Close," I replied, "but no cigar."

"Fourteen percent?" someone else ventured.

"No, you're getting colder."

After waiting another two or three minutes, I saw one student with her hand up. One student knew that the answer was almost 29 percent—*one* student in a class of 30.

When do they teach students how to do percentage changes? In high school? In middle school? Surely not in a college economics course.

How much of *your* time do you spend going over simple arithmetic and algebra? How much time do you spend going over simple graphs? Wouldn't you rather be spending that time discussing economics?

Now you'll be able to do just that, because all the arithmetic and simple algebra that you normally spend time explaining are covered methodically in this book. All you'll need to do is tell your students which pages to look at.

The micro chapters offer scores of tables and graphs for the students to plot on their own; the solutions are shown in the book. Learning actively rather than passively, your students will retain a lot more economics.

As an economics instructor for more than 30 years at such fabled institutions as Brooklyn College, New York Institute of Technology, St. Francis College (Brooklyn), and Union County College, I have used a variety of texts. But each of their authors assumed a mathematical background that the majority of my students did not have. Each also assumed that his graphs and tables were comprehensible to the average student.

The biggest problem we have with just about any book we assign is that many of our students don't bother to read it before coming to class. Until now, no one has written a principles text in plain English. I can't promise that every one of your students will do the readings you assign, but at least they won't be able to complain anymore about not understanding the book.

Distinctive Qualities

My book has six qualities that no other principles text has.

1. **It reviews math that students haven't done since middle school and high school.**

2. **It's an interactive text, encouraging active rather than passive reading.** Students are expected to solve numerical problems, fill in tables, draw graphs, and do economic analysis as they read the text.

3. **It's a combined textbook and workbook.** Each chapter is followed by workbook pages that include multiple-choice and fill-in questions, as well as numerical problems.

v

4. **It costs substantially less than virtually every other text on the market.** And it has a built-in study guide.

5. **It's written in plain English without jargon.** See for yourself. Open any page and compare my writing style with that of any other principles author. This book is written to communicate clearly and concisely with the students' needs in mind.

6. **It is written with empathy for students.** My goal is to get students past their math phobias and fear of graphs by having them do hundreds of problems, step-by-step, literally working their way through the book.

Special Features

Four special features of my book are its integrated coverage of the global economy, its extra help boxes, its advanced work boxes, and its end-of-chapter current issues.

The Global Economy

Until the early 1970s our economy was largely insulated from the rest of the world economy. All of this changed with the oil price shock of 1973, our subsequent growing appetite for fuel-efficient Japanese compact cars, as well as for TVs, VCRs, camcorders, and other consumer electronics made in Asia. As our trade deficits grew, and as foreigners bought up more and more American assets, every American became quite aware of how integrated we had become within the global economy.

The eighth edition has three chapters devoted entirely to the global economy—Chapter 31 (International Trade), Chapter 32 (International Finance), and Chapter 8 (The Export-Import Sector). This chapter is part of the sequence (C, I, G, and X_n) leading up to the chapter on GDP. In addition, we have integrated a great deal of material dealing specifically with the global economy throughout the text.

Here are some of the things we look at:

- Shipbreaking (Ch. 4, p. 79)
- The "Isms": Capitalism, Communism, Fascism, and Socialism (Ch. 4, pp. 86–89)
- The Decline of the Communist System (Ch. 4, p. 89)
- The American Consumer: World-Class Shopper (Ch. 5, p. 114)
- Why Did Incorporation Come So Late to Islamic Middle-Eastern Nations? (Ch. 6, pp. 126–127)
- Foreign Investment in the United States (Ch. 6, p. 131)
- Are We Giving Away the Store? (Ch. 7, p. 149)
- Trillion Dollar Economies (Ch. 9, p. 202)

- Comparative Unemployment Rates (Ch. 10, p. 227)
- Surplus or Deficit as Percentage of GDP, Selected Countries (Ch. 12, p. 290)
- Independence of Central Banks (Ch. 14, p. 332)
- Economic Growth during the Last Millennium (Ch. 16, p. 386)
- The Corporate Hierarchy (Ch. 22, p. 557)
- The Dango (Ch. 24, p. 588)
- European Antitrust (Ch. 25, p. 613)
- American Wages versus Foreign Wages (Ch. 28, p. 672)
- Children Living in Poverty in Various Countries (Ch. 30, p. 722)

Extra Help Boxes

Students taking the principles course have widely varying backgrounds. Some have no problem doing the math or understanding basic economic concepts. But many others are lost from day one.

I have provided dozens of Extra Help boxes for the students who need them. They are especially useful to instructors who don't want to spend hours of class time going over material that they assume should be understood after one reading.

Of course these boxes can be skipped by the better prepared students.

Here are some of the topics covered in the Extra Help boxes:

- Finding the Opportunity Cost (Ch. 2, p. 34)
- How Changes in Demand Affect Equilibrium (Ch. 3, p. 52)
- How Changes in Supply Affect Equilibrium (Ch. 3, p. 54)
- Price Ceilings, Price Floors, Shortages, and Surpluses (Ch. 3, pp. 58)
- A Word about Numbers (Ch. 5, p. 96)
- How Did We Get an Average Tax Rate of 15%? (Ch. 7, p. 152)
- Reviewing the Two Approaches to GDP (Ch. 9, p. 196)
- Calculating Percentage Changes (Ch. 9, p. 198)
- Read Only if You're Not Sure How to Calculate the Unemployment Rate (Ch. 10, p. 224)
- Finding Percentage Changes in the Price Level (Ch. 10, p. 232)
- Finding Equilibrium GDP (Ch. 11, p. 265)
- Finding the Multiplier (Ch. 12, p. 282)
- Does Printing More Money Increase Our Money Supply? (Ch. 14, p. 345)

- Differentiating between Changes in Supply and Changes in Quantity Supplied (Ch. 17, p. 420)
- Calculating Marginal Utility and Total Utility (Ch. 19, p. 462)
- Finding Marginal Cost When the Output is 0 (Ch. 20, p. 478)
- What's the Difference between Shutting Down and Going Out of Business? (Ch. 20, p. 492)
- Accounting Profit vs. Economic Profit (Ch. 21, p. 508)
- Finding the Firm's Short-Run and Long-Run Supply Curves, and Shut-Down and Break-Even Points (Ch. 21, p. 515)
- How to Find the Monopolist's Price and Output (Ch. 22, p. 545)
- Productivity and Marginal Physical Product (Ch. 26, p. 628)
- Finding the Imperfect Competitor's MRP (Ch. 26, p. 632)
- Finding the Percentage of Income Share of the Quintiles in Figure 1 (Ch. 30, p. 711)
- Interpreting the Top Line in Figure 5 (Ch. 32, p. 779)

Advanced Work Boxes

There are some concepts in the principles course that many instructors will want to skip. (Of course, if they're not included in principles texts, this will make other instructors quite unhappy.) These boxes are intended for the better prepared students who are willing to tackle these relatively difficult concepts.

Here is a sampling of my Advanced Work boxes:

- Post-World War II Recessions (Ch. 1, p. 12)
- The Law of Increasing Costs (Ch. 2, p. 32)
- APCs Greater than One (Ch. 5, p. 99)
- Nominally Progressive, Proportional, and Regressive Taxes (Ch. 7, p. 154)
- Should Cigarettes Be Taxed? (Ch. 7, p. 158)
- Why NDP Is Better than GDP (Ch. 9, p. 194)
- Calculating Per Capita Real GDP (Ch. 9, p. 204)
- The Paradox of Thrift (Ch. 12, p. 283)
- Money versus Barter (Ch. 13, p. 303)
- Three Modifications of the Deposit Expansion Multiplier (Ch. 14, p. 337)
- Rational Expectations versus Adaptive Expectations (Ch. 15, p. 369)
- The Malthusian Theory of Population (Ch. 16, p. 402)
- Why We Don't Use a Simpler Elasticity Formula (Ch. 18, p. 434)

- Deriving the Shut-down and Break-even Points (Ch. 20, p. 495)
- Calculating a Firm's Total Loss (Ch. 21, p. 512)
- Maximizing Total Profit and Maximizing Profit per Unit (Ch. 21, p. 524)
- Who's Got the Flatter Demand Curve? (Ch. 23, p. 569)
- Perfect Price Discrimination (Ch. 23, p. 574)
- The Concept of Margin in Economic Analysis (Ch. 26, p. 627)
- Who Created the Land? (Ch. 29, p. 691)
- Usury in Ancient Times (Ch. 29, p. 693)

Current Issues

Students often ask, "How does any of this affect me?" Or, "Why do I have to study economics?" The Current Issues provide answers to those questions. Each is a practical application of at least one of the concepts covered in the chapter.

Chapter 1: America's Place in History (p. 17)

Chapter 2: Will You Be Underemployed When You Graduate? (p. 37)

Chapter 3: High Gas Prices: Something Only an Economist Could Love (p. 62)

Chapter 4: The Bridge to Nowhere (p. 91)

Chapter 5: The American Consumer: World-Class Shopper (p. 114)

Chapter 6: "Benedict Arnold Corporations"? (p. 139)

Chapter 7: Will Social Security Be There for You? (p. 165)

Chapter 8: Is Your School Sweatshirt Sewn in a Sweatshop? (p. 182)

Chapter 9: GDP or GPI? (p. 209)

Chapter 10: Where Are All the Jobs? (p. 243)

Chapter 11: Keynes and Say in the 21st Century (p. 268)

Chapter 12: Deficits as Far as the Eye Can See (p. 295)

Chapter 13: Overdraft Privileges (p. 323)

Chapter 14: Who Controls Our Interest Rates? (p. 349)

Chapter 15: Is George W. Bush a Supply-Sider or a Keynesian? (p. 372)

Chapter 16: Health Care Costs in the Coming Decades (p. 403)

Chapter 17: Why Can't I Sell My House? (p. 427)

Chapter 18: How Elastic Is Your Demand for Food? (p. 453)

Chapter 19: All-You-Can-Eat Buffets (p. 468)

Chapter 20: Wedding Hall or City Hall? (p. 498)

Chapter 21: The Internet Effect: A More Perfect Knowledge and Lower Prices (p. 530)

Chapter 22: Would You Allow Wal-Mart to Open a Supercenter in Your Community? (p. 559)

Chapter 23: Selling Status (p. 576)

Chapter 24: Cutthroat Competition in the College Textbook Market (p. 593)

Chapter 25: The Enron Case (p. 619)

Chapter 26: Washing Machines and Women's Liberation (p. 636)

Chapter 27: Will You Ever Be a Member of a Labor Union? (p. 656)

Chapter 28: The Education Gap (p. 679)

Chapter 29: Subprime, Fringe, and Payday Lending (p. 701)

Chapter 30: Will Social Security Be There for You? (p. 733)

Chapter 31: Buy American? (p. 763)

Chapter 32: Editorial: American Exceptionality (p. 786)

Changes in the Eighth Edition

There are two major changes in the eighth edition. A Current Issue section has been added to the end of each chapter. For example, "Will You Be Underemployed When You Graduate?" has been added to Chapter 2. Also, Parts II and III of the chapter on foreign trade were completely rewritten and simplified.

Some 120 pages were cut from the seventh edition; in the eighth I tried to simplify some of the more obscure passages and to provide more practical applications. Here are some of the new topics:

- Chapter 2: New Extra Help box, "Finding the Opportunity Cost."

- Chapter 4: Added section, "Government Failure."

- Chapter 8: Added discussion of comparative advantage.
  New section, "Outsourcing and Offshoring."

- Chapter 13: Added section, "How Do We Pay Our Bills?"

- Chapter 16: New box, "The Best and the Brightest."

- Chapter 20: Added Extra Help box, "Finding Marginal Cost When the Output Is 0."
  New section, "The Production Function and the Law of Diminishing Returns."

- Chapter 21: Added Extra Help box, "Accounting Profit versus Economic Profit."
  New section, "Alternative Calculation of Profit and Loss."

- Chapter 24: New box, "The Penalty Box."

- Chapter 27: Added box, "Sports Strikes and Lockouts."

- Chapter 28: Added box, "A College Degree Is the Ticket out of Poverty."
  New section, "The Effects of Employment Discrimination on Wages."
  Added Advanced Work box, "The Real Minimum Wage."

- Chapter 30: Added box, "Abortion, Crime, and Poverty."
  Added box, "Helping the Poor Get Money Back from the IRS."

- Chapter 31: Part II is almost completely rewritten mainly to simplify the explanation of comparative advantage. Part III has also been rewritten.

- Chapter 32: Added box, "Sending Money Home."
  Added section, "A Codependent Relationship."

Two basic ways this book is different from all other principles texts is that it is a smoother read and it is interactive. The eighth edition improves on these features.

Most of the really hard stuff is in Advanced Work boxes and appendices. This relatively difficult material can be skipped, or perhaps assigned for extra credit. The really easy stuff—for example, math that should have been learned in high school—is covered in Extra Help boxes. These boxes save professors hours of valuable class time.

The Supplement Package

In addition to the workbook, which is built in, *Economics* has a supplemental package to help students and instructors as they use the text.

Instructor's Manual

This provides instructors with ideas on how to use the text, includes a description of the text's special features, a chapter-by-chapter discussion of material new to the eighth edition, and a rundown of chapter coverage to help them decide what they can skip. Also found here are the answers to the workbook questions and questions for thought and discussion at the end of each chapter of the text, as well as chapter worksheets and worksheet solutions.

Mark Maier, who has used the text for several editions, took over the Instructor's Manual in the sixth edition, and has added sections on learning objectives, ideas for use in class, and homework questions and projects (including scores of very useful websites) for each chapter. The Instructor's Manual now provides a rich source of interesting ideas of classroom activities and discussions involving concepts and issues included in the text.

Test Bank (Micro and Macro Versions)

The test bank now includes over 9,000 multiple-choice questions, fill-in questions, and problems. Jim Watson, another long-time user of the text, took over the testbank for the sixth edition, and has kept it current, culling outdated questions and adding new ones.

Computerized Testing

The Micro and Macro test banks are available in computerized versions for PCs. Developed by EZ Test, this state of the art software has the capability to create multiple tests, "scramble," and produce high-quality graphs.

Teaching Transparencies

The most important graphs and tables from the text are reproduced as two-color transparencies. Use of these acetates will aid the instructor's classroom presentations and the students' understanding.

Videos

A selection of videos is available to adopters, including both tutorial lessons and programs that combine historical footage, documentary sequences, interviews, and analysis to illustrate economic theory. There is also a 15-minute video that explains how to get the most out of the book. This may be played during the first day of class.

A series of DVDs produced by Paul Solman, business and economics correspondent for the Lehrer News Hour and WGBH Boston, cover the core topics in economics.

Website

Some of the text's unique qualities are incorporated in a dynamic new website. Its remedial nature, with attention toward helping students further overcome math anxiety and graphing difficulties, will take on a self-help orientation for needy students. The quizzing practice offers questions not found in the Workbook or the Test Bank and serves to reinforce the material covered in every chapter. Instructors will find material from the IM and PowerPoints. Several sections, of interest to both instructors and students, provide useful and thought-provoking material and broaden understanding of the scope of economics. Deborah Figart of Richard Stockton College (NJ) was very helpful in providing Learning Tips and Teaching Tips.

One-Semester Courses from *Economics*, 8e

Here are some syllabi for one-semester courses with varying orientations:

Macro oriented:

> Chapters 1–9; 12–14; 28–31.
> Chapters 1–3; 10; 12–14; 16; 25; 27–32.
> Chapters 1–10; 16–17; 25; 30–32.

Micro oriented:

> Chapters 2–4; 10; 16–25.
> Chapters 1–4; 16–24; 31–32.
> Chapters 2–3; 17–21; 26–32.

Balanced approach:

> Chapters 1–9; 17–21; 31–32.
> Chapters 1–4; 16–21; 25–30.

Here's another possibility—a one-semester course that focuses on contemporary problems:

> Chapters 2–4; 10; 12–14; 16; 25; 28–32.

Acknowledgments

Over the years since the first edition, hundreds of people have helped in large and small ways to shape this text. Over the last three editions, Paul Shensa and Tom Thompson have been there every step of the way, offering advice and encouragement, and guiding the book through the long and complex editorial and production process.

Paul Shensa, my sponsoring editor, has been a great advocate of my book, both inside and outside the company. Paul, who may well be the most knowledgeable economics textbook editor in the industry, was especially helpful in getting the reviewers' suggestions incorporated into the text and the supplements. I also wish to thank Gary Burke, my publisher, and Brent Gordon, the editorial director, who put together the group that edited and produced the book.

Tom Thompson, the developmental editor, saw this project through from the first reviews, the chapter-by-chapter revisions, the Test Bank revisions, and the dozens of deadlines that we met, to the time the book finally went into production. Tom was great at keeping all the plates spinning, dealing with a diverse group of personalities, making sure that all the pieces fit, and seeing to it that the text and the supplements were ready to go. When Tom retired just months before the publication date, Sarah Ebel stepped in, making sure editorial, marketing, and production were on the same page, so to speak.

Senior project manager Laura Griffin, with whom I worked day to day, managed the copyediting, artwork, and page proofs, and saw to it that we stayed not just on schedule, but ahead of schedule. Karen Nelson did a very thorough copyediting job, finding errors and inconsistencies, some of which originated in earlier editions. Also, special thanks to proofreader Nym Pedersen for exceptional attention to detail. Adam Rooke oversaw the design of the book from cover to cover. Jackie Henry, the project manager at Techbooks-York delivered an attractive and accurately composed text. Lead media project manager Becky Szura made sure the supplement production process went smoothly.

For the first five editions, I managed to write not just the textbook, but the test bank and instructor's manual as well. Since then two long time users of the book have taken over these duties. Mark Maier, of Glendale Community College, has done an outstanding job expanding and rewriting the instructor's manual. And Jim Watson, of Jefferson College, has managed to make all the questions in the test bank actually match the material in the text. I suspect that these two know my book better than I do. And Max Tarpley (Dyersburg State Community College) competently prepared the PowerPoint presentation.

Brent Gordon, the editorial director, Doug Hughes, the sponsoring editor, and Angie Cimarolli, the developmental editor, all got involved when the book was already in production. In addition to making sure that the text and all the supplements were printed on schedule, they looked forward to hearing suggestions from instructors using the text. Douglas Reiner, the new marketing director, and Jennifer Jelinski, the marketing coordinator, have been working to help the book reach an even wider audience than the seventh edition.

Every economist knows that no product sells itself. Without major sales and marketing efforts, my text could not sell very well. Douglas Reiner, in his previous capacity as senior marketing manager, has done a great job publicizing my book, and he deserves a good deal of the credit for its expanding sales. But most of the credit goes to all the McGraw-Hill Irwin sales reps for all their efforts to sell my book. And I would especially like to thank the reps in Dubuque, Iowa, who have personally accounted for about a quarter of our sales.

Three sales reps, Brian Murray, Boyd Call, and Bonnie Varker, were very helpful in providing topics for the new series of current issues. Bonnie inspired "Wedding Hall or City Hall?" which appears near the end of Chapter 20.

Kunle Adamson (DeVry College of New Jersey), Ronald Picker (St. Mary of the Woods College), and Jim Watson (Jefferson College) very generously provided numerous suggestions which greatly improved the text. I want to thank Eleni Zimiles, a student at Macalester College, for correcting several of the graphs, some of which had errors going back several editions.

I'd also like to thank the many reviewers who helped improve this text over the last seven editions:

Shawn Abbott, *College of the Siskiyous (California)*
Kunle Adamson, *DeVry College of New Jersey*
Carlos Aguilar, *El Paso Community College*
Jim Angus, *Dyersburg State Community College (Tennessee)*
Lyndell L. Avery, *Penn Valley Community College (Missouri)*
James Q. Aylsworth, *Lakeland Community College*
Kathleen Bailey, *Eastern Arizona College*
Kevin Baird, *Montgomery Community College*
David Bennett, *Ivy Tech (Indiana)*
John Bethune, *Barton College (North Carolina)*
Robert G. Bise, *Orange Coast College*
Van Bullock, *New Mexico State University*
Gerard A. Cahill, *Florida Institute of Technology*
Perry A. Cash, *Chadwick University (Alabama)*
Michael Cohik, *Collin Community College*
Steve Cole, *Bethel College*
Ana-María Conley, *DeVry Institute of Technology—Decatur*
Dave Cook, *Western Nevada Community College*
Debra Cummings, *Fort Scott Community College (Kansas)*
Bill Demory, *Central Arizona College*
Craig Depken II, *University of Texas, Arlington*
Thomas O. Depperschmidt, *University of Memphis*
Stacey Edgington, *San Diego State University*
Deborah M. Figart, *Richard Stockton College (New Jersey)*
Daniel Fischer, *University of Arizona*
Russell L. Flora, *Pikes Peak Community College*
Arthur Friedberg, *Mohawk Valley Community College*
Harold Friesen, *Friends University*
Marilyn Fuller, *Paris Junior College (Texas)*
Frank Garland, *Tricounty Technical College (South Carolina)*
Eugene Gendel, *Woodbury University*
Jay Goodman, *Southern Colorado University*
Cindy Goodyear, *Webster University*
Mehdi Haririan, *Bloomsburg University (Pennsylvania)*
Charles W. Harrington Jr., *Nova Southeastern University (Florida)*
Gail Hawks, *Miami Dade Community College*
Sanford B. Helman, *Middlesex County College*
Janet Hunter, *Northland Pioneer College (Arizona)*
Robert Jakubiak, *Milwaukee Area Technical College*
Danny Jeftich, *Ivy Tech (Indiana)*
Mark G. Johnson, *Lakeland Community College*
Roger Johnson, *Messiah College*
George Jouganatos, *California State University, Sacramento*

James Kelly, *Rio Hondo College*

M. Moosa Khan, *Prairie View A&M University (Texas)*

Kenneth E. Kimble, *Sinclair Community College*

Sara Kiser, *Judson College*

Jack Klauser, *Chaminade University of Honolulu*

Wayne Klutarits, *Jefferson College*

Harry Kolendrianos, *Danville Community College*

Michael J. Kuryla, *SUNY-Broome Community College*

Alan Levinsohn, *SUNY-Morrisville*

Stephen E. Lile, *Western Kentucky University*

Paul Lockard, *Black Hawk College*

Mark H. Maier, *Glendale Community College (California)*

Eddi Marlow, *Dyersburg State Community College (Tennessee)*

Steven B. McCormick, *Southeastern Illinois College*

John E. Michaels, *University of Phoenix*

Green Miller, *Morehead State University*

Charles Myrick, *Dyersburg State Community College (Tennessee)*

Bill Nook, *Milwaukee Area Technical College*

Ronan O'Beirne, *American Institute of Computer Sciences (Alabama)*

Joan O'Brien, *Quincy College*

Alannah Orrison, *Saddleback College*

Michael L. Palmer, *Maple Woods Community College (Missouri)*

Craig Parmley, *Ivy Tech (Indiana)*

Thomas R. Parsons, *Massachusetts Bay Path Community College*

Louis A. Patille, *University of Phoenix*

Ronald Picker, *St. Mary of the Woods College (Indiana)*

George Radakovic, *Indiana University of Pennsylvania*

Eric Rahimian, *Alabama A&M University*

Judith K. Robinson, *Massachusetts Bay Path Community College*

Michael Rosen, *Milwaukee Area Technical College*

Rose M. Rubin, *University of Memphis*

Mourad Sebti, *Central Texas College*

W. H. Segur, *University of Redlands*

John Somers, *Portland Community College*

Don M. Soule, *University of Kentucky*

Karen Spellacy, *SUNY-Canton*

Rob Steen, *Rollins College*

Bruno Stein, *New York University*

Stephen Steller, *University of Phoenix*

Daniel Stern, *South Hills School of Business (Pennsylvania)*

Edward Stevens, *Nebraska College of Business*

Denver O. Swaby, *Columbia Union College (Maryland)*

Max Tarpley, *Dyersburg State Community College (Tennessee)*

Bette Lewis Tokar, *Holy Family College (Pennsylvania)*

Jim Watson, *Jefferson College (Missouri)*

Simone Wegge, *CUNY-Staten Island*

Marc Weglarski, *Macomb Community College*

Steven White, *Glendale Community College (California)*

Elaine Gale Wrong, *Montclair State College*

Sandy Zingo, *Rogers State University (Oklahoma)*

Finally, to all adopters of the past seven editions, thank you. Your comments and concerns have helped to make this the best edition yet.

—Stephen L. Slavin

Preface to the Student

What have you heard about economics? That it's dull, it's hard, it's full of undecipherable equations and incomprehensible graphs? If you were to read virtually any of the introductory economics textbooks, that's exactly what you would find.

How is this book different from all other books? Reading this book is like having a conversation with me. I'll be right there with you, illustrating various points with anecdotes and asking you to work out numerical problems as we go along.

Are you a little shaky about the math? Your worries are over. If you can add, subtract, multiply, and divide (I'll even let you use a calculator), you can do the math in this book.

How do you feel about graphs? Do you think they look like those ultramodern paintings that even the artists can't explain? You can relax. No graph in this book has more than four lines, and by the time you're through, you'll be drawing your *own* graphs.

In nearly every chapter you'll find one or two boxes labeled "Extra Help." Sometimes you can master a concept when additional examples are given. Don't be too proud to seek extra help when you need it. And when you don't need it, just skip the boxes.

Unlike virtually every other economics text, this one includes a built-in workbook. Even if your professor does not assign the questions at the end of each chapter, I urge you to answer them because they provide an excellent review.

I can't guarantee an *A* in this course, but whether you are taking it to fulfill a college requirement or planning to be an economics major, you will find that economics is neither dull nor all that hard.

—*Stephen L. Slavin*

Contents in *Brief*

1 A Brief Economic History of the United States 1

2 Resource Utilization 23

3 Supply and Demand 47

4 The Mixed Economy 71

5 The Household-Consumption Sector 95

6 The Business-Investment Sector 121

7 The Government Sector 145

8 The Export-Import Sector 171

9 Gross Domestic Product 189

10 Economic Fluctuations, Unemployment, and Inflation 217

11 Classical and Keynesian Economics 251

12 Fiscal Policy and the National Debt 275

13 Money and Banking 301

14 The Federal Reserve and Monetary Policy 329

15 A Century of Economic Theory 355

16 Economic Growth and Productivity 385

17 Demand, Supply, and Equilibrium 409

18 The Elasticities of Demand and Supply 433

19 Theory of Consumer Behavior 459

20 Cost 475

21 Profit, Loss, and Perfect Competition 505

22 Monopoly 541

23 Monopolistic Competition 565

24 Oligopoly 581

25 Corporate Mergers and Antitrust 607

26 Demand in the Factor Market 625

27 Labor Unions 643

28 Labor Markets and Wage Rates 661

29 Rent, Interest, and Profit 687

30 Income Distribution and Poverty 709

31 International Trade 741

32 International Finance 769

Expanded Contents

1 A Brief Economic History of the United States 1

Introduction 1

The American Economy in the 19th Century 2
- Agricultural Development 2
- The National Railroad Network 4
- The Age of the Industrial Capitalist 5

The American Economy in the 20th Century 6
- The Roaring Twenties 7
- The 1930s: The Great Depression 7
- The 1940s: World War II and Peacetime Prosperity 10
- The 1950s: The Eisenhower Years 13
- The Soaring Sixties: The Years of Kennedy and Johnson 13
- The Sagging Seventies: The Stagflation Decade 14
- The 1980s: The Age of Reagan 15
- The State of American Agriculture 15
- The "New Economy" of the Nineties 16

Current Issue: America's Place in History 17

2 Resource Utilization 23

Economics Defined 23

The Central Fact of Economics: Scarcity 24
- Scarcity and the Need to Economize 24
- The Economic Problem 24
- The Four Economic Resources 24
- Opportunity Cost 26

Full Employment and Full Production 26

The Production Possibilities Curve 30

Productive Efficiency 35

Economic Growth 35

Current Issue: Will You Be Underemployed When You Graduate? 37

3 Supply and Demand 47

Demand 47

Supply 48

Equilibrium 50
- Surpluses and Shortages 50

Shifts in Demand and Supply 51

Price Ceilings and Price Floors 55

Applications of Supply and Demand 60
- Interest Rate Determination 60
- College Parking 61
- The Rationing Function of the Price System 61

Last Word 62

Current Issue: High Gas Prices: Something Only an Economist Could Love 62

4 The Mixed Economy 71

The Three Questions of Economics 71
- What Shall We Produce? 71
- How Shall These Goods and Services Be Produced? 72
- For Whom Shall the Goods and Services Be Produced? 72
- To Sum Up 73

The Invisible Hand, the Price Mechanism, and Perfect Competition 73
- The Invisible Hand 73
- The Price Mechanism 74
- Competition 74
- Trust 75
- Equity and Efficiency 75

The Circular Flow Model 76

The Economic Role of Government 77

Market Failure 78
- Externalities 78
- Curbing Environmental Pollution 80
- Lack of Public Goods and Services 81

Government Failure 82

Capital 84

The "Isms": Capitalism, Communism, Fascism, and Socialism 86
- The Decline and Fall of the Communist System 89
- Transformation in China 89

Current Issue: The Bridge to Nowhere 91

5 The Household-Consumption Sector 95

GDP and Big Numbers 95

Consumption 96

Saving 97

xvi *Expanded Contents*

Average Propensity to Consume (APC) 97

Average Propensity to Save (APS) 98

Marginal Propensity to Consume (MPC) 100

Marginal Propensity to Save (MPS) 101

Graphing the Consumption and Saving
  Function 101
    Reading a Graph 101

The Consumption Function 102

The Saving Function 104

Autonomous Consumption and Induced
  Consumption 104

What the Consumer Buys 107

Determinants of the Level of Consumption 108
    The Level of Disposable Income 109
    Credit Availability 109
    Stock of Liquid Assets in the Hands of Consumers 109
    Stock of Durable Goods in the Hands of Consumers 110
    Keeping Up with the Joneses 110
    Consumer Expectations 110

The Permanent Income Hypothesis 111

Is the Consumer Really King? 111

Why Do We Spend So Much and Save So
  Little? 112

Total Saving: Individual Saving + Business
  Saving + Government Saving 113

Current Issue: The American Consumer:
  World-Class Shopper 114

6 The Business-Investment Sector 121

Proprietorships, Partnerships, and Corporations 121
    The Proprietorship 121
    The Partnership 122
    The Corporation 122
    Stocks and Bonds 125
    Capitalization and Control 125
    The Business Population 126

Investment 126

How Does Savings Get Invested? 130

Gross Investment versus Net Investment 131

Building Capital 132

The Determinants of the Level of Investment 132
    (1) The Sales Outlook 132
    (2) Capacity Utilization Rate 133
    (3) The Interest Rate 134
    (4) The Expected Rate of Profit 134
    Why Do Firms Invest? 135

Graphing the C + I Line 136

The Summing Up of Investment 137

Current Issue: "Benedict Arnold
  Corporations"? 139

7 The Government Sector 145

Introduction: The Growing Economic Role of
  Government 145

Government Spending 146
    Federal Government Spending 146
    State and Local Government Spending 148
    Government Purchases versus Transfer Payments 149

Graphing the C + I + G Line 150

Taxes 150
    The Average Tax Rate and the Marginal Tax Rate 151
    Types of Taxes 153
    Sources of Federal Revenue 155
    Recent Tax Legislation 159
    Sources of State and Local Revenue 160
    The State and Local Fiscal Dilemma 160
    Comparison of Taxes in the United States and Other
        Countries 161

The Economic Role of Government 162
    (1) Provision of Public Goods and Services 163
    (2) Redistribution of Income 163
    (3) Stabilization 163
    (4) Economic Regulation 164
    Conclusion 164

Current Issue: Will Social Security Be There for
  You? 165

8 The Export-Import Sector 171

The Basis for International Trade 171

Specialization and Exchange 172

U.S. Exports and Imports 173

Outsourcing and Offshoring 175

A Summing Up: C + I + G + X_n 176

World Trade Agreements and Free Trade Zones 176
    Free Trade Zones 177
    World Trade Agreements 178

Current Issue: Is Your School Sweatshirt Sewn in a
  Sweatshop? 182

9 Gross Domestic Product 189

What Is Gross Domestic Product? 189

How GDP Is Measured 191
    The Expenditures Approach 191
    The Flow-of-Income Approach 192

Two Things to Avoid When Compiling GDP 195
    Multiple Counting 195
    Treatment of Transfer Payments and Financial
        Transactions 197

Nominal GDP versus Real GNP 197

International GDP Comparisons 202

Per Capita Real GDP 202

Shortcomings of GDP as a Measure of National
Economic Well-Being 205
Production That Is Excluded 205
Treatment of Leisure Time 207
Human Costs and Benefits 208
What Goes into GDP? 209

Current Issue: GDP or GPI? 209

10 Economic Fluctuations, Unemployment, and Inflation 217

Economic Fluctuations 217
Is There a Business Cycle? 217
Cycle Turning Points: Peaks and Troughs 218
The Conventional Three-Phase Business Cycle 219

Business Cycle Theories 220
Endogenous Theories 220
Exogenous Theories 221

Business Cycle Forecasting 221

Unemployment 223
The Problem 223
How the Unemployment Rate Is Computed 223
How Accurate Is the Unemployment Rate? 225
Types of Unemployment 226
Natural Unemployment Rate 229

Inflation 229
Defining Inflation 229
Deflation and Disinflation 231
The Post–World War II History of Inflation 233
The Construction of the Consumer Price Index 234
Anticipated and Unanticipated Inflation: Who Is Hurt by
Inflation and Who Is Helped? 236
What's a Dollar Worth Today? 237
Theories of the Causes of Inflation 238
Inflation as a Psychological Process 240
Creeping Inflation and Hyperinflation 241

The Misery Index 242

Current Issue: Where Are All the Jobs? 243

11 Classical and Keynesian Economics 251

Part I: The Classical Economic System 251
Say's Law 251
Supply and Demand Revisited 253

The Classical Equilibrium: Aggregate Demand
Equals Aggregate Supply 255
The Aggregate Demand Curve 255
The Long-Run Aggregate Supply Curve 257
The Short-Run Aggregate Supply Curve 258

Part II: The Keynesian Critique of the Classical
System 260

Part III: The Keynesian System 263
The Keynesian Aggregate Expenditure Model 263

Disequilibrium and Equilibrium 266
(1) Aggregate Demand Exceeds Aggregate Supply 266
(2) Aggregate Supply Exceeds Aggregate Demand 267
(3) Summary: How Equilibrium Is Attained 267

Keynesian Policy Prescriptions 267

Current Issue: Keynes and Say in the 21st
Century 268

12 Fiscal Policy and the National Debt 275

Putting Fiscal Policy into Perspective 275

Part I: The Deflationary Gap and the Inflationary
Gap 276
The Deflationary Gap 276
The Inflationary Gap 277

Part II: The Multiplier and Its Applications 278
The Multiplier 279
Applications of the Multiplier 280

Part III: The Automatic Stabilizers 282
Personal Income and Payroll Taxes 283
Personal Savings 284
Credit Availability 284
Unemployment Compensation 284
The Corporate Profits Tax 284
Other Transfer Payments 285

Part IV: Discretionary Fiscal Policy 285
Making the Automatic Stabilizers More Effective 286
Public Works 286
Changes in Tax Rates 286
Changes in Government Spending 287
Who Makes Fiscal Policy? 287

Part V: The Deficit Dilemma 288
Deficits, Surpluses, and the Balanced Budget 288
Deficits and Surpluses: The Record 288
Why Are Large Deficits So Bad? 289
Must We Balance the Budget Every Year? 290

Part VI: The Crowding-Out and Crowding-In
Effects 290

Part VII: The Public Debt 292

Conclusion 295

Current Issue: Deficits as Far as the Eye Can
See 295

13 Money and Banking 301

Money 301
The Three Jobs of Money 301
Medium of Exchange 302
Standard of Value 302
Store of Value 302
Money versus Barter 302
Our Money Supply 303
How Do We Pay Our Bills? 304

M1, M2, and M3 304
Our Growing Money Supply 306
The Demand for Money 306
The Demand Schedule for Money 309
The Liquidity Trap 310
Determination of the Interest Rate 310

Banking 311
A Short History of Banking 311
Modern Banking 314

The Creation and Destruction of Money 318
The Creation of Money 318
The Destruction of Money 319
Limits to Deposit Creation 319

Bank Regulation 319
Branch Banking and Bank Chartering 319
The Federal Deposit Insurance Corporation 321
The Savings and Loan Debacle 321
Wal-Mart Bank? 322

Current Issue: Overdraft Privileges 323

14 The Federal Reserve and Monetary Policy 329

The Federal Reserve System 329
The Federal Reserve District Banks 330
The Board of Governors 330
Independence of the Board of Governors 332
Legal Reserve Requirements 332
Primary and Secondary Reserves 334

Deposit Expansion 335
How Deposit Expansion Works 335
The Deposit Expansion Multiplier 335
Cash, Checks, and Electronic Money 336

The Tools of Monetary Policy 339
How Open-Market Operations Work 339
The Federal Open-Market Committee 340
Discount Rate and Federal Funds Rate Changes 342
Changing Reserve Requirements 344
Summary: The Tools of Monetary Policy 344

The Fed's Effectiveness in Fighting Inflation and Recession 346

The Depository Institutions Deregulation and Monetary Control Act of 1980 347

The Banking Act of 1999 348

Fiscal and Monetary Policies Should Mesh 349

Current Issue: Who Controls Our Interest Rates? 349

15 A Century of Economic Theory 355

The Equation of Exchange 355
The Quantity Theory of Money 357
Classical Economics 358
Keynesian Economics 360

The Monetarist School 361
The Importance of the Rate of Monetary Growth 361
The Basic Propositions of Monetarism 362
The Monetary Rule 364
The Decline of Monetarism 364

Supply-Side Economics 365
The Work Effect 365
The Saving and Investment Effect 365
The Elimination of Productive Market Exchanges 366
The Laffer Curve 366

Rational Expectations Theory 367
The Three Assumptions of Rational Expectations Theory 368

21st Century Economic Theory 370
Supply-Side Revival? 370
The Economic Behaviorists 371

Conclusion 371

Current Issue: Is George W. Bush a Supply-Sider or a Keynesian? 372

Appendix: A Guide to Macropolicy 377

Conventional Macropolicy 377
Fighting Recessions 377
Conventional Fiscal Policy 377
Conventional Monetary Policy 378
Two Policy Dilemmas 378

Fighting Inflation 378
Conventional Fiscal Policy 378
Conventional Monetary Policy 378

Fighting Inflationary Recessions: Two More Policy Dilemmas 378

Fiscal and Monetary Policy Lags 379
The Lags 379
Fiscal Policy Lags 379
Monetary Policy Lags 380

The Limits of Macropolicy 381

16 Economic Growth and Productivity 385

The Industrial Revolution and American Economic Development 385

The Record of Productivity Growth 387
How Saving and Investment Affect Productivity Growth 388
How Labor Force Changes Affect Productivity Growth 390
(1) The Average Workweek and Workyear 390
(2) Our Declining Educational System 391
(3) The Permanent Underclass: Poverty, Drugs, and Crime 393
(4) Restrictions on Immigration 393

The Role of Technological Change 394

Rising Health Case Costs and the Shift to a Service Economy 396

Additional Factors Affecting Our Rate of Growth 398

Summary 399

Economic Growth in the Less Developed
   Countries 401

Current Issue: Health Care Costs in the Coming
   Decades 403

17 Demand, Supply, and Equilibrium 409

Demand Defined 409

Individual Demand and Market Demand 410

Changes in Demand 411
   Increases in Demand 411
   Decreases in Demand 412
   Problems 412
   What Causes Changes in Demand? 415

Supply Defined 417

Individual Supply and Market Supply 417

Changes in Supply 418
   What Causes Changes in Supply? 420

Graphing the Demand and Supply Curves 421
   Graphing the Demand Curve 422
   Graphing the Supply Curve 423

Equilibrium 424

Finding Equilibrium Price and Quantity 426

Current Issue: Why Can't I Sell My House? 427

18 The Elasticities of Demand and Supply 433

The Elasticity of Demand 433
   Measuring Elasticity 435
   The Meaning of Elasticity 435
   Determinants of the Degree of Elasticity of Demand 440
   Advertising 443

Elasticity and Total Revenue 445
   Elastic Demand and Total Revenue 445
   Inelastic Demand and Total Revenue 445

Elasticity of Supply 446
   Elasticity over Time 447

Tax Incidence 449

Last Word 452

Current Issue: How Elastic Is Your Demand for
   Food? 453

19 Theory of Consumer Behavior 459

Utility 460
   What Is Utility? 460
   Marginal Utility 460
   Total Utility 461
   Maximizing Utility 461

The Water–Diamond Paradox 463
Some Limitations of Utility Applications 464

Consumer Surplus 464

Do Price Gougers Rip Us Off? 468

Current Issue: All-You-Can-Eat Buffets 468

20 Cost 475

Costs 475
   Fixed Costs 476
   Variable Costs 476
   Total Cost 476
   Marginal Cost 476

The Short Run and in the Long Run 479
   The Short Run 479
   The Long Run 479

Average Cost 479
   Average Fixed Cost 480
   Average Variable Cost 480
   Average Total Cost 481
   Graphing the AFC, AVC, ATC, and MC Curves 482
   Why Are the AVC and ATC Curves U-Shaped? 485
   The Production Function and the Law of Diminishing
      Returns 487
   Economies of Scale 489
   Diseconomies of Scale 490
   A Summing Up 491
   The Decision to Operate or Shut Down 492
   The Decision to Go Out of Business or Stay in Business 494
   Choosing Plant Size 497

Current Issue: Wedding Hall or City Hall? 498

21 Profit, Loss, and Perfect Competition 505

Total Revenue and Marginal Revenue 505
   Graphing Demand and Marginal Revenue 506

Economic and Accounting Profit 507

Profit Maximization and Loss Minimization 507
   A Summing Up 510

Efficiency 514
   Review of Efficiency and Profit Maximization 515

Do You Really Need to Make a Profit? 516

Definition of Perfect Competition 516

The Perfect Competitor's Demand Curve 519
   The Short Run 520
   The Long Run 522

Alternative Calculation of Profit and Loss 527

The Perfect Competitor: A Price Taker, Not a
   Price Maker 528

Efficiency, Price, and Profit 529

Current Issue: The Internet Effect: A More Perfect
   Knowledge and Lower Prices 530

22 Monopoly 541

Monopoly Defined 541
The Graph of the Monopolist 542
Calculating the Monopolist's Profit 544
Review of the Monopolist's Economic Analysis 545
The Monopolist in the Short Run and in the Long Run 548
Are All Monopolies Big Companies? 548
Barriers to Entry 549

Limits to Monopoly Power 553
Economies of Scale and Natural Monopoly 553
What Is Natural Monopoly? 553
Two Policy Alternatives 555

Is Bigness Good or Bad? 556
When Is Bigness Bad? 556
When Is Bigness Good? 558
The Economic Case against Bigness 558
Conclusion 558

Current Issue: Would You Allow Wal-Mart to Open a Supercenter in Your Community? 559

23 Monopolistic Competition 565

Monopolistic Competition Defined 565
The Monopolistic Competitor in the Short Run 565
The Monopolistic Competitor in the Long Run 567
Product Differentiation 568
The Typical Monopolistic Competitor 570
Price Discrimination 572
Is the Monopolistic Competitor Inefficient? 575
Current Issue: Selling Status 576

24 Oligopoly 581

Oligopoly Defined 581
Two Measures of the Degree of Oligopolization 582
Concentration Ratios 582
The Herfindahl-Hirschman Index (HHI) 583

The Competitive Spectrum 584
Cartels 584
Open Collusion 586
Covert Collusion 586
Price Leadership 587
Cutthroat Competition 589
Conclusion 592

Current Issue: Cutthroat Competition in the College Textbook Market 593
Appendix: The Four Types of Competition: A Review 601
Perfect Competition 601
Monopoly 602
Monopolistic Competition 602

Oligopoly 602
Perfect Competition versus Imperfect Competition 602
Summary Tables 603

25 Corporate Mergers and Antitrust 607

A Historical Perspective on Corporate Concentration 607
Antitrust 608
The Political Background 608
The Sherman Antitrust Act 608
The Clayton Antitrust Act 610
The Federal Trade Commission Act (1914) 610

Modern Antitrust 611
Partial Breakdown of the Rule of Reason 611
The 60 Percent Rule 612
Two Landmark Cases 612
European Antitrust 613

Types of Mergers 614
Horizontal Mergers 614
Vertical Mergers 614
Conglomerate Mergers 615

Deregulation 615
Corporate Misconduct 616
How Effective Is Antitrust? 617
The Trend toward Bigness 617
Current Issue: The Enron Case 619

26 Demand in the Factor Market 625

Derived Demand 625
Productivity 626
Prices of Substitute Resources 626
Marginal Revenue Product (MRP) 627
The MRP of the Imperfect Competitor 631

Changes in Resource Demand 632
Changes in Resource Demand versus Changes in Quantity of Resource Demanded 632
The Four Reasons for Changes in Resource Demand 633
Optimum Resource Mix for the Firm 635

Current Issue: Washing Machines and Women's Liberation 636

27 Labor Unions 643

A Short History of the American Labor Movement 643
The Early Years 643
Key Labor Legislation 644
Craft Unions versus Industrial Unions 645
Union Organizing since the 1950s 647

The Formation of Change to Win 649

Jobs: Exportable and Nonexportable 649

The Economic Power of Labor Unions 650

The Economic Power of Large Employers 650

Collective Bargaining 652
Strikes, Lockouts, and Givebacks 652
The Collective Bargaining Agreement 654
The Strike 654
Averting Strikes: Mediation and Arbitration 655

Current Issue: Will You Ever Be a Member of a Labor Union? 656

28 Labor Markets and Wage Rates 661

The Supply of Labor 661
Noncompeting Groups 661
The Theory of the Dual Labor Market 662
The Backward-Bending Labor Supply Curve 664

The Demand for Labor 665
The Marginal Revenue Product Schedule 665
Nonhomogeneous Jobs 666

The Effects of Employment Discrimination on Wages 667
Employment Discrimination against Women 667
Employment Discrimination against African Americans 669
Conclusion 670

The Wage Rate: Supply and Demand 670

High Wage Rates and Economic Rent 670

Real Wages versus Money Wages 672

The Minimum Wage and the Living Wage 676
The Minimum Wage Rate: 1938 to the Present 676
Should There Be a Minimum Wage Rate? 677
The Living Wage 679

Current Issue: The Education Gap 679

29 Rent, Interest, and Profit 687

Rent 687
What Is Land? 687
How Is Rent Determined? 689
Economic Rent 690
Are Prices High because Rents Are High, or Are Rents High because Prices Are High? 691

Interest 692
What Is Capital? 692
How Is the Interest Rate Determined? 692
Interest Rates and Consumer Loans 693
The Present Value of Future Income 695

Profits 698
How Are Profits Determined? 698
How Large Are Profits? 698

Theories of Profit 698
Conclusion 701

Current Issue: Subprime, Fringe, and Payday Lending 701

30 Income Distribution and Poverty 709

Income Distribution in the United States 709
The Poor, the Middle Class, and the Rich 709
Distribution of Wealth in the United States 714
Distribution of Income: Equity and Efficiency 714
What Determines Income Distribution? 716

Poverty in America 717
Poverty Defined 717
Who Are the Poor? 719
Child Poverty 721
The Main Government Transfer Programs 722
Theories of the Causes of Poverty 726
The Conservative View versus the Liberal View 728
Solutions 730

Current Issue: Will Social Security Be There for You? 733

31 International Trade 741

Part I: A Brief History of U.S. Trade 742
U.S. Trade before 1975 742
U.S. Trade since 1975 742
U.S. Government Trade Policy 743

Part II: The Theory of International Trade 745
Specialization and Trade 745
Comparative Advantage 745
Absolute Advantage versus Comparative Advantage 749
The Arguments for Protection 749
Tariffs or Quotas 754
Conclusion 755

Part III: The Practice of International Trade 756
What Are the Causes of Our Trade Imbalance? 756

Part IV: Our Trade Deficit with Japan and China 758
Japanese Trading Practices 758
Our Trade Deficit with China 760
Trading with China and Japan: More Differences than Similarities 761

Final Word 762
Free Trade in Word and Deed 762
Reducing Our Trade Deficit 763

Current Issue: Buy American? 763

32 International Finance 769

The Mechanics of International Finance 769
Financing International Trade 769
The Balance of Payments 770

Exchange Rate Systems 772

The Gold Standard 773
The Gold Exchange Standard, 1934–73 774
The Freely Floating Exchange Rate System, 1973 to the Present 775
How Well Do Freely Floating (Flexible) Exchange Rates Work? 777
The Euro 777
The Yen and the Yuan 777

Running Up a Tab in the Global Economy 780

From Largest Creditor to Largest Debtor 780

Living beyond Our Means 785
A Codependent Relationship 785
Why We Need to Worry about the Current Account Deficit 786

Current Issue: Editorial: American Exceptionality 786

Glossary 793

Index 803

About the Author

Stephen L. Slavin received his BA in economics from Brooklyn College and his MA and PhD in economics from New York University. He has taught at New York Institute of Technology, Brooklyn College, St. Francis College (Brooklyn), and in the MBA program at Fairleigh Dickinson University, at the New School University in New York City, and at Union County College in Cranford, New Jersey.

He has written eight other books: *The Einstein Syndrome: Corporate Anti-Semitism in America Today* (University Press of America); *Jelly Bean Economics: Reaganomics in the Early 1980s* (Philosophical Library); *Economics: A Self-Teaching Guide, All the Math You'll Ever Need, Math for Your First- and Second-Grader, Quick Business Math: A Self-Teaching Guide* (all four published by John Wiley & Sons); *Chances Are: The Only Statistics Book You'll Ever Need* (University Press of America); and *Everyday Math in 20 Minutes a Day* (LearningExpress). He is the coauthor of four other Wiley books, *Practical Algebra, Quick Algebra Review, Precalculus,* and *Geometry*. In addition he is also the coauthor of *Basic Mathematics*, a text published by Pi r squared Publishers.

Dr. Slavin's articles have appeared in *Studies in Family Planning, Economic Planning, Journal of BioSocial Science, Business and Society Review, Bankers Magazine, Education for Business, Public Management, Better Investing, Northwest Investment Review, U.S.A. Today Magazine, Patterns in Prejudice, Culturefront,* and *Conservative Review*. In addition, he has written more than 500 newspaper commentaries on public policy, demographic economics, politics, urban economics, international trade, investments, and economics fluctuations.

Chapter 1

A Brief Economic History of the United States

More than two centuries ago, some Americans believed it was "manifest destiny" that the 13 states on the eastern seaboard would one day be part of a nation that stretched from the Atlantic to the Pacific. Was it also our manifest destiny to become the world's economic superpower?

CHAPTER OBJECTIVES

In this chapter you'll learn:

- How we grew from a primarily agricultural nation of 4 million people to an industrial power of 300 million.
- How the Civil War, World War I, and World War II affected our economy.
- How our nation was shaped by suburbanization after World War II.

- What major factors affected our economic growth decade by decade from the 1920s into the new millennium.
- What the "new economy" is and how it differs from the "old economy."

Introduction

Our economy is a study in contrasts. We have poverty in the midst of plenty; we have rapidly expanding industries like computer software and medical technology, and dying industries like shipbuilding, textiles, and consumer electronics; we won the cold war against communism, but we may be losing the trade war against China.

Which country has the largest economy in the world, the United States, China, or Japan? Believe it or not, our national output is more than that of China and Japan combined.

America is the sole superpower and has one of the highest standards of living in the world. Communism—at least the version that was practiced in the Soviet Union and Eastern Europe—to borrow a phrase from Karl Marx, has been "swept into the dustbin of history."

The baby-boom generation has earned higher incomes than any other generation in history. Indeed, Americans once considered it their birthright to do better than their parents. But that ended about 35 years ago, and a lot of young people are worrying about their futures.

In the decade of the 1990s our economy generated more than 22 million new jobs. But since the millennium job growth has been lagging.

The year 2003 was not a good one for college graduates. Neither was 2002, for that matter. College job placement counselors said these two years were the worst in recent memory. During the boom years of the late 1990s, corporate recruiters visited college campuses in droves, offering jobs left and right. But these visits were much less frequent in the springs of 2002 and 2003. Although the job market for college graduates improved substantially in 2004 and 2005, hundreds of thousands of recent graduates are still living at home, sending out resumes, and often stuck in the same jobs they held while they were in college.

To sum up the good and the bad: We have the world's largest economy, and one of the world's highest standard of living, and, even though our recent economic performance has been less than stellar, most Americans have decent jobs paying decent wages. But there's the downside:

- Our federal budget deficit is at a record high and will remain high in the foreseeable future.
- Our trade deficit is at a record high and will remain high in the foreseeable future.
- We are borrowing more than $2 billion a day from foreigners to finance our trade and budget deficits.
- Unless Congress acts soon, our Social Security and Medicare trust funds will run out of money well before you reach retirement age.
- When you graduate, you may not be able to get a decent job.
- Our savings rate has fallen below zero.
- The real hourly wage (after inflation) of the average worker is 9 percent lower today than it was in 1973.

In these first four chapters, we'll be looking at how our economy uses its basic resources, at the workings of the law of supply and demand, and at how capitalism and other economic systems work. But first we need to ask how we got here. After all, the American economic system evolved over a period of more than 300 years.

Those who cannot remember the past are condemned to repeat it.

–George Santayana–

What did the great philosopher mean by this? Perhaps he meant that those who do not learn enough history the first time around will be required to repeat History 101. But whatever he meant, it is clear that to understand our economy today, we need to know how it developed over the years.

Did you see *Back to the Future*? You may have seen parts 1, 2, and 3, but let's stick with just part 1. Imagine being sent back to the 1950s. The way people lived then was very different from the way we live today—and the 1950s represented life in the fast lane compared to daily existence during the first decade of the 20th century. So before we worry about today's economy, we'll take a few steps back and look at life in this country about 200 years ago.

The American Economy in the 19th Century

Agricultural Development

America has always had a large and productive agricultural sector. At the time of the American Revolution, 9 out of every 10 Americans lived on a farm; 100 years later, however, fewer than 1 out of every 2 people worked in agriculture. Today, it's fewer than 2 in 100, but those 2 not only feed America but also produce a huge surplus that is sold abroad.

America had an almost limitless supply of land.

Unlike Europe, 200 years ago America had an almost limitless supply of unoccupied fertile land. The federal government gave away farmland—usually 160-acre plots (one-quarter of a square mile)—to anyone willing to clear the land and farm on it. Although sometimes the government charged a token amount, it often gave away the land for free.

The great abundance of land was the most influential factor in our economic development during the 19th century. Not only did the availability of very cheap or free land attract millions of immigrants to our shores, but it also encouraged early marriage and large families, since every child was an additional worker to till the fields and handle the animals. Even more important, this plenitude of land, compared to amount of labor, encouraged rapid technological development.

When George Washington was inaugurated in 1789, there were about 4 million people living in the United States. By the time of the War of 1812, our population had doubled. It doubled again to 16 million in 1835 and still again by 1858. Our numbers continued to grow, but at a somewhat slower pace, reaching the 100 million mark in 1915 and the 200 million mark in 1968, and 300 million in 2006.

Although all regions of the United States remained primarily agricultural in the years following the Civil War, New England, the Middle Atlantic states, and the Midwest—with their already well-established iron, steel, textile, and apparel industries—were poised for a major industrial expansion that would last until the Great Depression. In contrast, the South, whose economy was based on the cash crops of cotton, tobacco, rice, and sugar, as well as on subsistence farming, remained primarily an agricultural region well into the 20th century. The South continued to be the poorest section of the country, a relative disadvantage that was not erased until the growth of the Sun Belt took off in the 1960s. (See the box titled "Two Economic Conflicts Leading to the Civil War.")

Southern economic development remained agricultural.

Southern agriculture developed very differently from agriculture in the other regions of the nation. We know, of course, that most of the labor was provided by slaves whose ancestors had been brought here in chains from Africa. On the average, Southern farms were large. By 1860, four-fifths of the farms with more than 500 acres were in the South.

Two Economic Conflicts Leading to the Civil War

In the decades before the Civil War, the economic interests of the North and South came into sharp conflict. Northern manufacturers benefited from high protective tariffs, which kept out competing British manufacturers. The Southern states, which had only a small manufacturing sector, were forced to buy most of their manufactured goods from the North and to pay higher prices than they would have paid for British goods had there been no tariff.*

As the nation expanded westward, another conflict reached the boiling point: the expansion of slavery into the new territories. In 1860, when Abraham Lincoln had been elected president, most of the land between the Mississippi River and the Pacific Ocean had not yet been organized into states. As newly formed territories applied for membership in the Union, the big question was whether they would come in as "free states" or "slave states." Lincoln—and virtually all the other leaders of the new Republican Party—strenuously opposed the extension of slavery into the new territories of the West.

The Southern economy, especially cotton agriculture, was based on slave labor. The political leaders of the South realized that if slavery were prohibited in the new territories, it would be only a matter of time before these territories entered the Union as free states and the South was badly outvoted in Congress. And so, as Abraham Lincoln was preparing to take office in 1861, 11 Southern states seceded from the Union, touching off the Civil War, which lasted four years, cost hundreds of thousands of lives, and largely destroyed the Southern economy.

The two major consequences of the war were the freeing of 4 million black people who had been slaves and the preservation of the Union with those 11 rebel states. It would take the nation more than a century to overcome the legacies of this conflict.

---

*Tariffs are fully discussed in the chapter on international trade.

American Agricultural Technology

In the 19th century, a series of inventions vastly improved farm productivity. In the late 1840s, John Deere began to manufacture steel plows in Moline, Illinois. These were a tremendous improvement over the crude wooden plows that had previously been used.

Cyrus McCormick patented a mechanical reaper in 1834. By the time of the Civil War, McCormick's reaper had at least quadrupled the output of each farm laborer. The development of the Appleby twine binder, the Marsh brothers' harvesting machine, and the Pitts thresher, as well as Eli Whitney's cotton gin, all worked to make American agriculture the most productive in the world.

The mechanization of American agriculture, which continued into the 20th century with the introduction of the gasoline powered tractor in the 1920s, would not have been possible without a highly skilled farm workforce. Tom Brokaw described the challenge that farmers faced using this technology:

> Farm boys were inventive and good with their hands. They were accustomed to finding solutions to mechanical and design problems on their own. There was no one else to ask when the tractor broke down or the threshing machine fouled, no 1-800-CALLHELP operators standing by in those days.*

*Tom Brokaw, *The Greatest Generation* (New York: Random House, 1999), p. 92. The "greatest generation" was the one that came of age during the Great Depression and won World War II.

The plantation owners raised commercial crops such as cotton, rice, sugar, and tobacco, while the smaller farms, which were much less dependent on slave labor, produced a wider variety of crops.

In the North and the West, self-sufficient, 160-acre family farms were most common. Eventually, corn, wheat, and soybeans became important commercial crops. But in the years following the Civil War, increasing numbers of people left the farms of the North to take jobs in manufacturing.

Bad times for agriculture

Times were bad for agriculture from the end of the Civil War until the close of the century. The government's liberal land policy, combined with increased mechanization, vastly expanded farm output. The production of the nation's three basic cash crops—corn, wheat, and cotton—rose faster than did its population through most of that period. Why did production rise so rapidly? Mainly because of the rapid technological progress made during that period. (See the box titled "American Agricultural Technology.") This brings us to supply and demand, which is covered in Chapter 3 and explains why times were bad for agriculture despite expanded output. If the supply of corn increases faster than the demand for corn, what happens to the price of corn? It goes down. And this happened to wheat and cotton as well. Although other countries bought up much of the surpluses, the prices of corn, wheat, and cotton declined substantially from the end of the Civil War until the turn of the century.

Supply and demand

The National Railroad Network

The completion of the transcontinental railroads

The completion of a national railroad network in the second half of the 19th century made possible mass production, mass marketing, and mass consumption. In 1850, the United States had just 10,000 miles of track, but within 40 years the total reached 164,000 miles. The transcontinental railroads had been completed, and it was possible to get virtually anywhere in the country by train. Interestingly, however, the transcontinental lines all bypassed the South, which severely retarded its economic development well into the 20th century.

In 1836, it took a traveler an entire month to get from New York to Chicago. Just 15 years later, he or she could make the trip by rail in less than two days. What the railroads did, in effect, was to weave the country together into a huge social and economic unit, and eventually into the world's first mass market (see the box titled "Mass Production and Mass Consumption").

Mass Production and Mass Consumption

Mass production is possible only if there is also mass consumption. In the late 19th century, once the national railway network enabled manufacturers to sell their products all over the country, and even beyond our shores, it became feasible to invest in heavy machinery and to turn out volume production, which, in turn, meant lower prices. Lower prices, of course, pushed up sales, which encouraged further investment and created more jobs. At the same time, productivity, or output per hour, was rising, which justified companies in paying higher wages, and a high-wage workforce could easily afford all the new low-priced products.

Henry Ford personified the symbiotic relationship between mass production and mass consumption. Selling millions of cars at a small unit of profit allowed Ford to keep prices low and wages high—the perfect formula for mass consumption.

So we had a mutually reinforcing relationship. Mass consumption enabled mass production, while mass production enabled mass consumption. As this process unfolded, our industrial output literally multiplied, and our standard of living soared. And nearly all of this process took place from within our own borders with only minimal help from foreign investors, suppliers, and consumers.

After World War II, the Japanese were in no position to use this method of reindustrialization. Not only had most of their plants and equipment been destroyed by American bombing, but also Japanese consumers did not have the purchasing power to buy enough manufactured goods to justify mass production of a wide range of consumer goods. And so the Japanese industrialists took the one course open to them: As they rebuilt their industrial base, they sold low-priced goods to the low end of the American market. In many cases they sold these items—textiles, black-and-white TVs, cameras, and other consumer goods—at half the prices charged in Japan.

Japanese consumers were willing to pay much higher prices for what was often relatively shoddy merchandise, simply because that was considered the socially correct thing to do. Imagine American consumers acting this way! Within a couple of decades, Japanese manufacturers, with a virtual monopoly in their home market and an expanding overseas market, were able to turn out high-volume, low-priced, high-quality products. We will look much more closely at Japanese manufacturing and trade practices in the chapter on international trade.

John Steele Gordon describes the economic impact of the railroads:

> Most East Coast rivers were navigable for only short distances inland. As a result, there really was no "American economy." Instead there was a myriad of local ones. Most food was consumed locally, and most goods were locally produced by artisans such as blacksmiths. The railroads changed all that in less than 30 years.[1]

Before railroads, shipping a ton of goods 400 miles could easily quadruple the price. But by rail, the same ton of goods could be shipped in a fraction of the time and at one-twentieth of the cost.

The Age of the Industrial Capitalist

The last quarter of the 19th century was the age of the industrial capitalist. The great empire builders—Carnegie (steel), Du Pont (chemicals), McCormick (farm equipment), Rockefeller (oil), and Swift (meat packing), among others—dominated this era. John D. Rockefeller, whose exploits will be discussed in the chapter on corporate mergers and antitrust, built the Standard Oil Trust, which controlled 90 percent of the oil business. In 1872, just before Andrew Carnegie opened the Edgar Thomson works, the United States produced less than 100,000 tons of steel. Only 25 years later, Carnegie alone was turning out 4 million tons, almost half of the total American production. Again, as supply outran demand, the price of steel dropped from $65 to $20 a ton.

Andrew Carnegie, American industrial capitalist

---

[1]John Steele Gordon, "The Golden Spike," *Forbes ASAP,* February 21, 2000, p. 118.

The Development of the Automobile Industry

Nothing is particularly hard if you divide
it into small jobs.

–Henry Ford–

Who was the first automobile manufacturer to use a division of labor, to use a moving assembly line, and to bring the materials to the worker instead of the worker to the materials? Was it Henry Ford? Close, but no cigar. It was Henry Olds, who turned the trick in 1901 when he started turning out Oldsmobiles on a mass basis. Still another Henry, Henry Leland, believed it was possible and practical to manufacture a standardized engine with interchangeable parts. By 1908, he did just that with his Cadillac.

Henry Ford was able to carry mass production to its logical conclusion. His great contribution was the emphasis he placed on an expert combination of accuracy, continuity, the moving assembly line, and speed, through the careful timing of manufacturing, materials handling, and assembly. The assembly line speeded up work by breaking down the automaking process into a series of simple, repetitive operations.

Back in 1908, only 200,000 cars were registered in the United States. Just 15 years later, Ford built 57 percent of the 4 million cars and trucks produced. But soon General Motors supplanted Ford as the country's number one automobile firm, a position it continues to hold. In 1929, motor vehicle production peaked at 5.3 million units, a number that was not reached again until 1949.

The industrial capitalists not only amassed great economic power, but abused that power as well. Their excesses led to the rise of labor unions and the passage of antitrust legislation.[2]

The American Economy in the 20th Century

On the world's technological cutting edge

By the turn of the century, America had become an industrial economy. Fewer than 4 in 10 people still lived on farms. We were among the world's leaders in the production of steel, coal, steamships, textiles, apparel, chemicals, and agricultural machinery. Our trade balance with the rest of the world was positive every year. While we continued to export most of our huge agricultural surpluses to Europe, increasingly we began to send the countries of that continent our manufactured goods as well.

We were also well on our way to becoming the world's first mass-consumption society. The stage had been set by the late-19th-century industrialists. At the turn of the 20th century, we were on the threshold of the automobile age (see the box titled "The Development of the Automobile Industry"). The Wright brothers would soon be flying their plane at Kitty Hawk, but commercial aviation was still a few decades away.

American technological progress—or, if the South can forgive me, Yankee ingenuity—runs the gamut from the agricultural implements previously mentioned to the telegraph, the telephone, the radio, the TV, and the computer. It includes the mass-production system perfected by Henry Ford, which made possible the era of mass consumption and the high living standards that the people of all industrialized nations enjoy today. America has long been on the world's technological cutting edge, as well as being the world's leader in manufacturing.

This technological talent, a large agricultural surplus, the world's first universal public education system, and the entrepreneurial abilities of our great industrialists combined to enable the United States to emerge as the world's leading industrial power by the time of World War I. Then, too, fortune smiled on this continent by keeping it out of harm's way during the war. This same good fortune recurred during World War II; so, once again, unlike the rest of the industrial world, we emerged from the war with our industrial plant intact.

Henry Ford, American automobile manufacturer (The Granger Collection, New York)

---

[2]See the chapters on labor unions and antitrust in *Economics* and *Microeconomics*.

Agricultural conditions really turned around in the first two decades of the 20th century. Production stabilized, and agriculture enjoyed mild prosperity from 1900 to 1913. Then came World War I, which brought the farmer unprecedented prosperity despite a huge increase in output. Wheat production, for example, which exceeded 1 billion bushels in 1915, passed the 3-billion-bushel mark in 1920. But in the years immediately after the war, agriculture went into a terrible slump. It was not until the New Deal, World War II, and the massive federal farm subsidy program that followed the war that farmers finally were able to get on their feet again.

When did the United States emerge as a mature industrial economy? We'll take as our starting point the decade of the 1920s, when America truly became a mass-consumption economy. But that economy did not have any distinct time of departure. It evolved from a set of powerful forces that were described in the first part of this chapter.

America's large and growing population has been extremely important as a market for our farmers and manufacturers. After World War II, Japanese manufacturers targeted the American market, while the much smaller Japanese market remained largely closed to American manufactured goods. Japan—with less than half our population and, until very recently, much less purchasing power than the United States—has largely financed its industrial development with American dollars. (See again the box titled "Mass Production and Mass Consumption.")

The Roaring Twenties

World War I ended on November 11, 1918. Although we had a brief depression in the early 1920s, the decade was one of almost unparalleled expansion, driven largely by the automobile industry. Another important development in the 1920s was the spreading use of electricity. During this decade, electric power production doubled. Not only was industrial use growing, but by 1929 about two out of every three homes in America had been wired and were now using electrical appliances. The telephone, the radio, the toaster, the refrigerator, and other conveniences became commonplace during the 1920s.

The postwar boom

The spreading use of electricity

Between 1921 and 1929, national output rose by 50 percent and most Americans thought the prosperity would last forever. The stock market was soaring, and instant millionaires were created every day, at least on paper. It was possible, in the late 1920s, to put down just 10 percent of a stock purchase and borrow the rest on margin from a stockbroker, who, in turn, borrowed that money from a bank. If you put down $1,000, you could buy $10,000 worth of stock. If that stock doubled (that is, if it was now worth $20,000), you just made $10,000 on a $1,000 investment. Better yet, your $10,000 stake entitled you to borrow $90,000 from your broker, so you could now own $100,000 worth of stock.

How to become a millionaire in the stock market

This was not a bad deal—as long as the market kept going up. But, as they say, what goes up must come down. And, as you well know, the stock market came crashing down in October 1929. Although it wasn't immediately apparent, the economy had already begun its descent into a recession a couple of months before the crash. And, that recession was the beginning of the Great Depression.

...the chief business of the American people is business.
—President Calvin Coolidge

Curiously, within days after the crash, several leading government and business officials—including President Hoover and John D. Rockefeller—each described economic conditions as "fundamentally sound." The next time you hear our economy described in those terms, you'll know we're in big trouble.

The 1930s: The Great Depression

Once upon a time my opponents honored me as possessing the fabulous intellectual and economic power by which I created a worldwide depression all by myself.

–President Herbert Hoover–

By the summer of 1929, the country had clearly built itself up for an economic letdown. The boom in sales of cars and electrical appliances was over. The automobile market was saturated. Nearly three out of four cars on the road were less than six years old, and

The August 1929 recession

model changes were not nearly as important then as they are today. The tire industry had been overbuilt, and textiles were suffering from overcapacity. Residential construction was already in decline, and the general business investment outlook was not that rosy.

Had the stock market not crashed and had the rest of the world not gone into a depression, we might have gotten away with a moderate business downturn. Also, had the federal government acted more expeditiously, it is quite possible that the prosperity of the 1920s, after a fairly short recession, could have continued well into the 1930s. But that's not what happened. What did happen completely changed the lives of the people who lived through it, as well as the course of human history itself.

The Dust Bowl and the "Okies"

Prices began to decline, investment in plant and equipment collapsed, and a drought wiped out millions of farmers. In fact, conditions grew so bad in what became known as the Dust Bowl that millions of people from the Midwest just packed their cars and drove in caravans to seek a better life in California. Their flight was immortalized in John Steinbeck's great novel *The Grapes of Wrath,* which was later made into a movie. Although most of these migrants came from other states, they were collectively called Okies, because it seemed at the time as if the entire state of Oklahoma had picked up and moved west.

The bank failures

There had been widespread bank failures in the late 1920s and by the end of 1930, thousands of banks had failed and the generally optimistic economic outlook had given way to one of extreme pessimism. From here on, it was all downhill. By the beginning of 1933, banks were closing all over the country; by the first week in March, every single bank in the United States had shut its doors.

Hitting bottom

When the economy hit bottom in March 1933, national output was about one-third lower than it had been in August 1929. The official unemployment rate was 25 percent, but official figures tell only part of the story. Millions of additional workers had simply given up looking for work during the depths of the Great Depression, as there was no work to be had. Yet according to the way the government compiles the unemployment rate, these people were not even counted since they were not actually looking for work.[3]

Herbert Hoover, thirty-first president of the United States

The Depression was a time of soup kitchens, people selling apples on the street, large-scale homelessness, so-called hobo jungles where poor men huddled around garbage-pail fires to keep warm, and even fairly widespread starvation. "Are you working?" and "Brother, can you spare a dime?"[4] were common greetings. People who lived in collections of shacks made of cardboard, wood, and corrugated sheet metal scornfully referred to them as Hoovervilles. Although President Herbert Hoover did eventually make a few halfhearted attempts to get the economy moving again, his greatest contribution to the economy was apparently his slogans. When he ran for the presidency in 1928, he promised "two cars in every garage" and "a chicken in every pot." As the Depression grew worse, he kept telling Americans that "prosperity is just around the corner." It's too bad he didn't have Frank Perdue in those days to stick a chicken in every pot.

Herbert Hoover and the Depression

Why did the downturn reverse itself?

Why did the downturn of August 1929 to March 1933 finally reverse itself? Well, for one thing, we were just about due. Business inventories had been reduced to rock-bottom levels, prices had finally stopped falling, and there was a need to replace some plants and equipment. The federal budget deficits of 1931 and 1932, even if unwillingly incurred, did provide a mild stimulus to the economy.[5]

I see one-third of a nation ill-housed, ill-clad, ill-nourished.
—Franklin D. Roosevelt
Second Inaugural Address,
January 1937

Clearly a lot of the credit must go to the new administration of Franklin D. Roosevelt, which reopened the banks, ran large budget deficits, and eventually created government job programs that put millions of Americans back to work (see the box titled "The New Deal"). Recognizing a crisis in confidence, Roosevelt said, "The only thing we have

---

[3]How the Department of Labor computes the unemployment rate is discussed in the chapter on economic fluctuations in *Economics* and *Macroeconomics.* In Chapter 2, we'll be looking at the concept of full employment, but you can grasp intuitively that when our economy enters even a minor downturn, we are operating at less than full employment.

[4]"Brother, Can You Spare a Dime?" was a depression era song written by Yip Harburg and Jay Gorney.

[5]In Chapter 12 of *Economics* and *Macroeconomics* we'll explain how budget deficits stimulate the economy.

The New Deal

When Franklin D. Roosevelt ran for president in 1932, he promised "a new deal for the American people." Action was needed, and it was needed fast. In the first 100 days Roosevelt was in office, his administration sent a flurry of bills to Congress that were promptly passed.

The New Deal is best summarized by the three Rs: relief, recovery, and reform. Relief was aimed at alleviating the suffering of a nation that was, in President Roosevelt's words, one-third "ill-fed, ill-clothed, and ill-housed." These people needed work relief, a system similar to today's workfare (work for your welfare check) programs. About 6 million people, on average, were put to work at various jobs ranging from raking leaves and repairing public buildings to maintaining national parks and building power dams. Robert R. Russell made this observation:

> The principal objects of work-relief were to help people preserve their self-respect by enabling them to stay off the dole and to maintain their work habits against the day when they could again find employment in private enterprises. It was also hoped that the programs, by putting some purchasing power into the hands of workers and suppliers of materials, would help prime the economic pump.*

The economic recovery could not begin to take off until people again began spending money. As these 6 million Americans went back to work, they spent their paychecks on food, clothing, and shelter, and managed to pay off at least some of their debts. The most lasting effect of the New Deal was reform. The Securities and Exchange Commission (SEC) was set up to regulate the stock market and avoid a repetition of the speculative excesses of the late 1920s, which had led to the great crash of 1929. After the reform, bank deposits were insured by the Federal Deposit Insurance Corporation (FDIC) to prevent future runs on the banks by depositors, like those experienced in the early 1930s. Also, an unemployment insurance benefit program was set up to provide temporarily unemployed people with some money to tide them over. The most important reform of all was the creation of Social Security. Although even today retired people need more than their Social Security benefits to get by, there is no question that this program has provided tens of millions of retired people with a substantial income and has largely removed workers' fears of being destitute and dependent in their old age.

*Robert R. Russell, *A History of the American Economic System* (New York: Appleton-Century-Crofts, 1964), p. 547.

to fear is fear itself." Putting millions of people back to work was a tremendous confidence builder. A 50-month expansion began in March 1933 and lasted until May 1937. Although output did finally reach the levels of August 1929, more than 7 million people were still unemployed.

By far, the most important reason for the success of the New Deal's first four years was the massive federal government spending that returned millions of Americans to work. This huge infusion of dollars into our economy was just what the doctor ordered. In this case, the doctor was John Maynard Keynes, the great English economist, who maintained that it didn't matter *what* the money was spent on—even paying people to dig holes in the ground and then to fill them up again—as long as enough money was spent. But in May 1937, just when it had begun to look as though the Depression was finally over, we plunged right back into it again.

What went wrong? Two things: First, the Federal Reserve Board of Governors, inexplicably more concerned about inflation than about the lingering economic depression, greatly tightened credit, making it much harder to borrow money. Second, the Roosevelt administration suddenly got that old balance-the-budget-at-all-costs religion. The cost of that economic orthodoxy—which would have made sense during an economic boom—was the very sharp and deep recession of 1937–38. Tight money and a balanced budget are now considered the right policies to follow when the economy is heating up and prices are rising too quickly, but they are prescriptions for disaster when the unemployment rate is 12 percent.[6]

Franklin D. Roosevelt, thirty-second president of the United States

The recession of 1937–38

---

[6]These policies will be discussed in Chapters 12 and 14 of *Economics* and *Macroeconomics*.

The ensuing downturn pushed up the official unemployment count by another 5 million, industrial production fell by 30 percent, and people began to wonder when this depression would ever end. But there really *was* some light at the end of the tunnel.

In April 1938, both the Roosevelt administration and the Federal Reserve Board reversed course and began to stimulate the economy. By June, the economy had turned around again, and this time the expansion would continue for seven years. The outbreak of war in Europe, the American mobilization in 1940 and 1941, and our eventual entry into the war on December 7, 1941, all propelled us toward full recovery.

When we ask what finally brought the United States out of the Great Depression, there is one clear answer: the massive federal government spending that was needed to prepare for and to fight World War II.

For most Americans the end of the Depression did not bring much relief, because the nation was now fighting an all-out war. For those who didn't get the message in those days, there was the popular reminder, "Hey, bub, don't yuh know there's a *war* goin' on?"

The country that emerged from the war was very different from the one that had entered it less than four years earlier. Prosperity had replaced depression. Now inflation had become the number one economic worry.

 Globally, we were certainly at the top of our game. With just 7 percent of the world's population, we accounted for half the world's manufacturing output, as well as 80 percent of its cars and 62 percent of its oil. Our potential rivals, Japan, Germany, France, and the United Kingdom, would need at least 15 years to repair their war-damaged industrial plant and begin competing again in world markets.

The United States and the Soviet Union were the only superpowers left standing in 1945. When the cold war quickly developed, we spent tens of billions of dollars to prop up the sagging economies of the nations of Western Europe and Japan, and we spent hundreds of billions more to provide for their defense. In the four decades since the close of World War II we expended 6 percent of our national output on defense, while the Soviet Union probably expended at least triple that percentage. This great burden certainly contributed to the collapse of the Soviet Union in 1990–91, and our own heavy defense spending continues to divert substantial resources that might otherwise be used to spur our economic growth.

The 1940s: World War II and Peacetime Prosperity

Just as the Great Depression dominated the 1930s, World War II was the main event of the 1940s, especially from the day the Japanese bombed Pearl Harbor until they surrendered in August 1945. For the first time in our history, we fought a war that required a total national effort. Although the Civil War had caused tremendous casualties and had set the South back economically for generations, we had never before fought a war that consumed nearly half of our nation's total output.

At the peak of the war, more than 12 million men and women were mobilized and, not coincidentally, the unemployment rate was below 2 percent. Women, whose place was supposedly in the home, flocked to the workplace to replace the men who had gone off to war. Blacks, too, who had experienced great difficulty finding factory jobs, were hired to work in the steel mills and the defense plants in the East, the Midwest, and the West.

No more than 2 or 3 percent of the defense plant workers had any experience in this area, but thanks to mass production techniques developed largely by General Motors and Ford, these workers would turn out nearly 300,000 airplanes, over 100,000 tanks, and 88,000 warships. America clearly earned its title, "Arsenal of Democracy."

Between 1939 and 1944, national output of goods and services nearly doubled, while federal government spending—mainly for defense—rose by more than 400 percent. By the middle of 1942, our economy reached full employment for the first time since 1929. To hold inflation in check, the government not only instituted price and wage controls but also issued ration coupons for meat, butter, gasoline, and other staples.

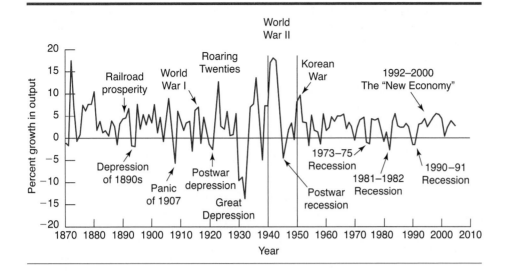

F*igure* 1

Annual Percentage Growth of U.S. Output of Goods and Services, 1870–2005

Although there were plenty of ups and downs, in most years output grew at a rate of between 2 and 5 percent. What stands out are the booms during World War I, the Roaring Twenties, the abortive recovery from the Great Depression (in the mid-1930s), World War II, and the relative prosperity since the beginning of World War II. The two sharpest declines in output occurred during the Great Depression and after World War II. The drop after World War II was entirely due to a huge cut in defense spending, but our economy quickly reconverted to producing civilian goods and services, so the 1945 recession was actually very mild.

Sources: U.S. Department of Commerce, and AmeriTrust Company, Cleveland.

During the war, 17 million new jobs were created, while the economy grew 10 or 11 percent a year. Doris Kearns Goodwin attributed "a remarkable entrepreneurial spirit" not only to the opportunity to make huge wartime profits but to a competitiveness "developed within each business enterprise to produce better than its competitors to serve the country." A sign hanging in many defense plants read: "PLEDGE TO VICTORY: The war may be won or lost in this plant."[7]

Figure 1 provides a snapshot of U.S. economic growth since 1870. You'll notice that our economy has been pretty stable since the end of World War II.

Within a year after the war ended, some 12 million men and several hundred thousand women returned home to their civilian lives. Very little housing had been built during the war and the preceding depressed period, so most veterans lived in overcrowded houses and apartments, often with three generations under one roof. The first thing veterans wanted was new housing.

The federal government obligingly facilitated this need for new housing by providing Veterans Administration (VA) mortgages at about 1 percent interest and often nothing down to returning veterans. The Federal Housing Administration (FHA) supplemented the VA program with FHA mortgages to millions of other Americans. Where were these houses built? In the suburbs. By 1945, little land was available in the cities, so suburbanization was inevitable.

The suburbanization of America

And how would these new suburbanites get to work? By car. So more highways were needed. Once again, the federal government stepped in. Before long a federally subsidized interstate highway network was being built, along with thousands of state and local highways, parkways, and freeways, as well as local streets and roads.

Hence the late 1940s and the 1950s were one big construction boom. Highway building and home construction provided millions of jobs. The automobile industry, too,

---

[7]Doris Kearns Goodwin, "The Way We Won: America's Economic Breakthrough during World War II," *The American Prospect,* Fall 1992, p. 68.

Post–World War II Recessions

Since World War II, the United States has had 10 recessions of varying length and severity. The longest was from 1973–75, but the most severe was the 1981–82 recession.

February 1945–October 1945

November 1948–October 1949

July 1953–May 1954

August 1957–April 1958

April 1960–February 1961

December 1969–November 1970

November 1973–March 1975   This one was set off by a fourfold increase in the price of oil engineered by the OPEC nations (which we'll talk a lot more about in the chapter on economic fluctuations in *Economics* and *Macroeconomics*). Simultaneously, there was a worldwide shortage of foodstuffs, which drove up food prices. To make matters worse in this country, we struck a deal to export about one-quarter of our wheat and other grains to the Soviet Union. Output fell about 5 percent, and, to make matters still worse, the rate of inflation remained unacceptably high.

January 1980–July 1980   A doubling of oil prices by OPEC and a credit crunch set off by the Federal Reserve Board of Governors, which had been alarmed by an inflation rate that had reached double-digit levels, pushed us into a very brief, but fairly sharp, recession. When interest rates rose above 20 percent, the Federal Reserve allowed credit to expand and the recession ended.

July 1981–November 1982   This downturn was also set off by the Federal Reserve, which was now determined to wring inflation out of our economy. By the end of the recession—which now held the dubious distinction of being the worst downturn since the Great Depression—the unemployment rate had reached almost 11 percent. But the inflation rate had been brought down, and in late summer 1982, the Federal Reserve once again eased credit, setting the stage for the subsequent recovery. At the same time, the federal government had been cutting income tax rates, further helping along the business upturn.

July 1990–March 1991   After the longest uninterrupted peacetime expansion in our history, a fairly mild downturn was caused by a combination of sharply rising oil prices (due to Iraq's invasion of Kuwait on August 2 and the ensuing Persian Gulf War), tight money, and a deficit-cutting budget agreement between President George Bush and Congress in October. President Bush himself termed the recovery "anemic," and its slow pace was largely responsible for his loss of the 1992 election to Bill Clinton.

March 2001–November 2001   By mid-2000, it had become apparent that many high-tech stocks in telecommunication, Internet, and computer software companies were overvalued, and consequently, investment in these industries began to sink very rapidly. Excess capacity needed to be worked off before investment would revive. What was very unusual for a recession was that consumer spending, buoyed by low interest rates, mortgage refinancing, and massive federal tax cuts, actually continued to rise throughout the recession. Then, just when recovery seemed likely, the terrorist attacks of 9/11 provided an additional economic shock, depressing the demand for air travel and hotel rooms. To counter the effects of the recession as well as to aid in the recovery from the attacks, the Bush administration pushed through Congress not only a major tax cut and tax refunds, but increased government spending. The recession was one of the mildest on record, and output began to rise in the fourth quarter of 2001.

was prospering after a total shutdown during the war. In the postwar era, we not only supplied all the new suburbanites with cars, but we also became the world's leading auto exporter.

The returning veterans had a lot of catching up to do. Couples had been forced to put off having children, but after the war the birthrate shot up and stayed high until the mid-1960s. This baby boom and low gasoline prices added impetus to the nation's suburbanization. Why continue to live in cramped urban quarters when a house in the suburbs was easily affordable, as it was to most middle-class and working-class Americans (see the box titled "Levittown, U.S.A.")?

The GI Bill of Rights

In 1944 Congress passed the GI Bill of Rights, which not only offered veterans mortgage loans, as well as loans to start businesses, but also provided monthly stipends for those who wanted help with educational costs. By 1956, when the programs ended, 7.8 million veterans, about half of all who had served, had participated. A total of 2.2 million went to college, 3.5 million to technical schools below the college level, and 700,000 to agricultural schools. The GI Bill made college affordable to men from

Levittown, U.S.A.

No man who owns his own house and lot can be
a communist.

–William Levitt–

Levittown, Long Island, a tract development of 17,000 nearly identical homes, was built right after World War II, largely for returning veterans and their families. These 800-square-foot, prefabricated homes sold for $8,000 with no down payment for veterans. William Levitt described the production process as the reverse of the Detroit assembly line:

> There, the car moved while the workers stayed at their stations. In the case of our houses, it was the workers who moved, doing the same jobs at different locations. To the best of my knowledge, no one had ever done that before.*

Levittown became the prototype of suburban tract development, and the Levitts themselves built similar developments in New Jersey, Pennsylvania, and Maryland. In 1963, civil rights demonstrations targeted William Levitt's housing development in Bowie, Maryland.

Levitt admitted he had refused to sell houses to black families, because, he said, integrating his developments would put him at a competitive disadvantage. Levitt's discriminatory sales policy was no different from most other developers, who did not relent until well into the 1960s, when government pressure forced them to do so.

Of course racism was hardly confined to developers like Levitt. James T. Patterson, a historian, wrote that the Federal Housing Administration "openly screened out applicants according to its assessment of people who were 'risks.'"[†] These were mainly blacks, Jews, and other "unharmonious racial or nationality groups." In so doing, FHA enshrined residential segregation as a public policy of the United States government.

In New York and northern New Jersey, fewer than 100 of the 67,000 mortgages insured by the GI Bill supported home purchases by nonwhites.

---

*Eric Pace, "William J. Levitt, 86, Pioneer of Suburbs, Dies," *New York Times,* January 29, 1994, p. A1.

[†]James T. Patterson, *Grand Expectations* (New York: Oxford University Press, 1997), p. 27.

---

working-class and lower-middle-class backgrounds and was almost entirely responsible for enrollments more than doubling between 1940 and 1949.

The 1950s: The Eisenhower Years

The economy was further stimulated by the advent of television in the early 1950s, as well as by the Korean War. It didn't really matter what individual consumers or the government spent their money on, as long as they spent it on something.

General Dwight D. Eisenhower, one of the great heroes of World War II, made two key promises in his 1952 campaign for the presidency: He would end the war in Korea, and he would end the inflation we had had since the close of World War II. Eisenhower made good on both promises. Although three recessions occurred during his eight years in office, economic growth, although not as fast as it had been in the 1940s, was certainly satisfactory (see the box "The Consequences of Suburbanization").

Eisenhower would end the war and end the inflation.

What may be most significant about the Eisenhower years is what *didn't* happen rather than what did. Eisenhower made no attempt to undo the legacies of the New Deal such as Social Security, unemployment insurance, or the regulatory reforms that had been instituted. The role of the federal government as a major economic player had become a permanent one. Twenty-eight years later, when President Ronald Reagan left office after having paid great lip service to "getting the government off the backs of the American people," that role had grown even greater.

The Soaring Sixties: The Years of Kennedy and Johnson

When John F. Kennedy ran for president in 1960, the country was mired in the third Eisenhower recession. Kennedy pledged to "get the country moving again." The economy *did* quickly rebound from the recession and the country embarked on an uninterrupted

The Consequences of Suburbanization

Suburbanization was the migration of tens of millions of middle-class Americans—nearly all of them white—from our nation's large central cities to newly developed suburban towns and villages. Instead of getting to work by public transportation, these commuters now went by car. Truck transport replaced railroads as the primary way to haul freight. Millions of poor people—the large majority of whom were black or Hispanic—moved into the apartments vacated by the whites who had fled to the suburbs.

Suburbanization left our cities high and dry. As middle-class taxpayers and millions of factory jobs left the cities, their tax bases shrank. There were fewer and fewer entry-level jobs for the millions of new arrivals, largely from the rural South. Throughout the 1950s, 1960s, and 1970s, a huge concentration of poor people was left in the cities as the middle-class workers—both black and white—continued to flee to the suburbs. By the mid-1970s, the inner cities were rife with poverty, drugs, and crime, and had become socially isolated from the rest of the country.

Still other consequences of suburbanization were our dependence on oil as our main source of energy and eventually, our dependence on foreign sources for more than half our oil. Indeed, America's love affair with the automobile has not only depleted our resources, polluted our air, destroyed our landscape, and clogged our highways but also has been a major factor in our imbalance of trade.*

---

*The damage we are doing to our nation's environment and to that of our planet is alarming, but discussing it goes beyond the scope of this book. However, in the chapter on international trade, we do have a lengthy discussion of our trade imbalance and how our growing oil imports have contributed to it.

---

eight-year expansion. An assassin shot Kennedy before he could complete his first term; he was succeeded by Lyndon Johnson, who in his first speech as president stated simply, "Let us continue." A major tax cut, which Kennedy had been planning, was enacted in 1964 to stimulate the economy. That and our growing involvement in the Vietnam War helped bring the unemployment rate down below 4 percent by 1966. But three major spending programs, all initiated by Johnson in 1965, have had the most profound long-term effect on the economy: Medicare, Medicaid, and food stamps.

Our rapid economic growth from the mid-1940s through the late 1960s was caused largely by suburbanization. But the great changes during this period came at a substantial price (see the box titled "The Consequences of Suburbanization"). Whatever the costs and benefits, we can agree that in just two and a half decades, this process made America a very different place from what it was at the close of World War II.

The Sagging Seventies: The Stagflation Decade

Stagnation + inflation = stagflation

The 1970s brought Americans crashing back to economic reality. In 1973, we were hit by the worst recession since the 1930s. This came on the heels of an oil price shock: The Organization of Petroleum Exporting Countries (OPEC) had quadrupled oil prices in the fall of 1973, and by then, too, we were mired in double-digit inflation, an annual rate of increase in prices of at least 10 percent. About the only good thing during this period was that we were able to add a new word to our vocabularies—*stagflation*. The first part of this word is derived from stagnation. Our rate of economic growth, which had been fairly rapid for 25 years after World War II, had slowed to a crawl. Usually when this happened, prices would stop rising or at least would slow their rate of increase. But now the opposite had happened: We had a bad case of inflation, which gave us the second part of the word *stagflation*.

Jimmy Carter's economic problems

The president who seemed to have the worst economic luck of all was Jimmy Carter. He presided over mounting budget deficits that, coupled with a rapid growth of the money supply, pushed up the inflation rate to nearly double-digit levels. And then suddenly, in 1979, the Iranian revolution set off our second oil shock. Gasoline prices went through the ceiling, rising from about 70 cents a gallon to $1.25.

Alarmed at the inflation rate, which had nearly doubled in just three years, the Federal Reserve literally stopped the growth of the money supply in October 1979. By the following January we were in another recession, while the annual rate of inflation reached 18 percent. Talk about stagflation!

The 1980s: The Age of Reagan

Ronald Reagan, who overwhelmingly defeated incumbent Jimmy Carter in the 1980 presidential election, offered the answers to our most pressing economic problems. For too long, he declared, we had allowed the federal government to "tax, tax, tax, spend, spend, spend." Big government was not the answer to our problems. Only private enterprise could provide meaningful jobs and spur economic growth. If we cut tax rates, said Reagan, people would have more incentive to work, output would rise, and inflation would subside. After all, if inflation meant that too many dollars were chasing too few goods, why not produce more goods?

This brand of economics, supply-side economics, was really the flip side of Keynesian economics. Both had the same objective: to stimulate output, or supply. The Keynesians thought the way to do this was to have the government spend more money, which, in turn, would give business firms the incentive to produce more. The supply-siders said that if tax rates were cut, people would have more of an incentive to work and would increase output.

Personal income taxes were cut by a whopping 23 percent in 1981 (stretched over a three-year period), and business taxes were also slashed. This was the heart of the supply-side program. As it happened, most of the tax cuts went to the wealthy.

In January 1981, it was Ronald Reagan's ball game to win or lose. At first he seemed to be losing. He presided over still another recession, which, by the time it ended, was the new postwar record holder, at least in terms of length and depth. The second-worst recession since World War II had been that of 1973–75. But the 1981–82 recession was a little longer and somewhat worse.

By the end of 1982, the unemployment rate reached nearly 11 percent, a rate the country had not seen since the end of the Depression. But on the upside, inflation was finally brought under control. In fact, both the inflation and unemployment rates fell during the next four years, and stagflation became just a bad memory.

Still, some very troubling economic problems surfaced during the period. The unemployment rate, which had come down substantially since the end of the 1981–82 recession, seemed stuck at around 6 percent, a rate that most economists consider to be unacceptably high. A second cause for concern were the megadeficits being run by the federal government year after year. Finally, there were the foreign trade deficits, which were getting progressively larger throughout most of the 1980s.

In 1988, George H. W. Bush, who had served as Reagan's vice president for eight years and claimed to be a convert to supply-side economics, made this famous campaign promise: "Read my lips: No new taxes." Of course, the rest is history. Bush won the election, and a couple of years later, in an effort to reduce the federal budget deficit, he agreed to a major tax increase. Not only did his words come back to haunt him when he ran for reelection in 1992, but the deficit continued to rise. And to completely ruin his party, we suffered a lingering recession that began in the summer of 1990 and from which we did not completely recover until the end of 1992, with the unemployment rate still hovering above 7 percent.

The State of American Agriculture

The story of American agriculture is the story of vastly expanding productivity. The output of farm labor doubled between 1850 and 1900, doubled again between 1900 and 1947, and doubled a third time between 1947 and 1960. In 1800 it took 370 hours to produce 100 bushels of wheat. By 1960 it took just 15 hours. In 1820 one farmer could feed 4.5 people. Today that farmer could feed about 100 people.

One of the most dramatic agricultural advances was the mechanical cotton picker, which was introduced in 1944. In an hour, a laborer could pick 20 pounds of cotton. The mechanical picker could pick one thousand pounds of cotton in the same length of time. Within just four years, millions of the Southern rural poor—both black and white—were forced off the farms and into the cities of the South, the North, and the Midwest.

While agriculture is one of the most productive sectors of our economy, only about 4.5 million people live on farms today, and less than half of them farm full time. Despite hundreds of billions of dollars in price-support payments to farmers for crops in the years since World War II, the family farm is rapidly vanishing. This is certainly ironic, since the primary purpose of these payments has been to save the family farm. During the more than seven decades that this program has been in operation, 7 out of every 10 family farms have disappeared, while three-quarters of the payments go to large corporate farms. One by one, the dairy farmers, the poultry farmers, the grain growers, and the feedlot operators are being squeezed out by the huge agricultural combines.

While we have lingering images of family farms, large farms—those with more than $250,000 in sales—now account for more than three-quarters of all agricultural sales. In the mid-1980s, their share was less than half. To keep costs down, especially when growing corn, wheat, and soybeans, a farmer needs a lot of expensive equipment and, consequently, must plant on a huge acreage.[8] In other words, you've got to become big just to survive.

Senator Dick Lugar, who owns a farm in Indiana that grows corn and soybeans, has long been a critic of huge agricultural subsidies. In a *New York Times* op-ed piece,[9] he blamed the federal government for creating and perpetuating the huge and growing mess in agriculture:

> Ineffective agricultural policy has, over the years, led to a ritual of overproduction in many crops and most certainly in the heavily supported crops of corn, wheat, cotton, rice, and soybeans and the protected speciality products like milk, sugar, and peanuts. The government has provided essentially a guaranteed income to producers of these crops. So those farmers keep producing more crops than the market wants, which keeps the price low—so low that these farmers continually ask the government for more subsidies, which they get.

The farm bill of 2002

In 2002 President George W. Bush signed a 10-year $190 billion farm bill that provides the nation's largest farmers with annual subsidies of $19 billion.[10] The law's defenders point out that the European Union gives its farmers $60 billion in annual subsidies, and that to compete in world markets, we need to keep our prices down. So what we and the Europeans are doing is subsidizing the overproduction of agricultural commodities so that we can compete against each other.

American farms are so productive that we often export more than one-third of our corn, wheat, and other crops. And yet millions of Americans go to bed hungry every night. Back in the depths of the Great Depression, hungry Americans resorted to soup kitchens for their only meals. Today some 35 million Americans make use of food pantries, soup kitchens, and other food distribution programs.

The "New Economy" of the Nineties

We've never been better off, but can America keep the party going?

—Jonathan Alter, *Newsweek,*
February 7, 2000

What exactly *is* the "new economy"? And is it really all that new? It is a period marked by major technological change, low inflation, low unemployment, and rapidly growing productivity. Certainly that is a fair description of the 1990s, but one may ask if other decades—the 1920s and the 1960s—might be similarly described. Perhaps judging the appropriateness of the term "new economy" might best be left to the economic historians of the future. But new or not new, the 1990s will surely go down in history as one of the most prosperous decades since the founding of the republic.

---

[8] The average farm has gone from 139 acres in 1910 to 435 acres today.

[9] Dick Lugar, "The Farm Bill Charade," *New York Times,* January 21, 2002, p. A15.

[10] The Environmental Working Group lists the subsidies paid to grain farmers by name and by zip code on its website. If you're interested in how much individual farmers are collecting, go to www.ewg.org, and click on Farm Subsidies and then on Farm Subsidy Database.

The new economy could trace its beginnings back to the late 1970s when the federal government began an era of deregulation, giving the market forces of supply and demand much freer reign. In the 1980s federal income tax rates were slashed, allowing Americans to keep much more of their earnings, thereby providing greater work incentives.

As the decade of the 1990s wore on, the economic picture grew steadily brighter. The federal deficit was reduced each year from 1993 through the end of the decade, by which time we were actually running budget surpluses. Inflation was completely under control, and an economic expansion that began in the spring of 1991 reached boom proportions toward the end of the decade. Optimism spread as the stock market soared, and by February 2000, the length of our economic expansion reached 107 consecutive months—an all-time record. This record would be extended to 120 months—exactly 10 years—before the expansion finally ended in March 2001.

The 1990s was the decade of computerization. In 1990 only a handful of households were on the Internet; by the end of 2000, about 40 percent were connected. Much more significant was the spread of computerization in the business world. Indeed, by the millennium there was a terminal on almost every desk. Planes, cars, factories, and stores were completely computerized. All this clearly has made the American labor force a lot more efficient. Economists, as well as ordinary civilians, believe that our rapid economic growth has been largely the result of computerization of the workplace.

California's Silicon Valley became a hotbed of entrepreneurial innovation. New companies, financed by local venture capitalists, sprang up to perform new economic roles—eBay, Amazon.com, Netscape, Google, Yahoo, and Excite! to name just a few. As these companies went public, their founders became not just millionaires, but often instant billionaires.

Back in 1941, Henry Luce, the founder of *Life Magazine,* wrote an editorial titled "The American Century." History has certainly proven Luce right. Not only had American soldiers and economic power won World Wars I and II, but we also contained communism from the mid-1940s through the 1980s. With the collapse of the Soviet Union, we were the only military and economic superpower left standing.

The American Century

Just as no man is an island, there are no longer any purely national economies. As we've seen, the United States, which began as 13 English colonies, expanded across the continent, attracted tens of millions of immigrants, and eventually became an economic superpower, importing and exporting hundreds of billions of dollars of goods and services. Over the last three decades, our economy has become increasingly integrated with the global economy.

First there was an exodus of jobs making shoes, cheap electronics, toys, and clothing to developing countries. Next to go were jobs in steel, cars, TV manufacturing, and furniture. Then simple service work like writing software code and processing credit card receipts was shifted from high-wage to low-wage countries.

Now white-collar jobs are being moved offshore. The driving forces are digitization, the Internet, and high-speed data networks that span the globe. In the 1990s, hundreds of thousands of immigrants helped ease our shortage of engineers, but now, we are sending routine service and engineering tasks to nations like India, China, and Russia where a surplus of educated workers are paid a fraction of what their American counterparts earn.

Current Issue: America's Place in History

America, America
God shed his grace on thee

–From the song, "America the Beautiful," by
Katherine Lee Bates–

In the early years of the 20th century, the United States emerged as the world's leading industrial power, with the largest economy and the largest consumer market. By the end of World War I, we had become the greatest military power as well.

Our economic and military roles grew during the next two decades, and by the close of World War II, the United States and the Soviet Union were the world's only military superpowers. Although Western Europe and Japan eventually recovered from the devastation of the war, the United States continued to be the world's largest economy. Henry Luce was certainly correct in calling the 20th century "The American Century."

At the end of that century, although some economic problems had emerged—namely our huge budget and trade deficits—we were clearly at the top of our economic game. The dot-com bubble had not yet burst, the new economy was in full flower, and most Americans were confident that the party would go on forever. Just 10 years earlier the Soviet Union had dissolved, its Eastern European empire largely allied itself with the West, and even the most ardent militarists agreed that the costly arms race was finally over. The resulting "peace dividend" enabled us to divert tens of billions of dollars a year from military spending to much more productive uses.

Back in the 19th century, the sun never set on the British Empire, but the drain of two world wars compelled the British to give up their empire. By the mid-20th century, American military bases dotted the globe, and today we have become, to a large extent, the world's policeman. Many observers believe we are overstretched both militarily and economically, and that, consequently, we will be compelled to cut back on these commitments.

Now, in the wake of the dot-com crash, the attacks on 9/11, the war in Iraq, rising budget and trade deficits, and a lagging job market, we may well wonder if the 21st, like the 20th, will be an American century. We wonder if Social Security and Medicare will even be there when we retire. And in the meanwhile, will we be able to live as well as our parents did?

I wish I could answer these questions, but as Benjamin Franklin once said, "A question is halfway to wisdom." As you continue reading, each of these questions will be raised again, and hopefully, we'll get closer to their answers.

Questions for Further Thought and Discussion

1. Describe, in as much detail as possible, the impact of the Great Depression on the lives of those who lived through it. If you know anyone who remembers the 1930s, ask him or her to describe those times.

2. What were the main agricultural developments over the last two centuries?

3. How have wars affected our economy? Use specific examples.

4. Inflation has been a persistent problem for most of the 20th century. What were some of its consequences?

5. In what ways were the 1990s like the 1920s, and in what ways were the two decades different?

6. When our country was being settled, there was an acute shortage of agricultural labor. Over the last 100 years millions of Americans have left the farms. How have we managed to feed our growing population with fewer and fewer farmers?

7. Today America has the world's largest economy as well as a very high standard of living. What factors in our economic history helped make this possible?

8. List the main ways the "new economy" (since the early 1990s) differs from the "old economy."

Workbook for Chapter 1

Name _____   Date _____

Multiple-Choice Questions

Circle the letter that corresponds to the best answer.

1. Which statement is true?
   a) Twenty-five million Americans were officially unemployed in 1933.
   b) Our economy expanded steadily from 1933 to 1945.
   c) Once the Great Depression began in 1929, our economy moved almost steadily downhill until the beginning of 1940.
   d) None of the above.

2. In the early 19th century, the United States suffered from a scarcity of _____.
   a) land and labor
   b) land—relative to labor
   c) labor—relative to land
   d) neither land nor labor

3. Which statement is false?
   a) President Eisenhower presided over three recessions.
   a) Our economy has not had an unemployment rate below 5 percent since the early 1940s.
   b) There were six straight years of economic expansion under President Reagan.
   c) None of the above. (All of the above are true.)

4. Which statement is true?
   a) There was a great deal of stagflation in the 1970s.
   b) We had full employment for most of the 1980s.
   c) We have had seven recessions since World War II.
   d) None of the above.

5. Each of the following were elements of the New Deal except _____.
   a) relief, recovery, reform
   b) a massive employment program
   c) unemployment insurance and bank deposit insurance
   d) a balanced budget

6. Which of these best describes the post-World War II recessions in the United States?
   a) They were all very mild, except for the 1981–82 recession.
   b) They were all caused by rising interest rates.
   c) None lasted more than one year.
   d) Each was accompanied by a decline in output of goods and services and an increase in unemployment.

7. At the time of the American Revolution, about _____ of every 10 Americans lived on a farm.
   a) one   c) five   e) nine
   b) three   d) seven

8. Between 1939 and 1944, federal government spending rose by more than _____.
   a) 100%   c) 300%   e) 500%
   b) 200%   d) 400%

9. Each of the following was a year of high unemployment except _____.
   a) 1933   c) 1944   e) 1982
   b) 1938   d) 1975

10. The year 2005 could be described as having had a relatively _____ unemployment rate and a relatively _____ rate of inflation.
    a) low, low   c) high, low
    b) high, high   d) low, high

11. Between 1929 and 1933, output fell _____.
    a) by about one-tenth   c) by about one-half
    b) by about one-third   d) by about two-thirds

12. The inflation rate declined during the presidency of _____.
    a) both Eisenhower and Reagan
    b) neither Eisenhower nor Reagan
    c) Reagan
    d) Eisenhower

13. Which of the following would be the most accurate description of our economy since the beginning of the new millennium?

    a) We have had virtually no economic problems.

    b) We are in the worst economic mess since the Great Depression.

    c) Aside from the federal budget deficit, we have no major economic problems.

    d) Our unemployment and inflation rates have generally been relatively low.

14. The transcontinental railroads completed in the 1860s, 1870s, and 1880s all bypassed the _____.

    a) Northeast   d) mountain states

    b) Midwest   e) Far West

    c) South

15. Compared to our economic history between 1870 and 1945, our economic history since 1945 could be considered _____.

    a) much more stable   c) much less stable

    b) about as stable

16. The longest economic expansion in our history began in _____.

    a) the spring of 1961

    b) the winter of 1982

    c) the spring of 1991

    d) the fall of 1993

17. The age of the great industrial capitalists like Carnegie, Rockefeller, and Swift was in the _____.

    a) second quarter of the 19th century

    b) third quarter of the 19th century

    c) fourth quarter of the 19th century

    d) first quarter of the 20th century

    e) second quarter of the 20th century

18. _____ completely changed the face of the United States in the 25 years following World War II.

    a) Almost constant warfare

    b) Suburbanization

    c) Welfare spending

    d) The loss of jobs to Japan, India, and China

19. Medicare and Medicaid were inaugurated under the administration of _____.

    a) Franklin D. Roosevelt

    b) Harry S. Truman

    c) Dwight D. Eisenhower

    d) John F. Kennedy

    e) Lyndon B. Johnson

20. Most of the recessions since World War II lasted _____.

    a) less than 6 months

    b) 6 to 12 months

    c) 12 to 18 months

    d) 18 to 24 months

    e) 24 to 36 months

21. Which statement is true?

    a) President Eisenhower attempted to undo most of the New Deal.

    b) There was a major tax cut in 1964.

    c) The federal budget deficit was reduced during President Lyndon Johnson's administration.

    d) None of the above.

22. There was a major tax cut in _____.

    a) both 1964 and 1981

    b) neither 1964 nor 1981

    c) 1964, but not in 1981

    d) 1981, but not 1964

23. Our economic growth began to slow markedly _____.

    a) in the early 1940s

    b) in the early 1960s

    c) in the early 1970s

    d) between 1982 and 1985

24. During World War II most of the people who got jobs in defense plants were _____ who had _____ experience building planes, tanks, and warships.

    a) men, substantial

    b) men, no

    c) women, substantial

    d) women, no

25. In the 1970s, our economy suffered from _____.
    a) inflation but not stagnation
    b) stagnation but not inflation
    c) inflation and stagnation
    d) neither inflation nor stagnation

26. There were no recessions during the administration of _____.
    a) Dwight D. Eisenhower
    b) Ronald Reagan
    c) Bill Clinton
    d) George W. Bush

27. Our longest uninterrupted economic expansion took place mainly in the decade of the _____.
    a) 1940s   c) 1960s   e) 1980s
    b) 1950s   d) 1970s   f) 1990s

28. In the 1990s our economy has generated more than _____ million additional jobs.
    a) 5   b) 10   c) 15   d) 20

29. Compared to today, in 1945, _____.
    a) our economy was plagued by high unemployment and slow economic growth
    b) we faced much greater competition from our economic rivals in Europe and Asia
    c) we were a much more dominant global economic power
    d) we accounted for almost one-quarter of the world's manufacturing output and slightly more than one-third of its output of automobiles

30. Which statement is the most accurate?
    a) The South had some very substantial economic grievances against the North in the years immediately preceding the Civil War.
    b) The South seceded from the Union when President Lincoln proclaimed that he was freeing the slaves.
    c) Aside from slavery, southern and northern agriculture were very similar.
    d) Most of the nation's industries were relocated from the North and Midwest to the South in the years immediately following the Civil War.

31. The massive shift of population and industry out of the large central cities from the late 1940s through the 1960s was caused by _____.
    a) wars
    b) the mechanization of agriculture
    c) suburbanization
    d) immigration
    e) fear of nuclear war

32. Each of the following was a major contributing factor to suburbanization except _____.
    a) low-interest federal loans
    b) a federal highway building program
    c) the pent-up demand for housing
    d) the baby boom
    e) federal subsidies for public transportation

33. Which statement is true?
    a) Subsidy payments to farmers were almost completely phased out in 2005.
    b) The so-called new economy of the 1990s was neither new, nor very different from the economy of the previous 25 years.
    c) Until the time of the Great Depression, the United States was primarily an agricultural nation.
    d) There were no recessions during the presidency of Bill Clinton (January 1993–January 2001).

34. Who made this statement? "Once upon a time my opponents honored me as possessing the fabulous intellectual and economic power by which I created a worldwide depression all by myself."
    a) Franklin D. Roosevelt
    b) Herbert Hoover
    c) John F. Kennedy
    d) Ronald Reagan
    e) Bill Clinton

35. Which statement is the most accurate?
   a) The 21st century will almost definitely be another "American Century."
   b) The 21st, rather than the 20th, will be called "The American Century."
   c) The 21st century will definitely not be an "American Century."
   d) Although we got off to a rocky start, this century may well turn out to be another "American Century."

36. Our most rapid job growth was in the period from _____.
   a) 2000 to 2005
   b) 1995 to 2000
   c) 1978 to 1983
   d) 1953 to 1958

Fill-In Questions

1. The low point of the Great Depression was reached in the year _____.

2. In 1790, about _____ of every 10 Americans lived on farms.

3. The worst recession we had since World War II occurred in _____.

4. The country with the world's largest output is _____.

5. In 1933, our official unemployment rate was _____ %.

6. Bills providing for Medicare and Medicaid were passed during the administration of President _____.

7. Today one American farmer feeds about _____ people.

8. During President Dwight D. Eisenhower's two terms, there were _____ recessions.

9. Rapid technological change in agriculture during the first half of the 19th century was brought on mainly by _____.

10. The main factor in finally bringing us out of the Great Depression was _____.

11. Since the end of World War II there have been _____ recessions.

12. The quarter century that was completely dominated by the great industrialists like Andrew Carnegie and John D. Rockefeller began in the year _____.

13. Passage of the _____ in 1944 enabled nearly 8 million veterans to go to school.

14. The _____ century was termed "The American Century."

Chapter 2

Resource Utilization

conomics is defined in various ways, but scarcity is always part of the definition. We bake an economic pie each year, which is composed of all the goods and services we have produced. No matter how we slice it, there never seems to be enough. Some people feel the main problem is how we slice the pie, while others say we should concentrate on baking a larger pie.

CHAPTER OBJECTIVES

In this chapter you'll learn:

- The definition of economics.
- The central fact of economics.
- The four economic resources.
- The concepts of full employment, full production, and underemployment.

- Productive efficiency.
- What enables an economy to grow.
- The law of increasing costs.
- The concept of opportunity cost.

Economics Defined

Economics is the efficient allocation of the scarce means of production toward the satisfaction of human wants. You're probably thinking, What did he say? Let's break it down into two parts. The scarce means of production are our resources, which we use to produce all the goods and services we buy. And why do we buy these goods and services? Because they provide us with satisfaction.

The only problem is that we don't have enough resources to produce all the goods and services we desire. Our resources are limited while our wants are relatively unlimited. In the next few pages, we'll take a closer look at the concepts of resources, scarcity, and the satisfaction of human wants. Keep in mind that we can't produce everything we'd like to purchase—there's scarcity. This is where economics comes in. We're attempting to make the best of a less-than-ideal situation. We're trying to use our resources so efficiently that we can maximize our satisfaction. Or, as François Quesnay put it back in the 18th century, "To secure the greatest amount of pleasure with the least possible outlay should be the aim of all economic effort."[1]

Economics is the efficient allocation of the scarce means of production toward the satisfaction of human wants.

Economics is the science of greed.

—F. V. Meyer

---
[1]François Quesnay, *Dialogues sur les Artisans,* quoted in Gide and Rist, *A History of Economic Doctrines,* 1913, pp. 10–11.

23

The Central Fact of Economics: Scarcity

Scarcity and the Need to Economize

He who will not economize will have to agonize.

—Confucius

Most of us are used to economizing; we save up our scarce dollars and deny ourselves various tempting treasures so we will have enough money for that one big-ticket item—a new car, a sound system, a trip to Europe. Since our dollars are scarce and we can't buy everything we want, we economize by making do with some lower-priced items—a Cadillac instead of a Rolls Royce, chicken instead of steak, a video rental instead of a neighborhood movie.

If there were no scarcity, we would not need to economize.

If there were no scarcity, we would not need to economize, and economists would have to find other work. Let's go back to our economic pie to see how scarcity works. Most people tend to see scarcity as not enough dollars, but as John Maynard Keynes[2] pointed out more than 70 years ago, this is an illusion. We could print all the money we want and still have scarcity. As Adam Smith noted in 1776, the wealth of nations consists of the goods and services they produce, or, on another level, the resources—the *land, labor, capital,* and *entrepreneurial ability*—that actually produce these goods and services.

John Kenneth Galbraith, American economist and social critic (UPI/Bettmann)

Our necessities are few but our wants are endless.

—Inscription found in a fortune cookie

The Economic Problem

In the 1950s, John Kenneth Galbraith coined the term *the affluent society,* which implied that we had the scarcity problem licked. Americans were the richest people in the world. Presumably, we had conquered poverty. But within a few years, Michael Harrington's *The Other America*[3] challenged that contention.

The economic problem, however, goes far beyond ending poverty. Even then, nearly all Americans would be relatively poor when they compared what they have with what they would like to have—or with what the Waltons, Gateses, Buffetts, Allens, and Ellisons have.

Human wants are relatively limitless. Make a list of all the things you'd like to have. Now add up their entire cost. Chances are you couldn't earn enough in a lifetime to even begin to pay for all the things on your list.

The Four Economic Resources

We need four resources, often referred to as "the means of production," to produce an output of goods and services. Every society, from a tiny island nation in the Pacific to the most complex industrial giant, needs these resources: *land, labor, capital,* and *entrepreneurial ability.* Let's consider each in turn.

Land

As a resource, land has a much broader meaning than our normal understanding of the word. It includes natural resources (such as timber, oil, coal, iron ore, soil, and water) as well as the ground in which these resources are found. Land is used not only for the extraction of minerals but for farming as well. And, of course, we build factories, office buildings, shopping centers, and homes on land. The basic payment made to the owners of land is rent.

Labor

Labor is the work and time for which employees are paid. The police officer, the computer programmer, the store manager, and the assembly-line worker all supply labor. About two-thirds of the total resource costs are paid to labor in the form of wages and salaries.

Capital

Capital is "man"-made goods used to produce other goods or services. It consists mainly of plant and equipment. The United States has more capital than any other country in the world. This capital consists of factories, office buildings, and stores. Our shopping

---

[2]Keynes, whose work we'll discuss in later chapters of *Economics* and *Macroeconomics,* was perhaps the greatest economist of the 20th century.

[3]Michael Harrington, *The Other America* (New York: Macmillan, 1962).

malls, the Empire State Building, and automobile plants and steel mills (and all the equipment in them) are examples of capital. The return paid to the owners of capital is interest.

Entrepreneurial ability is the least familiar of our four basic resources. The entrepreneur sets up a business, assembles the needed resources, risks his or her own money, and reaps the profits or absorbs the losses of this enterprise. Often the entrepreneur is an innovator, such as Andrew Carnegie (U.S. Steel), John D. Rockefeller (Standard Oil), Henry Ford (Ford Motor Company), Steven Jobs (Apple Computer), Bill Gates (Microsoft), and Sam Walton (Wal-Mart).

Entrepreneurial ability

We may consider land, labor, and capital passive resources, which are combined by the entrepreneur to produce goods and services. A successful undertaking is rewarded by profit; an unsuccessful one is penalized by loss.

In the American economy, the entrepreneur is the central figure, and our long record of economic success is an eloquent testimonial to the abundance of our entrepreneurial talents. The owners of the nearly 30 million businesses in this country are virtually all entrepreneurs. The vast majority either work for themselves or have just one or two employees. But they have two things in common: Each runs a business, and each risks his or her own money.

Sometimes entrepreneurs cash in on inventions—their own or someone else's. Alexander Graham Bell and Thomas Edison were two of the more famous inventors who *did* parlay their inventions into great commercial enterprises. As you know, tens of billions of dollars were earned by the founders of America Online, Amazon, eBay, Yahoo!, Google, and the thousands of other so-called dot-coms when they went public. These folks were all entrepreneurs. But have you ever heard of Tim Berners-Lee, the creator of the World Wide Web? Berners-Lee worked long and hard to ensure that the Web remained a public mass medium in cyberspace, an information thoroughfare open to all. He came up with the software standards for addressing, linking, and transferring multimedia documents over the Internet. And most amazing, Tim Berners-Lee did not try to cash in on his years of work.

Is this man an entrepreneur? Clearly he is not. He is an inventor of the first rank—like Bell and Edison—but the act of invention is not synonymous with being an entrepreneur.

Perhaps nothing more typifies American entrepreneurial talent than the Internet, which *The New York Times* termed the "Net Americana." Steve Lohr observed that "all ingredients that contribute to the entrepreneurial climate in the United States—venture capital financing, close ties between business and universities, flexible labor markets, a deregulated business environment, and a culture that celebrates risk-taking, ambition and getting very, very rich"—fostered the formation of the Internet.[4]

What factors explain why so many of the world's greatest innovations have originated in the United States? Thomas Friedman produces a summation:

> America is the greatest engine of innovation that has ever existed, and it can't be duplicated anytime soon, because it is the product of a multitude of factors: extreme freedom of thought, an emphasis on independent thinking, a steady immigration of new minds, a risk-taking culture with no stigma attached to trying and failing, a noncorrupt bureaucracy, and financial markets and a venture capital system that are unrivaled at taking new ideas and turning them into global products.[5]

Resources are scarce because they are limited in quantity. There's a finite amount of land on this planet, and at any given time a limited amount of labor, capital, and entrepreneurial ability is available. Over time, of course, the last three resources can be increased.

---

[4]Steve Lohr, "Welcome to the Internet, the First Global Colony," *New York Times,* January 9, 2000, Section 4, p. 1.

[5]Thomas Friedman, "The Secret of Our Sauce," *New York Times,* March 7, 2004, Section 4, p. 13.

Our economic problem, then, is that we have limited resources available to satisfy relatively unlimited wants. The reason why you, and everyone else, can't have three cars, a town house and a country estate with servants, designer clothing, jewelry, big screen TVs in each room, and a $50,000 sound system is that we just don't have enough resources to produce everything that everyone wants. Therefore, we have to make choices, an option we call opportunity cost.

Opportunity Cost

There was an accounting professor nicknamed "the phantom," who used to dash from his last class to his car, and speed off to his office. During tax season, he was almost never seen on campus, and certainly not during his office hours. One day a student managed to catch him in the parking lot. Big mistake. As he climbed into his car, the professor asked scornfully, "Do you realize how much money you're costing me?"

Unknowingly, the phantom was illustrating the concept of opportunity cost. "Every minute I waste answering your questions could be spent in my office earning money. So if I spend five minutes with you, that just cost me $10." Perhaps if the student had handed him a ten dollar bill, he could have bought a few minutes of his professor's time.

Because we can't have everything we want, we must make choices. The thing we give up (that is, our second choice) is called the opportunity cost of our choice. Therefore, *the opportunity cost of any choice is the forgone value of the next best alternative.*

Suppose a little boy goes into a toy store with $15. Many different toys tempt him, but he finally narrows his choice to a Monopoly game and a magic set, each costing $15. If he decides to buy the Monopoly game, the opportunity cost is the magic set. And if he buys the magic set, the opportunity cost is the Monopoly game.

If a town hires an extra police officer instead of repaving several streets, the opportunity cost of hiring the officer is not repaving the streets. Opportunity cost is the cost of giving up the next best alternative.

In some cases the next best alternative—the Monopoly game or the magic set—is virtually equal no matter what choice is made. In other cases, there's no contest. If someone were to offer you, at the same price, your favorite eight-course meal or a Big Mac, you'd have no trouble deciding (unless, of course, your favorite meal *is* a Big Mac).

What is the opportunity cost of the war in Iraq? Because the conduct of the war costs taxpayers about $5 billion a month, the opportunity cost of the war is how that $5 billion a month might have otherwise been spent. Possibilities include reducing the federal budget deficit, a tax cut, more students loans, research for a cure for breast cancer, and a high speed rail system between pairs of major cities.

Today, as we all know, people are living longer. This has set the stage for an ongoing generational conflict over how much of our resources should be devoted to Medicare, Social Security, nursing homes, and old age homes, and how much to child care, Head Start, and, in general, education. If we are to be a humane society, we must take care of our aging population. But if our economy is to be competitive in the global economy, we need to devote more dollars to education.

What are some of the opportunity costs *you* have incurred? What is the opportunity cost of attending college? Owning a car? Or even buying this economics text? There's even an opportunity cost of studying for an exam. How would you have otherwise spent those precious hours?

Full Employment and Full Production

Everyone agrees that full employment is a good thing, even if we don't all agree on exactly what full employment means. Does it mean that every single person in the United States who is ready, willing, and able to work has a job? Is *that* full employment?

Margin notes:

The opportunity cost of any choice is the forgone value of the next best alternative.

Even children learn in growing up that "both" is not an admissible answer to a choice of "which one?"
—President Warren G. Harding

The answer is no. There will always be some people between jobs. On any given day thousands of Americans quit, get fired, or decide that they will enter the labor force by finding a job. Since it may take several weeks, or even several months, until they find the "right" job, there will always be some people unemployed.

If an unemployment rate of zero does not represent full employment, then what rate does? Economists cannot agree on what constitutes full employment. Some liberals insist that an unemployment rate of 4 percent constitutes full employment, while there are conservatives who feel that an unemployment rate of 6 percent would be more realistic.

If economists were laid end to end, they would not reach a conclusion.
—George Bernard Shaw

Similarly, we cannot expect to fully use all our plant and equipment. A capacity utilization rate of 85 or 90 percent would surely employ virtually all of our usable plant and equipment. At any given moment there is always some factory being renovated or some machinery under repair. During wartime we might be able to use our capacity more fully, but in normal times 85 to 90 percent is the peak.

In a global economy, not only has it become increasingly difficult to define which goods and services are made in America and which originate abroad, but one may even question the relevance of a plant's location. If our steel industry were operating at full capacity, we could get still more steel from Germany, Japan, Korea, Brazil, and other steel-producing nations. In the context of the global economy, our capacity utilization ratio is clearly much less important than it was just a few decades ago.

As long as all available resources are fully used—given the constraints we have just cited—we are at our production possibilities frontier. A few additional constraints should also be considered because they too restrict the quantity of resources available. These are institutional constraints, the laws and customs under which we live.

The so-called blue laws restrict the economic activities that may be carried out in various cities and states, mainly on Sundays. Bars and liquor stores must be closed certain hours. In some places, even retail stores must be closed on Sundays.

State and federal law carefully restricts child labor. Very young children may not be employed at all, and those below a certain age may work only a limited number of hours.

Traditionally, Americans dislike working at night or on weekends, particularly on Sundays. Consequently, we must leave most of our expensive plant and equipment idle except during daylight weekday hours. We don't consider that plant and equipment unemployed, nor do we consider those whose labor is restricted by law or custom unemployed. All of this is already allowed for in our placement of the location of the production possibilities frontier (shown in Figure 1 in the next section).

By full production, we mean that our nation's resources are being allocated in the most efficient manner possible. Not only are we using our most up-to-date technology, but we are using our land, labor, capital, and entrepreneurial ability in the most productive way.

Full production: Our nation's resources are being allocated in the most efficient manner possible.

We would not want to use the intersection of Fifth Avenue and 57th Street in Manhattan for dairy farming, nor would we want our M.D.s doing clerical work. But sometimes we do just that.

Until very recently in our history blacks, Hispanics, and women were virtually excluded from nearly all high-paying professions. Of course, this entailed personal hurt and lost income; this discrimination also cost our nation in lost output. In the sports world, until 1947, when Brooklyn Dodger owner Branch Rickey defied baseball's "color line" and signed Jackie Robinson for the team, major league baseball was played by whites only (see box, "The Jackie Robinson Story"). At that time, only a tiny handful of Hispanic players were tolerated. Today there are several black and Hispanic players on every team. Today, professional basketball would hardly be described as a "white man's sport." Nor, for that matter, would the National Football League be accused of discrimination, at least at the level of player personnel. But until the late 1940s, blacks were almost entirely banned from those professional sports.

Employment discrimination

As late as the 1950s, only a few stereotypical roles were available to blacks in the movies and on TV. And, except for Desi Arnaz (Ricky Ricardo of "I Love Lucy"),

The Jackie Robinson Story

Blacks had always been banned from professional sports, but most notoriously by the "American sport"—major league baseball. For decades there was a parallel association for blacks called the Negro leagues. Finally, the color barrier was broken in 1947 when Jackie Robinson began playing for the Brooklyn Dodgers.

Looking back, then, to all those years when black ballplayers were not permitted to play major league baseball (and basketball and football), we see that hundreds of athletes were underemployed. Not only did they suffer economically and psychologically, but the American public was deprived of watching innumerable talented athletes perform.

Jackie Robinson
(Bettmann/CORBIS)

In 1991 I met a few of the men who played in the Negro leagues when I was visiting Kansas City, where the Negro League Baseball Museum is located. They all knew Satchel Paige, a legendary pitcher whose fastball was so fast, the batters often couldn't even see it, let alone hit it. Sometimes Paige would wind up and pretend to throw a pitch. The catcher pounded his glove and the umpire called a strike. Then the catcher, who had the ball all along, threw it back to Paige. As great as he was, Satchel Paige didn't play in the major leagues until the twilight of his career, when he was in his late forties.

there were virtually no Hispanic Americans in these entertainment media. That was America not all that long ago, when employment discrimination was the rule, not the exception.

Until recently only a tiny minority of women employed in the offices of American business were not typists or secretaries. In the 1950s and even into the 1960s, virtually every article in *Fortune* was written by a man and researched by a woman. What a waste of labor potential!

I can still picture one ad that appeared in several business magazines back in the 1950s. Four or five young women were on their knees on an office carpet sorting through piles of papers. This was an advertisement for a collator. The caption read, "When your office collator breaks down, do the girls have to stay late for a collating party?"

This ad said a great deal about those times. Forget about political correctness! Every woman (but almost no men) applying for office jobs was asked, "How fast can you type?" because those were virtually the only jobs open to women in corporate America—even to college graduates. Typing, filing, and other clerical positions were considered "women's work." The high-paying and high-status executive positions were reserved for men. So when the collator broke down, it seemed perfectly logical to ask the "girls" to stay late for a "collating party."

These are just a few of the most blatant examples of employment discrimination, a phenomenon that has diminished but has not yet been wiped out. Employment discrimination automatically means that we will have less than full production because we are not efficiently allocating our labor. In other words, there are millions of Americans who really should be doctors, engineers, corporate executives, or whatever but have been condemned to less exalted occupations solely because they happen not to be white Protestant males.

But, in the words of Bob Dylan, "the times, they are a' changin'." The civil rights revolution of the 1960s and the women's liberation movement a decade later did bring millions of blacks and women into the economic mainstream. Elite business schools began admitting large numbers of women in the mid-1970s, and today there are hundreds of women occupying the executive suites of our major corporations.

Perhaps the most visible evidence of the employment advances of minorities and women may be seen in President George W. Bush's cabinet. We have certainly come a long way since President Franklin Roosevelt appointed Labor Secretary Frances Perkins as the first woman cabinet member in history, and, some three decades later, when President Lyndon Johnson made Housing Secretary Warren Weaver the first black cabinet member. It would be a fair description to say that the Bush Administration represents the face of America a whole lot better than those of presidential administrations just one generation ago.

Finally, there is the question of using the best available technology. Historically, the American economy has been on the cutting edge of technological development for almost 200 years; the sewing machine, mechanical reaper, telephone, airplane, automobile, assembly line, and computer are all American inventions.

Using the best technology

Now it's the computer software industry. Not only are we on the cutting edge in this rapidly expanding industry, but we produce and export more software than the rest of the world combined. Microsoft, Cisco, Oracle, and a host of other American companies are household names not just in the United States but all across the globe.

We need to tie up one more loose end before moving on to the main focus of this chapter, the production possibilities frontier. We need to be clear about distinguishing between less than full employment and underemployment of resources.

Full employment and underemployment

If we are using only 70 percent of our capacity of plant and equipment, as we do during some recessions, this would be a case of our economy operating at less than full employment of its resources. Anything less than, say, an 85 percent utilization rate would be considered below full employment.

More familiarly, when the unemployment rate is, say, 10 percent, there is clearly a substantial amount of labor unemployed. But how much *is* full employment? We never really answered that one.

As a working definition, we'll say that an unemployment rate of 5 percent represents full employment. Why not use 4 percent, as the liberal economists suggest, or the 6 percent figure favored by the conservatives? Because 5 percent represents a reasonable compromise. So we'll be working with that figure from here on, but keep in mind that not everyone agrees that a 5 percent unemployment rate represents full employment.

Unemployment means that not all our resources are being used. Less than 95 percent of our labor force is working, and less than 85 percent of our plant and equipment is being used. It also means that our land and entrepreneurial ability are not all being used.

What is underemployment of resources? To be at full production, not only would we be fully employing our resources, we would also be using them in the most efficient way possible. To make all women become schoolteachers, social workers, or secretaries would grossly underuse their talents. Equally absurd—and inefficient—would be to make all white males become doctors or lawyers and all black and Hispanic males become accountants or computer programmers.

Similarly, we would not want to use that good Iowa farmland for office parks, and we would not want to locate dairy farms in the middle of our cities' central business districts. And finally, we would certainly not want to use our multimillion-dollar computer mainframes to do simple word processing.

These are all examples of underemployment of resources. Unfortunately, a certain amount of underemployment is built into our economy, but we need to reduce it if we are going to succeed in baking a larger economic pie.

The production possibilities frontier represents our economy at full employment and full production.

This brings us, at long last, to the production possibilities curve. As we've already casually mentioned, the production possibilities frontier represents our economy at full employment and full production. However, a certain amount of underemployment of resources is built into our model. How much? Although the exact amount is not quantifiable, it is fairly large. But to the degree that employment discrimination has declined since the early 1960s, underemployment of resources may still be holding our output to 10 or 15 percent below what it would be if there were a truly efficient allocation of resources.

The Production Possibilities Curve

Since scarcity is a fact of economic life, we need to use our resources as efficiently as possible. If we succeed, we are operating at full economic capacity. Usually there's some economic slack, but every so often we *do* manage to operate at peak efficiency. When this happens, we are on our production possibilities frontier (or production possibilities curve).

Often economics texts cast the production possibilities curve in terms of guns and butter. A country is confronted with two choices: It can produce only military goods or only civilian goods. The more guns it produces, the less butter and, of course, vice versa.

If we were to use all our resources—our land, labor, capital, and entrepreneurial ability—to make guns, we would obviously not be able to make butter at all. Similarly, if we made only butter, there would be no resources to make any guns. Virtually every country makes *some* guns and *some* butter. Japan makes relatively few military goods, while the United States devotes a much higher proportion of its resources to making guns.

You are about to encounter the second graph in this book. This graph, and each one that follows, will have a vertical axis and a horizontal axis. Both axes start at the origin of the graph, which is located in the lower left-hand corner and usually marked with the number 0.

In Figure 1 we measure units of butter on the vertical axis. On the horizontal axis we measure units of guns. As we move to the right, the number of guns increases—1, 2, 3, 4, 5.

The curve shown in the graph is drawn by connecting points A, B, C, D, E, and F. Where do these points come from? They come from Table 1. Where did we get the numbers in Table 1? They're hypothetical. In other words, I made them up.

Table 1 shows six production possibilities ranging from point A, where we produce 15 units of butter and no guns, to point F, where we produce 5 units of guns but no butter. This same information is presented in Figure 1, a graph of the production possibilities curve. We'll begin at point A, where a country's entire resources are devoted to producing butter. If the country were to produce at full capacity (using all its resources) but wanted to make some guns, they could do it by shifting some resources away from butter. This would move them from point A to point B. Instead of producing 15 units of butter, they're making only 14.

Guns and butter

Figure 1

Production Possibilities Curve
This curve shows the range of possible combinations of outputs of guns and butter extending from 15 units of butter and no guns at point A to 5 units of guns and no butter at point F.

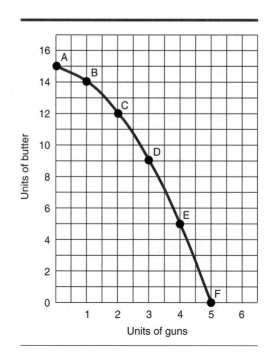

TABLE 1	Hypothetical Production Schedule for Two-Product Economy	
Point	Units of Butter	Unit of Guns
A	15	0
B	14	1
C	12	2
D	9	3
E	5	4
F	0	5

Before we go any further on the curve, let's go over the numbers at points A and B. We're figuring out how many guns and how much butter are produced at each of these points. Starting at the origin, or zero, let's check out point A. It's directly above the origin, so no guns are produced. Point A is at 15 on the vertical scale, so 15 units of butter are produced.

Now we'll move on to point B, which is directly above 1 unit on the guns axis. At B we produce 1 unit of guns and 14 units of butter (shown vertically). Incidentally, to locate any point on a graph, first go across, or horizontally, then up, or vertically. Point B is 1 unit to the right, then 14 units up.

Now locate point C: 2 units across and 12 up. At C we have 2 guns and 12 butters. Next is D: 3 across and 9 up (3 guns and 9 butters). At E: 4 across and 5 up (4 guns and 5 butters). And finally F: 5 across and 0 up (5 guns and no butter).

The production possibilities curve is a hypothetical model of an economy that produces only two products—in this case, guns and butter (or military goods and civilian goods). The curve represents the various possible combinations of guns and butter that could be produced if the economy were operating at capacity, or full employment.

The production possibilities curve represents a two-product economy at full employment.

Since we usually do not operate at full employment, we are seldom on the production possibilities frontier. So let's move on to Figure 2, which shows, at point X, where we generally are. Sometimes we are in a recession, with unemployment rising beyond 8 or 9 percent, represented on the graph by point Y. A depression would be closer to the origin, perhaps shown by point Z. (Remember that the origin is located in the lower left-hand corner of the graph.)

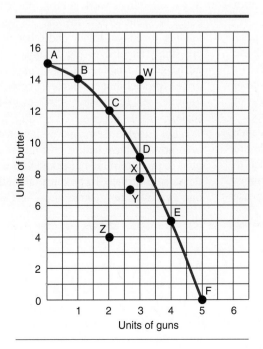

Figure 2

Points Inside and Outside the Production Possibilities Curve
Since the curve represents output of guns and butter at full employment, points X, Y, and Z, which lie inside or below the curve, represent output at less than full employment. Similarly, point W represents output at more than full employment and is currently unattainable.

The Law of Increasing Costs

The production possibilities curve below reproduces Table A. You may notice that, as we shift production from guns to butter, we have to give up increasing units of guns for each additional unit of butter. Or, shifting the other way, we would have to give up increasing units of butter for each additional unit of guns we produce.

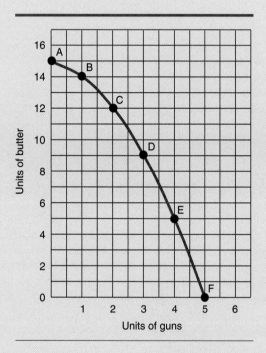

Note that as you move from A to B you produce an extra gun at the expense of 1 unit of butter, but when you move from E to F, you produce an extra gun at the expense of 5 units of butter.

We will be calling this "the law of increasing costs." Stated formally, this law says that *as the output of one good expands, the opportunity cost of producing additional units of this good increases*. In other words, as more and more of a good is produced, the production of additional units of this good will entail larger and larger opportunity costs.

The law of increasing costs is based on three concepts: (1) the law of diminishing returns, (2) diseconomies of scale, and (3) factor suitability. We've already alluded to factor suitability when we talked about using our resources in the most efficient way possible. One example was to use

our computer mainframe for sophisticated data analysis rather than for simple word processing.

The law of diminishing returns, which we'll take up more formally in a later chapter, is defined this way: *If units of a resource are added to a fixed proportion of other resources, eventually marginal output will decline*. Suppose one farmer working with one tractor can produce 100 bushels of wheat on one acre of land. Two farmers, working together, can produce 220 bushels. And three, working together, can produce 350.

The marginal output of the first farmer is 100. (In other words, the first farmer added 100 bushels to output.) The marginal output of the second farmer is 120. And the marginal output of the third farmer is 130. So far, so good. We call this increasing returns.

If we keep adding farmers, do you think we'll continue to enjoy increasing returns? Won't that single acre of land start getting a little crowded? Will that one tractor be sufficient for four, five, and six farmers? Suppose we did add a fourth farmer and suppose output rose from 350 to 450. By how much did marginal output rise?

It rose by only 100. So marginal output, which had been rising by 120 and 130, has now fallen to 100. We call this diminishing returns.

Diseconomies of scale is a new term. As a business firm grows larger, it can usually cut its costs by taking advantage of quantity discounts, the use of expensive but highly productive equipment, and the development of a highly specialized and highly skilled workforce. We call these *economies of scale*. But as the firm continues to grow, these economies of scale are eventually outweighed by the inefficiencies of managing a bloated bureaucracy, which might sometimes work at cross-purposes. Most of the day could be spent writing memos, answering memos, and attending meetings. Labor and other resources become increasingly expensive, and not only are quantity discounts no longer available, but now suppliers charge premium prices for such huge orders. As costs begin to rise, diseconomies of scale have now overcome economies of scale.*

Let's look at some increasing costs. We have already seen how we have had to give up the production of some guns to produce more butter and vice versa. We'll now take this a step further. To produce additional units of guns—one gun, two guns, three guns—we will have to give up

Table A   Production Shifts from Butter to Guns

Shift from Point to Point	Change in Gun Production	Change in Butter Production
A to B	+1	−1
B to C	+1	−2
C to D	+1	−3
D to E	+1	−4
E to F	+1	−5

increasing amounts of butter. Similarly, to produce additional units of butter, we will have to give up increasing numbers of guns.

How many units of butter would we have to give up to produce each additional gun? This is shown in the table above, which is derived from the figure in this box, or, if you prefer, from Table 1 earlier in this chapter.

In the table above, as we begin to switch from butter to guns, we move from point A to point B. We give up just one unit of butter in exchange for one unit of guns. But the move from B to C isn't as good. Here we give up two butters for one gun. C to D is still worse: We give up three butters for one gun. D to E is even worse: We give up four units of butter for one gun. And the worst trade-off of all is from E to F: We lose five butters for just one gun.

This is why we call it the law of increasing relative costs. To produce more and more of one good, we have to give up increasing amounts of another good. To produce each additional gun, we have to give up increasing amounts of butter.

There are three explanations for the law of increasing relative costs. First, there's diminishing returns. If we're increasing gun production, we will need more and more resources—more land, more labor, more capital, and more entrepreneurial ability. But one or more of these resources may be relatively limited. Perhaps we will begin to run out of capital—plant and equipment—or perhaps entrepreneurial ability will run out first.

Go back to our definition of the law of diminishing returns. *If units of a resource are added to a fixed proportion of other resources, eventually marginal output will decline.* Had we been talking about farming rather than producing guns, the law of diminishing returns might

have set in as increasing amounts of capital were applied to the limited supply of rich farmland.

A second explanation for the law of increasing costs is diseconomies of scale. By shifting from butter to guns, the firm or firms making guns will grow so large that diseconomies of scale will eventually set in.

The third explanation, factor suitability, requires more extensive treatment here. We'll start at point A of Table A where we produce 15 units of butter and no guns. As we move to point B, gun production goes up by one, while butter production goes down by only one. In other words, the opportunity cost of producing one unit of guns is the loss of only one unit of butter.

Why is the opportunity cost so low? The answer lies mainly with factor suitability. We'll digress for a moment with the analogy of a pickup game of basketball. The best players are picked first, then the not-so-good ones, and finally the worst. If a couple of players from one side have to go home, the game goes on. The other side gives them their worst player.

If we're shifting from butter to guns, the butter makers will give the gun makers their worst workers. But people who are bad at producing butter are not necessarily bad at making—or shooting—guns.

When all we did was make butter, people worked at that no matter what their other skills. Even if a person were a skilled gun maker, or a gun user, what choice did he have? Presumably, then, when given the choice to make guns, those best suited for that occupation (and also poorly suited for butter making) would switch to guns.

As resources are shifted from butter to guns, the labor, land, capital, and entrepreneurial ability best suited to guns and least suited to butter will be the first to switch. But as more resources are shifted, we will be taking resources that were more and more suited to butter making and less and less suited to gun making.

Take land, for example. The first land given over to gun making might be terrible for raising cows (and hence milk and butter) but great for making guns. Eventually, however, as nearly all land was devoted to gun making, we'd be giving over fertile farmland that might not be well suited to gun production.

---

*Economies and diseconomies of scale are more fully discussed in a later chapter.

Finding the Opportunity Cost

Figure A shows us how many apples and oranges we can produce. The more apples we produce, the fewer oranges we can produce. Similarly, the more oranges we produce, the fewer apples we can produce.

Opportunity cost tells us what we must give up. So if we increase our production of oranges by moving from point B to point C, how many apples are we giving up?

We are giving up 1 apple. Next question: If we move from point F to point D, how many oranges are we giving up?

We are giving up 2 oranges. Now, let's take it up a notch. What is the opportunity cost of moving from A to D?

It's 3 apples, because at point A we produced 5 apples, but at point D we're producing only 2. One more question: What is the opportunity cost of moving from E to B?

It's 6 oranges, because at E we produced 10 oranges and at B, only 4.

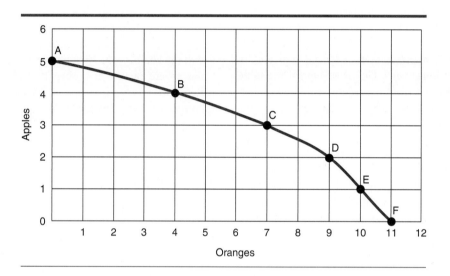

Figure A

What if we were at the origin? What would that represent? Think about it. What would be the production of guns? How about the production of butter? They would both be zero. Is that possible? During the Great Depression in the 1930s, the U.S. economy sank to point Z, but no economy has ever sunk to the origin.

Move back to the production possibilities curve, say, at point C, where we are producing 2 units of guns and 12 units of butter. Is it possible to produce more guns? Certainly. Just move down the curve to point D. Notice, however, that we now produce fewer units of butter.

At D we have 3 units of guns and 9 units of butter. When we go from C, where we have 2 guns, to D, where we have 3, gun production goes up by 1. But at the same time, butter production declines from 12 at C to only 9 at D (a decline of 3).

If we're at point C, then, we can produce more guns, but only by sacrificing some butter production. The opportunity cost of moving from C to D (that is, of producing 1 more gun) is giving up 3 units of butter.

Let's try another one, this time moving from C to B. Butter goes up from 12 to 14—a gain of 2. Meanwhile, guns go down from 2 to 1, a loss of 1. Going from C to B, a gain of 2 butters is obtained by sacrificing 1 gun. The opportunity cost of producing 2 more butters is 1 gun. If you need a little more practice, please work your way through the accompanying box.

Except at point A, we can go somewhere else on the production possibilities curve and increase our output of butter. Similarly, anywhere but at point F, we can go somewhere else on the curve and raise our output of guns. It is possible to increase our output of *either* guns *or* butter by moving somewhere else on the curve, but there is an opportunity cost involved. The more we produce of one (by moving along the curve), the less we produce of the other. It is not possible, then, if we are anywhere on the curve, to raise our production of both guns *and* butter. Of course, over time it is possible to produce beyond our current production possibilities curve as our economy grows. We'll get to economic growth in a few minutes.

What if we're somewhere inside the production possibilities curve? Would it be possible to produce more guns *and* more butter? The answer is yes. At point Z we have an output of 2 guns and 4 butters. By moving to point D we would have 3 guns and 9 butters. Or, by going to point E, output would rise to 4 guns and 5 butters.

We are able to increase our output of both guns and butter when we move from Z to D or E because we are now making use of previously unused resources. We are moving from depression conditions to those of full employment. But when we go from C to D, we stay at full employment. The only way we can produce more guns is to produce less butter, because resources will have to be diverted from butter to gun production. As we divert increasing amounts of resources to gun production, we will be able to understand the law of increasing costs (see box, "The Law of Increasing Costs").

Productive Efficiency

So far we've seen that our economy generally falls short of full production. Now we'll tie that failure in to our definition of economics.

At the beginning of this chapter, we defined economics as *the efficient allocation of the scarce means of production toward the satisfaction of human wants.* The scarce means of production are our resources, land, labor, capital, and entrepreneurial ability. So how efficiently do we use our resources?

An economy is efficient whenever it is producing the maximum output allowed by a given level of technology and resources. *Productive efficiency is attained when the maximum possible output of any one good is produced, given the output of other goods.* This state of grace occurs only when we are operating on our production possibilities curve. Attainment of productive efficiency means that we can't increase the output of one good without reducing the output of some other good.

As we've seen, our economy rarely attains productive efficiency, or full production. We have managed this state of grace from mid-1997 through mid-2001, when the unemployment rate dipped below 5 percent. Since the summer of 2005 it hovered around 5 percent. The previous time our economy actually operated on its production possibilities frontier was during the Vietnam War, in 1968 and 1969.

Productive efficiency is attained when the maximum possible output of any one good is produced, given the output of other goods.

Economic Growth

If the production possibilities curve represents the economy operating at full employment, then it would be impossible to produce at point W (of Figure 2). To go from C to W would mean producing more guns *and* more butter, something that would be beyond our economic capabilities, given the current state of technology and the amount of resources available.

Every economy will use the best available technology. At times, because a country cannot afford the most up-to-date equipment, it will use older machinery and tools. That country really has a capital problem rather than a technological one.

The best available technology

As the level of available technology improves, the production possibilities curve moves outward, as it does in Figure 3. A faster paper copier, a more smoothly operating assembly line, or a new-generation computer system are examples of technological

The Production Possibilities Frontier during World War II

World War II was a classic case of guns and butter, or, more accurately, guns *or* butter. Almost two years before we became actively involved in the war, we began increasing our arms production and drafting millions of young men into the armed services. Did this increase in military goods production mean a decrease in the production of consumer goods?

Gee, that's a very good question. And the answer is found when you go from point A to point B on the first figure shown here.

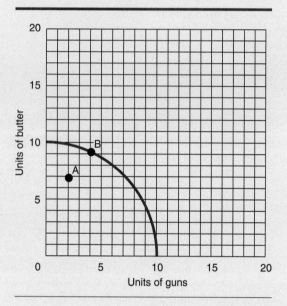

How were we able to increase the production of both guns and butter in 1940 and 1941? Because there was still a great deal of economic slack in those years. It was the tail end of the Great Depression described in Chapter 1, and there were still millions of people out of work and a great deal of idle plant and equipment that could be pressed into use.

Now we're in the war, and we're at point B in the first figure. Is it possible to further expand our output of both guns and butter? Think about it.

Is there any way we could do it? How about if there's economic growth? In the second figure shown here, we went from point B to point C by moving to a higher production possibilities curve. Is this *possible*? Over a considerable period of time, yes. But in just a couple of years? Well, remember what they used to say: There's a *war* going on. So a move from point B to point C in just a couple of years is possible during a war.

Now we're really going to push it. How about a move from point C to point D in the second figure?

Is *this* move possible? Can we raise our production of both guns *and* butter to a point beyond our production possibilities frontier without jumping to a still higher production possibilities curve?

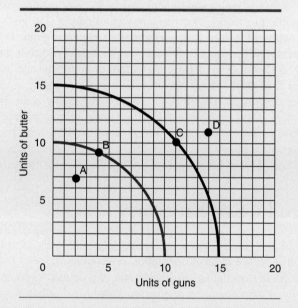

Well, what do *you* think? Remember, there's a war going on. The answer is yes. In 1942, 1943, and 1944 we did push our official unemployment rate under 3 percent, well below the 5 percent rate we would consider full employment today. Employers were so desperate for workers that they would hire practically anybody, and people who wouldn't ordinarily be in the labor market—housewives, retired people, and teenagers—were flocking to the workplace.

Meanwhile, business firms were pressing older machinery and equipment into use, because it was almost impossible to get new machinery and equipment built during the war. And so we were operating not only at full capacity but well beyond that point.

How long were we able to stay at point D? Only as long as there was a war going on. Point D represents an output of guns and butter that our economy can produce temporarily if it operates beyond its production possibilities curve. It's almost like bowling 300. You can't expect to go out and do it every night.*

---

*One can argue that we were temporarily operating on a higher production possibilities curve, and, at the end of the war, we returned to the lower production possibilities curve.

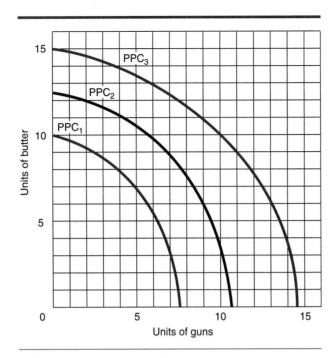

Figure 3
Production Possibilities Curves
A move from PPC$_1$ to PPC$_2$ and
from PPC$_2$ to PPC$_3$ represents
economic growth.

advances. And increasingly, industrial robots and bank money machines are replacing human beings at relatively routine jobs.

As you know, recent advances in information technology (or, IT, as it's often called) has boosted output per worker and cut costs. It costs FedEx \$2.40 to track a package for a customer who calls by phone, but only four cents for one who visits its website. FedEx now gets about 3 million online tracking requests a day, compared with only 30,000 or 40,000 by phone.

Our economic capacity also grows when there is an expansion of labor or capital. More (or better trained) labor and more (or improved) plant and equipment would also push the production possibilities curve outward. This is illustrated in Figure 3, as we go from PPC$_1$ to PPC$_2$, and from PPC$_2$ to PPC$_3$.

Imagine that in 1991 a hypothetical nation had two choices. It could either produce a preponderance of consumer goods or a preponderance of capital goods. Which choice would lead to a faster rate of growth?

On the left side of Figure 4 we see what would have happened to the nation if it had chosen to concentrate on producing consumer goods; on the right side we see what would have happened if it had concentrated on producing capital goods. Obviously by concentrating on capital goods production, that nation would have had a much faster rate of economic growth.

The main factors spurring growth are an improving technology, more and better capital, and more and better labor. Using our resources more efficiently and reducing the unemployment of labor and capital can also raise our rate of growth. This topic is discussed more extensively in Chapter 16 of *Economics* and *Macroeconomics*.

Current Issue: Will You Be Underemployed When You Graduate?

Every spring newspaper reporters ask college placement officials about the prospects of that year's graduating class. The recession of 2001 and the subsequent "jobless recovery" left hundreds of thousands of recent graduates without jobs. But 2004

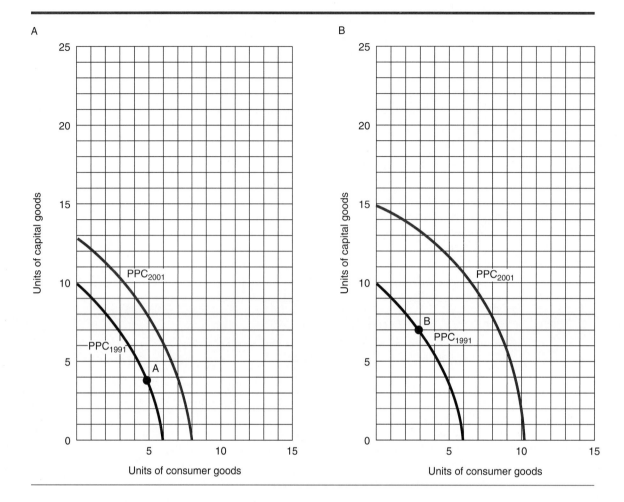

Figure 4

and 2005 were much better years, as corporate recruiters flocked back to college campuses.

I happened to graduate during a *bad* year. My only job offer was from the recruiter from Continental Baking Company to drive a bakery truck. "But how will I use my economics?" He told me I could economize on the gasoline.

Had I taken the truck-driving job, I would have been underemployed. When you graduate, you may face the same problem. It turns out that one in five college graduates ends up in a job that does not require a college degree. In addition, many employers require a degree just as a credential. So when you start working, ask yourself, "I need a degree to do *this*?"

From time to time you'll hear reports of PhD's driving cabs, lawyers typing their own briefs, and doctors bogged down in paperwork. Perhaps there's some degree of underemployment in almost everyone's future. All you can really do is avoid taking a job in which you are clearly underemployed. So when you're interviewing with prospective employers at your college placement office and that guy with the bakery truck shows up, just say no.

Questions for Further Thought and Discussion

1. If you were in a position to run our economy, what steps would you take to raise our rate of economic growth?

2. Under what circumstances can we operate outside our production possibilities curve?

3. Give an example of an opportunity cost for an individual and a nation.

4. Would it be harder for a nation to attain full employment or full production? Explain.

5. Could a nation's production possibilities curve ever shift inward? What might cause such a shift to occur?

6. What is the opportunity cost you incurred by going to college?

7. Although the U.S. is one of the world's wealthiest nations, some of the federal government's budget decisions are severely constrained by scarcity. Can you think of one such decision that was in the recent economic news?

8. Why is scarcity central to economics?

9. Can you think of any decisions you have recently made that incurred opportunity costs?

10. Do you know any entrepreneurs? What do they do?

11. Why is entrepreneurship central to every business firm?

12. Explain the law of increasing costs, using a numerical example.

13. Discuss the three concepts on which the law of increasing costs is based.

Workbook for Chapter 2

Name _____   Date _____

Multiple-Choice Questions

Circle the letter that corresponds to the best answer.

1. The word that is central to the definition of
   economics is _____.
   a) resource   c) scarcity
   b) wants   d) capital

2. We would not need to economize if _____.
   a) the government printed more money
   b) there was no scarcity
   c) there was less output of goods and services
   d) everyone received a big pay increase

3. Human wants are _____.
   a) relatively limited
   b) relatively unlimited
   c) easily satisfied
   d) about equal to our productive capacity

4. Which of the following is an economic resource?
   a) gold   c) labor
   b) scarcity d) rent

5. Each of the following is an example of capital except
   _____.
   a) land   c) a computer system
   b) an office building d) a factory

6. The opportunity cost of spending four hours studying
   a review book the night before a final exam would be
   _____.
   a) the cost of the review book
   b) missing four hours of TV
   c) a higher grade on the exam
   d) the knowledge gained from studying

7. An economy operating its plant and equipment at full
   capacity implies a capacity utilization rate of
   _____.
   a) 40 percent   c) 85 percent
   b) 70 percent   d) 100 percent

8. The full-production level of our economy implies
   _____.
   a) an efficient allocation of our resources
   b) zero unemployment
   c) our plant and equipment being operated at
      100 percent capacity
   d) a high unemployment rate

9. Underemployment means _____.
   a) the same thing as unemployment
   b) underutilization of resources
   c) a recession
   d) slow economic growth

10. The production possibilities curve represents
    _____.
    a) our economy at full employment but not full
       production
    b) our economy at full production but not full
       employment
    c) our economy at full production and full
       employment

11. If we are operating inside our production possibilities
    curve _____.
    a) there is definitely recession going on
    b) there is definitely not a recession going on
    c) there is definitely less than full employment
    d) there is definitely inflation

12. The closer we are to the origin and the farther away
    we are from the production possibilities curve
    _____.
    a) the more unemployment there is
    b) the less unemployment there is
    c) the more guns we are producing
    d) the more butter we are producing

13. Economic growth will occur if any of the following occur except _____.

    a) a better technology becomes available

    b) the level of consumption rises and the savings rate falls

    c) more capital becomes available

    d) more labor becomes available

14. To attain a higher rate of economic growth, we need to devote _____.

    a) a higher proportion of our production to capital goods and a lower proportion to consumer goods

    b) a higher proportion of our production to consumer goods and a lower proportion to capital goods

    c) a higher proportion of our production to both consumer goods and capital goods

    d) a lower proportion of our production to both consumer goods and capital goods

15. Which is the most accurate statement?

    a) Nearly every major economic innovation originated abroad and was then applied in the United States.

    b) The United States provides a poor environment for innovation.

    c) Freedom of thought, a risk-taking culture, and a noncorrupt bureaucracy have made the United States very hospitable to innovation.

    d) Although the United States was once the world's leading innovator, since we lost most of our manufacturing base, we are no longer a major innovator.

16. Which is the most accurate statement?

    a) Most Americans are underemployed.

    b) Employment discrimination causes underemployment of labor.

    c) It is impossible for an economy to operate outside its production possibilities curve.

    d) There is no longer employment discrimination.

17. Statement 1: The old Negro leagues provide an example of underemployment.
    Statement 2: Underemployment means basically the same thing as unemployment.

    a) Statement 1 is true and statement 2 is false.

    b) Statement 2 is true and statement 1 is false.

    c) Both statements are true.

    d) Both statements are false.

18. Employment discrimination is most closely related to _____.

    a) specialization   c) unemployment

    b) technology   d) underemployment

19. Miranda Bowman, a Harvard MBA, is almost definitely _____ if she is working as a secretary.

    a) unemployed   b) underemployed

    c) both unemployed and underemployed

    d) neither unemployed nor underemployed

20. On the following list, the most serious problem facing today's college graduate is _____.

    a) outsourcing of jobs to foreign countries

    b) employment discrimination

    c) unemployment

    d) underemployment

21. Which statement is true?

    a) America has always had a shortage of entrepreneurs.

    b) Our economic problem is that we have limited resources available to satisfy relatively unlimited wants.

    c) America has less economic resources today than we had 40 years ago.

    d) Aside from a few million poor people, we have very little scarcity in the United States.

22. Suppose you had $1,000 to spend. If you spent it on a vacation trip rather than on new clothes, your second choice, or 1,000 lottery tickets, your third choice, what was your opportunity cost of going on a vacation trip?

    a) $1,000

    b) the vacation trip itself

    c) not buying the new clothes

    d) not buying the lottery tickets

    e) missing out on the $10 million lottery prize

23. Which of the following best describes the role of an entrepreneur?

    a) the inventor of something with great commercial possibilities

    b) anyone who made a fortune by purchasing stock in a dot-com before its price shot up

    c) inventors who parlay inventions into commercial enterprises

    d) any employee earning at least $200,000 at a Fortune 500 company

24. As we produce increasing amounts of a particular good, the resources used in its production _____.

   a) become more suitable
   b) become less suitable
   c) continue to have the same suitability

25. The law of increasing costs is explained by each of the following except _____.
   a) the law of diminishing returns
   b) diseconomies of scale
   c) factor suitability
   d) overspecialization

26. As a firm grows larger, _____.
   a) economies of scale set in, then diseconomies of scale
   b) diseconomies of scale set in, then economies of scale
   c) economies of scale and diseconomies of scale set in at the same time
   d) neither economies of scale nor diseconomies of scale set in

27. The law of increasing costs states that, as _____.
   a) output rises, cost per unit rises as well
   b) the output of one good expands, the opportunity cost of producing additional units of this good increases
   c) economies of scale set in, costs increase
   d) output rises, diminishing returns set in

28. If Figure 1 shows our production possibilities frontier during World War II, at which point were we operating?
   a) point A
   b) point B
   c) point C
   d) point D

29. If Figure 1 shows our production possibilities frontier during the Great Depression, at which point were we operating?
   a) point A
   b) point B
   c) point C
   d) point D

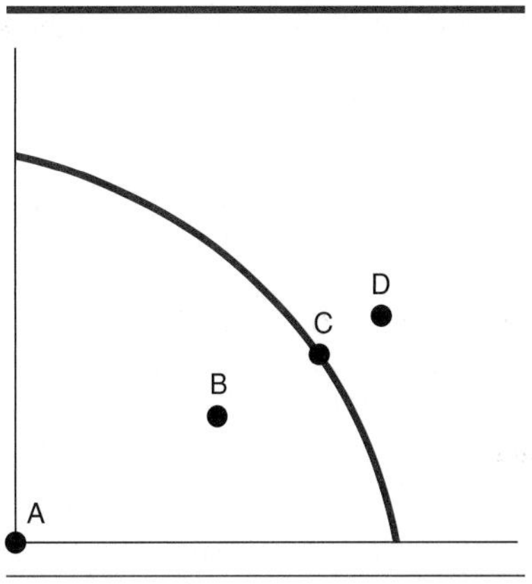

Figure 1

Fill-In Questions

1. A PhD driving a cab would be considered _underemployed_.

2. The central fact of economics is (in one word) _scarcity_

3. Human wants are relatively _unlimited_, while economic resources are relatively _scarce_.

4. The law of increasing costs states that, as the output of one good expands, _diminished returns set in_.

5. The law of diminishing returns, diseconomies of scale, and factor suitability each provide an explanation for the law of _increased costs_.

6. If you went into a store with $25 and couldn't decide whether to buy a pair of jeans or a jacket, and you finally decided to buy the jeans, what would be the opportunity cost of this purchase? _the jacket_

7. Full employment implies an unemployment rate of about _5_ percent.

8. List some constraints on our labor force that prevent our fully using our plant and equipment 24 hours a day, seven days a week.
   (1) _laws_;
   (2) _employee preference_;
   and (3) _wea maintenance on cap._

9. Employment discrimination results in the _underemployment_ of our labor force.

10. When we are efficiently allocating our resources and using the best available technology, we are operating on our _prod poss frontier_.

11. Most of the time our economy is operating _inside_ its production possibilities frontier.

12. Economic growth can be attained by:
    (1) _Capital production_ and
    (2) _the best available Technology_.

Problems

1. If we were at point C of Figure 2 below, could we quickly produce substantially more houses *and* more cars? _no_

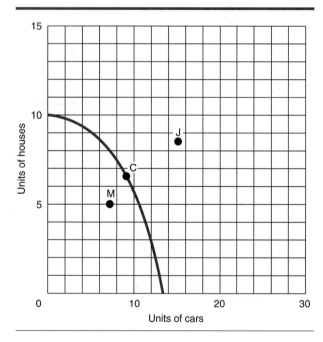

F*igure 2*

2. If we were at point M of Figure 2, could we quickly produce substantially more houses *and* more cars? _no_

3. If we were at point C on Figure 2, could we quickly go to point J? _no_

4. Fill in the following points on Figure 3.
   Point X: where our economy generally operates
   Point Y: a serious recession
   Point Z: a catastrophic depression
   Point W: economic growth

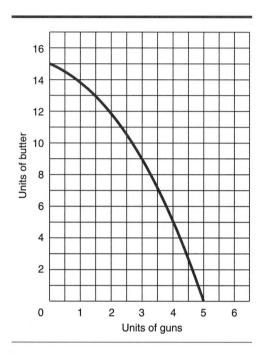

F*igure 3*

5. In Figure 4, fill in a new production possibilities frontier representing substantial economic growth.

6. In Figure 4, place point M where there is 100 percent unemployment.

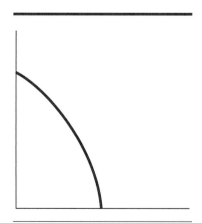

F*igure 4*

7. Fill in the following points on Figure 5.

   Point A: an unemployment rate of 100 percent

   Point B: an unemployment rate of 20 percent

   Point C: an unemployment rate of 2 percent

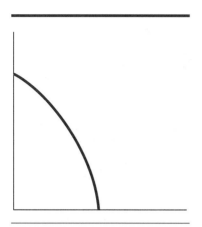

Figure 5

8. Given the information in Table 1, below, what is the opportunity cost of going from point B to point C? And of going from point D to point C?

TABLE 1	Hypothetical Production Schedule for Two-Product Economy	
Point	Units of Butter	Units of Guns
A	15	0
B	14	1
C	12	2
D	9	3
E	5	4
F	0	5

9. Use Figure 6 to answer these questions:

   a) What is the opportunity cost of going from point B to point C?

   b) What is the opportunity cost of going from point D to point C?

   c) What is the opportunity cost of going from point B to point A?

   d) What is the opportunity cost of going from point C to point D?

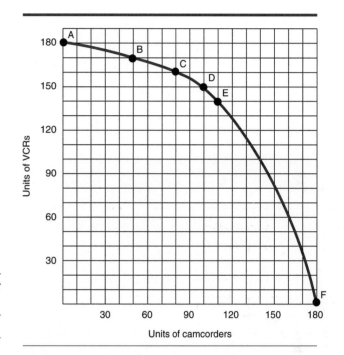

Figure 6

10. Use the data in Figure 6 to illustrate the law of increasing costs numerically. (Hint: Start at point E and move toward point A.)

Chapter 3

Supply and Demand

Should your college charge you for parking, or should parking be free? Should the federal government put a ceiling of, say, $2 a gallon on gas prices? And should drug companies be forced to make prescription drug prices affordable to senior citizens? Our price system is constantly sending buyers and sellers thousands of signals. Running an economy without that system would be like flying a jumbo jet plane without an instrument panel.

Our economy has a built-in guidance system that allocates resources efficiently. This guidance system, which includes the interaction of the forces of supply and demand in the marketplace, is known as the price system. How does it work? You're about to find out.

How are you at reading graphs? Economists love to draw them, so if you're going to get through this course, you'll need to be able to read them. The main graph we like to draw has just two curves: the demand curve and the supply curve. By observing where they cross, we can easily find not only the price of a good or service, but the quantity sold.

CHAPTER OBJECTIVES

In this chapter you'll learn how to:

- Define and explain *demand* in a product or service market.
- Define and explain *supply*.
- Determine the equilibrium point in the market for a specific good, given data on supply and demand at different price levels.

- Explain what causes shifts in demand and supply.
- Explain how price ceilings cause shortages.
- Explain how price floors cause surpluses.

Demand

We define *demand as the schedule of quantities of a good or service that people are willing to buy at different prices.* And as you would suspect, the lower the price, the more people will buy.

How much would people living in Denver or in Chicago be willing to pay for a round-trip plane ticket for weekday travel between the two cities? Suppose we conducted a survey and were able to draw up a demand schedule like the one shown in Table 1.

Definition of demand: the schedule of quantities of a good or service that people are willing to buy at different prices.

TABLE 1	Hypothetical Daily Demand for Coach Seats on Round-Trip Weekday Flights between Denver and Chicago
Price	**Quantity Demanded**
$500	1,000
450	3,000
400	7,000
350	12,000
300	19,000
250	30,000
200	45,000
150	57,000
100	67,000

F*igure* 1

Hypothetical Daily Demand for Coach Seats on Round-Trip Weekday Flights between Denver and Chicago

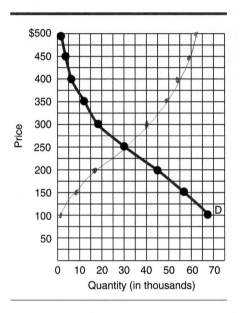

Note that, as the price declines, increasing quantities of tickets are demanded. Now look at Figure 1 to see how a graph of this demand schedule actually looks.

The demand curve slopes downward and to the right. That's because of the way we've set up our graph. Prices are on the vertical axis, with the highest price, $500, at the top. From here on, the vertical axis of every graph in this book will be measured in terms of money. The horizontal axis of Figure 1 measures the quantity sold, beginning with zero, at the origin of the graph, and getting to progressively higher quantities as we move to the right. In all the demand and supply graphs that follow, price will be on the vertical axis, and quantity on the horizontal.

Supply

Definition of supply: the schedule of quantities of a good or service that people are willing to sell at different prices.

Supply is defined as *the schedule of quantities of a good or service that people are willing to sell at different prices.* If you compare the definition of supply with that of demand, you'll find that only one word is changed. Can you find that word?

If you are a supplier, then you are willing to *sell* a schedule of quantities at different prices; if you are a buyer, then you are willing to *buy* a schedule of quantities at different prices. What's the difference, then, between supply and demand? At higher prices the suppliers are willing to sell larger and larger quantities, while the buyers are willing to buy smaller and smaller quantities. Similarly, as price declines, buyers are willing to buy more and sellers are willing to sell less. But we're getting a little ahead of ourselves, since you haven't yet been formally introduced to a supply schedule. So first check out Table 2, and then Figure 2, which is a graph drawn from the numbers in the table.

What happens, then, to quantity supplied as the price is lowered? It declines. It's as simple as that.

In our definitions of demand and supply, we talked about a schedule of quantities of a good or service that people are willing to buy or sell at different prices. But what if some buyers just don't have the money? Then those buyers are simply not counted. We say that they are not in the market. Similarly, we would exclude from the market any sellers who just don't have the goods or services to sell. I'd *love* to sell my services as a $500-an-hour corporate lawyer, but quite frankly, I just don't have those services to sell.

That brings us to a second factor not included in our definitions of supply and demand. The supply and demand for any good or service operates within a specific market. That market may be very local, as it is for food shopping; regional, as it is for used cars; national, as it is for news magazines; or even international, as it is for petroleum.

TABLE 2	Hypothetical Daily Supply for Coach Seats on Round-Trip Weekday Flights between Denver and Chicago
Price	Quantity Supplied
$500	62,000
450	59,000
400	54,000
350	48,000
300	40,000
250	30,000
200	16,000
150	7,000
100	2,000

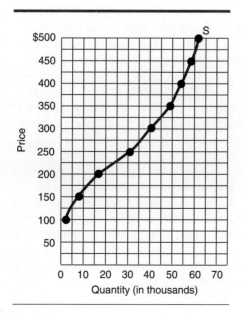

Figure 2

Hypothetical Daily Supply for Coach Seats on Round-Trip Weekday Flights between Denver and Chicago

Equilibrium

You've heard a lot about supply and demand—or is it demand and supply? It doesn't matter whether you put demand or supply first. What *does* matter is placing them together on the same graph. Look at Figure 3.

Can you find the equilibrium price? Did you say $250? Good! And how much is equilibrium quantity? Right again! It is 30,000.

Let's step back for a minute and analyze what we've just done. We've figured out the equilibrium price and quantity by looking at the demand and supply curves in Figure 3. So we can find equilibrium price and quantity by seeing where the supply and demand curves cross.

Equilibrium price is the price at which quantity demanded equals quantity supplied.

What is equilibrium price? It's the price at which quantity demanded equals quantity supplied. What is equilibrium quantity? It's the quantity sold when the quantity demanded is equal to the quantity supplied.

Surpluses and Shortages

Is the actual price, or market price, always equal to the equilibrium price? The answer is no. It could be higher and it could be lower. Suppose the airlines were selling tickets for $400. How many tickets would be demanded? Look back at Table 1 or, if you prefer, Figure 1 or Figure 3.

A total of 7,000 tickets would be demanded. And at a price of $400, how many tickets would be supplied?

A surplus occurs when the market price is above the equilibrium price.

The quantity supplied would be 54,000. What we've got here is a surplus. This occurs when the actual price, or the market price, is greater than the equilibrium price. How much is that surplus? You can measure it by finding the horizontal distance between quantity demanded and quantity supplied in Figure 3. Or, you can subtract the quantity demanded that you found in Table 1 (at a price of $400) from the quantity supplied in Table 2 (also at a price of $400). Either way, the surplus comes to 47,000.

The quantity that sellers are willing to sell (54,000) is much greater than the quantity buyers are willing to buy (7,000). This difference (54,000 − 7,000) is the surplus (47,000). The amount that sellers can sell is restricted by how much buyers are willing to buy.

What happens when there's a surplus? The forces of demand and supply automatically work to eliminate it. In this case, some of the airlines, which would be very unhappy about all those empty seats, would cut their prices. If the market price fell to $300, would there still be a surplus?

A glance at Figure 3 tells us that there would be. And how much would that surplus be? It would be 21,000 seats. So *then* what would happen?

Some of the airlines would cut their prices to $250, and the buyers would flock to them. The other airlines would have no choice but to cut their price—or stop flying the Denver–Chicago route altogether. At $250, we would be at the equilibrium point. There would be no tendency for the price to change.

A shortage occurs when the market price is below the equilibrium price.

What if the market price were below equilibrium price? Then we'd have a shortage. How much would that shortage be if the market price in Figure 3 were $200?

At a price of $200, quantity demanded would be 45,000, while quantity supplied would be just 16,000. So the shortage would be 29,000.

This time the buyers would be unhappy, because they would be quite willing to pay $200 for a round-trip ticket, but most would be unable to get one without waiting for months. Many of the buyers would be willing to pay more. So what do you think would happen?

You guessed it! The market price would rise to $250. At that price—the equilibrium price—quantity demanded would equal quantity supplied, and the shortage would be eliminated.

Thus we can see that the forces of demand and supply work together to establish an equilibrium price at which there are no shortages or surpluses. At the equilibrium price, all the sellers can sell as much as they want and all the buyers can buy as much as they want. So if we were to shout, "Is everybody happy?" the buyers and sellers would all shout back yes!

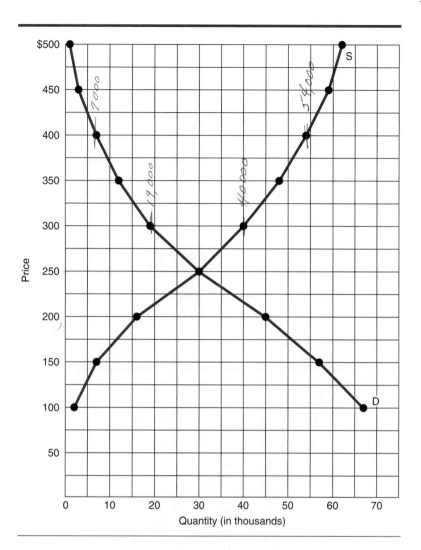

Figure 3
Hypothetical Demand and
Supply Curves

Shifts in Demand and Supply

So far we've seen how the forces of demand and supply, or the price mechanism, send signals to buyers and sellers. For example, the surplus that resulted from a price of $400 sent a clear signal to sellers to cut their prices. Similarly, a price of $200 was accompanied by a shortage, which made many buyers unhappy. And sellers quickly realized that they could raise their price to $250 and *still* sell all the tickets they wanted to sell.

Now we'll see how shifts in supply curves and shifts in demand curves change equilibrium price and quantity, thereby sending new sets of signals to buyers and sellers. Figure 4 has a new demand curve, D_2. This represents an increase in demand because it lies entirely to the right of D_1, the original demand curve. There has been an increase in demand if the quantity demanded is larger at every price that can be compared.

Why did the demand for airline tickets increase? Let's say that newer planes were introduced that cut travel time by 30 percent.

I'd like you to find the new equilibrium price and the new equilibrium quantity. When you do, please write down your answers.

The new equilibrium price is $300, and the new equilibrium quantity is 40,000. So an increase in demand leads to an increase in both equilibrium price and quantity.

Next question: What would happen to equilibrium price and quantity if there were a decrease in demand?

There would be a decrease in both equilibrium price and quantity. Need a little extra help? Then see the box, "How Changes in Demand Affect Equilibrium."

HELP

How Changes in Demand Affect Equilibrium

If demand falls and supply stays the same, what happens to equilibrium price and equilibrium quantity? To answer those questions, sketch a graph of a supply curve, S, and a demand curve, D_1. Then draw a second demand curve, D_2, representing a decrease in demand. I've done that in this figure.

The original equilibrium price was $50, and the original equilibrium quantity was 10. Equilibrium price fell to $35, and equilibrium quantity fell to 8. So a decrease in demand leads to a decrease in equilibrium price and quantity.

What would happen to equilibrium price and equilibrium quantity if demand rose and supply stayed the same? Equilibrium price and quantity would rise.

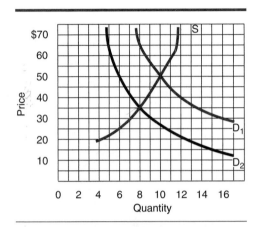

Figure 4

Increase in Demand

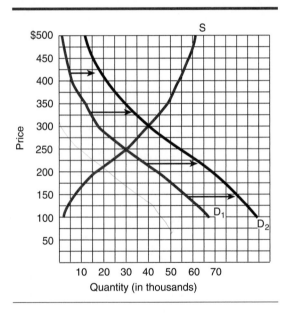

OK, one more set of shifts and we're out of here.

Figure 5 shows an increase in supply. You'll notice that the new supply curve, S_2, is entirely to the right of S_1. There has been an increase in supply if the quantity supplied is larger at every price that can be compared.

Why did supply increase? Let's assume that the cost of jet fuel fell by 50 percent. In response, the airlines scheduled more flights. Please find the new equilibrium price and quantity, and write down your answers.

An increase in supply lowers equilibrium price and raises equilibrium quantity.

The new equilibrium price is $200, and the new equilibrium quantity is 45,000. So an increase in supply lowers equilibrium price and raises equilibrium quantity. One last question: If supply declines, what happens to equilibrium price and equilibrium quantity?

When supply declines, equilibrium price rises and equilibrium quantity declines. As you make your way through this text, supply and demand graphs will pop up from time to time. In every case you'll be able to find equilibrium price and quantity by locating the point of intersection of the demand and supply curves. If you need extra help, see the box, "How Changes in Supply Affect Equilibrium."

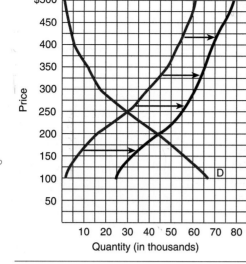

Figure 5
Increase in Supply

Was
    $250 /30,000

Now
    $200 /45,000

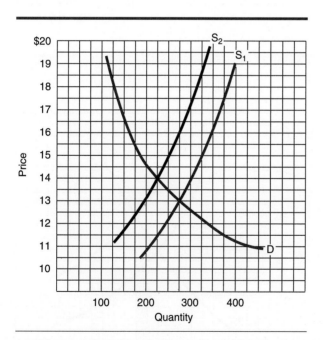

Figure 6

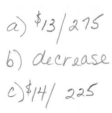

a) $13/275
b) decrease
c) $14/ 225

Now let's work out a couple of problems. First, look at Figure 6 and write down your answers to this set of questions: (*a*) If the supply curve is S_1, how much are the equilibrium price and quantity? (*b*) If supply changes from S_1 to S_2, does that represent an increase or decrease in supply? (*c*) How much are the new equilibrium price and quantity?

Here are the answers: (*a*) $13; 275; (*b*) decrease; and (*c*) $14; 225.

Next problem: Use Figure 7 to answer these questions: (*a*) If the demand curve is D_1, how much are the equilibrium price and quantity? (*b*) If demand changes from D_1 to D_2, does that represent an increase or decrease in demand? (*c*) How much are the new equilibrium price and quantity?

EXTRA HELP

How Changes in Supply Affect Equilibrium

If supply rises and demand stays the same, what happens to equilibrium price and equilibrium quantity? Again, to answer those questions, sketch a graph of a demand curve, D_1, and a supply curve, S_1. Then draw a second supply curve, S_2, representing an increase in supply. I've done that in this figure.

The original equilibrium price was $12, and the original equilibrium quantity was 20. Equilibrium price fell to $9, and equilibrium quantity rose to 26. So an increase in supply leads to a decrease in equilibrium price and an increase in equilibrium quantity.

What happens to equilibrium price and equilibrium quantity if supply falls and demand stays the same? Equilibrium price rises and equilibrium quantity falls.

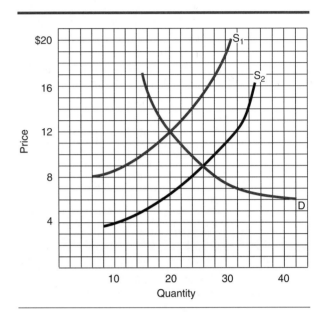

Figure 7

26/120
decrease
24.50/100

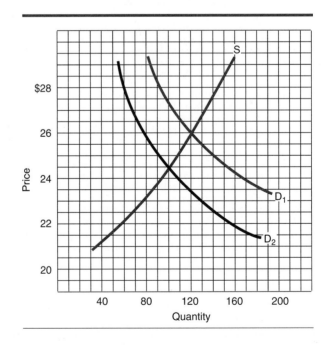

Here are the answers: (*a*) $26; 120; (*b*) decrease; and (*c*) $24.50; 100.

OK, you're taking an exam, and here's the first question: Demand rises and supply stays the same. What happens to equilibrium price and quantity? Just sketch a graph (like the one in Figure 4). Then you'll see that an increase in demand raises equilibrium price and quantity.

What happens to equilibrium price and quantity when there's a decrease in demand? Again, just sketch a graph, and you'll see that a decrease in demand lowers equilibrium price and quantity.

Next question: What happens to equilibrium price and quantity when there's an increase in supply? If your sketch looks like the one in Figure 5, you'll see that an increase in supply leads to a lower equilibrium price and a higher equilibrium quantity.

And finally, how does a decrease in supply affect equilibrium price and quantity? A decrease in supply leads to a higher equilibrium price and a lower equilibrium quantity.

Now let's return to that exam. When you're asked: How does an increase or decrease in demand affect equilibrium price and quantity, what do you do?

You just sketch a graph of a demand curve and a supply curve, and then another demand curve representing an increase or decrease in demand. Similarly, if you're asked how an increase or decrease in supply affects equilibrium price and quantity, just draw a sketch. It leads you to the right answers.

Price Ceilings and Price Floors

One of the most popular sayings of all time is "You can't repeal the law of supply and demand." Maybe not, but our government sure has a lot of fun trying. Price floors and price ceilings, which Washington has imposed from time to time, have played havoc with our price system. And taxes on selected goods and services have also altered supply and demand.

You can't repeal the law of supply and demand.

What's the difference between a floor and a ceiling? If you're standing in a room, where's the floor and where's the ceiling? As you might expect, economists turn this logic upside down. To find floors, we need to look up. How high? Somewhere above equilibrium price. And where are ceilings? Just where you'd expect economists to place them. We need to look down, somewhere below equilibrium price. A *price floor* is so named because that is the lowest the price is allowed to go in that market. Similarly, a *price ceiling* is the highest price that is allowed in that market.

Figure 8 illustrates a price floor. Equilibrium price would normally be $10, but a price floor of $15 has been established. At $15 businesses are not normally able to sell everything they offer for sale. Quantity supplied is much larger than quantity demanded. Why? At the equilibrium price of $10, sellers are willing to sell less while buyers are willing to buy more.

At a price of $15, there is a surplus of 30 units (quantity demanded is 20 and quantity supplied is 50). The government has created this price floor and surplus to keep the price at a predetermined level. This has been the case for certain agricultural commodities, most notably wheat and corn. It was hoped that these relatively high prices would encourage family farms to stay in business. That the bulk of farm price support payments has gone to huge corporate farms has not discouraged Congress from allocating billions of dollars a year toward this end.

Floors and surpluses

The way the government keeps price floors in effect is by buying up the surpluses. In the case of Figure 8, the Department of Agriculture would have to buy 30 units.

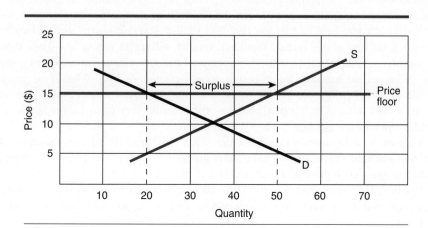

F*igure* 8

Price Floor and Surplus
The price can go no lower than the floor. The surplus is the amount by which the quantity supplied is greater than the quantity demanded.

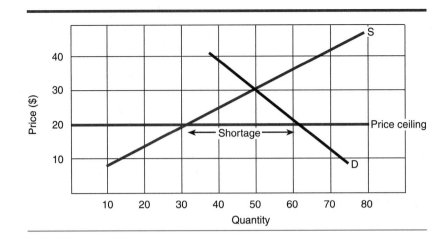

Another important price floor is the minimum wage. Today the vast majority of Americans are guaranteed a minimum of $5.15 an hour. Thus the wage rate, which is the price of an hour's labor, is, in effect, at least $5.15.

Price ceilings are the mirror image of price floors. An example appears in Figure 9. Price ceilings are set by the government as a form of price control. "No matter what," the government tells business firms, "don't charge more than this amount."

Ceilings and shortages

A ceiling prevents prices from rising. The last time we had widespread price ceilings was during World War II. Because ceilings cause shortages, a rations system was worked out to enable everyone to obtain their "fair share" of such commodities as butter, meat, and sugar.

I remember World War II. I remember the ration books and the coupons you'd tear out when you went to the store. But chances are, even your parents don't remember the war, with its attendant shortages and rationing.

Ceilings and gas lines

Those over 35 may remember the gas lines we had in 1979, and real old-timers even recall the ones we had back in 1973. If not, imagine waiting a couple of hours in a line of cars six blocks long just to fill up your tank. What was the problem? In 1973 it was the Arab oil embargo, while the crisis in 1979 was set off by the Iranian Revolution.

How shortages are eliminated

In both cases, there was ostensibly an oil shortage. But according to the law of supply and demand, there can't really *be* any shortages. Why not? Because prices will rise. For example, in Figure 9, at a price of $25, there's a shortage. But we know the price will rise to $30 and eliminate that shortage. Why? Who drives it up? The dissatisfied buyers (the people who would rather pay more now than wait) drive it up because they are willing to pay more than $25. Note that as the price rises, the quantity demanded declines, while the quantity supplied rises. When we reach equilibrium price, quantity demanded equals quantity supplied, and the shortage is eliminated.

Now, I left you back in that gas line, and I know you don't want to wait two hours until it's your turn at the pump. Wouldn't you be willing to pay a few cents more if that meant you didn't have to wait? Let's suppose the gas station owner posted a higher price. What would happen? Some people would get out of line. What if he posted a still higher price? Still more people would leave the line. And as gas prices rose, more stations would miraculously open, and the others would stay open longer hours. What would happen to the gas lines? They'd disappear.

Who actually caused the shortages?

So now, let's ask the obvious question: What *really* caused the gasoline shortages? Who was the *real* villain of the piece? You guessed it! It was the federal government, which had set a ceiling on gasoline prices.

Let's return once more to Figure 9, the scene of the crime. What crime? How could you forget? Our government was caught red-handed, trying to violate the law of supply and demand.

In Figure 9, when a ceiling of $20 is established, there is a shortage of about 30 units. Had price been allowed to stay at the equilibrium level of $30, there would have been no shortage. However, at this lower price, business firms would be willing to sell about 18 units fewer than they'll sell at equilibrium, and consumers would demand about 12 units more than they would at equilibrium. This explains the shortage.

One way the market deals with a government-imposed shortage is to create what is known as a black market. Products subject to the price ceiling are sold illegally to those willing to pay considerably more. During World War II there was an extensive black market.

Two important price ceilings are rent control laws (see the box, "Rent Control: The Institution People Love to Hate") and usury laws, which put a ceiling on interest rates. Usury laws go back to biblical times when the prophets debated what, if anything, was a "fair" rate of interest. This same debate was carried on more than two millennia later by Christian scholars. And to this day we ask whether it is "moral" to charge high interest rates.

Usury laws put a ceiling on interest rates.

Rent Control: The Institution People Love to Hate

I grew up in a rent-controlled apartment and still believe that rent control worked very well at the time it was instituted. Very little new housing had been built during the 1930s because of the Great Depression and during the first half of the 1940s because of World War II. If rents had been allowed to rise to their market value in the late 1940s, my family, and hundreds of thousands— if not millions—of other families would have been forced out of their apartments.

Rent control is an institution that landlords, economists, libertarians, and nearly all good conservatives just love to hate. In fact, about the only folks who still seem to support rent control are the tenants whose rents are below what the market would have set and the politicians who voted for these laws in the first place.

Rent controls establish ceilings for how much rent may be charged for particular apartments and how much, if at all, these rents may be raised each year. The case for rent control is that it keeps down housing costs for the poor and the elderly. Actually, it keeps down housing costs for a lot of middle-class and rich people as well. Because the rent ceiling is established for each apartment regardless of who is living there, many people are paying a lot less than they could afford.

One of the perverse effects of rent control is to reduce vacancy rates. First, those paying low rents don't want to move. Second, real estate developers are reluctant to build apartment houses if their rents will be subject to controls. Still another perverse effect has been the large-scale abandonment of apartment buildings, especially in the inner cities, when landlords find that it makes more sense to walk away from their buildings than to continue losing money. These landlords had been squeezed for years by rising maintenance costs and stagnant rent rolls.

Richard Arnott has noted that "Economists have been virtually unanimous in their opposition to rent control." Why? Arnott provides a full list of reasons:

There has been widespread agreement that rent controls discourage new construction, cause abandonment, retard maintenance, reduce mobility, generate mismatch between housing units and tenants, exacerbate discrimination in rental housing, create black markets, encourage the conversion of rental to owner-occupied housing, and generally short-circuit the market mechanism for housing.*

After rent control was imposed in New York City in 1943, many landlords stopped taking care of their buildings and eventually walked away from 500,000 apartments.

Today nearly 200 cities, mostly in New York, New Jersey, and California, have some form of rent control. It is clear that this price ceiling has kept rents well below their equilibrium levels and consequently has resulted in housing shortages.

From a policy standpoint, do we want to eliminate rent controls? Would skyrocketing rents drive even more families into the ranks of the homeless? Perhaps a gradual easing of rent controls and their eventual elimination in, say, 10 or 15 years would send the right message to builders. But because these are local laws, only local governments can repeal them. And because the name of the political game is getting reelected, it is unlikely that many local politicians will find it expedient to repeal these popular laws.

*Richard Arnott, "Time for Revisionism on Rent Control?" *Journal of Economic Perspectives,* Winter 1995, p. 99.

EXTRA
HELP

Price Ceilings, Price Floors, Shortages, and Surpluses

Let's look at Figure 1. See if you can answer these three questions: (1) Is $10 a price ceiling or a price floor? (2) Is there a shortage or a surplus? (3) How much is it?

Let's look at Figure 2. We see that the quantity demanded is 75 and the quantity supplied is 45. The shortage is equal to quantity demanded less quantity supplied (75 − 45 = 30).

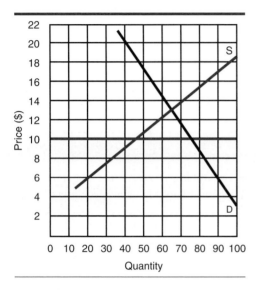

Figure 1

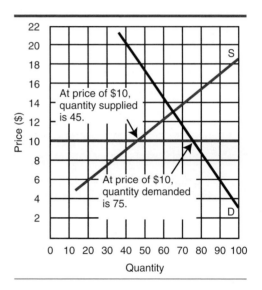

Figure 2

Solution: (1) $10 is a price ceiling because it is below equilibrium price: The ceiling is holding the market price *below* equilibrium price. (2) There is a shortage because quantity demanded is greater than quantity supplied. (3) The shortage is 30.

One dictionary definition of usury is "an unconscionable or exorbitant rate or amount of interest."[1] Many states have usury laws that prohibit banks, savings and loan associations, and certain other financial institutions from charging above specified rates of interest. What effect, if any, do these laws have?

Until the late 1970s interest rates were well below their legal ceilings. But then came double-digit inflation rates, sharply rising interest rates, and, as these interest rates reached their legal ceilings, a full-fledged credit crunch. In other words, these interest rate ceilings created a shortage of loanable funds—which is exactly what one would expect to happen when a price ceiling is set below the market's equilibrium price. In this case we're talking about the market for loanable funds and their price, the interest rate.

The confusion over the location of price floors and ceilings on the graph may be overcome by considering what the government is doing by establishing them. Normally, price would fall to the equilibrium level, but a price floor keeps price artificially high.

[1]*Webster's Collegiate Dictionary,* 10th ed., p. 1302.

Moving right along, answer these three questions with respect to Figure 3. (1) Is $40 a price ceiling or a price floor? (2) Is there a shortage or a surplus? (3) How much is it?

Let's look at Figure 4. We see the quantity supplied is 130 and quantity demanded is 80. The surplus is equal to quantity supplied less quantity demanded (130 − 80 = 50).

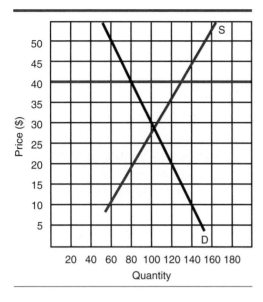

F*igure* 3

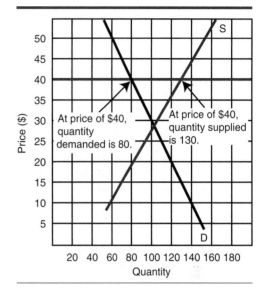

F*igure* 4

Solution: (1) $40 is a price floor because it is above equilibrium price: The floor is holding market price *above* equilibrium price. (2) There is a surplus because quantity supplied is greater than quantity demanded. (3) The surplus is 50.

Think of a floor holding price above equilibrium; therefore, a price floor would be located above equilibrium price.

By the same logic, a price ceiling is intended to keep price *below* equilibrium. If not for that ceiling, price would rise. Therefore, an effective price ceiling must be located below equilibrium to keep price from rising to that level.

Keep in mind, then, that the normal tendency of prices is to move toward their equilibrium levels. A price ceiling will prevent prices from rising to equilibrium, while a price floor will prevent prices from falling to equilibrium. If you need more information about ceilings, floors, shortages, and surpluses, see the box, "Price Ceilings, Price Floors, Shortages, and Surpluses."

Let's summarize: When the government sets a price floor above equilibrium price, it creates a surplus. That surplus is the amount by which the quantity supplied exceeds the quantity demanded. When the government sets a price ceiling below equilibrium price, it creates a shortage. That shortage is the amount by which the quantity demanded exceeds the quantity supplied.

Applications of Supply and Demand

Throughout this book we encounter many applications of supply and demand—so many, in fact, that I'm going to give you a quiz. But it will be an extremely easy quiz. There's just one answer to all these questions. Are you ready?

1. Interest rates are set by _____.
   Did you answer "supply and demand"? Good.

2. Wage rates are set by _____.

3. Rents are determined by _____.

4. The prices of nearly all goods are determined by _____.

5. The prices of nearly all services are determined by _____.

Occasionally, however, government intervention interferes with the price mechanism and imposes price floors (or minimums) or price ceilings (or maximums). This gets economists very upset because it not only prevents the most efficient allocation of resources. It also makes it much harder to read our supply and demand graphs.

Interest Rate Determination

Let's take a closer look at the determination of the interest rate. I want to state right up front that there is no "interest rate" but rather scores of interest rates, such as mortgage rates, commercial loan rates, and short-term and long-term federal borrowing rates, as well as the interest rates paid by banks, credit unions, and other financial intermediaries. Figure 10 shows a hypothetical demand schedule for loanable funds and a corresponding hypothetical supply schedule.

We can see that $600 billion is lent (or borrowed) at an interest rate of 6 percent. In other words, the market sets the price of borrowed money at an interest rate of 6 percent. What would happen to the interest rate and to the amount of money borrowed if the supply of loanable funds increased?

Did you figure it out? If you did, then you can confirm your answers by glancing at Figure 11. A rise in the supply of loanable funds leads to a decrease in the interest rate to 4 percent and an increase in the amount of money borrowed to $800 billion.

Figure **10**

Hypothetical Demand for and Supply of Loanable Funds

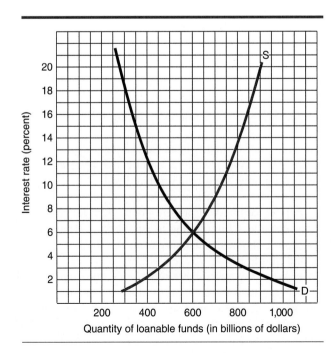

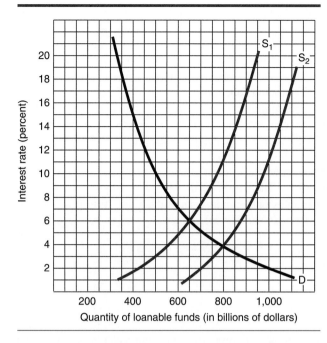

F*igure* 11

Hypothetical Demand for and Supply of Loanable Funds

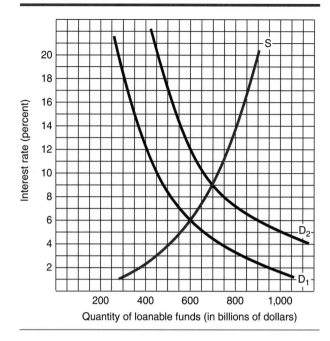

F*igure* 12

Hypothetical Demand for and Supply of Loanable Funds

One more question: What happens to the interest rate and to the amount of money borrowed if the demand for loanable funds rises?

Did you say that the interest rate would rise and the amount of money borrowed would also rise? Good. Then what you must have done was to have sketched a graph like the one shown in Figure 12. The interest rate rose to 9 percent, and the amount of money borrowed rose to $700 billion.

College Parking

One of the big complaints on college campuses is the scarcity of parking spots for students—which means that, if you get to school after 9 o'clock, you may have to walk a half mile or even more to get to class.

Should parking be free at your school?

Is parking free at your school? Although you may well believe it should be, let's look at the consequences of free parking. The school has set the price of parking at zero. That's a price ceiling of zero. We may conclude that this price ceiling has caused a shortage of available parking spots.

Suppose that the college administration decided to charge $25 a semester to students, faculty members, administrators, and other employees (and eliminated reserved parking as well). Would this fee eliminate the parking shortage? Surely it would cut down on the quantity of parking spots demanded. But if the shortage were not completely eliminated, perhaps a fee of $50 might do the trick. Or even $100. In short, if the price of parking were set high enough, the parking shortage would disappear.

The Rationing Function of the Price System

If gasoline went up to $8 a gallon, would you cut back on your driving? Maybe you would try to do all your shopping in one trip instead of in two or three. And if gasoline went still higher, maybe you would even agree to join a car pool.

The price system is constantly sending buyers and sellers thousands of signals. The price of *this* service has gone through the roof. *That* product is on sale. *This* good is over-priced and *that* one is a bargain. When something becomes very expensive, we generally cut back. We do this not because the government ordered us to do so or because it issued ration coupons entitling everyone to only three gallons a week, but because the price system itself performed this rationing function.

At the beginning of Chapter 2, I defined economics as *the efficient allocation of the scarce means of production toward the satisfaction of human wants.* In a free-market, private-enterprise economy such as ours, we depend on the price mechanism, or the forces of supply and demand, to perform that job.

In the next chapter, we'll see how the price mechanism plays the central role in allocating resources under capitalism. The forces of demand and supply operate as an automatic guidance system that enables our economy, and others like it, to provide consumers with an endless stream of goods and services.

Last Word

We talked earlier of how the government sometimes interferes with the free operation of markets by imposing price floors and price ceilings. But the government may also ensure the smooth operation of markets by protecting property rights, guaranteeing enforcement of legal contracts, and issuing a supply of money that buyers and sellers will readily accept. Economist John McMillan has emphasized the historic importance of property rights:

Mohammed on supply and demand and property rights

> The prophet Mohammed was an early proponent of property rights. When a famine in Medina brought sharp price increases, people implored him to lessen the hardship by fixing prices. He refused because, having once been a merchant himself, he believed the buyers' and sellers' free choices should not be overridden. "Allah is the only one who sets the prices and gives prosperity and poverty," he said. "I would not want to be complained about before Allah by someone whose property or livelihood has been violated."[2]

So while governmental interference with the market system can have adverse effects, the government does have a substantial supportive role to play in a market economy. In the next chapter we'll consider the role of government under economic systems ranging from capitalism to communism.

Current Issue: High Gas Prices: Something Only an Economist Could Love

On the Labor Day weekend of 2005, gas prices reached nearly $6 in some parts of the South. Customers groused about "price gouging," and many even limited their purchases to "just" $30 or $40, rather than filling their tanks.

What drove prices so high—*besides* the greed of the sellers? As you'll remember, Hurricane Katrina, in addition to devastating New Orleans and its neighboring Gulf Coast communities, also temporarily shut down offshore oil wells which accounted for 25 percent of our domestic oil production. The storm also briefly put about 10 percent of our refineries out of commission.

What we had was a sudden drop in supply. When that happens, of course, price will go up sharply. Which is exactly what happened.

---

[2]John McMillan, *Reinventing the Bazaar* (New York: W. W. Norton, 2002), p. 90.

So what is there to love about high gas prices? Consider the alternative. Back in 1973 and 1979 we had similar supply problems, when shipments from the Middle East were curtailed. Although prices rose sharply, there were gas lines, sometimes six or eight blocks long. In 1979, various states imposed odd and even days to buy gas. If your license plate ended with an even number, you could buy gas on Monday, Wednesday, and Friday. If it ended with an odd number, then you were a Tuesday, Thursday, Saturday buyer.

The government's solution to the gasoline shortage in the 1970s was to restrict purchases and to hold down price increases. But in 2005, the government basically took a hands-off attitude to the gasoline shortage. Prices certainly *did* go up, but there were few gas lines. Everyone could buy as much gas as they wanted, albeit at perhaps $3.50 or $3.75 a gallon. So the price system performed its rationing function very, very well. Although there were widespread complaints about prices, nearly everyone was much happier to pay, say, a dollar a gallon more, and not have to wait in line for an hour or two to buy gas.

Most economists believe price ceilings do more harm than good. In the short run, at least we don't have to wait in gas lines. Furthermore, because of high prices in the summer and fall of 2005, many people cut back on their driving. And in the long run, they will trade in their SUVs for more gas efficient cars. Also, higher prices encourage greater exploration for oil, as well as the development of alternative energy sources. To sum up, rather than impose price controls, we should let the market forces of supply and demand reduce the shortage of gasoline.

Questions for Further Thought and Discussion

1. a. If market price is above equilibrium price, explain what happens and why.
    b. If market price is below equilibrium price, explain what happens and why.

2. a. As the price of theater tickets rises, what happens to the quantity of tickets that people are willing to buy? Explain your answer.
    b. As the price of theater tickets rises, explain what happens to the quantity of tickets that people are willing to sell. Explain your answer.

3. Where is a price ceiling with respect to equilibrium price? What will be the relative size of quantity demanded and quantity supplied?

4. How is equilibrium price affected by changes in (*a*) demand and (*b*) supply?

5. What are the two ways to depict a demand schedule? Make up a demand schedule for some good or service you often buy.

6. What is equilibrium? Why is it advantageous for the market price to be at equilibrium?

7. If you were a landlord, why would you be against rent control? A shortage occurs when the market price is below the equilibrium price.

W*orkbook*   for Chapter 3

Name _____   Date _____

Multiple-Choice Questions

Circle the letter that corresponds to the best answer.

1. When demand rises and supply stays the same, _____.

   a) equilibrium quantity rises

   b) equilibrium quantity declines

   c) equilibrium quantity stays the same

2. When supply rises and demand stays the same, _____.

   a) equilibrium quantity rises

   b) equilibrium quantity falls

   c) equilibrium quantity stays the same

3. At equilibrium price, quantity demanded is _____.

   a) greater than quantity supplied

   b) equal to quantity supplied

   c) smaller than quantity supplied

4. When quantity demanded is greater than quantity supplied, _____.

   a) market price will rise

   b) market price will fall

   c) market price will stay the same

5. What happens to quantity supplied when price is lowered?

   a) It rises.

   b) It falls.

   c) It stays the same.

   d) It cannot be determined if it rises, falls, or stays the same.

6. What happens to quantity demanded when price is raised?

   a) It rises.

   b) It falls.

   c) It stays the same.

   d) It cannot be determined if it rises, falls, or stays the same.

7. When market price is above equilibrium price, _____.

   a) market price will rise

   b) equilibrium price will rise

   c) market price will fall

   d) equilibrium price will fall

8. At equilibrium, quantity demanded is _____ equal to quantity supplied.

   a) sometimes

   b) always

   c) never

9. Market price _____ equilibrium price.

   a) must always be equal to

   b) must always be above

   c) must always be below

   d) may be equal to

10. A demand schedule is determined by the wishes of _____.

    a) sellers

    b) buyers

    c) buyers and sellers

    d) neither sellers nor buyers

11. In Figure 1, if market price were $110, there would be _____.

    a) a shortage

    b) a surplus

    c) neither a shortage nor a surplus

12. In Figure 1, if market price were $140, there would be _____.
   a) a shortage
   b) a surplus
   c) neither a shortage nor a surplus

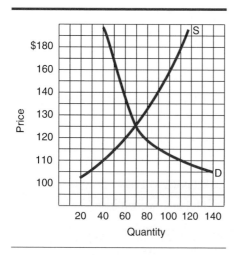

F*igure* 1

13. Market price may not reach equilibrium if there are _____.
   a) both price ceilings and price floors
   b) neither price ceilings nor price floors
   c) only price ceilings
   d) only price floors

14. Gas lines in the 1970s were caused by _____.
   a) price floors
   b) price ceilings
   c) both price floors and price ceilings
   d) neither price floors nor price ceilings

15. Statement 1: Price ceilings cause shortages.
   Statement 2: Interest rates are set by supply and demand, but wage rates are not.
   a) Statement 1 is true and statement 2 is false.
   b) Statement 2 is true and Statement 1 is false.
   c) Both statements are true.
   d) Both statements are false.

16. If the equilibrium price of corn is $3 a bushel, and the government imposes a floor of $4 a bushel, the price of corn will _____.
   a) increase to $4
   b) remain at $3
   c) rise to about $3.50
   d) be impossible to determine

17. Usury laws tend to _____.
   a) create a shortage of loanable funds
   b) create a surplus of loanable funds
   c) make it easier to obtain credit
   d) have no effect on the amount of loanable funds available

18. If the price system is allowed to function without interference and a shortage occurs, quantity demanded will _____ and quantity supplied will _____ as the price rises to its equilibrium level.
   a) rise, rise   c) rise, fall
   b) fall, fall   d) fall, rise

19. Which statement is true?
   a) A price floor is above equilibrium price and causes surpluses.
   b) A price floor is above equilibrium price and causes shortages.
   c) A price floor is below equilibrium price and causes surpluses.
   d) A price floor is below equilibrium price and causes shortages.

20. An increase in supply while demand remains unchanged will lead to _____.
   a) an increase in equilibrium price and a decrease in equilibrium quantity
   b) a decrease in equilibrium price and a decrease in equilibrium quantity
   c) an increase in equilibrium price and an increase in equilibrium quantity
   d) a decrease in equilibrium price and an increase in equilibrium quantity

21. A decrease in demand while supply remains unchanged will lead to _____.
    a) an increase in equilibrium price and quantity
    b) a decrease in equilibrium price and quantity
    c) an increase in equilibrium price and a decrease in equilibrium quantity
    d) a decrease in equilibrium price and an increase in equilibrium quantity

22. As price rises, _____.
    a) quantity demanded and quantity supplied both rise
    b) quantity demanded and quantity supplied both fall
    c) quantity demanded rises and quantity supplied falls
    d) quantity demanded falls and quantity supplied rises

23. When quantity demanded is greater than quantity supplied, there _____.
    a) is a shortage
    b) is a surplus
    c) may be either a shortage or a surplus
    d) may be neither a shortage nor a surplus

24. When quantity supplied is greater than quantity demanded _____.
    a) price will fall to its equilibrium level
    b) price will rise to its equilibrium level
    c) price may rise, fall, or stay the same, depending on a variety of factors

Use Figure 2 to answer questions 25 and 26.

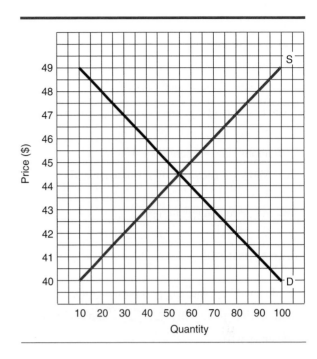

Figure 2

25. At a market price of $47, there is _____.
    a) a shortage
    b) a surplus
    c) both a shortage and a surplus
    d) neither a shortage nor a surplus

26. At a market price of $42, there is _____.
    a) a shortage
    b) a surplus
    c) both a shortage and a surplus
    d) neither a shortage nor a surplus

27. If the government set a price ceiling of 25 cents for a loaf of bread, the most likely consequence would be _____.
    a) a surplus of bread
    b) no one would go hungry
    c) most Americans would put on weight
    d) a shortage of bread

28. Usury laws and rent control are examples of

    _____.

    a) price floors
    b) price ceilings
    c) rationing
    d) the law of supply and demand

29. The best way to eliminate gas lines would be to
    a) impose government price ceilings.
    b) Impose government price floors.
    c) Allow the forces of supply and demand to function.
    d) Put price gougers into jail.

Fill-In Questions

1. If demand falls and supply stays the same, equilibrium price will _____, and equilibrium quantity will _____.

2. If supply rises and demand stays the same, equilibrium price will _____, and equilibrium quantity will _____.

3. If quantity supplied were greater than quantity demanded, market price would _____.

4. Equilibrium price is always determined by _____ and _____.

5. As price is lowered, quantity supplied _____.

6. Shortages are associated with price _____; surpluses are associated with price _____.

7. If supply falls and demand remains the same, equilibrium price will _____, and equilibrium quantity will _____.

8. Price floors and price ceilings are set by _____.

9. Interest rates are set by _____ and _____.

10. What happens to interest rates when the demand for money rises? _____

11. When the supply of money falls, interest rates _____.

Use Figure 3 to answer questions 12 through 15.

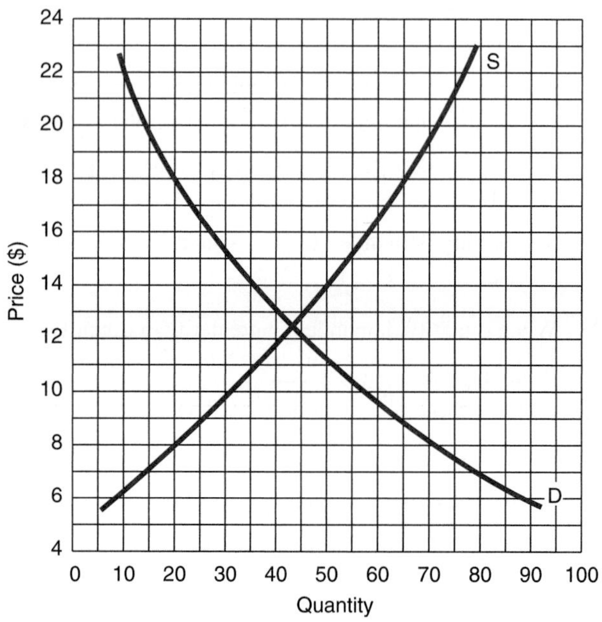

Figure 3

12. Equilibrium price is about $ _____.

13. Equilibrium quantity is about _____.

14. If price were $20, there would be a (shortage or surplus) _____ of _____ units of quantity.

15. If price were $8, there would be a (shortage or surplus) _____ of _____ units of quantity.

16. Price floors keep prices _____ equilibrium price; price ceilings keep prices _____ equilibrium price.

Problems

1. In Figure 4, find equilibrium price and quantity (in dollars and units, respectively).

2. Draw in a new demand curve, D₁, on Figure 4, showing an increase in demand. What happens to equilibrium price and quantity?

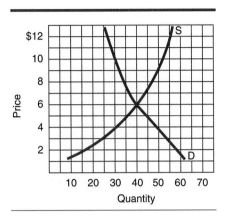

F*igure* 4

3. In Figure 5, find equilibrium price and quantity (in dollars and units, respectively).

4. Draw in a new supply curve, S₁, on Figure 5, showing a decrease in supply. What happens to equilibrium price and quantity?

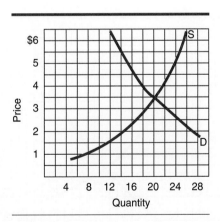

F*igure* 5

5. a) In Figure 6, if the demand curve is D₁, how much are equilibrium price and quantity? b) If demand changes from D₁ to D₂, does that represent an increase or decrease in demand? c) How much are the new equilibrium price and quantity?

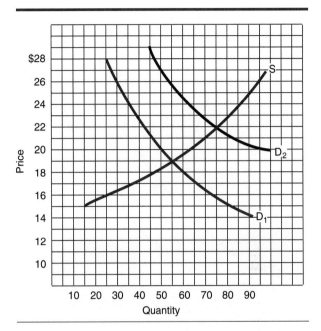

F*igure* 6

6. a) In Figure 7, if the supply curve is S_1, how much are equilibrium price and quantity? b) If the supply changes from S_1 to S_2, does that represent an increase or decrease in supply? c) How much are the new equilibrium price and quantity?

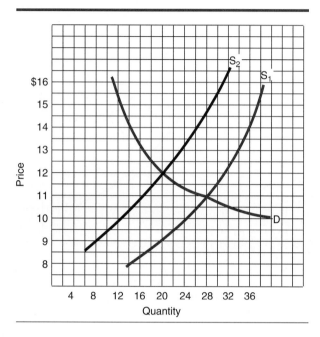

Figure 7

7. Given the information in Figure 8: a) Is $12 a price ceiling or a price floor? b) Is there a shortage or a surplus? c) How much is it (in units of quantity)?

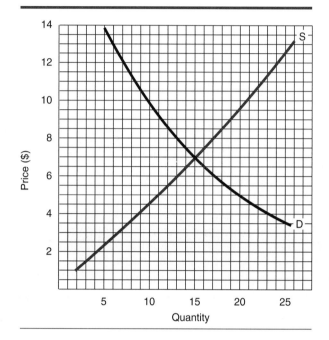

Figure 8

8. Given the information in Figure 9: a) Is $16 a price ceiling or a price floor? b) Is there a shortage or a surplus? c) How much is it (in units of quantity)?

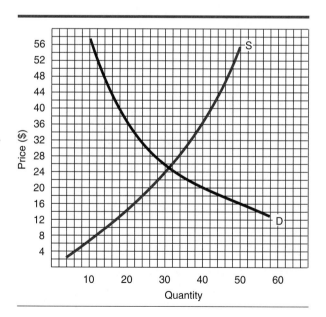

Figure 9

Chapter 4

The Mixed Economy

Ours is a mixed economy because there is a private sector and a public sector. Close to 90 percent of our goods and services originate in the private sector, although the government co-opts some of this production for its own use. China also has a mixed economy; the public sector produces about one-third the goods and services. Every economic system needs to put bread on the table, clothes on people's backs, and a roof over their heads. The question is how resources are used to attain these goods and services.

CHAPTER OBJECTIVES

In this chapter we'll cover:

- The three questions of economics.
- The concepts of the profit motive, the price mechanism, competition, and capital.
- The circular flow model.
- Market failure and externalities.
- Government failure.

- The economic role of capital.
- The "isms": capitalism, fascism, communism, and socialism.
- The decline and fall of the communist system.
- Transformation in China.

The Three Questions of Economics

Because every country in the world is faced with scarce (limited) resources, every country must answer three questions: (1) What shall we produce? (2) How shall these goods and services be produced? (3) For whom shall the goods and services be produced? We'll take up each in turn.

What Shall We Produce?

In the United States, most of our production is geared toward consumer goods and services. About 4 percent goes toward defense. In the former Soviet Union, a much higher proportion was devoted to armaments, with a proportionately smaller percentage devoted to consumer goods and services. Japan has concentrated on building up its plant and equipment but devotes just 1 percent of its production to defense.

Military, consumption, or capital goods?

Who makes these decisions? In the United States and Japan there is no central planning authority, but rather a hodgepodge of corporate and government officials, as well as individual consumers and taxpayers. The Soviets *did* have a central planning authority.

F*igure* 1

Sector Employment as
Percentage of Total
Employment, 1940–2004
The service sector, which accounted
for less than half the jobs in our
economy in 1940, now accounts for
82 percent.
Source: U.S. Census Bureau, *Statistical
Abstract of the United States,* 2006.

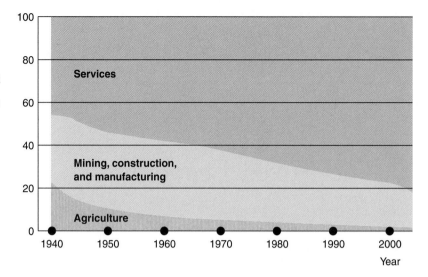

In fact, every five years the Soviet government used to come up with a new plan that set goals for its economy in numbers of cars, TVs, factories, and bushels of wheat and corn to be produced.

As a nation matures, its economy shifts from agricultural to manufacturing, and then to services. This shift is reflected in employment (see Figure 1). Until about 150 years ago, most Americans worked on farms. But today, only 1 in 40 still does. Today, four out of every five workers produce services.

How Shall These Goods and Services Be Produced?

In our country—and in most others as well—nearly everything is produced by private businesses. Not only are all the goods and services that consumers purchase produced by businesses, but so are most of what the government purchases. For example, when our astronauts landed on the moon, a long list of contractors and subcontractors was released. It read like a who's who in American corporations.

In socialist countries, of course, the government is the main producer of goods and services. But even in a communist country, China, there is still a substantial role for private enterprise.

For Whom Shall the Goods and Services Be Produced?

For whom shall the goods be produced?

Economics may be divided into two parts: production, which we dealt with in the first two questions, and distribution. In the first question, we asked what the economic pie should be made of; in the second, we talked about how the pie would be made. Now we are ready to divide up the pie.

Our distribution system is a modified version of one dollar, one vote. In general, the more money you have, the more you can buy. But the government also has a claim to part of the pie. Theoretically, the government takes from those who can afford to give up part of their share (taxes), spends some of those tax dollars to produce various government goods and services, and gives the rest to the old, the sick, and the poor. (Nevertheless, the rich reap a major share of the subsidies to airlines, shipping companies, defense contractors, and agriculture.)

Henry Fairlie has come up with a capitalist credo: From each according to his gullibility. To each according to his greed.

In theory, the Soviets' distributive system was diametrically opposed to ours. The communist credo "From each according to his ability, to each according to his needs" was something the Soviet leaders claimed to follow, and it does have a nice ring to it. But in actuality, their income distribution system, with its jerry-built structure of wage incentives, bonus payments, and special privileges, was probably no more equitable than our own.

To Sum Up

In a mixed economy, both the government and the market have roles in answering: (1) What shall we produce? (2) How shall these goods and services be produced? (3) For whom shall these goods and services be produced? In nearly all mixed economies the government plays a relatively minor role in production, but may play a relatively strong role in distribution.

The Invisible Hand, the Price Mechanism, and Perfect Competition

We have just set the stage for a comparison between our economic system and those of several other countries. We'll start with the competitive economic model, which is based on the law of supply and demand, and then talk about the economic roles of government and of capital. These concepts, common to all economies, need to be understood before we can make comparisons among the economies of different nations.

The Invisible Hand

When Adam Smith coined this term in 1776, he was thinking about an economic guidance system that always made everything come out all right. He believed that if people set out to promote the public interest, they will not do nearly as much good as they would if they pursued their own selfish interests. That's right! If all people are out for themselves, everyone will work harder, produce more, and we'll all be the richer for it. And that premise underlies the free-enterprise system.

Smith said that the entrepreneur is motivated by self-interest:

> He generally, indeed, neither intends to promote the public interest, nor knows how much he is promoting it. By preferring the support of domestic to that of foreign industry, he intends only his own gain, and he is in this, as in many other cases, led by an invisible hand to promote an end which was no part of his intention. . . . By pursuing his own interest he frequently promotes that of the society more effectually than when he really intends to promote it.[1]

Adam Smith, Scottish professor of philosophy (Historical Pictures Stock Montage)

Whenever a businessperson runs for public office, he or she invariably brings up the fact that his or her opponent never met a payroll. This businessperson, motivated solely by a quest for profits, provided jobs for perhaps hundreds, or even thousands, of people. His or her firm produced some good or service so desirable that buyers were willing to pay for it. And so, this aspiring politician, who went into business solely to make money, now claims credit for creating jobs and promoting the public interest. And not a word of thanks to the invisible hand.

Greed makes the world go round.

Less than 20 years ago, about one-third of the food in the Soviet Union was produced on just 2 percent of the land under cultivation. That 2 percent was made up of small, privately owned plots; the other 98 percent was in the form of large collective farms. Obviously, the same farmers worked much harder on their own land than on the land whose produce was owned by the entire society. As Adam Smith said, a person pursuing his own interest "frequently promotes that of society more effectively than when he really intends to promote it."

The invisible hand is really the profit motive.

---

[1]Adam Smith, *The Wealth of Nations,* Book IV (London: Methuen, 1950), chap. II, pp. 477–78.

The Chinese communists, too, forced hundreds of millions of peasants to work on huge collective farms, and like the Soviet agricultural experiment, it had disastrous results. Robert Shiller wrote about the first American experiment in collective ownership:

> When they arrived in the New World, in 1620, the Pilgrims of Plymouth Colony tried communal ownership of the land. It didn't work: crops were not well cared for and the result was a severe food shortage. So in 1623 each family was given a private plot of land along with responsibility for maintaining it. This worked much better. As William Bradford, the second governor of Plymouth Colony, recounted in *Of Plymouth Plantation,* people worked harder when they had private plots, and the crop yield was much higher. The moral of this story—at least according to the proponents of private ownership who like to quote from it—is simple: people take better care of things they own individually than of things they hold in common.[2]

The Price Mechanism

It is often said that everyone has a price, which means that nearly all of us, for a certain sum of money, would do some pretty nasty things. The key variable here is *price*. Some of us would do these nasty things for $100, others for $1,000, others perhaps only for $1 million.

Not only does every*one* have a price, but every*thing* has a price as well. The price of a slice of pizza or a gallon of gasoline is known to all consumers. Although they vary somewhat, gas prices rarely fall below $1.50 and hardly anyone would pay $10 for a slice of pizza.

Prices send signals to producers and consumers.

Just as prices send signals to consumers, they also signal producers or sellers. If pizza goes up to $10 a slice, I'll put an oven in my living room and open for business the next day.

When consumers want more of a certain good or service, they drive the price up, which, in turn, signals producers to produce more. If the price rise is substantial and appears permanent, new firms will be attracted to the industry, thereby raising output still further.

During the 1970s, when we experienced some of the worst inflation in our history, many people called for price controls. These were very briefly and halfheartedly instituted by President Nixon, and their results in controlling inflation were decidedly mixed. Critics of controls believe they interfere with our price mechanism and the signals that mechanism sends to producers and consumers. Others, most notably John Kenneth Galbraith, have argued that the prices of our major products are administered or set by the nation's largest corporations rather than in the marketplace. What this disagreement boils down to is whether our economic system is basically competitive, with millions of buyers and sellers interacting in the marketplace, or whether our economy is dominated by a handful of corporate giants who have subverted the price system by setting prices themselves.

Competition

Competition makes the price system work.

What is competition? Is it the rivalry between Burger King and McDonald's? GM and Ford? Wal-Mart and Target? Most economists will tell you that to have real competition, you need many firms in an industry. How many? So many that no firm is large enough to have any influence over price. So, by definition, an industry with many firms is competitive.

When GM or Ford announces its new prices, *those* are the prices for American cars. Of course, when Microsoft talks about the price of its latest version of Windows, everyone listens. No ifs, ands, or buts. No give-and-take in the marketplace. And the price mechanism? It just doesn't apply here.

To allow the price mechanism to work, we need many competing firms in each industry. There are entire industries—autos, computer software, oil refining, pharmaceuticals, retail bookstores, breakfast cereals, and long distance phone calls—which are dominated by just one or two firms.

---

[2]Robert J. Shiller, "American Casino," *The Atlantic Monthly,* March 2005, p. 33.

If large sectors of American industry are not very competitive, then the price system doesn't work all that well, and the invisible hand becomes even more invisible. However, even without a perfectly competitive economic system, we can't just toss the price mechanism out the window. The forces of supply and demand, however distorted, are still operating. With all their price manipulation, even the largest corporations must guide themselves by the wishes of their consumers. In conclusion, then, let's just say that we have an imperfectly functioning price system in a less than competitive economy that is guided by a not too vigorous invisible hand.

Trust

You'll find the saying, "IN GOD WE TRUST," printed on the back of our currency. Some cynic made up another saying, "In God we trust; all others pay cash"—which means, we suspect that your check might bounce, so we insist on being paid right now in cash.

But despite our cynicism, capitalism is based on trust. Lenders expect borrowers to pay them on time and in full. Sellers ship goods or provide services in advance of payment. And although all businesses guard against theft, the presumption is that the people you deal with are not out to steal from you. Indeed, we build up business relationships over time, and those relationships are based largely on trust.

Capitalism is based on trust.

Because of that underlying trust, business flows smoothly in virtually all capitalist societies. Although the parties to major transactions are bound by formal legal contracts, day-to-day business is usually conducted in person, by phone, by fax, or by e-mail.

Imagine doing business in a socialist or communist economy. You need to order a pencil. So you make out a purchase order, hand it to your supervisor, the purchase order goes up through five more levels of authority, and is then sent to a government purchasing agency where it might sit for several months before some bureaucrat gets around to taking the necessary action. If you're lucky, you'll have your pencil by the end of the year.

Of course government agencies are not all so inefficient, but the reason they are often so bound by rules and regulations is the presumption that bureaucrats can't be trusted to make any business decisions on their own. Under capitalism, we assume that individuals will do the right thing, and because most people are quite trustworthy, the system works very efficiently.

Equity and Efficiency

Under our economic system, most of the important decisions are made in the marketplace. The forces of supply and demand (that is, the price system) determine the answers to the three basic questions we raised at the beginning of the chapter: What? How? And for whom? Most economists would agree that this system leads to a very efficient allocation of resources, which, incidentally, happens to conform to our definition of economics: *Economics is the efficient allocation of the scarce means of production toward the satisfaction of human wants.*

So far, so good. But does our system lead to a fair, or equitable, distribution of income? Just look around you. You don't have to look far to see homeless people, street beggars, shopping-bag ladies, and derelicts. Indeed, there are about 38 million Americans whom the federal government has officially classified as "poor." Later in this chapter, we'll see that one of the basic functions of our government is to transfer some income from the rich and the middle class to the poor. Under the capitalist system, there are huge differences in income, with some people living in mansions and others in the streets. One of the most controversial political issues of our time is how far the government should go in redistributing some of society's income to the poor.

Is our income distributed fairly?

Very briefly, the case for efficiency is to have the government stand back and allow everyone to work hard, earn a lot of money, and keep nearly all of it. But what about the people who don't or can't work hard, and what about their children? Do we let them starve to death? The case for equity is to tax away some of the money earned by the relatively well-to-do and redistribute it to the poor. But doing so raises two questions:

(1) How much money should we redistribute? and (2) Won't this "handout" just discourage the poor from working? We'll discuss this further in the chapter on income distribution and poverty toward the end of the book.

The Circular Flow Model

In Chapter 2 we talked about the four basic resources—land, labor, capital, and entrepreneurial ability. Who owns these resources? We all do. Nearly all of us sell our labor, for which we earn wages or salaries. In addition, many people own land or buildings for which they receive rent. A landlord may have just one tenant paying a few hundred dollars a month, or she may own an office building whose rent is reckoned by the square foot.

We also may receive interest payments for the use of our funds. Since much of the money we put into the bank is borrowed by businesses to invest in plant and equipment, we say that interest is a return on capital.

Finally, there are profits. Those who perform an entrepreneurial function (that is, own and run a business) receive profits for income.

What do people do with their incomes?

The question we are asking here is: What do people *do* with their incomes? What happens to the tremendous accumulation of rent, wages and salaries, interest, and profit? Mostly, it is spent on consumer goods and services, which are produced by private businesses.

This is the essence of what economists call the *circular flow model*. A model is usually a smaller, simplified version of the real thing. (Think of a model plane, a model ship, a map, or a globe.) An economic model shows us how our economy functions, tracing the flow of money, resources, and goods and services. Let's take the circular flow model step by step.

First we have some 113 million households receiving their incomes mainly from the business sector. A household may be a conventional family—a father, mother, and a couple of children—it may be a person living alone, or it may be two cohabiting adults. Any combination of people under one roof—you name it—is defined as a household.

Who owns our resources? It is not the employer who pays wages—he only handles the money. It is the product that pays wages.

—Henry Ford

We diagram the household income stream in Figure 2. Businesses send money income (rent, wages and salaries, interest, and profits) to households. We've ignored the government sector (that is, Social Security checks, welfare benefits, food stamps) and the foreign trade sector.

In Figure 3 we show where this money goes. It goes right back to the businesses as payment for all the goods and services that households buy. In sum, the households provide business with resources—land, labor, capital, and entrepreneurial ability—and use the income these resources earn to buy the goods and services produced by these same resources.

In effect, then, we have a circular flow of resources, income, goods and services, and payments for these goods and services. By combining Figures 2 and 3, we show this circular flow in Figure 4.

There are two circular flows.

We can distinguish two circular flows in Figure 4. In the inner circle, we have resources (land, labor, capital, and entrepreneurial ability) flowing from households to business firms. The business firms transform these resources into goods and services, which then flow to the households.

The outer circular flow is composed of money. Households receive wages and salaries, rent, interest, and profits from business firms. This money is spent on goods and services, so it is sent back to business firms in the form of consumer expenditures.

Thus we have two circular flows: (1) money and (2) resources, and goods and services. These two flows represent the economic activities of the private sector. Whenever any transaction takes place, someone pays for it, which is exactly what *does* happen whenever we do business.

Although the circular flow model may appear fairly complex, it actually oversimplifies the exchanges in our economy by excluding imports, exports, and the government sector. I leave it to your imagination to picture the additional flow of taxes, government purchases, and transfer payments such as unemployment and Social Security benefits. We shall now look at the government's economic role, but our analysis will be separate from our analysis of the private sector.

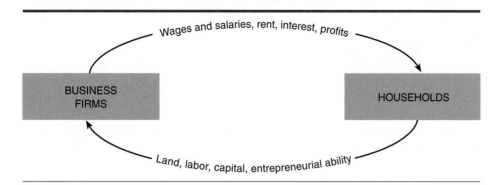

F*igure* 2
The Flow of Resources and Payments for Them

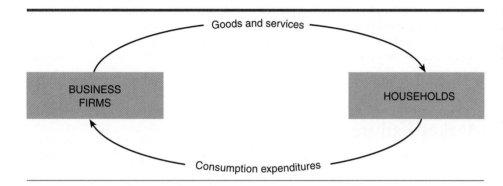

F*igure* 3
The Flow of Goods and Services, and Payments for Them

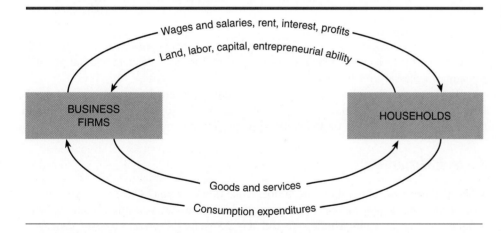

F*igure* 4
The Circular Flow

The Economic Role of Government

The government under our federal system has three distinct tiers. At the top is the federal, or national, government, which we generally refer to as "the government." There are also 50 state governments and tens of thousands of local governments.

Each of these units of government collects taxes, provides services, and issues regulations that have a profound effect on our economy. By taxing, spending, and regulating, the government is able somewhat to alter the outcome of the three questions: What? How? and For whom?

The government provides the legal system under which our free enterprise economy can operate. It enforces business contracts and defines the rights of private ownership. Our legal system works so well that bribery is the very rare exception, rather than the rule, as it is in so many other countries, especially in Asia and Africa.

The government also maintains our competitive system and ensures the relatively unfettered operation of the law of supply and demand. Barriers to competition are sometimes broken down by the government, particularly when a few large firms attempt to squeeze their smaller competitors out of a market. We'll discuss those efforts more fully in the chapter on corporate mergers and antitrust in *Economics* and in *Microeconomics*.

Some of what we produce is done in response to government demand for roads, schools, courthouses, stamp pads, and missile systems. Government regulations have prevented business firms from producing heroin, cyclamates (from the mid-1960s to the late 1970s), and alcoholic beverages (from 1920 to 1933), as well as prostitutes' services (except in part of the state of Nevada, where they are legal).

How things are produced is also influenced by child labor laws, health and safety regulations, and pollution control. And finally, the government, by taking over $3 trillion away from wage earners in taxes, redistributes some of these funds to the old, the disabled, and the poor, thus strongly altering the outcome of the question "For whom?"

The government must provide the infrastructure for a market system to function efficiently. In addition to ensuring that competition flourishes, the government must see that information flows freely, that property rights are protected, and that unpleasant side effects such as pollution are minimized.

Market Failure

Markets don't always provide the most desirable economic outcomes. For example, we assume a great deal of competition among firms, but what happens when some firms grow larger and larger, driving out their smaller competitors? What if one giant firm like Microsoft corners almost the entire market? In the chapter on corporate mergers and antitrust in *Economics* and *Microeconomics,* we'll see how the government has intervened to preserve competition.

When our resources are not allocated efficiently, we have market failure. So while we might prefer to leave as much as we can to the forces of demand and supply, it is sometimes necessary for the government to take action.

We'll examine three basic classes of market failure: externalities, environmental pollution, and the lack of public goods and services. Each provides the government with the opportunity to improve on the work of Adam Smith's invisible hand.

Externalities

When you drive to school, how much does your ride cost you? Once you figure in the cost of gas, oil, insurance, and the depreciation on your car, you might come up with a figure of, say, 25 cents a mile. We call that 25 cents the *private cost* of driving to school.

External cost

But there's also an *external cost*. You cause a certain amount of pollution and congestion, and we could even factor in the cost of highway construction and maintenance. It would be hard to actually come up with a monetary figure, but there is no question that your drive to school imposes a definite social, or external, cost on society.

You probably never thought that driving to school was such a terrible thing, especially if there is no convenient public transportation. But you will be happy to know that you are capable of doing many socially beneficial things as well. If you paint your house and plant a beautiful garden in your front yard, you will not only add to the beauty of your neighborhood, but you will also enhance its property values. So now you are

External benefit

providing an *external benefit*.

Definition of external cost and benefit

Let's define *external cost* and *external benefit*. *An external cost occurs when the production or consumption of some good or service inflicts costs on a third party without compensation. An external benefit occurs when some of the benefits derived from the production or consumption of some good or service are enjoyed by a third party.*

Shipbreaking

When ships grow too old and expensive to run—usually after about 25 or 30 years—their owners sell them on the international scrap market, where the typical freighter may bring a million dollars for the weight of its steel. Are the ship owners behaving in an environmentally correct manner, like those of us who return our soda cans to the grocery or deposit them in recycling bins? It turns out that they are not.

About 90 percent of the world's annual crop of 700 condemned ships are sailed right up on the beaches of China, Pakistan, India, and Bangladesh, where they are dismantled. Predictably, these once pristine beaches have become an environmental wasteland. In an *Atlantic Monthly* article, William Langewiesche describes the risks to which the workers are exposed: "falls, fires, explosions, and exposure to a variety of poisons from fuel oil, lubricants, paints, wiring, insulation, and cargo slop. Many workers are killed every year."*

What the United States and other industrial nations have done is exported our environmental problems to the less developed countries of the world. Langewiesche explains how this came about:

Shipbreaking was performed with cranes and heavy equipment at salvage docks by the big shipyards of the United States and Europe until the 1970s, when labor costs and environmental regulations drove most of the business to the docksides of Korea and Taiwan. Eventually, however, even these entrepreneurial countries started losing interest in the business and gradually decided they had better uses for their shipyards. This meant that the world's shipbreaking business was again up for grabs. In the 1980s enterprising businessmen in India, Bangladesh, and Pakistan seized the initiative with a simple, transforming idea: to break a ship they did not need expensive docks and tools; they could just wreck the thing—drive the ship up onto a beach as they might a fishing boat, and tear it apart by hand.[†]

*William Langewiesche, "The Shipbreakers," *The Atlantic Monthly,* August 2000, p. 34.
[†]Ibid., p. 33.

The private market, governed solely by the forces of supply and demand, does not take into account external costs and external benefits. This is market failure. When the market failure imposes a high cost on society, we demand that the government do something about it.

Basically, the government can take three types of action. If you are doing something that provides an external benefit, such as running a family farm, the government may provide you with a subsidy to encourage you to continue farming. As we saw back in Chapter 1, although the federal government has paid out hundreds of billions of dollars in farm subsidies since World War II, not only have most family farms disappeared, but huge corporate farms have gotten most of the subsidies.

If you are incurring external costs, the government can discourage these activities in two ways. It can tax you, or it can impose stringent regulations.

Let's consider what the government can do about air and water pollution. It could tax these activities highly enough to discourage them. A hefty tax on air pollution will force the biggest offenders to install pollution-abatement equipment. What about the disposal of nuclear waste? Do we let nuclear power plants dump it into nearby rivers but make them pay high taxes for the privilege? Hardly. The federal government heavily regulates nuclear plants.

Basically, we want to encourage activities that provide external benefits and discourage those that incur external costs. One method now used in many states is the five-cent deposit on cans and bottles. Millions of people have a monetary incentive to do the right thing by returning these bottles and cans for recycling.

A major part of the external costs of manufacturing and commerce affect our environment. Obvious examples include strips of tires along the highways, abandoned cars, acid rain, and toxic waste. The accompanying box discusses an international example of external costs—shipbreaking.

Air pollution and water pollution are perhaps the two greatest external costs of industrial economies. Let's see how the government can curb pollution.

Curbing Environmental Pollution

The incentive to pollute is much stronger than the incentive to curb pollution.

Left to its own devices, private enterprise creates a great deal of pollution. After all, it's a whole lot easier—and cheaper—to dump waste products into nearby rivers and streams, or send them up a smokestack. The government, most notably the federal Environmental Protection Agency, has taken two types of measures to lower pollution levels—command-and-control regulations and incentive-based regulations.

Command-and-Control Regulations   Automobile fuel-burning emissions are a major cause of air pollution. The federal government has imposed three regulations which have substantially reduced these emissions—mandating the use of catalytic converters on all new vehicles, fuel economy standards for all new cars, and a ban on leaded gasoline. Overall, these regulations have greatly reduced air pollution from motor vehicles. However, fuel economy standards were supposed to be raised periodically (more miles per gallon), but these increases have been periodically postponed. Furthermore, these standards are applied just to new cars, exempting minivans and sports utility vehicles (SUVs), which are classified as light trucks, and not subject to the fuel standards. Today cars are just half of all new passenger vehicles.

Since the passage of the Clean Air Act in 1972, which requires companies to reduce air pollution, there has been a marked improvement in air quality throughout much of the United States. During the decade of the 1990s alone, concentrations of sulfur dioxide and carbon monoxide decreased by 36 percent, and lead by 60 percent.

Do command-and-control regulations work? Clearly they do. But can we do better? Nearly all economists would agree we can do better using incentive-based regulations.

Incentive-Based Regulations   How can we give people an incentive to cause less air pollution? How about taxing gasoline? In addition to a federal tax on gasoline, there are also state and local taxes. Using the supply and demand graph shown in Figure 5A, let's trace the effect of gasoline taxes on the purchase of gasoline.

These taxes lower the supply of gasoline from S_1 to S_2. The price of gasoline consequently rises from $1.00 to $1.80 per gallon. And the number of gallons purchased falls from 900 million to 820 million per week.

The less gasoline purchased, the less people drive and the lower the level of air pollution. In most other economically advanced countries, gasoline taxes are much higher—sometimes more than $4 a gallon. The effect of a $4 per gallon tax is shown in Figure 5B. The price of gasoline rises from $1.00 to $4.20 per gallon. And the number of gallons purchased falls from 900 million to just 580 million.

It's obvious that a $4 per gallon tax would result in a much lower level of air pollution than a $1 per gallon tax. So why don't we raise gasoline taxes to the same levels as in Western Europe? Can you guess why we don't? Imagine that you are a member of Congress getting ready to vote on raising the federal tax on gasoline to $4 a gallon. Your constituents back home would not be very happy campers, and, if you were planning any kind of political future, you would not vote for this tax increase.

Emissions rights trading

Perhaps the most promising approach to incentive-based regulations is emissions rights trading, which originated as a result of the 1990 Amendments to the Clean Air Act. The government determines the permissible level of pollution and issues permits to each polluting firm. These permits allow up to a certain level of pollution, and the firms are allowed to buy or sell the permits.

Although the markets for emissions permits are in their early stages, there have already been some notable transactions. The Times Mirror Company purchased from other polluters the right to discharge 150 tons of hydrocarbons annually before completing an expansion of its paper plant near Portland, Oregon. In a three-party trade, the city of Torrence, California, acquired the rights from General Motors to dump 900 pounds of reactive vapors per day. Torrence then sold these rights to Mobil Oil (now ExxonMobil) for $3 million. And since 1994 there has been trading in pollution permits on the Chicago Board of Trade.

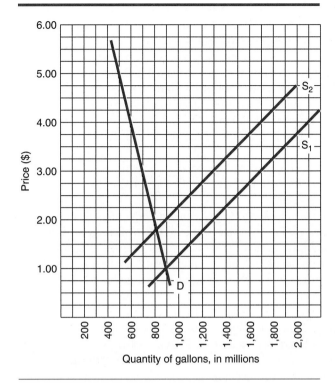

F*igure* 5A

Hypothetical Weekly Demand for and Supply of Gasoline, with $1 Tax

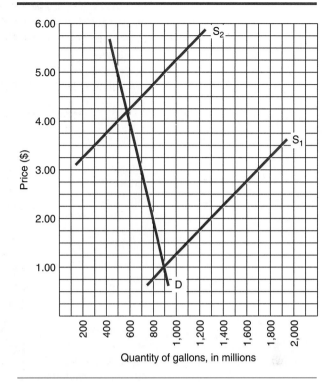

F*igure* 5B

Hypothetical Weekly Demand for and Supply of Gasoline, with $4 Tax

What level of pollution is acceptable to you? Would you be willing to give up driving to reduce auto emissions to zero? Would you be willing to use a lot less electricity to curb emissions of electrical power plants? In general, would you be willing to accept a substantially lower standard of living if that would result in substantially less pollution? I think it's a pretty safe bet that your answer is "No!" to all three questions.

Lack of Public Goods and Services

A wide range of goods and services is supplied by our federal, state, and local governments. These include national defense; a court system; police protection; the construction and maintenance of streets, highways, bridges, plus water and sewer mains; environmental protection; public parks; and public schools. Few of these would be supplied by private enterprise because entrepreneurs would not be able to make a profit.

Interestingly, many of these goods and services *were* once supplied by private enterprise. The nation's first toll road, Pennsylvania's Lancaster Turnpike, was built two centuries ago. Private toll bridges were constructed all over the country. Even today, there are more than twice as many people who work in private security ("rent-a-cops," store and hotel detectives, building security, campus security, and private investigators, for example) than there are city and state police. Our national rail lines were once privately owned, with such fabled names as the Pennsylvania (or Pennsy) Railroad; the Baltimore and Ohio (you'll still find the B&O on the Monopoly board); the Seaboard; the Southern; the Great Northern; the New York Central; the New York, New Haven, and Hartford; the Boston and Maine; the Southern Pacific; and the storied Atchison, Topeka, and the Santa Fe.

Let's talk about the difference between *public* goods and *private* goods. Private goods are easy. You buy a car. It's your car. But a public good is something whose consumption by one person does not prevent its consumption by other people. Take our national defense. If you want to pay to have your home defended from nuclear attack,

Difference between public and private goods

then everyone on your block is defended as well, even though they don't chip in a cent. Or, if your block association hires a private security firm to patrol your neighborhood, even your neighbors who were too cheap to pay their dues are protected.

Not everything produced by the public sector is a public good. We mentioned defense as a public good—something whose consumption by one person does not prevent its consumption by other people. What about a ride on a public bus? Or driving on the Jersey Turnpike? These are not public goods because only those who pay get to ride.

The two defining characteristics of public goods and services

Public goods and services have two defining characteristics. First, they are *nonexcludable,* which means that once it exists, everyone can freely benefit from it. You can benefit from unpolluted air whether or not you helped pay for it. Second, public goods and services are *nonrivalrous,* which means that one person's benefiting from it does not reduce the amount of it available for others. Police protection for you does not prevent others from also enjoying that protection.

Public goods tend to be indivisible; they usually come in large units that cannot be broken into pieces for purchase or sale in private markets. Often there is no way they can be produced by private enterprise because there is no way to exclude anyone from consuming the goods even if she or he did not pay for them. National defense is a classic example. Could you imagine putting *that* service on a pay-as-you-go basis? "I think this year I'll just skip being defended." We can't exactly move the nuclear umbrella away from my house while continuing to shield those of all my neighbors.

Not everyone favors an expansion of public goods. Aristotle observed that "What is common to many is taken least care of, for all men have a greater regard for what is their own than for what they possess in common with others." Public property is often not as well maintained as private property, because, as Aristotle noted, people will take better care of their own property than of property held in common.

Government Failure

The United States is the only country where it takes more brains to figure your tax than to earn the money to pay it.
—Edward J. Gurney

Just as the market sometimes fails us, so does the government. Below is a short list of some of the more blatant forms of government failure. Keep in mind, however, that in most cases the government performs its functions reasonably well, so these failures should be considered exceptions and not the norm.

Let's start with an obvious failure—our complex and confusing federal tax code. University of Michigan economist Joel Slemrod estimates that it costs taxpayers (in accounting fees as well as in the value of their own time) about $100 billion a year to complete their tax returns. According to the Internal Revenue Service it takes 28 and a half hours to complete an average tax return with itemized deductions. Even the simplest form, 1040EZ, takes on average 3 hours and 43 minutes to fill out.

The hardest thing in the world to understand is the income tax.
—Albert Einstein

Closely related are the forms the government sends all large and most medium-sized companies. It takes hundreds of hours a year to fill out these monthly, quarterly, and annual forms. The government compiles copious statistics on the economy, which it then publishes in thousands of monthly, quarterly, and annual reports. I enjoyed dropping in to my local federal bookstore to peruse these publications and would usually buy a few. But the stores were closed in 2003 to save money. Question: Wouldn't it then have made sense to cut down on the number of these publications? And maybe not collect so much data, thereby freeing up tens of thousands of corporate employees?

Another abject government failure is its agricultural price support program, which currently costs the taxpayers $19 billion a year, and, since its inception more than seven decades ago, has cost hundreds of billions of dollars. What is the main purpose of this program? Ostensibly the purpose is to save the family farm. But since the 1930s millions of family farms have gone out of business; most of the payments now go to huge corporate farms.

A society should be judged largely by how it treats its children. Of the 38 million Americans living in poverty, more than half are children. In the 1960s President Lyndon Johnson declared a massive war on poverty, and some 30 years later came the Welfare Reform Act of 1996. And yet, today, one of every six American children is growing up poor.

Our public education system, once the envy of the world, is now the laughingstock. While we still have some of the finest schools of higher education, our elementary, middle, and high schools have been deteriorating for decades. The fact that we need to teach the three r's—reading, writing, and arithmetic—to millions of college students pretty much says it all. While all the blame for our failing educational system cannot be placed on the government's doorstep, the fact remains that getting a decent education has become a difficult challenge for most children. I am old enough to remember when high school graduates could actually read, write, and do some algebra and geometry.

Since 2001 the federal government has failed to keep its financial house in order. In just six short years we have swung from a budget surplus of $236 billion to a deficit approaching $500 billion. Most of the deficit is financed by foreigners, mainly the Chinese and Japanese. Instead of calling for further tax cuts, we need to bring down the deficit and eventually begin to pay off the national debt.

Hurricane Katrina is still fresh enough in our memory that if I asked you to grade the government's response, I'm sure you would have a pretty strong opinion. You might give a failing grade to the state and local authorities, to the federal government, or to all three. But regardless of how the blame is apportioned, Hurricane Katrina provides a very clear example of government failure.

Millions of Americans helped the hurricane victims, directly or indirectly. But these private efforts were directed at ameliorating the suffering, rather than preventing it. In hindsight, New Orleans and its suburbs should have been fully evacuated, and once the flooding took place, those left behind should have been quickly rescued. Those were not jobs for individuals, voluntary organizations, or business firms, but mainly for the federal government.

Local and state officials, as well as the Army Corps of Engineers, knew only too well that New Orleans' levees would not be able to hold back the floodwaters produced by a major hurricane. Once the city began to flood, only federal agencies such as FEMA (Federal Emergency Management Agency) had the resources to deal with a catastrophe of this magnitude. While there are plenty of places to spread the blame of the slow and halting rescue and recovery effort, maybe someone should send President Bush a copy of the placard President Harry Truman kept on his desk. It read: "The buck stops here."

Like you, I have a pretty strong opinion of which government officials should be blamed. Dealing with hurricanes, other natural disasters, as well as terrorist attacks is very clearly a government function. In late August and early September of 2005 our government very badly failed the people on the Gulf Coast. Will our government be better prepared when the next disaster strikes?

In contrast to government failure, large companies such as Wal-Mart, Home Depot, and FedEx were the first responders in the wake of Hurricane Katrina. The October 3, 2005 issue of *Fortune* sings the praises of these companies, which had, as our army generals like to say, boots on the ground. While the government took precious days to act, these and other large companies made plans days in advance, and put them into effect hours after the hurricane made landfall.

Just by staying open for business, these and other companies provided a lifeline to hurricane victims. Jessica Lewis, the co-manager of the Waveland, Mississippi Wal-Mart, had to deal with two feet of water and tons of damaged stock. Here is an account of what she saw and how she reacted:

> As the sun set on Waveland, a nightmarish scene unfolded on Highway 90. She saw neighbors wandering around with bloody feet because they had fled their homes with no shoes. Some wore only underwear. "It broke my heart to see them like this," Lewis recalls. "These were my kid's teachers. Some of them were *my* teachers. They were the parents of the kids on my kid's sports teams. They were my neighbors. They were my customers."
>
> Lewis felt there was only one thing to do. She had her stepbrother clear a path through the mess in the store with a bulldozer. Then she salvaged everything she could and handed it out in the parking lot. She gave socks and underwear to shivering Waveland police officers who had climbed into trees to escape the rising water. She handed out shoes to her barefoot neighbors and diapers for their babies. She gave people bottled water to drink and sausages,

stored high in the warehouse, that hadn't been touched by the flood. She even broke into the pharmacy and got insulin and drugs for AIDS patients. "This is the right thing to do," she recalls thinking. "I hope my bosses aren't going to have a problem with that."[3]

While all Wal-Mart managers might not have acted as altruistically as Jessica Lewis, the company made a major difference simply by staying open, keeping their stores stocked with food and water, and, in keeping with their slogan, charging low, everyday prices. Unlike price gougers who drove into the disaster area to sell portable generators for $1,500, Wal-Mart sold theirs at their regular $300 price.

Finally, let's talk about the Medicare drug prescription plan, which was rammed through Congress in 2005 by President George W. Bush and Republican Congressional leaders and has caused mass confusion among senior citizens, pharmacists, doctors, nursing home administrators, and the dozens of participating insurance companies. When the new plan went into effect in January, 2006, hundreds of thousands of senior citizens were turned away by their pharmacies when they came in to have their prescriptions filled. It would be charitable to say that the system had some glitches that needed to be worked out. Writing in *The New York Times,* Jane Gross described some of the complexities of the drug prescription plan, and the problems they have caused:

> Even those who received their new prescription drug cards on time are not home free. Each person has an ID number, an Issuer number, an Rx Bin number, an Rx PCN number and an Rx Group number. Type one digit wrong when ordering medications and the computer flashes an error message.
>
> ...
>
> Each plan also has tiered subplans, labeled bronze, silver or gold. And each of those has its own formulary, the list of drugs that are covered, and its own appeals process for those that are not. But search the plans' Web sites looking for instructions for appeals. "Sorry, the document you request doesn't exist," comes the mannerly reply.[4]

Capital

Capital is the crucial element in every economic system. Karl Marx's classic *Das Kapital* examined the role of capital in the mid-19th-century industrializing economy of England. According to Marx, the central figure of capitalism is the capitalist, or business owner, who makes huge profits by exploiting his workers. Capital consists of plant and equipment. Marx said that whoever controlled a society's capital controlled that society.

Furthermore, Marx observed that one's social consciousness was determined by one's relationship to the means of production. Inevitably, he believed, there would be a clash between the capitalists and the workers, leading to an overthrow of capitalism and the establishment of a communist society. Then the workers would own the means of production. In the Soviet Union, incidentally, the means of production *were* owned by the workers, but the ruling elite, the top Communist Party officials, had real economic and political control.

The role of capital in the production process is central to why our country is rich and most of the rest of the world is poor. The reason an American farmer can produce 10 or 20 times as much as a Chinese farmer is that the American has much more capital with which to work—combines, tractors, harvesters, and reapers. And the reason the American factory worker is more productive than the Brazilian factory worker is that our factories are much better equipped. We have a tremendous stock of computers, assembly lines, warehouses, machine tools, and so on.

Take the example of the word processor and its successor, the personal computer. In the past, a lot of business letters had to be personally or individually typed, although

Karl Marx, German economist, historian, and philosopher (Historical Pictures/Stock Montage)

Capital consists of plant and equipment.

The central economic role of capital

---

[3]Devin Leonard, "The Only Lifeline Was the Wal-Mart," *Fortune,* October 3, 2005, p. 75.

[4]Jane Gross, "Nursing Homes Confront New Drug Plan's Hurdles," *The New York Times,* January 15, 2006, p. 16.

Where Capital Comes From

The following hypothetical situation will illustrate the value of capital. Suppose it takes a man 10 hours to make an optical lens, while someone working with a machine can make one in just 5 hours. Let's assume that it would take 1,000 hours to build such a machine.

Assume, however, that a person working 10 hours a day is barely able to support himself and his family. (Karl Marx observed that, in most working-class families, not only did wives work, but they didn't have to worry about day care centers or baby-sitters for the children because factories employed six- and seven-year-olds.) If he could not afford to spend 100 days (1,000 hours) building the machine, he still had two choices. He could cut back on his consumption—that is, lower his family's standard of living—by working nine hours a day on the lenses and one hour a day on building the machine. Or he could work, say, an extra hour a day on the machine.

In either case, it would take 1,000 days to build the machine. If he cut back on his consumption *and* worked an extra hour a day, it would take him 500 days to build the machine.

Once he had the machine, he'd *really* be in business. He could double his daily output from one lens a day to two a day (remember that a person working with a machine can turn out a lens in just 5 hours).

Each day, if he held his consumption to the same level, he would produce two lenses and sell one for food, rent, and other necessities. The other lens he'd save. At the end of just 100 days, he'd have saved 100 lenses. Those 100 lenses represent 1,000 hours of labor, which is exactly the same amount of labor that went into building a machine. He would probably be able to buy another machine with those 100 lenses.

Now he's *really* a capitalist! He'll hire someone to run the second machine and pay him a lens a day. And in another 100 days, he'll have a surplus of 200 lenses, and he'll be able to buy two more machines, hire a foreman to run his shop, retire to a condominium in Miami Beach at the age of 36, and be the richest kid on the block.

---

they were really only form letters. Today we have a PC that can be programmed to print identical texts with different addresses at the rate of one letter every couple of seconds.

Our stock of capital enables us to turn out many more goods per hour of labor than we could produce without it. Much backbreaking as well as tedious labor has been eliminated by machines. Without our capital, we would have the same living standard as that of people living in the poorer countries of Asia, Africa, and Latin America.

Where did capital come from? Essentially from savings. Some people would set aside part of their savings, go into business, and purchase plant and equipment (see the box, "Where Capital Comes From"). But we're really skipping a step.

Initially there was no capital, except for some crude plows and other farm tools. People worked from sunrise to sunset just to produce enough food to put on the table. But a few farmers, a little more prosperous than their neighbors, were able to spare some time to build better farm tools. Or they might have had enough food stored away to employ someone to build these tools. Either way, some productive resources were diverted from producing consumer goods to producing capital goods.

The factory conditions of the 19th-century England that Marx described in *Das Kapital* were barbaric, but the end result was that a surplus of consumer goods was produced. The factory owner, by paying his workers meager wages, was able to use this surplus to buy more capital goods. These enabled his factory to be more productive, creating still greater surpluses that were used to purchase still more plant and equipment.

Under Joseph Stalin, the Russians devoted a large part of their production to capital goods, literally starving the Russian population of consumer goods. To this day there is a great shortage of consumer goods in the former Soviet Union. But this shortage is no longer due to diversion of resources from production of consumer goods to the production of capital goods. It is due to the inefficiencies of the economic system itself—something we'll be looking at more closely in the closing pages of this chapter.

In the years following World War II, Japan and the countries of Western Europe, struggling to rebuild their shattered economies, held down their consumption as they

Where did capital come from?

Capital is past savings accumulated for future production.
—Jackson Martindell

concentrated on building new plant and equipment. The South Koreans and Taiwanese later followed this model of building capital.

Capital is the key to our standard of living.

The world's developing nations face nearly insurmountable obstacles—rapidly growing populations and very little plant and equipment. The experience of the industrializing nations in the 19th century was that, as people moved into cities from the countryside and as living standards rose, the birthrate invariably declined. But for industrialization to take place, capital must be built up. There are two ways to do this: Cut consumption or raise production. Unfortunately, most developing nations are already at subsistence levels, so no further cuts in consumption are possible without causing even greater misery. And production cannot easily be raised without at least some plant and equipment.

With the exception of the OPEC nations, which have been able to sell their oil in exchange for plant and equipment, the poorer nations of Africa, Asia, and Latin America have little hope of rising from extreme poverty. A supposed exchange of letters that took place between Mao Tse-tung and Nikita Khrushchev when China and the Soviet Union were allies in the early 1960s illustrates the futility of a third way out—foreign aid.

> Mao: Send us machinery and equipment.
> Khrushchev: Tighten your belts.
> Mao: Send us some belts.

 # The "Isms": Capitalism, Communism, Fascism, and Socialism

Q: What is the difference between capitalism and socialism?
A: Under capitalism, man exploits man. Under socialism, it's just the opposite.

–Overheard in Warsaw–[5]

Property is the exploitation of the weak by the strong.
Communism is the exploitation of the strong by the weak.

–Pierre-Joseph Proudhon–[6]

Capitalism

During the 20th century, perhaps no three opprobriums have been hurled more often at political opponents than those of Communist! Capitalist! and Fascist! Let's compare the four great economic systems. Capitalism, as we've already seen, is characterized by private ownership of most of the means of production—that is, land, labor, capital, and entrepreneurial ability. Individuals are moved to produce by the profit motive. Production is also guided by the price system. Thus, we have millions of people competing for the consumer's dollar. The government's role in all of this is kept to a minimum; basically, it ensures that everyone sticks to the rules.

Since the early 1980s there has been a huge swing throughout much of the world towards capitalism. First capitalism took root in China, and a decade later in the former Soviet Union and in what had been its satellite empire in Eastern Europe as well. Today the great preponderance of the world's output of goods and services is produced under capitalism.

Capitalism is often confused with democracy. A democracy has periodic elections in which the voters freely choose their rulers. Most capitalistic nations—for example, the United States, Japan, and the members of the European Union—are democracies.

---

[5]Lloyd G. Reynolds, *Microeconomic Analysis and Policy,* 6th ed. (Burr Ridge, IL: Richard D. Irwin, 1988), p. 435.
[6]Pierre-Joseph Proudhon, *What Is Property?* chap. V, Part II.

On the opposite end of the political spectrum is the dictatorship, under which the rulers perpetuate themselves in power. Their elections do not have secret ballots, so predictably the rulers always win overwhelmingly. Indeed, Saddam Hussein received 100 percent of the vote in Iraq's 2002 presidential election.

Sometimes capitalistic dictatorships evolve into capitalistic democracies. Taiwan, South Korea, Indonesia, the Philippines, and Chile are recent examples. The Soviet Union, which has been going through a painful conversion from communism to capitalism, now holds relatively free elections, and could be considered a democracy. There are hopes that China will also evolve into a democracy. But the leaders of the Communist Party, who have handed power down from one generation to the next, show no signs of allowing free elections.

"The theory of the Communists may be summed up in the single sentence: Abolition of private property," declared Karl Marx and Friedrich Engels in *The Communist Manifesto*. Who would own everything? The state. And eventually the state would wither away and we would be left with a workers' paradise.

In the Soviet version of communism, under which the state had evidently not yet withered away, most of the capitalist roles were reversed. Instead of a guidance system of prices to direct production, a government planning committee dictated exactly *what* was produced, *how* it was produced, and *for whom* the goods and services were produced. After all, the state owned and operated nearly all of the means of production and distribution.

All of the resources used had to conform to the current five-year plan. If the goal was 2 million tractors, 100 million tons of steel, 15 million bushels of wheat, and so on, Soviet workers might have expected to be putting in a lot of overtime.

The big difference between the old Soviet economy and our own is what consumer goods and services are produced. In our economy, the market forces of supply and demand dictate what gets produced and how much of it gets produced. But a government planning agency in the Soviet Union dictated what and how much was made. In effect, central planning attempted to direct a production and distribution process that works automatically in a market economy.

How well did the Soviet communist system work? Remember the chronic shortages of consumer goods we mentioned earlier in the chapter? Although Soviet president Mikhail Gorbachev went to great lengths to shake up the bureaucracy and get the economy moving again, his efforts were futile. To raise output, he found he needed to somehow remove the heavy hand of bureaucracy from the economic controls. But as he stripped away more and more of the Communist Party's power, he found that his own power had been stripped away as well.

If the Soviet Union did not exemplify pure communism, then what country did? In the box "Real Communism," you'll read that we have had pure communism right under our noses for many years.

Communism

Communism doesn't work because people like to own stuff.
—Frank Zappa, Musician

Communist: A fellow who has given up all hope of becoming a capitalist.
—Orville Reed

They pretend to pay us, and we pretend to work.
—Polish folk definition of communism

Communism was a great system for making people equally poor.
—Thomas Friedman

Real Communism

Several years ago, I knew a history professor at St. Francis College in Brooklyn who loved to shock his students by telling them that he had been a communist. As a young man, he had joined a Catholic religious order, lived in a commune, and shared all his possessions with his fellow seminarians. "What could be more communist than living in a commune with no private property?" he asked his students.

And so we may ask whether what they had in the Soviet Union and in Eastern Europe was really communism. How would Karl Marx have reacted to those huge bureaucratic dictatorships? Marx had foreseen "the withering away of the state," until all that was left was a society of workers who followed his credo "From each according to his ability; to each according to his needs." This sounds a lot more like that history professor's seminary than what was passing for communism in the old Soviet empire.

The Soviet regime collapsed not just because of its bureaucratic inefficiencies but also because it supported a huge military establishment that claimed between one-fifth and one-quarter of its resources and national output.

One of the fundamental economic problems with *any* economy that attempts to substitute government planning for the price system (or to replace the law of demand and supply with government decrees) is that changes in price no longer help producers decide what and how much to produce. In a capitalist country, higher microwave oven prices would signal producers to produce more microwave ovens. But in the Soviet Union, there was very little inflation even though there were widespread shortages of consumer goods. In fact, the Soviets came up with a great cure for inflation. Just let everyone wait in line.

The entire Soviet economy was a Rube Goldberg contraption[7] of subsidies, fixed prices, bureaucratic rules and regulations, special privileges, and outright corruption. Had Gorbachev not acted, the entire Soviet system might well have come apart by itself over another couple of generations.

A joke that circulated in the late 1980s went like this: Under communism your pockets are full of money, but there isn't anything in the stores you can buy with it. Under capitalism, the stores are full, but you have no money in your pockets.

Fascism

Fascism hasn't been in vogue since Hitler's defeat in 1945, but it does provide another model of an extreme. In Nazi Germany the ownership of resources was in private hands, while the government dictated what was to be produced.

The problem with describing the fascist economic model is that there really *is* no model. The means of production are left in private hands, with varying degrees of governmental interference. Generally those in power are highly nationalistic, so a high proportion of output is directed toward military goods and services.

Fascists have been virulently anticommunist but have also been completely intolerant of any political opposition. The one-party state, suppression of economic freedom, and a militaristic orientation have been hallmarks of fascism.

The early 1940s were evidently the high-water mark of fascism. Although from time to time a fascist state does pop up, it appears to be a temporary phenomenon. With the possible exception of Hitler's Germany, which did put most Germans back to work after the Great Depression, albeit largely at military production, most fascist states have been economic failures that apparently collapsed of their own weight.

Socialism

Socialism has not gotten the bad press that capitalism, fascism, and communism have received, perhaps because those who dislike the socialists prefer to call them communists. In fact, even Soviet government officials used to refer to themselves as socialists and their country, the U.S.S.R., was formally called the Union of Soviet Socialist Republics, although President Ronald Reagan referred to the Soviet Union as the evil empire. And the countries with socialist economies were our military allies.

It is a socialist idea that making profits is a vice; I consider the real vice is making losses.

—Winston Churchill

The economies of such countries as Sweden, Canada, Great Britain, and, recently, France and Greece have been described as socialist, not only by government officials in those countries but by outside observers as well. In general, these economies have three characteristics: (1) government ownership of some of the means of production; (2) a substantial degree of government planning; and (3) a large-scale redistribution of income from the wealthy and the well-to-do to the middle class, working class, and the poor.

One of the most familiar characteristics of socialist countries is cradle-to-grave security. Medical care, education, retirement benefits, and other essential needs are guaranteed to every citizen. All you need to do is be born.

The vice of capitalism is that it stands for the unequal sharing of blessings; whereas the virtue of socialism is that it stands for the equal sharing of misery.

—Winston Churchill

Where does the money to pay for all of this come from? It comes from taxes. Very high income taxes and inheritance taxes fall disproportionately on the upper middle class and the rich. In Israel several years ago, a joke went around about a man who received an unusually large paycheck one week. He couldn't figure out what had happened until his wife looked at his check stub and discovered that he had been sent his deductions by mistake. Only the very wealthy must give the government more than half their pay in socialist countries, but the story *did* have a ring of truth to it.

Rather than allow the market forces to function freely, socialist governments sometimes resort to very elaborate planning schemes. And since the government usually owns

---

[7]Such a device is designed to accomplish by complex means what seemingly could be done simply.

the basic industries and provides the basic services, this planning merely has one hand directing the other.

Sweden is often considered the archetypal socialist country, although perhaps 90 percent of the country's industry is privately owned. It is the government's massive intervention in the private economy that gives Swedish society its socialist tone. Not only has the Swedish government kept the unemployment rate generally below 3 percent for several decades by offering industry and workers a series of subsidies and incentives, but it provides one of the most elaborate cradle-to-grave programs in the world. The government doles out $100 monthly allowances for each child and provides day care centers, free education from nursery school through college, free medical care, and very generous unemployment and retirement benefits. Women may take a year off work after the birth of a child while receiving 80 percent of their pay.

But Sweden's brand of socialism pales in comparison to that of Norway, its Scandinavian neighbor. In addition to free day care, subsidized housing and vacations, and free medical care, Norwegians receive annual stipends of more than $1,600 for every child under 17, retirement pay for homemakers, and 42 weeks of fully paid maternity leave. How do they pay for all of this? Not only does Norway have the world's highest income tax rates, but it has a 23 percent sales tax and a gasoline tax of about $5 a gallon. Hallmarks of Norwegian society are a great disdain for the trappings of wealth and power and a profound sense of equality, which militate against a wide disparity in pay.

Perhaps this joke, which has made its rounds on the Internet, may best sum up the four isms:

> Socialism: You have two cows. State takes one and gives it to someone else.
> Communism: You have two cows. State takes both of them and gives you milk.
> Fascism: You have two cows. State takes both of them and sells you milk.
> Capitalism: You have two cows. You sell one and buy a bull.

Swedish socialism

Norwegian socialism

The Decline and Fall of the Communist System

Under Joseph Stalin and his successors, from the late 1920s through the 1960s, Soviet economic growth was very rapid, as government planners concentrated on building the stock of capital goods, largely neglecting consumer goods. The government purposely set prices on consumer goods very low, often not changing them for decades. They wanted even the poorest people to be able to afford the basic necessities.

By the late 1970s, China began reforms, very gradually evolving into a market economy. However the Soviet Union, through the 1980s, continued to stagnate, devoting most of its talent and capital to its military establishment. Most of its armed forces served, basically, as an army of occupation in Eastern Europe. By the time that army was withdrawn, in 1989, and defense expenditures slashed, the Soviet Union was in political turmoil. Within two years the communists, along with the huge central planning apparatus, were gone, and the Soviet Union was dismembered into 15 separate nations, the largest of which was Russia.

Transformation in China

For decades before they attained power, the Chinese communists depicted themselves as agrarian reformers who would provide hundreds of millions of landless peasants with their own farms. But soon after attaining power they abolished virtually all private property and forced about 90 percent of the population to live and work on huge collective farms.

The communists came to power in 1949, taking over one of the world's poorest nations. For the first three decades, largely under Mao Tse-tung (his friends called him Chairman Mao, and he liked the rest of the Chinese to refer to him as "the Great Helmsman"), the Chinese economy was dominated by Soviet-style central planning.

Even though the economy absorbed two extremely disruptive setbacks—the Great Leap Forward (1958–60), during which perhaps 30 million people starved to death, and the Cultural Revolution (1966–75), both of which Mao used to consolidate power—economic growth may have averaged 9 percent a year. China was pulled up from a backward country plagued by periodic famine to one in which everyone had enough to eat and many could afford to buy TVs, refrigerators, cameras, and some of the other amenities we in the United States take for granted. In 1978 there were 1 million TV sets in China; by 1998 there were nearly 300 million.

The shift toward capitalism

In China, as in the former Soviet Union, the big boss of a province, or of the entire country, has held the modest title of First Secretary of the Communist Party. Back in 1978 a man named Zhao Ziyang was the First Secretary in Szechuan province, which was becoming world famous for its wonderful cuisine. Until 1978, the highly centralized Chinese planning system had slowed economic growth. Zhao issued an order that year freeing six state-owned enterprises from the control of the central planners, allowing the firms to determine their own prices and output, and even to keep any profits they earned. In just two years some 6,600 firms had been cut loose, Zhao had become the Chinese head of state, and China was well on its way to becoming a market, or capitalist, economy.

The farmers employed by the huge collective farms had little incentive to work hard. As John McMillan noted, "It made little difference whether a farmer worked himself to exhaustion or dozed all day under a tree. Either way, the amount he took home to feed his family was much the same."[8]

Beginning in 1979 many provincial leaders across China, independent of the central authorities in Beijing, shifted the responsibility of operating huge collective farms to the families that lived on the farms. Although each family was given a production quota to meet, any additional output could be sold at a profit. By 1984 more than 90 percent of China's agricultural land was farmed by individual households. In just six years food output rose by 60 percent.

In the late 1970s and early 1980s, reform began to take hold in the industrial sector as well. State firms were free to sell any surplus output, after having met their quotas. Simultaneously millions of tiny family-run enterprises were springing up all across the land, ranging from street peddlers, owners of tiny restaurants, and bicycle repair shops, to large factories and international trading companies. By the late 1980s, many of these large private factories were at least partially owned by Chinese businessmen from Hong Kong and Taiwan, as well as by investors from Japan, other Asian countries, and even some from Western Europe and the United States. China's southern provinces, and especially her coastal cities, have become veritable "export platforms," sending out a stream of toys, consumer electronics, textiles, clothing, and other low-tech products mainly to consumers in Japan, Europe, and North America. Between 1978 and 2000, Chinese exports rose from $5 billion to more than $200 billion.

The agricultural and industrial reforms diluted the ideological purity that had marked the first 30 years of communist rule. In 1984 the Communist Party's Central Committee went so far as to depart from the traditional communist credo "From each according to his ability, to each according to his needs." The new slogan was "More pay for more work; less pay for less work." What this did, implicitly, was to say to budding entrepreneurs, "It's OK if you get rich—you worked hard for your money."

To get rich is glorious.
    —Deng Xiaoping

Although average family income has at least quintupled since 1978, China remains a relatively poor agricultural nation with two-thirds of its population living in rural areas. But it has 1.3 billion people (one out of every five people on this planet lives in China), and it has become a middle-rank industrial power. Should its economy continue to grow at 8 or 9 percent a year, within a decade China may well replace Japan as our most formidable economic rival.

---

[8]John McMillan, *Reinventing the Bazaar* (New York: W. W. Norton, 2002), p. 94.

Current Issue: The Bridge to Nowhere

If the quest for profits motivates business owners, then what motivates members of Congress? They want to get reelected. And they're quite good at it: Over 98 percent of our representatives get reelected every two years.

The most effective campaign issue of every member of Congress is that they can bring home the bacon. They can point to the highways, bridges, rapid transit systems, military bases, and courthouses for which the federal government shelled out hundreds of millions of dollars. Never mind that, in the process, we have been running record federal budget deficits. The important thing is that your representative delivers.

Every member of Congress has a very strong incentive to bring home as much federal money as possible. So we have 435 Congressional districts competing for this money. It doesn't matter whether the projects are good or bad as long as the money is being spent. So what we have here is systematic government failure.

A handful of states, Alaska among them—are so sparsely populated that they have just one member of the House of Representatives. Alaska, for example, the third least populated state, is represented by Don Young, who happens to be the chairman of the House Committee on Transportation and Infrastructure. So perhaps it was no coincidence that when the Transit Act of 2005 was passed, Alaska got $941 million, the fourth largest amount received by any state. The two key projects funded were $231 million for a bridge near Anchorage called the "bridge to nowhere" and $233 million for another bridge connecting the tiny village of Ketchikan to an island with 50 inhabitants.

The "bridge to nowhere," to be formally called "Don Young's Way," will connect Anchorage with a swampy undeveloped port. The Ketchikan bridge will carry an estimated 100 cars a day, saving them a seven-minute ferry ride. So if the federal government will foot the bill, Alaska will take the money and run.

Questions for Further Thought and Discussion

1. The circular flow model is a simplified version of our economy. Describe how this model works.

2. What are the three basic economic questions that all economies must answer? Describe the differences in the ways capitalism and socialism answer these questions.

3. What was Adam Smith's invisible hand, and what economic function did it serve?

4. What are the two basic classes of market failure? What would be an example of each?

5. Can you think of any other government failures in addition to those listed in the chapter?

6. How far has China evolved into a market economy? To what degree has this evolution contributed to China's economic growth?

7. For many years Americans referred to the People's Republic of China as "Communist China." Why would that label be misleading today?

8. Explain why you would prefer to live in a socialist or a capitalist country.

Workbook for Chapter 4

Name _____   Date _____

Multiple-Choice Questions

Circle the letter that corresponds to the best answer.

1. We have a mixed economy because _____.
   a) we produce guns and butter
   b) we consume domestically produced goods as well as imports
   c) we consume both goods and services
   d) there is a private sector and a public sector

2. Which does not fit with the others?
   a) competition
   b) government planning and regulation
   c) the invisible hand
   d) the price mechanism

3. Adam Smith believed the best way to promote the public interest was to _____.
   a) have the government produce most goods and services
   b) let people pursue their own selfish interests
   c) wait for individuals to set out to promote the public interest
   d) get rid of the price mechanism

4. Our economy does a very good job with respect to _____.
   a) both equity and efficiency
   b) equity, but not efficiency
   c) efficiency, but not equity
   d) neither equity nor efficiency

5. Which is the most accurate statement?
   a) No country could be classified as having a communist economic system.
   b) It could be argued that every nation has a mixed economy.
   c) The United States is basically a socialist economy.
   d) The Chinese economy is evolving away from capitalism and toward pure communism.

6. Adam Smith believed people are guided by all of the following except _____.
   a) the profit motive
   b) self-interest
   c) the public good
   d) the invisible hand

7. The price system is based on _____.
   a) government regulation (i.e., the government sets most prices)
   b) the individual whim of the businessperson who sets it
   c) the feelings of the individual buyer
   d) supply and demand

8. Which one of the following would be the best public policy?
   a) Zero tolerance for pollution
   b) Allow private business firms to curb their own pollution.
   c) Provide business firms with incentives to curb their pollution.
   d) Hold economic growth to a minimum until pollution levels are reduced substantially.

9. In the United States, nearly all resources are owned by _____.
   a) the government
   b) business firms
   c) individuals
   d) foreigners

10. The pilgrims who settled Plymouth, Massachusetts, concluded that _____.
    a) only a social society of collective ownership would make economic sense.
    b) a capitalist society with large industrial corporations would make economic sense
    c) private ownership worked better than collective ownership
    d) from each according to his ability to each according to his wants was the best course to follow

11. Wages, rent, interest, and profits flow from _____.
    a) business firms to households
    b) households to business firms
    c) business firms to the government
    d) the government to business firms

12. Private ownership of most of the means of production is common to _____.
    a) capitalism and communism
    b) capitalism and fascism
    c) capitalism and socialism
    d) fascism and communism

13. The price mechanism is least important under _____.
    a) capitalism
    b) socialism
    c) fascism
    d) communism

14. The five-year plan had been the main economic plan of _____.
    a) the United States
    b) Sweden
    c) Nazi Germany
    d) the Soviet Union

15. Fascism peaked in the _____.
    a) 1920s
    b) 1930s
    c) 1940s
    d) 1950s

16. The strongest criticism of Sweden's economic system has been that _____.
    a) it provides too many benefits
    b) its taxes are too high
    c) its taxes are too low
    d) it doesn't provide enough benefits

17. The strongest indictment of the capitalist system was written by _____.
    a) Adam Smith
    b) John Maynard Keynes
    c) Rose D. Cohen
    d) Karl Marx

18. Karl Marx said that _____.
    a) whoever controlled a society's capital controlled that society
    b) in the long run, capitalism would survive
    c) the U.S.S.R.'s communist system was "state capitalism"
    d) capitalists and workers generally had the same economic interests

19. The main reason the American farmer can produce more than the farmer in China is that he _____.
    a) has more land
    b) has more capital
    c) has more labor
    d) is better trained

20. Capital comes from _____.
    a) gold
    b) savings
    c) high consumption
    d) the government

21. An individual can build up his/her capital _____.
    a) by working longer hours only
    b) by cutting back on consumption only
    c) by both cutting back on consumption and working longer hours
    d) only by borrowing

22. Which is the most accurate statement about shipbreaking?
    a) It is generally done in a manner that is environmentally sound and that minimizes dangers to workers.
    b) It is an extremely profitable activity that is sought after by the world's largest shipbuilders.
    c) Ship owners whose boats have grown too old and expensive to run usually abandon them at sea or sink them.
    d) The United States and other industrial nations have exported their environmental problems like shipbreaking to less developed countries such as India, Bangladesh, and Pakistan.

Fill-In Questions

1. The invisible hand is generally associated with (a) the _____ and (b) _____.

2. Adam Smith believed that if people set out to promote the public interest, they will not do nearly as much good as they will if they _____.

3. Defense spending and police protection are examples of _____.

4. Painting the outside of your house and planting a garden in your front yard are _____ to your neighbors.

5. When you drive, rather than walk or take public transportation, you incur social costs such as _____.

Chapter 5

The Household-Consumption Sector

C hances are you've never been to the South Street Seaport Museum in New York City, a combination museum-shopping center, with some great shops and restaurants. When it opened in 1983, Christopher Lowrey, its director, said, "The fact is that shopping is the chief cultural activity in the United States." So the next time you want to sop up some culture, instead of attending a concert or play, just head over to the mall.

In this chapter we begin our examination of the four sectors of gross domestic product (GDP): C (consumption), I (investment), G (government spending), and Xn (net exports). We look at consumption: why people spend money, what they buy, and why they save so little of their incomes. We will also introduce graphing techniques as a tool for macroeconomic analysis, which will be covered in Chapters 11 and 12.

Anyone who says money doesn't buy happiness doesn't know where to shop.

—Anonymous

CHAPTER OBJECTIVES

In this chapter we will introduce eight economic concepts:

- The average propensity to consume.
- The average propensity to save.
- The marginal propensity to consume.
- The marginal propensity to save.

- The consumption function.
- The saving function.
- The determinants of consumption.
- The permanent income hypothesis.

GDP and Big Numbers

Consumption, investment, and government spending are the three main sectors of GDP. But what, exactly, is GDP? Gross domestic product is a term that you'll find quite frequently in the financial section of your newspaper, as well as in *The Wall Street Journal, BusinessWeek, Fortune,* and other financial publications. Gross domestic product, which is the subject of Chapter 9, is the *nation's expenditure on all the final goods and services produced during the year at market prices.*

I'm going to be throwing very large numbers at you—millions, billions, and trillions. The box titled, "A Word about Numbers" provides a lucid explanation of how to deal with these numbers; so if you don't know your billions from your trillions, you definitely need to read the box.

Speaking of numbers, so they don't have to write out 12 zeros, economists write one trillion dollars like this: 1,000, or sometimes, 1000. It's a lot faster than writing, $1,000,000,000,000.

What's the difference between mathematics and economics? Mathematics is incomprehensible; economics just doesn't make sense.

A Word about Numbers

The time has come to talk about numbers—big numbers. We need to keep our thousands, millions, billions, and trillions straight, so here's a way to sort out big numbers.

1. Thousands come after the first comma: for example, 17,000 (seventeen thousand); 391,000 (three-hundred ninety-one thousand).

2. Millions come after the second comma: for example, 6,000,000 (six million); 410,000,000 (four-hundred ten million).

3. Billions come after the third comma: for example, 924,500,000,000 (nine-hundred twenty-four billion, five-hundred million); 86,000,000,000 (eighty-six billion).

4. Trillions come after the fourth comma: for example, 31,000,000,000,000 (thirty-one trillion); 570,000,000,000,000 (five-hundred seventy trillion).

How would they write $100 billion? See if you can do it. The answer is 100. How would you write $5 trillion? The answer is 5000 or 5,000.

Consumption

The average American spends virtually all of her income after taxes. The total of everyone's expenditures is consumption, designated by the letter C. The largest sector of GDP, C, now accounts for 7 out of every 10 dollars.

Consumers spend 59 percent of their money on services such as medical care, eating out, video rentals, life insurance, and legal fees. The rest is spent on durable goods, such as television sets and furniture, or on nondurable goods, such as food and gasoline. All consumption falls into one of the two categories of goods or services.

Until the late 1990s, consumption was usually between 90 and 95 percent of disposable income. John Maynard Keynes (pronounced "canes") noted that consumption is a stable component of income. His theory, called the consumption function, states that *as income rises, consumption rises, but not as quickly.*[1] For example, if a country's disposable income rises by 300 (from 2,000 to 2,300), its C will rise, but by less than 300. If C were 1,800, it might rise by 250 to 2,050.[2]

The consumption function is illustrated by the hypothetical figures in Table 1. We'll start with a disposable income of 1,000 (read as $1,000 billion, or $1 trillion) and consumption of 1,400 ($1,400 billion, or $1.4 trillion). Now let's move up to a disposable income of 2,000. You'll notice that C rose to 2,200. So an increase of 1,000 (from 1,000 to 2,000) in disposable income pushes up C by 800 (from 1,400 to 2,200). This relationship remains the same as we raise disposable income to 3,000, 4,000, and 5,000. Each 1,000 increase in disposable income gives us an 800 increase in C.

So, as disposable income rises in increments of 1,000, C rises in increments of 800, which conforms to the consumption function: *As income rises, consumption rises, but not as quickly.*

When we say, then, that consumption is a function of disposable income, we mean that it *varies* with disposable income. When disposable income goes up, so does consumption, though by a smaller amount. And when disposable income declines, so does consumption, but again, by a smaller amount.

> The consumption function states that as income rises, consumption rises, but not as quickly.

---

[1] His exact words were, "Men are disposed, as a rule and on the average, to increase their consumption as their income increases, but not by as much as the increase in their income."

[2] The number 2,050 represents $2,050 billion (or $2.05 trillion). Remember that 2,000 represents $2,000 billion, or $2 trillion. This is a convention economists use when writing about billions and trillions of dollars.

TABLE 1	Consumption and Disposable Income	
Disposable Income	**Consumption**	
1,000	1,400	
2,000	2,200	
3,000	3,000	
4,000	3,800	
5,000	4,600	

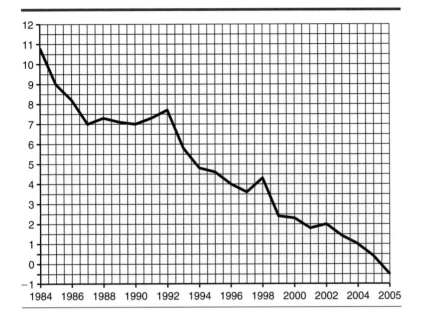

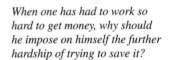

Figure 1

Savings as a Percentage of Disposable Personal Income, 1984–2005

Our savings rate fell quite steadily from the early 1980s into the new millennium. By 2005 our savings rate was −0.5 percent.

Source: Economic Report of the President, 2006; Survey of Current Business, March 2006.

Saving

Saving is simply not spending. Since the early 1990s our savings rate seems to be performing its own version of the limbo. In answer to the question, "How low can you go?" you'll see by glancing at Figure 1 that it fell from 10.5 in 1984 to around 5 in the late 1990s. By 2005 our savings rate actually turned negative—for the first time in 73 years. Indeed we have not experienced a negative savings rate since the depths of the Great Depression in 1932 and 1933.

During the depression many families had little or no income. They survived by digging into their savings, borrowing, and receiving private and public assistance. So their negative savings was no great surprise. But in these times of relative prosperity, Americans are spending more than they're earning. Unlike during the 1930s, when people spent most or all of their incomes just to put some food on the table and a roof over their heads, today Americans are buying a lot of things they want, but don't necessarily need. Our spending seems driven by a pervasive sense of entitlement.

How does our saving rate stack up against those of other leading developed economies? As you can see from a glance at Figure 2, we are near the bottom of the heap. Savings rates in virtually all these countries have fallen sharply over the last 10 years.

When one has had to work so hard to get money, why should he impose on himself the further hardship of trying to save it?
—Don Herold

Average Propensity to Consume (APC)

The average propensity to consume is the percentage of disposable income spent. Using the data in Table 2, let's calculate the APC.

Figure 2

Household Saving as a
Percentage of Disposable
Income, 2006 Forecast
Source: OECD, *The Economist,*
February 4, 2006, p. 93.

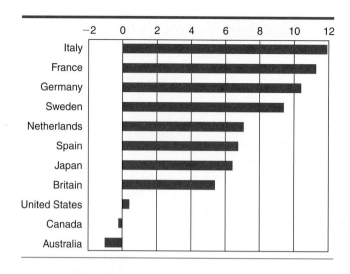

TABLE 2	
Disposable Income	Consumption
$40,000	$30,000

$$APC = \frac{Consumption}{Disposable\ income}$$

To find the percentage of disposable income spent, we need to divide consumption by disposable income.

$$APC = \frac{Consumption}{Disposable\ income} = \frac{\$30,000}{\$40,000} = \frac{3}{4} = 0.75$$

Let's review how this is done. We use the three-step method of solving this problem. First, write the formula. Then, substitute the numbers into the formula. Finally, solve the formula.

Average Propensity to Save (APS)

The APS is the mirror image of the APC. It is the percentage of disposable income saved. Using the data in Table 2, calculate the APS.

Use the same three-step method we used to calculate the APC: (1) Write the formula, (2) plug in your numbers, and (3) solve. Do it right here.

Now we'll check your work. The formula is:

$$APS = \frac{Saving}{Disposable\ income}$$

Next we'll substitute into the formula. You already know from Table 2 that disposable income is $40,000. How much is saving? It's not in Table 2, but since consumption is $30,000, we can find saving by subtracting consumption from disposable income: $40,000 − $30,000 = $10,000. Now we can complete the problem.

$$APS = \frac{Saving}{Disposable\ income} = \frac{\$10,000}{\$40,000} = \frac{1}{4} = 0.25^3$$

Note that the APC and the APS add up to 1. Let's work out another one, using the data in Table 3.

---

[3]To convert ¼ into a decimal, we must divide the bottom number, 4, into the top number, 1.

ADVANCED WORK

APCs Greater than One

Is it possible to have an APC greater than one? You bet it is! How much would your APC be if you had a disposable income of $10,000 and your consumption was $12,000? Figure it out:

$$APC = \frac{Consumption}{Disposable\ income} = \frac{\$12,000}{\$10,000} = \frac{12}{10} = 1.2$$

Where would this extra $2,000 come from? Let's round up the usual suspects. You might take money out of the bank, borrow on your credit cards, take out a car loan or a home equity loan, or buy on the installment plan. The bottom line is that many people find it quite easy to spend more than they earn year after year, whether by drawing down their savings, borrowing money, or some combination thereof.

Incidentally, if your APC *were* 1.2, how much would your APS be? Work it out right here:

$$APC = \frac{Saving}{Disposable\ income} = \frac{-\$2,000}{\$10,000} = \frac{-2}{10} = -0.2$$

Is it possible to have a negative APS? If your savings happens to be negative (that is, you spend more than your income), then your APS will definitely be negative. And you'll notice that your APC (1.2) plus your APS (−0.2) add up to 1.0.

TABLE 3

Disposable Income	Saving
$20,000	$1,500

Use the space below to calculate the APC and the APS.

Solutions:

$$APC = \frac{Consumption}{Disposable\ income} = \frac{\$18,000}{\$20,000} = \frac{185}{200} = \frac{37}{40} = 0.925$$

$$APS = \frac{Saving}{Disposable\ income} = \frac{\$1,000}{\$20,000} = \frac{15}{200} = \frac{3}{40} = 0.075$$

Note that once again APC (.925) and APS (.075) add up to 1. This is your check to ensure that you haven't made a mistake in your calculations. (But can the APC ever be greater than 1? See the box, "APCs Greater than One.")   APC + APS = 1

Now that we've done all this work, what does it mean to say that a person has an APC of .925 and an APS of .075? Think about the APC and the APS as percentages of disposable income. A person with an APC of 0.925 spends 92.5 percent of her disposable income and saves 7.5 percent of it. Go back to the formulas for the APC and the APS.

Just two more questions: How much is the current APC for the United States? How much is the country's APS? For the last few years it's averaged about 0.98. In other words, Americans spend about 98 percent of their disposable incomes and save the remaining 2 percent.

Figure 3

Average Propensity to
Consume, Selected Countries,
2006 Forecast

For 2006 Australia and Canada are
forecast to have APCs greater than 1,
while the U.S. is expected to have
an APC of just under 1. Among the
countries shown here, Italy, France,
and Germany are expected to have
APCs of less than 0.9.
Source: OECD.

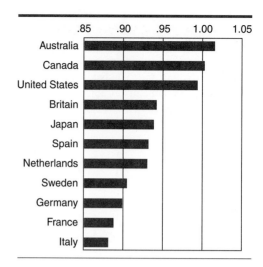

How does our APC compare with those of other countries. As you can see at a glance from Figure 3, we're number three, just behind Australia and Canada. To call Americans world-class consumers would be quite an understatement.

Marginal Propensity to Consume (MPC)

When income changes, so does consumption. When income rises, consumption also rises, but by less than does income. This is the consumption function, introduced at the beginning of the chapter.

The formula for calculating the MPC is:

$$\frac{\text{Change in C}}{\text{Change in income}}$$

$$MPC = \frac{\text{Change in C}}{\text{Change in income}}$$

TABLE 4		
Year	Disposable Income	C
2000	$30,000	$23,000
2001	40,000	31,000

Using the data in Table 4, calculate the MPC in the space below.

Solution:

$$MPC = \frac{\text{Change in C}}{\text{Change in income}} = \frac{\$8,000}{\$10,000} = \frac{8}{10} = 0.8$$

Marginal Propensity to Save (MPS)

When income changes, not only does consumption change, but so does saving. When income rises, both consumption and saving will rise. Similarly, when income falls, both consumption and saving fall.

The formula for calculating the MPS is:

$$MPS = \frac{\text{Change in saving}}{\text{Change in income}}$$

$$MPS = \frac{\text{Change in saving}}{\text{Change in income}}$$

Using Table 4 again, calculate the MPS. (Note: Remember how to find saving when you have disposable income and consumption.)[4]

Solution:

$$MPS = \frac{\text{Change in saving}}{\text{Change in income}} = \frac{\$2,000}{\$10,000} = \frac{2}{10} = 0.2$$

We'll be using the APC, APS, MPC, and MPS later in this chapter, and occasionally in later chapters.

Graphing the Consumption and Saving Functions

Reading a Graph

The key to reading economic variables from a graph is knowing where to look for them; so before we even look at graphs, let's just talk about them for a moment. There is a vertical line on the left side of every graph called the *vertical scale,* and there is a horizontal line on the bottom side of every graph called the *horizontal scale.* Take a peek at Figure 4 to see what I'm talking about.

Every graph you will ever see in an economics text will have these two dimensions: the horizontal and the vertical. The vertical scale is almost always measured in dollars. In Figure 4 we have an expenditures scale with the numbers 2,000, 4,000, and 6,000, which represent expenditures of $2 trillion, $4 trillion, and $6 trillion, respectively. Note that the distances between each of the successive numbers are equal. The horizontal axis in Figure 4 measures disposable income, also in units of 2,000, 4,000, and 6,000. This graph has only one line: a 45-degree line. This line has one purpose: to equate the horizontal scale with the vertical scale, that is, expenditures with disposable income.

Expenditures are measured on the vertical scale and disposable income along the horizontal scale.

---

[4]From Table 4: Disposable income − Consumption = Savings
(2000) $30,000 − $23,000 = $7,000
(2001) $40,000 − $31,000 = $9,000

F*igure* 4

Disposable Income and
Expenditures
The 45-degree line equates
expenditures and disposable income.
For example, when disposable
income is 4,000, expenditures are
4,000.

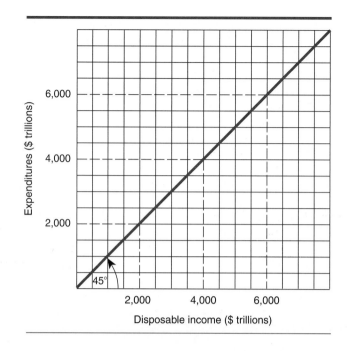

Note the dotted line rising from a disposable income of 2,000. It meets the 45-degree line and then moves horizontally to the left to the vertical scale. For a disposable income of 4,000, there is another dotted line rising to the 45-degree line and then moving straight across to the vertical scale. The same pattern occurs at a disposable income of 6,000.

The Consumption Function

Now we're ready to graph the consumption function. First we'll review it: *As income rises, consumption rises, but not as quickly.* How should it look on a graph? It is represented by the C line in Figure 5.

F*igure* 5

Consumption and Disposable
Income
At a disposable income of $3
trillion the C line crosses the
45-degree line. So consumption
expenditures are equal to disposable
income at $3 trillion.

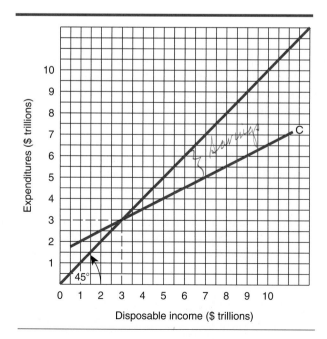

Now we're ready to read the graph in Figure 5. How much is consumption when disposable income is $3 trillion? This question is so easy, you should be able to answer it by just glancing at the graph.

When disposable income is $3 trillion, consumption is also $3 trillion. You'll notice that the C line and the 45-degree line cross at that point. To answer the question, just follow the dotted lines. Move up vertically from a disposable income of $3 trillion to the 45-degree line. Then move horizontally to the left to a consumption of $3 trillion on the vertical axis.

Next question: How much is consumption when disposable income is $6 trillion?

The answer is $4.5 trillion. Again, go straight up from $6 trillion on the horizontal axis to the C line, and then straight across to the left to $4.5 trillion on the vertical axis.

Last question: How much is consumption when disposable income is $1 trillion?

C is $2 trillion. How can our nation have a disposable income of just $1 trillion and manage to consume $2 trillion worth of goods and services? We can dig into our savings and we can borrow from banks and other lenders. And as a nation, we can borrow from foreigners.

Moving right along, let's use Figure 5 to find the nation's marginal propensity to consume and its average propensity to consume. See if you can do it on your own beginning with the MPC formula. Do your work right here:

Solution:

Let's say that disposable income rises from $3 trillion to $5 trillion. By how much does C rise?

At a disposable income of $3 trillion, C = $3 trillion. At a disposable income of $5 trillion, C = $4 trillion. So when disposable income rises from $3 trillion to $5 trillion, C rises by $1 trillion.

Now we can substitute numbers into the MPC formula and solve:

$$\text{MPC} = \frac{\text{Change in consumption}}{\text{Change in disposable income}} = \frac{\$1 \text{ trillion}}{\$2 \text{ trillion}} = \frac{1}{2} = 0.5$$

Now find the average propensity to consume when disposable income is $5 trillion.

Solution:

$$\text{APC} = \frac{\text{Consumption}}{\text{Disposable income}} = \frac{\$4 \text{ trillion}}{\$5 \text{ trillion}} = \frac{4}{5} = 0.8$$

The Saving Function

The saving function is virtually the same as the consumption function: *As income rises, saving rises, but not as quickly.*

The following equation summarizes some very basic relationships:

$$\text{Disposable income} = \text{Consumption} + \text{Saving}$$

If disposable income is $12 trillion and savings is $2 trillion, how much is consumption?

Consumption is $10 trillion. If disposable income is $5 trillion and consumption is $8 trillion, how much is saving?

Saving is −$3 trillion. Remember that disposable income ($5 trillion) = consumption ($8 trillion) + saving (−$3 trillion). When savings is negative, we call it "dissaving."

Let's turn back again to Figure 5 and find how much this nation saves at various levels of disposable income. Here's an easy one: How much is saving when disposable income is $3 trillion?

You can see that it's zero, because at the intersection of the C line and the 45-degree line, consumption = disposable income. Next, find savings when disposable income is $9 trillion.

Saving is $3 trillion. It's measured by the vertical distance between the C line and the 45-degree line. Incidentally, how much is C when disposable income is $9 trillion?

C is $6 trillion. To prove your answers, just substitute them into the formula:

$$\text{Disposable income} = \text{Consumption} + \text{Saving}$$
$$\text{\$9 trillion} \quad\quad = \text{\$6 trillion} \quad + \text{\$3 trillion}$$

Now find consumption and savings when disposable income is $2 trillion.

Solution:

$$\text{Disposable income} = \text{Consumption} + \text{Saving}$$
$$\text{\$2 trillion} = \text{\$2.5 trillion} \quad + (-\text{\$0.5 trillion})$$
$$\text{\$2 trillion} = \text{\$2.5 trillion} \quad - \text{\$0.5 trillion}$$

How are you doing? If you're getting the right answers, then you're ready to tackle autonomous consumption and induced consumption. But if you'd like a little more practice finding consumption, saving, and the MPC and APC by reading a graph, please work your way through the accompanying extra help box.

Autonomous Consumption and Induced Consumption

Autonomous consumption is our level of consumption when disposable income is 0. It is called autonomous consumption because it's autonomous, or independent, of changes in the level of disposable income. People will spend a certain minimum amount on the necessities of life—food, clothing, and shelter—even if they have low incomes or no incomes. Whether they have to beg, borrow, or steal, people will spend some minimum amount.

Finding Consumption, Savings, the MPC, and the APC on a Graph

See if you can find savings and consumption when disposable income is $8 trillion in Figure A.

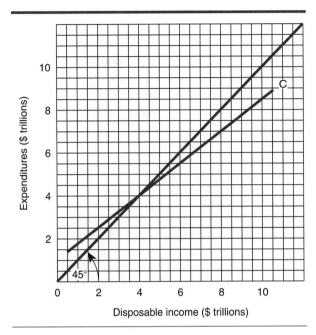

Figure A

Consumption is $7 trillion and savings is $1 trillion. Note that consumption ($7 trillion) and savings ($1 trillion) = disposable income ($8 trillion).

Now do this three-part problem by filling in the table below:

	Disposable income	Consumption	Savings
(a)	$2 trillion		
(b)	$4 trillion		
(c)	$6 trillion		

You'll find the answers in Figure B.

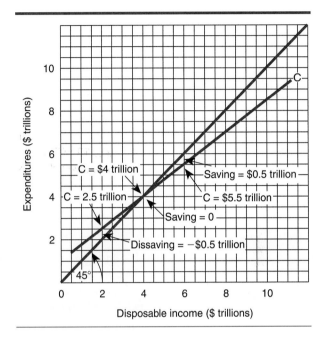

Figure B

See if you can find the MPC (use either graph).

Solution:

We'll go from a disposable income of $4 trillion to one of $8 trillion. When disposable income is $4 trillion, C is $4 trillion. When disposable income is $8 trillion, C is $7 trillion.

$$\text{MPC} = \frac{\text{Change in consumption}}{\text{Change in disposable income}} = \frac{\$3 \text{ trillion}}{\$4 \text{ trillion}}$$

$$= \frac{3}{4} = 0.75$$

One more problem: Find the APC when disposable income is $8 trillion.

Solution:

$$\text{APC} = \frac{\text{Consumption}}{\text{Disposable income}} = \frac{\$7 \text{ trillion}}{\$8 \text{ trillion}} = \frac{7}{8} = 0.875$$

Figure 6

Finding Autonomous
Consumption and Induced
Consumption

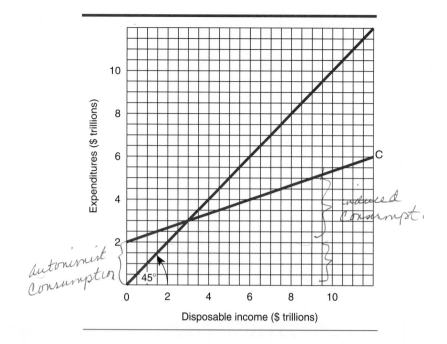

In Figure 6, can you find the level of autonomous consumption? Write down your answer.

Autonomous consumption is $2 trillion. Even if disposable income is 0, consumption will be $2 trillion. Therefore, when disposable income is 0, autonomous consumption is equal to total consumption.

Induced consumption is that part of consumption which varies with the level of disposable income. As disposable income rises, induced consumption also rises; when disposable income falls, induced consumption also falls. Changes in the level of disposable income induce changes in the level of consumption.

We had said that when disposable income is 0, autonomous consumption is equal to total consumption. A disposable income level of 0 cannot induce any consumption.

Consumption = Autonomous consumption + Induced consumption

The consumption function tells us that as income rises, consumption rises, but not as quickly. If consumption rises and autonomous consumption (by definition) stays the same, then what happens to induced consumption?

Obviously, it rises. In fact we can make two stronger statements: When consumption rises, induced consumption rises by the same amount; when consumption falls, induced consumption falls by the same amount.

OK, let's go to the graph in Figure 6. For disposable income levels of $3 trillion, $6 trillion, and $9 trillion, find autonomous consumption and induced consumption. Write your answers here:

Solution:
We know that autonomous consumption is $2 trillion. That's the level of consumption when disposable income is 0. So at disposable income levels of $3 trillion, $6 trillion, and $9 trillion, autonomous consumption remains $2 trillion.

When disposable income is $3 trillion, C is $3 trillion. We know that autonomous consumption is $2 trillion. Therefore, induced consumption must be $1 trillion:

Consumption = Autonomous consumption + Induced consumption
$3 trillion = $2 trillion   + $1 trillion

When disposable income is $6 trillion, C = $4 trillion.

Consumption = Autonomous consumption + Induced consumption
$4 trillion = $2 trillion   + $2 trillion

When disposable income is $9 trillion, C = $5 trillion.

Consumption = Autonomous consumption + Induced consumption
$5 trillion = $2 trillion   + $3 trillion

What the Consumer Buys

Consumption is traditionally divided into three categories: durables, nondurables, and services. Durables are things that last a while—say, at least three years. Nondurables, such as food, gasoline, and children's clothing, don't last long. (In fact, a case could be made that the clothing worn by fashion-conscious adults doesn't last either, although the reason it doesn't last is that fashions change rather than that it wears out.)

Durable goods include appliances, cars, and furniture. They last—or, at least, they're supposed to last. The big change in our economy since World War II has been in the service sector, which now produces over half of what consumers buy. Medical care, education, legal and financial services, and entertainment are some of the fields that have grown rapidly in the last five decades.

Figure 7 summarizes where the consumer's dollar went in 1955 and where it went in 2005. There has been a huge shift from expenditures on durables and nondurables to expenditures on services.

In 1955 Americans spent only 36 cents out of every consumer dollar on services; but today 59 cents goes toward services. Why this massive shift? For one thing, Americans are spending a much larger part of their incomes on medical care than they did in the 1950s. This trend has been reinforced as our population grows older. More Americans are going to college, eating out, travelling, and suing one another than ever before. Computer

The consumer buys durables, nondurables, and services.

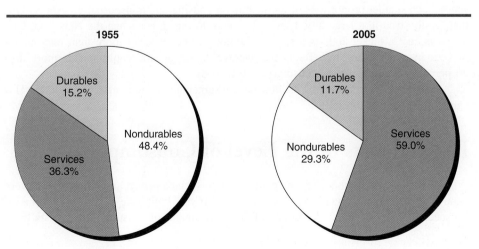

F*igure* 7

Consumer Spending, 1955 and 2005 ($ billions)
The major change in consumer spending has been a massive shift from nondurables to services.
Source: Economic Report of the President, 2006.

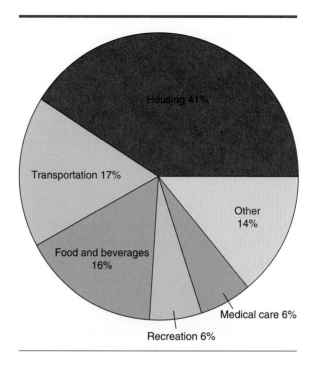

services, financial services, and personal services have expanded rapidly. Basically, we're paying people to do things for us that we either did for ourselves in the 1950s or didn't do at all.

Do you bring your lunch to school every day? Do you know anyone who does? Had you gone to college in the 1950s, the chances are you would have brown-bagged it. How does a homemade lunch go into GDP? It goes into the category of nondurable goods. But the lunch you buy in the cafeteria or at Burger King is classified as a service. Similarly, if you buy lettuce, tomatoes, carrots, and other raw vegetables, cut them up at home, and eat a salad, the components of that salad classify as nondurables. But if you stop at a salad bar and buy the identical components, which have been cut up for you—and pay about 10 times as much per pound—then this expenditure would count as a service.[5]

The Bureau of Labor Statistics has found that the average American family spends nearly three-quarters of its income on housing, transportation, food, and beverages (see Figure 8). Much of this spending is needed to support the suburban lifestyle that is so common throughout the United States. Sixty or seventy years ago, the average family spent much smaller proportions of its income on housing and transportation, especially if that family lived in a large city. I am old enough to remember when the New York City subways cost a nickel and, as a rule of thumb, you never spent more than one-quarter of your income on housing. Today the average American household spends more than 40 percent of its income on housing (see Figure 8).

Americans spent over $8.7 trillion on consumer goods and services in 2005. This came to 70 percent of GDP.

Determinants of the Level of Consumption

A budget tells us what we can't afford, but it doesn't keep us from buying it.
—William Feather

Why do people spend money? Some people hate to spend a penny, and others spend every penny they can lay their hands on. The aphorism, "If you don't have it, you can't spend it," is especially relevant to any discussion of the determinants of consumption. The six basic

---

[5]In 1970 about one-quarter of the average household's food budget was spent outside the home. Today it's more than one-half. Did someone say McDonald's?

determinants are listed below. (As we shall see, however, a person's level of spending is determined largely by how much money he or she has.)

1. Disposable income.
2. Credit availability.
3. Stock of liquid assets in the hands of consumers.
4. Stock of durable goods in the hands of consumers.
5. Keeping up with the Joneses.
6. Consumer expectations.

The Level of Disposable Income

Many factors influence how much money people spend; by far the most important is disposable income. As illustrated with the consumption function, as income rises, consumption rises, but not as quickly.

> The most important determinant of consumption is the level of disposable income.

At very low income levels, people not only don't save, they actually dissave. That is, their saving is negative. Suppose, for example, you lose your job. Do you simply stop spending money? If you did, you'd sure lose a lot of weight. How do you get by? If you collect unemployment benefits, then that's your disposable income. But the chances are, you would spend more each week than your unemployment checks, especially if you support a family. You still have to pay rent, car payments, other installment payments, utilities, and food bills, as well as the cost of looking for another job.

To manage all this you might borrow—if you can get credit—and you will go into your savings. So, at very low levels of income, you tend to spend more than your disposable income.

> *I don't think you can spend yourself rich.*
> —George Humphrey, Treasury Secretary in Eisenhower Administration

The more you've got, the more you spend. Or, alternatively, if you ain't got it, you can't spend it. So you can be sure that the working-class family spends more than the poor family. And that the upper-middle-class family spends more than the working-class family. Almost every family spends most of its income, so clearly the level of disposable income largely determines the level of consumption.

The main point here is that rich people spend a lot more money than do poor people. Why? Because they *have* more money. What is the most important determinant of consumption? Disposable income.

> *Live within your income, even if you have to borrow money to do so.*
> —Josh Billings

Credit Availability

You can't borrow money if you don't have credit. The most popular ways of borrowing are credit cards, especially VISA and MasterCard. Bank loans, home mortgages, home equity loans, and auto loans are other ways of borrowing. When credit is eased, people tend to borrow more.

> *Remember when people worried about how much it took to buy something, instead of how long?*
> —Earl Wilson

For example, suppose a furniture store, which had been asking its customers to put down 50 percent of their purchases in cash and pay out the balance in six months, now offered new terms: nothing down and two years to pay. Many more people would buy furniture on these terms. This is not to say that everyone stretches his or her credit to the limit, although some people do.

> *Never spend your money before you have it.*
> —Thomas Jefferson

Credit availability varies inversely with the level of consumer debt. That is, the more you owe, the less credit available. If your credit card limit is $5,000 and you already owe $4,900, you have only $100 of credit available. Furthermore, people who owe a great deal are somewhat reluctant to take on still more debt.

Stock of Liquid Assets in the Hands of Consumers

People own things that can be quickly turned into cash. These are called liquid assets. Prime examples include government and corporate bonds, corporate stocks, savings accounts, bank certificates of deposit (CDs), and money market funds.

> *The chief enjoyment of riches consists in the parade of riches.*
> —Adam Smith

In the United States today, people hold a stock of liquid assets of a few trillion dollars. This makes some people feel rich. Suppose, for example, you hold 1,000 shares of IBM stock and the price of that stock rises $2. You are $2,000 richer (at least on paper). This may induce you to go out and spend some of that money you just made.

Economists estimate that consumers cut back spending by about 4 cents for every dollar's worth of wealth they lose in the market, so a $1 trillion stock market plunge would cause about a $40 billion drop in annual consumption, or less than one-half of one percent of total spending. Of course, if the market were to continue to rise, we would see a corresponding *increase* in consumption.

In addition to *feeling* rich, if your liquid assets rise, you do indeed have more money to spend. That is, you can quickly convert some of these assets into money, then go out and spend it. Economists have found that there is some correlation between consumption and the amount of liquid assets held. The reasoning here is that if you don't have it, you can't spend it, and if you do have it, you will spend some of it.

Thorstein Veblen, American sociologist and economist (Historical Pictures/Stock Montage)

Stock of Durable Goods in the Hands of Consumers

In 1929, radios, phonographs, toasters, vacuum cleaners, waffle irons, and other appliances were relatively new because most of the country had been electrified only over the last decade and a half. More than 95 percent of the cars on the road were less than 10 years old. By 1930, the market for consumer durables was temporarily saturated.

When few people own items such as personal computers, DVD players, flat screen TVs, or video games, sales will rise. But when the market is saturated (and people own relatively late models), it will be some time before sales pick up again.

Consumer durables are now a relatively small part of total consumption—only 11.7 percent of all goods and services sold to consumers in 2005. However, their sales are somewhat erratic, largely because they vary inversely with the stock of consumer durables in the hands of consumers. When people hold a large stock of consumer durables, consumer durable sales tend to be low; when that stock is low, sales tend to be high.

Keeping Up with the Joneses

Wealth has never been a sufficient source of honor in itself. It must be advertised, and the normal medium is obtrusively expensive goods.
—John Kenneth Galbraith,
The Affluent Society

Conspicuous consumption

I shop. Therefore I am.
—Anonymous

Most of us, at least a few times in our lives, have been guilty of showing off our expensive clothes, our jewelry, our cars, or even our Florida tans. And most of us have been tempted to keep up with our neighbors, relatives, and friends. When the Joneses buy something, we have to go out and buy one, too—even if we can't afford it—because if we don't buy it, we won't be keeping up.

Why do some people spend $10,000 on a wristwatch, $200 for a pair of sneakers, or $5,000 for an evening gown? To a large degree, they're showing off. I have so much money, they seem to be saying, that I can afford these indulgences.

Almost a century ago Thorstein Veblen coined the term *conspicuous consumption*. In a marvelous book titled *The Theory of the Leisure Class,* Veblen stated, "Conspicuous consumption of valuable goods is a means of reputability to the gentleman of leisure." He went on to say, "With the exception of the instinct of self-preservation, the propensity for emulation is probably the strongest and most alert and persistent of the economic motives proper."[6]

Consumer Expectations

When people expect inflation, they often buy consumer durables before prices go up. On the other hand, when they expect recession, they tend to reduce their purchases of such big-ticket items as cars, furniture, and major appliances. Many people fear being

---

[6]Thorstein Veblen, *The Theory of the Leisure Class,* Chapters 4 and 5.

laid off or having their income reduced because of recessions, so they tend to postpone major purchases until times get better.

The Permanent Income Hypothesis

According to Milton Friedman, a prominent conservative economist, the strongest influence on consumption is one's estimated average lifetime income. No one knows what his or her average lifetime income will actually be, but people can generally figure out if they are earning more or less than that average.

If a factory worker earning $35,000 a year expects to remain a factory worker, she can estimate her future earnings until she retires. According to Friedman, people gear their consumption to their expected earnings more than to their current income.

Suppose someone's income temporarily contracts, say, because of a factory lay-off. Would the person cut back very sharply on her consumption? No, she would not, says this theory, since she knows she will be back on the job within a few months. She has to continue paying her rent, meeting her car payments, and eating three times a day.

Milton Friedman, winner of Nobel Prize, 1976, for work on monetary theory (The Nobel Foundation)

Earnings tend to rise until late middle age (about 55 or so) and then decline. Therefore the permanent income hypothesis would predict that most people's consumption is greater than their income until their mid- or late 20s. From the late 20s to the early 60s, current disposable income is usually greater than consumption. In old age, the relationship between consumption and current disposable income is again reversed, so consumption is greater than income.

Thus, our consumption is determined by our average expected income, or permanent income. That income is a constant; consumption is a constant percentage of that income. For most Americans, consumption would be more than 95 percent of permanent income.

According to Friedman's hypothesis, if you suddenly win the lottery, you will spend *some* of it because it will raise your permanent income, but you will spend only a small part of it. Is this how most lottery winners have handled their windfalls? Certainly not. But even though the permanent income hypothesis does not always hold true, it is still useful in predicting lifetime spending patterns.

Is the Consumer Really King?

Before we even receive our paychecks today, nearly all those dollars already have someone else's name on them. *Think* about it. How much of *your* family's paychecks goes toward paying off your mortgage, credit card debt, your cars, school tuition, insurance, medical bills, and home repair? Of course you would have had a lot more to spend if the government hadn't already taken *its* share of your pay before you even saw your paycheck.

Let's start with what is, by far, our most important purchase—a home. Once that purchase is made, you're committed to making mortgage payments, real estate taxes, heating bills, homeowner's insurance, upkeep, and repairs. Back in 1949, the average 30-year-old head of household needed to spend just 14 percent of his paycheck to make the payments on his home. By 1970 it took more than 21 percent of his paycheck to pay for that home. And today the average 30-year-old has to shell out more than 40 percent of his take-home pay.

The American dream has gradually become a financial nightmare. I recently asked my students how many cars their families owned. The majority owned three or four.

Suburban sprawl has almost completely obviated the use of mass transit. The trip to work, to school, to the store, to little league practice, and to virtually anywhere else must be made by car. The cost of car payments, insurance, gas, maintenance, and repairs takes another large chunk—often more than 25 percent—out of the typical suburban family's income. So it's no wonder that most households depend on two full-time incomes, and often one or two additional part-time incomes as well.

Elizabeth Warren and Amelia Warren Tyagi maintain that most middle-class families with children are caught in *The Two-Income Trap*. Even with two wage earners, families today are worse off than families supported by just one wage earner 30 years ago.

> The average two-income family earns far more today than did the single-breadwinner family of a generation ago. And yet, once they have paid the mortgage, the car payments, the taxes, the health insurance, and the day-care bills, today's dual-income families have *less* discretionary income—and less money to put away for a rainy day—than the single-income family of a generation ago.[7]

Elizabeth Warren and Amelia Warren Tyagi (Frank Carrere)

What happened between the early 1970s and today? Warren and Tyagi explain that millions of stay-at-home moms were compelled to enter the labor force to ensure that their children would live in safe neighborhoods and go to decent schools. A bidding war for housing in desirable suburban neighborhoods drove up the price of housing by 70 percent after allowing for inflation. So even though the two-wage-earner families today are bringing home 75 percent more than what one-wage-earner families brought home 30 years ago, they have less discretionary income. Nearly three-quarters of their income is earmarked for fixed expenses—mortgage, child care, health insurance, car(s), and taxes. Back in the early 1970s, the single-income family devoted just 54 percent of its income to fixed expenses, leaving the rest for discretionary spending. In addition, the stay-at-home mom spent a lot more time with her children.

Who was better off, ask Warren and Tyagi, the one-wage-earner family of the early 1970s or the two-wage-earner family today?

Today's family needs at least two paychecks just to maintain yesterday's standard of living.

—John J. Sweeney
President, AFL–CIO

> A generation ago, a single breadwinner who worked diligently and spent carefully could assure his family a comfortable position in the middle class. But the frenzied bidding wars, fueled by families with two incomes, changed the game for single-income families as well, pushing them down the economic ladder. To keep Mom at home, the average single-income family must forfeit decent public schools and preschools, health insurance, and college degrees, leaving themselves and their children with a tenuous hold on their middle-class dreams.[8]

So what do *you* think? Were families better off in the good old days back in the early 1970s than they are today? How well off are *your* parents compared to their own parents 30 years ago?

Murray Weidenbaum, President Reagan's first chief economic advisor (1993 Susan Muniak)

Why Do We Spend So Much and Save So Little?

> It may sometimes be expedient for a man to heat the stove with his furniture. But he should not delude himself by believing that he has discovered a wonderful new method of heating his premises.
>
> –Ludwig von Mises, early 20th-century Austrian economist–

Americans have been on a spending binge these last 30 years. In fact, the national motto might well be "Buy now, pay later," "Shop till you drop," or "We want it all, and we want it now!" The "me generation" has had a fascination for every conceivable type of electronic gadget, has had to buy new wardrobes every six months as the fashions change, and has had to drive the latest-model, fully loaded luxury foreign car. In fact, much of what we buy is made by foreigners. Murray Weidenbaum, who

---

[7]Elizabeth Warren and Amelia Warren Tyagi, *The Two-Income Trap* (New York: Basic Books, 2003), p. 8.
[8]Warren and Tyagi, *op. cit.,* p. 9.

served as President Ronald Reagan's first chief economic advisor, summed up our profligacy this way:

> As citizens of the United States, we are consuming more than we are producing, borrowing more than we are saving, and spending more than we are earning. We are rapidly approaching the time when we will have to pay the piper.

The federal government has actually underwritten our spending binge. Mortgage interest and property taxes are fully deductible. So buy a home and charge part of your costs to Uncle Sam. And if you need to borrow still more money, just take out a second mortgage and use this money to finance your ever-growing consumption expenditures.

The tremendous expansion of bank credit cards, installment credit, and consumer loans has further fueled the consumer binge of the last dozen years. Every day Americans are offered millions of credit cards, whether they asked for them or not. In fact, from 1990 to 2000 household debt doubled to $7 trillion and topped $11 billion at the end of 2005. Some people call credit cards "mall money."

Our saving rate might not have been so low were it not for two factors that have become increasingly important over the last five decades—Social Security and widespread home ownership. Most Americans do not feel the pressing need to save for their old age because they will receive Social Security benefits, not to mention private pensions. Similarly, home ownership is seen as a form of saving, especially during a period of rising real estate prices.

Bruce Steinberg, a Merrill Lynch economist, takes a contrarian view, by claiming that the savings rate is badly biased downward. His view was summarized by *BusinessWeek:*[9]

> In calculating the rate, he notes, the government inconsistently subtracts capital-gains taxes from income while failing to count as income the gains on which those taxes are paid.
>
> If realized capital gains were counted as income (which is how most people see them), Steinberg figures the current savings rate would be 10 percent—close to its historic level. In other words, people have not been dipping into their unrealized capital gains, as some charge.

How *have* we been able to put off paying the piper for so long? By borrowing. As individual consumers, we borrow; as giant corporations, we borrow; and as the federal government, we borrow. And who lends us this money? Increasingly, the answer is foreigners.

So far I've described the American consumer as someone who leaves the mall only to work and sleep. But most middle-class Americans, especially couples with children, are hard-pressed to make ends meet. They might have a nice suburban house and a couple of cars, but they may have a real struggle to make ends meet. And so we ask, Is the consumer really king?

Total Saving: Individual Saving + Business Saving + Government Saving

Every economy depends on saving for capital formation. That saving is the total of individual saving, business saving, and government saving.[10] We've seen that individual saving has dwindled in recent years. Businesses set aside savings in the form of depreciation allowances and retained earnings, while our local, state, and federal governments save by running surpluses and dissave by running deficits.

As you can see in Figure 9, the decline in household saving between 1993 and 2000 was offset by a sharp rise in government saving and business saving. But since 2001,

It seems a lot of trouble if, instead of having to earn money and save it, you can just go and borrow it.
—Winston Churchill

Nobody goes to the mall anymore because they're too crowded.
—Standard retail industry joke

A penny saved is a penny earned.
—Benjamin Franklin

---

[9]"Are Americans Spendthrifts?" *BusinessWeek,* November 22, 2000, p. 18.

[10]Government saving = federal surplus (or deficit) + state and local surplus.

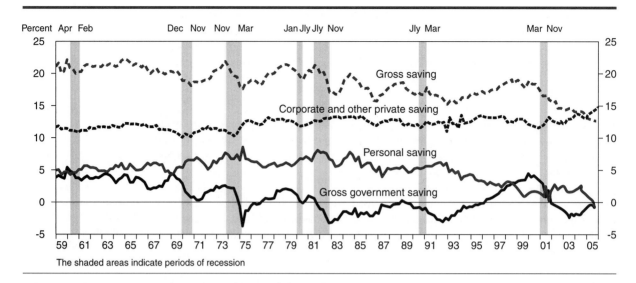

Percent Apr Feb   Dec Nov Nov Mar   Jan Jly Jly Nov   Jly Mar   Mar Nov

The shaded areas indicate periods of recession

F*igure* 9

The Three Components of National Saving, 1960–2005

Personal saving has been on the decline since the mid-1980s, while government saving (by the federal, state, and local governments), which was negative for most of the 1980s and 1990s, became positive in the late 1990s when the federal government went from huge budget deficits to huge surpluses. Now, as the federal budget deficits mount, government saving is once again in the red. By far, the most important component of national saving is business saving.

Source: Survey of Current Business, January 2006.

while personal savings continued its decline, government saving fell too. Indeed, both government and personal saving were both negative in 2005, dragging down the gross savings rate.

Until the recession of 1981–82, as a nation we generally saved about 20 percent of our gross national income. Except for a surge in gross saving in the mid-to-late 1990s, it has trended downward. By 2005 our gross saving rate was just 13 percent. This was not nearly enough to fund business investment needs as well as to finance the federal budget deficit. Since Americans were not saving enough, we have needed to borrow $2 billion a day from foreigners. But what if some day foreigners refuse to lend us any more money? Clearly we cannot continue spending more than we earn, whether as individuals or as a nation.

Current Issue: The American Consumer: World-Class Shopper

There is no question but that the American consumer is the prime mover not just of our economy, but of the world economy as well. As any business owner will tell you, you can't run a business without buyers for your goods or services.

So despite all the terrible things I've said about the spendthrift American consumer in this chapter—Born to shop. Shop till you drop—it's the consumer who makes our economy go.

Because the United States has the largest consumer market in the world, it has been targeted by foreign sellers, especially the Japanese and Chinese. Selling to America made possible the Japanese economic miracle in the decades after World War II, when Japanese industry was being rebuilt and its home market had relatively low purchasing power. Japan was able to sell us black and white TVs, then color TVs, cameras, VCRs, stereos, and cars. The American consumer helped finance the Japanese recovery.

China, which had maintained a growth rate of about 10 percent over the last 20 years, also hitched its economic wagon to the American market. Again, it was the American consumer buying microwave ovens, TVs, apparel, shoes, toys, personal computers, and consumer electronics that enabled China to lift itself by its own bootstraps. Today, the Chinese run such huge trade surpluses with us that they can finance most of our federal budget deficit.

So while all this spending may not be so great for the American economy, it is doing wonders for China, Japan, Korea, Canada, Mexico, and other countries running large trade surpluses with the United States. Were you to ask economists in these nations about the level of consumption spending in the United States, most of them would probably say it was just fine, thank you.

Questions for Further Thought and Discussion

1. Explain the relationship between consumption and saving.
2. Explain the difference between autonomous consumption and induced consumption.
3. Explain how the stock of consumer durables in the hands of consumers and credit availability each affect the level of consumption.
4. Since the 1950s a massive shift in consumption patterns with respect to nondurable goods and services has taken place. What is this shift and how can it be explained?
5. How little do Americans save? Why do they save so little?
6. How is it possible for a nation's consumption to sometimes exceed its disposable income?
7. The marginal propensity to consume (MPC) for a nation is .85. Explain what this means.
8. Why is the demand for consumer nondurable goods more stable than that for consumer durable goods?
9. How much was our APC and APS in 2005? (Hint: Look at Figure 1 near the beginning of this chapter.)

Workbook for Chapter 5

Name _____ Date _____

Multiple-Choice Questions

Circle the letter that corresponds to the best answer.

1. Since 1955 Americans have been spending _____.

   a) a larger percentage of their incomes on services
   b) a smaller percentage of their incomes on services
   c) about the same percentage of their incomes on services

2. When the C line crosses the 45-degree line, saving is _____.

   a) positive
   b) negative
   c) zero
   d) impossible to calculate because there is not enough information to know

3. When disposable income is zero, _____.
   a) autonomous consumption is equal to induced consumption
   b) autonomous consumption is equal to total consumption
   c) induced consumption is equal to total consumption

4. The minimum amount that people will spend even if disposable income is zero is called _____ consumption.
   a) autonomous
   b) induced
   c) total

5. According to the permanent income hypothesis, if a person received a windfall of $100,000, he would spend _____ that year.
   a) some of it   c) nearly all of it
   b) most of it   d) all of it

6. As disposable income rises, _____.
   a) autonomous C rises   c) induced C rises
   b) autonomous C falls   d) induced C falls

7. The largest component of GDP is _____.
   a) net exports   c) consumption
   b) investment   d) government purchases

8. The largest component of C is _____.
   a) durable goods
   b) services
   c) nondurable goods

9. The consumption function tells us that, as income rises, consumption _____.
   a) declines
   b) remains the same
   c) rises more slowly than income
   d) rises more quickly than income

10. When income levels are very low, C is _____.
    a) zero
    b) lower than income
    c) higher than income

11. When income is equal to consumption, saving is _____.

    a) negative
    b) zero
    c) positive
    d) impossible to calculate because there is insufficient information

12. Which of the following relations is *not* correct?
    a) MPC + MPS = 1   d) 1 − APS = APC
    b) APC + APS = 1   e) 1 − MPC = MPS
    c) MPS = MPC + 1

13. Induced consumption expenditures _____.
    a) fall as income rises
    b) are always equal to autonomous consumption expenditures
    c) plus saving equals total consumption expenditures
    d) represent consumption that is independent of income
    e) are influenced mainly by income

14. Autonomous consumption expenditures are

    _____.

    a) equal to induced consumption expenditures
    b) proportional to disposable income
    c) not influenced by income
    d) influenced primarily by the saving function

15. The average propensity to save _____.
    a) is disposable income divided by savings
    b) is a measure of the additional saving generated by additional income
    c) is negative at very high income levels
    d) varies directly with income; as income rises, the APS rises

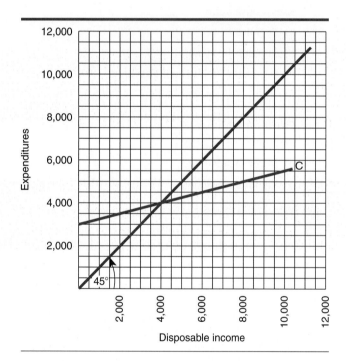

Figure 1

Use the data in Figure 1 to answer questions 16–18.

16. Savings is equal to zero at a disposable income of

    _____.

    a) 0   d) 6,000
    b) 2,000   e) 8,000
    c) 4,000

17. Consumption is equal to 5,000 at a disposable income
    of _____.

    a) 2,000   d) 8,000
    b) 4,000   e) 10,000
    c) 6,000

18. When disposable income is 2,000, consumption is

    _____.

    a) −3,500   d) 3,500
    b) 0   e) 4,000
    c) 2,000

19. Which is the most accurate statement?
    a) The American personal savings rate would be higher if we counted capital gains as income which is not spent.
    b) An average propensity to save of .02 means that only 2 percent of the population is saving any of their income.
    c) Our low savings rate is not considered a problem by many economists.
    d) Our government savings rate is always negative.

20. Our consumption spending tends to rise as the stock of liquid assets in the hands of consumers

    _____ and credit availability _____.

    a) rises, rises   c) rises, falls
    b) falls, falls   d) falls, rises

21. Boyd and Dianne Call earn $100,000 a year. They went deeply into debt after paying $75,000 for their daughter Chelsea's wedding and $50,000 for their daughter Kaylynne's sweet sixteen party. Their behavior might best be described by _____.
    a) Milton Friedman
    b) John Maynard Keynes
    c) Bruce Steinberg
    d) Thorstein Veblen

22. As a nation's income falls, induced consumption

    _____.

    a) rises
    b) falls
    c) remains the same

23. Twenty years from now our disposable income will rise from $30 trillion to $31 trillion. What would your best guess be as to how much consumption will rise?

    a) $50 billion   c) $950 billion

    b) $500 billion   d) $1.05 trillion

24. Which one of the following statements is the most accurate?

    a) The American consumer was largely responsible for Japan's economic resurgence since World War II.

    b) China, as the world's most populous country, has the world's largest consumer market.

    c) Although there are some who call the American consumer a world-class shopper, most Americans save substantial parts of their incomes.

    d) Since we import most of our goods, the American economy has only a small impact on the world's other large economies.

25. Which statement is true?

    a) Americans save much more of their incomes than they did 20 years ago.

    b) In 2005 our disposable income was smaller than our consumption spending.

    c) Although the U.S. does not have the highest saving rate in the world, Americans save more money than the citizens of every other country.

    d) Our APS has been negative since the early 1990s.

Fill-In Questions

1. About _____ percent of what Americans spend on consumption is spent on services.

2. The average propensity to consume is found by dividing _____ by _____.

3. The APS + the APC = _____.

4. The consumption function states that _____.

5. Dissaving takes place when _____.

6. Induced consumption is induced by _____.

7. According to the saving function, as disposable income rises, _____.

8. The most important determinant of the level of consumption is _____.

9. The average propensity to consume in the United States today is about _____.

10. 1 − MPS = _____.

11. When the C line crosses the 45-degree line, saving is equal to _____.

Problems

1. Given the information shown in Table 1, calculate the APC and the APS.

TABLE 1

Disposable Income	Consumption
$10,000	$8,400

2. Given the information shown in Table 2, calculate the MPC and MPS. (Assume disposable income rises from $35,000 to $37,000.)

TABLE 2

Year	Disposable Income	Saving
2002	$35,000	$4,600
2003	37,000	5,300

3. Using the information in Figure 2, how much are consumption and saving when disposable income is:

	C	Saving
a) 1,000	_____	_____
b) 2,000	_____	_____
c) 3,000	_____	_____

4. Using your answers from question 3a, calculate the APC and the APS.

119

5. Using your answers from questions 3*a* and 3*b*, calculate the MPC and the MPS when disposable income rises from 1,000 to 2,000.

6. Using the data in Figure 2, how much is autonomous consumption?

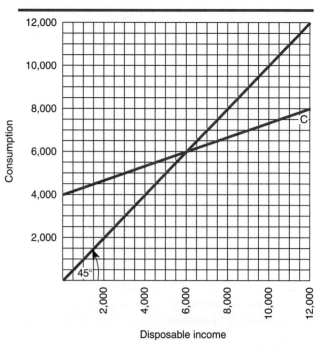

F*igure* 3

Use the data in Figure 3 to answer questions 9–12.

9. Determine induced consumption when disposable income is:
   a) 0
   b) 6,000
   c) 12,000

10. When disposable income is 9,000:
   a) How much is autonomous consumption?
   b) How much is total consumption?
   c) How much is saving?

11. When disposable income is 12,000:
   a) How much is the APC?
   b) How much is the APS?

12. In problem 11:
   a) How much is the MPC?
   b) How much is the MPS?

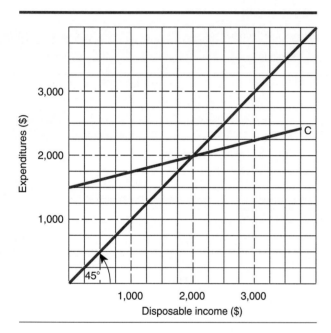

F*igure* 2

7. Using the data in Figure 2, determine induced consumption when disposable income is:
   a) 1,000
   b) 2,000
   c) 3,000

8. If C is $4 trillion, disposable income is $5 trillion, and autonomous consumption is $3 trillion:
   a) How much is saving?
   b) How much is induced consumption?
   c) How much is the APS?
   d) If the APS falls by .01, how much (in dollars) does saving fall?

Chapter 6

The Business-Investment Sector

Are you ready for two very easy questions? (1) Which country produces more goods and services than any other? (2) Which country has more capital than any other country? The answer to each question is the United States. Do you think there's some kind of connection between our having the most capital and producing the most output? The connection is very simple: The main reason we are able to produce so much is because we have so much capital.

Unlike in Vietnam, Cuba, North Korea, and dozens of other communist and socialist nations, most investment in the United States is carried out by private business firms rather than by the government. That investment consists of the production of new plant and equipment, residential housing, and additions to our inventories.

CHAPTER OBJECTIVES

In this chapter you'll learn:

- The three types of business firms.
- How investment is carried out.
- The difference between gross investment and net investment.
- How capital is accumulated.
- The determinants of the level of investment.
- The graphing of the C + I line.

Proprietorships, Partnerships, and Corporations

There are three types of business firms in the United States. Proprietorships are owned by individuals and are almost always small businesses. Partnerships, which are also usually small, are owned by two or more people. There are relatively few large businesses in our country, and virtually all of them are corporations. Most corporations, like most businesses, are small.

Most businesses are small.

The Proprietorship

A typical proprietorship would be a grocery, a barbershop, a candy store, a restaurant, a family farm, or a filling station. Chances are, nearly all of the places in the neighborhood where you shop are proprietorships.

To start a proprietorship, a person simply decides to go into business, either opening a new firm or taking over an existing one. With a proprietorship, there are fewer legal complications than with any other form of business organization. Another advantage is that you are your own boss. You don't have to consult with other owners, partners, or stockholders. Finally, there are tax advantages. A proprietor's income is taxed only once—when she or he pays personal income tax. But if the same firm were to incorporate, its income would be taxed twice—once as the income of the firm (the corporate income tax) and again as the personal income of the owner.

A proprietorship has three disadvantages. First, the entire burden of running the company falls on one person's shoulders. Second, the owner may be sued for everything she has if the business is sued. And third, it's a lot harder for one person, rather than two or more people, to raise capital.

The Partnership

Advantages of a partnership

Two or more people can form a partnership. Although the typical partnership has two people, some law and accounting firms have hundreds of partners. Two key advantages of forming a partnership are being able to raise more capital and to divide the work and responsibility of running the business.

A typical division of labor between partners would be production and sales, or, in the parlance of business, inside and outside. The advantages of forming a partnership must be weighed against two basic disadvantages. The first is that the partnership must be dissolved when one of its members dies or wants to leave the business. A second disadvantage is that of unlimited liability.

Disadvantages of a partnership

Both proprietors and partners are liable for all debts incurred by their businesses. For example, if the firm is sued for negligence, the owners are personally liable to pay the amount awarded if the firm cannot do so. If one partner absconds with funds, the other partners may lose their homes and cars even though they were innocent victims. The way to avoid ever having to face this dilemma is to incorporate.

The Corporation

The main advantage to incorporating is limited liability.

The key advantage of the corporation is limited liability. That is, each owner's liability is limited to the amount of money he has invested in the business. If there's a negligence suit or someone absconds with funds, the most you can lose is your investment. No one can touch your house, car, or any other personal property.

Corporation: An ingenious device for obtaining individual profit without individual responsibility.

—Ambrose Bierce,
The Devil's Dictionary

A corporation is a legal person. As such, it can sue and be sued. What is significant about this attribute is that the people who own the corporation—the stockholders—cannot be sued no matter how grievous the transgressions of the corporation. However, the courts have, on occasion, found stockholders liable (for example, when stockholders form a corporation for fraudulent purposes).

A second advantage of a corporation is its potentially perpetual life. While a partnership must be dissolved when one of the partners leaves the business, a corporation can continue indefinitely: The stock owned by the principal who wants to pull out is purchased by someone else. In the case of large, publicly held corporations, such transactions take place routinely at the major stock exchanges.

A third advantage is paying lower federal personal income tax. If you're a small business owner making at least $40,000, says Judith McQuown, author of *Incorporate Yourself,*[1] you can actually save on your taxes by incorporating.[2] You can find all of this spelled out in McQuown's book, and, if you decide to incorporate, you'll want to hire an accountant to calculate your tax savings.

---

[1]Judith McQuown, *Inc. Yourself: How to Profit by Setting Up Your Own Corporation,* 9th ed. (New York: Broadway Books, 1999).

[2]In 2003 Congress passed a law which largely eliminated "double taxation" of corporate profits (until then corporate profits were subject to the federal corporate income tax and the federal personal income tax).

Small Corporations

The typical corporation is very small, like the old North American Uniform Cap Corporation. Although the company had a rather impressive name, its officers were Jonas Lewy, president; Nadja Lewy, vice president; and their son, Henry Lewy, secretary-treasurer. They ran their business out of a tiny loft in Manhattan's garment district, sewing up work caps, military caps, and what are now called "gimme caps." They had about a half-dozen sewing machines, and Henry's parents—the president and the vice president—operated two of them.

During the "busy season," they hired another three or four operators.

The North American Uniform Cap Corporation never grew into a large enterprise, although the Lewys were always waiting for that one big order—like maybe a few million caps for the Chinese Peoples Liberation Army. But the big order never came, and, like 85 percent of all corporations, North American Uniform Caps never managed to do a million dollars worth of business in a single year.

TABLE 1	The Top Ten in U.S. Sales, 2005	
RANK 2005		(in billions of $)
1	EXXONMOBIL	$340
2	WAL-MART STORES	316
3	GENERAL MOTORS	193
4	CHEVRON	189
5	FORD MOTOR	177
6	CONOCOPHILLIPS	167
7	GENERAL ELECTRIC	157
8	CITIGROUP	131
9	AIG	109
10	IBM	91

Source: Fortune, April 17, 2006.

Still another advantage of incorporating is that the company can sell stock to the public to raise more money. Because the owners have limited liability and the firm itself has ongoing life, the corporation is in a better position than the proprietorship or partnership to go to the public to raise funds.

Of course, only a tiny fraction of all corporations ever go public. Nearly all are relatively small businesses that are completely owned by a few individuals. (See the box, "Small Corporations.")

Most corporations are small firms.

The largest 10 corporations are shown in Table 1. Who's number one? It's Exxon-Mobil, with sales of $340 billion.

How do the largest American firms stack up against the largest firms in the world? As you can see in Table 2, ExxonMobil is the world's largest company, and overall, there are six American firms among the top ten.

There are two disadvantages to incorporating. First, you have to have papers drawn up and pay a fee for a charter. The expense of doing this varies, but most states charge filing fees of less than $200. A second disadvantage is that you will have to pay federal, and possibly state, corporate income tax. Although the rates are very low for small corporations, those with profits of more than $10 million must pay 35 percent of anything above that amount to the Internal Revenue Service.[3] Because most corporations are very small, 60 percent paid no corporate income tax in 2005.

Two disadvantages to incorporating

---

[3]Corporations earning smaller profits pay lower rates.

ADVANCED WORK

The New Hybrid Varieties

Some companies seem to fall into the cracks between partnerships and corporations. There are limited partnerships, which not only avoid paying corporate income taxes but, as their name implies, also minimize legal risk to their investors. There are S corporations—named after the subchapter of the Internal Revenue Code that authorizes them—which offer their shareholders limited liability and pay no corporate income tax. Since 1988, the Internal Revenue Service has also authorized limited liability companies, which have the legal insulation of a corporation and the preferred tax treatment of a limited partnership.

You can also form a limited liability company, or limited liability partnership, to protect your personal assets if your business is sued. A suit can place only the assets of your business at risk. Between 1992 and 1994 more than 40 states—with California a prominent exception—passed limited liability legislation. A limited liability company carries the same benefits as the S corporation, with taxes assessed solely at the individual level; the owners pay personal income tax on their profits but do not have to pay corporate income tax.

But all of this said, these are still the exceptions that prove the rule. The vast majority of businessowners incorporate to secure limited liability, and are then subject to paying corporate income taxes. The hybrid entities do provide loopholes, but so far only a small minority of businessowners have crawled through.

TABLE 2	The Top Ten in World Sales, 2005	
RANK 2005		**(in billions of $)**
1	**EXXONMOBIL** U.S.	$340
2	**WAL-MART STORES** U.S.	316
3	**BRITISH PETROLEUM** Britain	310
4	**ROYAL DUTCH/SHELL** Britain/Netherlands	307
5	**GENERAL MOTORS** U.S.	193
6	**CHEVRON** U.S.	189
7	**DAIMLERCHRYSLER** Germany	180
8	**FORD MOTOR** U.S.	177
9	**TOTAL** France	173
10	**CONOCOPHILLIPS** U.S.	167

Source: Fortune, April 17, 2006; en.wikipedia.org.

The box titled "The New Hybrid Varieties" describes companies that are a cross between partnerships and corporations.

Given the advantages of incorporating, one may ask (as I did in the accompanying box), "Why Did Incorporation Come So Late to Islamic Middle-Eastern Nations?" As you'll see, the reasons may be traced back many centuries.

How easy is it to form a corporation? In most states it can be done in a matter of days and might cost a few hundred dollars. But in Austria, setting up any new business takes about six months and costs nearly $12,000 in official fees. In Mexico, it takes "only" four months and costs about $2,500. And in Egypt and Bolivia, the cost of setting up a business adds up to more than double the per capita income, while in Chad it's triple that figure.

It takes about five days to register and launch a new business in the United States, but considerably longer in most poorer nations. For example, it takes an average of 79 days in Belarus, 146 days in Angola, and an average of 203 days in Haiti. And once a business has managed to open, the regulatory burdens that poor countries have in place make it difficult to get credit, register property, or hire and fire employees. So despite our governmental reputation for red tape, you *ain't* seen nothing until you try starting a business in Chad, Burkina Faso, or Bangladesh.

Stocks and Bonds

Stockholders are owners of a corporation. Bondholders lend money to a company and are therefore creditors rather than owners. This distinction becomes important when we consider the order in which people are paid off when the corporation is doing well and when it goes bankrupt.

There are two types of corporate stock: common and preferred. The advantage of owning preferred is that you will receive a stipulated dividend, say 6 percent of the face value of your stock, provided there are any profits out of which to pay dividends. After you are paid, if some profits remain, the common stockholders will be paid.

Two types of stock

Why bother to own common stock? Mainly because only common stockholders may vote on issues of concern to the corporation as well as on who gets to run the corporation. Both preferred and common stockholders own the corporation, or hold equity in the company, but only common stockholders vote.

Bondholders are creditors rather than owners of a corporation. Like the preferred stockholders, they must be paid a stipulated percentage of the face value of their bonds, say 8 percent, in the form of interest, but they must be paid whether or not the company makes a profit. In fact, the interest they receive is considered one of the costs of doing business. And should a company go bankrupt, the bondholders, as creditors, have to be paid off before the owners of preferred and common stock see any money.

Bondholders are creditors—not owners.

Capitalization and Control

A corporation's total capital, or capitalization, consists of the total value of its stocks and bonds. For example, a $4 billion corporation may have $1 billion in bonds, $500 million in preferred stock, and $2.5 billion in common stock. Similarly, a corporation with $200 million in bonds, $100 million in preferred stock, and $300 million in common stock would be capitalized at $600 million.

One might ask how much money would be needed to gain control of a large corporation. Let's consider a corporation that's capitalized for $500 million—$300 million in bonds, $120 million in preferred stock, and $80 million in common stock. Theoretically, you would need slightly over $40 million, or 50 percent plus one share of the common stock.

But most large corporations are rather widely held; that is, there are many stockholders with only a few holding even 1 percent. Furthermore, many stockholders either don't bother to vote their shares or they give proxies to others who will. Usually, then, holding about 5 percent of the common stock of a company will be sufficient for control. So, in this case, by holding $4 million worth of common stock (5 percent of $80 million), you should be able to control this $500 million corporation.

Now let's work out a problem testing your knowledge of capitalization and control: If the XYZ corporation has $4 billion in preferred stock, $6 billion in common stock, and $3 billion in bonds: (*a*) How much is its capitalization? (*b*) Theoretically, how much would it take to control it? (*c*) Practically speaking, it may take only about how much to control it?

Work out your answers here:

Solutions: (*a*) $4 billion + $6 billion + $3 billion = $13 billion
(*b*) $6 billion × .50 = $3 billion, or, technically speaking, $3 billion + $1
(*c*) $6 billion × .05 = $300 million

Why Did Incorporation Come So Late to Islamic Middle-Eastern Nations?

While the corporation is the dominant form of enterprise in the industrialized world, it is a very new development in the Islamic Middle East, where small and very temporary partnerships have been the dominant business form for centuries. This raises two questions: (1) Why did corporations develop earlier in Western Europe and North America? (2) What have been the consequences of these very different histories?

The rules set forth by Islamic lawmakers for forming and executing partnerships were shaped by the needs of the mercantile class during the 7th to 10th centuries. These rules strongly affected Middle-Eastern economic development—or the lack thereof—over the next millennium. Timur Kuran explained this long-lasting effect:

> [T]he Islamic jurists treated the needs of the mercantile community as fixed. Given the sacredness of Islamic law the presumption of fixity meant that while several generations of merchants left their mark on Islamic commercial law, later generations were effectively prevented from revising the corpus of that law in accordance with changing economic conditions.*

Because every Islamic partnership ended with the death of any of its members, after each death a new partnership had to be negotiated. As Kuran noted, "Every additional partner raised the risk of premature liquidation by increasing the probability of a partner dying before the termination of the contract period. This situation obviously fostered [an] incentive to keep partnerships small."†

Such a firm would have great difficulty hiring employees, borrowing money, or raising capital from its partners. And so, the typical Islamic partnership consisted of just two members, who pooled their resources for perhaps a single trade mission. This tradition continued throughout most of the Middle East until well into the 20th century.

By the 13th century, Italian financiers were forming partnerships that lasted for many years, and did not dissolve with the death of a member. Between the 16th and 18th centuries, the great European trading organizations evolved from large and durable partnerships into joint-stock companies, the forerunners of the modern corporation.

Large accumulations of wealth were channeled into large European corporations. These accumulations were made possible by the inheritance laws of Western Europe. Let's see how Islamic and Western inheritance laws differed.

The Koran specified that at least two-thirds of an estate be divided among the deceased's spouse, sons and daughters, parents and grandparents, brothers and sisters, and possibly even distant blood relatives. This led to an equalization of wealth. On the downside, it

---

Many economists believe that you really need to hold about 10 percent of the common stock to be assured of control. In *that* case, we have: $6 billion $\times$ .10 = $600 million. So to be fair, we would have to accept an answer to question (c) of either 5 percent of the common stock or 10 percent of the common stock. Or, for that matter, any percentage between 5 and 10.

The Business Population

There are some 30 million business firms in the United States—almost one business for every ten people. As you'll notice in panel (*a*) of Figure 1, 72 percent of all American businesses are proprietorships. In panel (*b*), you'll see that corporations account for 84 percent of sales.

Investment

Investment is really the thing that makes our economy go. When we have prosperity, investment is high and rising. And when we're in a recession, it is low and falling. Let's define investment and then see how it varies.

hindered efforts to keep property intact over time, and also prevented great accumulations of wealth, which might have been channeled into capital formation.

Although there was a wide diversity of inheritance rules throughout pre-modern Europe, Timur Kuran wrote that these rules differed from the Islamic system in two critical respects.

> *First, none define the family as broadly as did the Koran; usually they limited the legal heirs to the kinship group now known as the nuclear family. Second, because Christian canon law did not standardize the law of inheritance, practices were easier to modify, and attempts at reform were less likely to be challenged as sacrilegious. Consequently, barriers to keeping estates intact across generations were considerably lower in relation to the Middle East. From the Middle Ages to recent times, the un-Islamic—and un-modern—devices of primogeniture (the preference in inheritance given to the oldest son) and and ultimogeniture (the preference given to the youngest son) enjoyed legal recognition in broad stretches of Europe.‡*

Islamic inheritance laws were consistent with the economic realities of that time. Most wealth was in the hands of traders and nomads, whose possessions consisted of movable and relatively easily partitioned goods, such as animal herds and cash. These could be quickly and easily divided among the heirs. By contrast, Roman and Germanic law developed in heavily agricultural

societies, whose members sought to keep land in units of sufficient size to sustain a family. Indeed, it was the quest for farmland that drove millions of Europeans to America, especially during the 19th century.

Basically, the very different histories of economic development in the Middle East and in Western Europe and North America can be largely explained by the development of very different economic institutions. As we've seen, the inheritance laws of the West enabled the accumulation of large fortunes, which were then invested in corporate capital. In the Middle East, while the inheritance laws encouraged economic equality, they discouraged the accumulation of capital. In addition, the Islamic laws governing partnerships discouraged the formation of large business enterprises and prevented the advent of corporations until well into the 20th century. In Western Europe and the United States, unfettered by such laws, the corporation became the dominant form of business enterprise by the second half of the 19th century. It was the large corporation that became the engine of economic growth and the facilitator of the economy of mass production and mass consumption.

*Timur Kuran, "The Islamic Commercial Crisis: Institutional Roots of the Delay in the Middle East's Economic Modernization," Research Paper No. C01–12, University of Southern California Law School, Center for Law, Economics, and Organization Research Paper Series, March 2001, p. 7 (http://papers.ssrn.com/abstract_id=276377).

†Ibid., pp. 12–13.

‡Ibid., pp. 29–30.

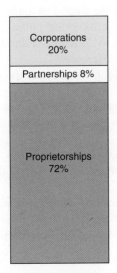
(a) Percentage of firms

(b) Percentage of sales

F*igure* 1

The Business Population and Shares of Total Sales, 2002

Source: Statistical Abstract of the United States, 2006.

TABLE 3	Hypothetical Inventory Levels of General Motors
Date	Level of Inventory
January 1, 2003	$120 million
July 1, 2003	145 million
December 31, 2003	130 million

TABLE 4	Hypothetical Inventory Levels of Shell Oil
Date	Level of Inventory
January 1, 2004	$230 million
May 15, 2004	215 million
September 1, 2004	240 million
December 31, 2004	220 million

Investment is any new plant, equipment, additional inventory, or residential housing.[4] Plant includes factories, office buildings, department and other retail stores, and shopping malls. Examples of equipment are assembly lines, machine tools, display cases, cash registers, computer systems, and office furniture—as long as businesses purchase them. For example, if you buy a car for your personal use, it's a consumption expenditure. But if Shell Oil buys a car for its executives to ride around in (on company business), then it's an investment. The key question we must ask is whether the purchase adds to a company's plant, equipment, or inventory. If not, then it's not investment. What if your town buys a new police car or a new PC or puts up a new school? Is this investment? Close, but no cigar. When the government makes these purchases, it's government spending rather than investment. This may sound arbitrary, but it's part of the rules of national income accounting, which we discuss fully in Chapter 9.

What if you were to purchase 100 shares of Intel stock? Would that be investment? Does that add (directly) to Intel's plant, equipment, or inventory? It doesn't? Then it isn't investment. It's merely a financial transaction. When Intel uses those funds to buy plant, equipment, or inventory, *then* it's investment.

Inventory includes goods on store shelves waiting to be sold, cars in a showroom or car lot, finished goods in a factory waiting to be shipped, and even parts of a product ready to be assembled. Business firms do not want to hold more inventory than they need because that inventory ties up money and also incurs storage costs. Suppose you owned a toy store and had sales of $10,000 a week. Would you want to carry an inventory of $100,000 toys? Today, with inventory computerization, many firms use the just-in-time method of inventory control. Stores and factories, many tied to the Internet, have found they can cut costs by shrinking the warehouses where they store the materials they use in production or the goods they sell later to consumers.

Calculating inventory investment is a little tricky. We include only the net change from January 1 to December 31 of a given year. For example, how much was inventory investment for General Motors in 2003 (using the figures in Table 3)?

How much was GM's inventory investment in 2003? $25 million? Nope. $395 million? Nope. The answer is $10 million. All you have to do is look at the levels of inventory on January 1 and December 31 and calculate the difference.

Let's try another one. Using the data in Table 4, calculate the inventory investment for Shell Oil in 2004.

Your answer should be −$10 million. Between the first day of the year and the last day of the year, the level of Shell's inventory went down by $10 million. In other words, inventory investment was negative.

The fact that we can have negative inventory investment is significant. Because investment is one sector of GDP, declining inventories will be a drag on GDP. That's what happens during recessions.

A glance at Figure 2 shows just how unstable inventory investment has been over the last 45 years. In fact, you've probably never been on a roller coaster that had as many steep ups and downs as inventory investment. Most of the steep drops are associated with

You are investing if you are adding to your firm's plant, equipment, or inventory.

How to calculate inventory investment

---

[4]Residential construction does not properly belong in a chapter on business investment, but I am prepared, just this once, to dispense with propriety, because I don't know where else to put it.

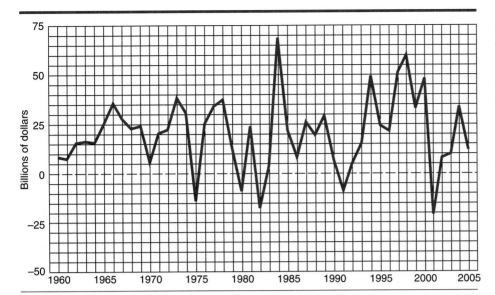

Figure 2
Inventory Investment, 1960–2005 (in billions of 1987 dollars)
This is the most volatile sector of investment. Note that inventory investment was actually negative during recessions in 1975, 1980, 1982, 1991, and 2001. Notice how pronounced the drop was in 2001.
Source: Economic Report of the President, 2001; Economic Indicators, February 2006.

recessions, and the years of negative investment (when inventories were being depleted) all occurred during recession years—1975, 1980, 1982, 1990–91, and 2001.

Investment in plant and equipment, or capital spending, represents the total cost of all the new factories and office buildings, machinery, software, computers, and other equipment that companies acquire to produce their goods and services. In the year 2005, capital spending was over $1.3 trillion, almost 60 percent higher (in 2005 dollars) than it had been just 10 years earlier. Almost half of today's fixed investment is in information processing equipment and software, in contrast to less than 10 percent in the mid-1980s.

Investment in plant and equipment, while it has its ups and downs, is more stable than inventory investment. Unlike inventory investment, even in a bad year companies will still invest a substantial amount in new plant and equipment, mainly because old and obsolete factories, office buildings, and machinery must be replaced. This is the depreciation part of investment.

A second reason for the stability of plant and equipment investment is that most of it is planned years ahead and will be carried out on schedule regardless of what phase the business cycle is in. Since this plant and equipment is being built to meet the needs of the years ahead, little would be gained by postponing construction for the duration of a recession.

A final reason for carrying out capital investment during a recession is that interest rates tend to come down at that time. As the cost of borrowing money is a major part of construction costs, it can be advantageous to carry out construction projects during times of recession. Other resources, too, would tend to be available at lower costs. Each of these factors places a floor under investment spending during recessionary years.

The three reasons for the stability of investment during business downturns were overwhelmed by the general economic collapse of the Great Depression. Why replace worn-out or obsolete plant and equipment when your plant is half idle? Why carry out long-term investment plans when your firm may not survive the next few weeks? Why bother to borrow at low interest rates when your expected rate of profit is negative?

Investment in plant and equipment plummeted over 70 percent between 1929 and 1933. While some people believe another depression could happen at any time, we shall see in subsequent chapters the country has several safeguards built into its economy to prevent a collapse of such proportions. Nevertheless, investment remains the loose cannon on our economic deck, a destabilizing element that tends to push our economy to its highs and lows.

For a majority of American families, their home is, by far, their largest asset. Not only is it their largest purchase, but they spend, on average, about 40 percent of their income on mortgage payments, real estate taxes, heating fuel, repairs, and upkeep.

Residential construction involves replacing our aging housing stock as well as adding to it. During the 25 years following World War II, the United States had a tremendous spurt in residential building, as nearly half of the American population moved to the suburbs. Today there is continued building, particularly in the outlying areas of the suburbs (the exurbs) 50 to 100 miles from the nearest city, but the postwar housing boom has been over for more than 35 years.

Residential home building fluctuates considerably from year to year. Mortgage interest rates play a dominant role. For example, from 1979 to 1982, when mortgage rates reached 15 and 16 percent in most parts of the country, new housing starts plunged by nearly 40 percent. Another factor that causes steep declines in home construction is periodic overbuilding. Once the surplus of new homes on the market is worked off, residential construction goes into another boom period.

Since the new millennium there was a widespread and growing perception that tens of millions of Americans were using their home equities as ATMs to finance a huge buying spree. As long as residential real estate prices were increasing—often at annual rates of over 10 percent—homeowners could take out larger and larger home equity loans.

But would home prices keep rising at such a fast pace? By mid-2005 there were signs that prices were leveling off, and that the so-called housing bubble was about to burst. In the face of rising mortgage interest rates, millions of homeowners would be unable to meet their monthly payments, and some would even lose their homes. By the time you read these words—written in the spring of 2006—you'll know if the housing bubble actually *did* burst, or if we somehow managed to muddle through.

Investment is very unstable.

What this all comes down to is that investment is the most volatile sector in the economy. Fluctuations in GDP are largely fluctuations in investment. More often than not, the country's recessions are touched off by declines in investment, and recoveries are brought about by rising investment.

How Does Savings Get Invested?

How *does* savings get invested? A good question. Well, for starters, what do *you* do with the money you save? Put it in the bank? Buy stocks? Buy corporate bonds?

Nearly all the money that flows into the stock market buys stock that has already been issued. So you might buy 500 shares of Cisco, but someone else has sold those 500 shares. However, initial public offerings (IPOs) and new issues of stock raise more than $200 billion a year, all of which goes directly to the corporations issuing stock. And most of that money finances capital spending.

If you deposit your money in a bank, much of it will end up being invested by large business borrowers. What the banks do is package a large number of deposits into a much smaller number of substantial business loans. When IBM, Dell, General Motors, and Verizon come calling on their bankers, they're going to borrow hundreds of millions or even billions of dollars—so much, in fact, that loan syndicates of dozens of banks are often formed to raise the total amount needed.

Corporations also raise a substantial portion of their investment funds internally through retained earnings and depreciation (or capital consumption) allowances. Retained earnings are the portion of profits not paid to the owners of the business. Depreciation allowances are the tax-deductible funds that have been set aside to replace worn-out or obsolete plant and equipment. Still another important source of investment funds comes from abroad (see the box, "Foreign Investment in the United States").

Let's make a clear distinction between "financial" investment and "real" investment. When you buy corporate stocks and bonds, a bank certificate of deposit (CD), or any other financial security, you may consider that an investment. But economists will tell you that while you made a personal financial investment, it was not a "real" investment. The only investment that is real to economists is the purchase of a new home or the purchase by a business firm of new plant, equipment, or inventory. Only "real" investment is counted in GDP. Suppose you bought 100 shares of Amazon.com, or you invested

---

Foreign Investment in the United States

Why have foreigners been so happy to invest in America? Mainly because of our relatively high interest rates. As our trade deficit topped $300 billion in 2000, foreigners have found themselves awash in U.S. dollars. Many of those dollars were recycled through the purchase of U.S. government securities, corporate stocks and bonds, real estate, and an increasing amount of direct investment, which entailed setting up shop in the United States. A prime example of foreign direct investment is the Japanese automobile transplants, most significantly Honda, Toyota, and Nissan.

Given our shortage of savings, this inflow of foreign investment has been a tremendous help. Not only has it provided needed funds to corporate borrowers and helped finance most of the federal deficit, but it has kept interest rates from going sky-high. However, a significant side effect, which we'll examine closely in the chapter on international finance, is the implication of foreign ownership on our national economic sovereignty.

$10,000 in a U.S. Treasury bond, or you bought part of Rockefeller Center. These were all investments, right? Wrong!

Remember that in economics there are only two types of investment: the purchase of (1) new plant, new equipment, and new residential housing, and (2) additional inventory. What about all that money you "invested" in stocks, bonds, and real estate? If those aren't investments, what *are* they? They are financial transactions—mere exchanges of assets. Now, there's nothing wrong with these transactions, but they don't go into GDP. And if they don't, then they're not investments.

Gross Investment versus Net Investment

In Chapter 9 we will be distinguishing between gross domestic product (GDP) and net domestic product (NDP): GDP − Depreciation = NDP.

We can even do a little generalizing now. *Gross domestic product is the sum of consumption, gross investment, government purchases, and net exports.* And how about net national product? *Net domestic product is the sum of consumption, net investment, government purchases, and net exports.* This leaves us with two simple relationships:

1. GDP − Depreciation = NDP

2. Gross investment − Depreciation = Net investment

Most of us are painfully familiar with the distinction between gross income (what your boss says you are earning) and net income (what you actually take home after taxes and other deductions). Gross and net investment are parallel concepts. In fact, when you subtract depreciation from gross investment, you get net investment.

Gross investment − Depreciation = Net investment

We've said that investment is our nation's expenditure on any new plant, equipment, additional inventory, or residential housing. That's *gross* investment. To get net investment we need to subtract depreciation on plant and equipment and residential housing. (There is no depreciation on inventory accumulation.)

Each year our stock of residential housing depreciates by a certain percentage, say 2 or 3 percent. This depreciation takes place every year even though the market value of that housing stock may be rising. What we're really doing is accounting for the physical deterioration of those buildings. Now we'll take a closer look at depreciation on plant and equipment.

Let's say you started the year with 10 machines and bought another 6 during the year. Your gross investment would be 6. If 4 machines (of your original 10) wore out or became obsolete during the year, your depreciation would be 4. Therefore, your gross investment (6) − depreciation (4) = net investment (2). In other words, you added 2 machines during the year, raising your total from 10 to 12.

In Chapter 8 we'll be using an equation for GDP: GDP = C + I + G + X_n, where C is consumption, I is investment, G is government spending, and X_n is net exports (exports minus imports). I represents gross investment. From now on, I'll often refer to gross investment with the letter I.

Building Capital

At the end of Chapter 4, I stressed that capital (plant, equipment, and inventory) is built up by producing more, consuming less, or some combination thereof. Suppose you want to open a factory with one machine. You have various alternatives.

You might be able to borrow the money to buy the machine. But the person from whom you borrow has saved this money by not consuming all of his or her income. And someone else, who built the machine, spent many hours working on it.

Investment, or the building up of capital, takes sacrifice. If you decide to save the money yourself, you may have to work overtime, take on a second job, or cut back on your lifestyle.

Finally, if you decide to build the machine yourself, think of all the hours this might take you. These are hours you could be working at a paid job, or maybe just lying around watching TV. So no matter how you go about building up capital, there's a great deal of sacrifice involved.

Essentially, then, to build up our plant, equipment, and inventory, we need to work more and consume less. On this all economists agree. But Karl Marx parted company with the classical economists of the 19th century when he wrote his landmark *Das Kapital*. Capital, according to Marx, is created by labor but expropriated by the capitalist, the factory owner. He wrote:

> The owner of the money has paid the value of a day's labour-power; his, therefore, is the use of it for a day; a day's labour belongs to him.... On the one hand the daily sustenance of labour-power costs only half a day's labour, while on the other hand the very same labour-power can work during a whole day, that consequently the value which its use during one day creates, is double what he pays for that use.[5]

In other words, if it costs three shillings to keep a person alive for 24 hours and this person produces three shillings' worth of cloth in six hours, pay him three shillings for 12 hours of work. And if he objects, just tell him to look out the window at the factory gate where hundreds of people stand waiting for a chance to have his job. Marx called them the reserve army of the unemployed.

Investment involves sacrifice.

To invest we must work more and consume less.

The Determinants of the Level of Investment

Many factors determine the level of investment. We'll confine ourselves to four.[6]

(1) The Sales Outlook

You won't invest if your sales outlook is bad.

If you can't sell your goods or services, there's no point in investing, so the ultimate determinant of the level of investment is the business firm's sales outlook. If business is

---

[5]Karl Marx, *Das Kapital*, Vol. 1 (New York: International Publishers, 1967), pp. 193–94.

[6]Additional factors are corporate income tax rates, depreciation allowances, the level of technology, and the cost of constructing new plant and equipment.

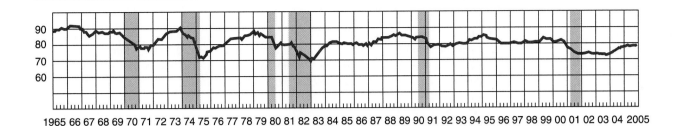

Figure 3
Capacity Utilization Rate in Manufacturing, 1965–2005
Since the mid-1980s, our capacity utilization rate has been below 85. Note that it fell during each recession, which is indicated by a shaded area.
Source: Survey of Current Business, March 2001; *Business Cycle Indicators,* December 2005.

good and sales are expected to be strong for the next few months, then business firms will be willing to take on more inventory. And if sales look good for the next few years, additional plant and equipment will probably be purchased.

(2) Capacity Utilization Rate

The capacity utilization rate is the percentage of plant and equipment that is actually being used at any given time. Since it would be virtually impossible to use every single factory, office, and piece of machinery day in and day out, we will always have *some* idle plant and equipment.

Generally, manufacturing firms use about 80 to 85 percent of their capacity. When business really gets good, the capacity utilization rate approaches 90 percent; during severe recessions, like those of 1974–75 and 1981–82, this rate dips close to 70 percent (see Figure 3). In early 2001 it fell below 80 as the economy slowed and remained there through 2005.

For our purposes, we can count on the capacity utilization rate as an important influence on the level of investment in plant and equipment. At high rates, companies have considerable incentive to build more plant and equipment because sales are pressing against factory capacity. During really bad recessions, when demand is slack, one-third of our factories and equipment may be idle. Why build more?

> You won't invest if you have a lot of unused capacity.

We must temper this analysis by taking note of three additional factors. First, it is likely that we are understating the capacity utilization rate by counting much obsolete or unusable capacity.[7] For example, steel mill and auto plant closings in the early 1980s indicated that some of the plant and equipment in those industries had been counted for several years when their use was economically unfeasible. Second, manufacturing has been a shrinking part of our economy for at least four decades. It now accounts for just one out of every ten jobs in our economy.

Third, the growing importance of imports—along with increasing investment in overseas manufacturing facilities by U.S. multinational corporations—has reduced the significance of our capacity utilization rate. To illustrate, let's suppose that our economy is approaching full capacity. Although we may invest in new capacity, we may also increase our imports and our multinational corporations may build new manufacturing capacity abroad.

---

[7]Suppose our capacity utilization rate is 80 percent, but 10 percent of our plant and equipment is obsolete or unusable. Then our true capacity utilization would be 89 percent (80/90).

(3) The Interest Rate

The interest rate is the cost of borrowing money. There are actually many different interest rates, depending on a firm's creditworthiness and the size of the loan.

Suppose you want to borrow $1,000 for one year and the bank will charge you 12 percent interest. How much interest will you have to pay if you borrow the $1,000 for one year?

Go ahead. Work it out.

I hope your answer is $120. If it isn't, here's how to calculate the interest:

$$\text{Interest rate} = \frac{\text{Interest paid}}{\text{Amount borrowed}}$$

$$.12 = \frac{x}{\$1,000}$$

Now, multiply both sides by $1,000:

$$\$120 = x$$

You won't invest if interest rates are too high.

In general, the lower the interest rate, the more business firms will borrow. But to know how much they will borrow—or whether they will borrow at all in any particular instance—we need to compare the interest rate with the expected rate of profit on the investment.

(4) The Expected Rate of Profit

Economists are not happy unless they give virtually the same concept at least three different names. Therefore, the expected rate of profit is sometimes called the marginal efficiency of capital or the marginal efficiency of investment. We'll define it this way:

$$\text{Expected rate of profit} = \frac{\text{Expected profits}}{\text{Money Invested}}$$

Now, of course, we have to work out a problem. Here's an easy one: How much is the expected profit rate on a $10,000 investment if you expect to make a profit of $1,650? You know how things work around here. Do it yourself, then check your result against mine. I'm always right. But you can't be right unless you try.

$$\begin{aligned}
\text{Expected rate of profit} &= \frac{\text{Expected profits}}{\text{Money invested}} \\
&= \frac{\$1,650}{\$10,000} \\
&= 16.5 \text{ percent}
\end{aligned}$$

The relationship between the interest rate and the expected profit rate was underscored by John Maynard Keynes in his landmark *The General Theory of Employment, Interest, and Money*. Keynes said that every profit opportunity would be exploited as long as the expected profit rate (which he called the "marginal efficiency of capital") exceeded the interest rate: "The rate of investment will be pushed to... where the marginal efficiency of capital in general is equal to the market rate of interest."[8]

Suppose your business firm is interested in borrowing $100,000 at the going interest rate of 15 percent to buy inventory. If your expected profit rate is 18 percent, would it pay to borrow? In other words, after you paid off the interest, how much money would you have left? ($18,000 − $15,000 in interest = $3,000.) You would stand to make $3,000 profit. Of course you would borrow the money.

Now we're ready for an easy three-part problem. Suppose you could borrow money at 20 percent interest and someone offered to buy 100 pounds of a certain substance from you at $1,300 a pound. It costs you only $1,000 a pound to grow this substance. The only problem is that the money you borrow will be tied up for a year until you are able to pay it back.

Answer yes or no to each of these three questions:

1. Would you accept the deal as it stands?
2. Would the deal be acceptable if the interest rate were 10 percent?
3. Would the deal be acceptable if the interest rate were 30 percent?

You stand to make a profit of 30 percent using borrowed money. From those profits, you need to pay interest on your loan. If you borrowed the money at (*a*) 20 percent interest, you would still have money left over (net profit) after you paid the interest, so it would pay to accept the deal. If you borrowed money at (*b*) 10 percent interest, it would be even more profitable than at 20 percent interest. But if you accepted the deal at (*c*) 30 percent interest, after you paid the interest from your 30 percent profit, there would be no money left over from your sales.

Business firms do not always borrow the money that they use for investment projects. Actually, American businesses invest hundreds of billions of dollars a year that they have accumulated in depreciation allowances and retained earings.

Why Do Firms Invest?

Firms tend to invest when (1) their sales outlook is good; (2) their capacity utilization rate is high; (3) interest rates are low; and (4) their expected profit rate is high. But *why* do they invest?

Some firms invest merely to replace worn-out equipment. A related purpose is to replace this equipment with equipment that is more technologically advanced. For example, an old photocopy machine that did 10 copies a minute may be replaced with a high-speed machine that can do more tricks than Houdini. In effect, then, we are replacing machinery and equipment that may not only be dilapidated but obsolete as well. A firm may have to do this just to keep up with the competition. So, in a large sense, just keeping up with current technology requires a substantial amount of investment.

A business may also invest to become larger. Of course, the incentive to invest is based on the sales outlook. No one will want to grow if it means operating at only 50 percent of capacity. In that case, you might be the biggest kid on the block, but you would certainly not be the richest—*or* the smartest.

> You won't invest unless the expected profit rate is high enough.

---

[8]John Maynard Keynes, *The General Theory of Employment, Interest, and Money* (New York: Harcourt Brace Jovanovich, 1958), pp. 136–37.

Graphing the C + I Line

Do you remember the consumption function from Chapter 5? As income rises, consumption rises, but not as quickly. Do you remember induced consumption? As income rises, more consumption is induced.

Figure 4 here reproduces the consumption function graphed in Figure 3 in Chapter 5. You'll note that, as income rises, the C line slopes upward. Higher income levels induce higher levels of consumption.

Would it be reasonable to assume that there is a parallel concept of induced investment? That as income rises, the level of investment rises as well? What do *you* think?

At very low levels of income, the country is in a depression. Nobody invests. At somewhat higher levels of income, more and more investment takes place, because people are able to save *some* money and those funds are invested. So it would be reasonable to say that as income rises, higher levels of investment are induced.

That would be a reasonable assumption, but we need to keep things simple here, because we want to be able to read our graphs easily. So we're going to assume the level of investment stays the same for all levels of income. We know that in the real world, as income rises, I rises, but we're going to trade off some reality for some simplicity.

So far we've had a graph with just two lines—the 45-degree line and the C line, or consumption function. From this two-line graph, C and savings could be calculated. To calculate I (actually the C + I line), a third line is necessary. Figure 5 graphs a C + I line, which is drawn parallel to the C line. This is the same graph as in Figure 4, with the C + I line added.

The question for you to solve has three parts: How much is I when disposable income is (*a*) 1,000, (*b*) 2,000, and (*c*) 3,000? Look at the graph and figure out the answers. Keep in mind that the C line and the C + I line are parallel.

Figure 4
The Consumption Function

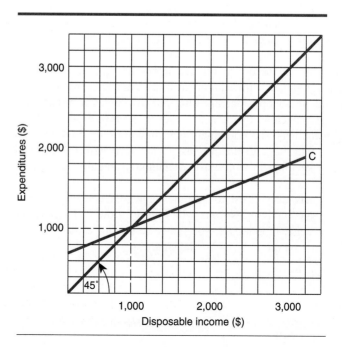

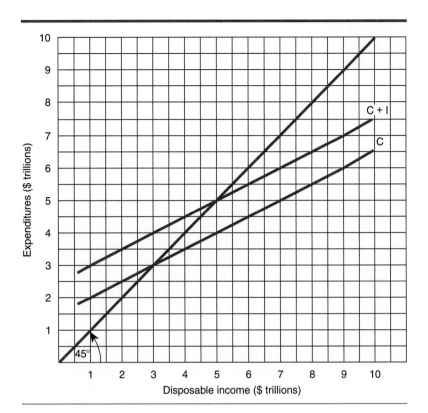

Figure 5
Measuring the Level of
Investment

The answer to the question "How much is I when disposable income is (*a*) $1 trillion, (*b*) $4 trillion, and (*c*) $8 trillion. Since the C line and the C + I line are parallel, the vertical distance between them remains the same. So I is 500 at every level of disposable income.

We're about halfway through our graphs. Before you go any further, you need to ask yourself this question: Self, do I really know how to measure I, or investment, in Figure 5? If the answer is a definite yes, then go directly to the next and final section of this chapter, The Summing Up of Investment. If you'd like a little extra help, you'll find it in the box "Reading the C + I Graph."

The Summing Up of Investment

We're finally ready to include the last part of investment: residential construction spending. The data shown in Table 5 indicate the relative size of the components of investment.

We mentioned previously that investment is the most volatile sector of GDP. Between 1991 (a recession year) and early 2000 (about 12 months before 2001 began), real gross investment (removing the effects of inflation) rose every year. Over this 10-year period real gross investment climbed by 90 percent. But from mid-2000 to late 2001 fell by over 15 percent (see top line of Figure 6).

Figure 6 summarizes the behavior of the three components of gross investment. During the recession of 2001 inventories declined as did nonresidential fixed investment, while residential fixed investment, stimulated by low mortgage interest rates, rose slightly. But the main thing to notice is that gross investment began falling sharply in early 2000 and did not begin to recover until late 2001 when the recession ended.

Reading the C + I Graph

Do you remember how, in the last chapter, we found C, or consumption, at various levels of disposable income? All we did was take the vertical distance between

the horizontal axis and the C line. For example, in the figure shown here, how much is C at a disposable income of $4 trillion? It's just a tad over $2.75 trillion—say $2.8 trillion.

How do we find I? Well, you tell *me*. How much is I, or investment, at a disposable income of $4 trillion? If you're not sure, just guess. Did you come up with about $500 billion, or $0.5 trillion? The way we measure I is to take the vertical distance between the C line and the C + I line. At a disposable income of $4 trillion, that vertical distance is about two boxes. Since each box counts for one-quarter of a trillion dollars (because there are four boxes between each trillion dollars), then two boxes equal half a trillion dollars, or $500 billion. Incidentally, if you're still having trouble distinguishing between millions and billions, and between billions and trillions, then you definitely need to reread the box "A Word about Numbers," which appears near the beginning of Chapter 5.

Now we'll do one more. How much is I when disposable income is $2.5 trillion? Did you get $500 billion, or $0.5 trillion? I certainly hope so. Just remember that we measure I by taking the vertical distance between the C line and the C + I line. It's as easy as counting the boxes.

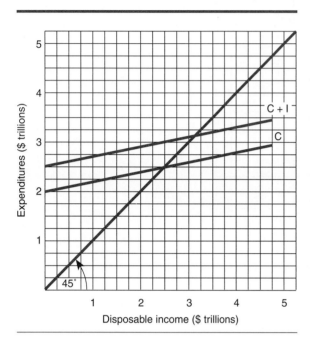

Figure 1

TABLE 5	Gross Investment, 2005
Equipment and software	994
Nonresidential structures	335
Inventory change	15
Residential structures	756
Total	2100

Source: Economic Report of the President, 2006.

At the beginning of the chapter we said that the reason the United States is able to produce so much is that we have so much capital. But because we save very little, our rate of capital formation has been lagging. We have been able to make up for most of our savings shortfall by borrowing hundreds of billions of dollars a year from foreigners. Not only have they been providing much needed funding for investment, but they have also been financing most of our huge and growing federal budget deficits. In the next chapter, we'll be looking at government spending and taxation.

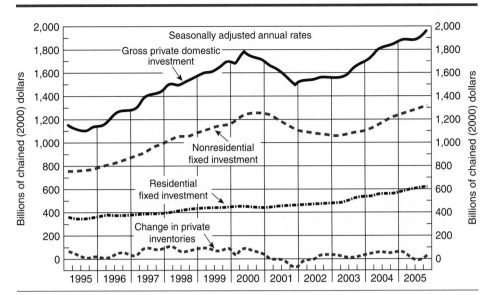

Figure 6

Gross Investment and Its Components, 1995–2005, in 2000 Dollars
Overall investment, nonresidential fixed investment, and inventories fell during the 2001 recession.
Source: Economic Indicators, February 2006.

Current Issue: "Benedict Arnold Corporations"?

During the 2004 presidential campaign, John Kerry castigated the many large companies that were shifting production and jobs abroad, calling them "Benedict Arnold corporations." As you'll recall, General Benedict Arnold betrayed his country by defecting to the British during the American Revolution. Where is the loyalty, Kerry asked, of companies that laid off longtime employees, often with little or no notice, so that they could cut costs by having their products made in Mexico, China, and other low-wage countries?

Clearly their loyalty was not to America. So it would be fair to ask: To whom *are* our corporate leaders loyal?

You can probably guess the answer. They're loyal to their bottom line. They're in business to not just make profits, but to maximize those profits. The chief executive officer of every large corporation serves at the pleasure of that company's board of directors, which, in turn, is elected by the common stockholders.

So what do these folks want above all else? I'll give you three choices: (1) to be fair to their employees; (2) to provide their customers with a great product or service; or (3) to maximize their profits.

Since we all know the answer is number three, it follows that if shifting production and jobs abroad is what it takes to maximize profits, then that's what nearly every firm will do.

So *are* these really Benedict Arnold corporations, betraying loyalties? That depends on where a corporation's loyalties lie. But one thing is perfectly clear: If a corporation does not maximize its profits, then it is disloyal to its owners.

Questions for Further Thought and Discussion

1. What are the advantages and disadvantages of the corporation as a form of business organization?
2. Explain how the capacity utilization rate and the interest rate affect the level of investment.
3. Explain why building up capital takes a great deal of sacrifice.

4. The Carolina Textile Corporation is capitalized at $200 million. If you wanted to buy control of this company, how much money would you have to spend? Since you don't have nearly enough information to make this decision, just make some reasonable assumption about its bonds, preferred stock, and common stock.

5. What has happened to our personal savings rate in recent years, and how has that affected our level of investment?

6. If you owned a business and were considering increasing your level of investment, what would be the most important factor you would consider in determining how much you planned to invest? Explain why you chose that factor.

7. Why are virtually all large business firms corporations?

8. The Swanson Company, a partnership, was formed in 1999 by Jill Swanson, Jenne Swanson, Duke Swanson, Gage Swanson, and Maggie Swanson. In 2000 Holly Swanson and Missy Swanson were taken into the partnership. In 2001 Duke Swanson left the partnership and Brenda Swanson and Jerry Swanson joined it. In 2002 Jill Swanson left the partnership and Buddie Swanson joined it. In 2003 Forrest Swanson joined the partnership. Explain why it would have been easier for this company to have begun as a corporation rather than as a partnership.

Workbook for Chapter 6

Name _____   Date _____

Multiple-Choice Questions

Circle the letter that corresponds to the best answer.

1. In the United States, investment is done _____.
   a) entirely by the government
   b) mostly by the government
   c) about half by the government and half by private enterprise
   d) mainly by private enterprise

2. Which of these is not investment?
   a) additional inventory
   b) the building of a county courthouse
   c) the building of a shopping mall
   d) the building of an automobile assembly line

3. There are about _____ business firms in the United States.
   a) 2 million   c) 30 million
   b) 12 million   d) 42 million

4. A business firm with one owner is _____.
   a) a proprietorship   c) a corporation
   b) a partnership   d) none of these

5. A partnership _____.
   a) must have exactly two owners
   b) must have more than two owners
   c) must have more than one owner
   d) may have more than one owner

6. A key advantage of a partnership over a proprietorship is _____.
   a) limited liability
   b) division of responsibility
   c) perpetual life of the business firm
   d) none of these

7. A _____ is a legal person.
   a) proprietorship   c) corporation
   b) partnership   d) business firm

8. Most corporations are _____.
   a) publicly held   c) very small
   b) very large   d) none of these

9. Corporations collect about _____ percent of all business receipts.
   a) 10   c) 61
   b) 32   d) 84

10. A key disadvantage of incorporating is that _____.
    a) you will have to pay corporate income tax
    b) you will have to charge sales tax
    c) you will have to sell stock
    d) you will have to reorganize the corporation whenever an officer resigns or dies

11. Corporations are controlled by the _____.
    a) employees   c) common stockholders
    b) bondholders   d) preferred stockholders

12. The last to be paid off, whether the corporation does well or goes bankrupt, are the _____.
    a) employees   c) common stockholders
    b) bondholders   d) preferred stockholders

13. Ownership of a corporation is based on _____.
    a) whether you work for the company
    b) whether you buy from the company
    c) whether you hold the bonds of the company
    d) whether you hold stock in the company

14. A corporation's capitalization is based on all of the following except _____.
    a) preferred stock   c) bonds
    b) common stock   d) sales

15. Which is not investment?
    a) the purchase of 100 shares of IBM
    b) the construction of a new factory
    c) the purchase of a new delivery truck
    d) the purchase of inventory

16. Inventory investment is _____.

    a) always positive

    b) always negative

    c) can be either positive or negative

    d) can be neither positive nor negative

17. Inventory investment is _____.

    a) very stable   c) fairly unstable

    b) fairly stable   d) very unstable

18. During severe recessions, inventory investment is

    _____.

    a) negative   c) fairly high

    b) stable   d) very high

19. Gross investment _____.

    a) plus depreciation equals net investment

    b) minus depreciation equals net investment

    c) plus net investment equals depreciation

    d) equals net investment minus depreciation

20. Each of the following might be used to acquire

    capital except _____.

    a) working more   c) borrowing

    b) consuming less   d) consuming more

21. Karl Marx said that capital is produced by _____.

    a) the worker   c) the government

    b) the capitalist   d) money

22. Which is the least stable?

    a) investment in plant and equipment

    b) investment in residential housing

    c) investment in inventory

    d) overall investment

23. Business firms invest in plant and equipment during
    recession years for each of these reasons except.

    a) interest rates are lower.

    b) it has been planned years ahead.

    c) it replaces worn-out plant and equipment.

    d) it is needed because capacity may be fully
       utilized.

24. During bad recessions, investment in plant and

    equipment will _____.

    a) be negative   c) fall somewhat

    b) fall by around 15–20 percent   d) rise

25. Each of the following is business investment except

    _____.

    a) inventory investment

    b) investment in new plant

    c) investment in new equipment

    d) investment in new residential housing

26. Investment will be high when the capacity utilization

    rate is _____ and the interest rate is _____.

    a) high, high   c) high, low

    b) low, low   d) low, high

27. Our capacity utilization rate is usually between

    _____.

    a) 10 and 30   c) 50 and 70

    b) 30 and 50   d) 70 and 90

28. Firms will most likely borrow money for investment

    when _____.

    a) interest rates are low

    b) interest rates are high

    c) the interest rate is higher than the expected profit
       rate

    d) the expected profit rate is higher than the interest
       rate

29. Which statement is the most accurate?

    a) Almost all corporations are very large.

    b) If you want to be your own boss and don't want to
       share any of the decision making, the business
       form that would best suit you is a proprietorship.

    c) It is very expensive to form a corporation.

    d) Most business firms are partnerships.

30. Statement I. Inventory computerization has tended to
    reduce inventory levels.
    Statement II. Inventory investment tends to rise
    during recessions.

    a) Statement I is true and statement II is false.

    b) Statement II is true and statement I is false.

    c) Both statements are true.

    d) Both statements are false.

31. Which is the most accurate statement?
    a) In Middle-Eastern Islamic countries, the typical partnership consisted of just two members, who pooled their resources for perhaps a single trade mission.
    b) In virtually all countries, partnerships dissolve with the death of a member.
    c) Inheritance laws in Western Europe and in Islamic Middle-Eastern countries each have the effect of keeping large fortunes intact.
    d) The large partnership became the engine of economic growth in the second half of the 19th century throughout Western Europe.

Fill-In Questions

1. Of the big three spending sectors of GDP, the least stable is _____.

2. There are about _____ million business firms in the United States.

3. A partnership is owned by _____ people.

4. The key advantage of incorporating is _____.

5. The two main disadvantages of incorporating are (1) _____ and (2) _____.

6. A corporation is owned by its _____ and its _____.

7. A corporation is controlled by its _____.

8. The creditors of a corporation are mainly its _____.

9. Theoretically, you would need an investment of about $_____ to control a corporation that had $100 million in preferred stock, $50 million in common stock, and $350 million in bonds.

10. The least stable form of investment is _____ investment.

11. Gross investment − _____ = Net investment.

12. According to Karl Marx, capital was created by the _____ and expropriated by the _____.

13. In Marx's terms, the people who wait outside the factory gates for work are the _____.

14. During severe recessions, our capacity utilization rate falls to around _____ percent.

15. The expected profit rate is found by dividing _____ by _____.

16. An investment will be undertaken if the expected profit rate is higher than the _____.

17. Total investment is found by adding (1) _____; (2) _____; and (3) _____.

Problems

1. If a corporation has $100 million in preferred stock, $150 million in common stock, and $250 million in bonds:
    a) How much is its capitalization?
    b) Theoretically, how much would it take to control it?
    c) Practically speaking, it may take only about how much to control it?

2. If a corporation has gross investment of $150 million and depreciation of $40 million, how much is its net investment?

3. Given the information in Table 1, find inventory investment in 2005.

TABLE 1	
Date	Level of Inventory
January 1, 2005	$500 million
July 1, 2005	530 million
December 31, 2005	485 million

4. Use the information in Figure 1 to fill in Table 2:

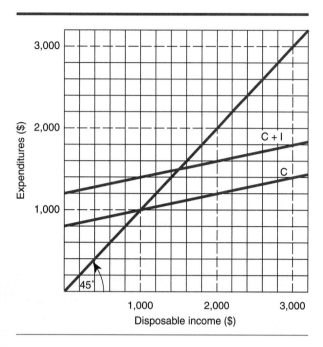

Figure 1

TABLE 2

Disposable Income	Consumption*	Savings*	Investment
(a) 1,000	——	——	——
(b) 2,000	——	——	——
(c) 3,000	——	——	——

*If you don't remember how to find consumption and savings, you'll need to review parts of Chapter 5.

5. If a corporation has $2 billion in common stock, $1 billion in preferred stock, and $4 billion in bonds: a) How much is its capitalization? b) Theoretically, how much would it take to control it? c) Practically speaking, it may take only about how much to control it?

6. If net investment is 400 and depreciation is 175, how much is gross investment?

7. Given the information in Table 3, find inventory investment in 2006.

TABLE 3 — Colin Noel Manufacturing Corp.

Date	Level of Inventory
January 1, 2006	$2.0 billion
May 1, 2006	2.1 billion
Sept. 1, 2006	1.8 billion
Dec. 31, 2006	2.3 billion

8. Suppose Colin Noel could borrow $200,000 for one year at an interest rate of 10 percent. He is virtually certain that he can invest this money in inventory that he could sell over a year for $300,000. If his selling costs were $50,000 and he were to pay his interest out of his profits, how much would Colin Noel's expected profit rate be on his investment?

9. Art Levine, Phyllis Levine, Leah Levine, and Suzannah Levine would like to gain control of the Sports Trading Card Corporation of America. If that corporation has $200 million in common stock, $300 million in preferred stock, and $500 million in bonds: a) Theoretically, how much would they need to invest to control it? b) Practically speaking, how much would they need to invest to control it?

Chapter 7

The Government Sector

In the wake of 9/11, no one is talking anymore about getting the government off the backs of the American people. Indeed, nearly everyone supported the creation of a federal Department of Homeland Security, as well as additional funding for the FBI, local police forces, airport security, and protection of thousands of potential targets that terrorists might strike.

CHAPTER OBJECTIVES

We'll be looking at these topics:

- Government spending.
- The graphing of the C + I + G line.
- Types of taxes.
- The average and marginal tax rates.

- Sources of government revenue.
- Principles of taxation.
- The economic role of the government.

Introduction: The Growing Economic Role of Government

The role of government has grown tremendously over the past seven decades. Actually, most of that growth took place between 1933 and 1945, during the administration of Franklin Delano Roosevelt. The two major crises of that period—the Great Depression and World War II—dwarfed anything our nation has faced since. In fact, we would have to go back to the Civil War to find an event as cataclysmic as either the Depression or what people over 65 still refer to as "the war."

> Most of the growth was due to the Depression and World War II.

Since 1945, the roles of government at the federal, state, and local levels have expanded, but the seeds of that expansion were sown during the Roosevelt administration. Americans seem determined never to experience again the traumatic events that overtook us during the 30s and 40s. *Never again* will we leave ourselves vulnerable to a depression or a military attack by another nation.

> *Government is not the solution to our problem. Government is the problem.*
>
> —Ronald Reagan

The government exerts four basic economic influences: It spends trillions of dollars, levies trillions of dollars in taxes, redistributes hundreds of billions of dollars, and regulates our economy. What does the government *do* with all our money? Some of it is spent on goods and services (that is, highways, police protection, defense), and some of it is redistributed to the poor, to retirees, and to the holders of government bonds.

What does the government do
with all our money?

The government also has an important regulatory role in our economy. We are subject to myriad local, state, and federal laws governing how business may be conducted. These will be examined toward the end of this chapter.

Government Spending

Federal Government Spending

While virtually all private businesses issue financial statements based on a normal calendar year—January 1 to December 31—the federal government's financial, or fiscal, year begins on October 1 and runs through September 30 of the following year. For example, fiscal year 2004 began on October 1, 2003.

In fiscal year 2007 the federal government plans to spend almost $2.8 trillion. Who gets the biggest bite of the pie? As you can see from Figure 1, there's a tie between Social Security and defense. In the accompanying box we spell out the chronology of the budget's preparation.

During the last 35 years, federal transfer payments have gone through the roof. How come? There are several explanations for this huge increase in social spending. Much of it reflects continued expenditures on the Great Society programs of the 1960s, particularly Medicare, Medicaid, and food stamps. A second reason for the increase is that the prosperity our nation has enjoyed in recent years has not spread to tens of millions of poor Americans. Consequently, spending on public assistance, unemployment insurance benefits, and food stamps has shot up since the early 1970s. Finally, in 1955 relatively few people were collecting full Social Security benefits, because that program was then only 20 years old. Today, however, the number of retired people on the rolls is more than twice that of 1955, and benefits have gone up substantially because they are indexed for inflation.

F*igure* 1

The Federal Government Dollar—Fiscal Year 2007 Estimate
Eighty-four cents of each dollar of federal revenue comes from individual income taxes and social insurance receipts, while slightly more than half of all federal expenditures goes for direct benefit payments for individuals. While national defense is budgeted at $537 billion, sometime after the budget is passed by Congress the Bush administration will make a request for supplementary funds to cover expenditures in Iraq and Afghanistan. National defense expenditures will probably reach $600 billion in fiscal year 2007.
Source: Economic Report of the President, 2006; *Survey of Current Business,* February 2006; www.whitehouse.gov/omb/budget.

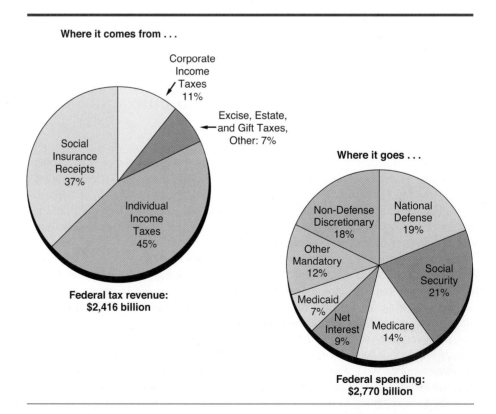

Where it comes from . . .

Corporate Income Taxes 11%

Excise, Estate, and Gift Taxes, Other: 7%

Social Insurance Receipts 37%

Individual Income Taxes 45%

**Federal tax revenue:
$2,416 billion**

Where it goes . . .

Non-Defense Discretionary 18%

National Defense 19%

Other Mandatory 12%

Social Security 21%

Medicaid 7%

Net Interest 9%

Medicare 14%

**Federal spending:
$2,770 billion**

The Chronology of Federal Budget Preparation

Preparation of the budget begins about two years before the beginning of the fiscal year. We'll be looking at the timetable for the preparation of the budget for fiscal year 2007, which began on October 1, 2006.

During early 2005, after months of internal studies, each department presented its budget for fiscal year 2005 to the Office of Management and Budget (OMB). That agency has the job of coordinating all budget requests to ensure that they are consistent with the president's economic program. The OMB then puts together a tentative budget for the president.

President George W. Bush was concerned not just with individual spending programs—foreign aid, defense, food stamps, Social Security—but with the bottom line, or total spending. The president and the director of the OMB then established spending ceilings for each department and the federal agencies, which were then asked to prepare a second round of expenditure plans over the summer.

During the fall of 2005 the OMB reviewed these revised programs, and in the late fall the budget was presented to President Bush for final approval. The final budget message was then drafted for submission to Congress in January 2006.

Over the next eight months the ball was in Congress's court. Both houses of Congress have budget committees that prepare "concurrent resolutions" to be reported to their respective houses by April 15. These resolutions contain two key figures: overall expenditures and overall revenue. By May 15 Congress must pass a single concurrent resolution.

Between May 15 and October 1, Congress passed various appropriations bills—agricultural subsidies, veterans' benefits, aid to mass transit, public assistance—while trying to stay within the limits set by the concurrent resolution. Finally, a second budget resolution had to be passed by October 1, the first day of the fiscal year.

That's the chronology of federal budget preparation in theory. But in practice, the 13 required spending bills, which are the heart of the budget, are not passed until months after the fiscal year begins. It wasn't until February, 2003, that Congress got around to passing the last spending bill for the fiscal year 2003, which began on October 1, 2002. The start of fiscal year 2004 was just a bit better. Instead of passing none of the 13 appropriations bills by the deadline, as happened in 2002, Congress had passed a grand total of three.

The next big-ticket item is defense expenditures, which will come to about $600 billion. This comes to $2,000 for each person in the United States. Today we spend as much on defense as the rest of the world combined. Are we spending too much? Before 9/11, many Americans saw no need to erect expensive defenses against nonexistent enemies. However, since the terrorist attacks, it has become a lot more difficult to argue against spending still more on defense.

One of the fastest-growing federal expenditures in the 1980s and early 1990s was interest on the national debt. The national debt is about ten times its 1980 size. When you owe ten times as much, you have to pay a lot more interest.

The 800-pound budgetary gorilla is medical care, namely Medicare and Medicaid. Back in 1966, just a year after President Lyndon Johnson pushed these programs through Congress, they accounted for just 2 percent of all federal spending (see Figure 2). Forty years later, in 2006, they accounted for 22 percent. And according to the Congressional Budget Office's projection, the share of Medicare and Medicaid will reach 35 percent of the federal budget in 2046.

If you're like most taxpayers, you'd like to see the government trim some of the fat from its budget. So I'd like you to pick up your heaviest ax and start hacking away at Figure 1. But be careful—as soon as you lift your ax, a lot of people will start howling.

Begin with defense. You'll not only make the president unhappy, but you'll incur the wrath of the secretary of defense, the armed forces' top brass, and thousands of defense contractors—not to mention the millions of your fellow citizens who think any cut in the defense budget is the same as just handing the country over to our enemies.

OK, let's cut Social Security and Medicare. Just try it! There are more than 48 million recipients of these benefits, and nearly all of them vote. What about federal pensions? First, we're legally obligated to pay pensions and other benefits to retired federal employees and

Government is the great fiction, through which everybody endeavors to live at the expense of everybody else.

—Frédéric Bastiat, *Essays on Political Economy*, 1872

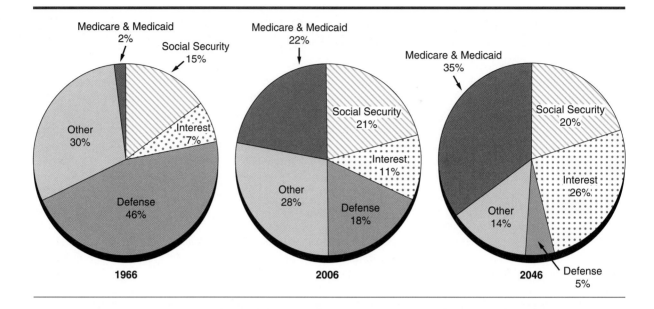

F*igure* 2

Federal Spending, 1966, 2006, and 2046*

As a share of federal spending, Social Security, Medicare, and Medicaid have more than doubled in 40 years and will continue to grow, according to the Congressional Budget Office's "intermediate" projections.
*Percentages may not add to 100.0 percent due to rounding.
Source: Congressional Budget Office.

veterans. Second, there's a political problem. Veterans' benefits have a powerful constituency. Just drop by your local American Legion hall and ask the people there how *they* would feel about the government cutting these benefits.

Many Americans feel we're giving away too much money to foreigners (see the box, "Are We Giving Away the Store?"). But this might be termed "chump change" compared to our big ticket budgetary items such as defense, Social Security, and Medicare.

State and Local Government Spending

Big state and local expenditures are education, health, and welfare.

State and local government spending has been rising rapidly since World War II, but it is still less than half the level of federal spending. Well over half of all state and local government expenditures goes toward education, health, and welfare. One of the problems faced by these governments is that they are expected to provide more and more services with limited tax bases. For example, more than 20 million teenagers are currently attending high school or college. Seventy years ago most people were working by the time they were 14, but now they are still in school. Supporting public education has traditionally been the role of the state and local governments, although in recent years Washington has provided supplementary funds covering about 6 percent of the costs of educating children through high school.

Another expenditure that has increased enormously is police protection. Although this is a function of local government, rising crime and the deterioration of neighborhoods have made it necessary to hire many more police officers. Until the 1950s, neighborhoods largely policed themselves informally, mainly because people spent a great deal of time on the street, most urban areas were more densely populated, and people tended to know one another. All this has changed, and now the police are being called on to perform functions that neighborhoods used to handle themselves.

Sometimes local government and private businesses perform the same tasks. In New York and other major cities, the local sanitation department picks up residential garbage, while private carters pick up garbage from stores, restaurants, and other commercial

Are We Giving Away the Store?

For many Americans, "foreign aid" sounds suspiciously like "welfare for foreigners."

–James Traub, *The New York Times* columnist, 2/13/05–

Many taxpayers are asking whether it makes sense to be spending so much money to help foreigners when we have so many poor people in the United States. During fiscal year 2006, we provided our friends, our allies, and many of the poorer nations of the world with about $25 billion in economic and military aid. About half went to Israel, Egypt, Russia, and the other states of the former Soviet Union.

Recent polls found that two out of five Americans believe foreign aid is the largest single item in the federal budget.

Many Americans ask if we should be building schoolhouses in Iraq instead of in storm ravaged Louisiana and Mississippi. Indeed, we are spending $6 to $7 billion a month in Iraq, but just a small fraction could be considered foreign aid. The lion's share, of course, is being spent on fighting the insurgency.

Our foreign aid bill comes to less than 1 percent of the federal budget, or less than 0.2 percent of our GDP. Twenty-one billion dollars is a lot of money. The chart shows how U.S. foreign aid, as a percentage of GDP, compares with that of other leading international aid-givers. As you can see, the U.S. is near the bottom of the list.

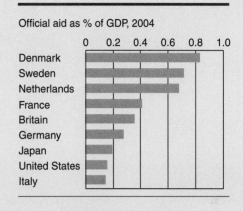

Source: OECD, *The Economist*, May 28, 2005, p. 77.

establishments. While the police provide basic protection and apprehend criminals, private security guards are employed by stores and by more affluent neighborhoods. There are public and private hospitals, schools, and colleges.

Government Purchases versus Transfer Payments

The federal, state, and local governments spend about $4 trillion a year. Nearly half goes to individuals as transfer payments, and the rest is government purchases. We represent these purchases by the letter G, and they go into our GDP equation: $GDP = C + I + G + X_n$.

$$GDP = C + I + G + X_n$$

What do you think the biggest government purchase is? It's defense, which accounts for 23 cents out of every dollar that goes into G. Other biggies are education, police, health, and highway construction. A government purchase is the spending of government funds to purchase or provide the public with some good or service.

Transfer payments cannot be counted in G because they do not represent that kind of spending. What is the largest government transfer payment? I'm sure you know that it's Social Security. Of the $1.5 trillion that the federal, state, and local governments pay out in transfer payments, $581 billion goes to Social Security recipients.

You may want to ask why we bother to distinguish between government purchases and transfer payments. OK, go ahead and ask. The reason is that we need to come up with a figure for GDP—the nation's expenditures on all final goods and services produced during the year at market prices. So we want to add in only what we produced and purchased that year. Don't people receiving transfer payments spend that money on consumer goods and services, or C in our GDP equation? Yes, they do. When they spend those Social Security, public assistance, or government employees' retirement and veterans' benefits, that money will go into GDP.

*F*igure 3
Measuring Government
Spending

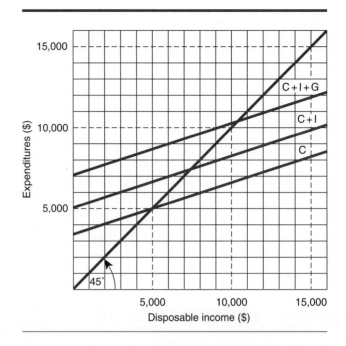

Federal and state and local transfer payments have grown from just 6 percent of GDP in 1960 to more than 13 percent today. Most of the impetus has come from two of President Lyndon Johnson's Great Society programs of the 1960s—Medicare and Medicaid—and from the rising proportion of retirees who are now collecting Social Security. It is conceivable that, in 25 years, when virtually all the baby boomers will have retired, total government transfer payments will be more than one-quarter of GDP.

Let's make sure we're clear on the difference between government spending and government purchases. Government spending is the total that the federal, state, and local governments spend on everything—transfer payments to individuals as well as purchases of goods and services. Which goes into GDP—transfer payments or government purchases? *Only government purchases are counted in GDP.* Now let's see how they're added in.

Graphing the C + I + G Line

In Chapter 5 we graphed the C line. In the last chapter we graphed the C + I line. Now we add another line to our graph: the C + I + G line. By now this should be old hat to you, so I'm going to ask you to figure out how much G is in Figure 3 (assuming the C + I + G line is parallel to the C + I line).

What did you get? You should have gotten 2,000. You'll notice that the level of G remains at 2,000 no matter what the level of disposable income. The main reason for doing this is to keep our graph as simple as possible.

We're not quite finished with our graphs. We still need to draw the C + I + G + X_n line, but that won't happen until the beginning of the next chapter.

A fine is a tax for doing wrong.
A tax is a fine for doing right.
        —Anonymous

The point to remember is that what the government gives it must first take away.

        —John S. Coleman

Taxes

Presidents Ronald Reagan and George W. Bush will go down in history as two of our greatest tax cutters. Before we even begin to consider how high our taxes are and how much they've been cut, we'll need to understand something about tax rates and the types of taxes that exist. Once that's done, we'll see just how onerous the American tax system really is.

The Average Tax Rate and the Marginal Tax Rate

If someone asked you what your tax rate was, would you have a ready answer? Generations of attorneys have taught us that the best answer to any question (and especially those to which you don't know the answer) is another question. So the answer to the question "What's your tax rate?" is "Which tax rate are you referring to? My average tax rate or my marginal tax rate?"

But what if your questioner replies, "What is your average tax rate?" What do you do then? You tell her. And if she then happens to ask you your marginal tax rate, you tell her that as well.

The average rate is the overall rate you pay on your entire income, while the marginal rate is the rate you pay on your last few hundreds (or thousands) of dollars earned. Your marginal rate is often referred to as your tax bracket. In nearly all cases, I'm talking about the average and marginal rates that you're paying in personal income tax, but I'll apply the average tax rate to the Social Security tax as well.

The art of taxation consists in so plucking the goose as to obtain the largest possible amount of feathers with the smallest amount of hissing.

—Jean-Baptiste Colbert

The Average Tax Rate   I kind of left you hanging there, didn't I? How do you answer the question "What is your average tax rate?"

Let's try a simple problem. The average tax rate is calculated by dividing taxes paid by taxable income:

$$\text{Average tax rate (ATR)} = \frac{\text{Taxes paid}}{\text{Taxable income}}$$

Suppose a person paid $3,000 on a taxable income of $20,000. How much is the average tax rate? Do your calculations right here:

$$\text{Average tax rate} = \frac{\text{Taxes paid}}{\text{Taxable income}} = \frac{\$3,000}{\$20,000} = 0.15 \text{ or } 15\%$$

$$\text{ATR} = \frac{\text{Taxes paid}}{\text{Taxable income}}$$

If you correctly calculated 15 percent, go on to the marginal tax rate in the next section. If not, let's go over all the steps in finding the average tax rate in the accompanying Extra Help box.

The Marginal Tax Rate   The average tax rate is the overall rate you pay on your entire income, while the marginal tax rate is the rate you pay on the last few hundred dollars you earned. Suppose you made $100 in overtime and the government took $70. Would you work overtime? Chances are you wouldn't, and that supposition forms a cornerstone of supply-side economics. The supply-siders' basic belief is that our high marginal tax rates rob people of the incentive to work as hard and as long as they would with a lower tax burden.

The marginal tax rate is calculated by dividing additional taxes paid by additional taxable income:

$$\text{Marginal tax rate (MTR)} = \frac{\text{Additional taxes paid}}{\text{Additional taxable income}}$$

How Did We Get an Average Tax Rate of 15%?

How do we get from $^{\$3,000}/_{\$20,000}$ to 0.15? First, reduce the fraction to $^3/_{20}$. Whatever you do to the top of the fraction, you do to the bottom. Get rid of the three zeros on top and get rid of three zeros on the bottom. (While you're at it, you can get rid of the dollar signs as well.)

The next step is to divide 3 by 20. Remember, whenever you have a fraction, you may divide the bottom number into the top number. If you divide the top into the bottom, you will not only violate a basic law of arithmetic, but you will also get the wrong answer. $20\overline{)3}$ is the same as $20\overline{)3.00}$. We are allowed to put a decimal point after any whole number. And we are allowed to put zeros after the decimal point, because they don't change the number's value. These are more laws of arithmetic.

$$20\overline{)3.00} = 20\overline{)3.00}^{.15}$$

The average tax rate is 0.15, or 15 percent. Our final law of arithmetic is that, whenever you want to convert a decimal into a percentage, you move the decimal point two places to the right and write a percent sign after the number. Examples would be 0.235 = 23.5%; or, 0.71 = 71%; or, 0.406 = 40.6%. If a baseball player is hitting .406, he is getting a hit 40.6 percent of the times he bats. And if your average tax rate comes to .406, it means you are paying 40.6 percent of your taxable income to the Internal Revenue Service.

Let's try one more problem. Suppose you pay $12,000 on a taxable income of $50,000. How much is your average tax rate? To solve this problem: (1) write the formula, (2) substitute numbers into the formula, and (3) solve.

$$\text{Average tax rate} = \frac{\text{Taxes paid}}{\text{Taxable income}}$$

$$= \frac{\$12,000}{\$50,000} = \frac{12}{50} = \frac{6}{25}$$

$$25\overline{)6.00}^{.24} = 24\%$$

Suppose you had to pay an additional $420 on an additional taxable income of $1,000. How much is your marginal tax rate?

$$\text{MTR} = \frac{\text{Additional taxes paid}}{\text{Additional taxable income}}$$

$$= \frac{\$420}{\$1,000} = \frac{42}{100} = 0.42 = 42\%$$

Now we'll get a little fancier. Suppose your taxable income rose from $20,000 to $22,000 and the taxes you paid rose from $4,500 to $5,200. How much is your marginal tax rate?

$$\text{MTR} = \frac{\text{Additional taxes paid}}{\text{Additional taxable income}}$$

$$\text{Marginal tax rate} = \frac{\text{Additional taxes paid}}{\text{Additional taxable income}}$$

$$= \frac{\$700}{\$2,000} = \frac{7}{20} = 0.35 = 35\%$$

Again, if you need a little help with the math, see the accompanying Extra Help box.

Types of Taxes

There are two basic divisions of taxes. First we'll be looking at the difference between direct and indirect taxes. Then we'll take up progressive, proportional, and regressive taxes.

Direct Taxes   A direct tax is a tax with your name written on it. The personal income and Social Security taxes are examples. They are taxes on particular persons. If you earn a certain amount of money, you must pay these taxes.

The corporate income tax is also a direct tax. You might not think so, but a corporation is considered a legal person. For example, in court, you would sue a corporation rather than its owners or officers. Thus, if a corporation makes a profit, it must pay a corporate income tax, and this is a direct tax.

Indirect Taxes   These are not taxes on people but on goods or services that we purchase. Taxes on things include sales and excise taxes. Examples are a state sales tax on most retail purchases and the excise taxes on tires, gasoline, movie tickets, cigarettes, and liquor.

The distinction between direct and indirect taxes was made by John Stuart Mill more than a century ago:

> A direct tax is one which is demanded from the very persons who, it is intended or desired, should pay it. Indirect taxes are those which are demanded from one person in the expectation and intention that he shall indemnify himself at the expense of another.[1]

Now we shall take up, in turn, progressive, proportional, and regressive taxes. The key variable we use to differentiate them is where the tax burden falls.

Progressive Taxes   A progressive tax places a greater burden on those best able to pay and little or no burden on the poor. The best example is, of course, the federal personal income tax. For the vast majority of American taxpayers today, the more they earn, the higher percentage they pay. In terms of the average tax rate, then, people in higher income brackets pay a substantially higher average tax rate than those in lower brackets.

Proportional Taxes   Proportional taxes place an equal burden on the rich, the middle class, and the poor. Sometimes a flat tax rate is advanced as a "fair" or proportional tax, but it is neither. For example, a flat income tax rate of, say, 15 percent with no deductions, would place a much greater burden on the poor and the working class than on the rich.[2] (See the box, "Nominally Progressive, Proportional, and Regressive Taxes.") It would be much harder for a family with an income of $10,000 to pay $1,500 in income tax (15 percent of $10,000) than it would be for a family with an income of $100,000 to pay $15,000 (15 percent of $100,000).

Several Eastern European countries have adopted the flat tax, especially since the turn of the century. Russia (13 percent), Ukraine (13 percent), Serbia (14 percent), and Romania (16 percent) are the largest countries having flat taxes. These countries have greatly simplified their income taxes, but at the price of giving up nearly all their deductions. Many Americans want to have it both ways—a flat tax, while retaining most of the deductions. Which would leave us right where we started—a tax code in great need of simplification.

Regressive Taxes   A regressive tax falls more heavily on the poor than on the rich. An example is the Social Security tax. In 2006 the rate was 6.2 percent on all wages

In this world nothing can be said to be certain, except death and taxes.

—Benjamin Franklin

John Stuart Mill, English philosopher and economist (Brown Brothers)

Where there is an income tax, the just man will pay more and the unjust less on the same income.

—Plato

People want just taxes more than they want lower taxes. They want to know that every man is paying his proportionate share according to his wealth.

—Will Rogers

A regressive tax falls mainly on the poor.

---

[1] John Stuart Mill, *Principles of Political Economy,* Book IV, ed. William J. Ashley (Philadelphia: Porcupine Press, 1979), p. 823.

[2] Steve Forbes, whose net worth is estimated to be about $400 million, made his flat tax proposal the major issue in his campaigns for the Republican presidential nomination in 1996 and 2000. He advocated a flat tax on wages and salaries, exempting profits, interest, and dividends. And for good measure, Forbes, who inherited his wealth, would abolish the federal tax on inheritances.

We have already defined these taxes in accordance with their effect, or burden, on taxpayers in different income groups. The burden of a progressive tax falls most heavily on the rich; the burden of a proportional tax falls equally on all income groups; and the burden of a regressive tax falls most heavily on the poor.

This three-part graph presents an alternative view of these types of taxes. I'll tell you up front that I strongly disagree with the implications of this view. Let's look at each part of this graph and see how *you* feel.

The graph in part (*a*) is nominally progressive because higher-income people pay a higher tax rate than lower-income people. For example, those earning $10,000 pay only 4 percent of their incomes, while those earning $100,000 pay 8 percent. But is this, in effect, a progressive tax? Is it as easy for a poor family to pay $400 as it is for a relatively rich family to pay $8,000? We could argue it either way. And, unfortunately, economic analysis cannot supply an answer. Now, I happen to feel that a $400 tax bill imposes a greater burden on a family earning

$10,000 than an $8,000 tax bill imposes on a family earning $100,000. What do *you* think?

Let's move on to the next part of the graph, (*b*), which shows a nominally proportional tax rate of 10 percent. Here's the question: Is it as easy for a poor family to hand over 10 percent of its income to the IRS as it is for a middle-class family, or a rich family? What do *you* think? My own view is that it isn't and that this nominally proportional tax is, in effect, a regressive tax.

The last part, (*c*), is easy. This is a nominally regressive tax because the tax rate declines as income rises. Obviously, by any measure, the burden falls most heavily on the poor.

Economists should avoid making value judgments, so perhaps I have gone a bit too far in claiming that nominally progressive taxes *could* be regressive in effect. And that nominally proportional taxes *are* regressive in effect (although this is somewhat less controversial). So if you disagree with my conclusions, that doesn't make one of us wrong and the other right. It means only that our values are different.

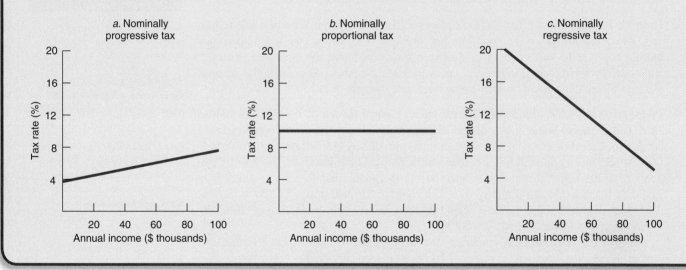

and salaries up to $94,200. The maximum you had to pay was $5,840.40. Where did this figure come from? I'll give you some space to come up with the answer:

That's right: multiply $94,200 by 6.2 percent, or 0.062. This comes to $5,840.40.

Now that I've had you do all these calculations, I have some bad news for you. The 6.2 percent of your wages deducted from your paycheck is not *all* the government takes. The Medicare tax of 1.45 percent is also taken out, but, unlike the Social Security tax, there's no wage-base limitation. If you earned $1 million, you'd pay a Medicare tax of $14,500.

TABLE 1	The Incidence of the Social Security Tax at Various Income Levels in 2006*		
Level of Earned Income		Taxes Paid	Average Tax Rate
$ 10,000		$ 620.00	6.20%
94,200		5,840.40	6.20
100,000		5,840.40	5.84
1,000,000		5,840.40	0.58

*The Social Security tax rate is set by law at 6.2 percent. Each year, however, the inflation rate of the previous year raises the wage base.

So let's go back to the drawing board. The deduction from your pay is 7.65 percent (6.2 percent for Social Security and 1.45 percent for Medicare). How much, then, is deducted per year for these programs from the pay of a person earning $10,000? Work it out right here:

No taxation without representation!
—Revolutionary War Slogan

Taxation with *representation ain't much fun either.*
—unknown

The answer is $765 ($10,000 × .0765). Of course, your employer also withholds money from your check for personal income taxes. But guess what! Seventy-five percent of all taxpayers pay more in payroll taxes (that is, Social Security and Medicare) than they do in personal income tax.

Table 1 shows the Social Security taxes paid by people with various incomes. Only earned income (wages and salaries) is subject to this tax; rental income, interest, dividends, and profits are not. It might appear at first glance that the Social Security tax is proportional; but as you examine Table 1, you should observe that it is not only regressive in effect, but nominally regressive as well.

Table 1 shows the Social Security taxes paid on earned income, which provides over 90 percent of the income of nearly everyone but the rich. The primary income sources of the rich are dividends, interest, and profit, none of which is subject to the Social Security tax. *Think* about it: Nearly all of the income of the non-rich is subject to the Social Security tax, but only a tiny fraction of the income of the rich is taxed. All the more reason to label the Social Security tax as regressive.

Today three-quarters of all taxpayers pay more in Social Security tax than in federal personal income tax. Indeed, this holds true for nearly everyone with an income below $75,000.

Sources of Federal Revenue

The Personal Income Tax   As we indicated in Figure 1 near the beginning of the chapter, individual income taxes account for 45 percent of all federal tax revenue. It has long been the most important revenue source, although it may soon be outstripped by social insurance receipts, which pay for Social Security and Medicare. In general, the middle class and the rich pay nearly all federal income taxes.

The largest source of federal revenue is the personal income tax.

You don't pay tax on all of your income. You may subtract various deductions and exemptions, and, consequently, very few people with low incomes have to pay any federal income tax. In 2005 a single person paid a marginal tax rate of just 10 percent on

The Economic Recovery Tax Act of 1981

Figure 4

Federal Personal Income Tax:
The Top Marginal Tax Rate,
1954–2006

The top rate today is less than half the
top rate in 1962, but it is substantially
higher than the top rate in the late 1980s.

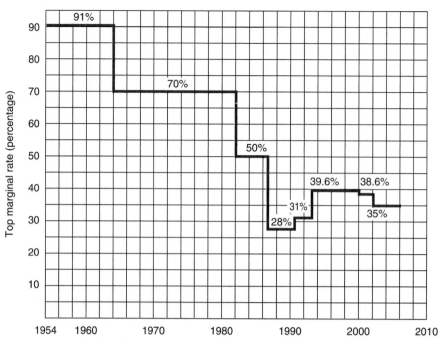

Note: During World War II the top MTR was 94%.

*The United States is the only
country where it takes more
brains to figure your tax than to
earn the money to pay for it.*
—Edward J. Gurney,
U.S. senator

*That which angers men most
is to be taxed above their
neighbors.*
—Sir William Petty, *A Treatise
of Taxes and Contributions,*
1662

her first $7,300 of taxable income, and 15 percent on the next $22,400. A married couple filing jointly paid 10 percent on their first $14,600 of taxable income and 15 percent on the next $44,800.[3] In 2005 the marginal tax rates were 10, 15, 25, 28, 33, and 35 percent. Two-thirds of all taxpayers have MTRs of either 15 percent or 10 percent.

Anyone with a taxable income of over $326,450 paid a marginal tax rate of 35 percent. Figure 4 shows the maximum marginal tax rate since 1954. The federal personal income tax is considered progressive because the burden falls mostly on the rich. Some would disagree, saying that many rich people pay no taxes. We won't go there, except to mention that only an infinitesimal fraction of the rich pay no income tax. Others say that the rich are unfairly called upon to pay the lion's share of this tax. We'll come back to that argument toward the end of the chapter, when we discuss recent federal tax laws.

We have mentioned that you don't have to pay tax on your entire income. In fact, a married couple with children earning less than $20,000 pays no federal income tax at all, because of a combination of deductions, exemptions, and child care tax credits. Randy Day is single and earns $10,000. If he is entitled to $9,000 in deductions and exemptions, how much federal personal income tax does he pay? Work it out right here:

Solution:
$10,000 − $9,000 = $1,000 taxable income. Since he is in the lowest income tax bracket, 10 percent, he would pay $100 in federal personal income tax ($1,000 × .10).

How does our top marginal tax rate compare with those of other wealthy countries? Would you believe it's the lowest in the group shown in Figure 5?

---

[3]Every year these tax brackets are adjusted upward for inflation. For example, in 2002 a single person paid 10 percent on her first $6,000 of taxable income, but by 2005 she had to pay 10 percent on her first $7,300 of income.

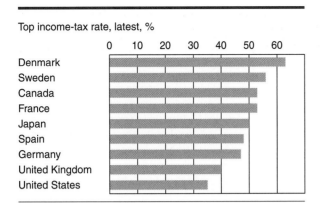

Top income-tax rate, latest, %

Figure 5
Top Marginal Income Tax Rates
in 9 Leading Wealthy Nations,
2003
The United States has the lowest
top personal income tax rate among
these nine nations. While our most
affluent taxpayers pay a marginal
tax rate of just 35 percent, those in
Denmark, Sweden, Canada, and
France all pay over 50 percent.
Source: OECD.

The Payroll Tax   What's the payroll tax? Remember the Social Security and Medicare taxes that you pay? What you pay is matched by your employer. When you pay 7.65 percent of your wages (6.2 percent for Social Security and 1.45 percent for Medicare), your employer also pays 7.65 percent of your wages. The payroll tax is the federal government's fastest-growing source of revenue and now stands second in importance to the personal income tax.

Let's make sure we're clear on what the Social Security, Medicare, and payroll taxes are. Our employers deduct 6.2 percent of our pay (up to $94,200) in Social Security taxes and 1.45 percent of our pay in Medicare taxes. In other words, we pay 7.65 percent in payroll tax on wages of up to $94,200, and 1.45 percent on all wages. The employer matches the employee's payments dollar for dollar. So how much payroll tax would the government collect all together on wages of $20,000?

Giving money and power to the government is like giving whiskey and car keys to teenage boys.
—P. J. O'Rourke

Solution: It would collect $3,060 ($20,000 × 0.153). Where did we get 0.153? We added the 0.0765 that the employee paid to the 0.0765 that the employer paid. The employee would pay $1,530 ($20,000 × .0765), and this would be matched by the employer.

The Corporate Income Tax   The corporate income tax is a tax on a corporation's profits. Those who believe profits provide our economy with its main incentive to produce goods and services are uneasy that they are so heavily taxed. However, corporate income taxes are now just 11 percent of all federal tax revenue and the maximum rate is 35 percent.[4]

The power to tax involves the power to destroy.
—Chief Justice John Marshall

Excise Taxes   An excise tax is a sales tax, but it is aimed at specific goods and services. The federal government taxes such things as tires, cigarettes, liquor, gasoline, and phone calls. Most excise taxes are levied by the federal government, although state and local governments often levy taxes on the same items. Cigarettes and gasoline, for example, are subject to a federal excise tax as well as to excise taxes in many states. In fact, the differential in state excise taxes encourages many people to "smuggle" cigarettes from North Carolina into New York.

Excise taxes, which account for about 4 percent of federal revenue, have another purpose beside serving as a source of revenue. They tend to reduce consumption of certain products of which the federal government takes a dim view. The surgeon general not only warns us about cigarettes but looks on approvingly as the government taxes them.

---

[4]All corporations earning profits of at least $335,000 pay an average tax rate of 35 percent. Of course, using loopholes in the tax law, virtually all major corporations are legally able to report much lower profits, and consequently, pay much lower taxes.

ADVANCED WORK

Should Cigarettes Be Taxed?

Should cigarettes be taxed? Why not? If the tax is high enough, it will discourage smoking. Of course, we don't want to make it too high, or nobody will smoke, and the federal government will be out about $8 billion a year.

But there are two good reasons why a tax on cigarettes is inequitable. First, it's regressive. We can see that it's harder for a poor person to pay $4 dollars a pack (or $1,460 a year, if that person has a two-pack-a-day habit) than it is for a rich person to pay $4 dollars a pack. But if you're poor, you're much more likely to smoke than if you're rich.

In 2006 it cost as much as $8 for a pack of cigarettes in New York City (where, in addition to the federal tax, there is a very high state and local tax on cigarettes). There are people selling individual cigarettes on the street for 40 or 50 cents. It's poor people who can't afford to buy an entire pack who are buying cigarettes on the street, which shows quite vividly just how regressive cigarette taxes are.

According to the U.S. Centers for Disease Control in Atlanta (where I once worked as a management trainee), 16 percent of all college graduates smoke, while 36 percent of all high school dropouts continue to puff away. Your average college graduate is much more affluent than your average high school dropout, which means a cigarette tax is almost targeted at the poor.

We single out relatively poor people, we tax them on something they really like to do, and then, to add insult to injury, we make them stand outside the building.

Should Our Gasoline Taxes Be Raised?

 Are our gas taxes too high? They certainly are not too high relative to the taxes paid in other industrial countries. The table below shows gasoline prices per gallon before and after taxes in selected industrial countries for the week ending February 11, 2006.

	Price per gallon of gas	Taxes as a percentage of price	
United Kingdom	$5.89	68.0%	
Germany	5.57	66.3	
France	5.37	65.1	
Italy	5.50	61.8	
Spain	4.16	54.1	
Japan	5.68	44.8	
Canada	4.01	33.1	
U.S.A.	2.45	17.1	

Sources: International Energy Agency; Energy Information Agency

Excise taxes are usually regressive.

Excise taxes are generally regressive because they tend to fall more heavily on the poor and working class. The tax on a pack of cigarettes is the same whether you're rich or poor, but it's easier for the rich person to handle $3 or $4 a day than it is for a poor person. The same is true of liquor and gasoline. In fact, a tax on most consumer goods is regressive because the poor tend to spend a higher proportion of their incomes on consumption than the rich (who save 20 to 25 percent of their incomes). (See the nearby boxes regarding cigarette and gasoline excise taxes.)

Would a tax on jewelry be progressive or regressive? Clearly it would be progressive since the rich spend a much higher proportion of their income on jewelry than the poor.

The Estate Tax   A tax on estates of people who die has been termed by its opponents as the "death tax." It is a graduated tax that rises to 55 percent but is levied only on estates valued at $1,000,000 or more. It accounts for about one and a half percent of federal tax revenue and is triggered by only 2 percent of all deaths. Most important, it falls on the relatively rich. More than 90 percent of estate taxes are paid by the estates of people with incomes exceeding $200,000 a year at the time of death.

Recent Tax Legislation

Kemp-Roth Tax Cut of 1981   This law, which lowered the average citizen's tax bill by 23 percent over a three-year period, was strongly supported by President Ronald Reagan. The top marginal income tax rate was cut from 70 percent to 50 percent.

Tax Reform Act of 1986   This cut personal income taxes still further. The maximum rate was lowered to 28 percent, and millions of poorer families were taken off the income tax rolls entirely.

In 1990 the top marginal rate was raised to 31 percent, and in 1993 to 39.6 percent. There were no more changes until 2001.

The Tax Cut of 2001   This law, passed at the behest of President George W. Bush, immediately lowered the minimum marginal tax rate from 15 percent to just 10 percent, and gradually lowered the other marginal tax rates over the next 10 years. By the end of the decade the top marginal tax rate would fall to 33 percent. In addition, the inheritance tax would be phased out completely. Weirdly, however, unless Congress made this law permanent, it would expire in 2011, and we would revert to the tax rates that were in effect in 2001.

The two main criticisms of this tax cut were that most of the benefits would go to the rich and that it would push up the federal budget deficit. President Bush countered that the rich paid most of the taxes, so it would be only fair that they should receive most of the benefits of a tax cut. The top 5 percent of all households pay 51 of the federal income tax, while the poorest 50 percent pay just 4 percent. Still, one must wonder why nearly *every* one of the president's tax proposals seems to be skewed toward helping the rich.

President Bush also maintained that a tax cut would give people more incentive to work, the economy would grow faster, and the budget deficit would subsequently shrink. Again, critics note that after we enacted massive tax cuts in 1981, the federal budget deficit almost tripled by the end of the decade.

The Tax Cut of 2003   This law, passed by Congress with strong support from President Bush, had three main provisions: The top federal personal income tax rate paid by stockholders on corporate dividends and on capital gains was lowered to 15 percent, but in 2009 the rate would revert back to the current higher rate.

- The child income tax credit was raised from $600 to $1,000.

- The highest income tax brackets were reduced as follows: 38.6 to 35 percent; 35 to 33 percent; 30 to 28 percent; and 27 to 25 percent.

- Dividends became 50 percent tax-free in 2003; 100 percent tax-free in 2004–6; fully taxable again in 2007.

Are you wondering why the measures were temporary? The Republicans, who narrowly controlled both houses of Congress, needed to compromise in order to pick up enough votes to pass these tax cuts. Congressional leaders, along with President Bush, hope to extend these cuts, perhaps even making them permanent.

It is generally allowed by all, that men should contribute to the publick charge but according to the share and interest they have in the public peace; that is, according to their estates or riches.
—Sir William Petty, *A Treatise of Taxes and Contributions*, 1662

Only the little people pay taxes.
—attributed to Leona Helmsley, billionaire who went to jail for tax evasion

Sources of State and Local Revenue

The Personal Income Tax   Almost half of all state revenue comes from personal income taxes. Generally these are progressive taxes, falling most heavily on the rich. However, high tax states like New York and California run the risk of driving their richest residents to other states. States with no personal income taxes are Alaska, Florida, Nevada, New Hampshire, South Dakota, Texas, Washington, and Wyoming.

The Sales Tax   Almost half the taxes collected by the states come from the sales tax. This is a highly regressive tax. Although most food items are exempt, the poor consume a higher proportion of their incomes than the rich, who are able to save. In other words, a higher proportion of poor people's income is subject to this tax.

Furthermore, the rich can avoid or evade a large proportion of the sales tax by buying their big-ticket items—furniture, stereos, TVs, cars, and so on—in states that have low or no sales tax. They can also evade the sales tax by buying expensive items with cash (an option not feasible for the poor) from merchants who don't declare their cash incomes.

Still another problem with the sales tax is that it can distort business decisions about where to locate. Why did Amazon.com buy warehouses in Nevada near the California border to serve its West Coast market, when warehouses in California's Central Valley would probably have been more cost-effective? Because a physical presence in California would make Amazon responsible for collecting sales taxes on items sold to Californians, something which Amazon wants to avoid. According to the U.S. Constitution, one state cannot require businesses in another state to collect taxes for it.

You probably never heard of the Internet Tax Freedom Act, which declared a tax moratorium for online sales, exempting buyers from paying state and local sales taxes. As these sales multiply, the states stand to lose an increasing proportion of their most important source of revenue. This loss was estimated at $20 billion in 2006. However, there will apparently be no Internet sales tax in the foreseeable future.

The Property Tax   About 80 percent of all local tax revenue is derived from the property tax. There is some disagreement about whether this is a regressive tax, but it is a deduction that you may take on your federal income tax. For example, if you paid $3,000 in property tax, you are entitled to a $3,000 deduction on your federal income tax return.

Are State and Local Taxes Regressive?   Yes! The people with the lowest 20 percent of household incomes—below $18,000—pay 11.4 percent of their income for state and local taxes. Those in the top 1 percent—earning over $350,000—pay just 5.2 percent. The prize for most regressive taxes goes to the state of Florida, where the lowest-income families pay 14.4 percent of their income for state and local taxes, while the top 1 percent pay just 2.7 percent. But Washington state can certainly make a valid claim that *it* has the most regressive state and local taxes. These taxes cost the poor 17.6 percent of their income, while the families in the top 1 percent income bracket pay just 3.1 percent.

The State and Local Fiscal Dilemma

Since World War II, state and local governments have been expected to provide an increasing number of services, most notably health, welfare, education, and police protection. According to the 1940 census, just one-third of all Americans who were 25 or older had gone beyond the eighth grade. Today more than 85 percent of those 25 or older are at least high school graduates. Education is perhaps the main job of local government, but it is paid for not just by local taxes, but by state and federal taxes as well. In 1945 state and local taxes were about 5 percent of GDP; now they are 9 percent (see Figure 6).

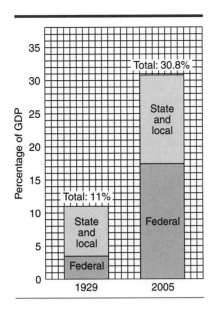

Figure 6
Government Tax Receipts as Percentage of GDP, 1929 and 2003
Taxes today are about two and a half times as high as they were in 1929.
Source: Economic Report of the President, 2003; *Survey of Current Business,* May 2003, www.bea.gov.

Furthermore, under our federal system, neighboring states and local governments are in direct competition with one another for tax dollars. If one government's tax rates—particularly the sales and property taxes—rise too far above the levels of its neighbors, its citizens will vote with their feet. They will shop or even move to the areas that have lower tax rates. Were there a uniform national sales or property tax, it could be more easily raised when necessary. As long as neighboring government units are in direct competition, raising the necessary tax revenues will be difficult.

The federal government has piled new obligations on state and local government, without providing nearly enough money to pay for them. The largest unfunded mandate is the No Child Left Behind Act of 2001, which requires all public schools to test students, in order to improve their education. In theory, the act fully finances the new tests, but in practice, say local officials, implementing the act requires changes in the whole educational system, not just adding a few extra tests. The cost, they say, is $35 billion a year more than the act provides.

The Department of Homeland Security requires states and localities to hire new police officers, but provides no money to pay their salaries. You may remember the Bush-Gore presidential election fiasco in Florida in 2000. The Bush administration now insists on nationwide election reform—a state responsibility—but does not provide the funding.

Through the 1970s, the 1980s, and the 1990s, the states ran substantial surpluses. But the 2001 recession, the events of 9/11, and the recent federal government spending mandates have driven many states governments—and with them thousands of local governments—into very serious financial difficulty. Faced with sharply rising projected budget deficits, every state but Vermont was legally obligated to balance its budget. In 2002 and 2003, state after state slashed services and raised taxes. College tuitions were raised in some states by over 20 percent, tens of thousands of state employees were laid off, prisoners were released early, and sales, personal income, and property taxes were increased across the nation.

Comparison of Taxes in the United States and Other Countries

Contrary to popular opinion, Americans are not heavily taxed in comparison with the citizens of other industrial countries. As we see in Figure 7, our taxes were at the low end of the world's leading rich countries. Keep in mind that these taxes include

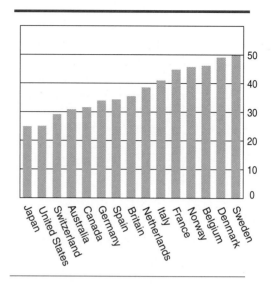

Figure 7

Tax Receipts as a Percentage of GDP in United States and Selected Countries, 2004
American taxpayers have a relatively low burden in comparison to taxpayers in other rich nations.
Source: Organization for Economic Cooperation and Development.

federal, state, and local taxes, and that almost half of that total is redistributed in the form of transfer payments, such as Social Security, public assistance, food stamps, and unemployment insurance payments.

Who pays the highest taxes in North America? OK, I'll give you a hint: In which *province* do they pay the highest taxes? In case you didn't know, it's Quebec, which boasts a 51.7 percent tax bite, which includes a sales tax of about 15 percent. So the next time you hear someone complaining about high taxes, just tell them to move to Quebec.

So what's our problem? Why all this whining and carrying on about our high taxes when people in other countries pay so much more? Much of the dissatisfaction has to do with the lack of tangible benefits we get in return for our taxes. In many European countries medical care is free, college is free, and day care is heavily subsidized. Indeed, parents of young children receive $1,000 or more every year in child care allowances from their governments. So the United States would definitely have many more happy campers if its citizens got to see more of what they've been paying for.

Do you remember the concept of *opportunity cost,* which we covered in Chapter 2? Because we're always having to make choices, *the opportunity cost of any choice is the foregone value of the next best alternative.* The tax cut debate is really over opportunity cost: What do we need to *give up* in exchange for lower taxes? How about a cut in Social Security benefits? A smaller armed forces? Lower pay for teachers, firefighters, and the police? Just as you can't have your cake and eat it too, the concept of opportunity cost shows us that we can't cut taxes *and* maintain the level of government spending that we would like.

A tax is a compulsory payment for which no specific benefit is received in return.
—U.S. Treasury

The Economic Role of Government

This chapter has talked a lot about taxes and government spending. In short, the government giveth and the government taketh away.

One fact that should be readily apparent is that the federal government and, to a lesser degree, state and local governments have a tremendous impact on the economy. This analysis, however, will be confined to the federal government. Although there is a great deal of overlap, we are going to consider, sequentially, four specific economic functions of government: provision of public goods and services, redistribution of income, stabilization, and economic regulation. We covered some of these functions back in Chapter 4, but now we'll talk about them in greater detail.

(1) Provision of Public Goods and Services

Government provides a wide range of goods and services. Private enterprise would supply few of these because they are not profitable. Back in the 1950s, most of the country was served by private intercity bus lines. In New Jersey, when these companies began losing money, the state had to subsidize them just to keep the buses running. Finally, more than 25 years ago the state was forced to take over all the remaining private bus lines. Other states and regions were also forced to form public transportation authorities, while the federal government formed Amtrak to take over the national rail lines. Add to these all the other government operations and you're talking about some $2.5 trillion of public goods and services.

Some of the main services our government provides include defense of the country, maintenance of internal order and a nationwide highway network, and provision of a money supply to facilitate exchanges of goods and services. While certain services, such as public education and the running of the criminal justice system, are very obvious, others, such as bank inspections, environmental protection, and the carrying out of scientific research are less visible to most citizens.

Our interstate highway network is an excellent example of the social infrastructure that our government provides. Imagine how much lower our standard of living would be without it. Compare our infrastructure with that of a poor country and you'll have a much better appreciation of the economic role of the government.

(2) Redistribution of Income

The government is sometimes seen as a modern-day Robin Hood, redistributing money from rich taxpayers to poor welfare recipients, or from huge corporations to unemployment benefit recipients. Food stamps, Medicaid, and disability payments are all programs aimed mainly at the needy, while the relatively well-to-do taxpayer foots the bill.

Some would argue that there is also welfare for the rich, whether in the form of subsidies to corporate farmers and shipbuilders; tax breaks for defense contractors, oil companies, and other large corporations; or huge government contracts for missile systems, aircraft, and highway construction.

A great example of corporate welfare is the "American Jobs Creation Act" of 2004. American corporations, which earned some $850 billion in foreign profits during the previous decade, were allowed to bring back that money to the United States while avoiding most of their tax liabilities. Instead of being taxed at the normal 35 percent rate, these foreign profits were taxed at a rate of just 5.25 percent. Companies were given about a year to bring back the money. The *Chicago Tribune* reported that "though billed as a jobs program, rules developed to implement the law by the Treasury Department don't require companies to create any new jobs with the money they bring back."[5]

Regardless of whether the rich or the poor are on the receiving end, one thing is perfectly clear: The government does redistribute a lot of money. The federal, state, and local governments combined provide Americans with $1.5 trillion a year in the form of transfer payments such as Social Security, veterans' pensions, public assistance, and unemployment insurance benefits.

Does the government take from the rich and give to the poor— or is it the other way around?

A government which robs Peter to pay Paul can always depend on the support of Paul.
—George Bernard Shaw

(3) Stabilization

Two basic goals of the federal government are stable prices and low unemployment. Stated somewhat differently, the goals may be seen as a fairly high rate of economic growth (which would hold the rate of unemployment to a minimum) with no inflation.

How the government might go about attaining these goals is the subject of Chapters 10 through 16. But at this time we can already gauge some of the economic impact of the federal budget and how that budget might affect the stability of our economy.

It is the aim of good government to stimulate production, of bad government to encourage consumption.
—Jean-Baptiste Say

[5]John Schmeltzer, "Money Washed Ashore, Not Jobs," *Chicago Tribune*, May 22, 2005, pp. 1, 10.

The almost $2.8 trillion that the federal government now dispenses annually puts a floor under our economy's purchasing power. During the early stages of the Great Depression, the federal government was only a minor economic player. The total federal budget was less than 5 percent of GDP. Now it's nearly 22 percent. Thus, no matter how bad things get, at least the government will provide a floor under total spending.

(4) Economic Regulation

Another important function of government is to provide the economic rules of the game and, somewhat more broadly, the social and political context in which the economy operates. Some of these rules are easily understood: the fostering of competition among business firms, environmental protection laws, child labor laws, the setting of a minimum hourly wage rate, consumer protection laws, and a court system to adjudicate disputes and punish offenders. Beyond these, the government helps provide the social and political framework within which individuals and business firms are able to function smoothly.

In Chapter 4 we talked about the role of competition and the price mechanism in our economic system. A competitive system will function only as long as there is competition. If there are only a handful of firms in several industries, there is no competition. The government's job is to make sure this doesn't happen.

Government provides the legal framework that enables private ownership and the enforcement of contracts. These protections are generally absent in primitive economies which lack entrepreneurs willing to create business firms. The government also provides a reliable money supply, which facilitates specialization and exchange, the development of financial markets, and a smoothly functioning banking system.

Within our political and social framework, the government must also allow individuals and business firms to operate with the maximum degree of freedom. There are those who consider the current level of government regulation blatant interference with their economic freedom.

Does that freedom imply the right to pollute the environment or to monopolize an industry by driving competitors out of business? Perhaps Justice Oliver Wendell Holmes put it best when he noted that a person's freedom to swing his fist extended only as far as his neighbor's nose. Unfortunately, in the economic environment, there is little agreement as to how far economic freedom may be extended without interfering with society as a whole or the economic rights of specific individuals or business firms.[6]

Conclusion

Adam Smith's dos and don'ts

Adam Smith, in his monumental *The Wealth of Nations,* published in 1776, summed up the dos and don'ts of economic endeavor: "Every man, as long as he does not violate the laws of justice, is left perfectly free to pursue his own interest his own way, and to bring both his industry and capital into competition with those of any other man, or order of men."[7]

Smith went on to define the economic role of government:

According to the system of natural liberty, the sovereign has only three duties to attend to; three duties of great importance, indeed, but plain and intelligible to common understandings: first, the duty of protecting the society from the violence and invasion of other independent societies; secondly, the duty of protecting, as far as possible, every member of the society from the injustice or oppression of every other member of it, or the duty of establishing an exact administration of justice; and, thirdly, the duty of erecting and maintaining certain public works and certain public institutions, which it can never be for the interest of any individual, or small number

---

[6]We discuss these issues in the chapter on corporate mergers and antitrust in *Economics* and in *Microeconomics.*

[7]Adam Smith, *The Wealth of Nations* (London: Methuen, 1950), p. 208.

of individuals, to erect and maintain; because the profit could never repay the expense to any individual or small number of individuals, though it may frequently do much more than repay it to a great society.[8]

If we were to take Adam Smith's description of the government's economic role as our starting point, let's see how far it might be expanded. Should the government try to curb air and water pollution? What about prohibiting the dumping of toxic waste or regulating the disposal of nuclear waste? One can only wonder what Smith would have said about Medicare's drug prescription program.

How much should the government be involved in helping the homeless and the 38 million Americans officially classified as poor?[9] Or the 45 million people without medical insurance? And what more should be done about crime and drugs? The government's economic role has grown tremendously these last seven decades, and it will continue to grow in coming years. Indeed, when your children take macroeconomics, the author of their textbook may look back at the first decade of the 21st century as a period when the economic role of government was still relatively small.

Current Issue: Will Social Security Be There for You?

Please answer these two questions:

1. Do you believe in flying saucers?
2. Do you believe you will be able to collect Social Security benefits when you're 65?

Surveys conducted over the last dozen years found that more people in their 20s believe that there are flying saucers than that they will be able to collect Social Security benefits.

When you reach the age of 65, will you be able to collect Social Security benefits? After all, you will pay Social Security taxes your entire working life. And ditto for Medicare. There's no question that you're entitled. But will you be able to *collect*?

My own guess is that before mid-century there will be a watered down version of both programs. You'll receive *some* benefits, but not at nearly the level that your grandparents received.

Right now we're paying about $150 billion more in Social Security taxes than we're spending on Social Security benefits. That surplus is deposited in the Social Security trust fund, which consists of trillions of dollars of U.S. government securities. But what's also happening is that the government, which has been running humongous budget deficits, is using the Social Security surpluses each year to offset the deficits. Each year, then, the U.S. Treasury spends the surplus and places its i.o.u.'s into the Social Security trust fund.

In 2011 the baby boomers (born between 1946 and 1964) will begin retiring, and by 2017, the annual Social Security surplus will disappear. But don't worry, because we can just draw down the trust fund until it runs out of money around 2042. The only problem is that the trust fund consists of U.S. treasury bills, bonds, notes, and certificates. The trust fund administrators aren't going to send people these U.S. government securities every month instead of checks. No problem, the administrators can just go out and sell the securities to the public. But they'd soon be selling hundreds of billions of U.S. government securities on top of financing our huge—and probably growing—federal budget deficit.

---

[8]Ibid., pp. 208–9.

[9]Poverty is the subject of a later chapter.

Long before the trust fund runs out of money around 2042, this massive government borrowing will very likely push up interest rates to record levels and possibly precipitate a financial crisis. That's if no strong measures are taken to raise Social Security taxes and lower benefits.

OK, that's the good news. The bad news is Medicare, which is even more seriously underfunded than Social Security. By 2018, Medicare spending will surpass Social Security spending. Remember all those retiring baby boomers? Medicare is a lot more complex than Social Security, so I promise that you'll soon be hearing more about an impending Medicare crisis.

Questions for Further Thought and Discussion

1. If a political candidate said that if she were elected to Congress, she would work toward cutting federal government spending by one-third over the next four years, would she stand much chance of fulfilling her promise? Why or why not?

2. When you retire, will you be able to collect Social Security benefits? Give the reasons why you might not be able to collect.

3. Discuss the pros and cons of having a high cigarette excise tax.

4. Make up a numerical example to show why the Social Security tax is regressive.

5. If Adam Smith were alive today, to what degree would he approve of the present economic role of the American government?

6. What additional goods and services do we expect from government today as opposed to 60 years ago?

7. Some politicians say that Americans pay too much in taxes. Explain why you agree or disagree with them.

8. Describe the growth of the economic role of the federal government since the 1930s.

9. Explain the difference between government spending and government purchases of goods and services.

10. Give two examples of public goods or services that you use.

Workbook for Chapter 7

Name _____

Multiple-Choice Questions

Circle the letter that corresponds to the best answer.

1. The role of government grew most rapidly during the period _____.
   - a) 1920–1933
   - b) 1933–1945
   - c) 1945–1960
   - d) 1960–1975

2. The seeds of the expansion of the federal government's economic role were sown during the administration of _____.
   - a) Franklin Roosevelt
   - b) Dwight Eisenhower
   - c) Richard Nixon
   - d) Ronald Reagan

3. Which couple pays the most in federal taxes?
   - a) Todd Lhuillier and Stacey Lhuillier derive their entire $100,000 income from dividends and have two young children, Chloe Lhuillier and Taylor Lhuillier.
   - b) Eric Church and Kim Swanson Church each have jobs that pay $50,000; they have no children.
   - c) Teodor Barnett and Miriam Barnett each have jobs that pay $51,000 and have two dependent grandchildren living with them—Sarah Jones and Emma Jones.
   - d) Patricia Judge has a job paying $55,000 and her husband, John Judge, has one that pays $52,000. They have five dependent grandchildren living with them—Jack Alaska Watt, William Watt, Matthew Watt, Blake Armstrong, and Susan Armstrong.

4. Which is the most accurate statement?
   - a) The rich pay most of the federal personal income tax.
   - b) President George W. Bush raised taxes that the poor must pay.
   - c) As a result of the events of 9/11, Americans are very supportive of tax cuts.
   - d) Government spending on defense declined between 2001 and 2006.

5. The federal government's fiscal year begins on _____.
   - a) January 1
   - b) July 1
   - c) October 1
   - d) November 1

6. Transfer payments to individuals are _____ percent of the federal budget.
   - a) 25
   - b) 50
   - c) 65
   - d) 85

7. Which statement is true?
   - a) Bill Gates pays more Social Security tax than most American workers.
   - b) The rich pay a higher proportion of their income in Social Security tax than in federal personal income tax.
   - c) Most wage earners pay more in federal personal income tax than in Social Security tax.
   - d) The rich pay Social Security tax on nearly their entire income.

8. Compared to federal spending, state and local spending is _____.
   - a) almost twice as large
   - b) about the same
   - c) half as large
   - d) one-quarter as large

9. The largest federal government purchase of final goods and services is _____.
   - a) Social Security
   - b) defense
   - c) interest on the national debt
   - d) foreign aid

10. If Kathie Barnes earns $10,000 and Katie Harvey earns $100,000 a year, they both will pay Social Security tax _____.
    a) at the same average tax rate
    b) but Kathie Barnes will pay at a higher average tax rate
    c) but Katie Harvey will pay at a higher average tax rate
    d) but it is impossible to tell what their average tax rates are

11. The most progressive tax listed here is the _____.
    a) Social Security tax
    b) federal personal income tax
    c) federal excise tax
    d) state sales tax

12. Each of the following is a direct tax except the _____ tax.
    a) Social Security   c) corporate income
    b) federal personal income   d) federal excise

13. Which is true?
    a) The rich are hurt more than the poor by regressive taxes.
    b) The poor are hurt more than the rich by progressive taxes.
    c) The federal personal income tax is a regressive tax.
    d) None of these statements is true.

14. A tax with an average rate of 20 percent for the rich and 2 percent for the middle class is _____.
    a) progressive   c) proportional
    b) regressive   d) none of these

15. In 2006 Brian Murray earned $200,000; he paid Social Security tax on _____.
    a) none of his income
    b) all of his income
    c) nearly all of his income
    d) less than half of his income

16. Which statement is true?
    a) There is no overlap between the duties of local government and private businesses.
    b) Medicare and Medicaid spending account for over 20 percent of the federal budget.
    c) We spend as much on defense than do the rest of the world's nations combined.
    d) Although President Bush has cut the tax rates of the rich, they generally end up paying more taxes because they are willing to work more hours.

17. Which would be the most accurate description of the top marginal tax rate of the federal income tax?
    a) It is higher than it has ever been.
    b) It is lower than it has ever been.
    c) It is much lower than it was in 1980.
    d) It is much higher than it was in 1980.

18. The most important source of federal tax revenue is the _____.
    a) personal income tax
    b) corporate income tax
    c) federal excise tax
    d) payroll tax

19. Until 1981 the maximum marginal tax rate on the federal income tax was _____ percent.
    a) 70   c) 40
    b) 50   d) 33

20. Taxes (including federal, state, and local) are about _____ of our GDP.
    a) 10 percent
    b) 20 percent
    c) 30 percent
    d) 40 percent

21. The most important source of local tax revenue is the _____ tax.
    a) property   c) excise
    b) income   d) sales

22. Compared with the citizens of other rich countries, Americans are _____.

    a) much more heavily taxed

    b) somewhat more heavily taxed

    c) taxed at about the same rate

    d) not as heavily taxed

23. Adam Smith endorsed each of the following roles of government except _____.

    a) providing for defense

    b) establishing a system of justice

    c) erecting a limited number of public works

    d) guaranteeing a job to every person ready, willing, and able to work

24. An example of a public good is _____.

    a) a Honda Accord   c) a Boeing 747

    b) a movie theater   d) a lighthouse

25. Which statement is true?

    a) Americans pay the highest taxes in the world.

    b) Public goods are provided by private enterprise.

    c) The economic role of the federal government has shrunk over the last 30 years.

    d) In 1990 and in 1993 taxes for the rich were increased substantially.

26. Major league baseball stars like Derek Jeter, Alex Rodriguez, and Pedro Martinez all pay _____.

    a) more Social Security tax than Medicare tax

    b) more Medicare tax than Social Security tax

    c) neither Medicare tax nor Social Security tax

27. Gasoline taxes in the United States are _____ than they are in other leading industrial nations.

    a) much higher

    b) a little higher

    c) a little lower

    d) much lower

28. State and local taxes are basically

    a) progressive.

    b) proportional.

    c) regressive.

Fill-In Questions

1. The economic role of the federal government began to get very large in the year _____.

2. Name basic economic influences of the federal government: (1) _____; (2) _____; and (3) _____.

3. Fiscal year 2007 began on _____ (fill in month, day, and year).

4. The largest federal government transfer payment is _____.

5. The average tax rate is found by dividing _____ by _____.

6. Progressive taxes place the greatest burden on the _____.

7. Examples of regressive taxes include _____ and _____.

8. In 2006 the Social Security tax rate was _____ percent.

9. The most important source of federal tax revenue is the _____ tax.

10. The maximum marginal tax rate of the federal personal income tax today is _____ percent.

11. If you earned $10,000 in 2006, how much did the federal government collect in payroll tax? $ _____.

(Hint: both you and your employer pay this tax.)

12. If Adam Smith were alive today, he would say that our government is too _____.

Problems

1. If Cayden Noel earned $80,000 in 2006, how much Social Security tax did he pay?

2. If Haley My Hang Althaus earned $10,000 in 2006; how much Social Security tax did she pay?

3. If Taryn Goulding had earned a taxable income of $20,000 and paid $1,000 in federal income tax, how much was her average tax rate?

4. If Mike DelMastro had a marginal tax rate of 28 percent and earned an extra $10,000, how much tax would he pay?

5. If Alex Lawson Ballard earned an extra $1,000 and paid $150 in taxes on that income, how much would his marginal tax rate be?

6. If Kyle Rollings Cavedo were in the lowest personal income tax bracket, how much personal income tax would he have to pay on $5,000 of taxable income?

7. Suppose that Bill Gates's income were to increase by $100 million. How much more personal income tax would he have to pay?

8. If Christian Collins' taxable income rose from $30,000 to $40,000 and his tax bill rose from $4,500 to $7,000, how much is his marginal tax rate?

9. If Terry Horn pays $5,000 on a taxable income of $40,000, how much is her average tax rate?

10. The Speedy Delivery Service paid its 10 drivers $30,000 each. How much did the company owe in payroll tax?

11. If Tanner Church earned $100,000, how much would he pay in Social Security tax and in Medicare tax?

12. Prove that a married person with three dependents (including himself) and an income of $12,000 pays more in Social Security tax than in federal income tax.

13. If Cynthia Moore were the only working member of a family of a husband, wife, and their two children and earned $15,000, (a) approximately how much federal personal income tax would she pay? (b) How much Social Security and Medicare tax would she pay?

14. If Jack Swanson paid $1,000 in federal income tax, how much is his marginal tax rate and his total tax rate? (There is enough information for you to figure out the answer.)

15. Caroline Krause earned a salary of $1,000,000. (a) How much Social Security tax did she pay? (b) How much Medicare tax did she pay? (c) What is her marginal tax rate on her federal personal income tax?

170

grain of salt.

The Export-Import Sector

The American economy is, by far, the largest and most productive in the world. Consequently, we are by far, the world's largest importer of goods and services. Until 2004, when Germany overtook the U.S., we were also the largest exporter. Yet foreign trade is less important to the U.S. economy than it is to those of nearly all other industrial nations. But in spite of the relatively small percentage of U.S. GDP accounted for through foreign trade, we have become thoroughly integrated into the global economy.

So far we've looked at the three main sectors of GDP—C (consumption), I (investment), and G (government spending). Now let's consider X_n (net exports). X_n = exports − imports.

CHAPTER OBJECTIVES

In this chapter we'll cover:

- The basis for international trade.
- U.S. imports and exports.
- A summing up: $C + I + G + X_n$.
- Specialization and exchange.

- The world's leading trading nations.
- World trade agreements and free-trade zones.
- Outsourcing and offshoring.

The Basis for International Trade

Let's look at trading, first between individuals, and then between nations. There are a lot of people who like to putter around the house, doing their own repairs. So how would you feel about doing a really *big* job, like building a $12' \times 20'$ deck in your backyard? If you're really good with tools, it might take you 60 hours from start to finish.

Let's say you're a very successful attorney, who earns $300 an hour. Now you could hire a carpenter to do the deck for you at $20 an hour. And to make things interesting, let's say that this person will also need 60 hours to complete the deck. Question: Should you hire him or her or build the deck yourself?

I'm sure that, unless you would rather do carpentry than anything else in the world, you would hire this person to build your deck. The labor will cost you $1,200. You could make $1,200 in just four hours by practicing law.

By the way, can you figure out the opportunity cost of building the deck yourself? It would be $18,000 (60 hours × $300). So you would save yourself $16,800 (the $18,000 that you earned − the $1,200 you paid the deckbuilder). If this sounds at all familiar, it may be because we talked about this in the section on specialization and exchange in Chapter 4.

Back in 1776 Adam Smith made *this* observation:

It is the maxim of every prudent master of a family, never to attempt to make at home what it will cost him more to make than to buy. The taylor does not attempt to make his own shoes, but buys them of the shoemaker. The shoemaker does not attempt to make his own clothes, but employs a taylor. The farmer attempts to make neither the one nor the other, but employs those different artificers....

What is prudence in the conduct of every private family, can scarce be folly in that of a great kingdom. If a foreign country can supply us with a commodity cheaper than we can make it, better buy it of them with some part of the produce of our own industry, employed in a way in which we have some advantage.[1]

Specialization and Exchange

We could not have a modern, highly productive economy without specialization and exchange. Imagine if we all had to be self-sufficient. Each of us would live on a farm where we would grow our own food, weave our own cloth, build our own homes, make our own tools and clothes—even our own pins and needles and nails.

In modern economies, virtually everyone specializes. We can sell whatever good or service we produce. By specializing, we get good at producing something, and we are able to sell it for a relatively low price. So instead of spending hours trying to make your own nails, you can buy all the nails you need at the hardware store for less than a dollar.

When people specialize, they are usually far more productive than if they attempt to be generalists. Doctors, lawyers, accountants, engineers, and, of course, college professors, all specialize.

People specialize in every field of learning. Your economics professor, for example, may have specialized in banking, and not only can tell you all the dirt on the 1980s savings and loan scandal, but can explain exactly how banks operate, how they determine the creditworthiness of borrowers, and even how you can wire money to other countries.

We've seen that, when you specialize in a certain type of work, you can get very good at it and have a much higher standard of living than you would as a jack-of-all-trades. In this case, what makes sense for individuals also makes sense for nations. Nations generally export the goods and services they can produce efficiently (that is, cheaply), and they import the goods and services that other nations produce more efficiently.

Because of our abundant fertile farmland and eventually our tremendous stock of farm equipment, we have been a major exporter of wheat, corn, cotton, and soybeans since colonial times. Today we are the world's leading exporter of computer software and entertainment goods and services. We were a major exporter of steel and textiles, but now that other nations can produce these more cheaply, we are a major importer of these products. Similarly, immediately after World War II we produced more than 60 percent of the world's oil, much of which we exported. Now that we have exhausted most of our easily extractable reserves, we import over 60 percent of our oil.

Tables 1, 2, and 3 provide a hypothetical example of two countries that can benefit from specialization and trade. Assume that both Algeria and Zaire produce just two goods—planes and trains. Table 1 shows how many trains and planes both countries currently produce.

TABLE 1	Production of Trains and Planes before Specialization	
	Trains	Planes
Algeria	5	10
Zaire	10	5

---

[1]Adam Smith, *The Wealth of Nations* (New York: Modern Library, 1937), p. 424. (Originally published in 1776.)

The citizens of Algeria and Zaire spend all of their income taking train trips and plane trips. Now suppose that Algeria decided to devote all its resources to building planes, while Zaire used all its resources to build trains. Their new production totals are shown in Table 2.

TABLE 2	Production of Trains and Planes with Specialization	
	Trains	Planes
Algeria	0	20
Zaire	20	0

Algeria specializes in building planes because it is especially good at it. Similarly Zaire specializes in building trains at which it excels.

What if in the world market trains and planes were sold for an identical price? Then Zaire could trade one train for each plane it received from Algeria. Suppose, then, that Zaire traded 10 trains for 10 of Algeria's planes. Table 3 shows how the two countries would end up.

TABLE 3	Consumption of Planes and Trains after Trade	
	Trains	Planes
Algeria	10	10
Zaire	10	10

Compare the numbers in Tables 1 and 3. Did both nations gain from specialization and trade? They certainly did.

This extremely simplified model makes the case for free trade. In Chapter 31 you'll find a more detailed presentation of the argument for free trade.

U.S. Exports and Imports

From the earliest days of our nation's history, we engaged in trade. As colonies of England in the 17th and 18th centuries, Americans were expected to provide her with raw materials and to buy England's manufactured goods. Indeed, we were largely prohibited from competing with her own manufacturers.

However, after independence, we became increasingly self-sufficient. As we noted back in Chapter 1, we were not only self-sufficient agriculturally, but by the time of the Civil War we had built a powerful manufacturing base in the North.

Our self-sufficiency in food production and our huge manufacturing base were important factors in helping us win World Wars I and II. America was called "the arsenal of democracy" because of the vast quantity of armaments we sent our allies, especially Great Britain and the Soviet Union during World War II. This self-sufficiency continued until well into the 1970s, when our relatively small export-import sector began to grow significantly.

Figure 1 provides a summary of our changing relationship to the global economy. For the first three-quarters of the 20th century we exported more than we imported virtually every year. But then we began importing more than we exported. You'll notice also that trade has become much more important to our economy than it was in 1970. In that year, our imports and exports together were just over one-tenth of our GDP; now they are over one-quarter of our GDP. In 2005 our imports were 16.2 percent of our GDP, while our exports were just 10.4 percent.

F*igure* 1

F*igure* 1

U.S. Imports and Exports as
Percentage of GDP, 1970–2005
Note the growing gap between
imports and exports. In 2005
imports were 16.2 percent of GDP,
while exports were just 10.4
percent.
*Source: Economic Report of the
President,* 2006.

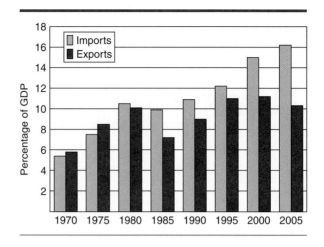

We're going to be using a couple of new terms: positive balance of trade and negative balance of trade. *We run a positive balance of trade when we export more than we import.* You can easily figure out, then, what a negative balance of trade is. *We run a negative balance of trade when we import more than we export.* In recent years the United States has been running huge and growing negative trade balances. We have been buying a lot more goods and services from foreigners than they have been buying from us. Sometimes we refer to a negative trade balance as a trade deficit.

What do we import and what do we export? We import and export both goods and services. The goods we import include cars, DVD players, TVs, microwave ovens, computer chips, cameras, wine, oil, toys, clothing, and steel. Among the goods we export are cotton, wood, wheat, cars, chemicals, computer software, cigarettes, pharmaceuticals, tractors, and airplanes. In 2005 we imported $783 billion more in goods from foreigners than we exported to them.

We import and export services such as hotel stays, restaurant meals, and car rentals for tourists, plane trips, movies, TV programming, compact discs, banking, insurance, legal, and accounting services. In recent years we have been running a large positive balance of trade in services. In 2005 we exported $57 billion more in services to foreigners than we imported from them.

When foreign tourists fly to the United States on U.S.-owned airlines and spend billions of dollars on hotels, meals, and local transportation, they are contributing to our positive balance of trade in services. That spending is added to our export of services. So the next time you see Japanese tourists snapping pictures of one of our national monuments, please thank them. They might even ask you to pose with them.

In the final chapter of this book we'll talk quite extensively about foreign exchange rates, but for now, let's consider how they might affect you. If you happen to be planning a trip to Europe, you'll certainly be very concerned about the exchange rate between dollars and euros. Let's say that on your first night in Paris, your restaurant bill comes to 40 euros. The exchange rate between dollars and euros has fluctuated between about $0.85 to about $1.30 for 1 euro. So do the math and figure out how much that meal would have cost at each of these exchange rates.

Solution:
If you could get 1 euro for $0.85, then your meal would have cost you just $34 (0.85 × 40). But if the euro were exchanged for $1.30, that same meal would have set you back $52.

TABLE 4	U.S. Balance of Trade, 2005 *(in billions of dollars)**		
Exports of goods	$893	Imports of goods	$1676
Exports of services	$379	Imports of services	$322
Exports of goods and services	$1271	Imports of goods and services	$1997

$$X_n = -\$726$$

*Numbers do not add up due to rounding.
Source: www.bea.gov.

The cost of all the foreign goods and services will vary with the dollar's exchange rate with euros, Japanese yen, British pounds, Canadian dollars, Mexican pesos, Chinese yuan, and a variety of other currencies. The financial section of most daily newspapers lists these exchange rates.

One of the services we provide to foreigners is education. There are more than 500,000 foreign college students in the United States spending over $13 billion, 75 percent of which is funded by overseas sources. Over half of these foreign students are studying management, mathematics, the sciences, or computer science. At some of our leading engineering schools, such as New Jersey Institute of Technology and Stevens Institute of Technology, over 70 percent of the doctoral degrees are awarded to foreigners. At the Polytechnic University of New York, one of the nation's leading engineering schools, the Russian students often complain that they cannot understand the English spoken by their Chinese professors.

Our balance of trade in goods is a completely different story. From the outbreak of World War I until 1970 we maintained a positive trade balance in merchandise. By the late 1970s we were beginning to run substantial deficits.

Table 4 summarizes our balance of trade in 2005. As you'll notice, we imported more goods than we exported. And we exported more services than we imported. But our positive balance of trade in services (+$57 billion) was far outweighed by our negative balance of trade in goods (−$783 billion). That left us with a balance of trade in goods and services, X_n, of −$726 billion.

Outsourcing and Offshoring

Many companies contract out some of their jobs to other firms. For example, Wal-Mart hires local janitorial firms to clean their stores at night. Magazine and newspaper subscriptions are sold by telemarketers who are employed by companies that specialize in telephone soliciting. Briefs for law firms may be typed by people in the West Indies.

All of these jobs are outsourced. But if they are performed abroad, then they are also offshored. When a company shuts down a textile mill in South Carolina and replaces it with one in China, those jobs were not just outsourced but off-shored as well.

As long as outsourced jobs remain in the United States, one American's job loss is another American's job gain. But when a job is off-shored, our employment goes down by one. While most of those whose jobs are off-shored do eventually find other jobs, it may take them months or even years to do so, and then the new job will generally pay less than the job that was lost.

Since 1970 at least five million relatively high-paying factory jobs—in autos, steel, textile, apparel, and consumer electronics—have been offshored. Today nearly 85 percent of our labor force is employed in the service sector, and now these jobs, too, are being sent abroad. Huge call centers are springing up in India to provide American customers with technical support. When you need help with your computer, you may get to talk with "Randy" in Bangalore, or perhaps "Samantha" in New Delhi.

A survey by McKinsey and Robbins indicates only about 10 percent of all service jobs are vulnerable to offshoring, and only a small fraction of these will actually be offshored in the foreseeable future. Still, who would have ever imagined that physicians

F*igure* 2
Hypothetical C + I + G + X$_n$
Line

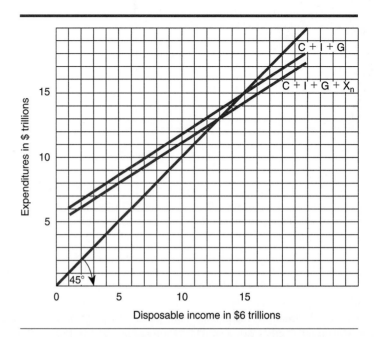

in India would be reading MRIs sent over the Internet, and doing so at just one-tenth the price charged by American physicians.

And yet, in the whole scheme of things, how much do we really have to fear off-shoring? Every year about 40 percent of all the jobs in our economy change hands. Since only a fraction of one percent is sent offshore every year, it is certainly something that we can live with. But if *your* job is offshored, then that's another story.

A Summing Up: C + I + G + X$_n$

Subtract imports from exports to get net exports.

X$_n$ = Exports − Imports

The last three chapters examined the three main components of GDP: C, or consumption; I, or investment; and G, or government spending. One more variable goes into GDP—net exports, or X$_n$. *Net exports = Exports − Imports.* If we subtract all the money the United States spends on foreign goods and services from what foreigners spend on U.S. goods and services, we get net exports. This number represents the difference between what we sell to foreigners and what they sell to us.

Until recently many economists more or less ignored this last item in the GDP equation. The figure for net exports, while positive, was usually less than 1 percent of GDP. For the first seven decades of the 20th century, we sold more to foreigners every single year than they sold to us. But in the early 1970s our balance of trade turned negative, with net exports reaching −$726 billion in 2005. Why did net exports turn negative in the early 1970s, and what accounts for our growing negative trade balance since then? You'll find out when you reach the next-to-last chapter, "International Trade."

Why is the C + I + G + X$_n$ line drawn below the C + I + G line?

Now we're going to graph the C + I + G + X$_n$ line. Keep in mind that X$_n$ has been negative since the early 1970s and will probably continue to be negative for decades. In Figure 2, why did we draw the C + I + G + X$_n$ line *below* the C + I + G line? Because X$_n$ is a negative number, so the sum of C + I + G + X$_n$ is *less* than the sum of C + I + G.

World Trade Agreements and Free Trade Zones

Since the end of World War II in 1945 there has been an accelerating movement toward free trade. The formation of the European Common Market, renamed the European Union, and of NAFTA (the North American Free Trade Agreement) has placed most of the industrial world within two virtual free trade zones. In addition, the General Agreement on Trade and Tariffs (GATT), now the World Trade Organization, has reduced trade barriers worldwide.

Free Trade Zones

NAFTA   The North American Free Trade Agreement, which was ratified by Congress in 1993, created a free trade area including Canada, the United States, and Mexico, a market of over 400 million consumers. Here is how the agreement is described in the 1994 *Economic Report of the President:*

> In addition to dismantling trade barriers in industrial goods, NAFTA includes agreements on services, investment, intellectual property rights, agriculture, and strengthening of trade rules. There are also side agreements on labor adjustment provisions, protection of the environment, and import surges.[2]

How well has the agreement worked so far? Has a flood of cheap Mexican goods resulted in "the sound of jobs being sucked out of the United States"? Hardly. But the threat of moving operations to Mexico, where hourly wages and fringe benefits average about $1.50 an hour, has had a depressing effect on American factory wages. But there is little evidence that the agreement has cost more than 200,000 jobs, which is less than 2 one-thousandths of our total employment. Nevertheless, our trade deficits with both Mexico and Canada have gone up substantially since the passage of NAFTA.

Mexico is becoming a manufacturing export platform. Currently over 60 percent of all U.S. exports to Mexico are eventually re-exported back to the United States—up from 40 percent before NAFTA. Mexican autoworkers performing sophisticated, highly productive manufacturing work that used to be done in America do it at one-eighth the U.S. wage.

Currently the United States absorbs over 80 percent of Mexico's exports. This figure should fall substantially during the next decade, especially after the trade deal negotiated between Mexico and the European Union, which will abolish most tariffs between them by 2007. Volkswagen, which makes the New Beetle solely in Mexico, currently pays a 7 percent duty when it ships to Europe, but under the new pact, these cars will be shipped to Europe duty-free.

NAFTA was an extension of an earlier trade agreement with Canada. We import more from Canada than any other country, and we export more to Canada than any other country. Because of our mutual interdependence—and because of the integration of our economies—it would be unthinkable for either country to erect trade barriers to keep out imports from the other. Under the agreement, duties on most goods will be phased out within the next few years.

Canada is our most important trading partner.

Table 5 summarizes the change in our trade position with Mexico and Canada between 1993 (the year before NAFTA went into effect) and 2005. While our trade with both nations expanded sharply, our trade deficit with both nations went up still faster. During this same period, however, our trade deficit with the rest of the world also rose very rapidly.

Our trade deficit with China reached $201 billion in 2005, which was, by far, our largest deficit in history with any nation, more than double our recent deficits with Japan. Just as many Americans engaged in Japan-bashing in earlier years, now Chinese trade practices have been targeted. One wonders if our trade deficits with Mexico and Canada continue to mount, whether there will be more demands that we disband NAFTA.

There has been talk of expanding NAFTA to include all 34 nations of the Western Hemisphere (except Cuba), a grouping tentatively called the "Free Trade Area of the Americas." The leaders of these nations met in Quebec in April 2001 at the third summit of the Americas, and agreed in principle to put the pact into operation no later than 2005. But we're still waiting.

---

[2]See page 225 of the *Report.*

TABLE 5	U.S. Trade with Mexico and Canada, 1993 and 2005 *(in billions of U.S. dollars)*		

Year	Exports to Mexico	Imports from Mexico	U.S. Trade Balance with Mexico
1993	42	40	2
2005	120	170	−50

Year	Exports to Canada	Imports from Canada	U.S. Trade Balance with Canada
1993	100	111	−11
2005	258	369	−111

Source: Office of Trade and Economic Analysis, U.S. Dept. of Commerce.

CAFTA The Central American–Dominican Republic Free Trade Agreement is a trade agreement between the U.S. and the Dominican Republic as well as five small Central American nations—Costa Rica, El Salvador, Guatemala, Honduras, and Nicaragua. Pushed through Congress by President George W. Bush, this agreement will eventually eliminate all tariffs among the seven nations. But its immediate impact will be very small, since 80 percent of Central American products were already entering the U.S. duty-free.

The European Union (EU) Although this free trade association of 25 nations (see Figure 3) can trace its origins back to the 1950s, it wasn't until 1992 that a truly common market was formed. Freight was now able to move anywhere within the EU without checkpoint delays and paperwork. So-called "quality" codes such as German beer-purity regulations and Belgian chocolate-content restrictions were ended. Workers from any EU country could work in any other member country.

With a population and GDP comparable to those of the United States, the EU is already an economic powerhouse. In 1999, 11 EU countries formed the European Monetary Union, which established the euro as a common currency,[3] making trade among participating member nations much easier to conduct. A German tourist buying a meal in a Parisian restaurant no longer has to convert her marks into francs, and a Dutch businessman buying Italian wine no longer has to convert his guilders into lira.

Mercosur Much less well known than NAFTA and the EU, this free trade zone includes Argentina, Brazil, Paraguay, and Uruguay and associate members Bolivia, Peru, and Chile.[4] It is the fourth largest integrated market after NAFTA, the EU, and Japan. Mercosur is an acronym for Mercado Común del Sur, or Common Market of the South. Formed in 1991, it has succeeded in eliminating all internal tariffs while imposing a common external tariff on goods imported from countries outside the union. However, some trade restrictions—especially between Brazil and Argentina—still persist.

World Trade Agreements

GATT The General Agreement on Trade and Tariffs was drafted in 1947 and has since been signed by more than 150 nations. GATT is a uniform system of rules for the conduct of international trade. Its latest version, which was ratified by Congress in 1994, was the culmination of years of negotiations. It will reduce tariffs worldwide by an average of 40 percent, lower other barriers to trade such as quotas on certain products, and provide patent protection for American software, pharmaceuticals, and other industries.

---

[3]Twelve countries are now members.

[4]Venezuela was in the process of becoming an associate member in 2006.

Figure 3

European Union: Member Countries and Candidates for Membership, 7/1/06
Members: Austria, Belgium, Cyprus, Czech Republic, Denmark, Estonia, Finland, France, Germany, Greece, Hungary, Ireland, Italy, Latvia, Lithuania, Luxembourg, Malta, Netherlands, Poland, Portugal, Slovakia, Slovenia, Spain, Sweden, and United Kingdom. Bulgaria and Romania are set for membership on January 1, 2007. Croatia, Macedonia, and Turkey are membership candidates.

Will GATT hurt our trade balance, unleash a flood of cheap foreign imports, and result in the loss of millions of American jobs? Although some industries will be affected adversely, the positive appears to outweigh the negative. First of all, on the average, foreign countries have more trade restrictions and tariffs on U.S. goods than we have on theirs, so GATT should help us much more than it hurts us. For the first time intellectual property rights like patents, trademarks, and copyrights will be protected. GATT will also open markets for service industries such as accounting, advertising, computer services, and engineering—fields in which Americans excel.

Finally, GATT brings agriculture under international trade rules for the first time. Many countries heavily subsidize their farmers (in 2005 the United States spent over $20 billion in crop subsidies), but European subsidies dwarf those paid to American farmers. President Clinton's Council of Economic Advisors noted that, "Since the United States has a strong underlying comparative advantage in agriculture, the mutual reduction in trade barriers and subsidization will be to the distinct advantage of U.S. producers."[5] Proportionately, the Europeans will have to reduce their subsidies a lot more than we'll have to, making American crop exports even more competitive.

WTO   The World Trade Organization has sometimes been confused with the International Monetary Fund (IMF) and with the World Bank. Each has been the target of massive protests against globalization. The accompanying box provides a brief description of the purposes and functions of each of these organizations.

The World Trade Organization was set up in 1995 as a successor to GATT. It is based on three major principles: (1) liberalization of trade; (2) nondiscrimination—the most-favored-nation principle; and (3) no unfair encouragement of exports. Let's consider each principle in detail.

Trade barriers, which were reduced under GATT, should continue to be reduced. Incidentally, barriers have been falling *within* free trade zones such as NAFTA and the European Union.

Under the most-favored-nation principle, members of the WTO must offer all other members the same trade concessions as any member country. Which is a lot like when the teacher says that if you bring candy to class, you must bring some for *everyone*.

Finally, no unfair encouragement of exports encompasses export subsidies, which are considered a form of unfair competition. American and European governments have long subsidized their farmers, who, in turn, have exported much of their crops. Subsidies enable American and European producers to sell their crops well below their cost of production. This sets the world price of corn and other agricultural staples so low that small farmers in developing countries can't compete. How bad *is* this problem? Three-quarters of the world's poor scratch out a living working small farms. As they are forced off their land by subsidized grain imports, they have no means to survive.

At the WTO meeting in Cancun, Mexico, in September 2003, the world's poor nations demanded that the richer nations cut their agricultural subsidies to create a more level playing field. But the United States, the European Union, Japan, and the other rich nations refused to lower their subsidies and the meeting ended abruptly. Since then there have been a few more unsuccessful attempts to lower subsidies.

The WTO has a Dispute Settlement Body to handle trade disagreements among member nations. Many of the disputes involve the charge of the dumping of products below cost. Although many politicians in the United States have very reluctantly accepted the jurisdiction of the WTO, we have won almost all the more than two dozen cases in which we have been the complaining party.

If you've ever been to a major protest demonstration, it's usually pretty clear what all the demonstrators are *against*. Beginning with the Seattle protest in late 1999 during the WTO meeting, there have been major protests in Washington, Prague, Quebec City, Genoa, and elsewhere targeting the WTO, the IMF, the summit of the Americas, and the World Bank.

BusinessWeek outlined the reasons for the protests:

> Environmentalists argue that elitist trade and economic bodies make undemocratic decisions that undermine national sovereignty on environmental regulation. Unions charge that unfettered trade allows unfair competition from countries that lack labor standards. Human rights and student groups say the IMF and the World Bank prop up regimes that condone sweatshops and pursue policies that bail out foreign lenders at the expense of local economies.[6]

---

[5]*Economic Report of the President*, 1995, p. 208.

[6]*BusinessWeek*, April 24, 2000, p. 40.

The WTO, the IMF, and the World Bank

What do the WTO and the IMF stand for, and what do they do? And what is the World Bank? You don't have a clue? Don't worry—you are not alone.

The WTO stands for the World Trade Organization, which was set up to encourage world trade by bringing down existing trade barriers.

The International Monetary Fund (IMF), an organization of more than 150 nations, was set up in 1944 as a lender of last resort to discourage member nations from devaluating their currency. For example, the IMF would lend dollars to Japan if the Japanese yen were falling relative to the dollar. Let's say that 100 yen were trading for one dollar and the yen fell to 105 for one dollar, and then to 110 for one dollar. The IMF would lend reserves to Japan to stabilize the yen.

The IMF has played an increasing role in providing loans to countries in financial crisis. For example, in 1997, when it became clear to international lenders that Korean banks and corporations were unable to repay the loans they had taken on, the IMF arranged for $55 billion in loans. But IMF loans do come with certain strings attached, such as a balanced budget and a tight monetary policy.* Some critics feel that by standing by as an international lender of last resort, the IMF actually encourages irresponsible behavior. Borrowers may take risks they would have otherwise not taken, knowing that the IMF stood ready to bail them out.

The World Bank, also created in 1944, makes long-term, low-interest loans to developing countries, mainly to build highways, bridges, dams, power generators, and water supply systems. In addition, it acts as a guarantor of repayment to encourage some private lending.

Joseph Stiglitz, a Nobel Prize–winning economist and former chief economist for the World Bank, wrote a highly critical book about the practices of the IMF, and, to a lesser degree, the World Bank and the WTO.

> *Over the years since its inception, the IMF has changed markedly. Founded on the belief that markets often worked badly, it now champions market supremacy with ideological fervor. Founded on the belief that there is a need for international pressure on countries to have more expansionary economic policies—such as increasing expenditures, reducing taxes, or lowering interest rates to stimulate the economy—today the IMF typically provides funds only if countries engage in policies like cutting deficits, raising taxes, or raising interest rates that lead to a contraction of the economy.†*

Since countries approach the IMF only when they are desperate for money, the fund has a good deal of leverage, which it uses to force governments to cut their budget deficits and shut down or sell off government enterprises. While these reforms are sometimes necessary, Stiglitz maintains that the IMF's representatives are often oblivious to the human suffering they cause.

---

*Tight monetary policy and a balanced budget will be discussed in Chapters 12 and 14, respectively.

†Joseph Stiglitz, *Globalization and Its Discontents* (New York: W. W. Norton, 2002), pp. 12–13.

The most potent argument against globalization is that workers in poorer countries are exploited to produce goods that are shipped to the United States and other relatively rich countries. This view was summarized by Tina Rosenberg.

> In many of the factories in Mexico, Central America and Asia producing American-brand toys, clothes, sneakers and other goods, exploitation is the norm. The young women who work in them—almost all sweatshop workers are young women—endure starvation wages, forced overtime and dangerous working conditions.[7]

Many Americans, as well as citizens of other leading industrial nations, have strong reservations about ceding their national sovereignty to international organizations, especially the WTO. Much of their concern centers on the possible loss of jobs and the reduction of wages in their countries if their workers were forced to compete with low-wage workers in the world's poorer countries, most of whom earn just one or two dollars a day. Is it fair to make American factories, which uphold relatively high environmental standards, compete with Third World factories that are not similarly burdened? If the United States

---

[7]Tina Rosenberg, "Globalization, the Free-Trade Fix," *New York Times Magazine,* August 18, 2002, p. 32.

and other industrial countries were subject to the rules and regulations of the WTO, their own governments would be unable to prevent a flood of cheap imports.

Most economists as well as most business leaders supported the establishment of NAFTA as well as of GATT. Like rock n' roll back in the 1950s, globalization is here to stay. Still, there are growing reservations about some of its outcomes, even among those who call themselves "free traders."

Tim Harford, in *The Undercover Economist,* agrees that sweatshop employees endure terrible working conditions, long hours, and pitiful wages. *But* sweatshops are the symptom, not the cause, of shocking global poverty. Workers go there voluntarily, which means—hard as it is to believe—that their alternatives are even worse. Turnover rates of multinational-owned factories are low, because conditions and pay, while bad, are better than those in factories run by local firms.[8]

Current Issue: Is Your School Sweatshirt Sewn in a Sweatshop?

Your school does not manufacture any of the products bearing its name. College names are licensed to apparel makers and other companies for a royalty of about 7 percent of the retail price of each T-shirt, sweatshirt, or key chain. Indeed, no one at your school has any idea of just who makes the products that bear the school's name. A global supply chain stretches from the licensee companies to large-scale factories in China, Mexico, Thailand, Indonesia, and dozens of other low-wage countries, to small-scale subcontractor factories everywhere in between, and in some cases, all the way to women stitching garments in their living rooms.

There are two questions that colleges have only begun to ask. How well are these workers paid and how decent are their working conditions? If well under a dollar an hour is satisfactory—the prevailing wage rate in these countries—then few college administrators are losing much sleep over this issue. Even the fact that many workers are forced to work over 300 hours a month—in violation of local law—does not seem to be too much cause for concern.

Various colleges as well as other organizations have banded together to inspect the actual factories. In addition, Nike, Adidas, Levi-Straus, Liz Claiborne, and Philips Van Heusen use monitors to check up on the factories producing their goods. But the inspectors rarely witness day-to-day conditions in these factories. Often the managers are tipped off about impending inspections and sometimes the contractors themselves choose the factories to be visited. Nevertheless here are some of the common working conditions inspectors have found:

- Lack of guards on sewing and cutting machines.
- High levels of cotton dust.
- Blocked aisles and fire exits.
- No running water in toilets.
- No information about hazardous chemicals workers are using.
- Restricted bathroom break times.

College administrators and the students themselves are indirectly responsible for these abysmal working conditions—not to mention the measly pay—of the workers making their college paraphernalia. In the words of Bob Dylan's 1962 classic folk song, *Blowin' in the Wind:*

> An' how many times can a man turn his head,
> An' pretend that he just doesn't see?

---

[8]Tim Harford, *The Undercover Economist* (New York: Oxford University Press, 2006), p. 222.

Questions for Further Thought and Discussion

1. Explain how and why trade barriers have come down in recent decades.
2. Do you think we should have joined NAFTA? Try to argue this question from both sides.
3. List the reasons why our trade deficit has grown so quickly since the mid-1990s. What can we do to help bring it down?
4. Identify the goods and services that you purchase that are imported. How would your lifestyle change if these imports were unavailable?
5. How would your life change if the United States were no longer the world's leading exporter?
6. Explain how international trade (exports and imports) affects a nation's output, employment, and income.

Workbook for Chapter 8

Name _____ Date _____

Multiple-Choice Questions

Circle the letter that corresponds to the best answer.

1. Today world trade is regulated by _____
   a) NAFTA   c) WTO
   b) GATT   d) EU

2. Which statement is true?
   a) Off-shoring is a type of outsourcing.
   b) Outsourcing is type of off-shoring.
   c) Outsourcing and off-shoring are identical concepts.
   d) Outsourcing is the opposite of off-shoring.

3. Which is the most accurate statement?
   a) Our trade deficit has narrowed since 1995.
   b) We export more merchandise than services (in terms of dollars).
   c) The largest service purchase that foreigners make from the United States is educational services.
   d) In recent years foreigners have generally refused to accept U.S. dollars in payment for their goods and services.

4. Since the early 1990s our trade deficit has _____.
   a) fallen substantially   c) risen slightly
   b) fallen slightly   d) risen substantially

5. In the 20th century our balance of trade was positive until the _____.
   a) 1950s   c) 1970s   e) 1990s
   b) 1960s   d) 1980s

6. Statement I: The European Union was formed as a trading counterweight to NAFTA.
   Statement II: Since the formation of NAFTA, the United States has lost millions of jobs to Mexico.
   a) Statement I is true, and statement II is false.
   b) Statement II is true, and statement I is false.
   c) Both statements are true.
   d) Both statements are false.

7. The basis for international trade is that _____.
   a) a nation can import a particular good or service at a lower cost than if it were produced domestically
   b) we stand to gain if we can sell more to other nations than they buy from us
   c) there are winners and losers
   d) it pays to trade, provided we remain independent by producing all our necessities

8. Adam Smith believed that _____.
   a) people should never buy anything if they can make it themselves
   b) what makes sense in the conduct of a private family's economic endeavors also makes sense in those of a nation
   c) trading with other nations promotes full employment
   d) a nation will gain if its citizens trade among themselves, but it will probably lose if it trades with other nations

9. GDP = C + I + G + X_n. If X_n were not included, our GDP would be _____.
   a) higher
   b) about the same
   c) lower

10. The most-favored nation clause of the WTO agreement stipulates that _____.
    a) no member nation may impose a tariff on the goods of any other member nation
    b) all member nations must offer all other member countries the same trade concessions as any member country
    c) each member may designate another member as a favored nation, providing that nation with trade concessions
    d) all member nations must sell their goods to other member nations at cost

11. Statement I: The United States has a much larger population and GDP than the European Union.
Statement II: The European Union has attained a higher degree of economic integration than NAFTA.

    a) Statement I is true, and statement II is false.

    b) Statement II is true, and statement I is false.

    c) Both statements are true.

    d) Both statements are false.

12. Statement I: Our trade deficit, although still high, is lower than it was five years ago.
Statement II: Taken together, our imports and exports are over one-quarter of our GDP.

    a) Statement I is true, and statement II is false.

    b) Statement II is true, and statement I is false.

    c) Both statements are true.

    d) Both statements are false.

13. Most economists and people in the business community supported the establishment of

    _____.

    a) both NAFTA and GATT

    b) neither NAFTA nor GATT

    c) NAFTA but not GATT

    d) GATT but not NAFTA

14. Which statement is true?

    a) X_n has always been positive.

    b) X_n has always been negative.

    c) X_n had been positive from the turn of the century until the 1970s.

    d) X_n had been negative from the turn of the century until the 1970s.

    e) None of these statements is true.

15. Statement I: Since the late 1990s, our negative balance of trade has become much larger.
Statement II: The United States has the world's largest negative balance of trade.

    a) Statement I is true, and statement II is false.

    b) Statement II is true, and statement I is false.

    c) Both statements are true.

    d) Both statements are false.

16. In 2005 which number is closest to our balance of trade?

    a) $725 billion

    b) $350 billion

    c) 0

    d) −$350 billion

    e) −$725 billion

17. Since the passage of NAFTA our trade deficit with Mexico has gone _____ and our trade deficit with Canada has gone _____.

    a) up, up   c) up, down

    b) down, down   d) down, up

18. Statement I: The United States has a much less self-sufficient economy than those of countries in Western Europe.
Statement II: Mexico sends the United States more than 80 percent of its exports.

    a) Statement I is true, and statement II is false.

    b) Statement II is true, and statement I is false.

    c) Both statements are true.

    d) Both statements are false.

19. Which one of these statements is true?

    a) To save money, most colleges manufacture their own sweatshirts.

    b) Most college administrators are well informed about the pay and working conditions of the people who sew their college's sweatshirts.

    c) Most of the people who sew college sweatshirts work in what may be termed sweatshops.

    d) Manufacturers of college sweatshirts in poor countries are usually under strict supervision to ensure that they don't violate local laws regulating pay, overtime hours, and working conditions.

20. Each of the following is a characteristic of the European Union EXCEPT that _____.

    a) workers from any EU country can seek work in any other member country

    b) the euro replaced the domestic currencies (for example, francs, marks, lira) in 1999

    c) its population and GDP are comparable to those of the United States

    d) freight is able to move anywhere within the EU without checkpoint delays and paperwork

21. The trading bloc that has eliminated all internal tariffs is _____.

    a) the European Union

    b) NAFTA

    c) Mercosur

    d) the World Trade Organization

22. Which one of these statements best describes the complaints of the protesters at meetings of the WTO, IMF, and World Bank?

    a) They opposed military aid to Third World dictatorships.

    b) They opposed trade with poor countries because of the exploitative nature of that trade.

    c) They opposed free trade with nations whose people worked under sweatshop conditions and opposed ceding national sovereignty to an international group.

    d) They opposed strict environmental standards, which they felt would increase our cost of living.

23. Which was NOT an argument of the protesters against the IMF, WTO, and World Bank?

    a) We are exploiting factory workers in poor countries.

    b) Our subsidized grain exports are sold below cost in poor countries, driving local farmers out of business.

    c) Globalization is hurting the American standard of living.

    d) Globalization is lowering American wages and exporting high-paying jobs.

24. Which statement would best describe the situation of the American economy?

    a) We are more dependent on foreign trade than most other nations.

    b) We are much more dependent on foreign trade than we were 30 years ago.

    c) We are much less dependent on foreign trade than we were 30 years ago.

    d) We are virtually self-sufficient.

25. Which statement is false?

    a) During World War I and World War II, the sum of our imports and exports as a percent of GDP rose sharply.

    b) Foreign trade in goods is much more important to the American economy than foreign trade in services.

    c) Because the American economy is much larger than any other economy, we can continue running larger and larger trade deficits for as long as we like.

    d) We pay for a large chunk of our trade deficit with U.S. dollars.

26. The main criticism Joseph Stiglitz levels at the IMF is that _____.

    a) it provides too many loans that are not repaid

    b) it no longer promotes economic growth, but rather contraction

    c) it does not provide enough loans

    d) it does not sufficiently promote the market system

27. Of the policy actions by richer countries shown below, which one would be most favored by poor countries?

    a) The elimination of agricultural subsidies

    b) The elimination of tariffs on industrial goods

    c) More vigorous enforcement of environmental laws

    d) Government promotion of labor union membership

28. Which would be the most accurate statement?

    a) Globalization has helped almost everyone and hurt almost no one.

    b) Aside from a few malcontents who turn up at demonstrations, there is almost no opposition to globalization in the United States.

    c) It can be argued that globalization has hurt many poorer countries.

    d) Globalization is an unmitigated economic disaster and should be reversed.

29. A characteristic of a modern economy is _____.

    a) Self-sufficiency

    b) Specialization and exchange

    c) A high percentage of people who make their living as jacks-of-all-trades

    d) A high proportion of people employed in agriculture

30. Which statement is true about the European Union?

 a) It has not taken in any new member nations since its formation.

 b) All of its members must use the euro as its official currency.

 c) It is essentially a free trade area.

 d) It has been basically a failure.

31. Which is the most accurate statement?

 a) The agricultural subsidies paid to American and European farmers have benefited farmers in poorer countries as well.

 b) Agricultural subsidies have been largely phased out since the turn of the century.

 c) Agricultural subsidies are a matter of great contention between rich and poor nations.

 d) Agricultural subsidies are paid by rich nations to poor nations.

32. Specialization and exchange can result in each of the following except _____.

 a) a higher standard of living.

 b) free trade.

 c) more output.

 d) more national self-sufficiency.

33. Which statement would you agree with?

 a) The exchange rate between the dollar and foreign currencies has no effect on our standard of living.

 b) The exchange rate between the dollar and foreign currencies affects our standard of living only when we travel abroad.

 c) Our standard of living is raised when we can get more yen, yuan, pounds, and euros for our dollars.

 d) Most Americans closely follow changes in the exchange rate between the dollar and foreign currencies.

Fill-In Questions

1. X_n = _____ − _____.

2. The three members of NAFTA are _____, _____, and _____.

3. In the year 2005 we ran a trade deficit of $_____ billion.

4. Farmers in poor countries with foreign grain imports have been most hurt by American and European _____.

5. Our exports of goods and services are about _____ percent of our GDP.

6. The only trading bloc that has eliminated all its internal tariffs is _____.

7. The main concern of the labor union members who were protesting against the WTO, the IMF, and the World Bank was _____.

Chapter 9

Gross Domestic Product

I magine that you're at a college football game and your school has just won the national championship. Tens of thousands of fans are jabbing their index fingers in the air and chanting, "We're number *one*! We're number *one*!"

Well, it just so happens that the United States has had the largest GDP in the world for probably 100 years. We're so used to being number one that we kind of take it for granted. But we may not be number one for too much longer. China, with more than four times our population, has been rapidly gaining on us, and may pass us in another 25 or 30 years.

CHAPTER OBJECTIVES

When you have finished this chapter, you will know the answers to these questions:

- What is GDP?
- How is GDP measured?
- What are the national income accounts?
- What is the difference between nominal GDP and real GDP?

- How does our GDP compare to those of other nations?
- How is per capita GDP calculated?
- What are the shortcomings of GDP as a measure of national economic well-being?
- What is the Genuine Progress Index?

What Is Gross Domestic Product?

What is GDP? *It is the nation's expenditure on all the final goods and services produced during the year at market prices.* For example, if we spent $18,000 per car on 10 million American cars, that $180 billion would go into GDP. We'd add in the 15 billion Big Macs at $3 for another $45 billion, and the 1.8 million new homes at $175,000 each for $315 billion. Then, for good measure, we'd add the 5 billion visits to doctors' offices at $75 apiece for $375 billion and the 20 billion nightclub admissions at $15 each for $300 billion. Add everything up and we'd get nearly $12,479,400,000,000 in the year 2005.

Definition of GDP

Did you notice the word *final* in the definition of GDP? We include only those goods and services that consumers, businesses, and governments buy for their own use. So when you buy a telephone answering machine or you get your hair cut, or if the government repaves a highway, we count those goods and services in GDP. But if Liz Claiborne buys 10,000 yards of fabric to make dresses, that purchase is not recorded in GDP. When the dresses are sold, *then* they're counted in GDP.

F*igure* 1
Hypothetical $C + I + G + X_n$
Line

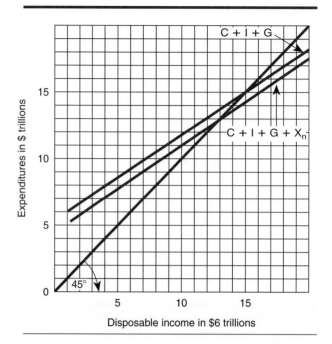

Why is the $C + I + G + X_n$ line *below* the $C + I + G$ line? It's because X_n is negative, so when it's added to $C + I + G$, it reduces its value.

Over the last four chapters we worked our way toward the graph in Figure 1 that depicts GDP. We began with the consumption function in Chapter 5, added investment in Chapter 6, government spending in Chapter 7, and finally, net exports in Chapter 8.

An alternate definition of GDP is *GDP is the value of all goods and services produced within a nation's boundaries during the year.* This would include the wages, rent, interest, and profits earned by the few million foreigners who work in the United States. For example, there are a lot of Japanese in Tennessee and a lot of Germans in South Carolina who make cars. But our GDP would not include the wages, rent, interest, and profits earned by Americans living abroad.

$GDP = C + I + G + X_n$

Let's get back to our GDP equation:

$$GDP = C + I + G = X_n$$

Substituting the year 2005 data into this equation, we get:

$$GDP^{[1]} = 8,746 + 2,100 + 2,360 - 726$$
$$GDP = 12,479$$

In 2005 we produced nearly \$12.5 trillion worth of final goods and services (see Table 1). Seventy percent were consumer goods and services, followed in size by government purchases, investment spending, and, finally, net exports, which were negative. Now we'll draw a few graphs and then move on to how GDP is measured.

Table 1 offers a detailed compilation of the components of GDP in 2005. As you can see, C was the largest, followed by G, I, and then X_n, which was negative.

About seven out of every ten dollars of our GDP is spent on consumer goods. Figure 2 shows the percentage share of each of the four components of GDP. You'll notice that X_n is negative.

---

[1]The numbers don't add up exactly because of rounding.

TABLE 1	The Components of GDP, 2005 (in $ billions)*		
Consumption:			
Durable goods	1,026		
Nondurable goods	2,564		
Services	5,156		
C	8,746	8,746	
Investment:			
Plant and equipment	1,328		
Residential housing	756		
Inventory change	15		
I	2,100	2,100	
Government purchases:			
Federal	875		
State and local	1,485		
G	2,360	2,360	
Net exports:			
Exports	1,299		
−Imports	2,025		
X_n	−726	−726	
GDP		12,479	

*Figures may not add up due to rounding.
Source: Economic Report of the President, 2006; Survey of Current Business, February 2006.

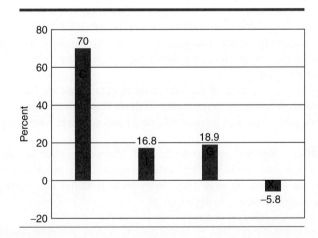

Figure 2
The Components of GDP as a Percentage of GDP*
*Figures may not add up to 100.0 percent due to rounding.
Source: See Table 1.

How GDP Is Measured

There are two basic ways to measure GDP: the flow-of-income approach and the expenditures approach (which happens to be *my* favorite). The expenditures approach is shown in the outer ring of Figure 3; the income approach is shown in the inner ring.

Two ways to measure GDP are the flow-of-income approach and the expenditures approach.

The Expenditures Approach

From time to time we will go back to the definition of GDP: *the nation's expenditure on all the final goods and services produced during the year at market prices.* Only "final" goods and services are counted. These include those goods and services

GDP is the nation's expenditure on all the final goods and services produced during the year at market prices.

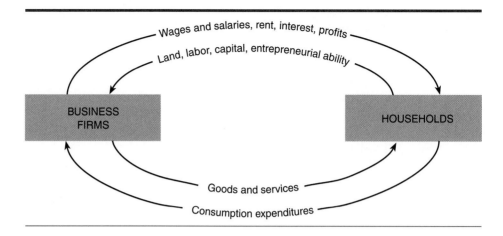

purchased by their ultimate consumers. They are represented by the variables in our equation:

$$GDP = C + I + G + X_n$$

Substituting the year 2005 data for these variables, we get:

$$12,479 = 8,746 + 2,100 + 2,360 - 726$$

The Flow-of-Income Approach

Business firms produce nearly all our goods and services. The firms pay people wages to get them to turn out these goods and services. Those who own the land and buildings used are paid rent, and those who supply the capital are paid interest. Add up all the goods and services produced and you have GDP. Or, alternatively, add up the incomes received by the factors of production (plus a couple of other things we'll be talking about) and you have GDP.

We need to look at the flow of income in more detail than we looked at the expenditures flow because it has more components. Indeed, this approach is so complex, we'll divide it into two parts: national product (Table 2) and national income (Figure 4).

GDP − Depreciation = NDP   **National Product**   Now we come to the fun part. Many economists are unhappy with the concept of gross domestic product. It's simply too gross. They much prefer net domestic product (NDP) (see the box on page 194, "Why NDP Is Better than GDP"). What's the difference? The main difference is depreciation.

Gross domestic product − Depreciation = Net domestic product

GDP includes, among other things, $1,328 billion worth of plant and equipment spending (see Table 1). This is money spent on new office buildings, shopping malls, factories, stores, assembly lines, office machines, computers, computer software, and a host of other machinery and equipment.

Why are we so anxious to get rid of depreciation? Depreciation represents the buildings and machinery (plant and equipment) that have worn out or become obsolete over the course of the year. Usually these are replaced with new plant and equipment, but this doesn't represent a net gain because the company ends up right where it started. For example, if a firm begins the year with eight machines and replaces three that wore out during the year, it still has eight machines at the end of the year.

Similarly, when we measure a nation's GDP, one of the things we are counting is the replacement of plant and equipment, which can lead to some dubious conclusions about a nation's economic well-being. For example, suppose Sweden and Canada each

TABLE 2	GDP and GNP, 2005 (*billions of dollars*)*
Consumption:	8,746
Investment	2,100
Government spending	2,360
Net exports	−726
GDP	12,479
(Plus) Receipts of factor income from rest of world	507
(Less) Payments of factor income to rest of world	−474
GNP	12,512
(Less) Depreciation	−1,574
Net domestic product	10,938
(Less) Indirect business taxes (plus) subsidies	−34
National income	10,904

*The figures do not add up exactly because of rounding. Because subsidies are relatively small, we'll ignore them.
Source: *Economic Report of the President*, 2006; *Survey of Current Business*, February 2006.

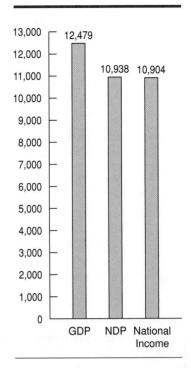

F*igure* 4

National Product and Income, 2005
Our GDP, which is nearly 12.5 dollars, is the largest of these three variables, and national income is the smallest.
Source: *Survey of Current Business*, February 2006.

have a GDP of 200, but depreciation in Sweden is 50, while in Canada it is only 30. The NDP of Sweden would be 150 (GDP of 200 − Depreciation of 50); Canada's NDP would be 170 (GDP of 200 − Depreciation of 30). A more elaborate example appears in the box, "Why NDP Is Better than GDP."

Are you ready for a big question? All right then, here it comes. What's the difference between gross investment and net investment? *Gross* investment is the total amount we invest in new plant and equipment (as well as new residential housing and additional inventory). *Net* investment is the additional plant and equipment with which we end up by the end of the year. So we have this equation:

$$\text{Gross investment} - \text{Depreciation} = \text{Net investment}$$

The *I* in the equation GDP = C + I + G + X_n is *gross* investment. We distinguished between *gross* investment and *net* investment back in Chapter 6.

Let's go over the arithmetic. In Table 2, we have a GDP of $12,479 billion (the sum of C + I + G + X_n). We add net receipts of factor income from the rest of the world ($33 billion) and subtract depreciation ($1,574 billion) from GDP to get net domestic product ($10,938 billion). Are you ready to take up national income? All right then, here it comes.

National Income Now we need to subtract indirect business taxes (mainly general sales taxes and taxes on specific items such as gasoline, liquor, and cigarettes) and add subsidies (such as government payments to farmers).

$$\text{NDP} - \text{Indirect business taxes and subsidies} = \text{National Income}$$
$$10,938 - \qquad\qquad 34 \qquad\qquad = \qquad 10,904$$

Why NDP Is Better than GDP

Although people commonly use GDP when they talk about national output, most economists prefer NDP. Why? Because it allows for depreciation of plant and equipment. Let's illustrate this with two hypothetical countries in the table below:

North Atlantis		South Atlantis	
GDP	500	GDP	500
−Depreciation	50	−Depreciation	100
NDP	450	NDP	400

We see that North Atlantis and South Atlantis had identical GDPs, but that North Atlantis had depreciation of $50 billion while South Atlantis's depreciation was $100 billion.* Consequently, North Atlantis ended up with an NDP of $450 billion, while South Atlantis had an NDP of just $400 billion.

This distinction is important. North and South Atlantis had the same GDP, but North Atlantis's NDP was $50 billion greater than that of South Atlantis. Why? Because South Atlantis had to replace $100 billion of worn-out or obsolete plant and equipment that year, while North Atlantis had to replace just $50 billion of plant and equipment.

In 1930 Babe Ruth held out for a salary of $80,000. A reporter asked him if it would be fair for a baseball player to earn more than Herbert Hoover, the president of the United States. "Why not? I had a better year than he did," the Babe replied. And so, we too may ask, who had a better year, North or South Atlantis? Based on GDP, they did equally well; based on NDP, North Atlantis did better.

South Atlantis had a lower NDP because it had to devote twice as much production to replacing worn-out and obsolete plant and equipment as did North Atlantis. When you are devoting such a large portion of your resources to replacing plant and equipment, these resources can't go toward adding to your stock of plant and equipment or, for that matter, to producing consumer goods and services.

Suppose North Atlantis devoted that extra $50 billion to production of more plant and equipment. It would now have $50 billion worth of additional plant and equipment. Or if it had produced $50 billion worth of consumer goods and services, its citizens would have enjoyed a much higher standard of living.

So who enjoyed a better year? Virtually every economist would tell you that North Atlantis did because it had a higher NDP. Stated differently, it's not as significant to know how much a country grossed as to know how much it netted.

---

*Economists use this shorthand way of writing billions (for example, 50 = $50 billion: 100 = $100 billion).

NDP − Indirect business taxes and subsidies = National Income

The big three of domestic product—GDP, NDP, and National Income—are lined up by size in Figure 4 for the year 2005. For other years, could they be in some other order? Could NDP, for example, be larger than GDP? The answer is no. Since GDP − Depreciation = NDP, the only way for NDP to be larger would be if depreciation were negative.[2]

Our National Income was $10,904 billion in the year 2005. The largest part, by far, was compensation of employees (see Figure 5). This compensation includes wages, salaries, and fringe benefits (such as medical insurance and sick, holiday, and vacation pay). Corporate profits are either paid out as dividends or plowed back into the corporation. Net interest is the total interest income of individuals minus interest paid by consumers to businesses and net interest paid by the government. (No one ever asks you to define net interest on an economics exam.) Rental income is the rent received by individuals (rent received by businesses is counted elsewhere). And finally, we have the fifth part of National Income: proprietors' income. This includes the total incomes of all unincorporated businesses (that is, rent, interest, profits, and compensation for labor).

National Income, then, is the sum of compensation to employees, corporate profits, net interest, rental income, and proprietors' income. These are all resource payments for the use of land, labor, capital, and entrepreneurial ability. Need a little extra help? Then see the box, "Reviewing the Two Approaches to GDP," on page 196.

---

[2]Negative depreciation is a logical absurdity. It would mean that plant and equipment have somehow become *less* obsolete and *less* worn out during the year. Negative depreciation is actually appreciation.

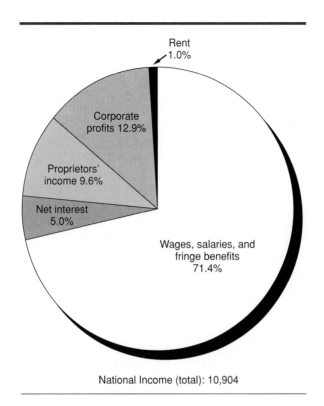

National Income (total): 10,904

Figure 5
Distribution of National
Income, 2005*
Wages, salaries, and fringe benefits
account for more than 70 cents of
every dollar of our domestic
income.
*Percentages may not add up to
100.0 percent due to rounding
Source: Survey of Current Business,
March 2006.

Two Things to Avoid When Compiling GDP

Two mistakes are commonly made when GDP is compiled. First we'll talk about multiple counting, that is, counting a particular good at each stage of production. Then we'll look at the inclusion of transfer payments. To compile GDP correctly, we count each good or service only once, and we don't count transfer payments as part of GDP.

Multiple Counting

We need to avoid multiple counting when we compile GDP. Only expenditures on final products—what consumers, businesses, and government units buy for their own use— belong in GDP. This is clearly illustrated by the journey wheat makes from the farm to the supermarket.

The farmer gets about 2 cents for the wheat that goes into a loaf of bread. This wheat is ground into flour at a mill and is now worth, say, 4 cents. When it is placed in 100-pound packages, it is worth 5 cents, and when it is shipped to a bakery, it is worth 10 cents. Baked bread is worth 20 cents, packaged baked bread is worth 23 cents, and bread delivered to the supermarket is worth 35 cents. The supermarket sells it for 89 cents.

How much of this goes into GDP? Do we add up the 2 cents, 4 cents, 5 cents, 10 cents, 20 cents, 23 cents, 35 cents, and 89 cents? No! That would be multiple counting. We count only what is spent on a final good, 89 cents, which is paid by the consumer. Of this entire process, only 89 cents goes into GDP.

GDP, then, counts only what we spend on final goods and services—not those of an intermediate nature. We are not interested in the money spent on wheat or flour, but only that which the buyer of the final product, bread, spends at the supermarket. If we count intermediate goods, we will greatly inflate GDP by counting the same goods and services over and over again.

GDP counts only what we spend on final goods and services.

First we'll go over the flow-of-income approach. If wages and salaries are $4.7 trillion, rent is $.1 trillion, interest is $.7 trillion, profits are $.5 trillion, indirect business taxes are $.8 trillion, and depreciation is $.6 trillion, find National Income, NDP, and GDP:

Solution:

Wages and salaries	$4.7 trillion
Rent	0.1
Interest	0.7
Profits	0.5
Domestic income	6.0
+ Indirect business tax	0.8
NDP	6.8
+ Depreciation	0.6
GDP	7.4

Now we'll do a problem that starts off with GDP and works its way down to domestic income. Given: GDP = 6,700, Indirect business taxes = 500, Depreciation = 700, and Direct taxes = 500. Find NDP and National Income.

Solution:

GDP	6,700
Depreciation	−700
NDP	6,000
−Indirect taxes	−500
National Income	5,500

Reviewing the Two Approaches to GDP

I hope you didn't try to use direct taxes. Clearly, they don't belong in our calculations. Just because they're listed doesn't mean we should use them. Suppose you were baking a cake and you had placed your flour, sugar, butter, and other ingredients on a counter. If someone left out a can of turpentine there, would you pour it into your mixing bowl? I hope not, especially if you were planning to offer me a slice of that cake.

Well, then, why did I put direct taxes into the last problem? Because I wanted to see what you would do with it. Remember, just because something is there doesn't mean we have to use it.

Moving right along, let's work out a problem using the expenditures approach to GDP. Given: C = 4,100, I = 900, G = 1,200, Imports = 750, Exports = 650. Find GDP:

Solution: First we'll find net exports:

$$X_n = \text{Exports} - \text{Imports}$$
$$X_n = 650 - 750$$
$$X_n = -100$$

Next we'll write down our equation:

$$\text{GDP} = C + I + G + X_n$$

Then we substitute numbers, for the letters:

$$\text{GDP} = 4,100 + 900 + 1,200 - 100$$

And finally, we solve:

$$\text{GDP} = 6,200 - 100$$
$$\text{GDP} = 6,100$$

We'll follow this general procedure for problem solving throughout the book: (1) Write down the equation, (2) substitute, and (3) solve.

Just as we don't include intermediate goods in GDP, we don't count used goods either. If you buy a used car, a 10-year-old house, or almost anything at a flea market or on eBay, your purchase does not go into GDP. Remember, we count only final goods and services that were purchased in the current year.

However, anything done this year to make a used product salable is counted (for example, a paint job for a used car). What if you add a room to your house? If you do it yourself, then the cost of materials will be included in GDP. If you pay someone to build the addition, then we'll include the full cost of the job.

Treatment of Transfer Payments and Financial Transactions

At first glance, transfer payments appear to belong in GDP. When the government issues a Social Security or unemployment insurance check, isn't this a form of government spending? Shouldn't it be part of G, like defense spending or the salaries paid to government employees?

GDP includes only payments for goods and services produced this year. A person receiving a Social Security check is not being reimbursed for producing a good or service this year. But a government clerk or the employee of a defense contractor *is* providing a good or service this year so their pay would therefore be included under government purchases, designated by the letter G.

Because Social Security, public assistance, Medicare, Medicaid, and other government transfer payments—which now make up more than half of the federal budget—are not payments for currently produced goods and services, they are not included in GDP. However, those who receive these payments will spend nearly all of that money, so, ultimately, the payments will go toward GDP in the form of consumer spending for the purchase of final goods and services produced in the current year.

Transfer payments don't go directly into GDP.

Something else not counted in GDP is financial transactions. The purchase of corporate stocks and bonds does not add anything to GDP. Isn't it an investment? It certainly is from an individual's point of view; but in strictly economic terms, the purchase of corporate stocks and bonds, government securities, real estate, and other financial assets does not constitute investment because it does not represent the purchase of new plant and equipment. But aren't these funds used to buy new plant and equipment? Perhaps. If and when they are, those purchases qualify as investment and therefore as part of GDP.

Financial transactions don't go into GDP.

Nominal GDP versus Real GDP

Every July 4 we order a large pizza. After all, what could be more American? In 2002 the pie cost $8. Each year it went up a dollar, so by 2006 we were paying $12 for the same size pizza. Question: If the price of pizza went from $8 to $12, by what percentage did it go up?

Solution:

$$\text{Percentage change} = \frac{\text{Current price} - \text{Original price}}{\text{Original price}}$$

$$= \frac{\$12 - \$8}{\$8} = \frac{\$4}{\$8} = \frac{1}{2} = 0.50 = 50\%$$

Calculating Percentage Changes

When we go from 100 to 120, that's an increase of 20 percent. From 150 to 200 is an increase of $33\frac{1}{3}$ percent. When we go from 50 to 25, that's a percentage decline of 50 percent. How do we know? We use this formula:

$$\% \text{ change} = \frac{\text{Change}}{\text{Original number}}$$

Using the first example, from 100 to 120 is a change of 20, and as our original number is 100, we have $\frac{20}{100}$. Any number divided by 100 may be read as a percentage—in this case, 20 percent.

Another way of figuring this out—and we'll need this method most of the time because 100 will rarely be the original number—is to divide the bottom number into the top number. Remember, whenever you have a fraction, you may divide the bottom number into the top:

$$\frac{\text{Change}}{\text{Original number}} = \frac{12}{50} = 0.24$$

0.24 = 24 percent. Any decimal may be read as a percent if you move the decimal point two places to the right and add the percent sign (%).

Now let's do the other two. First, the percentage change when we go from 150 to 200. Work it out yourself in the space provided here, and then go on to the last one—when we go from 50 to 25.

$$\frac{\text{Change}}{\text{Original number}} = \frac{50}{150} = \frac{5}{15} = \frac{1}{3} = 33\frac{1}{3}\%$$

Finally, find the percentage change when we go from 50 to 25.

$$\frac{\text{Change}}{\text{Original number}} = -\frac{25}{50} = -\frac{1}{2} = -0.50 = -50\%$$

You're going to have to calculate percentage changes in this chapter and the next, so please work your way through the accompanying box, "Calculating Percentage Changes," if you need some extra help.

Think of our GDP as a pizza. In this example our GDP went up a dollar a year from 2002 through 2006. We'll call that our nominal GDP. Our real GDP would be the actual pizza we produce each year. Between 2002 and 2006 we produced the same size pizza each year. So real GDP stayed the same.

Nominal GDP goes up virtually every year and real GDP goes up almost every year, except during recessions. Suppose nominal GDP grew by 8 percent in 2019 and there was a 3 percent rate of inflation. Can you guess by how much real GDP grew that year?

It grew by 5 percent. All we did was subtract the inflation rate (3%) from the GDP growth rate (8%). We can say, then, that nominal GDP rose by 8 percent but real GDP rose by just 5 percent.

GDP is the basic measure of how much the country produced in a given year. However, comparisons of GDP from one year to the next can be misleading. We need to be able to correct GDP for price increases so we can measure how much actual production rose. To do this we use the GDP deflator, which is calculated quarterly by the Department of Commerce.

The GDP deflator

In the base year the GDP deflator is 100. If the GDP deflator is 120 in the current year, prices have risen 20 percent since the base year.

Problem: GDP rises from \$10 trillion in 2004, the base year, to \$15 trillion in 2009, the current year. If the GDP deflator is 125 in 2009, find real GDP in 2009.

Solution:

$$\text{Real GDP} = \frac{\text{Nominal GDP}}{\text{GDP deflator}} \times 100$$

$$= \frac{15{,}000}{125} \times 100 = \frac{120}{1} \times 100 = 12{,}000$$

Next question: Find the percentage increase in real GDP between 2004 and 2009.

Solution:

$$\text{Percentage change} = \frac{\text{Current real GDP} - \text{Original real GDP}}{\text{Original real GDP}}$$

$$= \frac{(12{,}000 - 10{,}000)}{10{,}000} = \frac{2{,}000}{10{,}000} = 0.20 = 20\%$$

Here's one more problem: GDP rises from \$3 trillion in 1982 to \$6 trillion in 1988. The GDP deflator in 1988 is 150. Find the real GDP in 1988. Find the percentage increase in real GDP between 1982 and 1988.

Solution:

$$\text{Real GDP} = \frac{\text{Nominal GDP}}{\text{GDP deflator}}$$

$$= \frac{6{,}000}{150} \times 100 = \frac{40}{1} \times 100 = 4{,}000$$

$$\text{Percentage change} = \frac{\text{Current real GDP} - \text{Original real GDP}}{\text{Original real GDP}}$$

$$= \frac{4{,}000 - 3{,}000}{3{,}000} = \frac{1{,}000}{3{,}000} = \frac{1}{3} = 33\frac{1}{3}\%$$

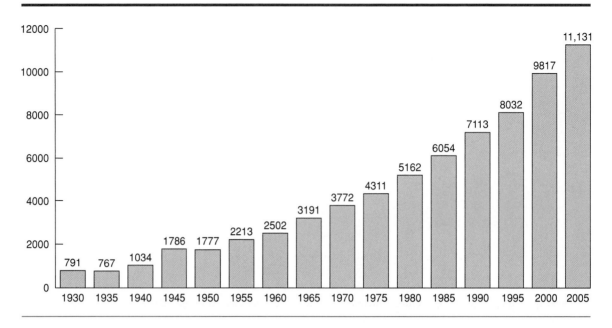

F*igure* 6
GDP, 1930–2005, in billions of 2000 dollars
Real GDP fell during the Great Depression and again after World War II. Since the late 1940s there has been a steady upward climb of real GDP.
Source: Statistical Abstract of the United States: 2006.

Figure 6 provides a 75-year record of real GDP. According to U.S. government measurements, we produce about 14 times as much as we did in 1930 and about 5 times as much as we did in 1955. Although real GDP comparisons over 50- and 75-year periods cannot be made with precision, they certainly give us a fair approximation of the growth of our national output.

Real GDP measures our output, or production. Output, or real GDP, falls during recession years. But GDP, by definition, is *the nation's expenditure on all final goods and services produced during the year at market prices.* If prices rise by a larger percentage than output falls, then GDP will increase. For example, if output goes down by 4 percent and prices go up by 7 percent, by what percentage does GDP go up?

It goes up by 3 percent. GDP measures changes in output *and* prices. Real GDP measures just changes in output.

Now let's see if you can work out some verbal GDP problems. If GDP rose and real GDP fell, explain what happened.

Answer: The GDP deflator (or, rate of inflation) rose more than real GDP fell. For instance, if GDP rose by 3 percent, while real GDP fell by 2 percent, then the GDP deflator must have risen by 5 percent.

Next problem: Real GDP remains unchanged, while GDP falls. What happened?

Answer: What happened was deflation, or a decline in the price level (that is, the GDP deflator dropped below 100). While those of us born after the administration of Herbert Hoover never experienced deflation, it *does* happen. In the next chapter we'll consider whether we might soon be seeing some deflation.

One more problem: GDP doubles and the price level doubles. What happened to real GDP?

Read Only if You're Still Confused about the Difference between a Change in GDP and Real GDP

From August 1981 through November 1982 we suffered our worst recession since the Great Depression of the 1930s. But GDP actually rose in 1981 and 1982. And what happened to real GDP?

Real GDP went down in 1982. How can you explain a rise in GDP accompanied by a decline in real GDP, or actual output?

Prices, measured by the GDP deflator, must have gone up at a higher rate than output declined. In the accompanying chart you'll see that GDP rose by 4.1 percent and that real GDP declined by 2.1 percent.

By how much did the price level rise from 1981 to 1982? This rise, measured by the GDP deflator, was 6.2 percent.

There's a very simple relationship among percentage changes in GDP, real GDP, and the GDP deflator from one year to the next:

Percentage change in GDP = Percentage change in real GDP + Percentage change in GDP deflator

Question: If real GDP rose by 3 percent and the GDP deflator fell by 1.2 percent, what was the percentage change in GDP?

Solution: Percentage change in GDP = Percentage change in real GDP (3%) + Percentage change in GDP deflator (−1.2%).

$$\text{Percentage change in GDP} = 3\% + (-1.2\%)$$
$$= 3\% - 1.2\% = 1.8\%$$

One more question: If GDP rose by 3.8 percent and the GDP deflator rose by 2.5 percent, find the percentage change in real GDP.

Solution: Percentage change in GDP = Percentage change in real GDP + Percentage change in GDP deflator.

$$3.8\% = \text{Percentage change in real GDP} + 2.5\%$$
$$1.3\% = \text{Percentage change in real GDP}$$

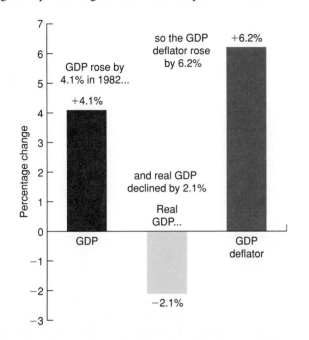

Answer: Real GDP stayed the same. Let's make up a problem with real numbers: GDP rises from 1000 to 2000, and the GDP deflator is 200 in the current year. What happened to real GDP?

$$\text{Real GDP} = \frac{\text{Nominal GDP}}{\text{GDP deflator}} \times 100$$

$$= \frac{2,000}{200} \times 100 = 100 \times 100 = 1,000$$

Real GDP remained at a level of 1000. If you're still confused about the difference between a change in GDP and a change in real GDP, please see the Extra Help box, "Read Only if You're Still Confused."

In recent years which grew faster—GDP or real GDP? *Think* about it. OK, what's your answer?

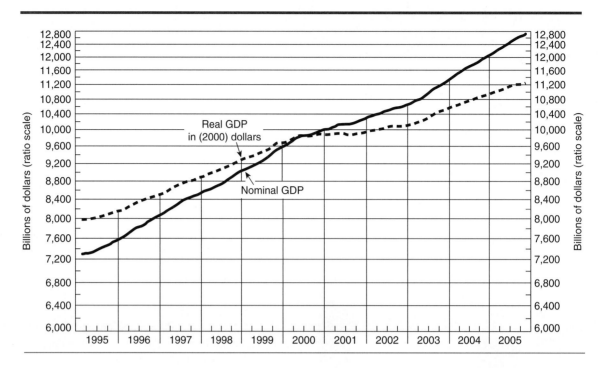

F*igure* 7

Nominal GDP and Real GDP, 1995–2005
Source: Economic Indicators, January 2006.

I hope you said, "GDP." That's because GDP was pushed up not just by rising output but by rising prices as well. Figure 7 illustrates that point. Because real GDP is measured in dollars of the year 2000, GDP and real GDP are equal in that year. You'll notice that in the years preceding 2000, real GDP was higher than GDP, and that after 2000, GDP was higher.

Here's a trick question. Suppose way in the future, the base year is 2050. In 2051 GDP rises more slowly than real GDP. What must have happened?

If GDP measures changes in output and prices, and real GDP measures changes in output, what *must* have happened to prices in 2051? They must have fallen. When there's a widespread decline in prices (which is called deflation), then GDP rises more slowly than real GDP.

International GDP Comparisons

Which country has the world's largest GDP? I hope you didn't forget that the United States does. Figure 8 shows the 2005 GDPs of the world's nine trillion-dollar economies.

Different countries use different national income accounting systems, and international exchange rates fluctuate (we'll take up international exchange rates in the last chapter of this book). Hence GDP comparisons among countries cannot be made with great precision. Yet it's reasonable to say that such comparisons do give us fairly close approximations.

Per Capita Real GDP

You may still be wondering, how are we doing in comparison to other countries? And how are we doing right now, compared to how we were doing 15 years ago—or 50 years ago?

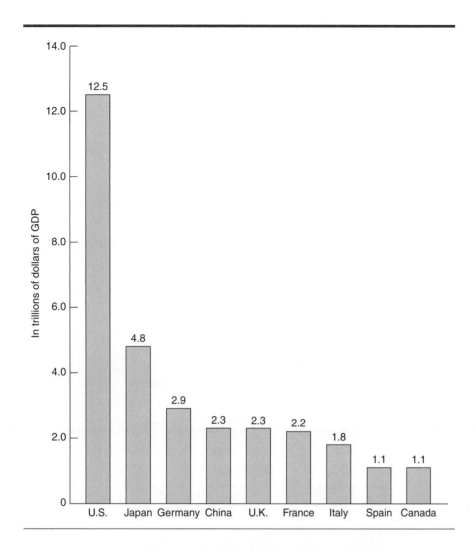

F*igure* 8

Trillion Dollar Economies, 2005
China, which has the most secretive
national income accounting system
of these trillion dollar economies,
may well have a much larger GDP
than shown here. By some measures
it is even larger than Japan's.
Source: http://en.wikipedia.org/wiki/
List_of_countries_by_GDP_(nominal).

GDP may be used to compare living standards among various countries or living standards during different time periods within one country. Such comparisons would usually be on a per capita (or per person) basis. Per capita GDP = GDP/Population. In the United States, per capita GDP in 2005 was:

$$\text{Per capita GDP} = \frac{\text{GDP}}{\text{Population}} = \frac{\$12,479,000,000,000}{300,000,000} = \$41,597$$

This means that in 2005 we produced \$41,597 worth of final goods and services for every man, woman, and child in this country.

To compare 2005 per capita GDP with that of another year, we would have to correct for inflation. In other words, we really need to revise our formula:

$$\text{Per capita real GDP} = \frac{\text{Real GDP}}{\text{Population}}$$

Per capita real GDP = Real GDP/Population

How does our per capita real GDP compare with earlier years? Just take a look at Table 3. Since World War II per capita real GDP has tripled. The calculation of per capita real GDP is shown in the accompanying Advanced Work box.

How valid are per capita real GDP comparisons over time? Over the short run, say, up to 10 years, they are quite valid. But comparisons over 20, 30, or 40 years become

Per capita real GDP comparisons over time

ADVANCED WORK

Calculating Per Capita Real GDP

Earlier in the chapter we worked out several problems in which we converted GDP into real GDP. And we've just done some per capita GDP problems. So what's left to do? Calculating per capita real GDP.

Suppose our GDP were to rise from $12 trillion in 2006 to $18 trillion in 2016, when the GDP deflator is 120. And suppose that our population rose from 280 million in 2006 to 300 million in 2016. What we want to find is (1) How much is per capita real GDP in 2016, and (2) By what percentage did per capita real GDP rise between 2006 and 2016?

See if you can work this out. I would suggest doing this problem in four steps: (1) Find real GDP in 2016; (2) find per capita real GDP in 2016; (3) find per capita real GDP for 2006; and (4) find the percentage rise in per capita real GDP between 2006 and 2016.

Solution:

(1) $\text{Real GDP}_{2016} = \dfrac{\text{Nominal GDP}}{\text{GDP deflator}} \times 100$

$= \dfrac{\dfrac{150}{\cancel{18,000}}}{\dfrac{\cancel{120}}{1}} \times 100$

$= 15,000$

(2) $\begin{aligned}\text{Per capita}\\ \text{real GDP}_{2016}\end{aligned} = \dfrac{\text{Real GDP}_{2016}}{\text{Population}_{2016}} = \dfrac{15,000}{.3} = \$50,000$

(3) $\begin{aligned}\text{Per capita}\\ \text{real GDP}_{2006}\end{aligned} = \dfrac{\text{Real GDP}_{2006}}{\text{Population}_{2006}} = \dfrac{12,000}{.280}$

$= \dfrac{6000}{.14} = \dfrac{3000}{.07} = \$42,857$

(4) $\begin{aligned}\text{Percentage}\\ \text{change}\end{aligned} = \dfrac{\text{Change}}{\text{Original number}} = \dfrac{\$7,143}{42,857} = 16.7\%$

TABLE 3	Per Capita Real GDP, Selected Years, 1776–2005 (*in 2005 dollars*)	
Year	Period	
1776	Revolutionary War	$ 1,630
1917–19	World War I	7,094
1941–45	World War II	13,183
1969	Vietnam War	21,140
1989	Pre-1990s boom	28,370
2005	Latest year available	41,597

Sources: *Economic Report of the President*, 2006; *Survey of Current Business*, February 2006; *Federal Reserve Bank of Dallas Annual Report*, 2001.

---

more and more like comparing apples and oranges, or, more to the point, like comparing video games and pocket calculators with nine-inch RCA TVs and those big old office adding machines whose lever you pulled every time you entered a number. Or like comparing Ford T-birds with Model-T Fords. Yale economists have calculated that under 30 percent of the goods and services consumed at the end of the 20th century were variants of the goods and services produced 100 years earlier.

International per capita real GDP comparisons

Per capita real GDP is not an accurate measure of international differences in production levels, but it does provide a rough measure. Comparisons of countries at similar stages of economic development are much more accurate, however, than comparisons of countries at different stages.

How does our per capita GDP compare with those of other leading industrial nations? Thirty years ago, we were clearly number one. By the late 1980s, however,

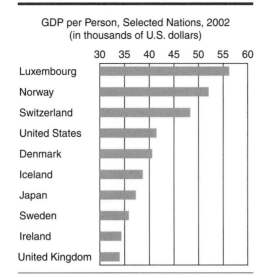

GDP per Person, Selected Nations, 2002
(in thousands of U.S. dollars)

Figure 9

Per Capita GDP of the World's
Ten Richest Countries, 2005
Although the United States is not
number one, we clearly have one of
the highest living standards in the
world. International comparisons for
per capita GDP are at least
somewhat suspect because of
varying national income accounting
systems as well as fluctuations of
foreign exchange rates.
Source: http://www.finfacts.com/biz10/
globalworldincomepercapita.htm.

we had probably lost our lead. As you can see in Figure 9, Luxembourg, Norway, and Switzerland have surpassed us. But using an alternate measure, the World Bank placed the United States second behind Luxembourg in terms of actual living standard.

Shortcomings of GDP as a Measure of National Economic Well-Being

Production That Is Excluded

Household Production   Household production consists mainly of the work done by homemakers—care of children, cleaning, shopping, and cooking. Were a housekeeper hired to do these tasks, this would be counted in GDP. Were two homemakers to work for each other as housekeepers (why, I don't know), their work would be counted in GDP. So why not count homemakers' work in their own homes? Because no money changes hands. No payments are recorded.

If a man marries his housekeeper or his cook, the national dividend is diminished.

—A. C. Pigou,
Economics of Welfare

Food grown in backyard plots, home repairs, clothes made at home, and any other do-it-yourself goods and services that people make or do for themselves, their families, or their friends are not counted in GDP. (The National Gardening Association reports that about 35 million households have garden plots that produce over $1 billion worth of food. The most popular crop is tomatoes, which are grown on 85 percent of the plots.) When you buy these goods and services from other people, the goods and services are counted (assuming they are reported by the sellers as income).

For decades, market production has been replacing household production because of two trends. As more and more women with children have been joining the labor force, some household production has shifted to the marketplace. Mothers' child care has been replaced by daycare and preschool. Five decades ago the large majority of children and adults brought their lunch to school or work. Now, of course, when away from home, the overwhelming majority of Americans eat out, mainly at fast food restaurants. So what had been two mainstays of household production (and not counted in GDP)—child care and home-cooked meals—have been largely replaced by paid child care and restaurant meals (which *are* counted in GDP).

Closely related to household production is bartering, or exchange of services. I'll tutor your children in math if you fix my car. Or you'll paint your friend's house in exchange for her free legal advice. We're performing useful services, but no money is exchanged. While there's no way of quantifying how much all these services are worth, they surely must be worth tens of billions of dollars. But none of this is counted in our GDP.

Illegal Production   Illegal goods and services are not counted in GDP. The big three—dope, prostitution, and gambling—are ignored even though people spend hundreds of billions on these goods and services. Of course, if you place a bet at a racetrack or an offtrack betting parlor, it is legal and counts in GDP. But a bet placed with a bookie is illegal. If you play the state lottery, your bet is counted toward GDP, but not if you play the numbers.

California is our leading agricultural state. Do you know its number one crop? Lettuce? Grapes? Citrus fruit? Sorry, it's none of the above. California's number one crop is grass—that's right, grass, as in marijuana. It is also the number one cash crop in Kentucky, Tennessee, and West Virginia. How much do Americans spend on illegal drugs? Estimates vary widely, but it is likely that more than $100 billion a year is spent on heroin and cocaine alone.

The Underground Economy   In every large city, on country roads, in flea markets, and even in suburban malls, there are people selling everything from watches to watermelons, and from corn to collectibles. Chances are, the proceeds of these sales are not reported to the government. Not only are no taxes paid, but the sales are not reflected in GDP.

Some of the items sold were stolen, but most are simply goods produced without the government's knowledge. Together with illegal goods and services, these markets form a vast underground economy. How vast? Maybe 10 or 15 percent of GDP. Who knows? How much of *your* income is spent in the underground economy? Or perhaps I should be asking, how much of your income *comes* from the underground economy? (See the box, "Pirated CDs and Videos.")

Our underground economy is not composed of only the street peddlers, cabdrivers, and low-life entrepreneurs who underreport their incomes. Oh no. The underground economy gets a very nice class of people—doctors, dentists, lawyers, and even, heaven forbid, accountants. In fact, there is a whole branch of accounting dedicated to the underground

Pirated CDs and Videos

Not everything sold on the street "fell off the truck."* A lot of those "designer" clothing items are illegal "knockoffs" of the real thing. What about those $5 CDs and $10 videos? Where do *they* come from?

Hollywood producers were amazed to find videos of their films being sold in the street just days after they opened and months before their own videos were released. The mystery was easily solved. When the films opened, people with camcorders would seat themselves just off the center aisles of the theaters and tape the films. These tapes would then be reproduced in quantity, put in authentic-looking jackets, and sold on the street.

Pirating CDs is even easier. For an investment of about $3,000, anyone can buy a "CD burner" and copy CDs onto blank disks called CD-recordables, or CD-Rs, through a digital process that maintains the quality of the recording. Since CD-Rs cost just a dollar, there's a nice

$4 markup when the CDs are sold by street peddlers. Meanwhile the customer gets a $15 CD of Britney Spears, TLC, the Backstreet Boys, or Puff Daddy for just five bucks. The only ones who lose are the record companies, the recording artists, and the government (assuming that no income is declared and no sales taxes are paid).

If you download music on your computer, especially if you use the popular file-sharing program called KaZaA, you may be guilty of copyright infringement. And what if you share these files with your friends? Then welcome to the underground economy. It would be a fair assumption that millions of American families have at least one member employed in the underground economy.

*A euphemism for goods that are stolen.

economy. It's called creative accounting. Often it involves keeping three separate sets of books—one for your creditors (showing an inflated profit), one for the government, and one for yourself, so you know how you're doing.

The underground economy adds hundreds of billions of dollars of goods and services to our national output. In addition, it is a safety valve, a generator of jobs and business opportunities that provide a great deal of economic support to the poor and near-poor. Go into any low-income housing project and you'll discover that many people are engaged in some underground economic activity—whether doing hairstyling, fixing cars, or providing child care.

Illegal immigrants are heavily employed in activities that can easily be conducted off the books. Tens of thousands of women work in garment sweatshops, often for substantially less than the legal minimum wage of $5.15 an hour. In New York you'll often find illegal immigrants peddling T-shirts and mood rings on the sidewalk in front of the Immigration and Naturalization Service office.

If our underground economy is, say, 10 or 15 percent of our GDP, we are underestimating our GDP by as much as 15 percent. But that's tiny compared to the underground economies of such countries as Egypt, Nigeria, and Thailand, which are about three-quarters the size of the official GDP. In other countries, such as Mexico, the Philippines, Peru, and Russia, the underground economy is about half the size of the official economy. So when we make international comparisons, we are seriously underestimating the GDP of these countries.

Let's step back for a minute and look once again at our definition of GDP: *the nation's expenditure on all the final goods and services produced during the year at market prices.*

What exactly is production? What we produce? For once economists are in agreement and quite clear about what something means. *Production is any good or service that people are willing to pay for.* And that means anything!

You go to a concert and fall asleep. How much was your ticket? $20? That was $20 worth of production.

You went to a brilliant lecture on the future of the universe. It was free. The speaker wasn't paid. No production.

You grow tomatoes in your backyard for your family's consumption. No production.

You take a course in philosophy. The professor walks into the room and lies down on the floor in the front of the class. This happens all term. How much tuition did you pay to take this course? That's how much production took place.

Let's put a number on the production of the underground economy. Edgar L. Feige, a retired economics professor at the University of Wisconsin, is an authority on the underground economy. He estimates that unreported income in the U.S. more than doubled during the 1990s, reaching $1.25 trillion in 2000, more than one-seventh of our national income.

The problem we have, then, is an inconsistency between the definition of GDP and the way it is compiled by the U.S. Department of Commerce. There's a lot of stuff going on out there that the department misses. The government not only refuses to count the underground economy—legal *or* illegal—but it will not even admit its existence. The bottom line is that it does not go into GDP, even as an estimate. So we are grossly (no pun intended) undercounting GDP.

Production is any good or service that people are willing to pay for.

Treatment of Leisure Time

GDP does not take leisure time into account. We have no way of telling if the people of a country enjoy a 30-hour week or have to work 60 hours a week. In the United States recent immigrant groups, whether the Mexicans or Pakistanis in the 1990s, the Vietnamese and Koreans in the 1970s and 1980s, the Cubans in the 1960s, the eastern and southern Europeans from the 1880s to the 1920s, or the Irish in the 1840s, have been resented for putting in longer hours than native-born Americans. For these immigrants long hours were necessary for survival, not only in America, but in their native lands.

The rice farmer in Egypt, the factory worker in Mexico, and the manual laborer in India do not have seven-hour workdays, paid sick leave, long vacations, 10 paid holidays, and a couple of days off for Christmas shopping.

Until the close of World War II, most workers still put in five and a half or six days a week. In 1900 the 10-hour day was common, and when you wanted to take a vacation, if your boss liked you, he reached into his pocket and gave you $5 spending money. The average workweek in the United States, as in the rest of the industrial world, has gradually declined.

The decline in the average workweek

In his novel, *The Plot Against America,* Philip Roth described the daily lives of people in the years before World War II. For most adults in those times, there *was* no such thing as leisure time.

> The men worked fifty, sixty, even seventy or more hours a week; the women worked all the time, with little assistance from labor-saving devices, washing laundry, ironing shirts, mending socks, turning collars, sewing on buttons, mothproofing woolens, polishing furniture, sweeping and washing floors, washing windows, cleaning sinks, tubs, toilets, and stoves, vacuuming rugs, nursing the sick, shopping for food, cooking meals, feeding relatives, tidying closets and drawers, overseeing paint jobs and household repairs, arranging for religious observances, paying bills and keeping the family's books while simultaneously attending to their children's health, clothing, cleanliness, schooling, nutrition, conduct, birthdays, discipline, and morale. A few women labored alongside their husbands in the family-owned stores on the nearby shopping streets, assisted after school and on Saturdays by their older children, who delivered orders and tended stock and did the cleaning up.[3]

While the average workweek has declined, many more mothers with young children have gone to work. Back in 1960, 79 percent of all families with children had at least one stay-at-home parent. Forty years later, this percentage had fallen to just 28.

Human Costs and Benefits

Another problem with comparing our GDP with those of other countries, or with our own GDP in previous years, is that the physical and psychological costs of producing that GDP and any human benefits associated with producing it are ignored.

First the costs. The strain of commuting long distances along congested routes, the tedium, the dangers, the low status, and other unpleasant factors associated with certain jobs are some of the costs. Other jobs cause anxiety because the worker is always worrying about getting ahead or just getting along. Advertising account executives, air traffic controllers, and bomb squad members are all under the gun, so to speak, during most of their working hours. Economists call the psychological strain associated with work *psychic cost*. Psychic costs detract from one's enjoyment of a job, while *psychic income* adds to that enjoyment.

Psychic cost

There are also physical strains and benefits associated with work. Not only have we shifted nearly completely from human power to mechanical power, but the nature of work has also changed from farming and manufacturing to service jobs, most of which require no physical labor. This is not to say that there are no longer any jobs requiring physical labor or being performed under unpleasant circumstances. Just ask the people who work in toy, handbag, textile, or automobile factories. Or talk to coal miners, sandhogs, day laborers, printing plant employees, migrant farm workers, slaughterhouse workers, and police officers. Or watch the mail sorters who work the graveyard shift in a large post office.

Some people, on the other hand, really enjoy their jobs. Take actors. They are willing to hold all kinds of stopgap jobs—waitress, hotel clerk, theater doorman, short-order cook, office temporary—while waiting for that big chance. For most, of course, it never comes. In New York, where there are no more than 2,000 people who earn their entire livelihood from acting, there are tens of thousands of aspiring actors. Why are they

---

[3]Philip Roth, *The Plot Against America* (New York: Vintage Books, 2004), p. 3.

willing to buck such outrageous odds? Because they love acting. The *psychic income* from working in the theater—the roar of the grease paint, the smell of the crowd, the adulation, the applause—is the compensation they seek.

Finally, let's consider the physical benefits from work. Literally. My friend Marty, the gym teacher, is always in great shape. What do you expect? But I really want to talk about Mr. Spalter, a little bald-headed man who taught gym (how can you *teach* gym?) at Brooklyn's James Madison High School in the 1950s. The guy had to be at least 80. Anyway, Mr. Spalter could go up a 30-foot rope in less than 15 seconds—and do it in perfect form, with his legs exactly perpendicular to his body. The physical benefits of being a gym teacher, farmer, or a health club employee are obvious.[4]

Today's GDP is produced by an entirely different type of labor force doing different work from that of 50 or 100 years ago. And our labor force works very differently from those of developing countries. This makes GDP comparisons that much less valid.

What Goes into GDP?

Other problems with GDP as a measure of national economic well-being have to do with what goes into GDP. When a large part of our production goes toward national defense, police protection, pollution control devices, repair and replacement of poorly made cars and appliances, and cleanups of oil spills, a large GDP is not a good indicator of how we're doing. And if a large part of our labor force staffs the myriad bureaucracies of state, local, and federal governments, as well as those of the corporate world, we're not all that well off. GDP tells us how much we produce. We need to ask: How much of *what?*

We also need to ask about the production of new goods and services and about the improvement of product quality. Let's use television sets as an example. Very few American families had TV sets before the late 1940s, and those who did had 9″, 13″, or the "big screen" 17″ black-and-white sets. We counted the $600 17″ black-and-white Philco, RCA, or Dumont (American TV-makers back in prehistoric times) at its selling price in the 1948 GDP. But the $600 Samsung 28″ ultra-flat-screen stereo color TV also counts for just $600 in the 2006 GDP, even though television sets today are vastly superior to those of the late 1940s. Of course the entire mix of goods and services that go into GDP is very different from what was available just 20 or 30 years ago. Personal computers, cell phones, DVD players, MRIs, laser surgery, CDs, disposable contact lenses, and faxes were not yet even part of our vocabulary, let alone available to the American consumer.

In general, the problem with using GDP as a measure of national economic well-being is that GDP is just one number, and no single number can possibly provide us with all the information we need. Just as a single number—whether it's your pulse, your weight, your cholesterol, or your blood sugar level—cannot provide a comprehensive measure of your health, neither can a single number such as GDP, accurately measure our economic well-being. So the next time you hear economists chanting "We're number *one*," with respect to our GDP, just remind them that GDP is only a partial and imperfect measure of our economic performance.

Current Issue: GDP or GPI?

As you remember, Hurricane Katrina not only caused a huge loss of life, property, and jobs on the Gulf Coast, but it disrupted our oil supply and wreaked havoc with shipping. So you would think it slowed the growth of real GDP. But the massive federal spending on hurricane relief and recovery far outweighed the negative economic effects of the

---

[4]Mr. Spalter must have been doing *something* right. Two Madison graduates have won the Nobel Prize in economics. Robert Solow, who graduated in 1940, won it in 1987, and Gary Becker, class of 1948, won it in 1992. Thus the high school I attended has had more economics Nobel Prize winners than any other high school in the country. And who knows, maybe lightning will strike a third time. If you're curious, I graduated in 1957.

storm. So if we went strictly by our real GDP figures, we might conclude that the worst natural disaster in U.S. history was actually good for our economy.

There is something wrong with our national income accounting system if a natural disaster like Hurricane Katrina ends up being recorded as a positive, despite the suffering and material loss left in its wake. Similarly, the $6–7 billion a month we spend on the Iraq War is simply added into our GDP, although it certainly builds no schools, highways, or oil refineries on American soil.

GDP is compiled from our recorded market transactions. But as we noted earlier in this chapter, there are a lot of activities that don't go through the marketplace, and often are not recorded. There is no accounting for leisure time, household production, underground economic production, and the psychic costs and benefits of various jobs. In addition, the environmental damage committed not just by our production of goods and services, but our very lifestyle, don't figure in the calculation of GDP. Nor are the nation's health or its distribution of income. What GDP measures as growth is merely increased spending, but it doesn't indicate whether the spending is good or bad. GDP rises with every oil spill, increase in air pollution, and nearly every other environmental disaster.

The Genuine Progress Index (sometimes called the Genuine Progress Indicator) is an alternate measure of our national well-being. Using GDP as its starting point, the GPI adds in sectors usually excluded from the market economy such as housework and volunteer work, and subtracts crime, natural resource depletion, and the loss of leisure time. It also adds in crucial contributions of the environment, such as clean air and water, moderate climate, and protection from the sun's burning rays. Agricultural activity that uses replenishing water resources, such as river runoff, will score a higher GPI than the same level of agricultural activity that drastically lowers the water table by pumping irrigation water from wells.

One of the developers of the GPI, Philip Lawn, came up with this list of the "costs" of economic activity, which need to be subtracted from GDP:

- Cost of resource depletion.
- Cost of crime.
- Cost of ozone depletion.
- Cost of family breakdown.
- Cost of air, water, and noise pollution.
- Loss of farmland.
- Loss of wetlands.

The next step in the calculation of the GPI is to come up with dollar figures for all the costs and benefits of economic activity. Reasonably accurate estimates may be made for housework, child- and elder-care, home repairs, and volunteer work by determining how much people are paid to do this work in the private sector. But how do you quantify the cost of ozone depletion or of family breakdown?

According to GPI calculations, our per capita GPI was less than one quarter of the official 2005 per capita GDP of $41,597. And real per capita GPI has fallen by about 40 percent since the early 1970s. What do *you* think about these conclusions?

Questions for Further Thought and Discussion

1. Suppose we want to compare this year's GDP with those of previous years. As we go back in time—to 1980, to 1970, to 1960, and to still earlier years—what happens to the validity of these comparisons? Why does this happen?

2. If our GDP rose from 11,000 to 11,500, there could be a few different explanations. List each of these possibilities.

3. Which has been increasing faster, GDP or real GDP? Explain your answer.

4. GDP is not an ideal measure of national economic well-being. Make a list of all the things you would do to improve this concept. Include in your list the goods and services that GDP does not count.

5. "Americans enjoy the highest standard of living in the world." Discuss why this statement is not perfectly accurate.

6. Under what circumstances could real GDP for a given year be greater than GDP for that same year? For example, if 2015 were the base year and 2016 were the current year, how could real GDP in 2016 exceed GDP for 2016?

7. Explain how GDP is affected by the sale of
   a. a new house.
   b. an hour session with a physical trainer.
   c. 1,000 shares of AT&T.
   d. an antique rolltop desk.

8. If you were comparing the economic well-being of two countries and had a choice of using one of the following four measures, which one would you choose and why would you choose it?
   a. GDP
   b. Real GDP
   c. Per capita GDP
   d. Per capita real GDP

9. Do you think we should switch from using GDP to GPI as our basic measure of national well-being?

W*orkbook*   for Chapter 9

Name _____   Date _____

Multiple-Choice Questions

Circle the letter that corresponds to the best answer.

1. Nearly all of our output is produced by _____.
   a) the government
   b) private business firms
   c) individual consumers

2. GDP may be found by _____.
   a) adding together money spent on goods and services and incomes received by the factors of production
   b) subtracting incomes received by the factors of production from the money spent on goods and services
   c) subtracting the money spent on goods and services from the incomes received by the factors of production
   d) adding the money spent on final goods and services

3. Which equation is correct?
   a) GDP − Depreciation = NDP
   b) NDP − Depreciation = GDP
   c) GDP + NDP = Depreciation

4. Each of the following is an indirect business tax except _____.
   a) sales tax
   b) excise tax
   c) business property tax
   d) corporate income tax

5. If Mexico had a GDP of 700 and depreciation of 100, while Italy had a GDP of 710 and a depreciation of 180, most economists would say that _____.
   a) Italy had a better year
   b) Mexico had a better year
   c) there is no way of determining which country had a better year

6. Pirated CDs and videos are _____.
   a) part of the underground economy
   b) sold only in other countries
   c) sold by recording studios and Hollywood movie producers
   d) encouraged by the federal government because their manufacture and sale provides tens of thousands of jobs to marginal workers

7. In declining order of size, which of these is the proper ranking?
   a) GDP, NDP, national income
   b) NDP, GDP, national income
   c) National income, GDP, NDP
   d) National income, NDP, GDP
   e) GDP, national income, NDP
   f) NDP, national income, GDP

8. Wages, salaries, and fringe benefits constitute about _____ of domestic income.
   a) 25 percent   c) 70 percent
   b) 50 percent   d) 95 percent

9. The largest sector of GDP is _____.
   a) investment   c) net exports
   b) government spending   d) consumer spending

10 Which is not counted in GDP?
   a) A Social Security check sent to a retiree
   b) Government spending on highway building
   c) Money spent on an airline ticket
   d) Money spent by a company to build a new office park

11. Which one of these goes into the investment sector of GDP?
   a) The purchase of a new factory
   b) The purchase of 100 shares of Intel stock
   c) The purchase of a 10-year-old office building
   d) The purchase of a U.S. savings bond

12. When there is inflation _____.

    a) real GDP increases faster than GDP

    b) GDP increases faster than real GDP

    c) GDP and real GDP increase at the same rate

    d) there is no way of telling whether GDP or real GDP increases faster

13. If GDP rose from $6 trillion to $9 trillion and prices rose by 50 percent over this period, _____.

    a) real GDP fell by 100 percent

    b) real GDP fell by 50 percent

    c) real GDP stayed the same

    d) real GDP rose by 50 percent

    e) real GDP rose by 100 percent

14. Which of the following is counted in GDP?

    a) Household production   c) Leisure time

    b) Illegal production   d) Government spending

15. Which statement is true?

    a) There is an inconsistency between the definition of GDP and the way it is compiled by the U.S. Department of Commerce.

    b) GDP is an accurate measure of production in the United States.

    c) U.S. GDP figures include estimates for production in the underground economy.

    d) Our GDP would grow faster if we had less inflation.

16. Suppose the GDP of Argentina were 10 times that of Uruguay. Which statement would be most accurate?

    a) There is no way of comparing the output of Argentina and Uruguay.

    b) Argentina's output is greater than that of Uruguay.

    c) Argentina's output is probably around 10 times that of Uruguay.

    d) Argentina's output is 10 times that of Uruguay.

17. Which statement is true?

    a) GDP tells us how much we produce as well as what we produce.

    b) GDP tells us neither how much we produce nor what we produce.

    c) GDP tells us what we produce.

    d) GDP tells us how much we produce.

18. We would like to compare real per capita GDP. Which would be the most valid comparison?

    a) China in 2004 and Thailand in 2004

    b) Germany in 2002 and 2004

    c) The United States in 1980 and 2004

    d) Nigeria in 1960 and the United Kingdom in 1990

19. Per capita real GDP is found by _____.

    a) dividing population by real GDP

    b) dividing real GDP by population

    c) adding population to real GDP

    d) multiplying real GDP by population

20. Which statement is true?

    a.) Over longer and longer periods of time, comparisons of real per capita GDP become increasingly valid.

    b) Over the short run, say, up to 10 years, comparisons of per capita real GDP are quite valid.

    c) International comparisons of per capita real GDP may be made with less caution than comparisons over time within a given country.

    d) None of these statements is true.

21. Since World War II our per capita real GDP has _____.

    a) stayed about the same

    b) risen by 50 percent

    c) tripled

    d) risen by almost 700 percent

22. Which statement is true?

    a) The Japanese have a higher standard of living than we do.

    b) The Japanese have a larger GDP than we do.

    c) The typical Japanese family has more living space than the typical American family.

    d) None of these statements is true.

23. $C + I + G + X_n$ is _____ approach(es) to GDP.

    a) the flow-of-income

    b) the expenditures

    c) both the expenditures and the flow-of-income

    d) neither the expenditures nor the flow-of-income

24. Which statement is true?

   a) Consumption as a percentage of GDP is higher today than it was in 1979.

   b) Government purchases are about 30 percent of GDP.

   c) Real GDP has risen faster than GDP since 1999.

   d) Consumption is a little over half of GDP.

25. Which is the most accurate statement about the underground economy?

   a) It adds hundreds of billions of dollars to our GDP.

   b) It provides employment to hundreds of thousands of illegal immigrants.

   c) It is run almost entirely by organized crime.

   d) It makes the rich richer and the poor poorer.

26. Which would be the most valid statement?

   a) The American standard of living is, by far, the highest in the world.

   b) The standard of living of the average American is about twice that of the average Russian.

   c) The standard of living of the average American is comparable to that of the average person in Switzerland, Germany, and Japan.

   d) If the underground economy, illegal production, and household production were accurately measured and added to GDP, our GDP would probably rise by less than 1 percent.

27. Which is the most accurate statement?

   a) We may be underestimating our GDP by as much as 50 percent by not taking into account the underground economy.

   b) Bartered goods and services are generally counted in GDP.

   c) Within the next five years, China will have a larger GDP than the United States.

   d) Although GDP has many shortcomings, it is still a very useful economic concept.

28. GDP is _____ GDI.

   a) much higher than

   b) about the same size as

   c) much lower than

29. Which of the following is the most accurate statement?

   a) On a per capita basis, GPI is greater than GDP.

   b) GPI has more than doubled over the last 40 years.

   c) The difference between GDP and GPI is the annual rate of inflation.

   d) GPI is about one quarter of GDP on a per capita basis.

30. Which one of the following statements would you agree with?

   a) GDP includes only market transactions, while GPI includes both market transactions and other factors affecting our national well-being.

   b) GPI is a very accurate measure of national well-being.

   c) As a measure of national well-being, GDP has no major shortcomings.

   d) GDP takes into account many more economic, social, and environmental activities than GPI.

Fill-In Questions

1. The nation's expenditure on all the final goods and services produced during the year at market prices is _____.

2. Nearly all our goods and services are produced by _____.

3. GDP − _____ = NDP.

4. NDP − _____ = national income.

5. A tax with your name on it is a(n) _____ tax.

6. A sales tax is a(n) _____ tax.

7. GDP includes only payments for _____ _____.

8. _____ measures total production in one year.

9. Goods and services produced without the government's knowledge are part of the _____ economy.

10. Economists call any good or service that people are willing to pay for _____.

11. Economists call the psychological strain associated with work _____.

12. Per capita real GDP is found by dividing _____ by _____.

13. Over time, per capita real GDP comparisons become _____ valid.

14. If Diane Hilgers had been alive during the American Revolution, her standard of living would have been about _____ percent of what it would be today.

15. Had Anne Gindorff Heinz been alive during World War I, her standard of living would have been about _____ percent of what it would be today.

Problems

1. Given the following information, calculate NDP and national income: GDP = $5 trillion, Indirect business taxes = $300 billion, and Depreciation = $500 billion.

2. If national income is $3 trillion, depreciation is $400 billion, and indirect business taxes are $300 billion, how much are NDP and GDP?

3. If wages, salaries, and fringe benefits are $4 trillion, profit is $500 billion, interest is $300 billion, rent is $100 billion, and depreciation is $600 billion, how much is National Income?

4. If wages, salaries, and fringe benefits are $3 trillion, profit is $400 billion, interest is $200 billion, rent is $100 billion, depreciation is $400 billion, and indirect business taxes are $300 billion, how much is National Income, NDP, and GDP?

5. If consumption spending is $3 trillion, investment is $800 billion, government spending is $1 trillion, imports are $1.2 trillion, and exports are $900 billion, how much is GDP?

6. If consumption is $3.8 trillion, investment is $1.1 trillion, government spending is $1.1 trillion, imports are $1.6 trillion, and exports are $1.4 trillion, how much is GDP?

7. GDP rises from $4 trillion in 1986, the base year, to $5 trillion in 1989. The GDP deflator in 1989 is 120. Find real GDP in 1989. Find the percentage increase in real GDP between 1986 and 1989.

8. GDP rises from $5 trillion in 1990, the base year, to $7 trillion in 1994. The GDP deflator in 1994 is 140. Find real GDP in 1994. Find the percentage increase in real GDP between 1990 and 1994.

9. GDP rises from $20 trillion in 2017 to $21 trillion in 2018, but the price level remains the same. (a) How much is real GDP in 2018? (b) By what percentage did real GDP rise between 2017 and 2018?

10. Find per capita GDP when population is 100 million and GDP is $2 trillion.

11. Find per capita GDP when GDP is $1.5 trillion and population is 300 million.

12. Suppose our GDP were to rise from $10 trillion in 2007 to $20 trillion in 2027, when the GDP deflator is 125. And suppose that our population rose from 300 million in 2007 to 330 million in 2027. (a) How much is per capita real GDP in 2027? (b) By what percentage did per capita real GDP rise between 2007 and 2027? [Hint: Do the problem in four steps: (1) Find real GDP in 2027; (2) find per capita real GDP in 2027; (3) find per capita real GDP for 2007; and (4) find the percentage rise in per capita real GDP between 2007 and 2027.]

13. Suppose the GDP of South Korea were to rise from $600 billion in 2005 to $1.5 trillion in 2015, when the GDP deflator is 150. And suppose that Korea's population rose from 40 million in 2005 to 50 million in 2015. (a) How much is per capita real GDP in 2015? (b) By what percentage did per capita real GDP rise between 2005 and 2015?

14. If GDP rises from $10 trillion to $10.4 trillion and real GDP rises from $10 trillion to $10.3 trillion, find the percentage change in the GDP deflator.

15. If real GDP goes up by 3.7 percent and the GDP deflator goes up by 1.6 percent, find the percentage change in GDP.

16. Suppose that in 2007 we were to have a deflationary recession. If GDP in 2006 were $12 trillion predict GDP and real GDP in 2007.

Chapter 10

Economic Fluctuations, Unemployment, and Inflation

Economics is not called the dismal science for nothing. Right now we'll be examining some of the problems that have contributed to this reputation—recessions, inflation, and unemployment. It would be wonderful if our economy could grow steadily at, say, 3 percent a year, with no recessions, no inflation, and no unemployment. But as you know, the real world is a lot more dismal.

Still, for every problem, there may be a solution. For much of the following six chapters, we'll consider how to ameliorate, if not solve, the problems of recession, inflation, and unemployment.

CHAPTER OBJECTIVES

In this chapter we will:

- Examine the business cycle.
- Consider various business cycle theories.
- Show how economic forecasting is done.
- Learn how the unemployment rate is computed.

- Look at the types of unemployment.
- Construct a consumer price index.
- Consider the theories of inflation.
- Learn about the misery index.

Economic Fluctuations

Figure 1 shows the country's economic record since 1960, but before we are in a position to analyze that record, we need a little background information on the business cycle.

Is There a Business Cycle?

Economists and noneconomists have long debated whether there is a business cycle. It all depends on what is meant by the term. If *business cycle* is defined as increases and decreases in business activity of fixed amplitude that occur regularly at fixed intervals, then there is no business cycle. In other words, business activity does have its ups and downs, but some ups are higher than other ups and some downs are lower than others. Furthermore, there is no fixed length to the cycle. For example, as Figure 1 shows, the United States went for nearly the entire decade of the 1960s without a recession but had back-to-back recessions in 1980 and 1981.

Q: Why did God create economists?
A: In order to make weather forecasters look good.

217

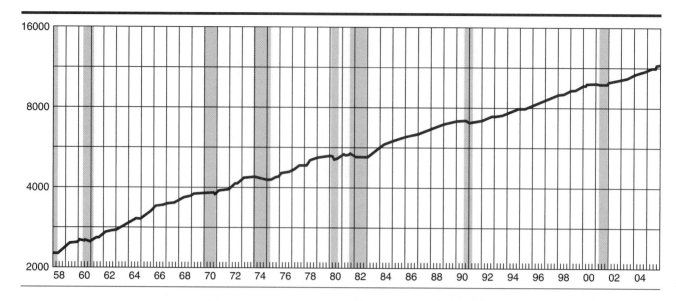

F*igure* 1
Real GDP 1958–2005, in 2000 dollars
Source: U.S. Dept. of Commerce, in *Business Cycle Indicators,* March 2006.

Upswings don't die of old age.
    —Economics saying

Since November 1982 we have had only two recessions (through 2003). The economic expansion that began in March 1991 is the longest in history. Can we say that our economy is finally recession-proof and that the business cycle is obsolete? I'm going to really stick my neck out on *this* one and make a prediction. Every expansion will end. The only question is when.

If we define the business cycle as alternating increases and decreases in the level of business activity of varying amplitude and length, then there is definitely a business cycle. What goes up will eventually come down, and what goes down will rise again.

Cycle Turning Points: Peaks and Troughs

Peaks

Troughs

At the end of economic expansion, business activity reaches a peak. At the peak real GDP, or output, reaches a maximum and then begins to fall. When the economy bottoms out, a trough occurs. From this low point, economic recovery sets in, and eventually most sectors share in the expansion.

Business cycles may be measured from peak to peak, or trough to trough. As we have noted, these cycles vary greatly in amplitude and length. Note the severity of the 1973–75 and 1981–82 recessions in Figure 1 and the varying lengths of the cycles shown in the same graph.

Since the end of World War II, the economy's expansions have been as brief as 16 months or as long as 10 years. The contractions fall into a much narrower range—from 6 to 16 months (see Table 1). And so we may conclude that, like snowflakes, no two business cycles are exactly alike. Most of the 10 post-World War II recessions have been mild and brief. But two of them—November 1973–March 1975 and July 1981–November 1982—were relatively severe and lengthy. Both were 16 months long, while every other recession lasted less than a year. During both recessions, real GDP fell by about 3 percent. In the aftermath of these two recessions, our unemployment rate reached its highest levels since the Great Depression.

A recession is when you get socks and underwear for Christmas.
    —Bob Rogers, cartoonist

When does an economic downturn qualify as a recession? In general if real GDP declines for two consecutive quarters, that's a recession. But it's not officially a recession until the Business Cycle Dating Committee of the National Bureau of Economic Research (a private research organization whose members include many prominent economists) says it is. These six gentlemen take a much more nuanced approach than just waiting for two quarterly declines in real GDP.

TABLE 1 Post-World War II Recessions*

Recession dates	Duration (months)	Percentage decline in real GDP	Peak unemployment rate
Nov. 1948–Oct. 1949	11	−1.7%	7.9%
July 1953–May 1954	10	−2.7	5.9
Aug. 1957–Apr. 1958	8	−1.2	7.4
Apr. 1960–Feb. 1961	10	−1.6	6.9
Dec. 1969–Nov. 1970	11	−0.6	5.9
Nov. 1973–Mar. 1975	16	−3.1	8.6
Jan. 1980–July 1980	6	−2.2	7.8
July 1981–Nov. 1982	16	−2.9	10.8
July 1990–Mar. 1991	8	−1.3	6.8
Mar. 2001–Nov. 2001	8	−0.5	6.0

*The February 1945–October 1945 recession began before the war ended in August 1945.

The committee uses four crucial barometers to determine if the economy has reached a peak, and will look at other data. The main measure is employment, based on nonfarm payrolls. The second is industrial production. The third is personal income minus government transfer payments, and the fourth is manufacturing and trade revenue.

Since October 2003 the committee began using estimates of monthly GDP. Figure 2 provides another look at the 10 recessions since World War II. As you can see, they vary in length from just 6 months up to 16 months. In fact, except for the 1973–75 and 1981–82 recessions, each lasted less than a year. And since 1982 we've had just two recessions.

The Conventional Three-Phase Business Cycle

We'll begin our analysis with the first peak in Figure 3. The decline that sets in after the peak is called a recession, which ends at the trough. Occasionally there is a false recovery when business activity turns upward for a few months but then turns down again. If the next low point is the lowest since the previous peak, then *that* is the trough.

Recovery begins at the trough, but the expansion must eventually reach the level of the previous peak. Occasionally business activity rises without reaching the previous peak; unless it does, it does not qualify as a recovery.

Once recovery definitely *has* set in, real GDP moves upward until it passes the level of the previous peak, when it enters the third phase of the cycle: prosperity. This phase does not necessarily mean there is full employment, or even that we are approaching full employment. As long as production (real GDP) is higher than it was during the previous peak, we are in the prosperity phase.

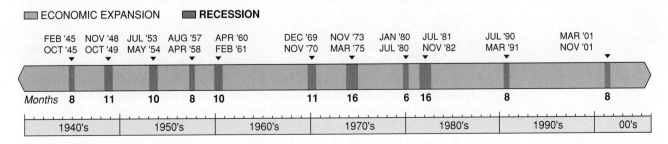

Figure 2

Recessions since 1945

Source: National Bureau of Economic Research.

Figure 3
Hypothetical Business Cycles
The three-phase business cycle runs from peak to peak, beginning with a recession, which ends at a trough, followed by a recovery. When the level of the previous peak is attained, prosperity sets in, continuing until a new peak is reached.

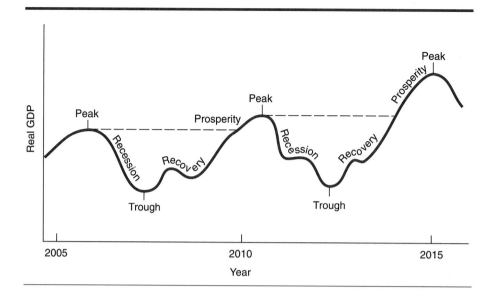

Some people say prosperity is when the prices of the things that you are selling are rising, and inflation is when the prices of things that you are buying are rising.

—Anonymous

What is the dividing line between recession and depression?

Prosperity is the second part of the economic expansion and is accompanied by rising production, falling unemployment, and often accelerating inflation. Sooner or later we reach a peak and the process starts all over—recession, recovery, and prosperity.

This is the conventional three-phase cycle. Some people talk of a fourth phase: depression. Although depressions are relatively rare—we have not had one since the 1930s—there is always talk about the possibility that a recession could turn into a depression.

What is the dividing line between a recession and a depression? There is no agreed-on or official definition. Obviously, an unemployment rate of 20 percent would be a depression. But would 10 percent qualify?

Perhaps the best definition was proposed by, among others, the late George Meany, longtime president of the AFL-CIO. He said that if his neighbor were unemployed, it would be a recession. If *he* were unemployed, it would be a depression!

Business Cycle Theories

I have stated that business cycles are inevitable; what goes up must come down, and what goes down must come back up. Although economists generally agree that business cycles exist, they have many competing theories explaining their causes. We'll briefly consider two types of theories: endogenous (internal) and exogenous (external).

Endogenous Theories

Innovation theory

These theories place the cause of business cycles within rather than outside the economy. We'll consider first the theory of innovations, which was advanced primarily by Joseph Schumpeter.

When a businessman attempts to market a new product such as a car or a television set, at first he will encounter resistance ("Get that contraption off the road—it's frightening my horses!"). But when others perceive the profits being made by the innovator, they will imitate his new product with their own versions, and production will soar. Eventually the market will be saturated—as it was by cars in 1929 and televisions in 1953—and an economic downturn will occur. The downturn continues until a new innovation takes hold and the process begins anew.

Psychological theory

A second endogenous theory is the psychological theory of alternating optimism and pessimism, which is really an example of a more general theory of the self-fulfilling prophecy. If businessowners are optimistic, they will invest in plant, equipment, and inventory. This will provide more jobs and result in more consumer spending, justifying still more investment, more jobs, and more spending. But eventually businessowners will turn pessimistic, perhaps because they figure this prosperity can't continue. As pessimism sets in, investment, jobs, and consumer spending all decline, and a recession begins. The contraction continues until businessowners figure that things have gone down so far, there's no place to go but back up again.

Still another endogenous theory is that of the inventory cycle. During economic recovery, as sales begin to rise, businessowners are caught short of inventory, so they raise their orders to factories, thus increasing factory employment. As factory workers are called back to work, they begin to spend more money, causing businessowners to order still more from factories. Eventually the owners are able to restock their inventories, so they cut back on factory orders. This causes layoffs, declining retail sales, further cutbacks in factory orders, and a general economic decline. The decline persists until inventory levels are depleted low enough for factory orders to increase once again.

Inventory cycle theory

Yet another endogenous theory of the business cycle is the monetary theory. When inflation threatens, the monetary authorities slow or stop the growth of the money supply. This causes a recession. When they are satisfied that inflation is no longer a problem—or if the recession they have caused has become even more of a concern than inflation—the monetary authorities allow the money supply to grow at a faster rate, which brings about economic recovery. The monetary theory may well explain the 1980 and 1981–82 recessions, when the Federal Reserve stepped heavily on the monetary brakes, as well as our subsequent recoveries, when monetary growth was increased. We'll have a lot more to say about monetary policy in Chapter 14.

Monetary theory

One last theory and we're out of here. The underconsumption or overproduction theory stipulates that our economy periodically produces more goods and services than people want or can afford. A variant is the overinvestment theory, which says that business firms periodically overinvest in plant and equipment.

Underconsumption theory

Exogenous Theories

Just as endogenous theories place the causes of the business cycle within the economy, exogenous theories place the causes of the business cycle outside the economy.

It has long been said that if the American economy catches a cold, many other economies catch pneumonia. The Chinese, Mexican, and Canadian economies are very dependent on American imports of their goods. If an American recession caused us to cut back sharply on imports, this could cause their own economies to go into recession. Let's call this the external demand shock theory.

Another external theory is the war theory. The production surge caused by preparation for war and war itself causes prosperity, and the letdown after war causes a recession. Our experiences before, during, and after World War II, the Korean War, and the Vietnam War seem to validate this theory.

The war theory

Although nearly all recessions have endogenous causes, the quadrupling of oil prices by the OPEC cartel in 1973 was the prime cause of the 1973–75 recession. We can call this the price shock theory. In this particular case, the price shock was exogenous.

Perhaps no single explanation, whether exogenous or endogenous, can explain each of the cycles we have experienced. The best we can do, then, is to treat each cycle separately, seeking causes that apply.

Business Cycle Forecasting

Who was the first person to forecast a business cycle? Here are a couple of hints. You can find him in the Book of Genesis and he made his forecast by interpreting the Pharaoh's dreams.

The Ten Leading Economic Indicators

1. **Average workweek of production workers in manufacturing**   When workers get less overtime, output may be declining.

2. **Average initial weekly claims for state unemployment insurance**   When first-time claims for unemployment insurance benefits rise, employment may be falling.

3. **New orders for consumer goods and materials**   When manufacturers receive smaller orders, they may cut back on output.

4. **Vendor performance (companies receiving slower deliveries from suppliers)**   Better on-time delivery by suppliers means they have a smaller backlog of orders.

5. **New orders for capital goods**   If these orders drop, then businesses are planning less output.

6. **New building permits issued**   This provides a good indication of how much construction activity there will be three or four months from now.

7. **Index of stock prices**   Declining stock prices may reflect declining prospects for corporate sales and profits.

8. **Money supply**   If the Federal Reserve slows the growth of the money supply, interest rates will rise, and it will be harder for businesses and individuals to borrow money.

9. **Spread between rates on 10-year Treasury bonds and Federal funds**   Long-term interest rates are usually much higher than short-term interest rates. Federal reserve policies designed to slow the economy raise short-term interest rates with little effect on long-term rates. So a smaller spread between short-term and long-term interest rates implies a restrictive monetary policy and a decline in output.

10. **Index of consumer expectations**   As consumers grow less confident about the future, they plan to make fewer major purchases.

An economist is an expert who will know tomorrow why the things he predicted yesterday didn't happen today.

—Laurence J. Peter,
Peter's Quotations

To err is human; to get paid for it is divine.

—William Freund,
economic consultant

We have two kinds of forecasters: Those who don't know . . . and those who don't know they don't know.

—John Kenneth Galbraith

In those dreams the Pharaoh saw seven fat cows and then seven lean cows. Joseph told the king that there would be seven fat years—years of good harvests—followed by seven lean years—years of very poor harvests. And sure enough, there were seven straight good harvests. During this period, some of the grain was set aside. When seven years of poor harvests followed, the Egyptians survived by consuming the grain they had stored.

Business cycle forecasting has come a long way over the intervening millennia, but its objective remains the same—forecasting the turning points of the business cycle.

The most widely used forecasting device is the index of leading economic indicators, which is compiled monthly by the Conference Board, a private business group. This series, which is a weighted average of 10 variables, is a valuable forecasting tool, particularly when used with caution.

The 10 leading indicators consist of variables that "lead" general economic activity by several months. (See the box, "The Ten Leading Economic Indicators.") When the index turns downward, particularly for two or three months in a row, there is a good chance the economy may be heading into a recession. However, as some pundits have put it, the index has predicted 13 of the last 5 recessions. In other words, the index may have turned downward for three or four months a total of 13 times, but in only 5 instances did a recession follow.

If the index moves steadily upward, there is virtually no chance of a recession in the next few months. But when it begins to move downward, watch out! A downturn *may* be at hand.

Similarly, when the index of leading economic indicators moves down steadily for 11 months in a row, as it did from April 1981 through March 1982, we were in a recession, but there was virtually no chance of an upturn until later in the year. And that's exactly what happened.

If economists could accurately forecast business cycle turning points—the peaks and troughs—then they're doing their job. But in a March 2001 survey, 95 percent of American economists said there would not be a recession. Then, in late 2001, that same gang predicted that real GDP would grow by just 0.1 percent in the first quarter of 2002, but it actually grew at an annual rate of 5 percent. It would be fair to say that economic forecasters aren't always right on the money.

Unemployment

The Problem

One of the most devastating experiences a person can have is to be out of work for a prolonged period. Most of us have been unemployed once or twice, but only those who have been unable to find work after looking for six to eight months, or even longer, really know that feeling of hopelessness and self-doubt, not to mention a depressed standard of living.

The Bureau of Labor Statistics (BLS) defines "discouraged workers" as those who have given up looking for work and have simply dropped out of the labor force. Where have all the discouraged workers gone?

Walk around the slums of our great cities. Walk through East St. Louis, Camden (New Jersey), Watts, Bedford-Stuyvesant, and the Hough district of Cleveland. Walk through Flint, Michigan, Gary, Indiana, or central Newark, or through most of our nation's capital. Walk through any of these places in midafternoon and you'll see block after block of teenagers and adults hanging around with nothing to do.

Ask them what they want more than anything else. A bigger welfare check? More food stamps? A big-screen TV? Most of them would tell you that all they want is a decent job. Not a dead-end, minimum-wage, low-status, menial job, but a *real* job.

Are these people unemployed? No, these people have given up, dropped out, and are, for all intents and purposes, no longer living in the United States. They may reside here physically, but they are not part of our society.

How can you expect somebody who's warm to understand somebody who's cold?
—Aleksandr Solzhenitsyn, *One Day in the Life of Ivan Denisovich*

Wanted: a *real* job

How the Unemployment Rate Is Computed

The Bureau of Labor Statistics (BLS) is in charge of compiling statistics on the number of Americans who are employed and unemployed. Where does it get its data? Most people believe it gets statistics from unemployment insurance offices, but if you stop and think about it, less than 40 percent of all unemployed Americans were collecting unemployment insurance benefits in 2006. The BLS gets its unemployment statistics by conducting a random survey of more than 60,000 households.

Essentially, the bureau asks a series of questions: (1) Are you working? If the answer is no, (2) Did you work at all this week—even one day? Anyone who has answered yes to questions 1 or 2 is counted as employed. For those who have not been working the BLS has one more question: (3) Did you look for work during the last month (that is, did you go to an employment agency or union hall, send out a résumé, or go on an interview)? If your answer is yes, you're counted as unemployed. If your answer is no, you're just not counted; you're not part of the labor force. If you want to work but have given up looking for a job, you're a "discouraged worker," but you are not in the labor force and you are not considered "unemployed."

Are people collecting unemployment insurance counted among the unemployed? Yes! To be able to collect unemployment insurance benefits, you must be ready, willing, and able to work. In addition, you are expected to be actively seeking work. As someone who collected unemployment insurance twice for the full 26 weeks, I kept a list of companies where I had looked for a job to prove that I was making an effort to find work.

The labor force consists of the employed and the unemployed. For example, in May 2003, 137,487,000 Americans were employed and 8,998,000 were unemployed. We can compute the unemployment rate by using this formula:

Where unemployment data comes from

$$\text{Unemployment rate} = \frac{\text{Number of unemployed}}{\text{Labor force}}$$

$$\underset{\text{rate}}{\text{Unemployment}} = \frac{\text{Number of unemployed}}{\text{Labor force}}$$

Read Only if You're Not Sure How to Calculate the Unemployment Rate

In January 1995, 7,500,000 Americans were unemployed and 124,600,000 held jobs. Go ahead and calculate the unemployment rate:

$$\text{Unemployment rate} = \frac{\text{Number of unemployed}}{\text{Labor force}}$$

$$= \frac{7,500,000}{132,100,000}$$

OK, where did we get the 132,100,000? That's the labor force—the number of unemployed (7,500,000) plus the number of employed (124,600,000).

The next step is simple division: 132,100,000 into 7,500,000, which gives us an unemployment rate of 5.7 percent.

Incidentally, a common mistake in this type of problem is to divide 7,500,000 into 132,100,000. Some people insist on dividing the smaller number into the larger number. But the rule we must always follow is to divide the bottom number into the top number.

How much was the unemployment rate in May 2003? Work it out right here.

When you lose your job, the unemployment rate is not 5.2 percent; it's 100 percent.

—Thomas Friedman

Did you get 6.1 percent? The key here is to figure out how many people are in the labor force. Add the employed (137,487,000) and the unemployed (8,998,000), and you'll get a labor force of 146,485,000. So in May 2003 the official unemployment rate was 6.1 percent. (If you need more practice, see the accompanying Extra Help box.)

It's been said that when there's a recession for whites, it's a depression for blacks. As you can see from the unemployment rates in Table 2, there was certainly no recession taking place in February 2006. The overall unemployment rate was just 4.2, and for whites it was 4.1 percent. But the unemployment rate for blacks was 9.3. During our worst recessions since World War II the overall unemployment rate only rarely got that high. If you traced the unemployment rates for blacks and whites over the last six decades, you find that the rate for blacks was consistently double the rate for whites.

TABLE 2	Unemployment Rate for Selected Groups of American Workers, February 2006
	Unemployment rates
All workers	4.8
Adult men	4.2
Adult women	4.3
Teenagers	15.4
White	4.1
Black or African American	9.3
Hispanic or Latino ethnicity	5.5

*Teenagers and African Americans have much higher unemployment rates than the average for all workers.

Source: Bureau of Labor Statistics: http://www.bls.gov/ces/

How Accurate Is the Unemployment Rate?

When the Bureau of Labor Statistics announces that the unemployment rate dipped from 5.0 percent in November 2005 to 4.9 percent in December, most of us think that the BLS is so accurate that it can calculate our unemployment rate to within one-tenth of a percent of its actual rate. But many liberal economists believe the actual unemployment rate is substantially *higher* than the official rate, while many conservative economists believe the actual rate is substantially *lower*. Obviously they can't *both* be right.

The liberal economists (does anyone still call herself a "liberal"?) would say that the true rate of unemployment is 2 or 3 percent higher because we should count all the jobless people who are ready, willing, and able to work. Let's ask about the 3 or 4 million people who are not working but are not officially unemployed. If we asked the BLS, it would tell us that they are discouraged workers.

The liberals have a couple of additional bones to pick with the BLS definition. A person who worked one day in the last month is counted as employed. Also, someone who works part-time but wants to work full-time is counted as employed. The liberals ask, "Doesn't this sort of measurement overstate the number of employed?" When you put it all together, they maintain, the BLS is overstating employment and understating unemployment. The result is an unemployment rate that is perhaps a couple of points too low.

That's the liberal view. As you would expect, the conservatives say the official unemployment rate *over*estimates the true rate of unemployment. Using the BLS definition of an unemployed person—someone who has not worked this month and who has actively sought work—the conservative focuses on those who are required to report to state employment or other government employment offices to remain eligible for unemployment insurance, welfare, or food stamps. Is this, asks the conservative, really an effort to look for work, or are these guys just going through the motions?

Some conservatives also cite the huge numbers of Americans—as well as illegal immigrants—working in the underground economy (see the section on this near the end of the previous chapter). There are a few million people out there working as hair dressers, livery cab operators, unlicensed plumbers, carpenters, electricians, and auto mechanics, as well as street peddlers, day laborers, and sewing machine operators in illegal garment sweat shops. All these people are employed off the books, do not report their income, and are not counted as employed by the Bureau of Labor Statistics.

The bottom line, according to the conservatives, is that perhaps a couple of million of the "officially" unemployed are not really looking for work. The liberal bottom line is that at least a couple of million people out there want to work but aren't being counted.

For decades the unemployment rate for blacks has been double that of whites. During recessions, the black unemployment rate is rarely below 10 percent. They also make up a disproportionate share of discouraged workers.

Two major changes have pushed down the unemployment rate—the work requirements under the 1996 Welfare Reform Act and the more than doubling of the U.S. prison population since 1985.

Over 2.1 million Americans are currently occupying cells in federal, state, or local prisons. The average convict has a much lower IQ and is considerably less educated than the average American. If these folks were not imprisoned, would they be legitimately employed? Most would not be. So keeping these people incarcerated has probably lowered our unemployment rate by about one percent.

The welfare work requirements have moved perhaps two million single mothers into low-wage jobs. Although few of these women previously had been in the labor force, they have been added to the ranks of the officially employed.

Illegal immigrants are about 5 percent of our labor force, most of whom are working off the books for employers who appreciate cheap, compliant labor free of employment regulations and payroll taxes. They make up at least one in four farm workers, one in six cleaning workers, and about one in seven construction workers. And then too, many

The liberals say the true unemployment rate is higher than the official rate.

Who are the discouraged workers?

The conservatives say the true unemployment rate is lower than the official rate.

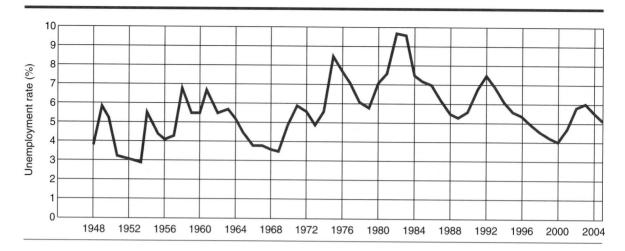

F*igure* 4

The Unemployment Rate, 1948–2005
Unemployment trended upward between 1969 and 1982 and trended downward after that.
Source: Economic Report of the President, 2006.

illegal immigrants are self-employed as street peddlers, handymen, car service drivers, or small business owners, all part of the underground economy. Were all these people counted as employed, the unemployment rate would be much lower.

In recent years the children of the baby boomers have been entering the labor force. Young adults tend to have a relatively high unemployment rate because, like homemakers returning to work, they need time to find a job. Because so many live at home or receive help from their parents, there is less pressure to take the first job that comes along. Then, they tend to drift from job to job, until, like Goldilocks, they find a position that is "just right."

Clearly it would go down. The number of unemployed would remain the same, the number of employed would go up, the labor force would go up, so the unemployment rate would go down.

The next time someone asks you if the official unemployment rate is an accurate measure of unemployment, just tell them that even economists can't agree on whether it's too high, too low, or just right.

Figure 4 is a record of the official unemployment rate from 1948 through 2002. You'll notice a marked upward trend from the late 1960s through the mid-1980s. But the trend seems to have reversed since then, heading back down again.

How does our unemployment rate compare to those of other industrial nations? It's relatively low. The "Comparative Unemployment Rates" box shows these rates and provides an explanation for our relatively low unemployment rate.

Types of Unemployment

Frictional Unemployment   Our economy is far from a well-tuned, efficient, smoothly functioning machine. When a job opening occurs somewhere, it is rarely filled instantaneously, even when there is someone ready, willing, and able to fill it. In a word, our economy has a certain degree of friction.

The frictionally unemployed are people who are between jobs or just entering or reentering the labor market. Because our system of filling jobs—newspaper classified ads, employment agencies, corporate recruiters, executive headhunters, help-wanted signs, Internet postings, and word of mouth—is imperfect, usually weeks or months pass before positions are filled.

The rate of unemployment is 100 percent if it's you who is unemployed.

—David L. Kurtz

The final solution for unemployment is work.

—Calvin Coolidge

Comparative Unemployment Rates

Why are the American and Japanese unemployment rates so low compared to those of other industrial nations in Western Europe? Europe's cradle-to-grave safety net means not only that being out of work has become a viable way of making a living but that there is no longer much stigma attached to joblessness. In Denmark workers can collect up to 90 percent as much as they could earn working, while in Spain it's 70 percent, and in France and Germany, 60 percent. But, in the United States and Japan, which also has a low unemployment rate, unemployment benefits are less than 50 percent of what workers would earn on the job.

Less than one-half of workers who are out of work qualify for benefits in the United States and Japan, where newer members of the labor force and temporary workers are ineligible. Compare that with 89 percent of unemployed workers in Germany and 98 percent in France. While the limit for collecting unemployment benefits in the United States and Japan is 26 weeks, German unemployed workers can collect for at least five years, and in Britain, unemployed people can collect practically forever.

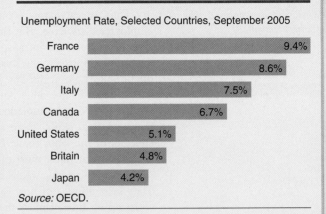

Unemployment Rate, Selected Countries, September 2005

France	9.4%
Germany	8.6%
Italy	7.5%
Canada	6.7%
United States	5.1%
Britain	4.8%
Japan	4.2%

Source: OECD.

And then too, Western Europe is much more heavily unionized than the United States. Often, by law, their collective bargaining agreements (including job security) are extended to all firms in the industry, whether or not they are unionized. In addition, business firms are so tied up by government rules and regulations that they find it nearly impossible to dismiss employees.

At any given time, about 2 or 3 percent of the labor force is frictionally unemployed. Students who are looking for their first full-time jobs, homemakers reentering the labor market after 5, 10, or 20 years, and servicemen and -women who have recently been discharged by the armed forces are frictionally unemployed until they find jobs. In addition, there are those who leave their jobs voluntarily, perhaps so they can spend all their time looking for better jobs. Maybe they're looking in another part of the country. Add to these the people who get fired or quit. These people, too, are between jobs, or frictionally unemployed.

> About 2 to 3 percent of our labor force is always frictionally unemployed.

When people change jobs, they may have time between jobs, or they may leave one job on a Friday and start a new one on Monday. Officials at the Labor Department estimate that 40 percent of the labor force, or roughly 50 million workers, change jobs within a year. But if you happen to be applying for a civil service job, whether with the federal, state, or local government, you may need the patience of Job. The time interval from when a job is advertised, a test is given and marked, a list is established, applicants are interviewed, a job offer is made and accepted, and the employee reports to work is often between one and two years.

Structural Unemployment Former U.S. Attorney General Robert F. Kennedy[1] once asked, "Have you ever told a coal miner in West Virginia or Kentucky that what he needs is individual initiative to go out and get a job where there isn't any?" A person who is out of work for a relatively long period of time, say, a couple of years, is structurally unemployed. The economy does not have any use for this person. The steelworker in Youngstown, Ohio, the autoworker from Flint, Michigan, and the coal miner from Kentucky are no longer needed because the local steel mills, auto plants, and coal mines have closed. And the skills of clerical workers, typists, and inventory control clerks who

> About 2 to 3 percent of our labor force is always structurally unemployed.

---

[1]Robert Kennedy also served as a U.S. senator from 1965 to 1968 and was the brother of President John F. Kennedy.

once staffed corporate offices have been made obsolete by computer systems. Add to these the people whose companies have gone out of business or whose jobs have been exported to low-wage countries and you've got another 2 to 3 percent of the labor force structurally unemployed.

Ours is a dynamic economy, and the opportunities for retraining and subsequent employment *do* exist. But the prospects for a 50- or 60-year-old worker embarking on a second career are not auspicious. To compound the problem, most of the structurally unemployed reside in the Rust Belt of the East and Midwest, while most of the new career opportunities are in the Sun Belt and in several states on the East and West coasts.

The "unemployables"

One out of five adult Americans is functionally illiterate. These people cannot read, write, or do simple numerical computations. In a workplace that increasingly demands these minimal skills, more and more of these people are finding themselves virtually shut out of the labor force. Each year our educational system turns out 1 million more functional illiterates, most of whom will face long periods of structural unemployment. Many of these young adults come from very poor families where no one has held a job. They have no idea of how to dress for a job interview, what to say, or even the need to show up on time. Unless these people are given some kind of vocational training and provided with entry-level jobs, they will be out of work for most of their lives.

What if someone were "between jobs" for six months, or a year, or even two years? When someone is out of work for a long period of time, he or she is classified as "structurally unemployed." But where do we draw the line between frictional and structural unemployment? The answer is that we don't. There *is* no clear dividing line.

Cyclical Unemployment   As you know, our economy certainly has its ups and downs, a set of fluctuations known as business cycles. During a recession, the unemployment rate sometimes rises to 8, 9, or even 10 percent. During the Great Depression, the "official" unemployment rate hit 25 percent, which definitely understated the true unemployment picture.

Fluctuations in our unemployment rate are due to cyclical unemployment.

If we allow for a certain amount of frictional and structural unemployment, anything above the sum of these two would be cyclical unemployment. Let's say that the sum of frictional and structural unemployment is 5 percent. If the actual rate of unemployment is 7.7 percent, then the cyclical rate is 2.7 percent.

If we take a 5 percent unemployment rate as our working definition of full employment, anything above 5 percent would be cyclical unemployment. You may wonder whether 5 percent is a reasonable level for full employment. Surely we can never expect our unemployment rate to reach zero, since we'll always have some frictionally and structurally unemployed people. Our unemployment rate did get down to 1.2 percent in 1944, but as they said back then, "There's a war going on." With 12 million men in the armed forces and the economy going full-steam ahead, employers were desperate for help, and anyone who could walk and spell his or her name had no trouble finding a job.

There are liberal economists who insist that we could realistically get the unemployment rate down to 4 percent, while there are conservative economists who consider 6 percent the lowest attainable rate. As I've said before, we'll split the difference and call 5 percent full employment.

Seasonal Unemployment   At any given time a couple of hundred thousand people may be out of work because this is their "slow season." The slack seasons in the ladies' garment industry are in the spring and fall after those seasons' new fashions have been shipped to the stores. The tourist season is slow all summer in Florida, and elsewhere some employees at Carvels and Dairy Queen are laid off in the winter. My aunt Betty, who worked in the garment industry for nearly 60 years, turned her seasonal unemployment to her advantage by arranging to get laid off each year in early November, registering for unemployment insurance benefits, and then taking off for Florida.

Seasonal unemployment is not nearly as large as frictional, structural, or cyclical unemployment, so it hasn't figured in our discussion of total unemployment. But if it weren't mentioned here, someone would be sure to ask why it wasn't included.

Natural Unemployment Rate

As the unemployment rate falls, and it becomes increasingly difficult to find employees, employers will bid up wage rates, pushing up the rate of inflation. Once the unemployment rate falls below its natural rate, which most economists estimate to be 5 or 6 percent, then inflationary wage pressure emerges.

Our unemployment rate fell below 6 percent in 1994, below 5 percent in 1997, and averaged just 4 percent in 2000 while the rate of inflation stayed below 4 percent. Could it be that the natural rate of unemployment was falling? There are at least five reasons to support this view.

First, the natural unemployment rate tends to fall when the proportion of youths in the labor force is shrinking. The youth contingent has been shrinking since the late 1970s from a post–baby boom peak of nearly 25 percent to just 16 percent in recent years.

A second factor is the doubling of the adult population in prison since 1985—with 2.3 percent of the male labor force behind bars at last count. Assuming a fair number of these inmates would be counted as unemployed if they weren't locked up, this too has pushed down our natural unemployment rate.

Worker insecurity, based on massive corporate downsizing and plant closings, has also tended to reduce the natural unemployment rate. Even though the unemployment rate peaked at just 6.4 percent after the 2001 recession and has since fallen, many workers have been willing to accept small pay increases, rather than risk the ire of their employers.

Next, there is the rapid growth of the temporary-help industry, whose share of employment has jumped from 0.5 percent in the early 1980s, to 2.2 percent today. Not only do many people who would otherwise be unemployed now work as temps as they look for permanent jobs, but the availability of temp agencies allows employers to fill vacancies more easily and, in some cases, to minimize wage pressures by keeping the new hires on temp payrolls.

Finally, the labor force has been expanding rapidly. The Census Bureau estimates that as many as 5 million illegal immigrants are working here today. In addition, many new workers are unmarried mothers with at least one child younger than three years old. The percentage of these women now in the labor force rose to 67 percent in 2006 from only 54 percent in 1995.

Inflation

> Inflation is like toothpaste. Once it is out of the tube, it is hard to get it back in again.
>
> –Karl Otto Pohl,
> former president of the
> German Bundesbank–

Defining Inflation

What exactly *is* inflation? It is a broadly based rise in the price level. *Generally, we consider inflation a sustained rise in the average price level over a period of years.* In our own lifetimes, we have known little *but* inflation.

If the rate of inflation had been 4 percent, would that mean the price of every good and service went up by 4 percent? Of course not! The prices of some things went up by much more than 4 percent, and the prices of others rose by less than 4 percent. The prices of some things may not have changed. And when the overall price level is rising, the prices of some goods and services are actually going down. Can you think of any examples? In the 1970s and 1980s color TV prices came way down. Average prices of 20-inch LCD TVs tumbled from more than $5,000 in 2000 to under $600 today. The prices of cell phones, fax machines, laser printers, DVD players, Ipods, and graphing calculators have also fallen substantially.

Inflation is not all that bad. After all, it enables us to live in a more expensive neighborhood without having to move.

—Anonymous

U.S. inflation has been persistent since World War II, particularly in the 1970s when, for some of the decade, it was at double-digit proportions. But since 1990, our rate of inflation has remained below 4 percent.

Ask the man on the street what inflation is and he'll tell you that everything costs more. To be more precise, the U.S. Department of Labor's Bureau of Labor Statistics compiles an average of all items that consumers buy—the prices of cars, gasoline, appliances, haircuts, TVs, contact lenses, dresses, steaks, medical services, plane tickets, motel rooms, and Big Macs—and figures out how much it costs the average family to live. Every month several hundred BLS employees around the country check the cost of 80,000 items—ranging from airline tickets to cat food. Let's say that in January 2003 it cost the Jones family $20,000 to maintain a certain standard of living. If it cost the Joneses $22,000 to buy the same items in January 2007, we would say that the cost of living went up 10 percent.

The consumer price index (CPI), which measures changes in our cost of living, is reported near the middle of every month by the Bureau of Labor Statistics. For example, you'll hear on the radio, "There was some good news today on the inflation front. Consumer prices rose just two-tenths of 1 percent last month, and the consumer price index now stands at 136.4." Before you have a chance to digest this information, the announcer is doing sports and weather.

Figure 5 provides a record of our year-to-year changes in the Consumer Price Index since the end of World War II. Although we suffered serious bouts of inflation, most recently from the late 1960s through the early 1980s, over the last 20 years, the inflation rate has generally stayed below 4 percent.

If our consumer price index is 136.4, what does that tell us? Unless you're familiar with the consumer price index, how it's constructed, and what it measures, you won't be able to fully appreciate the significance of that number. So let's see exactly what this index is all about.

The number 100 is a magic number. It lends itself well to calculating percentage changes. Suppose, for example, that we want to find out by what percentage prices rose since the base year for the consumer price index. The base year is set at 100. If the CPI were 136.4 today, by what percentage did prices rise since the base year?

> The consumer price index is based on what it costs an average family to live.

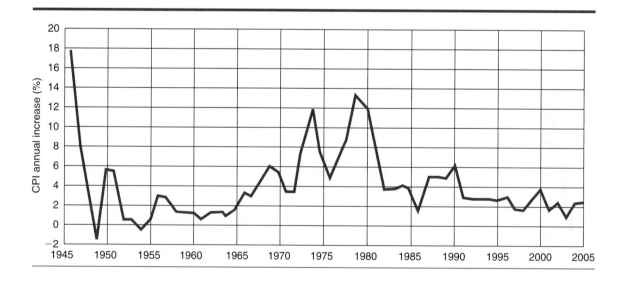

Figure 5

Annual Percentage Change in Consumer Price Index, 1946–2005
Since World War II we have had two periods of price stability—from 1952 through 1965, and from 1991 to the present.
Source: Economic Report of the President, 2006.

They rose by 36.4 percent. What I did was subtract 100 from 136.4. Try this one: If the CPI is now 201.6, by what percentage did prices rise since the base year? Work it out right here:

They rose by 101.6 percent (201.6 − 100). Now you're getting it—I hope. You'll notice that we take the CPI in the current year and subtract the CPI in the base year, which is always 100.

No one would complain if the cost of living rose 2 or 3 percent a year, but during the 10-year period from 1972 to 1982 the consumer price index rose from 125.3 to 289.1. By what percentage did the cost of living rise? Figure it out here:

Solution:

$$\text{Percent increase in CPI} = \frac{(\text{CPI in current year} - \text{CPI in previous year})}{\text{CPI in previous year}} \times 100$$

$$= \frac{(289.1 - 125.3)}{125.3} \times 100 = \frac{163.8}{125.3} \times 100 = 130.7\%$$

The cost of living rose by 130.7 percent, so it cost the typical American family more than twice as much to live in 1982 as it did just 10 years earlier.

That problem was so much fun, let's try one more. If the CPI rose from 114.3 in 2013 to 126.1 in 2020, by what percent did the CPI rise?

Solution:

$$\text{Percent increase in CPI} = \frac{(\text{CPI in current year} - \text{CPI in previous year})}{\text{CPI in previous year}} \times 100$$

$$= \frac{(126.1 - 114.3)}{114.3} \times 100 = \frac{11.8}{114.3} \times 100 = 10.3\%$$

If you had any trouble with these problems, then you can use some help calculating percentage changes. You'll find that help in the box, "Finding Percentage Changes in the Price Level."

Deflation and Disinflation

Deflation   *Deflation is a broadly based decline in the price level, not for just a month or two but for a period of years.* The last deflation the United States had was from 1929 to 1933, when prices fell 50 percent. Significantly, that deflation was accompanied by the Great Depression.

Finding Percentage Changes in the Price Level

Here's a chance to work out a few problems: Find the percentage change in price since the base year if the CPI is now 94.7.

The answer is −5.3 percent. The price level declined (94.7 − 100 = −5.3). By what percentage did prices rise since the base year if the CPI is now 485.2?

They rose by 385.2 percent (485.2 − 100 = 385.2). So when you're figuring out the percentage change in prices since the base year, all you have to do is subtract 100 from the current CPI.

Now try *this* one: If the CPI rises from 129.6 in 2029 to 158.3 in 2045, find the percentage increase in the CPI.

OOPS

Solution:

Percent increase in CPI

$$= \frac{\text{(CPI in current year − CPI in previous year)}}{\text{CPI in previous year}} \times 100$$

$$= \frac{(158.3 − 129.6)}{158.3} \times 100 = \frac{28.7}{158.3} \times 100 = 18.1\%$$

129.6

Until the inflationary recessions of the 1970s, business downturns were called deflations, for they were invariably accompanied by price declines. As much as business owners dislike inflation, particularly that of double-digit proportions, they hate deflation a lot more.

Suppose your store sells air conditioners, refrigerators, and other appliances. You place orders with manufacturers a few months before delivery and generally hold two months' worth of inventory in your warehouse. If there is a 2 or 3 percent rate of deflation, instead of the 2 or 3 percent rate of inflation you had been counting on, you'll probably have to charge 2 or 3 percent less than you had been planning to charge. You paid your suppliers more than you should have, and you'll collect less from your customers than you had expected to. So even a little deflation can be very bad news to business firms, especially retailers.

But deflation is great news to consumers, because it means that they'll be paying lower prices. If you happen to have a lot of money—in the form of currency or bank deposits—you will be sitting pretty, because each dollar that you hold will be going up in value. And if you're living on a fixed income, you'll be able to buy more for your money.

Deflation may sound like a very appealing state of affairs. Every time we visit supermarkets, department stores, and clothing shops, we find that prices have been reduced again and again. Doctors, lawyers, personal trainers, and beauticians charge us less and less. The only ones hurting are the business owners. But that's exactly why deflation is not such a wonderful thing.

Business owners would be losing money, cutting the wages of their employees, eventually laying them off, and even going out of business. Each wave of price and wage decreases would set off another wave of decreases, and soon we would be caught in a deflationary spiral. As prices drop, customers would delay their purchases, expecting further price cuts. As more and more businesses shut their doors and the unemployment rolls grow larger, we would end up with a depression like the one we suffered in the 1930s. In fact, well into the 1950s, many people still referred to the Great Depression as "the deflation."

Deflation has not been a concern in the United States since the 1930s, but it has been a problem in Japan where consumer prices fell virtually every month between April 1998 and the end of 2005. Deflation is chipping away at asset values, increasing credit risks,

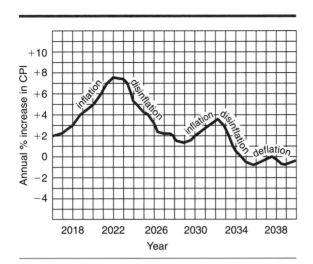

Figure 6
Hypothetical Annual Rate of
Increase of CPI, 2016–2040
Notice that after 2034 there was
deflation because the annual
percentage increase in the CPI
was 0.

pinching wages and salaries, and preventing the economy from generating any sustained growth after a decade of stagnation. Stocks were trading at the same prices in 2003 as they had been in the mid-1980s, and real estate prices had fallen for 10 consecutive years. Consumer prices were dropping at an annual rate of about 3 percent in 2003, and the Japanese economy was running the risk of getting caught in a deflationary spiral similar to the Great Depression when prices and wages fell sharply throughout the world.

Can deflation happen again in the United States? Remember, deflation is a *broad* decline in the price level. So while the prices of some goods and services are going up—gasoline, health care, and college tuition are prime examples—keep in mind that the prices of many other goods and services have been falling—personal computers, TVs, toys, long-distance phone calls, and audio equipment. *Will* there be deflation in our immediate future? It seems very unlikely. But it *can* happen here.

Disinflation   Immediately after World War II we had a great deal of inflation. But when recessions occurred, inflation would disappear and prices actually declined slightly. By the late 1950s, even though the rate of inflation was quite moderate, recessions no longer eliminated rising prices. They continued to rise, albeit at a slower rate. This gave us our definition of disinflation: *Disinflation occurs when the rate of inflation declines.*

For example, during the recession of 1981–82, the rate of inflation fell from about 12 percent to about 4 percent. And again, since the recession of 1990–91, the rate of inflation fell from a little more than 4 percent to less than 2 percent (see Figure 5).

In Figure 6 we've constructed a hypothetical graph illustrating inflations, disinflation, and deflation.

The Post-World War II History of Inflation

During every major war in U.S. history, prices rose sharply. Each war was accompanied by a combination of money supply increases and large budget deficits.

In 1945, as World War II ended, a tremendous pent-up demand for consumer goods was unleashed as price and wage controls were abolished. Consumer prices rose sharply. Too many dollars were chasing too few goods. Just as the inflation was being brought under control, the Korean War broke out. This brought on another wave of consumer spending and price increases.

President Dwight David Eisenhower took office in 1953, pledging to end the war in Korea and the inflation at home. It took him only a couple of months to end the war, but it wasn't until 1960, three recessions later, that inflation was finally brought under control. Until 1965, consumer prices rose at an annual rate of only 1 percent (see again Figure 5). Then the Vietnam War, accompanied by huge federal budget deficits, rekindled another inflationary fire.

At its present cost, life is worth about 30 cents on the dollar.
—Don Herold

Hobson's choice: You lose either way—more inflation or a possible recession.

By this time most Americans had become conditioned to rising prices; they seemed inevitable. When prices have been rising for some time, it is reasonable to assume they will keep rising. So what did we do? We ran out to buy still more goods and services before prices rose still further. And when businessowners saw that demand for their products was high, they were encouraged to raise *their* prices.

In 1971, in an effort to combat an escalating rate of inflation, President Richard Nixon imposed wage and price controls. But Nixon's wage and price freeze didn't really take, perhaps because it was applied only halfheartedly. When OPEC quadrupled oil prices in the fall of 1973, inflation accelerated (see Figure 5). The deep recession that followed did damp down the inflation, but in the late 1970s it returned with renewed vigor. Not until the back-to-back recessions of 1980 and 1981–82 was the rate of inflation finally brought down to acceptable levels.

In the 1970s we did get to add a new word to our vocabulary—*stagflation*—which is a contraction of the words *stagnation* and *inflation*. The new word got a great deal of use during the recessions of 1973–75, 1980, and 1981–82, when we experienced the worst of both worlds: declining output *and* inflation.

Since 1992, the inflation rate has stayed at or below 3 percent nearly every year. What accounts for this? Five factors come to mind. First is the rising tide of imported goods. When these imports compete with goods made in America, the competition drives down prices. Imported goods reduce our inflation rate by 1 or 2 percent.

A second factor is the rise of huge discounters, like Wal-Mart, Toys 'R' Us, Staples, and Price-Costco. In 2000, discount stores sold almost 50 percent of all general merchandise, up from 37 percent just 10 years earlier. Discounters work closely with suppliers to minimize distribution costs, and these savings are largely passed on to consumers as lower prices.

A third cause of our low rate of inflation is the advent of e-commerce, which has added a new layer of competition. Nearly every item that can be purchased at a traditional retail store is available on the Web, and for cost-conscious consumers, this provides unparalleled leverage, because buyers can comparison-shop across dozens of stores at the click of a mouse. Books, for example, cost about 20 percent less online than in bookstores. For sellers, savings come via lower real estate and rental costs, as well as reduced outlays for advertising, inventory, and transportation—items that ordinarily account for some 40 percent of the consumer price of goods.

A fourth cause is the accelerating pace of technological advance. When color TV appeared in 1956, it took two decades before the price dropped in half. It took a decade for VCR prices to halve. In contrast, prices for DVD players, launched in 1997 for $700, halved in about two years, and now they sell for under $80.

Finally, the efforts of business firms to become leaner and meaner have been paying off in rising efficiency and productivity. Wage increases have been held down, millions of workers have been discharged, and, again, savings have been passed on to consumers. Are the bad old inflationary days of the 1970s and early 1980s behind us, or will inflation come roaring back again?

The Construction of the Consumer Price Index

The most important measure of inflation is the consumer price index. Now we'll see how the Bureau of Labor Statistics goes about constructing this index.

First a base year is picked. In early 1998 we used the period 1982–84 as our base, setting the average price level of those years equal to 100. By December 1997 the CPI stood at 161.3, which meant, of course, that the price level had risen 63.1 percent since 1982–84. So the CPI measured the rise in the cost of living from the base years to December 1997.[2]

If you're *really* curious about the mechanics of how the CPI is constructed, it's worked out in the box, "Construction of the Consumer Price Index." Of course, this is

So far I haven't heard of anybody who wants to stop buying on account of the cost.

—Frank McKinney Hubbard

To find the CPI in the current year, divide the cost of living in the current year by the cost of living in the base year and multiply by 100.

---

[2]The Bureau of Labor Statistics overhauls the CPI periodically, doing a survey of some 10,000 families to find out what they're buying and how much they're paying.

Construction of the Consumer Price Index

We're going to calculate how much it cost a family to live in March 1987 and in March 1995. In the tables below showing hypothetical costs of living for these months, Table A has a month's expenditures for 1987, the base year. To find these expenditures, we multiply quantity purchased by price. Then, adding up the money spent on each item, we find the total amount of money spent in March 1987.

Now we'll compare that amount with the amount spent in March 1995, which is shown in Table B.* What happened, then, was that the family spent $848 for these six items in 1987 and $994 for these same items in 1995. Obviously, their cost of living went up. But by how much?

To find out, we'll construct a consumer price index. To do this, divide the cost of living in the base year, 1987, into the cost of living in the current year, 1995. After you've done that multiply your answer by 100 to convert it into an index number.

Do your work in the space provided and then check it with the calculations shown.

$$994/848 = 1.172$$
$$1.172 \times 100 = 117.2$$

That's our consumer price index for 1995. You'll notice that we've carried it to one decimal place, which is exactly how the Bureau of Labor Statistics does it and how you'll find it listed in the newspaper.

One last question. By what percentage did prices rise between 1987 and 1995? The envelope please. Prices rose by 17.2 percent (117.2 − 100).

If you're still having trouble figuring out percentage changes, reread the box titled, "Finding Percentage Changes in the Price Level," a little earlier in this chapter.

Table A   March 1987

Item	Quantity	Price	Quantity × Price
Loaf of bread	10	.70	7.00
Quart of milk	15	.60	9.00
Pair of jeans	2	28.00	46.00
New car	0.02	7800.00	156.00
Mortgage payment	1	590.00	590.00
Movie admission	8	5.00	40.00
Total			848.00

Table B   March 1995

Item	Quantity	Price	Quantity × Price
Loaf of bread	10	.90	9.00
Quart of milk	15	.80	12.00
Pair of jeans	2	31.00	62.00
New car	0.02	9000.00	180.00
Mortgage payment	1	675.00	675.00
Movie admission	8	7.00	56.00
Total			994.00

*We're assuming family has not altered its consumption pattern.

a very simplified version containing just six items. The Bureau of Labor Statistics compiles a market basket of 80,000 goods and services that the typical urban family buys in 1987. Assuming they buy that same market basket of goods and services in 1995, the BLS figures out how much that family would have had to spend. It then comes up with an index number for 1995. In fact, it does this every month.

The consumer price index tends to overstate the actual rate of inflation by failing to account completely for gains in the quality of the goods and services that people buy as well as improvements in technology. Back in 1987, when there were personal computers in just 18 percent of all American households, you would have paid a lot more and gotten a lot less computing power than you would today. But the CPI utterly fails to take into account such improvements in product quality. In the accompanying box, we consider an alternate cost of living measure. (See "The Declining *Real* Cost of Living.")

Suppose that in 2004 the CPI is recalculated so that the rate of inflation is adjusted downward by 1 percent. Because Social Security benefits are raised by the same percent

The Declining Real Cost of Living

The CPI measures the cost of living in money terms. "The real cost of living," say W. Michael Cox and Richard Alm, "isn't measured in dollars and cents, but in the hours and minutes we must work to live."* For example, back in 1916, you would have needed to work 3,162 hours to buy a refrigerator, 333 hours in 1958, and just 68 hours in 1997. And the 1997 model could do a lot more tricks. In 1919 you would have worked 80 minutes to buy a dozen eggs, but by 1997 you would have worked just 5 minutes.

Of course not everything is cheaper, when measured in hours worked. Take private college tuition. Today it costs about 1500 hours of work; in the mid-1960s, it cost just 500 hours of work. But if you happen to attend the University of Texas, the cost today of just over 200 hours' work is only a bit higher than it was in the mid-1930s.

*W. Michael Cox and Richard Alm, "Time Well Spent," *1997 Annual Report of the Federal Reserve Bank of Dallas.*

that the CPI rises, the average Social Security recipient would get about $100 less that year. In Chapter 12 we'll look at the effects of an adjustment in the CPI on government spending and tax receipts.

Anticipated and Unanticipated Inflation: Who Is Hurt by Inflation and Who Is Helped?

Why farmers like inflation

Traditionally, inflation has hurt creditors and helped debtors. Throughout our history, the farmers have been debtors. During times of deflation or stable prices, the farmers' anguished cries were heard loud and clear all the way to Washington; but during times of inflation, there was scarcely a peep out of them.

Creditors have better memories than debtors.

—James Howell, 1659

It is easy to see why. Suppose a farmer borrows $100, which he agrees to repay in one year along with 4 percent interest ($4). In one year he pays back $104. But what if, during the year, prices double? The money he pays back is worth half as much as the money he borrowed.

Let's say that when the farmer borrowed the money, wheat was selling at $2 a bushel. He would have been able to buy 50 bushels of wheat ($100/$2). But farmers don't buy wheat; they sell it. So one year later, this farmer harvests his wheat and pays back the loan. If the price level doubles, assume the price of wheat doubles. How much wheat would the farmer need to sell at $4 a bushel to pay off the $104 he owes? He would need to sell only 26 bushels ($104/$4).

This farmer, who is a debtor, benefits magnificently from unanticipated inflation because he has borrowed money worth some 50 bushels of wheat and pays back his loan—with interest—in money worth only 26 bushels of wheat. Debtors, in general, gain from unanticipated inflation because they repay their loans in inflated dollars.

The issuers may have, and in the case of government paper, always have, a direct interest in lowering the value of the currency, because it is the medium in which their own debts are computed.

—John Stuart Mill

Just as obviously, those hurt by unanticipated inflation are people who lend out the money—the creditors. We generally think of creditors as banks, but banks are really financial middlemen. The ultimate creditors, or lenders, are the people who put their money in banks, life insurance, or any other financial instrument paying a fixed rate of interest. And the biggest debtor and gainer from unanticipated inflation has been the U.S. government. The national debt, which is approaching $9 trillion, would be a lot easier to pay off if there were a great deal of inflation.

Another group helped by unanticipated inflation is businessowners. Just as businesses suffer losses on their inventory during periods of deflation, during inflations they obtain inventory price windfalls. Between the time inventory is ordered and the time it is sold, prices have crept upward, swelling profits.

Who is hurt by inflation?

Among those who are hurt by unanticipated inflation are people who live on fixed incomes, particularly retired people who depend on pensions (except Social Security) and those who hold long-term bonds, whether corporate or U.S. government bonds. Finally, people whose wages are fixed under long-term contracts and landlords who have granted long-term leases at fixed rent are hurt by unanticipated inflation. In other words, under unanticipated inflation, some people gain and others lose. In fact, the gains and losses are exactly equal.

When inflation is fully anticipated, there are no winners or losers. The interest rate takes into account the expected rate of inflation. Normally, without anticipated inflation, the interest rate would be around 3 or 4 percent. In 1980, and again in 1981, when the rate of inflation ran at close to 15 percent, the prime rate of interest (paid by top credit-rated corporations) soared over 20 percent.

If all prices and incomes rose equally, no harm would be done to anyone. But the rise is not equal. Many lose and some gain.
—Irving Fisher, 1920

For inflation to be fully anticipated and built into interest rates, people need to live with it for several years. Although the country had relatively high inflation for most of the 1970s, it was only in 1979 that the prime interest rate (which top credit-rated corporate borrowers pay) finally broke the 12 percent barrier. Today, however, unanticipated inflation is largely a thing of the past.

Creditors have learned to charge enough interest to take into account, or anticipate, the rate of inflation over the course of the loan. This is tacked onto the regular interest rate that the lender would charge had no inflation been expected. In addition borrowers have been issuing inflation-indexed bonds.

We'll work out a few examples. If the real rate of interest (the rate that would be charged without inflation) were 5 percent, and there was an expected rate of inflation of 3 percent, then obviously the creditors would charge 8 percent.

Real rate of interest

If the real rate of interest were 4 percent and the expected inflation rate were 6 percent, how much would the nominal rate (the rate actually charged) be? Good! I know you said 10 percent. Thus, the real rate of interest plus the expected rate of inflation equals the nominal rate of interest.

Are you ready for a tricky one? If the nominal interest rate is 6 percent and the expected rate of inflation is 8 percent, how much is the real rate of interest? Have you found it yet? The real rate of interest is −2 percent. How can a real rate of interest be negative? It can be negative if the rate of inflation is greater than the rate of interest that you pay or receive (that is, the nominal rate of interest).

If the nominal interest rate accurately reflects the inflation rate, then the inflation has been fully anticipated and no one wins or loses. This is a good thing for the economy because it means no one is hurt and no one is forced out of business because of inflation.

But if the rate of inflation keeps growing—even if it is correctly anticipated—our economy will be in big trouble. In a hyperinflation there are ultimately only losers.

Social Security benefits are indexed for inflation, protecting those who collect Social Security from inflation. Many wage-earners, too, are protected against inflation by cost-of-living adjustment clauses (called COLA agreements) in their contracts.[3] One way or another, many sectors of our society have learned to protect themselves from at least the short-term ravages of inflation.

What's a Dollar Worth Today?

What this country needs is a good five-cent cigar.

–Franklin Pierce Adams–

Some people say that today a dollar is worth only fifty cents. Others say a dollar today is worth only a quarter. And real old-timers claim that a dollar isn't worth more than a nickel.

When you lament the decline of the dollar's purchasing power, you need to specify which year's dollar you're comparing with today's dollar. Figure 7 shows us the five-year

---

[3]About one worker in four is covered by a COLA. See Chapter 29 of *Economics* (or Chapter 17 of *Macro-economics*).

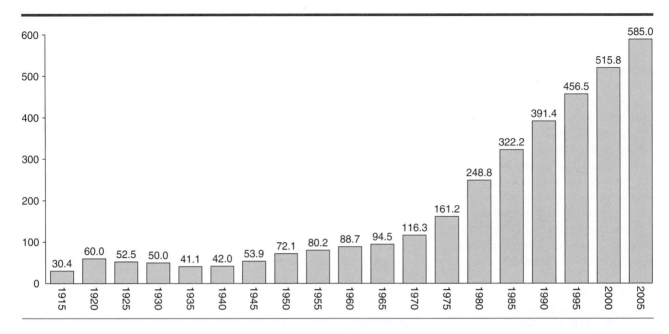

F*igure* 7

Consumer Price Index, 1915–2002 (1967 = 100)
Source: U.S. Bureau of Labor Statistics.

changes in the CPI since 1915. Let's compare prices in 1945 with those in 2005. How much higher was the cost of living in 2005? Since the CPI rose from 53.9 in 1945 to 585.0, the cost of living was about 11 times as high in 2005. So we could say that a dollar today could buy less than what a dime could buy in 1945.

Theories of the Causes of Inflation

Excessive demand causes demand-pull inflation.

Demand-Pull Inflation   When there is excessive demand for goods and services, we have demand-pull inflation. What is excessive? When people are willing and able to buy more output than our economy can produce. Something's gotta give. And what gives are prices.

Demand-pull inflation is often summed up as "too many dollars chasing too few goods." The problem is that we can't produce any more goods because our economy is already operating at full capacity.

What happens next if demand keeps rising? What if people have money in their pockets and the desire to spend it? Again, something's gotta give. Output can't rise any more. There's only one thing that can go up: prices.

Inflation is a form of taxation that can be imposed without legislation.

—Milton Friedman

This usually happens during wars. The government spends a lot of money on uniforms, tanks, planes, rifles, bullets, bombs, and missile systems. Private citizens want more consumer goods and services. Business firms are also bidding for resources to build more plant and equipment, expand their inventories, buy more raw materials, and hire more employees. So everyone's out there spending a lot of money to buy what they want.

At very low levels of output—depression levels—it is easy to increase output without raising prices. After all, with high unemployment and idle plant and equipment those resources can be put back to work without raising costs much. For example, if a person who has been out of work for several months is offered a job at the going wage rate, she will jump at the chance to get back to work.

As output expands, most of the idle resources will be back in production. Firms that need more plant and equipment will have to buy them. Employers will have to raise wages to induce new employees to work for them. In effect, then, businesses will have to bid for resources, and in doing so, they will bid up the prices of land, labor, and capital.

As their costs go up, business firms will be forced to raise their prices. We're moving closer and closer to full employment. It becomes increasingly difficult to get good help. New workers have to be lured away from other employers. There's only one way to do this—pay them more.

This pushes costs up still further until finally we've reached the full-employment level of output. Any further spending on goods and services will simply bid up prices without any corresponding increase in output.

Both depressions and runaway inflations are relatively rare occurrences, though they *do* happen. The twin goals of macroeconomic policy are to avoid these extremes, or anything approaching them. But runaway inflations in particular are sometimes unavoidable. This happens when macroeconomic policy must subordinate itself because of military necessity. During World War II, for example, the federal government bought up almost half the national output for military use. The only problem was that private citizens had plenty of money to spend and not enough output to spend it on. So civilians and the government had a bidding war for the country's limited resources. It was a classic case of too much money chasing too few goods.

It would not be unreasonable to ask, Just *where* did all this money come from? Milton Friedman, a Nobel laureate in economics and the world's leading exponent of monetary economics, has long been rounding up the usual suspects: the seven governors of the Federal Reserve System, which controls the money supply's rate of growth. Chapter 14 provides a detailed account of how the Board of Governors exercises that control.

Cost-Push Inflation   There are three variants of cost-push inflation. Most prominent is the wage-price spiral. Because wages constitute nearly two-thirds of the cost of doing business, whenever workers receive a significant wage increase, this increase is passed along to consumers in the form of higher prices. Higher prices raise everyone's cost of living, engendering further wage increases.

The wage-price spiral

Imagine a 3 percent rise in the cost of living. Labor unions will negotiate for a 3 percent catch-up increase and a 3 percent increase on top of that for an anticipated cost-of-living increase *next* year. That's 6 percent. If every labor union gets a 6 percent increase, prices will undoubtedly rise not 3 percent but you guessed it—6 percent! In the next round of labor negotiations, the unions might want not just a 6 percent catch-up but 12 percent, to take care of next year as well.[4]

All of this can be described as the wage-price spiral. Regardless of who is to blame for its origin, once it gets started the wage-price spiral spawns larger and larger wage and price increases. Round and round it goes, and where it stops, nobody knows.

One man's wage rise is another man's price increase.
—Sir Harold Wilson, 1970

This variant of cost-push inflation may well explain a great deal of the inflation the country experienced through the early 1970s. However, in recent decades the membership and bargaining power of U.S. labor unions have been sharply declining, so the wage-price spiral would serve today, at best, as a partial explanation for inflation.

The second variant of cost-push inflation is profit-push inflation. Because just a handful of huge firms dominate many industries (for example, computer software, publishing, cigarettes, detergents, breakfast cereals, cars, and oil), these firms have the power to administer prices in those industries rather than accept the dictates of the market forces of supply and demand. To the degree that they are able to protect their profit margins by raising prices, these firms will respond to any rise in costs by passing them on to their customers.

Profit-push inflation

Finally, we have supply-side cost shocks, most prominently the oil price shocks of 1973–74 and 1979. When the OPEC nations quadrupled the price of oil in the fall of 1973, they touched off not just a major recession but also a severe inflation. When the price of oil rises, the cost of making many other things rises as well, for example, electricity, fertilizer, gasoline, heating oil, and long-distance freight carriage. And as we've

Supply-side cost shocks

---

[4]Labor unions are covered in Chapter 27 of *Economics* and Chapter 15 of *Microeconomics*.

Graphing Demand-Pull and Cost-Push Inflation

Demand-pull inflation is set off by an increase in demand for goods and services without any increase in supply. The left graph shows how prices rise.

Cost-push inflation happens when production costs rise. Sellers can no longer supply the same output at current prices. This results in a decrease in supply. We see how prices go up in the right graph.

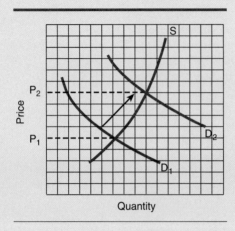

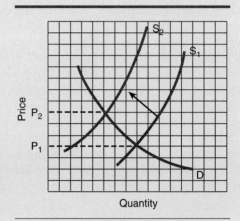

seen again and again, cost increases are quickly translated into price increases. Cost-push inflation is shown graphically in the Advanced Work box, "Graphing Demand-Pull and Cost-Push Inflation."

Inflation as a Psychological Process

Inflation takes on a life of its own.

Once inflation gets under way, the initial cause is of little consequence because the process takes on a life of its own. If people believe prices will rise, they will act in a way that keeps them rising. The only way to curb inflation is to counter inflationary psychology. Various things can set off an inflationary spiral—wars, huge federal budget deficits, large increases in the money supply, sudden increases in the price of oil—but once the spiral begins, inflationary psychology takes over.

When prices have been jolted upward, the original cause no longer matters; other forces are activated. Labor unions seek catch-up wage increases. Businesspeople raise their prices to keep up with costs—primarily wage increases. Consumers with money in their pockets spend it before prices rise further. To stop inflation, then, we need to convince workers, businesspeople, and consumers that prices will stop rising. If we can do that, prices *will* stop rising.

Once we attain a period of price stability, the psychology of inflation will be destroyed. We will enjoy that stability as long as we can avoid triggering another round of inflation. In the early 1960s we attained such a period of stability, but then came the Vietnam War and its attendant federal budget deficits.

Breaking the back of the inflationary psychology

To break the back of the inflationary psychology is to bring down the rate of inflation for a sufficiently long period of time for people actually to expect price stability to continue. It took four recessions over a 13-year period (1969–1982) to wring inflation out of the economy. To date, this has been the only cure we've come up with, and obviously it's a cure with some unpleasant side effects, particularly for those who lose their jobs during these recessions. After we examine creeping inflation and hyperinflation, we'll return to the problem of unemployment.

Creeping Inflation and Hyperinflation

An annual rate of increase in the consumer price index of 1 or 2 percent is something that virtually everyone would agree is creeping inflation. Very few people would be alarmed by this price-level increase. Businesspeople would generally like it because it would swell profits and be good for business. And as we have seen, many wage-earners and all Social Security recipients are protected from inflation by cost-of-living increases.

Creeping inflation in one country would be hyperinflation in another.

While there is no clear dividing line between creeping inflation and hyperinflation, why don't we say that once the annual rate of inflation reaches double digits, say 10 or 12 percent, *that's* hyperinflation. Once hyperinflation sets in, it becomes increasingly difficult to conduct normal economic affairs. Prices are raised constantly. It becomes impossible to enter into long-term contracts. No one is sure what the government might do.

Having a little inflation is like being a little pregnant.
—Leon Henderson

Prices serve as a signal system for business firms. If prices are rising, business firms will produce more goods and services. But what if costs are rising faster?

Suppose Nucor Steel agrees to supply General Motors with 50,000 tons of steel at $300 a ton. Suddenly Nucor's costs rise by 50 percent. Would GM go along with a $150 increase, raising the price from $300 to $450 a ton? Would *you*? Not if you had signed a contract calling for only $300 a ton.

Meanwhile, the government—meaning Congress, the president, and the Federal Reserve Board[5]—may decide to act precipitously. On August 15, 1971, President Nixon suddenly announced the imposition of wage and price controls—based on a law he said he would never use. In October 1979 the Federal Reserve Board suddenly stopped monetary growth, sending interest rates through the roof and touching off a sharp recession.

The classic hyperinflation took place in Germany after World War I. You may think that double-digit inflation (10 percent or more per year) is hyperinflation, but in Germany prices rose 10 percent an hour! The German government had to print larger and larger denominations—100-mark notes, then 1,000-mark notes, and, eventually, 1 million-mark notes. The smaller denominations became worthless; parents gave them to children as play money.

The German inflation

The German inflation eventually led to a complete economic breakdown, helped touch off a worldwide depression, and paved the way for a new chancellor named Adolf Hitler. No wonder the Germans get nervous whenever their inflation rate begins to inch up.

Another classic example is what happened in Hungary during and after World War II. Before the war, if you went into a store with a pengö, you had some money in your pocket. In those days a pengö was a pengö. But by August 1946, you needed 828 octillion pengös—that's 828 followed by 27 zeros—to buy what one pengö bought before the war.

Hungary's pengö provides an example of inflation.

More recently, there have been runaway inflations in Nicaragua (a 12 billion percent rise in prices between June 1986 and March 1991), and in Bolivia, which attained an annual inflation rate of 116,000 percent in 1985. Here is how the Bolivian inflation was described by a *Wall Street Journal* article:[6]

> *A courier stumbles into Banco Boliviano Americano, struggling under the weight of a huge bag of money he is carrying on his back. He announces that the sack contains 32 million pesos, and a teller slaps on a notation to that effect. The courier pitches the bag into a corner. "We don't bother counting the money anymore," explains Max Lowes Stah, a loan officer standing nearby. "We take the client's word for what's in the bag." Pointing to the courier's load, he says, "That's a small deposit."*

When inflation really gets out of hand, people begin to refuse to accept money as a means of payment. Society is reduced to a state of barter, making it extremely difficult for the economy to function. If you don't have what I want or I don't have what you want, we can't do business.

---

[5]Technically, the Federal Reserve Board is not part of the government. We'll consider its role in regulating the rate of growth of our money supply in Chapter 14.

[6]Sonia L. Nazario, "When Inflation Rate is 116,000 Percent, Prices Change by the Hour," *The Wall Street Journal*, February 7, 1985, p. 1.

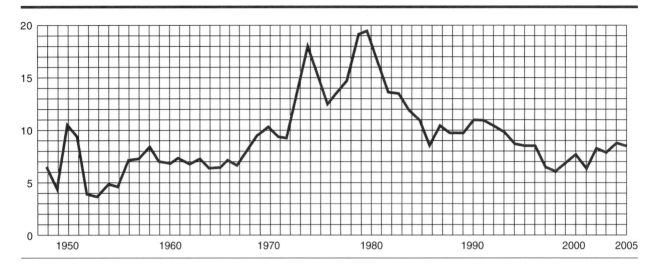

F*igure* 8

The Misery Index, 1948–2005
You'll note that this combined rate of unemployment and inflation rose to a peak in 1979 and has declined substantially since then.
Source: Economic Report of the President, 2006.

Those of us old enough to remember the relatively high rates of inflation in the 1970s and early 1980s tend to worry that such inflationary times may return. Is there any reason to worry? During wartime and during times of very heavy government borrowing, we have tended to have inflation. But not during the current war and the current record-setting government deficits. Maybe history is not repeating itself—at least not yet—because the massive influx of low-priced imported goods has held down inflation. And then, too, the hundreds of billions of dollars that foreigners lend us each year have held down interest rates, and indirectly, the cost of buying a home, a car, and the cost of other interest-sensitive goods and services.

So the big question is this: Will our luck continue to hold—or will we soon be seeing another bout of inflation? What do *you* think? And what does your professor think?

The Misery Index

One thing the economy has rarely been able to attain simultaneously is a low unemployment rate and stable prices. A British economist, A. W. Phillips, even had a curve named after him illustrating that there is a trade-off between price stability and low unemployment.

The misery index

As Phillips showed, in the 1950s and 1960s we attained price stability at the cost of higher unemployment and vice versa. In the 1970s, though, we had high unemployment *and* rapidly rising prices. During the presidential campaign of 1976, Jimmy Carter castigated President Gerald Ford with his "misery index," which was the inflation rate and the unemployment rate combined.[7] Anything over 10 was unacceptable, according to Carter.

During the 1980 presidential debates, Ronald Reagan resurrected the misery index for the voters, reminding them that it had gone from 10, when President Carter took office, all the way up to 20.

Although the misery index has obvious political uses, it also provides us with a snapshot view of our economic performance over the last four decades. From Figure 8 we can gauge just how stable our economy has been during this period. Which were the

---

[7]During the 1960s Arthur Okun, while he was President Lyndon Johnson's chairman of the Council of Economic Advisors, coined the term *economic discomfort index,* which Jimmy Carter renamed the *misery index.*

best two extended periods? I would say from the late 1950s through the late 1960s and since 1993. During both stretches our misery index stayed well below 10.

Whatever else might be said about Bill Clinton's two terms as president (January 1993–January 2001), he enjoyed great popularity and was overwhelmingly reelected in 1996. Why was he so popular? We need look no further than Figure 8. Both inflation and unemployment were not only quite low during his presidency, but the misery index declined almost steadily during both his terms.

Whatever else might be said about President George W. Bush's economic steward-ship, he would receive an "A" for keeping the misery index under 10 since he took office in January, 2001.

Current Issue: Where Are All the Jobs?

Every month at least 150,000 people enter or reenter the labor force, so we need to create that many new jobs. During the first five years of the presidential administration of George W. Bush, we averaged a monthly gain of 60,000 jobs. So we need to ask: Where are all the jobs?

A large part of the explanation is that during this period, we lost some 3 million manufacturing jobs. For decades, these jobs have been sent abroad to low-wage countries or eliminated through automation. The problem is that, at least since the new millennium, factory jobs have not been replaced by service sector jobs paying comparable wages.

Many Americans believe that there has been a great offshoring of jobs in recent years, but this is a case of perception leading reality. While the loss of manufacturing jobs has been very real, to date relatively few service jobs have been sent abroad. While we hear about all those calling centers in India, in fact we are losing just a few hundred thousand jobs a year to offshoring. But these numbers will very likely increase over the next few years as employers scramble to cut labor costs.

The March–November, 2001 recession, although quite mild, gave way to what was termed a "jobless recovery." And then, too, the terrorist attacks of 9/11 and the vast destruction wrought by Hurricane Katrina in the late summer of 2005 also depressed employment.

High productivity rates and soaring health costs may also have contributed to the slow pace of hiring new workers. Employers, especially during the jobless recovery, managed to squeeze more production from their current workers, rather than hire new ones. And they were also reluctant to take on the expensive healthcare insurance pay-ments for new employees. But high productivity growth and rapidly rising health costs are nothing new. Still, during the administration of Bush's predecessor, Bill Clinton, we added an average of 230,000 jobs per month.

So where *are* all the jobs? And to what extent is the Bush administration to blame for our poor record of job creation? If you look at the opinion polls about the president's economic stewardship, you'll see that we don't all agree. Fortunately we have presiden-tial elections every four years.

Questions for Further Thought and Discussion

1. Why is a high rate of inflation bad for the economy?

2. Right now, our economy is going through what phase of the business cycle? How do you know this?

3. Explain the difference between deflation and disinflation.

4. Being unemployed means different things to different people. Illustrate this by making up examples of three different unemployed people.

5. How would you improve upon the way the Bureau of Labor Statistics computes the unemployment rate?

6. How much is our misery index right now? How did you compute it?

7. Leo Krause is laid off. How does he make ends meet until he finds another job?

8. If we succeeded in setting up a computer-based national job bank with listings of virtually every job opening, what type of unemployment would this nearly eliminate? Explain how this would happen.

9. How were you and your family affected by the recession of 2001?

Workbook for Chapter 10

Name _____   Date _____

Multiple-Choice Questions

Circle the letter that corresponds to the best answer.

1. If the CPI rose from 160.5 in 1998 to 168.7 in 1999 to 173.4 in 2000, this would be an example of _____.

   a) deflation

   b) disinflation

   c) inflation

2. Disinflation generally occurs during _____.

   a) recessions

   b) economic booms

   c) periods of hyperinflation

   d) times of deflation

3. In the three-phase business cycle, the prosperity phase is always followed immediately by _____.

   a) recovery   c) depression

   b) the trough   d) recession

4. If our economy is at full employment, the cyclical rate of unemployment would be _____.

   a) 0   c) 5 percent

   b) 2 percent   d) impossible to find

5. During the Great Depression most unemployment was _____.

   a) frictional   c) cyclical

   b) structural   d) seasonal

6. If the CPI rose from 100 to 500, the price level rose by _____.

   a) 100 percent   d) 400 percent

   b) 200 percent   e) 500 percent

   c) 300 percent

7. Which would be the most accurate statement?

   a) Most business owners prefer deflation to inflation.

   b) In recent years Japan has suffered from deflation.

   c) Deflation is very likely in the United States over the next few years.

   d) Deflation is a form of disinflation

8. If there are 90 million people employed, 10 million unemployed, 5 million collecting unemployment insurance, and 5 million discouraged workers, there are _____ in the labor force.

   a) 90 million   d) 105 million

   b) 95 million   e) 110 million

   c) 100 million

9. During the 1970s, we experienced _____.

   a) high inflation and high unemployment

   b) low inflation and low unemployment

   c) high inflation and low unemployment

   d) low inflation and high unemployment

10. The misery index was highest in which of these years?

    a) 1960   d) 1990

    b) 1970   e) 2000

    c) 1980

11. The last time we had full employment was in _____.

    a) 1945   c) 1969

    b) 1957   d) 2001

12. We have business cycles of _____.

    a) the same length and amplitude

    b) the same length but different amplitudes

    c) the same amplitude but different lengths

    d) different lengths and amplitudes

13. During business cycles _____.
    a) troughs are followed by recessions
    b) troughs are followed by peaks
    c) peaks are followed by troughs
    d) peaks are followed by recessions

14. The second part of the expansion phase of the cycle is _____.
    a) recovery   c) recession
    b) prosperity   d) depression

15. An example of an exogenous business cycle theory would be _____.
    a) overinvestment c) money
    b) inventory   d) war

16. In 2025 the CPI rose 10 percent; in 2026 it rose 6 percent; and in 2027 it rose 2 percent. We could describe 2027 as a year of _____.
    a) inflation
    b) disinflation
    c) deflation

17. The Business Cycle Dating Committee of the national Bureau of Economic Research most likely classifies which of the following as a recession?
    a) A one-tenth of 1 percent decline in real GDP for two consecutive quarters
    b) An increase in the unemployment rate for two consecutive months
    c) A decline in nonfarm payrolls, industrial production, and personal income over six months
    d) A 1 percent rate of deflation over at least three months accompanied by rising interest rates

18. Which one of the following best describes a recession?
    a) A slowing of real GDP growth
    b) A rise in unemployment accompanied by a decline in total employment
    c) A decline in real GDP for two consecutive quarters
    d) A decline in GDP for two consecutive quarters

19. The unemployment rate is computed by the _____.
    a) nation's unemployment insurance offices
    b) Bureau of Labor Statistics
    c) Department of Commerce
    d) Office of Management and Budget

20. If the number of unemployed stays the same and the number of people in the labor force rises, _____.
    a) the unemployment rate will rise
    b) the unemployment rate will fall
    c) the unemployment rate will stay the same
    d) there is not enough information to determine what will happen to the unemployment rate

21. Which statement is true?
    a) Both liberals and conservatives feel that the official unemployment rate is too high.
    b) Both liberals and conservatives feel that the official unemployment rate is too low.
    c) The liberals believe that the official unemployment rate is too high, and the conservatives feel that it is too low.
    d) The conservatives feel that the official unemployment rate is too high, and the liberals feel that it is too low.

22. Which is the most accurate statement?
    a) Business cycle forecasting dates back to biblical times.
    b) Business cycle forecasts are nearly always inaccurate.
    c) Business cycle forecasts are almost always accurate.
    d) It is virtually impossible to forecast business cycle turning points.

23. Which statement is false?
    a) Over the last two decades there has been an upward drift in the unemployment rate.
    b) The unemployment rate for blacks is about twice that for whites.
    c) The official unemployment rate includes "discouraged" workers.
    d) None of the above is false.

Answer questions 24 through 29 by using one of these three choices:

   a) frictionally unemployed

   b) structurally unemployed

   c) cyclically unemployed

24. Ella Jillian Fosnough, an autoworker who is still out of work two years after her plant closed, is _____.

25. Sophia King, a homemaker returning to the labor market after an absence of 10 years and looking for work, is _____.

26. Brian Horn, a factory worker who is laid off until business picks up again, is _____.

27. Austin Noorda, Mark Noorda, and Debbie Noorda are "between jobs." They are _____.

28. Brad Peterson, a man in his mid-50s whose skills have become obsolete, would be _____.

29. When the unemployment rate goes above 5 percent, anything above that 5 percent level is _____.

30. An example of deflation since the base year would be a CPI in the current year of _____.

   a) 90   c) 110

   b) 100   d) 200

31. Inflation generally occurs _____.

   a) during wartime   c) during recessions

   b) before wars   d) during peacetime

32. The period of greatest price stability was _____.

   a) 1950–56   c) 1968–76

   b) 1958–64   d) 1976–82

33. Traditionally, those hurt by inflation have been _____.

   a) creditors and people on fixed incomes

   b) debtors and people on fixed incomes

   c) debtors and creditors

34. Farmers have generally been _____ by inflation.

   a) hurt

   b) helped

   c) neither helped nor hurt

35. Creditors generally do better when inflation is _____.

   a) anticipated

   b) unanticipated

   c) neither anticipated nor unanticipated

36. Businesspeople generally like a little _____ but dislike a little _____.

   a) inflation, deflation

   b) deflation, inflation

37. Inflationary recessions first occurred in the _____.

   a) 1950s   c) 1970s

   b) 1960s   d) 1980s

38. Most post-World War II recessions lasted less than _____.

   a) three years

   b) two years

   c) one year

   d) six months

39. According to the Book of Genesis, Joseph may have been the first person to _____.

   a) forecast a business cycle

   b) collect unemployment insurance benefits

   c) formulate the misery index

   d) differentiate between demand-pull inflation and cost-push inflation

40. The 1996 Welfare Reform Act has pushed _____ our unemployment rate; our high prison population has pushed _____ our unemployment rate.

   a) up, up

   b) down, down

   c) down, up

   d) up, down

41. During the mid-1980s, both Bolivia and Nicaragua experienced _____.

   a) creeping inflation

   b) hyperinflation

   c) disinflation

   d) deflation

42. The rate of job creation during the first 5 years of the administration of George W. Bush has been _____.

    a) relatively low

    b) relatively high

    c) about average

43. There are over 2 million Americans in prison. This tends to _____ the official unemployment rate.

    a) raise

    b) lower

    c) to have no effect on

44. Which is the most accurate statement?

    a) The monthly rate of job creation during the first five years of the administration of George W. Bush has been faster than that during Bill Clinton's first five years in office.

    b) We need to create at least 150,000 new jobs every month to accommodate the people entering or re-entering the labor force.

    c) Every year millions of American jobs are off-shored.

    d) There are as many manufacturing jobs in the United States today as there were when George W. Bush became president.

Fill-In Questions

1. The worst recessions since World War II began in the year _____ and the year _____.

2. Stagflation is a contraction of the words _____ and _____.

3. To find the number of people in the labor force we need to add the _____ and the _____.

4. To find the unemployment rate we need to divide the _____ by the _____.

5. A person who is functionally illiterate faces long periods of _____ unemployment.

6. When the overall unemployment rate is 6.5 percent, the cyclical unemployment rate is _____.

7. The upper turning point of a business cycle just before the onset of a recession is called the _____.

8. In the year _____ the OPEC nations quadrupled the price of oil.

9. The low point of a business cycle is the _____; the high point is the _____.

10. Theories that place the cause of business cycles within the economy rather than outside are known as _____ theories.

11. According to the inventory theory of the business cycle, a recession is set off when retailers _____.

12. The monetary theory of the business cycle hypothesizes that recessions are set off when _____ and recoveries begin when the monetary authorities _____.

13. Liberals say the unemployment rate is actually _____ than the BLS says it is; conservatives say it is really _____.

14. Between the mid-1970s and the mid-1980s, our unemployment rate never dipped below _____ percent.

15. The unemployment rate for blacks is about _____ times the white unemployment rate.

16. The misery index is found by adding the _____ and the _____.

17. Since President George W. Bush took office the misery index has been below _____.

18. During a very severe recession when more than 11 percent of the labor force is out of work, most of the unemployment is _____ unemployment.

19. Two exogenous business cycle theories are the _____ theory and the _____ theory.

20. According to A. W. Phillips, there is a trade-off between ＿＿＿＿ and ＿＿＿＿.

21. If the consumer price index rises from 150 to 180, the cost of living rose by ＿＿＿＿ percent.

22. Once inflation is under way, a(n) ＿＿＿＿ takes over.

23. To stop inflation, we need to convince people that ＿＿＿＿.

Problems

1. If the unemployment rate is 7 percent, how much is cyclical unemployment?

2. Compute the unemployment rate given the following information: 8 million unemployed, 117 million employed.

3. Given the following information, how many people are in the labor force? 3 million people are collecting unemployment insurance; 7 million people are officially unemployed; 2 million people are discouraged workers; and 110 million people are employed.

4. How much would the nominal interest rate be if the real rate of interest were 6 percent and the expected rate of inflation were 7 percent?

5. How much would the real rate of interest be if the nominal interest rate was 12 percent and the expected rate of inflation was 4 percent?

6. If the CPI is currently 178.9, by what percentage did prices rise since the base year?

7. If the CPI rose from 200 in 1991 to 240 in 1997, by what percentage did prices increase?

8. If the rate of inflation is 5 percent, the prime rate of interest is 6 percent, and the unemployment rate is 7 percent, how much is the misery index?

9. If the overall rate of unemployment is 8.3 percent, what is the rate of cyclical unemployment?

Figure 1

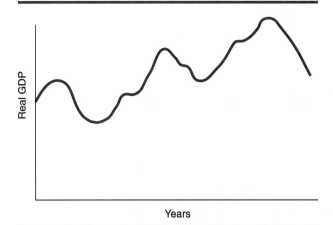

10. Label the graph in Figure 1 with respect to the three phases of the business cycle and the cycle turning points.

11. Answer these questions, given the information that follows: (a) How many people are in the labor force? (b) What is the unemployment rate?
Employed: 90 million; discouraged workers: 4 million; unemployed: 10 million; people collecting unemployment insurance: 8 million.

12. (a) If the CPI fell from 180 to 150, by what percentage did the price level fall? (b) If the CPI rose from 150 to 180, by what percentage did the price level rise?

13. In which year was the misery index (a) the highest? (b) the lowest?

Year	Unemployment Rate (percent)	Inflation Rate (percent)
1948	8.0	3.0
1949	5.9	−2.1
1950	5.3	5.9
1951	3.3	6.0
1952	3.0	0.8
1953	2.9	0.7
1954	5.5	−0.7
1955	4.4	0.4
1956	4.1	3.0
1957	4.3	2.9
1958	6.8	1.8
1959	5.5	1.7
1960	5.5	1.4
1961	6.7	0.7

14. If the unemployment rate is 10 percent, there are 150 million people in the labor force, and there are 5 million discouraged workers, how many people are unemployed?

15. (a) In which year did disinflation set in? (b) In which year did deflation set in?

Year	CPI
2010	100.0
2011	104.0
2012	110.2
2013	121.7
2014	129.4
2015	132.0
2016	133.5
2017	134.0
2018	133.8
2019	133.0
2020	131.6

16. If cyclical unemployment is 6 percent, how much is the unemployment rate?

17. If the unemployment rate is 10 percent and 90 million people are working, how many people are unemployed?

18. Cameron Amundson and Carter Amundson reside in Eagle's Nest, Iowa, which has an unemployment rate of 6 percent and a labor force of 100. Cameron is a senior at the University of Dubuque and Carter is unemployed. Cameron graduates and finds a job; Carter gives up looking for work and enrolls in Loris College. Compute the new unemployment rate of Eagle's Nest.

19. In which year and quarter did the prosperity phase of the business cycle begin?

Year	Quarter	Real GDP
2020	I	18,215
2020	II	18,703
2020	III	19,496
2020	IV	19,002
2021	I	18,771
2021	II	18,563
2021	III	18,428
2021	IV	18,737
2022	I	19,114
2022	II	19,385
2022	III	19,739
2022	IV	20,058

Chapter 11

Classical and Keynesian Economics

The first commandment of medicine is, "Do no harm." Until the Great Depression, the even stricter first commandment of economics was, "Do nothing." The workings of the price system would ensure that our economy be at, or moving toward, full employment. In the immortal words of Thomas Jefferson, "The government that governs least, governs best." But as the depression got worse, it became clear that the government needed to take very decisive measures to get the economy moving again. John Maynard Keynes outlined just what measures were needed.

This chapter is divided into three parts: (1) the classical economic system, (2) the Keynesian critique of the classical system, and (3) the Keynesian system. The basic difference between Keynes and the classicals is whether our economy tends toward full employment.

CHAPTER OBJECTIVES

In this chapter we shall take up:

- Say's law.
- Classical equilibrium.
- Real balance, interest rate, and foreign purchases effects.
- Aggregate demand.
- Aggregate supply in the long run and short run.

- The Keynesian critique of the classical system.
- Equilibrium at varying price levels.
- Disequilibrium and equilibrium.
- Keynesian policy prescriptions.

Jean Baptiste Say, French economist and entrepreneur (Historical Pictures Stock Montage)

Part I: The Classical Economic System

Say's Law

The centerpiece of classical economics is Say's law. Named for Jean Baptiste Say, a late-18th-century (the late 1700s) French economist, the law stated, *"Supply creates its own demand."* Think about it. Somehow what we produce—supply—all gets sold.

A few years later the great English economist David Ricardo elaborated on Say's law:

> No man produces but with a view to consume or sell, and he never sells but with an intention to purchase some other commodity which may be immediately useful to him or which may contribute to future production. By producing, then, he necessarily becomes

Say's law

Man produces in order to consume.

—Claude-Frédéric Bastiat, French economist

251

either the consumer of his own goods, or the purchaser and consumer of the goods of some other person.[1]

People who produce things are paid. What do they do with this money? They spend it. On what? On what *other* people produce.

We can illustrate Say's law using the production figures in Table 1. Let's look at Table 1. Everyone eats tomatoes, bread, and butter, and wears tee shirts and wooden shoes. Joe sells eight bushels of tomatoes, keeping two for his own use. Sally wears one of her tee shirts and sells the other four. And so forth.

What do they do with the proceeds from their sales? They use them to buy what they need from each of the others. Joe, for example, buys a tee shirt from Sally, four loaves of bread from Mike, two pounds of butter from Bill (they all like to put a lot of butter on their bread), and a pair of wooden shoes from Alice.

"Why does anybody work?" asked Say. People work to make money with which to buy things. Why do *you* work?

As long as everyone spends everything that he or she earns, we're OK. But we begin having problems when people start saving part of their incomes.

TABLE 1	Production in a Five-Person Economy
Joe	10 bushels of tomatoes
Sally	5 tee shirts
Mike	20 loaves of bread
Bill	10 pounds of butter
Alice	5 pairs of wooden shoes

Basically, producers need to sell everything they produce. If some people save, then not everything produced will be sold. In a world with large companies instead of self-employed producers, some workers must be laid off when demand for production falls. In fact, as unemployment mounts, demand falls still further, necessitating further cutbacks in production and employment.

The villain of the piece is clearly saving. If only people would spend their entire incomes, we'd never have unemployment. But people do save, and saving is crucial to economic growth. Without saving we could not have investment.

Think of production as consisting of two products: consumer goods and investment goods (for now, we're ignoring government goods). People will buy consumer goods; the money spent on such goods is designated by the letter C. Money spent by businesses on investment goods is designated by the letter I.

If we think of GDP as total spending, then GDP would be C + I. Once this money is spent, other people receive it as income. And what do they do with their income? They spend some of it and save the rest.

If we think of GDP as income received, that money will either be spent on consumer goods, C, or saved, which we'll designate by the letter S. If we put all this together, we have two equations:

$$GDP = C + I$$
$$GDP = C + S$$

These two equations can be simplified to one short equation. First, because things equal to the same thing are equal to each other:

$$C + I = C + S$$

---

[1]David Ricardo, *The Principles of Political Economy and Taxation* (Burr Ridge, IL: Richard D. Irwin, 1963), p. 166.

This step is justified because C + I and C + S are both equal to GDP. Therefore, they are equal to each other.

Next, we can subtract the same thing from both sides of an equation. In this case we are subtracting C:

$$C + I = C + S$$
$$I = S$$

$$C + I = C + S$$
$$I = S$$

Going back to Say's law, we can see that it holds up, at least in accordance with classical analysis. Supply *does* create its own demand. The economy produces a supply of consumer goods and investment goods. The people who produce these goods spend part of their incomes on consumer goods and save the rest. Their savings are borrowed by investors who spend this money on investment goods. The bottom line is that everything the economy produces is purchased.

This is a perfect economic system. Everything produced is sold. Everyone who wants to work can find a job. There will never be any serious economic downturns, so there is no need for government intervention to set things right.

Supply and Demand Revisited

How much is the equilibrium price in Figure 1? Good. And the equilibrium quantity? Good—you got that right, too. You followed the horizontal dotted line to a price of about $7.20 and the vertical dotted line to a quantity of 6.

Incidentally, we call the price that clears the market *equilibrium price* and the quantity purchased and sold *equilibrium quantity*. At the equilibrium price the quantity that buyers wish to purchase is equal to the quantity that sellers wish to sell.

Now let's see how the classical economists applied the law of supply and demand to help prove Say's law and, more specifically, to prove that I = S (Investment = Saving). This is done in Figure 2, which graphs the demand for investment funds and the supply of savings.

What if savings and investment were not equal? For instance, if savings were greater than investment, there would be unemployment. Not everything being produced would be purchased.

There's nothing to worry about, according to the classical economists. And they proved this by means of the two curves in Figure 2. If savings were greater than investment, the interest rate would fall. Why? Because some savers would be willing to lend at lower interest rates and some investors would be induced to borrow at lower interest rates.

The classical economists had a fallback position. Even if lower interest rates did not eliminate the surplus of savings relative to investment, price flexibility would bring about equilibrium between saving and investing. Business firms, unable to sell their entire output, would simply lower prices. And then people would buy everything produced.

Margin notes:

Equilibrium price and quantity

Savings and investment will be equal.

Prices and wages will fall to bring about equilibrium between saving and investing.

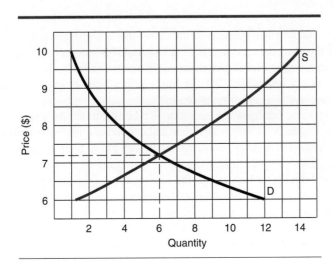

Figure 1
Demand and Supply Curves
The curves cross at a price of $7.20 and a quantity of 6.

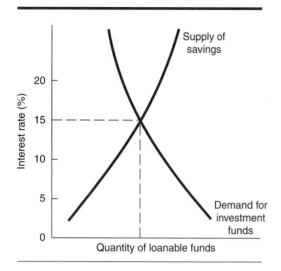

F*igure* 2

The Loanable Funds Market

The demand and supply curves cross at an interest rate of 15 percent.

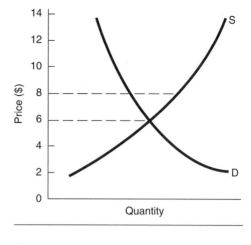

F*igure* 3

Market for Hypothetical Product

If the quantity supplied is greater than the quantity demanded at a certain price (in this case, $8), the price will fall to the equilibrium level ($6), at which quantity demanded is equal to quantity supplied.

F*igure* 4

Hypothetical Labor Market

If the wage rate is set too high ($9 an hour), the quantity of labor supplied exceeds the quantity of labor demanded. The wage rate falls to the equilibrium level of $7; at that wage rate the quantity of labor demanded equals the quantity supplied.

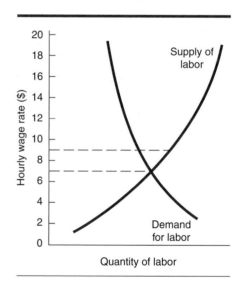

One might ask whether business firms could make a profit if prices were reduced. Yes, answered the classical economists, if resource prices—especially wages—were also reduced. Although output and employment might decline initially, they would move back up again once prices and wages fell. At lower prices people would buy more, and at lower wages employers would hire more.

Falling prices and falling wage rates can also be illustrated by a supply and demand graph. Look at Figure 3. If sellers of a particular good are not selling all they wish to sell *at the current market price,* some of them will lower their price. In Figure 3 the price falls from $8 to $6, which happens to be the equilibrium price.

Exactly the same thing happens in the labor market (see Figure 4). At a wage rate of $9 an hour, there are many unemployed workers. Some are willing to accept a lower wage rate. When the wage rate falls to $7 an hour, everyone who wants to work at that rate can find a job, and every employer willing to hire workers at that rate can find as many workers as she wants to hire.

The Classical Equilibrium: Aggregate Demand Equals Aggregate Supply

What exactly *is* equilibrium GDP? We've seen, on a microeconomic level, that when quantity demanded equals quantity supplied, we're at equilibrium. Similarly, on a macroeconomic level, when aggregate demand equals aggregate supply, we're at equilibrium. At equilibrium there is a state of balance between opposing forces such that there is no tendency for change.

The classical economists believed our economy was either at, or tending toward, full employment. So at the classical equilibrium—the GDP at which aggregate demand was equal to aggregate supply—we were at full employment. And as long as aggregate demand and aggregate supply did not change, our economy would continue operating at full employment.

Our economy is either at or tending toward full employment.

We've been weaving back and forth between macro and micro analysis. From here on it's going to be macro. We'll begin with the economy's aggregate demand curve, go on to the economy's aggregate long-run and short-run supply curves, and finally put these curves together to derive the economy's equilibrium GDP.

The Aggregate Demand Curve

The aggregate demand curve of Figure 5 depicts an inverse relationship between the price level and the quantity of goods and services demanded: As the price level declines, the quantity of goods and services demanded rises. Similarly, as the price level rises, the quantity of goods and services demanded declines. This relationship is illustrated by an aggregate demand curve that slopes downward to the right.

The aggregate demand curve shows that as the price level declines, the quantity of goods and services demanded rises.

What does this curve tell us? We'll begin by defining aggregate demand as *the total value of real GDP that all sectors of the economy are willing to purchase at various price levels.* You'll notice that as the price level declines, people are willing to purchase more and more output. Alternatively, as the price level rises, the quantity of output purchased goes down.

Definition of aggregate demand

There are three reasons why the quantity of goods and services purchased declines as the price level increases: (1) An increase in the price level reduces the wealth of people holding money, making them feel poorer and reducing their purchases; (2) the

There are three reasons why the quantity of goods and services purchased declines as the price level increases.

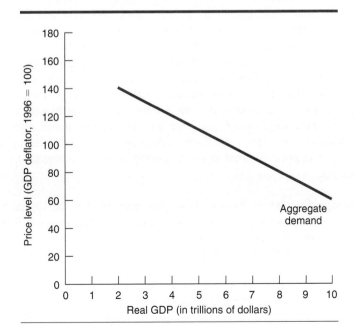

Figure 5

Aggregate Demand Curve (in trillions of dollars)
The level of aggregate demand varies inversely with the price level: As the price level declines, people are willing to purchase more and more output. Alternatively, as the price level rises, the quantity of output purchased goes down.

higher price level pushes up the interest rate, which leads to a reduction in the purchase of interest-sensitive goods, such as cars and houses; and (3) net exports decline as foreigners buy less from us and we buy more from them at the higher price level.

(1) The Real Balance Effect   When the price level goes up, your purchasing power goes down. The money you have in the bank, your stocks and bonds, and all your other liquid assets shrink in terms of what they can buy. You *feel* poorer, so you'll tend to spend less.

The *real balance effect* is the influence of a change in your purchasing power on the quantity of real GDP that you are willing to buy. Here's how it works. Suppose you are holding $800 in money and your only other asset is $200 worth of CDs. Now, what if the prices of most goods and services fell, among them those of CDs. The $800 that you're holding now buys more CDs than before. You've got a larger real balance.

Before prices fell, you were very happy holding 80 percent of your assets in the form of money ($800 of $1,000) and 20 percent in the form of CDs ($200 of $1,000). But now those CDs you're holding are worth less than $200 because their price has fallen, while your money is worth more. Let's say there was so much deflation that the purchasing power of your money doubled, to $1,600, while the value of your CDs fell to $100. Question: Wouldn't you like to take advantage of the price decrease to buy more CDs? Of course you would. And how many more dollars' worth of CDs would you buy if you wanted to keep 20 percent of your assets in the form of CDs (and 80 percent in the form of money)? Answer: Your total assets are now $1,700 ($1,600 in money and $100 in CDs), so you'd want to hold 20 percent of the $1,700, or $340, in CDs. In other words, you'd buy $240 worth of CDs.

Let's sum up. A decrease in the price level increases the quantity of real money. The larger the quantity of real money, the larger the quantity of goods and services demanded. Similarly, an increase in the price level decreases the quantity of real money. The smaller the quantity of real money, the smaller the quantity of goods and services demanded.

(2) The Interest Rate Effect   A rising price level pushes up interest rates, which in turn lowers the consumption of certain goods and services and also lowers investment in new plant and equipment. Let's look more closely at this two-step sequence.

First, during times of inflation, interest rates rise, because lenders need to protect themselves against the declining purchasing power of the dollar. If you lent someone $100 for one year and there was a 10 percent rate of inflation, you would need to be paid back $110 just to be able to buy what your original $100 would have purchased.

Second, certain goods and services are more sensitive to interest rate changes than others. Can you name some especially sensitive ones? Try auto purchases and home mortgages. Clearly, then, when interest rates rise, the consumption of certain goods and services falls, and when interest rates fall, their consumption rises.

Now let's see how a rising price level (which pushes up interest rates) affects investment spending. We saw in Chapter 6 that rising interest rates choke off investment projects that would have been carried out at lower rates. Some projects, especially in building construction, where interest is a major cost, are particularly sensitive to interest rate changes. So we know that a rising price level pushes up interest rates and lowers both consumption and investment. Similarly, a declining price level, which pushed down interest rates, encourages consumption and investment. Clearly the interest rate effect can be very powerful.

(3) The Foreign Purchases Effect   When the price level in the United States rises relative to the price levels in other countries, what effect does this have on U.S. imports and exports? Because American goods become more expensive relative to foreign goods, our imports rise (foreign goods are cheaper) and our exports decline (American goods are more expensive).

In sum, when our relative price level increases, this tends to increase our imports and lower our exports. Thus, our net exports (exports minus imports) component of GDP declines. When our relative price level declines, the net exports component (and GDP) rises.

The Long-Run Aggregate Supply Curve

First I'll define aggregate supply as *the amount of real output, or real GDP, that will be made available by sellers at various price levels.* Next let's see what the long-run aggregate supply curve looks like. It looks like the vertical line in Figure 6.

Definition of aggregate supply

This curve is based on two assumptions of the classical economists. First, in the long run, the economy operates at full employment. (In Chapter 10 we decided that, because there would always be frictional and structural unemployment totaling about 5 percent of the labor force, a 5 percent unemployment rate meant the economy was operating at full employment.) Second, in the long run, output is independent of prices.

Ready for a little action? We're going to put the aggregate demand curve and the long-run aggregate supply curve together on one graph and see what happens. Figure 7 does this.

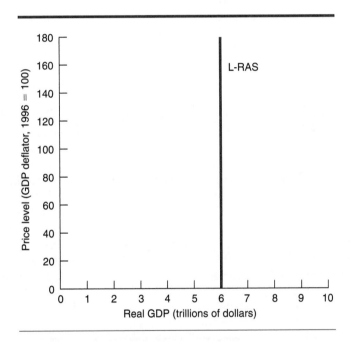

Figure 6

Long-Run Aggregate Supply Curve (in trillions of dollars) Why is this curve a vertical line? The classical economists made two assumptions: (1) In the long run, the economy operates at full employment; (2) in the long run, output is independent of prices.

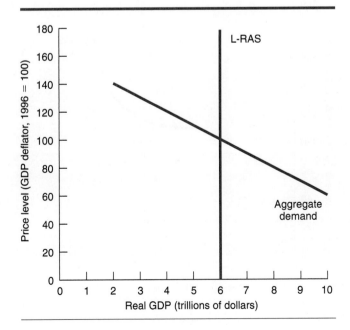

Figure 7

Aggregate Demand and Long-Run Aggregate Supply (in trillions of dollars) The long-run equilibrium of real GDP is $6 trillion at a price level of 100.

The equilibrium full-
employment level of real GDP

What happens is that we find two things: (1) the equilibrium full-employment level of real GDP and (2) the corresponding price level, which happens to be 100.

What does this *mean*? It means that in the long run our economy will produce the level of output that will provide jobs for everyone who wants to work (that is, the unemployment rate will be 5 percent). In other words, in the long run our economy will produce at full-employment GDP. And how much *is* full-employment GDP, according to Figure 7? It comes to exactly $6 trillion.

This is what the classical economists predicted and is completely consistent with Say's law: Supply creates its own demand. Our economy, then, will always be at full employment in the long run. But what about in the short run?

The Short-Run Aggregate Supply Curve

The economy may operate below full-employment GDP in the short run.

In the short run, according to the classical economists, some unemployment *is* possible. Some output *may* go unsold. And the economy *may* operate below full-employment GDP. Figure 8 shows all of this.

Why does the short-run aggregate supply curve sweep upward to the right? Because business firms will supply increasing amounts of output as prices rise. Why? Because wages, rent, and other production costs are set by contracts in the short run and don't increase immediately in response to rising prices. Your landlord can't come to you while your lease still has two years to go and tell you that he must raise your rent because *his* costs are going up. Your employees who are working under two- and three-year contracts can't ask you to renegotiate. (They can *ask* you to, but you probably won't.) And your suppliers may also have agreed contractually to send you their goods at set prices. So, in the short run, higher prices mean higher profit margins, which give business firms like yours an incentive to increase output.

As output rises, costs rise.

As output continues to rise, land, labor, and capital become more expensive and less-efficient resources are pressed into service. To get homemakers to work, employers need to make wage rates attractive enough (and some even go to the expense of setting up child care facilities) to entice them back into the labor force. As output approaches full employment, antiquated machinery and less-productive facilities must be used. And

F*igure* 8
Short-Run Aggregate Supply Curve (in trillions of dollars)
Why does the short-run aggregate supply curve sweep upward to the right? Because business firms will supply increasing amounts of output as prices rise.

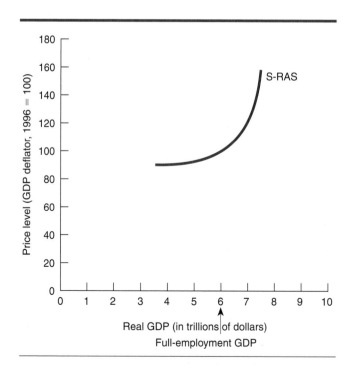

so, as the full-employment level of GDP is approached, the short-run aggregate supply curve is becoming steeper and steeper. You'll notice that full-employment GDP is still $6 trillion, as in Figure 7.

You'll also notice in Figure 8 that output continues to rise even after we've exceeded full-employment GDP. Is this *possible*? Can our real GDP ever exceed our full-employment GDP? Yes, it can. But only in the short run.

Let's extend the example of luring homemakers into the labor force with better pay. How about enticing full-time college students who are working part-time to give up their education (or perhaps switch to night school) and work full-time? Or how about persuading retired people, or those about to retire, to take full-time jobs? How would we do this? By paying attractive wage rates and providing whatever other incentives are necessary. We can also keep putting back into service aging or obsolete plant and equipment, and make use of marginal land as well.

Why, then, does the short-run aggregate supply curve eventually become vertical? Because there is a physical limit to the output capacity of the economy. There is just so much land, labor, and capital that can be put to work, and when that limit is reached, there is no way to increase production appreciably. During World War II, U.S. factories ran 24 hours a day, and millions of people worked 50 or 60 hours a week. But everyone simply could not have kept up this effort year after year. As Americans said at the time, "There's a war going on." Just in case someone hadn't noticed.

So, in the short run, we can push our output beyond the level of full-employment GDP and get our economy to operate beyond full employment. But this is possible only in the short run. In the long run, we're back at the long-run aggregate supply curve.

Figure 9 puts this all together for you. You see the point at which the short- and long-run aggregate supply curves intersect the aggregate demand curve? That's the long-run equilibrium level of GDP. At that point, the price level happens to be 100 and GDP is $6 trillion.

In the classical system, all the parts fit together neatly. The long-run aggregate supply curve, the short-run aggregate supply cost curve, and the aggregate demand curve come together at full employment. If there *is* some unemployment in the short run, it will automatically be eliminated as the economy returns to its long-run, full-employment equilibrium. And if there is more than full employment, this is again only a temporary phenomenon that will end as the level of economic activity returns to its full-employment level. In short, the economy can temporarily slide up and down its short-run aggregate supply curve, but it inevitably returns to its long-run equilibrium at full employment.

Beyond full employment

Why does the short-run aggregate supply curve eventually become vertical?

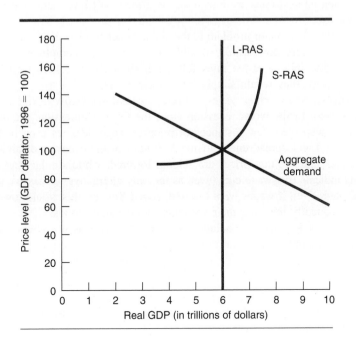

Figure 9

Aggregate Demand, Long-Run and Short-Run Aggregate Supply (in trillions of dollars)
The long-run aggregate supply curve, the short-run aggregate supply curve, and the aggregate demand come together at full employment.

Part II: The Keynesian Critique of the Classical System

> Our free enterprise system has rightly been compared to a gigantic computing machine capable of solving its own problems automatically. But anyone who has had some practical experience with large computers knows that they do break down and can't operate unattended.
>
> –Wassily Leontief, March 1971–

Until the Great Depression, classical economics was the dominant school of economic thought. Adam Smith, credited by many as the founder of classical economics, believed the government should intervene in economic affairs as little as possible. Indeed, laissez-faire economics was practiced down through the years until the time of President Herbert Hoover, who kept predicting that prosperity was just around the corner. John Maynard Keynes finally proclaimed the end of the classical era when he advocated massive government intervention to bring an end to the Great Depression.

John Maynard Keynes, a prominent classically trained economist, spent the first half of the 1930s writing a monumental critique of the classical system.[2] If supply creates its own demand, he asked, why are we having a worldwide depression? Keynes set out to learn what went wrong and how to fix it.

Keynes posed this problem for the classical economists: What if saving and investment were not equal? For instance, if saving were greater than investment, there would be unemployment. Not everything being produced would be purchased.

No problem, said the classicals, pointing back to Figure 2, which showed that the interest rate would equilibrate savings and investment. If the quantity of savings exceeded the quantity of loanable funds demanded for investment purposes, the interest rate would simply fall. And it would keep falling until the quantity of savings and the demand for investment funds were equal.

Keynes disputed this view. Saving and investing are done by different people for different reasons. Most saving is done by individuals for big-ticket items, such as cars, stereo systems, and major appliances, as well as for houses or retirement. Investing is done by those who run business firms basically because they are trying to make a profit. They will borrow to invest only when there is a reasonably good profit outlook. Why sink a lot of money into plant and equipment when your factory and machines are half idle? Even when interest rates are low, business firms won't invest unless it is profitable for them to do so.

Even *this* posed no major problem to the classical economists, because they assumed wages and prices were downwardly flexible. If there were unemployment, the unemployed would find jobs as wage rates fell. And, similarly, if sellers were stuck with unwanted inventory, they would simply lower their prices.

Keynes questioned whether wages and prices *were* downwardly flexible, even during a severe recession. In the worst recession since the Great Depression, the downturn of 1981–82, there were very few instances of price or wage declines even in the face of falling output and widespread unemployment. Studies of the behavior of highly concentrated industries indicate that prices are seldom lowered, while similar studies of large labor unions indicate that wage cuts (even as the only alternative to massive layoffs) are seldom accepted. Even if wages *were* lowered, added Keynes, this would lower workers' incomes, consequently lowering their spending on consumer goods.

All of this led Keynes to conclude that the economy was not always at, or tending toward, a full-employment equilibrium. Keynes believed three possible equilibriums

demand oriented

Keynes asked, "What if saving and investment were not equal?"

Keynes: Saving and investing are done by different people for different reasons.

We are not always at, or tending toward, full employment.

---

[2]*The General Theory of Employment, Interest, and Money* is considered one of the most influential books of the 20th century.

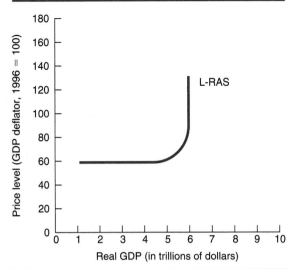

F*igure* **10**

Modified Keynesian Aggregate Supply Curve
As an economy works its way out of a depression, output can be raised without raising prices, so the aggregate supply curve is flat. However, as resources become more fully employed and bottlenecks develop, costs and prices begin to rise. When this happens the aggregate supply curve begins to curve upward. When we reach full employment (at a real GDP of $6 trillion), output cannot be raised any further.

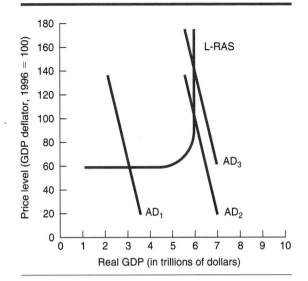

F*igure* **11**

Three Aggregate Demand Curves
AD_1 represents aggregate demand during a recession or depression; AD_2 crosses the long-run aggregate supply curve at full employment; and AD_3 represents excessive demand.

existed—*below* full employment, *at* full employment, and *above* full employment. Using the same demand and supply analysis as the classicals, Keynes showed that full employment was hardly inevitable.

The Keynesian long-run aggregate supply curve was really a hybrid of the classical short-run and long-run aggregate supply curves. It is drawn in Figure 10.[3] At extremely low levels of real GDP, when output is at, say, $3 trillion, our economy is in a catastrophic depression. As the economy begins to recover, output can be raised to about $4.7 trillion without any increase in prices. Why? Because millions of unemployed workers would be happy to work for the prevailing wage, so wage rates would certainly not have to be raised to entice people back to work. Furthermore, businessowners would also be happy to sell additional output at existing prices. But as real GDP continues to rise above $4.7 trillion, costs begin to rise, and bottlenecks eventually develop in certain industries, making greater and greater price increases necessary. Eventually, of course, at a real GDP of $6 trillion, we are at full employment and cannot, in the long run, raise output above that level. (See the box, "The Ranges of the Aggregate Supply Curve.")

So, for all intents and purposes, the Keynesian and classical aggregate supply analyses are virtually identical. But they are completely at odds with respect to aggregate demand. Figure 11 shows three aggregate demand curves. AD_1 represents a very low level of aggregate demand, which, Keynes believed, was the basic problem during recessions and depressions. The AD_2 curve shows the same full-employment equilibrium shown in Figure 9. And finally, AD_3 represents excessive demand, which would cause inflation.

The Keynesian and classical aggregate supply analyses are virtually identical.

[3]The curve shown in Figure 10 is actually a slightly modified Keynesian aggregate supply curve. Keynes originally assumed prices would not rise at all until full employment was attained (when real GDP was $6 trillion), but we've allowed here for an accelerating rise in prices from a real GDP of about $4.7 trillion to one of $6 trillion.

The Ranges of the Aggregate Supply Curve

The curve shown in the figure to the right is just slightly more elaborate than that in Figure 10. Here we have the three ranges: Keynesian, intermediate, and classical. The Keynesian range is thus named because John Maynard Keynes was writing during the Great Depression. People were so anxious to find work that they were happy to take a job—virtually any job—at the going wage rate. Thus, business firms could easily expand output without encountering rising wages.

Would they raise prices? Not for quite a while. After suffering through a few years of extremely low sales, they would be grateful for more business, albeit at the same price.

As the economy expanded, bottlenecks would begin to develop, shortages of resources (especially labor) would occur here and there, and costs would begin to rise in some sectors and eventually spread throughout the economy. And then business firms would begin raising their prices as well.

Eventually the economy would reach the maximum output level, at which point the only give would be in the form of higher prices. This would be the classical range of the aggregate supply curve. Remember that the classical economists believed that full employment was our normal state of affairs.

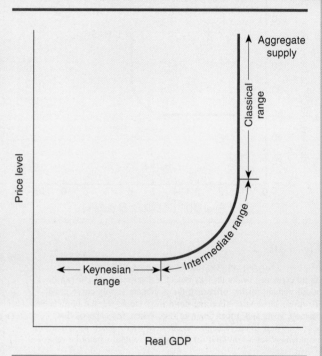

In the last chapter we talked about demand-pull inflation, which was described as "too much money chasing too few goods." Demand-pull inflation occurs in the intermediate range of the aggregate supply curve in the figure in the box, "The Ranges of the Aggregate Supply Curve." Or, looking at Figure 11, start with an aggregate demand of AD_1 and imagine a series of higher and higher aggregate demand curves. At first we would have increases in real GDP without any price increases, but as aggregate demand moved closer to AD_2, we would eventually be able to keep pushing up real GDP only at the cost of some inflation. And as aggregate demand approached AD_2, we would be obtaining smaller and smaller increments of added output at the cost of larger and larger rises in the price level.

So we see that increases in aggregate demand will eventually lead to inflation. Applying this same analysis but moving in the opposite direction, we'll observe that decreasing aggregate demand leads to declining output and a decline in the rate of inflation. Starting at AD_2 and moving toward AD_1 in Figure 11, we see that real GDP is declining. As we noted toward the beginning of the last chapter, a decline in real GDP for two consecutive quarters is, by definition, a recession. And if continued decreases in aggregate demand pushed real GDP down still further, the recession would deepen and we might even sink into a depression.

Under this Keynesian analysis, we have three distinct possible equilibriums—below full employment, at full employment, and above full employment (with respect to prices, not output). Our economy, according to Keynes, does not necessarily tend toward full employment, as the classicals maintained.

John Maynard Keynes, British economist (The Bettmann/Archives)

Our economy, said Keynes, can get stuck at an equilibrium that is well below full employment:

> Indeed it seems capable of remaining in a chronic condition of subnormal activity for a considerable period without any marked tendency either toward recovery or toward complete collapse. Moreover, the evidence indicates that full, or even approximately full, employment is a rare and short-lived occurrence.[4]

Let's examine the Keynesian system in more detail. Then we'll be ready to consider what the government should (or should not) do to prevent or to moderate recessions and inflations.

Part III: The Keynesian System

The classical theory of equilibrium was great at explaining why we would be either at full employment or tending toward it. But it wasn't much good at explaining why, in the 1930s, the entire world was in a depression. We needed a new theory to explain what was happening, and we needed a policy prescription to bring us out of this depression. John Maynard Keynes provided both.

The classical equilibrium could not explain the Great Depression.

Keynes used the same aggregate demand and supply apparatus as the classicals had, but he came up with very different conclusions. The key to his analysis was the role of aggregate demand. According to Keynes, the equilibrium level of GDP was determined primarily by the volume of expenditures planned by consumers, business firms, governments, and foreigners. Keynes concentrated on aggregate demand because he viewed rapid declines in this variable as the cause of recessions and depressions. Changes in aggregate supply—changes brought about by new technology, more capital and labor, and greater productivity—came about slowly and could therefore be neglected in the short run.

What about Say's law that "Supply creates its own demand"? Keynes stood Say's law on its head. In fact, we can summarize Keynesian theory with the statement, "Demand creates its own supply."

Aggregate demand, said Keynes, is our economy's prime mover. Aggregate demand determines the level of output and employment. In other words, business firms produce only the quantity of goods and services they believe consumers, investors, governments, and foreigners plan to buy.

Keynes: Aggregate demand is our economy's prime mover.

The centerpiece of his model was the behavior of the consumer. If consumers decide to spend more of their incomes on goods and services—or less, for that matter—then the effect on output and employment can be substantial.

The Keynesian Aggregate Expenditure Model

Since the Keynesian model assumes a constant price level, we'll return to our original graphic presentation, which we began in Chapter 5. We'll be on familiar ground because we'll be using some of the concepts covered in Chapters 5 through 9. You already have quite a bit of Keynesian analysis under your belt without knowing it.

In a nutshell, here's what we're going to be working with: (1) the consumption function; (2) the saving function; and (3) investment, which will be held constant. To keep things as simple as possible, we are including only the private sector, so government purchases (and net exports, as well) are excluded from our model. This means changes in aggregate demand are brought about only by changes in C. So the centerpiece of the Keynesian model was the behavior of the consumer.

---

[4]John Maynard Keynes, *The General Theory of Employment, Interest, and Money* (New York: Harcourt Brace Jovanovich, 1958), pp. 249–50.

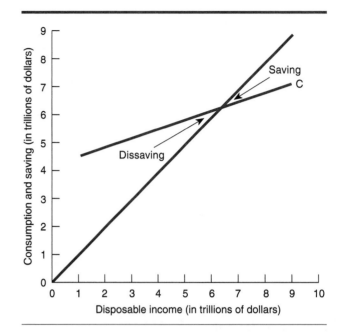

Figure 12

Disposable Income (in trillions of dollars)
When consumption is greater than disposable income, savings is negative; when disposable income is greater than consumption, savings is positive.

The Consumption and Saving Functions Here's the consumption function: *As income rises, consumption rises, but not as quickly*. It is a "fundamental psychological law," said Keynes "that men are disposed, as a rule and on the average, to increase their consumption as their income increases, but not by as much as the increase in their income."[5]

So what people do, then, as incomes rise, is spend some of this additional income and save the rest—which brings us to the saving function: *As income rises, saving rises, but not as quickly*. No surprises here.

Hypothetical consumption and savings functions appear in Figure 12. As disposable income rises, consumption and saving rise as well. Because disposable income rises as output, or real GDP rises, we can say that as real GDP rises, consumption and saving rise. What about investment?

Investment is unstable.

The Investment Sector We learned in Chapter 6 that investment is the loose cannon on our economic deck. Keynes was well aware of this. What causes recessions in the Keynesian model? A decline in profit expectations causes recessions, or as Keynes puts it, the marginal efficiency of capital. Although rising interest rates may play an important role in setting off recessions, Keynes stressed profit expectations:

> But I suggest that a more typical, and often the predominant, explanation of the crisis is, not primarily a rise in the rate of interest, but a sudden collapse in the marginal efficiency of capital.[6]

How do we allow for planned investment in the Keynesian model? We've seen that planned consumption rises with disposable income and real GDP. What about planned investment? It, too, probably varies directly with disposable income and real GDP. But we need to keep things simple. So we're going to come up with an arbitrary figure for planned investment—$500 billion—and keep it constant for all levels of real GDP.

---

[5]Ibid., p. 96.
[6]Ibid., p. 315.

Finding Equilibrium GDP

Finding equilibrium GDP is as easy as finding the level of spending at which saving and investment are equal. Try to find that level of spending in Figure A.

What did you get? Equilibrium real GDP is $5.5 trillion. Now, how much is saving? At equilibrium GDP, saving—the vertical distance between the C line and the 45-degree line—is about $1.7 trillion. And how much is I? It's the vertical distance between the C line and the C + I line—also about $1.7 trillion. And so, at an equilibrium

GDP of $5.5 trillion, saving and investment are equal at $1.7 trillion.

In Figure B we come back to the $C + I + G + X_n$ graph from Chapter 8. $C + I + G + X_n$ is aggregate demand, or GDP. We've simply added the government and foreign sectors to the consumption and investment sectors.

How much is equilibrium GDP in Figure B? It's $5 trillion. We'll be making good use of this type of graph at the beginning of the next chapter.

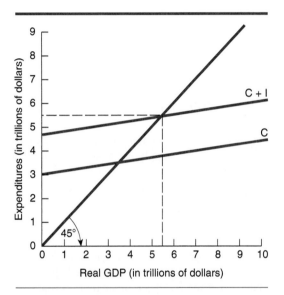

Figure A

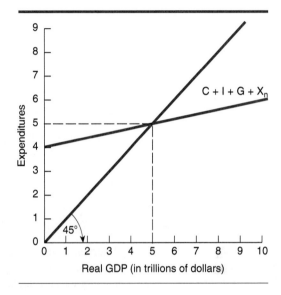

Figure B

We'll add just one line to our graph, the C + I line, and then we'll be able to wind up our analysis. We've done that in Figure 13. Assuming C + I constitutes aggregate demand, how much is equilibrium GDP? It comes out to $7 trillion.

And how much is investment? Also $500 billion.

So, at equilibrium GDP, all our ducks are in a line, so to speak. Aggregate demand, C + I (measured vertically), is equal to aggregate supply, or real GDP (measured on the horizontal scale). The level of output produced is exactly equal to the amount that buyers wish to purchase.

Also, saving and investment are equal. Saving is the vertical distance between the C line and the 45-degree line. The vertical distance between the C line and the C + I line is I. Therefore, the vertical distance between the C line and the 45-degree line must be equal to (actually, identical to) the vertical distance between the C line and the C + I line. (For extra help with finding equilibrium GDP, see the box, "Finding Equilibrium GDP.")

Figure 13
Real GDP (in trillions of dollars)
When C + I represents aggregate demand, how much is equilibrium GDP? It's $7 trillion.

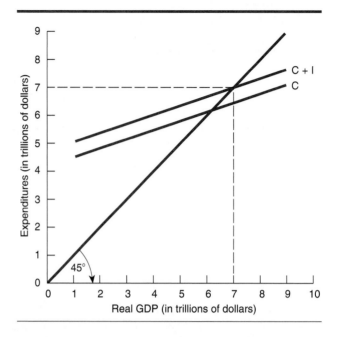

Disequilibrium and Equilibrium

In both Keynesian and classical economic systems, the economy is always tending toward equilibrium, where aggregate demand and aggregate supply are equal. Let's look at this process from two perspectives: first, when aggregate demand is larger than aggregate supply and second, when aggregate supply is larger than aggregate demand.

(1) Aggregate Demand Exceeds Aggregate Supply

When aggregate demand exceeds aggregate supply, inventories decline.

When aggregate demand exceeds aggregate supply, a chain reaction is set off and continues until the economy is back in equilibrium. The first thing that happens is that inventories start declining. What do business firms do? They order more inventory. Consequently, orders to manufacturers rise, and, of course, production rises. Manufacturers will hire more labor, and eventually, as plant utilization approaches capacity, more plant and equipment are ordered.

Suppose you own an appliance store. You have been ordering 50 blenders a month because that's about how many you sell. But during the last month your blender sales doubled, so you decide to order 100 blenders instead of your usual 50. Think of what this does to the production of blenders, assuming the other appliance stores double their orders as well.

As more people find employment, they will consume more, raising aggregate demand. Business firms may also begin raising their prices. Retailers may perceive that their customers are willing to pay more. Eventually, the manufacturers may have trouble increasing output much farther because of shortages in labor, raw materials, plant and equipment, or the funds to finance expansion. These shortages will occur at some point—and consequently, most prices will rise—because what is happening in the appliance industry is probably happening in the rest of the economy. As the economy approaches full capacity (and full employment), prices will have begun to rise.

We started with aggregate demand exceeding aggregate supply, but this disparity told manufacturers to increase aggregate supply. First, output was increased; eventually, so were prices. As final GDP (which is identical to aggregate supply) is defined as the nation's output of goods and services at market prices, it appears that there are two ways to raise aggregate supply—by increasing output and by increasing prices. By doing this, we raise aggregate supply relative to aggregate demand and quickly restore equilibrium.

(2) Aggregate Supply Exceeds Aggregate Demand

When aggregate supply is greater than aggregate demand, the economy is in disequilibrium. Aggregate supply must fall. Because aggregate supply is greater than aggregate demand, production exceeds sales, and inventories are rising. When retailers realize this, what do they do? They cut back on orders to manufacturers. After all, if you found you were accumulating more and more stock on your shelves, wouldn't you cut back on your orders? Remember, not only does it cost money to carry large inventories—shelf space as well as money is tied up—but also there is always the risk that you may not be able to sell your stock.

When manufacturers receive fewer orders, they reduce output and consequently lay off some workers, further depressing aggregate demand as these workers cut back on their consumption. Retail firms, facing declining sales as well as smaller inventories, may reduce prices, although during recent recessions price reductions have been relatively uncommon. Eventually, inventories are sufficiently depleted. In the meantime, aggregate supply has fallen back into equilibrium with aggregate demand.

When aggregate supply exceeds aggregate demand, inventories rise.

(3) Summary: How Equilibrium Is Attained

We can make an interesting observation about the entire process. When the economy is in disequilibrium, it automatically moves back into equilibrium. It is always aggregate supply that adjusts. When aggregate demand is greater than aggregate supply, the latter rises, and when aggregate supply exceeds aggregate demand, aggregate supply declines.

Please keep in mind that aggregate demand (C + I) must equal the level of production (aggregate supply) for the economy to be in equilibrium. When the two are not equal, aggregate supply must adjust to bring the economy back into equilibrium.

When the economy is in disequilibrium, it automatically moves back into equilibrium.

Keynesian Policy Prescriptions

Let's summarize the classical position. Recessions are temporary because the economy is self-correcting. Declining investment will be pushed up again by falling interest rates, while, if consumption falls, it will be raised by falling prices and wages. And because recessions are self-correcting, the role of government is to stand back and do nothing.

Keynes's position was that recessions were not necessarily temporary, because the self-correcting mechanisms of falling interest rates and falling prices and wages might be insufficient to push investment and consumption back up again. The private economy does not automatically move toward full employment. Therefore, it would be necessary for the government to intervene.

What should the government do? Spend money! How *much* money?[7] If the economy is in a bad recession, it will be necessary to spend a lot of money. And if it's in a depression, then it must spend even more.

Aggregate demand is insufficient to provide jobs for everyone who wants to work; thus it is necessary for the government to provide the spending that will push the economy toward full employment. Just spend money; it doesn't matter on what. Keynes made this point quite vividly:

The classicals believed recessions were temporary because the economy is self-correcting.

> If the Treasury were to fill old bottles with banknotes, bury them at suitable depths in disused coal mines which are then filled up to the surface with town rubbish, and leave it to private enterprise on well-tried principles of laissez-faire to dig the notes up again..., there need be no more unemployment.... It would, indeed, be more sensible to build houses and the like; but if there are political and practical difficulties in the way of this, the above would be better than nothing.[8]

---

[7]We'll be much more specific in the next chapter. But let's be clear now that, when the government *spends* more money, that's not the same thing as *printing* more money. Generally it borrows more money and then spends it.

[8]Keynes, *The General Theory of Employment, Interest, and Money*, p. 129.

Why didn't New Deal spending
get us out of the economic
crisis of the 1930s?

If all it takes is government spending to get us out of a depression, then why didn't President Franklin Roosevelt's massive New Deal spending get us out of the Great Depression? First of all, it *did* succeed in bringing about rapid economic growth between 1933 and 1937. But then, just when the economy seemed to be coming out of its depression, Roosevelt suddenly tried to balance the federal budget; he got Congress to raise taxes and cut government spending. On top of this, the Federal Reserve sharply cut the rate of growth of the money supply. So back down we went, with output plunging sharply and the unemployment rate soaring once again.

Not until the huge World War II armaments expenditures in the early 1940s did the United States finally emerge from the Depression. So what, then, did we learn from all of this? One possibility is that the only way to end a depression is to go to war. But what I hope you learned is that massive government spending of *any* kind—whether on highways, school construction, AIDS research, crime prevention, space exploration, *or* on soldiers' salaries—will pull us out of a depression.

In recent times, the most expensive application of Keynes's policy prescription for recessions has been carried out by Japan. For nearly the entire decade of the 1990s, the Japanese economy was mired in recession. During this period Japan spent more than $1 trillion, much of it on bridges, tunnels, airports, concert halls, and highways. Although none of these projects was as unproductive as burying bottles of banknotes, the new $10 billion Tokyo subway line, which was supposed to provide a direct route from the northern part of the city to the southwest, does not do so. It was just one of many Japanese public works projects that seem extravagant, wasteful, or even pointless.

But the million-dollar question—or, in this case, the trillion-dollar question—is how this giant public works program benefited the Japanese economy. Clearly it has kept a lingering recession from slipping into a more severe one, or even into a depression. Maybe the Japanese government, like the American New Deal of the 1930s, just did not spend enough for long enough. Or just maybe, what really counts is not just how *much* you spend, but *how* you spend it.

Over the last eight decades, our economy has been racked by repeated bouts of inflation, recession, and, of course, the decade-long Great Depression. According to John Maynard Keynes, our problem during periods of recession and depression has been insufficient aggregate demand. And though he died in 1946, before we encountered periods of sustained inflation, he would have prescribed lowering aggregate demand to bring down the inflation rate.

In the next chapter we shall deal specifically with this Keynesian manipulation of the level of aggregate demand to deal with inflation and recession. Fiscal policy, which is the name that has been assigned to Keynesian taxation and government spending prescriptions, became the basic government policy tool to ensure price stability and high employment from the 1930s through the 1960s.

Current Issue: Keynes and Say in the 21st Century

Until the 1970s the American economy was essentially a closed system. Mass production and mass consumption fed off each other. We made it and then we bought it. Our system was best described by Say's law: Supply creates its own demand.

There was no problem as long as American workers used their wages to buy up the goods and services they produced. Henry Ford recognized this truth back in 1914 when he doubled the wages of his semiskilled assembly line workers to the unheard sum of $5 a day. He recognized that every worker was a potential customer.

When our economy collapsed in the 1930s, John Maynard Keynes declared that our problem was inadequate aggregate demand for goods and services. Standing Say's law on its head, Keynes believed that demand creates its own supply. If individual consumers, business firms, and the government spent a lot more money, then a lot more goods and services would be produced.

The next three decades were quite prosperous as consumers, businesses, and the government spent enough money to buy up a steadily growing supply of goods and services. Almost every year we spent more and we produced more. We churned out suburban homes, station wagons, highways, TVs, furniture, clothing, school buildings, shopping malls, and foodstuffs, not to mention a vast array of weaponry.

During those decades we were nearly self-sufficient. But after Japan, Germany, and the rest of the industrial world rebuilt their war-devastated economies, American manufacturers began to face competition. In foreign markets, and even on our home turf, foreign manufactures of TVs, cars, clothing, and other consumer goods began eating our lunch.

Things went from bad to worse as manufacturing employment fell from 22 percent of total employment in 1979 to just 10 percent today. As demand for American manufactures declined, so too did its supply. We no longer were operating a closed system in which we bought up our own output.

Neither Say nor Keynes are giving us the answers we need. Supply is certainly *not* creating its own demand. Nor is a robust aggregate demand preventing our manufacturing base from eroding. To sum up: Because we consume much more than we produce, our aggregate demand is much greater than our aggregate supply. As a result, we are running huge and growing trade deficits. These deficits will be a major topic of the next to last chapter of this book.

Questions for Further Thought and Discussion

1. The classical economists believed that our economy was always at full employment or tending toward full employment. If our economy were operating below full employment, what would happen, according to the classicals, to move the economy back toward full employment?
2. When the price level increases, the quantity of goods and services purchased declines. Why does this happen?
3. Explain the difference between the long-run aggregate supply curve and the short-run aggregate supply curve.
4. What were the major areas of disagreement between John Maynard Keynes and the classical economists?
5. Describe the chain reaction that is set off when (a) aggregate demand exceeds aggregate supply; (b) aggregate supply exceeds aggregate demand.
6. If you lived in a village cut off from the rest of the world, show how Say's law would apply to your village's economy.

Workbook for Chapter 11

Multiple-Choice Questions

Circle the letter that corresponds to the best answer.

1. Until the Great Depression, the dominant school of economic thought was _____.
   a) classical economics
   b) Keynesian economics
   c) supply-side economics
   d) monetarism

2. The classical economists believed in _____.
   a) strong government intervention
   b) laissez-faire
   c) a rapid growth in the money supply
   d) none of these

3. Say's law states that _____.
   a) we can have an inflation or a recession, but never both at the same time
   b) the normal state of economic affairs is recession
   c) demand creates its own supply
   d) supply creates its own demand

4. People work, according to Jean Baptiste Say, so that they can _____.
   a) consume   c) stay busy
   b) save   d) none of these

5. According to the classical economists, _____.
   a) people will always spend all their money
   b) any money that is saved will be invested
   c) saving will always be greater than investment
   d) saving will always be smaller than investment

6. Keynes believed _____.
   a) recessions were temporary
   b) once a recession began, it would always turn into a depression
   c) the real problem that modern economies faced was inflation
   d) none of these

7. "Our economy is always at full employment" was a claim made by _____.
   a) both Keynes and the classicals
   b) neither Keynes nor the classicals
   c) Keynes but not the classicals
   d) the classicals but not Keynes

8. According to the classical economists, if the amount of money people are planning to invest is greater than the amount that people want to save, _____.
   a) interest rates will rise and saving will rise
   b) interest rates will fall and saving will fall
   c) interest rates will fall and saving will rise
   d) interest rates will rise and saving will fall

9. Each of the following supports the classical theory of employment except _____.
   a) Say's law
   b) wage-price flexibility
   c) the interest mechanism
   d) government spending programs

10. Our economy is definitely at equilibrium in each case except when _____.
    a) saving equals investment
    b) aggregate demand equals aggregate supply
    c) the amount people are willing to spend equals the amount that producers are producing
    d) equilibrium GDP equals full-employment GDP

11. That we are always tending toward full employment is a belief of _____.
    a) Keynes
    b) the classicals
    c) the supply-siders
    d) the monetarists

12. Keynes said _____.
    a) the expected profit rate was more important than the interest rate
    b) the interest rate was more important than the expected profit rate
    c) the expected profit rate and the interest rate were equally important
    d) neither the expected profit rate nor the interest rate was important

13. John Maynard Keynes is most closely associated with the _____.
    a) American Revolution
    b) French Revolution
    c) Great Depression
    d) inflation

14. The classical economists' aggregate supply curve is vertical _____.
    a) both in the short run and in the long run
    b) in neither the short run nor the long run
    c) in the short run, but not in the long run
    d) in the long run, but not in the short run

15. To end a bad recession, we need to _____.
    a) go to war
    b) spend a lot of money
    c) balance the federal budget

16. Which statement best describes the classical theory of employment?
    a) We will always have a great deal of unemployment.
    b) We will usually have a great deal of unemployment.
    c) We will occasionally have some unemployment, but our economy will automatically move back toward full employment.
    d) We never have any unemployment.

17. According to Keynes, our economy always tends toward _____.
    a) equilibrium GDP
    b) full-employment GDP
    c) recessions
    d) inflations

18. When saving is greater than investment, we are _____.
    a) at equilibrium GDP
    b) at full-employment GDP
    c) below equilibrium GDP
    d) above equilibrium GDP

19. Keynes considered full-employment GDP to be _____.
    a) the normal state of economic affairs
    b) a rare occurrence
    c) an impossibility
    d) none of these

20. Keynes was concerned mainly with _____.
    a) aggregate supply
    b) aggregate demand
    c) the interest rate
    d) inflation

21. When aggregate demand is greater than aggregate supply, _____.
    a) inventories get depleted and output rises
    b) inventories get depleted and output falls
    c) inventories rise and output rises
    d) inventories rise and output falls

22. When the economy is in disequilibrium, _____.
    a) production automatically rises
    b) production automatically falls
    c) it automatically moves back into equilibrium
    d) it stays in disequilibrium permanently

23. As the price level rises, _____.
    a) the quantity of goods and services demanded falls
    b) the quantity of goods and services demanded rises
    c) the quantity of goods and services demanded stays the same
    d) none of the above is correct

24. The slope of the aggregate demand curve is explained by each of the following except _____.
    a) the real balance effect
    b) the interest rate effect
    c) the foreign purchases effect
    d) the profit effect

25. Which of the following antirecession (or antidepression) programs would not be one that John Maynard Keynes would have prescribed?

   a) The New Deal under President Franklin Roosevelt

   b) The one-trillion-dollar Japanese public works program of the 1990s

   c) Letting the forces of supply and demand allow the economy to reattain full employment

   d) Burying bottles containing banknotes

26. Which of the following is the most accurate statement about meeting our current economic needs?

   a) John Maynard Keynes, rather than Jean Baptiste Say, is providing the economic answers we need.

   b) Say, rather than Keynes, is providing the economic answers we need.

   c) Neither Keynes nor Say is providing the economic answers we need.

   d) Together, Keynes and Say are providing the economic answers we need.

Fill-In Questions

1. Laissez-faire was advocated by the _____ school of economics.

2. Say's law states that _____ _____.

3. According to Say's law, people work so that they can _____.

4. According to Say's law, people spend _____ _____.

5. The classical economists believed savings would equal _____.

6. If supply creates its own demand, asked Keynes, why are we having a _____?

7. If saving were greater than investment, said the classical economists, they would be set equal by the _____.

8. The classical economists believed that wages and prices were _____ flexible.

9. The classical economists believed recessions were _____.

10. During recessions, said the classical economists, the government should _____.

11. Aggregate supply is _____ _____.

12. Aggregate demand is _____ _____.

13. At equilibrium GDP, _____ will be equal to _____.

14. Our economy always tends toward _____ _____ GDP.

15. When investment is greater than savings, we are _____ equilibrium GDP.

16. Full-employment GDP and equilibrium GDP are _____ equal.

17. Keynes was most concerned with one main variable, _____.

18. According to John Maynard Keynes, the level of aggregate supply is determined by the _____ _____.

19. When we are far below the full-employment level of GDP, Keynes policy prescription was _____ _____.

20. When aggregate supply is greater than aggregate demand, the economy is in _____.

21. When aggregate demand is greater than aggregate supply, inventories will _____ and output will _____.

22. When individuals, business firms, and the government are spending just enough money to provide jobs for everyone willing and able to work, we are at _____ GDP.

23. The real balance effect states that _____
_____
_____.

24. The two reasons why the aggregate supply curve
moves upward to the right are: (1) _____ and
(2) _____.

25. The interest rate effect states that _____
_____
_____.

26. The three reasons why the aggregate demand curve
slopes downward are (1) _____;
(2) _____;
and (3) _____.

27. The foreign purchases effect states that _____
_____
_____.

Problems

1. If GDP = C + I and if GDP = C + S, then
_____ = _____.

2. Given the information in Figure 1, and assuming an
interest rate of 15 percent: (a) Will the economy be at
equilibrium? (b) Will savings equal investment?

(c) What will happen, according to the classical
economists?

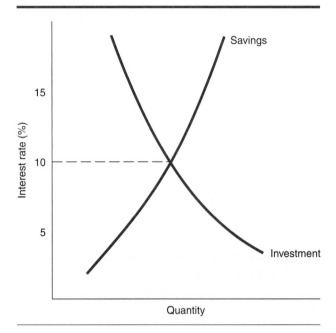

F*igure* 1

3. Given the information in Figure 2: (a) If aggregate
demand shifts from AD_1 to AD_2, what happens to the
level of prices and to output? (b) If aggregate demand
shifts from AD_2 to AD_3, what happens to the level of
prices and to output? (c) If aggregate demand shifts
from AD_3 to AD_4, what happens to the level of prices
and to output?

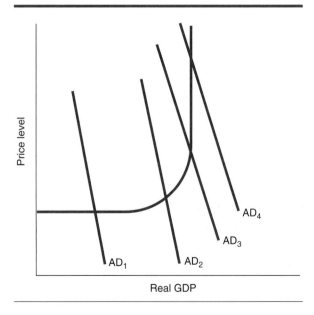

F*igure* 2

Chapter 12

Fiscal Policy and the National Debt

These are exciting times—at least for economists. In 2000 we had the largest federal government surplus in our history; in 2006 we had the largest deficit.

Fiscal policy is *the manipulation of the federal budget to attain price stability, relatively full employment, and a satisfactory rate of economic growth*. To attain these goals, the government must manipulate its spending and taxes. Later, in Chapter 14, we'll look at monetary policy, which uses very different means to promote the same ends.

CHAPTER OBJECTIVES

In this chapter you will learn about:

- The deflationary gap.
- The inflationary gap.
- The multiplier and its applications.
- Automatic stabilizers.

- Discretionary fiscal policy.
- Budget deficits and surpluses.
- The public debt.
- Crowding-in and crowding-out.

Putting Fiscal Policy into Perspective

Until the time of the Great Depression, the only advice economists gave the government was to try to balance its budget every year and to not interfere with the workings of the private economy. Just balance the books and then stay out of the way. There was no such thing as fiscal policy until John Maynard Keynes invented it in the 1930s.

He pointed out that there was a depression going on and that the problem was anemic aggregate demand. Consumption was lagging because so many people were out of work. Investment was extremely low because businessowners had no reason to add to their inventories or build more plant and equipment. After all, sales were very low and much of their plant and equipment was sitting idle. So the only thing left to boost aggregate demand was government spending.

What about taxes? Well, certainly, we would not want to *raise* them. That would push aggregate demand even lower. We might even want to *cut* taxes to give consumers and businesses more money to spend. OK, now if we were to follow this advice, would the government be able to balance its budget? No way! But if we ran a big enough budget deficit, we could jump-start the economy and, in effect, spend our way out of this depression.

You don't have to be a great economist to see that we haven't been too successful at attaining our fiscal policy goals, particularly since the mid-1960s. It's important that the aggregate supply of goods and services equals the aggregate demand for goods and services at just the level of spending that will bring about full employment at stable prices.

Equilibrium GDP tells us the level of spending in the economy. Full-employment GDP tells us the level of spending necessary to get the unemployment rate down to 5 percent (which we have been calling full employment). We'll see how fiscal policy is used to push equilibrium GDP toward full-employment GDP.

In terms of equilibrium GDP, sometimes we are spending too much, and at other times we are spending too little. When equilibrium GDP is too big, we have an inflationary gap, and when it's too small, a deflationary gap. Remember Goldilocks and the Three Bears? Remember the porridge that was too hot and the porridge that was too cold? Like Goldilocks seeking the perfect porridge, our policy objective is to find a level of GDP that is just right. We will deal with deflationary and inflationary gaps and GDPs that are just right in the next few pages.

Part I: The Deflationary Gap and the Inflationary Gap

Equilibrium GDP is the level of output at which aggregate demand equals aggregate supply.

Before we go to the gaps, we need to review some terms from Chapter 11. First: *equilibrium GDP*. Our economy is always at equilibrium GDP or tending toward it. *Equilibrium GDP is the level of output at which aggregate demand equals aggregate supply.* What is *aggregate demand*? It's *the sum of all expenditures for goods and services* (that is, $C + I + G + X_n$). And what is *aggregate supply*? Aggregate supply is *the nation's total output of final goods and services*. So at equilibrium GDP, everything produced is sold.

Full employment GDP is the level of spending necessary to provide full employment of our resources.

We need to review one more term: *full-employment GDP*. Full employment means nearly all our resources are being used. For example, if our plant and equipment is operating at between 85 and 90 percent of capacity, *that's* full employment. Or if only 5 percent of our labor force is unemployed, then *that's* full employment. So, what's full-employment GDP? Full-employment GDP is *the level of spending necessary to provide full employment of our resources*. Alternatively, it is the level of spending necessary to purchase the output, or aggregate supply, of a fully employed economy.

The Deflationary Gap

A *deflationary gap occurs when equilibrium GDP is less than full-employment GDP.* Equilibrium GDP is the level of spending that the economy is at or is tending toward. Full-employment GDP is the level of spending needed to provide enough jobs to reduce the unemployment rate to 5 percent. When too little is being spent to provide enough jobs, we have a deflationary gap, which is shown in Figure 1.

How much is equilibrium GDP in Figure 1? Write down the number. What did you get? Did you get $5 trillion? That's the GDP at which the $C + I + G + X_n$ line crosses the 45-degree line.

How can we close the deflationary gap?

How do we close this gap? We need to raise spending—consumption (C) or investment (I) or government expenditures (G)—or perhaps some combination of these. John Maynard Keynes tells us to raise G. Or we may want to lower taxes. Lowering business taxes might raise I; lowering personal income taxes would increase C.

How much would we have to raise spending to close the deflationary gap shown in Figure 1? Would you believe $1 trillion? That's right! This is *some* deflationary gap. There would have to be a depression going on, so we would need to raise spending by $1 trillion. Anything less would reduce, but not eliminate, the gap.

Note that equilibrium GDP is $2 trillion less than the full-employment GDP of $7 trillion. In a few pages we'll do some multiplier analysis. This analysis will show us

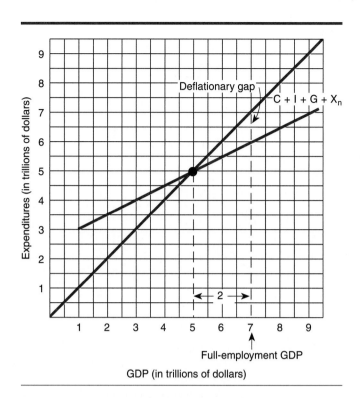

Figure 1
The Deflationary Gap
When full-employment GDP is greater than equilibrium GDP, there is a deflationary gap. How much is it in this graph? The deflationary gap is $1 trillion.

that raising G by $1 trillion will raise equilibrium GDP by $2 trillion and eliminate the deflationary gap. But let's not get ahead of ourselves.

Note how the points in Figure 1 line up. Equilibrium GDP is to the left of full-employment GDP. The deflationary gap is directly above the full-employment GDP. It is the vertical distance between the 45-degree line and the C + I + G + X_n line.

The Inflationary Gap

Figure 2 shows the inflationary gap. The key difference between this graph and that of the deflationary gap is the position of equilibrium GDP. When there is an inflationary gap, equilibrium GDP is to the right of full-employment GDP. It is to the left when there's a deflationary gap. *Equilibrium GDP is greater than full-employment GDP when there's an inflationary gap.* When there's a deflationary gap, full-employment GDP is greater than equilibrium GDP.

In both graphs the gap is the vertical distance between the C + I + G + X_n line and the 45-degree line, and in both graphs the gap is directly above full-employment GDP. In short, when there's a deflationary gap, equilibrium GDP is too small; when there's an inflationary gap, it's too big. To eliminate an inflationary gap, Keynes would suggest cutting G and raising taxes. Both actions are aimed at reducing spending and, therefore, equilibrium GDP.

In Figure 2 the inflationary gap is $200 billion ($1,200 billion − $1,000 billion). If we cut spending by $200 billion, it would have a multiplied effect on GDP. Equilibrium GDP would decline by $500 billion ($1,500 billion − $1,000 billion) to the full-employment level.

I'm tossing around billions and trillions as if they were pocket change. Remember that 1,000 billion equals 1 trillion. If you need a fast review, reread the box, "A Word about Numbers," near the beginning of Chapter 5.

To summarize, if spending is too high, equilibrium GDP is above the full-employment level. To eliminate the inflationary gap, we cut G and/or raise taxes. If equilibrium GDP is less than full-employment GDP, we eliminate the deflationary gap by raising G and/or cutting taxes.

Deflationary gap: Equilibrium GDP is too small.

Inflationary gap: Equilibrium GDP is too large.

Figure 2

The Inflationary Gap
When equilibrium GDP is greater
than full-employment GDP, there is
an inflationary gap. How large is
the inflationary gap in this graph?
The inflationary gap is $200 billion.

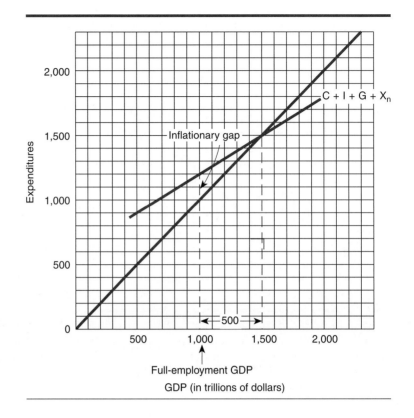

Over the 25 years Republicans have labeled every Democratic presidential candidate a "tax and spend liberal." And by inference these Republicans wanted to be called "low-tax and low-spend conservatives." To generalize, liberals would seem to favor a high-spending, high-taxing, big government, and conservatives a low-spending, low-taxing, relatively small government. How would these philosophies lend themselves to fiscal policy?

If there were a recession, conventional fiscal policy calls for tax cuts and more government spending. If the liberal could choose just one of these measures, which would she favor? And which one would the conservative favor? The liberal would choose higher government spending (which would increase the role of government), while the conservative would cut taxes, thereby reducing the government's role.

Now figure out the liberal's and conservative's respective policy prescriptions for dealing with inflation. Write them down right here:

The liberal would raise taxes, and the conservative would cut government spending. To generalize—or perhaps overgeneralize—the liberal tends to favor bigger government, and the conservative, smaller government.

Part II: The Multiplier and Its Applications

We're going to put together some concepts introduced in earlier chapters: aggregate demand (Chapters 9 and 11), the marginal propensity to consume (Chapter 5), and equilibrium GDP (Chapter 11). We know that an increase in G will raise aggregate demand, but by how much? We also know that a tax increase will lower aggregate demand, but, again, by how much? The multiplier will tell us by just how much.

The Multiplier

The multiplier is based on two concepts covered in Chapter 9: (1) GDP is the nation's expenditure on all the final goods and services produced during the year at market prices. (2) GDP $= C + I + G + X_n$.

It is obvious that if C goes up, GDP will go up. Or if I goes down, so will GDP. Now we'll add a new wrinkle. When there is any change in spending, that is, in C, I, G, or X_n, it will have a multiplied effect on GDP.

When money is spent by one person, it becomes someone else's income. And what do we *do* with most of our income? We spend it. Once again, when this money is spent, someone else receives it as income and, in turn, spends most of it. If a dollar were initially spent, perhaps someone who received that dollar would spend 80 cents, and of that 80 cents received by the next person, perhaps 64 cents would be spent. If we add up all the spending generated by that one dollar, it will add up to four or five or six times that dollar. Hence, we get the name *the multiplier.*

Any change in spending (C, I, or G) will set off a chain reaction, leading to a multiplied change in GDP. How *much* of a multiplied effect? A $10 billion increase in G might increase GDP by $50 billion. In that case, the multiplier is 5. If a decline of $5 billion in I causes GDP to fall by $40 billion, then the multiplier would be 8.

First we'll concentrate on calculating the multiplier, for which we'll use the formula:

$$\frac{1}{1 - MPC}$$

$$Multiplier = \frac{1}{1 - MPC}$$

Then we'll see how it is used to predict changes in GDP. (A reminder: MPC is marginal propensity to consume.)

The formula above is the same as 1/MPS. Remember, MPC + MPS = 1 (or 1 − MPC = MPS). Because the multiplier (like C) deals with spending, 1/(1 − MPC) is a more appropriate formula.

The MPC can thus be used to find the multiplier. If the MPC were .5, find the multiplier. Work this problem out in the space below. Write down the formula first, then substitute and solve.

Solution:

$$Multiplier = \frac{1}{1 - MPC} = \frac{1}{1 - .5} = \frac{1}{.5} = 2$$

Many students get lost at the third step. How do we get .5? How come 1 − .5 = .5? Look at it this way:

$$\begin{array}{r} 1.0 \\ -.5 \\ \hline .5 \end{array}$$

If it's still not clear, then think of 1 as a dollar and .5 (or .50) as 50 cents. How much is a dollar minus 50 cents?

Step four is just as easy. How many times does 50 cents go into a dollar? Or, you can just divide .5 into 1.0. Either way, it comes out to 2.

Let's try another problem. When the MPC is .75, how much is the multiplier?

Solution:

$$\text{Multiplier} = \frac{1}{1 - \text{MPC}} = \frac{1}{1 - .75} = \frac{1}{.25} = 4$$

After you've substituted into the formula, think of 1 as a dollar and .75 as 75 cents. From there (1/.25) we divide .25 into 1, or a quarter into a dollar.

Applications of the Multiplier

The multiplier is used to calculate the effects of changes in C, I, and G on GDP.

Knowing the multiplier, we can calculate the effect of changes in C, I, and G on the level of GDP. If GDP is 2,500, the multiplier is 3, and C rises by 10, what is the new level of GDP?

A second formula is needed to determine the new level of GDP:

New GDP = Initial GDP + (Change in spending × Multiplier)

Note the parentheses. Their purpose is to ensure that we multiply before we add. In arithmetic you must always multiply (or divide) before you add (or subtract). Always. The parentheses are there to make sure we do this.

Copy down the formula, substitute, and solve.

Solution:

(1) New GDP = Initial GDP + (Change in spending × Multiplier)

(2)   = 2,500 + (10 × 3)

(3)   = 2,500 + (30)

                = 2,530

Here are a few variations of this type of problem. Suppose that consumer spending rises by $10 billion and the multiplier is 3. What happens to GDP?

(See solution on the next page.)

Solution: It rises by $30 billion: $10 billion × 3.

Try this one: Government spending falls by $5 billion with a multiplier of 7.

Solution: −$5 billion × 7 = −$35 billion. In other words, if government spending falls by $5 billion with a multiplier of 7, GDP falls by $35 billion.

Two more multiplier applications and we're through. First, how big is the multiplier in Figure 1? If you're not sure, guess. What's your answer? Is it 2? We can find the multiplier by using deductive logic. We know the deflationary gap is $1 trillion. We also know that equilibrium GDP is $2 trillion less than full-employment GDP. (Equilibrium GDP is $5 trillion and full-employment GDP is $7 trillion.) Suppose we were to raise G by $1 trillion. What would happen to the gap? It would vanish! And what would happen to equilibrium GDP? It would rise by $2 trillion and become equal to full-employment GDP.

Still not convinced? Let's redraw Figure 1 as Figure 3 and add $C_1 + I_1 + G_1 + X_{n_1}$. You'll notice that $C_1 + I_1 + G_1 + X_{n_1}$ is $1 trillion higher than $C + I + G + X_n$. You'll also notice that the deflationary gap is gone. And that equilibrium GDP equals full-employment GDP.

One more question: How big is the multiplier in Figure 2? Again, if you're not sure, guess. Is your answer 2.5? How do we get 2.5? OK, we know that the inflationary gap is 200, and we know equilibrium GDP is 500 greater than full-employment GDP. So if we lower G by 200, the inflationary gap disappears. And now equilibrium GDP falls by 500 and is equal to full-employment GDP.

Here's a formula you can use to find the multiplier whether you have an inflationary gap or a deflationary gap:

$$\text{Multiplier} = \frac{\text{Distance between equilibrium GDP and full-employment GDP}}{\text{Gap}}$$

In Figure 4 the distance is 500 and the inflationary gap is 200. So 500/200 = 2.5. You can also use this formula to find the multiplier if there is a deflationary gap. For

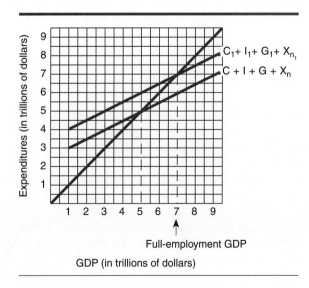

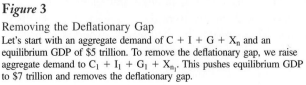

Figure 3

Removing the Deflationary Gap

Let's start with an aggregate demand of $C + I + G + X_n$ and an equilibrium GDP of $5 trillion. To remove the deflationary gap, we raise aggregate demand to $C_1 + I_1 + G_1 + X_{n_1}$. This pushes equilibrium GDP to $7 trillion and removes the deflationary gap.

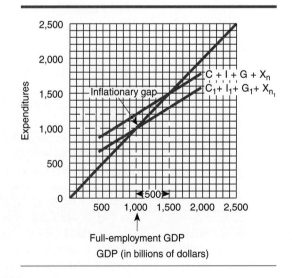

Figure 4

Removing the Inflationary Gap

We'll start with an aggregate demand of $C + I + G + X_n$ and an equilibrium GDP of 1,500. To remove the inflationary gap, we lower aggregate demand to $C_1 + I_1 + G_1 + X_{n_1}$. This pushes equilibrium GDP down to 1,000 and removes the deflationary gap.

Finding the Multiplier

Let's assume that the full-employment GDP is $4 trillion in Figure 3 (use the $C + I + G + X_n$ line; ignore the $C_1 + I_1 + G_1 + X_{n_1}$ line). See if you can answer these three questions:

1. Is there an inflationary gap or a deflationary gap?
2. How much is the gap?
3. How much is the multiplier?

Solution:

1. There is an inflationary gap because full-employment GDP is less than equilibrium GDP. If aggregate demand, or total spending, is greater than the spending necessary to attain full employment, that excess spending will cause inflation.

2. The inflationary gap is measured by the vertical distance between the 45-degree line and the $C + I + G + X_n$ line at full-employment GDP. It appears to be half a trillion, or $500 billion, which we can write as 500.

3. Multiplier = $\dfrac{\text{Distance between equilibrium GDP and full-employment GDP}}{\text{Gap}}$

   $= \dfrac{1{,}000}{500} = 2$

Now let's assume that full-employment GDP is $6 trillion. Please answer the same three questions.

Solution:

1. There is a deflationary gap.
2. It is $500 billion, or 500.
3. Multiplier = $\dfrac{1{,}000}{500} = 2$

example, in Figure 3 the distance between equilibrium GDP and full-employment GDP is $2 trillion, which we can express as 2,000. And the deflationary gap is $1 trillion, or 1,000. Using the formula:

$$\text{Multiplier} = \frac{\text{Distance between equilibrium GDP and full-employment GDP}}{\text{Gap}} = \frac{2{,}000}{1{,}000} = 2$$

If you are still a bit uncertain and want a little more practice, then do the work in the Extra Help box, "Finding the Multiplier." The box on the paradox of thrift also provides some insight on how the multiplier works.

Part III: The Automatic Stabilizers

Have you ever been on an airborne plane when the pilot took a stroll through the cabin and you asked yourself, Who's flying the plane? Let's hope it's the copilot. Or, if there's no turbulence, maybe the plane is flying on automatic pilot. If it does get turbulent, then the pilot takes over the manual controls.

An analogy can be made with our economy. Our automatic stabilizers enable us to cruise along fairly smoothly, but when we hit severe economic turbulence, then we hope the president and Congress take the controls. Right now, we'll examine our automatic stabilizers, and in Part IV, we'll talk about discretionary fiscal policy, which is our manual control system.

In the 1930s the government built a few automatic stabilizers into the economy, mainly to prevent recessions from becoming depressions. Today, when the country hits routine economic turbulence, Congress does not need to pass any laws, and no new bureaucracies have to be created. All the machinery is in place and ready to go.

Each of these stabilizers protects the economy from the extremes of the business cycle—from recession and inflation. They are not, by themselves, expected to prevent booms and busts, but only to moderate them. To do still more, we need discretionary economic policy, which we'll discuss in the next section.

The automatic stabilizers protect us from the extremes of the business cycle.

The Paradox of Thrift*

Since childhood we have been taught that saving is good. Benjamin Franklin once said, "A penny saved is a penny earned." Franklin, it turns out, never followed his own advice. It also turns out that if we all try to save more, we'll probably end up with a really bad recession. This outcome is explained by the paradox of thrift.

You have probably heard that the sum of the parts does not necessarily add up to the whole. Consider, for example, what you would do if you were in a room full of people and that room suddenly burst into flames. Would you politely suggest to your companions that everyone file out of the room in an orderly fashion? Or would you bolt for the door?

What if the door opened inward (that is, into the room)? Whoever got there first would attempt to pull open the door. But if everyone made a dash for the door, they would all arrive at just about the same time. The person trying to pull open the door wouldn't have space to do this because everyone else would be pushing him against the door. Several people would get injured in the crush. Unless they backed off, no one would get out of the room.

We call this an example of the fallacy of composition. What makes perfect sense for one person to do—rush to the door and pull it open—makes no sense when everyone tries to do it at the same time.

The paradox of thrift is a variant of the fallacy of composition. *If everyone tries to save more, they will all end up saving less.* Let's say that every week you save an extra $10 from your paycheck. At the end of a year, you will have saved an extra $520. Right? Right! Now, what if everyone tries saving an extra $10 a week? At the end of a year, we should have tens of billions in extra savings. Right? Wrong!

How come? Because what makes sense for one person to do does not make sense for everyone to do. If everyone tries to save more, everyone is cutting back on consumption. Business sales fall by hundreds of millions of dollars a week. If 130 million people each cut back by $10 a week, that comes to a weekly reduction of $1.3 billion. Over the course of a year, this will add up to $67.6 billion!

This $67.6 billion decline in consumption will have a multiplied effect on GDP. If the multiplier is 4, GDP will decline by $270.4 billion; if it is 6, GDP will decline by $405.6 billion. So we'd be in a recession.

When retailers get the idea that business will be off over the next few months, they do two things: lay off employees and let their inventory run down. The workers who lose their jobs cut back on their consumption. Meanwhile, the retailers have begun canceling their orders for new inventory, prompting factories to lay off people and lower their orders for raw materials.

As the recession spreads, more and more people get laid off, and each will cut back on his or her consumption, further aggravating the decline in retail sales.

Now we come back to saving. Millions of people have been laid off and millions more are on reduced hours. Still others no longer get overtime. Each of these people, then, has suffered substantially reduced income. Each is not able to save as much as before the recession. Savings decline.

And so we're back where we started. We have the paradox of thrift: *If everyone tries to save more, they all will end up saving less.*

One of the biggest problems we have had since the early 1980s has been our low savings rate. So one may ask: If our savings rate is too low, don't we really need to save more, and will more saving really lead to a recession? One way that this dilemma can be resolved is to have a growing economy. Everyone's income goes up, everyone saves more and consumes more, and there's no recession.

---

*The paradox of thrift is not relevant today because, as a nation, we actually have a negative rate of personal saving. That is, we spend more than we earn. Then why talk about it? Because it does a great job of illustrating how the multiplier works.

Personal Income and Payroll Taxes

During recessions the government collects less personal income tax and Social Security tax than it otherwise would. Some workers who had been getting overtime before the recession are lucky to be hanging on to their jobs even without overtime. Some workers are less lucky and have been laid off. That's the bad news. The good news is that they don't have to pay any personal income tax or payroll tax because they have no income.

> During recessions, tax receipts decline.

During prosperous times our incomes rise, and during times of inflation our incomes tend to rise still faster. As our incomes rise, we have to pay more taxes. These taxes tend to hold down our spending, relieving inflationary pressures.

> During inflations, tax receipts rise.

During recessions, as incomes fall, federal personal income and Social Security tax receipts fall even faster. This moderates economic declines by leaving more money in taxpayers' pockets.

Personal Savings

During recessions, saving declines.

During prosperity, saving rises.

As the economy moves into a recession, saving declines. Many Americans lose their jobs and others earn less overtime. As incomes fall, savings must fall as well. Looked at from another perspective, consumption rises as a percentage of income.

Just as the loss of income is cushioned by a fall in saving, the reverse happens when the economy picks up again. Like higher taxes, during times of rapid economic expansion, increased saving tends to damp down inflationary pressures.

Credit Availability

Credit availability helps get us through recessions.

Because most Americans now hold bank credit cards, mainly MasterCard and VISA, we may think of these as automatic stabilizers that work in the same way that personal savings does. During good times, we should be paying off the credit card debts that we run up during bad times.

Although many of us are quite good at running up credit card debt during good times as well as bad, our credit cards, as well as other lines of credit, may be thought of as automatic stabilizers during recessions because they give us one more source of funds with which to keep buying things. You may have lost your job and have no money in the bank, but your credit cards are just as good as money.

Most Americans can take out home equity loans if they're short of cash. Even if you've lost your job, the bank may not care since they've got your home as collateral. Best of all, you'll pay a much lower interest rate than you would on your credit card debt.

Unemployment Compensation

During recessions, more people collect unemployment benefits.

Reason to study economics: When you are in the unemployment line, at least you will know why you are there.

During recessions, as the unemployment rate climbs, hundreds of thousands and then millions of people register for unemployment benefits. The tens of billions of dollars of unemployment benefits being paid out establish a floor under purchasing power. People who are, they hope, only temporarily out of work will continue spending money. This helps keep retail sales from falling much, and even without further government help, the economy has bought some time to work its way out of the recession. As the economy recovers and moves into the prosperity phase of the cycle, people find jobs more easily and unemployment benefit claims drop substantially.

In neighborhoods hard hit by recessions, friends would often great each other with the question, "Are you collecting?" In other words, are you getting unemployment benefits checks? As someone who has "collected" twice for the full 26 weeks, I would answer, "Yes. And how about you?" In 2005, the average weekly benefit was $265. Average benefits varied from state-to-state, from $351 in Massachusetts to $172 in Mississippi.

Other countries are much more generous. Swedes, Danes, and Norwegians, for example, receive as much as 90 percent of prior earnings for up to a year after losing a job. In the United States, by contrast, unemployment insurance replaces less than one-third of prior earnings and eligibility is so restricted that nearly two-thirds of unemployed workers receive no benefits at all.

The Corporate Profits Tax

During recessions, corporations pay much less corporate income taxes.

Perhaps the most countercyclical of all the automatic stabilizers is the corporate profit (or income) tax. Corporations must pay 35 percent of their net income above $10 million to the federal government. During economic downturns, corporate profits fall much more quickly than wages, consumption, or real GDP; and, of course, during expansions, corporate profits rise much more rapidly.

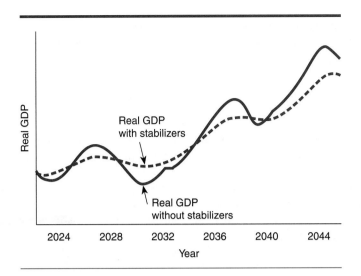

Part of this decline is cushioned by the huge falloff of federal tax collections from the corporate sector. This leaves more money to be used for investment or distribution to shareholders in the form of dividends. And when corporate profits shoot up during economic booms, the federal government damps down economic expansion by taxing away 35 percent of the profits of the larger corporations.

Other Transfer Payments

Some people think that when a recession hits, the government automatically raises Social Security benefits. This might make sense, but it doesn't happen. Congress would have to pass special legislation to do so.

Three important payments do rise automatically because of laws on the books. Each is aimed at helping the poor. These are welfare (or public assistance) payments, Medicaid payments, and food stamps.

A safety net for the poor

These programs are important for two reasons. Not only do they alleviate human suffering during bad economic times, but they also help provide a floor under spending, which helps keep economic downturns from worsening.

The automatic stabilizers smooth out the business cycle, keeping the ups and downs within a moderate range. Since the Great Depression, we have had neither another depression nor a runaway inflation. But the stabilizers, by themselves, cannot altogether eliminate economic fluctuations.

Figure 5 shows the workings of the stabilizers. The solid line shows real GDP in an economy with no automatic stabilizers. The dotted line shows real GDP in an economy such as ours, which does have automatic stabilizers. The latter part of the expansions are held down in the hypothetical business cycle with stabilizers in place, and the contractions are less severe. Basically, then, the automatic stabilizers smooth out the business cycle but don't eliminate it.

The automatic stabilizers may be likened to running our economy on automatic pilot—not well suited for takeoffs and landings, but fine for the smooth part of the flight. However, when the going gets rough, the economy must resort to manual controls. Discretionary policy is our manual control system.

Part IV: Discretionary Fiscal Policy

Among the first words of this chapter were *Fiscal policy is the manipulation of the federal budget to attain price stability, relatively full employment, and a satisfactory rate of economic growth.* The automatic stabilizers, which swing the federal budget into substantial deficits during recessions and tend to push down those deficits during periods of inflation, would appear to be part of fiscal policy. Because they are built into our economy, one might call them a passive fiscal policy. But our automatic stabilizers are now taken for granted; therefore we consider fiscal policy to be purely discretionary. Let's now consider the discretionary fiscal policy tools that are available to the federal government.

Making the Automatic Stabilizers More Effective

One problem with unemployment benefits is that they run out in six months while a recession can drag on for more than a year and its effects can last still longer. After the 1990–91 recession ended, the unemployment rate continued rising and did not begin to decline until a full year after the start of the recovery. Extending the benefit period is an example of discretionary fiscal policy because benefits are not extended automatically. In 2002, President George W. Bush signed into law a bill that extended unemployment benefits an additional 13 weeks. An increase in the benefit ceiling or a widening of eligibility standards are other ways of making this stabilizer more effective.

Public Works

The main fiscal policy to end the Depression was public works.

During the Great Depression, the Roosevelt administration set up several so-called alphabet agencies to provide jobs for the long-term unemployed. Among them, the Works Progress Administration (WPA), the Civilian Conservation Corps (CCC), and the Public Works Administration (PWA) put millions of people to work doing everything from raking leaves to constructing government buildings.

One of the problems in getting these public works projects off the ground was a lack of plans. Not only did the government lack ready-to-go blueprints, but it did not even have a list of the needed projects. If the country is ever again to institute a public works program, it needs to be much better prepared than it was in the early 1930s. If not, by the time the program gets started, the recession will be over.

Although criticized as "make-work projects," the public works projects gave jobs to millions of the unemployed. These workers spent virtually their entire salaries, thereby creating demand for goods and services in the private sector, thus creating still more jobs. Public works is probably not the answer to recessions unless the downturns last so long that the projects can be carried out. Yet one might ask, if public works are so necessary, why wait for a recession to carry them out?

It seems ideally conceivable that the state… should undertake public works, that must be executed some time, in the slack periods when they can be executed at least expense, and will, at the same time, have a tendency to counteract a serious evil.

—Philip H. Wicksteed,
The Common Sense of
Political Economy

Changes in Tax Rates

So far, the discretionary policy measures have dealt exclusively with recessions. What can we do to fight inflation? We can raise taxes.

This was done in 1968 when Congress, under President Lyndon Johnson, passed a 10 percent income tax surcharge. If your income was $15,000 and your federal income tax was listed in the tax table as $2,300, you had to pay a $230 surcharge, which raised your taxes to $2,530.

In the case of a recession, a tax cut would be the ticket. The recession of 1981–82 was somewhat mitigated by the Kemp-Roth tax cut, which called for a 5 percent cut in personal income taxes in 1981 and a 10 percent cut in July 1982. However salutary its effects, Kemp-Roth was seen by its framers as a long-run economic stimulant rather than an antirecessionary measure. Similarly, President George W. Bush billed his $1.35 trillion tax cut in 2001 as both an immediate economic stimulus to fight the current recession as well as a long-term boost to economic growth. And during the jobless recovery that followed, he referred to the tax cuts of 2001 and 2003 as a "jobs program."

Corporate income taxes, too, may be raised during inflations and lowered when recessions occur. The investment tax credit, first adopted by the Kennedy administration, is another way of using taxes to manipulate spending.

A key advantage to using tax rate changes as a countercyclical policy tool is that they provide a quick fix. We have to make sure, however, that temporary tax cuts carried out during recessions do not become permanent cuts.

During the recession of 2001, at the behest of President George W. Bush, Congress passed a one-time tax refund of $300 to individuals and $600 to married couples who filed jointly. Everyone got their checks within months, providing the economy with a much needed stimulus.

Changes in Government Spending

Discretionary fiscal policy dictates that we increase government spending and cut taxes to mitigate business downturns, and that we lower government spending and raise taxes to damp down inflation. In brief, we fight recessions with budget deficits and inflation with budget surpluses.

Who Makes Fiscal Policy?

Making fiscal policy is like driving a car. You steer, you keep your foot on the accelerator, and occasionally you use the brake. Basically, you should not go too fast or too slow, and you need to stay in your lane.

Would you mind letting someone else help you drive? Suppose you had a car with dual controls, like the ones driving schools have. Unless you and the other driver were in complete agreement, not only would driving not be much fun, but you'd be lucky to avoid having an accident.

So, if making fiscal policy is like driving a car, let's ask just who is doing the driving. Is it the president? Or is it Congress? The answer is yes to both questions. In other words, the conduct of our fiscal policy is a lot like driving a dually controlled car. Further complicating maneuvers, sometimes one political party controls Congress while the president belongs to the other party. In October 1990 the federal government all but shut down while President George Bush struggled with Congress in an effort to pass a budget. And in 1993, even though President Bill Clinton and a substantial majority of members of both houses were Democrats, each house passed a budget by just one vote. (See the box, "The Politics of Fiscal Policy.")

Fiscal policy is indeed a powerful tool that may be used to promote full employment, stable prices, and a satisfactory rate of economic growth. But no one seems to be in charge of *making* fiscal policy. Nor is there widespread agreement among economists

liberals - spend more
conservatives - tax less

The Politics of Fiscal Policy

In a sense there really *is* no fiscal policy, but rather a series of political compromises within Congress and between the president and Congress. The reason for this lies within our political system, especially the way we pass laws.

To become a law, a bill introduced in either house of Congress must get through the appropriate committee (most bills never get that far) and then receive a majority vote from the members of that house. It must get through the other house of Congress in the same manner. Then a House–Senate conference committee, after compromising on the differences between the two versions of the bill, sends the compromise bill to both houses to be voted on once again. After receiving a majority vote in both houses, the bill goes to the president for his signature.

If the president does not like certain aspects of the bill, he can threaten to veto it, hoping Congress will bend to his wishes. If he gets what he wants, he now signs the bill and it becomes law. If not, he vetoes it. Overriding a veto takes a two-thirds vote in both houses—not an easy task.

as to what effect any given fiscal policy measure has on our economy. Perhaps the words of Robert J. Gordon lend just the right perspective:

> Unfortunately, policymakers cannot act as if the economy is an automobile that can quickly be steered back and forth. Rather, the procedure of changing aggregate demand is much closer to that of a captain navigating a giant super-tanker. Even if he gives a signal for a hard turn, it takes a mile before he can see a change, and 10 miles before the ship makes the turn.[1]

Part V: The Deficit Dilemma

Deficits, Surpluses, and the Balanced Budget

A deficit is created when the government is paying out more than it's taking in.

A billion here, a billion there, and pretty soon you're talking about real money.

—Everett Dirksen,
U.S. Senator from Illinois
in the 1960s and 1970s

To understand how fiscal policy works, we need to nail down three basic concepts. First, the deficit. *When government spending is greater than tax revenue, we have a budget deficit.* The government is paying out more than it's taking in. How does it make up the difference? It borrows. Deficits have been much more common than surpluses. In fact, the federal government ran budget deficits every year from 1970 through 1997.

Second, budget surpluses are the exact opposite of deficits. They are prescribed to fight inflation. *When the budget is in a surplus position, tax revenue is greater than government spending.*

Finally, *we have a balanced budget when government expenditures are equal to tax revenue.* We've never had an exactly balanced budget; in many years of the 19th and early 20th centuries, we had small surpluses or deficits. Perhaps if the deficit or surplus were less than $20 billion, we'd call that a balanced budget.

Deficits and Surpluses: The Record

A budget tells us what we can't afford, but it doesn't keep us from buying it.

—William Feather

Back in Chapter 7, we talked about federal government spending and federal government tax receipts. Let's put all that data together and focus on how well the government has covered its spending with tax revenue. Let's look at the record since 1970 (see Figure 6).

How do we interpret the data? On the surface, it's obvious that the deficit went through the roof in the 1980s. Indeed, during the late 1940s the government ran three surpluses, in the 1950s it ran four, it ran just one in the 1960s, and it ran none between 1970 and 1997. We ran surpluses from 1998 through 2001, but we've returned to deficits since 2002.

What brought the deficit down after 1992? Congress passed two huge deficit reduction packages in 1990 and in 1993. To secure the spending cuts he wanted in 1990, George ("Read my lips: No new taxes") H. W. Bush agreed with the Democratic leaders of Congress to a tax increase, which probably cost him reelection in 1992. The $492 billion five-year deficit reduction package had a major impact. Then, three years later, President Clinton pushed a five-year $433 billion deficit reduction package through Congress. About half this package was tax increases and half was government spending reductions. From 1993 through 1997 the deficit fell every year, and in 1998 we had our first federal budget surplus since 1969. By 2000 we were running a record surplus of $236 billion. What, then, accounts for our spectacular fall from budgetary grace after 2000?

There were several major causes: the bursting of the high-tech bubble and the subsequent stock market crash of 2000–2001; the March–November 2001 recession; the events of 9/11; our weak and slow recovery from that recession; the economic disruption caused by the war in Iraq; higher military spending for that war, its aftermath, and the war on terror; and the massive tax cuts of 2001 and 2003.

---

[1]Robert J. Gordon, *Macroeconomics* (Boston: Little, Brown, 1978), p. 334.

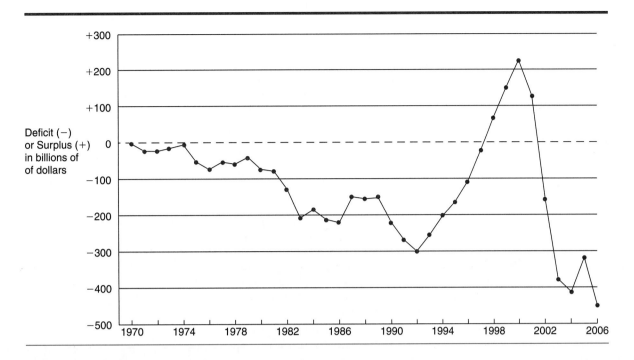

Figure 6

The Federal Budget Deficit, Fiscal Years 1970–2006
There were mounting deficits through most of the 1980s and early 1990s, followed by steadily declining deficits
beginning in 1993. Finally in 1998 we had our first surplus since 1969. The 2006 deficit is the author's estimate.
Sources: Economic Report of the President, 2006: www.omb.gov.

A law enacted in 2004 and valid only in 2005 allowed companies to bring about
$300 billion in untaxed foreign profits back into the United States at a special low rate of
just 5.25 percent, compared with the normal corporate tax rate of 35 percent. That inflated
tax revenues by over $15 billion in 2005.

Other short-term tax breaks also swelled tax revenue in fiscal year 2006. So while the
deficit did shrink substantially in 2005, it went right back up again to well over $400 billion
in fiscal year 2006, and may continue rising for the rest of the decade. It appears very likely
that we will be running very large deficits well into the future. As the baby boomers (the
generation born between 1946 and 1964) begin to collect Social Security benefits starting
around 2011, we may face still larger deficits.

How does our deficit compare with those of other relatively rich nations? As you can see
by glancing at Figure 7, only Japan's deficit, as a percentage of GDP, is larger. But by the next
edition of this book, I predict we will have overtaken Japan.

Why Are Large Deficits So Bad?

Let us count the ways. Number one: They tend to raise interest rates, which, in turn,
discourages investment. The Bush administration, which has been running huge and
growing deficits, disputes whether these deficits raise interest rates. In early 2003, the
mortgage rate as well as a few other rates were at 20-year lows. However, the last word
on the effect of deficits on interest rates seems to be a paper by William Gale and Peter
Orszag, which is based on 58 earlier studies.[2] Their conclusion: A projected rise in the
budget deficit of 1 percent of GDP raises long-term interest rates by 0.4 to 0.6 percentage points. Since we are predicting deficits of about 4 percent of GDP, Gale and Orszag
would project a rise in long-term interest rates of about 2 percent.

There is no practice more
dangerous than that of
borrowing money.
—George Washington

---

[2]William Gale and Peter Orszag, "The Economic Effects of Long-Term Fiscal Discipline," available at
www.brook.edu/dybdoctoot/views/papers/gale/20021217.pdf.

Figure 7

The Surplus or Deficit as a Percentage of GDP, Selected Countries, 2006

The figures, which are based on an OECD forecast, show that next to Japan, the U.S. has the largest budget deficit relative to the size of its GDP.

Source: OECD; *The Economist,* December 17, 2005, p. 93.

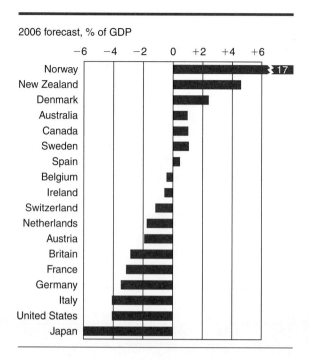

Number two: The federal government has become increasingly dependent on foreign savers to finance the deficit. How likely is it that foreigners might suddenly sell hundreds of billions of dollars worth of U.S. government securities because they disagreed with some of our foreign policy measures? When France opposed our 2003 war with Iraq, some Americans were so angry with the French they even renamed french fries "freedom fries" and French's mustard found it necessary to proclaim that only its name was French. Fortunately French, German, and other foreign investors did not dump their portfolios of U.S. government securities. Had they done so, interest rates would have shot up.

Number three: The deficit sops up large amounts of personal savings in this country, making that much less savings available to large corporate borrowers seeking funds for new plant and equipment. We'll talk about this when we discuss the crowding-out effect in one more page.

Must We Balance the Budget Every Year?

In a word, "no!" First of all, we couldn't, even if we tried. During recessions, the budget will automatically go into deficit. And as we saw after 9/11, events well beyond our control will force the federal government to spend great sums of money to deal with unforeseen problems.

But there are those who believe that, barring national emergencies and possibly recessions, the government should be legally bound to balance its budget every year. During the 1990s, several attempts were made to pass a constitutional amendment which would have required just that. None was successful.

Part VI: The Crowding-Out and Crowding-In Effects

The great debate: Monetarists: Deficits cause crowding-out. Keynesians: Deficits cause crowding-in.

Welcome to a debate we are going to be sponsoring between the monetarists and the Keynesians. In this debate the monetarists will argue in favor of the crowding-out effect, while the Keynesians will take the side of the crowding-in effect.

The monetarists maintain that Keynesian deficits designed to raise aggregate demand will have little, if any, positive effect. First, budget deficits drive up interest rates, thus discouraging investment. Second, the more money the government borrows to finance the deficit, the less will be available to private borrowers.

If the proper fiscal policy during recessions is a large budget deficit, one would wonder where the Treasury will get all this money. Presumably it will go out and borrow it. But from whom?

If it borrows funds from individuals who would have otherwise made this money available for business investment, won't business borrowers be "crowded out" of the financial markets by the government? And won't interest rates be driven up in the process, further discouraging investment? Won't increased government spending financed by borrowing be replacing private investment spending?

The answer is yes to all three questions. Yes—but to what degree?

During recessions business firms cut back on their investing, so the government would be tapping a relatively idle source of funds, and during recessions interest rates tend to fall.

Even during relatively prosperous times, such as the mid-1980s, there is enough money to go around if the Federal Reserve allows the money supply to grow at a fairly rapid clip and if foreign investors are willing to make a few hundred billion dollars available each year to major corporations as well as to the U.S. Treasury.

Nevertheless, the crowding-out effect cannot be dismissed out of hand, particularly during times of tight money, such as the late 1970s and early 1980s. That any borrower as big as the U.S. government crowds other borrowers out of financial markets is a fact (see the box, "Was the Federal Government Crowding Out Private Borrowers?"). And as the late Israeli defense minister Moshe Dayan once put it, "You can't argue with a fact."

Let's take a closer look at the Keynesian position. When there is substantial economic slack, one would not expect increased government borrowing to have much impact in financial markets. Not only would there be little effect on interest rates, but the Treasury would be sopping up funds that would otherwise go unclaimed. When orthodox Keynesian fiscal policy is followed, it is precisely during times of economic slack that large budget deficits are incurred.

One might also mention a possible "crowding-in" effect caused by deficit financing. This results from the stimulative effect that the deficit has on aggregate demand. If a massive personal income tax cut causes the deficit, consumption will rise, pulling up

Was the Federal Government Crowding Out Private Borrowers?

In the late 1980s and early 1990s the government was running massive budget deficits, although the unemployment rate was hovering around 5 percent. The Treasury was sopping up over half of all personal saving just to finance these deficits. But foreigners were also financing just over half of the deficit. Because virtually all our personal savings was indeed available to private borrowers, it could be argued that there was no crowding-out effect.

However, had the Treasury not been borrowing so heavily from foreigners, *that* money would have been available to American corporations seeking funds to replace and expand their plant and equipment. Furthermore, because of the huge deficits the Treasury was financing, real interest rates were much higher than they would have otherwise been. These high rates further discouraged private borrowing.

In sum, there definitely *was* a large crowding-out effect in the late 1980s. But it would have been a lot larger had it not been for the great inflow of foreign funds.

In the aftermath of the recession of 1990–91, not only did the government run the two largest budget deficits in U.S. history until then, but the Federal Reserve tried to accommodate private borrowers by pushing interest rates down to 15-year lows. And still the first President Bush was forced to term the recovery "anemic." One of the problems was that many banks were happy to pay only 2 or 3 percent interest for deposits and then buy U.S. government securities of varying maturities paying more than 5 percent interest. What we had here was a classic crowding-out effect at a time when it clearly hurt our economy.

So in the late 1980s and early 1990s, the conservative critics of an expansionary fiscal policy could point to a tangible crowding-out effect.

aggregate demand and inducing more investment. Similarly, increased government spending will raise aggregate demand, also inducing more investment. In other words, any rise in aggregate demand will induce a rise in investment.

This leaves us with one last question: which is larger, the crowding-in or the crowding-out effect? It doesn't really matter. The point is that as long as there is a sizable crowding-in effect, every dollar the government borrows will not crowd out a dollar of private borrowing. Thus, all we need to demonstrate is that there is a substantial crowding-in effect.

It appears that if we accept one fact—that the total amount of loanable funds is not fixed—there probably will be a substantial crowding-in effect. If there is indeed a fixed pool of saving, then it follows that every dollar the government borrows is one less dollar available to private savers. But *is* this total pool of saving fixed? If aggregate demand, stimulated by massive budget deficits, *does* rise, won't people save more money (as well as spend more)?

Therefore, as more saving becomes available, not every dollar borrowed by the government will actually be taken from private borrowers. Furthermore, as aggregate demand rises, more investment will be stimulated. If the crowding-in effect dominates the crowding-out effect, not only will government borrowing rise but so will private borrowing and investing. All we need to show is that total borrowing—government and private—rises.

You can see for yourself if there is much of a crowding-in effect. At the behest of President George W. Bush, Congress passed massive tax cuts in 2001 and in 2003. Although huge budget deficits were expected, Bush administration economists predicted that the tax cuts would stimulate economic growth, push up tax revenue, and actually shrink the deficits. They called this process "dynamic scoring." Were they right?

What do *you* think? Are the monetarists right in saying that government borrowing crowds out private borrowing? Or are the orthodox Keynesians correct in saying that the crowding-in effect may dominate the crowding-out effect? The betting here is that the truth lies somewhere between these two extremes.

Part VII: The Public Debt

The attractiveness of financing spending by debt issue to the elected politicians should be obvious. Borrowing allows spending to be made that will yield immediate payoffs without the incurring of any immediate political cost.

—James Buchanan,
The Deficit and American Democracy

The debt is like a crazy aunt we keep down in the basement. All the neighbors know she's there, but nobody wants to talk about her.

–Ross Perot–

The public, or national, debt is the amount of currently outstanding federal securities that the Treasury has issued. It is what the federal government owes to the holders of Treasury bills, notes, bonds, and certificates.

In 1981 the public debt went over the $1 trillion mark. Do you remember how much money $1 trillion is? Write it out with all the zeros right here:

Written out, it looks like this: $1,000,000,000,000.[3] In 1986 the national debt broke the $2 trillion mark. That means it took the federal government just five years to

---

[3]If big numbers still make you nervous, you would do well to review the box "A Word about Numbers," near the beginning of Chapter 5.

accumulate as much debt as it had accumulated between 1776 and 1981. Our national debt passed $8 trillion in 2005 (see Figure 8).

Exactly what is the national debt? It is *the cumulative total of all the federal budget deficits less any surpluses.* Much of it was run up during recessions and wars. It is owed to the holders of Treasury bills, notes, certificates, and bonds. For example, if you own any of these, you are holding part of the national debt.

Who holds the national debt? First we need to differentiate between the publicly held debt and the debt held by U.S. government agencies, mainly the Federal Reserve and the Social Security Trust Fund. Figure 9 shows how much of the national debt is held by U.S. government agencies, the American public, and by foreigners.

Exactly what is the national debt?

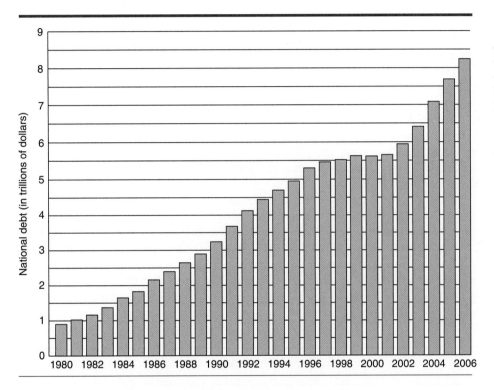

F*igure* 8

National Debt, 1980–2006*
The steady rise in the national debt through the 1980s and almost the entire 1990s was caused by the federal budget deficits that we ran each year. And when we finally began running surpluses in the late 1990s, we were able to start paying down the debt. Then deficits reappeared in 2002, and once again the national debt began to rise.
*Debt on January 1 of each year.
Source: Economic Report of the President, 2006.
www.whitehouse.gov/omb.

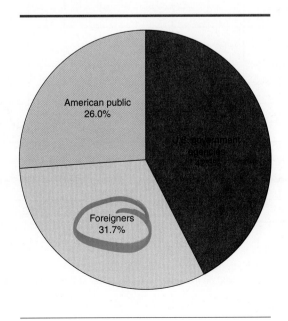

F*igure* 9

Holders of National Debt, January 2006
The main U.S. government agencies holding the national debt are the Social Security Trust Fund and the Federal Reserve (which, technically is a quasi-government agency?). Foreigners include private investors and central banks, most notably those of Japan and China. The American public includes households, mutual funds, banks, insurance companies, and other American private firms.
Source: www.publicdebt.treas.gov/opd/opdpdodt.htm.

Although the national debt has been increasing at an alarming pace since 2002, is this really something we should worry about? After all, don't we owe it to ourselves? Until the 1970s foreigners owned no more than 5 percent of the publicly held debt, but today they hold over 50 percent. Figure 10 shows that their holdings rose sharply in the early 1970s and again since the mid-1990s. How much more of our debt will foreigners need to buy up before we allow that perhaps we don't really owe it to ourselves?

To summarize, foreigners hold 54 percent of the outstanding national debt (see Figure 10), and 31.7 percent of the entire national debt (see Figure 9). So while foreigners *do* hold more than half the outstanding national debt, they hold less than a third of the entire national debt.

Blessed are the young, for they shall inherit the national debt.
—Herbert Hoover

Is the national debt a burden that will have to be borne by future generations? As long as we owe it mainly to ourselves, the answer is no. If we did owe it mainly to foreigners, and if they wanted to be paid off, it could be a great burden. While that is certainly not the case at this point, stay tuned, because in another few years foreigners may own over half our national debt.

The national debt rose substantially during wars. We paid for these wars partly by taxation and partly by borrowing. In wartime a nation will invest very little in plant and equipment; all available resources must go toward the war effort. As a result, during the first half of the 1940s, we built no new plant, equipment, and residential housing. Had there been no war, hundreds of billions of dollars' worth of plant, equipment, and housing would have been built. The generation that came of age after the war inherited less capital and housing than it would have had no war been fought. To that degree, a burden was placed on their shoulders.

Those who would point at the huge increase in the national debt during the war as the cause of our having less plant and equipment have misplaced the blame. It was the war, not the increase in the debt, that prevented wartime construction of capital goods.

When do we have to pay off the national debt?

When do we have to pay off the debt? We don't. All we have to do is roll it over, or refinance it, as it falls due. Each year about $3 trillion worth of federal securities fall due. By selling new ones, the Treasury keeps us going. But there is no reason why the national debt ever has to be paid off. Besides, as long as we continue running huge deficits, any discussion of paying off the debt is moot.

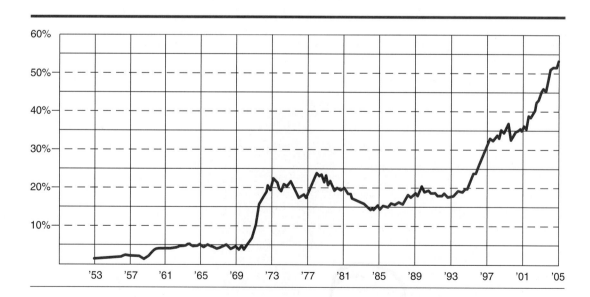

F*igure* **10**

Percentage of Outstanding National Debt Held by Foreigners, 1953–2005
Before the early 1970s, foreigners held no more than about 5 percent of the outstanding debt; today they hold over 50 percent.

Source: Haver Analytics; Floyd Norris, "More Than Ever, the U.S. Spends and Foreigners Lend," *The New York Times,* October 1, 2005, p. C4.

To the degree that the debt is being held increasingly by foreigners, we can no longer say we owe it (only) to ourselves. In the future, even if we never pay back one penny of that debt, our children and our grandchildren will have to pay foreigners hundreds of billions of dollars a year in interest. At least to that degree, then, the public debt *will* be a burden to future generations.

You may have heard about the national debt clock high above Manhattan's Times Square. It's a digital clock that updates the national debt every few seconds. Would you believe that it's running out of space? It has 13 digits, which can accommodate numbers no larger than $9,999,999,999,999. What happens when the debt reaches $10 trillion, probably sometime in late 2008? It will be time to build a larger clock.

A nation is not in danger of financial disaster merely because it owes itself money.
—Andrew W. Mellon, Secretary of the Treasury in the 1920s

Conclusion

As a self-confessed deficit hawk, I was quite pleased with the successful efforts of the first President Bush, President Bill Clinton, and the Congresses that served through the decade of the 1990s to eventually turn a record deficit into a record surplus. Obviously, those of us who dislike large deficits are growing increasingly alarmed with the current huge and growing deficits. Laura D'Andrea Tyson, the Chair of President Clinton's Council of Economic Advisors, writing in *BusinessWeek,* has summarized this view:

> When George W. Bush became President, the federal government enjoyed a projected 10-year budget surplus of $5.6 trillion. Today, less than three years later, Washington confronts sizable annual budget deficits regardless of the cyclical ups and downs of the economy. A growing number of several private forecasters now predict a 10-year deficit of around $4 trillion—$6.7 trillion excluding the Social Security surplus. Government debt and interest payments are slated to double as a share of the economy over the next decade, crowding out private investment and government spending on anything else.[4]

Defenders of the Bush administration's fiscal policy strenuously oppose Tyson's view. The president, several of his cabinet members, and Republican Congressional leaders have all contended that their program would create more jobs, faster economic growth, and eventually shrinking deficits. Were they right or wrong? You know what *I* think. But what do *you* think?

Fiscal policy, however, is just half the story. Monetary policy, which is controlling the rate of growth of our money supply, will be covered in Chapter 14.

Current Issue: Deficits as Far as the Eye Can See

From 1930 through 1945 we averaged just 1 million births a year. But from 1946 through 1964, this average shot up to 3 million. How do you explain this change?

OK, *I'll* explain it. In the 1930s, couples could not afford to have many children because of the Great Depression. And the birthrate stayed low for the first half of the 1940s because so many married men were sent abroad during World War II. But as soon as the war ended, 12 million men came home. I'll let you take it from there.

We called the period of high birthrates from the mid-1940s through the mid-1960s the "baby boom." Now fast forward to the second and third decades of the current century. The baby boomers will be retiring, and when they do, the federal government is going to have to shell out hundreds of billions in Social Security and Medicare payments. So if you think the federal budget deficits have been big—you ain't seen nothin' yet.

---

[4]Laura D'Andrea Tyson, "The Bush Tax Cuts Are Sapping America's Strength," *BusinessWeek,* August 11, 2003, p. 22.

In 2006 we took in $150 billion more in Social Security taxes than we paid out in Social Security benefits. Similarly, we ran a Medicare surplus of $20 billion. By the middle of the next decade these positive cash flows will turn negative—unless Congress takes decisive action well before then—and we can expect federal budget deficits to climb beyond the trillion dollar mark.

In January, 2006, we had a national debt of over $8 trillion on which we paid about $370 billion a year in interest. For the rest of the decade we will almost certainly run deficits of over $400 billion, and we can also look forward to rising interest rates. Let's move on to 2011, when the publicly held national debt will reach around $11 trillion, with interest rates at, say, 6 percent. How much interest will we have to pay on the debt that year? Do the math.

That's right! $660 billion! So in 2011 we'll be adding $660 billion to the debt in interest payments alone. And as the U.S. Treasury needs to borrow more and more, that will drive interest rates up still further.

In the second decade of this century huge and growing Social Security and Medicare expenditures along with rising interest payments will drive up the deficit. Each year's deficit will be tacked on to the national debt. A higher debt will mean still higher interest payments. So we can look forward to a vicious spiral of rising debt and deficits, each feeding off the other. Ten years from now we'll be looking back at the good old days of $400-billion deficits.

Questions for Further Thought and Discussion

1. Describe the differences between an inflationary gap and a deflationary gap.
2. Explain why large deficits are so bad.
3. It can be argued that there really is no fiscal policy. How would you make this argument?
4. To what degree is the public debt a burden to future generations?
5. Explain how, in general, the automatic stabilizers work. Then use one automatic stabilizer to illustrate this.
6. Suppose income taxes and unemployment compensation were cut by an equal amount. How would aggregate demand be affected?
7. Right now is there an inflationary gap or a deflationary gap?
8. Can you remember the last good or service you purchased? Explain how the money you spent will lead to a multiplied chain of increased income and spending.
9. As late as 1992 we were running budget deficits of nearly $300 billion. How do you explain the decline in the deficits through the rest of the decade of the 1990s?
10. Explain the crowding-in and crowding-out effects. How valid are these two concepts?

Workbook for Chapter 12

Name _____   Date _____

Multiple-Choice Questions

Circle the letter that corresponds to the best answer.

1. In the late 1970s and early 1980s, the goals of fiscal policy were _____.
   a) completely attained
   b) largely attained
   c) largely unattained
   d) completely unattained

2. When equilibrium GDP is too small, we have _____.
   a) a deflationary gap
   b) a depression
   c) an inflationary gap
   d) none of these

3. There is an inflationary gap when _____.
   a) equilibrium GDP is equal to full-employment GDP
   b) equilibrium GDP is smaller than full-employment GDP
   c) equilibrium GDP is larger than full-employment GDP
   d) none of these occur

4. Fiscal policy and monetary policy are _____.
   a) different means used to attain different goals
   b) different means used to attain the same goals
   c) the same means to attain the same goals
   d) the same means to attain different goals

5. Budget surpluses are most appropriate during _____.
   a) depressions
   b) recessions
   c) inflations

6. Each of the following is an automatic stabilizer except _____.
   a) unemployment compensation
   b) direct taxes
   c) welfare payments
   d) Social Security benefits

7. The crowding-out effect is _____.
   a) much stronger during a recession than during prosperity
   b) much stronger during prosperity than during a recession
   c) equally strong during a recession and prosperity

8. When there is a recession, the biggest decline is in _____.
   a) Social Security tax receipts
   b) personal income tax receipts
   c) consumer spending
   d) corporate aftertax profits

9. The automatic stabilizers _____.
   a) help smooth out the business cycle
   b) make the business cycle worse
   c) eliminate the business cycle

10. Each of the following is an example of discretionary fiscal policy except _____.
    a) public works spending
    b) making the automatic stabilizers more effective
    c) changes in tax rates
    d) the unemployment insurance program

11. Which of the following is an example of crowding out?
    a) Federal government spending causes changes in state and local government spending.
    b) Government spending reduces private spending.
    c) Tax changes perceived as temporary are largely ignored.
    d) Government spending causes the price level to rise.

12. Fiscal policy is made by _____.
    a) the president only
    b) Congress only
    c) both the president and Congress
    d) neither the president nor Congress

13. The requirement to override a presidential veto is
    _____.

    a) a majority vote in each house of Congress

    b) a two-thirds vote in each house of Congress

    c) a three-quarters vote in each house of Congress

    d) a majority vote of both houses of Congress
       combined

14. The crowding-out effect cancels out at least part of
    the impact of _____.

    a) expansionary fiscal policy

    b) expansionary monetary policy

    c) restrictive fiscal policy

    d) restrictive monetary policy

15. If equilibrium GDP is $5.5 trillion and full
    employment GDP is $5 trillion, there is _____.

    a) definitely an inflationary gap

    b) probably an inflationary gap

    c) definitely a deflationary gap

    d) probably a deflationary gap

16. Statement 1: A tax cut will have the same impact on
    the deflationary gap as an increase in G only if people
    spend the entire tax cut.
    Statement 2: The paradox of thrift is more relevant
    today, when savings are so low, than it was back in
    the 1950s and 1960s.

    a) Statement 1 is true and statement 2 is false.

    b) Statement 2 is true and statement 1 is false.

    c) Both statements are true.

    d) Both statements are false.

17. Statement 1: We ran large federal budget deficits
    from the early 1980s through the early 1990s.
    Statement 2: The federal budget deficit reached
    $8 trillion in 2005.

    a) Statement 1 is true and statement 2 is false.

    b) Statement 2 is true and statement 1 is false.

    c) Both statements are true.

    d) Both statements are false.

18. Which statement is true?

    a) About one-third of the national debt is rolled over
       (or refinanced) every year.

    b) The national debt is doubling every 10 years.

    c) Unless we balance the budget within the next five
       years, the United States stands a good chance of
       going bankrupt.

    d) None of these statements is true.

19. Between 2002 and 2006 the federal budget deficit
    _____ and the national debt _____.

    a) increased, increased

    b) decreased, decreased

    c) increased, decreased

    d) decreased, increased

20. Which statement is true?

    a) The national debt is larger than GDP.

    b) The national debt will have to be paid off
       eventually.

    c) Most of the national debt is held by foreigners.

    d) None of these statements is true.

21. If the federal government attempts to eliminate a
    budget deficit during a depression, this will
    _____.

    a) alleviate the depression

    b) contribute to inflation

    c) make the depression worse

    d) have no economic effect

22. During times of inflation, we want to _____.

    a) raise taxes and run budget deficits

    b) raise taxes and run budget surpluses

    c) lower taxes and run budget surpluses

    d) lower taxes and run budget deficits

23. Which statement is true?

    a) The public debt is larger than our GDP.

    b) The public debt is the sum of our deficits minus
       our surpluses over the years since the beginning of
       the country.

    c) We have had budget deficits only during recession
       years and wartime.

    d) None of these statements is true.

24. Through the 1970s, 1980s, and most of the 1990s, the public debt _____; from 1998 to 2000 the public debt _____.
    a) fell, rose
    b) rose, fell
    c) fell, fell
    d) rose, rose

25. A major advantage of the automatic stabilizers is that they _____.
    a) simultaneously stabilize the economy and tend to reduce the size of the public debt
    b) guarantee that the federal budget will be balanced over the course of the business cycle
    c) automatically produce surpluses during recessions and deficits during inflations
    d) require no legislative action by Congress to be made effective

26. The most valid argument against the size of the national debt is that it _____.
    a) will ruin the nation when we have to pay it back
    b) is owed mainly to foreigners
    c) leaves future generations less plant, equipment, and housing than would be left had there been a smaller debt
    d) will bankrupt the nation because there is a limit as to how much we can borrow

27. Assuming that present trends continue, the best estimate of our national debt on January 1, 2011 would be _____.
    a) $4 trillion
    b) $6 trillion
    c) $8 trillion
    d) $11 trillion
    e) $15 trillion

28. Currently we have a _____.
    a) a deflationary gap
    b) neither an inflationary gap nor a deflationary gap
    c) an inflationary gap

29. Between 1998 and 2000 the federal budget surplus _____ and the national debt _____.
    a) rose, rose
    b) fell, fell
    c) rose, fell
    d) fell, rose

30. Dynamic scoring is closely related to _____.
    a) the crowding-out effect
    b) the crowding-in effect
    c) both the crowding-out and crowding-in effect
    d) neither the crowding-out nor crowding-in effect

Fill-In Questions

1. The means that fiscal policy uses to attain its goals are the manipulation of _____ and _____.

2. We could eliminate inflationary gaps and deflationary gaps by making _____ GDP equal to _____ GDP.

3. The two ways of eliminating an inflationary gap are
   (1) _____
   and (2) _____.

4. The two ways of eliminating a deflationary gap are
   (1) _____
   and (2) _____.

5. Welfare spending, unemployment compensation, and direct taxes are all examples of _____.

6. The crowding-out effect states that when the Treasury borrows a lot of money to finance a budget deficit, _____.

7. Perhaps the most countercyclical of all the automatic stabilizers is the _____.

8. In addition to the automatic stabilizer, we have _____ fiscal policy.

9. Fiscal policy was invented by _____.

10. When equilibrium GDP is equal to full-employment GDP, we have an inflationary gap equal to _____.

Problems

1. (a) In Figure 1, is there an inflationary gap or a deflationary gap? (b) How much is it? (c) How much is the multiplier?

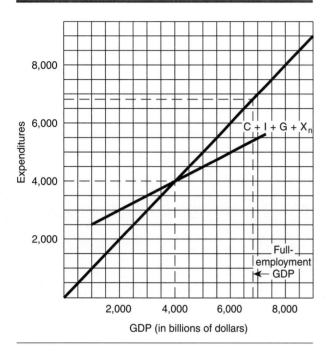

Figure 1

2. To remove the gap in Figure 1, what two fiscal policy measures would you recommend?

3. When the MPC is .8, how much is the multiplier?

4. If the MPC is .6, how much is the multiplier?

5. If C rises by $10 billion and the multiplier is 4, what happens to the level of GDP?

6. If I falls by $20 billion and the multiplier is 5, what happens to the level of GDP?

7. If GDP is 3,400, the multiplier is 5, and I rises by 15, what is the new level of GDP?

8. If GDP is 3,900, the multiplier is 8, and G falls by 10, what is the new level of GDP?

9. Suppose that Derek Bowman and Nicole Bowman each have MPCs of .5. If Derek receives one dollar of income, how much of that dollar would he be expected to spend? If Nicole receives all of the money that Derek spent, how much would Nicole be expected to spend?

10. If equilibrium GDP is $400 billion greater than full-employment GDP and there is an inflationary gap of $50 billion, how much is the multiplier?

11. If the full-employment GDP is $1 trillion greater than equilibrium GDP and the multiplier is 5, how much is the deflationary gap?

12. If Guy Barnes receives $1,000 from his newly created government job and gives $900 to Jingles Althaus for writing him a speech, and then Jingles gives $810 to Alayna Noel for installing a computer system, assuming everyone else in the nation has the same spending pattern: (a) How much is the multiplier? (b) If $10 billion of new investment had been made, by how much would our GDP rise?

13. Suppose that in the year 2020 our national debt were $10 trillion and our budget deficit were $300 billion. If a plan to gradually reduce the deficit and to balance the budget in the year 2030 were successful, make an estimate of the national debt in 2030.

14. In Figure 2: (a) Is there an inflationary gap or a deflationary gap? (b) How much is it? (c) How much is the multiplier?

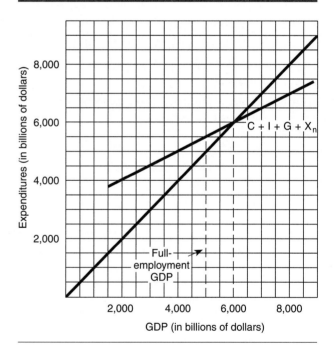

Figure 2

15. In fiscal year 2029 there is a budget deficit of $1 trillion. The fourth Bush administration, which believes in dynamic scoring, gets Congress to pass a tax cut of $500 billion a year for the next 20 years. How much will the Bush administration's economists predict the deficit will be in fiscal year 2034?

300

Chapter 13

Money and Banking

Why would it be a dumb idea to keep your money under your mattress, especially during times of inflation? What backs up our money supply? How much is a dollar worth today? What would happen if everyone tried to get their money out of the bank at the same time? By the time you've gotten to the end of the chapter, you'll know the answers to these questions.

Banks create money. The rate of monetary growth itself is controlled by the Federal Reserve, which serves as our nation's central bank. In this chapter we'll look at our country's money supply and banking system, and in the next, at the Federal Reserve System.

First we'll talk about the money supply in the United States and the jobs it does. Next we'll work in a little monetary theory; we'll look at the demand for money and how interest rates are set. Then we'll turn to banking, beginning with its origins in medieval times; moving right along, we'll look at modern banking. So fasten your seat belt; in the words of the late Jackie Gleason, "And away we go!"

CHAPTER OBJECTIVES

We will discuss the following interesting topics:

- The three jobs of money.
- What money is.
- M1, M2, and M3.
- The demand for money.
- The origins of banking.
- The creation and destruction of money.
- Branch banking and bank chartering.
- The FDIC.
- The savings and loan debacle.

Money

The Three Jobs of Money

How important *is* money? Imagine trying to get by without any. How well would you manage if you were dropped off in some strange town with no money, no credit cards, and no friends or family? What if there were no such thing as money? If you were hungry, maybe you could find a place where you'd be able to trade your wristwatch for a meal. But then, how would you pay for your *next* meal? And where would you sleep that night? And the next?

The three jobs of money are (1) medium of exchange, (2) standard of value, (3) store of value.

So wouldn't you agree that money is pretty important? Sometimes we don't know quite *how* important until we're caught without it. Money is important to us as individual consumers, and it is also essential to our economy. It performs three important jobs that enable our economy to function smoothly and productively.

Medium of Exchange

Money's most important job

Money is a terrible master but an excellent servant.

—P. T. Barnum,
Circus owner

By far the most important job of money is to serve as a medium of exchange: When any good or service is purchased, people use money.

Money makes it much easier to buy and to sell because money is universally acceptable. With money I can go out and buy whatever I want—provided, of course, I have enough of it. Similarly, a seller will sell to anyone who comes along with enough money; he won't have to wait for a buyer who's willing to trade something the seller needs.

Money, then, provides us with a shortcut in doing business. By acting as a medium of exchange, money performs its most important function.

Standard of Value

A currency, to be perfect, should be absolutely invariable in value.
—David Ricardo,
Works

Is money a good standard of value?

Wanna buy a brand name DVD player? A new sports car? A Swiss watch?

"Sure," you say. "How much?"

Thus money performs well at its second job—as a standard of value. If I told you that I got gasoline at $1 a gallon, you'd want to know the exact location of that gas station. But if I said that I bought a cheeseburger at a fast-food place for $10, you might wonder whether I have both oars in the water. A clerical job that pays $2 an hour would be nearly impossible to fill, while one paying $50 an hour would be swamped with applicants.

Does money work well as a standard of value? You tell *me*.

Store of Value

I measure everything I do by the size of a silver dollar. If it don't [sic] come up to that standard, then I know it's no good.
—Thomas A. Edison

Is money a good store of value?

Imagine that in 1986 you put $100 under your mattress and took out that same hundred dollars in 2006. How much was that $100 worth?

In other words, if you could buy 100 units of goods and services with your $100 in 1986, how many units could you buy with $100 in 2006? Eighty? No, fewer. Seventy? No, but very close. OK, I'll put you out of your misery. You could have bought just 55 units.

Did someone sneak into your bedroom in the middle of the night and steal most of your money? No; but over the years, inflation took its toll. During this 20-year period, inflation robbed the dollar of almost half of its purchasing power.

This brings us back to the third job of money. Is money a good store of value or wealth? Over the long run, and particularly since World War II, it has been a very poor store of value. However, over relatively short periods of time, say, a few weeks or months, money does not lose much of its value. More significantly, during periods of price stability, money is an excellent store of value. Of course, the best time to hold money is during deflation because the longer you hold it, the more it's worth. For example, if you held money under your mattress from late 1929 to early 1933, it would have doubled in value during those years.

Money versus Barter

Try to imagine how hard it would be to do business without money. Whenever you shopped, you'd have to have something to trade that the shopkeeper wanted. Your employer would have to pay you with something that you could trade for at least some of the things you needed. You'd have to find a way to make your car payments and your rent or mortgage payments, and pay for electricity, gasoline, food, clothing, appliances, and anything else you needed. In short, to carry out every transaction, you would need to find someone with whom you had a double coincidence of wants.

ADVANCED WORK

Money versus Barter

Imagine living in a country with no money. Every time you needed something, you would have to find someone who had what you wanted and was willing to trade for something that you had.

But if there were money, a widely accepted medium of exchange, you wouldn't need to barter. You could just go out and buy what you wanted without having to find someone willing to trade.

Money also provides a standard of value. Every good and service has a price that's expressed in terms of dollars and cents. If there were no money, then everything we traded would be valued in terms of what we traded for. For example, a haircut might trade for three movie tickets. Suppose there were just three goods and services in our economy, a, b, and c. The price of a would be expressed in terms of b and c, and the price of b would be expressed in terms of c. If there were four goods and services—a, b, c, and d—then the price of a would be expressed in terms of b, c, and d, the price of b would be expressed in terms of c

and d, and the price of c would be expressed in terms of d. So four goods would have six prices in a barter economy.

As the number of goods and services in a barter economy increases, the number of prices increases exponentially (see the table below). It sure is hard to do business when you have to keep track of so many prices.

Number of Goods and Services	Number of Prices in a Money Economy	Number of Prices in a Barter Economy
2	2	1
3	3	3
4	4	6
10	10	45
100	100	4,950
1,000	1,000	499,500

Without money, the only way to do business is by bartering. "How many quarter sections of beef do you want for that car?" or "Will you accept four pounds of sugar for that 18-ounce steak?"

For barter to work, I must want what you have and you must want what I have. This makes it pretty difficult to do business. (See the Advanced Work box, "Money versus Barter.")

Everything, then, must be assessed in money; for this enables men always to exchange their services, and so makes society possible.

—Aristotle,
Nicomachean Ethics

Our Money Supply

What does our money supply consist of? Gold? No! U.S. government bonds? No! Diamonds? No! Money consists of just a few things: coins, paper money, demand (or checking) deposits, and checklike deposits (sometimes called NOW—or negotiable order of withdrawal—accounts) held by the nonbank public. Coins (pennies, nickels, dimes, quarters, half-dollars, silver dollars, and other dollar coins) and paper money (dollar bills, fives, tens, twenties, fifties, and hundreds) together are considered currency. (By the way, where did the *dollar* come from? See the box on this topic.)

Five out of every 10 dollars in our money supply are demand deposits and other checkable deposits. Virtually all the rest is currency. We have to be careful, however, to distinguish between checks and demand (or checking) deposits. Jackie Gleason used to tell a story about two guys who get into an argument in a bar about who is more miserly (or cheaper). Suddenly one of them pulls out a dollar bill and a book of matches, lights the bill on fire, and lets it burn to a crisp. Not to be outdone, the other guy pulls out a five, lights it, and watches it burn to a crisp. So then the first guy does the same thing with a $10 bill. Well, the other guy doesn't want to look bad, so he reaches into his pocket, pulls out his checkbook, writes out a check for $1,000, lights it, and watches it burn to a crisp.

Checks are *not* money. Checking deposits *are*.

Incidentally, demand deposits are so named because they are payable "on demand." When you write a check, your bank must honor it, provided, of course, that you have enough money in your account to cover the check. Banks also insist that a certain number of business days go by before they will cash a specific check. It is usually 5 days for a

What does our money supply consist of?

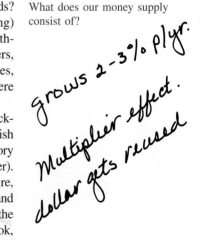
grows 2-3% p/yr.
Multiplier effect.
dollar gets reused

Where Did the Dollar Come From?

The U.S. dollar traces its roots back to the old Spanish-milled silver dollar. You didn't think it was based on the old British system, did you? You'd really have to be crazy to try to copy a system that uses pence, shillings, guineas, and pounds.

Are you any good at trivia questions? In Robert Louis Stevenson's *Treasure Island,* there was a parrot who, as parrots will do, kept repeating the same phrase over and over. OK, what was the phrase? You have eight seconds to answer the question. What was the phrase that the parrot, who, by the way, was acquainted with Long John Silver, kept repeating? Did you guess? Sorry—time's up.

The answer is "Pieces of eight. Pieces of eight." See that? You learn something every day.

By the way, how much money is two bits? It's a quarter. And four bits? That's right—50 cents. Eight bits? A dollar.

What was that parrot getting at with his "Pieces of eight. Pieces of eight"? He was talking dollars, Spanish-milled silver dollars. Those dollars were milled in such a way, that eight pieces—or bits—could be torn from each dollar, like perforated slices in a metal pie. That way, if you had a dollar and wanted to spend just 25 cents, you tore off two pieces or bits. To this day, some South American countries have coins worth $12\frac{1}{2}$ centavos.

local check and 7 to 10 days for an out-of-town check. Banks call this waiting period the time it takes for a check to clear. But any money in your checking account that has been cleared is available to depositors on demand.

Our currency is legal tender for all debts, public and private. But don't take *my* word for it. You'll find those words written just to the left of George Washington's portrait on the one dollar bill, or to the left of Abraham Lincoln's on the five. So the government says that your money must be accepted for payment of all debts. Does the government say that about checks and credit cards? No! (See the accompanying box.) Now what does it say on the back of each dollar just below "THE UNITED STATES OF AMERICA"? It says, "IN GOD WE TRUST." And as many people say: "In God we trust—all others pay cash."

How Do We Pay Our Bills?

There are many ways to pay for things—cash, check, credit card, debit card, prepaid or stored-value cards, and electronic fund transfers. Checks are the most important, but we have been moving rapidly toward a relatively checkless economy.

Credit cards, and especially debit cards, increasingly are used to pay for goods and services. And prepaid cards, which have long been issued by phone companies, have replaced food stamps, and are even being issued by employers in place of paychecks.

More and more people are paying their bills with electronic fund transfers—movements of funds directly from one bank account to another. Many people have arrangements with the phone and electric companies to have their bills automatically deducted from their bank accounts. Similarly, some employers deposit paychecks electronically. And every month, the Social Security Administration sends out tens of millions of benefit payments electronically. As electronic payments become more widespread, their share of total payments will continue to grow very rapidly.

M1, M2, and M3

M1 = currency, demand deposits, traveler's checks, and other checkable deposits

Our money supply includes currency, demand deposits, traveler's checks, and what the Federal Reserve terms "other checkable deposits," which include the NOW accounts and "share draft accounts," or checking accounts issued by credit unions.

According to the Federal Reserve there is almost $750 billion in currency in the hands of the public (see Figure 1). But the U.S. Treasury estimates that between two-thirds and three-quarters of U.S. currency is held outside the United States. Foreigners,

Are Credit Cards Money?

The answer is no. Credit cards are ID cards that enable you to buy a whole range of goods and services without having to pay until the end of the month. Who pays? The bank that issued your credit card pays the merchant; then, a few weeks later, you repay the bank.

What the bank would really like you to do is run up a large balance and pay 18 or 20 percent interest on that balance for years and years. That's the main reason they will give you a credit line of $5,000, $10,000, or even more.

Credit cards are a convenient way to buy things and account for nearly one-quarter of the dollar value of all purchases. They provide short-term loans from the financial institutions that issued the cards.

Bank of America issued the first bank credit cards in 1958, but most people didn't begin using them regularly until the 1970s. Through the 1960s people used cash and checks to pay for nearly all purchases.

American households, on average, possess nearly eight major bank cards—or 17, including store and gas cards.

Bank credit cards like VISA, MasterCard, and American Express have become extremely important in our economy. Not only can you travel and make major purchases without having to carry hundreds or thousands of dollars in cash, but you won't be able to rent a car, stay in some hotels, or transact certain types of business without such a card. But remember, they're only pieces of plastic—not money.

Debit cards look like credit cards. They're not money either. When you buy something, the sales clerk asks you, "Credit or debit?" If you have a debit card, the money comes right out of your checking account. Suppose you've got $1,000 in your checking account and use your debit card to pay for a $200 purchase. Before you've left the cash register, your checking account balance has already gone down to $800.

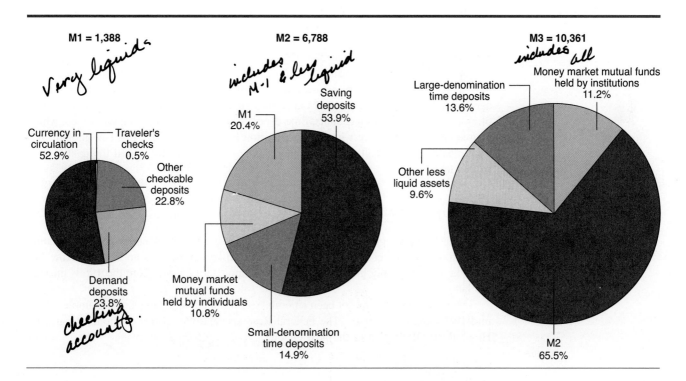

Figure 1

M1, M2, M3, February 27, 2006*

By adding savings deposits, small-denomination time deposits, and money market mutual funds held by individuals to M1, we get M2. Adding large-denomination time deposits (of $100,000 or more) and money market mutual funds held by institutions, we get M3.

*Percentages may not add to 100.0 percent due to rounding.

Source: Federal Reserve Statistical Release, March 9, 2006.

especially Russians, consider American dollars—especially one hundred dollar bills—as a much better medium of exchange and standard of value than their own currencies. So the bottom line is that our money supply, M1, may be as much as $500 billion lower than the official figure shown in Figure 1.

M1 is shown, along with M2 and M3, in Figure 1. As of February 2006, our money supply totaled $1,388 billion. Nearly everyone considers M1 our money supply, but we're going to consider two broader measures of money, M2 and M3.

By adding savings deposits, small-denomination time deposits, and money market mutual funds held by individuals to M1, we get M2. You know what savings deposits are. Time deposits hold funds that must be left in the bank for a specified period of time—a week, a month, three months, a year, five years, or even longer.

Remember the bank ads that warn, "There is a substantial penalty for early withdrawal"? These warnings are another way of saying that under the conditions of a time deposit, you are legally required to leave your money in the bank for a specified period of time. And so, unlike a demand deposit, time deposits are not payable until a certain date.

Technically, the money held in time and savings deposits does not have to be paid to the depositors "on demand." When you fill out a withdrawal slip to take money out of your savings account, you are completely confident that you will walk out of the bank with your money. Legally, however, your bank can require up to 30 days' written notice before giving you these funds. In practice, of course, no bank ever does this. Although nearly every bank in the country is insured by the Federal Deposit Insurance Corporation, it is quite possible that, if a 30-day waiting period were enforced, many nervous depositors would rush into their banks to get their money while they could. Money market mutual funds are issued by stockbrokers and other institutions, usually pay slightly higher interest rates than banks, and offer check-writing privileges.

We get from M2 to M3 by adding large-denomination time deposits, money market mutual funds held by institutions, and other less liquid assets. How large is large? The dividing line between small-denomination and large-denomination time deposits is $100,000. Any deposit of less than $100,000 is small.

A strong case can be made to designate M2 as our basic money supply rather than M1. First, it is the monetary measure most closely watched by the Federal Reserve, the agency that controls the growth of our money supply. Second, with the enormous growth of money market deposit accounts, time deposits, and money market mutual funds, which people can quickly convert into cash, attention has shifted to M2. But I'm enough of a traditionalist to keep calling M1 our basic money supply—at least until the next edition of this text.

M1 + savings, small-denomination time deposits, and money market funds = M2

M2 + large-denomination time deposits = M3

Our Growing Money Supply

Our money supply grows from year to year as the amount of currency in circulation goes up and as our checking deposits and checklike deposits go up as well. How fast does the money supply grow? Figure 2 shows monetary growth from the 1960s through the late 1990s.

Monetary growth has not been smooth. You'll notice huge jumps, for example, in the mid-1980s and early 1990s. The Federal Reserve controls the rate of monetary growth. How? Read all about it in the next chapter.

The Demand for Money

How much of *your* assets do you hold in the form of money? A typical middle-class family might own a home, two cars, several thousand dollars' worth of corporate stock, and perhaps one or two U.S. Treasury bonds. Of course, none of that is money. But the same family may also have a couple of bank accounts and $800 in cash. Let's consider the reasons why people hold some of their assets in the form of money.

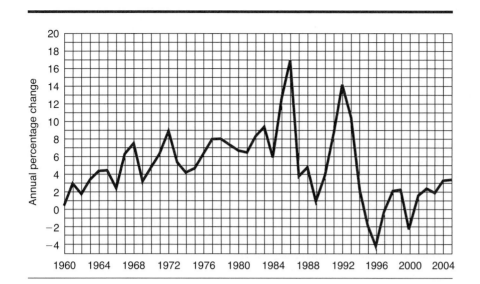

F*igure* 2

Annual Percentage Change in the
Money Supply, M1, 1960–2005
Between 1960 and 1983, there was
a fairly steady upward trend in the
annual growth of M1 from less than
1 percent to just over 9 percent.
But since then there have been
extremely sharp fluctuations,
ranging from an annual increase of
17 percent to a decrease of about
4 percent.

*Sources: Economic Report of the
President,* 2006; *Federal Reserve
Bulletin,* March 2006.

Economists recognize that people hold money for a variety of purposes. John Maynard Keynes noted that people had three reasons for holding money: to make transactions, for precautionary reasons, and to speculate. After we discuss the Keynesian motives for holding money, we shall look at the influences that shape the demand for holding money.

Why do people hold money?

The Keynesian Motives for Holding Money   John Maynard Keynes said people have three motives for holding money. Instead of holding their assets in other forms—stocks, bonds, real estate, commodities—everyone opts to hold at least some of their assets in the form of currency or demand deposits. First we'll look at the transactions motive.

Individuals have day-to-day purchases for which they pay in cash or by check. You take care of your rent or mortgage payment, car payment, monthly bills, and major purchases by check. Cash is sometimes needed for groceries, gasoline, restaurant meals, the movies, and nearly every other small purchase. Businesses, too, need to keep substantial checking accounts to pay their bills and to meet their payrolls. Individuals and businesses, then, both need to hold a certain amount of money for regular expenses. Keynes called this the transactions motive for holding money.

Transactions motive

Next we have the precautionary motive. People will keep money on hand, sometimes called a rainy-day fund, just in case some unforeseen emergency arises. They do not actually expect to spend this money, but they want to be ready if the need arises.

Precautionary motive

Finally, there is the speculative motive for holding money. When interest rates are very low—as they were during the Great Depression when Keynes was writing—you don't stand to lose much by holding your assets in the form of money. Alternatively, by tying up your assets in the form of bonds, you actually stand to lose money should interest rates rise, because you'd be locked into very low rates. In effect, the speculative demand for money is based on the belief that better opportunities for investment will come along and that, in particular, interest rates will rise.

Speculative motive

Four Influences on the Demand for Money   The amount of money we hold is influenced by four factors: (1) the price level, (2) income, (3) interest rates, and (4) credit availability. Changes in these factors change how much money we hold.

(1) The Price Level   As prices rise you need more money to take care of your day-to-day transactions. During those prosperous years before World War I, you didn't need to carry much money around. After all, those were the days, my friend. The days of nickel beer and nickel hot dogs. And, believe it or not, two kids could see a movie for a nickel.

A popular mid-1950s Broadway musical, *The Most Happy Fella,* had a hit song, "Standin' on the Corner,"[1] which had this couplet:

Saturday and I'm so broke
Couldn't buy a girl a nickel Coke.

Almost everything costs a lot more than it did 50 years ago. As the price level went up, so did the demand for money balances. Nobody leaves home with just a nickel anymore.

Today we must pay a substantial penalty for holding our assets in the form of money. In fact, there are two closely related penalties. First, there's inflation. If the inflation rate is 5 percent, then $100 held for a year will be worth only about $95. That is, $100 will buy as much as $95 bought one year ago.

During times of inflation, then, we don't want to hold more than is necessary in currency or checking deposits. We want to get some kind of return on our money, or in some other way protect its purchasing power.

By holding our assets in the form of money, not only would we be forgoing interest, but our money would be losing its purchasing power from month to month. Therefore, in times of high interest rates and inflation (the two generally go together), people prefer to hold as little as possible of their assets in the form of money.

We should distinguish between two contradictory influences on money balances with respect to the price level. As the price level rises, people need to hold higher money balances to carry out their day-to-day transactions. But as the price level rises (that is, with inflation), the purchasing power of the dollar declines; so the longer you hold money, the less that money is worth.

A distinction between short run and long run would be helpful. Assume a constant inflation rate of 10 percent so that the price level rises by exactly 10 percent every year. The cost of living would double every seven years.[2] So you would need to carry double the money balance in 2007 that you did in 2000 to handle exactly the same transactions.

However, with a 10 percent rate of inflation, the longer you hold assets in the form of money, the less that money will buy. Even though there is an inflation penalty for holding money for relatively long periods of time, you will surely keep enough on hand to take care of your day-to-day transactions. And if you compared your money balance in 2000 with that of 2007, you'd find that in 2007 you would be holding about double what you held in 2000, all other things remaining the same.

We are left with this conclusion: Even though people tend to cut down on their money balances during periods of inflation, as the price level rises they will hold larger money balances.

Money is the poor people's credit card.

    —Marshall McLuhan

(2) Income   Poor people seldom carry around much money. Check it out. The more you make, the more you spend, and the more you spend, the more money you need to hold as cash or in your checking account. Even if you use a credit card, you still have to pay your bill at the end of the month. As income rises, so does the demand for money balances.

(3) The Interest Rate   So far we've had two positive relationships: the quantity of money demanded rises with the level of prices and income. Are you ready for a negative relationship? All right, then. The quantity of money demanded goes down as interest rates rise.

Until recently people did not receive interest for holding money. Cash that you keep in your wallet or under your mattress still pays no interest, and until the late 1970s neither did checking deposits. Even today nearly all checking deposits pay less than 2 percent interest, and some don't pay any interest whatsoever. Alternatives to holding your assets

---

[1]This song actually made the charts on three different occasions, with versions by the Four Lads, the Four Freshman, and the Four Aces.

[2]Any number that increases by 10 percent a year will double in seven years. This is an application of the rule of 70: Any number that increases by 1 percent a year doubles in 70 years. You can check this out on your calculator or by consulting a book of compound interest tables.

in the form of money are to hold them in the form of bonds, money market funds, time deposits, and other interest-bearing securities. As interest rates rise, these assets become more attractive than money balances. Thus, there is a negative relationship between interest rates and money balances.

Do you remember the concept of opportunity cost, which was introduced in Chapter 2? What is the opportunity cost of holding money? It's the interest that you forgo.

(4) Credit Availability   If you can get credit, you don't need to hold so much money. Forty years ago most Americans paid cash for their smaller purchases and used checks for big-ticket items. The only form of consumer credit readily available was from retail merchants and manufacturers. The last four decades have seen a veritable explosion in consumer credit in the form of credit cards and bank loans. Over this period increasing credit availability has been exerting a downward pressure on the demand for money.

We can now make four generalizations:

1. As interest rates rise, people tend to hold less money.
2. As the rate of inflation rises, people tend to hold more money.
3. As the level of income rises, people tend to hold more money.
4. People tend to hold less money as credit availability increases.

The Demand Schedule for Money

For purposes of analysis, we shall use the Keynesian motives for holding money to derive the demand schedule for money. This schedule, when brought together with the money supply schedule in the next section, will enable us to derive the interest rate. Right now we'll be combining the transactions, precautionary, and speculative demands for money.

How much money individuals and business firms need to hold for their transactions really depends on the size of GDP, or total spending. The more we spend, the more we need to hold at any given time. The transactions demand for money is somewhat responsive to interest rate changes (see Figure 3A). Corporate comptrollers used to leave relatively large balances in their checking accounts in the 1950s when interest rates were very low and checking accounts paid zero interest. Today those funds might be held in the form of seven-day certificates of deposit or other very short-term, very liquid assets to take advantage of the relatively high interest rates. Individuals, too, because of today's

The transactions demand

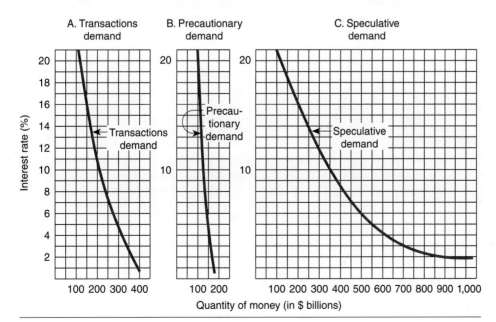

Figure 3

The Three Demands for Money
The amount of money that people hold for precautionary reasons has almost no responsiveness to interest rate changes, while the amount held for day-to-day transactions is somewhat responsive to interest rate changes. However, the speculative demand for money is very responsive, and, at relatively low interest rates, people wish to hold very large money balances.

higher interest rates as well as the widespread use of credit cards, carry much smaller money balances than they would have back in the 1950s.

The precautionary demand

The precautionary demand for money is least responsive to interest rate changes (see Figure 3B) because people have a specific purpose for holding these funds. However, even these funds would be at least partially converted into other assets at extremely high interest rates.

The speculative demand

The speculative demand for money is, as we would expect, the most responsive to interest rate changes (see Figure 3C). The people who are holding these funds would obviously hold a lot more at low interest rates than they would at higher rates.

The Liquidity Trap

At very low interest rates, people don't lend out their money.

When John Maynard Keynes carried his speculative motive for holding money to its logical conclusion, he determined that at very low interest rates people would not lend out their money, would not put it in the bank, would not buy bonds with it, but would simply hold it. That's right—they'd sit on it, they'd hoard it, but they wouldn't spend it or make it available to anyone else.

Why should they? When the interest rate declines to, say, 2 percent, why would people risk their money for such a low rate of return? And why would they tie it up at such a low interest rate when within a few months the interest rate might rise? *Then* they would sink it into interest-bearing assets, not now. This reasoning is reflected by the horizontal section of the Keynesian money demand curve (which he called a liquidity preference curve) shown in Figure 4.

This demand curve is the sum of the three demand curves shown in Figure 3—the transactions demands, precautionary demands, and speculative demands for money. In the next section we combine this curve with the money supply curve to determine the interest rate.

Since the late 1990s, Japan has been caught in a liquidity trap. The Bank of Japan has pushed interest rates to virtually 0, while Japanese citizens are sitting on personal savings of over $1 trillion. But the banks were not lending out enough of these funds to boost economic growth. And mid-decade the Japanese economy has finally begun to grow again.

Determination of the Interest Rate

The demand for and the supply of money determine the interest rate.

In Figure 4 we assumed various interest rates and determined that as the interest rate declined, the amount of money that the public wished to hold went up. But what determines the interest rate? If we think of the interest rate as the price of money,

Figure 4

Total Demand for Money
This is the sum of the transactions demands, precautionary demands, and speculative demands for money shown in Figure 3.

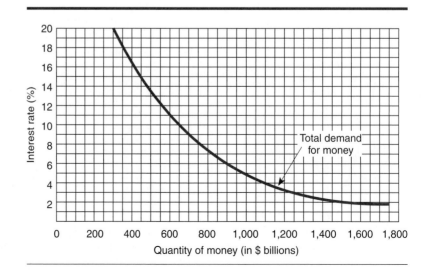

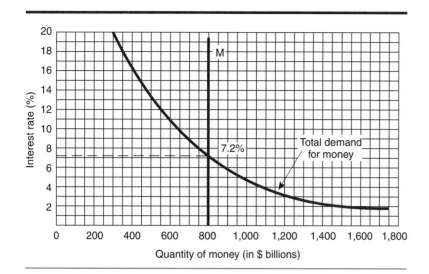

F*igure* 5
Total Demand for Money and
Supply of Money
The interest rate of 7.2 percent is
found at the intersection of the total
demand for money and the supply
of money (M). We used the total
demand for money curve shown in
Figure 4 and added a vertical M
curve. Since at any given time the
supply of money is fixed, it can be
represented as a vertical line.

then the interest rate, like the price of anything else, is set by the forces of supply
and demand.

At any given time supply is fixed, so we'll represent it as a vertical line at 800 in
Figure 5. Taking the demand curve from Figure 4, we find that it crosses the money supply
curve in Figure 5 at an interest rate of about 7.2 percent. It's as simple as that. Find the point
at which the demand curve and supply curve cross, and you've got the interest rate.

Of course, both our demand and supply curves are hypothetical, so the interest rate
we've found is hypothetical as well. OK, then, let's get real. How much is the interest
rate right now? 5 percent? 8 percent? 10 percent? How much *is* it? How much is it on
what? On passbook savings? On home mortgages? On Treasury bills? Are we talking
about the interest rate that you *get* for your money or the interest rate that you *pay*?
Guess which is always higher?

There are literally scores of interest rates. People may receive between 2 and 5 percent
on their savings, and a lot more during times of inflation, and may have to pay somewhere between 6 and 15 percent on a home mortgage. Large corporations with good
credit ratings pay the prime rate, while smaller and less creditworthy firms might pay 1
or 2 percent above prime.

Interest rates may vary from day to day, and there may be considerable variation
over the course of a year or two. Figure 6 shows the prime rate of interest that banks
charged on short-term business loans from 1978 through 2005. Because all interest rates
move up and down together, you can easily observe their cyclical nature. This particular
rate (along with the prime rate, which is generally slightly lower) rose from 10 percent
in 1980 to 22 percent in 1981 and then fell to 10 percent in early 1983.

Who controls interest rates? Is it the people who borrow money? Is it the banks? Is
it the Federal Reserve? The answer is yes to all three questions. But most experts say
the Federal Reserve Board of Governors plays the dominant role. In the next chapter
we'll see how the Federal Reserve controls the rate of growth of the money supply and
greatly influences interest rates.

*If you would know the value of
money, go and borrow some.*
    —Benjamin Franklin

*In banking it is axiomatic that
the richest customers paid the
least for borrowed money;
highest interest rates were for
the poor.*

    —Arthur Hailey,
    The Moneychangers

Who controls interest rates?

Banking

A Short History of Banking

There are just under 7,500 commercial banks in the United States. These are defined as
banks that hold demand deposits, but other banks—mutual savings banks, savings and loan
associations, credit unions, and mutual money market funds—also issue checking accounts.
The distinction between commercial banks and other savings institutions is blurring.

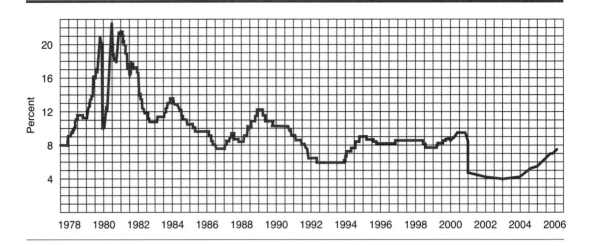

F*igure* 6

The Prime Rate of Interest Charged by Banks on Short-Term Business Loans, 1978–2006
Although the prime rate is set by the nation's largest banks, it is strongly influenced by the actions of the Federal Reserve Board of Governors.
Source: Federal Reserve Bulletin, 1978–2006; http://research.stlouisfed.org/fred2/data/PRIME.txt.

We'll talk about the origins of banking before we discuss how banking is conducted today in the United States. The first banks were run by goldsmiths back in the Middle Ages. We'll see that these fellows invented not only banking, but paper money as well.

The origins of banking

In medieval times, about the only secure place for your money was in the safes of the goldsmiths, so anybody who was anybody kept his money with the local goldsmith. These gentlemen would give receipts that possibly looked a little like the hatcheck slips you get at some of the fancier restaurants. If you left 10 gold coins with the smith, he wrote 10 on your receipt. If you happened to be rich, it was very important to be able to count past 10.

Although no one is quite sure who was the first to accept paper money—that is, goldsmiths' receipts—it might well have happened this way:

A knight was having his castle completely redone—new wallpaper, new bearskin rugs, new dungeon, new drawbridge—the works! When the job was finally completed, the contractor handed him a bill for 32 gold pieces.

The knight told the contractor, "Wait right here. I'll hitch up the team and take the oxcart into town. I'll get 32 gold coins from the goldsmith. I shouldn't be gone more than three days."

"Why bother to go all the way into town for the 32 gold coins?" asked the contractor. "When you give them to me, I'll have to ride all the way back into town and deposit the coins right back in the goldsmith's safe."

"You mean you're not going to charge me for the job?" The knight, while able to count past 10, came up short in certain other areas.

"Of course I want to get paid," replied the contractor. "Just give me your receipt for 32 gold coins."

It took the knight a little while to figure this out, but after the contractor went over it with him another six or eight times, he was finally able to summarize their transaction: "If I give you my receipt, we each save a trip to the goldsmith." And with that, paper money began to circulate.

The goldsmiths were not only able to count higher than anyone else in town, but they generally had a little more upstairs as well. Some of them began to figure out that they could really start to mint money, so to speak. First, they recognized that when people did

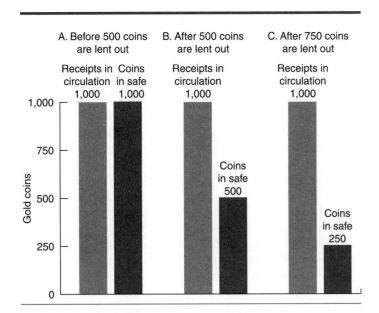

F*igure* 7

Goldsmith's Receipts and Reserves

Three questions: What is the goldsmith's reserve ratio when there are (a) 1,000 receipts in circulation and 1,000 coins in his safe? (b) 1,000 receipts in circulation and 500 coins in his safe? (c) 1,000 receipts in circulation and 250 coins in his safe? Answers: (a) 100 percent; (b) 50 percent; (c) 25 percent.

come in to retrieve their gold coins, they did not insist on receiving the identical coins they had left. Second, they noticed that more and more people were not bothering to come in at all to get their money because they were paying their debts with the receipts. And so, the goldsmiths were struck with this evil thought: Why not lend out some of these gold coins just sitting here in the safe?

This was the moment modern banking was born. As long as the total number of receipts circulating was equal to the number of gold coins in the safe, there was no banking system, but when the number of receipts exceeded the number of coins in the safe, a banking system was created. For example, if a goldsmith had 1,000 coins in his safe and receipts for 1,000 coins circulating, he wasn't a banker. What if he knew that his depositors would never all come at the same time for their money and he decided to lend out just 10 gold coins? He would then still have receipts for 1,000 coins circulating, but he'd have only 990 coins in his safe.

The "paper money" issued by the goldsmith is no longer fully backed by gold, but there's really nothing to worry about because not everyone will show up at the same time for their gold. Meanwhile, the goldsmith is collecting interest on the 10 gold pieces he lent out.

"But why stop there?" asks the goldsmith. "Why not lend out 100 gold coins, or even 500?" And so he does. With 500 coins lent out, he still has 500 in his safe to cover the 1,000 receipts in circulation. And what are the chances that half his depositors will suddenly turn up demanding their coins?

Now we have 500 coins backing up 1,000 receipts, or a reserve ratio of 50 percent. As long as no panics occur, 50 percent is certainly a prudent ratio. As the ratio declines (from 100 to 50 percent), let's see what happened to the money supply, the gold coins, and the goldsmith's receipts in the hands of the public (Figure 7).

Initially the goldsmith has 1,000 coins in the safe (or bank) and 1,000 receipts circulating. The reserve ratio is 100 percent (1,000 coins backing 1,000 receipts). Next he has 500 coins in the safe and 500 circulating, along with the 1,000 receipts in the hands of the public. His reserve ratio is 50 percent (500 coins backing 1,000 receipts). And the money supply? It's grown to 1,500—1,000 receipts and 500 coins in circulation. Thus, as the reserve ratio declines, the money supply rises.

Let's go a step further and have the goldsmith lend out an additional 250 gold coins. See if you can figure out the reserve ratio and the size of the money supply.

Because there are now 250 coins backing 1,000 receipts, the reserve ratio is 25 percent. Meanwhile the money supply has grown from 1,500 to 1,750, because in addition to the 1,000 receipts, 750 coins are in the hands of the public.

Moment at which modern banking was born

If the goldsmith were to continue lending out gold coins, he would end up with none in his safe. His reserve ratio would sink to zero, and the money supply would be 2,000 (1,000 receipts and 1,000 coins).

Being such a clever fellow, the goldsmith has noticed that his receipts circulate as easily as gold coins. And so, long before he has lent out all his coins, which he really needs as reserves (or backing for his receipts), he begins to make loans in the form of his receipts. For example, suppose you need to borrow 10 gold coins. The goldsmith merely writes up a receipt for 10 gold coins and off you go with your money.

What is to prevent the goldsmith from writing up receipts every time someone wants to borrow? We call this printing money. For example, with his original 1,000 gold coins tucked away in his safe, the goldsmith prints up 1,000 receipts (in addition to the 1,000 receipts he already gave to the owners of the 1,000 gold coins). How much would the reserve ratio be and what would be the size of the money supply?

With 1,000 coins backing up 2,000 receipts, the reserve ratio is 50 percent. The money supply consists of the 2,000 receipts in the hands of the public. Suppose the goldsmith lent out another 2,000 (units) in the form of receipts. The reserve ratio would be 25 percent (1,000 coins backing 4,000 receipts), and the money supply would be the 4,000 receipts.

If the goldsmith so chose, he could even print up 10,000 receipts, which would bring about a reserve ratio of 10 percent (1,000 coins backing 10,000 receipts) and a money supply of 10,000 receipts. Or he could lend out 100,000, bringing the reserve ratio down to 1 percent (1,000 coins backing up 100,000 receipts) and creating a money supply of 100,000 receipts.

The system worked as long as the goldsmiths did not get too greedy and as long as the depositors maintained their confidence in their goldsmith's ability to redeem his receipts in gold coins. From time to time, however, individual goldsmiths went too far in lending out money, whether in the form of gold coins or receipts. When depositors began to notice so many receipts in circulation, they asked themselves whether the goldsmith could possibly have enough coins in his safe to redeem them all. And when they thought he might not, they rushed into town to withdraw their gold coins before everyone else tried to.

If too many people reached the same conclusion, a panic ensued and the goldsmith could not possibly meet the demands of his depositors. In effect, then, he went bankrupt, and those left holding his receipts found them worthless. Of course, that was all before the days of the Federal Deposit Insurance Corporation (FDIC), so there was no one to whom depositors could turn.

The system worked as long as the goldsmiths did not get too greedy.

Modern Banking

Like the early goldsmiths, today's bankers don't keep 100 percent reserve backing for their deposits. If a bank kept all its deposits in its vault, it would lose money from the day it opened. The whole idea of banking is to borrow money at low interest rates and then lend out that same money at high interest rates. The more you lend, the more profits you make.

Banks would like to keep about 2 percent of their deposits in the form of vault cash. As long as depositors maintain confidence in the banks—or at least in the FDIC—there is really no need to keep more than 2 percent on reserve.

Unhappily for the banks, however, they are generally required to keep a lot more than 2 percent of their deposits on reserve. All the nation's commercial banks, credit unions, savings and loan associations, and mutual savings banks now have to keep up to 10 percent of their checking deposits on reserve. (See Table 1 of Chapter 14.)

Let's take a closer look at our banks. A bank as a financial institution accepts deposits, makes loans, and offers checking accounts.

Commercial Banks   These 7,500 banks account for the bulk of checkable deposits. Until the passage of the Depository Institutions Deregulation and Monetary Control Act of 1980, which is outlined near the end of the next chapter, only commercial banks were legally allowed to issue checking deposits, and they were the only institutions clearly recognized as "banks." Usually they have the word "bank" in their names. Traditionally, banks lent money for very short-term commercial loans, but in the last few decades they have branched out into consumer loans, as well as commercial and residential mortgages, and many offer brokerage services.

Savings and Loan Associations   Although originally established to finance home building, these associations also offer most of the services offered by commercial banks. The nearly 500 S&Ls invest more than three-quarters of their savings deposits in home mortgages. Later in the chapter we'll cover the savings and loan debacle of the 1980s, which ultimately reduced the number of S&Ls by almost two-thirds.

Mutual Savings Banks   Mostly operated in the northeastern United States, these institutions were created in the 19th century to encourage saving by the "common people." They traditionally made small personal loans, but today, like savings and loan associations, they offer the same range of services as commercial banks. There are about 1,000 mutual savings banks, all of which are located in New York, Massachusetts, Connecticut, Pennsylvania, and New Jersey.

Credit Unions   Although there are close to 10,000 credit unions in the United States, they hold less than 5 percent of total savings deposits. While these banks, like the others we've mentioned, do offer a full range of financial services, they specialize in small consumer loans. They are cooperatives that generally serve specific employee, union, or community groups.

The Banking Act of 1980 blurred the distinctions between commercial banks and the three other depository institutions. The main distinction—before 1980 only commercial banks were legally allowed to issue checking accounts—was swept away in 1980.

The Big Banks   Figure 8 lists our country's top 10 banks by size of assets in 2005. Nearly all are familiar names. You may notice that the top two, Citigroup and J. P. Morgan Chase, are located in New York City. Although it remains the financial capital of America, New York has been superseded by Tokyo as the preeminent financial center of the world.

The top 10 banks hold about two-thirds of all U.S. bank deposits. That's certainly a lot of money in the hands of a relatively small number of institutions. There has been a trend toward consolidation of financial institutions for more than 20 years, and that consolidation means a lot less competition in the industry. Since competition is what drives firms to be efficient, we certainly have cause for concern.

This disturbing trend has been largely offset by the growing presence of foreign banks in the United States. For example, HSBC (Hong Kong and Shanghai Bank Corporation), a British bank, purchased two major New York banks, Marine Midland and Republic National, and is the third largest bank in New York state. In California, Japanese banks hold more than one-third of that state's banking assets. Clearly, banking has become a global industry.

Consolidation has also brought about huge economies of scale—most notably ongoing computerization and the spreading network of ATMs—efficiencies that are necessary for American banks to compete in global markets. Considering the trend toward financial supermarkets providing one-stop shopping, the efficiencies from consolidation may even outweigh the efficiency losses resulting from diminished competition.

How do the banks listed in Figure 8 rank internationally? Of the top 10 commercial banks (ranked by size of assets as of February 2005), 3 are British, 3 are American, and there are 2 each from France and Japan. We've listed the top 10 American banks in Figure 8, and the world's top 10 banks in Table 1.

Bank Lending   Banking is based on one simple principle: Borrow money at low interest rates and lend that money out at much higher interest rates. Even when interest rates are very low, as they were in 2003, banks charge their borrowers a lot more than they pay their depositors. Just look at the rates that banks post in their windows or in their lobbies. They

A banker is a fellow who lends his umbrella when the sun is shining and wants it back the minute it begins to rain.

—Mark Twain

Figure 8

The Top Ten American Banks, Ranked by Assets, February 2005

Total bank assets were roughly 8.2 trillion. What percentage of those assets were held by (a) the top three banks? (b) the top ten banks?

Source: The World Almanac, 2006; Forbes.com.

Answers:
(a) 45%
(b) 66%

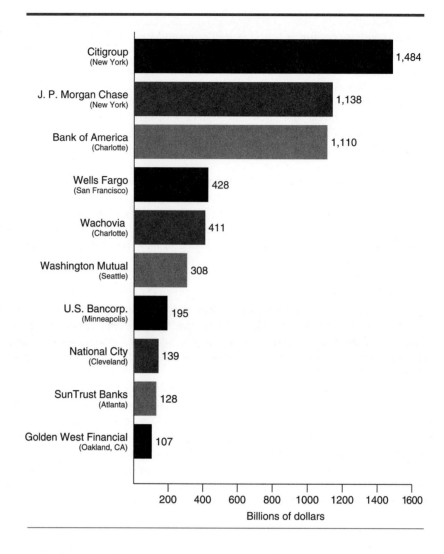

TABLE 1 The World's Top Ten Banks, Ranked by Assets, February 2005

Bank	Country	Total Assets (in billions)
Citigroup	United States	$1,484
Mizuho Financial	Japan	1,307
BNP Paribas	France	1,228
J. P. Morgan Chase	United States	1,138
Royal Bank of Scotland	United Kingdom	1,120
Bank of America	United States	1,110
HSBC Group	United Kingdom	1,031
Mitsubishi Tokyo	Japan	1,015
Barclays	United Kingdom	1,002
Credit Agricole	France	988

Sources: The World Almanac, 2006; www.Forbes.com.

come right out and admit that they pay either zero or up to maybe 3 percent interest on most deposits—and perhaps 1 or 2 points more if you leave your money on deposit for a few years—but they charge about 7 percent for fixed-rate mortgages, a bit more for most business loans, and about 18 percent on credit card loans. (See the box, "Welfare Banks.")

"Welfare Banks"

Most of us take for granted the services provided by our neighborhood banks. They cash our paychecks; they operate 24-hour cash machines; and, if we need the money to buy a new car or even a house, they lend it to us.

But where do poor people do their banking? Chances are, they go to the "welfare bank," which is what the check-cashing stores are called. You'll find at least one in virtually every poor neighborhood. Where did the name come from? Well, on "check day," which almost always falls on the 1st and the 16th of every month, 6 million Americans receiving public assistance get their checks in the mail. Why don't they cash them at their neighborhood banks? First of all, many poor neighborhoods don't have banks. Second, you usually need to have a minimum balance of at least $1,500 or the bank will charge you some pretty stiff fees for its services. Third, people receiving public assistance are not allowed to have bank accounts; they have no choice but to find someplace else to cash their checks.

The check-cashing outlets not only cash checks but also sell money orders. Who pays their bills by money order? Poor people do. And, of course, a money order may cost $1, or $2, or even more. To cash a check, you usually pay a fee of $5 or 1 to 6 percent of the value of the check, but some check-cashing stores will charge you as much as 20 percent.

You may ask why banks almost always require a minimum balance on checking accounts in the first place. The reason is that every banking transaction—depositing money, withdrawing money, processing checks, even posting interest—costs the banks money. However, the poor, especially those on welfare, can least afford to pay the fees charged by check-cashing services. Congress, as well as state legislatures, has considered passing laws requiring banks to cash welfare and Social Security checks, and to provide other banking services to people who cannot afford to keep the stipulated minimum balances, but the American Bankers Association, one of the nation's most powerful special interest groups, has easily beaten back this legislation.

In the 1990s the number of check-cashing outfits tripled to 7,000 and reached 11,000 in 2006. These outfits charged poor people between 4 and 10 times what they would have paid for the same services at a bank. And yet most poor people are unaware that several states (including Illinois, Massachusetts, New Jersey, New York, Rhode Island, Vermont, and Minnesota) have laws that require banks to offer accounts with minimum deposits of $100 or less and monthly fees of no more than $3. Although banks are often required to post information about low-cost checking accounts, few actually do, because these laws are rarely enforced.

Financial Intermediaries Financial intermediaries channel funds from savers to borrowers. Basically they repackage the flow of deposits, insurance premiums, pension contributions, and other forms of savings into larger chunks—$10,000, $1 million, $50 million, or even more—for large business borrowers. And, of course, they pay relatively low rates of interest to their lenders and charge relatively high rates to their borrowers. We're all familiar with banks, but this function is performed by a variety of other financial intermediaries (see the box, "Nonbank Financial Intermediaries").

Sometimes business borrowers dispense with financial middlemen altogether by borrowing directly from savers. The U.S. Treasury does this every month by issuing new bonds, certificates, notes, and bills. And increasingly, large business borrowers are doing the same thing by issuing relatively short-term commercial paper and long-term bonds.

One way that banks and other financial intermediaries differentiate between the relatively well off and the less fortunate is in the home mortgage market. Just over two-thirds of all American families own their home, nearly all of which have outstanding mortgages.

There are two distinct mortgage markets. The conventional market, in which commercial banks, savings banks, savings and loan associations, and credit unions provide middle class and relatively well off homeowners conventional mortgages at interest rates which hovered just below 6 percent through most of 2005 and were on track to reach 7 percent before the end of 2006. The subprime market caters to poorer homeowners, and has interest rates that are double what they are in the conventional market. Banks generally do not lend directly to homeowners in the subprime market, but they either provide the funds to consumer lending companies like Countrywide Credit or Household

Nonbank Financial Intermediaries

Banks offer their customers checking deposits that are included in M1. Some nonbank financial intermediaries may come close, but no cigar. Money market mutual funds, for instance, often allow their investors to write checks on their balances, but usually only a few a month, and for at least $500 or $1,000.

Pension funds, generally set up by large corporations, are another major form of financial intermediary. TIAA-CREF, which nearly all college professors have joined, is the largest, with a stock and bond portfolio worth several hundred billion dollars. Where did it get all this money? From our paychecks, with matching contributions from our employers.

Insurance companies collect billions of dollars in premiums every year, which they invest in real estate, stocks and bonds, and mortgages. Consumer finance companies—such as Beneficial Finance and Household Finance—borrow at very low rates, because they have excellent credit ratings, and charge their customers 25, 30, or even 40 percent interest rates. Why are these people willing to pay so much? Because they don't have much choice—if their credit ratings had been better, they could have borrowed from a bank.

International, that provide the actual mortgages, or else huge banks, such as Bank of America and Citicorp own these subprime lenders outright.

There have been moves on the local, state, and federal levels to more closely regulate these subprime lenders. Their defenders point out that without this market, millions of relatively poor families would be unable to own homes. However, the high interest rates and other financial charges have caused hundreds of thousands of families to lose their homes each year. The case of Veronica Harding, which was reported in *The New York Times,* illustrates the plight of relatively poor homeowners. Ms Harding "... bought a row house in North Philadelphia for $7,500 in 1980, but now owes about $35,000 after refinancing five times in four years. The last loan generated $5,600 in fees, or 16 percent of the loan value.[3]

In 2002 Household International paid a record $484 million fine to settle allegations that it had misled borrowers in more than a dozen states into paying mortgage rates that in some cases were almost twice what was promised. Household also agreed to stop allowing loan officers to persuade customers to refinance home loans to take advantage of lower rates without advising them about other fees they would have to pay.[4]

The Creation and Destruction of Money

The Creation of Money

Money consists of checking deposits, checklike deposits, and currency in the hands of the public. To create money, banks must increase either currency held by the public or checkable deposits. The way banks do this is by making loans.

Banks create money by making loans.

A businessperson walks into Bank of America and requests a loan of $10,000. Later that day she calls the bank and finds out that her loan is granted. Because she already has a checking account at Bank of America, the bank merely adds $10,000 to her balance. In return she signs a form promising to pay back the loan with interest on a specified date. That's it. Money has been created. Checking deposits have just increased by $10,000.

---

[3]Richard A. Oppel, Jr. and Patrick McGeehan, "Lenders Try to Fend Off Laws on Subprime Loans," *New York Times,* April 4, 2001, p. C17.

[4]Subprime lending is discussed more extensively in the chapter, "Rent, Interest, and Profit," in *Economics* and *Microeconomics.*

If, for some reason, the businessperson had asked to be paid in cash, the public would have held $10,000 more in currency. And the bank? The $10,000 it loaned out was merely inventory; it was not counted as part of our money supply.

The point is that the bank just created $10,000. Whether checkable deposits or currency held by the public rose by that amount, our money supply rose by $10,000.

This may sound like a license to print money. It is, but it's a very restricted license. A bank may make loans only if it has some available reserves. And who determines whether banks have these reserves? You guessed it—the Federal Reserve. So we really have three parties involved in the creation of money: the person who wants to borrow the money, the bank that creates the money, and the Federal Reserve, which allows this creative act to take place.

The Destruction of Money

Whoever creates can usually destroy as well. That's what happens when the businessperson pays back her loan. She'll probably write a check on her account for $10,000 plus the interests she owes, and when the bank deducts that amount from her account, down goes the money supply. Or if she pays back the loan in cash, again—down goes the money supply. In this case the currency leaves the hands of the public (literally) and goes into the bank's inventory. The bank will stamp the loan agreement form "paid," and the transaction is completed.

The creation and destruction of money is a major function of banking. The basic way this is done is through loans. The most important commercial bank loans are commercial and industrial loans, although consumer loans have grown considerably in importance since the 1970s.

> Money is destroyed when a loan is repaid to the bank.

Limits to Deposit Creation

Most bank loans involve giving the borrower an additional deposit in his or her checking account; therefore, it would appear that banks can create all the money they wanted by doing this. All you need is a simple bookkeeping operation. A $20,000 loan means you increase that customer's account by $20,000 by a computer entry.

Remember the goldsmith who kept writing receipts until there were 1,000 gold coins in his safe backing 100,000 receipts? Why can't bankers keep issuing loans by increasing the checking accounts of their customers?

The first limit would be prudence. Most banks would try to keep about 2 percent of their demand deposits on reserve in the form of vault cash; in case some of their depositors came in to cash checks, there would be enough money on hand to pay them. But no banker has that choice. The Federal Reserve sets legal requirements to which the banks must adhere, and, as I've already mentioned, these limits are substantially higher than those that might be set by the most prudent of bankers.

Bank Regulation

Branch Banking and Bank Chartering

Branch Banking versus Unit Banking   Banking is legally defined as accepting deposits. Branch banking, therefore, would be the acceptance of deposits at more than one location. Branch banking rules are set by the state in which a bank is located. Bank of America, for example, is subject to North Carolina banking law, while Citibank and J. P. Morgan Chase are regulated by New York banking law.

Three types of branch banking have evolved under various state laws. First is unrestricted branch banking, under which a bank may open branches throughout the state. Golden West Financial and Wells Fargo have branches all over California.

The three types of branch banking are
(1) unrestricted branching,
(2) limited branching,
(3) unit banking.

A second variation is restricted, or limited, branch banking. For example, a bank may be allowed to open branches only in contiguous communities. What is permissible varies from state to state.

Finally, there is unit banking, in which state law forbids any branching whatsoever. A bank that opens an office that receives deposits at a particular location cannot open any other branches. This obviously restricts the size of banks in those states. In fact, banks in unit banking states are, on the average, about one-fifth the size of banks in states that permit unrestricted branching.

Right now two out of five states, nearly all in the East and Far West, have unlimited branching. Another two out of five states, mainly in the Midwest and the South, allow limited branching. And finally, the remaining states, mostly in the Midwest, permit only unit banking.

There are 75,000 bank branches throughout the nation—an increase of 15,000 since 1985—but some banks are closing branches and replacing them with automated teller machines. Why the shift to ATMs? Processing a teller transaction costs more than double what an ATM transaction costs. By the end of 2003 there were about 425,000 ATMs in the United States doing more than 14 billion transactions a year. But banks have new competitors. In 1996 7 percent of all ATMs were privately owned (i.e., by individual entrepreneurs rather than banks); in 2003 37 percent were privately owned.

Now, you can withdraw money from your checking account at hundreds of thousands of retail outlets with a debit card. The vast majority of the 75 million debit cards in circulation were issued by MasterCard and VISA. But instead of getting a month to pay off your balance, as you would on your credit card, your money is automatically withdrawn instantly from your checking account to pay for your purchases. Like the advent of the ATM the debit card promises to make personal banking almost obsolete.

The ATM Wars   Should banks be allowed to charge fees—usually $1 to $2—to noncustomers? Virtually all bankers and most economists (including the author) would answer "yes!"

First, there's the issue of fairness. Six out of seven ATM users don't pay surcharges. The fees hit only users who go to "foreign" ATMs—machines not owned by their own bank. Why should a bank's customers underwrite the noncustomers who demand access to cash wherever they are? And why should a bank provide a free service to people who do not otherwise patronize it? Indeed, after Santa Monica and San Francisco banned the fees, Bank of America and Wells Fargo briefly stopped allowing noncustomers in those cities to use their machines.

Second, we need to think of an ATM as a convenience. We pay more to shop at a "convenience store" than at a supermarket. We pay more for soda from a vending machine than at a grocery. Why not charge people for the convenience of withdrawing cash at an airport, at a shopping mall, or even in another state?

And finally, banning the surcharges would leave consumers with fewer choices. It would presumably become unprofitable to operate the machines in some out-of-the-way places that didn't have them before the fees. Perhaps banks won't continue to serve out-of-town travelers. We'll all have to make do with fewer cash machines and longer lines.

Most banks have state charters.

State and Nationally Chartered Banks   To operate a bank, you must get a charter. More than two-thirds of the nation's banks have state charters; the rest have national charters. National charters are issued by the comptroller of the currency and are generally harder to obtain than state charters. Each of the 50 states issues state charters.

To get a bank charter you need to demonstrate three things: (1) that your community needs a bank or an additional bank; (2) that you have enough capital to start a bank; and (3) that you are of good character.

Most large banks are nationally chartered. Often the word *national* will appear in their names, for example, First National City Bank or Mellon National Bank. Incidentally, all nationally chartered banks must join the Federal Reserve. About three-quarters of all banks have state charters.

To summarize, all nationally chartered banks must join the Federal Reserve System. All Federal Reserve member banks must join the FDIC. Only a small percentage of the state-chartered banks are members of the Federal Reserve. Nearly all banks are members of the FDIC.

Interstate Banking   Until 1994 interstate banking was technically illegal, although banks managed to engage in the practice by buying banks in other states and operating them as separate entities. But the passage of the Riegle-Neal Interstate Banking and Branching Efficiency Act of 1994 swept away the last barriers to opening branches in different states. Until this law was passed, for example, a customer of a bank branch in North Carolina was not permitted to make a deposit at one of the same bank's South Carolina branches.

The Federal Deposit Insurance Corporation

After the massive bank failures of the 1930s, Congress set up the FDIC—another case of closing the barn door after the horses had run off. The amount insured has progressively been raised, the last time in 1980, when the ceiling was raised from $40,000 to $100,000.

The whole idea of the FDIC is to avert bank panics by assuring the public that the federal government stands behind the bank, ready to pay off depositors if it should fail. The very fact that the government is ready to do this has apparently provided enough confidence in the banking system to avoid any situation that could lead to widespread panic.

The whole idea of the FDIC

The FDIC would rather have another bank take over an ailing institution than be forced to pay off its depositors. Often, to encourage such takeovers, the FDIC will actually give the cooperating bank up to several hundred million dollars to take certain white elephants off its hands.

The FDIC prefers takeovers to payoffs.

Is the FDIC in any danger of running out of money? Not really. The Congress, the Federal Reserve, the Treasury, and all the financial resources of the U.S. government are committed to the preservation of this institution.

Will the FDIC run out of money?

More than 99 percent of all banks are members of the FDIC. If you want to make sure that yours is, first check to see whether there's a sign in the window attesting to this fact. If there isn't, ask inside, and if the answer is no, then very calmly walk up to the teller and withdraw all your money. Membership in the FDIC means that your money is safe and that we will probably never have a repetition of what happened back in the 1930s when there were runs on the banks, culminating in the Great Depression.

The Savings and Loan Debacle

In early 1990 the financial press was calling this the greatest financial scandal in the history of the United States. How could it have happened? How bad *was* it? The roots of the problem date to the 1950s and 1960s, when the nation's 3,000 savings and loan associations were handing out millions of 30-year mortgages at 4, 5, and 6 percent fixed interest rates. This was good business—at that time—because the S&Ls were paying just 2 or 3 percent interest to their shareholders.[5]

The origins

When interest rates went through the roof from the late 1970s through the early 1980s, the shareholders rushed in to withdraw their money. But their money wasn't just sitting there in the vaults. It was already lent out to homeowners. It was being paid back, a little each month, over a 30-year period.

Why did the shareholders want to take their money out? Because they could get much higher interest rates by purchasing Treasury bills, certificates of deposit, money market mutual funds, corporate bonds, or other financial instruments. Why didn't the

---

[5]Technically, people who deposit their money in savings and loan associations are shareholders, but if you'd rather call them depositors, that's fine with me.

savings and loan associations simply pay them more interest? Because they were legally barred from doing so.

In 1980 the law was changed to allow the savings and loan associations to pay much higher rates of interest.[6] In addition, they were freed from making primarily home mortgage loans. What the S&Ls did, then, with their newfound freedom was go out and borrow funds at very high interest rates and lend them out at still higher interest rates. The only trouble was that the loans they tended to make were very risky ones.

Dangerous speculation

Money was lent to farmland speculators in the Midwest and to people buying up oil properties in the Southwest. These seemed like reasonably safe loans because the prices of this land had been rising very rapidly. But what goes up must come down. At least it did during the severe recession of 1981–82. And what was a bad situation nationwide got to be a worse situation in the Southwest and the Midwest as declining oil prices and drought depressed land prices still further. Borrowers defaulted on their loans, and the S&Ls were stuck with large holdings of real estate, which they had to sell in a depressed market. In short, scores of S&Ls—most notably in Texas and Oklahoma—lost their shirts.

And that was just *part* of the problem. Real estate developers, many of them based in California, Florida, and Texas, bought control of many S&Ls and poured billions of dollars into shopping malls, office parks, condos, and other ventures of dubious merit (dubious during a time of sinking real estate prices, anyway). And so another wave of S&Ls was taken to the cleaners.

Junk bonds

Still another aspect of the S&L debacle revolved around junk bonds, which were used extensively to finance corporate takeovers or, alternatively, to stave off hostile takeovers. To raise billions of dollars quickly, corporate raiders—or the boards of the corporations facing hostile bids—would issue bonds given very low credit ratings. Why did anyone want to buy them? Because they paid relatively high interest rates.

Among the biggest buyers of these junk bonds were failing S&Ls. And so, using their shareholders' money, they helped feed the speculative corporate takeover frenzy that dominated Wall Street during the 1980s. When the prices of many of these bonds plunged steeply in the late 1980s, in the wake of the stock market crash of October 1987, several hundred more S&Ls were ruined.

Organized crime

So far we've been talking about the nice guys. Now let's talk about organized crime. Stephen P. Pizzo, who extensively studied the downfall of the S&L industry,[7] had *this* to say about the role that organized crime played:

> Coast to coast, mob families and their associates bellied up to thrifts and sucked out hundreds of millions of dollars. One New York mob associate turned up in the records of 130 thrifts; 125 of those failed. Another organized crime figure, now in jail, was in the federal witness protection program while he defrauded thrifts of tens of millions of dollars. The longer list of those who showed up at now-dead thrifts reads like a Mafia Who's Who.[8]

The federal government ended up paying perhaps $200 billion to clean up the mess. Depositors were paid off, hundreds of failed S&Ls were shut down, and the surviving S&Ls were now more closely supervised.

Wal-Mart Bank?

Since 1999 Wal-Mart has been attempting to get government approval to set up its own in-house banking unit, which it now claims will have only one purpose—to process credit and debit card transactions for its 3,500 U.S. stores. This would save the company most

---

[6]Insurance coverage was raised at that time from $40,000 to $100,000 on savings and loan shares and on bank deposits.

[7]Stephen P. Pizzo is coauthor of *Insider Job: The Looting of America's Savings and Loans* (New York: McGraw-Hill, 1990).

[8]Stephen P. Pizzo, "The Real Culprits in the Thrift Scam," *New York Times,* April 2, 1990.

of the 1.75–2.0 percent "interchange" fee it now pays to credit card companies every time a shopper pays with plastic. Wal-Mart already does, directly or indirectly, provide some banking services. It sells low-price money orders, and provides check cashing and money wiring services. And some 1,400 Wal-Mart stores have partnerships with banks, some with leases running for another 15 years.

What worries local banks most is the thought that Wal-Mart will get into true branch banking by issuing checking accounts. There is no question that the nation's banks, large and small, oppose new competition from the world's largest retailer. But who would be the *real* losers? They would be VISA, MasterCard, American Express, Discovery, and the other credit card companies, which handled more than $2 trillion in consumer transactions and took in nearly $30 billion in fees in 2005.

In an editorial, *The Wall Street Journal* fully supported Wal-Mart's effort to enter the banking industry:

> At issue is whether Wal-Mart should be granted the authority to establish an Industrial Loan Company (ILC) in Utah. ILCs are state-chartered, quasi-banks that were originally designed a century ago to help low-income workers get cheap loans. ILCs can provide most banking services, such as check cashing, lending, and credit card processing. Target and General Electric have been granted an ILC with little controversy. But because Wal-Mart has been portrayed as America's latest corporate villain, its political hurdles are much higher.[9]

In hearings before the FDIC in April 2006 Jane Thompson, the store's president of financial services, offered a pledge, in writing, that Wal-Mart would open bank branches to process credit card charges, but not to accept deposits. A decision by the FDIC was expected by mid-2006.

Current Issue: Overdraft Privileges

When you don't have enough money in your account to cover a check you wrote, your check will bounce. This can be very embarrassing, so banks now grant overdraft privileges to their depositors. If you overdraw your account, your check won't bounce, but you *will* have to pay an overdraft fee.

Each time a person overdraws her account, she's charged a fee of $15 to $35, and she must pay back the overdraft within a week or two. When an overdraft occurs as a result of a debit card or ATM transaction, banks generally don't immediately inform their customers or give them the option of reversing the transaction. Instead they mail out a notice. So a person may incur several overdrafts before realizing how many fees she's incurred.

Here's what happened to one college student who took advantage of his overdraft privileges:

> Chris Keeley went on a shopping spree last Christmas Eve, buying $230 in gifts with his debit card. But the New York University student's holiday mood soured a few days later when he received a notice from Pittsburgh's PNC Bank that he had overdrawn the funds in his checking account. While PNC allowed each of his seven transactions to go through, it charged him $31 for each overdraft—or a hefty $217 in fees for his $230 worth of purchases.[10]

Would *you* agree to pay $217 in interest on a two-week $230 loan? Did Chris Keeley know how much he would be paying for overdrawing his checking account? It all comes down to the issue of truth-in-lending, and the banks could certainly be more forthcoming about the cost of the overdraft privileges they so freely extend.

---

[9] *The Wall Street Journal,* "Banking Against Wal-Mart," January 4, 2006, p. A10.
[10] See *BusinessWeek,* May 2, 2005, p. 68.

Questions for Further Thought and Discussion

1. When would you expect to find barter used instead of money?

2. What happens to the demand for money as (a) the price level rises; and (b) the availability of credit rises? Explain your answers.

3. Describe the conditions that were necessary for modern banking to be born.

4. What were the conditions that led to the savings and loan debacle?

5. How could rapid inflation undermine money's ability to perform each of its four basic jobs?

6. What distinguishes money from other assets, such as corporate stock, government bonds, and expensive jewelry?

7. Our money supply is defined as M1. But the Board of Governors of the Federal Reserve and many others believe M2 would better define our money supply. Can you think of one reason to support M1 and one reason to support M2?

8. Why do most interest rates go up and down together over time?

9. Financial intermediaries perform an important job. What is that job, and how do they perform it?

10. What percentage of your money balance do you hold for transactions purposes, precautionary purposes, and speculative purposes?

11. What percentages of your or your family's bills are paid by cash, by check, and by credit card?

Workbook for Chapter 13

Name _____

Date _____

Multiple-Choice Questions

Circle the letter that corresponds to the best answer.

1. Each of the following except _____ is a job of the money supply.
   a) medium of exchange
   b) store of value
   c) standard of value
   d) receipt for gold

2. Which is the most important job of money?
   a) Medium of exchange
   b) Store of value
   c) Standard of value
   d) Receipt for gold

3. The basic alternative to money in the United States would be _____.
   a) gold   c) stealing
   b) barter   d) the underground economy

4. Barter involves _____.
   a) money
   b) specialization
   c) a double coincidence of wants
   d) demand deposits

5. Which one of the following is not part of our money supply?
   a) Dollar bills   c) Traveler's checks
   b) Demand deposits   d) Gold

6. Which statement is true?
   a) M1 is larger than M2.
   b) M1 + M2 = M3.
   c) M2 + large-denomination time deposits + money market mutual funds held by institutions = M3.
   d) M1 × M2 = M3.

7. Which statement is true?
   a) Checks are not money.
   b) A small part of our money supply is silver certificates.
   c) Most of our money supply is in the form of currency.
   d) None of these statements is true.

8. The U.S. dollar is based on _____ currency.
   a) British   c) Dutch
   b) French   d) Spanish

9. Which is not in M2?
   a) Currency
   b) Demand deposits
   c) Small-denomination time deposits
   d) Large-denomination time deposits

10. Which statement is true?
    a) Credit cards are a form of money.
    b) M1 is closer to the size of M2 than M2 is to the size of M3.
    c) M2 is about five times the size of M1.
    d) M3 is about $2 trillion.

11. When you buy something with a credit card _____ and when you buy something with a debit card _____.
    a) you owe money; you owe money
    b) you owe money; money is taken out of your checking account
    c) money is taken out of your checking account; money is taken out of your checking account
    d) money is taken out of your checking account; you owe money

12. In February 2006 M1 was more than $_____ billion.
    a) 600   c) 1,300
    b) 900   d) 1,700

13. Over the last three decades our money supply _____.
    a) grew steadily at about the same rate
    b) fell steadily at about the same rate
    c) rose steadily through the 1970s and fell steadily through the 1980s and 1990s
    d) fell steadily through the 1970s and rose steadily through the 1980s and 1990s
    e) grew most years, but at widely varying rates

14. The interest rate on business loans _____ the interest rate that banks pay their depositors.
    a) is higher than
    b) is lower than
    c) has no relationship to

15. The most important way of paying for goods and services is _____.
    a) electronic fund transfers
    b) gold
    c) checks
    d) cash
    e) prepaid or stored-value cards

16. If Wal-Mart does get FDIC approval to enter the banking industry, the clearest immediate consequence would be
    a) most small banks and some larger ones would soon be driven out of business.
    b) MasterCard, VISA, and other credit card companies would be driven out of business.
    c) Wal-Mart would quickly begin accepting deposits and become the nation's largest bank.
    d) Wal-Mart would save a significant amount of money by not having to pay "interchange" fees when their shoppers pay with credit or debit cards.

17. John Maynard Keynes identified three motives for holding money. Which motive listed below did Keynes not identify?
    a) Transactions
    b) Precautionary
    c) Psychological
    d) Speculative

18. As the price level rises, the amount of money demanded for transactions purposes _____.
    a) rises
    b) falls
    c) remains about the same

19. As the interest rate rises, the quantity of money demanded _____.
    a) rises
    b) falls
    c) remains about the same

20. People tend to hold more money as _____.
    a) incomes rise and credit availability rises
    b) incomes fall and credit availability falls
    c) incomes rise and credit availability falls
    d) incomes fall and credit availability rises

21. The distinction between commercial banks and other banks is _____.
    a) very clear
    b) becoming blurred
    c) nonexistent
    d) none of these

22. Which statement is true?
    a) Most U.S. currency is held by foreigners.
    b) We have greatly underestimated the amount of currency circulating in the U.S.
    c) Russians hold virtually no U.S. currency.
    d) About 10 percent of our currency is held by foreigners.

23. What led to the bankruptcy of many goldsmiths was that they _____.
    a) had a reserve ratio that was too high
    b) had a reserve ratio that was too low
    c) lent out gold coins instead of receipts
    d) lent out receipts instead of gold coins

24. Which statement is false?
    a) About 99 percent of all banks are members of the FDIC.
    b) If the FDIC runs out of money, the federal government will supply it with more funds.
    c) The FDIC would rather have another bank take over an ailing institution than be forced to pay off its depositors.
    d) None of these statements is false.

25. Which statement is true?
    a) Most states allow only unit banking.
    b) Most states allow unlimited branching.
    c) Most banks have national charters.
    d) None of these statements is true.

26. To get a bank charter, you need to demonstrate each of the following, except _____.
    a) that your community needs a bank or an additional bank
    b) that you have sufficient banking experience
    c) that you have enough capital to start a bank
    d) that you are of good character

27. Money is created when someone _____.
    a) takes out a bank loan
    b) pays back a bank loan
    c) spends money
    d) saves money

28. Bank deposit creation is limited by _____.
    a) reserve requirements
    b) the interest rate
    c) whether a bank is nationally or state chartered
    d) whether a bank is in a large city or a rural area

29. Which statement is true?
    a) About half the savings and loan associations went bankrupt in the early 1980s.
    b) The savings and loan associations were helped by high interest rates in the late 1970s and early 1980s.
    c) Most savings and loan associations were locked into low-interest-rate mortgages in the 1950s and 1960s.
    d) None is true.

30. Suppose you had no money in your checking account and your bank granted you overdraft privileges. You then went out and charged $20 on your debit card. How much would your bank charge you in fees for using your overdraft privileges?
    a) 0
    b) $5
    c) $10–$15
    d) $15–$35
    e) $50

Fill-In Questions

1. The most important job of money is as _____. The other two jobs of money are _____ and _____.

2. The alternative to money would be _____. To do this, you would need a _____.

3. The U.S. dollar is based on the _____.

4. The basic function of credit cards is _____.

5. To get from M2 to M3, we add _____.

6. M2 is almost _____ times the size of M1.

7. About _____ percent of the states allow only unit banking.

8. About _____ percent of all banks have state charters.

9. The main way that banks create money is by _____; the main way that money is destroyed is when _____.

10. The interest rate is set by the _____ and the _____.

11. People hold more money for their _____ motive than for the other two motives.

12. According to Keynes's liquidity trap, at very low interest rates, people would _____.

13. The world's first bankers were the _____.

14. Modern banking was born when the first bankers noticed two things: (1) _____ and (2) _____.

15. The world's first paper money was in the form of _____.

16. If a goldsmith had 100 gold coins sitting in his safe and lent out 50 of them, this would imply a reserve ratio of _____ percent.

17. The bankruptcy of the goldsmiths who lent out part of the gold they were safekeeping was caused by _____.

18. Most bankers today would like to hold a reserve of about _____ percent.

19. Banks are very heavily regulated. The main reason for this is that _____.

20. The FDIC insures all bank deposits of up to $ _____.

21. Rather than pay off depositors of a failed bank, the FDIC would prefer that _____ _____.

Problems

1. If M2 were 2,500, small-denomination time deposits were 250, large-denomination time deposits were 300, and money market mutual funds held by institutions were 200, how much would M3 be?

2. (a) A goldsmith has 1,000 gold coins in his safe and 1,000 receipts circulating. How much are his outstanding loans and what is his reserve ratio?
(b) The goldsmith then lends out 100 of the coins. What is his reserve ratio?

3. A goldsmith has 100 gold coins in his safe. If there are 500 receipts in circulation, how much is his reserve ratio?

4. (a) A banker lends a businessowner $100,000. How does this affect the money supply? (Hint: You need to have a dollar amount in your answer.)
(b) The businessowner pays back the loan. How does this affect the money supply?

5. How much would M2 be if M1 were 500; small-denomination time deposits, savings deposits, and money market mutual funds held by individuals totaled 1,200; and large-denomination time deposits were 300? How much would M3 be?

6. (a) Initially M1 is 1,000; M2 is 4,000; and M3 is 6,000. Find the size of M1, M2, and M3 if demand deposits rise by 100.
(b) Initially M1 = 2,000; M2 = 7,000; and M3 = 9,000. Find the size of M1, M2, and M3 if large-denomination time deposits rise by 300.

7. State numerically what would happen to M1 if:
(a) Ashley Whittingham brought $1,000 to her bank and deposited it in her checking account; (b) Arthur Sotak took $500 out of his checking account and put it in his savings account; (c) Richard Barnett bought $700 of traveler's checks for which he paid by check.

Chapter 14

The Federal Reserve and Monetary Policy

W̶ho wields the most power over our economy? Congress? The president? For many years some believed it was a man named Alan Greenspan, who served as Federal Reserve chairman from 1987 to 2006. When things were not working out, some people asked, "Who elected that guy?" It turns out that no one elected Dr. Greenspan. He was appointed by four presidents and confirmed by the Senate.

In the first part of the chapter, we'll examine the organization and management of the Federal Reserve System (the Fed), especially how it uses open-market operations, changes in the federal funds and discount rates, and changes in reserve requirements to control the rate of growth of the money supply.

Monetary policy is the manipulation of the money supply. The Federal Reserve determines how much money should be circulating in our economy. The goals of monetary policy are price stability, relatively full employment, and a satisfactory rate of economic growth. If you go back to the first page of Chapter 12, you'll see that the goals of fiscal and monetary policy are identical. The melodies are the same, but the lyrics are quite different. Fiscal policy is the use of government spending and taxation to affect the overall economy, while monetary policy controls the growth of the money supply.

CHAPTER OBJECTIVES

The main topics of this chapter are:

- The organization of the Federal Reserve System.
- Reserve requirements.
- The deposit expansion multiplier.

- The tools of monetary policy.
- The Fed's effectiveness in fighting inflation and recession.
- The Banking Acts of 1980 and 1999.

The Federal Reserve System

Unlike most other industrial nations, the United States was without a central bank until 1913.[1] While the Bank of England and the Bank of France acted, respectively, as England's and France's central banking authority, Americans were left defenseless when financial panics set in. Every few years in the 1880s, 1890s, and early 1900s, financial crises developed and eventually receded until, finally, we had the Panic of 1907.

---

[1]There had been a First United States Bank (1791–1811) and a Second United States Bank (1816–36), but the charters of both had been allowed to lapse, mainly for political reasons.

During this panic, people rushed to their banks to take out their money, and business was severely disrupted. The public demanded that the government take steps to prevent this from ever happening again. After six years of intermittent debate, Congress finally passed the Federal Reserve Act of 1913. One of the hopes of its framers was that the 12 Federal Reserve District Banks would, at times of crisis, act as a "lender of last resort." In other words, if U.S. bankers were caught with their pants down, someone stood ready to give them a little time to get their affairs back in order.

In the very first paragraph of the Federal Reserve Act, Congress outlined its main objectives:

> An Act to provide for the establishment of Federal reserve banks, to furnish an elastic currency, to afford means of rediscounting commercial paper, to establish a more effective supervision of banking in the United States, and for other purposes.

What's an elastic currency? It's a money supply that expands when the economy is growing rapidly and businesses need more money. Rediscounting, which we'll talk about later in the chapter, is a way for the Federal Reserve to lend money to banks, which, in turn, would lend that money to businesses.

The Federal Reserve has five main jobs:

1. Conduct monetary policy, which is, by far, the most important job. Monetary policy is the control of the rate of growth of the money supply to foster relatively full employment, price stability, and a satisfactory rate of economic growth.

2. Serve as a lender of last resort to commercial banks, savings banks, savings and loan associations, and credit unions.

3. Issue currency (see the box, "Who Issues Our Currency?").

4. Provide banking services to the U.S. government.

5. Supervise and regulate our financial institutions.

The Federal Reserve District Banks

The 12 Federal Reserve District Banks

There are 12 Federal Reserve District Banks, one in each of the nation's Federal Reserve districts. These are shown in the map in Figure 1. Each of these banks issues currency to accommodate the business needs of its district.[2] (To learn who actually issues our currency, see box.)

You'll notice in Figure 1 that the Federal Reserve District Banks are concentrated in the East and Midwest. This reflects the concentration of banks and business activity in 1913. Each Federal Reserve District Bank is owned by the several hundred member banks in that district. A bank becomes a member by buying stock in the Federal Reserve District Bank, so the Fed is a quasi public–private enterprise, not controlled by the president or by Congress. However, effective control is really exercised by the Federal Reserve Board of Governors in Washington, D.C.

The Board of Governors

The seven members of the Federal Reserve Board

The seven members of the Board of Governors are nominated by the president, subject to confirmation by the Senate. Each is appointed for one 14-year term and is ineligible to serve a second term. The terms are staggered so that vacancies occur every two years. That way, in every four-year term, a president appoints two members of the Board of Governors.

---

[2]The Bureau of Engraving in Washington does the actual printing, but why be picky?

Who Issues Our Currency?

The U.S. Treasury issues it, right? Wrong! Our currency is issued by the 12 Federal Reserve District Banks.* Check it out. Pull a dollar out of your wallet and look at it. What does it say right near the top, about a half inch above George Washington's picture? That's right—"Federal Reserve Note."

If you thought the Treasury issues our currency, it used to (and the secretary of the Treasury still signs every bill). The last thing it issued, until the mid-1960s, was $1 and $5 silver certificates. These certificates are now out of circulation, snapped up by collectors. The Treasury still issues our pennies, nickels, dimes, quar-ters, half dollars, and metal (no longer silver) dollars, but, as you might have suspected, that's just the small change of our money supply.

And what about the backing for the dollar? Look on the back of the bill just above the big "ONE." What's the backing for our currency? That's right—"In God We Trust." Actually, there is backing for our currency—the government's word, as well as its general acceptability.

---

*As noted in footnote 2, the actual printing is done by the Federal Bureau of Engraving.

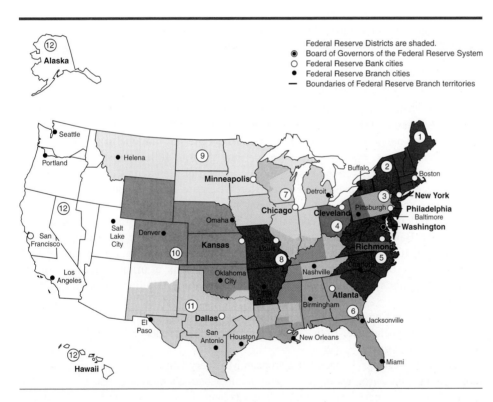

Figure 1
The Federal Reserve System

Usually, however, a president gets to appoint three or even four members during a single executive term because many Governors do not serve their full 14-year terms. Why not? Mainly because they could make much more money "on the outside." Serving on the Board looks great on your résumé, and it's done in the spirit of serving one's country, but 14 years is a bit long to live on a government paycheck.

All seven members of the Board that was serving in the spring of 2006 had been appointed by President George W. Bush, and five have PhDs in economics.

The chairman of the Board, who generally exercises considerable influence, serves a 4-year term, which is part of his or her 14-year tenure as a member of the Board. He or she is also appointed by the president and may serve more than one term as chairman.

Independence of the Board of Governors

Should the Board of Governors be controlled by or answerable to anyone else?

Does the president "control" the Board of Governors and its chairman? The answer is, generally, no. First, unless there is a vacancy caused by death or resignation, the president would have to serve two terms to appoint four members to the Board. Second, once someone is appointed to the Board, there is no reason to expect that person to do the president's bidding.

The president does get to appoint a chairman sometime during his or her term. There have been proposals that the president be allowed to appoint his own chairman at the beginning of the executive term so that monetary and fiscal policy can be coordinated, but no action has been taken thus far.

During the 18 years that Alan Greenspan served as chair, he largely shaped monetary policy with little interference from the president, Congress, or other Board members. It remains to be seen if his successor, Ben Bernanke, who had earlier served three years as a Board member, would retain most of Mr. Greenspan's powers. His immediate challenge, when his term began in January 2006, was to deal with an inflation rate, which while still relatively low, had been accelerating during the past year.

Once a Board member or chairman is confirmed by the Senate, she or he is not answerable to the president or Congress. Some feel that for a group of unelected officials, the members of the Board have too much power. When interest rates soar or inflation rages out of control, these rascals cannot be turned out of office by an angry electorate. About all we can do is hope that better people will eventually be appointed to the Board.

Others feel that the difficult, unpopular decisions of monetary policy must be made by those who are insulated from the wrath of the voters. Tight money is hardly a popular policy, but when the Federal Reserve Board members think it will help control inflation, why should they be inhibited by fears of political reprisal?

While the members of the Board of Governors are not immune to the reactions of their fellow citizens, their independence permits them to follow unpopular policies if they feel that doing so is in the best economic interest of the nation. Attempts have been made in recent years to make the Federal Reserve Board more responsive to the wishes of Congress and the administration, but none has been successful.

How independent is our central bank in comparison to other leading central banks? The Bank of England has relatively little independence from political control. The British government sets a specific numerical target for inflation each year which the bank tries to hit. Consequently, the bank is often under pressure to increase the money supply and stimulate the economy, leading to relatively high inflation rates.

The Bank of Canada and the Bank of Japan are in the middle rank of central banks in terms of independence. Both enjoy considerable independence but still come under some political pressure.

You may recall the 12-member European Monetary Union from Chapter 8. Its common currency, the euro, has replaced each member nation's currency. The euro is issued by the European Central Bank, which coexists with Deutsche Bundesbank, La Banca d'Italia, and each of the other nations' central banks. The ECB is perhaps the most independent central bank in the world, and has been very effective in limiting inflation.

Legal Reserve Requirements

The Federal Reserve's most important job

The Federal Reserve has various jobs, the most important of which is to control the money supply. When it was set up in 1913, the framers of the Federal Reserve Act envisaged the Fed as a "lender of last resort." Obviously, the record of widespread bank failures in the early 1930s is a sad commentary on how well the Fed was able to do that job.

Before we consider how the Fed works today, we will look at the focal point of the Federal Reserve's control of our money supply–legal reserve requirements. Every financial institution in the country is legally required to hold a certain percentage of its

TABLE 1	Legal Reserve Requirements for Checking Accounts,* May 1, 2006**
$0 million − $7.8 million	0%
$7.8 million − $48.3 million	3
over $48.3 million	10

*Time deposits have a 0% reserve requirement.
**The numerical boundaries of these limits are revised annually.
Source: http://woodrow.mpls.frb.fed.us/info/policy/res-req.cfm.

deposits on reserve, either in the form of deposits at its Federal Reserve District Bank or in its own vaults. As neither Federal Reserve deposits nor vault cash pays interest, no one is very happy about holding 10 percent of most demand deposits on reserve (see Table 1).

We'll be using some technical terms, so let's be very clear about their meanings. *Required reserves* is the minimum amount of vault cash and deposits at the Federal Reserve District Bank that must be held by the financial institution. *Actual reserves* is what the bank is holding. If a bank is holding more than required, it has excess reserves. Therefore, *actual reserves − required reserves = excess reserves.*

If a bank had $100 million in checking deposits, how much reserves would it be required to hold? Work it out right here, using the information in Table 1:

Solution:

First $7.8 million of deposits: 0% reserve requirement

Next $40.5 million: $40,500,000 × .03 = $1,215,000

Next $51.7 million: $51,700,000 × .10 = 5,170,000

Required reserves $6,385,000

If this bank happened to be holding reserves of, say, $9 million, find its excess reserves.

Solution:

Actual reserves − Required reserves = Excess reserves

$9,000,000 − $6,385,000 = $2,615,000

Because banks earn no interest on their reserves, they try to keep them down to a bare minimum. In fact, a bank ideally holds no excess reserves whatsoever; its goal is zero excess reserves.

Let's try another question. If a bank had demand deposits of $1 billion and held $120 million in actual reserves (in the form of deposits at the Federal Reserve

District Bank and vault cash), calculate (1) its required reserves and (2) its excess reserves.

Solution:

$$
\begin{array}{rl}
(1)\ 0\%\ \text{of}\ 7.8\ \text{million} = & 0 \\
3\%\ \text{of}\ \$40.5\ \text{million} = & \$1,215,000 \\
10\%\ \text{of remaining}\ \$951.7\ \text{million} = & \underline{95,170,000} \\
\text{Required reserves} = & \$96,385,000
\end{array}
$$

$$
\begin{array}{c}
(2)\ \text{Actual reserves} - \text{Required reserves} = \text{Excess reserves} \\
\$120,000,000 - \$96,385,000 = \$23,615,000
\end{array}
$$

Can a bank ever end up with negative excess reserves? Think about it. Time's up: what do you think? If actual reserves are less than required reserves, then excess reserves are negative. Or, in simple English, the bank is short of required reserves. If a bank does find itself short, it will usually borrow reserves from another bank that has some excess reserves. The reserves it borrows are called *federal funds,* and the interest rate charged for them is called the *federal funds rate.* A bank short of reserves may also borrow at the discount window of its Federal Reserve District Bank, a process we'll discuss later in the chapter.

In *Money Makes The World Go Around,* Barbara Garson provides a succinct description of the role of federal funds in helping banks meet their reserve requirements.

Barbara Garson

> Every bank that does business in the United States is required to keep an account with a certain minimum deposit at the Federal Reserve Bank. This account doesn't receive any interest, so banks don't like to keep more money, more Federal funds, as this money is called, in their Federal Reserve accounts than they have to. On the other hand, if they fall below their reserve requirement, there are severe penalties. Being overdrawn at the Fed is such a taboo that no banker I asked even knew what the penalties were.
>
> The goal of every bank, therefore, is to meet its reserve requirement (which changes with each day's inflows and outgoes) while having as little extra in the account as possible. It's tricky. One way banks solve the problem is to lend and borrow (sell and buy) the uninvested money among themselves. In other words, there's a market among banks for their extra federal funds.[3]

The Monetary Control Act of 1980 (which will be discussed in detail toward the end of this chapter) called for uniform reserve requirements for all financial institutions—commercial banks, savings banks, savings and loan associations, money market mutual funds, and credit unions. You'll notice in Table 1 that the reserve requirement for time deposits is zero. Because time deposits, by definition, are held for relatively long periods of time, the Federal Reserve Board eliminated reserve requirements for all time deposits in 1992.

Primary and Secondary Reserves

A bank's *primary reserves are its vault cash and its deposits at the Federal Reserve District Bank.* These reserves pay no interest; therefore the banks try to hold no more than the Federal Reserve requires. Ideally, then, they hold *zero* excess reserves.

---

[3]Barbara Garson, *Money Makes The World Go Around* (New York: Viking, 2001), pp. 22–23. Garson is the author of the Vietnam War era play, *MacBird!* which helped turn public opinion against the war.

Bankers are, if nothing else, prudent. Their main aims, other than making high profits, are to protect their depositors and to maintain liquidity. Liquidity is the ability to convert assets quickly into cash without loss.

Even without legal reserve requirements, bankers would keep some cash on reserve to meet the day-to-day needs of their depositors as well as to meet any unforeseen large withdrawals. The cash that banks do keep on hand, together with their deposits at the Federal Reserve District Banks, is sometimes called primary reserves. In addition, every bank holds secondary reserves, mainly in the form of very short-term U.S. government securities.

Treasury bills, notes, certificates, and bonds (that will mature in less than a year) are generally considered a bank's secondary reserves. These can quickly be converted to cash without loss if a bank suddenly needs money, whether because of increased withdrawals or perhaps a shortage of primary reserves. Generally, in the case of a shortage of primary reserves, a bank will borrow on a daily basis from other banks in the federal funds market.

What are the three main aims of bankers?

Deposit Expansion

How Deposit Expansion Works

To see how deposit expansion works, we'll assume a 10 percent reserve ratio because that's an easy number with which to work. And we'll assume everyone uses just one bank. Suppose someone comes into a bank and deposits $100,000.

We know that banks don't like to have idle reserves because they don't earn any interest on them. So what does the bank do with the $100,000? It lends out as much as it can. Let's assume it lends $90,000 to a single business firm.

Normally, the bank would need an additional $9,000 in reserves to cover the new $90,000 demand deposit. But why did the company borrow $90,000? Obviously it was needed for certain business expenses; no one pays interest on borrowed money just to sit on it.

Again, keeping things simple, suppose this company wrote a check for $90,000 to pay for additional inventory. The company receiving the check deposits it in its bank, and the process is repeated. The bank keeps the required 10 percent ($9,000) on reserve and lends out the remaining $81,000. This money is spent and eventually deposited in a third bank, which keeps 10 percent ($8,100) on reserve and lends out $72,900.

We could go on and on. Indeed, we have in Table 2. Were we to continue the process with an infinite number of banks, we would eventually end up with $1 million in deposits and $100,000 in reserves.

The Deposit Expansion Multiplier

Remember the multiplier in Chapter 12? Now we'll look at the deposit expansion multiplier, which is based on the same principle and nearly the same formula.

Any new money injected into the banking system will have a multiplied effect on the money supply. How large this multiplied effect will be depends on the size of the multiplier. In general, when the reserve ratio is low, the multiplier will be high and vice versa.

The formula for the deposit expansion multiplier is:

$$\frac{1}{\text{Reserve ratio}}$$

$$\text{Deposit expansion multiplier} = \frac{1}{\text{Reserve ratio}}$$

If the reserve ratio is .10, we substitute and solve to find the multiplier:

$$\frac{1}{\text{Reserve ratio}} = \frac{1}{.10} = 10$$

Remember, how many dimes are in a dollar?

TABLE 2	Hypothetical Deposit Expansion with 10 Percent Reserve Requirement

Deposits	Reserves
$100,000.00	$10,000.00
90,000.00	9,000.00
81,000.00	8,100.00
72,900.00	7,290.00
65,610.00	6,561.00
59,049.00	5,904.90
53,541.00	5,354.10
48,186.90	4,818.69
43,368.21	4,336.82
39,031.39	3,903.14
35,128.25	3,512.83
31,615.43	3,161.54
28,453.89	2,845.39
25,608.50	2,560.85
23,047.65	2,304.76
20,742.89	2,074.29
18,668.60	1,866.86
16,812.00	1,681.20
15,130.80	1,513.08
13,617.72	1,361.77
—*	—*
—	—
—	—
$1,000,000.00	$100,000.00

*To save space, the rest of the calculations are omitted.

If the reserve ratio is .25, find the deposit expansion multiplier. Do it right here.

Using the formula, we get:

$$\frac{1}{\text{Reserve ratio}} = \frac{1}{.25} = 4$$

How many times does .25 go into 1? How many times does a quarter go into a dollar?

Now that I've made you do these calculations, a confession is in order. The deposit expansion multiplier is a bit less wonderful than I led you to believe. It's just too big. You can probably get on with your life just accepting this fact, but if you happen to be from Missouri (the Show Me State), then you can check out the Advanced Work box, "Three Modifications of the Deposit Expansion Multiplier."

Cash, Checks, and Electronic Money

One of the jobs of the Federal Reserve is called check clearing. Through this process, once the checks you write are deposited by the people you gave them to, they make their way through our financial system, facilitated by the Fed, and eventually wind up

Three Modifications of the Deposit Expansion Multiplier

Not every dollar of deposit expansion will actually be redeposited and lent out repeatedly. Some people may choose to hold or spend some of their money as currency. For example, an individual receiving a $300 check may deposit $200 and receive $100 back as cash.

This cash leakage tends to cut down on the deposit expansion multiplier because not all the money lent out is redeposited. For example, if $90,000 is lent out but only $81,000 is redeposited, this would have the same effect on the multiplier as a 10 percent increase in the reserve ratio.

It is also possible, although unlikely in times of inflation, for banks to carry excess reserves. To the degree that they do, however, this cuts down on the deposit expansion multiplier. Why? Because it, in effect, raises the reserve ratio. For example, if the reserve ratio rose from .20 to .25 because banks were carrying a 5 percent excess reserve, the multiplier would fall from 5 ($1/_2 = 5$) to 4 ($1/_{25} = 4$). These leakages take place during times of recession and low interest rates, when banks may carry excess reserves. One might also keep in mind that during recessions, banks might carry excess reserves because of a scarcity of creditworthy borrowers.

Finally, there are leakages of dollars to foreign countries caused mainly by our huge foreign trade imbalance. Our imports far exceed our exports, so there is a large drain of dollars to foreigners. And then, too, there is all the currency that American tourists spend abroad, plus the tens of billions sent covertly to international drug traffickers. Some of these dollars return to the United States in the form of various investments (particularly in U.S. government securities, corporate securities, and real estate), but there is a definite net outflow of dollars, which, in turn, depresses still further the deposit expansion multiplier.

Where does all this leave us? It leaves us with the conclusion that the deposit expansion multiplier is, in reality, quite a bit lower than it would be if we based it solely on the reserve ratio. In other words, if the reserve ratio tells us it's 10, perhaps it's only 6.

photocopied to the back of your monthly bank statement. How did they get there? Read the box, "Check Clearing."

In 2004 Congress passed the Check Clearing for the 21st Century Act, often called Check 21, which is intended to hasten the adoption of electronic check processing. The main effect of this law will be that bank statements will carry photocopies of checks, not originals saving banks from having to fly checks across the country. The new system allows the bank that first receives the check to create an electronic image for transmission through the system. Will this law ultimately lead to the elimination of paper checks? Maybe, but probably not for quite a few years.

If your company in Boston needs to pay $937,042.91 to my company in St. Louis, does it send a check? Chances are, it will wire the money. To pay your phone bill, do you still send a check, or have the payment deducted electronically from your bank account? An increasing number of Americans no longer receive paychecks. Instead their pay is deposited electronically into their bank accounts. And when you buy things and pay with your debit card, a few seconds after your card is swiped by the sales clerk, the amount of your purchase has been deducted from your checking account.

Increasingly, money is changing hands electronically rather than in the form of checks. Trillions of dollars a day are transferred electronically—80 percent of the total payments made worldwide in dollars. About one-third of these transfers are carried out by the Federal Reserve's electronic network, while most of the other two-thirds are done by the Clearing House Interbank Payments System (CHIPS), which is owned by 10 of the world's largest banks.

Does all this mean that we are well on our way to a checkless, cashless society? Yes and no. We still carry out about 80 percent of our monetary transactions in cash—everything from paying for our groceries to tipping the hairdresser. But when we consider the total dollars actually spent, cash covers less than 1 percent of the total value of transactions, while electronic transfers account for five out of every six dollars that move in the economy.

If you buy things on the Internet, you probably have heard of Paypal (a company now owned by eBay). When you make a purchase, Paypal deducts the money from your bank account in the same way that it happens with a debit card.

Check Clearing

If you have a checking account at your local bank, at the end of each month you receive a statement listing all your deposits and withdrawals. On your statement, your bank includes tiny photocopies of the checks you wrote that month.

Did you ever wonder how, if you wrote a check, it ended up on your statement at the end of the month? No? Well, I'm going to tell you anyway. The whole process is called check clearing, and it is a service provided by the Federal Reserve System.

In 1976 we had a series of birthday parties for the nation. The United States of America was 200 years old that year. I was visiting some friends out in San Francisco at the time, and one of them, Bob, sold me a beat-up old bugle, which actually *looked* like it might have dated from the American Revolution.

This bugle has come in quite handy at my 8:00 A.M. classes. At the time I bought it, though, the big question was how I would pay for it. I didn't have $50 in cash,

so I gave Bob my check for $50. It was written on Citibank back in Brooklyn. Bob deposited it in his account at Bank of America. From there it went to Bank of America's main office in San Francisco, which, in turn, sent it on to the San Francisco Federal Reserve District Bank. Bank of America's reserves were raised by $50 (the amount of the check). Doing this was a simple bookkeeping operation.

The check was sent to the New York Federal Reserve District Bank, which deducted $50 from the reserves of Citibank. The check then went to Citibank's main office in Manhattan, and then to my branch out on Flatbush Avenue in Brooklyn. The $50 was then deducted from my account, and at the end of the month, the canceled check was mailed to me with my statement.

All of these transactions are shown pictorially in the diagram below. The check I gave Bob in San Francisco was sent back to me by my Brooklyn bank with my statement at the end of the month.

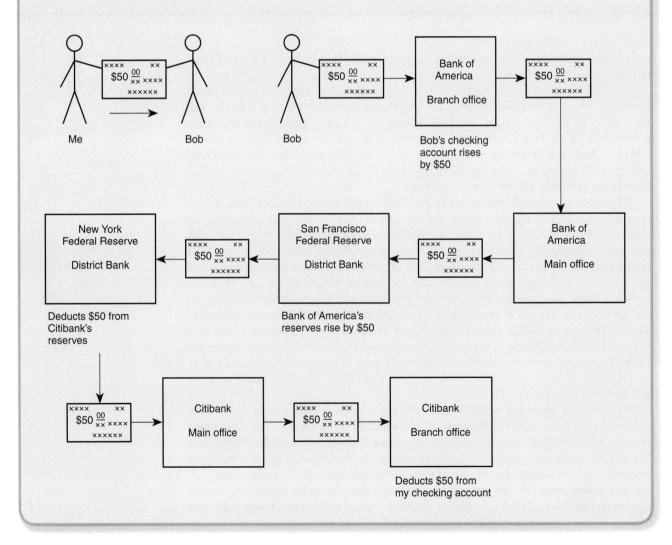

The Tools of Monetary Policy

The most important job of the Fed is to control the growth of the money supply; its most important policy tool to do that job is open-market operations.

How Open-Market Operations Work

Open-market operations are the buying and selling of U.S. Treasury bills, notes, and bonds. The Fed does not market new securities.[4] That's the Treasury's job. Rather, the Fed buys and sells securities that have already been marketed by the Treasury, some of which might be several years old.

What are open-market operations?

The total value of all outstanding U.S. government securities is more than $4 trillion. What open-market operations consist of, then, is the buying and selling of chunks of the national debt. The Fed does this by dealing with government bond houses, which are private bond dealers. If the Fed wants to buy $300 million of Treasury notes that will mature within the next three months, it places an order with a few of these bond houses, which then buy up the securities for the Fed. When the Fed wants to sell securities, it again goes to the government bond houses and has them do the actual selling.

When the Fed wants to increase the money supply, it goes into the open market and buys U.S. government securities. You might ask, "What if people don't want to sell?" Remember the line from *The Godfather,* "I'll make you an offer you can't refuse"? Well, that's exactly what the Fed does. It tells the government bond houses, "Buy us 30,000 Treasury bills no matter what the price."

How the Fed increases the money supply

Question: What do you get when you cross the Godfather with an economist? Answer: An offer you can't understand.

If the Fed goes on a buying spree in the open market, it will quickly drive up the prices of U.S. government securities. All this buying will push down interest rates. Let's see why.

Suppose a bond is issued by the Treasury with a face value of $1,000 and an interest rate of 8 percent. This means the bond costs the initial buyer $1,000 and pays $80 interest a year. The price of the bond will fluctuate considerably over its life; but when it matures, the Treasury must pay the owner $1,000, its face value. And every year the Treasury must pay the owner $80 interest.

Using the formula

$$\text{Interest rate} = \frac{\text{Interest paid}}{\text{Price of bond}}$$

$$\frac{\text{Interest}}{\text{rate}} = \frac{\text{Interest paid}}{\text{Price of bond}}$$

we can observe that a $1,000 bond paying $80 interest pays an interest rate of 8 percent:

$$\frac{\$80}{\$1,000} = 8 \text{ percent}$$

This is sometimes called the stated rate or face rate.

We have been talking about the Fed going into the open market and buying government securities. Suppose the Fed bought enough securities to bid up their price to $1,200. Remember, these securities still pay $80 interest a year. Let's calculate their new interest rate:

$$\text{Interest rate} = \frac{\text{Interest paid}}{\text{Price of bond}} = \frac{\$80}{\$1,200} = 6\frac{2}{3} \text{ percent}$$

Gov't Buying bonds raises int rate
puts $ into the economy

You see that, as previously noted, when the Fed goes into the open market to buy securities, it bids up their price and lowers their interest rates. In the process, as we shall soon see, this also expands the money supply.

---

[4]The Fed is legally limited to buying no more than $5 billion in newly issued government securities a year, which is less than 1 percent of what the Treasury issues.

The 6$\frac{2}{3}$ percent is the effective, or market, rate of interest. Although the U.S. Treasury is still paying 8 percent ($80) on the face value ($1,000) of the bond, the Federal Reserve has effectively lowered the market rate of interest to 6$\frac{2}{3}$ percent. Incidentally, if the Treasury were to issue new bonds that day, it would need to pay an interest rate of just 6$\frac{2}{3}$ percent (that is, $66.67 on a $1,000 bond).

When the Fed wants to contract the money supply, or at least slow down its rate of expansion, it goes into the open market and sells securities. In the process, it lowers bond prices and raises interest rates.

When selling securities, the Fed also uses the "Godfather principle." Again, it makes an offer that can't be refused (in this case, an offer to sell securities at low enough prices to get rid of a certain amount).

If the Fed bids bond prices down to $800, we use the same formula to find that the interest rate has risen to 10 percent.

$$\text{Interest rate} = \frac{\text{Interest paid}}{\text{Price of bond}} = \frac{\$80}{\$800} = 10 \text{ percent}$$

When the Fed sells securities on the open market to contract the money supply, bond prices fall and interest rates rise. Falling bond prices and rising interest rates generally accompany a tightening of the money supply.

You should note that although the Fed deals only with U.S. government securities, interest rates and bond prices move together in a broad range. When the Fed depresses the prices of U.S. government securities, all government and corporate bond prices tend to fall. And when the Fed pushes up the interest on U.S. government securities, all interest rates tend to rise.

Let's try another interest rate problem. Find the interest rate on a bond that pays $100 a year in interest and is currently selling for $800. Work it out right here:

Solution:

$$\text{Interest rate} = \frac{\text{Interest paid}}{\text{Price of bond}} = \frac{\$100}{\$800} = 12.5 \text{ percent}$$

Figure 2A and Figure 2B show how open market operations affect interest rates. We'll begin at equilibrium point E in Figure 2A. If the Fed buys a huge amount of U.S. Treasury securities on the open market, this purchase raises the money supply from MS_1 ($3 trillion) to MS_2 ($4 trillion) pushing the equilibrium point from E_1 to E_2, and driving down the interest rate from 8 percent to 6 percent.

Figure 2B illustrates what happens when the Fed sells a huge amount of U.S. Treasury securities on the open market. Money supply falls from MS_1 ($3 trillion) to MS_2 ($2 trillion) pushing the equilibrium point from E_1 to E_2, and driving the interest rate up from 5 percent to 8 percent.

The Federal Open-Market Committee

Open-market operations are conducted by the Federal Open-Market Committee (FOMC), which consists of 12 people. Eight are permanent members—the seven members of the Board of Governors and the president of the New York Federal Reserve District Bank (he or she is a permanent member because nearly all open-market purchases are made in the New York federal securities market). The other four members of the FOMC are presidents of the other 11 Federal Reserve District Banks; they serve on a one-year rotating basis.

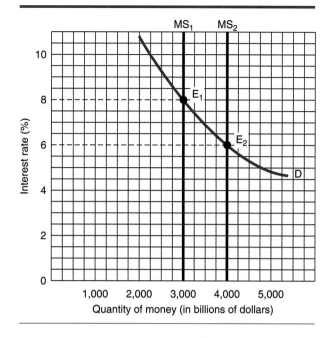

F*igure* 2A
Increase in Money Supply

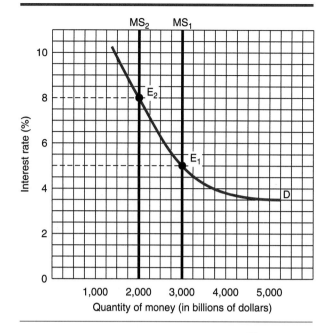

F*igure* 2B
Decrease in Money Supply

The FOMC meets eight times a year to decide what policy to follow. This is not to say that every six weeks the committee changes directions from buy to sell to buy again.

Assume the FOMC decides to ease credit a bit, perhaps because of the threat of a recession. It might decide to buy $100 million of securities on the open market. The New York Bank, as agent of the Federal Reserve, places an order with several government bond houses. The bonds are paid for by checks written on various Federal Reserve District Banks. Each government bond house deposits the checks in its own commercial bank. From there the checks are sent to the New York Federal Reserve District Bank, which adds the amount of the checks to the banks' reserves.

Say, for example, the Fed gives a $10 million check to bond house number one, which deposits it in its account at Commerce Bank. From there the check is sent a few blocks away to the New York Federal Reserve District Bank, which adds $10 million to the reserves of Commerce Bank.

What does Commerce Bank do with $10 million of reserves? Assuming it now has excess reserves of $10 million, it will lend most of it out. Up goes the money supply! As we have noted, banks seldom keep excess reserves because they don't earn interest. Thus we have a multiple expansion of deposits.

The process works the same way if the government bond houses are not the ultimate sellers of the securities. Usually those sellers are individuals, corporations, or banks. If an individual sells a $10,000 bond to the government bond house, which, in turn, sells it to the Fed, the government bond house is only the middleman. When the Fed pays the government bond house, this money will be turned over to the person who sold the bond. When she deposits her check at her local bank, say the National State Bank of New Jersey, the check will still be sent to the New York Federal Reserve District Bank. Ten thousand dollars will be added to the reserves of the National State Bank, which is now free to lend it out.

When banks lend out money, the money supply increases. When the Fed buys $100 million of securities, it is making $100 million of reserves available to the banking system. Most of this money will be lent out, and through the deposit expansion multiplier, it will create a multiplied deposit amount. For example, if the reserve ratio were 10 percent, the multiplier would be 10 (Multiplier = 1/Reserve ratio = $1/_{.10}$ = 10). However, allowing for currency leakages and bank holdings of some excess reserves, we'll say that the multiplier is actually

To fight recessions, the FOMC buys securities.

only 6. A $100 million open-market purchase will lead to about a $600 million expansion of deposits (and, therefore, a $600 million expansion of the money supply).

To fight inflation, the FOMC sells securities.

During periods of inflation, when the FOMC decides to sell securities, we have exactly the opposite set of events. If the FOMC were to give the government bond houses $100 million of securities with orders to sell them at whatever the market will bring, we can easily trace the steps.

Customers will be found, and they will pay by check. For example, a corporation with an account at SunTrust Bank in Atlanta might buy $50,000 of securities. When its check reaches the Atlanta Federal Reserve District Bank, $50,000 is deducted from the reserves of SunTrust Bank. Similar reserve deductions occur around the country. Soon reserves for the entire banking system are reduced by $100 million.

That's just the first step. The banks will probably be short of reserves as they carry little, if any, excess. Where do they get the money? They can borrow from their Federal Reserve District Bank's discount windows, but this will only tide them over temporarily, and they're reluctant to do this anyway. They can go into the federal funds market, which is an overnight market in which banks borrow from each other on a day-to-day basis if they are short of reserves. But because most banks are short because of FOMC sales, this source of funds has constricted.

Ultimately, the banks will have to curb their loans, which is what the FOMC wanted all along. Initially, then, we would expect that $100 million less reserves will mean $100 million less in loans. But *had* those loans been made, with a multiplier of six, there would have been some $600 million worth of loans, and the money supply would have been $600 million higher.

We're saying that if reserves are reduced by $100 million, this will, with a multiplier of six, ultimately reduce the money supply by $600 million. Or, put slightly differently, when reserves are reduced, the money supply will end up being lower than it would otherwise have been.

Are you ready to apply your knowledge of the monetary multiplier to determine the potential effect of the sale of some securities on the open market? Suppose the Fed buys $200 million of securities and the monetary multiplier is 5. By how much could our money supply increase?

Solution:

$$\frac{\text{Excess}}{\text{reserves}} \times \frac{\text{Monetary}}{\text{multiplier}} = \frac{\text{Potential expansion of}}{\text{the money supply}}$$

$$\$200 \text{ million} \times 5 = \$1,000,000,000$$

Discount Rate and Federal Funds Rate Changes

The discount rate is the interest rate paid by member banks when they borrow at the Federal Reserve District Bank. The main reason today's banks borrow is that they are having trouble maintaining their required reserves.

The original intent of the Federal Reserve Act of 1913 was to have the District Banks lend money to member banks to take care of seasonal business needs. In the busy period before Christmas, firms would borrow money from their banks, which would, in turn, borrow from the Federal Reserve District Banks. Borrowing, then, was really note discounting.

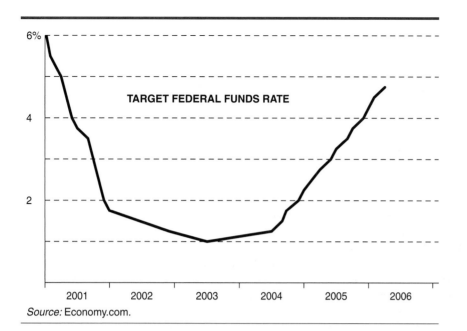

Figure 3
The Target Federal Funds Rate,
1954–2006
This rate was pushed to a 45-year
low of just 1 percent on June 25,
2003. In June 2004 the Open
Market Committee began raising
the rate in quarter of a percent
increments. By January 2006 it had
reached 4.5 percent.

You technically borrowed $1,000, but if the interest rate was 8 percent, the interest—$80 for a one-year loan—was deducted in advance. All you got was $920; you paid back $1,000.

This was called discounting. When the commercial banks took these IOUs or commercial paper to the Federal Reserve District Bank, they would borrow money to cover these loans. This was called rediscounting.

How discounting works

Today banks no longer rediscount their commercial paper. Instead, they borrow directly from the Federal Reserve and call the interest they pay the discount rate. Although each of the 12 District Banks sets its own discount rate, they agree virtually all the time—perhaps with an occasional prod from the Board of Governors—to charge the same rate.

On any given day, banks rarely owe the Fed more than a couple of hundred million dollars. But remember that the Fed does stand ready in times of emergency, as a lender of last resort. The last such emergency was set off by the terrorist attacks of 9/11. On September 12, 2001, banks borrowed $45.5 billion from the Fed. Had those funds not been available, there is no telling if a financial panic might have taken place, possibly with depositors all over the country rushing to their banks to withdraw their money.

Rather than borrow from the Fed, banks usually borrow excess reserves from each other, usually for no more than a few days at a time. The interest rate they pay is called the federal funds rate. Kathleen Madigan of *BusinessWeek* describes what happens when the Fed changes the discount rate and the federal funds rate simultaneously:

> The Fed can also change the discount rate when it alters the federal funds rate, a
> one-two punch called "banging the gong" because it reverberates across global
> markets. The discount rate is charged when a member bank borrows from the Fed,
> a move done when the bank can't borrow anywhere else. The discount rate is
> usually set equal to or a half-point below the funds rate.[5]

Figure 3 provides a record of the federal funds rate between 1954 and 2006. Why did the Fed lower the rate 13 times between the beginning of 2001 and mid-2003? Because the economy had entered a recession and had lost more than two and a half million jobs since January 2001.

The federal funds rate hit 20 percent twice in the late 1970s and early 1980s. At that time the Fed was worried mainly about double digit inflation, so it pursued a very stringent tight money policy. Consequently the economy had back-to-back recessions in

[5]Kathleen Madigan, *BusinessWeek,* February 7, 2000, pp. 124 and 126.

1980 and 1981–82. When the Fed was convinced it had broken the back of the inflation, it eased money growth in late 1982, the federal funds rate—and all other interest rates—fell sharply, and the recession ended.

The federal funds rate is actually set by the forces of supply and demand, but the Federal Open-Market Committee sets a federal funds rate target and then makes sure that target is hit. When the committee raised the federal funds rate target from 3 percent to 3.25 percent in July 2005, it sold billions of dollars worth of U.S. government securities. Setting the target federal funds rate is the FOMC's primary policy instrument. Indeed, setting that target rate *is,* in effect, monetary policy.

Changing Reserve Requirements

The Fed's ultimate weapon

A changing of reserve requirements is really the ultimate weapon of the Federal Reserve System. Like nuclear weapons, which are rarely—if ever—used, it can be nice to know that the mechanism is there.

The Federal Reserve Board has the power to change reserve requirements within legal limits, but in practice it does this perhaps once in a decade. The limits for checkable deposits are between 8 and 14 percent.[6]

The basic reserve rate was set at 12 percent in 1980 for most checking deposits; in 1992 it was lowered to 10 percent. The Board of Governors took this strong measure to help the economy recover from the lingering effects of the 1990–91 recession. In banking circles this 10 percent rate is often referred to as the *reserve ratio,* ignoring the fact that there is, in effect, a 0 percent reserve requirement for the first $7.8 million of checking deposits and a 3 percent requirement on the next $40.5 million (see Table 1 on page 333).

This weapon is so rarely used because it is simply too powerful. For example, if the Federal Reserve Board raised the reserve requirement on demand deposits by just one half of 1 percent, the nation's banks and thrift institutions would have to come up with nearly $4 billion in reserves.

Why does the Fed rarely change reserve requirements?

Reserve requirements, then, are raised reluctantly by the Board of Governors, and only after all else fails. However, when the economy is gripped by recession, the Fed becomes less reluctant to turn to its ultimate weapon; but even then, reserve requirement changes are a last resort.

The Fed has three ways of increasing our money supply: lowering reserve requirements, lowering the discount rate, and buying government securities on the open market. What about printing currency? Does *this* raise our money supply? If you think the answer is yes, then you definitely should read the box, "Does Printing More Money Increase Our Money Supply?"

Favorite test question: Of the three main monetary policy instruments, which is the most important?

The correct answer is "open-market operations." It has the advantage of flexibility, since government securities can be bought or sold in large or small amounts. In addition, its impact on bank reserves is prompt. So the buying and selling of U.S. government securities is, by far, the most important monetary policy weapon in the Fed's arsenal.

A relatively minor Federal Reserve policy tool is raising and lowering the stock market margin requirement, which is discussed in the accompanying box.

Summary: The Tools of Monetary Policy

What three things can the Fed do to fight a recession? List them right here:

1.

2.

3.

---

[6]If five members of the Board deem it desirable, the maximum can be raised to 18 percent, and if conditions are extraordinary, any rate whatsoever may be set.

Does Printing More Money Increase Our Money Supply?

When the Federal Reserve Banks issue currency, doesn't this increase our money supply? Surprisingly, the answer is no, Now I'm going to prove it.

What is the money supply? It's currency, demand deposits, and other checkable deposits held by the public. So the question is, When the Fed prints currency, how does it get into the hands of the public?

Suppose the Federal Reserve Bank of San Francisco issues 10 one-hundred-dollar bills and gives them to Security Pacific Corp., which pays by having its reserves lowered by $1,000. (Actually, its reserves stay the same, because this money goes into its vault.) Next, a local businesswoman writes a check for $1,000 on her account at Security Pacific and walks out of the bank with the 10 one-hundred-dollar bills.

Did that transaction increase the money supply? What do you think? On the one hand, when the teller gave the woman the cash, that increased the amount of money in the hands of the public by $1,000. But what the bank gave with that one hand, it took away with the other by decreasing her checking account by $1,000.

To recap: When the Federal Reserve Bank of San Francisco issued $1,000 in currency, did that lead to an increase in the money supply? No, it did not. When the Fed prints money, it does so to accommodate the needs of the public. If the public wishes to hold more of its money in the form of currency—and, parenthetically, less in the form of checking deposits—the Fed will accommodate these wishes. So the next time someone walks up to you on the street and asks you whether the Fed increases the money supply by issuing currency, tell him no.

Margin Requirements

The Federal Reserve Board has the power to set margin requirements in the stock market. In Chapter 1 we talked about how in the 1920s stock market speculators could borrow 90 percent of the price of a stock from a stockbroker and put up just 10 percent of their own money. If the stock went up, they made a lot of money. But when the market crashed in 1929, not only were these speculators wiped out but so were their stockbrokers, who were not repaid. They, in turn, could not repay the banks all they had borrowed.

Today the margin requirement is set by the Federal Reserve Board, which has pegged it at 50 percent since 1974. This means that, if you wanted to invest $10,000 in the stock market, you would need to put up $5,000 of your own money. When Alan Greenspan, who had repeatedly expressed concern about the "irrational exhuberance" of the stock market, was asked why he didn't raise the margin requirement, he replied that an increase would be unfair to small investors. Perhaps, but margin debt has grown at an alarmingly rapid rate since 1990. In that year margin debt was just over 4 percent of all consumer debt. By the end of 2000 it was more than 16 percent.

If—or perhaps one should say when—the market turns down sharply, the stockbrokers will ask their margin customers to put up more money, or else they will sell their stocks. Most won't have the money, so their stocks will be sold, driving stock prices down still further. Although we are not nearly as vulnerable as we were in 1929, the huge and growing overhang of margin debt makes it increasingly likely that a sharp decline in stock prices could lead to a stock market crash.

The answers are (1) lower the discount rate, (2) buy securities on the open market, and, ultimately, if these two don't do the job, (3) lower reserve requirements.

What three things can the Fed do to fight inflation? List them here:

1.

2.

3.

The Effectiveness of Monetary Policy in an Open Economy

Suppose the Fed tightens money and interest rates rise. Investors all over the world will be attracted to the higher interest rates they can earn by purchasing U.S. bonds, corporate bonds, and other assets. But in order to invest, they will need to exchange their money for U.S. dollars.

This will drive up the dollar relative to foreign currencies. In other words, you will now be able to get more euros, yen, and pounds for your dollars. Foreign goods will become cheaper to Americans and our imports will soar. Meanwhile, foreigners will be getting fewer dollars for their euros, yen, and pounds, so they will find American goods more expensive. And they will cut back on their purchases of those goods.

Let's recap: Tight money drives up interest rates, making American investments more attractive to foreigners.

They will bid up the dollar, thus lowering our exports and raising our imports. So tight money works to lower our net exports (exports minus imports).

Did you get all that? We've really gotten a bit ahead of ourselves, because the effects to exchange rate changes on foreign trade are not analyzed until the last chapter of this book. But while we're at it, how would an expansionary monetary policy affect our net exports?

It would have just the opposite effect of a contractionary policy. Monetary expansion would lower our interest rates. Lower interest rates are not attractive to foreign investors, whose demand for U.S. dollars will drop. If the dollar falls relative to foreign currencies, that makes our exports cheaper and our imports more expensive. Thus, an expansionary monetary policy will raise our net exports and further stimulate our economy.

The answers are (1) raise the discount rate, (2) sell securities on the open market, and, ultimately, if these two don't do the job, (3) raise reserve requirements. (For further results of monetary policy, see the Advanced Work box, "The Effectiveness of Monetary Policy in an Open Economy.")

The Fed's Effectiveness in Fighting Inflation and Recession

The Fed is more effective in fighting inflation than recession.

Federal Reserve policy in fighting inflation and recession has been likened to pulling and then pushing on a string. Like pulling on a string, when the Fed fights inflation, it gets results—provided, of course, it pulls hard enough.

Fighting a recession is another matter. Like pushing on a string, no matter how hard the Fed pushes, it might not get anywhere.

First we'll consider fighting inflation. Assume all three basic policy tools have been used: Securities have been sold on the open market, the discount and federal funds target rates have been raised, and, ultimately, reserve requirements have been raised. The results are that bond prices have plunged, interest rates have soared, and money supply growth has been stopped dead in its tracks. Banks find it impossible to increase their loan portfolios. There's a credit crunch and there's credit rationing. Old customers can still borrow, but their credit lines are slashed. (My own line of credit, for example, was cut by Citibank during the 1980 credit crunch from $3,500 to $500.) Nearly all new customers are turned away.

The government fighting inflation is like the Mafia fighting crime.
—Laurence J. Peter

During times like these, the rate of inflation has got to decline. It's hard to raise prices when no one is buying anything. No one can buy because no one has any money. Of course, the Fed is somewhat reluctant to tighten up too much or too long because such a policy generally brings on recessions.

The Fed has a far harder time dealing with a recession. Again, assume the standard tools have been used: Securities have been purchased on the open market, the discount and federal funds target rates have been lowered, and reserve requirements have been lowered. All this creates excess reserves for the banks. But now the $1,000,000 question: What do they *do* with these reserves?

Do they lend them out? Is that your final answer? Yes! To whom should they lend them? To a businessowner who needs a loan to keep going? To a firm that can't meet its next payroll without a loan? To an individual who has just lost her job and can't meet her car payments?

All these examples bring to mind the first law of banking: Never lend money to anyone who needs it. If you ever want a bank loan, you've got to convince the loan officer that you don't really need the money. I don't mean to make the banks sound bad, but from their point of view, they simply can't afford to take the risks inherent in these loans. A banker's first concern must be "Will the bank be paid back?"

Never lend money to anyone who needs it.

Businesses that were good credit risks during prosperity become poor risks during recessions. Individuals, too, lose creditworthiness during recessions, particularly if they've just been laid off. So the very segment of the economic community most in need of help during recessions is least likely to be accommodated.

Meanwhile, many of the top credit-rated corporations are not coming in to borrow large sums of money. During recessions the companies to whom the banks will lend money are not borrowing. Why? Because business isn't so great for them either. Would you borrow to buy more equipment—even at low interest rates—if your equipment was one-third idle? Would you expand your factory if sales were down 20 percent—even if the interest rate fell to 4 percent?

In fact, in October 1982 the economy's capacity utilization rate had fallen to just 68.4 percent—an all-time low since this statistic was first compiled in 1948.[7] The Fed had by then loosened credit, but not until sales finally picked up in early 1983 did investments begin to rise appreciably.

All of this said, may we conclude that easy money has little or no effect in ending a recession? Not at all! It's like the adage "You can lead a horse to water, but you can't make him drink." But if that horse happens to be thirsty, just try to *stop* him from drinking.

During the recession of 1990–91 the Fed used all three of its policy tools to at least cushion the economic decline—buying securities on the open market, lowering the discount rate eight times, and, in early 1992, lowering the reserve requirement on demand deposits from 12 percent to 10 percent. The ensuing recovery was weak and slow. Similarly the Fed made all the right moves during the recession of 2001, but once again, the recovery was weak and slow.

The Fed was able to help end the recessions of 1980 and 1981–82 by relaxing credit and driving down interest rates. However, the excruciatingly slow and halting recovery of 1991–92 was not very responsive to the lowest interest rates in 15 years. Furthermore, even though the banks had plenty of money that they could have loaned out to individuals and business firms, many banks preferred to purchase short-term U.S. government securities.[8]

The Depository Institutions Deregulation and Monetary Control Act of 1980

Economic historians will mark the 1970s and 1980s as decades of swift and significant change in American banking. During this period, the distinction between commercial banks and thrift institutions (savings banks, savings and loan associations, and credit unions) became blurred to the point where it's hard to tell what is a bank and what isn't.

What is a bank and what isn't?

Until 1980 there was a clear line of demarcation between commercial and thrift institutions. Banks (meaning commercial banks) could issue checking deposits; savings banks, savings and loan associations, and credit unions could not. The only problem was that more

---

[7]The capacity utilization rate is the percentage of the nation's plant and equipment that is being used. The full-employment and full-production section of Chapter 2 indicated that a capacity utilization rate of 85 to 90 percent would employ virtually all our usable plant and equipment.

[8]Do you recall the crowding-out effect discussed in Chapter 12? It shows how private borrowers are crowded out of financial markets by the U.S. Treasury, thus offsetting some of the effects of an expansionary fiscal policy.

and more of the thrifts were doing just that. The way they got around the law was to call those checking deposits something else—namely, negotiable order of withdrawal accounts (or NOW accounts). Thus, technically, people who had deposits at these thrift institutions were not writing checks; they were writing negotiable orders of withdrawal.

While Federal Reserve regulation prohibited commercial banks from paying any interest on checking deposits, the thrifts were paying their depositors about 5 percent interest on their NOW accounts. Because these were technically savings accounts rather than checking accounts, it was OK to pay interest. Therefore, the thrifts had it both ways: They were able to give their depositors checking accounts and pay interest on them—which gave them a considerable competitive advantage over commercial banks.

The commercial banks complained to the Fed and to anyone else who would listen, but to little avail. Finally Congress took matters into its own hands and passed the Depository Institutions Deregulation and Monetary Control Act of 1980. It had three key provisions:

The three key provisions of the Banking Act of 1980

1. All depository institutions are now subject to the Fed's legal reserve requirements. Before this act, only those commercial banks that were members of the Federal Reserve—about one-third of all commercial banks were members—were subject to these requirements. The other commercial banks and thrift institutions were subject to state reserve requirements, which were substantially lower.

2. All depository institutions are now legally authorized to issue checking deposits. Furthermore, they may be interest bearing. Previously, commercial banks were forbidden to pay interest on checking accounts, while the thrift institutions claimed to be paying interest on savings accounts.

3. All depository institutions now enjoy all the advantages that only Federal Reserve member banks formerly enjoyed—including check clearing (see the box, "Check Clearing," earlier in this chapter) and borrowing from the Fed (discounting).

Remember that the main job of the Federal Reserve is to control the money supply. By bringing all depository institutions—especially the nonmember commercial banks and the savings banks that had NOW accounts—under the Fed's control, the Monetary Control Act made this job a lot easier.

The number of financial institutions is shrinking quickly.

Another important consequence of this law is that by the end of the 1990s, intense competition reduced the 40,000-plus financial institutions that existed at the beginning of the 1980s to just 20,000 today. The lifting of the prohibition against interstate banking, combined with further advances in electronic banking, will create greater consolidation, with perhaps just 30 or 40 giant financial institutions doing most of the business.

The Banking Act of 1999

In 1980 the jurisdiction of the Federal Reserve had been extended to all commercial banks and thrift institutions. In 1999 it was further extended to insurance companies, pension funds, investment companies, securities brokers, and finance companies.

The new law repealed sections of the Glass-Steagall Act of 1933, which was based on the premise that America's financial house could best be restored if bankers and brokers stayed in separate rooms. It was thought that this could reduce the potential conflicts of interest between investment banking[9] and commercial banking, which had contributed to the speculative frenzy leading to the stock market crash of 1929. Under Glass-Steagall, commercial banks could receive no more than 10 percent of their income from the securities markets, a limit so restrictive that most simply abandoned business on Wall Street selling stocks and bonds to their customers. Over time, Federal judges and regulators chipped away at Glass-Steagall and other restrictions on cross-ownership

---

[9]Investment banks sell new stock and new bonds for existing companies and help arrange corporate mergers.

of banks, insurance companies, and securities firms, enabling, for instance, Citibank to merge with Travelers in 1998 to form Citigroup, the world's largest financial services company. Indeed, this merger helped secure the scrapping of Glass-Steagall.

One purpose of the 1999 law was to give all financial firms, including banks, the chance to sell all sorts of investments. In this way they would be similar to banks in other countries that already provide such services. According to *The Economist,* "Banks in America and Japan—where laws based on Glass-Steagall were imposed by the Americans during the post-war occupation—suffered from a lack of diversification compared with 'universal' banks in continental Europe."[10] The law allows banks, securities firms, and insurance companies to merge and to sell each other's products, and has enabled a wave of mergers as companies compete to build financial supermarkets offering all the services customers need under one roof.

Fiscal and Monetary Policies Should Mesh

It should be apparent that until the early 1990s there was little coordination in the making of fiscal and monetary policies. Indeed, there is little fiscal policy as such, but rather a series of compromises within Congress and between Congress and the president. Further, given the independence of the Federal Reserve Board, different groups of people are responsible for monetary and fiscal policy.

Because of the need for these policies to mesh rather than work at cross-purposes (as they sometimes have), we should consider ways to unify monetary and fiscal policy. One step in this direction would be to allow each newly elected president to appoint a new chairman of the Board.

Current Issue: Who Controls Our Interest Rates?

Who controls our interest rates? The Fed, right? Well, it turns out the Chinese and Japanese governments, which have been buying hundreds of billions of dollars in U.S. government securities, now play a large and growing role. In recent years both nations have tried to hold down the exchange rate of their currencies to dollars. They've done this by buying dollars, mainly by financing our huge federal budget deficits. What would happen to our interest rates if the Chinese and Japanese stopped buying our government securities? Or even worse, what if they began selling them off?

As you probably guessed, the prices of these securities would plummet and interest rates would shoot up. Consider what we can expect for the remaining years of this decade. The federal budget deficit will probably rise above $500 billion, Americans will continue to spend their entire incomes, and the U.S. Treasury will become still more dependent on the kindness of foreigners to finance the deficit.

And the Fed? From mid-2004 through early 2006 it raised the federal funds rate by quarter point increments from just 1 percent to 4.75 percent and was on track to raise it to 5 percent or even higher if deemed necessary. While the Fed was quite successful in increasing short-term interest rates, long-term interest rates (most notably on home mortgages and 10-year Treasury bonds) remained fairly flat. Why couldn't the Fed push up long-term rates? Mainly because foreigners, especially the Chinese government, were buying hundreds of billions of dollars of U.S. government securities.

So who *does* control our interest rates? While the Fed still is, by far, the biggest kid on the block, it no longer calls all the shots. And if our financial dependency on foreigners continues to grow, then in the not-too-distant future, our monetary policy will originate more and more in Shanghai, Tokyo, London, Frankfurt, and other financial capitals.

---

[10]"The Wall Falls," *The Economist*, October 30, 1999, p. 79.

Questions for Further Thought and Discussion

1. Should the Federal Reserve Board of Governors remain independent? What is the strongest argument on either side?

2. Is the Federal Reserve more effective in fighting recessions or inflations? Explain your answer, if possible, using a flow chart.

3. What is the most important job of the Federal Reserve? What makes it so important?

4. What are open-market operations? How are they conducted to fight inflation and recession?

5. Draw a diagram showing the impact on bond prices, interest rates, and the level of investment of (a) an expansionary monetary policy; (b) a contractionary monetary policy.

6. Distinguish between the prime interest rate and the federal funds rate.

7. Why has the power to set the discount rate become a less effective monetary policy tool over the last eight decades?

8. In 1980 and in 1999 two major banking laws were passed. Explain how each law affects bank consolidation.

9. What is the current macroeconomic situation in the United States? What should the Fed do about it?

10. What monetary policy tools should the Fed use to achieve the result you recommended in question 9?

11. How is money created and destroyed? Explain the concept of the money multiplier, and discuss the factors that influence its size.

Workbook for Chapter 14

Name _____   Date _____

Multiple-Choice Questions

Circle the letter that corresponds to the best answer.

1. Fiscal and monetary policy have _____.
   a) the same means and ends
   b) different means and ends
   c) the same means and different ends
   d) different means and the same ends

2. Which statement is true?
   a) The United States has always had a central bank.
   b) The United States has never had a central bank.
   c) The United States had a central bank until 1913.
   d) The United States has had a central bank since 1913.

3. The most important Federal Reserve policy weapon is _____.
   a) changing reserve requirements
   b) changing the discount rate
   c) moral suasion
   d) open-market operations

4. To restrict monetary growth, the Federal Reserve will _____.
   a) raise the discount rate and sell securities
   b) raise the discount rate and buy securities
   c) lower the discount rate and sell securities
   d) lower the discount rate and buy securities

5. Monetary policy is conducted by _____.
   a) the president only
   b) Congress only
   c) the president and Congress
   d) the Federal Reserve

6. Which statement about the Federal Reserve Board of Governors is true?
   a) They serve seven-year terms.
   b) There are 14 members.
   c) Every president appoints his own board.
   d) The members serve at the pleasure of the president, who can force their resignations at any time.
   e) None of these statements is true.

7. Control of the Federal Reserve System is vested in _____.
   a) the president   c) the Board of Governors
   b) Congress   d) the District Banks

8. Basically the Board of Governors is _____.
   a) independent
   b) dependent on the president and Congress
   c) powerless
   d) on a par with the District Banks

9. Legal reserve requirements are changed _____.
   a) very often   c) never
   b) on rare occasions   d) none of these

10. Which of these is a secondary reserve?
    a) Treasury bills
    b) gold
    c) vault cash
    d) deposits at the Federal Reserve District Bank

11. The larger the reserve requirement, the _____.
    a) smaller the deposit expansion multiplier
    b) larger the deposit expansion multiplier
    c) easier it is for banks to lend money

12. Each of the following is a leakage from the deposit expansion multiplier except _____.
    a) cash
    b) the foreign trade imbalance
    c) excess reserves
    d) all of these are leakages

13. Check clearing is done by _____.
    a) the bank where a check is deposited
    b) the bank on which a check is written
    c) the Federal Reserve System
    d) the comptroller of the currency

14. Open-market operations are _____.
    a) the buying and selling of U.S. government securities by the Fed
    b) borrowing by banks from the Fed
    c) the selling of U.S. government securities by the U.S. Treasury
    d) raising or lowering reserve requirements by the Fed

15. When the Fed wants to increase the money supply, it _____.
    a) raises the discount rate
    b) raises reserve requirements
    c) sells securities
    d) buys securities

16. To buy securities, the Fed offers _____.
    a) a low price and drives up interest rates
    b) a low price and drives down interest rates
    c) a high price and drives up interest rates
    d) a high price and drives down interest rates

17. Which statement is the most accurate?
    a) The federal funds rate and the discount rate generally rise and fall together.
    b) The prime rate of interest is usually about a half percentage point below the federal funds rate.
    c) The federal funds rate did not change at all during the late 1990s.
    d) The Federal Reserve has little influence on interest rates.

18. The original intent of the Federal Reserve Act was to have the District Banks lend money to _____.
    a) individual borrowers, particularly business firms
    b) member banks to take care of seasonal needs
    c) the U.S. Treasury
    d) none of the above

19. Which statement is true?
    a) The Fed is more effective at fighting inflation than fighting recession.
    b) The Fed is more effective at fighting recession than fighting inflation.
    c) The Fed is effective at fighting both recession and inflation.
    d) The Fed is effective at fighting neither inflation nor recession.

20. The Depository Institutions Deregulation and Monetary Control Act of 1980 had three key provisions, one of which was _____.
    a) uniform reserve requirements for all financial institutions
    b) zero reserve requirements for all time deposits
    c) that no interest may be paid on checking deposits
    d) that vault cash would no longer count toward reserves

21. The main job of the Fed is to _____.
    a) control the rate of growth of the money supply
    b) to manage the national debt
    c) provide low-interest loans to all financial institutions
    d) raise and lower tax rates

22. One of the main results of the Depository Institutions Deregulation and Monetary Control Act of 1980 may be to _____.
    a) lessen the number of financial institutions in the United States
    b) increase the number of financial institutions in the United States
    c) discourage the formation of big, nationwide, all-purpose financial institutions
    d) make it easier for the member banks to borrow money from the Federal Reserve District Banks

23. Reserve requirements are changed _____.
    a) once a week
    b) three or four times a year
    c) once every two or three years
    d) once every ten or fifteen years
    e) only if Congress passes a new law

24. Suppose that the deposit expansion multiplier were 7. After taking into account its three modifications, we might estimate the true deposit multiplier to be _____.

a) 14
b) 9
c) 7
d) 4
e) 1

25. Statement 1: Currency leakages take place especially during times of recession and low interest rates. Statement 2: The process of check clearing is being partially replaced by the electronic transferring of money.

a) Statement 1 is true and statement 2 is false.
b) Statement 2 is true and statement 1 is false.
c) Both statements are true.
d) Both statements are false.

26. Which is the most accurate statement? The Federal Reserve _____.

a) markets new Treasury bills, notes, certificates, and bonds
b) runs a check clearing operation for U.S. government checks, but does not handle checks written by private individuals or business firms
c) Open-Market Committee is part of the U.S. Treasury
d) buys and sells chunks of the national debt

27. The limits set by law for reserves on checking accounts are between _____.

a) 0% and 9%
b) 3% and 12%
c) 8% and 14%
d) 12% and 18%

28. Which of the following is the most accurate statement?

a) We will have a checkless economy before 2010.
b) Your bank must return the checks you wrote with your monthly statement.
c) The Fed uses open-market operations to hit its target federal funds rate.
d) When the Fed pushes up the money supply, interest rates tend to rise.

29. The repeal of Glass-Steagall in 1999 _____.

a) had the objective of allowing banks, securities firms, and insurance companies to merge and to sell each others' products
b) will result in a huge expansion in the number of financial institutions doing business in the United States
c) will result in the same abuses that led to the passage of the original act in 1929
d) will make it much harder for U.S. financial institutions to merge

30. If the equilibrium rate of interest is 7 percent and market price of a U.S. government bond is $1,000, what is the most likely interest rate and bond price if the Fed increases the money supply by a substantial amount?

a) 8 percent; $1,100
b) 8 percent; $1,000
c) 8 percent; $900
d) 6 percent; $1,100
e) 6 percent; $1,000
f) 6 percent; $900

31. Who will control interest rates in the United States in 2015? The best guess would be _____.

a) the Federal Reserve
b) the Japanese government
c) the Chinese government
d) the governments of China and Japan
e) the Federal Reserve and the governments of China and Japan

32. Which would be the most accurate statement?

a) The Federal Reserve Board of Governors has more power than the monetary authorities of any other country.
b) The Deutsche Bundesbank has more power than the Federal Reserve.
c) The Bank of England and La Banca d'Italia are two of the most powerful central banks.
d) The European Central Bank is one of the most powerful central banks in the world.

Fill-In Questions

1. The Federal Reserve System was established in the year _____.

2. There are _____ Federal Reserve districts.

3. The members of the Board of Governors are appointed by _____, subject to confirmation by the _____.

4. Control of the Federal Reserve is held by _____.

5. At the present time, nearly all checking deposits are subject to a legal reserve requirement of _____ percent.

6. Time deposits are subject to no reserve requirement because _____ _____.

7. All reserves pay an interest rate of _____ percent.

8. If the Fed wants to increase the money supply, it will follow these two steps: (1) _____ _____; (2) _____ _____ ; and if these do not prove sufficient, it may _____.

9. It has been much easier for the Fed to fight _____ than _____.

10. Our paper currency is issued by _____.

11. Our currency is backed by _____.

Problems

1. If you ran a bank with checking deposits of $20 million, you would need to hold reserves of how much? (Use Table 1 on page 333.)

2. If you ran a bank with checking deposits of $400 million, you would need to hold reserves of a little less than how much (assuming you don't remember the cutoff point)?

3. If the reserve requirement were 15 percent, how much would the deposit multiplier be?

4. Using your answer from the previous problem, if the Federal Reserve increased bank reserves by $100 million, by how much would the money supply rise?

5. How much is the effective, or market, interest rate on a bond that has a face value of $1,000 and a selling price of $1,200 and that pays $120 interest?

6. If a bank has reserves of $21 million and demand deposits of $200 million, how much are the bank's: (a) required reserves? (b) excess reserves?

7. Approximately how much in reserves does a bank with $5 billion in demand deposits have to hold?

8. If a bank has reserves of $100 million and checking deposits of $700 million, how much are the bank's: (a) required reserves? (b) excess reserves?

9. How much reserves would a bank have to hold on: (a) $1 billion of time deposits that will mature in less than 18 months? (b) $1 billion of time deposits that will mature in more than 18 months? (Hint: see Table 1 on page 333.)

10. Use the information in Table 1 to find this bank's required reserves.

TABLE 1

Checking deposits: $1 billion
Time deposits: $300 million

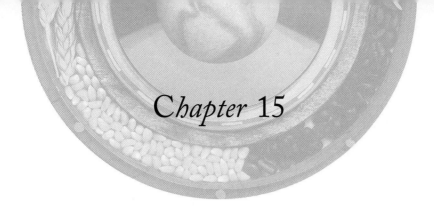

Chapter 15

A Century of Economic Theory

The First Law of Economics: For every economist, there exists an equal and opposite economist.
The Second Law of Economics: They're both wrong.

conomists are not easy to follow when they talk about familiar, day-to-day events like unemployment rate changes and the rising consumer price index. But when they talk theory, however, even their fellow economists have difficulty understanding what they are saying to each other. I'll repeat the words of George Bernard Shaw: "If all economists were laid end to end, they would not reach a conclusion."

John Maynard Keynes put all of this into perspective much more elegantly:

> The ideas of economists and political philosophers, both when they are right and when they are wrong, are more powerful than is commonly understood. Indeed, the world is ruled by little else. Practical men, who believe themselves to be quite exempt from any intellectual influences, are usually slaves of some defunct economist.

What conclusion will you reach at the end of this chapter? If you're like my fellow economists, you will choose one school of economic thought to defend, while attacking each of the others. I hope you'll take each economic theory with a grain of salt, disregarding what you can't accept while appreciating the cogency of the arguments that have been advanced. No attempt is being made to do more than outline some of the underlying ideas of each of the five main schools of the last one hundred years.

An economist is someone good with numbers who didn't have the personality to become an accountant.
—Anonymous

CHAPTER OBJECTIVES

After you've read this chapter, you will have a better understanding of the basics of:

- The equation of exchange.
- The quantity theory of money.
- Classical economics.
- Keynesian economics.
- The monetarist school.
- Supply-side economics.
- The rational expectations theory.

The Equation of Exchange

Much of the Keynesian-Monetarist debate revolves around the quantity theory of money, which itself is based on the equation of exchange. So in the first two sections let's look at these two concepts before we deal specifically with any of the schools of economic thought. The equation of exchange and the quantity theory of money are easily confused, perhaps because the equation of exchange is used to explain the quantity

Don't get the equation of exchange mixed up with the quantity theory of money.

[Handwritten margin notes:]
V Velocity - $ turnover
M Money in the economy
P = Price level, average price of everything produced in a year
Q = Quantity of production in a year
MV ≠ PQ

MONEY (Velocity) = Price Level (Quantity)

P·L = GDP
So MV = GDP

theory. I warn my students every term about how easily the unwary test taker writes down the equation of exchange when asked for the quantity theory, or vice versa. Still, many of them remain faithful to the tradition of confusing the two concepts on the next exam.

The equation of exchange is

$$MV = PQ$$

What do these letters stand for? M represents the number of dollars in the nation's money supply—the currency, demand deposits, and checklike deposits.

The velocity of circulation, or the number of times per year that each dollar in our money supply is spent, is represented by V. If we were to multiply M times V, or MV, that would be our money supply multiplied by the number of times per year each dollar is spent—in other words, total spending. Total spending by a nation during a given year is GDP. Therefore:

$$MV = GDP$$

Now for the other side of the equation. P represents the price level, or the average price of all the goods and services sold during the year. Finally, there's Q, the quantity of goods and services sold during the year. Multiplying P times Q, we get the total amount of money received by the sellers of all the final goods and services produced by the nation that year. This is also GDP. Things equal to the same thing are equal to each other (MV = GDP; PQ = GDP); therefore MV = PQ.

We'll get a better idea of how this equation works by replacing the letters with numbers. For M we can substitute $900 billion, and we'll give V a value of 9.

$$MV = PQ$$
$$900 \times 9 = PQ$$
$$8{,}100 = PQ$$

This gives us a GDP of 8,100, or $8.1 trillion. As a form of shorthand, economists write billions of dollars without the dollar sign. The money supply of $900 billion becomes 900, and the GDP of $8,100 billion becomes 8,100.

So far we have MV = 8,100; therefore, PQ also = 8,100. How much are P and Q? We don't know. All we do know is that P × Q = 8,100.

What we'll do, so we can fool around with this equation, is arbitrarily assign values to P and Q. That might not be very nice or proper, but let me assure you that people do this sort of thing every day. Let's take P. Who can guess what the average price of all the final goods and services sold actually is? In other words, could you guess the average price of all those cars, houses, hot dogs, pairs of shoes, haircuts, cans of beer, cavity fillings, and so on? As there's no way of even guessing, we'll make the number $81. Why $81? Because it will be easy to work with. But perhaps $61.17 or $123.98 is the actual value of P. We'll never know.

Now we'll consider Q. How many final goods and services were sold during the year? 23 billion? 345 billion? Again, we can't possibly know, so we'll assign a number. If we've already picked $81 for P, and PQ = 8,100, then Q must equal 100 (meaning, in economists' shorthand, 100 billion). Therefore:

$$MV = PQ$$
$$900 \times 9 = 81 \times 100$$
$$8{,}100 = 8{,}100$$

That's the equation of exchange. It must always balance, as must all equations. If one side rises by a certain percentage, the other side must rise by the same percentage. For example, if MV rose to 9,000, PQ would also rise to 9,000.

The Quantity Theory of Money

The quantity theory of money has both a crude version and a more sophisticated version. The crude quantity theory of money holds that when the money supply changes by a certain percentage, the price level changes by that same percentage. For example, if the money supply were to rise by 10 percent, the price level would rise by 10 percent. Similarly, if M were to double, then P would double. Using the same figures we assigned to the equation of exchange, let's see what happens if M and P double.

The crude version of the quantity theory

$$MV = PQ$$
$$900 \times 9 = 81 \times 100$$
$$1,800 \times 9 = 162 \times 100$$
$$16,200 = 16,200$$

If we double M, then MV doubles, and if we double P, PQ doubles. Because both sides of the equation must be equal, it appears that the crude quantity theory of money works out.

There are only two problems here. We are assuming V and Q remain constant. Do they? If they do, the crude quantity theory is correct. But what if they don't? For example, what if M, P, and Q all double? For the equation to balance, V would have to double. Similarly, what if M doubles and V declines by 50 percent? In that case, the rise in M would be canceled by the decline in V. If M doubles and MV stays the same, can we expect an automatic doubling of P?

Let's take a closer look at V and then at Q. Since 1950 V has risen fairly steadily from about three to nearly seven. In other words, individuals and businesses are spending their dollars much more quickly. Alternatively, they are making more efficient use of their money balances.

During a period of very tight money in the late 1970s and early 1980s, V rose to nearly seven.

There are several explanations for the rise of V. First, there's inflation. Why hold large money balances when they lose their value over time? Second, why hold idle cash balances when they could be earning interest? Finally, the use of credit cards, debit cards, and automatic teller machines (ATMs), especially during the last 15 years, has allowed people to carry less cash. As a result, V has more than doubled since the mid-1950s.

Now let's see about Q, the quantity of final goods and services produced. During recessions, production, and therefore Q, will fall. For example, during the 1981–82 recession Q fell at an annual rate of about 4 percent during the fourth quarter of 1981 and the first quarter of 1982. During recoveries, production picks up, so we go from a declining Q to a rising Q.

Obviously, then, we cannot consider V or Q to be constants. Therefore, the crude version of the quantity theory is invalid.

The real problem with the early quantity theorists is that they overstated their case. Clearly, rapid monetary growth will invariably lead to inflation. But does a given rate of increase in the money supply lead to precisely the same rate of growth in the price level? Not in *my* book, nor in any other economics text.

Today's modern monetarists, those who believe the key economic variable is changes in M, have come up with a more sophisticated quantity theory. They assume any short-term changes in V are either very small or predictable. The situation with Q, however, is another story.

The sophisticated version of the quantity theory

Let's say M rises by 10 percent and V stays the same: MV will rise by 10 percent and PQ will rise by 10 percent. So far, so good. In fact, so far the crude and sophisticated quantity theories are identical. But what happens next is entirely up to the level of production, Q.

If there's considerable unemployment and we increase M, most, if not all, of this increase will be reflected in an increase in production, Q. Money flowing into the economy will lead to increased spending, output, and employment. Will it lead to higher prices as well? Probably not. It is reasonable to expect most of the rise in M to be reflected in a rise in Q.

The value of money ... varies inversely as its quantity; every increase of quantity lowering the value, and every diminution raising it, in a ratio exactly equivalent.

—John Stuart Mill,
Principles of Political Economy

F*igure* 1

Hypothetical Aggregate Supply Curve

Moving from the extreme left side of the aggregate supply curve, we can raise output without raising prices until we begin to approach full-employment GDP. After continuing to raise output, accompanied by a rising price level, we reach full-employment GDP, at which point any further movement along the aggregate supply curve will raise prices without increasing output.

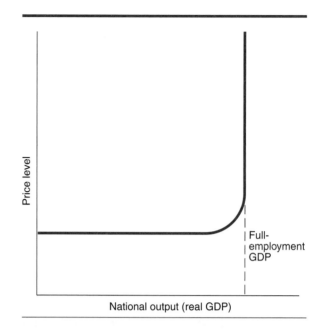

Sophisticated quantity theory in brief

As we approach full employment, however, further increases in M will begin to lead, more and more, to increases in P, the price level (see Figure 1). And it is there that the sophisticated quantity theory becomes operative. We therefore can make two statements summarizing the sophisticated quantity theory:

1. If we are well below full employment, an increase in M will lead mainly to an increase in Q.

2. If we are close to full employment, an increase in M will lead mainly to an increase in P.

That's the sophisticated quantity theory of money. Please don't confuse it with the crude quantity theory, and don't confuse either quantity theory with the equation of exchange.

What is the sophisticated quantity theory supposed to do? Like most theories, it makes a prediction. In its least rigorous version, it says that changes in M's rate of growth lead to similar changes in PQ's rate of growth. If M is increasing slowly, PQ will increase slowly; rapid growth in M leads to rapid growth in PQ. Although no precise mathematical relationship is claimed (as under the crude quantity theory), the monetarists say changes in M lead to predictable changes in PQ.

Classical Economics

The American economy suffered very bad recessions, even depressions, in the 1830s, 1870s, and 1890s, but eventually we always did manage to recover. If the government tried to get the country out of a recession, said the classicals, it only made things worse.

Recessions cure themselves.

The classical school of economics was mainstream economics from roughly 1775 to 1930. Adam Smith's *The Wealth of Nations,* a plea for laissez-faire (no government interference), was virtually the economics bible through most of this period. The classicals believed our economy was self-regulating. Recessions would cure themselves, and a built-in mechanism was always pushing the economy toward full employment.

Say's law

As we saw at the beginning of Chapter 11, the centerpiece of the classical system was Say's law: Supply creates its own demand. Everything produced gets sold. Why? Because people work so that they can spend.

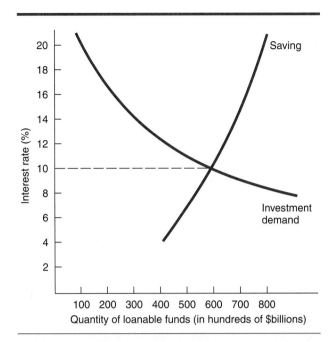

F*igure* 2
The Interest Rate Mechanism
An interest rate of 10 percent is found at the intersection of the saving curve and the investment demand curve.

What if people save some of their incomes? No problem, said the classicals, because that savings will be invested. With that, they pointed to Figure 2, which shows a graph of saving and investment. The two are equal at an interest rate of 10 percent.

Savings will be invested.

What if the amount of money people wanted to save at 10 percent interest were greater than the amount businesspeople wanted to invest? Still no problem, said the classicals. The interest rate would fall automatically. People would be inclined to save less at lower interest rates, and businesspeople would be inclined to invest more. Eventually, the interest rate would fall far enough so that savings and investment would be equal.

Interest rate mechanism

The classicals also assumed downwardly flexible wage rates and prices. If there happened to be a temporary recession and business firms could not sell their entire inventories, they would simply lower their prices until their inventories were depleted. Similarly, if some workers were unemployed, they would offer to work for lower wages and would find new jobs.

Flexible wages and prices

Another basic classical tenet was the quantity theory of money. Stated in its crudest version, when the money supply changes by a certain percentage, the price level changes by that same percentage. Thus, when the money supply is increased by 5 percent, the price level rises by 5 percent.

Quantity theory of money

Resorting once again to the equation of exchange:

$$MV = PQ$$

If M rises by 5 percent and P rises by 5 percent, that means V and Q remain constant. In the six decades since World War II V has generally been stable during nonrecession years and during peacetime. How stable has Q been? Q, the quantity of output of goods and services, rises during nonrecession years and falls during recession years.

V and Q are constant.

Q: How many conservative economists does it take to screw in a light bulb?

A: None. If the government would just leave it alone, it would screw in itself.

Where does all this leave us as regards the quantity theory? In its crude version, which the classicals espoused, we could hardly expect V *and* Q to stay constant from year to year. So much, then, for the crude quantity theory.

Finally, let's take a closer look at the classical contention that recessions are temporary phenomena, which, with the help of Say's law, the interest rate mechanism, and downwardly flexible wages and prices, cure themselves. This leads to the basic classical macroeconomic policy when there is a recession: Do nothing!

If the government attempted to cure a recession by spending more money or cutting taxes, these measures would not get the economy out of the recession. Why not?

Government can't cure recessions.

Because the recession would cure itself. Government intervention could not help, and it might even hurt.

What about monetary policy? If there were a recession, the standard monetary policy would be to increase the rate of growth of the money supply. What would this accomplish? Ask the classicals. Because the recession would be curing itself, output, Q, would go up automatically. Because V would be stable, a rise in M would simply be translated into a rise in P, so the attempt to cure the recession by means of monetary policy would only cause inflation.

The classical school dominated economic thought until the time of the Great Depression. If recessions cure themselves automatically, asked John Maynard Keynes in the 1930s, why is the entire world economy dragging along from year to year in unending depression? And if the economy isn't curing itself, said Keynes, government intervention is in order.

Keynesian Economics

Economics is the painful elaboration of the obvious.

—Anonymous

John Maynard Keynes wrote his landmark work *The General Theory of Employment, Interest, and Money* during the depths of the Great Depression. While President Herbert Hoover (perhaps the last political leader to uphold the theories of classical economics) was telling everyone who would listen that recovery was just around the corner, things were going from bad to worse. As the unemployment rate mounted, production plummeted, and soup kitchens proliferated, more and more Americans demanded that the federal government do something. When Franklin Roosevelt defeated Hoover by a landslide in 1932, he had a mandate to do whatever was necessary to bring about recovery.

Keynes: The problem with recessions is inadequate aggregate demand.

Keynes provided a blueprint. The problem, he said, was inadequate aggregate demand. People were just not buying enough goods and services to employ the entire labor force. In fact, aggregate demand was so low that only the government could spend enough money to provide a sufficient boost.

Keynes defined aggregate demand as consumer spending, investment spending, and government spending (plus net exports, which at that time were negligible). Consumption is a function of disposable income. When disposable income is low, said Keynes, consumption is low. And during the Great Depression disposable income was extremely low.

The cure for recession is government spending.

Investment, which is largely a function of the marginal efficiency of investment, or the expected profit rate, was not just low, but even negative. So we could not hope that an upturn in investment would lead the way out of the Depression. The only hope was for the government to spend enough money to raise aggregate demand sufficiently to get people back to work.

What type of spending was necessary? Any kind, said Keynes. Quantity is much more relevant than quality. Even if the government employed some people to dig holes, said Keynes, and others to fill up those holes, it would still be able to spend the country out of these economic woes.

Where would the government get the money? There were two choices: print it or borrow it. If the government printed it, wouldn't that cause inflation? Keynes thought this unlikely; during the Depression, the country had been experiencing *de*flation, or falling prices. Who would even *think* of raising prices when she was having trouble finding customers?

In a campaign speech in Brooklyn in the fall of 1932, Roosevelt castigated Hoover for not balancing his budget.

What about budget deficits? Nothing improper about these, said Keynes. Although the common wisdom of the times was that the government must balance its budget, there was absolutely nothing wrong with deficits during recessions and depressions. It was necessary to prime the pump by sucking up the idle savings that businesses were not borrowing and using those funds to get the economy moving again.

Once government spending was under way, people would have some money in their pockets. And what would they do with that money? You guessed it—they'd spend it. This money would then end up in other people's pockets, and they, in turn, would spend it once again. This is the fabled multiplier effect that we introduced in Chapter 12.

That money would continue to be spent again and again, putting more and more people back to work. As they began paying taxes, the deficit would melt away. The government could cut back on its spending programs while tax receipts swelled, so we could view the budget deficits as a temporary expedient to get the economy off dead center.

But what of the classical automatic mechanism that ensured that the economy always moved toward full employment? In the long run, Keynes conceded, maybe it really *did* work. But in the long run, noted Keynes, "we are all dead."

Why didn't the classical mechanism work in the short run? Keynes observed that interest rates fell to about 2 percent during the Great Depression, but business firms still were not borrowing all that much to build new plant and equipment. After all, who in his right mind would invest in new plant and equipment when his factory was operating at only 30 or 40 percent of capacity? Besides, said Keynes, at an interest rate of 2 percent, many people would not be willing to lend out their savings. Why tie up their money at such a low interest rate? Why not just sit on this money until interest rates rose again?

> Why invest in new plant and equipment when most of your capacity is idle?

So much for the interest rate mechanism. With respect to downwardly flexible wages and prices, there were institutional barriers. Labor unions would oppose lowered wage rates, while highly concentrated industries would tend to prefer output decreases to price cuts during recessions.

Keynes also raised some objections to the quantity theory of money. Most significant, he asked what would happen to the money that would be printed if the government did increase the money supply. The classicals had assumed it would be spent, thus pushing up the price level. This could happen, conceded Keynes, but during a bad recession perhaps people would just hold their money, waiting for interest rates to rise before they lent it out.

> If M rises, what if people don't spend additional money, but just hold it?

Wouldn't they spend it, as the classicals suggested? Poor people would. But if they were poor, what would they be doing with money in the first place? If the money supply were increased during a bad recession, said Keynes, that money would simply be held as idle cash balances by relatively well-to-do people. Nothing would happen to the money until the economy was well on its way toward recovery, interest rates rose, and more investment opportunities became available.

By the mid-1930s the classical school of economics had lost most of its adherents. Not everyone became a Keynesian. Conservative economists in particular could never fully reconcile themselves to the vastly increased economic role that the Keynesians awarded to the federal government. In fact, the remaining economic schools to be considered here—the monetarists, the supply-siders, and the rational expectationists—would all rail against the evils of big government.

But big government was here to stay. Although the massive spending programs of Franklin Roosevelt's New Deal did not get the country out of the Depression, the much bigger defense spending during World War II certainly did. There was no question that Keynes had been right, but since the war Americans had been plagued not just by periodic recessions but by almost unending inflation. There was growing feeling among economists that perhaps Keynesian economics was just recession and depression economics, that it could not satisfactorily deal with curbing inflation.

> Is Keynesian economics valid just during recessions?

The Monetarist School

The Importance of the Rate of Monetary Growth

Monetarism begins and ends with one obsession: the rate of growth of the money supply. According to monetarists, most of our major economic problems, especially inflation and recession, are due to the Federal Reserve's mismanagement of our rate of monetary growth.

> Monetarists are obsessed with the growth rate of M.

Milton Friedman, an economist who did exhaustive studies of the relationship between the rate of growth of the money supply and the rate of increase in prices, reached a couple of not surprising conclusions. First, the United States has never had a serious inflation that was not accompanied by rapid monetary growth. Second, when the money supply has grown slowly, the country has had no inflation.

In a study of the monetary history of the United States during the period of nearly a century after the Civil War, Friedman and his longtime collaborator Anna Jacobson Schwartz reached this conclusion: "Changes in the behavior of the money stock have been closely associated with changes in economic activity, money income, and prices."[1]

Building on the quantity theory of money, the monetarists agreed with the classicals that when the money supply grows, the price level rises, albeit not at exactly the same rate. But they refuted Keynes's argument that if the money supply were raised during a recession, people might just hold on to these added funds. Like the classicals, the monetarists assumed that to get it is to spend it—not necessarily on consumer goods, but on stocks, bonds, real estate, and other noncash assets.

If people *did* spend this additional money, the prices of what they bought would be bid up. In other words, the monetarists were saying that the quantity theory basically holds true.

So far, so good. Now for recessions. What causes them? When the Federal Reserve increases the money supply at less than the rate needed by business—say, anything less than 3 percent a year—the economy is headed for trouble. Sometimes, in fact, the Fed does not let it grow at all and may even cause it to shrink slightly.

By and large the facts have borne out the monetarists' analysis. Without a steady increase in the money supply of at least 3 percent a year, there is a high likelihood of a recession.

The Basic Propositions of Monetarism

(1) The Key to Stable Economic Growth Is a Constant Rate of Increase in the Money Supply
Has our economic history been one of stable growth? No inflation? No recessions? Since World War II alone, we've had four waves of inflation and 10 recessions.

The monetarists place almost the entire blame on the Federal Reserve Board of Governors. If only they had been increasing the money supply by a steady 3 percent a year, we could have avoided most of this instability.

Let's trace the monetarist reasoning by analyzing the Fed's actions over the course of a business cycle. As a recession sets in, the Fed increases the rate of growth of the money supply. This stimulates output in the short run, helping to pull the economy out of the recession. In the long run, however, this expanded money supply causes inflation. So what does the Fed do? It slams on the monetary brakes, slowing the rate of growth in the money supply. This brings on a recession. And what does the Fed do in response? It increases the rate of monetary growth.

"Is this stop-go, stop-go monetary policy any way to run an economy?" ask the monetarists. This type of policy inspires about as much confidence as the student driver approaching a red light. First he hits the brakes about 100 yards from the corner. Then, overcompensating for his error, he hits the accelerator much too hard. When the car lurches forward, he hits the brakes again, bringing the car to a dead stop about 50 yards from the corner. Then he repeats the whole process.

In the late 1960s, an accelerating rate of monetary growth was accompanied by a rising rate of inflation, which, in the early 1970s, reached double-digit proportions. In 1973 the Federal Reserve Board put on the brakes, and we went into the worst recession

---

[1]Milton Friedman and Anna Jacobson Schwartz, *A Monetary History of the United States, 1867–1960* (Princeton, NJ: Princeton University Press, 1971), p. 676.

we had suffered since World War II. In 1975 the Fed eased up and we recovered. Then, in late 1979, the brakes were applied. The prime rate of interest soared to more than 20 percent, and in January 1980 we went into a sharp six-month recession. What happened next? You guessed it. The Fed eased up again. Interest rates came down, and economic recovery set in. But in 1981 the Fed, alarmed at the rising inflation rate, slammed on the monetary brakes, and we entered still another recession in August 1981. The prime once again soared to more than 20 percent. This recession proved even deeper than that of 1973–75. In summer 1982 the Fed once again eased up on the brakes; sure enough, by November of that year the recession had ended.

(2) Expansionary Monetary Policy Will Only Temporarily Depress Interest Rates   In the short run, when the Fed increases the rate of monetary growth, interest rates decline. If the interest rate is the price of money, it follows that if the money supply is increased and there is no change in the demand for money, then its price (the interest rate) will decline.

The monetarists tell us that in the long run an increase in monetary growth will not lower interest rates; the increased money supply causes inflation. Lenders will demand higher interest rates to compensate them for being repaid in inflated dollars.

In the long run, a rise in M pushes up inflation and interest rates.

Let's say, for example, there's no inflation and the interest rate is 5 percent. This is the real rate of interest. The rate of inflation then rises to 8 percent; that means if it cost you $10,000 to live last year, your cost of living is now $10,800. If lenders can anticipate the rate of inflation, they will insist that they be paid not just for the real interest rate of 5 percent but also for the anticipated inflation of 8 percent. This raises the interest rate from 5 percent to a nominal rate of 13 percent.

When the Federal Reserve allows the money supply to grow quickly, interest rates are kept down for a while until lenders realize the rate of inflation (caused by faster monetary growth) is rising. They will then demand higher interest rates. Thus, a higher rate of monetary growth in the short run will keep interest rates low, but in the long run it will lead to higher interest rates.

(3) Expansionary Monetary Policy Will Only Temporarily Reduce the Unemployment Rate   The first two basic propositions partially explain the third. First, when monetary growth speeds up, output is expanded, but in the long run only prices will rise. Because rising output would lower the unemployment rate, in the short run unemployment is reduced. But in the long run, an increase in the rate of monetary growth will raise prices, not output, so the unemployment rate will go back up. We'll come back to why this happens.

The second basic proposition states that expansionary monetary policy only temporarily depresses interest rates. In the short run, more money means lower interest rates. These lower interest rates encourage more investment and, consequently, less unemployment.

But in the long run the added money in circulation causes inflation, which, in turn, raises interest rates. As interest rates rise, investment declines and the unemployment rate goes back up.

The monetarists have explained the temporary reduction in the unemployment rate more directly. As labor union members begin to anticipate inflation, they will demand higher wage rates. New labor contract settlements will reflect the higher cost of living, but these higher wage settlements will price some workers out of the market, thus raising the unemployment rate.

(4) Expansionary Fiscal Policy Will Only Temporarily Raise Output and Employment   Here we have another conflict—this time a basic one—between the monetarists and the Keynesians. The Keynesians believe fiscal policy, particularly heavy government spending, will pull us out of a recession. But how is this spending going to be financed? By borrowing. The Treasury goes into the market for loanable funds and borrows hundreds of billions of dollars to finance the deficit.

Crowding-out effect

The monetarists point out that such huge government borrowing comes directly into conflict with the borrowing of business firms and consumers. Not only will it be harder for these groups to borrow, but interest rates will be driven up. This crowding-out effect represents, according to the monetarists, a substitution of public for private spending. All we're really doing is spending more on government goods and services and less on consumer and investment goods and services. Aggregate demand is not increased.

How well would a budget surplus restrain inflation? Not very, say the monetarists. The Treasury would be repaying part of the national debt, which would tend to push down interest rates and make borrowing easier. Private borrowing would replace public borrowing. The hoped-for restraint would not materialize because private borrowers would now be spending these borrowed funds on goods and services. In effect, then, we would still have the same level of spending.

The Monetary Rule

Increase the money supply at a constant rate.

The policy prescription of the monetarists is simply to increase the money supply at a constant rate. When there is a recession, this steady infusion of money will pick up the economy. When there is inflation, a steady rate of monetary growth will slow it down. So one size of monetary growth fits all economic occasions.

You might ask why the money supply should be increased at all during inflation. There are two answers. First, the monetarists would tell you that if we didn't increase the money supply at all, we would be going back to the old, failed discretionary monetary policies of the past—the start-and-stop, start-and-stop policies that only made the business cycle worse. Second, over the long run the economy does need a steady infusion of money to enable economic growth.

The monetarists' steady monetary growth prescription is analogous to the feeding policy of the American Army. Every day, in every part of the world, at every meal, the soldiers walk along the chow line and receive, in addition to the main course and dessert, two pieces of white bread, two pats of butter, and one pint of whole milk. The main course is also dished out in equal portions. The food servers do not dole out portions whose sizes vary with that of the eater. They look from the serving pan to the eater's tray, slopping out serving spoonfuls of whatever it is that the Army decided to cook that day.

So, we have a 6-foot 6-inch 300-pound person getting the same size portion as does a 5-foot 6-inch 130-pound person. My theory is that the Army wants everyone to be the same size—a theory that also seems to be borne out by the single uniform size that is issued. If everyone eats the same portion, presumably they will all end up this same size.

Perhaps the monetarists got the idea of increasing the money supply by a constant percentage by observing Army chow lines. They believe our economic health will be relatively good—if not always excellent—if we have a steady diet of money. No starts and stops, no extreme ups and downs, and, to complete the analogy, no very fat years and no very lean years.

The Decline of Monetarism

It's interesting that when the Fed really began to pay attention to what the monetarists were saying, this may have led to the ultimate decline of the monetarist school. In October 1979 Federal Reserve Chairman Paul Volcker announced a major policy shift. No longer would the Fed focus only on keeping interest rates on an even keel. From now on the Fed would set monetary growth targets and stick to them.

This new policy was followed for most of the next three years. The double-digit inflation that prevailed in 1979 and 1980 was finally brought under control by late 1982—but not until we had gone through a period of sky-high interest rates, very high unemployment, and back-to-back recessions.

Even though the Fed had finally followed the advice of the monetarists—at least to a large degree—and even though the nagging inflation of the last 15 years had finally been wrung out of the economy, people began to look elsewhere for their economic gurus. They looked to the White House, which had become a stronghold of the latest school of economics, the supply-side school.

Supply-Side Economics

Supply-side economics came into vogue in the early 1980s when Ronald Reagan assumed the presidency. Supply-siders felt that the economic role of the federal government had grown much too large and that high tax rates and onerous government rules and regulations were hurting the incentives of individuals and business firms to produce goods and services. President Reagan suggested a simple solution: get the government off the backs of the American people. How? By cutting taxes and reducing government spending and regulation.

Cut tax rates, government spending, and government regulation.

The objective of supply-side economics, then, is to raise aggregate supply, the total amount of goods and services the country produces. The problem, said the supply-siders, is that high marginal tax rates are hurting the incentive to work and to invest. All the government needs to do is cut tax rates, and *voilà!* Up goes production.

Raise aggregate supply.

Many of the undesirable side effects of high marginal tax rates are explained by the work effect, the savings and investment effect, and the elimination of productive market exchanges, which we shall take up in turn.

The Work Effect

People are often confronted with work–leisure decisions. Should I put in that extra couple of hours of overtime? Should I take on a second job? Should I keep my store open longer hours? If you answer yes to any of these, you'll have to give the government a pretty big slice of that extra income. At some point you may well conclude, "I'd have to be nuts to take on any extra work; I'd only be working for the government."

Work–leisure decisions

At what point do *you* start working for the government? When it takes 20 cents out of each dollar of extra income (a marginal tax rate of 20 percent)? When it takes 30 cents? Or 40 cents? If you are a wage-earner, you will have to pay Medicare and Social Security tax, federal income tax, and, probably, some state income tax. Back in 1980, before the passage of the Kemp-Roth tax cut and the tax cuts that came under the Tax Reform Act of 1986, people earning more than $50,000 a year often had marginal tax rates of more than 50 percent. If you paid more than half of your overtime earnings in taxes, would you consider yourself to be working for the government?

Facing high marginal tax rates, many people refuse to work more than a certain number of hours of overtime or take on second jobs and other forms of extra work. Instead, they opt for more leisure time. In sum, high marginal tax rates rob people not only of some potential income but of the incentive to work longer hours. People working shorter hours obviously produce less, so total output is lower than it might have been with lower marginal tax rates.

Why work if the government gets most of your money?

The Saving and Investment Effect

When people save money, they earn interest on their savings. But a high marginal tax rate on interest income will provide a disincentive to save, making less savings available for investment purposes.

High marginal tax rates discourage working, saving, and investing.

Similarly, people who borrow money for investment purposes—new plant and equipment and inventory—hope that this will lead to greater profits. But if those profits are subject to a high marginal tax rate, once again there is a disincentive to invest.

Supply-side economists point to the economic stagnation of the late 1970s and early 1980s as proof of the basic propositions of their theory. On the other hand, the economic record during the Reagan years, particularly with respect to saving, investment, and economic growth, was nothing to write home about.

The Elimination of Productive Market Exchanges

Most people have jobs at which they are good; if an accountant, a carpenter, an automobile mechanic, and a gourmet chef are all relatively good at their professions, that's probably why they chose those lines of work to begin with—and all that on-the-job training didn't hurt either.

When you need your taxes prepared—especially if you stand to save several thousand dollars—you go to an accountant. When you need your transmission fixed, unless you're a skilled mechanic, you'll certainly be better off going to someone who is. In fact, one of the main reasons our standard of living is so high in the United States is because a large proportion of our labor force is composed of individuals with specialized skills.

What happens when your roof must be reshingled? Do you hire a roofer, or do you do it yourself? Do you do it yourself because it's cheaper?

Well, maybe it's cheaper and maybe it isn't. Suppose you can reshingle your roof in 100 hours and a roofer can do the job in 60 hours. If the roofer charges you $12 an hour (in addition to materials), it will cost you $720. How many hours would you have to work to earn $720? Suppose your clerical job pays $10 an hour and you are in the 40 percent marginal tax bracket. You take home only $6 an hour (that is, 60 percent of $10).

Do you hire the roofer or do it yourself? If you do it yourself, it will take you 100 hours. If you hire the roofer, you must pay him $720. How many hours would you have to work to bring home $720? Figure it out: $720/$6 = 120 hours. I think even *I* would rather spend 100 hours on my roof than 120 hours in front of a class. And I'm afraid of heights!

There is a serious misallocation of labor when the productive market exchange—your clerical work for your roofer's labor—is eliminated; but because of the high marginal tax rate, it pays for you to work less at your regular job (at which you are presumably good) and more at household tasks (at which you are not so good). When you add up all the productive market exchanges short-circuited by high marginal tax rates, you may well be talking about hundreds of billions of dollars in misallocated resources.

> High tax rates discourage productive market exchanges.

> Policy prescription: Cut taxes!

The Laffer Curve

Supply-side economists have one basic policy prescription: Cut tax rates! Won't federal tax revenue fall precipitously? But Arthur Laffer, an orthodox supply-side economics professor, said that cutting marginal tax rates could lead to an increase in government revenue. (See the box, "The Laffer Curve.")

Let's see how this works by looking at the case of a specific individual. Suppose this person pays $50,000 on an income of $100,000. If this person's tax rate were lowered to 40 percent, she would pay $40,000. Right? Wrong, say the supply-siders. She would now have an incentive to work harder. How *much* harder? Hard enough, say, to earn $130,000 by working every available hour of overtime or taking on a second job.

How much is 40 percent of $130,000? It comes out to exactly $52,000. How much did the government collect from her before the tax cut? Only $50,000. So by cutting tax rates, say the supply-siders, the government will end up collecting more revenue. But when the government cut tax rates in 1981 and 1982, tax revenue actually declined. Of course, there was a recession going on.

During the last two years of the Reagan administration, it had become apparent that supply-side economics was an idea whose time had gone. Although inflation had been brought under control and interest rates had declined as well (largely because of the efforts of the Federal Reserve), the supply-side policies had not yielded the rapid rate of economic growth that the public had been led to expect. Perhaps the greatest legacies of supply-side economics were huge budget deficits.

Arthur Laffer, American economist

> *Waiting for supply-side economics to work is like leaving the landing lights on for Amelia Earhart.*
> —Walter Heller

The Laffer Curve

Imagine that we're at point A on the Laffer curve drawn in Figure A. We cut the marginal tax rate from 50 percent to 40 percent, and lo and behold, tax revenue rises from $1,200 billion to nearly $1,400 billion. Is this sophistry? (That's Greek for "pulling a fast one.")

What if we were at, say, point C on the Laffer curve and we cut tax rates? What would happen to federal tax revenue? Obviously, it would decline.

The problem is to figure out where we are on the Laffer curve, or what the parameters of the curve itself are, before we start cutting taxes. There really *is* a Laffer curve out there. The trouble is we don't know exactly where, so when we try to use it as a policy tool, it's kind of like playing an economic version of pin the tail on the donkey. When you play a game blindfolded, you run the risk of looking a lot like the six-year-old kids who miss the donkey completely. And this game is for somewhat higher stakes.

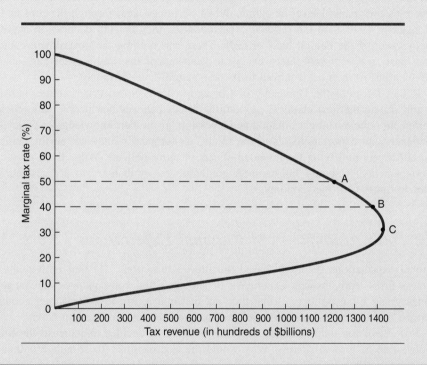

Figure A

The Laffer Curve

At a marginal tax rate of 0, tax revenues are 0. Tax revenue can be increased by raising the marginal tax rate to point C, at which they will be maximized. If marginal tax rates are raised still higher, tax revenue will decline. And, if the marginal tax rate were 100 percent, no one would work, and tax revenue would be 0. The rationale of the Laffer curve is that, when the marginal tax rate is too high, say, at 50 percent (see point A), we can raise tax revenue by lowering it to 40 percent (see point B).

Rational Expectations Theory

Whatever else you have learned about economic policy, you know that economists don't all agree on what policies we should follow. But most economists would more or less agree on two sets of policies. To fight inflation, you want to lower the rate of growth of the money supply and reduce federal government budget deficits. And to fight recessions, you want to do the opposite: increase the rate of growth of the money supply and increase the size of the deficits. But prominent among those who would disagree with these policies are the rational expectationists.

Most economists agree on two sets of policies.

You probably never saw *Monty Python and the Holy Grail*, but in that movie there was a group of knights who distinguished themselves solely by saying "Neee." No matter what questions they were asked, they would always answer "Neee." Assuming "Neee" was Middle English for nay or no, those knights were the rational expectations theorists, or the new classical economists of their day.

Like the "old" classical economists, today's rational expectationists say no to any form of government economic intervention. Such intervention, no matter how well intentioned, would do a lot more harm than good. In fact, they maintain that anti-inflationary and antirecessionary policies, at best, would have no effect whatsoever. More likely, say the new classical economists, these policies would end up making things worse.

It would be best for the government to do nothing, even if there were a recession or a substantial amount of inflation. The economy will automatically and quickly right itself, ending up again with full employment and little or no inflation. The reason that fiscal and monetary policy would have little effect, according to the rational expectationists, is that they affect mainly aggregate demand but that the prime economic mover is aggregate supply.

They argued that at any given time there was a natural level of real GDP, toward which the economy gravitated. The deflationary and inflationary gaps that so perplexed policymakers during the 1970s weren't gaps at all. Instead they reflected changes in the economy's own natural level of output. When oil prices went through the roof in 1973 and again in 1979, said the rational expectationists, they created declines in aggregate supply, lowering the natural level of GDP. There was nothing the government could do about these new economic facts, except to keep out of the way and let our economy quickly adjust to them as it moved to its new natural level of output.

The view of Robert Lucas

Robert Lucas of the University of Chicago, a 1995 Nobel Prize winner, is clearly top gun among the new classical economists. Lucas believes that people can anticipate government policies to fight inflation and recession, given their knowledge of policy, past experience, and expectations about the future. Consequently, they act on this anticipation, effectively nullifying the intended effects of those policies. What, then, should the government do? It should follow strict guidelines rather than try to use discretionary policy to tinker with the economy.

The Three Assumptions of Rational Expectations Theory

Rational expectations theory is based on three assumptions: (1) that individuals and business firms learn through experience to anticipate the consequences of changes in monetary and fiscal policy; (2) that they act instantaneously to protect their economic interests; and (3) that all resource and product markets are purely competitive.

Now we'll translate. Imagine the Federal Reserve decides to increase the money supply's rate of growth sharply. Why would the Fed do this? To stimulate output and raise employment.

An economist is someone who doesn't know what he's talking about—and makes you feel it's your fault.

—Anonymous

The scenario, according to the Fed, would be as follows: (1) the money supply rises; (2) business firms order more plant and equipment and more inventory; (3) more jobs are created and output rises; (4) wages do not rise right away, but prices do; (5) because prices rise and wages stay the same, profits rise; (6) eventually wages catch up to prices, profits go back down, and the expansion comes to an end.

This may have happened in the old days, say the rational expectations theorists, but surely people have learned something from all this experience. Everybody knows that when the Fed sharply increases the monetary growth rate, inflation will result. Business firms, of course, will raise prices. But what about labor? Anticipating the expected inflation, wage-earners will demand wage increases now. No more playing catch-up after the cost of living has already risen.

If wage rates are increased along with prices, do profits increase? No! If profits are not rising, there goes the main reason for increasing output and hiring more people—which, of course, was why the rate of monetary growth was raised in the first place.

Let's return to the rational expectations theorists' three assumptions. The first one is plausible enough—that through experience, we learn to anticipate the consequences of changes in monetary and fiscal policy. So, if a sharp increase in the rate of growth of the money supply always leads to inflation, eventually we will all learn to recognize this pattern. (See the box, "Rational Expectations versus Adaptive Expectations.")

Rational Expectations versus Adaptive Expectations

How do we predict the future? The simplest way is to assume that past trends will continue. The *adaptive expectations hypothesis* is based on the assumption that the best indicator of the future is what happened in the past.

Suppose the price level has been rising at an annual rate of 6 percent for the last three years. Under adaptive expectations, people will expect prices to rise about 6 percent in year 4. Now let's add a wrinkle. Suppose that in year 4 the rate of inflation rises to 9 percent. So what rate of inflation do people now predict for year 5? They predict 9 percent. Well, suppose that in year 5 it rises to 14 percent. What will everyone predict for year 6? Fourteen percent? Fine. Except that in year 6 it goes down to 10 percent. So for year 7 everyone predicts 10 percent. But in year 7 the inflation rate falls to just 5 percent.

Under adaptive expectations, forecasts of the future rate of inflation may be right on the money, but they may also exhibit systematic error. When inflation is accelerating, forecasts will tend to be too low. And when inflation is decelerating (that is, disinflation is taking place), then forecasts will tend to be too high.

The *rational expectations hypothesis* makes the assumption that people do not keep making the same mistakes over and over again when predicting future events. After getting burned once or twice, they do not systematically keep assuming that past trends will necessarily continue into the future.

The rational expectations hypothesis assumes that future expectations are based not just on past trends but on an understanding of how the economy works. For example, to form their expectation of the inflation rate, decision makers will use all available information, including past inflation rates, the impact of expected policy actions and their knowledge of macroeconomic relationships within our economy.

So which hypothesis is right—rational expectations or adaptive expectations? To the degree that people have a sense of how our economy operates—and to the degree that they don't just blindly assume that past trends will continue into the future—the rational expectations hypothesis appears to have greater validity. But it falls far short of its adherents' claim that it is so powerful that it nullifies descretionary monetary and fiscal policy.

It would follow from the next two assumptions that the intended results of macroeconomic policy shifts will be completely frustrated. Why? If you knew that prices would be increasing, would you be willing to sit back and passively accept a decline in your standard of living? Wouldn't you demand a higher wage rate to keep pace with rising prices? The rational expectations theorists say people can always be expected to promote their personal economic interests, and furthermore, in a purely competitive market, they are free to do so.

Most macroeconomic policy changes, say the rational expectations theorists, are readily predictable. When there's inflation, there are extended debates in Congress, demands for cuts in government spending and tax increases, and a slowdown in the rate of monetary growth. Both Congress and the Federal Reserve generally telegraph policy moves, often months in advance. So when these moves are made, no one is surprised. And because the public anticipates these policy changes, their intended effects are canceled out by the actions taken by individuals and business firms to protect their economic interests. In the case of policies aimed at raising output and employment, all the government gets for its efforts is more inflation.

Most macroeconomic policy changes are predictable.

What should the government do? It should do, say the rational expectations theorists, as little as possible. Like the classical economists and the monetarists, they believe the more the government tries to be an economic stabilizing force, the more it will destabilize the economy.

What should the government do?

Basically, then, the federal government should figure out the right policies to follow and stick to them. What *are* the right policies? As you might expect, they've taken up the conservative economists' agenda: (1) steady monetary growth of 3 to 4 percent a year (the monetarists' monetary rule) and (2) a balanced budget (favored by the classical economists, among others).

Criticism of the rational
expectations school

Is it reasonable to expect individuals and business firms to predict the consequences of macroeconomic policy changes correctly when economists themselves come up with widely varying predictions, most of which are wrong? Economists place little faith in each other's rationality; is it rational for them to ascribe a greater prescience to the general population than they give themselves?

In a world of constant change, is it possible for people to accurately predict the economic consequences of policy changes? Indeed, when a continually changing cast of policy makers, each with his or her own economic agenda, seems to be calling for entirely new economic approaches every few years, it's awfully hard to tell the players without a scorecard. It's even harder to predict the final score.

A second criticism of the rational expectations school is that our economic markets are not purely competitive; some are not competitive at all. Labor unions are not an economist's idea of purely competitive labor market institutions. Nor would industries such as those that produce automobiles, petroleum, cigarettes, and breakfast cereals, each of which has just a handful of firms doing most of the producing, be considered very competitive. How much competition does Microsoft Windows have?

Finally, critics raise the question of the rigidities imposed by contracts. The labor union with the two- or three-year contract cannot reopen bargaining with employers when greater inflation is anticipated because of a suddenly expansionary monetary policy. Nor can business firms that have long-term contracts with customers decide to charge higher prices because they perceive more inflation in the future.

An economist is someone who cannot see something working in practice without asking whether it would work in theory.
—Walter Heller

But this school is correct in calling their attention to how expectations may affect the outcome of macroeconomic policy changes. In recent years, then, economists have become more aware that to the degree policy changes are predictable, people will certainly act to protect their economic interests. Because they will succeed to some degree, they will partially counteract the effect of the government's macroeconomic policy.

This leaves us with a major economic policy disagreement: What should the government do when there's a recession? "Nothing," say the monetarists because policy makers are too incompetent to make the right decision. "Nothing," say the classical economists and the rational expectationists, since the economy will quickly and automatically move back to full employment. But this is definitely a minority view. Most economists today would agree that, since it might take years for our economy to work its way out of a recession, some monetary and fiscal policy actions would need to be taken.

In the event of inflation, this same policy dichotomy would be apparent. Although the monetarists might be somewhat amenable to a large degree of monetary restraint, the classical economists and rational expectationists would again suggest that the government do nothing. But the large majority of economists would again advocate some monetary and fiscal policy actions.

21st Century Economic Theory

In the first few years of the new century we've already had a mild revival of the supply-side school, and the rise of a completely new school of economic thought—economic behaviorism. Here are some preliminary observations.

The Supply-Side Revival?

Despite the fact that he [Labor Secretary John Dunlop] is an economist, basically I have great confidence in him.
—George Meany

By mid-2003 President George W. Bush had signed legislation passed by razor-thin Republican Congressional majorities which cut taxes by at least $2 trillion by the end of the decade. Just as in 1981 when Ronald Reagan signed the massive Kemp-Roth tax cut, the president maintained that the tax cut would spur economic growth, raise tax revenues, and consequently, shrink the federal budget deficit. Is this a resurrection of supply-side economics? Bush administration officials aren't *calling* it supply-side economics, but these tax cuts certainly do pass the smell test.

The basic premise of supply-side economics is that lower marginal tax rates would give people a greater incentive to work. Under President Bush's plan, for example, the top marginal tax rate of 39.6 percent would be cut to 33 percent, while taxpayers in each of the lower brackets—36 percent, 33 percent, 28 percent, and 15 percent—would also receive substantial tax cuts.

The question is: If your marginal tax rate is lowered (enabling you to keep more of your earnings), would you work more hours? The supply-siders say "Yes!"

The Economic Behaviorists

In economics, like in popular music, we often ask ourselves, who's hot and who's not? There's a hot new group of young economists, many of whom are barely out of graduate school and are complete newcomers to the economic theory scene. Their work is just beginning to appear in some of the big economics journals, so it may be a while yet before they work their way up to the top of the charts. They call themselves economic behaviorists, and they're definitely going to hit it big.

Until the behavioral economists arrived upon the scene, a core belief among economists of all schools of thought was that people's actions were guided by rational, unemotional self-interest. So if you won the lottery, you would put most of this money aside for the rest of your life. The behavioral economists observed that most lottery winners quickly spent most or all of their winnings. Maybe not very rational behavior, but very *human* behavior.

The behaviorist view of the business cycle also departs from mainstream economic thinking. When the good times are rolling, most people seem to think that they will continue indefinitely. Remember the stock market boom in the 1990s? People kicked themselves for not putting more of their money in the market. Then, when the market tanked, those who were most heavily invested were the ones kicking themselves. During the economic boom in the late 1990s, many people thought the "new economy" had ushered in permanent prosperity. The national psyche quickly swung from overly optimistic to overly pessimistic in the wake of falling stock prices, the events of 9/11, the 2001 recession, and the slow recovery.

One of the two 2002 Nobel Prize winners in economics was Daniel Kahneman, who is not even an economist. A cognitive psychologist, Kahneman described humans as shortsighted, overconfident in their predictive skills, and irrationally prone to buying insurance on cheap home appliances. The next time a salesperson tries to sell you a three-year warranty on an air conditioner, a vacuum cleaner, or a microwave oven, take Daniel Kahneman's advice and just say no.

In sum, the behavioral economists are not challenging the mainstream beliefs that rational behavior and economic self-interest are important motivators of economic behavior. But they *are* challenging the belief that these are the *only* motivating factors. Their goal is to apply a wider range of psychological concepts to economic theory.

Economics is the only field in which two people can share a Nobel Prize for saying opposing things.

—Roberto Alazar

Conclusion

Murray Weidenbaum, who served as chairman of President Reagan's Council of Economic Advisors, puts a lot of what we've been talking about in this chapter into perspective:

> Each of the major schools of economic thought can be useful on occasion. The insights of Keynesian economics proved appropriate for Western societies attempting to get out of deep depression in the 1930s. The tools of monetarism were powerfully effective in squeezing out the inflationary force of the 1970s. Supply-side economics played an important role in getting the public to understand the high costs of taxation and thus to support tax reform in the 1980s. But sensible public policy cannot long focus on any one objective or be limited to one policy approach.[2]

[2]Murray Weidenbaum, *Rendezvous with Reality* (New York: Basic Books, 1988), p. 23.

Current Issue: Is George W. Bush a Supply-Sider or a Keynesian?

Presidents do not often declare themselves members of any particular economic school, although Richard Nixon did once proclaim, "I am a Keynesian," and Ronald Reagan was a firm adherent of supply-side economics. While President George W. Bush has never said so in as many words, he has clearly placed most of his economic bets on the workings of supply-side economics by presiding over two massive tax cuts during his first term.

You'll recall that John Maynard Keynes advocated spending whatever it takes to bring us out of economic downturns, and indeed a downturn did take place in 2001. Largely in response to the recession, Congress boosted spending significantly in 2001, but spending continued to rise sharply over the next five years even though the recession had ended in November, 2001. Through his first five years in office, Bush did not veto even one congressional spending bill sent for his signature.

So would we call President Bush a supply-sider or a Keynesian? Those tax cuts certainly seem to qualify him as a supply-sider. And the spending he approved in 2001 might qualify him as a Keynesian as well. But Keynes would not have called for the huge spending increases in subsequent nonrecession years. In addition, supply-side economics holds that tax cuts should ultimately lead to reductions in government spending—and definitely not to huge spending *increases*. While President Bush did make supply-side tax cuts as well as Keynesian spending increases, he is neither a supply-sider nor a Keynesian.

Questions for Further Thought and Discussion

1. According to the classical economists, how did Say's law, the interest rate mechanism, and downwardly flexible wages and prices ensure that recessions would cure themselves?

2. According to John Maynard Keynes, what was the basic problem during recessions, and what was his solution?

3. What is the monetary rule and why is it favored by the monetarists?

4. What is the Laffer curve? How do supply-siders use it with respect to tax rates?

5. What are the three basic assumptions of the rational expectations theorists? Are they valid?

6. Is there any consensus among at least some of the different schools of economic thought with respect to the effectiveness of monetary and fiscal policy?

7. How does the crude quantity theory of money differ from the modern, sophisticated version?

8. When a recession begins, if the federal government spent tens of billions of dollars on a highway building program and consequently ran a large deficit, how would this fiscal policy measure be judged by each of the five main schools of 20th century economic thought?

Workbook for Chapter 15

Name _____   Date _____

Multiple-Choice Questions

Circle the letter that corresponds to the best answer.

1. Say's law states that _____.
   a) supply creates its own demand
   b) demand creates its own supply
   c) demand will always exceed supply
   d) supply will always exceed demand

2. According to the classical economists, if the quantity of money that people wanted to save was greater than the amount that people wanted to invest, _____.
   a) there would be a recession
   b) there would be inflation
   c) the interest rate would fall
   d) the interest rate would rise

3. The classical economists believed _____.
   a) both wages and prices were downwardly flexible
   b) neither wages nor prices were downwardly flexible
   c) wages, but not prices, were downwardly flexible
   d) prices, but not wages, were downwardly flexible

4. The classicals believed recessions were _____.
   a) impossible
   b) potential depressions
   c) temporary
   d) hard to end without government intervention

5. The problem during recessions, said John Maynard Keynes, was _____.
   a) inadequate aggregate supply
   b) inadequate aggregate demand
   c) too much inflation
   d) too much government intervention

6. According to Keynes, _____ was necessary to get us out of a depression.
   a) investment spending
   b) consumer spending
   c) foreign spending
   d) any kind of spending

7. Keynes believed budget deficits were _____.
   a) to be avoided at all costs
   b) bad during recessions
   c) good during recessions
   d) good all the time

8. The key to investment spending, said Keynes, was _____.
   a) the interest rate
   b) the expected profit rate
   c) foreign spending
   d) government spending

9. Classical economics lost most of its popularity in _____.
   a) the 1920s   c) the 1960s
   b) the 1930s   d) the 1980s

10. Big government was ushered in during the _____.
   a) 1920s   c) 1960s
   b) 1930s   d) 1980s

11. To the monetarists, the most important thing was _____.
   a) the rate of growth of the money supply
   b) balancing the federal budget
   c) raising the federal government's tax base
   d) giving the Federal Reserve free reign

12. During a recession, if the money supply were increased _____.

    a) the Keynesians and the monetarists agree that people would probably just hold on to these funds

    b) the Keynesians and the monetarists agree that people would spend this money on assets of one kind or another

    c) the Keynesians believe people would probably just hold on to these funds, while the monetarists believe people would spend this money on assets of one kind or another

13. Which of the following is a basic proposition of monetarism?

    a) The key to stable economic growth is a constant rate of increase in the money supply.

    b) Expansionary monetary policy will permanently depress the interest rates.

    c) Expansionary monetary policy will permanently reduce the unemployment rate.

    d) Expansionary fiscal policy will permanently raise output and employment.

14. The monetary rule states that _____.

    a) the federal budget must be balanced every year

    b) the money supply must increase at the same rate as the price level

    c) the money supply must remain a constant from year to year

    d) the money supply must be increased at a constant rate

15. The monetarists criticized _____.

    a) the stop-and-go policies of the Federal Reserve

    b) the ineffectiveness of monetary policy at fighting inflation

    c) the importance given to money by the Keynesians

    d) the Fed for keeping a heavy foot on the monetary brake and allowing the money supply to rise by only 3 percent a year

16. Supply-siders felt _____.

    a) the federal government played too large an economic role

    b) the federal government played too small an economic role

    c) tax rates were too low

    d) the federal government was not spending enough to meet the needs of the poor

17. According to the supply-siders, each of the following resulted from high marginal tax rates except _____.

    a) the work effect

    b) the savings-investment effect

    c) the elimination of productive market exchanges

    d) lagging demand for imported goods and services

18. According to the Laffer curve, when very high marginal tax rates are lowered, tax revenue will _____.

    a) decline considerably   c) stay the same

    b) decline slightly   d) increase

19. The rational expectations theorists said anti-inflationary policy will _____.

    a) generally work

    b) definitely do more harm than good

    c) either do no good or do harm

20. According to the rational expectations theorists, everyone learns that when the Fed sharply increases monetary growth _____.

    a) inflation will result and people must move to protect themselves

    b) a recession will result and people must move to protect themselves

    c) people will continue to make the same mistakes over and over again

21. The effects of most macroeconomic policy changes, say the rational expectations theorists, are _____.

    a) very hard to predict

    b) very easy to predict

    c) slow—that is, they take place over a period of many years

    d) irrational

22. The advice the rational expectations theorists give the federal government is to _____.

    a) change macropolicy often

    b) figure out the right policies to follow and stick to them

    c) figure out what the public is expecting and then do the opposite

23. Which school would advocate government spending to end a recession?
    a) Classical
    b) Keynesian
    c) Monetarist
    d) Supply-side
    e) Rational expectations

24. Which school would consider cutting tax rates as the cure for all our economic ills?
    a) Classical
    b) Keynesian
    c) Monetarist
    d) Supply-side
    e) Rational expectations

25. MV = PQ _____.
    a) all the time
    b) most of the time
    c) some of the time
    d) never

26. If MV rises, PQ _____.
    a) must rise
    b) may rise
    c) must stay the same
    d) must fall

27. The crude quantity theory of money states that if M rises by 20 percent, P will _____.
    a) fall by 20 percent
    b) fall
    c) stay the same
    d) rise
    e) rise by 20 percent

28. The modern monetarists believe _____.
    a) V is very unstable
    b) V never changes
    c) any changes in V are either very small or predictable
    d) if M rises, V will fall by the same percentage

29. As we approach full employment, what will probably happen?
    a) V will fall
    b) Q will fall
    c) Q will rise
    d) P will rise
    e) P will fall

30. Each of the following explains why wages are not downwardly flexible *except* _____.
    a) the efficiency wage theory
    b) the law of diminishing returns
    c) the insider-outsider theory
    d) labor contracts
    e) the minimum wage

31. The rational expectationists believe that fiscal and monetary policy are _____.
    a) most effective fighting recessions
    b) most effective fighting inflation
    c) more effective in influencing aggregate supply than aggregate demand
    d) not effective

32. The behaviorial economists believe that economic behavior is guided _____.
    a) entirely by rational, unemotional self-interest
    b) entirely by emotions
    c) by both rational self-interest and emotions
    d) by neither rational self-interest nor emotions

33. Which is the most accurate statement about President George W. Bush's economic policies?
    a) They are pure supply-side.
    b) They are pure Keynesian.
    c) They are pure monetarist.
    d) They are pure classical.
    e) They have some elements of supply-side and some elements of Keynesian economics.

Fill-In Questions

1. According to the classical economists, if there is a recession, the government should _____.

2. The classicals, applying Say's law, believed all our income would be _____; all our production would be _____; and all our savings would be _____.

3. The classicals said if the amount of money people wanted to save was greater than the amount businesspeople wanted to invest, _____ _____.

4. According to Keynes, the main institutional barriers to downward wage and price flexibility were (1) _____ and (2) _____.

5. Milton Friedman is a leader of the _____ school.

6. John Maynard Keynes said that during recessions and depressions, the main problem was _____ _____.

7. To solve that problem, Keynes suggested _____ _____.

8. Monetarism begins and ends with one obsession: _____.

9. Milton Friedman concluded that we have never had a serious inflation that was not accompanied by _____.

10. The monetarists believed that if the money supply were raised during a recession, people would _____.

11. According to the monetarists, recessions are caused by _____.

12. The key to stable economic growth, according to the monetarists, is _____.

13. The monetarists say expansionary monetary policy will _____ depress interest rates and the unemployment rate. They further say expansionary monetary policy will _____ raise output and employment.

14. The objective of supply-side economics is to _____ _____. The problem, said the supply-siders, was that _____ were hurting the incentive to work and invest.

15. The way to get people to work more, say the supply-siders, is to _____.

16. According to the Laffer curve, reducing very high marginal tax rates will result in _____ federal tax revenue.

17. Most macroeconomic policy changes, say the rational expectations theorists, are _____ _____.

18. The main criticism leveled at the rational expectations theorists is that _____ _____.

Problems

1. If M were 600 and V were 10, how much would PQ be?

2. According to the crude quantity theory of money, if M were to increase by 10 percent, what would happen to V, P, and Q?

3. If M were 800, P were 20, and Q were 400, how much would V be?

4. Initially M = 600, V = 8, P = 16, and Q = 300. According to the crude quantity theory of money, if M rose to 720, how much would P be?

5. If P were 7 and Q were 800, how much would MV be?

Appendix

A Guide to Macropolicy

The three main goals of macropolicy are stable prices, high employment, and a satisfactory rate of economic growth. All economists agree to these goals; they disagree about the means of achieving them.

APPENDIX OBJECTIVES

After you have read this appendix, you will have a better understanding of:

- Conventional fiscal and monetary policy to fight recession.
- Conventional fiscal and monetary policies to fight inflations.

- How to fight inflationary recessions.
- Fiscal and monetary policy lags.
- The limits of macropolicy.

Conventional Macropolicy

Is it possible, then, to formulate conventional economic policy to fight recessions and inflation? As you know, it would be impossible to obtain unanimous agreement for *any* given policy. But a majority of economists, with varying degrees of enthusiasm, would go along with the conventional fiscal and monetary policies summarized below.

Fighting Recessions

We're going to talk about the conventional fiscal and monetary policies that are advocated by most economists. But as we saw in the last chapter, a significant minority opinion—especially among the monetarists and rational expectationists—runs counter to the majority opinion on macropolicy. So if you happen to disagree with conventional fiscal and monetary policy, just grit your teeth, work your way through the next few pages, and be thankful that they will be short.

Conventional Fiscal Policy

The most conventional fiscal policy for fighting a recession is to run a budget deficit. Indeed, given the automatic stabilizers as well as our tax laws, deficits are virtually inevitable during recessions.

Run deficits to fight recessions.

Conventional Monetary Policy

Speed up M growth to fight recessions.

Were we to enter a recession, the conventional monetary policy would be to speed up the rate of growth of the money supply. Here we need to be careful: If we were to speed it up too much, we would have to worry about an inflation and possibly rising interest rates, which, in time, would kill off any recovery.

Two Policy Dilemmas

1. Huge budget deficits are financed by massive borrowings by the Treasury. As the economy begins to recover, business and consumer borrowing picks up as well. What does all this loan demand do to interest rates? It drives them up. And when interest rates, which were high even during the recession, rise still higher in the early stages of recovery, what happens next? The recovery collapses.

   Thus, a budget deficit, designed to stimulate the economy, necessitates massive Treasury borrowing, driving up interest rates and ultimately choking off recovery. Is there any way to resolve this dilemma? How about gradually reducing the deficit as the recovery progresses?

2. Let's consider rapid monetary growth. It stimulates recovery, making funds available to business firms and consumers. Interest rates may decline. So far, so good. But when we increase the money supply this rapidly, we also court inflation, and with inflation, people will demand more interest for their savings. With inflation and higher interest rates, it won't be long before the recovery sputters to a stop.

   Can you think of a way out of this dilemma? We could try to reduce the rate of monetary growth as recovery begins to set in.

Fighting Inflation

Conventional Fiscal Policy

To fight inflation, reduce the deficit.

To fight inflation, we would immediately want to try to reduce the size of the federal budget deficit—if we happen to be running one. It would be too much of a shock to reduce it too quickly, but in the face of persistent inflation, we would need to reduce the deficit year by year and ultimately run budget surpluses.

Conventional Monetary Policy

To fight inflation, slow the rate of M growth.

The obvious policy move here would be to slow down the rate of growth of the money supply, indeed; if inflation were beginning to rage out of control, not only would the Fed have to stop the money supply from growing, but it would have to cause it to contract slightly.

Fighting Inflationary Recessions: Two More Policy Dilemmas

Some people think of inflations and recessions as separate problems. They once were. However, beginning with the recession in 1957–58, the price level has risen during every recession. To add insult to injury, during three of the most recent recessions, 1973–75, 1980, and 1981–82, inflation was of double-digit proportions.

Let's review conventional fiscal policy to fight recession and inflation. To fight recession, we run budget deficits; to fight inflation, we run surpluses. Very well, then, what do we do to fight an inflationary recession? That's one dilemma.

We'll go on to the second dilemma. What is the conventional monetary policy to fight a recession? It's to speed up the rate of monetary growth. And to fight an inflation? Slow it down.

Here's the million-dollar question: How do we fight an inflation and a recession simultaneously using conventional fiscal and monetary policy? The answer: We can't.

Don't give up; there *is* hope.

One approach would be to try a combination of tight money to fight the inflation and a large budget deficit to provide the economic stimulus needed to fight the recession. We kind of stumbled onto this combination during the recession of 1981–82, but not until the Fed eased up on the tight money part did the economy finally begin to recover. By then, much of the inflation had been wrung from the economy.

This suggests a second approach. First deal with the inflation, then cure the recession. In the early 1950s the United States suffered from a surge of inflation brought on by the Korean War. Three recessions occurred over the course of just eight years. By the end of the third recession, the consumer price index was virtually stable. Then, through almost the entire decade of the 1960s, the economy went through a recession-free expansion.

Conventional monetary and fiscal policy tools are sufficient to deal with simple recessions or inflations, but inflationary recessions pose additional problems. Conventional macropolicy cannot cure them without a great deal of suffering, especially by those who lose their jobs, their businesses, and even their homes.

> Conventional policies are not ideal for fighting inflationary recessions.

Fiscal and Monetary Policy Lags

The Lags

Timing, in economic policy as in most other areas, is of utmost importance. The effectiveness of both monetary and fiscal policy depends greatly on timing. Unfortunately, both of these policies are subject to three lags: the recognition, decision, and impact lags.

> Recognition, decision, and impact lags.

Suppose our economy enters a recession and the government provides a counteracting stimulus. What if this stimulus does not have full impact until recovery has set in? The end result of this well-intentioned government policy will be to destabilize the economy by making the recovery and subsequent prosperity far too exuberant. Similarly, if the government were to try to damp down an inflation, but the effects of its policy were not felt until the economy had already entered a recession, the policy would end up making the recession that much worse.

The recognition lag is the time it takes for policy makers to realize that a business cycle's turning point has been passed, or that either inflation or unemployment has become a particular problem. The decision lag is the time it takes for policy makers to decide what to do and to take action. And finally, the impact lag is the time it takes for the policy action to have a substantial effect. The whole process may take anywhere from about nine months to more than three years.

Fiscal Policy Lags

The lengths of the three lags under fiscal policy are not well defined. First, the recognition lag is the time it takes the president and a majority of both houses of Congress to recognize that something is broken and needs fixing—either an inflation or a recession. You would be amazed at how long this can take. In August 1981 we entered a recession, but in the spring of the following year President Reagan still could not bring himself to admit that we were actually in a recession (which, incidentally, proved to be the worst downturn since the Great Depression).

> First, the president and Congress must recognize that there is a problem.

Congress, which at the time was divided between a Republican Senate and a Democratic House, also took some time to recognize the problem. This state of affairs was similar to that of 1967; inflation was beginning to get out of hand, but the president and Congress were reluctant to recognize the obvious.

Once the president *and* Congress recognize that something needs to be done about the economy, they must decide what action to take. After investigating the problem with his advisers, the president may make a fiscal policy recommendation to Congress. This recommendation, among others, is studied by appropriate subcommittees and committees, hearings are held, expert witnesses called, votes taken. Eventually bills may be passed by both houses, reconciled by a joint House-Senate committee, repassed by both houses, and sent to the president for his signature. This process usually takes several months. Finally, if the president likes the bill, he signs it. (If he doesn't, Congress may override his veto, but it usually doesn't.)

All this delay is part of the decision lag. We still have the impact lag. Once a spending bill, say a highway reconstruction measure, has been passed for the purpose of stimulating an economy that is mired in recession, a year may pass before the bulk of the appropriated funds is actually spent and has made a substantial economic impact. By then, of course, the country may already have begun to recover from the recession.

Monetary Policy Lags

One would expect monetary policy time lags to be somewhat shorter than fiscal policy time lags. The Board of Governors, which always has at least three or four professional economists among its membership, continually monitors the economy. Further, because the Board has only seven members, with the chair playing the dominant role, a consensus with respect to policy changes is reached far more easily than it is under our political method of conducting fiscal policy. While the legislative wrangling among the members of each house of Congress, between the two houses, and between the president and Congress may take several months, consensus among the seven members of the Fed is reached relatively quickly. The decision lag is thus fairly short.

How long is the impact lag—the time until monetary policy changes have a substantial effect? Economists estimate this time as anywhere from nine months to about three years. Further, there is some agreement that a tight money policy will slow down an inflation more quickly than an easy money policy will hasten a recovery. Still, there is no general agreement on whether monetary policy or fiscal policy is faster—or more effective.

While the goals of monetary policy and fiscal policy are identical—low unemployment and stable prices—the effects of each are felt in different economic sectors. Fiscal policy is generally directed toward the consumer sector (tax cuts) or the government sector (spending programs). Monetary policy, however, has its strongest impact on the investment sector. In brief, tight money discourages investment, and a rapidly growing money supply has the opposite effect. The only question, then, is how long it takes before the investment sector feels the impact of monetary policy changes.

Corporate investment does not fall off precipitously when the interest rate rises, nor does it shoot up when the interest rate falls. Although investment in plant and equipment becomes more attractive when the interest rate declines, as a rule large corporations take months, and sometimes years, to formulate investment plans. Therefore, transitory changes in the availability of investment funds or the rate of interest do not have a substantial impact on the level of investment in the short run. However, over a two- or three-year period, it's another story.

During a period of inflation, the proper monetary policy for the Fed to pursue is to slow down or even halt the growth of the money supply. But what if, by the time this is done and has had any impact, the economy has already entered a recession? Clearly it will make that recession even worse.

During a period of recession, what is the proper monetary policy? To speed up the rate of growth of the money supply. But suppose that by the time this policy has had any impact, recovery has begun? Oh no! Now this monetary expansion will fuel the next round of inflation.

To sum up, because of the recognition lag, the decision lag, and especially the impact lag, monetary policy is too slow to have its intended effect. By the time the monetary brakes are working to halt an inflation, the economy may have already entered a recession; and when an expansionary monetary policy is pursued to bring the economy out of a recession, recovery has already set in. Thus, because of the time lags, monetary policy may actually destabilize the economy. The Fed surely did not intend to have that effect, but the road to economic instability is often paved with good intentions.

The Limits of Macropolicy

There is no question that the federal government can easily alter the course of our economy; but during the last decade, substantial changes took place that sharply limited its power. The internationalization of our economy has completely altered the rules of the macroeconomic policy game.

Marc Levinson noted these changes:

> International capital flows ... have made it much more difficult for the central bank to plot the nation's monetary course.
>
> Suppose, for example, that the Fed wants to boost the economy's growth rate. When international capital flows were small, the central bank could stimulate borrowing by pumping up the money supply or cutting the discount rate. But now, lower real interest rates will spur investors to move their capital out of dollar-denominated investments. Economists can't even begin to estimate the likely extent of those capital flows.[1]

Levinson's analysis is supported by that of Kenichi Ohmae, who reasons that if the Fed tightens the money supply and pushes up interest rates, money will flow in from abroad, attracted by our relatively high interest rates. This will frustrate the tight-money and high-interest-rate objectives of the Fed, and, in effect, render the traditional instruments of monetary policy obsolete.[2]

As our economy becomes even more closely integrated into the world economy—a topic we'll pursue in the last two chapters in this book—it is clear that macropolicy will become less important. Still, while macropolicy may no longer be the only economic game in town, it is still, by far, the biggest game.

There is another limitation to macropolicy: our huge and growing deficits. Should we need to fight a new recession, can we cut taxes still further and push federal government spending even higher? Will members of Congress allow the deficit to reach 7 or 8 percent of GDP? When the last recession struck in early 2001, we actually had been running a budget surplus. It was a lot easier in 2001 to cut taxes and raise government spending than it would be when the deficit is $500 billion. Such a large deficit will limit our fiscal policy options when the next recession begins.

Question for Further Thought and Discussion

Outline the conventional monetary and fiscal policies for fighting an inflation. Then outline the conventional monetary and fiscal policies for fighting a recession. Why would an inflationary recession pose a dilemma for those who would attempt to apply conventional monetary and fiscal policies?

---

[1]Marc Levinson, "Economic Policy: The Old Tools Won't Work," *Dun's Business Month*, January 1987, pp. 30–33.

[2]Kenichi Ohmae, *The Borderless World* (New York: HarperCollins, 1990), p. xi.

Workbook for Appendix to Chapter 15

Name _____   Date _____

Multiple-Choice Questions

Circle the letter that corresponds to the best answer.

1. The conventional fiscal policy to fight a recession would be to _____.
   a) increase the rate of monetary growth
   b) decrease the rate of monetary growth
   c) run budget deficits
   d) run budget surpluses

2. The conventional monetary policy to fight inflation would be to _____.
   a) increase the rate of monetary growth
   b) decrease the rate of monetary growth
   c) run budget deficits
   d) run budget surpluses

3. One problem or dilemma we might face in fighting a recession is that _____.
   a) we might end up with budget surpluses
   b) output might rise too quickly
   c) interest rates might fall
   d) interest rates might rise

4. During recessions, we want _____.
   a) budget deficits and faster monetary growth
   b) budget deficits and slower monetary growth
   c) budget surpluses and faster monetary growth
   d) budget surpluses and slower monetary growth

5. During inflations, we want _____.
   a) budget deficits and faster monetary growth
   b) budget deficits and slower monetary growth
   c) budget surpluses and faster monetary growth
   d) budget surpluses and slower monetary growth

6. Which statement is true?
   a) In recent years inflation and recession have become separate problems.
   b) In recent years inflation and recession have become related problems.
   c) Inflation and recession have never been related problems.
   d) Inflation and recession have always been related problems.

7. In recent years macropolicy has _____.
   a) become more powerful
   b) become less powerful
   c) remained about as powerful as it was 15 years ago

8. Each of the following is a policy lag except the _____ lag.
   a) psychological   c) recognition
   b) impact   d) decision

9. The lags under fiscal policy are _____ the lags under monetary policy.
   a) more clearly defined than
   b) as well defined as
   c) less defined than

Fill-In Questions

1. The three main goals of macropolicy are
   (1) _____; (2) _____
   _____; and (3) _____.

2. The conventional fiscal policy to fight a recession is to _____ while the conventional monetary policy is to _____.

3. The conventional fiscal policy to fight an inflation is to _____, while the conventional monetary policy is to _____ _____.

4. One problem with both expansionary monetary and fiscal policies used to fight recessions is that they could lead to _____ _____.

5. The dilemma of fighting an inflationary recession with conventional fiscal policy would be _____ _____.

6. The dilemma of fighting an inflationary recession with conventional monetary policy would be _____ _____.

Chapter 16

Economic Growth and Productivity

The American worker has long been among the most productive in the world, turning out relatively large amounts of goods or services per hour. Our hourly output has been growing rapidly since the mid-1990s. The McKinsey Global Institute breaks the economy down into 60 sectors. U.S. workers are the most productive on Earth in at least 50 sectors. This, in turn, has driven our rate of economic growth, making us among the fastest growing mature economies in the world.

But there have been some very serious problems. Our extremely low savings rate has forced us to borrow some $2 billion dollars a day from foreigners to finance not just our federal budget and trade deficits, but also much of our investment in new plant and equipment. The quality of our labor force has declined in recent years, which reflects a failing educational system. And as globalization proceeds, there is growing concern about the migration of high-skilled, well-paying jobs, mainly to China, India, and other developing countries.

Our problems pale in comparison with those of the less developed countries of Asia, Africa, and Latin America. They are just beginning the journey to development that we undertook more than two centuries ago. But, unlike us, they are beginning from a base of such abject poverty that many of them may never get far.

CHAPTER OBJECTIVES

In this chapter your objective is to understand:

- Economic growth in the United States: The record.
- The role of productivity.
- The reasons our productivity growth has varied.
- The roles of savings, capital, and technology.
- The declining quality of our labor force.
- Economic growth in the less developed countries.
- The Malthusian theory of population.
- Baumol's Disease.

The Industrial Revolution and American Economic Development

Prior to the Industrial Revolution, about two and a half centuries ago, one generation lived about as well as the next—or as badly. Except for a few rich families, almost everyone was poor. Throughout the world, you were lucky if you had the basics—three square meals a day, some homespun clothes on your back, and a thatched roof over your head.

Economic Growth during the Last Millennium

For most of the last millennium, growth in world output per head averaged little more than 0.1 percent a year. But that growth accelerated to 1.2 percent a year around 1800. The accompanying chart shows that world GDP today is more than 30 times as great as it was 1,000 years ago.

The Industrial Revolution set off this great burst of sustained economic growth. But until the mid-20th century nearly all this growth was confined to Europe, the United States, Canada Australia, New Zealand, and Japan.

Source: The Economist, September 23, 2000, p. 7.

If you were *really* lucky, you might live to see your old age, which began around your 40th birthday. You lived and died within a few miles of where you were born, you spent most of your time farming, and you were illiterate. About the only good thing in life before the Industrial Revolution was that you never had to worry about finding a parking space.

The Industrial Revolution made possible sustained economic growth and rising living standards for the first time in history.

The Industrial Revolution made possible sustained economic growth and rising living standards for the first time in history (see the accompanying box, "Economic Growth during the Last Millennium"). The steam engine, the factory system, mass production, the mechanized cotton spindle, the blast furnace (for smelting iron), railroads, and scores of other innovations ushered in a massive increase in productivity and output.

Although living standards in the industrializing nations of Western Europe and in the United States rose steadily, not until the 1920s did the age of mass consumption truly arrive. Homes were electrified; electric appliances, telephones, and cars became commonplace; and most working people were even beginning to enjoy increasing amounts of leisure time. After the Great Depression and World War II, the industrialized nations were able to pick up where they had left off in 1930, and by 1990 living standards in most of these countries had tripled. Chapter 1 of this book traced American economic development over the last two centuries.

Starting in 1780, England needed 58 years to double its per capita GDP. The American industrial revolution following the Civil War was a bit faster, with per capita output doubling in 47 years. Beginning in 1885, Japan doubled its per capita GDP in 34 years.

But borrowing heavily on earlier technology and making use of a great influx of Japanese capital, South Korea doubled its per capita output in just 11 years, starting in 1966. And now, China is roaring along with its own industrial revolution, doubling its per capita output every 10 years.

The Industrial Revolution, which began in England around the middle of the 18th century, entered its second phase in America in the early years of the 20th century. It was based on the mass production of cars, electrical machinery, steel, oil, and chemicals. But in the last three decades, the third phase of the Industrial Revolution has taken hold in Japan, Western Europe, and newly industrialized countries of Southeast Asia, as well as in the United States. This phase is based largely on consumer electronics, computer systems, communications systems, computer software, and advances in manufacturing processes. Since the early 1990s we have been in the fourth phase of the Industrial Revolution—the information age. During this period nearly all business firms and most homes in the world's richest countries have been computerized.

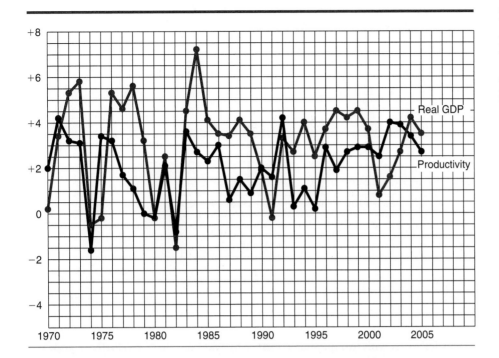

F*igure* 1

Annual Percentage Change in Productivity and Real GDP, 1970–2005

Source: Economic Report of the President, 2006; www.bls.gov/ news.release/prod2t01.htm.

The Record of Productivity Growth

In an extensive study of American economic growth over the 1929–82 period, Edward Denison attributed about half our growth to added inputs of labor and capital and the rest to increased productivity.[1] The main source of productivity growth was advances in knowledge obtained through research and development. A second major source was improvements in the quality of labor, primarily the consequence of improvements in education and training.

Productivity is output per unit of input. For example, a telephone switchboard operator handles 100 calls per hour. So the output is 100 calls handled, and input is one hour of labor. If, one year later, the switchboard operator handles 103 calls per hour, his productivity has grown 3 percent.

The faster our productivity grows, the faster our output, or real GDP will grow. (This relationship is shown in Figure 1.) New ways of doing things can sometimes drastically boost productivity. Before we began shipping freight in standard-sized containers in the 1960s, it would take 300 longshoremen 10 days to unload a large freighter. Today it takes 30 longshoremen just one and a half days to do the same job. Another example: I'm old enough to remember the photocopy machines that looked liked elongated toasters. You'd place the page to be copied in one slot and about 30 seconds later it would emerge from the other slot. And your copy would emerge from a third slot at the same time. Of course you'd have to wait another minute or so for that copy to dry. And if you weren't careful, you'd get chemicals all over your original. That happened to my friend when he tried to make a copy of a ten-dollar bill and it turned brown. Today, machines make hundreds of copies in a minute. So we could say that the productivity of photocopy machines—and longshoremen as well—has improved by several thousand percent since the 1950s.

Figure 2 provides a summary of productivity growth since the mid-1960s. As you'll notice, it lagged considerably from the mid-1970s through the mid-1990s.

One may also question whether our measure of productivity is all that accurate to begin with. Stephen S. Roach, chief economist for Morgan Stanley, has noted that the Labor Department reports that the average work-week has been virtually constant at 35.5 hours since 1988. But with the advent of laptops, cell phones, and personal digital

---

[1]Edward S. Denison, *Accounting for Slower Economic Growth* (Washington, D.C.: Brookings Institution, 1979).

Figure 2

Annual Productivity Percentage
Increase, 10-Year Periods,
1966–2005
*Source: Economic Report of the
President,* 2006.

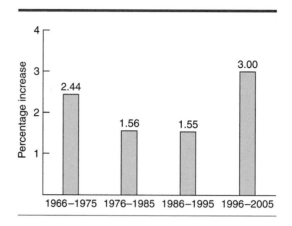

assistants, many information workers are on call 24/7. If the Labor Department is ignoring these extra, out of the office, hours that so many millions of workers are putting in, then it is overestimating productivity growth.

This leaves us with two questions. First, why was our rate of productivity growth so low from the mid-1970s through the mid-1990s? And second, why did it pick up again in the mid-1990s?

How Saving and Investment Affect Productivity Growth

We're looking for the factors that depressed our productivity growth from the mid-1970s through the early 1990s, and we're looking for those factors that pushed up our productivity growth beginning in the mid-1990s.

Low savings rate means low
productivity growth.

Our Low Savings Rate   There is no one clear reason why our rate of productivity increase slowed in the 1970s and 1980s, but a reason singled out by many economists is our low savings rate. Americans have been poor savers for generations, but through most years of the 1950s, 1960s, and 1970s, we still managed to put away around 7 to 8 percent of disposable income. This changed in the 1980s, however, when savings averaged just 5.4 percent of disposable income. In the second half of the 1990s it declined steadily, falling below 0 in 2005.

As a nation, we're spending more than we're earning. We made up the difference by borrowing from foreigners, taking out home equity loans, running up credit card debt, or digging in our savings. It boggles the mind that in a relatively poor country like China, people can save one quarter of their income, but in our own relatively rich country, we can't even make ends meet.

The generations that came of
age in the 1980s and 1990s
have not done as well as their
parents' generations.

Why do Americans save so little? Much of the blame is placed on the generations that came of age over the last few decades, whose rallying cries were, "Shop till you drop," "Born to Shop," and "I want it all and I want it now!" Their sense of entitlement was fostered by indulgent parents who did not want their children to go without. And, of course, the parents, themselves, did not go without either. The members of the baby-boom generation, unlike their middle-aged predecessors, have saved very little of their disposable incomes.

Although their savings rate is extremely low, Americans are putting away hundreds of billions for their retirement in the form of 401Ks, IRAs, and mutual funds, as well as the purchase of individual corporate stocks and bonds. Most of this does not count as personal savings, but a large chunk of these funds find their way into corporate investment.

Gross saving = personal +
business + government saving

Personal savings is just one part of the total amount saved by Americans, which we call *gross saving* (see Figure 3). Businesses save as well as does the government

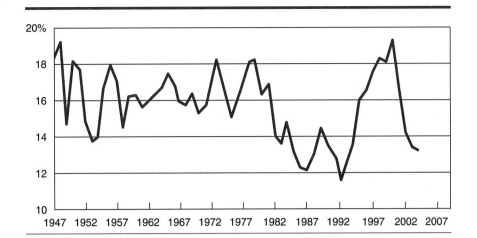

Figure 3
U.S. Gross Savings Rate: Gross
Saving as a Percentage of GDP,
1947–2005
For most of this period our gross
savings has been in the 14–18
percent range. There was a
downward trend from 1977 through
1992, an upward trend from 1993
to 2000, and a sharp downward
trend since then.
*Source: Economic Report of the
President,* 2001; Survey of Current
Business, March 2005.

(I'm lumping together the federal, state, and local governments). Businesses save money through retained earnings (that is, profits plowed back into the business), but most of their savings is in the form of depreciation (or capital consumption) allowances (which we talked about in Chapter 6). These funds are used to replace the plant and equipment that have worn out or become obsolete, and they are also used to purchase additional plant and equipment.

The federal government ran budget deficits from 1970 through 1997, while the state and local governments generally ran surpluses. Beginning in the late 1970s, the federal deficits far outweighed the state and local surpluses, so the government contribution to the gross savings rate became a big minus.

As we noted back in Chapter 7, the massive federal budget deficits of the early 1990s fell during the rest of the decade, and by 1998 we were running surpluses. But soon after the new millennium began things took a turn for the worse. In short order the stock market tanked, the telecommunications-led boom became a bust, a recession set in, and, of course, there were the terrorist attacks of 9/11. Although the economy did slowly recover from the recession, the federal, state, and local government surpluses disappeared, and by 2003, we were running a combined deficit of over $400 billion.

What does our gross savings rate look like? In Figure 4 you can see an unmistakable downward trend from the late 1970s to the early 1990s, and then an apparent reversal beginning in 1993. But since the beginning of the new millenium there has been another downward trend. Not only are we running huge and growing federal budget deficits but our lagging personal savings rate actually became negative in 2005.

Because we save so little, we generate a very low flow of funds for investment. Since the late 1990s we've been running huge trade deficits and foreigners have been recycling most of the dollars we sent them by making investments in the United States. Our investment is consequently much higher than it would otherwise have been due to this influx of dollars from abroad. For foreigners, the key attraction of investing in the United States is the relatively high interest rates that we pay.

Foreign investors have been attracted by our high interest rates.

Our Low Rate of Investment   To increase our output at a satisfactory rate, we need to keep replacing worn-out and obsolete capital with the most up-to-date and technologically advanced plant and equipment. And we need not only to replace the capital that we've cast off, but also to keep increasing our capital stock.

Do you recall the production possibilities curves from Chapter 2? Figure 4 reproduces a few of them. The production possibilities curve provides a snapshot of our economy at full employment producing just two types of goods. Here they're capital goods and consumer goods. A country that devotes a higher proportion of its resources to capital goods than to consumer goods will grow faster than another country that initially has the same production possibilities curve but emphasizes consumer goods.

*F*igure **4**

Capital Spending and Economic Growth

Panels A and B show identical production possibility curves in 1994. If a nation allocates its production of capital goods and consumer goods at point A of panel A, in 10 years it will be at PPC$_{2004}$. If it allocates its production of capital goods and consumer goods at point B of panel B, in 10 years it will be at much higher PPC$_{2004}$.

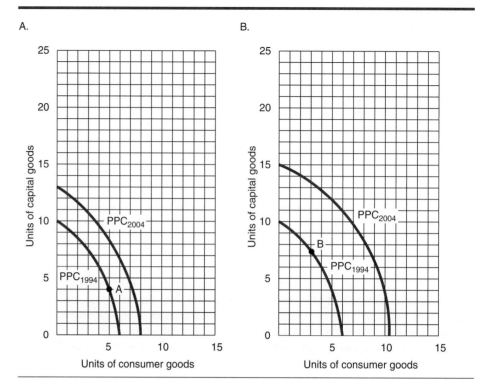

As you can see, the country shown in Figure 4B has a much higher rate of growth than the one in Figure 4A. And the reason why it has enjoyed this relatively high growth should be obvious. Perhaps the two countries in question are the United States and China (leaving aside the fact that China's economy is just a fraction of the size of ours). The lesson our nation must learn is that until we begin to devote more resources to capital goods production and less to consumer goods production, our growth rate will be lower than it would have otherwise been.

We have depended on foreign investors to provide us with some of *their* savings. And where did they get all those dollars? We supplied them ourselves by running massive trade deficits in recent years. As long as foreigners are willing to accept our dollars in payment for these trade deficits and to send most of them back to us in the form of investment, we can keep our financial heads above water. But as long-time Federal Reserve Chairman Alan Greenspan has repeatedly warned, foreigners will not be willing to accommodate us forever.

How Labor Force Changes Affect Productivity Growth

In 1870, American, German, French, Japanese, and British workers averaged nearly 3,000 hours a year on the job. Now it is less than 2,000 hours, with much of the decline having come since World War II. How does our labor force stack up against those of the rest of the industrial world? Are we growing flabby and complacent? Some things are easier to measure than others, so we'll start with the easiest: the declining average workweek.

(1) The Average Workweek and Workyear

The average workweek has declined from 60 hours in 1900 to less than 35 hours by the mid-1970s. Today most people put in the standard nine-to-five (or eight-to-four) with an hour for lunch. Until the 1920s most Americans were putting in a six-day week. From there we went to a standard Monday-to-Friday plus half a day on Saturday, and finally, by the late 1940s, we got it down to the five-day week.

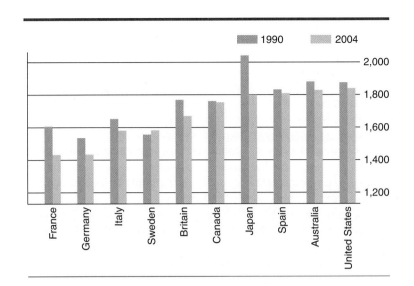

Figure 5

Average Number of Hours per Employed Person in Selected Countries, 1990 and 2004
Two things stand out here. First, in each of these countries, the average person worked fewer hours in 2004 than in 1990. And second, Americans worked longer hours than workers of each of the other countries. Indeed, the average American worker put in almost 400 hours a year more than the average French and German workers.

Source: OECD; *The Economist,* September 24, 2005, p. 124.

In the 1950s, if George Washington's birthday fell on a Saturday, you had to celebrate on your own time. But today his birthday (as well as several other holidays) is celebrated on Monday, ensuring that almost everyone not only has the day off but also gets to enjoy a three-day weekend. In fact, most full-time workers are guaranteed 10 paid holidays. When you figure in vacation time, paid sick leave, and personal leave, it's a wonder anyone ever has to show up to work at all. And if you run out of sick leave, you can always call in dead.

I really don't mean to give you the impression that Americans are a nation of slackers, because the average American works longer hours than her counterpart in every other large industrialized nation (see Figure 5). There was a significant drop-off in hours worked in each of these nations since 1990, but it is clear that Americans are among the world's hardest working people. While Americans average just two weeks of paid vacation a year, Western Europeans average five or six weeks. And then there are all those off-the-clock hours on company business that so many workers put in on the phone and at their home computers.

What is the effect of all these long working hours on productivity? Employers may be aware that after working more than a certain number of hours their employees becomes less productive. But in these times of fierce global competition, many employers squeeze their workers well beyond that point.

(2) Our Declining Educational System

"I didn't meet the bar. But I think truly and honestly it has no relevancy to what I do every day."—Wilfredo Laboy, the school superintendent of Lawrence, Mass., on failing a basic literacy test for the third time.

Business firms are having trouble finding secretaries who can spell and put together grammatically correct sentences. Law firms spend millions of dollars teaching their attorneys how to write. And fast-food restaurant chains have found it necessary to place pictures of burgers, fries, sodas, and other items on their cash registers because so many of their clerks are numerically challenged.

It is truly paradoxical that at a time when more people than ever are attending college and millions of them are graduating every year, our labor force is less well-educated than those of previous generations. So I'll resolve the paradox. Our educational leaders figured out that they could get more students through the educational system by lowering standards every 10 or 15 years—kind of like a reverse game of limbo. They kept lowering the limbo stick and letting people step *over* it instead of having to squeeze *under* it. Peer pressure ("Don't appear too smart, or we won't accept you"),

More people are going to college, but our labor force is less educated.

television (watching sitcoms rather than reading books), and less parental supervision (one-parent families or two parents holding down jobs) have also taken a toll. Did I leave out computer games?

Given the product of our educational system, it is no great surprise that the quality of our labor force has been derided, especially in comparison with those of other leading industrial nations. In an age when literacy, numerical skills, and problem-solving ability are crucial in the workplace, our schools are failing us.

Let no child be left behind.
—President George W. Bush

There is something very wrong with the way our children learn. By the time they reach high school, most of them still cannot do simple arithmetic without a calculator, and when they enter college, more than one out of three freshmen must enroll in at least one remedial course (at some community colleges, it's 9 out of 10). If this is called higher education, one shudders to think of what is happening on the lower levels.

A large and growing number of 18-year-olds are entering an increasingly high-tech labor market, unable to find jobs that pay much more than the minimum wage rate ($5.15 an hour). This is the other half—those who don't go to college. Several Western European nations, most notably Germany, have work-study programs for most teenagers who are not planning to enroll in college. They are awarded certificates of competence upon completing these programs, which often lead to relatively high-paying technical jobs.

Basically the dominant competitive weapon of the 21st century will be the education and skills of the work force.
—Lester Thurow, former dean, MIT Sloan School of Management

On the plus side, despite their lagging academic performance, our high school students have not suffered any loss of self-esteem. Our 12th graders rank in the 10th percentile (i.e., the lowest 10 percent) in math globally, but first in their opinion of their own math skills.

Despite all our educational problems, however, the United States must be doing something right. Although the United States has less than 5 percent of the world's population, in the 1990s Americans won 59 percent of the Nobel Prizes in economics, 59 percent in physics, and 60 percent in medicine. And the United States has captured sizable world leads in many knowledge industries—computers, telecommunications, and finance. Clearly, the upper strata of our work force is very smart and well educated. But what about the rest of us? (See the box, "The Best and the Brightest.")

The key to maintaining our technological edge is in continuing to produce sufficient numbers of engineers. In 2005 American colleges awarded 70,000 undergraduate degrees

The Best and the Brightest

The Intel Science Talent Search is an annual competition among the nation's brightest high school seniors. Ten of the 40 finalists in 2005 had perfect 1600 scores on their SATs. Of course those who made it into the final 40 did not receive even one-tenth of 1 percent of the media coverage of the NCAA basketball tournament's final four. But hey! This is America, where the jocks trump the nerds every day of the year. Not that I'm criticizing.

Craig R. Barrett, CEO of Intel, notes that even after decades of lamenting America's relatively poor skills in math, science, and engineering, "we still do a very, very poor job of educating our kids." Comparing high school graduates in the world's top 25 countries, he says, "an American kid is, on average, near the bottom 10 percent."*

Over the last decade about one-quarter of the Intel finalists were immigrants, and half were the children of immigrants. Research by the National Foundation for American Policy in Arlington, Virginia, indicates that 60 percent of the nation's top science and math students are children of immigrants. So, if you want to do well in these subjects, you would do well to be born in a foreign country, or at least have parents who were.

At the elite high schools around the country we have thousands of students doing research with atom smashers, fiber-optics, DNA, stem-cells, and nanotechnology. But what about the rest of us? What about the fact that half of all high school math and science teachers are unqualified to teach their subjects? And that about one-half of all American 18-year-olds cannot do simple arithmetic?

*Otis Port, with John Clary, "Meet the Best and Brightest," *BusinessWeek,* March 22, 2005, p. 88. See also, www.businessweek.com/go/sts.

in engineering, compared with 600,000 in China and 350,000 in India. About half of our graduating engineers were foreign-born. And American universities award 25 percent of all their PhDs in science and engineering to Chinese citizens.

Over the last 10 years many states have abolished automatic promotion, and several have introduced competency exams at various grade levels. Many school systems have gone "back to basics," a movement which stresses mastering reading, writing, and arithmetic in the early grades. The charter school movement (which provides autonomy from local school boards for individual schools) and the growing popularity of private schools (most notably the Edison project) are promising developments. There is also growing support for school vouchers—a very controversial initiative—which would give parents a range of choices of public and private schools, rather than having to send their children to the local public school. Whatever the results of these reforms, there is virtual agreement that an improving educational system holds the key to high productivity growth, and ultimately, to a high rate of economic growth.

(3) The Permanent Underclass: Poverty, Drugs, and Crime

One of the major factors holding down our growth rate is a permanent underclass of nearly 10 percent of our population. Most of these people are supported by our tax dollars, and many are members of third- and fourth-generation welfare families. No other industrialized nation in the world has such a large dependent population.

We have a permanent underclass constituting 10 percent of our population.

Closely associated with poverty are drugs and crime. Although poor people are much more likely than any other population group to be afflicted by both drugs and crime, these problems have affected the life of nearly every American. No community is free of either drugs or crime, and they have taken an enormous toll, both economically and socially. Although we cannot quantify how the related problems of poverty, drugs, and crime have affected our rate of economic growth, they have clearly played a major role in lowering productivity and output, as well as our quality of life.

Poverty amidst plenty is an apt description of America today. Although we try to avoid making value judgments in economics, it is amazing that so few Americans feel an urgent need to alleviate the poverty that is all around us. The homeless, especially in the downtown areas of large cities, have become invisible to most of us as we pass them by.

Poverty amid plenty

Just to begin to wipe out poverty and eradicate the epidemics of drugs and crime would take a massive effort. Somehow these 25 million Americans must be rewoven into our social fabric and become fully integrated, self-supporting members of our labor force. But there are signs since the mid-1990s that some of these disturbing trends have been reversed. The welfare rolls have been cut by more than 60 percent and the crime rate has fallen substantially all across the country.

(4) Restrictions on Immigration

To say this country was literally built by immigrants would be no exaggeration. Immigration has been a tremendous source of strength to our nation. Even though immigrant families were always willing to start out on the bottom rung of the economic ladder and work their way up, the rise of "native American" groups eventually led to severe restrictions on the number of people allowed into this country.

This country was built by immigrants.

The Daughters of the American Revolution, many of whom trace their ancestry back to the Mayflower, used to invite the president of the United States to address them every year. In 1933 Franklin Roosevelt, whose forebears arrived in New York while it was still a Dutch colony, was invited to speak. His first words were, "Fellow immigrants." Needless to say, the Daughters never asked him back.

Roosevelt's point, of course, was that we are indeed a nation of immigrants—regardless of when our families arrived. And each new wave of immigrants—whether from Europe, Africa, Latin America, or Asia—worked hard so that their children would have a better life. Hard work and deferred gratification were the hallmarks of each immigrant group.

Before the early 1920s, when a series of increasingly restrictive immigration laws were passed, virtually anyone who wanted to come here was welcome.[2] In the early years of the 20th century, close to a million people came here each year, mostly from eastern and southern Europe. The prime motivation in restricting their numbers was to prevent further dilution of our vaunted northern European stock.

Immigrants are usually in their 20s or 30s, and they tend to be more adventurous, ambitious, and upwardly mobile than those who stay behind. As an added bonus, their educations have already been completed, so we reap the benefits while their native countries bear the costs. This phenomenon has been termed the *brain drain*.

Immigrants are often willing to work 14 to 16 hours a day, seven days a week. Within a couple of years, an immigrant has typically saved enough to open a small business. They may never get rich, but their children will go to college.

Until the 1920s immigrants were a tremendous source of economic strength. Not only did they help build the railroads, settle the West, staff the factories, and set up businesses, but they provided the energy, the ambition, and the drive that were often lacking in native-born Americans.

Today, with legal immigration restricted to slightly over 800,000 people a year, we are deprived of much of what made our economy go. There is no way to quantify how much this has cost us in terms of economic growth, but a remark overheard in the giant Hunts Point produce market in the Bronx sums it up well. An older man pointed at a hard-working Korean vegetable store owner and said to his friend, "*He* works like our *grandfathers* used to work."

Today nearly one-third of the entrepreneurs and higher-level employees in Silicon Valley come from overseas. Indians started some of the Valley's most famous companies—Vinod Khosla of Sun Microsystems and Sabeer Bhatia of Hotmail, for example—and together with Chinese entrepreneurs were responsible in 2005 for nearly one-third of the Valley's new start-ups, creating 60,000 jobs.

Because of much tighter entry restrictions since 9/11, people seeking to visit the United States have faced much longer waits for approval, and many more are refused visas. In the year 2000, we gave almost 300,000 temporary visas to people working and studying in scientific and technical areas; that number is down to half that today.

But our basic problem with respect to immigration dates back to 1965, when immigration policy became heavily titled toward reunited families. Since then more than 70 percent of each year's immigrant visas are granted to reunify families, while only 20 percent are reserved for professionals and other skilled workers. Still, there had been a temporary hike to 195,000 visas in 2001 for technical and professional workers for jobs that Americans could not fill, but by 2005 the cap dropped back to 95,000. If we are determined to restrict immigration, we would do well to follow Canada's example; 54 percent of its immigrants are skilled workers.

The Role of Technological Change

Way back in Chapter 2, we saw that there are two basic ways to attain economic growth: (1) more inputs of capital and labor and (2) technological change. So far we've been talking about capital and labor. Now we'll turn to technological change.

Economic growth rate is largely determined by the rate of technological change.

The rate of technological change may well be the single most important determinant of a nation's rate of economic growth. Technological change enables us to produce more output from the same package of resources or, alternatively, to produce the same output

---

[2]Everyone, that is, except people from China and Japan. Fewer than 100 a year were allowed in under law and by the so-called Gentlemen's Agreement as well as the Chinese Exclusion Act of 1882. Just to be even-handed (I'm saying this tongue-in-cheek), Congress enacted the Immigration Act of 1924, whose quotas tried to limit Italian and Jewish immigration. From 1924 until after World War II, no one from Japan or China was allowed to enter the United States.

with fewer resources. Technological change could be the creation of new or better goods and services. It also includes greater efficiency in market processes, improvements in the qualities of resources, improved knowledge about how to combine resources, and the introduction of new production processes.

A nation's educational system plays a basic role in promoting a high rate of technological change. How well trained are its scientists and engineers, and how many graduate each year? How well trained are its workforce, its industrial managers, and its marketing people?

Over the last 15 years computer literacy has increased exponentially. Today more than three-quarters of all American homes have at least one personal computer and most ten-year-olds can use computers for a multitude of activities. And so, as basic reading, writing, and math skills have declined, computer skills have increased dramatically.

How has computerization affected productivity? Two statements by Nobel Prize–winner Robert Solow may lend some insight. In 1987 he said, "You can see the computer age everywhere but in the productivity statistics." In 2000 he said, "You can now see computers in the productivity statistics." Between 1973 and 1995 the annual rate of productivity growth was about 1.5 percent, and it has since doubled. But how much of this increase was due to computerization? The most comprehensive study of this question was conducted by two economists at the Federal Reserve, Stephen Oliner and Daniel Sichel, who concluded that computers were responsible for as much as two-thirds of this increase.[3]

What is the tangible impact of the computer and the Internet? Many industries are benefiting: airlines and theaters through ticket sales on the Web, retailers through e-commerce, Wall Street through online trading. Perhaps most significant is business-to-business (B2B) commerce on the Internet, which has cut purchasing costs of some firms by as much as one-third. B2B transactions reached $2.4 trillion by mid-2003.

Here are a few tangible examples of how information technology has boosted productivity:

- It costs FedEx $2.40 to track a package for a customer who calls by phone, but just 4 cents for one who visits its website. The company now gets more than 3 million online tracking requests a day, compared with only 20 or 30 thousand by phone.

- Wal-Mart developed a system for tracking inventories for every store and automatically restocking the shelves.

- The airlines have installed ATM-like machines at airports that deliver boarding passes, making do with fewer counter clerks.

- Bar codes save customers, retailers, and manufacturers $40 billion a year in the supermarket and mass-merchandise sectors.

What took so long for the introduction of computers to have such a major impact on productivity? For one thing, it wasn't enough for a company to just buy a bunch of computers. Employees needed time to learn how to use them, and whole computer networks needed to be built up. The Internet, which has been so vital to computerization, was not all that widely used until the mid-1990s, when productivity growth doubled. Referring to the introduction of a new technology such as computerization, Thomas Friedman observed, "… it always takes time for all the flanking technologies, and the business processes and habits needed to get the most out of them, to converge and create that next productivity breakthrough."[4]

Globalization, of course, has had a profound effect on productivity. As lower-priced technology flooded the marketplace, it helped generate new jobs, as companies that snapped up computers suddenly required software and workers who could adapt the products to their needs. Furthermore, in order to continue to live and prosper in a global

---

[3]"Economic Focus: Productivity on Stilts," *The Economist*, June 10, 2000, p. 86.

[4]Thomas Friedman, *The World Is Flat* (New York: Farrar, Straus and Giroux, 2005), p. 177.

F*igure* 6

Health Spending as a
Percentage of GDP, Selected
Countries, 2003
Source: OECD; *The Economist,* June 18,
2005, p. 96

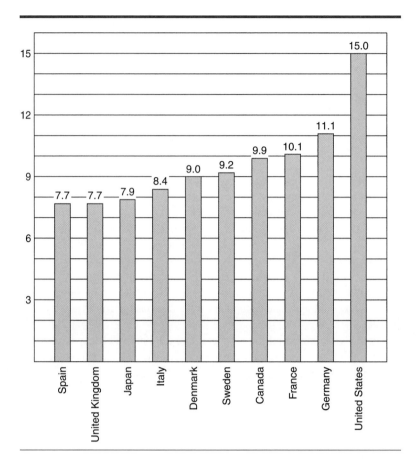

economy, American firms had to become much leaner and meaner. Their very survival
depended on significantly boosting productivity.

Rising Health Care Costs and the Shift to a Service Economy

Our rising health care costs claimed 16 percent of our GDP in 2005 and are on track to reach
20 percent by 2015. These impose a tremendous burden on taxpayers, who foot the bill for
Medicare and Medicaid, on private employers, who must shell out hundreds of billions of
dollars in medical insurance premiums, and on individual Americans who pay the balance.

The United States spends more on health care per capita (see Figure 6) than any
other industrial nation, but the quality of that care has come under heavy criticism,
and more than 45 million Americans have no medical insurance. Nearly one out of
every six dollars of our GDP goes toward health care, but we are clearly getting less
per dollar than the citizens of every other industrial country (see Figure 6). Again,
while there is no way of quantifying how much the inefficiencies of our health care
system have slowed our economic growth, they have clearly played a major role (see
the box, "Why Are Health Care Costs So High").

When labor and management negotiate a new collective bargaining agreement, the
most contentious issue is usually who is responsible for paying the workers' health insurance premiums. Companies like General Motors and Ford have asked their employees—
and retirees—to pay some, or even most, of their premiums. These companies pay $1,500
in health care cost for each car they make, while some competitors pay as little as $200.
By 2005 the average annual premium employers paid for employee family coverage was
$8,167. Since health insurance premiums have been rising two or three times as fast

Why Are Health Care Costs So High?

Are you ready for another "I am old enough to remember" story? When I was a kid, Dr. Rubinstein was our family doctor, and his nurse was Mrs. Plotkin. Perhaps every other year, the third week in September, I would have such a bad asthma attack that I could barely breathe. My mother would be on the phone with Mrs. Plotkin, and within an hour, Dr. Rubinstein would come by, give me an injection, and in seconds I was able to breathe again. I think he charged around $10 for house calls.

Today, of course, few doctors make house calls. You have two options—drag yourself to the emergency room of the closest hospital, or call the EMS and go to the hospital by ambulance. Of course, if you're poor, you might well consider the hospital emergency room to be your family doctor's office.

Doctors' offices have changed radically in recent decades. No longer do you have just a doctor and nurse in a three-room office, with a reception area, an examination room, and the doctor's private office with all her diplomas. Now you've got three or four additional employees, who spend nearly all of their time filling out insurance forms or talking on the phone with insurance companies.

When you call for a doctor's appointment, what's the first question you're asked? You're asked, "What kind of insurance do you have?"

And when you're sitting there in the waiting room, you can hear someone on the phone talking to someone at Oxford, Blue Cross, or another insurance company discussing coverage and reimbursement. Multiply this conversation by the hundreds of thousands that are taking place between doctor's offices and insurance companies all over the country and think of the resources being used to fill out an unending stream of insurance forms. Back in the good old days, none of these jobs even existed and there were no forms to fill out, and no claims to be submitted. It was just the patients, the doctor, and the nurse in a quiet three-room office.

So exactly what's going on here? Why is medical care so different from back in the good old days? Why are doctors so harried, rushing from one examination room to another? Indeed, when did medical practices come to resemble factory assembly lines?

More than anything else, the advent of medical insurance has driven health care costs through the roof. Some doctors need to pay over $100,000 a year for malpractice insurance. But more visible to the patient, every medical office must employ people to deal with insurance companies. This necessitates not only putting more people on the payroll, but paying a higher rent for more office space. Because of this huge overhead, doctors are driven to work much longer hours and to see more patients per hour.

Think about just covering the rent. Fifty years ago, a doctor charged about $10 for an office visit and paid, say, $200 a month rent. So he could cover his rent by seeing 20 patients. Today, that doctor might get $60 per patient (including insurance company reimbursement and a patient's co-payment), but pays $3,000 in rent. Do the math.

Back in the 1950s, before Medicare, Medicaid, and before the rise of the huge private insurance bureaucracies, medical care was on a pay-as-you-go basis. Now, an operation or even a simple medical procedure unleashes a flood of paperwork. As you get older and your medical problems increase, you may need a secretary to handle all your insurance claims. That would free up more of your time to spend in your doctor's waiting room.

as the rate of inflation, employers have been very anxious to contain this cost. Indeed, medical insurance premiums have become such a large cost of doing business that many employers have become increasingly reluctant to hire new employees.

Through the 1970s and 1980s most of our productivity growth was in the manufacturing sector, which was being pushed to the wall by foreign competition. But productivity growth in services was low to nonexistent. Can you think of a service worker whose productivity has not grown at all over time? In a *New Yorker* piece, James Surowiecki observed that:

> In a number of industries, workers produce about as much per hour as they did a decade or two ago. The average college professor can't grade papers or give lectures any faster today than he did in the early nineties. It takes a waiter just as long to serve a meal, and a car-repair guy just as long to fix a radiator hose.[5]

---

[5]James Surowiecki, "What Ails Us," *The New Yorker,* July 7, 2003, p. 27.

New York University Professor William Baumol has argued that any service—health care, law, education, social work—is inherently labor intensive. He used as an example the playing of Mozart's string quartets, which have been performed countess times since the composer's death in 1791. Playing one of his quartets still requires four instruments and four players and the same number of minutes. No way has ever been found to make this process more efficient. Similarly, despite all the medical advances in recent decades, doctors still examine just one patient at a time, while surgeons perform just one operation at a time.

This phenomenon has been named "Baumol's Disease." He believed that because productivity growth in the labor-intensive service sector tends to lag behind manufacturing productivity growth, costs in service-related businesses end up increasing over time. Baumol predicted that the share of GDP spent on health care would rise from 11.6 percent in 1990 to 35 percent in 2040. By 2005, health care's share had already reached 16 percent. While the cost of many manufactured goods have declined, the cost of health care has increased much faster than the rate of inflation. Indeed, since 1948 the cost of a day in the hospital has risen 700 percent in dollars of constant purchasing power. If a cure is not found for Baumol's Disease, then the not-too-distant future shock of the baby boomers' health care needs may drag down productivity gains in the coming decades.

Additional Factors Affecting Our Rate of Growth

Factors retarding our growth rate are higher energy costs, environmental protection requirements, health and safety regulations, rising health care costs, the effects of 9/11, military spending, and others.

Since the early 1970s various other factors retarding our rate of economic growth have come into play: higher energy costs, environmental protection requirements, health and safety regulations, high military spending, the effects of 9/11, and the influence of special interest groups. When the OPEC nations quadrupled the price of oil in 1973, this not only set off a severe inflationary recession, but it permanently raised the cost of doing business and somewhat retarded our rate of growth. Similarly, environmental protection legislation requiring the expenditure of tens of billions of dollars to reduce air and water pollution also slowed economic growth. And then, too, new health and safety regulations—some of which were relaxed in the 1980s—ate up billions of dollars that would have otherwise been invested in plant and equipment or research and development.

None of this is to say that environmental protection and health and safety measures were not needed. Indeed, they probably reduced medical expenses and sick time significantly, while substantially improving the quality of our lives. But they did divert resources from investment, consequently slowing our rate of growth perhaps by as much as 1 percent a year.

The effect of military spending

Like soaring health care costs, high military spending has been a drag on our economic growth. Between the close of World War II in 1945 and the end of the cold war in 1990, we devoted about 6 percent of our GDP to defense. Japan, whose economy grew much more rapidly during this period, held military spending to less than 1 percent. Resources that would have otherwise been used to produce capital goods and consumer goods and services were instead expended on military salaries, weapons systems, guns, bullets, and bombs. With the collapse of the Soviet Union and its satellite empire in Eastern Europe, we were finally able to cut defense spending to just 3 percent of GDP by the start of the new millennium. But after 9/11 when the terrorists struck, our defense spending began going right back up again. In 2006 we devoted more than 5 percent of our GDP to military spending.

Finally, let's consider the more lasting effects of the events of 9/11 on our economy. Until that day, it had been business as usual. Now we anxiously await the next attack and the one after that. Will it take the form of anthrax, a small nuclear device, poison gas, or something we never anticipated? At a recent high school reunion, we reminisced about how, in elementary school, there were shelter drills, during which we would climb under our desks to protect ourselves against nuclear attack, one hand over the napes of our necks, the other shielding our eyes. Apparently those days are back again, only this time, we actually *have* been attacked.

The cost of doing business has gone up since September 11, 2001, which reduces productivity. Increased spending on security by the government and private businesses also reduces productivity. Richard Berner outlined some of the costs:

> But in the long term, terrorism is imposing new costs that are unlikely to go away. For every business, insurance and security costs will be higher. For many, the benefits of just-in-time management will be sacrificed as companies hold more inventory to guard against breaks in the global supply chain. The threat of cyberterrorism, which once seemed distant, will almost certainly lead to new measures for Internet security, slowing activity even for those operating in the supposedly frictionless world of cyberspace. And America's first experience with bioterrorism has thrown sand in the gears of commerce, government and everyday life, requiring new caution and precaution in once-mundane activities like mail sorting.[6]

Most developed nations have experienced an eventual slowing of their growth rate. Mancur Olson, in his study titled *The Rise and Decline of Nations,* concludes that special interest groups—particularly labor unions, farmers' cooperatives, and employers' associations—become stronger as the economy grows.[7] These groups then make it more difficult to introduce new technologies that could continue to increase growth. For example, the International Longshoremen's Union prevented the containerization of freight for years until the shippers offered them an extremely lucrative retirement plan. And the farmers have persuaded Congress to provide them with $19 billion dollars a year in price supports and subsidies. In 2005 these payments reached a record $23 billion.

How do we counteract the influence of these special interest groups? Olson suggests that we bring down the barriers to international trade. Look at what foreign competition has done for the automobile industry. The United Auto Workers Union has been forced to grant concessions to the big three automakers, resulting in lower costs and increased efficiency. And now Americans have a wider range of better-quality cars to choose from at lower prices.

Summary

We've talked about a multitude of factors affecting our productivity, but we need a more integrated explanation of why our productivity growth was so low from the mid-1970s to the mid-1990s and why it picked up again.

1. *Our low savings rate*   In addition to our low personal savings rate, the federal government ran huge deficits until the mid-1990s. Since 2001 we have had mounting federal deficits and extremely low personal savings.

2. *Our low rate of investment*   Net domestic investment trended downward from the late 1960s until 1992, when it began to rise sharply. So the downward trends in both savings and investment tended to depress productivity growth in the 1970s, 1980s, and the early 1990s.

3. *The rising quantity of labor*   The average workweek, which had been declining in the 1950s and 1960s, stopped falling in the 1970s and has increased over the last two decades. This may have depressed productivity growth since the 1970s.

4. *The declining quality of labor*   Although more people than ever before are going to college, our educational standards today—from the first grade through college—are well below the standards we maintained 40 or 50 years ago. I realize that this viewpoint is controversial (there are many people who disagree with me), but everyone would agree that a good education is crucial to performing most jobs in today's high-tech economy.

---

[6]Richard Berner, "The Terror Economy," *New York Times,* October 23, 2001, p. A23.

[7]Mancur Olson, *The Rise and Decline of Nations* (New Haven, CT: Yale University Press, 1982).

Although computer literacy is extremely high in this country, a high proportion of those entering the labor force are profoundly weak in reading, writing, and arithmetic—skills that are required in the workplace. So the declining quality of labor has had a long-term depressing effect on our productivity growth.

5. *The growth of the permanent underclass and its attendant problems of poverty, drugs, and crime*   This factor has also tended to depress productivity growth in the 1970s and 1980s. However, sharp declines in welfare dependancy and crime since the early 1990s may have contributed to productivity growth over the last decade.

6. *Restrictions on immigration*   Immigration restrictions dating back to the 1920s may have lowered productivity growth. In recent decades we have been allowing a fairly large flow of relatively low-skilled immigrants into the country. By 2006 Congress was debating what to do about the estimated 11 million illegal immigrants living here.

7. *Computerization*   The United States was computerized in the 1990s, and the long-awaited accompanying rise in productivity growth had apparently begun to materialize in the second half of that decade. We may eventually conclude that computers have had an increasingly salutary effect on productivity since the mid- to late-1980s. The 1999 *Economic Report of the President* noted that "although the electric dynamo was invented well before the turn of the century, it did not seem to fuel large gains in productivity until many years later."[8] Productivity growth actually slowed between 1890 and 1913, but it increased rapidly between 1919 and 1929. If history repeats itself we should experience rapid productivity growth well into the first decades of the 21st century because of computerization.

8. *Military and other security spending*   A large and growing share of our resources is being spent not just on weaponry and research, past, current, and future wars, and homeland security, but on private security as well. The loss of these resources, which would otherwise have been used to raise economic growth, is holding down productivity gains.

9. *Globalization*   The spur of foreign competition forced manufacturing companies into being much more efficient, especially in the 1970s and 1980s, and more recently it has boosted efficiency in those service industries that were vulnerable.

10. *Rising health care costs*   Because this sector suffers from "Baumol's Disease," as its share of GDP rises, it tends to hold down productivity gains.

Why did productivity growth slow in the early 1970s? Was this slowdown caused by the oil price shock of 1973? The tens of millions of young baby boomers who were entering the labor force? The decline of manufacturing and the accompanying rise of the service sector? My own pet theory that the slowdown may have been partially caused by the decline of our educational system? There is certainly no shortage of theories, and consequently, there is no clear consensus among economists. Although we don't know for sure why productivity growth declined in 1973, there is fairly widespread agreement about the causes of the sharp rise in productivity growth since 1995.

By 1995 the forces depressing our productivity growth were overwhelmed by the gains wrought by computerization and global competition. Computerization had reached the necessary critical mass to finally produce the long awaited burst in efficiencies. A large majority of adults had become computer proficient, and as the price of personal computer systems and other equipment such as smart cash registers fell sharply, virtually every business firm could afford them.

By the mid-1990s global competition, which had been confined mainly to manufacturing, was now affecting many of our service industries. In later chapters we'll discuss how legal, financial, medical, and customer service work has been flowing overseas. Like manufacturing firms in earlier decades, many service firms were now forced to compete, thus boosting their productivity.

---

[8]Page 77.

TABLE 1	The Poorest Countries in the World
Country	GDP Per Capita, 2004 ($)
Burundi	$ 90
Congo, Dem. Rep.	120
Eritrea	180
Ethiopia	110
Guinea-Bissau	160
Liberia	110
Malawi	170

Source: www.finfacts.com/biz10/globalworldincomepercapita.htm

But economists, by definition, are a pessimistic lot. Many of us look at rising military and other security spending, as well as the coming retirement of the baby boom generation and the projected rise in health care costs, and we think that these factors, among others, may slow productivity growth in future decades. But on the other hand, perhaps new innovations in such fields as nanotechnology, communications, medical research, or in some fields not yet imagined, will create the next wave of productivity growth.

Economic Growth in the Less Developed Countries

Well, enough about *our* problems. Now let's talk about other people's problems. Let's talk about people who *really* have problems—those who live in less developed countries (LDCs).

The world can be divided into three groups of countries: the industrialized nations, the newly industrializing countries (NICs), and the less developed countries (LDCs). The big question, then, is how to get from LDC to NIC and, ultimately, to industrialized. And, parenthetically, at what cost?

The only way to industrialize is to build up capital in the form of new plant and equipment. There are two main ways of doing this: working more and consuming less. As some of the poor nations of the world are barely at subsistence level, it's pretty hard for them to consume less. And because there is often a great deal of unemployment in preponderantly agricultural economies, those who want to work more have a hard time finding work.

The only way to industrialize

Each of the LDCs shown in Table 1 has a per capita GDP of less than $200. Not all the LDCs have per capita incomes as low as $200, but nearly half the world's population lives on less than $2 a day.

Compounding the problems of the LDCs are rapidly growing populations. More than 200 years ago, an English economist named Thomas Robert Malthus predicted that the world's growth of food production would not be able to keep up with the growth of population (see the box, "The Malthusian Theory of Population"). The Malthusian dilemma—a food supply growing at an arithmetic rate and a population growing at a geometric rate—is becoming a reality in some of the nations of sub-Saharan Africa, as well as in a few countries in Asia and in Latin America. Hundreds of millions face starvation, with virtually no chance to substantially raise their food output. The recurrent famines in sub-Saharan Africa may be mere dress rehearsals for a future crisis of much greater dimension.

Even more alarming in the long run, the birthrates of less developed nations show little indication of declining. And unless they decline, the emergency shipments of foodstuffs from the rest of the world are merely postponing the inevitable.

One way out of this dilemma may be the family planning programs that have been attempting to lower birthrates in the LDCs. Supported by government funding as well as

Thomas Robert Malthus, English cleric and economist (The Granger Collection, New York)

The Malthusian Theory of Population

Economics is called the "dismal science" largely because of the Malthusian theory. As it was originally formulated, the theory predicted that famine and warfare would, within perhaps a few generations, beset the world. This was inevitable because of a tendency for the world's population to double every 25 years.

The Reverend Thomas Robert Malthus wrote the first edition of the *Essay on the Principle of Population* in 1798. His two main points were that population tended to grow in a geometric progression—1, 2, 4, 8, 16, 32—and that the only ways to stop population from growing this rapidly were the "positive checks" of pestilence, famine, and war. Not a very pleasant outlook.

In his second edition, Malthus held out slightly more hope for holding down the rate of the population increase. It could be contained by the "preventive check" of "moral restraint," which meant not getting married until one could support a family (and, it went without saying, no fooling around before you got married).

Malthus also noted that the food supply could not increase as rapidly as population tended to because the planet was limited in size and there was only a fixed amount of arable land. He felt the food supply would ultimately tend to grow in an arithmetic progression—1, 2, 3, 4, 5, 6—and it would not take a mathematical genius to conclude that we would be in trouble within a few generations. The relevant figures are shown in the table below.*

Year	Food Production	Population
1800	1	1
1825	2	2
1850	3	4
1875	4	8
1900	5	16
1925	6	32

The Malthusian theory is a variant of the law of diminishing returns. As increasing amounts of labor are applied to a fixed amount of land, eventually marginal output will decline.

Was Malthus right? Surely not in the industrialized countries, particularly the United States, Canada, and Australia, which are major exporters of wheat and other farm products. Two things happened in these countries to ward off Malthus's dire predictions. First, because of tremendous technological advances in agriculture—tractors, harvesters, better fertilizer, and high-yield seeds—farmers were able to feed many more people.† Second, as industrialization spread and more and more people left the countryside for the cities, the birthrate fell.

However, the less developed countries are caught in a double bind. The Malthusian positive check of a high death rate has been largely removed by public health measures, such as malaria control, smallpox vaccine, and more sanitary garbage disposal. But because these countries have not yet been able to industrialize and urbanize their populations, birthrates remain high. In most of Asia, Africa, and Latin America, populations are doubling every 30 to 35 years, putting hundreds of millions of people in peril of starvation. Famine is a reality in these countries, and it may well become even more widespread in the coming decades.

Many see the AIDS epidemic, which has swept through much of sub-Saharan Africa, as a fulfillment of the Malthusian prophecy. In some countries as many as one in five people is infected with the HIV virus and may eventually die of AIDS. Even if the governments of the developed world and the major pharmaceutical companies make cheap or free vaccines available and somehow bring this epidemic under control, according to the Malthusian theory people in these same countries will eventually die of starvation. The only long-term solution, according to the followers of Malthus, would be to somehow bring down the extremely high birthrates in these countries.

---

*Malthus did not use actual years in his predictions; the years in the table are purely hypothetical to illustrate his theory. Also, Malthus did not predict that this would actually happen. Rather, he indicated that these were the tendencies, but that population increases could be checked by war, pestilence, famine, or moral restraint.

†Some observers have been encouraged by the so-called Green Revolution, which has enabled many large growers to double and triple yields by using better seeds and fertilizer. However, the prime beneficiaries have been the wealthy farmers and a few multinational agribusinesses, such as Dole, Del Monte, and Ralston Purina. They have profited by producing for export such crops as sugar, soybeans, bananas, and peanuts. But they have also forced millions of small farmers off the land and actually caused the production of indigenous food staples to decline, making these countries even more dependent on food imports.

grants from the Population Council, the International Planned Parenthood Federation, and the United Nations, the programs have had great success in lowering birthrates. In 1970 families in LDCs had an average of 6 children. Today that average is just 3. With fewer mouths to feed, these countries now have more savings available for development.

Even *with* family planning programs, the populations of most LDCs continue to grow between 2 and 3 percent a year, and these countries must struggle to increase their food supplies at that rate just to keep pace. To industrialize, they would need to attain a high enough economic growth rate to be able to produce capital goods as well as the basic consumer necessities. Thus many LDCs clearly will never be able to begin industrializing without outside help.

There *is* one additional source of capital: grants and loans from the industrialized nations. Over the last four decades hundreds of billions of dollars have been provided by the United States, the Soviet Union, Western Europe, and Japan. But now that many LDCs are deeply in debt (some have defaulted on their loans), it is unlikely that more credit will be extended. In fact, the interest that must be paid out each year by the LDCs has become a tremendous burden.

Grants and loans from industrialized nations

During the 1980s some nations *did* attain the status of NIC. The "four tigers" of Asia—South Korea, Taiwan, Hong Kong, and Singapore—as well as Malaysia, Brazil, Indonesia, and Thailand have done this, largely through foreign investment.

Still another problem is that virtually all LDCs spend a major part of their budgets on armaments, which diverts desperately needed funds from development. Warfare in Southeast Asia, Afghanistan, the Congo, Ethiopia, Sudan, Peru, Somalia, and the Persian Gulf has further exacerbated the situation. The United States, the former Soviet Union, China, and several European nations have encouraged this unfortunate tendency by selling—or even giving—arms to developing nations.

Military spending and wars

China and India, the world's most populous nations, have made impressive strides toward development. Today almost one-half of the people in the world live in LDCs, and in those countries about half live at or near the subsistence level. Most live out their lives in abject poverty, with no hope that they or their children will have better lives.

Current Issue: Health Care Costs in the Coming Decades

It is said that we have the greatest healthcare system in the world, but maybe we need to take another look. Leaving aside the Medicare prescription drug benefit fiasco and skyrocketing medical bills, let's compare the results of our system with those of other industrialized countries.

- American life expectancy is lower than average.
- Childhood immunization rates in the U.S. are lower than average.
- Infant mortality rates are higher than in 80 percent of the other countries.
- We have fewer doctors per capita and have fewer doctor visits per year.
- We are admitted to the hospital less frequently.

Does *this* sound like better medical care? The next question: Do we get what we pay for? Not really. The U.S. spends more than $1,000 per year per capita just for health-care-related paperwork and administration. Canada, where medical care is provided by the government, spends just $300 per person. And, of course, every other industrialized country insures all its citizens. Although we spend a lot more per capita on medical care, more than 45 million Americans are uninsured.

But that's the *good* news. The *bad* news begins when the baby boom generation enters retirement over the next two decades. That's when our health care bill will *really* go through the roof. And if you think we need to worry about the Social Security trust fund going bust, just wait till you see what happens to the Medicare trust fund.

An inefficient health care system and escalating health care costs will be a tremendous drag on productivity growth, and consequently on our economic growth. Unless we fix this malfunctioning system very soon, we will see the continued spread of Baumol's Disease.

Here's my own suggestion for a partial quick fix. By introducing what's called a single payer system, we could eliminate most of the wasteful paper work, phone calls, and the multitude of forms. That single payer would replace the hundreds of private insurance companies, managed care organizations, and government agencies. It could be a private company, or, more likely, a government agency.

This would relieve private employers of a tremendous financial obligation—insurance premiums that now average over $10,000 for each employee's family. Not only are huge and growing health care premiums a disincentive to hiring additional employees, but they create a tremendous competitive disadvantage to American companies. If General Motors and Ford could shed their extremely burdensome health care obligations to current and retired employees, they would once again become profitable companies.

Questions for Further Thought and Discussion

1. How has our educational system affected the quality of our labor force?

2. Explain the Malthusian theory of population. Is it relevant today anywhere in the world? Explain where and why.

3. How does the American savings rate compare to that of other leading industrial nations? What accounts for the difference?

4. What changes took place during the Industrial Revolution that made possible sustained economic growth?

5. Why did our rate of productivity growth slow from the mid-1970s through the mid-1990s?

6. Why did our rate of productivity growth speed up in the late 1990s? Is this higher growth rate just temporary, or will it be sustained over the next 10 or 15 years?

7. Should we remove all barriers to immigration into the United States? What would be the consequences?

8. If we could let in an extra hundred thousand immigrants every year, should we favor certain immigrants over others? Why?

Workbook for Chapter 16

Name _____ Date _____

Multiple-Choice Questions

Circle the letter that corresponds to the best answer.

1. Our rate of productivity increase in the 1980s was

   _____ the rate of productivity increase in the

   1960s.
   a) faster than
   b) about
   c) slower than

2. Which one of the following statements is true?
   a) America's immigration policies are much less restrictive today than they were 100 years ago.
   b) The fewer immigrants we let into the United States, the better off we'll be.
   c) The colleges in the United States graduate fewer engineers than those in China, India, and Japan.
   d) The United States and Canada have virtually identical immigration policies.

3. Each of the following except _____ slowed our

   rate of economic growth in the 1970s.
   a) research and development spending
   b) pollution regulations and requiring pollution reduction
   c) health and safety regulations
   d) rising energy costs

4. The key to productivity growth is _____.
   a) an increasing labor force
   b) technological change
   c) expansion of land under cultivation
   d) the use of deteriorating and obsolete capital

5. Rising productivity could be each of these except

   _____.
   a) more units of output from more units of input
   b) more output per unit of input
   c) the same output from fewer units of input

6. Edward Denison attributes about _____ percent

   of our economic growth to increases in productivity.
   a) 10   d) 70
   b) 30   e) 90
   c) 50

7. Almost half of the people in the world live in

   _____.
   a) LDCs
   b) NICs
   c) industrialized countries

8. The Malthusian theory appears to be coming true in

   _____.
   a) sub-Saharan Africa
   b) the United States
   c) China
   d) the entire world

9. Which one of the following factors contributed most to our economic growth between 1995 and today?
   a) Our high rate of savings
   b) Our educational system
   c) Technological change
   d) Our high rate of investment

10. Sustained economic growth did not begin anywhere

    in the world until around _____.
    a) 1450   c) 1750
    b) 1600   d) 1900

11. Which is the most accurate statement?
    a) We are spending more on defense (as a percentage of our GDP) than at any previous time in our history.
    b) We are spending less on defense (as a percentage of GDP) than at any previous time in our history.
    c) Defense spending (as a percentage of GDP) is declining.
    d) Defense spending (as a percentage of GDP) is rising.

12. Which statement is true?

    a) Immigration has long been a tremendous drain on our economy and has slowed our rate of economic growth.

    b) Hundreds of thousands of immigrants come here every year on work visas.

    c) Our immigration policies in the 19th century favored Chinese immigrants.

    d) Very few immigrants have found employment in California's Silicon Valley.

13. Which is the most accurate statement?

    a) Americans work fewer hours per year than the citizens of virtually every other developed country.

    b) Americans work about the same number of hours as French and German workers.

    c) Americans work more hours than the citizens of virtually every other developed country.

14. The events of 9/11 had _____.

    a) the long-term effect of raising our rate of productivity growth

    b) the long-term effect of lowering our rate of productivity growth

    c) virtually no effect on our rate of productivity growth

15. All other things remaining equal, which country in the figure below would you expect to have a higher growth rate?

    a) Country A

    b) Country B

    c) They would have the same growth rate.

    d) There is no way of telling which would have the higher growth rate.

16. Which one of the following has not slowed our productivity growth?

    a) high military spending

    b) high health care costs

    c) immigration

    d) low savings

    e) technological change

17. Which statement best reflects the role of our educational system in preparing students for the workforce?

    a) More people than ever are attending college, so our labor force is better educated than at any time in our history.

    b) Business firms are having trouble finding secretaries who can spell and put together grammatically correct sentences.

    c) Most people in our labor force are unable to perform their jobs because of their educational shortcomings.

    d) Increased spending on teachers' salaries, science labs, and computer facilities will completely solve any educational problems this nation has.

18. Which statement is true?

    a) The permanent underclass is basically an economic asset because it is a cheap source of labor.

    b) The permanent underclass has slowed our rate of economic growth.

    c) About 2 percent of all Americans are members of the permanent underclass.

    d) Because the United States is a socially mobile society, there is no such thing as a permanent underclass.

19. Which is the most accurate statement?

    a) The tremendous surge of immigrants into the United States has slowed our economic growth.

    b) Most high-tech employers oppose increasing immigration quotas.

    c) In the late 1990s the flood of immigrants willing to take low-paying jobs has caused millions of Americans to be unemployed.

    d) Very few businesses are owned by immigrants.

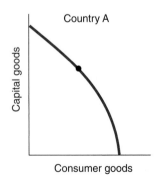

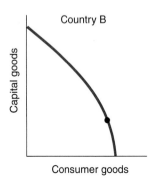

20. A major reason why health care costs are so high is
_____.

a) doctors must not only pay high malpractice insurance premiums, but employ people just to deal with health care insurance payments

b) doctors have become very greedy

c) Medicaid and Medicare have forced up doctors' fees

d) doctors are spending so much time with each patient.

21. Mancur Olson suggests that the best remedy for overcoming the economic influence of special interest groups is _____.

a) bringing down the barriers to international trade

b) having the federal government curb the influence of special interest groups

c) raising tariffs on all imports that are putting American workers out of work

d) having the federal government nationalize all industries dominated by special interest groups

22. Which of the following statements is true?

a) The American health care system is run very efficiently.

b) About one out of every six dollars of our GDP goes toward health care.

c) The United States spends less per person on health care than most other developed nations.

d) Health insurance premiums are an insignificant cost of doing business for most large companies.

23. Rapid population growth _____ the economic development of LDCs.

a) severely hampers

b) slightly hampers

c) slightly helps

d) greatly helps

24. Malthus may have been correct in his predictions for _____.

a) at least some industrial countries and some LDCs

b) at least some industrial countries but no LDCs

c) at least some LDCs but no industrial countries

d) neither the LDCs nor the industrial countries

25. Since 1995 our productivity rose by more than 2.5 percent in _____.

a) just one year

b) two years

c) three years

d) more than 3 years

26. FedEx, Wal-Mart, and the airlines have

a) not taken advantage of the information technology revolution.

b) used the information technology revolution mainly to lay off employees.

c) used the information technology revolution to cut costs.

d) all experienced lower productivity growth due to the information technology revolution.

27. Which statement is true?

a) Americans are the most productive workers in the world.

b) In most economic sectors Americans are less productive than workers in other mature economies.

c) The official average workweek for most American information workers greatly overestimates the hours they really work.

d) Productivity growth in the United States has slowed since the mid-1990s.

28. Each of the following countries *except* _____ is extremely poor.

a) Malawi   c) Burundi

b) Brazil   d) Ethiopia

29. Which one of the following statements would you agree with?

a) By the mid-1990s computerization had reached the critical mass necessary to significantly raise our rate of productivity growth.

b) Globalization has slowed our rate of productivity growth.

c) High military and homeland security spending since 9/11 has helped raise our rate of productivity growth.

d) Since 2001 the United States has been able to meet nearly all its financial needs from government and individual savings.

30. Which one of the following is the most accurate statement?

    a) Baumol's Disease explains most of our loss of manufacturing jobs to foreign competitors.

    b) The productivity of many workers in the service sector cannot be increased.

    c) William Baumol believes that the expansion of the health care industry will greatly increase our productivity growth rate in the coming decades.

    d) The sharp increase in productivity growth since 1995 proves that Baumol's Disease has been cured.

31. Which statement is true?

    a) Americans unquestionably receive the best health care in the world.

    b) Americans have the highest life expectancy and the lowest infant mortality rate in the world.

    c) More than $1,000 per capita in the U.S. is spent on health-care-related paperwork and administration.

    d) The U.S. has more doctors per capita than any other nation.

Fill-In Questions

1. Productivity is defined as _____ _____.

2. Most Americans, French, Germans, Japanese, and British work less than _____ hours a year.

3. The Industrial Revolution began over _____ centuries ago in _____.

4. Edward Denison attributes about _____ percent of our economic growth to increases in labor and capital and about _____ percent to increases in productivity.

5. Sustained economic growth was made possible by the _____.

6. The threat of terrorist attacks has tended to _____ our rate of productivity growth.

7. Compared to the 1970s and 1980s, our rate of productivity growth is _____.

8. By the year 2015 we may be spending about _____ percent of our GDP on health care.

Problem

1. Given the information in Table 1, fill in Malthus's predictions for the years 2025, 2050, and 2075.

TABLE 1		
Year	Food Production	Population
2000	1	1
2025	_____	_____
2050	_____	_____
2075	_____	_____

2. If real GDP rose by 4 percent and the productivity rate rose by 2 percent, by how much would employment rise?

3. Productivity has been rising by about 3 percent a year. By how much would real GDP need to rise to increase employment?

Chapter 17

Demand, Supply, and Equilibrium

hy do people like Oprah Winfrey, Alex Rodriguez, Derek Jeter, Jay Leno, Shaquille O'Neal, Angelina Jolie, Eddie Murphy, and Julia Roberts earn so much more than other athletes, actors, and entertainers, let alone the rest of us? What makes the price of gasoline go up and down? Why have PCs, palm pilots, and DVD players come down so much in price? The answer is that each is subject to the workings of supply and demand.

In Chapter 3 we showed how the interaction of supply and demand resulted in an equilibrium price and quantity. Now let's examine the workings of supply and demand much more closely and look at the factors that influence them.

Supply and demand change over time, causing changes in equilibrium price and quantity. We'll examine what causes these changes, and by the end of the chapter you'll be drawing supply and demand graphs. Before we begin, you'll need to buy at least one package of graph paper.

CHAPTER OBJECTIVES

In this chapter you will find out everything you always wanted to know about:

- Individual and market demand.
- Changes in demand.
- Individual and market supply.
- Changes in supply.

- Graphing supply and demand curves.
- Finding equilibrium price and quantity.

Demand Defined

Demand is *the schedule of quantities of a good or service that people will purchase at different prices.* Let's look at the demand for sirloin steak. At $1 a pound, it would create traffic jams as people rushed to the supermarket; but at $3 a pound, sirloin steak would be somewhat less of a bargain. At $4 a pound, it would lose many of its previous buyers to chicken, chuck steak, and other substitutes.

As the price of an item goes up, the quantity demanded falls, and as the price comes down, the quantity demanded rises. This inverse relationship may be stated as the law of demand: *When the price of a good is lowered, more of it is demanded; when it is raised, less is demanded.* There is an implicit assumption that there is no change in any other factors. The law of demand holds an honored place in the history of economic thought. (See box, "The Work of Alfred Marshall.")

Definition of demand

The law of demand: When the price of a good is lowered, more of it is demanded; when it is raised, less is demanded.

409

There are many factors besides price that influence demand, including income, the prices of related goods and services, tastes and preferences, and price expectations. We'll discuss each of these factors a little later in the chapter.

Individual Demand and Market Demand

The law of demand holds for both individuals and markets. Individual demand is the schedule of quantities that a person would purchase at different prices. Market demand is the schedule of quantities that everyone in the market would buy at different prices.

Table 1 shows four examples of individual demand and then adds them up to total market demand. We add straight across. For example, at a price of $30, the quantity demanded on an individual basis is 0, 1, 2, and 1. Adding them together, we get total or market demand of 4. In the same way, by adding the individual quantities demanded at a price of $25, we get 9 (2 plus 1 plus 3 plus 3). And so forth.

TABLE 1 Hypothetical Individual Demand and Market Demand Schedules

		Quantity Demanded by					
Price	Venus	+	Martina	+	Serena	+	Lindsay	=	Total
$30	0		1		2		1		4
25	2		1		3		3		9
20	3		2		5		4		14
15	3		3		6		6		18
10	4		5		7		7		23
5	5		6		7		8		26

There is one interesting question about market demand: What is the market? The market is where people buy and sell. Generally there is a prevailing price in a particular market. Take gasoline. In New York City the price of regular unleaded gas at most gas stations varied between $2.25 and $2.75 in January 2006. But just across the bay in New Jersey most stations charged between $2.00 and $2.20.

What is the market?

New York City and New Jersey are two separate markets for gasoline. People in New York would not go to New Jersey to save 15 or 20 cents a gallon because the trip would not only be inconvenient, it would cost them a $5 toll.

The market for gasoline is very local because the money you'd save by driving to the next market would be more than offset by the money it would cost you to go there. Another local market is for groceries. Again, you wouldn't drive to the other side of your city or perhaps three towns down the highway just to save a dollar or two.

The market for automobiles is regional. If you live in Boston and can save a couple of hundred dollars by going to a dealer in Providence, you might make the trip, but if you live in Chicago you won't go to San Francisco to save $200 on a car.

On a very local basis, then, prices for most goods will not vary much, but as the area covered grows larger, so do price variations. If people are willing to travel to get a bargain, the market will be much larger.

The market for some goods and services may be national or even international. A company shopping for a sophisticated computer system will look all over the world for the right system at the right price. And a man who needs brain surgery or a heart transplant will not go to his local doctor and ask her to operate in her office.

I have strongly implied that a market is at a specific location. But does it *have* to be? What about business conducted over the phone or over the Internet? A market for a good or service might be local, regional, national, or global, but business in that market may well be conducted just about anywhere—even in cyberspace.

In the year 2000 two major markets *were* created in cyberspace. Fourteen of the world's largest mining and metals companies created a single procurement marketplace on the Internet, which has cut the industry's $200 billion-a-year supply bill. And 14 leading oil and gas companies joined forces in a similar project designed to put $125 billion a year of procurement spending on a common website. Other exchanges have been introduced for industries as diverse as retail and autos.

eBay has created a global market for goods that previously had mainly local markets. Its popularity induced others to start offering Internet auctions. Now, at thousands of different auction sites, people bid for computer equipment, antiques, fine art, coins, stamps, toys, comic books, jewelry, travel services, and even real estate.

Here's a two-question pop quiz. Name the leading U.S. used-car dealer? Would you believe eBay? Second question: Name the biggest leisure travel agency. You have 30 seconds. All right, is that your final answer? If you said Expedia, then you're right!

Changes in Demand

The definition of demand is our point of departure, so to speak, when we take up changes in demand. Once again, demand is the schedule of *quantities* that people purchase at different prices. A change in demand is a change in, or a departure from, this schedule.

Increases in Demand

Using the market demand schedule in Table 1, let's say the product in question becomes much more desirable, perhaps because it is suddenly discovered that it slows the aging process. The people listed in Table 1 might well decide they are willing to pay even more for each unit.

This takes us from Table 1 to Table 2, and it involves an increase in market demand. At each price, buyers are willing to buy more. Thus, by definition, there is an increase

An increase in demand is an increase in the quantity people are willing to purchase at all prices.

TABLE 2	Hypothetical Market Demand Schedule Illustrating an Increase in Demand	
Price	(1) Quantity Demanded	(2) Quantity Demanded
$30	4	5
25	9	11
20	14	18
15	18	28
10	23	38
5	26	50

Figure 1

Increase in Demand
Note that D₂ lies to the right of D₁.
At each price people buy a larger
quantity.

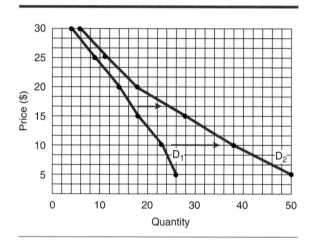

in demand. It is important to emphasize that *an increase in demand is an increase in the quantity people are willing to purchase at each price.*

It will be helpful to illustrate this increase by means of a graph. This is done in Figure 1, which is drawn from the data in Table 2. Note that the second demand curve, D_2, representing the increase in demand, is to the right of D_1. You should also note that at each price, the quantity demanded in D_2 is greater than the quantity demanded in D_1.

Decreases in Demand

A decrease in demand means people are willing to buy less at each price.

Now we're ready for a decrease in demand, also illustrated in Figure 1. You should be able to guess what the decrease would be. After all, there are only two curves on the graph, and if going from D_1 to D_2 is an increase—that's right!—going from D_2 to D_1 is a decrease.

A decrease in demand means people are willing to buy less at each price. In Figure 1, D_1 lies entirely to the left of D_2. If the curves were to cross, we would have neither an increase nor a decrease in demand; rather, we would have a change in demand.

Problems

Figure 2 illustrates a change in demand, whether we go from D_1 to D_2 or from D_2 to D_1. My students often dispute this point. In Figure 2, they argue, when price is more than $5.25, going from D_1 to D_2 represents an increase in demand because people are

Figure 2

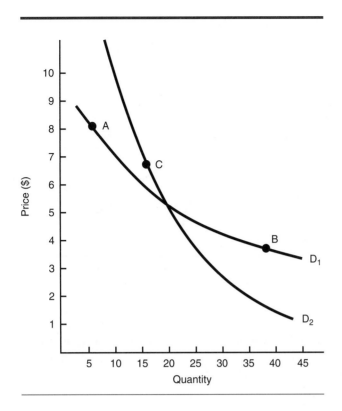

willing to purchase more. And, they add, when we go from D_1 to D_2 at prices below $5.25, there is a decrease in demand.

Let's go back to our definitions: An increase in demand is an increase in the quantity people are willing to purchase at each price. When we go from D_1 to D_2, are people willing to purchase a larger quantity at *each* price? No! So going from D_1 to D_2 is not an increase in demand.

Maybe it's a *decrease* in demand. A decrease in demand is a decrease in the quantity people are willing to purchase at each price. When we go from D_1 to D_2, are people willing to purchase a smaller quantity at *each* price? No! So going from D_1 to D_2 is not a decrease in demand.

So if going from D_1 to D_2 is not an increase in demand nor a decrease in demand, what *is* it? It's a *change* in demand. Why a change? Because we moved from one demand curve to another. In this case, we went from demand schedule D_1 to demand schedule D_2.

Look again at Figure 2. Does going from point A to point B represent a change in demand? Going back once more to our definition of demand—the schedule of quantities that people will purchase at different prices—when we go from A to B, has there been any change in the demand schedule? If both A and B are on that same schedule, there has been no change in demand.

On the graph we can easily see that both A and B are on the same demand curve. For a change in demand to have taken place, you would have to move off the demand curve. If you moved from point A on D_1 to point C on D_2 that would be a change in demand.

If the move from A to B is not a change in demand, what is it? It's simply a change in quantity demanded in response to a price change. Price fell, and quantity demanded rose. Incidentally, a favorite exam question is: If price falls and in response quantity demanded rises, does this represent a change in demand? *Please* answer no.

Here are some problems to see whether you're following what I'm talking about. Each is based on Figure 3. There are four possible answers: (*a*) a change in quantity

Figure 3

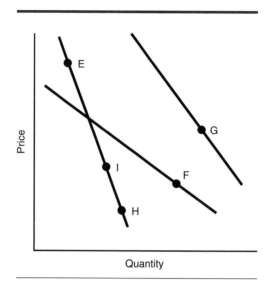

demanded, (*b*) a change in demand, (*c*) an increase in demand, and (*d*) a decrease in demand.

1. When we move from E to F, it is _____.
2. A move from F to G is _____.
3. A move from G to H is _____.
4. A move from H to I is _____.

Now we will go over each of the answers.

1. (b)   Moving from E to F is a change in demand because these points are on different demand curves that cross; neither is a higher demand curve because they cross. A higher demand would mean people would buy more at every price. When two curves cross, they don't fulfill this condition.

2. (c)   From F to G is an increase in demand because the demand curve on which G is situated is to the right of F's demand curve. Note that there is an increase in demand because people are willing to buy more at all prices on G's demand curve.

3. (d)   From G to H is a decrease in demand for the same reason. On H's demand curve, people are willing to buy *less* for every price than on G's curve.

4. (a)   From H to I is a change in the quantity demanded. As long as we remain on the curve, there's no change in demand.

Now we'll try another set of problems using the same four possible answers. These are based on Figure 4.

5. A move from J to K is _____.
6. A move from K to L is _____.
7. A move from L to M is _____.

5. (a)   This is a change in quantity because we stay on the same demand curve.

6. (c)   The L's demand curve is situated entirely to the right of K's demand curve.

7. (d)   A move from L to M is the reverse of a move from K to L.

Figure 4

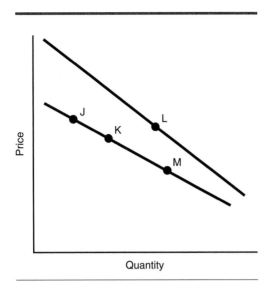

What Causes Changes in Demand?

Changes in Income   When your income goes up, you can afford to buy more goods and services. Suppose the incomes of most Americans rise. That means a greater demand for cars, new homes, furniture, steaks, and motel rooms. Similarly, if incomes decline, as they do during recessions, there will be a smaller demand for most goods and services.

Most goods are *normal goods*. The demand for these goods varies directly with income: When income goes up, the demand for these goods goes up. When incomes decline, the demand for these goods declines as well.

> The demand for normal goods varies directly with income.

However, certain goods are *inferior goods* because the demand for them varies inversely with income. For example, as income declines, the demand for potatoes, spaghetti, rice, and intercity bus rides increases. Why? Because these are the types of goods and services purchased by poorer people, and if income declines, people are poorer. As incomes rise, the demand for these inferior goods declines because people can now afford more meat, cheese, and other relatively expensive foods, and they'll take planes rather than ride in buses.

> The demand for inferior goods varies inversely with income.

Changes in the Prices of Related Goods and Services   Suppose tunas suddenly discovered a way to evade tuna fishermen, the supply of tuna fish drastically declined, and the price of tuna fish shot up to $3 a can. What do you think would soon happen to the price of salmon, chicken, and other close substitute goods? Obviously, they would be driven up.

Let's see why this happens. First, the supply of tuna fish goes down and its price goes up. Most shoppers would say to themselves, "Three dollars a can! I've had tuna fish sandwiches for lunch every day of my life, but I'm not going to pay three dollars!" And so the former tuna fish buyers end up buying salmon and chicken. What has happened to the demand for salmon and chicken? It has gone up. And when the demand for something goes up, what happens to its price? It too goes up.

Many power plants can burn either natural gas or oil, so the prices tend to be linked. When one becomes scarce, the price of both tends to rise.

Now we can generalize. The prices of substitute goods are directly related. If the price of one good goes up, people will increase their purchases of close substitutes, driving their prices up. If the price of one good comes down, people will decrease their purchases of close substitutes, driving *their* prices down.

> The prices of substitute goods are directly related.

The prices of another set of goods and services, those with complementary relationships, are inversely related. That is, when the price of one goes down, the price of the other goes up, or vice versa.

> The prices of complementary goods are inversely related.

Suppose the price of DVD rentals falls from $2 a day to 50 cents a day. Many people will rush out to buy DVD players, driving up their prices. But what will happen if gasoline goes up to $5 a gallon? People will drive a lot less. This will lower the demand for tires, pushing down their prices.

Changes in Tastes and Preferences   Suppose the American Cancer Society and the surgeon general mounted a heavy TV campaign with rock stars, professional athletes, movie actors and actresses, and other celebrities. The message: Stop smoking. Imagine what a successful campaign would do to cigarette sales.

Sometimes tastes and preferences change by themselves over time. Over the last two decades Americans have opted for smaller cars and less-fattening foods, and growing numbers of people have become more fashion conscious, buying only designer clothing and accessories. No member of *my* generation would have guessed that children would one day demand "fashionable" sneakers at more than $150 a pair.

Patterns of food consumption have changed over time. Beginning in the 1950s, Americans became increasingly conscious of being overweight, and very soon the supermarket shelves began filling with dietary products. As each new dietary fad took hold, our preferences shifted from low calories to low carbohydrates, to low fat, to whatever the next fad dictates. And there was even a papal decree which had a major effect on eating patterns. (See box, "The Pope and the Price of Fish.")

Changes in Price Expectations   If people expect the price of a product to rise, they rush out to stock up before the price goes up. However, if the price is expected to fall, they will tend to hold off on their purchases.

When it appears that a major war will break out, people will stock up on canned food, appliances, and anything else they think may be hard to buy in the coming months. On the other hand, when prices seem inordinately high, as the Manhattan co-op and condominium market did in early 1985, potential buyers will hold out for lower prices. Incidentally, the prices of co-ops and condominiums *did* come down considerably in 1985 and 1986, partly because buyers expected a decline and waited for it to happen.

Changes in Population   As the nation's population increases, the demand for a particular good or service tends to increase. Mainly because of immigration—both legal and illegal—our population has been growing by more than 3 million each year, adding to the demand for food, housing, automobiles, medical care, and tens of thousands of other goods and services. Contrary to common opinion among many native-born Americans, immigration creates jobs and profit opportunities.

The changing age distribution of our population also affects demand. During the baby boom, 1946 to 1964, there was a tremendous rise in the demand for housing, and later, as these babies became teenagers, there was more demand for rock concert tickets, stereo systems, and designer jeans. In the second, third, and fourth decades of the 21st century, there will be a higher demand for retirement homes, nursing homes, wheelchairs, and bifocal glasses.

The Pope and the Price of Fish

In 1966 Pope Paul VI issued a decree allowing American Catholic bishops to end year-round meatless Fridays, except during Lent. So what did this decree have to do with the price of fish?

A lot, as it turns out. Until 1966 Catholics across the nation generally ate fish every Friday. Since one of every four Americans was Catholic, that was a whole lot of fish. In an article published in the December 1968 *American Economic Review,* Frederick Bell showed that the papal/bishop action caused the average price of seven kinds of fish to fall by 12.5 percent.* The declines ranged from 21 percent for large haddock to 2 percent for scrod.

What this all came down to was a substantial decline in the demand for fish. And when demand falls, while supply remains the same, price will fall. If a future pope were to nullify this decree, it would be interesting to see how high the price of fish would rise.

---

*F.W. Bell, "The Pope and the Price of Fish," *The American Economic Review* (1968), vol. 58, no. 5, pp. 1346–50.

Supply Defined

Supply is *a schedule of quantities of a good or service that people are willing to sell at various prices.* As prices rise, they are willing to sell more.[1] Thus we have a positive or direct relationship between price and quantity: As price rises, quantity supplied rises; as price falls, quantity supplied falls.

Definition of supply

You may ask *why* quantity supplied rises as price rises. Let me answer by asking *you* a question. Can you type? I mean, can you type at all? Even using the two-finger method with four mistakes on each line? Most people can type at least that well.

What happens when your professor wants a term paper typed? "I don't own a PC." "My PC is down." "My printer ran out of ink." "I don't know how to type." "I have a broken hand—tomorrow I'll bring in the cast."

But if the professor insists on a typed term paper, somehow everyone eventually comes up with one. Some students pay people to type the papers. Some students even pay people to *write* them. If the going rate were $2 a page and you were a terrible typist, you might well go out and hire a typist.

What if suddenly millions of term papers were assigned and, because of the unprecedented demand for typists, the price was bid up to $20 a page. Would *you* pay someone $20 a page to do what you could do yourself? Why stop there? Twenty dollars a page! Why not set yourself up in business as a typist?

Let's analyze what has happened. At very low prices, many students are willing to hire typists; but at very high prices, they'd not only do their own typing, but they'd hire themselves out as typists. This helps explain why, at very high prices, the quantity supplied will be high.

Try *this* one on for size. Over the last 20 or 30 years doctors have become very reluctant to make house calls. "You broke your leg, have a 108-degree fever, and you're hallucinating? You must be hallucinating if you think I make house calls. Why don't you hop right over to the office and we'll have a look at you?" How do you get this joker to make a house call? Do what you do when you want a ringside table at a club; grease the guy's palm. Tell your doctor there's an extra $100 in it for him if he can make it over to your place before your mortician. If $100 doesn't do it, try $200. Almost everyone can be bought for a price. The only question is: How much?

Individual Supply and Market Supply

Individual supply is *the supply schedule of a single firm.* As we've seen, the higher the price, the greater the quantity of output supplied by an individual firm.

There are many influences on supply, including the cost of production, technological advance, the number of suppliers, the expectation of future price changes, and taxes on the good or service being sold. Each of these factors will be discussed a little later in the chapter.

Market supply is the sum of the supply schedules of all the individual firms in the industry. Table 3 presents a simplified supply schedule for the American automobile industry (excluding imports).

There are two main simplifications in this supply schedule. Obviously, Lincoln Town Cars, Ford Mustangs, Dodge Challengers, and Honda Accords, as well as the whole range of Chryslers, Chevys, and Buicks, vary greatly in price, so we'll assume each of these nine American car manufacturers produces an identical car. A second simplification is that these companies would actually be willing to sell *any* car at relatively low prices.

---

[1] We're assuming there is no change in any of the factors that influence supply. These factors are listed later in the chapter in the section, "What Causes Changes in Supply?"

TABLE 3	Hypothetical Supply of American Cars, 2007 (*in thousands*)				
			Quantity Supplied by		
Price	GM +	Ford +	Daimler-Chrysler +	Japanese-Owned Firms =	Total
$20,000	5,311	2,356	1,245	535	9,447
18,000	4,617	1,984	991	384	7,976
16,000	4,002	1,584	762	270	6,618
14,000	3,623	1,216	601	208	5,648
12,000	3,190	996	491	181	4,858

F*igure* 5

Hypothetical Supply of American Cars, 2004
Note: We don't go down to 0 on the price scale; we don't go down to 0 on the output scale. We don't need those figures, so why put them in the graph?

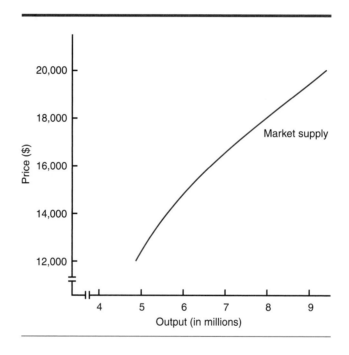

The right-hand column of Table 3 gave us the market supply. It is, of course, the sum of the individual supplies of the nine companies; and, as we see in Figure 5, the market supply curve, like each individual supply curve, moves upward to the right. At higher and higher prices the market will supply an increasing number of cars.

Changes in Supply

Earlier in this chapter we solved a series of problems dealing with changes in demand. This section presents a similar group of problems, this time dealing with changes in supply. The first set is based on Figure 6. You have four choices: (*a*) a change in quantity supplied, (*b*) a change in supply, (*c*) an increase in supply, and (*d*) a decrease in supply.

1. A move from E to F is _____.

2. A move from F to G is _____.

3. A move from G to H is _____.

4. A move from H to I is _____.

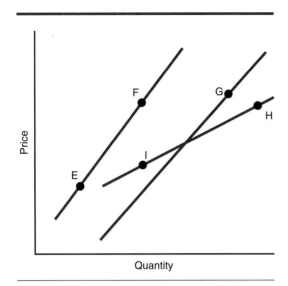

Figure 6

1. (a) When we go from E to F, there is merely a change in the quantity supplied because we never leave the supply curve.

2. (c) The move from F to G is an increase in supply. Why an increase? Because we are going to a higher supply curve; G is situated on a supply curve that provides greater quantities at *all* prices than the one on which F is located.

3. (b) The move from G to H is a change in supply. Although we leave G's supply curve—that's the change—we cannot say whether the change is an increase or a decrease because H is located on a supply curve that crosses G's.

4. (a) Finally we have the move from H to I, which is similar to the move from E to F. It is also a change in the quantity supplied.

Now we'll do another set of problems, using Figure 7.

5. A move from J to K is _____.
6. A move from K to L is _____.
7. A move from L to M is _____.

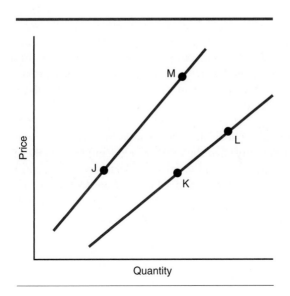

Figure 7

Differentiating between Changes in Supply and Changes in Quantity Supplied

Let's go back to the definition of supply, which is *the schedule of quantities of a good or service that people will sell at various prices*. So a change in supply is a departure from that schedule. A move from K to L on the higher supply curve in Figure 7 is *not* a change in supply. Why not? Because we stay on that supply curve. A move from K to L is a change in quantity supplied. When we leave that supply curve, as we do when we go from point L to point N, a change in supply has taken place.

The supply curve is the graphic representation of the supply schedule. Any departure from that schedule is a change in supply. But if we just slide along the supply curve, in response to a change in price, then what we have is a change in the quantity supplied.

Let's move on to Figure 8. When we go from S_2 to S_1, we say that there has been an *increase* in supply. But doesn't S_2 look higher than S_1? It may *look* higher, but what's important here is that S_1 lies entirely *to the right* of S_2. And so, at every price, sellers on S_1 are willing to sell larger quantities than sellers on S_2 will sell.

5. (c) The move from J to K is an increase in supply because we have moved to a higher supply curve (at *every* price, more is offered for sale).

6. (a) When we go from K to L we stay on the same supply curve, so it is just a change in the quantity supplied.

7. (d) The move from L to M is the opposite of that from J to K, so it is a decrease in supply.

It's easy to confuse a change in supply with a change in the quantity supplied. If the price of gold rises from $450 an ounce to $500 an ounce, sellers will put more gold on the market. Is that an increase in supply or an increase in the quantity supplied?

It's an increase in the *quantity* supplied. If you'd like a little more practice differentiating between changes in supply and changes in the quantity supplied, please see the accompanying box.

What Causes Changes in Supply?

Changes in the Cost of Production   The main reason for changes in supply is changes in the cost of production. If the cost of raw materials, labor, capital, insurance, or anything else goes up, then supply goes down. For example, consider what happened when oil prices rose to record levels in mid-2005. Within months electricity bills went up sharply. Why?

Oil is the most important energy source for generating electricity. So, when the price of oil went up, so did the cost of producing electricity. Electric utilities were no longer willing to supply as much electricity at any given price as they had been before the oil price hike. In effect, then, the rise in the price of oil lowered the supply of electricity, resulting in higher electric bills.

Let's analyze this electricity price increase with a simple supply and demand graph. Figure 8 shows that the sudden sharp increase in the cost of oil (which is used to generate much of our electricity) had the effect of reducing our supply of electricity from S_1 to S_2, which, in turn, pushed up the price of electricity from P_1 to P_2.

The same analysis applies to changes in other costs of doing business—for example, interest, rent, and wages. An increase in these costs tends to reduce supply, while a decrease in costs pushes up the supply of that good or service.

Technological Advance   A technological improvement will increase supply. For example, look at the improvements in personal computers over the last 15 years. In addition, we are able to build PCs at much lower cost.

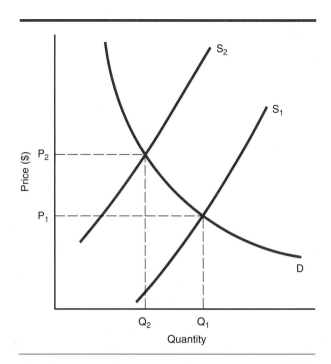

F*igure* 8
Hypothetical Demand and
Supply for Electricity
We're getting a little ahead of
ourselves here since we haven't
gotten to finding equilibrium price
yet. This concept was covered
thoroughly in Chapter 3; we'll
come back again to finding
equilibrium price in just a couple
of pages.

Prices of Other Goods   Changes in the prices of other goods can shift the supply curve for a product. If the price of corn rises, a farmer may cut back on the production of wheat. Or if the price of hair transplants declines, some dermatologists may do more face-lifts.

Change in the Number of Suppliers   When more sellers enter an industry, supply rises. Consider, for example, the proliferation of video rental stores over the last 20 years, as the VCR, and, more recently, the DVD player have become increasingly popular. Personal trainers, health clubs, stores that do nails, and the newly minted dot-coms have seemingly materialized out of thin air. When new firms enter an industry, supply rises; when firms leave, supply falls.

Changes in Taxes   Still another factor that affects supply is taxes. The basic effect of a tax increase is to reduce supply. For example, a move from S_1 to S_2 in Figure 8 might reflect a tax increase. The effect of taxes on supply will be taken up in the next chapter.

Expectation of Future Price Changes   We'll consider one more influence on supply: the expectation of future price changes. If prices are expected to rise sharply, suppliers will try to hold current production off the market in anticipation of these higher prices. Suppose you make hula hoops and you have inside information that their price will triple in a few weeks. What do you do? You hold your hoops off the market, thereby reducing supply and driving up price. On the other hand, if you expect a steep drop in prices, what will you do? You'll try to offer your entire inventory at lower prices, which thereby increases supply.

Graphing the Demand and Supply Curves

From here on we're going to be drawing a lot of graphs. Once we set up a graph, we plot demand and supply curves by connecting the dots. You will find it a lot easier to draw your graphs on graph paper, and your answers will be much more accurate. So if you have not yet purchased a package of graph paper, please go out right now and buy one. In fact, buy two, because you'll run through a couple of packages over the next few weeks.

TABLE 4	Hypothetical Demand Schedule
Price	Quantity Demanded
$10	1
9	2
8	4
7	7
6	12

Graphing the Demand Curve

Graphing step by step

This is a hands-on approach to economics. What we're going to do now is graph the demand schedule shown in Table 4. I'm going to talk you through this step-by-step. The first step is to set up the axes of the graph. The vertical axis measures price, and the horizontal axis measures quantity. This is a convention that we follow consistently in economics—price (or some other variable measured in money) goes on the vertical axis, and quantity (often output) is measured on the horizontal axis.

Setting up the vertical axis

Step 2 is to figure out our scales of measurement. On the vertical axis we measure price from $10 down to $6. There's a temptation to go all the way down to a price of zero, but that just wastes your time. Ideally a graph should take up about two-thirds of a sheet of graph paper.

Setting up the horizontal axis

Step 3 is to set up the horizontal axis, or quantity scale.

Ready for the third step? All right, then, here it comes. Put numbers on your quantity scale. Here you can start with 0 directly under the price scale and work your way across to the right. Go ahead and put in the numbers on your horizontal axis. Did you number the quantities consecutively from 0 to 12? That is not a good idea because consecutive numbering—one number to each line (or box) on your graph—makes it hard to read.

You'd be much better off numbering by twos or fours. It's easier to read a scale that has numbers that are an inch apart, rather than just ¼-inch apart.

Remember, you have to be able to read your graph and to reach accurate conclusions on the basis of your observations.

Plotting the demand curve

Step 4: Place dots for each of the points (or coordinates) of your demand curve on the graph. Use the data from Table 4.

Step 5: Connect the dots. Wait! I almost forgot to tell you something. Don't connect the dots with a ruler or any type of straightedge. Connect the dots freehand. Let your eyes guide you into drawing a smooth curve. Wait! I almost forgot to tell you something else. Use a pencil to draw your curve. Always draw your graphs in pencil. Can you guess why? You guessed it! If you mess up, you can erase your mistake and not have to start all over again. Before exams I warn my students about never drawing their graphs in ink. But about midway through the exam I hear paper being crumpled and students muttering under their breath. And they're the ones who tell me at the end of the test that I didn't give them enough time.

Now connect your dots and then see if your graph looks like the one I drew in Figure 9. If it does, great! If it doesn't, then check each of your dots with each of mine and see where you went astray. Throughout the next 8 chapters, I'll be asking you to do calculations and to draw graphs, and then to check your work. You'll be getting most things right, but remember that you can learn a lot from your mistakes.

The law of demand is this: The lower the price of a good or service, the greater the quantity that people will buy.

Notice that the demand curve slopes downward and to the right as quantity rises. At high prices people buy little, but as price declines they buy more. We have an inverse relationship: As price comes down, quantity purchased goes up. This is the law of demand. More formally stated, *the law of demand tells us that the lower the price of a good or service, the greater the quantity that people will buy.* So the demand curve's downward slope reflects the law of demand.

So much for demand. Now we're ready for supply. We'll follow exactly the same procedure we followed for demand: We'll use data from a table to draw a graph of a

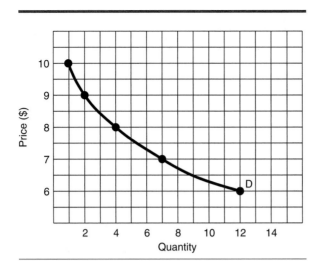

Figure 9
Demand Curve

supply curve. Then we'll put our two curves together in one graph to see one of the longest-playing acts in the entire history of economic thought: the law of demand and supply. Or is it the law of supply and demand? Actually, either one is fine.

Graphing the Supply Curve

Now use the data in Table 5 to draw the graph of a supply curve. Use a separate piece of graph paper, set up your axes, plot out each of the five points, and connect them to obtain your supply curve. Remember to do it in pencil and to draw a smooth freehand curve. Then see whether it came out like mine in Figure 10.

TABLE 5	Hypothetical Supply Schedule
Price	Quantity Supplied
$10	14
9	12
8	9
7	5
6	1

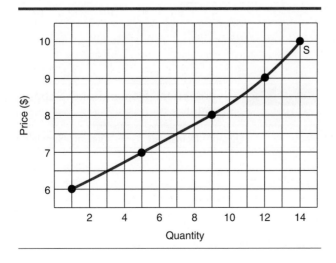

Figure 10
Supply Curve

The law of supply: The higher the price of a good or service, the greater the quantity that people will sell.

You'll observe that the supply curve slopes upward and to the right as quantity rises. As price rises, then, quantity supplied rises as well. This is a direct relationship: Price and quantity supplied move in the same direction—which happens to be the law of supply. In more formal terms, *the higher the price of a good or service, the greater the quantity that people will sell.* So the upward slope of the supply curve reflects the law of supply.

Equilibrium

At equilibrium, quantity demanded and quantity supplied are equal. At a certain price, all buyers who are willing to buy will be able to. And all sellers who are willing to sell will also be able to. That price is the equilibrium price.

The equilibrium point is where the demand and supply curves cross.

To find the equilibrium price and quantity, let's draw our demand and supply curves on the same graph. In Figure 11 we can find our equilibrium point by noting exactly where the curves cross. That tells us equilibrium price and quantity.

Where the demand and supply curves cross is a price of about $7.20, and the quantity is about 5. As a check, go back to the tables, which, if anything, are more accurate than the graph. This is because the graph is derived from the tables. Table 6 combines Table 4 and Table 5.

At a price of $8 in Table 6, the quantity demanded is 4 and the quantity supplied is 9. The difference between quantity demanded (4) and quantity supplied (9) is 5. At a price of $7, quantity demanded is 7 and quantity supplied is 5. At $7, quantity demanded (7) and quantity supplied (5) are only 2 apart. A price of $7 is much closer to equilibrium price than is $8. Remember that at equilibrium, quantity demanded equals quantity

Figure 11

Demand, Supply, and Equilibrium

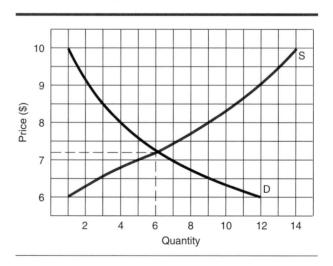

TABLE 6	Hypothetical Demand and Supply Schedules	
Price	Quantity Demanded	Quantity Supplied
$10	1	14
9	2	12
8	4	9
7	7	5
6	12	1

supplied. Because quantity demanded and quantity supplied are 2 apart at $7 and 5 apart at $8, $7 is much closer to equilibrium than $8.

If price is determined by supply and demand, we may ask whether one or the other is more important. More than a century ago the great classical economist Alfred Marshall wrote, "We might as reasonably dispute whether it is the upper or the under blade of a pair of scissors that cuts a piece of paper" as whether price is set by demand or supply.[2] In short, supply and demand are equally important in setting price.

Price always tends toward its equilibrium level. If it should happen to be set higher, say $9, it will fall to $7.20. And if it's set lower than $7.20, it will rise.

Let's say the price is $9. A lot of unhappy sellers will say, "Here I go without a sale when I would have been willing to settle for a lower price." What do they do? They lower their price. And when they do—to, let's say, $8—most of the other sellers follow suit. Why? Because otherwise they'd sell nothing. Why would any buyers pay any sellers $9 when the others are selling for $8?

As the price falls to $8, a few sellers—3, to be exact—will leave the market. In Table 6 we see that at $9 there are 12 sellers, but at $8 there are only 9. At the same time the number of buyers rises from 2 to 4.[3]

We're not yet at equilibrium, but we're getting closer. At $9 sellers outnumbered buyers 12 to 2. At $8 sellers outnumber buyers just 9 to 4. The price must be lowered to $7.20 for 6 buyers and 6 sellers to do business.

If price were below equilibrium, say at $6, the dissatisfied buyers would bid the price up. At $6 there would be 12 people willing to buy, but only 1 seller. Some of the buyers—7, in fact—would be willing to pay $7. So they'll say to the sellers, "Let's make a deal." These buyers will bid the price up to $7 and find 5 sellers willing to do business. We're still not quite at equilibrium. The price will be bid up slightly more to $7.20, bringing in one more seller and causing one more buyer to drop out of the market. At $7.20 there are 6 buyers and 6 sellers.

An alternative way to look at prices above and below equilibrium is in terms of surpluses and shortages. When the price is above $7.20, there is a surplus. Quantity supplied is greater than quantity demanded, and this difference is the surplus. For example, at a price of $9, the surplus is 10. How is the surplus eliminated? As we've just seen, by letting the price fall. The surplus, then, eliminates itself through the price mechanism.

When the price is too low, there is a shortage. A shortage of 11 units occurs when the price is $6. But the shortage disappears when the price rises automatically to its equilibrium level of $7.20.[4]

Equilibrium price is the result of the forces of supply and demand. Together they determine equilibrium price. There will be no tendency for a price to change once it has reached its equilibrium. However, if either demand or supply (or both) changes, there will be a new equilibrium price.

A price is pushed toward equilibrium by the market forces of supply and demand. In other words, the price of any good or service is set by the law of supply and demand. That makes things easy for economists. Why are Rolls Royces so expensive? Supply and demand. Why is rice so cheap? Supply and demand. As long as the government does not interfere with the private market, the forces of supply and demand set the prices of everything. Or, as the popular saying goes, you can't repeal the law of supply and demand.

At equilibrium everyone is happy. Buyers can buy as much as they want. Sellers can sell as much as they want. Quantity demanded equals quantity supplied, and the market is said to *clear*.

It's easy to train economists. Just teach a parrot to say "supply and demand."

—Thomas Carlyle

Above equilibrium price there are surpluses.

Below equilibrium price there are shortages.

---

[2]See Alfred Marshall, *The Principles of Economics,* 8th ed., 1920, p. 348. The first edition came out in 1890.

[3]I have oversimplified here by assuming that each seller has one unit to sell and that each buyer buys just one unit. In real life buyers may purchase many units and sellers may supply many units.

[4]Shortages and surpluses were discussed much more extensively in Chapter 3.

TABLE 7	Hypothetical Demand and Supply Schedules	
Price	Quantity Demanded	Quantity Supplied
$15	2	19
14	4	17
13	7	12
12	12	6
11	20	3

F*igure* 12

Demand and Supply

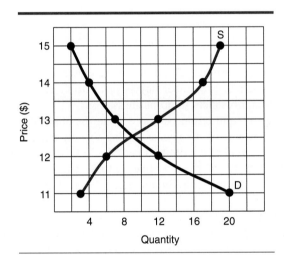

Finding Equilibrium Price and Quantity

If we draw our graphs accurately, we can usually find equilibrium price and quantity in a couple of seconds, especially if we've used graph paper. But sometimes we need to do further analysis to find really accurate equilibrium prices and quantities.

First, please draw a graph of the demand and supply curves for the information shown in Table 7.

Finding equilibrium price from the table

If you did a good job, your graph probably looks a lot like mine in Figure 12. Now comes the analysis. How much is equilibrium price? Go ahead and write down your best guess. What did you get? Maybe $12.50? I hate to tell you, but $12.50 is not the right answer. The way to find the right answer is to go back to Table 7 and do a little analysis. We want to find the price that is closest to equilibrium price. Is it $12 or $13? Take your time. Don't let me rush you. OK, time's up. Equilibrium price is a little closer to $13 than to $12.

How do I *know* this? Easy. At a price of $13, quantity demanded is 7 and quantity supplied is 12. So they're 5 units apart. Now check out the quantity demanded and the quantity supplied at a price of $12. Quantity demanded is 12 and quantity supplied is 6; they're 6 units apart. In other words, we are a little closer to equilibrium at a price of $13 than at a price of $12.

So what *is* the equilibrium price? Would $12.60 be correct? Sure. How about $12.58? Yes! $12.56? $12.61? $12.62? Any one of these is a fine answer, because each is a little closer to $13 than to $12. Anything between $12.55 and $12.65 is fine. We're not talking about economics being an exact science here, but more of an art.

TABLE 8		
Price	Quantity Demanded	Quantity Supplied
$15	5	10
14	10	4

You don't have to draw a graph to find the equilibrium price and quantity. There's enough information in Table 8 to find them. See what you can do.

At a price of $15 quantity demanded is 5 and quantity supplied is 10, so they are 5 apart. At a price of $14 quantity demanded is 10 and quantity supplied is 4, so they are 6 apart. We are a little closer to equilibrium at a price of $15 than a price of $14. Let's call our equilibrium price $14.60 (or anything between $14.55 and 14.65).

Current Issue: Why Can't I Sell My House?

My neighbors, the Fergusons, had lived on our block for over 30 years. The Fergusons' children had grown up, gotten married, and had started their own families. So Mr. and Mrs. Ferguson decided to sell their house and move to a smaller house about 50 miles away.

Most of the houses in our neighborhood were sold over the last 10 years for two main reasons. Like the Fergusons, the owners didn't need such large houses any more. And because real estate prices had risen very rapidly, they could sell their homes for eight or ten times what they had paid for them.

The Fergusons had not sold their house by the time they moved. No problem, their broker said, indicating there were plenty of interested buyers. Yeah, the house needed a little work, but so did most of the other houses in our neighborhood. Mr. Ferguson would come by every couple of weeks to mow the lawn and spruce things up.

In the meanwhile, real estate prices stopped climbing. Still, each month, a few more houses were sold, as old families moved out and new ones moved in. But the Ferguson house stood empty.

Question: Why couldn't they sell their house? Think about this question for a minute and then, even if you're not sure, just guess at the answer.

OK, time's up. Did you say that maybe their price was too high? Then you're right!

The Fergusons could have sold their house two years ago if they would have been willing to accept about $20,000 less than they were asking. In fact, when they finally *did* sell, that's about what they took. The Fergusons' mistake, of course, was thinking that real estate prices would keep going up. But they guessed wrong.

As sellers, we can learn a valuable lesson from the Fergusons' experience. If someone were to ask them today, "What would you have done differently?" They'd answer, "We would have accepted a lower price."

So now we can make a general observation. You can sell virtually any good or service for which there is a demand. As long as people are willing and able to pay you for that good or service, you can sell it. If you want to sell something pretty quickly and get no bites, what do you do?

You lower your price. And if there are *still* no buyers willing to pay your price? You keep lowering it until you make a sale.

So the next time you hear someone say, "I can't sell my house," or better yet, "No one wants to buy my house," you know just what to tell him.

Questions for Further Thought and Discussion

1. Suppose a nearby concert hall booked a different one of your favorite performers every night for the next month. Make up a table showing your demand schedule for tickets.

2. What inferior goods do you buy? Would you continue to buy them if your income doubled?

3. Explain how the price of a good you buy is affected by changes in the prices of (a) substitute goods; (b) complementary goods.

4. Use examples from your own experience to illustrate (a) a change in demand; (b) a change in the quantity demanded. Draw a graph for each example showing what happened to prices.

5. Give one example from actual firms or industries for each of the factors that cause changes in supply. Draw a graph for each example showing what happens to price and quantity supplied.

6. It has just been reported that Happy Smile toothpaste reduces your cavities by 70 percent, while whitening your teeth and freshening your breath. Using supply and demand curves, demonstrate the report's likely effect on the price and quantity of this toothpaste's sales.

7. Do you agree with this statement: "As price goes up, demand goes down"? Explain your answer.

8. Why does the demand curve slope downward?

9. Why does the supply curve slope upward?

10. If you were a seller, why would you want to limit supply—either by keeping out new market entrants or by establishing production quotas for everyone? Show this graphically. And why would you hate that if you were a consumer?

11. How could an economic crisis in Southeast Asia cause the price you pay for gasoline to fall? Show this graphically.

12. If marijuana were legalized, what do you think would happen to the supply and demand curves and the price? Show this graphically.

13. You're moving into a new house one week from today. Checking the local newspaper and the phone book, you find 10 movers. Each one of them gives you a quote at least $1,000 more than you think you should pay. Explain what you will do in terms of demand and supply.

Workbook for Chapter 17

Name _____   Date _____

Multiple-Choice Questions

Circle the letter that corresponds to the best answer.

1. As price rises _____.
   a) supply rises
   b) supply falls
   c) quantity supplied rises
   d) quantity supplied falls

2. Goods for which demand is directly (positively) related to income are called _____.
   a) substitute goods
   b) complementary goods
   c) inferior goods
   d) normal goods

3. Change in which of the following would not quickly cause a shift in demand?
   a) Number of buyers
   b) Tastes
   c) Buyers' perception of quality of product
   d) Income
   e) Price

4. A shift in the supply curve for gasoline in the United States would result if _____.
   a) people decided to travel more by automobile
   b) the OPEC nations decided to stop sales of crude oil to the United States
   c) the price of gasoline increased
   d) the price of gasoline decreased
   e) the price of mass transit increased

5. If the price of a product rises and as a result businesses increase their production, then _____.
   a) supply has increased
   b) supply has decreased
   c) quantity supplied has increased
   d) quantity supplied has decreased
   e) both supply and quantity supplied have increased

6. Changes in supply may be caused by changes in _____.
   a) the cost of factors of production
   b) the level of technology
   c) the number of suppliers
   d) all of the above
   e) none of the above

7. Each of the following may lead to a change in the demand for product A except _____.
   a) a change in the price of product A
   b) a change in people's taste for product A
   c) a change in people's incomes
   d) a change in the price of product B (a substitute for product A)

8. The retail market for gasoline is _____.
   a) local   c) national
   b) regional   d) international

9. Suppose the price of a service falls and people buy more of that service. What has happened?
   a) Quantity demanded changed.
   b) Demand changed.
   c) Demand increased.
   d) Demand decreased.

10. An increase in the wage rate paid to construction workers will tend to _____.
    a) decrease the demand for homes
    b) cause a movement along the supply curve for new homes
    c) decrease the supply of new homes
    d) increase the supply of new homes

11. If the price of laser surgery to correct near-sightedness falls by 50 percent, _____.
    a) industry supply will rise
    b) industry supply will fall
    c) industry demand will rise
    d) industry demand will fall

12. An increase in the demand for steak could be caused quickly by a(n) _____.
    a) fall in the price of steak
    b) increase in the supply of steak
    c) expectation of a future cutback in the supply of steak
    d) a decline in the price of chicken

13. The demand for an inferior good is _____.
    a) positively related to its own price
    b) negatively related to income
    c) unaffected by consumer tastes and preferences
    d) insensitive to changes in prices of its complements

Use Table 1 to answer questions 14 and 15.

TABLE 1

Price	Quantity Demanded	Quantity Supplied
$12	10	15
11	14	10
10	20	5

14. The equilibrium price is about _____.
    a) $11.25   d) $11.60
    b) $11.40   e) $11.75
    c) $11.50

15. Equilibrium quantity is about _____.
    a) 12   d) 12.8
    b) 12.3   e) 13
    c) 12.5

16. Demand for a good or service may be depicted in _____.
    a) a table, but not a graph
    b) a graph, but not a table
    c) both a graph and a table
    d) neither a graph nor a table

For questions 17 through 22, use choices a) through d) and Figures 1 and 2. Each choice may be used more than once.

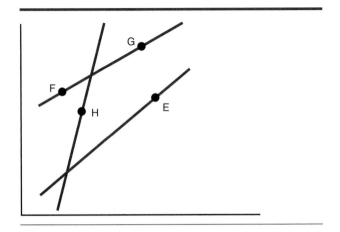

Figure 1

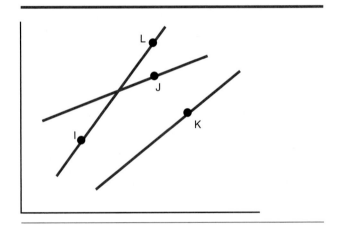

Figure 2

    a) change in quantity supplied
    b) change in supply
    c) increase in supply
    d) decrease in supply

____ 17. A move from E to F

____ 18. A move from F to G

____ 19. A move from G to H

____ 20. A move from I to J

____ 21. A move from J to K

____ 22. A move from K to L

430

23. If the price of cameras falls, there will be a(n)

    _____.

    a) decrease in the demand for film
    b) decrease in the quantity of cameras demanded
    c) decrease in the supply of cameras
    d) increase in the demand for cameras
    e) increase in the quantity of cameras demanded

24. The market demand for a good will decrease

    _____.

    a) as income decreases if the good is an inferior good
    b) if the market price of a substitute good increases
    c) as income decreases if the good is a normal good
    d) if the market price of a complementary good decreases
    e) as the number of consumers in the market increases

25. A decrease in demand means that the quantity

    demanded _____.
    a) does not fall at any price
    b) falls only at the equilibrium price
    c) falls at a few prices
    d) falls at most prices
    e) falls at all prices

For questions 26 through 31, use choices a) through d) (the same choice may be used more than once) and refer to Figures 3 and 4.

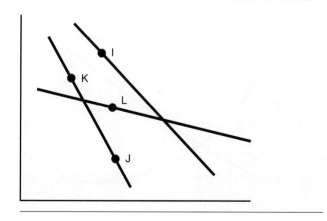

Figure 3

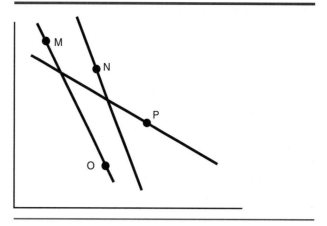

Figure 4

    a) change in quantity demanded
    b) change in demand
    c) increase in demand
    d) decrease in demand

____ 26. A move from I to J

____ 27. A move from J to K

____ 28. A move from K to L

____ 29. A move from M to N

____ 30. A move from N to O

____ 31. A move from O to P

Fill-In Questions

1. As price rises, quantity supplied _____.

2. At _____, quantity demanded equals quantity supplied.

3. As price falls, quantity demanded _____.

4. An increase in supply is shown graphically by a shift of the supply curve to the _____.

5. The main reason for changes in supply is changes in the _____.

6. If business owners expected a steep drop in prices, they would take action which would tend to _____ supply.

Problems

1. Given the information in Table 2, draw a graph of the demand and supply curves on a piece of graph paper.

TABLE 2

Price	Quantity Demanded	Quantity Supplied
$20	1	25
19	3	24
18	6	22
17	10	18
16	16	10
15	24	2

2. Equilibrium price is $_____; equilibrium quantity is _____.

3. Given the information in Table 3, draw a graph of the demand and supply curves on a piece of graph paper.

TABLE 3

Price	Quantity Demanded	Quantity Supplied
$15	1	27
14	4	25
13	9	21
12	16	12
11	22	6
10	26	2

4. Equilibrium price is $_____; equilibrium quantity is _____.

5. Draw a demand curve, D_1. Then draw a second demand curve, D_2, that illustrates a decrease in demand.

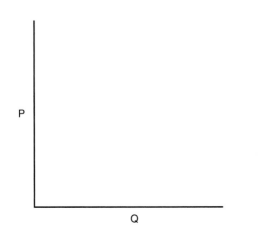

6. Draw a supply curve, S_1, and a second supply curve, S_2, that represents an increase in supply.

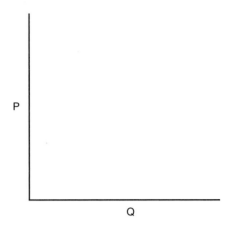

7. Given the information in Table 4, make your best estimate of equilibrium price and quantity. You don't need to draw a graph.

TABLE 4

Price	Quantity Demanded	Quantity Supplied
$6	12	19
5	18	13

8. A major technological improvement leads to a large decrease in the cost of production. Using Figure 5 draw a new supply curve, S_2, to reflect this change. Then state the new equilibrium price and quantity.

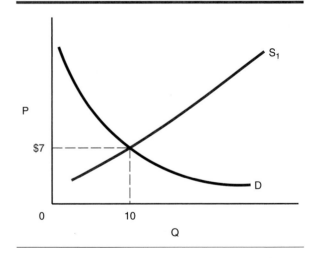

Figure 5

432

Chapter 18

The Elasticities of Demand
and Supply

If the government wants to discourage teen smoking by raising the price of cigarettes with a hefty tax, will it work? How big would the price increase need to be to induce, say, a 50 percent drop in teen smoking? Would such a price increase affect teens and adults equally? Lawmakers rely on economists to answer such questions by estimating elasticities.

In this chapter we'll continue our analysis of supply and demand to include *how much* of the quantity demanded responds to a change in price—what economists call *elasticity of demand*. Similarly, *elasticity of supply* measures responsiveness of the quantity supplied to change in price. These concepts are useful economic tools because they allow us to make predictions about what will happen in markets when prices or quantities change.

CHAPTER OBJECTIVES

In this chapter you will find out everything you always wanted to know about:

- The elasticity of demand.
- The determinants of elasticity.
- Elasticity and total revenue.

- The elasticity of supply.
- Tax incidence.

The Elasticity of Demand

The elasticity of demand for a good or service measures the change in quantity demanded in response to change in price. In other words, elasticity measures the sensitivity (measured in percentage change) of quantity demanded because of a change (percentage) in price. When price goes up, we know that quantity demanded declines. But by how much? Elasticity provides us with a way of measuring this response. And we measure the responsiveness of quantity demanded to a change in price by calculating the coefficient of price elasticity of demand (E_p) as follows.

Measuring Elasticity

$$E_p = \frac{\text{Percentage change in quantity demanded}}{\text{Percentage change in price}}$$

We'll start with this problem. A business firm has been selling 100 kitchen chairs a week. It runs a sale, charging $8 instead of the usual $10. People recognize this great

Why We Don't Use a Simpler Elasticity Formula

Considering that elasticity is the percentage that quantity sold changes in response to a 1 percent change in price, wouldn't it be a lot easier to use the formula *percentage change in quantity divided by percentage change in price?* Let's try it for this problem. Price drops from $10 to $9, and quantity demanded rises from 100 to 120.

Using the formula:

$$\frac{\text{Percentage change in quantity}}{\text{Percentage change in price}}$$

we get:

$$\frac{20\%}{10\%} = 2$$

So far, so good. Now let's look at the same price range but reverse the direction so that price rises from $9 to $10 and quantity demanded falls from 120 to 100. Here our percentage change in quantity divided by percentage change in price would be:

$$\frac{16\frac{2}{3}\%}{11\frac{1}{9}\%} = 1.5$$

That's quite a discrepancy for the range of the demand schedule between $9 and $10. When price is lowered from $10 to $9, elasticity is 2, but when it is raised from $9 to

$10, elasticity is only 1.5. Therefore, the same formula measuring elasticity over the same range of the demand curve yields two very different answers.

Let's try the more complex formula on the same data. Go ahead and do it in the space provided below, first trying the price decrease and then the price increase.

Solution: $P_1 = \$10$; $P_2 = \$9$; $Q_1 = 100$; and $Q_2 = 120$.

$$\frac{120 - 100}{120 + 100} \cdot \frac{9 + 10}{9 - 10} = \frac{\overset{1}{\cancel{20}}}{\underset{11}{\cancel{220}}} \cdot \frac{19}{1} = \frac{19}{11} = 1.72727*$$

(when price rises from $9 to $10)

$P_1 = \$9$; $P_2 = \$10$; $Q_1 = 120$; and $Q_2 = 100$.

$$\frac{100 - 120}{100 + 120} \cdot \frac{10 + 9}{10 - 9} = \frac{20}{220} \cdot \frac{19}{1} = 1.72727*$$

---

* You may round off at one decimal place for elasticity problems (1.72727 = 1.7) or at two places (1.73).

Elasticity formula

Above 1 elastic

Vertical-perfectly inelastic
horizontal - perfectly elastic

bargain, and sales go up to 140 chairs. If P_1 is the initial price charged and P_2 is the sale price, Q_1 the initial quantity sold and Q_2 the quantity sold during the sale, we can calculate the coefficient of price elasticity of demand as follows:

$$E_p = \frac{\text{Percentage change in quantity demanded}}{\text{Percentage change in price}} = \frac{Q_2 - Q_1}{Q_2 + Q_1} \cdot \frac{P_2 + P_1}{P_2 - P_1}$$

This formula looks a lot more complicated than it is (see the box, "Why We Don't Use a Simpler Elasticity Formula"). It simply calls for finding the percentage change in quantity and the percentage change in price, and then dividing the former by the latter. Go ahead and substitute into the formula in the space below and then solve.

Solution: $P_1 = 10$; $P_2 = 8$; $Q_1 = 100$; and $Q_2 = 140$.

$$\frac{140 - 100}{140 + 100} \cdot \frac{8 + 10}{8 - 10} = \frac{40}{240} \cdot \frac{18}{-2} = \frac{1}{6} \cdot \frac{9}{-1} = \frac{9}{6} = \frac{3}{-2} = 1.5$$

Elasticity comes to -1.5, but by convention we ignore the sign (which, by the way, will always be negative for price elasticity of demand). In this case our answer is 1.5. A coefficient of 1.5 for price elasticity of demand means that for every 1 percent change in price, there will be a corresponding 1.5 percent change in quantity demanded.

Most students initially have some difficulty calculating elasticity, so we'll work out a few more problems. When you become confident that you can do this type of problem, you may skip the remaining problems and begin the next section.

Problem: Price is raised from $40 to $41, and quantity sold declines from 15 to 12. Solve in the space below.

Solution: $P_1 = \$40$; $P_2 = \$41$; $Q_1 = 15$; and $Q_2 = 12$.

$$\frac{12-15}{12+15} \cdot \frac{41+40}{41-40} = \frac{3}{27} \cdot \frac{\overset{3}{\cancel{81}}}{1} = \frac{9}{1} = 9$$

Problem: Price is lowered from $5 to $4, and quantity demanded rises from 80 to 82.

Solution: $P_1 = \$5$; $P_2 = \$4$; $Q_1 = 80$; and $Q_2 = 82$.

$$\frac{82-80}{82+80} \cdot \frac{4+5}{4-5} = \frac{2}{\underset{18}{\cancel{162}}} \cdot \frac{\overset{1}{\cancel{9}}}{1} = \frac{2}{18} = \frac{1}{9} = 0.11$$

Problem: Price is raised from $30 to $33, and quantity demanded falls from 100 to 90.

Solution: $P_1 = \$30$; $P_2 = \$33$; $Q_1 = 100$; and $Q_2 = 90$.

$$\frac{90-100}{90+100} \cdot \frac{33+30}{33-30} = \frac{10}{190} \cdot \frac{63}{3} = \frac{1}{19} \cdot \frac{21}{1} = 1.11$$

The Meaning of Elasticity

What does all this mean? First, we say that when elasticity is greater than 1, demand is elastic. Remember, elasticity is the percentage change in quantity demanded brought about by a price change. It is percentage change in quantity divided by percentage change in price. For elasticity to be greater than 1, percentage change in quantity must be greater than percentage change in price. A price change of a certain percentage causes quantity to change by a larger percentage. When this happens, we say demand is elastic. For example, if the coefficient of price elasticity of demand is 10, that means for every 1 percent change in price, there will be a corresponding 10 percent change in quantity demanded. In this example, we would say demand is very elastic. We mean that the quantity demanded is responsive to price changes.

F*igure* **1**
Perfectly Elastic Demand Curve

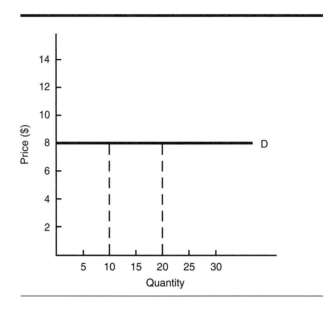

When demand is elastic, the quantity demanded is very responsive to price changes.

When demand is elastic, it stretches as price changes. And when demand is not very elastic, it does not stretch much.

Elasticity is a simple number—2, 3.5, or 0.5, for example. It's a number that represents the percentage change in quantity demanded of a good resulting from each 1 percent change in that good's price. So an elasticity of 2 means that a 1 percent price change leads to a 2 percent change in quantity. What about elasticities of 3.5 and 0.5?

When elasticity is 3.5, a 1 percent change in price results in a 3.5 percent change in quantity demanded. And when elasticity is 0.5, a 1 percent change in price leads to an 0.5 percent change in quantity demanded.

Inelastic demand is defined as an elasticity of less than 1; anything from 0 to 0.99 is inelastic. We can also make somewhat finer distinctions. An elasticity of 0.1 or 0.2 would be very inelastic, while one of 0.8 or 0.9 would be slightly inelastic. Similarly, an elasticity of 1.5 or 2 would be slightly elastic. And one of 8 or 10 would be very elastic.

The border between elastic and inelastic is 1. We call this *unit elastic.* Thus, if elasticity is less than 1, it is inelastic. If it is exactly 1, it is unit elastic. If elasticity is more than 1, it is elastic.

Now we'll deal with perfect elasticity and perfect inelasticity. Figure 1 shows a perfectly elastic demand curve. It is horizontal. Go ahead and calculate its elasticity from a quantity of 10 to a quantity of 20. Note that price remains fixed at $8.

Solution: $P_1 = \$8$; $P_2 = \$8$; $Q_1 = 10$; and $Q_2 = 20$.

$$\frac{20 - 10}{20 + 10} \cdot \frac{8 + 8}{8 - 8} = \frac{10}{30} \cdot \frac{16}{0} = \frac{1}{3} \cdot \frac{16}{0} = \infty$$

How big is infinity? Big. Very, very big. How elastic is the demand curve in Figure 1? Very, very elastic. Infinitely elastic, or as we say here, perfectly elastic.

Now we'll move on to perfect inelasticity. If perfect elasticity is ∞, how large is perfect inelasticity? $-\infty$? Nope. Go back to what I said about the range of inelasticity—anything from 0 to 0.99. The lowest it can go is 0. That's perfect inelasticity.

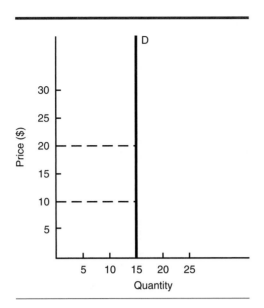

F*igure* 2
Perfectly Inelastic Demand
Curve

Using the data in Figure 2, calculate the elasticity of the vertical demand curve. Quantity stays put at 15, but price varies. Let's say the price has fallen from 20 to 10. Calculate the elasticity. Again, use the formula, substitute, and solve below.

Solution: $P_1 = 20$; $P_2 = 10$; $Q_1 = 15$; $Q_2 = 15$.

$$\frac{15 - 15}{15 + 15} \cdot \frac{10 + 20}{10 - 20} = \frac{0}{\cancel{30}} \cdot \frac{\cancel{30}^{\,1}}{10} = \frac{0}{10} = 0$$

How many times does 10 go into 0? None. You can't divide *any* number into 0. Therefore, elasticity is 0. The elasticity of a perfectly inelastic line is 0.

Next we'll consider relative elasticity. If a vertical line is perfectly inelastic and a horizontal line is perfectly elastic, what about lines that are somewhere in between? Figure 3 has two such lines. The question here is, which of the two is more elastic, D_1 or D_2?

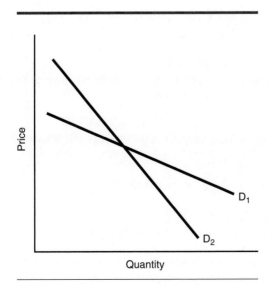

F*igure* 3
Relative Elasticity of Demand
Curves

Figure 4
Straight-Line Demand Curve

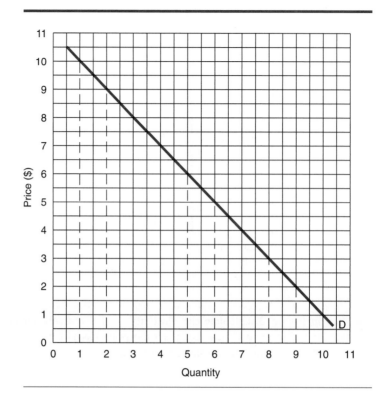

D₁ is more elastic because it is closer to being horizontal. Remember, the more horizontal the demand curve is, the more elastic it is; and the more vertical the curve, the more inelastic it is.

Finally, we'll calculate the elasticity of a straight line. Surprisingly, it is not constant. Using Figure 4, let's calculate the elasticity at three points. First, do the calculations when price falls from $10 to $9 and quantity rises from 1 to 2.

Solution: $P_1 = \$10$; $P_2 = \$9$; $Q_1 = 1$; and $Q_2 = 2$.

$$\frac{2-1}{2+1} \cdot \frac{9+10}{9-10} = \frac{1}{3} \cdot \frac{19}{1} = \frac{19}{3} = 6.33$$

An elasticity of 6.33 is fairly high.

Moving right along, let's calculate the elasticity when price falls from $6 to $5 and the quantity demanded rises from 5 to 6.

Solution: $P_1 = \$6$; $P_2 = \$5$; $Q_1 = 5$; and $Q_2 = 6$.

$$\frac{6-5}{6+5} \cdot \frac{5+6}{5-6} = \frac{1}{11} \cdot \frac{11}{1} = 1$$

What we have here is unit elasticity, when a price change causes quantity demanded to change by the same percentage. Note that in Figure 4 this occurs at the middle of the demand curve.

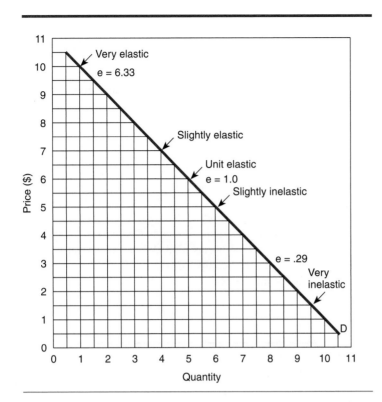

Now let's calculate the elasticity when price falls from $3 to $2 and quantity demanded rises from 8 to 9.

Solution: $P_1 = \$3$; $P_2 = \$2$; $Q_1 = 8$; and $Q_2 = 9$.

$$\frac{9-8}{9+8} \cdot \frac{2+3}{2-3} = \frac{1}{17} \cdot \frac{5}{1} = \frac{5}{17} = 0.29$$

The answer, 0.29, is rather inelastic. When we compare the three elasticities we calculated, this time moving to Figure 5, we reach this conclusion: A straight-line demand curve that moves downward to the right is very elastic at the top and progressively less elastic as we move down the curve. As we approach the lower right end of the curve, demand becomes more and more inelastic.

In 2005 the Federal Trade Commission issued a report which concluded that a 10 percent increase in the price of gasoline could ultimately result in a daily decline of 550,000 barrels of oil demanded. At that time the U.S. consumed 20 million barrels a day. Calculate the elasticity of demand for gasoline and state if it is elastic, unit elastic, or inelastic.

Solution:

$$\text{elasticity} = \frac{\text{percentage change in quantity}}{\text{percentage change in price}}$$

$$\text{elasticity} = \frac{2.75}{10.00}$$

$$\text{elasticity} = 0.275$$

The demand for gasoline is inelastic.

Do Higher Cigarette Prices Stop Smoking?

Let's face it: smokers have less fun. Everywhere they go there are No Smoking signs and they're usually forced to stand outside even in the rain and snow. To add insult to injury, the price of a pack of cigarettes has doubled in just a few years.

Now you would think that an awful lot of people must have given up smoking. A study by Michael Grossman, Gary Becker, and Kevin Murphy found that a 10 percent increase in cigarette prices reduced current consumption among adults by 4 percent, and over a five-year period cigarette consumption fell by 7.5 percent.

Another study by the U.S. General Accounting Office revealed that the elasticity of demand for cigarettes among teenagers was somewhat higher—between 0.76 and 1.2. In a survey tracking 25,000 eighth-graders since 1988, Donna B. Gilleskie and Koleman S. Strumpf of the University of North Carolina found that raising taxes by $1 per pack would reduce the likelihood of smoking by half.

This raises an interesting public policy issue. The surgeon general keeps reminding us on every pack of cigarettes as well as in newspaper and magazine cigarette ads about all the terrible things smoking will do to us. But even more effective would be a hefty tax of two or three dollars on every pack, as there is in Canada, Great Britain, Ireland, Denmark, Norway, and a few other countries. Canada's tax of $3 per pack has helped cut per capita consumption by more than 50 percent since 1980.

Figure 6
Relatively Inelastic Demand
Curve

Do you smoke? Well, whether you do or you don't, do you think the demand for cigarettes is elastic or inelastic? Are cigarettes a necessity? I'll let the smokers answer that one. Are there any close substitutes? Lollipops? Chewing gum? Hey, if these were such wonderful substitutes, you wouldn't have nearly so many smokers.

In general, it would be safe to say that the demand for cigarettes is inelastic. How inelastic? If you're really curious, then check out the box, "Do Higher Cigarette Prices Stop Smoking?"

Determinants of the Degree of Elasticity of Demand

The demand for certain goods and services is relatively elastic, while that for others is relatively inelastic. Consider heart medicine, for example. Suppose this medicine keeps you alive, and suppose its price doubles. Would you cut back on your purchases? Your demand curve would probably look like the one in Figure 6.

Do you think that a person who needs heart medicine would cut back on the quantity she buys because its price doubles? A few people might do this. Why? Because they might not be able to afford it. Maybe one or two poor souls would say it's just not worth what they're being charged.

TABLE 1	Elasticity of Demand of Selected Goods and Services		
Household electricity	0.13	Gasoline	0.60
Bread	0.15	Milk	0.63
Telephone service	0.26	Beer	0.90
Medical care	0.31	Motor vehicles	1.14
Legal services	0.37	Restaurant meals	2.27
Clothing	0.49		

Source: Compiled from numerous sources.

When AZT was first sold to people who are HIV-positive, plenty of people simply couldn't afford to pay $800 to $1,000 a month. As its price came down, the quantity purchased rose somewhat. And so, Figure 6 might well represent the demand for a life-extending drug. It's not perfectly elastic because at extremely high prices some people just can't afford the drug.

How elastic is the demand for gasoline? In the mid-1970s, when the price of oil more than tripled, American consumption of gasoline fell sharply. But when gasoline prices again tripled in 1999 and 2000, there was no appreciable cutback in gasoline sales. Instead, some people switched from using expensive premium gasoline to regular. And sales of the very largest sports utility vehicles (SUVs) fell somewhat.

One might reason that the demand for gasoline has become more inelastic since the mid-1970s. But there are two major differences between now and the mid-1970s. First, gasoline is much cheaper today, after you adjust its price for inflation. So why cut back, when you can still afford a full tank? And second, there are no gas shortages or long gas station lines as there were back in the 1970s. Back then plenty of drivers refused to spend hours waiting on a gas line, and there were others who couldn't find a nearby station that was open.

Our experience was similar when the average retail gasoline price jumped from $1.87 a gallon in September 2004 to $2.90 a year later—a 55 percent increase. Yet gasoline consumption dropped only 3.5 percent. But there were a couple of extenuating circumstances. First, many consumers probably viewed recent price increases as temporary, so why trade in that SUV for a more fuel-efficient vehicle? And then, too, most people's incomes are much higher than they were back in the 1970s, so gasoline—even at $3 a gallon—is still a relative small expense relative to buyers' incomes.

We can conclude that the demand for gasoline today is indeed inelastic (see Table 1). But, in the long run, more and more Americans may be shopping for fuel-efficient vehicles.

Can you think of any good or service for which demand is exactly unit elastic? OK, that's really an unfair question. You'll find the answer in the box, "The Cookie Monster's Unit Elasticity of Demand."

What about relatively elastic demand? Take steak, for example. When its price goes too high, we substitute chicken, fish, and other meats for our steak dinners. The demand curve for steak might look something like the one in Figure 7.

The Cookie Monster's Unit Elasticity of Demand

The easiest example to use to understand elasticity is the behavior of the Cookie Monster on *Sesame Street*. As nearly every American under the age of thirty-five knows, the Cookie Monster (CM) eats only cookies. Assume that his income is $100 per week and that the price of a cookie is $1. If the price doubles, he cuts his consumption in half; the amount that he spends on cookies stays constant at $100. This means that CM's **price elasticity of demand** for cookies is exactly –1. His demand is **unit-elastic.***

*Excerpted from Daniel S. Hamermesh, *Economics Is Everywhere* (New York: McGraw-Hill, 2004), p. 49.

Figure 7
Relatively Elastic Demand
Curve

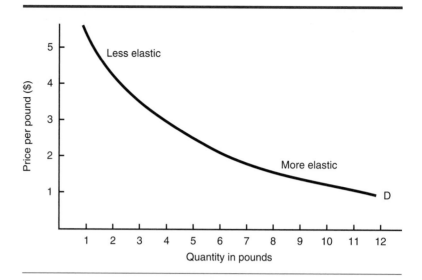

The most important influence
on the elasticity of demand is
availability of substitutes.

What makes demand elastic or inelastic? By far the most important influence is the availability of substitutes. Steak has a number of reasonably close substitutes. If its price gets too high, people will buy other cuts of beef or fish and fowl instead. A relatively small percentage increase in price leads to a large percentage decline in quantity demanded.

In the case of heart medicine, demand is quite inelastic; there are no close substitutes. If price rises, quantity sold will not fall much.

Is the product a necessity rather
than a luxury?

There are other influences on the degree of elasticity in addition to the availability of substitutes. If the product is a necessity rather than a luxury, its demand will tend to be more inelastic. When the price of a movie ticket goes up by a dollar, you might stay home and watch television; but if the price of gasoline goes up by, say, 50 percent, you'll still buy it because you need to drive places. (Luxuries and necessities are further discussed in the Current Issue at the end of this chapter.)

Product's cost relative to
buyer's income

In downtown London two Marks and Spencer stores are just 500 yards of each other. In one, every item is about 15 percent cheaper than the other. Big salads are $5.65, rather than $6.60, while sandwiches are $3.55, rather than $4.15. One would think, then, that the more expensive store would be empty and the cheaper store full of customers. If you're on your lunch break, would *you* be willing to walk a few extra blocks to save a dollar? So another factor, then, affecting elasticity, is the product's price relative to the buyer's income.[1]

Suppose you make $20,000 a year and you're interested in a used car selling for $5,000. If the seller were willing to drop the price by 5 percent to $4,750, that small percentage price cut might be enough to induce you to buy that car.

The passage of time

Over time the demand for a particular good often becomes more elastic. Take gasoline. If its price doubles, will people stop driving to work? To school? To the store? For the first year or two, there may be little you can do except cut back on your less essential driving. But when it comes time to buy a new car, you're likely to look for one that gives really good gas mileage. You may look for a job that's closer to home. Also, over time, the high price of gas may lead to the development of substitute fuels.

Number of uses

Finally, the number of uses a product has affects the elasticity of its demand. The more uses, the higher the elasticity. Salt, for example, has two main uses: to season food and to make your sidewalk less slippery when it snows. At $30 a pound, salt will still be purchased by most people to season food, but only when the price gets down to around 30 cents a pound will salt be used on the sidewalks.

---

[1]See Tim Harford, *The Undercover Economist* (New York: Oxford University Press, 2006), p. 41.

You Don't Have to Be Jewish to Eat Kosher

Only 8 percent of those buying kosher food do so for religious reasons. Most of the rest buy it for health-related reasons—they are vegans, vegetarians, Muslims, or Seventh Day Adventists with similar dietary laws, are lactose-intolerant, or have other food allergies.

Sales of kosher food shot up from just $45 billion in 1996 to $165 billion in 2002. Albertsons, Pathmark, ShopRite, Kmart, Wal-Mart, and other chains all have aggressively retooled their kosher offerings.

Question: What has this tremendous expansion of the kosher food market done to the elasticity of demand for kosher food? Clearly the more uses a product has, the higher its elasticity of demand.*

---

*Sherri Day, "Forget Rye Bread, You Don't Have to Be Jewish to Eat Kosher," *The New York Times*, June 28, 2003, p. B1.

Does a food that's kosher (i.e., something that observant Jews are allowed to eat) have a higher elasticity of demand than one that isn't (for example, ham, pork, shellfish)? Does being kosher help sales? As you'll see in the accompanying box, it doesn't hurt.

What makes demand elastic?

- Close substitutes are available.
- The product is a luxury rather than a necessity.
- The price of the product is high relative to buyers' incomes.
- Over time, the demand for a product becomes more elastic.
- The more uses for a product, the greater its elasticity.

Advertising

What is the purpose of advertising? Everyone knows it's supposed to get the consumer to buy more of a product. Some industries (such as tobacco, toothpaste, breakfast cereals, and liquor) spend very heavily on advertising. In terms of what we've already discussed, we'll talk about how advertising affects demand.

In a nutshell, advertisers try to make demand for their products greater but, at the same time, less elastic. They want to push their firm's demand curve over to the right; but they also want to make it steeper or more vertical.

First, advertising seeks an increase in demand. A second way in which advertising can influence a product's demand curve is by making it more inelastic. This is often done by means of brand identification. (See the box, "When Advertisers Go Too Far.")

Two similar products, Bayer aspirin and St. Joseph's aspirin for children, have been extremely well advertised. The fact that both are familiar product names alone attests to their popularity. If you go into the drugstore and see Squibb, Johnson & Johnson, and Bayer aspirin, which do you buy? Do you buy Bayer even if it's more expensive?

Aspirin is aspirin. What's in the Squibb and Johnson & Johnson bottles is identical to what Bayer puts in its bottles. But Bayer has convinced large numbers of people that somehow its aspirin is better, so people are willing to pay more for it. Right on the bottle it says "Genuine Bayer Aspirin," which may raise doubts about the genuineness of the aspirin sold by the competition. Bayer's advertising has been able to make its demand curve more inelastic. This company could raise its price, yet not lose many sales. That is the essence of inelastic demand.

Advertising attempts to change the way we *think* about a product. It tries to make us think a product is more useful, more desirable, or more of a necessity. Ideally, an ad will make us feel we *must* have that product. To the degree that advertising is successful, the demand curve is made steeper and is pushed farther to the right, as in Figure 8.

> *Yes, I sell people things they don't need. I can't, however, sell them something they don't want. Even with advertising. Even if I were of a mind to.*
> —John O'Toole, Chairman, Foote Cone & Belding (advertising agency)

> *Advertising is legalized lying.*
> —H. G. Wells

> *Advertising may be described as the science of arresting the human intelligence long enough to get money from it.*
> —Stephen Leacock, economist

When Advertisers Go Too Far

Advertisers go to great lengths to build brand loyalty, thereby making the demand for their products more inelastic. Many years ago the makers of Camel cigarettes spent millions on an ad that said, "I'd walk a mile for a Camel." And millions more were spent on ads showing Tareyton smokers with black eyes. The smokers were saying, "I'd rather fight than switch." But sometimes, in their attempts to build and maintain the brand loyalty of their customers, advertisers went too far and engaged in false advertising.

What is false advertising? It's any claim made by an advertiser that a court rules is false or misleading. A January 2000 ruling by a Texas federal magistrate, William Sanderson Jr., was so upsetting to publisher (and erstwhile presidential candidate) Steve Forbes, that it was criticized twice in the same issue of *Forbes*. Sanderson forbade a pizza chain, Papa John's International, to continue using its slogan, "Better ingredients.

Better pizza," which he termed "false and misleading." In addition, $468,000 in damages was awarded to the plaintiff, Pizza Hut.

Columnist Michael Fumento raised *this* point: Burger King claims its hamburger, "just tastes better." Can McDonald's litigate the point? Snapple brags it's "made from the best stuff on earth." Will its owner have to prove that claim?* The real issue, Fumento claims, is free speech.

An editorial by Steve Forbes concludes, "Next thing you know, judges will require producers to put warning labels on their products: 'This may not be as good as a competing product.'"†

---

*Michael Fumento, "Free-a the Papa!" *Forbes*, February 21, 2000, p. 53.

†Steve Forbes, "What Crust," *Forbes*, February 21, 2000, p. 40.

Figure 8

An Increased and Less Elastic Demand

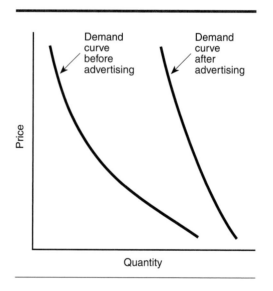

An advertising campaign may attempt to convince consumers that a certain good or service is not only unique but actually a necessity. If you were running the advertising campaign for a medical group doing hair transplants, you would try to convince millions of middle-aged men that a transplant would not only change their lives, but that only *your* doctors could do it right. If your ads were completely successful, the demand curve for hair transplants from your firm would be very inelastic.

Price elasticity of demand is closely related to the total revenue earned by a firm. We'll examine that relationship in the next section.

Elasticity and Total Revenue

Elastic Demand and Total Revenue

If you owned a haircutting salon and gave 20 haircuts at a price of $10, how much would your total revenue be? It would be $200 ($10 × 20). *Total revenue is price times output sold.*

Suppose price were raised from $10 to $12 and quantity demanded fell from 20 to 12. Let's try a three-part question: (1) calculate elasticity; (2) state whether demand is elastic, unit elastic, or inelastic; and (3) calculate total revenue where price is $10 and $12. (See Table 2.)

[handwritten note in right margin: If elastic a price increase will make a fall in total revenue. inelastic (insulin) a raise in price will create raise in Total revenue]

Solution: $P_1 = \$10$; $P_2 = \$12$; $Q_1 = 20$; and $Q_2 = 12$.

$$\frac{12 - 20}{12 + 20} \cdot \frac{12 + 10}{12 - 10} = \frac{\overset{1}{\cancel{8}}}{\underset{4}{\cancel{32}}} \cdot \frac{\overset{11}{\cancel{22}}}{\underset{1}{\cancel{2}}} = \frac{11}{4} = 2.75$$

The coefficient of elasticity being greater than 1, demand is elastic. What happened to total revenue when price is raised from $10 to $12? It fell from $200 to $144.

We see, then, that *when demand is elastic, if we were to raise price, total revenue would fall.* This would make another good exam question: "If price rises and demand is elastic, total revenue will (*a*) rise, (*b*) fall, or (*c*) remain the same."

What do most students do when their instructor goes over this problem and tells them it might make a good exam question? They write down what appears in italic type in the previous paragraph. Then, on the exam, if they happen to remember that rule—there will be about 20 such rules to memorize—they'll get it right. After the test, the rule is forgotten along with 99 percent of the other material that was memorized.

In this course you can figure out a lot of the answers to exam questions right on the spot. Take the exam question I quoted: "If price rises and demand is elastic, total revenue will (*a*) rise, (*b*) fall, or (*c*) remain the same." To figure this out, make up a problem like the one we just did. The key here is that you want demand to be elastic. That means percentage change in quantity is greater than percentage change in price.

To derive our next rule, we'll use the same problem we've just solved (when elasticity was found to be 2.75). Try this question: "If price declines and demand is elastic, total revenue will (*a*) rise, (*b*) fall, or (*c*) remain the same." In that problem, when price dropped from $12 to $10, what happened to total revenue?

Seeing that total revenue rose from $144 to $200, we can state our second rule. *When demand is elastic, if we were to lower price, total revenue would rise.*

Inelastic Demand and Total Revenue

Now we're ready for the third and fourth rules. What happens to total revenue when demand is inelastic and price is raised? You can make up your own problem, or if you

If demand is elastic, a price increase will lead to a fall in total revenue.

TABLE 2	Hypothetical Revenue Schedule	
Price	Quantity Demanded	Total Revenue
$10	20	$200
12	12	144

TABLE 3	Elasticity of Demand and Total Revenue

If demand is elastic:

when price is raised, total revenue falls.

when price is lowered, total revenue rises.

If demand is inelastic:

when price is raised, total revenue rises.

when price is lowered, total revenue falls.

If demand is inelastic, a price increase will lead to an increase in total revenue.

like, use the data from our straight-line graph in Figure 5. When price was raised from $2 to $3, quantity demanded declined from 9 to 8. How much, then, is total revenue at a price of $2 and at a price of $3?

At a price of $2, it is $18 ($2 × 9); at a price of $3, it is $24 ($3 × 8). We now have our third rule. *When demand is inelastic, if we were to raise price, total revenue would rise.*

Can you guess the fourth rule? Using the same data but reversing the process (that is, lowering price), we find: *When demand is inelastic and price is lowered, total revenue will fall.* (Price goes from $3 to $2, and total revenue falls from $24 to $18.)

As a businessperson facing an inelastic demand curve, you would never lower your price, because your total revenue would decline. You would be selling *more* units and getting *less* revenue. If someone offered to buy 8 units from you for $24, would you agree to sell 9 units for $18? *Think* about it. What would happen to your total revenue? What would happen to your total cost? Obviously, your total revenue would decline from $24 to $18. And your total cost? Surely it would cost you more to produce 9 units than 8 units. If your total revenue goes down and your total cost goes up when you lower your price, it would hardly make sense to do so (see Table 3).

Elasticity of Supply

Elasticity of supply is the responsiveness of quantity to changes in price.

Our analysis of the elasticity of supply parallels our analysis of the elasticity of demand. This time around we'll take some shortcuts. Let's begin with the formula for the price elasticity of supply. Because it's identical to the formula for the elasticity of demand, I won't even repeat it.

Next, let's discuss the meaning of the elasticity of supply. Not surprisingly, it has pretty much the same meaning as the elasticity of demand. It measures the responsiveness of the quantity supplied to changes in price. A high elasticity of, say, 10 means a 1 percent change in price brings about a 10 percent change in quantity supplied. And, similarly, an elasticity of 0.2 means a 10 percent change in price gives rise to just a 2 percent change in quantity supplied.

Now we'll look at a few graphs illustrating elasticity of supply. We'll start with perfect elasticity, then look at perfect inelasticity, and close with relative elasticity.

Figure 9 shows a perfectly elastic supply curve, which is exactly the same as a perfectly elastic demand curve. Figure 10 shows a perfectly inelastic supply curve, which would be identical to a perfectly inelastic demand curve.

Supply tends to be inelastic during very short periods of time. In the United States right after World War II, it was nearly impossible to get a car at *any* price. It took time to convert from tank, jeep, and plane production back to turning out those shiny new Hudsons, Studebakers, Kaiser-Fraisers, Nashes, and Packards. Even if you were willing to part with a big one—that's right, a thousand bucks—you still had to put your name on a year-long waiting list. Supply became more elastic after a few years, as more firms entered the industry and existing firms increased their output.

As you might even know from personal experience, Americans don't like to wait. Why didn't we just import the cars we needed from Japan, Korea, Germany, and other automobile-producing nations? After all, today, barely half of all the cars we buy are made by American firms. Back in 1945, though, the United States was the only large industrial

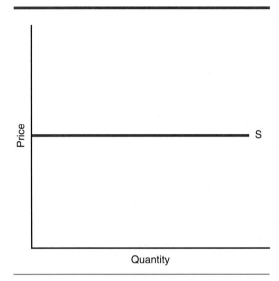

F*igure* 9
Perfectly Elastic Supply Curve

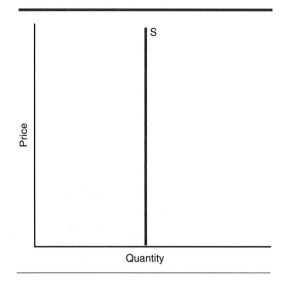

F*igure* 10
Perfectly Inelastic Supply Curve

nation with its factories still intact. Those of Japan, Germany, Italy, the United Kingdom, and most other advanced economies had been largely destroyed by wartime bombing. So in the late 1940s if you wanted to buy a car, you bought one made in Detroit.

Finally, take a look at relative elasticities of supply in Figure 11. Which curve is more elastic? You should recognize S_2 as the more elastic because it is closer to horizontal and quantity supplied would be fairly responsive to price changes.

Elasticity over Time

We've mentioned that supply grows more elastic over time, especially when enough time has passed for new firms to enter the industry and for existing firms to increase their output. Economists have identified three distinct time periods, which we'll look at now.

(1) The Market Period   The *market period* is the time immediately after a change in market price during which sellers can't respond by changing the quantity supplied.

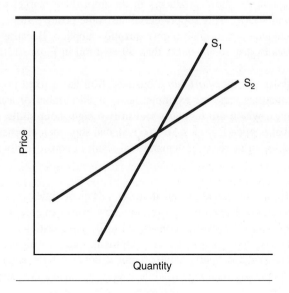

F*igure* 11
Relative Elasticities of Supply

*F*igure 12

The Market Period
(a) Initially the price is $5 (where S and D$_1$ cross). Demand increases to D$_2$, raising price to $9. Supply is perfectly inelastic, so suppliers cannot sell more even though they want to.
(b) When demand rises from D$_1$ to D$_2$, price increases from $5 to $8.40. Sellers are able to raise their output just slightly, as indicated by the very inelastic supply curve.

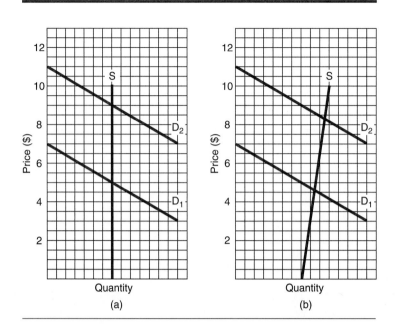

The classic example is the strawberry farmer who arrives at a farmers' market with 100 buckets of strawberries. These are her entire inventory of ripe strawberries. What does her supply curve look like?

It looks like the one in Figure 12(a). So, even though the price rose from $5 a bucket to $9 a bucket, she cannot add to her supply of 100 buckets. The farmer's supply curve is perfectly inelastic. She has no time to respond to this increase in demand and its resulting price increase.

We know that ripe strawberries are perishable: They need to be sold before they go bad. So let's say that, instead of rising, demand fell in Figure 12(a) from D$_2$ to D$_1$. The seller would be forced to accept the lower price of $5. She would not be in a position to withhold any of her supply of strawberries because they will spoil in another few days. Under such circumstances, at the end of the day, sellers of perishable goods often discount their prices by 50 percent or even more.

Does this mean that in the market period, all supply curves are perfectly inelastic? While they may well be for those selling perishables as well as products that will soon be obsolete (like today's newspapers and this week's news magazines), other producers might be able to carry an inventory of goods that they could sell if the price went up unexpectedly. The supply curve for those producers in the immediate market period might look like the one in Figure 12(b). This supply curve has some positive slope, indicating that a higher price *does* induce a somewhat higher quantity supplied. Because of this, the price in Figure 12(b) rises to just $8.40, rather than $9 as it did in Figure 12(a).

(2) The Short Run   In the *short run* a business firm has a fixed productive capacity. A firm that manufactures cars, for example, has a fixed number of assembly lines, but those assembly lines, which are regularly run in two eight-hour shifts, can be extended to three. A store that is open from 8 A.M. to 6 P.M. can stay open another couple of hours each evening. And so, an increase in demand will result in considerably more output [see Figure 13(a)].

(3) The Long Run   In the *long run* there is sufficient time for a firm to alter its productive capacity, it can leave the industry, and new firms can enter the industry. When demand rises—and when that rise is considered to be long lasting—then at least some existing firms will add to their plant and equipment, and new firms, attracted by the higher price, will enter the industry. Alternatively, if demand falls, some or all firms will cut back on their plant and equipment, while others may leave the industry.

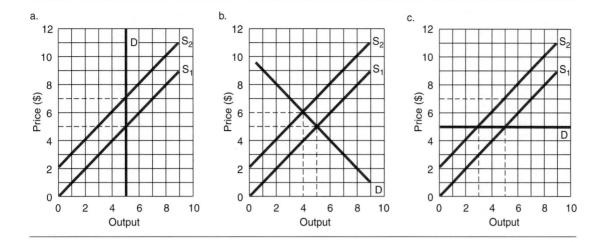

Figure 15

Decreases in Supply Due to Tax

(a) When demand is perfectly inelastic, a decrease in supply from S_1 to S_2 represents a tax of $2, which is borne entirely by the buyer. We see that because the price rises from $5 to $7.

(b) When the elasticities of demand and supply are equal, the burden of the $2 tax is borne equally by the buyer and the seller; each pays $1. We can see that because the price rises from $5 to $6.

(c) When demand is perfectly elastic, a tax increase of $2 is borne entirely by the seller. Note that price remained at $5.

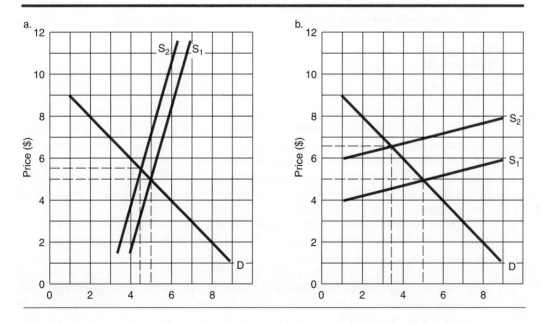

Figure 16

Decreases in Supply Due to Tax

In the left graph (panel a), a $2 tax increase pushes up price from $5 to $5.50. How much of this tax is borne by the buyer and how much by the seller?

The buyer pays $0.50 and the seller pays $1.50. In the right graph (panel b), a $2 tax pushes up price from $5 to $6.50. How much of this tax is borne by the buyer and how much by the seller?

The buyer pays $1.50 and the seller pays $0.50.

Death and Taxes

In 2001, at President George W. Bush's behest, Congress voted to phase out the federal estate tax, which falls on estates valued at more than $1.5 million. All estates will be tax-free in 2010.* Question: Would some of those who were dying hang on for a few more days or weeks, so that their heirs would reap a substantial tax savings?

The answer is "Yes!" according to a study by University of Michigan economists Wojciech Kopczuk and Joel Slemrod. Their findings were reported by *BusinessWeek:*

> *... they examined death rates of those affected by 13 estate-tax changes from 1917 to 1984. Somewhat to their surprise, they found that in cases where tax rates were raised, death rates tended to be higher in the weeks before the rise went into effect. And in*

cases where tax rates were cut, death rates were higher in the weeks following the cut.

The researchers estimate that a $10,000 tax saving seems to boost the probability of someone dying just before a tax increase by 1 percent, while the same saving increases the probability of dying just after a tax cut by almost 2.5 percent. "Evidently," says Slemrod, "some people are able to will themselves to survive a bit longer if it will enrich their heirs."

---

*Unless a new law is passed, in 2011 the estate tax will be reinstated.
Source: BusinessWeek, April 9, 2001, p. 24.

Once you're really good with tax burdens, all you'll need to do is glance at a graph and you'll know the relative tax burdens of the buyer and the seller. Then, if you find yourself in a juice bar and the guy next to you starts complaining about taxes, you can whip out some graph paper and show him all about the relative elasticities of supply and demand. And, who knows, he might even buy you a glass of carrot juice.

You have probably heard the aphorism that the only sure things in life are death and taxes. In the accompanying box, we reveal an actual relationship between these two great inevitabilities.

Last Word

From the fall of 1999 to the spring of 2000 the price of oil more than tripled. Tracing the oil supply from the market period through the short run and into the long run, it was clear that oil production would be increased considerably within weeks and that over a period of years new oil exploration and increased flows from producing oil fields could raise supply much more. Over time, then, the supply of oil becomes more elastic.

What about the elasticity of demand for oil? The two main consumer uses are gasoline for cars and home heating oil. In the very short run, the demand for these products is almost perfectly inelastic. In the long run, however, when people are buying new cars, many more will opt for more fuel-efficient vehicles, just as they did after the two oil crises in 1973 and 1979. From the mid-1970s through the mid-1980s American car buyers traded in their American-made gas guzzlers for Japanese-made compacts and subcompacts.

There were similar results in the heating oil market. Although home heating oil prices went through the roof, so to speak, in the spring of 2000, few people sold their homes or switched from oil to gas heat. But in the long run, we can expect fewer oil furnaces to be installed in new homes and gas heat to become considerably more popular. Indeed, you may even notice a few more solar panels on the roofs of your neighborhood houses.

Current Issue: How Elastic Is Your Demand for Food?

No matter how low your income, you still have to eat. When told that the people of France had no bread, Queen Marie Antoinette reportedly replied, "Let them eat cake!" Maybe not the best answer, but she did have a point. When your income falls, and you can't afford even bread, look for some *less* expensive food. Had the queen gone to a supermarket back in the 1780s, she probably would have found cake was more expensive than bread.

If *your* income went all the way down, what would *you* do? You might eat a lot more rice, potatoes, and spaghetti. During a couple of my bouts with extreme poverty, I bought huge jars of peanut butter and of marmalade, which I would spread on white bread. In addition to always having something to eat, I never needed to plan meals.

So as your income falls, you buy more and more low-priced foods. And, of course, less higher-priced foods like filet mignon and caviar. In fact you'd think of rice and potatoes as necessities and filet mignon and caviar as luxuries. Now we're ready for a sweeping generalization: A good or service is a necessity if its share of your budget falls as your income rises; it's a luxury if its share of your budget rises as your income rises.

Questions for Further Thought and Discussion

1. As you move down a straight-line demand curve, what happens to its elasticity? Can you prove this with a numerical example?

2. If demand is elastic and price is raised, what happens to total revenue? Can you prove this?

3. Estimate your elasticity of demand for (a) gasoline; (b) cigarettes; (c) video rentals.

4. Why is industry supply more elastic in the long run than in the short run, and more elastic in the short run than in the market period?

5. How do the relative elasticities of demand and supply affect the relative tax burdens of the buyer and the seller?

6. What are the major determinants of the elasticity of demand?

7. When would you want to own a business that sells price-elastic products? Why?

8. Draw a demand curve with unitary elasticity everywhere. (Hint: Think about total revenue.)

9. You live in a drafty old house that was once owned by your great grandparents. When the price of home heating oil triples, it now costs you over $2,000 a month to heat your house, which is a lot more than you can afford. What would you do in the market period, the short run, and the long run?

Workbook for Chapter 18

Name _____ Date _____

Multiple-Choice Questions

Circle the letter that corresponds to the best answer.

1. If demand is inelastic and price is raised, total revenue will _____.
   a) rise
   b) fall
   c) stay the same
   d) possibly rise or possibly fall

2. If demand is elastic and price is lowered, total revenue will _____.
   a) rise
   b) fall
   c) stay the same
   d) possibly rise or possibly fall

3. Over time the supply of a particular good or service tends to _____.
   a) become more elastic
   b) become less elastic
   c) stay about the same

4. Demand is elastic when _____.
   a) percentage change in price is greater than percentage change in quantity
   b) percentage change in quantity is greater than percentage change in price
   c) the demand curve is vertical
   d) price increases raise total revenue

5. A perfectly elastic supply curve is _____.
   a) a horizontal line
   b) a vertical line
   c) neither a horizontal nor a vertical line

6. A 5 percent increase in the price of sugar causes the quantity demanded to fall by 15 percent. The demand for sugar is _____.
   a) perfectly elastic   d) inelastic
   b) elastic   e) perfectly inelastic
   c) unit elastic

7. Which statement is true about the graph in Figure 1?
   a) Demand is perfectly elastic.
   b) Demand is perfectly inelastic.
   c) Demand is more elastic at point X than at point Y.
   d) Demand is more elastic at point Y than at point X.

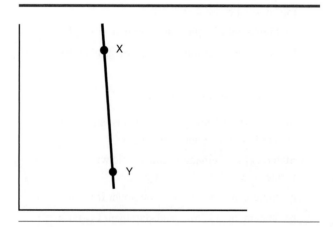

Figure 1

8. The advertiser wants to push her product's demand curve _____.
   a) to the right and make it more elastic
   b) to the right and make it less elastic
   c) to the left and make it more elastic
   d) to the left and make it less elastic

9. Demand is elastic if _____.

   a) percentage change in quantity is greater than percentage change in price

   b) percentage change in price is greater than percentage change in quantity

   c) percentage change in quantity demand is zero

   d) percentage change in price is zero

   e) percentage change in quantity is equal to percentage change in price

10. The most important determinant of the degree of elasticity of demand is _____.

    a) whether the item is a big-ticket item

    b) whether the item is a luxury

    c) how many uses the product has

    d) the availability of substitutes

11. Statement I. A perfectly elastic demand curve has an elasticity of zero.

    Statement II. When demand is elastic and price is raised, total revenue will fall.

    a) Statement I is true, and statement II is false.

    b) Statement II is true, and statement I is false.

    c) Both statements are true.

    d) Both statements are false.

12. Statement I. When demand is inelastic and price is lowered, total revenue will rise.

    Statement II. Demand is unit elastic when elasticity is one.

    a) Statement I is true, and statement II is false.

    b) Statement II is true, and statement I is false.

    c) Both statements are true.

    d) Both statements are false.

13. When demand is perfectly elastic, a tax increase is borne _____.

    a) only by the buyer   c) mostly by the buyer

    b) only by the seller   d) mostly by the seller

14. If supply is perfectly inelastic, a tax increase is borne _____.

    a) only by the buyer

    b) only by the seller

    c) mostly by the buyer

    d) mostly by the seller

15. A tax will _____.

    a) lower price and raise supply

    b) lower price and lower supply

    c) raise price and lower supply

    d) raise price and raise supply

16. When demand is relatively inelastic and supply is relatively elastic, the burden of a tax will be borne _____.

    a) mainly by sellers

    b) mainly by buyers

    c) equally between sellers and buyers

    d) it is impossible to determine the relative burdens of the tax

Use Figure 2 to answer questions 17 through 20.

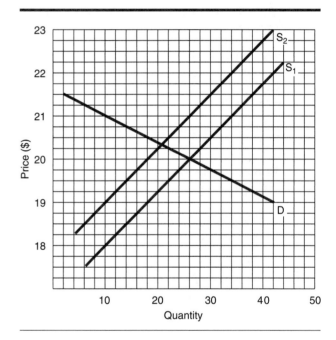

Figure 2

17. How much is the tax?

    a) $.35   d) $1.00

    b) $.50   e) $1.50

    c) $.65

18. About how much of the tax is paid by consumers in the form of higher prices?

    a) 10 cents   d) 50 cents

    b) 20 cents   e) 65 cents

    c) 35 cents

19. About how much of the tax is paid by the sellers?
    a) 80 cents   d) 35 cents
    b) 65 cents   e) 10 cents
    c) 50 cents

20. As a result of the tax, the consumption of this good

    falls by about _____.
    a) 4   d) 7
    b) 5   e) 8
    c) 6

21. The imposition of a tax _____.
    a) raises both supply and demand
    b) lowers neither supply nor demand
    c) lowers only supply
    d) lowers only demand

22. Supply is most elastic in _____.
    a) the market period
    b) the short run
    c) the long run

23. Which is the most accurate statement?
    a) The demand for gasoline is very elastic.
    b) The demand for home heating oil is very inelastic.
    c) The seller of a perishable commodity has a
       relatively elastic supply.
    d) Most firms can double their output in the short run.

Fill-In Questions

1. Elasticity of demand is a measure of the

   responsiveness of _____ to changes in price.

2. Over time the elasticity of supply for a particular

   good or service tends to become _____.

3. A tax on a service that has a relatively elastic demand

   and a relatively inelastic supply will be borne mainly

   by the _____.

4. A perfectly elastic supply curve can be shown

   graphically as _____.

5. A tax cut _____ supply.

Problems

1. Draw a perfectly elastic supply curve.

P

Q

2. Draw a perfectly inelastic supply curve.

P

Q

3. Draw a supply curve, S_1. Then draw a more elastic
   supply curve, S_2.

P

Q

4. If price were increased from $40 to $42 and quantity demanded fell from 50 to 45, calculate elasticity; state whether demand is elastic, unit elastic, or inelastic; and find how much total revenue was when price was $40 and $42.

5. If price were lowered from $50 to $43 and quantity demanded rose from 15 to 16, calculate elasticity; state whether demand is elastic, unit elastic, or inelastic; and find how much total revenue was when price was $50 and $43.

6. Draw a demand curve, D_1. Then draw a second demand curve, D_2, that is less elastic.

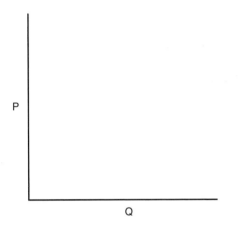

7. Draw a perfectly elastic demand curve and state its elasticity.

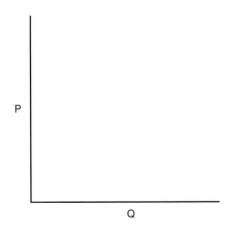

8. On the demand curve shown in Figure 3, label the curve where it is very elastic, unit elastic, and very inelastic.

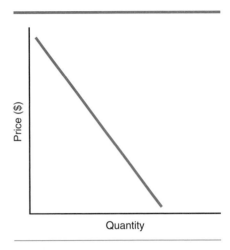

Figure 3

9. If elasticity of demand is 2 and price is raised from $10 to $11, by what percentage will quantity demanded fall?

10. If elasticity of demand is .5 and price is lowered from $20 to $19, by what percentage will quantity demanded rise?

11. In Figure 4: (a) How much is the tax? (b) How much of this tax is borne by the buyer and how much is borne by the seller?

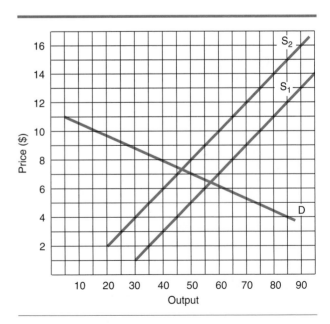

Figure 4

Chapter 19

Theory of Consumer Behavior

Aren't you tired of getting ripped off by unscrupulous merchants who overcharge their customers? Don't you agree that the prices of so-called designer jeans, designer sun glasses, and even designer bottled water are ridiculous? Aren't you so fed up that you're just not going to *take* it anymore? Well, I've got some good news and some bad news. The bad news is that sellers will keep charging whatever outrageous prices they feel like charging. And the good news? You don't have to pay those prices. Because if you look around, none of these sellers is exactly putting a gun to your head.

There's a rest stop on the Belt Parkway at Plum Beach, which, of course, is in Brooklyn. The water fountains are usually not working, but there's a guy in a truck selling cans of soda for $1.50. If you were really thirsty, would you pay $1.50? If you did, would you feel that you were being ripped off? By the time you have finished this chapter, you may have changed your mind. In the strange and wonderful world of utility, no buyer is ever ripped off.

Why do people buy goods and services? Because they derive some utility or value from them. We measure that utility by how much consumers are willing to pay.

CHAPTER OBJECTIVES

When you have completed this chapter you will know everything you'll ever need to know about:

- Marginal utility.
- The law of diminishing marginal utility.
- Total utility.

- Maximizing utility.
- The water–diamond paradox.
- Consumer surplus.

You may recall from earlier chapters that Adam Smith established that individuals act in their own self-interest. The 19th-century British economist, Jeremy Bentham, applied this observation to human behavior: Individuals make choices in order to promote pleasure and to avoid pain. In sum, we make our choices in a way that *maximizes* the degree of satisfaction we gain from our activities. So what are we waiting for? Let's maximize our pleasure and minimize our pain.

Utility

What Is Utility?

> Everything is worth what its purchaser will pay for it.
>
> –Publilius Syrus (1st century B.C.E.)–

Utility is measured by how much you are willing to pay for something.

People often confuse utility and usefulness. "Why did he buy that thing? It has no utility." In economics that would be a self-contradicting statement. Utility means only that you think enough of something to buy it.

Suppose you were ravenously hungry and came upon a hamburger stand. If the attendant told you that he had just one hamburger left—you're hungry enough to put away four—and that you'd have to pay $3 for it, would you buy it?

If you did, that hamburger would have given you at least $3 worth of utility. What if you had refused to pay $3, but when he lowered the price to $2.75 you bought it? Then that hamburger's utility would have been $2.75.

You were still hungry and soon came upon a second hamburger stand. You said to yourself as you approached, "I'd be willing to spend $2 on a second hamburger." Why not $2.75? Because you're not as hungry as you were before you wolfed down that $2.75 hamburger.

Suppose you spent $2 on a second hamburger and would be willing to pay just $1 for a third. Notice how the utility derived from consuming that third hamburger is much less than what the second one was worth.

If you managed to find someone who would let you have that third hamburger for no more than a dollar, what then? You'd try to get a fourth hamburger for a quarter. Why only a quarter? Because you're feeling a little piggy, and besides, I need you to be a little hungry still so I can illustrate a couple of things.

Table 1 sums things up. That's your demand schedule for hamburgers when you're ravenously hungry.

Marginal Utility

You've seen that the first hamburger you consumed had a utility of $2.75, the second had a utility of $2, the third, $1, and the fourth, 25 cents. Thus you just derived your marginal utility schedule. It appears in Table 2.

Marginal utility

Marginal utility is the additional utility derived from consuming one more unit of some good or service. What happens to your marginal utility as you consume more and more hamburgers? It declines from $2.75 to $2 to $1 to 25 cents.

The law of diminishing marginal utility

We've come to the *law of diminishing marginal utility.* As we consume more and more of a good or service, we like it less and less. That might be OK for an exam answer, but I have to be a bit more elegant here, so let's restate the law as follows. *As we consume increasing amounts of a good or service, we derive diminishing utility, or satisfaction, from each additional unit consumed.*

TABLE 1	Hypothetical Demand Schedule for Hamburgers
Price	Quantity Demanded
$2.75	1
2.00	2
1.00	3
.25	4

TABLE 2	Hypothetical Marginal Utility Schedule
Units Purchased	Marginal Utility
1	$2.75
2	2.00
3	1.00
4	.25

Think about it. How many movies would you want to go to in a day? In a week? How many plane trips to Europe would you want to take in a month? How many times do you want to take this economics course?

Total Utility

Are you ready to put all of this together? Let's hope everything *will* come together when we look at total utility. *Total utility is the utility you derive from consuming a certain* *number of units of a good or service.* To get total utility, just add up the marginal utilities of all the units purchased. Table 3 does this for your hamburgers.

Total utility

Let's go over Table 3 column-by-column. The first two columns come from Table 1, which is your hypothetical demand schedule for hamburgers. The third column, "Marginal Utility," shows how much utility you derive from the first, second, third, and fourth hamburgers.

Can you figure out how we got the fourth column, "Total Utility"? Start with a total utility of $2.75. That's the marginal utility of the first hamburger. How much is the second hamburger worth to you? It's worth $2; so what's the total utility of two hamburgers? It's $4.75—$2.75 for the first hamburger plus $2 for the second.

How much is the total utility of three hamburgers? It's $5.75—$2.75 for the first plus $2 for the second plus $1 for the third. And finally, how much is the total utility of four hamburgers? It comes to $6 ($2.75 + $2 + $1 + $.25).

There are two ways to find total utility. First, we can add up the marginal utilities of the items purchased, in this case hamburgers. A shortcut would be to add the marginal utility of the last hamburger purchased to the total utility of the previous hamburgers purchased. For example, the total utility of three hamburgers is $5.75. The marginal utility of the fourth hamburger is $.25; just add that to the $5.75 to get a total utility of $6 for four hamburgers.

Are you comfortable calculating marginal utility and total utility? If you are, please go directly to the next section, on maximizing utility. But if you need more practice, then you'll find help in the box "Calculating Marginal Utility and Total Utility."

Maximizing Utility

How much we buy of any good or service depends on its price and on our marginal utility schedule. Go back to the hamburger example. We can see in Table 3 how many hamburgers we'd buy at each price. Unlike that example, however, in real life there's

TABLE 3	Hypothetical Utility Schedules		
Price	Units Purchased	Marginal Utility	Total Utility
$2.75	1	$2.75	$2.75
2.00	2	2.00	4.75
1.00	3	1.00	5.75
.25	4	.25	6.00

HELP

Calculating Marginal Utility and Total Utility

We'll start with a demand schedule for College of Staten Island sweatshirts, shown in Table A. We can use this demand schedule to derive a marginal utility schedule and a total utility schedule for Karen Jones. How much utility does she derive from that first sweatshirt? Obviously, she gets $15 worth. So now you have her marginal utility and total utility from one sweatshirt. Put those numbers in Table A below and then complete the table.

The second table shows Karen Jones's marginal utility and total utility schedules. Make sure that your figures in Table A match mine in Table B.

Did you get everything right? If you did, you may skip the rest of this box. But stay with it if you need more help.

Look at the marginal utility column. Now look at the price column (to the far left on Table B). You'll notice

that they're identical. Check back to Table 3. You see that the price column and the marginal utility column are also identical. So when you're filling in the marginal utility column, just copy the price column.

Now let's tackle total utility. Marginal utility and total utility are identical at a quantity of one. At a quantity of two, total utility is found by adding the marginal utility at quantity one plus the marginal utility at quantity two. So total utility ($27) = $15 + $12. How do we find total utility at a quantity of three? We add the first three marginal utilities: $15 + $12 + $10 = $37.

At a quantity of four, total utility ($44) = $15 + $12 + $10 + $7. At a quantity of five, total utility ($49) = $15 + $12 + $10 + $7 + $5. And at a quantity of six, total utility ($53) = $15 + $12 + $10 + $7 + $5 + $4.

Table A

Price	Quantity Demanded	Marginal Utility	Total Utility
$15	1	------	------
12	2	------	------
10	3	------	------
7	4	------	------
5	5	------	------
4	6	------	------

Table B

Price	Quantity Demanded	Marginal Utility	Total Utility
$15	1	$15	$15
12	2	12	27
10	3	10	37
7	4	7	44
5	5	5	49
4	6	4	53

usually only one price. No one will offer us that first hamburger at $2.75, the second at $2, the third at $1, and the fourth at a quarter. For every good or service at any given time, there's just one price.

What we do, then, with our limited incomes is try to spend our money on what will give us the most satisfaction or utility. Keep in mind that as we consume more and more of any good or service, according to the law of diminishing marginal utility, its marginal utility declines. How much do we buy? We keep buying more and more until our marginal utility declines to the level of the price.

Because we buy a good or service up to the point at which its marginal utility is equal to its price, we could form this simple equation:

$$\frac{\text{Marginal utility}}{\text{Price}} = 1$$

$$\frac{\text{Marginal utility}}{\text{Price}} = 1$$

For example, if the price of hamburgers were 25 cents, we'd buy four hamburgers. The marginal utility of the fourth hamburger would be 25 cents. So

$$\frac{\text{Marginal utility}}{\text{Price}} = \frac{25¢}{25¢} = 1$$

If we buy hamburgers up to the point where $\dfrac{\text{MU of hamburgers}}{\text{P of hamburgers}} = 1$, we will do the same with everything else we buy. How many CDs do we buy? We keep buying them until their MU falls to the level of their price. If there are 93 different CDs we like equally, do we buy them all, even if we have the money? Maybe we buy two or three. The first one we buy is worth more to us than the price if we go ahead and buy a second one; and that second one is worth more than the price if we buy a third CD. If we stop at three, the third CD is worth the price, but a fourth would not be.

We keep buying CDs until their MU declines to the price level. In fact, the same thing can be said about everything we buy. To generalize,

$$\frac{MU_1}{P_1} = \frac{MU_2}{P_2} = \frac{MU_3}{P_3} = \frac{MU_n}{P_n}$$

General utility formula

A person distributes his income in such a way as to equalize the utility of the final increments of all commodities consumed.

—W. Stanley Jevons,
Theory of Political Economy

We have been making an implicit assumption throughout our discussion of utility: We are getting bargains on each unit we purchase until the last one. The MU of that last one is just equal to price, but the MU of the earlier units purchased is greater than price. This is the assumption on which consumer surplus is based.

Suppose that a good or service were free. How many units would you consume? You would keep consuming units until the item's marginal utility fell to zero.

If movies were free, you might go to three or four a week. I once knew a guy who went to four a day. Not only did he love movies, but he didn't work, go to school, or engage in any other productive activity.

We have seen that as we consume more units, not only does marginal utility decline, but total utility keeps rising. But what happens when marginal utility falls to zero? At that point we don't consume any more of that good or service. And our total utility is at a maximum.

If, for some reason, we consumed still another unit, our marginal utility would become negative. That unit would be worth less than zero. An extra hamburger that would make us sick or a movie that we didn't have time to see or didn't really *want* to see would decrease total utility. And so, in conclusion, we maximize our total utility when our marginal utility falls to zero.

The Water–Diamond Paradox

How come water, which is essential to life, is so cheap, while diamonds, which are not at all essential, are so expensive? We now have enough utility theory under our belts to resolve this apparent paradox.

First, the law of diminishing marginal utility tells us that as we consume increasing amounts of a good or service, we derive decreasing utility (or satisfaction) from each additional unit consumed. Second, we know from the general utility formula that we'll keep buying more of a good or service until its marginal utility falls to the level of its price. Therefore:

$$\frac{\text{MU of water}}{\text{P of water}} = \frac{\text{MU of diamonds}}{\text{P of diamonds}}$$

The price of water in most parts of the world is low because it is abundant. But the price of diamonds is high because they are not abundant.

We consume a great deal of water, so the marginal utility of the last gallon consumed is as low as its price. But we buy very few diamonds, so the marginal utility of the last carat purchased is very high.

Imagine what would happen if diamonds were to become plentiful and water were to become scarce. The marginal utility of water would go way up, along with its price. And the marginal utility and price of diamonds would fall. Not only that, but there would no longer be a water–diamond paradox.

Some Limitations of Utility Applications

What is the utility of an hour with a personal trainer? What is the utility of a ballpoint pen? What is the utility of the economics course you're taking?

The answer to each of these questions is that there *is* no answer, because utility is not inherent in a particular good or service. It is simply a measure of what the buyer is willing to pay. So an hour with a personal trainer may be worth $100 to Becky Sharp, but only $40 to Alexei Karamazov. One of your classmates might have been willing to pay $5,000 to take this economics course, but perhaps you would not pay one penny more than you had to.

So it would be meaningless to state that a certain good is worth, say, $10. Or that a certain service has a value of $50. We *may* say that a particular good is worth $10 to Margaret Thatcher. Or that a service is worth $50 to John Galt.

One of the basic functions of our federal government is to transfer money from most taxpayers to the poor in the form of welfare payments, food stamps, Medicaid, free school lunches, and housing assistance. One may draw the inference that the poor would derive more utility from the goods and services they now can afford than would the more affluent taxpayers. Is this a correct assumption?

Well, it *sounds* reasonable. But we can't make that assumption. We can't assume, for example, that if a poor person found a 10-dollar bill, he would derive more utility spending it than a rich person. It would seem *reasonable* that the poor person would derive more utility, but we can't make interpersonal utility comparisons. We *can* observe *one* person's spending behavior and determine *her* utility schedule, but we have no basis on which to compare that of two or more people.

We also need to consider that a person's utility schedule can change over time. If you decided to lose some weight, or you wanted to eat better, then surely your demand for Godiva chocolates would go down. And that would lower your utility schedule for those chocolates. Similarly, if you suddenly got a yen for travel, there would be a major upward shift in your utility schedule for airplane tickets.

Consumer Surplus

You may remember the great English economist Alfred Marshall from the last chapter. Here's his description of consumer surplus:

> The price which a person pays for a thing can never exceed, and seldom comes up to, that which he would be willing to pay rather than go without it, so that the satisfaction which he gets from its purchase generally exceeds that which he gives up in paying away its price; and he thus derives from the purchase a surplus of satisfaction. It may be called consumer's surplus.

Definition of consumer surplus

[margin handwritten note: Difference between what you were willing to pay and what you actually did pay.]

Today we define consumer's surplus, or consumer surplus, a little more succinctly: *Consumer surplus is the difference between what you pay for some good or service and what you would have been willing to pay.*

I used to live in a very classy neighborhood. In fact, this neighborhood was so classy that none of the supermarkets bothered to stay open on Sunday. One tiny grocery store was open all the time, and I made a point of never shopping there because the place was an unbelievable rip-off.

As fate would have it, a friend who was visiting on a Sunday wanted meatballs and spaghetti. I warned her that the only place to buy it was at that store. She went there and came back with an eight-ounce can. "How much?" I asked.

"Don't ask," she replied.

Later I saw the price on the can. It was $5.99.

Was my friend ripped off? The answer, surprisingly, is no. Forget about the store being open on Sunday, the convenience, and all the rest. The bottom line is my friend

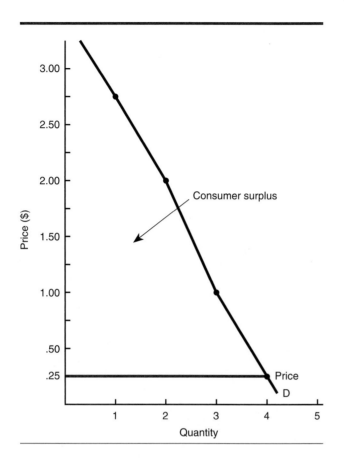

F*igure* 1

Consumer Surplus
Since the consumer's surplus is the
difference between the price you
pay and the price you would have
been *willing* to pay, then the
consumer surplus in this graph
would be represented by the area to
the left of the demand curve (what
you would have been willing to
pay) and above the price line.

bought that can of meatballs and spaghetti. If it wasn't worth at least $5.99 to her, she wouldn't have bought it.

When you're really thirsty, wouldn't you be willing to pay $3 for a bottle of water if you had to? You might be very angry, but as we like to say here in Brooklyn, no one was twisting your arm.

In the previous section, we said a person keeps buying more and more of a good or service until that person's marginal utility for that item falls to the price level. Therefore, each unit purchased except the last one was a bargain because MU was greater than price. This can be seen in Figure 1, where we once again use the hamburger example from the beginning of the chapter.

If the price of hamburgers were a quarter, you would purchase four and the consumer surplus would be the triangular area above the price line in Figure 1. The total consumer surplus would be based on the difference between what you paid for each hamburger (25 cents) and what you would have been willing to pay. You would have been willing to pay $2.75 for the first one, so your consumer surplus on the first hamburger is $2.50. You would have been willing to pay $2 for the second, so on that one your consumer surplus is $1.75. Similarly, on the third hamburger your consumer surplus is $1.00 − .25 = $.75. On the fourth hamburger, MU = Price (25 cents = 25 cents), so there is no consumer surplus. Your total consumer surplus would be $2.50 + $1.75 + $.75 = $5. Looked at another way, your total utility derived from the four hamburgers is $6, and if you pay 25 cents for each of four hamburgers, $6 minus $1 equals a consumer surplus of $5.

The next time you go shopping, don't complain about being ripped off. No one ever paid more than he or she was willing to pay; no one ever bought anything whose price exceeded its utility; and anyone who ever bought several units of the same product at a fixed price enjoyed a consumer surplus.

Let's calculate another consumer surplus. I'm getting a little tired of hamburgers, so let's do exercise sessions with a personal trainer. Enough sessions and you'll be on

TABLE 4	Hypothetical Demand Schedule for Sessions with a Personal Trainer		
Price	Quantity Demanded	Marginal Utility	Total Utility
$50	1	——	——
40	2	——	——
30	3	——	——
25	4	——	——
20	5	——	——
15	6	——	——

TABLE 5	Hypothetical Utility Schedule for Sessions with a Personal Trainer		
Price	Quantity Demanded	Marginal Utility	Total Utility
$50	1	$50	$ 50
40	2	40	90
30	3	30	120
25	4	25	145
20	5	20	165
15	6	15	180

the next U.S. Olympic team. Use just the information in Table 4 to find the consumer surplus you'll enjoy by purchasing four sessions.

The key thing to remember in solving this problem is the definition of consumer surplus: the difference between what you pay for something and what you would have been willing to pay. How much did you pay for four sessions? If you bought four, then the price must have been $25; so you paid $100 (4 × $25). Now, how much would you have been *willing* to pay for these four sessions? In other words, how much total utility do you derive from four personal training sessions? To find that out, we need to fill in Table 5.

We see from Table 5 that four sessions have a total utility of $145. If you have to pay only $100 for these sessions, then your consumer surplus is $45 ($145 − $100).

Next question: How much would your consumer surplus be if you purchased six sessions? Work it out right here:

You would have been willing to pay $180 for the six sessions, as that's the total utility you would derive from these sessions. But you would buy six sessions only if the price were $15 per session. So you would have to pay $90 (6 × $15) for these sessions. Your consumer surplus would be $180 − $90 = $90.

Need a little more practice? You'll get it in the Extra Help box, "Finding the Consumer Surplus."

Use the demand schedule in Table A to find the consumer surplus if a quantity of six is purchased.

Table A

Price	Quantity Demanded	Marginal Utility	Total Utility
$100	1	------	------
80	2	------	------
65	3	------	------
55	4	------	------
50	5	------	------
45	6	------	------

How much do we have to pay for six units? The answer is $270 (6 × 45). Next, how much would we be willing to pay for these six units? Your filled-in table should look like Table B, which indicates that the total utility of six units is $395.

Table B

Price	Quantity Demanded	Marginal Utility	Total Utility
$100	1	$100	$100
80	2	80	180
65	3	65	245
55	4	55	300
50	5	50	350
45	6	45	395

Finding the Consumer Surplus

Now all we have to do is simple subtraction. We start with what we are willing to pay for six units, a total utility of $395, and subtract what we have to pay, $270. The calculation is $395 − $270 = $125. Thus $125 is our consumer surplus.

Can you find how much the consumer surplus would be if we purchased five units? Figure it out in this space.

Total utility of five units is $350. We would have to pay $250 (5 × $50). Consumer surplus is $350 − 250 = $100.

How much would the consumer surplus be if we bought three units?

Total utility of three units is $245. We would have to pay $195 (3 × $65). Consumer surplus is $245 − $195 = $50.

If you were a seller, is there anything you could do about cutting down on the consumer surplus of each of your customers? Not as long as you charged only one price. Now the Coca-Cola Company has begun testing a vending machine that can automatically raise prices for its drinks in hot weather. Actually in Japan, some vending machines already use wireless modems to adjust their prices based on the temperature outside.

Do Price Gougers Rip Us Off?

Let's go back to a couple of questions we asked at the beginning of the chapter: If you were really thirsty, would you pay $1.50 for a can of soda? And if you paid $1.50, were you ripped off?

If you answered "yes" to the first question, did you also answer "yes" to the second question? I hate to tell you, but if you agreed to pay $1.50 for the soda, then you were *not* ripped off. Nobody held a gun to your head, forcing you to buy that soda. You derived at least $1.50 of utility from the can of soda or you never would have spent the money. So no, you were *not* ripped off.

So we can derive this rule of thumb: *Even if you pay a very high price for a good or service, you are not getting ripped off.* But maybe there *is* an exception to this rule. Maybe during disasters, whether natural or man-made, this rule doesn't always hold.

Disasters usually bring out the best and the worst in us. The attacks of 9/11 induced an almost unprecedented outpouring of volunteers, food, protective clothing, and equipment. But disaster victims have also been subject to widespread price gouging and profiteering.

In the summer and early fall of 2004, Florida was pounded by one major hurricane after another. Here's the opening paragraph of a *New York Times* article describing price gouging in the aftermath of Hurricane Charley:[1]

> Greg Lawrence talks about the $10 bag of ice. Kenneth Kleppach says he was clipped for nearly three times the advertised price for a hotel room. And a man with a chain saw told Jerry Olmstead that he could clear the oak tree off his roof, but it would cost $10,500.

It would appear that the hotel was guilty of deceptive advertising, which is illegal. If it had openly advertised its actual room prices, then if you paid that price, you were not overpaying. If there's one thing you should remember from this chapter it's this: Nobody overpays.[2]

Do you remember the great blackout of 2003? At about 4 o'clock on an otherwise pleasant August afternoon, most of the East Coast experienced a power failure that lasted over 12 hours. There were instant entrepreneurs out on the streets of New York and other cities hawking tiny votive candles for $2, bottled water for $5, and flashlights for $10. Were these people unscrupulous price gougers or just businesspeople providing the supply of goods for which there was an increased demand? In economics, we can't make moral judgments. But we *can* ask whether their customers were being ripped off. The answer is "no."

Current Issue: All-You-Can-Eat Buffets

All-you-can-eat buffets are great places to do utility experiments because you can always identify the dividing line between positive and negative marginal utility. Let's suppose that you love pizza and there's an all-you-can-eat pizza buffet just down the block from you. So you're in there almost every night. And when you arrive, you're ravenously hungry. Question: How many slices do you eat?

Let's say that you always have four slices. In fact, you can't quite finish that fourth slice. Next question: How much marginal utility would you have gotten from a fifth slice?

---

[1] Joseph B. Treaster, "With Storm Gone, Floridians Are Hit with Price Gouging," *The New York Times,* August 18, 2004, P. Al.

[2] Some of the most outrageous price gouging took place soon after Hurricane Katrina devastated parts of the Gulf Coast in August, 2005. Six-dollar-a-gallon gasoline, $300 generators selling for $1,500, and dozens of other necessities selling for three, four, or five times their normal prices were quite common. For more on this, see the end of the section, "Government Failure," in Chapter 4.

Answer: Less than zero. Your marginal utility from that fifth slice would have been negative. How much marginal utility do you get from the fourth slice?

Answer: Not a lot, since you can't finish it. But that fourth slice provided you with *some* marginal utility.

So the next time you go to an all-you-can-eat restaurant, keep in mind that you're there to carry out a marginal utility experiment. If your friends don't believe you, just bring along this book and I'll vouch for you.

Questions for Further Thought and Discussion

1. Explain the law of diminishing marginal utility, and give an example to illustrate it.
2. If you were to consume five hamburgers at Wendy's, would you enjoy a consumer surplus? Explain your answer.
3. How do we measure utility? Are interpersonal comparisons valid? Why or why not?
4. Why would Tommy Watson eventually reach the point of negative marginal utility at an all-you-can-eat restaurant?
5. Explain the water–diamond paradox.

Workbook for Chapter 19

Name _____   Date _____

Self-Review Examination

Questions 1–8: Answer true or false.

_____ 1. The water–diamond paradox has never been resolved.

_____ 2. Total utility will rise as long as marginal utility is rising.

_____ 3. The concept of consumer surplus was formulated by Alfred Marshall.

_____ 4. Total utility is at a maximum when marginal utility is zero.

_____ 5. We are maximizing our utility when the marginal utility of each good or service we purchase is equal to its price.

_____ 6. Utility is measured by a product's usefulness.

_____ 7. As increasing amounts of a product are consumed, marginal utility will decline.

_____ 8. If Matthew Avischious were to purchase five drinks at $1 each, he would enjoy a consumer surplus.

9. State the general utility formula.

10. Define marginal utility.

11. Explain the law of diminishing marginal utility.

12. What is a consumer surplus?

Multiple-Choice Questions

Circle the letter that corresponds to the best answer.

1. If we know Olivia King's demand schedule, we can find _____.
   a) her marginal activity, but not her total utility
   b) her total utility, but not her marginal utility
   c) both her total utility and her marginal utility
   d) neither her total utility nor her marginal utility

2. If a service is free, you will consume more and more of it until _____.
   a) your marginal utility is zero
   b) your total utility is zero
   c) both your marginal utility and your total utility are zero
   d) neither your marginal utility nor your total utility is zero

3. A product's utility to a buyer is measured by

   _____.
   a) its usefulness
   b) its price
   c) how much the buyer is willing to pay for it
   d) none of the above

4. As the price of a service rises, _____.
   a) the consumer surplus decreases
   b) the consumer surplus increases
   c) the consumer surplus may increase or decrease

5. In Figure 1 (price is OA) consumer surplus is bounded by _____.
   a) OBD   c) ABC
   b) OACD   d) none of these

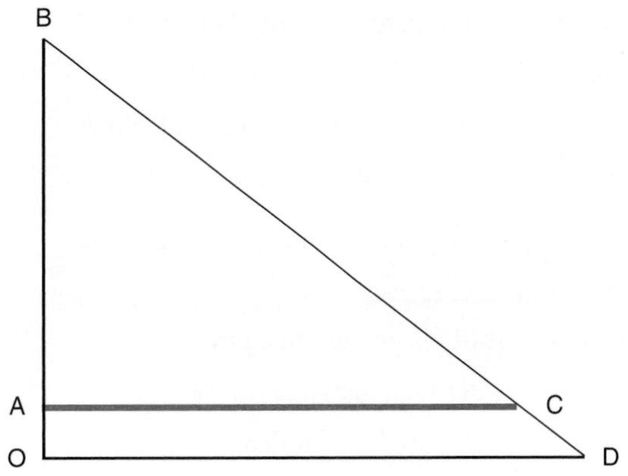

Figure 1

6. When Kelly Ziegenfuss buys five units of a particular good or service, _____.

a) she has no consumer surplus

b) she has a consumer surplus

c) there is no way of knowing whether she has a consumer surplus

7. Lauren Elise Ballard would be maximizing her total utility when _____.

a) she had a consumer surplus

b) her marginal utility was zero

c) her marginal utility was equal to her total utility

d) she had no consumer surplus

8. Which statement is true?

a) Most people have the same utility schedules.

b) Most people enjoy a consumer surplus for at least some of the things they buy.

c) We will consume additional units of a product until our consumer surplus is zero.

d) The utility of a product is measured by its usefulness.

9. Which statement is false?

a) The water–diamond paradox can be resolved with the help of the law of diminishing marginal utility.

b) We will consume a service when its marginal utility is equal to its price.

c) The law of diminishing marginal utility has little validity today.

d) None is false.

10. As Keith Collins buys more and more of any good or service, his _____.

a) total utility and marginal utility both decline

b) total utility and marginal utility both rise

c) total utility rises and marginal utility declines

d) total utility declines and marginal utility rises

11. Doug Horn will buy more and more of a good or service until _____.

a) marginal utility is greater than price

b) price is greater than marginal utility

c) price is equal to marginal utility

12. In Figure 2 (price is JK) consumer surplus is bounded by _____.

a) JKMN   c) JLN

b) KLM   d) none of these

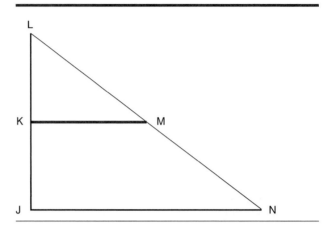

Figure 2

13. If the marginal utility you derived from the last video game you played was $1.75 and the game cost 50 cents to play, _____.

a) you have been playing the game too long

b) you haven't been playing the game long enough

c) there is no way to determine whether you have played the game long enough

14. If a 10-dollar bill was found lying on the sidewalk, _____.

a) if a rich person found it, she would get more utility from what she could buy with it than a poor person

b) if a poor person found it, she would get more utility from what she could buy with it than a rich person

c) there is no way to determine whether a rich person or a poor person who found the money would get more utility from what she could buy with it

472

15. Which statement is the most accurate?

   a) Your utility schedule for chewing gum can never change, since it is based on your demand schedule for chewing gum.

   b) Interpersonal utility comparisons cannot be made unless people buy that good at the same price.

   c) Everyone gets the same utility from taking a biology course.

   d) A good or service does not have any inherent utility, so we cannot say that a day at a beauty spa is worth $250.

16. You are definitely enjoying a consumer surplus when you _____.

   a) go on an amusement park ride 10 times in the row

   b) go to the same amusement park once a summer for 10 years in a row

   c) take 10 courses a year at your college

   d) take 10 friends to the movies

17. Haley Megan Fosnough–Biersmith goes shopping for shoes and has plenty of money with her. She will keep buying shoes until _____.

   a) her total utility equals the price

   b) her marginal utility equals the price

   c) she runs out of money

   d) the store runs out of shoes

18. Colin Kelley maximizes his utility when _____.

   a) the marginal utility of everything he buys is equal to its price

   b) the marginal utility of everything he buys is zero

   c) he no longer enjoys a consumer surplus

   d) he buys only the lowest-priced goods and services

19. Which statement is true?

   a) The utility of a plasma TV is greater than the utility of a 2001 Honda Accord.

   b) A $50 ticket to a Broadway show provides the ticket-holder with more utility than a $100 ticket to a different Broadway show.

   c) No one would pay for a service that provided him with no utility.

   d) A one-hour dance lesson would provide ten different people with exactly the same utility.

20. If this year's Nobel Prize winner in physics gives a free lecture at your school and just eight people attend, you may conclude that _____.

   a) no one derived any utility from his lecture

   b) none of the people who attended would have come if there had been an admission fee

   c) the lecture must have been at an inconvenient time.

   d) at least some of the people who attended enjoyed a consumer surplus.

21. Which statement would be true about a person who goes to an all-you-can-eat restaurant?

   a) She will never eat more food than she would at a regular restaurant.

   b) She will eat until closing time.

   c) She will eat until the marginal utility of the last portion of food is zero.

   d) She will keep eating while her marginal utility is rising.

22. Price gouging can take place only when _____.

   a) there is a natural disaster

   b) buyers are poorly informed about market conditions

   c) some buyers are willing to pay the asking price, however high

   d) the forces of supply and demand are not operating

23. Price gouging will _____.

   a) raise consumer surplus

   b) lower consumer surplus

   c) have no effect on consumer surplus

24. If food were free in your school cafeteria, you would keep eating until _____.

   a) your total utility was zero

   b) your marginal utility was zero

   c) your consumer surplus was zero

   d) you were sick

Problems

1. Suppose Table 1 shows your demand schedule for cans of soda. (a) What is your total utility from three cans of soda? (b) What is your marginal utility from the third can of soda? (c) If price were $1.50, how much would your consumer surplus be?

TABLE 1

Price	Quantity Demanded
$3.00	1
2.00	2
1.50	3

2. Suppose Table 2 shows your demand schedule for CDs. (a) What is your total utility from four CDs? (b) What is your marginal utility from the fourth CD? (c) If the price is $2, how much will your consumer surplus be?

TABLE 2

Price	Quantity Demanded
$10	1
8	2
6	3
4	4
2	5

3. Suppose that at three units purchased, marginal utility is $8 and total utility is $30. If the marginal utility of the fourth unit purchased is $6, how much is the total utility of four units?

4. You're in the desert on an extremely hot day and become quite thirsty. Luckily you come upon a stand where they're selling bottled water. You would be willing to pay $10 for the first bottle, $5 for the second bottle, and $1 for the third. Luckily they're charging just a dollar. (a) How many bottles do you buy? (b) How much is your marginal utility from the third bottle? (c) How much is the total utility you will get from the three bottles? (d) How much is your consumer surplus?

Chapter 20

Cost

There are about 27 million business firms in the United States, so it would not be a stretch to say that sometime in your life you may own or at least help run a business. The most important equation of any business firm is Total revenue − Total cost = Profit. In Chapter 17 (Chapter 5 of *Microeconomics*) we looked at total revenue, and now we'll look at total cost. In the next chapter we'll find profit.

CHAPTER OBJECTIVES

This chapter introduces these concepts:

- Fixed costs, variable costs, and total cost.
- Marginal cost.
- Short run and long run.
- Shut-down and go-out-of-business decisions.
- Average cost.

- Graphing the AFC, AVC, ATC, and MC curves.
- The production function.
- The law of diminishing returns.
- Economies and diseconomies of scale.

Costs

In a business firm costs are half the picture. The other half is sales or total revenue. The equation that every businessperson knows better than anything else in the world is

Revenue

$$\text{Sales} - \text{Costs} = \text{Profit}$$

It can also be stated this way:

$$\text{Total Revenue} - \text{Total Costs} = \text{Profit}$$

If you write it vertically—

$$
\begin{array}{r}
\text{Total Revenue} \\
-\text{Total Cost} \\
\hline
\text{Profit}
\end{array}
$$

—you can quickly grasp what is meant by looking at "the bottom line."

We are going to analyze costs in two ways. First we'll divide them into fixed and variable costs. A little later we'll divide them into costs in the short and long runs.

Fixed Costs

Fixed costs stay the same no matter how much output changes.

Examples of fixed costs are rent, insurance premiums, salaries of employees under guaranteed contracts, property taxes, interest payments, and most of the depreciation allowances on plant and equipment. Even when a firm's output is zero, it incurs the same fixed costs.

Fixed costs are sometimes called *sunk costs* because once you've obligated yourself to pay them, that money has been sunk into your firm. Fixed costs are your firm's overhead. The trick, as we'll see in the next chapter, is to spread your overhead over a large output.

Variable Costs

Variable costs vary with output.

When output rises, variable costs rise; when output falls, variable costs fall. What are examples of variable costs? The most important is wages, particularly the wages of production workers. If you cut back on output, you lay off some of these people. If you reduce output to zero, none of them will be paid.

Another variable cost is fuel. When you raise or lower output, you vary your fuel bill. The same is true with raw materials (for example, steel, glass, and rubber in automobile production). Electricity, telephone use, advertising, and shipping are other variable costs.

Some costs can have a component or part that is fixed and part that is variable. Take electricity. The more you use, the higher your bill—so we would generally consider electricity a variable cost. But, even if your output fell to zero and you never turned on a light, you would still have to pay a minimum bill. The same with your phone bill. It could vary substantially with your firm's output, but even if you don't make one call, you'll have to pay a minimum bill.

Total Cost

Total cost is the sum of fixed cost and variable cost.

The data in Table 1 illustrate total cost, fixed cost, and variable cost. Note that as output rises, fixed cost stays the same and variable cost rises. Note also how the increase in total cost is due to the increase in variable cost. These relationships may also be observed in Figure 1, which is based on Table 1.

Marginal Cost

Marginal cost is the cost of producing one additional unit of output.

Marginal cost is the cost of producing one additional unit of output. The concept of margin is extremely important in economic analysis, so I've listed the main examples that you'll encounter in this course in the box, "The Concept of Margin."

TABLE 1	Hypothetical Cost Schedule for a Business Firm		
Output	Fixed Cost	Variable Cost	Total Cost
1	$1,000	$ 400	$1,400
2	1,000	700	1,700
3	1,000	1,100	2,100
4	1,000	1,700	2,700
5	1,000	2,700	3,700
6	1,000	4,500	5,500
7	1,000	7,500	8,500

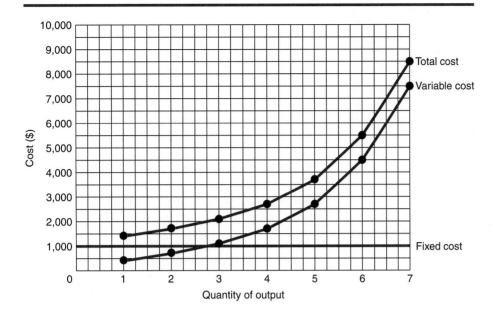

Figure 1
Fixed, Variable, and Total Cost
Since the fixed cost is $1,000, the
total cost curve is $1,000 higher
than the variable cost curve for
each unit of output. Note, also, that
total cost and variable cost rise with
output, while fixed cost is constant.

Using the data in Table 1, see if you can find the marginal cost of producing the first unit of output. Go ahead and write down your answer.

Did you get $400? If you did, that's great. If not, then you need to read the Extra Help box, "Finding Marginal Cost When the Output is 0."

Now find the marginal costs of producing the second, third, fourth, fifth, sixth, and seventh units of output. Write down your answers here:

Solution:
Marginal cost of second unit = $1,700 − $1,400 = $300
Marginal cost of third unit   = $2,100 − $1,700 = $400
Marginal cost of fourth unit = $2,700 − $2,100 = $600
Marginal cost of fifth unit   = $3,700 − $2,700 = $1,000
Marginal cost of sixth unit   = $5,500 − $3,700 = $1,800
Marginal cost of seventh unit = $8,500 − $5,500 = $3,000

The Concept of Margin

In economics the word *marginal* means "additional" or "incremental." So a *marginal cost is the cost of producing one additional unit of output*. A parallel concept, which we'll be using in the next chapter, is *marginal revenue. Marginal revenue is the additional revenue derived from selling one more unit of output.*

In Chapter 5 of *Economics* and *Macroeconomics* we used the marginal propensities to consume and save.

The marginal propensity to consume tells us what percentage of each dollar of additional income we spend; the marginal propensity to save tells us what percentage of each dollar of additional income we save. And, in Chapter 7 of *Economics* and *Macroeconomics,* we worked with the marginal tax rate, which tells us what percentage of each dollar of additional income we pay in taxes.

Finding Marginal Cost When the Output is 0

Finding the marginal cost of the first unit of output is a little tricky. You need to subtract the total cost of producing 0 units of output from the total cost of producing 1 unit of output.

Reading from Table 1, we see that total cost at an output of 1 is $1,400. OK, how much is total cost when the output is 0? Remember that total cost = fixed cost + variable cost. How much is fixed cost in Table 1?

It's $1,000. And how much is variable cost when the output is 0? Variable cost is always 0 when the output is

0. So total cost at an output of 0 is equal to the fixed cost of $1,000.

Here's one more problem to work out. Suppose that fixed cost is $500, and at an output of 1, total cost is $800. How much is marginal cost at an output of 1?

The answer is $300. Total cost at an output of 1 − total cost at an output of 0 = $800 − $500 = $300. Remember that at an output of 0, total cost = fixed cost, which, in this case is $500.

TABLE 2	Hypothetical Cost Schedule for a Firm			
Output	Fixed Cost	Variable Cost	Total Cost	Marginal Cost
0	$500	$ 0	____	____
1		200	____	____
2		300	____	____
3		450	____	____
4		650	____	____
5		950	____	____
6		1,500	____	____

TABLE 3	Hypothetical Cost Schedule for a Firm			
Output	Fixed Cost	Variable Cost	Total Cost	Marginal Cost
0	$500	$ 0	$ 500	____
1		200	700	$200
2		300	800	100
3		450	950	150
4		650	1,150	200
5		950	1,450	300
6		1,500	2,000	550

Here's another problem to work out. Fill in the columns for total cost and marginal cost in Table 2. After you've done this problem, you can check your answers against those in Table 3.

Before we get into the short run and the long run, I'd like to go back over fixed cost, variable cost, and total cost when the output is 0. Suppose that at an output of 0 fixed cost is $200. How much is variable cost and total cost?

At an output of 0, variable cost is always 0. Therefore the total cost (fixed cost + variable cost) is $200. At an output of 0, total cost is equal to fixed cost. Let's do one more. At an output of 0, if fixed cost is $1,000, how much is variable cost and total cost?

Variable cost is 0 and total cost is $1,000.

The Short Run and the Long Run

The present time is always in the short run. The short run extends for some time into the future—sometimes a few weeks, possibly a few years. During the short run a firm has two options: It can continue operating, or it can shut down and produce no output. In the long run a firm also has two options: to stay in business or to go out of business.

The short run is the length of time it takes all fixed costs to become variable costs.

The Short Run

As long as there are any fixed costs, we are in the short run. How long is the short run? In some businesses, only a couple of minutes.

When I was growing up in New York during the years immediately following the Civil War, there was a guy who would make an announcement on the subway train as it went over the Manhattan Bridge. Then he'd open his raincoat; he had hundreds of ballpoint pens hanging in rows from the lining of the coat. He was selling pens. He would tell us that he had a short-term lease, which was true. It took the train about five minutes to go over the bridge, and then his lease was up. That was the length of his short run.

Most firms have considerably longer short runs. A steel firm might need a couple of years to pay off such fixed costs as interest and rent. Even a grocery store would need several months to find someone to sublet the store and to discharge its other obligations.

The Long Run

The long run is the time at which all costs become variable costs. But the long run never exists except in theory. Why not? Because you'll never have a situation in which all your costs are variable. It would mean no rent, no interest, no insurance, no depreciation, and no guaranteed salaries. That would indeed be a hard way to do business.

Toward the end of the short run, as the times for paying off various fixed costs approach, you have to decide whether you're going to stay in business. If you are, when your lease is up, you sign a new one. When a machine wears out, you replace it. And so forth.

You never really reach the long run. Like Moses, you can see the mountains of Canaan from afar, but you never get to set foot in the promised land. On any given day you can gaze out beyond your short run to your long run, but as you proceed through the short run, you have to make decisions that will push your long run farther and farther into the future.

Average Cost

Suppose you're interested in selling hot dogs at the beach. There are dozens of other hot dog venders, each of whom charges $1.50 for each hot dog. You tote up all your costs, including the rent for a cart, the cost of hot dogs, buns, mustard, sauerkraut, relish, heating fuel, and napkins. Your total cost is $250 and you expect to sell 200 hot dogs a day. How much is your average cost per hot dog?

It's $1.25. So you'd make a 25 cent profit on each hot dog. What if your total cost came to $300? Find your average cost and your profit per hot dog.

Your average cost would be $1.50. Since you'd be charging $1.50 per hot dog, you'd make zero profit.

In this section we'll find average fixed cost, average variable cost, and average total cost. To get each, we do simple division, dividing by output.

Average Fixed Cost

Average fixed cost (AFC) is fixed cost divided by output.

Average fixed cost gets progressively smaller as output rises because we are dividing a larger and larger denominator into a numerator that stays the same. If fixed cost is $1,000 how much will average fixed cost be at one unit of output?

$$AFC = \frac{Fixed\ cost}{Output}$$

$$Average\ fixed\ cost\ (AFC) = \frac{Fixed\ cost}{Output} = \frac{1,000}{1} = 1,000$$

Now figure out AFC at two units of output. Just plug the numbers into the formula.

$$AFC = \frac{Fixed\ cost}{Output} = \frac{1,000}{2} = 500$$

Calculate AFC for three, four, five, and six units of output to the nearest dollar in the space below. Use your figures to fill the AFC column of Table 4.

Solutions:

$$AFC = \frac{Fixed\ cost}{Output}$$

$$\frac{1,000}{3} = 333; \quad \frac{1,000}{4} = 250; \quad \frac{1,000}{5} = 200; \quad \frac{1,000}{6} = 167$$

Average Variable Cost

Average variable cost (AVC) is variable cost divided by output.

Unlike fixed cost, variable cost rises with output. What about AVC? Usually it declines for a while as output increases. Eventually, however, AVC will level off and begin to rise.

Table 4 shows a variable cost schedule. I've worked out the AVC for 1 and 2 units of output. I'd like you to work out the rest and fill in that column of the table.

$$AVC = \frac{Variable\ cost}{Output}$$

$$Average\ variable\ cost\ (AVC) = \frac{Variable\ cost}{Output} = \frac{500}{1} = 500$$

$$\frac{800}{2} = 400$$

			Average	Average	Average
Output	Variable Cost	Total Cost	Fixed Cost	Variable Cost	Total Cost
1	$ 500	$1,500	——	$500	$1,500
2	800	1,800	——	400	900
3	1,000	2,000	——	——	——
4	1,300	2,300	——	——	——
5	1,700	2,700	——	——	——
6	2,400	3,400	——	——	——

TABLE 4 Hypothetical Cost Schedule

Average Total Cost

Like AVC, ATC declines with output for a while but eventually levels off and then begins to rise. We'll see that ATC lags slightly behind AVC, leveling off when AVC begins to rise and not rising until after AVC is well on the way up.

We'll use Table 4 to get in some practice. I'll work out ATC for the first two outputs, and you work out the rest.

$$\text{Average total cost (ATC)} = \frac{\text{Total cost}}{\text{Output}} = \frac{1,500}{1} = 1,500$$

$$\frac{1,800}{2} = 900$$

Average total cost (ATC) is total cost divided by output.

$$\text{ATC} = \frac{\text{Total cost}}{\text{Output}}$$

You'll find everything worked out in Table 5. I'd like you to note that AFC and AVC add up to the ATC at each output. You can use this as a check on your work. If they don't add up, you've made a mistake.[1]

We'll work out one more table and then move on to a graph. Table 6 has all the numbers you'll need to calculate AFC, AVC, and ATC. Please fill in Table 6, including the marginal cost (MC). Work out your answers this time to the nearest cent. Assume fixed cost is $500. Check your work using Table 7.

TABLE 5 Hypothetical Cost Schedule

Output	Variable Cost	Total Cost	Average Fixed Cost	Average Variable Cost	Average Total Cost
1	$ 500	$1,500	$1,000	$500	$1,500
2	800	1,800	500	400	900
3	1,000	2,000	333	333	667
4	1,300	2,300	250	325	575
5	1,700	2,700	200	340	540
6	2,400	3,400	167	400	567

TABLE 6 Hypothetical Cost Schedule

Output	Variable Cost	Total Cost	AFC	AVC	ATC	Marginal Cost
1	$ 200	___	___	___	___	___
2	300	___	___	___	___	___
3	420	___	___	___	___	___
4	580	___	___	___	___	___
5	800	___	___	___	___	___
6	1,200	___	___	___	___	___
7	1,900	___	___	___	___	___

[1]You may have noticed that AFC and AVC don't add up to ATC when the output is 3. This slight discrepancy is actually due to rounding: 333⅓ + 333⅓ = 666⅔. I rounded 333⅓ down to 333 and 666⅔ up to 667, so when the sum of AFC and AVC doesn't exactly equal ATC, it is probably due to rounding.

TABLE 7	Hypothetical Cost Schedule					
Output	Variable Cost	Total Cost	AFC	AVC	ATC	Marginal Cost
1	$ 200	$ 700	$500	$200	$700	$200
2	300	800	250	150	400	100
3	420	920	166.67	140	306.67	120
4	580	1,080	125	145	270	160
5	800	1,300	100	160	260	220
6	1,200	1,700	83.33	200	283.33	400
7	1,900	2,400	71.43	271.43	342.86	700

Graphing the AFC, AVC, ATC, and MC Curves

Much of microeconomic procedure involves three steps: filling in a table, drawing a graph based on that table, and doing an analysis of the graph. We're ready for the second step.

When you draw a graph, you should plan it first. Label both axes. Figure out how high you'll need to go. Then figure out your scale. Will each box on your graph paper represent $5, $10, or $20? To draw a proper graph, you need graph paper. If you *still* haven't purchased at least one package of graph paper, you need to go out right now to get one or two packages.

Plan your graph before you draw it.

Your output will be from 1 to 7. What will be the highest point on your graph? Both ATC and MC have highs of $700. So the vertical axis should go up to $700. When students begin to draw graphs, they connect all the points with straight lines, often using rulers. For starters, don't use a ruler to connect the points. You're drawing curves, not a series of straight lines that meet each other at odd little angles.

The AFC curve, which is not used very often in microeconomic analysis, is plotted in the accompanying box, "Distinguishing between Fixed Cost and Average Fixed Cost." I'd like you to draw a graph of the AVC, ATC, and MC curves. If you've drawn them correctly, they'll come out like those in Figure 2.

The most important thing is the shape of the AVC and ATC curves. Both are U-shaped, and both are intersected by the MC curve at their minimum points.

Why does the MC curve pass through the AVC and ATC curves at their minimum points?

Why does the MC curve pass through the AVC and ATC curves at their minimum points? The basic reason is that each marginal value changes the average value. If you *really* want to know why, see the box, "Computing Your Exam Average."

Incidentally, when you draw the curves, if you start with the MC curve, it will be much easier to draw in the AVC and ATC curves.

We'll try another problem. First fill in Table 8. A completed version appears in Table 9. Assume here that fixed cost is $400. Work out each answer to the nearest dollar.

I hope your table matches Table 9. Now we're ready for the graph. We'll use only three of the curves in the analysis that comes a little later in the chapter—the AVC, ATC, and MC. The AFC curve doesn't serve any analytic purpose, so from here on we won't draw it.

Now I'd like you to draw a graph of the AVC, ATC, and MC curves on a piece of graph paper. Remember, start with the MC curve because you need that curve to help you plot the minimum points of the AVC and ATC curves. Still not convinced? Then just trust me.

Compare your graph with the one in Figure 3. How did your minimum points come out on the AVC and ATC curves? If you drew your curves in the order I suggested—MC first, then AVC and ATC—your MC should have intersected both the AVC and ATC curves at their minimum points.

Distinguishing between Fixed Cost and Average Fixed Cost

Using a piece of graph paper, see whether you can draw the average fixed cost curve, using the data in Table 7. Then on the same graph, draw the fixed cost curve. If your graph looks like the one in this box, then you don't need any extra help.

If your AFC curve looks different, make sure you plotted each point correctly. If you're having trouble plotting points, you definitely need to reread the early sections of Chapter 17 (Chapter 5 in *Microeconomics*), where I went over how to plot graphs.

The AFC curve sweeps downward to the right, getting closer and closer to the output axis. When drawn correctly, it should be a very smooth curve.

The fixed cost curve is always a perfectly horizontal line. In this case, fixed cost is $500, so the fixed cost

curve runs straight across the graph at a cost of $500. It stays fixed at $500 no matter what the output.

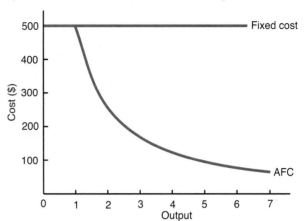

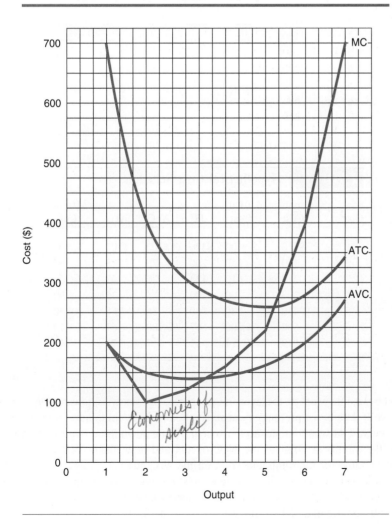

Figure 2

Average Total Cost, Average Variable Cost, and Marginal Cost

The marginal cost curve intersects the ATC and the AVC at their minimum points.

Computing Your Exam Average

We'll digress for a moment by discussing grades on exams. Suppose you took three exams and scored 80, 70, and 60. Your average would be 70. What if, on the next exam, you got a 66? What would your average be? It would be 276/4 = 69.

Suppose on the next exam you got a 67? Now what would your average be? It would be 343/5 = 68.6.

If you got a 68 on the next exam, what would happen to your average? 411/6 = 68.5.

If your next exam mark was exactly 68.5? 479.5/7 = 68.5. No change.

If you scored a 69 on the next exam, what would your average be? 548.5/8 = 68.56.

All of this is meant to show you how the marginal score affects the average score. Note that as long as the marginal score is below the average score, the latter is declining, but when the marginal score is 68.5, it is equal to the average score. And the average score is neither rising nor falling; it is at its minimum point.

Similarly, when MC intersects AVC and ATC, it does so at their minimum points. As long as MC is below AVC, AVC must be falling. Once MC cuts through the AVC curve, the latter begins to rise. The same is true of the relationship between MC and ATC.

TABLE 8 Hypothetical Cost Schedule

Output	Variable Cost	Total Cost	AFC	AVC	ATC	Marginal Cost
1	$100	——	——	——	——	——
2	150	——	——	——	——	——
3	210	——	——	——	——	——
4	300	——	——	——	——	——
5	430	——	——	——	——	——
6	600	——	——	——	——	——
7	819	——	——	——	——	——

TABLE 9 Hypothetical Cost Schedule

Output	Variable Cost	Total Cost	AFC	AVC	ATC	Marginal Cost
1	$100	$ 500	$400	$100	$500	$100
2	150	550	200	75	275	50
3	210	610	133	70	203	60
4	300	700	100	75	175	90
5	430	830	80	86	166	130
6	600	1,000	67	100	167	170
7	819	1,219	57	117	174	219

Before we move on to the even more spectacular analysis toward the end of the chapter, we'll do a bit of preliminary analysis. Read off the minimum points of the AVC and ATC curves. At what outputs do they occur? Write down these two values: the output at which the minimum point of the AVC occurs and how much AVC is at that point. Then do the same for the minimum point on the ATC curve.

Your answers should be within these ranges: For AVC, your output should be somewhere between 3.3 and 3.4. AVC is a bit less than $70. How *much* less? Probably around $69, or $69 and change. Where do we get these numbers? If you were careful when

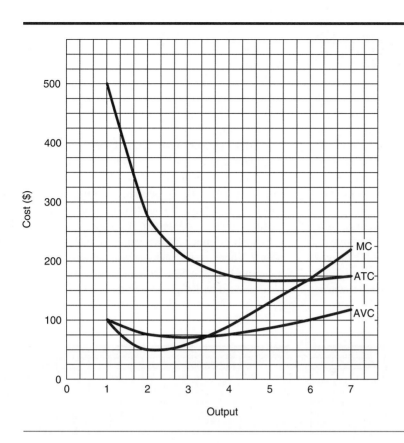

F*igure* 3
Average Variable, Average
Total, and Marginal Cost
How much is the minimum point of
this firm's ATC curve? Answer: a
bit less than $166 (I'll call it $165).
You can't really tell just by looking
at the graph: You have to look at
the ATC figures in Table 9 at
outputs of 5 and 6 and then, since
we're looking for a minimum point,
come up with a number slightly
less than $166.

you drew your graph—if you weren't, use mine—AVC is $70 at an output of 3. MC is still a bit below AVC at $60. As output goes beyond 3, MC continues to rise while AVC declines slightly.

For the minimum point of the ATC curve, your output should be around 5.8. ATC is between $165 and $165.90. Notice that the MC curve intersects the ATC curve between outputs of 5 and 6, but closer to 6. Note that at an output of 5, ATC is $166, and at an output of 6, it is $167, but because the MC curve cuts the ATC curve at its minimum point, ATC must be *less* than $166.

It might seem to you that we are reading Figure 3 with great precision, perhaps a little too *much* precision. For example, to the naked eye, is it really clear that the minimum point of the ATC curve is between $165 and $165.90? Hardly. But we use Table 9 to guide us. We want a number that is slightly less than $166. Why not $164.25? All right, all right—you're twisting my arm. I personally think $164.25 is a bit low. On an exam I'd mark it right, but I can't vouch for *your* professor.

The most difficult part of graphing the ATC and AVC curves is making sure that they are crossed at their minimum points by the MC curve. You can get a little more help with this in the accompanying box.

Why Are the AVC and ATC Curves U-Shaped?

As output rises, initially both average variable cost and average total cost decline, reach minimum points, and then begin to rise. This makes these curves U-shaped. Before we tackle the question of *why* they are U-shaped, let's ask and answer a related question. Why does the AVC curve reach a minimum before the ATC curve?

Average total cost is the sum of average fixed cost and average variable cost. We know that, as long as output is expanding, AFC is declining. But, as you can see from Figures 2 and 3, AFC declines at a declining rate (that is, more and more slowly) as

Graphing the Average Total Cost Curve

The points shown in Figure A—$50.00, $32.50, $25.00, etc.—are points on a firm's average total cost curve. Very carefully connect all these points; this will give us the firm's average total cost curve.

Now we come to one of the most crucial questions of this course. How much is the minimum point of the ATC curve you've just drawn? Please write down your answer in dollars and cents.

Let's see how you did. Does your ATC curve look like the one I drew in Figure B? Does it continue to decline from $22.50 until it touches the MC curve? And after reaching a minimum at that point, does your ATC curve begin to rise again as it moves towards $22.00?

Next question: What is the minimum point of your ATC curve in dollars and cents? *I* see it as $21.80. What did *you* get?

Your answer *must* be a little lower than $22.00, because $22.00 is *not* the minimum point of the ATC curve. That occurs when the MC and the ATC curves intersect. The ATC is declining until it crosses the MC and then it begins to rise. It rises from an output of 120 to an output of 140, where it reaches a value of $22.00.

So how much *is* the value of ATC at its minimum point? There *is* no one correct answer. I would accept anything between $21.25 and $21.99. And if you got me on a good day, I'd go as low as $21.00.

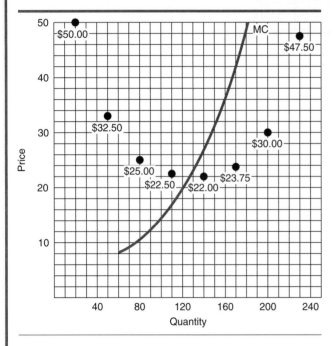

Figure A

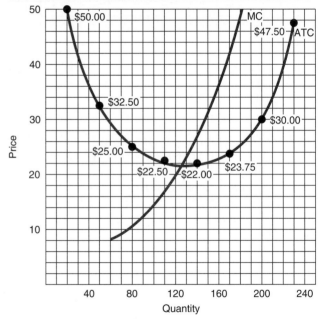

Figure B

output rises. Average variable cost, in contrast, declines at a declining rate, reaches a minimum, and then begins to rise at an increasing rate (faster and faster). Eventually the increase in AVC outweighs the decrease in AFC. At that point ATC begins to rise.

Now we know why AVC begins to rise before ATC begins to rise. And we also know that it is the rise in AVC that ultimately pushes up ATC. Do you follow so far? OK, then *why* does AVC begin to rise? *That* is the $1 million question. To answer that question we'll need to look at three related concepts—the law of diminishing returns, economies of scale, and diseconomies of scale.

The Production Function and the Law of Diminishing Returns

A business owner tries to keep her costs down by getting the maximum output from using the best combination of the factors of production—land, labor, and capital. To do so, she may try different production functions, which would tell her how much output she can produce with varying amounts of factor inputs. *A production function is the relationship between the maximum amounts of output a firm can produce and various quantities of inputs.*

Resources may be used in various proportions. For example, a farmer may either plant crops on 400 acres or cultivate 200 more intensively. Similarly, a bank may either install hundreds of ATMs or hire hundreds of real tellers. Using resources in different proportions will yield varying amounts of output.

Using the data in Table 10, we see that one person working alone turns out two log cabins a month, while two people working together can turn out five per month. If you've ever attempted to move a 500-pound log, you know it's easier to have someone at the other end of the log. Perhaps three people can work together even more efficiently.

The first three workers give us increasing returns (or increasing marginal returns). Working together, they can get a lot more done than if each worked alone. But note what happens when we hire a fourth worker. This person raises output, but only by 3. With the fourth worker we have the onset of diminishing returns (or diminishing marginal output).

Diminishing marginal output

Why is this so? Because three people may be an ideal number to move and lift 400-pound logs. The fourth worker is certainly a help, but proportionately, she doesn't add as much as the third worker.

A fifth worker adds still less to output (2 units) and a sixth worker even less (1 unit). In other words, five people can manage building log cabins almost as well as six. As we add the seventh worker, we find that he is superfluous. From the fourth to the seventh worker, we have *diminishing returns*.

The eighth worker is actually in the way, having a marginal output of minus one. Returns become negative when this eighth worker is added. A ninth worker gets in the way even more. The eighth and ninth workers have negative returns.

Negative returns

TABLE 10 The Law of Diminishing Returns: Building Log Cabins

Number of Workers	Total Output	Marginal* Output	
0	0	0	
1	2	2	Increasing returns
2	5	3	Increasing returns
3	9	4	Increasing returns
4	12	3	Diminishing returns
5	14	2	Diminishing returns
6	15	1	Diminishing returns
7	15	0	Diminishing returns
8	14	−1	Diminishing and negative returns
9	11	−3	Diminishing and negative returns

*Marginal output is the additional output produced by the last worker hired. Thus the first worker adds 2 units to output, so his marginal output is 2. The second worker hired adds 3 units of output (output has risen from 2 to 5), so his marginal output is 3. When a third worker is hired, total output jumps to 9. Marginal output has therefore risen by 4.

*F*igure 4

Building Log Cabins: Total
Output and Marginal Output

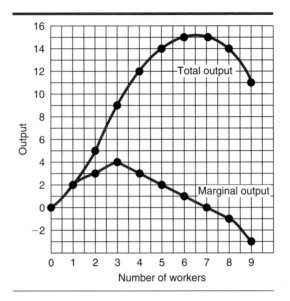

What would be the maximum number of workers you would hire? The answer is six. If the wage rate were very low, you would hire up to six. The seventh worker, however, adds nothing to output, and the eighth and ninth get in the way, thereby reducing output.

Let's see how all this looks graphically. We see in Figure 4 how total output and marginal output rise as more workers after the first three workers are added. But after the third worker, total output begins to rise more slowly. And marginal output? It begins to decline. Hence, diminishing returns.

Total output reaches a maximum with the addition of the sixth worker, then levels off, so that the seventh worker adds 0 output. And what is the marginal output of the seventh worker?

The marginal output of the seventh worker is 0. If we add an eighth and ninth worker, what happens to total output? It declines. And marginal output? It becomes negative.

The law of diminishing returns states that, *as successive units of a variable resource (say, labor) are added to a fixed set of resources (say, land and capital), beyond some point the extra, or marginal, product attributable to each additional unit of the variable resource will decline.* So if we added more and more farm workers to an acre of land, beyond some point (say, after the third worker), the extra output that that fourth worker added would be less than the extra output that the third worker added. We'll consider how this law applies to agricultural production and to office work.

Let's now apply the law of diminishing returns to an office. You're working in an office that is 15 feet long and 10 feet wide. Your job is to type, run a small switchboard, act as a receptionist, and do filing. You really could use some help because the phone keeps ringing, visitors keep arriving, you keep getting more papers to file, and you've got a whole pile of correspondence to type. So a second worker is hired, and you divide up the work. That way neither of you will have your work constantly interrupted. On the down side, you now have to share your office. But the two of you working together produce three times as much work as you did working alone.

Let's say that a third person was hired to work in your office. Would output go up? Yes. But now the office is *really* getting crowded. Suppose that a fourth, fifth, sixth, seventh, and eighth worker were hired. Imagine how crowded your office would be. Indeed, you'd end up sitting on one another's desks, maybe on one another's laps. At some point total output would begin to decline, and *negative returns* would set in.

It would be absurd for a company to have workers beyond the point of negative returns, or even to approach that point. However, we would certainly want to keep hiring workers who yielded *increasing returns*. And, if the firm found it profitable to increase output still further, it would keep hiring workers even though their returns were diminishing.

Declining ATC in Drugs

Here is an excerpt from the 1999 annual report of the Federal Reserve Bank of Dallas:

It takes roughly $350 million to bring the average new drug to market. That's just for the first pill. Making the second costs closer to a penny. Clearly, nobody's going to pay $350 million for that first pill. So to make medicine affordable, drug companies have to spread the cost of developing their products over years and years of sales. The larger the sales, the less each unit can cost the consumer. Assuming $350 million in development costs and 1¢ marginal production cost thereafter, the average cost of making a pill would fall from $350 million for producing just one to $350.01 each for making a million to 4¢ each for sales of 10 billion. Prices fall in inverse proportion to the size of the market. This example illustrates that for pharmaceuticals demand is not the enemy of price but its friend. The higher the demand, the lower the price because, after all, you can't have quantity discounts without quantity.

Average Cost of a Pill	
Quantity	Cost
1	$350,000,000.00
10	35,000,000.01
100	3,500,000.01
1,000	350,000.01
10,000	35,000.01
100,000	3,500.01
1,000,000	350.01
10,000,000	35.01
100,000,000	3.51
1,000,000,000	.36
10,000,000,000	.04

Economies of Scale

Economies of scale are the economies of mass production, which drive down average total cost. They are largely responsible for the declining part of the ATC curve. Large-scale enterprise is expected to be more efficient than small business. And in general, we expect large firms to be able to undersell small firms. One reason for this belief is that large firms can often get quantity discounts when they buy raw materials or inventory (Safeway, Target, and Wal-Mart, for example, use a system of central buying and warehousing). A manufacturer will be able to give you a better price if she can deliver 10,000 cartons of tuna fish to one warehouse rather than 100 cartons to 100 different stores. Also, it costs less to sell your final product in quantity than to sell it piece by piece. For this reason, a wholesaler has much lower prices than a retailer. Buying and selling in large quantities, then, is one reason for economies of scale.

Quantity discounts

As a firm grows, it takes advantage of being established. Its salespeople are known, it has established outlets and delivery routes, and its brand name becomes familiar. These advantages will mount as the firm continues to grow.

Economies of being established

When a company has a very high fixed cost and a low marginal cost, its ATC curve will slope downward almost indefinitely. Software, CDs, DVDs, and drugs are some of the products in this category. In addition, economies of scale tend to dominate industries that deliver their goods or services through a network, such as telephone, television, radio, fax, e-mail, the Internet, package delivery, and pipelines. In the box, "Declining ATC in Drugs," you'll see the economies of scale realized in the pharmaceutical industry.

Spreading fixed cost

Economies of scale in computer software are almost mind-boggling. The cost of producing copies of a software program is virtually zero. Microsoft merely licenses its computer code to PC makers, who then install it. Whether Microsoft sells 100 million or 200 million copies, its costs are all in developing the code to begin with. As in the case of the drug companies, there are very high fixed costs and minimal marginal costs.

Economies of Scale in Entertainment and Communications

In entertainment and the Internet, where there are huge fixed costs, the cost of serving additional customers is generally very small. These points are illustrated in an article by Robert H. Frank, a Cornell University economics professor.

> The cost of producing a movie or writing Internet access software, for example, is essentially the same whether the product attracts one million buyers or 100 million.
>
> So the more customers a company serves, the more cheaply it can sell its product and still make money...

So the trick is to make a big investment that will attract millions of customers, spreading that fixed cost over millions of units of output.

> If Time Warner's Home Box Office bids for star performers or spends more on elaborate special effects for its made-for-TV movies, it can attract more subscribers, yet it will not have to charge each customer a higher price to cover its increased costs. And having a better product would help HBO lure subscribers away from Showtime and Cinemax, reinforcing the initial advantage.
>
> Similar forces govern the contest to provide Internet access. Because many of the biggest costs of delivering Internet service are fixed, the average cost per subscriber declines sharply with the number of subscribers served.*

*Robert H. Frank, "A Merger's Message: Dominate or Die," *New York Times,* January 11, 2000, p. A25.

Adam Smith's pin factory

In 1776 in *The Wealth of Nations,* Adam Smith noted three other advantages. When a firm is large enough to provide specialized jobs for its workers, economies of scale will follow. He used a pin factory as an example.

One worker, said Smith, "could scarce, perhaps, with his utmost industry, make one pin in a day, and certainly could not make twenty." He then described how pin making has become specialized: "One man draws out the wire, another straights it, a third cuts it, a fourth points it, a fifth grinds it at the top for receiving the head."[2]

There are three distinct advantages to producing pins in this manner. First, the workers become good at their jobs—better than they would be if they went from one function to another. Second, they don't waste time going from one task to another. Third, the factory can employ specialized and expensive equipment because it will be fully used. For example, a special die to draw the wire can be purchased because it will be used continually; and a machine to cut the wire can be purchased for the same reason.

Ten pin makers, working on their own, could turn out at most a total of 200 pins. Smith estimated that 10 people working together in a factory could produce 48,000 pins a day, which is a prime example of economies of scale.

Economies of scale enable a business firm to reduce its costs per unit of output as output expands (see the box, "Economies of Scale in Entertainment and Communications"). Often these cost reductions can be passed on to the consumer in the form of lower prices. One outgrowth of expansion is increasing specialization. People's jobs become more and more specialized, as they did in Adam Smith's pin factory. But with the growth of specialization are sown the seeds of inefficiency, rising costs, and diseconomies of scale.

If a company gets too large, break it into smaller parts. Once people start not knowing the people in the building and it starts to become impersonal, it's time to break up a company.
—Richard Branson, founder, Virgin Group

Diseconomies of Scale

Diseconomies of scale are the inefficiencies that become endemic in large firms. Diseconomies of scale are evidenced by the rising part of the ATC curve.

The growing bureaucracy

As a business grows larger, it will create a bureaucracy. Early in the company's history, the founder hired all her employees personally. As the firm grew, she had her

---

[2]Adam Smith, *The Wealth of Nations* (London: Methuen, 1950), Book 1, Chapter 1, pp. 8–9.

foreman do the hiring. Today, if you try to get a job at a large company, you have to go through the personnel (or human resources) department, then meet your prospective supervisor, then meet your prospective supervisor's supervisor, and perhaps meet several other members of "the team"—or work your way through some other variation of this process. In the early days of the company, there was no such thing as a third interview.

A huge hierarchy of corporate authority is established—a hierarchy that might have once made sense, but that now may either have little relevant function or actually work at cross-purposes. The American automobile industry is a good case in point. Fewer than half the employees of GM, Ford, and Chrysler actually make cars. The rest do sales, advertising, market research, litigation, accounting, personnel work, budgeting, or public relations and the like for their companies—anything but make cars.

You may have heard of C. Northcote Parkinson, who formulated Parkinson's Law: "Work expands so as to fill the time available for its completion." Just picture all those seemingly busy bureaucrats scurrying around, firing off memos, talking on the phone, and rushing off to meetings. But no discernible output results. Parkinson added a corollary: "Work expands to occupy the people available for its completion." If Parkinson is right, then large organizations are filled with important-looking people who appear very busy but are doing virtually no real work.

Even the quantity discounts enjoyed by large firms will eventually disappear as the firms use up so many resources that they bid up their prices. If a company rents office space, it can save money by renting several floors in a building. But if the firm needs much of the downtown office space in a city, it will end up paying more per square foot. Similarly, suppliers who gladly give quantity discounts for large orders will have to raise their prices to a customer who purchases their entire output. Furthermore, other customers will bid up prices rather than see their own supplies cut off.

Depicting the stages of growth of several large corporations, we start with the initial spurt, during which economies of scale are operative and unit costs are declining. As the companies mature and output continues to rise, unit costs stay about the same. This stage is sometimes called *proportional returns to scale*.

In the final stage, which many large corporations have reached, diseconomies of scale set in. The corporate dinosaurs, beset with rising unit costs, are now so huge that they may no longer be able to compete.

When I had a prescription filled at Rite Aid, I received a circular listing an 800 number to call about getting a flu shot. I called that day, and after the standard runaround, finally got through to a customer service representative. He informed me that they had run out of vaccine, so Rite Aid was no longer providing flu shots. So why, I asked, was the store still giving out these notices? The poor guy didn't have a clue.

It would be fair to assume that a small neighborhood pharmacy would not be making this systematic error. But when you've got a nationwide chain, the left hand does not always know what the right hand is doing.

Expansion means complexity, and complexity means decay.

Parkinson's Law

Big business breeds bureaucracy and bureaucrats act exactly as big government does.
—Theordore K. Quinn, General Electric officer in the 1920s and 1930s

Size works against excellence.
—Bill Gates, cofounder and chairman, Microsoft

A Summing Up

At the beginning of this section we asked why the AVC and ATC curves are U-shaped. Now that we have covered the law of diminishing returns, economies of scale, and diseconomies of scale, we can answer this question.

ATC is the sum of AFC and AVC. AFC declines by smaller and smaller increments as output rises. So, as output rises, ATC is pushed down by smaller and smaller increments.

Remember that we often have the sequence of increasing returns, diminishing returns, and negative returns. Increasing returns would initially drive down AVC. But eventually diminishing returns would drive up AVC. We won't worry about negative returns, because no firm would hire workers or engage other resources that would cause output to decline.

Economies of scale drive down AFC, but at smaller and smaller increments. Diseconomies of scale drive up AVC as output rises and eventually exceed economies of scale, at which point AVC begins to rise.

What's the Difference between Shutting Down and Going Out of Business?

One big difference between shutting down and going out of business is that after you've shut down you're still paying bills, but when you've gone out of business you're "free at last!"* That's right! Once you've legally left the industry, you have no more bills to pay because you have no more costs—fixed *or* variable.

When you've shut down operations, you may still owe money on your lease, insurance premiums may be due, and you may still be paying off a loan. There may be employees under contract who have been guaranteed salaries even if there is no work for them. In addition, if you have a shut-down plant, you might need employees to maintain the equipment, keep the pipes from freezing, and keep out intruders. And if there are hazardous waste materials on the premises, these may have to be disposed of before you can legally go out of business.

---

*This was the conclusion of Dr. Martin Luther King, Jr.'s stirring 1963 "I Have a Dream" speech. He was not, of course, discussing the difference between shutting down and going out of business.

To sum up, the overlapping forces of increasing returns and economies of scale drive down ATC, but eventually the overlapping forces of diminishing returns and diseconomies of scale push ATC back up again.

The U-shaped ATC is very important not only in economic analysis but also in business strategy, especially in answering questions such as: What size factory or store or office should we build? How many workers should we hire? What would be the output at which our firm would operate most efficiently? We'll answer the first of these questions in the next section and answer the others in later chapters.

The Decision to Operate or Shut Down

A firm has two options in the short run.

A firm has two options in the short run: It can either operate or shut down. If it operates, it will produce the output that will yield the highest possible profits; if it is losing money, it will operate at that output at which losses are minimized.

If the firm shuts down, its output is zero. Shutting down does not mean zero total costs. The firm must still meet its fixed costs. Look at Table 1 again. At an output of zero, fixed costs—and therefore total costs—are $1,000.

Why can't the firm go out of business in the short run? Because it still has fixed costs (see the box, "What's the Difference between Shutting Down and Going Out of Business?"). These obligations must be discharged. Any plant, equipment, inventory, and raw materials must also be sold off. All of this takes time. How long? In some types of business, such as retail food, garment manufacturing, TV production, and most service industries, it would be a matter of two or three months. But in heavy industry, such as iron and steel, nonferrous metals, automobiles, oil refining, and other types of manufacturing, it might take a couple of years.

We'll work out some problems involving the shut-down decision. If a firm has fixed costs of $5 million, variable costs of $6 million, and total revenue of $7 million, what does it do in the short run? It has a choice: (1) operate or (2) shut down.

If you owned this firm, what would *you* do? No matter what you do, you'll lose money. If you operate, your total cost will be $11 million ($5 million fixed cost plus $6 million variable cost). Total Revenue − Costs = Profit, so $7 million − $11 million = −$4 million. That's not too good.

How much will you lose if you shut down? You will still have to pay out $5 million in fixed costs. Your variable cost will be zero. How much will your sales be? Zero. If you shut down, you produce nothing. If you shut down, your fixed and total costs are the same—$5 million. As total revenue is zero, you lose $5 million by shutting down.

What do you do? Shut down and lose $5 million, or operate and lose $4 million? Remember, in the short run, these are your only options. What you then do is operate. It's a lot better to lose $4 million than to lose $5 million. Can you go on month after month—and possibly year after year—losing so much money? You can't. In the long run you have the added option of going out of business.

Here's another problem. What does this firm do in the short run if its fixed costs are $10 million, its variable costs are $9 million, and its total revenue is $8 million? Will the firm operate or shut down? Back up your answer with numbers after you've figured out the right choice.

If the firm shuts down, it will lose its $10 million in fixed costs. If it operates, it will have total revenue of $8 million and total costs of $19 million ($10 million fixed plus $9 million variable). If the firm operates, it will lose $11 million (total revenue of $8 million minus costs of $19 million). So the firm will shut down because it's obviously better to lose $10 million than $11 million.

We'll try one more problem. What does a firm do in the short run with total revenue of $10 million, variable costs of $12 million, and fixed costs of $8 million?

If the firm shuts down, it will lose its $8 million in fixed costs. If it operates, it will lose $10 million (total revenue of $10 million minus total costs of $20 million). Clearly, it shuts down.

We are now ready for another rule. When does a firm operate in the short run? *A firm will operate in the short run when total revenue exceeds variable costs.* Go back to the first problem. Total revenue was $7 million, and variable costs were $6 million. By operating, it added $7 million in total revenue and had to pay out only an additional $6 million in costs. By operating, it cut its losses by $1 million.

A firm will shut down when variable costs exceed total revenue. Check back to the second and third problems. In the second problem, when variable costs are $9 million and total revenue is $8 million, the firm saves $1 million by shutting down. In the third problem, variable costs are $12 million and total revenue $10 million, so $2 million is saved by shutting down.

Stop! We need to pause, catch our breath—and summarize the last three problems. Table 11 provides that summary.

In the short run a firm has two options: (1) operate or (2) shut down. It operates when total revenue exceeds variable costs. And when variable costs are greater than total revenue, it shuts down. What if variable costs equal total revenue? Flip a coin.

> A firm will operate in the short run when prospective sales exceed variable costs.

> A firm will shut down in the short run when variable costs exceed prospective sales.

TABLE 11	Summary Table of Last Three Problems *(All dollar figures in millions)*		
	Problem 1	Problem 2	Problem 3
Fixed costs	5	10	8
Variable costs	6	9	12
Total revenue	7	8	10
Decision	Operate	Shut down	Shut down

Case Study: The πr^2 Publishing Company

The chances are pretty good that someday you will start your own business. You'll probably start out with an idea, a specific skill, a knowledge of an industry, a few connections, and whatever money you'll need not just to start the business but to live on until you're making a profit.

Ginny Crisonino and I had written a precalculus book, which John Wiley and Sons had published in 1999. Why not write a basic mathematic book for college students? So we did. After having a compositor whip our manuscript into shape, we had 10,000 copies printed. Those two fixed costs set us back close to $70,000.

We then did a mailing to 26,000 math professors offering them a free examination copy of our book and some 1,300 replied. Our fulfillment house in New Hampshire sent out the books. Within a couple of months we started getting book orders. In our first year we had sales of $56,000, fixed costs of $73,000, and variable costs of $18,000.

So how did we do? On the one hand, we did lose $35,000. Should we have shut down? I'm sure you said no, since our sales were more than three times our variable costs. And, as it happened, we still had about 6,500 books left, so it was a no-brainer to stay in business for at least another year. In the second year, we had sales of $65,000, fixed costs of $4,000, and variable costs of $22,000. That left us with a profit of $39,000.

Neither Ginny or I have been able to quit our day jobs yet, but our book is in a second edition, and πr^2 Publishing Company is still turning a profit.

Does Everybody Who's Losing Money Go Out of Business?

Mom and Pop run a little grocery in a tiny town somewhere in northwestern Nebraska. You can go there anytime between 6:00 A.M. and midnight to buy some of the stuff you forgot to pick up at the supermarket. And if you forget your wallet, no problem. Your credit is good there.

If Mom and Pop ever sat down and figured out how much money was coming in each week and how much they were paying out, they'd probably close up their store and go to work for someone else. Or maybe not. There's a lot to be said for being your own boss and making your own hours, even if they do happen to be from 6:00 A.M. to midnight.

Now according to our analysis, if sales are lower than variable costs, the firm will shut down. And if sales do not cover total costs in the long run, the firm will go out of business. But maybe Mom and Pop's store is the exception that proves the rule. The rule says you go out of business if you're not at least breaking even. But if you look hard enough, you'll almost always be able to find some people who don't follow this rule.

If you were to go into business, perhaps your two biggest worries would be having enough money to live on while you're launching your business, and then, in the short run, covering your variables. If you need to quit your day job to have enough time to run your company, then you better have enough money socked away to last you at least until you can begin taking some money out of the business. While you're still in the short run, your sales should be greater than your variable costs, or you should shut down operations. In the accompanying box, you can read about my own recent experience starting the πr^2 Publishing Company.

The Decision to Go Out of Business or Stay in Business

In the short run the businessowner must decide whether to operate or shut down. In the long run the owner is faced with two different options. The long-run choices are easier: (1) stay in business or (2) go out of business. If a firm has total revenue of $4 million, fixed costs of $3 million, and variable costs of $2 million, what does it do in the long run?

Deriving the Shut-down and Break-even Points

The firm can make the same shut-down or operate decision on the basis of price and average variable cost. Let's see why. Total revenue is the product of price times output. In order words, Total revenue = Price × Output. Average variable cost is equal to variable cost divided by output. We can put it this way:

$$\text{Average variable cost} = \frac{\text{Variable cost}}{\text{Output}}$$

If we're at the shut-down point, then Total revenue = Variable cost. If we divided total revenue by output and variable cost by output, we'd get this:

$$\frac{\text{Total revenue}}{\text{Output}} = \frac{\text{Variable cost}}{\text{Output}}$$

$$\frac{\text{Price} \times \cancel{\text{Output}}}{\cancel{\text{Output}}} = \text{Average variable cost}$$

$$\text{Price} = \text{Average variable cost}$$

Now we can restate our rules: If price is greater than average variable cost, the firm will operate. If average variable cost is greater than price, the firm will shut down.

Moving right along, let's take another look at the decision to stay in business or go out of business. We know that average total cost is equal to total cost divided by output, which we can put this way:

$$\text{Average total cost} = \frac{\text{Total cost}}{\text{Output}}$$

If we're at the break-even point, then Total revenue = Total cost. If we divided total revenue by output and total cost by output, we'd get this:

$$\frac{\text{Total revenue}}{\text{Output}} = \frac{\text{Total cost}}{\text{Output}}$$

$$\frac{\text{Price} \times \cancel{\text{Output}}}{\cancel{\text{Output}}} = \text{Average total cost}$$

$$\text{Price} = \text{Average total cost}$$

Again, we can restate our rules: If price is greater than average total cost, the firm will stay in business. If average total cost is greater than price, the firm will shut down.

This firm will go out of business because in the long run it will be losing money. Total revenue of $4 million − Total costs of $5 million ($3 million fixed + $2 million variable) = −$1 million profit.

What would you do in the long run if your firm's total revenue were $8 million, fixed costs were $4 million, and variable costs were $3 million?

You would stay in business because you would make a profit of $1 million (total revenue of $8 million minus costs of $7 million).

In summary, then, we have two long-run options: (1) stay in business or (2) go out of business. If a firm's total revenue is greater than its total costs (variable cost plus fixed cost), it will stay in business. But if total costs exceed total revenue, the firm will go out of business.

We'll need to qualify this. If a firm lost one dollar, that loss would obviously be unlikely to drive it out of business. Some very large firms have lost hundreds of millions of dollars for several years running and *still* have not gone out of business. Fine. They are the exceptions that prove the rule (see the box, "Does Everybody Who's Losing Money Go Out of Business?"). The rule is that if your total costs exceed your total revenue, you'll go out of business in the long run.

We can illustrate the shut-down or operate decision graphically. In the accompanying box, we derived the shut-down point and concluded that if price is greater than average variable cost, the firm will operate, but if average variable cost is greater than price, the firm will shut down.

Exactly where on a firm's average variable cost curve do you think you'd find the shut-down point? At its minimum point? Is that your final answer? Then you're right! Please turn back to Figure 2 and tell me how much the output is at the shut-down point.

It looks like 3.4. Now what would be the lowest price the firm would accept in the short run?

It appears to be about $140. Well, I hate to tell you, but it's *not* $140. How can I possibly tell? Remember what we said about tables and graphs—that if a graph is drawn from the data in a table, it cannot be more accurate than the table? So let's go back to Table 7, which was used to draw Figure 2. How much is AVC at an output of 3? It's $140. OK, go back to Figure 2 and you'll see that the minimum point of the AVC is at an output of 3.4. So if AVC is $140 at an output of 3, it must be a little lower at an output of 3.4. So we'll say that it's $139 (or $139.50, or even $139.99).

What is the lowest price the firm can accept in the short run and still operate? It's $139. What would the firm do if the price were $138? It would shut down.

What is the lowest price the firm would accept in the short run and still operate if we use the information in Figure 3 (based on data from Table 9)?

The answer is $69 (or $69.50, or $69.99). If the price were $70, what would the firm do in the short run? It would operate. If the price were $68, what would the firm do in the short run? It would shut down.

So, if the price is above the shut-down point, in the short run the firm will operate. But if, in the short run, the price is below the shut-down point, the firm will shut down.

We'll use the same analysis to find out how the firm will behave in the long run with respect to the break-even point. Using the information from Figure 2 and Table 7, what is the lowest price the firm can accept in the long run and stay in business?

It would be $259 (or $259 and change, for example, $259.75). What would the firm do in the long run if the price were $265? It would stay in business. What would it do in the long run if the price were $250? It would go out of business.

Now look at Figure 3 and Table 9. What is the lowest price the firm can accept in the long run? It would be $165.90. This is a judgment call. I personally would not be comfortable going as low as $165. But I would mark $165 right on an exam. How about $164? Don't push it.

OK, what would the firm do in the long run if the price were $162? It would go out of business. And if it were $170? It would stay in business.

Just to wrap things up, in Figure 5, we've labeled the shut-down and break-even points. Inspecting them visually, what is the lowest price the firm can accept in the short run (and still operate) and in the long run (and stay in business)?

F*igure* 5

Average Total Cost, Average Variable Cost, and Marginal Cost
The shut-down point is at the minimum point of the AVC curve and the break-even point is at the minimum point of the ATC curve.

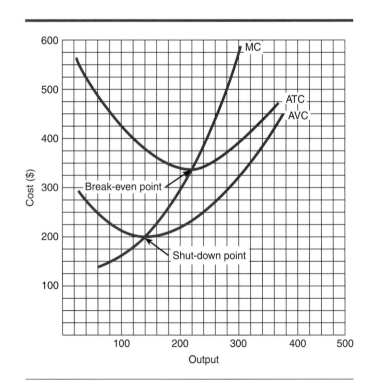

F*igure* 6
Varying Factory Capacities
Each of these ATCs represents a
different size factory, with a
different optimum level of output
represented by the minimum point
on the ATC curve. ATC_1 has the
lowest capacity, while ATC_5 has the
highest. Which size factory would a
firm choose to build to produce
400 units of output? The answer is
ATC_4.

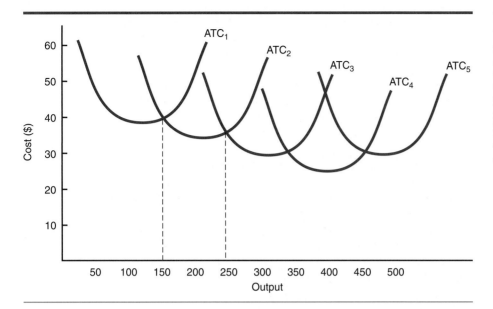

The lowest price the firm will accept in the short run is $200. The lowest price it will accept in the long run is $336.

Choosing Plant Size

We have been making an implicit assumption about the business firm. We've assumed it has been operating with a plant of given size. What's wrong with assuming that? Nothing, unless the firm alters the size of its plant.

What is a plant? It's a factory, office, store, or any combination of factories, offices, or stores. The plant used by Procter & Gamble consists of hundreds of factories and offices. The plant of General Motors consists of hundreds of car lots, factories, and offices, and the plant of Kone's ice-cream parlor on Kings Highway in Brooklyn consists of that one store (and, some would say, of the Kone "boys," who must now be in their 80s).

What is a plant?

If a firm were to build a larger factory, it might be able to lower its costs. For example, looking at Figure 6, ATC_2 reflects lower costs than does ATC_1 for outputs greater than 150. And ATC_3 reflects lower costs than does ATC_2 for outputs of more than 250.

How much would it cost to produce at ATC_1's break-even point? How much would it cost to produce at the break-even points of ATC_2 and ATC_3?

Note we have declining costs: $39 at the break-even point of ATC_1, $34 at that of ATC_2, $30 at that of ATC_3, and $26 at that of ATC_4. Why are costs declining? For a variety of reasons, which could be lumped under the heading of economies of scale. These economies include quantity discounts by making massive purchases from trade suppliers and the three economies noted in Adam Smith's discussion of mass production in a pin factory. These economies are specialization at a particular job, the use of specialized machinery, and the time saved by not having workers go from job to job.

Just as a firm may realize economies of scale as output rises, a certain point is reached when ATCs begin to rise. Here the diseconomies of scale set in. Basically, the firm grows so large that management becomes inefficient. One hand does not know what the other is doing. Divisions of a corporation begin to work at cross-purposes.

Thus, as the firm grows in size and output, it increases its plant. ATC will fall through a certain range of output, but eventually it will begin to rise. This is seen in Figure 6. Costs decline from ATC_1 to ATC_2 to ATC_3 to ATC_4. After ATC_4, they begin to rise.

When a firm grows, it increases its plant.

In the short run, a firm is stuck with a certain size plant. If output were 175 and the firm were operating with ATC_1, the firm could do nothing about it in the short run. But in the long run, it would expand so it could operate a plant that would be better suited to producing at 175. That plant would be signified by ATC_2. If it were producing in plant ATC_5 with an output of 500, if output should decline to 275 and that decline were perceived as a permanent decline, the firm would contract its plant size to ATC_3.

These changes in the size of plant are long-run changes; they take time. New factories, offices, and stores would have to be constructed. Old ones would have to be sold or sublet. In the long run, a firm could be virtually any size, provided, of course, it had the requisite financing to expand.

Current Issue: Wedding Hall or City Hall?[3]

You don't need an economist to tell you that deciding to have a big wedding is, among other things, an economic decision. Because there's no way you can have a big wedding for less than, what, $20,000? Unless, of course, you get married at home, order take-out, and let your Uncle Al tend bar.

Whether your wedding is big or small, you're going to incur certain fixed costs—the flowers, the photographer, the videographer, the wedding hall, the gowns, the tux rentals, and the clergyman or clergywoman. Your variable costs will include the food and drinks. And what you have to pay for the wedding hall will vary with the number of guests.

A larger, more expensive wedding, of course, will increase the value of the gifts you receive. Think of that as your revenue.

Let's suppose that a small wedding—just 100 close friends and family members—at the Elks or the American Legion Hall—costs you $20,000. And you pull in $10,000 in gifts. A large wedding—300 guests at the country club—runs you $100,000. And you get gifts worth $50,000.

OK, do you go for the small wedding or the large one? You'll lose $10,000 by having the small one and $50,000 by having the large one. Most brides would probably opt for the large one. Hey, you get married only once, or maybe twice.

Questions for Further Thought and Discussion

1. What happens to the difference between ATC and AVC as a firm's output expands? Explain.
2. How would you distinguish between the short run and the long run?
3. What are economies of scale? Please give an example. What are diseconomies of scale? Please give an example.
4. Your rich uncle died and left you $100,000, which you decided to use for your own Internet business. What business will you go into, and what will be your fixed and variable costs? Show how your business can take advantage of economies of scale.
5. Can a firm losing money go out of business in the short run? If it can't, explain why not.
6. Why are there no fixed costs in the long run?
7. Why is a business firm never in the long run?
8. On what basis does a firm decide whether or not to shut down? On what basis does it decide whether or not to go out of business?
9. What are the fixed and variable costs for a car wash? Is it likely to experience economies of scale?

---

[3]Bonnie Varker, a McGraw-Hill sales rep based in California, suggested this topic.

W*orkbook*   for Chapter 20

Name _____   Date _____

Multiple-Choice Questions

Circle the letter that corresponds to the best answer.

1. Al and George's used car lot has total revenue of $5 million, fixed costs of $8 million, and variable costs of $4 million. In the short run the firm will _____, and in the long run it will _____.
   a) shut down, go out of business
   b) shut down, stay in business
   c) operate, stay in business
   d) operate, go out of business

2. The decision to shut down is made in _____.
   a) both the short run and the long run
   b) neither the short run nor the long run
   c) the long run
   d) the short run

3. When MC is rising but still below ATC, then _____.
   a) ATC is declining
   b) ATC is constant
   c) ATC is rising
   d) there is no way of determining what ATC is doing

4. In general a firm's _____.
   a) total cost rises as output rises up to a certain point and then begins to decline
   b) marginal cost rises as output rises up to a certain point and then begins to decline
   c) average total cost declines as output rises up to a certain point and then begins to rise

5. If AVC is declining, then _____.
   a) marginal cost must be less than AVC
   b) marginal cost must be greater than ATC
   c) AVC must be greater than AFC

6. Which of the following is most likely to be a variable cost?
   a) Real estate taxes
   b) Rental payments of IBM equipment
   c) Interest on bonded indebtedness
   d) Fuel and power payments

7. When output is 0, fixed cost is _____ and variable cost is _____.
   a) 0, 0
   b) 0, more than 0
   c) more than 0, 0
   d) 0, more than 0

8. Which of these statements is false?
   a) When the firm shuts down, output is zero.
   b) When variable cost is zero, output is zero.
   c) When output is zero, total cost is zero.
   d) None of these is false.

9. Total cost is the sum of _____.
   a) marginal cost and fixed cost
   b) marginal cost and variable cost
   c) variable cost and fixed cost

10. In the short run, _____.
    a) all costs are fixed costs
    b) all costs are variable costs
    c) some costs are fixed costs
    d) all costs are marginal costs

11. Which statement is true?
    a) A firm will operate in the short run when total revenue exceeds fixed costs.
    b) A firm will operate in the short run when total revenue exceeds variable costs.
    c) A firm will shut down when total cost exceeds total revenue.
    d) None of these statements is true.

12. A firm has a fixed cost of $100,000, and variable cost is $90,000 at an output of one. How much is marginal cost at an output of one?

    a) $10,000

    b) $90,000

    c) $100,000

    d) $190,000

    e) There is insufficient information to answer the question.

13. Parkinson's Law is an example of _____.

    a) economies of scale

    b) diseconomies of scale

    c) Adam Smith's pin factory

    d) the firm's search for its most profitable output

14. In the short run, a firm has two options: _____.

    a) stay in business or go out of business

    b) stay in business or shut down

    c) operate or go out of business

    d) operate or shut down

15. As output expands to larger and larger numbers, _____ continues to decline.

    a) AFC

    b) AVC

    c) ATC

    d) MC

16. As output increases, eventually _____.

    a) economies of scale become larger than diseconomies of scale

    b) diseconomies of scale become larger than economies of scale

    c) economies of scale and diseconomies of scale both increase

    d) economies of scale and diseconomies of scale both decrease

17. The salaries paid to people who are in the middle of three-year guaranteed contracts are _____.

    a) a fixed cost

    b) a variable cost

    c) a fixed cost or a variable cost

    d) neither a fixed cost nor a variable cost

18. The marginal cost curve intersects _____ at its/their minimum point(s).

    a) the ATC, but not the AVC

    b) the AVC, but not the ATC

    c) both the ATC and the AVC

    d) neither the ATC nor the AVC

19. Average variable cost is found by dividing _____.

    a) variable cost by output

    b) output by variable cost

    c) marginal cost by output

    d) output by marginal cost

20. Statement 1: AVC can never be higher than ATC. Statement 2: AVC and marginal cost are equal at an output of one.

    a) Statement 1 is true, and statement 2 is false.

    b) Statement 2 is true, and statement 1 is false.

    c) Both statements are true.

    d) Both statements are false.

21. In Figure 1, if you want to produce an output of 100, in the long run you will choose a plant whose size is represented by _____.

    a) ATC_1

    b) ATC_2

    c) ATC_3

    d) ATC_4

    e) ATC_5

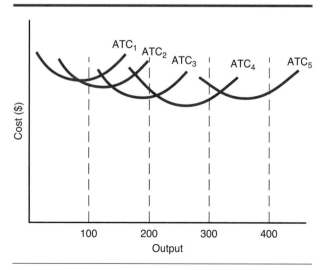

Figure 1

22. In Figure 1, if you want to produce an output of 200, in the long run you will choose a plant whose size is represented by _____.
    a) ATC_1
    b) ATC_2
    c) ATC_3
    d) ATC_4
    e) ATC_5

23. Which statement is false?
    a) AFC plus AVC equals ATC.
    b) Marginal cost equals AVC at an output of one.
    c) AVC equals ATC at an output of one.
    d) None is false.

24. As output rises, the difference between ATC and AVC _____.
    a) rises
    b) stays the same
    c) falls

25. Adam Smith noted each of the following economies of scale except _____.
    a) specialization
    b) employment of expensive equipment
    c) saving of time that would otherwise be spent going from one task to another
    d) diminishing returns

26. In general, as output rises you first attain _____.
    a) increasing returns, then diminishing returns, then negative returns
    b) diminishing returns, then negative returns, then increasing returns
    c) negative returns, then increasing returns, then diminishing returns
    d) increasing returns, then negative returns, then diminishing returns

27. The law of diminishing returns may also be called the law of _____.
    a) diminishing marginal output
    b) diminishing positive returns
    c) negative returns
    d) increasing returns

28. Each of the following provides an example of economies of scale *except* _____.
    a) the computer software industry
    b) the pharmaceutical industry
    c) Adam Smith's pin factory
    d) movie and TV production
    e) the services of psychiatrists, personal trainers, barbers, and beauticians

29. We find price by dividing _____.
    a) total revenue by output
    b) output by total revenue
    c) total cost by output
    d) output by total cost

30. The marginal cost curve intersects the average variable cost curve at the _____.
    a) shut-down point
    b) break-even point
    c) maximum profit point

31. If price is above ATC, the firm will _____.
    a) shut down in the short run and go out of business in the long run
    b) shut down in the short run and stay in business in the long run
    c) operate in the short run and go out of business in the long run
    d) operate in the short run and stay in business in the long run

32. A production function shows a firm how to _____.
    a) maximize profit
    b) maximize output
    c) minimize losses
    d) minimize output

33. When total output is maximized, marginal output is _____.
    a) rising
    b) falling
    c) positive
    d) negative
    e) zero

34. Which of the following is the most accurate statement?

    a) Virtually no one getting married thinks that considering whether or not to have a large wedding is mainly an economic decision.

    b) Most American families holding large weddings get by for less than $2,000.

    c) When making a wedding, it is impossible to think in terms of fixed costs and variable costs.

    d) Whether to hold a wedding in city hall or in a wedding hall is at least partially an economic decision.

Fill-In Questions

1. In the long run a business has two options: to _____ or to _____.

2. Variable costs change with _____.

3. At zero units of output, total cost is equal to _____.

4. The short run is the length of time it takes all fixed costs to become _____.

5. In the short run a firm has two options: (1)_____ or (2) _____.

6. A firm will operate in the short run as long as _____ are greater than _____; a firm will operate in the long run as long as _____ are greater than _____.

7. When AVC is less than price, in the short run the firm will _____.

8. Total revenue divided by output equals _____.

Problems

1. Fill in Table 1.

TABLE 1

Output	Fixed Cost	Variable Cost	Total Cost	Marginal Cost
0	$800	——	——	——
1		$100	——	——
2		150	——	——
3		200	——	——
4		270	——	——
5		360	——	——

2. If a firm's total revenue is $5 billion, its fixed costs are $3 billion, and its variable costs are $1.5 billion, what does it do: (a) in the short run? (b) in the long run?

3. If a firm's total revenue is $20 million, its fixed costs are $12 million, and its variable costs are $22 million, what does it do: (a) in the short run? (b) in the long run?

Answer Questions 4 through 7 using Table 2.

TABLE 2

Output	Variable Cost	Total Cost	AVC	AVC	Marginal Cost
1	$ 400	——	——	——	——
2	700	——	——	——	——
3	900	——	——	——	——
4	1,350	——	——	——	——
5	2,000	——	——	——	——
6	3,000	——	——	——	——

4. Given: Fixed cost = $500. Fill in Table 2.

5. On a piece of graph paper, draw a graph of the ATC, AVC, and MC curves.

6. State the minimum point of the ATC curve in dollars and cents.

7. State the minimum point of the AVC curve in dollars and cents.

8. a) Fill in the marginal output column of Table 3.

TABLE 3

Number of Workers	Total Output	Marginal Output
0	0	
1	1	_____
2	3	_____
3	6	_____
4	9	_____
5	11	_____
6	13	_____
7	14	_____
8	14	_____
9	13	_____
10	11	_____
11	8	_____

b) Diminishing returns set in with the _____ worker.

c) Negative returns set in with the _____ worker.

9. a) Fill in the marginal output column of Table 4.

TABLE 4

Number of Workers	Total Output	Marginal Output
0	0	
1	3	_____
2	7	_____
3	10	_____
4	12	_____
5	13	_____
6	13	_____
7	12	_____
8	10	

b) Given the information in Table 3, diminishing returns set in with the _____ worker.

c) Negative returns set in with the _____ worker.

10. A Toyota plant has fixed costs of $300 million and variable costs of $540 million. If it produces 60,000 cars, how much is the average total cost of producing one car?

11. If it cost Amazon.com $10 million to set up a database of potential customers and $100,000 each time it e-mailed them an advertising message, what would be the average total cost of sending out 10 e-mails? What would be the average total cost of sending out 100 e-mails?

Use Figure 2 to answer problems 12 through 15.

12. If the price is below $11, what will the firm do: (a) in the short run? (b) in the long run?

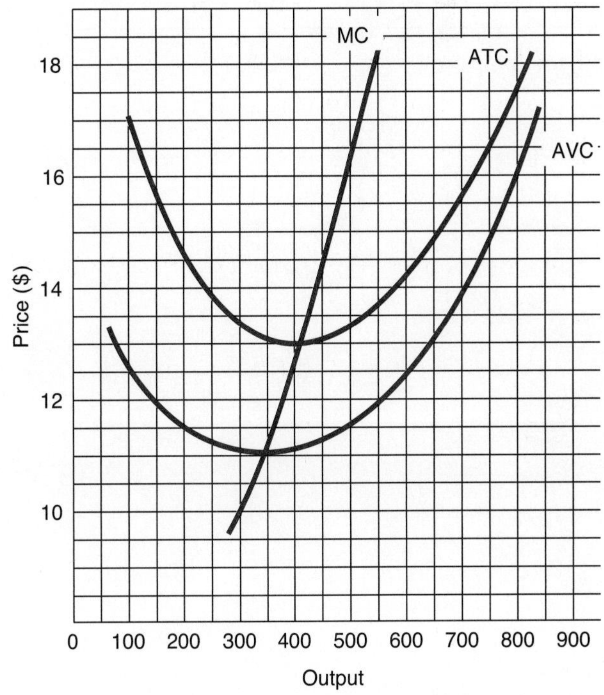

Figure 2

503

13. If the price is between $11 and $13, what will the firm do: (a) in the short run? (b) in the long run?

14. If the price is above $13, what will the firm do: (a) in the short run? (b) in the long run?

15. Please label the firm's break-even point and shut-down point in Figure 2.

Use the information in Figure 3 to answer problems 16 through 18.

16. What is the lowest price the firm would accept in the short run?

17. What is the lowest price the firm would accept in the long run?

18. On Figure 3, label the shut-down and break-even points.

19. You just got closed out of an economics course you need to graduate and need to persuade the department chair to open another section. She tells you that the school will have to pay a part-time instructor $3,000 to teach the course, and that there will be an additional $50 in administrative costs per student to run the course. If tuition is $600 for the course, how many students would you need to sign up for the course to run?

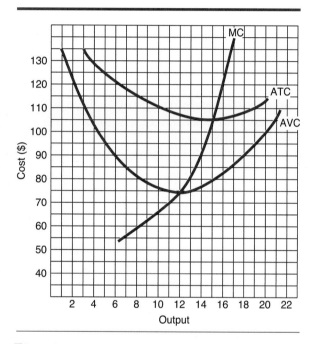

Figure 3

Chapter 21

Profit, Loss, and Perfect Competition

A sk any businessowner why she went into business and the chances are she'll answer, "To make money." If she's from Brooklyn, she might add, "I didn't go into business for my health." This is not to say that every businessowner spends every waking hour chasing down every last penny of profit. But we can say that making money, or, more specifically, making a large profit, is the driving force in our economy.

We can say, then, that every businessowner tries to maximize her profits, and, if needed, minimize her losses. Later in the chapter we'll introduce the concept of perfect competition—in which many firms sell the same good or service. We'll see that this fierce competition forces the firms to produce at peak efficiency.

CHAPTER OBJECTIVES

After reading this chapter you will be familiar with:

- Marginal revenue.
- Profit maximization and loss minimization.
- The characteristics of perfect competition.
- The perfect competitor in the short run and long run.

- The short-run and long-run supply curves.
- Economic efficiency.
- Economic profits and accounting profits.

Total Revenue and Marginal Revenue

In the last chapter we introduced the concept of marginal cost. Marginal revenue is a parallel concept. Using both concepts, we'll be able to find the output at which a firm maximizes its profit and to calculate that profit.

If your firm sold four workstations at $3,200 each, calculate your total revenue. The answer is $12,800. *Total revenue is price times output sold.*

Now let's do marginal revenue. Suppose you sold five workstations instead of four. How much would your total revenue be? It would be $16,000 (5 × $3,200). Your marginal revenue from selling that fifth workstation would be $3,200. *Marginal revenue is the increase in total revenue when output sold goes up by one unit. We can also say that marginal revenue is the additional revenue derived from selling one more unit of output.*

We'll be assuming for the next two chapters that a seller can sell as much output as he or she wants at the market price. Thus, if the market price is $5, we can easily

Total revenue is price times output sold.

Marginal revenue is the increase in total revenue when output sold goes up by one unit.

Marginal Revenue & demand is the same thing in the short run

TABLE 1	Revenue Schedule for Jill Peterson and Kaitlyn Ziegenfuss, Fashion Consultants		
Output	Price	Total Revenue	Marginal Revenue
1	$5	_____	_____
2	5	_____	_____
3	5	_____	_____
4	5	_____	_____
5	5	_____	_____
6	5	_____	_____

TABLE 2	Revenue Schedule for Jill Peterson and Kaitlyn Ziegenfuss, Fashion Consultants		
Output	Price	Total Revenue	Marginal Revenue
1	$5	$ 5	$5
2	5	10	5
3	5	15	5
4	5	20	5
5	5	25	5
6	5	30	5

calculate the total revenue and marginal revenue. I'd like you to do that by filling in Table 1. Then you can check your work by looking at Table 2.

Graphing Demand and Marginal Revenue

Now we're ready to draw the graph of the demand and marginal revenue curves. The demand curve for this firm is the output, which runs from 1 to 6, at a price of $5. And the marginal revenue curve is the output, from 1 to 6, at whatever the price happens to be. Go ahead and draw a graph of the firm's demand and MR curves on graph paper.

Check your work against Figure 1. You should have drawn just one line, perfectly elastic, which serves as the firm's demand and MR curves. When price is constant, so is MR, and MR and demand are identical.

Figure 1

Demand and Marginal Revenue Curves

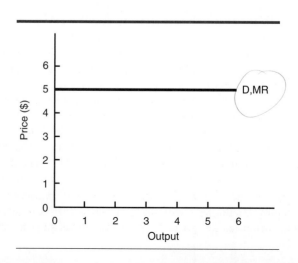

Economic and Accounting Profit

To find a firm's profit, we use this simple formula:

$$\text{Total Profit} = \text{Total Revenue} - \text{Total Cost}$$

If your company had a total revenue of $4,300,000 and a total cost of $3,750,000, how much would its total profit be?

It would be $550,000 ($4,300,000 − $3,750,000). Your accountant would tell you that your total profit is $550,000. So we'll call that your accounting profit.

Accounting profit is what's left over from sales after the firm has paid all its explicit, or dollar, costs—rent, wages, cost of goods sold, insurance, advertising, fuel, taxes. What the businessowner keeps is the accounting profit. But the economist makes some additional deductions, called "implicit costs."

Implicit costs are a business firm's *opportunity costs*. What is an *opportunity cost*? Near the beginning of Chapter 2, I said: *The opportunity cost of any choice is the forgone value of the next best alternative*. If you work for yourself, the opportunity cost of that choice is the income you forgo by not doing the same work for someone else. And what is the opportunity cost of investing $1 million of your own money in your business? It's the interest you could have earned on your money by investing it in an equally risky business owned by someone else.

What, then, are the implicit (or opportunity) costs of a family business? These costs include a return on your investment, wages that you and your family members could have earned doing the same work for another firm, rent on the space used in your house, and wear and tear on your car when it is used for your business. Your accountant will probably include these last two costs but will not deal with the first two.

OK, you and your spouse start a business and your accountant says you made a profit of $85,000. Suppose you've invested $100,000 of your own money in your business. You could have earned $15,000 in interest had you lent these funds to another business of comparable risk. If you and your spouse, instead of working 12 hours a day for your business, had worked for another firm, the two of you would have earned $70,000. The economist will subtract this $85,000 in implicit costs from your $85,000 in accounting profits. And poof—your economic profit is zero.

Why, you ask, should implicit costs be subtracted from accounting profits? Because they represent alternatives that you have forgone to have your own business. You *could* have earned $15,000 interest on your $100,000 by investing it elsewhere, and you and your spouse *could* have earned $70,000 by working for someone else. The cost of forgoing these opportunities—your opportunity cost—is $85,000. Being in business for yourselves cost you $85,000.

Why stay in business if your economic profit is zero? Because you *are* still making accounting profit. And you wouldn't do any better if you invested your money elsewhere and worked for someone else; you'd be in exactly the same economic situation. And, of course, by having your own business, you're your own boss.

When economic profit becomes negative—particularly if these losses are substantial and appear permanent—many people will close their businesses and go to work for other companies. Going back to our example, they will then be able to earn $85,000 a year ($15,000 in interest and $70,000 in wages). If you'd like more practice finding economic and accounting profit, see the accompanying box, "Accounting Profit versus Economic Profit."

Even going to college has both implicit and explicit costs. Do you know how much going to college *really* costs you? Read the box, "What Is the Cost of a College Education?"

Accounting profit

Economic profit

Being in your own business is working 80 hours a week so that you can avoid working 40 hours a week for someone else.

—Ramona E. F. Arnett, President, Ramona Enterprises

Profit Maximization and Loss Minimization

Now we're ready to do some marginal analysis, which is the basis of much of microeconomic decision making. The big decision we'll be making here is choosing the output at which the business firm should produce. If we choose correctly, profits will be maximized (or losses minimized).

Accounting Profit versus Economic Profit

Let's compare the accounting profit of Bonnie's Bargain Bazaar.

Item	Accounting Profit	Economic Profit
Total revenue	$700,000	$700,000
Less explicit costs:		
Wages and salaries	200,000	200,000
Cost of goods sold	150,000	150,000
Advertising	50,000	50,000
Phone, electricity, and other office expenses	20,000	20,000
Less implicit costs:		
Foregone salaries	0	120,000
Foregone interest	0	10,000
Foregone rent	0	20,000
Equals profit	$280,000	$130,000

As you can see, when figuring accounting profit, we subtract explicit costs from total revenue. But to find economic profit, we subtract both explicit and implicit costs from total revenue.

What Is the Cost of a College Education?

How much does it cost you to go to college? If you attend a public college or university, your out-of-pocket expenses might come to between $5,000 and $15,000, depending largely on whether you live on campus and are an in-state or out-of-state resident. Attending a private college might set you back over $40,000 a year.

But those are your explicit costs. What about your implicit costs? Like dozens of college athletes who forego their senior year to join the pros, what if you quit college and got a full-time job? How much could you earn? Let's suppose you're currently working part-time and summers for a software firm, earning $15,000. You're offered a full-time job at a starting salary of $40,000. What would you do?

Let's get back to our original question: What is the cost of a college education? Suppose that you live at home and pay $7,000 for tuition, fees, books, and other college expenses. You earn $15,000 working part-time and summers, but you could earn $40,000 by working full-time. What is it costing you to go to college? Do the math and write down your answer.

Solution: Cost of going to college = explicit cost ($7,000) + implicit cost ($40,000 − $15,000 = $25,000) = $32,000. If you were to take the full-time job, you would have $32,000 more than if you stayed in college.

It should be clear that going to college involves not just an explicit cost, but an implicit cost, which would be your foregone income. The foregone income of a college athlete good enough to play pro ball is often enough to induce him to leave school before graduation. But unless you expect to be a first- or second-round draft choice, you might not want to give up college for a day job.

I'd like you to fill in the columns in Table 3 corresponding to total revenue, marginal revenue, average total cost (ATC), marginal cost, and total profit. Make sure your work matches that in Table 4. Once you've done that, see if you can figure out the output at which the firm maximizes its total profit.

Did you get an output of 5? At that output total profit is $200. But we can do even better. The maximum profit point in this problem is actually between two outputs. How do we know? We can find out by drawing a graph of the firm's ATC, MC, and demand curves. (The firm's demand and marginal revenue curves are identical—in this case a horizontal line drawn at a price of $500.) So go ahead and draw this on a piece of graph paper, and then see if your graph looks like Figure 2.

Are you ready for some marginal analysis? All right, then, we're going to start with a very important rule: *A firm will maximize its profit or minimize its loss at the output where MC = MR*. Now let's see how this rule applies to Figure 2. At what output does MC = MR?

MC = MR at an output of 5.75. (Your estimate may be slightly different.) Let's calculate total profit at that output. We'll use this formula:

$$\text{Total profit} = \text{Output (Price} - \text{ATC)}$$

We can substitute actual numbers for output, price, and ATC. So substitute and then solve for total profit. Do your work right here:

TABLE 3 Cost and Revenue Schedule for Sam and Rachel Whittingham, Clothiers

Output	Price	Total Revenue	Marginal Revenue	Total Cost	ATC	Marginal Cost	Total Profit
1	$500			$1,000			
2	500			1,500			
3	500			1,800			
4	500			2,000			
5	500			2,300			
6	500			2,850			
7	500			3,710			

TABLE 4 Cost and Revenue Schedule: Solution

Output	Price	Total Revenue	Marginal Revenue	Total Cost	ATC	Marginal Cost	Total Profit
1	$500	$ 500	$500	$1,000	$1,000	—	−$500
2	500	1,000	500	1,500	750	500	−500
3	500	1,500	500	1,800	600	300	−300
4	500	2,000	500	2,000	500	200	0
5	500	2,500	500	2,300	460	300	200
6	500	3,000	500	2,850	475	550	150
7	500	3,500	500	3,710	530	860	−210

Figure 2

Hypothetical D, MR, MC, and ATC Curves

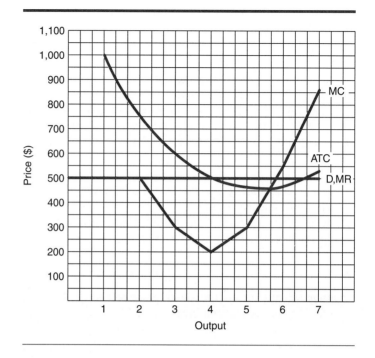

What did you get? I got $201.25. Here's my work:

$$\text{Total profit} = \text{Output (Price} - \text{ATC)}$$
$$= 5.75\ (\$500 - \$465)$$
$$= 5.75\ (\$35)$$
$$= \$201.25$$

The numbers I substituted for output and ATC are not written in stone. Two people with perfect vision could look at Figure 2 and see slightly different outputs and ATCs. But we *do* know that we are maximizing our profit at the output at which the MC and MR curves cross. So when we calculate total profit, we *should* get something a little higher than $200.

Using the same analysis and the same formula, we can calculate a firm's total loss. We've done that in the accompanying box, "Calculating a Firm's Total Loss."

The most important thing we've covered so far in this chapter is that the firm will always produce at the output at which MC = MR. At that output it will be maximizing its profit or minimizing its losses. Using this information, we can now derive the firm's short-run and long-run supply curves (see the box "Calculating a Firm's Total Loss").

A Summing Up

We're going to do a little more graphical analysis. I'll supply the graph (Figure 3), and you supply the analysis. Figure 3 is based on Table 5.

First, calculate total profit. Follow our usual three-step method: (1) write down the formula, (2) plug in the numbers, and (3) solve.

Solution:

$$\text{Total profit} = (\text{Price} - \text{ATC}) \times \text{Output}$$
$$= (\$130 - \$126) \times 5.1$$
$$= \$4 \times 5.1$$
$$= \$20.40$$

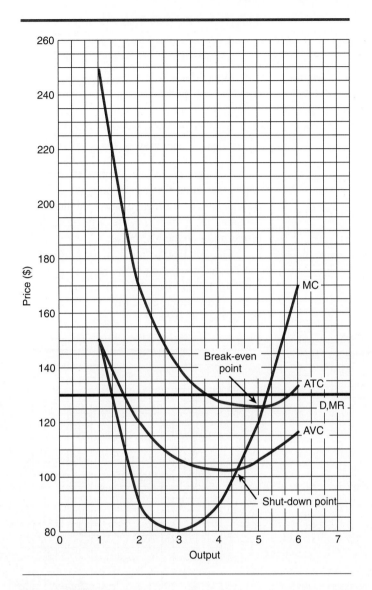

Figure 3
The Shut-Down and Break-Even Points
What is the lowest price this firm will accept in the short run and in the long run? In the short run, the firm will not accept any price below $101, the shut-down point. If the price is below $101, the firm will shut down in the short run. In the long run, the firm will not accept any price below $125.50. If price is below $125.50, the firm will go out of business in the long run.

TABLE 5						
Output	Variable Cost	Total Cost	Average Variable Cost	Average Total Cost	Marginal Cost	Total Profits
1	$150	$250	$150	$250	$150	−$120
2	240	340	120	170	90	−80
3	320	420	106.67	140	80	−30
4	410	510	102.50	127.50	90	+10
5	530	630	106	126	120	+20
6	700	800	116.67	133.33	170	−20

You'll want to watch out for a couple of things here. First, when you're picking an ATC, remember it will be the ATC at the output at which you are maximizing your total profit. That output looks like 5.1 or so. At *that* output, ATC is *more* than it is at the break-even point (that is, the minimum point of the ATC curve). I see it as $126. *You* may see it as $125.90 or $126.10.

A D V A N C E D <u>WORK</u>

Calculating a Firm's Total Loss

We're going to use the same analysis, the same formula, and the same data that we did when we calculated the firm's total profit. This time, however, let's assume that the price is just $400. We've shown this in Figure A. Let's calculate the firm's loss.

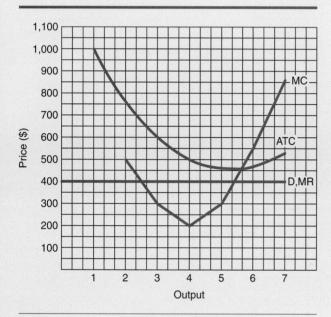

Figure A
Hypothetical D, MR, MC, and ATC Curves

Because ATC will be greater than price, total profit will be a negative number, which means the firm is losing money.

$$\text{Total profit} = \text{Output (Price} - \text{ATC)}$$
$$= 5.35 \ (\$400 - \$456)$$
$$= 5.35 \ (-\$56)$$
$$= -\$299.60$$

The firm has minimized its losses at an output of 5.35, because that's where the MC and MR curves cross. Any other output would result in still greater losses.

At any given time, a business firm will have a certain set of cost curves: AVC, ATC, and MC. These curves are determined mainly by the firm's capital stock—its plant and equipment. Over time the curves can change; but at any given time they're fixed. What concerns us here is the MC curve. We can assume it doesn't change.

What about MR? That changes with price. Because the firm will always operate where MC equals MR, there is an infinite number of possible prices and therefore an infinite number of MRs, but only one MC curve. It follows, then, that we could slide along the MC curve so that no matter what the MR, MC would equal MR.

Let's go over these points. MC must equal MR. MC stays the same. MR can change—to any value. Whenever price changes we have a new MR line, but the MC curve remains the same. The MC will equal MR, but at some other point on the MC curve.

This can be illustrated. In the graph in Figure B, based on the accompanying table, we'll start with MC = MR at an output of 9. MR = $43. At an output of 8, MC = MR = $28. At an output of 7, MC = MR = $19. And so forth down the MC curve.

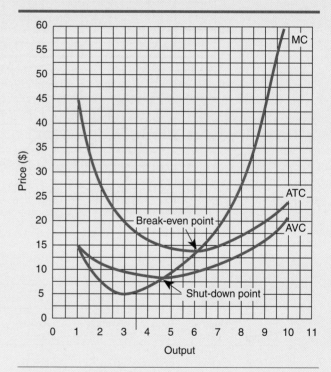

Figure B
Derivation of Firm's Short-Run and Long-Run Supply Curves

When we get below an output of about 6.1, we run into a problem. We're losing money. In the long run no firm will stay in business if it's losing money, so for every output above 6.1 we can just move along the MC curve and, in effect, we will be moving along the firm's long-run supply curve.

Hypothetical Schedule of Costs*

Output	Variable Cost	Total Cost	AVC	ATC	Marginal Cost
1	$ 15	$ 45	$15	$45	$15
2	22	52	11	26	7
3	27	57	9	19	5
4	34	64	8.50	16	7
5	44	74	8.80	14.80	10
6	58	88	9.67	14.67	14
7	77	107	11	15.29	19
8	105	135	13.33	16.88	28
9	148	178	16.23	19.78	43
10	210	240	21	24	62

*Fixed cost = $30.

Now hold it right there! *What* did I just say? I said, "We can just move along the MC curve and, in effect, we will be moving along the firm's long-run supply curve." So now I'm calling the firm's MC curve (above a certain output) its long-run supply curve. Where did *that* come from? It came from our definition of supply, which was given at the beginning of Chapter 3: *Supply is a schedule of quantities of a good or service that people are willing to sell at various prices.* This is exactly what we've derived by examining the firm's MC curve at various prices.

At outputs below 6.1, the firm is losing money because ATC is above price. Remember that price and MR are the same. Below an output of 6.1, MC is less than ATC; and because the firm will produce where MC equals MR, it should be obvious that below an output of 6.1, MR is less than ATC. In other words, the firm would be receiving less for each unit sold than the cost of producing that unit.

This is consistent with what we concluded toward the end of the last chapter—that in the long run a firm will go out of business if total cost is greater than sales. It is exactly the same thing to say that a firm will go out of business if ATC is greater than price (or MR). Why? Because if we divide total cost by output, we get ATC. If we divide total revenue by output, we get price.* In other words, since we would go out of business if total cost were greater than sales, we'd also go out of business if ATC were greater than price.

Let's go on to the firm's short-run supply curve. If we continue our way down the firm's MC curve below an output of 6.1, we find that at an output of 5, MC = MR = $10. At an output of 4, MC = MR = $7. But we see that at an output of about 4.6, the MC curve passes through the AVC curve, signifying the minimum point of the AVC. This means any price (and MR) below that point (about $8.25) will be below AVC.

In the last chapter we introduced two sets of rules for the firm in the short run and in the long run. In the short run, the firm will (a) shut down if AVC is greater than price; (b) operate if price is greater than AVC. In the long run the firm will (a) go out of business if ATC is greater than price; (b) stay in business if price is greater than ATC.

Thus the firm's short-run supply curve does not go below the point at which MC is lower than AVC. In this case, the short-run supply curve does not go below an output of 4.6. We call this the shut-down point. *The firm's short-run supply curve begins at the shut-down point and moves up the firm's MC curve as far as it goes.* It does *not* stop at the point at which the MC curve intersects the ATC curve. The short-run supply curve runs all the way up the firm's MC curve.

The firm's long-run supply curve also runs up the MC curve, beginning at the point at which the MC curve intersects the ATC curve. That is called the break-even point. In this case, it is at an output of 6.1. *A firm's long-run supply curve begins at the break-even point and runs all the way up the MC curve.*

*Total revenue = Price × Output. Total revenue/Output = Price.

A second thing to watch out for is that your total profit *must* come out to more than any total profit shown in Table 5. Why? We are maximizing our total profit at an output of 5.1, so the profit we calculate must be larger than the profit at any other output. Because the largest profit shown in the table is $20 (at an output of 5), *your* total profit *must* be larger than $20. Even if it comes out to $20.01, that's big enough.

Ready for some more analysis? What is the lowest price the firm will accept in the short run? If price is less than that figure, what will the firm do?

The firm will not accept a price lower than $101 in the short run (you may see this as $100.50 or $101.25, which is fine). If the price is less, the firm will shut down. So if price is lower than the firm's shut-down point, it shuts down.

What is the lowest price the firm will accept in the long run? If price is less than that figure, what will the firm do?

The firm will not accept a price of less than $125.50 in the long run. Why can't we use $126? Because the *minimum* point on the firm's ATC curve—the break-even point—occurs at an output of slightly more than 5, and we know from Table 5 that ATC is $126 at an output of 5. Therefore, if price is less than $125.50 (I'll take anything from $125.90 down to $125), the firm will go out of business in the long run.

Here is one last set of questions. How much will the firm's output be in the short run and the long run if the price is $170? In both the short run and the long run, the output will be 6. At an output of 6, MC is $170, so MC equals MR, and the firm is maximizing its profit.

If the price is $115, find output in the short run and the long run. In the short run output will be about 4.75 (MC equals MR). How much will output be in the long run? This is a trick question. The answer is zero. Why? Because $115 is below the firm's break-even point, so it is less than the lowest price the firm would accept in the long run (that is, the lowest price that could induce the firm to stay in business).

And finally, if the price is $90, what will the firm's output be in the short run and the long run? The answer to both questions is zero. In the short run, because the price is lower than the shut-down point, the firm will shut down and produce nothing. And in the long run the firm will go out of business.

If all of this is not perfectly clear, then work out the problems in the box, "Finding the Firm's Short-Run and Long-Run Supply Curves, and Shut-Down and Break-Even Points."

Efficiency

So far, we've concentrated on a firm's most profitable output. But we are concerned with more than just profits in economics. We are also concerned with efficiency.

Efficiency is such an important economic concept that it is part of the definition of economics: *Economics is the efficient allocation of the scarce means of production toward the satisfaction of human wants*. It's time to explain just what the word *efficient* means.

We say that a firm is operating at peak efficiency if its average total cost is held to a minimum.* How much would that output be in Figure 4? The answer is 10. You'll notice that the peak efficiency output is also where the break-even point is located.

How much is the most profitable output in Figure 4? It is 11. OK, if you owned this firm, would you produce at an output of 10 or 11? I hope you said 11. Given the choice of operating at peak efficiency or most profitably, we assume that every businessowner would choose the latter.

---

*We are confining our definition to productive efficiency, which means producing output at the least possible cost. We are not considering allocative efficiency, which occurs when firms produce the output that is most valued by consumers. Allocative efficiency is covered in a more advanced course.

Finding the Firm's Short-Run and Long-Run Supply Curves, and Shut-Down and Break-Even Points

First I'd like you to label the firm's short-run and long-run supply curves in Figure A. Then label the shut-down and break-even points.

Once you've done that, check your work against mine in Figure B. Next I'd like you to write down the lowest price this firm would accept in the short run and the lowest price it would accept in the long run.

The lowest price the firm would accept in the short run is $28; the lowest price it would accept in the long run is $48.

Last set of questions: (1) If the price is $50, what will the firm's output be in the short run and in the long run?

(2) If the price is $40, what will the firm's output be in the short run and in the long run?

Answers: (1) If the price is $50, the firm will have an output of 10.1 (you might even call it 10) in both the short run and the long run. (2) If the price is $40, the firm will have an output of 9.1 in the short run. In the long run it will go out of business; so its output will be 0.

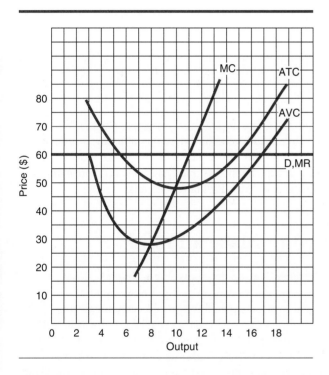

Figure A

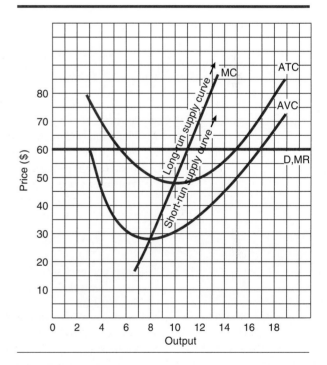

Figure B

This is not to say that a businessowner may ignore efficiency. Indeed, we shall see later in this chapter that the perfect competitor is driven to produce at peak efficiency in the long run.

Review of Efficiency and Profit Maximization

If *you* were running a business, would you try to run it at peak efficiency or would you try to maximize your profits? It is a basic assumption of microeconomics that businessowners would choose profitability over efficiency every time. Using graphic analysis, we know we're operating most efficiently when our output is at the break-even point,

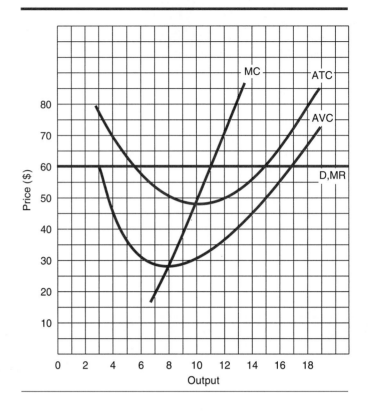

Figure 4

The Most Efficient Output
How much is this firm's most
efficient output? This occurs at an
output of 10, which is the minimum
point (the break-even point) on the
ATC.

where the MC intersects the ATC curve. And we know we're operating most profitably if we're at the output at which the MC and MR curves cross. If you'd like to take a closer look at the most efficient and most profitable outputs, please see the accompanying box, "A Closer Look at the Most Efficient and Most Profitable Outputs."

Do You Really Need to Make a Profit?

Have you ever wondered how all those start-up dot-coms stay in business losing money year after year? Look at Amazon.com, the world's largest online bookstore, which lost hundreds of millions of dollars and kept on expanding. An old economists' joke is that some firms may lose money on each item they sell, but they make up for it in volume.

Of course that's absurd: As its losses mounted, Amazon.com continued to expand. And, as long as its stock went up, who cared? But, after its stock price tanked in 1999, financial analysts began having second thoughts about the company's long-term viability. Amazon's rationale for expansion was to capture more and more market share and eventually become profitable. Eventually the company *did* make a small profit.

Definition of Perfect Competition

Perfect competition, as economists wistfully point out, is an ideal state of affairs, which, unfortunately, does not exist in any industry. So if it doesn't exist, why do you need to read about it? Just look at Judeo-Christian tradition. We're all sinners, but we still need to know right from wrong. Perfect competition fulfills the ideal of always being right. It's a goal we should strive to approach, even if we can never hope to attain its state of grace. But who knows—maybe we'll get lucky.

How wonderful *is* the perfect competitor? In the long run, the perfectly competitive firm is forced to operate at the break-even point in order to survive. This means that it

A Closer Look at the Most Efficient and Most Profitable Outputs

Figure A highlights two relationships. First, we can see that the output at which the firm operates at peak efficiency, 5.67, is clearly less than the output at which it maximizes its profit (5.7). And second, the ATC at output 5.67 ($53.00) is just a drop lower than it is at an output of 5.7 ($53.20).

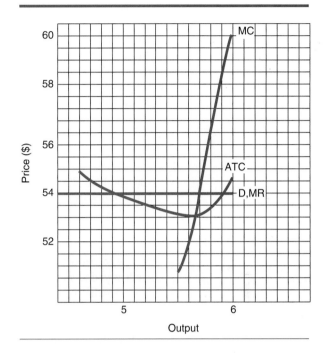

Figure A

is operating at peak efficiency. In addition, the price it gets is just equal to the minimum point of its ATC (in other words, the break-even point), so it charges the lowest possible price it can, while remaining in business. When we've gotten through this chapter and the next three, we'll see that in the long run, the perfect competitor charges the lowest price and operates most efficiently.

For our purposes, perfect competition will be considered an unattainable standard by which the other forms of competition—monopoly, monopolistic competition, and oligopoly—will be judged. Thus, even though it doesn't exist, perfect competition has its uses.

Perfect competition is a market structure with many well-informed sellers and buyers of an identical product and no barriers to entering or leaving the market. Let's deal with these characteristics one at a time.

Definition of perfect competition

Under perfect competition, there are so many firms that no one firm is large enough to have any influence over price. What is influence? If any action taken by the firm has any effect on price, that's influence. If a firm, by withholding half of its output from the market, were able to push up price, that would be influence. If a firm doubled its output and forced down price, that too would be influence. Even if a firm made prices go up by leaving the industry, *that* would be influence on price.

The industry operating under perfect competition includes many firms. How many? So many that no single firm has any influence on price. How many would *that* be? There's no exact answer, but we can agree on some numbers. Would a million firms be many? Obviously, yes. Would 80,000? Definitely. Ten thousand? Yes. Would three be many? No! Ten? No! Seventeen? No.

There's no clear dividing line. Students don't seem very happy with "more than 17 but fewer than 10,000." If you want my guess—and it's only an arbitrary number—I'd

Identical Products Are in the Minds of the Buyers

Are all hamburgers identical? Is the Whopper identical to the Big Mac? Are Wendy's hamburgers identical to those of White Castle? Maybe *you* can differentiate among these choices, but what if every buyer in the market considered them identical? Then they *would* be identical.

This identity takes place in the minds of the buyers. If they think all cars—Toyotas, Fords, Volkswagens, Lincolns, and Cadillacs—are the same, they're the same. If all buyers are indifferent about whether they're offered station wagons, stretch limos, or subcompacts, all cars are identical. A car is a car. Remember: the customer is always right.

---

say perhaps 200 firms would constitute many. But that's just *my* guess, and in microeconomics there's no one correct answer to this question of how many is many.

We're assuming, too, that no firm has more than, say, 1 percent of market share. Our definition of perfect competition would go right out the window if one of the many firms sold half the industry output.

The perfect competitor is a price taker rather than a price maker. Price is set by industrywide supply and demand; the perfect competitor can take it or leave it.

Another part of the definition of perfect competition has to do with the product. *For perfect competition to take place, all the firms in the industry must sell an identical, or standardized, product.* That is, those who buy the product cannot distinguish what one seller offers from what another seller offers. So, in the buyer's mind, the products are identical. The buyer has no reason to prefer one seller to another (see the box, "Identical Products Are in the Minds of the Buyers").

> A perfectly competitive industry has many firms selling an identical product.

Now we can define perfect competition. A perfectly competitive industry *has many firms selling an identical product.* How many is many? So many that no one firm can influence price. What is identical? A product is identical in the minds of buyers if they have no reason to prefer one seller to another.

> Two additional characteristics are perfect mobility and perfect knowledge.

We've already discussed the two most important characteristics—actually, requirements—of perfect competition: many firms and an identical product. Two additional characteristics are perfect mobility and perfect knowledge.

Firms must be free to move wherever there's an opportunity for profits. Land, labor, and capital will move where they can secure the highest possible return. An entrepreneur will give up his or her business and work for someone else if the wage offered is higher than the firm's profit.

> Perfect mobility

Usually certain barriers to entry in various markets inhibit mobility. Licenses, long-term contracts, government franchises, patents, and control over vital resources are some of these barriers. Under perfect competition, there would be perfect mobility, and none of these barriers could exist. As in an open game of poker, anyone with a sufficient stake is welcome to play. In fact, hundreds of firms are entering or leaving each year. There are no significant barriers to entry, with the possible exception of money.[1]

> Perfect knowledge

Perfect knowledge or information is another characteristic. Everyone knows about every possible economic opportunity. One example would be the market for audiologists in New York; everyone knows every job that exists and every opening when it occurs. In fact, if one person leaves one job for another, several other people become involved in a game of musical chairs as each fills the next vacated position. The audiologist from New York Eye and Ear who fills the position at Brooklyn Jewish Hospital leaves a position vacant at

---

[1]To go into any business these days, you not only need to lay out several thousand dollars for rent, inventory, equipment, advertising, and possibly salaries, but you also need money on which to live for at least six months.

More Perfect Knowledge

The computerization of the business world in the 1980s and 1990s, and the advent of the Internet in the second half of the 1990s, has brought wide sectors of business very close to a state of perfect knowledge. Tens of thousands of stockbrokers and millions of investors are hooked into the world's leading stock exchanges and have up-to-the-second information on stock prices, bids, and shares sold.

BusinessWeek reports that "business-to-business auction site Free Markets Inc. says that purchasers are saving anywhere from 2 percent to 25 percent by letting suppliers bid for business online."* And, of course, Price.com, eBay, and a host of other online websites provide the consumer with an incredible mass of information on where to purchase everything from the cheapest airline tickets to the cheapest groceries.

*Jennifer Reingold and Marcia Stepanek, *BusinessWeek*, February 14, 2000, p. 114.

New York Eye and Ear. His or her position is taken by someone from Long Island College Hospital, which now leaves that person's position open. And so forth. See the boxes, "More Perfect Knowledge," and "You get what you pay for. Right?" for two more examples.

You get what you pay for. Right?*

Do you believe in the old adage, "You get what you pay for?" So the more you pay, the better the good or service? Let's use reading glasses as an example, because they range in price from just $1 at bargain stores like Dollar Tree to about $10 or $15 at most drugstores, to perhaps $100 at your optometrist's office.

Well, you might ask, are the reading glasses that you can buy in the drugstore or at a Dollar Tree as good as the ones your optometrist prescribes for you? Yes, they are. Of course not everyone knows that, so many people just assume that if they pay more, they are getting a better product.

Those of us who have attained middle age can tell you how easy it is to misplace or lose a pair of reading glasses. So we buy several pairs, sometimes keeping a pair in every room. At $100 a pair, or even $10 or $15, that can really add up.

So why doesn't everyone pay just a dollar for reading glasses? First, many people don't realize that all reading glasses are basically the same. And second, they don't realize how much prices vary among sellers. But in a world of perfect information, the market price of reading glasses would be $1, and most people who needed them would keep a pair in every room.

*Some of the information was supplied by Harriet DeVeto of the *Brooklyn Daily Eagle*.

Agriculture, particularly wheat growing, has been held up as an example of perfect or near-perfect competition. The rise of the giant corporate farm may make this example somewhat obsolete, but economists haven't been able to come up with any other examples of perfect competition. If you can come up with a good example, then I suggest you become an economics major, go on to graduate school for your PhD, and write your doctoral dissertation on perfect competition.

The Perfect Competitor's Demand Curve

The perfect competitor faces a horizontal, or perfectly elastic, demand curve (see Figure 5). As we noted in the last chapter, a firm with a perfectly elastic demand curve has an identical MR curve. This is significant because the firm can sell as much as it wants to sell at the market price. It's not necessary to lower price to sell more.

Horizontal demand curve

Why the Firm's Demand Curve Is Flat

Look at the scale of industry output in Figure 5; it's in the millions. The output scale of the individual firm goes up to 30. When the industry demand curve slopes downward to the right, it does so over millions of units of output. For example, as the price falls from $6 to $5, output goes from 4 million to 5.5 million. In fact, it takes a price change of just $1 to bring about a change in the quantity demanded of 1.5 million units.

The graph on the right side of Figure 5 deals with output changes between 0 and 30 units. It would take a far greater change in output to change price, even by one cent. That's why the demand curve of the individual firm is seen as flat; and that's why the firm is too small to have any effect on price.

Theoretically, the firm's demand curve slopes ever so slightly downward to the right. But we can't see that slope, so we draw a perfectly horizontal curve and consider it perfectly elastic.

Figure 5

Perfect Competition: How Price Is Set

The intersection of the industry supply and demand curves sets the price that is taken by the individual firm, in this case, $6.

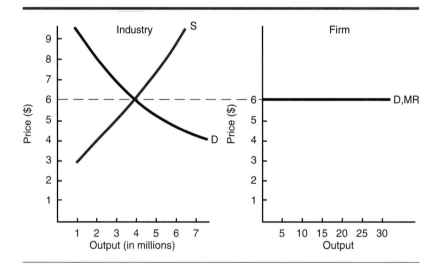

What determines the market price? Supply and demand. The graph on the left side of Figure 5 has a supply curve and a demand curve. Where they cross is the point of market price.

In our graph, the market price is $6. The firm can sell all it wants to sell at that price. What would happen if it should raise its price one penny to $6.01? It would lose all its sales to its many competitors who would still be charging $6, so the firm would never raise its price above market price.

Would a firm ever lower its price below market price, say to $5.99? Why would it do that? To get sales away from its competitors? There is no need to do this because the perfect competitor can sell as much as he or she desires at the market price. There is no point in charging less.

Why is the demand curve flat instead of curving downward to the right?

If the firm's demand curve is derived from the intersection of the industry demand and supply curves, why is it flat? Why isn't it sloping downward to the right like the industry demand curve? Actually, it is. I know it doesn't look that way, but it really is. If you'd like to know more about this, please see the Advanced Work box, "Why the Firm's Demand Curve Is Flat."

The Short Run

Short run: profit or loss

In the short run the perfect competitor may make a profit or lose money. In the long run, as we'll see, the perfect competitor just breaks even.

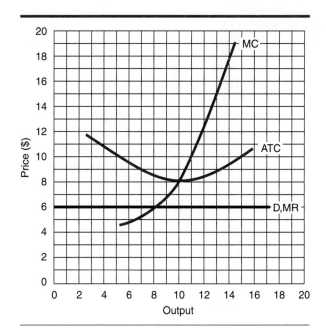

F*igure* 6
The Perfect Competitor in the Short Run

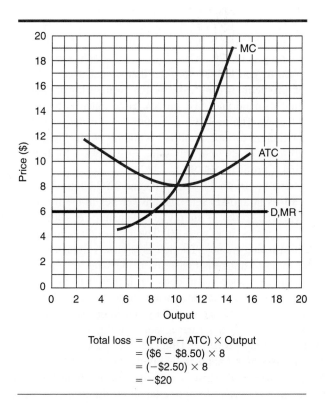

Total loss = (Price − ATC) × Output
= ($6 − $8.50) × 8
= (−$2.50) × 8
= −$20

F*igure* 7
The Perfect Competitor in the Short Run: Solution

Figure 6 shows one example of a perfect competitor in the short run. Is the firm making a profit or is it losing money? How do you know?

Long run: break even

You can always tell by looking at the demand curve and the ATC curve. If the demand curve is above the ATC curve at any point, the firm will make a profit. If the demand curve is always below the ATC curve, the firm will lose money.

In this case, the firm is losing money. How much? You should be able to figure that out for yourself. Go ahead. You'll find the solution in Figure 7.

Did you get a loss of $20? If you didn't, check your price and output. Clearly, the price is $6 and the output is 8. What about ATC? I saw it as $8.50. But suppose you saw

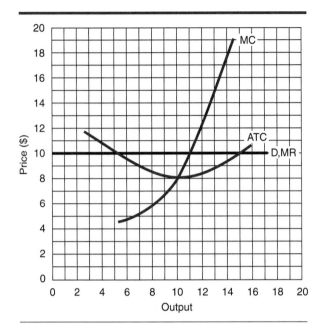

Figure 8

The Perfect Competitor in the
Short Run

it as $8.45. Then your total loss would have come to $19.60. Would this be wrong? It would be no more wrong than $20. When I drew this graph, I wanted ATC to be exactly $8.50, but if it looked to you like $8.45, then that's what it is.

Here's another problem. In this case, is the firm losing money or is it making a profit? Check out the demand and ATC curves. How much is the profit or loss? Figure it out; you have the tools. The problem is Figure 8; the solution is Figure 9.

Is this graph beginning to look familiar? It should be. In Figures 6 and 7 the firm is losing money—$20 to be exact—but this same firm looks a lot better in Figures 8 and 9, where it is turning a profit of $20.90.

How can this same firm with the same MC and ATC be making a profit in one set of graphs and taking a loss in another set? The answer lies in the forces beyond its control. What *kind* of forces? The forces of supply and demand. Let's look at them.

A double graph appears in Figure 10. The right side reproduces Figure 6 (or 7), which shows the firm losing money. The left side shows industry supply and demand.

Price is the same for the firm and the industry.

The important thing to notice is that price is the same for the firm and the industry. The price is set by industry supply and demand. It then becomes the demand/MR curve for the firm, which can sell as much as it wants at that price. Also note that the amount the firm does choose to sell is determined by the intersection of the firm's MC curve with its demand/MR curve. (For a further discussion of graphs, see the box, "Maximizing Total Profit and Maximizing Profit per Unit.")

The same analysis can be applied in Figure 11, the right side of which is taken from Figure 8 (or 9), where the firm is making a profit. Again, notice the price set in the industry market is identical to the price taken by the firm.

In the short run a firm will either make a profit or take a loss. There is a remote possibility that it will break even, but that possibility is about the same as the possibility of a tossed coin landing on its edge instead of on its head or tail. It's something you can count on happening about as often as white Christmases—in Hawaii.

The Long Run

In the long run, firms may enter or leave the industry.

In the long run there is time for firms to enter or leave the industry. This factor ensures that the firm will make zero profits in the long run. What was an unlikely outcome for the firm in the short run—zero profits—becomes an absolute certainty in the long run.

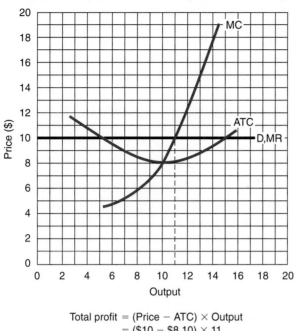

Figure 9
The Perfect Competitor in the
Short Run: Solution

Total profit = (Price − ATC) × Output
= ($10 − $8.10) × 11
= ($1.90 × 11)
= $20.90

If you read ATC as anywhere between $8.05 and $8.15 (and calculated a total profit of anything between $20.35 and $21.45), then you're right on the mark. But for analytic purposes, we'll need to show a profit of more than $20 (see the box, "Maximizing Total Profit and Maximizing Profit per Unit").

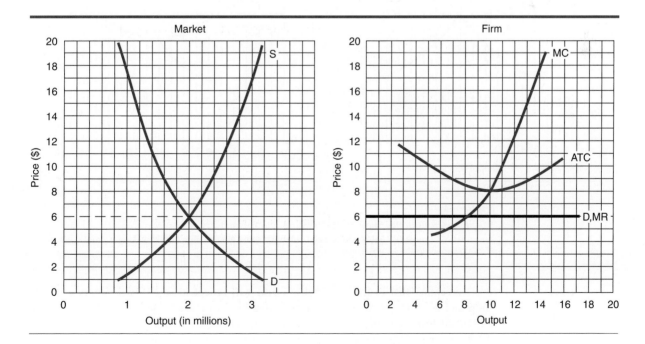

Figure 10

Taking a Loss in the Short Run: The Firm and the Industry
Since the ATC curve lies above the demand curve, the firm is losing money at a price of $6. Question: How do we get to the long run, where the firm is breaking even?

ADVANCED WORK

Maximizing Total Profit and Maximizing Profit per Unit

To find total profit we use the following formula: (Price − ATC) × Output. For instance, we calculated the total profit in Figure 5 to be $20.90 by using that formula. The formula for profit per unit of output is simple: Price − ATC.

To summarize, our total profit is the profit we make by selling our entire output. In other words, it's our profit per unit multiplied by our output. And our profit per unit is the profit we make on each unit of output sold.

When do we maximize our profit per unit? Obviously when the difference between price and ATC is at a maximum. This can be found by visually inspecting Figure 9. Price, which is read from the demand curve, is $10. At what output is ATC at a minimum? At the break-even point, where the MC curve crosses the ATC curve. The break-even point is at an output of 10.

How much is ATC at an output of 10? It's $8. How much is profit per unit at an output of 10? It's $2. Well, you may ask, why not produce at an output of 10 and maximize our profit per unit? That's a good question you're asking. Can you tell me why we are better off producing 11 units of output, even though we have a profit margin (or profit per unit) of only $1.90?

Think about it. All right, then, did you figure out that at 11 units of output we make a larger total profit ($1.90 × 11 = $20.90) than at 10 units of output ($2 × 10 = $20)? Remember, we assume that every businessowner has one main objective: to maximize profits. So if you have to choose between maximizing your total profit or maximizing your profit per unit, you'll go for total profit every time.

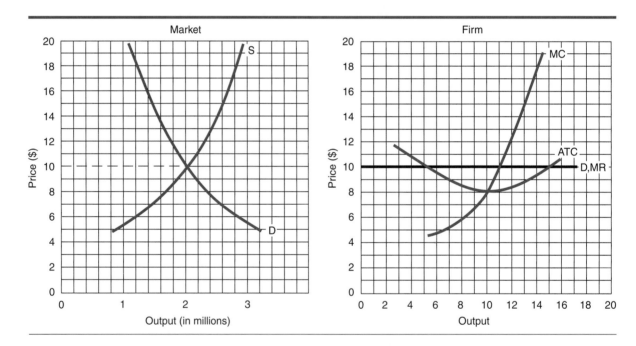

Figure 11

Making a Profit in the Short Run: The Firm and the Industry
Since the ATC curve lies below the demand curve for some outputs, this firm is making a profit. Question: How do we get to the long run, where the firm is breaking even?

Remember that in the long run, no firm will accept losses. It will simply close up shop and go out of business. Given the situation in Figure 6 (and 7 and 8), where the individual firm is losing money, it will leave the industry. But you'll remember from the beginning of the chapter, one firm cannot influence price. So if one firm leaves the industry, market price will not be affected.

If one firm is losing money, presumably others are, too; given the extent of the short-run losses this individual firm is suffering, chances are other firms are also ready to go out of business. When enough firms go out of business, industry supply declines from S_1 to S_2, which pushes price up from $6 to $8. This price rise is reflected in a new

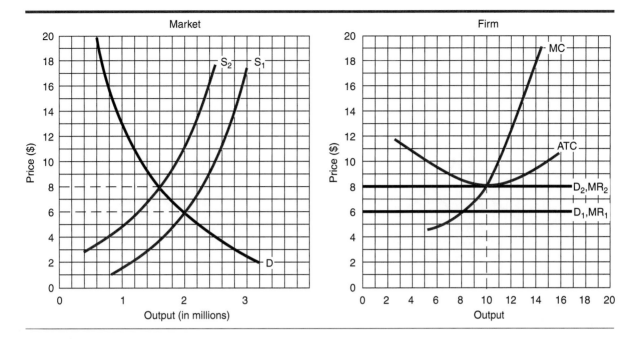

F*igure* 12

Going from Taking a Loss in the Short Run to Breaking Even in the Long Run
At a price of $6 the firm is losing money and so, too, are all the other firms in the industry. Some leave
the industry in the long run, pushing the supply down from S_1 to S_2, which, in turn, pushes up the industry
price to $8. At that price the firm breaks even.

demand curve for the firm on the right side of Figure 12. In short, a decline in industry
supply from S_1 to S_2 raises industry price from $6 to $8. This price increase pushes up
the firm's demand curve from D_1 to D_2 (in the right graph).

There is a secondary effect on the firms that remain in the industry. Each will expand
output slightly to the right. On the right side of Figure 12, we see that the firm's output
rises from 8 to 10.

Figure 13 is based on Figure 11. It shows the long-run effect of a short-run profit.
If one firm is making a profit, we can assume others are, too. New firms will spring up,
as entrepreneurs enter the industry to get their share of the profits. As more and more
firms enter the industry, market supply increases, pushing the supply curve up from S_1
to S_2 (see the left side of Figure 13). As market supply rises, market price comes down
until it reaches $8.

Here, once again, industry price and the price taken by the individual firm are identical. The output for the individual firm has been reduced slightly; but, more significantly,
the new firms that entered the industry have increased market supply. This, in turn,
reduced the price to $8, and profits for the individual firm are now zero. Along with this,
as we can see on the right side of Figure 13, output has fallen from 11 to 10.

The right side of Figure 12 and the right side of Figure 13 look identical. Notice
that the ATC and the demand/MR curves are tangent (just touching). At the point of
tangency, MC equals MR, so that is where the firm produces. ATC equals price at that
point, so profit is zero.

Still another way to find total profit and total loss is to draw a couple of dashed
lines on a graph to form a box. By multiplying the height and length of this box, or
rectangle, you can find a firm's total profit or total loss. This method is illustrated in the
box, "Showing Total Profits and Losses Graphically."

Let's slow down for a minute to catch our breath. We've talked about the firm
making a profit or taking a loss in the short run and just breaking even in the long run.
But to make sure that you're clear on what the firm's long-run situation looks like, I'm
going to draw yet another graph. Figure 14 shows the firm's demand and MR curve

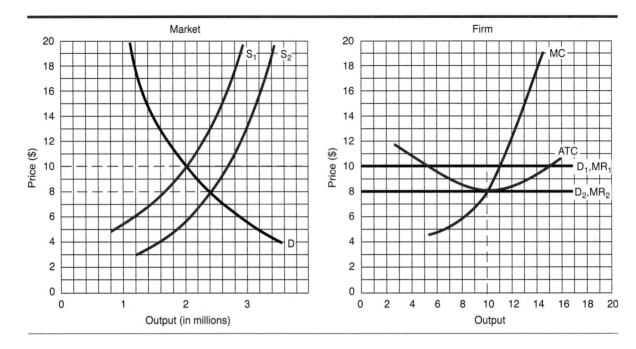

Figure 13

Going from Making a Profit in the Short Run to Breaking Even in the Long Run
At a price of $10 all firms in the industry are making a profit. New firms are attracted to the industry, pushing the supply drive up from S_1 to S_2. This reduces industry price to $8, at which all firms just break even.

Figure 14

The Perfect Competitor in the Long Run
In the long run the firm breaks even. The ATC curve is tangent to the demand curve at an output of $10 and a price of $18.50. Note that at that output, MC = MR.

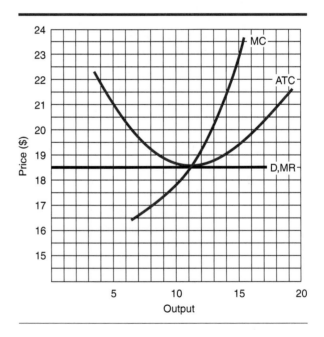

tangent to the ATC curve. So, what are the firm's long-run price and output? Have you figured them out? The price is $18.50, and the output is 11.

We need to be clear on just what we mean by profit. When we say that the perfect competitor earns zero profit in the long run, are we saying that she earns zero accounting profit or zero economic profit? We are talking about zero *economic* profit. We need to be very clear on this point. A firm that has $800,000 in sales, $600,000 in explicit costs, and

Face it. Economists sometimes like to show off a little, and one way we really get to shine is when we draw some truly elegant graphs. So buckle your seat belt because we are about to take off.

By drawing just a couple of dotted lines and then multiplying two numbers, you can quickly calculate a firm's total profit. In Figure A I drew a vertical dotted line down from the intersection of the MR and MC curves at 50 units of output. Then I drew a horizontal dotted line from the ATC curve at 50 units of output straight across to the price scale.

Of course, we could have used the tried-and-true method:

$$\begin{array}{rl} \text{Price} & \$10 \\ -\text{ATC} & \underline{-8} \\ & \$\ 2 \times \text{output (50)} = \$100 \end{array}$$

We can also find total loss graphically by drawing just two dotted lines and multiplying. I've worked out a problem in Figure B.

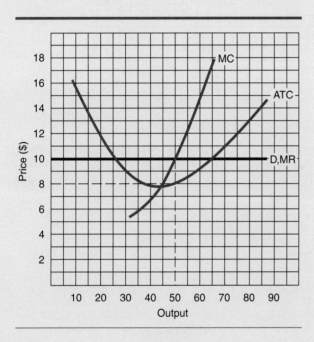

Figure A

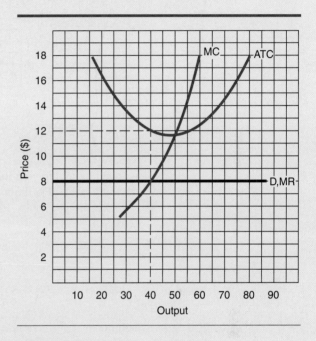

Figure B

Now it's easy to find total profit. It is the area of the box that is bounded by the two dotted lines, the demand curve, and the price scale. To find that area, simply multiply the distance of the vertical line ($2) and the horizontal line (50 units of output). How much is $2 × 50? It's $100.

Our loss box is $4 × 40, or a loss of $160. Just like our box for total profit, it is bounded by the two dotted lines, the demand curve, and the price scale. Again, we can find our loss (or negative profit) this way:

$$\begin{array}{rl} \text{Price} & \$\ 8 \\ -\text{ATC} & \underline{-12} \\ & \$\ 4 \times \text{output (40)} = \$160 \end{array}$$

$200,000 in implicit costs earns zero economic profits. So whenever we say that the perfect competitor earns zero profits in the long run, we're talking about zero economic profits.

Alternative Calculation of Profit and Loss

Sometimes we can calculate profit or loss by just glancing at a graph and doing some fast multiplication. In Figure 15, total profit is bounded by the rectangle EFGH. So total profit is represented by the area of that rectangle. As you know, the area of a rectangle

F*igure* **15**

Alternate Calculation of Profit
Profit per unit ($12.50) × quantity
sold (70) = $875.

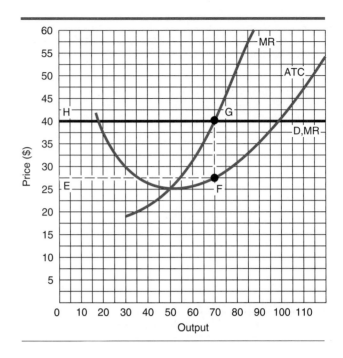

is found by multiplying its length times its width. The length of this rectangle is EF and its width is FG. Do the math and write down the total profit.

Use the profit box EFGH to find total profit. Profit per unit ($12.50) × quantity sold (70) = $875.

Solution:

$$EF\ (70) \times FG\ (\$12.50) = \$875 \text{ total profit}$$

In Figure 16 the firm is losing money. How much? Work it out by finding the area of rectangle JKLM.

Use the loss box JKLM to find total loss. Loss per unit ($2) × quantity sold (600) = total loss of $1,200.

Solution:

$$JK\ (600) \times KL\ (\$2) = \$1,200 \text{ total loss}$$

The Perfect Competitor: A Price Taker, Not a Price Maker

If you own a store, you get to decide how much to charge your customers. But if you happen to be a perfect competitor, you don't have that privilege; you're a price taker, not a price maker. What price do you take? You take the market price. In Figures 12 and 13, we showed how the market works. The industrywide supply and demand determine the

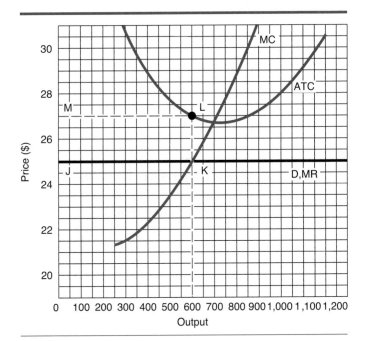

Figure 16
Alternate Calculation of Loss

market price. If you feel that price is too low, about the only thing you could do is to close up shop and leave the industry. Otherwise you have no choice but to charge what everyone else is charging.

Although you're way too young to remember the original Broadway musicals, there are lines from the songs of *South Pacific* and *Oklahoma!* that illustrate the plight of a farmer who grows corn. The lines from *South Pacific,* "I am corny as Kansas in August," and from *Oklahoma!,* "The corn is as high as an elephant's eye," attest to the abundance of our corn crop. If you were to drive through the Grain Plains in August, you'd see field after field of corn and wheat.

Grain farmers are about as close as we come to perfect competitors. And more likely than not, you'll hear them complaining about crop prices. If the price is just $3 a bushel, the farmer, as the price taker, has no choice but to sell his entire output at that price. The farmer, then, is the classic price taker.

Efficiency, Price, and Profit

You remember the concept of efficiency from earlier in the chapter. We define *efficient* as cheap. When a firm is an efficient producer, it produces its product at a relatively low cost. A firm operates at peak efficiency when it produces its product at the lowest possible cost. That would be at the minimum point of its ATC curve—the break-even point.

Efficiency defined

For the perfect competitor in the long run, the most profitable output is at the minimum point of its ATC curve. Check it out in Figure 14. At any other output, the firm would lose money; just to stay in business, it must operate at peak efficiency.

This is the hallmark of perfect competition. The firm, not through any virtues of its owners but because of the degree of competition in the marketplace, is forced to operate at peak efficiency. As we'll see in the next three chapters, the other forms of competition do not force peak efficiency.

Competition is the keen cutting edge of business, always shaving away at costs.

—Henry Ford

Perfect competition is very good for consumers; they can buy at cost. That's right, price is equal to ATC. Remember, there's no economic profit. And consumers have the firm's competitors to thank for such a low price. Competition will keep businessowners honest—that is, if there's enough competition.

In the next three chapters we'll introduce the three other forms of competition. But we can tell you in advance that in the long run the perfect competitor sells at a lower price and operates more efficiently. And, by selling at cost, the perfect competitor makes no economic profit. Under perfect competition you don't need a friend in the business to find someone who will sell to you at cost. In the long run, *every* perfect competitor sells at cost.

Current Issue: The Internet Effect: A More Perfect Knowledge and Lower Prices

You can now find almost anything on the Internet by using Google, Yahoo, or some other search engine. And, of course, like tens of millions of other buyers or sellers around the world, you can find a ready market on eBay. In sum, the Internet has moved entire markets much closer to the ideal of perfect knowledge. It's also lowered barriers to entry in many markets, bringing us much closer to perfect competition in the markets for many goods and services.

For example, I've recently started collecting silver dollars, primarily from the 1880s and 1890s. Sellers post pictures of coins on eBay, where people all over the world can place bids. Before the Internet, you might find just a couple of coin dealers nearby, and unless you were a coin expert, these dealers would know a lot more than you about how much these coins were worth.

Gasbuddy.com surveys 150,000 American and Canadian gas stations every week. When gas shot up to over $3 a gallon in the summer of 2005 the site got over 500,000 hits a day. Volunteers report the gas prices while visitors to the site enter their zip codes to find gas prices at nearby stations.

Finally let's look at the strange case of the price of term life insurance, which fell dramatically in the 1990s, while the prices of other types of insurance, including medical and automobile coverage, were certainly not falling. What happened? According to the authors of *Freakonomics,*

> The Internet happened. In the spring of 1996, Quotesmith.com became the first of several websites that enabled a customer to compare, within seconds, the price of term life insurance sold by dozens of different companies. For such websites, term life insurance was a perfect product. Unlike other forms of insurance—including whole life insurance, which is a far more complicated financial instrument—term life policies are fairly homogeneous: one thirty-year, guaranteed policy for $1 million is essentially identical to the next. So what really matters is the price. Shopping around for the cheapest policy, a process that had been convoluted and time-consuming, was suddenly made simple. With customers able to instantaneously find the cheapest policy, the more expensive companies had no choice but to lower their prices. Suddenly customers were paying $1 billion less a year for term life insurance.[2]

Questions for Further Thought and Discussion

1. How do you find the most efficient output, and how do you find the most profitable output?

2. At the output at which a firm maximizes its profits, what two variables are equal? At the output at which a firm minimizes its losses, what two variables are equal?

---

[2]Steven D. Levitt and Stephen J. Dubner, *Freakonomics* (New York: William Morrow, 2005), p. 66.

3. Is the analysis for maximizing profits the same as that for minimizing losses? Explain why it is or why it isn't.

4. What is the difference between the firm's short-run supply curve and its long-run supply curve? Make up an example to explain your answer.

5. At the output at which MC = MR, suppose that price were higher than AVC but lower than ATC. What should the firm do in the short run and the long run? Explain your answer.

6. Why might a firm produce at a loss in the short run rather than shut down? Make up an example to illustrate your answer.

7. Does the perfect competitor always break even in the long run? Explain why or why not.

8. If the perfect competitor is losing money in the short run, what happens in the market to drive up price?

9. Two characteristics of perfect competition are perfect mobility and perfect knowledge. Make up an example of each.

10. Can you think of any dot-coms that may be considered perfect competitors?

11. Although perfect competition may not exist, explain why it is relevant to the study of microeconomics.

12. How have you used the Internet to search for product information and lower prices?

13. Explain why a perfectly competitive firm won't advertise.

Workbook for Chapter 21

Name _____   Date _____

Multiple-Choice Questions

Circle the letter that corresponds to the best answer.

1. A firm with explicit costs of $2,000,000, no implicit costs, and total revenue of $3,000,000 would have _____.

   a) zero economic profit

   b) zero accounting profit

   c) an accounting profit and an economic profit of $1,000,000

   d) a higher economic profit than an accounting profit

   e) a higher accounting profit than economic profit

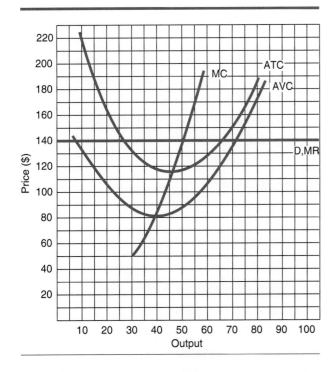

Figure 1

2. In Figure 1, at which output is the firm operating most efficiently?

   a) 30   c) 46

   b) 39   d) 50

3. The marginal cost curve intersects the ATC curve at its _____.

   a) minimum point, which is the break-even point

   b) maximum point, which is the break-even point

   c) minimum point, which is the shut-down point

   d) maximum point, which is the shut-down point

4. A profit-maximizing firm will increase production when _____.

   a) price is less than marginal cost

   b) price equals marginal cost

   c) price exceeds marginal revenue

   d) price exceeds marginal cost

5. The lowest point on a firm's short-run supply curve is at the _____.

   a) break-even point

   b) shut-down point

   c) most profitable output point

   d) lowest point on the marginal cost curve

6. A firm will operate at that output where MC equals MR _____.

   a) only when it is maximizing its profits

   b) only when it is minimizing its losses

   c) both when it is maximizing its profits and when it is minimizing its losses

   d) neither when it is maximizing its profits nor minimizing its losses

7. When marginal cost is rising but is less than average total cost, we are definitely below the _____.

   a) shut-down point

   b) break-even point

   c) maximum profit point

8. Which statement is true?

   a) Accounting profits are greater than economic profits.

   b) Economic profits are greater than accounting profits.

   c) Accounting profits are equal to economic profits.

9. Statement 1: Price is equal to total revenue divided by output. Statement 2: A firm never maximizes profits.
   a) Statement 1 is true, and statement 2 is false.
   b) Statement 2 is true, and statement 1 is false.
   c) Both statements are true.
   d) Both statements are false.

10. If a firm is producing a level of output at which that output's marginal cost is less than the price of the good, _____.
    a) it is producing too much to maximize its profits
    b) it is probably maximizing its profits
    c) higher profits could be obtained with increased production
    d) none of the above

11. The firm's long-run supply curve runs along its _____ curve.
    a) ATC   c) MC
    b) AVC   d) MR

12. A firm will operate at that output at which MC = MR _____.
    a) only in the short run
    b) only in the long run
    c) in both the short run and the long run
    d) in neither the short run nor the long run

13. At an output of 5, MC = $49 and ATC = $52. At an output of 6, MC = $59 and ATC = $53. At the break-even point, ATC is _____.
    a) above $53
    b) $53
    c) between $52 and $53
    d) $52
    e) less than $52

14. Statement 1: The firm's short-run supply curve runs up the marginal cost curve from the shut-down point to the break-even point.
    Statement 2: The firm will not accept a price below the break-even point in the short run.
    a) Statement 1 is true, and statement 2 is false.
    b) Statement 2 is true, and statement 1 is false.
    c) Both statements are true.
    d) Both statements are false.

15. A business firm is in the short run _____.
    a) virtually all the time   d) rarely
    b) most of the time   e) never
    c) occasionally

16. If the price is between the shut-down point and the break-even point, the firm is in the _____.
    a) short run making a profit
    b) short run taking a loss
    c) long run making a profit
    d) long run taking a loss

17. The most efficient output of a firm is located _____.
    a) at the shut-down point
    b) at the break-even point
    c) where MC = MR
    d) when the vertical distance between AVC and ATC is at a maximum

18. What would be the most accurate statement about Amazon.com?
    a) It is not an exception to the model of going out of business in the long run if you are losing money.
    b) It may be losing money, but it more than makes up for those losses in volume.
    c) It has been maximizing its profits for years.
    d) Its long-run strategy is to gain market share at the expense of relatively high short-term losses.

19. Perfect competition is _____.
    a) the prevalent form of competition in the United States
    b) the only form of competition in the United States
    c) found occasionally
    d) probably impossible to find

20. Under perfect competition, _____.
    a) many firms have some influence over price
    b) a few firms have influence over price
    c) no firm has any influence over price

21. Under perfect competition, there are _____.
    a) many firms producing an identical product
    b) a few firms producing an identical product
    c) many firms producing a differentiated product
    d) a few firms producing a differentiated product

22. The perfect competitor is _____.
    a) a price maker rather than a price taker
    b) a price taker rather than a price maker
    c) a price taker and a price maker
    d) neither a price maker or a price taker

23. The determination of whether two products are identical _____.
    a) is done by market research
    b) takes place in the minds of the buyers
    c) is done by the government
    d) is done by the sellers

24. The perfect competitor's demand curve is _____.
    a) always horizontal
    b) always vertical
    c) sometimes horizontal
    d) sometimes vertical

25. Which statement about the perfect competitor is true?
    a) She may charge a little below market price to get more customers.
    b) She may charge a little above market price to imply that her product is superior.
    c) She will always charge the market price.
    d) None of these statements is true.

26. Each of the following is a characteristic of perfect competition except _____.
    a) many firms
    b) identical products
    c) perfect mobility
    d) varying prices charged by different firms

27. In the short run the perfect competitor will probably _____.
    a) make a profit or break even
    b) take a loss or break even
    c) make a profit or take a loss

28. In the long run the perfect competitor will _____.
    a) make a profit
    b) break even
    c) take a loss

29. Under perfect competition _____ profits are always zero in the long run.
    a) accounting
    b) economic
    c) both economic and accounting
    d) neither accounting or economic

Use the choices below to answer questions 30 and 31.
    a) in the long run making a profit
    b) in the long run breaking even
    c) in the long run taking a loss
    d) in the short run making a profit
    e) in the short run breaking even
    f) in the short run taking a loss

30. Figure 2 shows the perfect competitor _____.

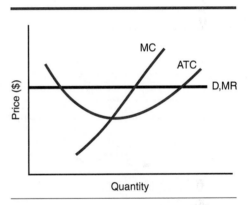

F*igure* **2**

31. Figure 3 shows the perfect competitor _____.

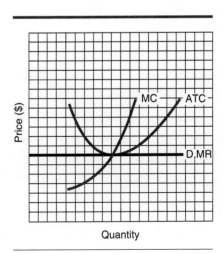

F*igure* **3**

32. The perfect competitor's demand and marginal revenue curves are _____.
    a) identical only in the long run
    b) identical only in the short run
    c) never identical
    d) always identical

33. The most efficient output _____.
    a) is always equal to the most profitable output for the perfect competitor
    b) is never equal to the most profitable output for the perfect competitor
    c) is equal to the most profitable output for the perfect competitor only in the long run
    d) is equal to the most profitable output for the perfect competitor only in the short run

Use Figure 4 to answer questions 34 through 37.

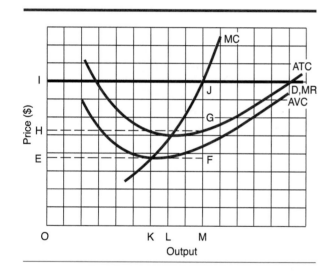

Figure 4

34. Total profit _____.
    a) is the rectangle bounded by EFJI
    b) is the rectangle bounded by EFGH
    c) is the rectangle bounded by HGJI
    d) cannot be found on this graph

35. Output _____.
    a) is OK
    b) is OL
    c) is OM
    d) cannot be found on this graph

36. Profit per unit is _____.
    a) MF   d) FJ
    b) MG   e) GJ
    c) MJ

37. The firm's most efficient output _____.
    a) is OK
    b) is OL
    c) is OM
    d) cannot be determined on this graph

38. Statement I: The advent of the Internet has brought "perfect knowledge" closer to reality.
    Statement II: The cost of businesses buying their supplies online is convenient, but they generally pay more than they would if they used customary channels.
    a) Statement I is true, and statement II is false.
    b) Statement II is true, and statement I is false.
    c) Both statements are true.
    d) Both statements are false.

39. Statement I: No firm will stay in business more than one year if it is losing large sums of money.
    Statement II: Many dot-coms have lost money in the short run.
    a) Statement I is true, and statement II is false.
    b) Statement II is true, and statement I is false.
    c) Both statements are true.
    d) Both statements are false.

40. When an industry is in long-run equilibrium economic profits are _____ and _____ will be entering or leaving the industry.
    a) zero, some
    b) zero, none
    c) positive, some
    d) positive, none

41. If a perfectly competitive firm sells 10 units of output at a price of $10 per unit, its marginal revenue per unit is _____.
    a) $1   d) more than $1, but less
    b) $10   than $10
    c) $100   e) more than $10, but less
                       than $100

Fill-In Questions

1. Under perfect competition there are so many firms that no one firm has any influence over _____.

2. The determination that a product is identical takes place in _____.

3. The perfect competitor's demand curve is a _____; the marginal revenue curve is a _____.

4. A perfect competitor would never charge more than market price because _____; the perfect competitor would never charge less than market price because _____.

5. In the short run the perfect competitor may make a _____ or take a _____; in the long run the perfect competitor will _____.

6. In a perfectly competitive industry, if firms are making profits, _____, which will result in zero profits in the long run; if there are losses in the short run, _____, resulting in zero profits (and losses) in the long run.

7. The perfect competitor operates at the _____ point of her average total cost curve in the long run.

8. If the firms in a competitive industry are earning profits, in the long run new firms will _____. But if most firms are losing money, then in the long run some of the firms will _____.

Problems

Use Figure 5 for problems 1–6.

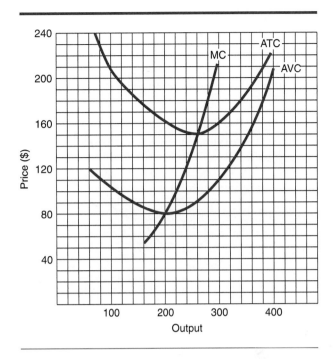

Figure 5

1. How much will output be in the short run if the price is (a) $70? (b) $120? (c) $160?

2. How much is the firm's most efficient output?

3. If price is $180, how much is total profit?

4. If price is $120, how much is total profit? (Hint: You might consider this a trick question.)

5. How much is output at (a) the break-even point? (b) the shut-down point?

6. How much is the lowest price the firm will accept in (a) the short run? (b) the long run?

Use Figure 6 for problems 7–12.

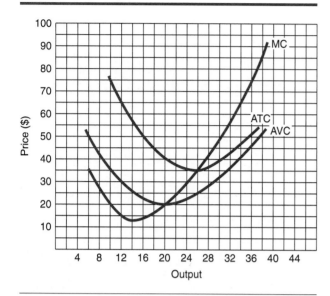

Figure 6

7. How much is the most efficient output?

8. a) If the. price is $55, how much is the most profitable output?
   b) Calculate total profit.

9. How much is output in the short run if price is (a) $65? (b) $30? (c) $15?

10. If price is $30, what will the firm do in (a) the short run? (b) the long run?

11. Label the break-even and shut-down points.

12. Label the short-run supply curve and the long-run supply curve.

13. At an output of 14, MC = $50 and ATC = $55. At an output of 15, MC = $65 and ATC = $56. Estimate the ATC at the break-even point.

14. At an output of 9, MC = $20 and AVC = $25. At an output of 10, MC = $32 and AVC = $26. What is the lowest price the firm will accept in the short run?

15. You should do this problem in four steps. First: Fill in Table 1. Assume fixed cost is $100 and price is $64.

TABLE 1

Output	Variable Cost	Total Cost	Average Variable Cost	Average Total Cost	Marginal Cost
1	$ 30	_____	_____	_____	_____
2	50	_____	_____	_____	_____
3	80	_____	_____	_____	_____
4	125	_____	_____	_____	_____
5	190	_____	_____	_____	_____
6	280	_____	_____	_____	_____

Second: Fill in Table 2.

TABLE 2

If Price Were	What Would the Firm Do in the:		How Much Would Output Be in the Short Run?
	Short Run?	Long Run?	
$90	_____	_____	_____
40	_____	_____	_____
20	_____	_____	_____

Third: Draw a graph of the firm's demand, marginal revenue, average variable cost, average total cost, and marginal cost curves on a piece of graph paper. Be sure to label the graph correctly. On the graph, indicate the break-even and shut-down points and the firm's short-run and long-run supply curves.

Fourth: Calculate total profit in the space below, then answer questions (a) through (d).

(a) The minimum price the firm will accept in the short run is $ _____. (b) The minimum price the firm will accept in the long run is $ _____.

(c) The output at which the firm will maximize profits is _____. (d) The output at which the firm will operate most efficiently is _____.

16. (a) Find the total profit or total loss of the firm shown in Figure 7. (b) Is the firm in the short run or the long run? (c) How much is the firm's most efficient output? (d) What is the lowest price the firm would accept in the long run?

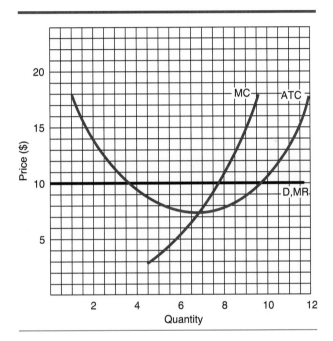

Figure 7

17. (a) Find the total profit or total loss of the firm shown in Figure 8. (b) Is the firm in the short run or the long run? (c) How much is the firm's most efficient output? (d) What is the lowest price the firm would accept in the long run?

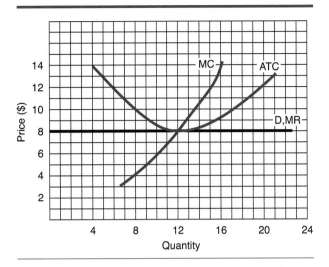

Figure 8

18. (a) Find the total profit or total loss of the firm shown in Figure 9. (b) Is the firm in the short run or the long run? (c) How much is the firm's most efficient output? (d) What is the lowest price the firm would accept in the long run?

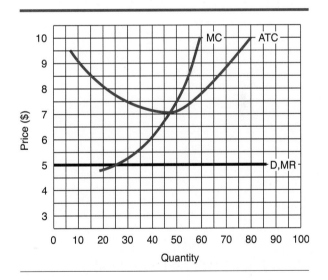

Figure 9

539

19. Given the industry supply and demand shown on the right side of Figure 10, use the left side of the figure to draw the perfect competitor's demand, marginal revenue, average total cost, and marginal cost curves for its long-run situation.

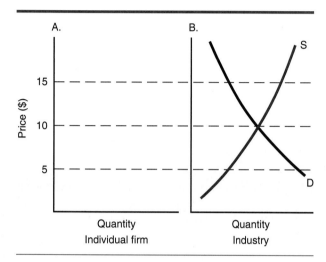

F*igure* 10

Chapter 22

Monopoly

We've talked enough about perfect competition, an ideal state that probably does not exist. Welcome to the real world of imperfect competition. We'll begin here with monopoly and then go on to monopolistic competition and oligopoly in the next two chapters. When we've completed our analysis of these competitive states, you will probably conclude what I concluded a long time ago: that nobody's perfect.

When you were a kid, did you ever play the game of Monopoly? The whole idea was to control strips of properties, such as Boardwalk and Park Place. Some people get to play Monopoly even after they've grown up—and they get to keep all the money. In this and the next three chapters, we'll see how this game is played by the big kids.

CHAPTER OBJECTIVES

We'll look at these topics:

- The graph of the monopolist.
- How the monopolist's profits are calculated.
- The monopolist in the short run and the long run.
- Barriers to entry.
- Limits to monopoly power.
- Economies of scale and natural monopoly.
- What makes bigness bad?

Monopoly Defined

A monopoly is the only firm in an industry. There's nobody else selling anything like what the monopolist is producing. In other words, there are no close substitutes.

Examples of monopoly include DeBeers diamonds, the local gas and electric companies, and your local phone company. During the years after World War II, IBM, Xerox, the International Nickel Company, and Alcoa (Aluminum Company of America) also had monopolies.

One might ask how close substitutes would need to be to disqualify firms from being monopolies. Surely a Cadillac Seville is a reasonably close substitute for a Lincoln Continental. Further, there are many close substitutes for a Xerox photocopying machine, but there are no close substitutes for diamonds, gas, electricity, and local phone calls.

We need to ask *why* there are no close substitutes for the monopolist's goods or services. Has the monopolist erected barriers to keep out potential competitors, or is there some other explanation as to why the monopolist is the sole producer? We'll talk about barriers to entry later in the chapter.

A monopoly is a firm that produces all the output in an industry.

What are close substitutes?

We should also distinguish between local and national monopolies. Someone may be the only doctor in the vicinity and have a local monopoly, but there are more than 700,000 doctors in the United States. A hardware store, grocery, drugstore, or dry cleaners may have a monopoly in its neighborhood, but each may have several competitors within a few miles.

The Graph of the Monopolist

The distinguishing characteristic of imperfect competition

The distinguishing characteristic of imperfect competition is that the firm's demand curve is no longer a perfectly elastic horizontal line; now it curves downward to the right. This means the imperfect competitor will have to lower price to sell more.

Using the data in Table 1, we'll draw our four standard curves: demand, marginal revenue, marginal cost, and average total cost. First, fill in Table 1 and check your figures against those in Table 2. Please observe that the demand and marginal revenue schedules no longer coincide.

A common mistake students make when filling out Table 1 is to use some number (in this case, 20) for MC at one unit of output. We'll review exactly what MC is; then we'll see why there's no way of finding MC at one unit of output.

Marginal cost is the additional cost of producing one more unit of output.

Do you recall the definition of marginal cost? *MC is the additional cost of producing one more unit of output.* Remember that as output rises, fixed cost stays the same and variable cost rises. So far, so good. The only problem is we don't know how much fixed cost is at one unit of output; nor do we know how much variable cost is at one unit of output. The MC of the first unit of output would be total cost at output one minus total cost at output zero. How much is total cost at output zero? It's fixed cost. But we don't know fixed cost, so we can't figure out MC at output one. For the remaining outputs, we *can* figure out MC because we know how much total cost rises. Now use the data

| TABLE 1 | Hypothetical Demand and Cost Schedule for a Monopoly |

Output	Price	Total Revenue	Marginal Revenue	Total Cost	ATC	MC
1	$16	——	——	$20	——	——
2	15	——	——	30	——	——
3	14	——	——	36	——	——
4	13	——	——	42	——	——
5	12	——	——	50	——	——
6	11	——	——	63	——	——
7	10	——	——	84	——	——

| TABLE 2 | Hypothetical Demand and Cost Schedule for a Monopoly |

Output	Price	Total Revenue	Marginal Revenue	Total Cost	ATC	MC	Total Profit
1	$16	$16	$16	$20	$20	——	−$ 4
2	15	30	14	30	15	$10	0
3	14	42	12	36	12	6	6
4	13	52	10	42	10.50	6	10
5	12	60	8	50	10	8	10
6	11	66	6	63	10.50	13	3
7	10	70	4	84	12	21	− 14

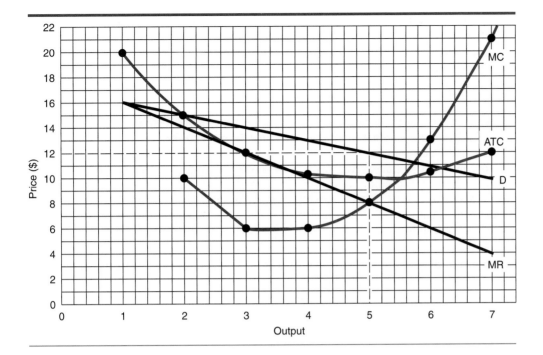

Figure 1

The Monopolist Making a Profit

The monopolist will make a profit if for some range of output her ATC lies below her demand curve. In this instance, the monopolist maximizes her profit at five units of output charging a price of $12.

you've written in Table 1 to draw a graph of the D, MR, MC, and ATC curves of the monopolist. Remember to use graph paper.

Look at the graph you drew and see whether it matches the one in Figure 1. The ATC and MC curves are the same as they were for the perfect competitor. I hope your MC intersects your ATC at its minimum point. Also note that the demand and marginal revenue curves slope downward to the right. At one unit of output, the demand and marginal revenue curves share the same point—$16—but the MR curve then slopes down much faster. In fact, when the demand curve is a straight line, the marginal revenue curve is also a straight line that falls twice as quickly. If you want to know why, take a look at the box, "Why the MR Curve Declines Faster than the Demand Curve."

Why the MR Curve Declines Faster than the Demand Curve

In Table 2, when the output is one, price is $16; but to sell two units of output, the seller must lower price to $15. Two units at $15 equals $30 (total revenue). Notice that the seller can't charge $16 for the first unit and $15 for the second. That's because the seller has to post one price. (If the seller manages to charge more than one price, we have price discrimination, which we'll talk about in the next chapter.)

When price is lowered to $15 total revenue is $30. Marginal revenue is $14 (total revenue of $30 at two units of output minus total revenue of $16 at one unit of output). At two units of output, because we charge a

price of $15, the point on the demand curve is $15. So, at two units of output, we have $15 on the demand curve and $14 on the MR curve.

To sell three units, the seller must lower price to $14. That yields a total revenue of $42 and an MR of $12 ($42 − $30). So, at three units of output, we're at $14 on the demand curve and $12 on the MR curve.

Let's summarize. If the seller lowers price to sell more output, the price is lowered on all units of output, not just on the last one. This drives down MR faster than price (which is read off the demand curve). Note also that the MR curve descends twice as quickly as the D curve.

When the demand curve falls $1 to $15 at two units of output, the MR curve falls $2 to $14. At three units of output, when the demand curve falls $1 to $14, the MR curve falls $2 to $12.

Calculating the Monopolist's Profit

At what output does the monopolist produce?

Now we'll get down to business. At what output does the monopolist produce? Go ahead and perform the marginal analysis to determine the most profitable output. I'll tell you the first step. Look at Figure 1 and find the point at which your marginal cost curve crosses your marginal revenue curve. That's your output. Do your calculations right here:

According to Figure 1, MC equals MR at 5 units of output. Using the formula for total profit, we find:

$$\text{Total profit} = (\text{Price} - \text{ATC}) \times \text{Output}$$
$$= (\$12 - \$10) \times 5$$
$$= \$2 \times 5$$
$$= \$10$$

Every firm produces where MC = MR.

We have a conflict here that didn't exist under perfect competition. The perfect competitor produced at the most profitable output, which in the long run always happened to be the most efficient output. But we see that the monopolist does not produce where output is at its most efficient level (the minimum point of the ATC curve). Remember, *every firm will produce at its most profitable output, where MC equals MR.* If that does not happen to be the most efficient output and if, for example, that firm is a bakery—get ready for a terrible pun—then that's the way the cookie crumbles. Finding the monopolist's price and output is a little harder than finding the price and output for the perfect competition. If you need more practice, see the box, "How to Find the Monopolist's Price and Output."

Looking at Figure 1, let's compare the price of the monopolist with that of the perfect competitor. In the very long run the perfect competitor would charge $9.90, the minimum point of its ATC curve, while the monopolist's price is $12. Next, let's compare output. The perfect competitor would produce at an output of 5.5, which is where ATC is at its minimum, but the monopolist's output is 5.

In the long run, the monopolist makes a profit, but the perfect competitor does not.

To summarize, the monopolist makes a profit, whereas in the long run the perfect competitor makes no profit. The monopolist operates at less than peak efficiency, while the perfect competitor operates at peak efficiency (the lowest point on the ATC curve). Finally, the perfect competitor charges a lower price and produces a larger output than the monopolist.[1]

This last point bears some explanation. The monopolist operates on a much larger scale than does the individual perfect competitor. But the sum of output under perfect competition would be larger than it would be under monopoly.

---

[1] In theory, the perfect competitor produces 5.5 units and the monopolist 5. But because the perfect competitor is a tiny firm, we can't really compare its output with that of the monopolist, who produces the industry's entire output. Thus, when we say the perfect competitor would produce an output of 5.5, we must realize that the firm would no longer be a perfect competitor. Do you follow this? If you don't, don't worry. This is only a footnote.

EXTRA
HELP

How to Find the Monopolist's Price and Output

Let's go over how the monopolist sets price step-by-step, using Figure 1. Step 1: The monopolist chooses her output by finding where the MC and MR curves cross. Step 2: By moving down along the dashed line, we find that the output she chose is 5.

Step 3: We move up the dotted line from MC = MR to the demand curve. Step 4: We move horizontally along the dotted line to a price of $12.

Here's another one for you to work out. How much is the output and price of the monopolist represented by Figure A?

If we move down from where the MC and MR curves cross, we find that the output is 20. To find price we go up from where the MC and MR curves cross to the demand curve, and then horizontally to the price axis. This gives us a price of $9.

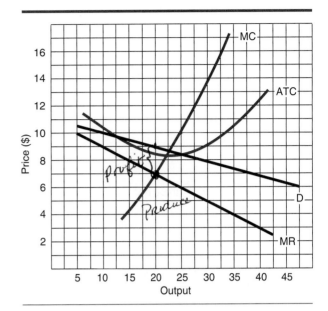

Figure **A**

I haven't bothered to distinguish between the short run and the long run mainly because the monopolist has no rivals. With perfect competition, the fact that the firms entered the industry (attracted by profits) or left the industry (driven out of business by losses) made the short run differ from the long run. Under monopoly, even larger profits wouldn't attract rival firms; otherwise, there would no longer be a monopoly. If a monopoly were losing money, in the long run it, too, would go out of business.

You might ask, How could a monopoly lose money? What if, given both the demand for its product and its ATC schedule, no matter what the output, the firm lost money?

How could a monopolist lose money?

I once started a mail-order business. I had invented a fantastic liquid diet. Interested? OK, here it is. Just drink these liquids—skim milk, Alba 70 shakes, clear soup, plain nonfat yogurt, grapefruit, watermelon, fruit pops, fruit juice, and vegetable juice (and take a daily vitamin pill)—and you'll lose about a pound a day. It also helps to run 25 to 30 miles a week.

I had what I thought was a great slogan: "What have you got to lose?" But I needed to advertise, rent a post office box, and print up my diet. I charged $2. What happened? What do you *think* happened? I spent about $350 and got 20 or 30 orders. If you happen to want to go into the diet business, I'll sell you *my* business—cheap. And then *you'll* have a monopoly (even though this diet has imitators, none comes close).

Review of the Monopolist's Economic Analysis

I've thrown a lot of new stuff at you, so let's step back for a few minutes and review the monopolist's table and graph. (For extra help, see the box, "How to Read a Graph.") Microeconomics is based largely on the three-step problems you've come to know and love: (1) filling in the table, (2) drawing the graph, and (3) doing the analysis.

You may begin by filling in Table 3 and then seeing whether your numbers correspond to the data in Table 4.

How to Read a Graph

Let's go over some of the points we've already covered. How much is the output of the monopolist shown in Figure B? Write down your answer. Next question. How much is price? Again, write down your answer. Finally, how much is total profit? Work it out in the space here.

Did you notice that once we find output (where MC = MR), everything else lines up? Price is located on the demand curve above the output of 4.2. ATC is on the ATC curve, also above an output of 4.2. When we find total profit, we plug price, ATC, and output into our formula.

We'll go over each of these questions in turn. First, *our output is always determined by the intersection of the MC and MR curves*. That occurs at an output of about 4.2.

How much is price? *Price is read off the demand curve*. Where on the demand curve—at what output? At the maximum profit output we just found—4.2. How much is price at that output? It appears to be about $9. And how much is ATC? Go straight up from where MC crosses MR to the ATC curve. It looks like about $7.50.

Next we calculate total profit.

$$\text{Total profit} = (\text{Price} - \text{ATC}) \times \text{Output}$$
$$= (\$9 - \$7.50) \times 4.2$$
$$= \$1.50 \times 4.2$$
$$= \$6.30$$

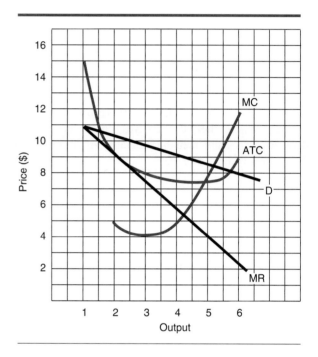

Figure B

Next comes the graph. Draw the demand, marginal revenue, marginal cost, and average total cost curves on a piece of graph paper. Then check your work with that in Figure 2.

Are you ready to do some analysis? We need to find the monopolist's total profit. Do that right here. Then check your work with the calculations that follow.

$$\text{Total profit} = (\text{Price} - \text{ATC}) \times \text{Output}$$
$$= (\$17 - \$14) \times 5$$
$$= \$3 \times 5$$
$$= \$15$$

TABLE 3

Output	Price	Total Revenue	Marginal Revenue	Total Cost	ATC	MC
1	$21	——	——	$30	——	——
2	20	——	——	40	——	——
3	19	——	——	48	——	——
4	18	——	——	57	——	——
5	17	——	——	70	——	——
6	16	——	——	93	——	——

TABLE 4

Output	Price	Total Revenue	Marginal Revenue	Total Cost	ATC	MC	Total Profit
1	$21	21	21	$30	30	——	−$ 9
2	20	40	19	40	20	10	0
3	19	57	17	48	16	8	9
4	18	72	15	57	14.25	9	15
5	17	85	13	70	14	13	15
6	16	96	11	93	15.50	23	3

I'm not going to let you off the hook just yet. Try these three questions.

1. At what output would the firm produce most efficiently?
2. At what output would the perfect competitor produce in the long run?
3. What price would the perfect competitor charge in the long run?

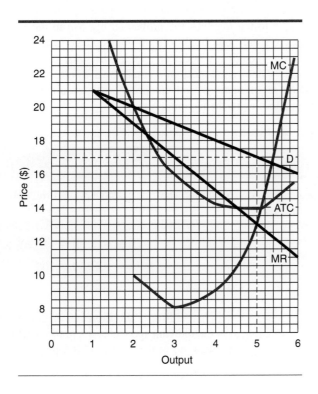

Figure 2
The Monopolist Making a Profit

Here are the answers.

1. The output at which the firm would produce most efficiently would be about 5.1, which is the minimum point of the ATC curve.

2. The perfect competitor would produce at an output of 5.1 in the long run.

3. In the long run the perfect competitor would charge a price of about $13.97 (the minimum, or break-even, point of the ATC curve). I'll take anything between $13.90 and $13.99.

The Monopolist in the Short Run and in the Long Run

There is no distinction between the short run and the long run for the monopolist.

No distinction is made for the monopolist between the short and long runs. Why not? Because no other firms will enter or leave the industry; by definition, the monopolist is the only firm.

If the firm is losing money, is it in the short run or the long run? What do *you* think?

It must be in the short run because no firm will stay in business if it's losing money. Not even the Chicago Cubs. For years the Wrigley family (as in Wrigley's chewing gum) lost money on the Cubs. It was an expensive hobby. Eventually it became too expensive even for the Wrigleys, who probably decided that they could double their pleasure *and* their fun by selling the team. (See box, "A Special Case: The Monopolist Losing Money.")

If the monopolist is making a profit, is it in the long run or the short run? Can you tell? Think about it.

If the firm were in the short run, would this monopolist stay in business? Yes! And so it would continue to make a profit. In the long run, then, it would still be making a profit. Therefore, there is no way to distinguish between the long run and the short run if the firm is making a profit.

Let's sum things up. If the firm is making a profit, for analytic purposes, it doesn't matter whether it's in the short run or the long run. If the firm is losing money, it must be in the short run; in the long run it will go out of business.

Are All Monopolies Big Companies?

The answer is no. Many monopolies are tiny firms operating in very tiny markets. What matters is size relative to the market—the proverbial big fish in the small pond.

Chances are there's only one bookstore on your college campus. That store would have a monopoly even though it's not nearly as big as some of the Barnes and Noble superstores. The only video rental store in a small town would have a monopoly. There are tens of thousands of gas stations, convenience stores, restaurants, cleaners, and repair shops that have monopolies in their communities.

A Special Case: The Monopolist Losing Money

If a monopolist *does* lose money, what would her graph look like? It might look like the one in Figure 3. Please find the firm's price, output, and total loss. Write your answers here:

Solution: The price is $18.50 and the output is 200.

$$\text{Total profit} = (\text{Price} - \text{ATC}) \times \text{output}$$
$$= (\$18.50 - \$20.40) \times 200$$
$$= -\$1.90 \times 200$$
$$= -\$380$$

Is this firm in the short run or the long run? Unless it's the old Chicago Cubs, it's in the short run. What will the firm do in the long run? It will go out of business.

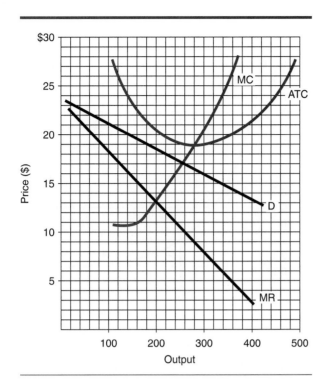

Figure 3
Monopolist Taking a Loss

Barriers to Entry

Does the cafeteria at your school have a monopoly? Does it serve either Pepsi or Coke, but not both? Have you noticed that Microsoft sells more computer operating systems than all its rivals put together? How do these companies manage to maintain their monopolies? In many cases, monopolies are protected by barriers to entry into their industries.

We'll consider each of five barriers to entry in turn: (1) control over an essential resource, (2) economies of scale, (3) legal barriers, (4) required scale for innovation, and (5) economies of being established.

Control over an Essential Resource   The Metropolitan Opera has a near monopoly because it has most of the world's opera stars (labor) under contract. Until the early 1960s the National Football League (NFL) had a monopoly, but this was challenged by the American Football League. The NFL had virtually all the established star football players under contract, so the AFL went after college stars. In 1965 the New York Jets signed University of Alabama star quarterback Joe Namath for the then unheard-of sum of $427,000; that action broke the back of the NFL's monopoly.

DeBeers Diamond Company in South Africa owns four-fifths of the world's diamond mines, and the International Nickel Company of Canada controls about 90 percent of the world's nickel reserves. The Standard Oil Company controlled the oil industry in the 1880s until the early 1900s because it owned more than 90 percent of the nation's oil fields and refineries. At that same time the American Tobacco Company controlled 90 percent of U.S. tobacco production.[2]

> Basic resources are land, labor, and capital.

Economies of Scale   Typically, heavy industry—iron and steel, copper, aluminum, and automobiles—has high setup costs. But once your plant and equipment are set up, you can take advantage of economies of scale by increasing your output. Thus we are

---

[2]In 1911 the Supreme Court broke up these monopolies. (See the chapter titled "Corporate Mergers and Antitrust.")

Figure 4

Hypothetical Production Costs
for Cars
This would be an example of
decreasing costs, where economies
of scale drive down ATC through
an output of at least 700,000 cars.

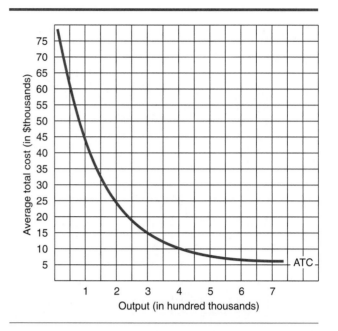

really talking about two necessary conditions for realizing economies of scale: having
the wherewithal to set up and having sufficient demand for your product.

Imagine how difficult it would be to set up a rival phone network or even a rival electric
company in a large city. What protects monopolies from potential rivals is that they're selling
enough units to have a relatively low ATC (see Figure 3). If you were to enter the industry,
how could you hope to have the capital to set yourself up to compete effectively?

Figure 4 illustrates the problem of economies of scale faced by the small producer
of cars. At relatively low levels of production, say 100,000 to 200,000 cars, the firm will
not be able to take advantage of the economies of mass production that are available to
rival firms. According to this illustration, ATC continues to decline appreciably through
an output of at least 700,000.

Legal barriers include licensing,
franchises, and patents.

Legal Barriers   These include licensing, franchises, and patents. The whole idea is for
the government to allow only one firm or a group of individuals to do business.

Licensing

Licensing prevents just anybody from driving a taxi, cutting hair, peddling on the
street, practicing medicine, or burying bodies. Often the licensing procedure is designed to
hold down the number of people going into a certain field to keep prices high. The state of
Arizona requires that hairstylists take 1,600 hours of classroom instruction at a cosmetology
school approved by the government. The cost? Ten thousand dollars. In Oregon hairstylists
are even better trained since they are required to received 2,500 hours of instruction.

Patents

Patents are granted to investors so that they have a chance to get rich before someone
else uses their ideas (see the box, "How Do You Stop Others from Stealing Your Idea?").
The patent holders have 20 years to get their act together. In some cases, perhaps most

How Do You Stop Others from Stealing Your Idea?

Two budding entrepreneurs in Houston noticed that people
who had put their drinks down at parties often forgot
which glass was theirs. So they set up a business selling
wineglass jewelry, which helped people identify their drink
glass. In their first year, they signed up 90 stores in Texas
to carry their product and racked up sales of $35,000.

But quite soon competing products selling for lower
prices drove them out of business. Should they have
patented their idea? While the idea could not qualify for
a patent, perhaps a trademark for their company logo
and a copyright for the design might have helped.

At Rutgers Coke Is the Only Choice

Outbidding Pepsi by about $2.5 million, the Coca-Cola Company paid Rutgers, the State University of New Jersey, some $10 million in 1994 for exclusive rights to sell its products to some 48,000 students on three campuses over the next decade. On-campus food and beverage vendors may sell only Coca-Cola Company beverages, which include Nestea iced tea, Sprite, Minute Maid drinks, and, of course, every variety of diet and regular Coke. The football coach will even be doused with Powerade, rather than Gatorade.

Rutgers, of course, is not the first school to sell an exclusive franchise to a private vendor. If you happen to visit any of Penn State's 21 campuses, you might think you're at Pepsi-Cola University. The school has a ten-year, $14 million dollar deal for exclusive rights for *that* company's products. The next time you're in *your* school cafeteria or snack bar, see whether it sells both Coke and Pepsi. If it doesn't, you'll know who's got the franchise.

notably U.S. Shoe Machinery Company, a firm buys up patents and uses them to prevent competition. A common practice is to obtain a patent on a new product or process and then, before the 20 years are up, obtain a new patent on some improvement or innovation. Japanese firms have been able to dominate the consumer electronics industry by successfully obtaining patents on each innovation to the original product.

Patents are essential to pharmaceutical companies, which may spend hundreds of millions of dollars developing a drug. They would be a lot less willing to spend so much money on research if their competitors could immediately capitalize on this research and sell close substitutes. By and large, it appears that patents do speed up technological advance and the consequent flow of new products to the consumer.

The most important legal barrier is the government franchise. And the most important form of local franchise is the public utility—your gas and electric companies. There's only one to a locality. The local government grants the franchise, and, like it or not, the company's got you. Monopolies don't have to worry about giving poor service at outrageous prices. Where else can you go? (See the box, "At Rutgers Coke Is the Only Choice.")

Government franchises

Required Scale for Innovation   Do you know anyone who's invented a board game? Have they thought of taking it to Parker Brothers, the company that sells Monopoly? Or someone who wants to sell a greeting card idea to Hallmark? Or a new toy to Mattel? Most inventors don't have the wherewithal to produce and market their ideas, but they would usually be quite happy to hand them over to one of the big guys for a slice of the sales or profits.

While individuals come up with all the great ideas, only large firms have the money and know-how to bring them to the marketplace. However, the vast proliferation of dot-coms, many of which have found venture capital to carry them until they are ready to go public (that is, sell stock to raise still more capital), certainly proves that you don't necessarily have to be big to innovate.

Economies of Being Established   Companies that have been operating for many years have recognizable brand names, and their sales representatives have established territories. Most important, the seller and buyer have a long-standing relationship. A retailer can count on her supplier for fast, reliable service.

A new company, with newly hired sales reps just learning their routes, will have a hard time prying customers from a well-established competitor. How can you convince a retailer to buy your product or service when she never saw you before and is unfamiliar with what you're selling? For these reasons, the economies of being established make it difficult to take market share from a company that may have been doing business before you were born.

But wait—there's more. Established firms selling to retailers, especially supermarkets, already have their products on the shelves. And just as possession is nine-tenths of the law, once a firm's products are on a shelf, it's very hard for newcomers to dislodge

Finding Space on the Shelf

Have you ever wondered why a bookstore places certain books in its window? Or right by the cash register? Or why certain publishers have their books piled on tables or on entire shelves? Chances are those publishers paid extra bucks for that placement. On the shelves of retail stores, just like in real estate, location is everything.

Consumer goods manufacturers pay over $100 billion a year for shelf space, of which food companies spend about $60 billion on what is termed givebacks or slotting fees. In 2001 Kellogg's shelled out $7.6 billion, followed by Kraft ($4.6 billion), Pepsico ($3.4 billion), and Coca-Cola ($2.6 billion).* Most large supermarket chains charge slotting fees, but significantly, Wal-Mart does not.

Until I started studying economics, I thought that the reason a refrigerated display case was filled with Carvel's ice cream was because Carvel's was nice enough to donate the display case. But Carvel's is paying for more than just the case.

Is paying for shelf space anticompetitive? After several small manufacturers complained about being shut out of stores, the Federal Trade Commission has been conducting an ongoing investigation.

---

*Julie Forster, "The Hidden Cost of Shelf Space," *BusinessWeek,* April 15, 2002, p. 103. See also, Bea Goldman, "Hitting the Salsa," *Forbes,* April 15, 2002, p. 134.

Setting the Standard

If you know how to type, then you've heard of the QWERTY keyboard, named for the first six letters in the upper row. The Remington Sewing Machine Company decided to make its typewriters with this configuration of keys. It made so many typewriters that, once all the typists got used to the layout, the less willing they were to switch to a different one. They were "locked in."

Customers are locked in even if the standard is inferior to alternatives. Remington designed its keyboard to slow down typists, who, it was feared, would make too many mistakes if they typed too fast. So whenever you sit down at your computer, you'll know who to blame.

In the computer software business, establishing a big user base is the key to success, writes James Aley. "It's the reason that Microsoft set a standard for personal computer operating systems that 'locked in' and consequently gave it a huge advantage in selling its spreadsheet and word processing software." Look at Windows 95. ". . . the more copies the company puts on the shelves, the more it sells, because the more people use Windows 95, the more software gets developed for it. The more software is available, the more people buy Windows 95."*

---

*James Aley, "The Theory That Made Microsoft," *Fortune,* April 29, 1996, pp. 65–66.

those products. In the box, "Finding Space on the Shelf," we see that the economies of being established include monopolizing shelf space.

Another advantage of being established is setting the industry standard, as does Microsoft in computer software and Matsushita in VCR format. Why does *your* VCR have a VHS format rather than a (Sony) Betamax format? Mainly because nearly all available tapes are VHS. Back in the late 1970s when Sony and Matsushita went head-to-head, Sony's one-hour tapes were too short for movies. Since Matsushita produced two-hour tapes, their VHS format very quickly became the industry standard (see the box, "Setting the Standard").

And talking about the advantages of being established, it's hard not to notice that virtually everyone drives a car powered by gasoline. Would you believe that the Stanley Steamer set a world speed record of 122 miles an hour way back in 1909? That's right—a steam-powered car. If the manufacturer had not priced it as a luxury vehicle and instead had striven for economies of scale as Henry Ford was doing, we might all be driving Stanley Steamers. And perhaps sometime soon, more and more of us will be driving electric cars. Which brings us to the limits of monopoly power.

Limits to Monopoly Power

First, we'll consider limits to the five barriers to entry. We saw how the National Football League lost its monopoly when it lost control over an essential resource—star football players. Similarly, Alcoa, which at one time controlled nearly all the world's known bauxite (aluminum ore) reserves, lost its monopoly when other reserves were discovered.[3]

Economies of scale and high capital requirements are a significant barrier to entry, but by 1990 Nissan, Honda, Toyota, Mazda, and Mitsubishi joined the parade of American automobile producers. Of course, each of these producers was set up by its friendly giant company back home.

Finally, even legal barriers have been overcome. Rival phone companies have gone to court to win the right to plug into local phone companies while providing a competing and generally lower-priced long-distance service. In general, however, government franchises are there for a reason: In some industries it makes economic sense to have only one firm in a given locality; so the franchise may well be a barrier we don't want to overcome.

The ultimate limit to monopoly power may come from the government or from the market itself. If a firm gets too big or too bad, the federal government may decide to trim that firm's sails. We'll examine this issue in the chapter, "Corporate Mergers and Antitrust."

Let's consider how the market limits monopoly power, basically through the development of substitutes. Take Kleenex, for example. To this day, some people call tissues "Kleenexes." In the late 1940s Kleenex was the only paper tissue on the market, so *tissues* and *Kleenexes* could properly be considered synonymous. But over the years scores of competitors have sprung up, and today the market share of Kleenex is very small indeed.

The market limits monopoly power through the development of substitutes.

Another interesting case is that of Xerox. Having invented the first "dry" photocopy machine, Xerox had the market all to itself during the late 1950s and early 1960s. Shortly thereafter, IBM, Savin, Canon, Sharp, Pitney-Bowes, Multilith-Addressograph, and a multitude of other firms began marketing their own photocopiers. Nonetheless, to this day when someone needs a photocopy, chances are he or she will ask you to "xerox" it—which is a lot easier than asking you to "multilith-addressograph" it.

You certainly weren't expecting to read about male impotence in an economics textbook, but I'm sure you know the name of the drug that treats it. Viagra is a household name. Since it was introduced by Pfizer in 1998, it had the market entirely to itself. But in 2004 two new drugs were introduced—Levitra (made by GlaxoSmithKline and Bayer) and Cialis (Eli Lilly). Although Viagra rivals Coca-Cola as one of the most widely known brands in the world, there goes its monopoly.

Economies of Scale and Natural Monopoly

There are really only two justifications for monopoly: economies of scale and natural monopoly. Economies of scale justify bigness because only a firm with a large output can produce near the minimum point of its long-run ATC curve. When the firm's output is so large that it is almost equal to the output of the entire industry, this state of monopoly is justified by calling it efficient. Of course, we have just seen that the firm is not operating at the minimum point of its ATC curve (see Figure 2), but that's another story.

Two justifications for monopoly

What Is Natural Monopoly?

Natural monopoly is closely related to economies of scale. Some think a natural monopoly occurs when someone gains complete control of the wheat germ supply or of the entire crop of Florida oranges. Close, but no cigar. Cigar? No, even Cuban cigars are not a natural monopoly.

---

[3]The Alcoa case is discussed in the chapter "Corporate Mergers and Antitrust."

Figure 5

One Electric Company Is Better than Four

Panel A shows a single electric transmission feeder cable serving all the homes on one block. Panel B shows four cables serving that same block. It is a lot more efficient (and cheaper) to have one cable than four.

A.

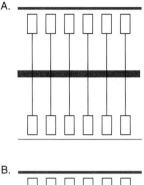

B.

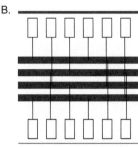

Examples of natural monopolies

Examples of natural monopolies are the local gas and electric companies, the local phone companies, and local cable TV companies. Why are these natural monopolies? Because they can provide cheaper service as monopolies than could several competing firms. Let's see why.

In Figure 5A, one electric company serves an entire suburban town. Pictured here is one street in that town, its houses lined up properly just as they might be anywhere in suburbia. Every house on the block uses the same company. After all, what choice do they have?

Figure 5B shows four competing electric companies on an identical street of an identical town somewhere else in suburbia. Notice the four power lines running along the street. In this town there's freedom of choice; you can hook up with any of these four companies.

There's only one problem with this arrangement. It's much more expensive. You see, each company, assuming customers are evenly distributed, does only one-quarter of the business that would be done by a company that had a monopoly. While it must construct the same system of power lines, it realizes only one-quarter of the output. Its costs are much higher than those of the monopoly.[4]

From society's viewpoint, these higher costs reflect a great waste of resources. Why construct four parallel power lines when one will do as nicely? And, one might add parenthetically, why dig up the street four times rather than once to lay and repair the cables?

This is the case for natural monopoly. It's cheaper, it's more efficient, and it's more convenient. The bottom line is that our bills are much lower.

Imagine if we had six or eight competing local phone companies.

Another case for natural monopoly can be made with respect to local telephone service. Imagine if we had four, six, or eight competing phone companies. Placing a call would be like playing Russian roulette. Imagine your surprise if you actually got through!

It would not be easy to conduct business. "Let's see now, I call this client on the orange phone, my lawyer on the gray phone, and my accountant on the yellow phone." And what if the president needs to reach his opposite number in the Kremlin in a hurry and can't remember: "Was it the red phone for the Kremlin and the green phone for McDonald's—or was it the other way around?" You can imagine the puzzlement in Moscow at getting an order for two Big Macs and a large order of fries.

---

[4]Technically, these are average fixed costs. They're four times as high as that of the electric company that has a monopoly. For example, if it cost $4 million to lay cable through a town, and if 40,000 families lived in the town, the monopoly would have an AFC of $100 ($4,000,000/40,000). Each of the four competing companies would have an AFC of $400 per family ($4,000,000/10,000).

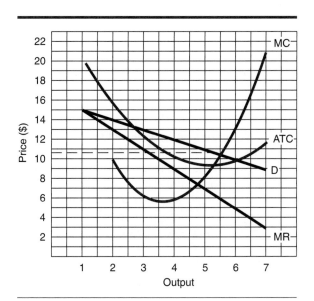

Figure 6
The Market Situation of the
Rochester Electric Company
If free to set its own price, the
company would charge $11.10. But
the New York State Public Service
Commission could set the price
lower, say at $10.75.

Speaking of fries, would you believe that the snack stand at a multiplex movie theater can be a natural monopoly? Surely the multiplex realizes great economies of scale by operating one large stand, which is busy all the time, rather than 20 separate stands in 20 scattered movie theaters. But unlike Wal-Mart and other big box stores, these folks don't often pass on their savings to their moviegoer customers in the form of lower prices.

The 1996 Telecommunications Act allowed the local phone companies into the long-distance market but only after they could prove that their local markets were open to competition. So *are* the Bells (among them Verizon, BellSouth, Qwest, and SBC) allowing local rivals into their markets by making their lines available? Under the Telecom Act, regulators in many states are finally forcing the Bells to lower wholesale rates for local service. Competitors such as Sprint, Talk America, Z-Tel, and Supra Telecom control about 15 percent of the local market.

Two Policy Alternatives

We have accepted certain instances of monopoly—mainly, local public utility companies. These companies are natural monopolies and provide the public with better and more cheaply priced service than it would get from most competing firms. How can we prevent these public utilities from taking advantage of their power and charging outrageous prices? There are two ways: (1) government regulation and (2) government ownership.

Two ways to prevent public utilities from charging outrageous prices are:
(1) government regulation and
(2) government ownership.

Government Regulation Suppose Figure 6 represents the market situation of the Rochester Electric Company, which is now regulated by the New York State Public Service Commission.

The commission would have two objectives: a lower price for electricity consumers and a higher output of electricity than we see in Figure 5. To accomplish both ends, the commission would set the price of electricity at about $10.75, which is lower than the current market price of $11.10. How much would output now be? How about total profit?

Using the formula for total profit, we get:

$$\text{Total profit} = (\text{Price} - \text{ATC}) \times \text{Output}$$
$$= (\$10.75 - \$9.30) \times 5.25$$
$$= \$1.45 \times 5.25$$
$$= \$7.61$$

This is illustrated in Figure 6. Consumers now pay a lower price and receive more electricity than they would have under an unregulated monopoly. But this is not a perfect solution because even the regulated natural monopoly does not necessarily produce at the minimum point of its ATC curve.

Government Ownership   The second option for a natural monopoly is government ownership. The post office, the Tennessee Valley Authority, Amtrak, the New York State Power Authority, the New Jersey Transit System, and the Metropolitan Transit Authority of Boston are all examples.

Are these inefficient government boondoggles whose jobs could be better done by private enterprise? Consider the origins of the New Jersey public transportation system. When the private bus lines were unable to operate even with massive public subsidies, the state of New Jersey reluctantly took them over.

The case of the Tennessee Valley Authority (TVA) is even stranger. TVA uses itself as a yardstick with which to measure the costs of power provided by privately owned utilities. The latter complain about "unfair" government competition, and they do have a point because TVA sometimes provides electricity at half the cost of that incurred by privately owned companies.

This is rather interesting when one considers the origins of TVA. Much of rural Tennessee, Arkansas, and Alabama, as well as parts of other states near the Tennessee Valley, were not provided with electricity by private power companies as late as the early 1930s because they were not deemed worthy customers. They were too poor, they lived too far apart, and it was simply not economically feasible to run transmission cables into this part of the country. So TVA, without competing with private companies, went into this area and provided it with electricity at half the going rate.

The general thrust of public policy in the area of natural monopoly is to let private enterprise do the job but to regulate prices closely. Only as a last resort, when private enterprise is unwilling or unable to do the job, does the government take on the job itself.

Are government-owned enterprises inefficient?

Let private enterprise do the job—if it can.

Is Bigness Good or Bad?

It's both. If you're a big company, do you necessarily behave badly? Why do big companies—Microsoft, Wal-Mart, General Motors, the oil, tobacco, and pharmaceutical companies, and the giant defense contractors—seem to have such bad reputations? And can a case be made that bigness is good?

When Is Bigness Bad?

From what we've seen so far, monopoly isn't *all* bad. At times only a monopolist can fully take advantage of economies of scale; and in certain instances, particularly with respect to local public utilities, there are natural monopolies. In the case of Xerox, Kleenex, and IBM, these innovative companies once had monopolies simply because each was the first to enter its field.

Why, then, do so many people dislike monopolies? For one thing, monopolies tend to be inefficient. As illustrated earlier in Figures 1 and 2, a monopoly does not produce at the minimum point of its ATC curve. Furthermore, by always restricting output to some point to the left of that minimum, the monopoly is preventing resources from being allocated in the most efficient manner. Land, labor, and capital that would have otherwise flowed into the monopolized industry are kept out and will eventually find their way into other industries where they will not be as efficiently used.

Bigness can also mean inefficiency. In the chapter before last, we talked about corporate bureaucracies and diseconomies of scale. This problem has become acute among the giant firms that are often referred to as "corporate dinosaurs." The box titled, "The Corporate Hierarchy" takes a critical look at this growing problem.

Bigness can also mean inefficiency.

The Corporate Hierarchy

Americans are fond of creating pecking orders, and the bureaucratic managerial structures set up to run America's large corporations are prime examples. In Japan and Germany where the corporate hierarchy is substantially flatter, chief executive officers earn 10 times what their average employees earn. But in the United States the average CEO pulls down more than 400 times the earnings of the average worker. In the chart you'll find that since 1980 the disparity between the salaries of CEOs and ordinary workers has increased almost tenfold.

porations have. The tip of the hierarchy passes orders down to the troops. The rank-and-file worker is rarely consulted and does not identify with the company or with the product it produces. Furthermore, the people who are making the decisions at the top have virtually no contact with their customers. The end result is often a high-cost, low-quality product.

The large college textbook publishers—McGraw-Hill (which publishes my book), International Thompson, Houghton-Mifflin, Pearson, John Wiley and Sons, and W. W. Norton—are major exceptions to the hierarchical

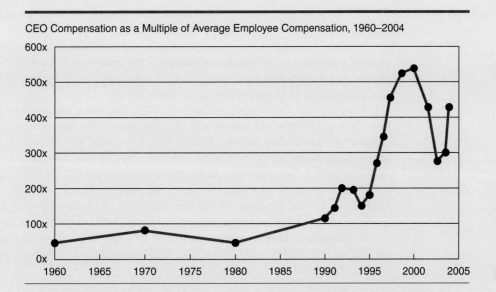

CEO Compensation as a Multiple of Average Employee Compensation, 1960–2004

Sources: G. William Domhoff, "Wealth, Income, and Power," September 2005, http://sociology.ucsc.edu/whorulesamerica/power/wealth.html; http://www.aflcio.org/corporatewatch/paywatch/pay/.

Our leading corporations have become so complex, so overmanaged, so distant from their customers, and so alienating to their rank-and-file employees that it is a wonder they have been able to function as well as they have. Perhaps the dilemma is best summed up by management consultant Ichak Adizes: "Good organizations should be structured by geniuses so that idiots can run them. Unfortunately, most American organizations are structured by idiots so that it takes a genius to run them."*

This structure is not efficient. It allows no feedback from consumers, no competition, and very few work incentives. But it's just the structure our own huge cor-

rule. Their sales representatives provide daily feedback from their customers, who happen to be your professors. Their editors, regional managers, marketing managers, as well as national sales managers have had years of selling experience themselves, and often accompany the sales reps on visits to colleges. Although these companies certainly do exhibit the trappings of corporate status and privilege, the decision makers are a lot closer to the customer than the rest of Corporate America.

---

*Quoted in Steven Schlosstein, *The End of the American Century* (New York: Congdon & Weed, 1989), p. 108.

When Is Bigness Good?

To be big is not necessarily to behave badly. Natural monopolies, for example, taking advantage of economies of scale, deliver services much more cheaply than could a multitude of competing firms. And in general, large firms can take advantage of economies of scale.

Sometimes a firm, such as Xerox, IBM, or Microsoft, is the first to enter an industry. Should we ask such a firm to wait until each of its competitors can catch up? Or do we allow them to grow very large? Perhaps the question we should ask is whether a firm is big because it is very bad or because it is very good.

Wal-Mart, while technically not a monopoly, is certainly the dominant retailer in the United States. Question: Is it good or bad? Read the Current Issue on page 559 and then decide for yourself.

The Economic Case against Bigness

The best of all monopoly profits is a quiet life.

—John Hicks

I'll start with the obvious. Does the monopolist operate at the minimum point of her ATC curve? No! Just glance back at Figure 1 and 2.

Because the monopolist is not pressed by competition, there is no great incentive to control costs or to use resources efficiently. Indeed, there is no need to spend much money on research and development, to improve manufacturing processes, to develop new products, or to be responsive to customer needs.

A monopolist can charge her customers higher prices and provide poorer service than she would if she had competitors. I mean, where else can you go? Have you ever lost your temper dealing with your local bank (assuming it's the only one in town), the phone company, or the gas or electric company? You've heard the phrase "The customer is always right"? Not when you're dealing with a monopoly.

One of the most important effects of the growing amount of foreign competition, especially from the Japanese, is the new emphasis on product quality. American cars, specialty steel, machine tools, and a whole host of consumer products have all enjoyed tremendous quality improvement over the last 15 years. It is a virtual certainty that without the spur of foreign competition, the quality standards of American products would not have improved nearly as much.

Conclusion

Is monopoly good, bad, or indifferent? One fair conclusion is that natural monopoly would be good, if only its power were not abused. But monopolies based on other factors—I refrain from calling them "unnatural monopolies"—must be looked on with suspicion. They may be up to no good, and they also may be illegal.

In a sense, virtually all firms are monopolies. The last gas station before the turnpike entrance, the only bar on your block, and the only grocery in your neighborhood that stays open until midnight are all monopolies. The test they must pass is whether or not there are close substitutes.

Who decides this? The buyers do. If the buyers in your local area think that your store is the only game in town—that no one else even comes close—then you have a monopoly. But let's not get carried away. No one is going to drive 50 miles just to buy your gas, drink your beer, or buy a quart of milk at your store. What you've got is a very local monopoly. You may even be earning an economic profit, but you're not exactly Exxon.

From this discussion we shall make a very neat segue into monopolistic competition, which is the subject of the next chapter. By blending some elements of monopoly and some elements of perfect competition, we will obtain a mixture of firms that we encounter every day in the real world.

Current Issue: Would You Allow Wal-Mart to Open a Supercenter in Your Community?[5]

Let's start with two facts almost everyone agrees on:

1. Wal-Mart lives up to the slogan printed right on every shopping bag, "Always low prices. *Always.*" After all, 20 million daily shoppers can't *all* be wrong.

2. Wal-Mart's full-time employees' average hourly wages are about $10 an hour—perhaps 30 percent lower than those paid by competitors.

These two facts create a personal conflict for many of us. After all, who can resist all those bargains? But those bargains are subsidized by low wages.

Here's another conflict to mull over. Wal-Mart imports $20 billion a year of microwave ovens, TVs, DVD players, toys, shoes, apparel and other goods from China. It then passes along the savings in the form of low prices. But these imports not only add to our trade deficit, they put some Americans out of work.

Is Wal-Mart anti-union? Not even one of its more than 4,000 stores is unionized. (See the chapter on labor unions in *Economics* and *Microeconomics*.) And a unionized Wal-Mart would pay higher wages and provide better medical benefits.

Wal-Mart relentlessly drives down its costs—not just by paying relatively low wages and squeezing its suppliers—but by running a ruthlessly efficient, lean and mean operation. Its customers have an average family income of $35,000, and save about $1,000 a year by shopping there, while more affluent families save even more. And while its wages are admittedly low, virtually each new store is flooded by job applicants. One may conclude, then, that Wal-Mart's low everyday wages are dictated more by supply and demand than by a desire to exploit its hired help.

When you factor in the price cuts other retailers must make to compete, Wal-Mart has saved consumers well over $100 billion a year. Far more than any other business firm, it has been responsible for holding down our rate of inflation.

In 2005 less than 45 percent of Wal-Mart's workers had company health insurance and 46 percent of their children were uninsured or on Medicaid. In October of that year, the company announced a new health plan with premiums as low as $11 a month, but still leaving many employees paying thousands of dollars in out-of-pocket medical expenses.

Does Wal-Mart discriminate against its female employees? (See the chapter on labor markets and wage rates in *Economics* and *Microeconomics*.) A huge class-action suit has been filed on behalf of 1.6 million past and current employees. The suit notes that women make up over 72 percent of all hourly employees, but just one-third of the store managers are women. The jury may be out on this case for some time to come.

In December 2005 the company was ordered by a California court to pay $172 million to 116,000 hourly workers in damages for failing to provide meal breaks. California law requires that employers provide a meal break of 30 minutes for every five hours on the clock. This class-action lawsuit is one of about 40 nationwide alleging workplace violations by Wal-Mart, and the first to go to trial.

Has Wal-Mart driven smaller retailers out of business? Clearly it has. Often, soon after a Wal-Mart supercenter opened, local supermarkets as well as smaller groceries were forced to close. Indeed, big box retailers as well as giant suburban shopping malls are responsible for the demise of downtown shopping areas, not just in cities, but in small towns as well.

Perhaps Wal-Mart attained its finest hour simply by remaining open for business in the wake of Hurricane Katrina. By keeping their stores stocked with food and water, it provided a lifeline to hurricane victims. Significantly, while some other sellers were price gouging, Wal-Mart lived by its motto, *"Always low prices. Always."* This is more fully discussed in Chapter 4.

---

[5]Full disclosure: The author owns 41 shares of Wal-Mart stock.

More and more communities have opposed the opening of new Wal-Marts. Other communities welcomed Wal-Mart, not just because of its low prices, but for the new jobs it provided. Would *you* allow Wal-Mart to open a supercenter in your community?

Questions for Further Thought and Discussion

1. Are very large firms economically justifiable? What are the pros and cons of bigness?
2. A monopolist can control her price or the quantity she sells, but she can't control both. Explain this statement.
3. Make the case for natural monopolies.
4. Are all monopolies large firms? Make up an example of a monopoly that is a small firm.
5. How does the demand curve faced by the monopolist differ from that confronting the perfect competitor? Why do they differ?
6. What are the main barriers to entry? Explain how each barrier can foster monopoly.
7. Pharmaceutical companies can turn out pills for pennies and sell them for dollars. Many people who need these drugs can't afford them. How can these companies justify charging so much?
8. Wal-Mart wants to open a superstore near you. List the reasons why you think they (a) should be allowed to do so; (b) should not be allowed to do so.

Workbook for Chapter 22

Name _____ Date _____

Multiple-Choice Questions

Circle the letter that corresponds to the best answer.

1. Which statement is true?
   a) All monopolists' products have close substitutes.
   b) Most firms in the United States are monopolies.
   c) There are no monopolies in the United States.
   d) A monopoly is a firm that produces all the output in an industry.
   e) None of these statements is true.

2. The monopolist is _____.
   a) an imperfect competitor and has a horizontal demand curve
   b) an imperfect competitor and has a downward sloping demand curve
   c) a perfect competitor and has a horizontal demand curve
   d) a perfect competitor and has a downward sloping demand curve

3. A downward sloping demand curve means _____.
   a) you have to lower your price to sell more
   b) demand falls as output rises
   c) demand rises as output rises
   d) total revenue declines as price is lowered

4. The monopolist's demand and marginal revenue curves _____.
   a) are exactly the same
   b) are completely different
   c) coincide only at one unit of output
   d) cross

5. The monopolist produces _____.
   a) where MC equals MR
   b) at the minimum point of ATC
   c) at maximum output
   d) when price is highest

6. If a monopolist has a straight-line demand curve, its marginal revenue curve _____.
   a) will be the same as the demand curve
   b) will fall twice as quickly as the demand curve
   c) will lie below the demand curve at all points
   d) will cross the demand curve

7. Which statement is true?
   a) The monopolist and the perfect competitor both produce where MC equals MR.
   b) Neither the monopolist nor the perfect competitor produce where MC equals MR.
   c) The monopolist, but not the perfect competitor, produces where MC equals MR.
   d) The perfect competitor, but not the monopolist, produces where MC equals MR.

8. Which statement is true about economic profit in the long run?
   a) Both the monopolist and the perfect competitor make one.
   b) Neither the monopolist nor the perfect competitor makes one.
   c) Only the perfect competitor makes one.
   d) Only the monopolist makes one.

9. Which statement is true?
   a) The monopolist cannot lose money.
   b) The monopolist always operates a large firm.
   c) The monopolist will not lose money in the short run.
   d) The monopolist will not lose money in the long run.

10. Price is always read off the _____ curve.
    a) MC   c) ATC
    b) MR   d) demand

11. The most efficient output is found _____.

    a) where MC and MR cross

    b) at the bottom of the ATC curve

    c) when the demand and MR curves are equal

    d) where the ATC and demand curves cross

12. When the monopolist is losing money, _____.

    a) we are in the short run

    b) we are in the long run

    c) it is impossible to tell if we are in the short run or the long run

    d) we have to go back and check our work because monopolists don't lose money

13. The basis for monopoly in the automobile industry would most likely be _____.

    a) control over an essential resource

    b) economies of scale

    c) legal barriers

14. Which statement is true?

    a) It is impossible for monopolies to exist in the United States.

    b) Once a monopoly is set up, it is impossible to dislodge it.

    c) Monopolies can be overcome only by market forces.

    d) Monopolies can be overcome only by the government.

    e) None of these statements is true.

15. Which of the following is a natural monopoly?

    a) The National Football League

    b) A local phone company

    c) DeBeers Diamond Company

    d) IBM

16. Each of the following is true about Wal-Mart EXCEPT that _____.

    a) it is the largest employer in the United States

    b) it is the largest company in the world

    c) it pays its employees, on average, about the same as its competitors

    d) it drives hard bargains with suppliers and passes along the savings to its customers

17. An example of government ownership of a monopoly is _____.

    a) the Tennessee Valley Authority

    b) the New York State Public Service Commission

    c) AT&T

    d) General Motors

18. Who said, "Good organizations should be structured by geniuses so that idiots can run them. Unfortunately, most American organizations are structured by idiots so that it takes a genius to run them"?

    a) Ichak Adizes

    b) Robert Frost

    c) John Hicks

    d) General Douglas MacArthur

    e) President Dwight D. Eisenhower

19. The average American CEO pulls down _____ times the earnings of the average worker.

    a) 10 to 15   d) 400 to 600

    b) 25 to 40   e) 1,000 to 1,200

    c) 100 to 150

20. Which statement is true?

    a) The monopolist is just as driven as the competitive firm to control costs and use resources efficiently.

    b) The monopolist often charges his customers higher prices and provides poorer service than he would if he had competitors.

    c) Growing foreign competition has had no effect on the quality of American products.

    d) None of these statements is true.

21. The monopolist produces at the minimum point of her ATC curve _____.

    a) all the time   c) some of the time

    b) most of the time   d) none of the time

22. Each of the following is an example of successfully setting a standard *except* _____.

    a) Windows 95   c) the VHS format

    b) QWERTY   d) the electric car

23. Which is the most accurate statement?

   a) The rationale for natural monopoly has been strengthened by deregulation.

   b) Your local phone and electric companies will probably continue to be monopolies for at least another 50 years.

   c) Deregulation and competition tend to lower costs.

   d) Natural monopoly never had any economic basis.

Use the graph in Figure 1 to answer questions 24 and 25.

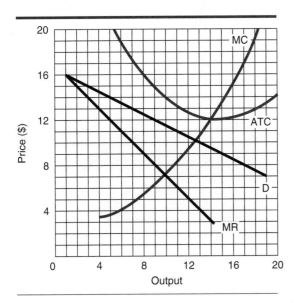

F*igure* 1

24. If this firm produced at optimum efficiency, it would have an output of _____.

   a) less than 10

   b) 10

   c) more than 10, but less than 14

   d) 14

   e) more than 14

25. This firm is _____.

   a) making a profit of $25

   b) making a profit of 0

   c) taking a loss of $25

   d) taking a loss of $30

   e) taking a loss of $50

Fill-In Questions

1. A monopoly is a firm that produces _____ _____.

2. A monopoly is a firm that has _____ _____ substitutes.

3. The demand curve of an imperfect competitor slopes _____.

4. The monopolist always produces at that output at which _____ is equal to _____.

5. If a firm's demand curve is a straight line sloping downward to the right, its marginal revenue curve will be a _____ _____.

6. In the long run the perfect competitor makes _____ profit; in the long run the monopolist makes _____ profit.

7. The five barriers to entering a monopolized industry are

   (1) _____;

   (2) _____;

   (3) _____;

   (4) _____;

   and (5) _____.

8. There are really only two justifications for monopoly:

   (1) _____.

   and (2) _____.

9. Local gas and electric companies, the phone company, and local cable TV companies are all examples of _____ monopolies.

10. The main economic criticism of monopolies and big business in general is that they are _____.

11. There are two ways to prevent public utilities from taking advantage of their power: (1) _____ and (2) _____

_____.

Problems

1. (a) Fill in Table 1. (b) Using your own piece of graph paper, draw a graph of the firm's demand, marginal revenue, marginal cost, and average total cost curves. (c) Calculate the firm's total profit. (d) If the firm operates at optimum efficiency, how much will its output be? (e) If the firm were a perfect competitor, how much would its price be in the long run?

TABLE 1

Output	Price	Total Revenue	Marginal Revenue	Total Cost	ATC	MC
1	$19	——	——	$25	——	——
2	18	——	——	40	——	——
3	17	——	——	50	——	——
4	16	——	——	58	——	——
5	15	——	——	65	——	——
6	14	——	——	74	——	——
7	13	——	——	87	——	——

2. (a) Fill in Table 2. (b) Using your own piece of graph paper, draw a graph of the firm's demand, marginal revenue, marginal cost, and average total cost curves. (c) Calculate the firm's total profit. (d) If the firm operates at optimum efficiency, how much will its output be? (e) If the firm were a perfect competitor, how much would its price be in the long run?

TABLE 2

Output	Price	Total Revenue	Marginal Revenue	Total Cost	ATC	MC
1	$22	——	——	$30	——	——
2	21	——	——	42	——	——
3	20	——	——	51	——	——
4	19	——	——	60	——	——
5	18	——	——	70	——	——
6	17	——	——	82	——	——
7	16	——	——	98	——	——

3. (a) Using the data from Figure 2, calculate the firm's total profit. (b) If the firm operates at optimum efficiency, how much will its output be? (c) If the firm were a perfect competitor, how much would its price be in the long run?

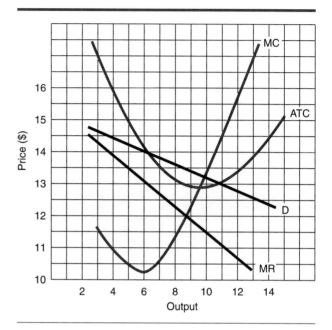

Figure 2

4. (a) Using the data from Figure 3, calculate the firm's total profit. (b) If the firm operates at optimum efficiency, how much will its output be? (c) If the firm were a perfect competitor, how much would its price be in the long run?

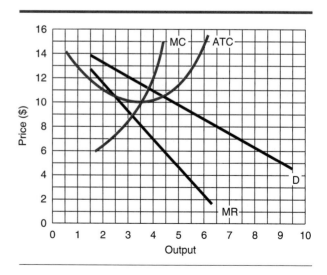

Figure 3

Chapter 23

Monopolistic Competition

Why do you shop at one drugstore rather than another? Why do you frequent particular restaurants, beauty parlors, video stores, and coffee shops? Do you always shop at the stores that charge the lowest prices? Let's examine these questions and see if we can come up with some answers.

More than 99 percent of the 30 million business firms in the United States are monopolistic competitors. So the least we can do is give them a chapter all to themselves.

CHAPTER OBJECTIVES

When you have completed this chapter you will be familiar with:

- The monopolistic competitor in the short and long runs.
- Product differentiation.

- The characteristics of monopolistic competition.
- Price discrimination.

Monopolistic Competition Defined

A monopolistically competitive industry has many firms selling a differentiated product. How many is many? So many that no one firm has any significant influence over price. Although this is our working definition, monopolistic competitors do have some influence over price because their products are differentiated. But it's a very *small* influence.

We now encounter a differentiated product for the first time. Note that the definition of monopolistic competition differs from that of perfect competition only in the element of a differentiated product. You'll remember that under perfect competition, all the sellers sold an identical product.

Why did we say the product was identical? Because none of the buyers differentiated among the products for sale. Each was considered the same: Number 2 wheat is number 2 wheat; a large grade A egg is a large grade A egg.

If the buyer doesn't differentiate among the versions of the product sold, the products are identical. If he does differentiate, the product is then differentiated. Who determines whether the product is differentiated or identical? The buyer—that's who.

Definition of monopolistic competition

The difference between identical and differentiated

The Monopolistic Competitor in the Short Run

Like the perfect competitor, the monopolistic competitor can make a profit or take a loss in the short run; but in the long run the firm will break even. The reason the monopolistic competitor makes zero economic profits in the long run is the same as that under perfect competition.

The monopolistic competitor can make a profit or take a loss in the short run.

F*igure* 1

Monopolistic Competitor Making
a Profit in the Short Run
The monopolistic competitor makes
a profit only in the short run. How
much is this firm's price and
output? The price is $15 and the
output is 60.

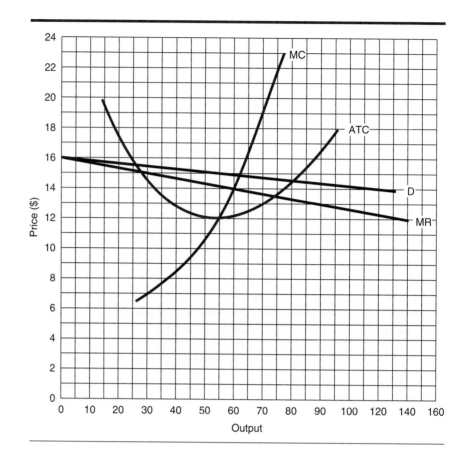

In the long run, if firms are losing money, many will leave the industry, lowering industry supply and raising market price. And if, in the long run, firms are realizing substantial profits, new firms will be attracted to the industry, thus raising supply and lowering market price. But we're getting ahead of ourselves.

Figure 1 shows a monopolistic competitor in the short run. Notice how its demand and MR curves slope downward, like those of the monopolist. Theoretically, we may opt for a somewhat more elastic demand curve for the monopolistic competitor than for the monopolist because the latter faces the demand curve for the entire industry. The monopolistic competitor, as only one firm in a crowded industry, must have a very elastic demand curve because there are many close substitutes for the firm's product. In fact, no one can get too far out of line with respect to price because buyers are always ready to purchase substitutes from a rival firm.

Very elastic demand curve

Getting back to Figure 1, how much is the firm's output? How much is its price? How much profit does it make? Work it out right here:

First the output. When MC equals MR, output is 60. We find that at an output of 60, the price, which we read off the demand curve, is $15, and the ATC is $12.10 or so. Now we can write down our standard equation, substitute, and solve:

$$\text{Total profit} = (\text{Price} - \text{ATC}) \times \text{Output}$$

$$= (\$15 - \$12.10) \times 60$$

$$= \$2.90 \times 60$$

$$= \$174$$

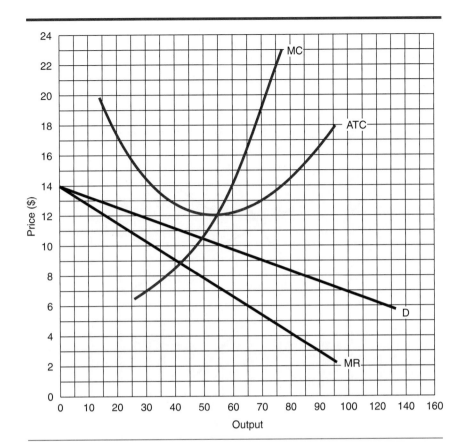

Figure 2
Monopolistic Competitor Taking
a Loss in the Short Run
The monopolistic competitor will
take a loss only in the short run.
How much is this monopolistic
competitor's price and output? Price
is $11 and output is 42.

Now we're ready for Figure 2, which also shows the monopolistic competitor in the short run. How much is output? Is the firm making a profit or taking a loss? How much is it?

$$\text{Total profit} = (\text{Price} - \text{ATC}) \times \text{Output}$$
$$= (\$11 - \$12.80) \times 42$$
$$= -\$1.80 \times 42$$
$$= -\$75.60$$

I'm not above admitting that even *I* cannot read my *own* graphs with any greater precision than the average reader. So, if your price, output, ATC, and, consequently, loss are a little different from mine—no problem. I'll accept any loss that's within the range of $70 to $80.

The Monopolistic Competitor in the Long Run

As I said earlier, in the long run the monopolistic competitor makes zero economic profits. If there are short-run profits, more firms will enter the industry, driving down market price and profits. If there are losses, some firms will leave the industry, pushing up market price and reducing losses.

Figure 3 is a model of the monopolistic competitor in the long run. Note how the point at which the MC and MR curves cross is directly below the price. Output is 40, and price is $12.25. Note also that price is equal to ATC at that output.

Were the firm to produce at any other output, what would happen to its profits? I'm sure you figured out that they would be losses. At any other output, the demand curve lies below the ATC curve, so price is less than ATC.

The monopolistic competitor
makes zero economic profits in
the long run.

Figure 3

Monopolistic Competitor
Breaking Even in the Long Run
In the long run, the monopolistic
competitor must break even. Note
that the ATC curve is tangent to the
demand curve and that at that same
output, MC = MR. How much is
price and output for this firm? Price
is $12.25 and output is 40.

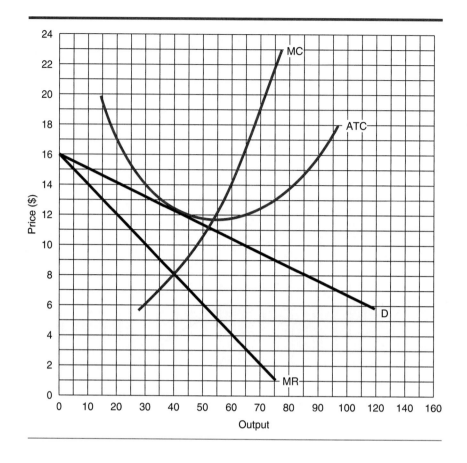

Note that the price in Figure 3 is higher than the minimum point of the ATC curve. This means that in the long run price is higher under monopolistic competition than it is under perfect competition.

What about output? Again, because the monopolistic competitor produces to the left of the minimum point of its ATC curve, output is lower than it is under perfect competition.

Finally, we have efficiency. Who is more efficient: the monopolistic competitor or the perfect competitor? There is one test for efficiency: What is your ATC? Because the perfect competitor produces at the minimum point of its ATC curve and the monopolistic competitor does not, clearly the perfect competitor is more efficient.

To sum up, both the monopolistic competitor and the perfect competitor make zero economic profits in the long run. The monopolistic competitor charges a higher price and has a lower output than the perfect competitor. And the perfect competitor is a more efficient producer than is the monopolistic competitor.

I'm going to make a confession now that may shake you up a little. The graphs drawn in Figure 1, 2, and 3 have demand curves that really should not be as inelastic as they appear. Nearly all economics textbook writers are guilty of this sin, so I didn't want to be left out. You'll probably be able to get through the rest of your life without being asked why these demand curves should be flatter, or more elastic. In the box, "Who's Got the Flatter Demand Curve?" I plead guilty to drawing demand curves of insufficient elasticity, but I *do* have an explanation.

Who is more efficient: the perfect competitor or the monopolistic competitor?

Product Differentiation

The crucial factor is product differentiation.

Product differentiation is crucial to monopolistic competition. In fact, the product differentiation is really what stands between perfect competition and the real world. People differentiate among many similar products.

Who's Got the Flatter Demand Curve?

Whose demand curve is flatter, the monopolistic competitor's or the monopolist's? Because the monopolist faces the industry's entire demand curve, its demand curve is less flat, or more inelastic, than that of the monopolistic competitor, which is one of many competing firms. Under monopolistic competition, even small price increases will drive many customers to rival firms.

In terms of elasticity, it is fair to say that the monopolistic competitor faces a more elastic, or flatter, demand curve than does the monopolist. But this difference in elasticity would not be apparent if you were to compare the graphs in this chapter with those in the previous chapter. For analytic purposes, I made the demand curves for the monopolistic competitor steeper, or more inelastic, than I should have. I wanted to be sure that these graphs looked notably different from those of the perfect competitor. But in the real world, in which nearly all firms happen to be monopolistic competitors, each firm's demand curve would be nearly horizontal. Such a demand curve is shown in the figure here.

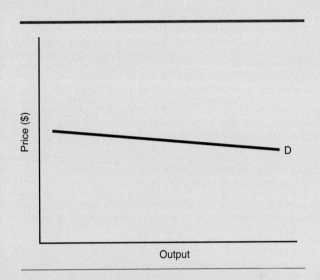

What makes one good or service differ from another? We need only for the buyer to believe there's a difference, because product differentiation takes place in the buyer's mind. What's the difference between a Toyota Camry and a Corvette? There is absolutely no difference between these two cars *if* the buyer sees no difference. Suppose someone is given the choice and says, "I don't care. They're both the same to me." To this buyer, the cars are identical. One is longer, maybe; one has nicer upholstery.

Americans are provided with a wide array of shampoos, breakfast cereals, candy bars, facial and bath soaps, soft drinks, ballpoint pens, and thousands of other consumer goods. Similarly, we can choose from among huge numbers of lawyers, accountants, physical therapists, chiropractors, advertising agencies, public relations firms, service stations, and restaurants. People living in most other countries don't have all the consumer choices that Americans do, so they don't engage in nearly as much product differentiation as Americans.

We're always differentiating, and our basis doesn't have to be taste, smell, size, or even any physical differences among the products. Two music shops might carry the same CDs; both shops charge exactly the same prices. Both shops are conveniently located. But one is usually crowded and the other is always empty.

We're always differentiating.

Why? Ambience. Perhaps one place lets you listen to a CD before you buy it. Perhaps one store will take special orders for you. Perhaps the salesclerks and owners are nice, helpful people, while in the other store they're all grouches.

Now we're dealing with a differentiated product. The CDs are the same. The prices are the same. But one store's got ambience up to here, and the other has to send out for it. The buyer prefers Mr. Nice Guy's store over the grouch's store, so we have a differentiated product.

When sellers try to get buyers to differentiate between their products and those of competitors, the sellers do so based on more than physical differences between their product and other versions of it. Also used are convenience, ambience, reputations of

Customization: Taking Product Differentiation One Step Further

The trend toward customization is taking product differentiation one step further. When you're buying a new car, you can pick something from the lot, or, if you don't mind waiting a few weeks, you can order a car customized to your specifications. Now, however, you can configure your vehicle to your specifications on the Internet and climb behind the wheel within just a few days. More and more, manufacturers like SONY, Dell, and Apple Computer are allowing customers to bypass retailers and buy direct. Toyota and other carmakers have equipped their showrooms in Japan with Internet terminals. And very soon you will be able to personalize almost any standardized product from your cell phone to your computer.

Publishers are at the forefront of product customization. Some publish books on demand. In other words, if there's some out-of-print book that you'd like to buy, they can just print it up for you. Very soon you'll be able to walk into a bookstore, ask them for virtually any book, and it will be waiting for you when you return from the coffee bar. College textbook publishers accommodate professors by custom publishing book-long collections of articles to be read by their students. And, finally, here's some news you may be able to use. If you, or anyone you know, should happen to have a novel you would like to have published—with an audience presumably limited to friends and family—there are new digital publishing houses (for example, iUniverse and Replica Books) that will get your book into print.

the sellers, and appeals to your vanity, unconscious fears, and desires, as well as snob appeal. To all that we can now add customizing products to suit individual tastes (see the box on customization).

Is McDonald's a monopolistic competitor? *Think* about it. First, does McDonald's produce a differentiated product? To answer one question with another, do customers differentiate between a Big Mac and Burger King's Whopper? To judge from their advertising, both companies seem to think so.

Next question: Is McDonald's one of many firms in the industry? Well, what's the industry? Ready-to-eat burgers and fries? Or fast food? What do *you* think? Fast food? I agree. So McDonald's 13,000 U.S. outlets compete with almost a quarter million other fast-food outlets. What percentage of fast-food outlets within five miles of your home are McDonald's? So McDonald's, although a huge chain, is basically a monopolistic competitor.

The Typical Monopolistic Competitor

Nearly all business firms in the United States are monopolistic competitors. They are monopolistic rather than perfect competitors because, in the mind of the buyer, their products are differentiated from one another. The monopolistic element is the uniqueness of each seller.

You walk into your neighborhood tavern. By the time you have bellied up to the bar, your drink is waiting for you. OK, so it's only a Diet Coke with a twist of lemon. It's the thought that counts. The bartender, by silently placing your usual in front of your spot at the bar has announced, "This woman is one of my regulars. She doesn't even have to say anything. I know what she drinks, and I know where she likes to sit."

The bartender has accorded you a certain status, a sense of belonging. It's something the perfect competitor can't provide, unless, of course, *all* bars happen to do this. Walk into a strange bar and see whether the bartender puts a drink down in front of you before you've ordered. If this happens—*and* if it's what you always order—then that drink's on me.

Each monopolistic competitor attempts to set his firm apart from the competition. The main way of doing this is through advertising. As we saw in the "Demand" chapter,

The monopolistic competitor tries to set his or her product apart from the competition.

Why Service Stinks*

How many times have you called a company's service number and gotten a prerecorded message when you needed to talk to a live person? How many times have you been put on hold for 20 minutes because "all our representatives are currently assisting other customers"?[†] Why *does* service stink? It's simple, explains *Business-Week:* Providing a live person costs a lot more than playing a recording.

And it's a question of who is calling. "The top 20 percent of customers at a typical commercial bank generate up to six times as much revenue as they cost, while the bottom fifth costs three to four times more than they make for the company."[‡] So you want to keep your best customers happy while sometimes doing everything you can to lose your least desirable customers. To do this, many large companies have set up two-tier, three-tier, or even four-tier customer service departments. For example, one New England electric utility provides its top 350 business clients with six customer-service representatives. The next tier of 700 is handled by six more, and the next 30,000 have just two reps to service their needs. And the remaining 300,000 residential customers at the lowest end? They get an 800 number with a recorded message.

---

*BusinessWeek, October 23, 2000, cover story.

[†]There's a great website which shows you how to cut through all those automated menus and talk directly with a fellow human. Go to www.gethuman.com and click on FAQ for a listing of the phone numbers of prompts of hundreds of large companies.

[‡]*BusinessWeek,* op. cit., p. 126.

---

when this is done successfully, the demand curve faced by the monopolistic competitor becomes more vertical or inelastic. Buyers are willing to pay more for this product because they believe it's wonderful. Or they'll undergo acts of great physical endurance: "I'd walk a mile for a Camel."

Typical monopolistic competitors are grocery stores, drugstores, restaurants and fast-food emporiums, gas stations, hardware stores, 99-cent stores, dry cleaners and laundries, (small) accounting and law firms, doctors, dentists, electricians, plumbers, and all the other small businesses you'd see along any Main Street, USA. Each has many competitors, and each produces a differentiated product.

Think of all the 7-Elevens, diners, coffee shops, greasy spoons, beauty parlors and barbershops, mom-and-pop groceries and general stores, bars, hamburger joints, and millions of other tiny retail stores where people spend time eating, drinking, getting groomed, or picking up a couple of everyday household items. Most of them dispense one thing, and you won't find it on the menu. It's local gossip. People stop by in the morning with last night's news, and later that afternoon they come to pick up that day's latest scoop. If you lived in a small town, where would *you* rather do business?

You eat in one luncheonette rather than any of the others because the counterman talks to you while you're having lunch or the waitress keeps your coffee cup filled. You prefer one grocery because they'll take your order over the phone. You'd rather shop in a particular drugstore because it has a much more cheerful atmosphere than all the other drugstores in town.

Small businesses often provide better service than larger businesses, mainly because they can provide personal contact (see the box, "Why Service Stinks"). When you have a problem, you can go right to the top and talk directly with the boss (which is especially easy when it's a one-person business). You are dealing with a live human being rather than a computer-based mailing, a recorded message, or an unnavigable website.

Ambience, cleanliness, personal attention, convenience of location, easy credit, free delivery service, and good service in general are all reasons why buyers might shop at one store rather than at its competitors. Thus product differentiation does not necessarily mean there are any physical differences among the products. They might all be the same, but how they're sold may make all the difference.

Why do business at one store rather than at its competitors?

On the other hand, there are, of course, some very real physical product differences. Different brands of orange juice, beer, cigars, ice cream, and hamburgers *do* taste different and *are* different in physical composition. Buyers often differentiate based on real physical differences among products. But differentiation takes place only in the buyer's mind, and it may or may not be based on real physical differences.

Price Discrimination

Price discrimination[1] sounds like a terrible thing, something that violates our basic constitutional rights. Sometimes it's bad, and other times it's not bad at all. In fact, price discrimination is often a disguised subsidy to the poor.

Price discrimination occurs when a seller charges two or more prices for the same good or service. Doctors often charge rich patients 10 times what they charge poor patients for the same service. Airlines sometimes allow riders under 16 years of age to fly for half the regular fair ("youthfare").

The most notorious example of price discrimination was probably that of A&P markets during the 1940s. A&P had three grades of canned goods: A, B, and C. Grade A was presumably of the highest quality, B was fairly good, and C was—well, C was edible. My mother told me that she always bought grade A, even though it was the most expensive. Nothing but the best for our family.

My parents were friendly with another family in the neighborhood. The husband, a man in his early 50s, found out he had stomach cancer. "Aha!" exclaimed my mother, "Mrs. S. always bought grade C!"

A few years later the Federal Trade Commission (FTC) prohibited A&P from selling grades A, B, and C. The FTC didn't do this because of Mr. S.'s stomach cancer, but because there was absolutely no difference among the grades.

Why did A&P go to all this trouble to concoct such an elaborate subterfuge? Because by creating separate grades of canned peas, corn, beans, and other foods, it was able to reap tens of millions of dollars in profits. If you'd like to see how they did this, we've done all the math in the box, "How A&P Created Grades A, B, and C to Raise Its Profits."

The firm that practices price discrimination needs to be able to distinguish between two or more separate groups of buyers. The doctor clearly does this when she sizes up the patient's ability to pay, so when you go to the doctor, wear your most raggedy clothes, ask whether food stamps are accepted, and be sure to say you're a college student.

In addition to distinguishing among separate groups of buyers, the price discriminator must be able to prevent buyers from reselling the product (i.e., stop those who buy at a low price from selling to those who would otherwise buy at a higher price).[2] If the 15-and-a-half-year-old buys an airline ticket at half fare and resells it to someone who is 35 years old, the airline loses money. Most 15-and-a-half-year-olds don't have lots of money, so the special fare is a way of filling an otherwise empty seat; but when the 35-year-old flies half-fare and would have been willing to pay full fare, the airline loses money. In the case of A&P, there was no problem preventing the grade C customers from reselling their food to the grade A customers because shoppers voluntarily separated themselves into these markets.

Let's return again to those airlines. How come a flight from New York to Houston costs three times as much if you don't stay over on Saturday night? You probably figured out that, since business travelers want to get home on weekends, the airlines can charge

---

[1]Although price discrimination is generally associated with monopolists, you don't have to be a monopolist—or even a very large firm—to engage in price discrimination.

[2]Remember when you passed your 12th birthday and could no longer get into the movies at the children's price? Did you ever get a younger-looking kid to buy your ticket for you and try to pass yourself off as under 12 to the ticket taker? What? You *still* do it?

Definition of price discrimination

To practice price discrimination, you need to be able to
(1) distinguish between at least two sets of buyers and
(2) prevent one set of buyers from reselling the product to another set.

How A&P Created Grades A, B, and C to Raise Its Profits

Let's start with the demand and total revenue schedules in Table A. If A&P had not created grades A, B, and C, it would receive a total revenue of $50 if it charged 50 cents for a can of peas. Similarly, it would receive a total revenue of $56 if it charged 40 cents and one of $51 if it charged 30 cents.

TABLE A Hypothetical Demand Schedule for Canned Peas

Price	Quantity Demanded	Total Revenue
$.50	100	$50
.40	140	56
.30	170	51

Now let's assume it cost A&P 20 cents for each can of peas. Let's take the data from Table A, add a total cost column and find total profit at prices of 50 cents, 40 cents, and 30 cents. That's done in Table B.

TABLE B Hypothetical Profit Schedule for Canned Peas

Price	Quantity Demanded	Total Revenue	Total Cost	Total Profit
$.50	100	$50	$20	$30
.40	140	56	28	28
.30	170	51	34	17

Which price would A&P charge—50 cents, 40 cents, or 30 cents? Well, all you have to do is look at the total profit column to see that the answer is obviously 50 cents. It makes a profit of $30.

Now we'll see that A&P can raise its profit by creating grades A, B, and C. In doing so it separates its buyers into three different markets. The grade A buyers are willing and able to pay 50 cents. They buy 100 cans. The grade B buyers, who buy 40 cans, would like to buy grade A, but they just can't afford to pay 50 cents. Finally, we have the poor, who can afford only grade C; they buy 30 cans.

All this is worked out in Table C. Total revenue now is $75 for the 170 cans sold, and total cost of 170 cans remains $34. This gives A&P a total profit of $41.

TABLE C Hypothetical Demand Schedule for Canned Peas, by Grades

Grade	Price	Quantity Demanded	Total Revenue	Total Cost	Total Profit
A	$.50	100	$50	$20	$30
B	.40	40	16	8	8
C	.30	30	9	6	3
			$75	$34	$41

Why is total profit so much greater under price discrimination ($41) than it is under a single price ($30)? Because the seller is able to capture some or all of the consumer surplus. (Consumer surplus was covered in the chapter entitled, "The Theory of Consumer Behavior.") People are willing to buy 100 cans at 50 cents, 40 more at 40 cents, and another 30 at 30 cents. But the people who buy only grade A will buy *all* their cans of green peas at that price, while those buying grade B will buy all their peas at 40 cents and grade C buyers will buy all their peas at 30 cents. By keeping its markets separate rather than charging a single price, A&P was able to make much larger profits.

them more. This is clear-cut price discrimination. But the airlines know they can get away with this because business travel and leisure travel are two separate markets. Imagine if the airlines and other practitioners of price discrimination knew their markets so well that each customer's demand schedule became a separate market. This would make possible *perfect price discrimination* (see the box, "Perfect Price Discrimination").

Before the advent of Medicare, Medicaid, HMOs, and private health insurance, doctors customarily practiced price discrimination. But they did so in a very good way. They usually charged their relatively rich patients as much as ten times more as they did their poorer patients. In essence, the rich were subsidizing the poor. Was their medical treatment the same? Pretty much, although maybe the doctors didn't always order expensive lab work for the poorer patients. And, of course, doctors may have spent a bit more time schmoozing with the wealthier patients.

To a lesser degree storeowners also practiced price discrimination—again in a good way. The poor were often extended credit, lower prices, and even freebies. This type

ADVANCED WORK

Perfect Price Discrimination

If price discrimination were carried to its logical conclusion, we would have perfect price discrimination. Every buyer in the market would lose his or her entire consumer surplus in the process.

Let's review the definition of consumer surplus, which was discussed in the "Theory of Consumer Behavior" chapter: *Consumer surplus is the difference between what you pay for some good or service and what you would have been willing to pay.* We'll start with a very simple situation. Amanda is willing to pay $30 for a pair of jeans, and Kristin is willing to pay $25. If the seller were to charge $20, then Amanda would enjoy a consumer surplus of $10 and Kristin would enjoy one of $5. But if the seller *knew* how much each woman was willing to pay for a pair of jeans, and if the seller were able to tell Amanda that the price was $30 and tell Kristin separately that the price was $25, he would completely eliminate their consumer surpluses.

Now we'll add another wrinkle. Suppose Amanda is willing to pay $30 for the first pair of jeans and $20 for the second. And suppose Kristin is willing to pay $25 for the first pair and $15 for the second. If the seller knew this and was able to take advantage of this information, he would charge Amanda $30 for the first pair and $20 for the second. And Kristin would be charged $25 for the first pair and $15 for the second.

Now we'll wind things up. Imagine there are 20 buyers in the market for jeans. The seller has somehow found out exactly how much each pair of jeans is worth to each of the buyers. By charging them *exactly* those prices, he will have managed to carry out perfect price discrimination. Of course, it would be virtually impossible to carry out price discrimination on such a large scale. But when you think about all those ridiculous sets of rules the airlines set up—tickets must be purchased 7 or 14 or 21 days in advance, no refunds, no changes, and you've got to stay over for at least one Saturday night—what they're really trying to do is squeeze out as much of their customers' consumer surpluses as they can.

of price discrimination is much less in evidence today. But you can get a pretty good idea of how it worked 60, 70, and 80 years ago by watching old movies like *The Last Angry Man* (in which Paul Muni played an aging doctor who continued practicing in a neighborhood that had grown increasingly poor) and *To Kill a Mockingbird* (in which Gregory Peck plays a depression-era Georgia lawyer who accepted farm produce for legal fees).

The next time you see or hear the words, new introductory offer, the chances are good that these are the words of a price discriminator. The company is offering new customers a special deal that is not available to old customers (see the box, "New Customers Get Better Deals than Old Customers").

New Customers Get Better Deals than Old Customers

There are many cases where new customers get a better deal than old customers do. This is true for sales from the Victoria's Secret catalog: The company's computerized records tell it when you last bought. The catalog offers lower prices if your last purchase was a long time ago. Similarly, this week Roadrunner cable modems are offering a $19.95 monthly price for three months (instead of the usual $44.95) if you sign on now. Both represent good examples of pure demand-based **price discrimination:** The good or service offered is identical, and the only difference between customers is how wedded to the good or service they appear to be. The companies assume that frequent buyers or long-term users will buy anyway and thus they have an **inelastic demand.** Another precondition for price discrimination is met too: The companies are sure beforehand that the low-priced good or service—the lingerie or the high-speed Internet connection—will not be resold.*

*Excerpted from Daniel Hamermesh, *Economics Is Everywhere* (New York: McGraw-Hill, 2004), pp. 150–51.

There are vending machines that now charge more for a can of soda on a hot day than on other days. Would *you* be willing to pay a higher price on a hot day? Because of consumer protests, the Coca-Cola Company put off installing these machines in the United States.

Price discrimination is woven into our economic fabric, and in most cases it is basically a mechanism for rationing scarce goods and services. For example, because nearly everyone seems to want to go to the movies at eight on Saturday night, the theaters encourage moviegoers to see films at other times by charging considerably less. But the main motivation for price discrimination is, of course, to raise profits. If price discrimination were carried to its logical conclusion, we would have perfect price discrimination.

Is the Monopolistic Competitor Inefficient?

It appears from our analysis of the long-run position of the monopolistic competitor in Figure 3 that the firm does not produce at the minimum point of its ATC curve. Economists criticize monopolistic competition as wasteful on two counts: too many firms in the industry and overdifferentiation.

Are there too many beauty parlors? Not if you want to get your hair done on Friday or Saturday afternoon. Too many gas stations? Not when there are gas lines. Too many Chinese restaurants? Not on Sundays. Are there too many grocery stores and too many real estate offices? Only when they're not busy. But most business firms, which apparently carry excess capacity during certain times of the day or the week, are set up to handle peak loads, so there aren't necessarily too many monopolistic competitors.

Are there too many firms in monopolistically competitive industries?

With respect to the second criticism, is there really overdifferentiation? Perhaps there don't seem to be substantial differences among grocery stores, drugstores, luncheonettes, dry cleaners, and ice-cream parlors, but consider the alternative. Consider the drab monotony of the stores in much of Eastern Europe, including the old Soviet Union. Maybe this lack of differentiation, this standardization, enables the sellers to cut costs somewhat. But is it worth it?

What are you *really* buying when you go to a fancy restaurant? Surely not just a meal. Undoubtedly you'll order something on a somewhat higher culinary plane than a Big Mac, large fries, and a Coke, but is that meal worth $80? It is when it is served by a waiter with a phony French accent, there are flowers on your table, a nice linen tablecloth, candlelight, soft music, and a solicitous maitre d', plus the restaurant is a restored 18th-century carriage house. (See Current Issue, "Selling Status," on the next page.)

A hamburger by any other name costs twice as much.
—Evan Esar

Monopolistic competition, with its attendant product differentiation, may be viewed as wasteful and inefficient, and a case can easily be made that it is. Think of all the money spent on advertising, packaging, marketing, and sales promotion, as well as interiors, facades, and window displays. These expenses add perhaps 10 or 20 percent to the prices of most things we buy; so we may well ask, Is it worth it? *You* decide.

Is monopolistic competition wasteful and inefficient?

I'll bet you're saying to yourself, "There he goes again, copping out and passing the buck." And you're right. You see, the buck stops with you because it's *your* buck and it's *your* decision about how to spend it.

Do you want to spend it on advertising, ambience, service, and convenience, or are you basically a no-frills person? Do you usually buy no-frills brands in the supermarket, fly coach rather than first-class, drive an economy car, and consider dinner in a fast-food emporium "eating out"? If you have answered yes to each of these questions, you are indeed a no-frills person who knows the value of a dollar.

However, if you answered no to all the above, you are clearly a person of refined taste and high style—a very *au courant* person (that's French for "up-to-date"). Whether we like it or not, product differentiation is the way monopolistic competitors compete. And whether we're aware of it or not, our entire environment is flavored by product differentiation. Imagine that next December every commercial Christmas display is done in black and white. Imagine what our supermarkets would look like with all black-and-white

Can you imagine a no-frills world?

boxes, jars, and cans. And imagine what people would look like if they all wore the same styles and colors. In a word, product differentiation adds flavor, texture, and variety to our lives. Whether we want to pay the price is a matter of individual taste.

The product differentiation engendered by monopolistic competition is a strong counterforce to the McDonaldization of America. In the opening paragraph of a book review, Karal Ann Marling paints a vivid picture of our country.

> One source of a pervasive millennial malaise is the perception that American life has come down to a couple of monster corporations selling the same Gap chinos and Egg McMuffins on every corner, from sea to shining sea—that the rich pageantry of the national folklife, in all its pungent variety, has played itself out in a roadside litter of discarded clamshell burger boxes and chicken buckets. Every city looks just the same, its presence marked upon the landscape not by impressive civic monuments but by a garishly lighted corridor of brand-name drive-ins, pointing the way from the Interstate to an all but abandoned urban center: McDonald's, Arby's, Wendy's, Taco Bell, Pizza Hut. Topeka or Syracuse, Cheyenne or Memphis—only the order of the pseudo-haciendas and the golden arches changes.[3]

Finally, let's consider the nature of competition. Monopolistic competitors *do* compete with respect to price, but they compete still more vigorously with respect to ambience, service, and the rest of the intangibles that attract customers. In this arena American business does engage in lively, innovative competition. The next time you're walking along a shopping street, take note of how the storekeepers try to entice you with their window displays. To the degree that they're successful, they have induced you to differentiate their products from all the others. That is what monopolistic competition is all about.

Current Issue: Selling Status

Starbucks does a great job selling status, along with its coffee and hot chocolate. You can pay $2.20 for a hot chocolate or $3.20 for a white chocolate mocha. Why the dollar price differential? After all, how much more does it cost to make the white chocolate mocha than to make the plain hot chocolate? Maybe a few cents. Tim Harford observes that "By charging wildly different prices for products that have largely the same cost, Starbucks is able to smoke out customers who are less sensitive about the price."[4]

Harford also asks why airport departure areas across the world are so shoddy. Or why the stewardesses stand ready to physically restrain coach passengers who attempt to leave a plane before the last first-class passenger has left the aircraft. The first-class passengers paid for first class treatment. If everyone is treated first class, there'd be no point in paying a premium price.

Have you ever thought about opening a restaurant? Restaurants are getting to be pretty complicated places considering that local laws usually dictate that you segregate your diners by smoking preference (pro or con). Why not segregate *your* diners by *status*?

That's *right*! We've got a table for two in our low-status section. What's that? Oh, there's a 15-minute wait for a high-status table. What's the difference? Well, if you need to ask, then you probably *belong* in the low-status section.

Do the high-status diners get better food? No, the food's the same. And the service? The same. Then what *is* the difference? Price. That's right—we charge twice as much for the same food and service in the high-status section as in the low-status section.

How can we get away with that? It's easy. Everyone knows who's in which section. We know the cheapos and the big spenders, the tightwads and the sports.

---

[3]Karal Ann Marling, "Sameness Is Glorious," *New York Times Book Review,* December 26, 1999, p. 34.
[4]Tim Harford, *The Undercover Economist* (New York: Oxford University Press, 2006), p. 35.

Why are people willing to pay twice as much for the same food and the same service? They're paying for status. And by selling status, you can really boost your profits. So go ahead and open your restaurant. And save a nice table for me. In which section? I'll give you three guesses.

Questions for Further Thought and Discussion

1. In what respects does a monopolistic competitor differ from a perfect competitor?
2. Explain why the monopolistic competitor breaks even in the long run.
3. Is the monopolistic competitor inefficient? Try to argue the question from both sides.
4. What are the two necessary conditions under which price discrimination can take place? Give an example of price discrimination.
5. Do monopolistically competitive industries have too many firms, each of which produces too little?
6. Make a list of five firms with whom you or your family members have done business this week. Which are monopolistic competitors?
7. Are you in favor of price discrimination or against it? Try to argue pro and con.
8. What are the ways in which a firm can differentiate its product from those of its competitors?

Workbook for Chapter 23

Name _____   Date _____

Multiple-Choice Questions

Circle the letter that corresponds to the best answer.

1. Monopolistic competition differs from perfect
   competition only with respect to _____.
   a) the number of firms in the industry
   b) product differentiation
   c) barriers to entry
   d) economies of scale

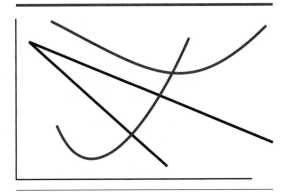

F*igure* 1

2. In the long run the monopolistic competitor in
   Figure 1 is _____.
   a) more efficient than the perfect competitor
   b) less efficient than the perfect competitor
   c) as efficient as the perfect competitor

3. In the short run the monopolistic competitor will
   be _____.
   a) definitely making a profit
   b) definitely taking a loss
   c) definitely breaking even
   d) either taking a loss or making a profit

4. In the long run the monopolistic competitor will
   be _____.
   a) making a profit
   b) taking a loss
   c) breaking even

5. The demand curve of a monopolistic competitor
   is _____.
   a) flatter than that of the perfect competitor and
      steeper than that of the monopolist
   b) flatter than that of the monopolist and steeper than
      that of the perfect competitor
   c) identical to the perfect competitor's demand curve
   d) identical to the monopolistic competitor's
      marginal revenue curve

6. Product differentiation can take place _____.
   a) only if there are physical differences among the
      products
   b) only if there are no physical differences among
      the products
   c) whether or not there are physical differences
      among the products

7. Which statement is true?
   a) When you decide which doctor to go to, your only
      concern is the quality of the medical service you
      will receive.
   b) People differentiate among goods and services
      based not only on physical differences but also on
      ambience, convenience, and service.
   c) Monopolistic competitors are usually large firms.
   d) None of these statements is true.

8. Which of the following would not be a monopolistic
   competitor?
   a) Thursa Sotak's hair salon
   b) Keith and Cathi Collins' mom-and-pop grocery store
   c) Adam Avischious, a storefront lawyer
   d) Kelley's family restaurant owned by Robin Kelley,
      Caroline Kelley, and Claire Kelley
   e) All are monopolistic competitors.

9. Which statement about price discrimination is true?
   a) It generally hurts the poor.
   b) It is inherently evil.
   c) It involves charging at least two separate prices for
      the same good or service.
   d) It generally involves deceiving the consumer.

10. Each of the following is an example of price discrimination except _____.
    a) airline "youthfares"
    b) higher-price movie tickets after 5:00 P.M. and on weekends
    c) doctors charging more to patients who need lab tests
    d) A&P's old grades A, B, and C

11. In the long run in monopolistic competition _____.
    a) most firms make a profit
    b) the absence of entry barriers ensures that there are no profits
    c) economies of scale ensure that there are no profits
    d) most firms lose money

12. Which statement is true?
    a) Most firms in the United States are monopolistic competitors.
    b) Most firms in the United States are perfect competitors.
    c) Most consumers would prefer lower prices and less product differentiation.
    d) None of these statements is true.

13. Perfect price discrimination eliminates _____ of the customer's consumer surplus.
    a) all   b) most   c) some   d) none

14. Which statement is true about perfect price discrimination?
    a) It is very common.
    b) It is illegal.
    c) The larger the market, the more likely one is to find it.
    d) None of these statements is true.

15. Price discrimination _____.
    a) often works to the advantage of the poor
    b) generally helps rich customers
    c) is very hard to find in the United States
    d) is illegal in the United States

16. Under perfect price discrimination _____.
    a) consumer surplus is zero
    b) consumer surplus is maximized
    c) consumer surplus is a constant no matter what price is charged
    d) consumer surplus rises as price is lowered

Fill-In Questions

1. The most crucial feature of monopolistic competition is _____.

2. A monopolistic competitor makes a profit only in the _____

3. The monopolistic competitor's demand curve slopes _____.

4. Price discrimination occurs when a seller charges _____ for the same good or service.

5. The monopolistic competitor _____ produces at the minimum point of his or her ATC curve.

Problems

1. Given the information in Figure 2, how much profit does this monopolistic competitor make?

2. Is the firm in Figure 2 operating in the short run or the long run? How do you know?

3. Draw a graph of a monopolistic competitor in the long run on a piece of graph paper.

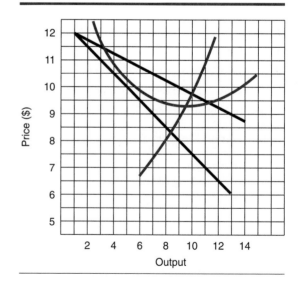

Figure 2

Chapter 24

Oligopoly

The prefix *oli* means "few." An oligarchy is a government controlled by only a few rulers. An oligopoly is an industry controlled by only a few firms.

CHAPTER OBJECTIVES

In this chapter you'll learn about these topics:

- Concentration ratios.
- The Herfindahl-Hirschman index.
- The competitive spectrum.

- The kinked demand curve.
- Administered prices.

Oligopoly Defined

An oligopoly is an industry with just a few sellers. How few? So few that at least one firm is large enough to influence price.

Oligopoly is the prevalent type of industrial competition in the United States as well as in most of Europe, Japan, and southeast Asia. Table 1 lists some of the more important American industries that are oligopolies. Perhaps two-thirds of our GDP is accounted for by firms in oligopolistic industries.

Is the product identical or differentiated? It doesn't matter. In the case of the steel, copper, and aluminum industries, the product happens to be identical; but in most other industries, the product is differentiated.

The crucial factor under oligopoly is the small number of firms in the industry. Because there are so few firms, every competitor must think continually about the actions of its rivals. What each does could make or break the others. Thus there is a kind of interdependence among oligopolists.

Because the graph of the oligopolist is similar to that of the monopolist, we will analyze it in exactly the same manner with respect to price, output, profit, and efficiency. Price is higher than the minimum point of the ATC curve, and output is somewhat to the left of this point. And so, just like the monopolist, the oligopolist has a higher price and a lower output than does the perfect competitor.

The oligopolist, like the monopolist and unlike the perfect competitor and monopolistic competitor, makes a profit. Because the oligopolist does not produce at the minimum point of its ATC curve, it is not as efficient as the perfect competitor.

An oligopoly is an industry with just a few sellers.

Is product identical or differentiated?

TABLE 1	Concentration Ratios in Selected Industries, 2000*	
Industry	Largest Firms	Concentration Ratio
Airlines	American, United, Delta, Northwest	56
Beverages	Coca-Cola, Pepsi, Anheuser-Busch, Coors	82
Computer Software	Microsoft, Oracle, Computer Assoc. Int., Compuware	60
Computers, Office Equipment	IBM, Hewlett-Packard, Compaq, Dell	71
Energy	Duke, Reliant, Utilicorp, Avista	45
Entertainment	Walt Disney, Viacom, Clear Channel, USA Networks	55
Food Production	IBP, Archer Daniels Midland, Farmland Industries, Tyson Foods	55
Food Services	McDonald's, Tricon, Darden, Wendy's	43
Forest and Paper Products	International Paper, Georgia-Pacific, Weyerhaeuser, Kimberly-Clark	58
Mail, Package, and Freight Delivery	United Parcel Service, FedEx, Pittston, Airborne Freight	85
Motor Vehicles	General Motors, Ford, DaimlerChrysler, Toyota	70
Petroleum Refining	ExxonMobil, Texaco, Chevron, USX	67
Pipelines	Enron, Dynegy, El Paso, Williams	82
Railroads	Union Pacific, Burlington No. Santa Fe, CSX, Norfolk Southwestern	80
Telecommunications	AT&T, Verizon, SBC, Worldcom	56
Tobacco	Philip Morris, R.J. Reynolds, Universal	96
Wholesalers: Food and Grocery	Supervalue, Sysco, Fleming, Genex	68
Wholesalers: Health Care	McKesson HBOC, Cardinal Health, Berger Brunswig, Amerisource Health	84

Source: Fortune, April 16, 2001.
*Concentration ratios for 2002 was due out in June 2006 at www.census.gov/epcd/www/concentration.html.

We're going to consider a whole range of oligopolistic models, from close collusion to cutthroat competition. But first, let's look at concentration ratios and the Herfindahl-Hirschman index, two measures of the degree of oligopoly in various industries.

Two Measures of the Degree of Oligopolization

Looking at the percentage share of sales of the leading firms is one way of measuring how concentrated an industry is. This is called the industry's concentration ratio. A second way to measure this is to calculate the Herfindahl-Hirschman index, which, it turns out, is a lot easier to do than to say.

Concentration Ratios

The total percentage share of industry sales of the four leading firms is the industry concentration ratio.

Economists use concentration ratios as a quantitative measure of oligopoly. *The total percentage share of industry sales of the four leading firms is the industry concentration ratio.* Industries with high ratios are very oligopolistic.

How much is the concentration ratio for an industry whose four largest firms produce, respectively, 10, 8, 7, and 5 percent of the industry's output? Work it out right here:

Just add them together to get 30.

The concentration ratios in Table 1 range from 43 in food services to 96 in tobacco. Railroads, pipelines, health care wholesalers, beverages, and mail, package, and freight delivery are all in the 80s. Remember that the concentration ratio is the total percentage share of industry sales of the four leading firms.

Two key shortcomings of concentration ratios should be noted. First, they don't include imports. For example, in the motor vehicle industry, with a concentration ratio of 76, imported cars and light trucks account for about one-third of the American market. Although Toyota is listed among the top four American automakers, the concentration ratio does not take into account over 1 million Japanese imports, not to mention the hundreds of thousands of Volkswagens, Saabs, BMWs, Audis, Jaguars, Porsches, and Rolls Royces the United States also imports.

Two key shortcomings

Concentration ratios have become less meaningful as foreign imports have increased. For instance, we get 80 percent of our consumer electronics and over 60 percent of our oil from abroad, so concentration ratios in these industries are meaningless. Perhaps in a world with unrestricted international trade, which would make our world a veritable global village, we could replace national concentration ratios with international concentration ratios. In the meantime we'll go with what we have in Table 1.

The second shortcoming is that the concentration ratios tell us nothing about the competitive structure of the rest of the industry. Are the remaining firms all relatively large, as in the cigarette industry, which has a total of just 13 firms, or are they small, as in the aircraft and engine parts industry, which totals about 190 firms? This distinction is important because when the remaining firms are large, they are not as easily dominated by the top four as are dozens of relatively small firms.

The American automobile industry, which was long a classic example of oligopoly, has been changing drastically in recent years (see the box, "Oligopoly in the Automobile Industry"). Not only have imports made a substantial impact, but foreign owned companies now make over half the cars made in the U.S.A. The imports have made the automobile industry's concentration ratio much less relevant, while the transplants have been reducing that ratio. But these developments have been an unmitigated boon to the car buyer, who is reaping the benefits of lower prices and much higher quality.

The Herfindahl-Hirschman Index (HHI)

The Herfindahl-Hirschman index (HHI) is *the sum of the squares of the market shares of each firm in the industry.* We'll start with a monopoly. One firm has all the sales, or 100 percent of the market share. So its HHI would be 100^2, or $100 \times 100 = 10,000$.

The Herfindahl-Hirschman index is the sum of the squares of the market shares of each firm in the industry.

Now that's some big Herfindahl-Hirschman index! In fact, they just don't come any bigger than that. What is the HHI of *every* monopoly? That's right—it's 10,000.

Now *you'll* get a chance to compute a few HHIs. Find the HHI of an industry with just two firms, both of which have 50 percent market shares. Work it out right here:

Solution: $50^2 + 50^2 = 2,500 + 2,500 = 5,000$.

Oligopoly in the Automobile Industry

The automobile industry has long been considered the archetypal American oligopoly. Until the arrival of Volkswagen in Pennsylvania (which closed up shop in 1988), followed by the six Japanese "transplants," the entire industry consisted of just four firms. More than 95 percent of our cars were made by the Big Three—General Motors, Ford, and Chrysler—and the rest by American Motors, which has since merged with Chrysler, which itself was swallowed by Daimler, a German company. So until very recently the American automobile industry had a concentration ratio of 100.

But there were two major changes during the last three decades. The first was set off by the gasoline shortages we had in 1973 (the Arab oil embargo) and in 1979 (the Iranian Revolution). The higher gas prices that followed made fuel-efficient cars—particularly Japanese cars—much more attractive to the American buyer. Imports, which had been limited to just 10 percent of the market, shot up to about 30 percent by the mid-1980s.

Of equal long-run significance to the industry has been the advent of the Japanese transplants, which began setting up assembly lines during the 1980s. Today these firms assemble four of every ten cars produced in the U.S. And once again, we're back to the Big Four—General Motors, Ford, DaimlerChrysler, and Toyota.

Table A   Market Share of Top Six U.S. Makers of Cars and Light Trucks, 2005

Company	Market Share
General Motors	26.0%
Ford	17.4
DaimlerChrysler	13.6
Toyota	13.3
Honda	8.6
Nissan	6.3
Other Companies	29.7

Source: http://www.detnews.com/apps/pbcs.dll/article?AID=20060105/AUT.

Now let's add another wrinkle. Find the HHI of an industry that has four firms, each with a 25 percent market share:

Solution: $25^2 + 25^2 + 25^2 + 25^2 = 625 + 625 + 625 + 625 = 2,500$.

Can you see where all this is going? The less concentrated an industry, the lower its HHI. And here's one last question. Imagine an industry with 100 firms, each with an equal market share. Without going through all the work, see if you can figure out the HHI.

It would come to 100: $1^2 + 1^2 + 1^2 \ldots + 1^2 = 100$.

The Justice Department uses the HHI to decide whether an industry is highly concentrated and considers an industry with an HHI of under 1,800 to be competitive. This measure is preferred to four-firm concentration ratios because the index is based on the shares of *all* firms in an industry.

The Competitive Spectrum

We shall now consider the possible degrees of competition, from cartels and open collusion down through cutthroat competition. These possibilities are shown in Figure 5, toward the end of this section.

Cartels

A cartel is an extreme case of oligopoly.

With so few firms in our basic industries, there is a strong temptation for the leading firms to band together to restrict output and, consequently, increase prices and profits. An extreme case is a cartel, where the firms behave as a monopoly in a manner similar to that

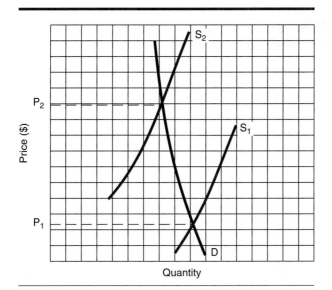

F*igure* 1
Withholding Supply to Raise Price
When supply is lowered from S_1 to S_2, price rises from P_1 to P_2.

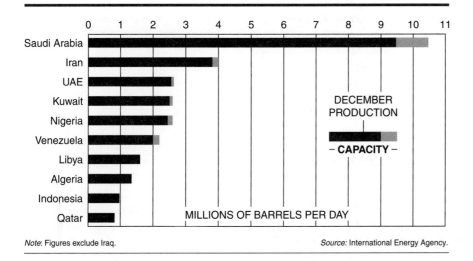

F*igure* 2
Daily Output and Capacity of 10 Members of OPEC, December 2005
Saudi Arabia is, by far, the largest producer, and has the most excess capacity.

of the Organization of Petroleum Exporting Countries (OPEC) in the world oil market. More formally, *a cartel is a combination of firms that acts as if it were a single firm.*

Given a certain market demand for a good or service over which an oligopoly exercises little control, firms that openly collude can control industry supply and, to a large degree, market price. For example, by withholding part or most of supply, the colluding firms can bid the market price way up. This was done by OPEC in 1973 when the price of oil quadrupled (see Figure 1).

If the cartel is able to operate successfully, securing the full support of all its members (who don't try to undercut the cartel price by selling some extra output under the table), its situation will approximate that of a monopoly. Just like a monopoly, which faces the entire market demand curve, the cartel will control the entire industry supply. OPEC, which controlled most of the world's oil exports, was able to take advantage of a relatively inelastic demand for oil by withholding supply in late 1973 and early 1974, thereby quadrupling world oil prices.

OPEC has a great deal of market power, but it is responsible for less than half the world's oil exports and less than one-third of all oil production. Who are its members? They are listed in Figure 2 and are mainly situated on the Persian Gulf, the world's largest known oil field. In addition to these 10 OPEC members, in recent years two other major oil exporters, Mexico and Norway, have raised and lowered production in step with the OPEC nations.

In 1999, when oil was selling at just \$10 a barrel, OPEC members agreed to cut production. At the same time, most of the economies of Europe and Asia, which had been stagnating, began a vigorous recovery, pushing up the worldwide demand for oil. The American economy, too, continued its rapid growth. A very cold winter further pushed up demand for oil. By March of 2000, the price of oil topped \$34 a barrel.

Cartels have also operated locally; perhaps the most notorious example is the mob-run New York trash cartel. After a 10-year investigation of the Mafia's longtime control of the garbage-hauling industry in New York City and its northern suburbs, three men, reputedly mobsters, and 14 hauling company owners, pleaded guilty to setting up a property rights system in which they claimed the permanent right to the locations where they picked up garbage, shared profits from their contracts, and disguised their profit sharing through sham transactions and false tax returns. Two years later, the cost of garbage removal tumbled 30 to 40 percent for most of the city's 200,000 commercial buildings, restaurants, stores, private hospitals, and private schools, which have to hire commercial haulers.

Open Collusion

Open collusion operates like the Mafia.

Slightly less extreme than a cartel would be a territorial division of the market among the firms in the industry. This would be a division similar to that of the Mafia, if indeed there really is such an organization. An oligopolistic division of the market might go something like this. All prostitution, dope, loan-sharking, and gambling in New England is run by Steve (The Fence); New York is run by Frankie (Big Frank); Philly and Atlantic City are run by Max (Tiny); the Midwest is run by Mike (The Banker); Florida by Joey (Three Fingers); the Gulf Coast by Paddy (The Professor); the mountain states by Benny (Dog Ears); and the West Coast by Anthony (Fat Tony).

Nobody messes with anyone else's territory. The arrangement will continue until there is a new power alignment within the family or a new firm tries to enter the industry.

This cozy arrangement would give each operation a regional monopoly. On a national basis, each operation's market situation is depicted by Figure 3.

You may have noticed that this graph is identical to that of a monopoly. Although the firm may have only 15 or 20 percent of the market, its pricing behavior is that of the monopolist, and the results are similar. Compared to the perfect competitor, the colluding oligopolist charges a higher price (not one equal to the minimum point of the ATC curve); has a higher ATC (and is therefore less efficient); restricts output (that is, operates to the left of the minimum point of the ATC); and finally, unlike the perfect competitor, makes a profit.

These are extreme cases, but they would be illegal, even during the last few years of less-than-stringent enforcement of the antitrust laws. Now, as we move to somewhat less extreme cases of collusion, we begin to enter the realm of reality. This brings us to the celebrated electric machinery conspiracy case.

Covert Collusion

A case of price-fixing

In the late 1950s officials of General Electric, Westinghouse, Allis-Chalmers, and other leading electrical firms met periodically at various hotels and motels around the country. These secret meetings were set up to fix the prices of electric transformers, turbines, and other electrical equipment. Although government contracts were awarded based on the lowest sealed bid, the conspirators rigged the bidding so that even the lowest bid would be extremely profitable. In fact, the firms took turns making low bids. The public, too, was bilked of hundreds of millions of dollars in higher prices.

Finally, in 1961, the U.S. Supreme Court found seven high-ranking company officials guilty of illegal price-fixing and market-sharing agreements. They were given fines,

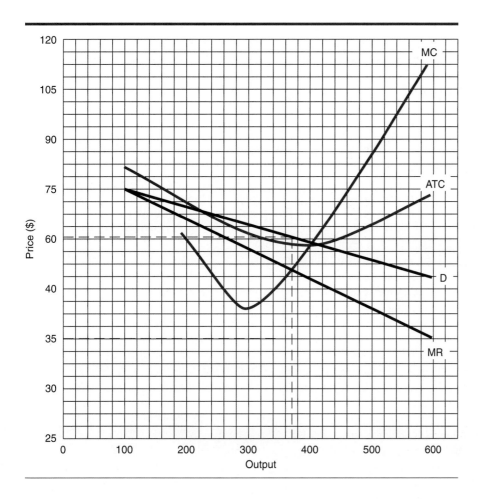

Figure 3
The Colluding Oligopolist
This graph could also belong to the monopolist or the monopolistic competitor in the short run.

which their companies took care of, and short jail sentences, during which time their salaries were paid. On release from jail each was given back his old job. Talk about tying yellow ribbons round the old oak tree!

As a footnote to this story, some 11 years later two of the companies involved in the 1961 case, General Electric and Westinghouse, were charged with fixing prices on turbine generators. Oh well, nobody's perfect.

Covert collusion, while frowned upon in the United States (see "The Penalty Box"), is often the way business is done in Asia. In Japan, the *dango* (see accompanying box) is a formal negotiating process, under which firms take turns making low bids on government construction projects. In contrast, in the United States, usually construction firms, without consulting among themselves, submit bids, and the lowest bidder will win.

Other cases of collusion

Price Leadership

Short of meeting in hotel rooms to set prices secretly, do oligopolists conspire in more overt fashion? Until the 1930s U.S. Steel exercised open price leadership in the steel industry. On one day U.S. Steel would post a price for a particular type of steel, and the next day Bethlehem, Republic, Armco, Inland, and the rest of the industry would post an identical price, down to the last hundredth of a cent.

Playing follow-the-leader

At the turn of the century the leaders of the major steel firms actually collectively agreed on prices at dinners held periodically by Judge Gary, president of U.S. Steel. Since those days, not only has it become much more difficult to get away with collusion, but the companies could no longer take the full cost of these dinners as tax write-offs because only 80 percent of business "entertainment" expenses are deductible.

The Penalty Box

When a hockey player commits a flagrant foul, he's asked to sit in the penalty box. As we'll see in the next chapter, a bunch of corporate executives have received substantial prison sentences for their crimes. But not everyone found guilty of serious corporate crime goes to prison. Sometimes their companies are merely fined and they promise to mend their ways.

That's how our system of justice generally deals with covert collusion, price fixing, and related crimes. In 1996 the Archer Daniels Midland Company pleaded guilty and paid a $100 million criminal fine for its role in two international conspiracies to fix prices to eliminate competition and allocate sales in the lysine and citric acid markets. Three former executives were sentenced to prison terms ranging from two to two-and-a-half years, and two of the three former executives were also fined $350,000 each.

In 1999 an arrangement was uncovered that fixed worldwide vitamin prices as much as 25 percent above the market level. Hoffmann-La Roche, a Swiss pharmaceutical conglomerate that controls about 40 percent of the worldwide vitamin market, settled with the U.S. Justice Department, paying a $500 million penalty. A second company, BASF AG of Germany, agreed to pay a $225 million fine for its role in the conspiracy. In 2001 the European Commission fined Hoffmann-La Roche an additional $752 million and BASF an additional $260 million.

In 2004 Schering-Plough agreed to pay $350 million in fines and plead guilty to criminal charges for selling its products to private health care providers for far less than it sold them to Medicaid. Indeed, we can probably look forward to a stream of cases involving overbilling of both Medicaid and Medicare.

The Dango

Covert collusion is the way much business is done in the Japanese construction industry. When the government asks for bids on a construction project, one firm will bid lower than its competitors. But they're not really competing. The firms negotiate among themselves to decide which firm will make the lowest bid and get the job. That negotiating process is *dango*.

Usually the firms take turns making the low bid. That way every company gets some of the business. But just to keep everyone happy, the low bidder actually pays each of its competitors thousands of dollars in compensation. In addition, government bureaucrats are paid off as well.

Here's how *dango* works. The government announces that it is accepting bids on a project and sets a ceiling price. After the so-called competitors confer among themselves, they make bids on the project. But the firm that has been designated to win the contract makes a bid just below the ceiling price.

What if a new firm enters the industry and bids lower? The government bureaucrats will say that this firm cannot be given the contract because it had not been awarded any previous contracts. How does the firm break in? It must pay its dues by joining the *dango*.*

---

*See John McMillan, *Reinventing the Bazaar* (New York: W. W. Norton, 2002), pp. 141–47.

The cigarette industry provided another instance of price leadership.

Between 1923 and 1941, virtual price identity prevailed continuously among the "standard" brands. During this period there were eight list price changes. Reynolds led six of them, five upward and one downward, and was followed each time, in most cases, within 24 hours of its announcement. The other two changes were downward revisions during 1933 led by American and followed promptly by the other standard brand venders.[1]

---

[1] F. M. Scherer, *Industrial Pricing: Theory and Evidence* (Skokie, IL: Rand McNally, 1970), p. 38.

Another form of price leadership that has sprung up in recent years is the setting of the prime rate of interest by the nation's leading banks. That rate might stay the same for several months until suddenly 2 of the top 10 banks raise their prime by a quarter of a percent, and within 24 hours, the rest of the nation's 7,000-odd banks raise theirs a quarter of a percent. What is interesting here is that rarely do the same banks change the rate two times in a row, but in virtually every instance the other 7,000-some banks play follow-the-leader. Bankers and other oligopolists engaging in price leadership would have us believe that they are "locked in competition" and that the forces of supply and demand dictate the same price to everyone. But this explanation strains credulity because no two firms—and certainly not 7,000—face exactly the same demand schedules or have the same cost schedules.

The prime rate set by big banks is a form of price leadership.

When is collusion most likely to succeed? Mainly when there are few firms in the industry and when there are high barriers to entry. Basically, it's much easier to keep secrets—when you're violating the antitrust laws, you have to keep secrets—when there aren't too many people to deal with. In a far-fetched example, in the 1950s the American Communist Party was considered a group of people conspiring to advocate the violent overthrow of the American government. It turned out that several thousand of their somewhat fewer than 20,000 card-carrying members were actually FBI agents or paid informers. Some conspiracy!

Collusion is most likely to succeed when there are few firms and high barriers to entry.

Conspiracies need to be kept very small. When entry barriers, particularly capital requirements, are high enough, conspirators don't have to worry about new firms entering the industry and, presumably, being taken into the conspiracy.

Cutthroat Competition

It is ridiculous to call this an industry. This is rat eat rat; dog eat dog. I'll kill 'em, and I'm going to kill 'em before they kill me. You're talking about the American way of survival of the fittest.

–Ray Kroc (founder of McDonald's)–

Welcome to the world of cutthroat competition, the world in which oligopolistic firms take no prisoners. Although we won't be getting into industrial espionage, you can be sure that industrial spies are lurking everywhere. Each firm wants to know exactly what its competitors are doing and how they will react to any changes in price that it might initiate. The dynamics of oligopoly under cutthroat competition are very different from those of oligopoly with collusion.

Now we deal with the extreme case of oligopolists who are cutthroat competitors, firms that do not exchange so much as a knowing wink. Each is out to maximize its profits. These oligopolists are ready to cut the throats of their competitors, figuratively speaking, of course.

Cutthroat competition: an extreme case

The uniqueness of this situation leads us to the phenomenon of the kinked demand curve, pictured in Figure 4. For the first time in this textbook, we have a firm's demand curve that is not a straight line.

Before changing price, a firm will try to gauge its competitors' reactions.

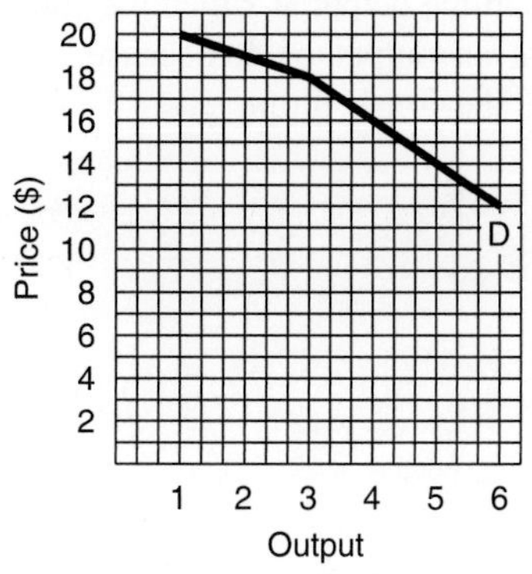

Figure 4
The Kinked Demand Curve

Why does the demand curve of the fiercely competing oligopolist have a kink? The answer is that it is based on the oligopolist's assumption about his rivals' behavior in response to his own actions. The oligopolist can make three possible pricing decisions: raise price, lower price, or not change price.

If I raise my price, they won't raise theirs.

Suppose the price has been the same for a fairly long period of time. The oligopolist thinks about raising price. If I raise my price, what will my competitors do? Who knows? What would *I* do if one of my rivals raised her price? If I did nothing, I would get some of my rival's customers, so I wouldn't change my price.

Even though I hate to admit it, my competitors are as smart as I am, so if *my* response to a rival's price increase is to keep my price the same and get some of my rival's customers, surely my rivals would respond in the same way to my price increase. Therefore, I don't raise my price.

If I lower my price, they lower theirs.

What about lowering my price and stealing some of my competitors' customers? Now I ask myself, how would *I* react? I'd immediately lower my price in response to a price cut by one of my competitors. And my competitors would lower their prices in response to my lowering mine. So I won't lower my price.

If I don't lower my price (because my competitors would follow) and if I don't raise my price (because my competitors won't follow), what *do* I do? Nothing. I leave my price where it is.

What makes sense for me also makes sense for my competitors. None of them will raise or lower price. We all keep price where it is, and that happens to be at the kink in the demand curve.

This explains why price does not change often under extremely competitive oligopoly. A firm is afraid to make a move for fear of what its rivals might or might not do. Underlying that fear is the memory of price wars touched off by one firm lowering its price. Hence it's better to leave well enough alone.

Fast food chains like McDonald's and Burger King are definitely cutthroat competitors. Daniel Hamermesh shows how their behavior is virtually predicted by the kinked demand curve.

> The major fast-food chains seem to be unable to break the ninety-nine-cent barrier for burger prices. The standard burger price goes above $1 occasionally, and then one of the major companies begins selling "Value Meals" or the equivalent, and the others have to cut back prices to attract customers. This is classic "kinked demand curve" behavior: If you raise your price in an oligopoly and the others don't, you lose lots of sales. (If the market were competitive, you couldn't raise price at all without losing all your sales.)[2]

Are Costco and Sam's Club cutthroat competitors? Definitely. Perhaps the classic case would be two or three gas stations located at the same intersection engaged in a price war. First one would cut its prices, and then, five minutes later, the others would go even lower. This might go on for just a few hours, or maybe even several days. Eventually the gas station owners would come to their senses and prices would go back up to their old levels.

Now you're going to catch a break. We're not going to make you fill in any more tables or draw any more graphs, at least in *this* chapter. Just glance at Figure 5, which is based on Table 2, and see if you can find the output at which the competitive oligopolist produces.

Clearly, she produces at an output of 4, because at that output the MC and MR curves cross. Next, calculate the firm's profit.

---

[2]Daniel Hamermesh, *Economics Is Everywhere* (New York: McGraw-Hill, 2002), pp. 161–62.

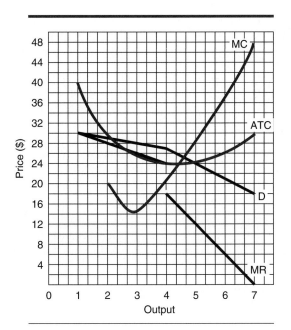

Figure 5
The Cutthroat Oligopolist
How much is the price and output of this firm? The price is $27 (at the kink of the demand curve), and the output is 4 (note that MC = MR at this output).

TABLE 2 Hypothetical Demand and Cost Schedules for a Competitive Oligopolist

Output	Price	Total Revenue	Marginal Revenue	Total Cost	ATC	Marginal Cost	Total Profit
1	$30	$ 30	$30	$ 40	$40	—	−$10
2	29	58	28	60	30	$20	− 2
3	28	84	26	75	25	15	9
4	27	108	24	96	24	21	12
5	24	120	12	125	25	29	− 5
6	21	126	6	162	27	37	− 36
7	18	126	0	210	13	48	− 84

Solution: Output, which is directly under the kink, is 4. Price, which is at the kink, is $27. Remember that price is *always* read off the demand curve. And now, total profit:

$$\text{Total profit} = (\text{Price} - \text{ATC}) \times \text{Output}$$
$$= (\$27 - \$24) \times 4$$
$$= \$3 \times 4$$
$$= \$12$$

Can you come up with an easier way of finding the firm's total profit? Look at Table 2 again. Did you figure it out yet? Just subtract total cost from total revenue at an output of 4 ($108 − $96 = $12). Once you know the output, all you need to do is subtract TC from TR.

In passing, let us note that the oligopolistic firm does not produce at the minimum point of its ATC curve, so we do not have peak efficiency even though there is considerable competition. Price tends to stay at $27. This is the main reason why, under competition,

Administered Prices

Administered prices are set by large corporations for relatively long periods of time, without responding to the normal market forces, mainly, changes in demand. For example, although demand fell substantially during the Great Depression, many firms, most notably the railroads, did not lower their prices.

We already saw how, under the constraints of fierce competition, the oligopolist is reluctant to raise or lower price. Prices are said to be sticky.

If we take the firm's MC curve as its supply curve, we will see that the oligopolist operates within a fairly wide range of possible MRs before it is necessary to change price. Look back at Figure 4. Because of the discontinuity of the MR curve (the vertical broken line), the firm will charge the same price at the same output no matter how much MC varies within the range of $18 to $24 and still equals MR.

Administered prices are peculiar to oligopoly. Perfect competitors and monopolistic competitors are too small to dictate price. Monopolists will change their output and price in response to changes in demand in order to maximize their profits. But under competitive oligopoly, the firms will rarely shift output or price because they will continue to maximize profit as long as MC is within the range of MR.

Figure 6

The Competitive Spectrum

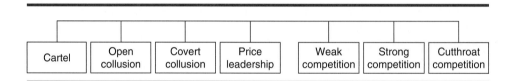

oligopolists' prices tend to be "sticky." We call such sticky prices *administered prices*, which is the topic of the box by that name.

Conclusion

Let's take a look at the chart in Figure 6. At one end we have the cartel, which no longer operates within the American economy although it may be found in world markets (most notably in the oil market). At the opposite end of the spectrum we have the cutthroat competitor, the firm that will stop at nothing to beat out its rivals. Industrial espionage and sabotage, underselling, disparaging of rival products, and other unfair competitive practices are the trademarks of such firms.

Near the middle are the mildly competing oligopolists and the occasionally cooperating oligopolists. Sometimes their leaders are called corporate statesmen.

Where on this spectrum is American industry?

Where on this spectrum is American industry? Where do we place the industries listed back in Table 1? Near the middle? Toward the cutthroat end of the spectrum? Or toward the cartel end?

The answer is that there *is* no answer. You won't pin me down on this one. There are two reasons why there is no answer to this question.

First, there is no one place where American industry is located because different industries have different competitive situations. In short, some oligopolistic industries are more competitive than others, so to say that *all* industries are located at a certain point on the spectrum—regardless of where—has got to be wrong.

Second, there is widespread disagreement about the degree of competition in any given industry. Take banking, for example. If one were to judge the degree of competitiveness among banks by all the newspaper advertising they do to attract depositors and to get people to take out car loans and mortgages, it would appear that this is a very competitive industry. But one would reach quite a different conclusion by observing that when one or two major banks change their prime rate of interest, within a day or so all the other major banks, not to mention the rest of the banks around the country, play follow-the-leader.

Current Issue: Cutthroat Competition in the College Textbook Market

Do you buy your books new or used? Textbook prices have been going up much faster than the rate of inflation. In fact, the typical college text now costs over $100. At many community colleges, students pay more for their books than they do for their tuition. And so, not surprisingly, they often try to buy used books.

Publishers get to play the role of bad guys. They're the ones charging those outrageous prices, and, on top of that, they seem to change editions every other year. While economics texts do need to be periodically updated, do math and chemistry books?

Let's consider a $100 textbook. In theory, your college bookstore is supposed to buy it back from you for half price, or $50, and then resell it as a $75 used book. But as you know, college bookstores often give you less than half price for the books they buy back.

Students will have the choice of buying a new book for $100 or a used book for $75. Bookstore managers usually prefer selling used books because they'll make a larger profit than on new books. Generally they'll have to pay the publisher over $75 for that new $100 book.

Why do publishers charge so much for their books? The main reason is that they are also providing several costly ancillary products—test banks, instructor's manuals, videos, computerized tutorials, PowerPoint lecture notes, overhead transparencies, and FastFax testing. Indeed, it cost publishers well over $1 million to launch a new major textbook.

Do professors use all of these ancillaries? Some professors use some of them, while others use none of them. Then why not publish some no-frills texts and charge no-frills prices? A few decades ago, there were over 20 major textbook publishers (today there are only three), and most textbooks came with no more than one or two supplements. Now, besides having much less competition, the major publishers seem to follow a herd mentality. If some professors want a video or a 10,000-question test bank, then we better provide these, because our competitors certainly will.

Let's suppose that one publisher actually *did* put out a textbook without ancillaries and cut the price by, say, 50 percent. Wouldn't a lot of professors order that book to save their students all that money? Well, the sad truth is that most professors have gotten quite used to all the ancillaries that come with their textbooks, so if one publisher stopped supplying them, the professors would just switch to another publisher who did.

In addition, the Big Three—McGraw-Hill (which publishes my book), Pearson, and International Thompson—have hundreds of sales reps who call upon your professors to drum up sales. It costs well over $100,000 a year to keep each sales rep out in the field. If one of the Big Three fired its sales reps, it could save a bundle of money, and maybe cut textbook prices by one-third. But what would happen to its sales?

Let's look at one more factor in the textbook business. Unlike nearly any other market, you, as the consumer, have only one choice to make: Do I buy my books new or used? Your professors decide which texts you'll buy, and even *they* generally get to pick that text from one of just three publishers. But if students could choose their own texts, you could bet that the publishers would start producing no-frills texts at much lower prices.

Questions for Further Thought and Discussion

1. The American automobile industry is an archetypical oligopoly. Show why this statement is true.

2. Where is American industry on the competitive spectrum? Instead of answering this question, you may criticize it.

3. What are the two measures of the degree of oligopolization? Work out a numerical problem using each of them.

4. Explain the cutthroat competitor's reasons for not raising or lowering his price, thereby accounting for the kink in his demand curve.

5. What are administered prices, and how are they set?

6. Should covert collusion be illegal?

Workbook for Chapter 24

Name _____   Date _____

Multiple-Choice Questions

Circle the letter that corresponds to the best answer.

1. Which statement is true?
   a) All oligopolies have only a few firms.
   b) Most oligopolies have only a few firms.
   c) Some oligopolies have only a few firms.

2. The auto industry has a concentration ratio of about _____ percent.
   a) 10   d) 70
   b) 30   e) 90
   c) 50

3. Administered prices are most likely to occur under _____.
   a) perfect competition   c) monopoly
   b) monopolistic competition d) oligopoly

4. Price is _____.
   a) always read off the demand curve
   b) sometimes read off the demand curve
   c) always read off the marginal revenue curve
   d) sometimes read off the marginal revenue curve

5. In the U.S. today collusion is _____.
   a) illegal and does not exist
   b) illegal and does exist
   c) legal and does not exist
   d) legal and does exist

6. Which statement is true?
   a) All firms in oligopolistic industries are large.
   b) Most firms in the United States are oligopolies.
   c) The crucial factor in oligopolistic industries is product differentiation.
   d) Most of our GDP is produced by oligopolies.

7. Which of the following is not an oligopolist?
   a) ExxonMobil
   b) General Motors
   c) Your local phone company
   d) Xerox

8. Which statement about oligopolies is false?
   a) They operate at the minimum points of their ATC curves.
   b) They charge higher prices than perfect competitors.
   c) They make profits in the long run.
   d) They cannot legally form cartels in the United States.

9. Which statement is false?
   a) The cigarette and auto industries have high concentration ratios.
   b) OPEC is a cartel.
   c) Most oligopolies engage in outright collusion.
   d) None of these statements is false.

10. The electric machinery case involved _____.
    a) a cartel   c) cutthroat competition
    b) covert collusion   d) none of the above

11. The least competitive industry is one that has _____.
    a) price leadership   c) overt collusion
    b) covert collusion   d) a cartel

12. Which one of these could not be considered cutthroat competitors?
    a) Members of Japanese dangos
    b) McDonald's and Burger King
    c) Costco and Sam's Club
    d) Gas stations on the same intersection

13. Which statement is true?

a) Most of American industry is engaged in cutthroat competition.

b) Most of American industry does not compete.

c) Some oligopolistic industries are more competitive than others.

d) None of these statements is true.

14. An industry that is highly concentrated might have a Herfindahl-Hirschman index of _____.

a) 20,000   d) 100

b) 2,000   e) 1

c) 800

15. An industry that has 100 firms, each with a 1 percent market share, would have a Herfindahl-Hirschman index of _____.

a) 1   d) 1,000

b) 10   e) 10,000

c) 100

Use Table 1 to answer questions 16 through 19.

TABLE 1

Industry X		Industry Y		Industry Z	
Firm	Market Share (%)	Firm	Market Share (%)	Firm	Market Share (%)
1	25	1	35	1	30
2	25	2	20	2	30
3	15	3	15	3	20
4	10	4	15	4	10
5	10	5	10	5	5
6	10	6	5	6	5
7	5				

16. The highest concentration ratio _____.

a) is in Industry X   c) is in Industry Z

b) is in Industry Y   d) cannot be determined

17. The highest Herfindahl-Hirschman index _____.

a) is in Industry X   c) is in Industry Z

b) is in Industry Y   d) cannot be determined

18. Which statement is true?

a) Industry X is more concentrated than Industry Y.

b) Industry Y is more concentrated than Industry Z.

c) Industry Z is more concentrated than Industry X.

d) Industries X, Y, and Z have the same concentration ratio.

19. Which statement is true?

a) Industry X has a higher Herfindahl-Hirschman index than Industry Y.

b) Industry Y has a higher Herfindahl-Hirschman index than Industry Z.

c) Industry Z has a higher Herfindahl-Hirschman index than Industry X.

d) Industries X, Y, and Z have the same Herfindahl-Hirschman index.

20. Which statement is true?

a) Most cars and light trucks sold in the United States are either imported or made by Japanese firms in this country.

b) Toyota and Honda are the largest makers of cars and light trucks in the United States.

c) Japanese companies make about 10 percent of all cars and light trucks in the United States.

d) None of these statements is true.

21. Imports have made the automobile industry's concentration ratio much _____ relevant, while the Japanese transplants have been _____ that ratio.

a) more, reducing   c) less, reducing

b) more, increasing   d) less, increasing

22. A monopoly would have a concentration ratio of _____ and a Herfindahl-Hirschman index of _____.

a) 100, 100   c) 10,000, 100

b) 10,000, 10,000   d) 100, 10,000

23. Which statement is true?

   a) The higher the Herfindahl-Hirschman index, the higher the degree of concentration.

   b) The lower the Herfindahl-Hirschman index, the higher the degree of concentration.

   c) The Herfindahl-Hirschman index remains constant as the degree of concentration rises.

   d) There is no relationship between the Herfindahl-Hirschman index and the degree of concentration.

24. Compared to the perfect competitor in the long run, the cutthroat oligopolist has a _____.

   a) lower price and lower profits

   b) higher price and higher profits

   c) higher price and lower profits

   d) lower price and higher profits

25. According to the theory of the kinked demand curve, if a firm were to raise its price, its competitors would _____.

   a) lower theirs

   b) raise theirs

   c) keep theirs the same

26. According to the theory of the kinked demand curve, if a firm were to lower its price, its competitors would _____.

   a) lower theirs

   b) raise theirs

   c) keep theirs the same

27. The kinked demand curve depicts _____.

   a) cutthroat competition   c) collusive oligopoly

   b) cartels   d) price leadership

28. The kinked demand curve is associated with _____.

   a) sticky prices   c) covert collusion

   b) OPEC   d) none of the above

29. The discontinuity in the oligopolist's marginal revenue curve occurs _____.

   a) to the right of the kink

   b) to the left of the kink

   c) directly below the kink

   d) at different places at different times

30. The Japanese *dango* is _____.

   a) a way to ensure that government construction contracts will always go to the low bidder

   b) a negotiating process under which construction firms take turns receiving government contracts

   c) a cartel whose sole purpose is to keep construction prices high

   d) an organization that helps new firms enter the construction industry

31. Which one of the following statements is true?

   a) Competition among college textbook publishers has kept prices from rising even further.

   b) The college textbook publishing industry is highly oligopolized.

   c) If it were not for the sale of used books, college textbook publishers would make much smaller profits.

   d) Because college textbooks are often accompanied by supplements, this has tended to keep their prices down.

Fill-In Questions

1. An oligopoly is an industry with _____ _____.

2. One measure of the degree of competitiveness (or of oligopoly) is called a _____.

3. The oligopolist _____ at the minimum point of her ATC curve.

4. The total _____ of industry sales by the four leading firms is the industry concentration ratio.

5. The most important cartel in the world today is _____.

6. An important Supreme Court case involving covert collusion was the _____ case.

7. U.S. Steel and a few cigarette companies were all engaged in _____ to attain their economic ends.

8. The sign of cutthroat competition on a graph would

   be the _____.

9. One of the outcomes of the kinked demand curve is

   _____ prices.

10. Administered prices are set by _____

    for _____ without responding to

    _____.

11. Administered prices are peculiar to _____

    _____.

Problems

1. Given the information in Table 2, calculate the
   concentration ratio of this industry. *Show your work.*

TABLE 2

Firm	Percent of Sales
A	14%
B	4
C	23
D	5
E	2
F	8
G	17
H	10
I	2
J	15
Total	100%

2. (a) How much is the concentration ratio in the
   industry shown in Table 3? (b) Calculate the
   Herfindahl-Hirschman index in this industry.

TABLE 3

Firm	Market Share
1	30%
2	20
3	20
4	10
5	10
6	5
7	5

3. (a) How much is the concentration ratio in the
   industry shown in Table 4? (b) Calculate the
   Herfindahl-Hirschman index in this industry.

TABLE 4

Firm	Market Share
1	40%
2	15%
3	10
4	10
5	10
6	5
7	5
8	5

4. Given the information in Figure 1, calculate the
   firm's profit.

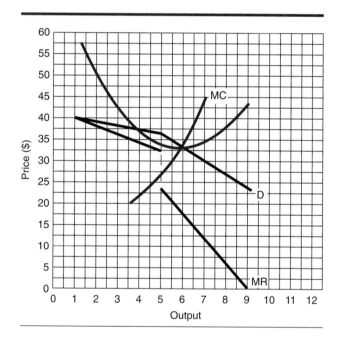

Figure 1

5. Given the information in Figure 2, answer these questions:

a) How much is the firm's output?

b) How much is the firm's profit?

c) What type of oligopolist is this?

d) If the firm were a perfect competitor, how much would its output be in the long run?

e) If the firm were a perfect competitor, how much would its price be in the long run?

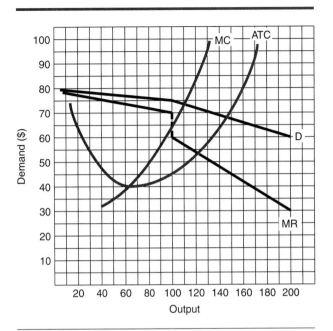

Figure 2

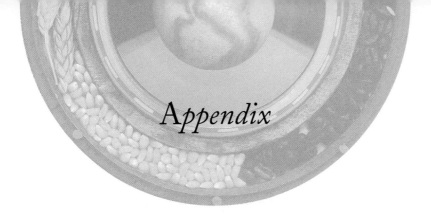

Appendix

The Four Types of Competition: A Review

This appendix will summarize some of the high points of the last four chapters, especially the graphs. No new material will be introduced.

APPENDIX OBJECTIVES

You will be able to review:

- Perfect competition.
- Monopoly.
- Monopolistic competition.
- Oligopoly.

Perfect Competition

A perfectly competitive industry has many firms selling an identical product. How many is many? So many that no one firm can influence price. What is identical? A product is identical in the minds of buyers when they have no reason to prefer one seller to another.

Definition of perfect competition

In the long run, if the firm has been losing money, it may well leave the industry. Enough firms will leave to reduce market supply and raise price enough to eliminate the economic losses of the firms that remain in the industry. Thus, in the long run, the perfect competitor will make zero economic profit.

The long run

In the long run, if the firm has been making a profit, additional firms will have been attracted to the industry, raising industry supply and reducing market price. Thus, in the long run, profit is reduced to zero.

In the long run the perfect competitor's price is equal to the low point on the firm's ATC curve. Because the firm produces at that output, it operates at peak efficiency. That is, it operates at the minimum point of its ATC curve, which means it produces at the lowest possible cost.

Here's a nice exam question: Draw the demand curve for the perfect competitor and state its elasticity.

You would draw a horizontal line. Its elasticity would be infinity or undefined. In other words, it would be perfectly elastic.

Are there any perfectly competitive industries? Perhaps not, but wheat, soybeans, and corn may come pretty close.

Monopoly

Definition of monopoly

There is no distinction between
the short run and the long run.

A monopoly is a firm that produces all the output in an industry. There's nobody else selling anything like what the monopolist is producing. In other words, there are no close substitutes.

There is no distinction between the short run and the long run under monopoly because the monopolist is the only firm in the industry. No firms enter or leave, as they do with perfect competition. The market demand curve *is* the monopolist's demand curve.

What does the monopolist's demand curve look like? It's a line that slopes downward to the right. So to sell additional output, the monopolist must lower her price.

What are examples of monopolies? Microsoft's near monopoly of computer operating systems comes to mind. Patented drugs for which there are no close substitutes. Viagra had a monopoly at least until 2004, when other male impotence drugs came on the market. Local phone, gas, electric, and cable TV service are also monopolies. Major league baseball, football, basketball, and hockey are certainly monopolies as well.

Monopolistic Competition

Definition of monopolistic
competition

The short run

The long run

A monopolistically competitive industry has many firms selling a differentiated product. How many is many? So many that no one firm has any significant influence over price.

If the buyer doesn't differentiate among the various products sold, the product is identical. If the buyer does differentiate, the product is differentiated. Who determines whether the product is differentiated or identical? The buyer does.

Like the perfect competitor, the monopolistic competitor can make a profit or take a loss in the short run, but in the long run, the firm will break even. The reason the monopolistic competitor makes zero economic profits in the long run is the same as that under perfect competition.

In the long run, if firms are losing money, then many will leave the industry, thus lowering industry supply and raising market price. If firms are realizing substantial profits in the long run, then new firms will be attracted to the industry, thus raising supply and lowering market price.

Like the perfect competitor, the monopolistic competitor is a small firm, one of many in its industry. But what's the main difference between the monopolistic competitor and the perfect competitor? Here's a hint: Go back to the definitions of perfect competition and monopolistic competition.

The main difference between them is that perfect competitors produce *identical* products while monopolistic competitors produce *differentiated* products.

Examples of monopolistic competitors are restaurants, convenience stores, haircutting salons, clothing stores, real estate brokers, law firms, medical offices, bars, and nearly all retail stores.

Oligopoly

Defenition of oliogopoly

An oligopoly is an industry with just a few sellers. How few? So few that at least one firm is large enough to influence price.

Examples of oligopolies are the automobile, breakfast cereal, airline, beverage, entertainment, aircraft, petroleum refining, and tobacco industries.

Perfect Competition versus Imperfect Competition

The perfectly competitive model is an ideal, rarely if ever attained in a world of imperfect competition. Indeed, more than 99 percent of the business firms in the United States are monopolistic competitors. Virtually all of the rest are oligopolies and monopolies.

TABLE A–1	The Four Types of Competition: Number of Sellers and Type of Product		

Type of Competition	Number of Sellers	Type of Product
Perfect competition	Many	Identical
Monopoly	One	—unique
Monopolistic competition	Many	Differentiated
Oligopoly	Few	Either identical or differentiated

TABLE A–2	The Four Types of Competition: Price and Output in Long Run

Type of Competition	Price	Output
Perfect competition	At minimum ATC	At minimum ATC
Monopoly	Higher than minimum ATC	Restricted (to left of minimum ATC)
Monopolistic competition	Higher than minimum ATC	Restricted (to left of minimum ATC)
Oligopoly	Higher than minimum ATC	Restricted (to left of minimum ATC)

TABLE A–3	The Four Types of Competition: Profit and Efficiency in Long Run

Type of Competition	Profit	Efficiency
Perfect competition	Zero economic profit	Peak efficiency
Monopoly	Makes an economic profit	Less than peak efficiency
Monopolistic competition	Zero economic profit	Less than peak efficiency
Oligopoly	Makes an economic profit	Less than peak efficiency

Now let's look at some tables listing the characteristics of perfect competition and imperfect competition, which includes monopoly, oligopoly, and monopolistic competition.

Summary Tables

Tables A–1, A–2, and A–3 summarize what we've covered here with respect to number of sellers, type of product, price, output, profit, and efficiency.

Questions for Further Thought and Discussion

1. How does perfect competition compare to monopolistic competition with respect to price, profit in the long run, average total cost, and output?
2. How does perfect competition compare to monopoly with respect to price, profit in the long run, average total cost, and output?
3. How does perfect competition compare to oligopoly with respect to price, profit in the long run, average total cost, and output?

Workbook for Appendix to Chapter 24

Name _____   Date _____

Multiple-Choice Questions

Write in the letter that corresponds to the best answer for questions 1 through 28, using choice a), b), c), or d).

   a) perfect competitor/competition

   b) monopolist/monopoly

   c) monopolistic competitor/competition

   d) oligopolist/oligopoly

1. A firm in an industry with many sellers selling a differentiated product would be a(n) _____.

2. A firm that faces the entire demand curve of an industry would be a(n) _____.

3. In the long run only a(n) _____ operates at the minimum point of its ATC curve.

4. The crucial factor in _____ is the low number of sellers.

5. The crucial factor in _____ is product differentiation.

6. Under _____ and _____, there are no profits in the long run.

7. A firm with many sellers and an identical product is a(n) _____.

8. The kinked demand curve takes place under competitive _____.

9. With respect to computer operating systems, Microsoft is a(n) _____.

10. A mom-and-pop grocery in Harlem is a(n) _____.

11. Most firms in the United States are _____.

12. Imperfect competition includes _____, _____, and _____.

13. A company making a profit in the long run would be a(n) _____ or a(n) _____.

14. If there are many firms in the industry, we are talking about either _____ or _____.

15. The most efficient producer is the _____.

16. Jennifer Ziegenfuss owns a firm that manufactures cell phones that double as garage door openers. Another firm, owned by Jared Collins, produces the same product. A third firm, owned by Daniel Quinn, also makes this product. The only other firm manufacturing cell phone–garage door openers is owned by Robert Roan. This industry is a(n) _____.

17. The airline industry is a(n) _____.

18. Ford Motor Company is a(n) _____.

19. Wheat growing is an example of _____.

20. A camera store in downtown Chicago is a(n) _____.

21. An industry with seven firms is a(n) _____.

22. A firm that faces a downward sloping demand curve is *not* a(n) _____.

23. An industry with 100,000 firms is either a (n) _____ or a(n) _____.

24. Most college bookstores are _____.

25. Major league baseball is a(n) _____.

26. A firm that operates at peak efficiency in the long run must be a(n) _____.

27. A firm that makes a profit in the long run must be either a(n) _____ or a(n) _____.

28. A firm producing a differentiated product must be either a(n) _____ or a(n) _____.

Fill-In Questions

1. How many firms is many? So many that _____ _____.

2. A product is identical in the _____.

3. Under any type of competition, if firms are losing money in the long run, _____ _____. If firms are making a profit in the long run, _____ _____.

4. In the long run the perfect competitor's price is equal to the _____ on the firm's ATC curve. Therefore, the firm is operating at _____ efficiency.

5. A monopolist's product has no _____.

6. The monopolist's price is _____ than the perfect competitor's; in the long run the monopolist's profit is _____ than the perfect competitor's.

7. A monopolistically competitive industry has _____ firms selling a _____ product.

8. Product differentiation takes place in the _____ _____.

9. In the long run the monopolistic competitor's price is _____ the minimum point on its ATC curve.

10. An oligopoly is an industry with _____ _____.

11. Only the _____ in the _____ produces at the minimum point of its ATC.

12. The perfect competitor has a _____ demand curve.

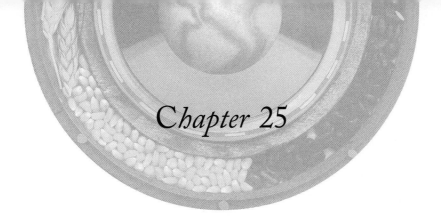

Chapter 25

Corporate Mergers and Antitrust

There has been an unmistakable trend toward bigness in business since the mid-1980s. Corporate mergers and takeovers have become so common that anything less than a $10 billion deal is not even considered financial news. Let's see how this trend developed and how the government has attempted to regulate it.

CHAPTER OBJECTIVES

When you complete this chapter you will have learned about each of the following:

- The explanation of antitrust.
- Major antitrust laws.
- Modern antitrust.
- Types of mergers.

- The effectiveness of antitrust.
- The trend toward bigness.
- The Microsoft case.
- Corporate corruption.

A Historical Perspective on Corporate Concentration

The history of the American economy since the Civil War has been one of growing corporate concentration. Like the tides, this concentration has had its ebbs and flows.

A high-water mark was reached in the early years of this century when J. P. Morgan put together a couple of huge deals with his fellow captains of industry, Andrew Carnegie, Edward Harriman, and John D. Rockefeller. Then, in the years before World War I, came the first trustbusters, Presidents Teddy Roosevelt and William Howard Taft. A new wave of corporate mergers took place in the 1920s, only to be succeeded by the antitrust enforcement policies of Presidents Franklin Roosevelt and Harry Truman in the 1930s and 1940s. After that, a new wave of mergers continued for the next five decades.

During the last century and a quarter, a few hundred huge companies came to dominate our economy. There have been a few reverses—the 1911 breakup of the Standard Oil and American Tobacco trusts, and the antitrust enforcement of the 30s and 40s, and the more recent breakup of AT&T—but the trend has been unmistakable.

> The nature of a market society is to push toward a higher degree of concentration, and the nature of antitrust is to push back toward a more deconcentrated, competitive environment.
>
> –Louis Galambos, business historian,
> Johns Hopkins University–

Antitrust

The Political Background

John D. Rockefeller, American oil magnate (The Granger Collection, New York)

What is a trust?

The common view is that during the 19th century the federal government rarely intervened in the economy, allowing businesses to go their own ways. There were, however, two major forms of intervention, both of which were key issues in the events leading up to the Civil War.

First, at various times the government passed a high protective tariff that generally made certain imports more expensive and greatly aided northern manufacturers. Second, the transcontinental railroad, which completely bypassed the South, was built with a tremendous amount of federal aid. This aid took the form of 10-mile strips of land on alternating sides of the track, so that for every mile of track built, the railroad received 10 square miles of land.

Both policies were benevolent with respect to big business, so few protests were raised about government intervention in that arena. Furthermore, with the election of Abraham Lincoln in 1860, the Republican Party would dominate the federal government for the next 70 years. This was the political backdrop in which the first antitrust legislation was passed in 1890. The Sherman Antitrust Act was passed by a Republican Congress and signed by a Republican president. For "the party of big business" to have passed a law such as this, the economic situation had to have been pretty desperate.

The late 19th century was the era of the "trust." Trusts were cartels that set prices and allocated sales among their member firms. In some cases, most blatantly oil, a single company was formed that controlled most or all production in the industry. The Standard Oil trust, which was carved out of 39 independent oil companies by John D. Rockefeller, controlled 90 percent of all U.S. oil production, refining, and marketing. In 1892, 40 independent sugar companies formed the American Sugar Refining Company. Still other trusts were formed in meat packing, cottonseed and linseed oil, lead, leather, whiskey, tobacco, electrical goods, coal, steel, and the railroads.

The Standard Oil trust was so powerful that it forced the railroads not only to grant it discounts, and not grant them to their competitors, but even to give it "drawbacks"—that is, payments on every shipment of oil refined by *rival* firms. This was such a blatant restraint of trade that it angered even the staunchest probusiness congressional Republicans.

In his landmark work on those times, Matthew Josephson pictured

> an America in which the citizen was born to drink the milk furnished by the milk Trust, eat the beef of the beef Trust, illuminate his home by grace of the oil Trust, and die and be carried off by the coffin Trust.[1]

Even more grating were the insults hurled at the public by those who ran these huge industrial empires. The great financier J. P. Morgan proclaimed, "I owe the public nothing." Probably the most famous was the remark by railroad tycoon Billy Vanderbilt: "The public be damned. I am working for my stockholders."[2]

The Sherman Antitrust Act

Sherman had mixed feelings about the growing concentration of corporate power and its abuses. After all, he was a leader of the Republicans, the party of big business. He hoped his law would slow the powerful trend toward monopolization of American industry, but the language of the law was left rather vague. In 1890 Congress passed the Sherman Antitrust Act to curb the trust movement. Named after Senator

---

[1]Matthew Josephson, *The Robber Barons* (New York: Harcourt Brace Jovanovich, 1962), p. 358.
[2]Ibid., p. 187.

The Breakup of Standard Oil

In 1911 the Supreme Court ordered the breakup of the Standard Oil Company for violating the Sherman Act. The five largest pieces were Standard Oil of New York, New Jersey, Ohio, Indiana, and California.

Standard Oil of New York evolved into Standard Oil Company of New York, into SOCONY-Mobil-Vacuum, and finally, into Mobil Oil, the nation's second-largest oil company.

Standard Oil of New Jersey became ESSO, and nearly twenty years ago it became Exxon, the largest oil company in the world.

Standard Oil of Ohio (Sohio), is still known by its original name, while Standard Oil of California, SoCal, became Chevron and is now ChevronTexaco.

Additional derivative firms include Continental Oil (now part of Du Pont), Marathon Oil (which merged with U.S. Steel), and Atlantic Richfield.

Exxon and Mobil, the world's two largest oil companies, both part of the original Standard Oil trust, merged in 1999, becoming ExxonMobil. And Atlantic Richfield (later known as ARCO) and Amoco (formerly Standard Oil of Indiana) are now both part of British Petroleum. So apparently the old Standard Oil trust is not dead after all.

John Sherman, this law remains the most important piece of antitrust legislation in our nation's history.

The key passage stated that "every contract, combination in the form of trust or otherwise, in restraint of commerce among the several states, or with foreign nations, is hereby declared illegal." It went on to state, "Every person who shall monopolize, or conspire with any other person or persons to monopolize any part of the trade or commerce of the several states, or with foreign nations, shall be guilty of a misdemeanor."

The key passage

Finally, after years of preparation by the Roosevelt and Taft administrations, suits were brought against two of the biggest trusts of the day, the Standard Oil and American Tobacco trusts. In the first case the Standard Oil Trust was split into 34 separately owned companies, the five largest of which were later known as Exxon, Mobil, Sohio (Standard Oil of Ohio), Amoco, and Chevron (see the box, "The Breakup of Standard Oil"). The American Tobacco Company was broken up into three companies: the American Tobacco Company, Liggett & Myers, and P. Lorillard.

Standard Oil and American Tobacco cases

Were these trusts broken up because they were big? No! Bigness per se did not offend the Court. The trusts were broken up because they had behaved badly.

What had the Standard Oil trust done that was bad? It had forced the railroads, which were then the basic means of shipping oil, to give it rebates or discounts not just on the oil it shipped but even on the oil shipped by its competitors. You can justify asking for a rebate on your *own* freight charges, but imagine forcing the railroads to pay you a rebate on your competitors' freight charges. Basically, it was using its tremendous market power to force its rivals out of business.[3]

The problem with the Supreme Court's interpretation of Sherman was that it did not prohibit monopoly per se, but prohibited only certain illegal tactics that had been practiced by Standard Oil and American Tobacco. Clearly the Court was even more conservative than other Republican branches of government—the president and Congress. Nevertheless, the breakup of these companies was a radical measure that indicated how serious the problem of monopolization had become to the rest of the business establishment. In a sense, then, their breakup was deemed necessary to preserve the status quo.

From this decision the Supreme Court formulated its "rule of reason," which set the tone for antitrust enforcement for the next two decades. Bigness itself was no offense as long as that bigness was not used against rival firms.

The rule of reason

---

[3]The Interstate Commerce Act of 1887 prohibited granting rebates to large shippers.

Mere size is no offense.

The rule of reason was applied in the *U.S. Steel* case of 1920 when President Woodrow Wilson's administration sought the same legal remedy against the steel trust that had been applied nine years earlier against the oil and tobacco trusts. The Court concluded that the U.S. Steel Corporation, which produced more than half of the nation's steel, did not violate the Sherman Act just because it was big. The Court pronounced: "The corporation is undoubtedly of impressive size. . . . But we must adhere to the law, and the law does not make mere size an offense, or the existence of unexerted power an offense." And the very existence of competitors disproved the contention that U.S. Steel had misused its power.

So not *all* trusts were illegal, but only *unreasonable* restraints of trade. Remember the fairy tale of the three little pigs accosted by the big bad wolf, who told them, "I'll huff and I'll puff and I'll blow your house down"? Well the Supreme Court's rule of reason said that the wolf not only had to be big and bad, but he actually had to blow that house down. Bigness and bad intentions alone were not illegal per se. So even though the folks running U.S. Steel had intended to drive out their competitors, the fact that they had not succeeded was proof enough that they had done nothing illegal.

The Clayton Antitrust Act

For the first time since before the Civil War, the Democrats finally sat in the driver's seat, with Woodrow Wilson occupying the White House and a Democratic majority in both houses of Congress. In 1914 they passed two laws aimed at bolstering the Sherman Act by specifically outlawing all the bad business practices that continued to go unpunished.

The Clayton Act prohibited practices that lessened competition or tended to create a monopoly.

The Clayton Antitrust Act prohibited five business practices when their effect was to "substantially lessen competition or tend to create a monopoly."

1. *Price discrimination.* This was introduced in the chapter, "Monopolistic Competition," using the examples of airlines charging half fare to teenagers, doctors charging widely varying rates based on patients' incomes, and the grades A, B, and C set up by A&P. Generally, the courts have not held price discrimination to be illegal.

2. *Interlocking stockholding.* This occurs when one firm buys the stock of another. Although this goes on every day, on occasion the courts will find it illegal. In the 1950s, Du Pont, together with Christiana Securities, both controlled by the Du Pont family, were forced to sell the huge block of General Motors stock they had accumulated.[4] The question is whether a stock acquisition is deemed to lessen competition.

3. *Interlocking directorates.* It is expressly forbidden for a person who is a director of one corporation to sit on the board of another corporation that is in the same industry. This obvious conflict of interest could easily be detected as corporate boards are widely published.

4. *Tying contracts.* It is illegal to sell one product on the condition that another product or products be purchased from the same seller. For example, the law prohibits General Electric from telling a buyer it can purchase GE toasters only if it also purchases GE lightbulbs.

5. *Exclusive dealings.* It is illegal to tell a retailer that he or she must not carry some rival firm's product line. For example, Panasonic cannot tell an appliance dealer that if he wants to carry Panasonic televisions and VCRs, he can't also carry Sony and Sharp competing products.

The Federal Trade Commission Act (1914)

FTC as a watchdog

The Federal Trade Commission (FTC) was set up as a watchdog against the anticompetitive practices outlawed by the Sherman and Clayton acts. Although empowered to investigate anticompetitive business practices and issue cease-and-desist orders, the

---

[4]Du Pont bought about 25 percent of General Motors's stock in 1919. Over the next four decades GM bought most of its seat-cover fabrics, paints, and glues from Du Pont. In 1957 the Supreme Court found that other firms had been unfairly excluded from selling paint, glues, and fabrics to GM and forced Du Pont to sell its GM stock.

courts stripped most of its powers by the 1920s. In 1938 the Wheeler-Lea Amendment gave the Federal Trade Commission what has become its most important job: preventing false and deceptive advertising.

In recent years the FTC has been playing a much more active role in approving or disapproving mergers. In 1995 it blocked the proposed merger of the Rite Aid and Revco drugstore chains, contending that the combination would leave millions of consumers with no low-cost outlet for prescription drugs. That same year, it did allow the merger of two pharmaceutical giants, Ciba-Geigy and Sandoz, but only after forcing them to divest themselves of $1 billion in assets to prevent the combined company from dominating several market segments.

When Staples and Office Depot proposed merging in 1997, they agreed to sell hundreds of their stores. Nevertheless the FTC did not approve the deal, arguing that the office supply superstores were a market in themselves, distinct from the much larger market for office goods sold through catalogues, discount chains, and stationery stores.

Another merger that never happened was Barnes & Noble's (the nation's largest bookstore chain) acquisition of the Ingram Book Group, the nation's biggest book wholesaler. The Federal Trade Commission chairman, Robert Pitofsky, voiced concern about the effect on the smaller, independent bookstores, who depended on Ingram for just-in-time delivery. Another concern was whether a new company, as Amazon.com had been in the mid-1990s, could now get started on the Internet if it depended on Ingram, whose new parent, Barnes & Noble, also sold books on the Internet. Barnes & Noble decided to back out of the deal to avoid a protracted legal battle.

Modern Antitrust

We understand that companies have to be of sufficient size and scope to play in the global marketplace.

–Joel Klein,
Chief, U.S. Justice Department
Antitrust Division during Clinton Administration–

Antitrust enforcement evolved over the last century, growing more stringent or lax, depending on the presidential administration as well as the political leanings of the Supreme Court justices and the judges sitting in the lower federal courts. In Europe, enforcement varied from country to country, but with the formation and consolidation of the European Union, a unified approach to antitrust has evolved, especially since 1997.

Partial Breakdown of the Rule of Reason

Keep in mind that the Supreme Court continued to be dominated, right into the 1940s, by a conservative majority who had been appointed by the almost unbroken string of Republican presidents who served from the Civil War to the Great Depression. To ensure that the Sherman Act was not applied too vigorously, the justices developed the "rule of reason" doctrine. First applied in the 1911 *Standard Oil* case and then refined in the 1920 *U.S. Steel* case, the rule prevailed until the Alcoa case of 1945. Until then, you had to be big *and* bad before the Court would find you guilty under Sherman.

The membership of the Supreme Court changed radically during the Roosevelt and Truman administrations, which extended from 1933 to 1953. In a landmark 1945 decision, the Court found that the Aluminum Company of America (Alcoa), which held   Alcoa case
90 percent of the aluminum market, was an illegal monopoly.

The two arguments that Alcoa presented in its defense were rejected. The first, based directly on the rule of reason, was that although it did have a nominal monopoly on aluminum production, it had not intended to exclude competitors and had not, in fact, behaved badly. This argument was rejected by the Court, which noted that the absence of competitors was itself proof of monopolizing.

The second argument advanced by Alcoa was to define the relevant market more broadly than just aluminum. Steel, copper, and even recycled aluminum should be included as well, which would reduce Alcoa's market share from 90 percent to about one-third. This argument, too, was rejected by the Court.

Judge Learned Hand said, "Congress did not condone 'good trusts' and condemn 'bad' ones; it forbade all." A 90 percent share of the market "is enough to constitute a monopoly; it is doubtful whether 60 or 64 percent would be enough, and certainly 33 percent is not."

The Alcoa decision eclipsed the rule of reason.

The *Alcoa* decision appeared to sweep away the last vestiges of the rule of reason, making monopoly itself, and not merely monopolization, illegal. This change was underscored by the fact that Alcoa had been big but hadn't been bad.

The *Alcoa* case represented the high-water mark of antitrust enforcement. Eight years later, in the *Du Pont* case, the defendant was able to use the relevant market argument that Alcoa had unsuccessfully raised. Du Pont and a licensee had 100 percent of the nation's cellophane market (and 75 percent of the market for transparent wrapping material). But the Court accepted the argument that the relevant market included all "flexible packaging materials," such as aluminum foil and waxed paper. Du Pont had only 18 percent of the flexible packaging materials market, which would hardly constitute a monopoly.

The 60 Percent Rule

A firm must be big and bad.

What has apparently evolved from these antitrust decisions is what might be called "the 60 percent rule." Should a firm have a share of at least 60 percent of the relevant market *and* should that firm have behaved badly toward its competitors, it would then be subject to prosecution. However, whether it would be prosecuted would depend on the political and economic outlook of the current administration, and whether it would be found guilty would depend on the outlook of the nine Supreme Court justices.

Two Landmark Cases

AT&T   AT&T was accused of having a monopoly on local phone service (which it could hardly contest) and of making it hard for its long-distance competitors (such as MCI and Sprint) to use its local phone network. In 1984 in exchange for giving up its 22 local phone companies, AT&T was not only allowed to keep its long-distance service, Bell Labs, and Western Electric, but it was allowed to enter the telecommunications-computer field.

Microsoft   Windows, the Microsoft operating system, runs on more than 90 percent of the 100 million PCs sold in the world each year. The Justice Department was concerned that the company would use this virtual monopoly to force computer makers to use software products it might create in the future, further extending that monopoly.

For two decades Microsoft has made computers more powerful and easier to use for millions of consumers by adding more to its program, from point-and-click icons to fax software. But its growing market power has enabled the company to crush competitors, thus eliminating competition and innovation and probably harming consumers. What were once separate products, such as Microsoft's Web browser, Internet Explorer, were pulled in to become features of Microsoft's Windows operating program.

By bundling Internet Explorer with Windows, PC manufacturers were given no choice but to use the Microsoft browser. Netscape's browser, Navigator, which at one time had had 80 percent of the market, saw its market share reduced to just 7 percent by 2002, and that company is now part of AOL Time Warner.

In 1995 Microsoft signed a consent decree with the government that prohibits the company from tying the purchase of one product to another but that does allow it to develop "integrated" products. In 1997 the Justice Department brought suit, contending that Microsoft was violating its consent decree by forcing PC makers to take Internet

Explorer as a condition of licensing Windows. The company contends that Explorer and Windows are not separate products but a single integrated product.

The case bounced back and forth between the Federal District Court and the Federal Court of Appeals, finally resulting in a 2002 settlement between the federal government and Microsoft. Here are the main terms of this settlement:

- Microsoft can add anything it wants to its Windows operating system.
- Microsoft cannot restrict the freedom of PC makers to install non-Microsoft software, and is prohibited from retaliating against PC makers for shipping machines with competing software.
- Microsoft must sell Windows under the same terms to all PC makers.
- Microsoft must disclose technical information of software to rivals so that their products run smoothly on Windows.
- Microsoft cannot retaliate against any software or hardware company for developing software that competes with Microsoft.
- A three-person technical committee with offices on the Microsoft campus will monitor compliance.

European Antitrust

Antitrust enforcement in the European Union is conducted by the European Commission, which not only approves or prohibits mergers between Europe-based corporations, but also plays an increasingly important antitrust role with respect to other corporations doing substantial business in Europe.

In recent years the European Commission has shifted the emphasis in antitrust policy from the fulfillment of legal requirements to an examination of the consequences on competition. In rejecting a combination of Volvo (which produces trucks in addition to its better-known cars) and Scania (another large Swedish truck-maker) announced in 1999, the Commission declared such a merger would dominate the Scandanavian market and hold a virtual monopoly for heavy trucks in Sweden.

In 1997 the Federal Trade Commission approved the merger of Boeing, which builds 60 percent of the world's commercial aircraft, and McDonnell Douglas, whose market share had shrunk to just under 10 percent (the remaining 30 percent is built by Airbus Industrie, the European consortium). One reservation the FTC had concerning the merger was Boeing's 20-year contracts to be sole supplier of new jets to American, Delta, and Continental airlines. The European Commission, which is the executive arm of the 25-nation European Union, considered these supply arrangements a threat to the survival of Airbus, and was set to reject the merger.

How, you may ask, can these European guys reject a merger between two American firms? Although the Commission could not technically block the deal, it could make it difficult for Boeing-McDonnell to do business in Europe by imposing fines of up to 10 percent of the company's worldwide revenues. One day before the Commission was to vote, Boeing-McDonnell blinked. It agreed to alter its use of the exclusive aircraft supply contracts.

In 1998 the European Commission, along with antitrust regulators in Australia and Canada, apparently forced the cancellation of an announced merger between two Big Six accounting firms, Ernst & Young and KPMG Peat Marwick. One of the concerns was that the merger would lead to the layoff of thousands of employees, this at a time of high unemployment in Europe.

Another deal that was blocked by the European Commission in 2000 was between Time Warner and EMI Group of Britain. This was to be a joint venture that would have created a giant in the music business—one with more than 2,500 musicians, including superstars like David Bowie and the Rolling Stones and accounting for more than 2,000 new albums a year. The commission thought that the Warner-EMI monolith could strangle Internet access by leveraging its media assets, especially in music. The more AOL Time Warner makes its music available online, the more Europeans become dependent on the

Americans for their Net-delivered entertainment. Also, other music companies may be forced to offer their wares on AOL's network to reach customers.

In 2004 the European Commission ruled that Microsoft had broken European Union law by using its "near monopoly" to squeeze out software rivals. In addition to paying a fine of $613 million, Microsoft was ordered to share details of its Windows operating system with rival software competitors allowing them to build programs that could work with Windows.

The Commission threatened to fine Microsoft over $2 million a day if it did not provide sufficient source code and technical support to ensure that the data-serving software made by rivals could work as easily with Microsoft's desktop operating system as Microsoft's server software does. In April 2006, Microsoft appealed the fine in the European Court of First Instance; a decision was not expected until sometime in 2007.

Types of Mergers

Horizontal mergers

Horizontal Mergers

A horizontal merger is the conventional merger. Two firms in the same industry form one larger company. Usually a larger firm swallows a smaller one. When John D. Rockefeller was running Standard Oil, he swallowed 39 competing firms.

Horizontal integration has become particularly prevalent among the airlines, oil companies, banks, and companies in the communications field. The legal problem with horizontal mergers is that they appear to violate the Sherman Act. Two competing firms that merge may well lessen competition. The question is, Where do the Justice Department and the courts draw the line? If the number-two firm merges with the number-three firm, does this lessen competition? The answer depends on the makeup of the administration at the time, which may vary from the relatively restrictive Roosevelt and Truman administrations to the relatively permissive Reagan administration, as well as on the makeup of the courts, which see personnel shifts as justices retire and presidents appoint new ones. In 1999, when the number-one and number-two oil companies, Exxon and Mobil, announced their plans to merge, there was scarcely a peep out of the Antitrust Division of the Clinton administration's Justice Department.

Vertical mergers

Vertical Mergers

When firms that have been engaged in different parts of an industrial process or in manufacturing and selling join together, we have a vertical merger. A maker of TVs and stereos that bought out a retail chain and marketed its TVs and stereos through this new outlet would be an example. If an auto company merged with a steel mill, a tire company, or a glass manufacturer, we would have a vertically integrated company.

Janet Lowe described this process in the entertainment field:

> The purchase of the entertainment giant MCA by Matsushita and Columbia
> Pictures by Sony represented an effort to complete a vertical structure by these two
> companies. They already produce much of the high-technology equipment used in
> the entertainment industry; the companies wanted to add to that the technology of
> programming that was transmitted by their own equipment.[5]

Walt Disney's 1995 acquisition of the ABC network provided Disney with a ready market in which to show its made-for-TV films. Similarly, the 1989 purchase of Time Inc.

---

[5]Janet Lowe, *The Secret Empire: How 25 Multinationals Rule the World* (Burr Ridge, IL: Business One Irwin, 1992), p. 65.

by Warner Communications (originally known as Warner Brothers, the filmmaker) gave it Time's book list, from which it has been making movies.

Despite some spectacularly large vertical mergers in recent years, including the largest in American corporate history—AOL and Time Warner, vertical mergers have generally not worked out too well, and appear to be losing their popularity. The AOL Time Warner vision of combining editorial content and Internet services under the same corporate roof has turned out to be an expensive folly. Nor have other media mergers based on the same theory, such as Disney's acquisition of ABC, done all that well.

Back in the great industrial age of the last quarter of the 19th century, manufacturers needed to control every aspect of their businesses—the acquisition of raw materials, shipping, manufacturing, and marketing—in order to assure reliability. But today that's no longer necessary. It's more flexible and efficient to specialize in one activity and then buy from or sell to a number of outside companies. So what we can look forward to is fewer and fewer vertical mergers.

Conglomerate Mergers

Two companies in unrelated fields

A conglomerate merger occurs between two companies in unrelated industries—telephones and hotels, real estate and auto parts, oil and steel. A conglomerate, the product of such mergers, is a group of unrelated companies under one corporate umbrella. The term comes from the Latin *conglomeraré,* meaning "to roll together."

The huge wave of conglomerate mergers in the 1960s was the cutting edge of the long-term trend toward corporate concentration. About 80 percent of the mergers during that decade were of the conglomerate variety. Firms that were minuscule in the 1950s became corporate giants over the course of 10 or 15 years.

Conglomerating has several advantages. In addition to providing ready-made markets for the goods and services produced by various divisions, the very diversity of the company is insurance against economic adversity. A downturn in one industry will not hurt too much because the firm is diversified into many industries. A strike in one component firm or division will shut down only a small part of the entire conglomerate because virtually all unions are organized along industry or craft lines. For example, if the Screen Actors Guild (Ronald Reagan was its first president) went on strike, Viacom, which owns Paramount, would hardly notice.

The king of conglomerates today is General Electric, a mix of manufacturing, finance, and broadcasting, including NBC. Although General Electric is considered one of the nation's best-run corporations, conglomeration sometimes does not work out well. The companies do not mesh, and inefficiencies often result. Despite the advantages of conglomeration, by the 1980s there were very few conglomerate mergers. It had been found that highly diversified companies were hard to manage, and there was a strong trend toward de-diversification through the 1980s and 1990s, as conglomerates spun off divisions and concentrated on their core businesses.

Deregulation

In the late 1970s a consensus had formed among government and corporate officials that regulations were holding down economic growth. Under Presidents Jimmy Carter and Ronald Reagan, regulations were cut back and government fiat was largely supplanted by the market forces of demand and supply.

Ronald Reagan spoke to the frustrations of millions of people who ran businesses of all sizes when he said back in 1980 that he would "get the government off the backs of the American people." Reagan estimated that American businesses spent upwards of $100 billion a year just to follow all the federal rules and regulations and to employ people to fill out all the required forms. Did he succeed in cutting the red tape? Not really, inasmuch as the pile of paperwork imposed by the federal government is now

Deregulation: The Record Since the Late 1970s

Under the administrations of Jimmy Carter and Ronald Reagan, a great deal of deregulation took place in banking, the airlines, long-distance trucking, and long-distance phone calling. In banking, the country ended up with the savings and loan debacle (discussed in Chapter 13 of *Economics* and *Macroeconomics*), costing American taxpayers almost $300 billion. But the effects of deregulation in the other industries have been much more salutary.

Until the passage of the Airline Deregulation Act in 1978, the Civil Aeronautics Board controlled fares, assigned routes, and controlled industry entry. Indeed, no new carriers had been permitted to enter major interstate routes since the board's creation in 1938. But by the early 1980s, the airlines were free to set their own prices and select their own routes. Perhaps a victim of its own success, deregulation accelerated the increasing volume of air traffic, resulting in greater delays and the possibility of more midair collisions. Although the industry is still in flux after a series of bankruptcies and mergers, labor productivity is up sharply, costs have been cut, and airfares have dropped by about a third, on an inflation-adjusted basis. However, they have risen substantially on routes of less than 750 miles.

Before deregulation, the Interstate Commerce Commission sometimes forced truckers to take roundabout routes and to return with empty trucks from long hauls. According to *The Economist,* "America's trucking industry was a cosy, regulated semi-cartel, with a few big companies dominating most regions." But after deregulation in the early 1980s, hundreds of thousands of small firms went into business, as the number of trucking firms shot up from 10,000 to 45,000. Most important for consumers, shipping prices dropped.*

You're probably not old enough to remember when, in the early 1980s, AT&T still had a monopoly on all phone calls—local *and* long distance. The 1984 breakup of AT&T left it with its long-distance business, but the regional Baby Bells spun off into independent companies that handle local and intrastate (within a state) calls.

---

*The Economist, June 3, 2000, p. 66.

higher than ever. The box, "Deregulation: The Record Since the Late 1970s" discusses the effects of the deregulation of three major industries—the airlines, long-distance trucking, and long-distance phone calling.[6]

At this juncture the results of deregulation have been quite good. Clearly prices have been held down by competition among the long-haul trucking firms, the long-distance phone companies, and the airlines. But fierce competition has driven several major airline carriers out of business and in the four years since 9/11 the airlines have lost a total of $32 billion.

Corporate Misconduct

Beware of false profits.

Corporate stockholders, employees, creditors, and customers have long assumed that our corporate leaders run their companies efficiently and honestly. They expected audited corporate financial statements to provide an accurate picture of each firm's sales, costs, profits, and financial viability. But when dishonest officials at firms like Enron (at the time, the nation's seventh largest company), WorldCom, Global Crossing, and Arthur Andersen (recently one the world's largest CPA firms) knowingly cheat and lie, the public begins to lose its confidence in the integrity of *all* corporations.

We have seen executives make hundreds of millions of dollars selling stock before their companies collapsed, as did Enron's chief executive officer, Kenneth Lay (nicknamed "Kenny Boy," by his old friend, President George W. Bush). They were not selling shares on which they had risked their *own* money. Most got shares from stock options, and some were given shares by their companies only weeks

---

[6]The railroads (1976–80) and the natural gas industry (1978) were also deregulated. In Chapter 13 (of *Economics* and *Macroeconomics*) we talked about the disastrous effects of deregulation on the savings and loan industry.

before they dumped them on public investors. Compounding the injustice at Enron, the company invested virtually all of its employees' pension funds in Enron stock, which became worthless in just a few months. Meanwhile Arthur Andersen, which was responsible for auditing the books, gave Enron repeated clean bills of financial health. Later Andersen was found guilty of obstruction of justice for shredding Enron-related documents, and was, like Enron, forced into bankruptcy (see the box, "The Scorecard for Scandal").

In an editorial *BusinessWeek* explained why corporate corruption hurts not just employees and stockholders, but our entire economy.

> The truth is economists don't usually compute the tax that is imposed on economic growth by corruption. They should. In the past few years, we have witnessed conflicts of interest and manipulation within the initial public offering, mutual-fund, investment banking, and insurance markets. These rigged markets stifle innovation, erode discipline in the markets, channel money into less productive activities, add expense, and undermine national competitiveness.[7]

How Effective Is Antitrust?

What do we want antitrust to do? If we want to create something approximating perfect competition, antitrust has failed miserably. If we would like to prevent further oligopolization of American industry, it has been a qualified success. *How* qualified?

Well, things could have been a lot worse. Without antitrust, there would have been no legal means for the government to curb even those mergers that most blatantly stifled competition. Furthermore, many firms hesitate to merge because they are fairly certain the Justice Department *would* take legal action.

What do we want antitrust to do?

Things could have been a lot worse without antitrust.

The Trend toward Bigness

One of the refreshing things about economics is that we can all look at exactly the same data and come to widely varying conclusions. One view is that economic competition has grown in recent years for three reasons. First, there's much more foreign competition. However, as huge foreign firms buy up American firms (we'll talk about this in the final chapter, "International Finance") or squeeze them out of business, we may end up with *less* competition than we had before the foreign firms began competing. The second reason is the declining importance of manufacturing (which is dominated by relatively large firms) relative to the service industries (where smaller firms prevail); this makes for a lot more competition. And third, the rise of new industries, such as production of microcomputers and computer software, has created many small, highly competitive firms.

All that said, as you can see in Table 1, 8 of the 10 largest mergers in U.S. history took place in 1998, 1999, and 2000. Six of these were in communications. All these mergers are part of a worldwide trend which shows no sign of slowing. Table 2 lists the world's largest mergers, including those involving American corporations.

Since every one of the companies listed in Tables 1 and 2 does business in many different countries, the distinction between American and foreign companies is becoming blurred. For example, we think of Honda and Toyota as Japanese firms, but they make a lot of their cars here—and in other countries as well. Two of the largest corporations in Canada are General Motors and Ford. The term for a firm that does business in many different countries is *multinational*. Perhaps in the not-too-distant future virtually all large

[7]"The High Cost of Corruption," *BusinessWeek*, November 29, 2004, p. 156.

The Scorecard for Scandal

As in baseball, it's sometimes hard to identify all the corporate crooks without a scorecard. Here's a very brief summary of whose been accused of doing what.

their shares before the price plunged to virtually zero. As of November 2003, 14 executives of HealthSouth agreed to plead guilty of conspiring to overstate earnings by

The Corporate Cheat Sheet

Company	Primary Allegations
Enron	Fraudently inflated financial results; conspiracy; money laundering
WorldCom	Fraud; improper profiting from IPOs; inappropriate company loans; conspiracy
Xerox	Fraudulently inflated financial results to profit from bonuses and stock sales
Adelphia	Fraud; misuse of corporate funds by founding family
Tyco	Tax evasion; misuse of company funds to inflate stock value; inappropriate company loans
ImClone	Insider trading; tax evasion; obstructing justice
Qwest	Improperly profited from IPOs; fraudulently inflated financial results
Global Crossing	Fraudulently inflated financial results; cashed in stock just before bankruptcy
HealthSouth	Fraudulently inflated financial results; conspiracy
Investment banks	Abuse of conflicts of interest
AIG	Used misleading accounting techniques to artificially bolster profits
KPMG	Tax-shelter fraud

Source: The Economist, June 28, 2003, p. 7; www.marketwatch.com.

What's the common thread running through all these charges? It's that the people running these companies used their insider knowledge for ill-gained profits. Saul Waksal, who headed ImClone, sold a huge bloc of his stock (and possibly alerted his friend, Martha Stewart, to sell her much smaller holdings), when he learned that an experimental drug his company produced to fight cancer would not be approved by the Federal Drug Administration. Sentencing Waksal to seven years in prison, Judge William H. Pauley III told him: "You abused your position of trust as chief executive officer of a major corporation and undermined the public's confidence in the integrity of the financial markets. Then you tried to lie your way out of it, showing a complete disregard for the firm administration of justice."

Several officers of Enron conspired to artificially inflate profits, pushing up the stock price, and then selling

about $2.5 billion to keep its stock price from collapsing. On the other side of the ledger, WorldCom officials managed to hide $3.8 billion in expenses.

As of April 1, 2006, here's the lineup of the corporate criminals drawing the longest sentences:

- Bernard Ebbers, former CEO of WorldCom, received a 25-year jail sentence for his role in an $11 billion accounting fraud.

- Jamie Olis, a Dynergy executive, got a 24-year jail sentence for devising a scheme to falsify his company's books.

- John Rigas got 20 years in prison, and his son, Timothy Rigas, got 15 years for looting hundreds of millions of dollars from Adelphia.

- Andrew Fastow received a 10-year sentence for disguising Enron's poor financial health and scheming to defraud the company.

corporations will be considered multinationals, and no one will bother mentioning their national origin.

Within this context one may begin to question the relevance of monopoly and antitrust enforcement. Because the markets are global, few companies are reaching the size and scale

TABLE 1	The Largest U.S. Corporate Mergers and Acquisitions		
Acquirer	Acquisition	Year	Value of Transaction in $ Billions
AOL (America Online)	Time Warner	2000	$183
Pfizer	Warner-Lambert	2000	90
Exxon	Mobil	1999	86
Travelers Group	Citicorp	1998	73
SBC	Ameritech	1998	72
Comcast	AT&T Broadband	2001	72
Bell Atlantic	GTE	1998	71
AT&T	Tele-Communications	1999	70
AT&T	BellSouth	2006	67
NationsBank	Bank America	1998	62
Pfizer	Pharmacia	2001	61
British Petroleum	Amoco	1998	59
JP Morgan Chase	Bank One Corp	2004	59
Qwest Communications	U.S. West	1999	56
Procter & Gamble	Gillette	2005	55
AT&T	MediaOne Group	2000	52

Source: Securities Data Corp.; *The World Almanac,* 2003; *The Wall Street Journal,* March 6, 2006, p. C1.

TABLE 2	The Largest Worldwide Corporate Mergers and Acquisitions		
Acquirer	Acquisition	Date Announced	Value ($ Billions)
Vodafone AirTouch	Mannesmann	2000	$203
America Online (AOL)	Time Warner	2000	183
Pfizer	Warner-Lambert	2000	90
Exxon	Mobil	1999	86
Glaxco Wellcome	SmithKline Beecham	2000	76
Royal Dutch Petroleum	Shell Transport & Trading	2004	74
Travelers Group	Citicorp	1998	73
SBC	Ameritech	1998	72
Comcast	AT&T Broadband	2001	72
Bell Atlantic	GTE	1998	71
AT&T	Tele-Communications	1999	70

Source: Thompson Financial Securities Data.

that should cause concern about monopolies. And how does one nation—even one with the economic clout of the United States—enforce its antitrust laws in the global marketplace?

Current Issue: The Enron Case

The corporate scandals of the early years of the new millennium culminated in the mother of all trials, which began the first week of February 2006. Ken Lay, who had been affectionately nicknamed Kenny Boy by his former friend, President George W. Bush, and Jeffrey Skilling, both former Enron chief executive officers, stood trial for fraud and conspiracy. The Justice Department had already obtained 16 guilty pleas from former Enron managers. Most were awaiting sentencing and stood ready to bear witness against Skilling and Lay.

Enron, the nation's seventh largest corporation, fell into bankruptcy during the last few months of 2001. Tens of thousands of employees lost not just their jobs, but their pensions as well, since they were invested mainly in worthless Enron stock. Did Lay and Skilling, both of whom sold off millions of shares, do so because they had inside knowledge of the impending bankruptcy? And while they were selling their stock, why were they telling stock analysts that the company was doing just great?

Several former Enron employees, most notably chief financial officer, Andrew Fastow, testified against Lay and Skilling, claiming that the two were well aware that the company had not only falsified its true financial condition, but that they actively encouraged these practices. Large losses were hidden to prevent the price of Enron's stock from falling, while, as it turns out, Lay and Skilling were selling off their holdings. But the defendants claimed that the company was truly in great shape, and that if not for Fastow's financial machinations, and the disparaging news articles printed in the *Wall Street Journal,* Enron would not have gone bankrupt. In addition, they argued, except for Fastow, who faced a 10-year prison sentence for, among other crimes, stealing $45 million from the company, most of the other 15 former officials had been forced by government prosecutors to admit committing crimes they had not committed, and had testified at this trial in exchange for shorter prison sentences.

On May 25, 2006, after a 56-day trial, a 12-person jury found both defendents guilty. Jeffrey Skilling was convicted of 18 counts of fraud and conspiracy and one count of insider trading, while Kenneth Lay was found guilty on six counts of fraud and conspiracy and four counts of bank fraud. The jurors, who were all interviewed by reporters immediately after delivering their verdict, said they had been persuaded that Lay and Skilling had perpetuated a far-reaching fraud by lying to investors and employees about Enron's performance. After posting millions of dollars in bail, the two remained free while awaiting sentencing on September 11, 2006. They faced a prison term of perhaps 10 years or more, and were expected to appeal the verdict.

While awaiting sentencing, Kenneth Lay died suddenly of coronary artery disease. His codefendant, Jeffrey Skilling, also awaiting sentencing, was expected to serve a long prison sentence.

Questions for Further Thought and Discussion

1. How effective is antitrust?

2. Trace the strength of the corporate merger movement since the early 1980s.

3. What was the historical and political background against which the Sherman Antitrust Act was passed?

4. Trace the use of the rule of reason since it was first applied in the *U.S. Steel* case.

5. Should the antitrust authorities stop more corporate mergers than they currently do? What are some of the pros and cons?

6. Suppose a proposed merger will simultaneously lessen competition and reduce unit costs through economies of scale. Do you think such a merger should be allowed?

7. Do you think the size of a firm's market share or its conduct is the more reasonable basis for antitrust regulation? Explain your answer.

8. Do you think Microsoft should be broken up into two or even three separate corporations? Give at least two reasons to support your conclusion.

9. Use the example of any industry to support the argument that the global economy is making monopoly and antitrust enforcement irrelevant.

10. Has deregulation been successful? Use examples of two industries to support your answer.

Workbook for Chapter 25

Name _____   Date _____

Multiple-Choice Questions

Circle the letter that corresponds to the best answer.

1. The Microsoft case ended with _____.
   a) a clear-cut win for the federal government
   b) a compromise settlement between Microsoft and the federal government
   c) a guilty plea by Microsoft, but no breakup of the company
   d) an abandonment of the case by the federal government

2. The first trustbusters were Presidents _____.
   a) Teddy Roosevelt and William Howard Taft
   b) Franklin Roosevelt and Harry Truman
   c) Dwight D. Eisenhower and John Kennedy
   d) Jimmy Carter and Ronald Reagan

3. A key passage of the _____ Act stated that "every contract, combination in the form of trust or otherwise, in restraint of commerce among the several states, or with foreign nations, is hereby declared illegal."
   a) Clayton
   c) U.S. Communications
   b) FTC
   d) Sherman

4. The trusts won only the _____ case.
   a) AT&T
   c) American Tobacco
   b) U.S. Steel
   d) Standard Oil

5. In 1911 the Supreme Court decided to _____.
   a) allow the trusts to keep functioning as they had in the past
   b) break up the trusts
   c) let the trusts off with small fines
   d) put the leaders of the trusts in jail

6. Until the *Alcoa* case, the Supreme Court generally held that _____.
   a) bigness was all right as long as the company wasn't bad
   b) bigness was all right under any circumstances
   c) a company could do as it pleased as long as it wasn't big

7. The Supreme Court's rule of reason was applied _____.
   a) from the time of the Civil War
   b) from 1911 to 1945
   c) after 1945
   d) after 1970

8. The high-water mark of antitrust enforcement was marked by the _____ case.
   a) *Alcoa*
   c) *Du Pont*
   b) *U.S. Steel*
   d) *Microsoft*

9. The Clayton Antitrust Act prohibited each of the following except _____.
   a) price discrimination
   b) interlocking stockholding
   c) interlocking directorates
   d) trusts

10. The most important job of the Federal Trade Commission today is to _____.
    a) prevent false and deceptive advertising
    b) break up unlawful trusts
    c) issue cease-and-desist orders when anticompetitive business practices occur
    d) promote commerce with foreign nations

11. The rule of reason today is _____.
    a) outlawed
    b) partially in force
    c) completely irrelevant

12. Antitrust today could best be summed up by the
_____.

   a) 90 percent rule
   b) 60 percent rule
   c) rule of reason
   d) one-year rule

13. Which would be the most accurate statement?

   a) The honesty of our corporate leaders is beyond question.
   b) Most corporate leaders are dishonest.
   c) Even if a corporation "cooks" its books, the CPA firm it hires to audit its books will quickly find out and blow the whistle.
   d) Enron was not the only American corporation in recent years to be guilty of corporate misconduct.

14. The merger between Exxon and Mobil was subject to antitrust regulation by _____.

   a) the Justice Department only
   b) the European Commission only
   c) both the Justice Department and the European Commission
   d) neither the Justice Department nor the European Commission

15. In the 1950s and 1960s the predominant form of merger was the _____ merger.

   a) horizontal
   b) vertical
   c) conglomerate
   d) diversifying

16. Which is the most accurate statement?

   a) Virtually no chief executive officers of large corporations have gone to prison in recent years.
   b) About one-quarter of the chief executive officers of the 500 largest American corporations have either gone to prison, paid large fines, or both.
   c) Although some chief executive officers of large corporations have received prison sentences, none has been longer than three years.
   d) Martha Stewart was the only person to do actual time in prison for corporate crime.
   e) In recent years some corporate executives have received prison sentences of over 5 years.

17. When two firms in the same industry form one larger company, this is a _____ merger.

   a) horizontal
   b) vertical
   c) conglomerate
   d) diversifying

18. Which statement is true?

   a) Conglomerate mergers are all vertical mergers.
   b) General Electric is the largest conglomerate in the United States.
   c) There is no discernable trend toward corporate bigness.
   d) Most of the largest corporate mergers in the world are between firms located outside the United States.

19. Which statement is true?

   a) Microsoft is subject to American antitrust laws, but not those of Europe, Asia, or elsewhere.
   b) Microsoft has never been involved in an antitrust suit.
   c) The European Commission fined Microsoft over $600 billion for its anticompetitive behavior.
   d) Microsoft has always gone out of its way to be helpful to its competitors.

20. Since the early 1980s the size of companies acquired in mergers has been _____.

   a) getting smaller
   b) staying about the same
   c) getting larger

21. In general, the deregulation of the airlines and interstate trucking led to _____.

   a) lower costs and lower prices
   b) higher costs and higher prices
   c) higher costs and lower prices
   d) lower costs and higher prices

22. The acquisitions of Time by Warner and ABC by Walt Disney were examples of _____ mergers.

   a) horizontal
   b) vertical
   c) conglomerate

23. Deregulation of the trucking industry resulted in
_____.

   a) many more firms and lower prices
   b) many more firms and higher prices
   c) fewer firms and lower prices
   d) fewer firms and higher prices

622

24. Which one of the industries listed below has had the largest mergers during the last five years?

a) Steel manufacturing

b) Automobile production

c) Communications

d) Trucking

25. Which one of these statements is false?

a) Most of the largest U.S. corporate mergers and acquisitions have occurred since 1995.

b) The U.S. government has not stopped any mergers from occurring.

c) There have been several large banking mergers in recent years.

d) Virtually all large mergers have transaction values of more than $100 billion.

26. Which statement is true?

a) Most of the largest corporate mergers in our history took place during the period 1998–2000.

b) There have been virtually no large mergers in banking or communications.

c) Nearly all large corporations are conglomerates.

d) Enron continues to be one of our largest corporations.

27. Which is the most accurate statement about the recent corporate scandals?

a) Although the companies involved got some bad publicity, none of the executives had to do jail time.

b) There were only two or three corporations that engaged in illegal behavior.

c) One of the main charges was fraudulently inflated financial results.

d) Virtually all large American corporations were caught in illegal insider dealings.

28. The most common corporate crime is _____.

a) taking advantage of insider knowledge for ill-gained profits

b) embezzlement

c) overstating costs

d) overcharging customers

29. The greatest damage caused by the corporate scandals of the last few years was to _____.

a) the employees of those companies

b) the U.S. Treasury, which was bilked out of billions of tax dollars

c) the customers of those companies

d) the public trust in financial markets

30. Which would be the most accurate statement about the recent wave of corporate corruption?

a) It has hurt employees, stockholders, and, in general, the entire economy.

b) It has actually been very healthy for our economy.

c) It has very little bearing on employees, stockholders, or the economy.

d) None of these statements is accurate.

Fill-In Questions

1. The first trustbuster presidents were _____ and _____.

2. In 1911 the Supreme Court broke up the _____ _____ and the _____.

3. In the late 19th century trusts were formed. They were _____; the largest trust was the _____ _____ trust.

4. "Every person who shall monopolize, or conspire with any other person or persons to monopolize, any part of the trade or commerce of the several states, or with foreign nations, shall be guilty of a misdemeanor" was a key passage of the _____ Act.

5. The first case to be tried under the Sherman Act was the _____ case; the companies were found guilty of _____.

6. In 1911 the Supreme Court broke up the _____ _____ trust into three component parts:
   (1) _____;
   (2) _____;
   and (3) _____.

7. The Supreme Court broke up the trusts in 1911 because they _____.

8. "Bigness was no offense" was the underpinning of the _____.

9. A _____ makes the sale of one product conditional on the purchase of another product or products from the same seller; _____ stipulate that a retailer must not carry some rival firm's product line.

10. Expressly forbidding a person who is a director of one corporation to sit on the board of another corporation in the same industry is a provision of the _____ Act.

11. _____ used the relevant market argument successfully in its case, just eight years after the *Alcoa* case.

12. By the 1950s and 1960s, the most prevalent type of merger was the _____ merger.

13. A vertical merger takes place when two firms that _____ join together, while a horizontal merger takes place when two firms that _____ _____ join together.

14. Had there been no antitrust, there probably would have been _____.

Chapter 26

Demand in the Factor Market

Every few chapters you can hear the gears grinding as we head off in another direction. So buckle up because here we go again. This time we're moving away from how businesses compete to how they manage their resources. In the preceding six chapters we analyzed the behavior of firms as sellers in the market for final goods and services; now we'll analyze how they behave in the market for factors of production.

Chapter 2 was about the factors of production, or resources. In this chapter we'll see how their prices are determined. We'll use the concept of marginal revenue product to determine how many units of a factor will be hired by perfect and imperfect competitors. As we shall see, the law of demand and supply plays a central role.

CHAPTER OBJECTIVES

We'll cover these important topics:

- Derived demand.
- Productivity.
- Marginal revenue product.

- Changes in resource demand.
- The substitution and output effects.
- Optimum resource mix for the firm.

Derived Demand

Demand for goods and services is sometimes called *final demand*. Examples of final demand are the demand for cars, TVs, haircuts, medical services, or gasoline.

Now we'll look at *derived demand*, which is the demand for the resources which are used to produce goods and services. There are four resources: land, labor, capital, and entrepreneurial ability. The demand for these resources is derived from the demand for the final products. For example, the demand for land on which to grow corn is derived from the demand for corn, and the demand for labor with which to produce cars is derived from the demand for cars.

A change in final demand brings about a change in derived demand. The Arab oil embargo and the quadrupling of oil prices in 1973 led to a decline in the demand for large cars. This caused massive layoffs in Detroit. Thus a decline in the demand for the final product, cars, led to a decline in the derived demand for the resource of autoworkers. Simultaneous with the falling demand for American cars, the Russian wheat crop

What is derived demand derived from?

It is not the employer who pays wages—he only handles the money. It is the customer who pays the wages.

—Henry Ford

failed and the Soviet Union made massive purchases of American wheat. This, in turn, drove up the demand for farm labor and farmland in the United States.

Productivity

In addition to the demand for the final product, two other factors influence the demand for the productive resources (land, labor, capital, and entrepreneurial ability). First we'll consider the productivity of the resource and then the relative prices of substitutable resources.

Productivity is output per unit of input.

Productivity is *output per unit of input.* What exactly is meant by *productivity* and *unit of input*? Productivity itself is really measured by how much is produced. "I had a productive night," my friend confided over a plate of lo mein in an all-night Chinese restaurant after a party. "Productive?" I asked. "Sure," he said, "I got 16 phone numbers." That's productive! Especially since he's 84 years old.

What about units of input? Inputs measure the quantities of the four resources—land, labor, capital, and entrepreneurial ability. Thus, a unit of input might be an hour of labor, an acre of land, or an automobile assembly line. We haven't yet figured a way of quantifying entrepreneurial ability.

Let's put these concepts together. Productivity is output per unit of input. If John produces 8 microchips per hour and Sally produces 16, Sally is twice as productive as John. If 30 bushels of wheat are harvested from acre one and 10 bushels from acre two, acre one is three times as productive as acre two.

The more productive a resource is, the more it will be in demand. Obviously, acre one is in much greater demand than is acre two. This would be reflected in both their prices and their rents. Similarly, Sally can obtain much higher wages than John because she is so much more productive.

Prices of Substitute Resources

A given good or service can usually be produced in many different ways. The producer can use various combinations of resources. The Chinese, for example, didn't have many capital goods available a few decades ago, so when they built a factory they used a very labor-intensive method of construction. Thousands of workers dug the hole for the foundation, carting off the dirt in wicker baskets. In the United States, where we have a great deal of capital equipment, we use a capital-intensive method of production. Bulldozers and other earth-moving equipment get the job done with much less labor.

Every country uses the cheapest production method.

In each country the cheapest production method available is used. Ethiopia happens to be a labor-intensive country because capital is relatively expensive. In the United States we use a capital-intensive method because labor is relatively expensive.

Photocopy machines are so expensive in Ethiopia that you won't find them in many neighborhood stores, and they certainly aren't standard equipment in home offices. Suppose you need to send out 50 copies of your résumé. Will you type out each copy or type one and photocopy the rest? Figure it out. Do you type individual résumés when you're looking for a job, or do you get a hundred photocopied or offset for 5 cents apiece? If the wage rate were just 10 or 15 cents an hour—as it still is in some of the poorer countries of the world—you'd be typing your résumés.

When wages rise, many companies seek to substitute machinery for relatively expensive labor. By automating, they will be able to lower their costs of production. If land became more expensive, farmers would work each acre much more intensively, substituting labor and capital for relatively more expensive land.

The demand for a resource is its marginal revenue product schedule. After we see how this schedule is derived, we'll return to our discussion of the determinants of the demand for a resource and how changes in those determinants change that demand.

The Concept of Margin in Economic Analysis

We discussed diminishing returns in Chapter 16 of *Economics* and *Macroeconomics*. If you were to glance back at that section, you'd see that the marginal physical product we're computing here is identical to the marginal output we computed there.

Indeed, all of our marginal concepts—marginal physical product, marginal output, marginal cost, marginal revenue, and the soon-to-be-introduced marginal revenue product—are cut from the same cloth, so to speak. Let's define each.

- Marginal output, or marginal physical product, is the additional output produced by one more unit of a resource.

- Marginal cost is the cost of producing one additional unit of output.
- Marginal revenue is the additional revenue for selling one more unit of output.
- Marginal revenue product is the additional revenue obtained by selling the output produced by one more unit of a resource.

The concept of margin is central to economic analysis. These marginal concepts enable us to figure out exactly what mix of resources we should use, what output we should produce, and what price we should charge in order to maximize our profits—which remains, of course, our bottom line.

Marginal Revenue Product (MRP)

The demand for resources is derived mainly from the demand for the final product. Resource productivity and the relative prices of substitutable resources also help determine price. Now we're ready to see how a firm decides how much of a resource to purchase.

How much of a resource a firm will purchase depends on three things: (1) the price of that resource, (2) the productivity of that resource, and (3) the selling price of the final product that the resource helps to produce. We'll go through a few numerical examples to find out how much land, labor, and capital will be purchased by a firm. Along the way, we'll introduce three new terms: *marginal physical product, marginal revenue product,* and *marginal revenue product schedule*. The last is the firm's demand schedule for a given resource. (See the Advanced Work box, "The Concept of Margin in Economic Analysis.")

How much of a resource is purchased depends on three things.

Table 1 has an output schedule for a firm that is using up to 10 units of labor. Fill in the column for marginal physical product. Do it in ink so we can sell a lot of new books. Just treat marginal physical product as you've treated marginal cost and marginal

TABLE 1	Hypothetical Output of Labor Hired by a Firm

Units of Labor	Output	Marginal Physical Product
1	15	_____
2	29	_____
3	41	_____
4	51	_____
5	58	_____
6	62	_____
7	63	_____
8	63	_____
9	62	_____
10	60	_____

Productivity and Marginal Physical Product

The relationship between productivity and marginal physical product, or marginal output, could stand some clarification. Suppose a machine operator produces 100 units per hour. That's her productivity. A second machine operator is hired. If their combined output is 198, then their average productivity is 99 (198/2 = 99).

We can also say that the marginal output, or marginal physical product, of the second worker is 98. However, we're not saying that the second worker is not as productive as the first worker, but just that if a second worker were added, output would rise by 98.

TABLE 2	Hypothetical Output of Labor Hired by a Firm	
Units of Labor	Output	Marginal Physical Product
1	15	15
2	29	14
3	41	12
4	51	10
5	58	7
6	62	4
7	63	1
8	63	0
9	62	−1
10	60	−2

revenue. Marginal physical product is simply the additional output produced by one more unit of input (in this case, one more unit of labor).[1]

I hope your marginal physical product schedule checks out with mine in Table 2. Notice that the marginal physical product is zero with the 8th worker and negative with the 9th and 10th workers. The 8th worker adds nothing to output, while the 9th and 10th workers are in the way. No business firm would hire more than seven workers under these circumstances, even if the wage rate were a penny an hour. (For extra help, see the box, "Productivity and Marginal Physical Product.")

Table 3 has a column for price. Why is it always the same no matter how large output is? Because in this case we're dealing with a perfect competitor. In a few pages we'll work with imperfect competitors.

Go ahead and fill in the third column of Table 3. That should be a cinch for you by this time. Now for the fifth column, total revenue product. Try your luck on this one.

Let's check your methodology. Did you multiply output (column 2) by price (column 4)? If you did, you definitely got total revenue product (column 5) right because it's pretty hard to multiply a number by 10 and get the wrong answer.

Oh yes, I almost forgot! How do we find marginal revenue product? First, we'll define it. MRP is *the additional revenue obtained by selling the output produced by one more unit of a resource.* To find MRP, just take the difference in total revenue product between

MRP is the additional revenue obtained by selling the output produced by one more unit of a resource.

---

[1]You'll notice that the second worker adds less to output than the first worker, and that the third adds less to output than the second. Why? Diminishing returns is why. If you're really interested in the whys and wherefores of diminishing returns, this topic was discussed toward the end of Chapter 16 of *Economics* and *Macroeconomics*.

| TABLE 3 | Hypothetical Marginal Revenue Product Schedule |

(1) Units of Land	(2) Output	(3) Marginal Physical Product	(4) Price	(5) Total Revenue Product	(6) Marginal Revenue Product
1	20	____	$10	____	____
2	38	____	10	____	____
3	53	____	10	____	____
4	65	____	10	____	____
5	73	____	10	____	____
6	78	____	10	____	____
7	80	____	10	____	____
8	80	____	10	____	____
9	79	____	10	____	____

| TABLE 4 | Hypothetical Marginal Revenue Product Schedule |

(1) Units of Land	(2) Output	(3) Marginal Physical Product	(4) Price	(5) Total Revenue Product	(6) Marginal Revenue Product
1	20	20	$10	$200	$200
2	38	18	10	380	180
3	53	15	10	530	150
4	65	12	10	650	120
5	73	8	10	730	80
6	78	5	10	780	50
7	80	2	10	800	20
8	80	0	10	800	0
9	79	−1	10	790	−10

units of land. We'll start with the first unit of land; it produces a total revenue product of $200. Because zero units of land produce no revenue, the MRP of the first unit of land is $200. How about the second unit of land? Just take the total revenue produced by two units of land and subtract the total revenue produced by one unit of land. And so forth. After you've done that for all nine units, check your results with those in Table 4.

You may have noticed that you can also find MRP by multiplying marginal physical product by price. In Table 4, one unit of land has MRP of 20 and a price of $10 (20 × $10 = MRP of $200). The second unit of land has MRP of 18 and a price of $10 (18 × $10 = $180). Can you use this shortcut to find MRP? You can when you're finding the MRP of the perfect competitor. But in another couple of pages we'll be finding the MRP of the imperfect competitor. To do that you'll have to use our original method—taking differences in total revenue product produced by additional units of a resource.

Now we're ready to do some marginal analysis using Table 4. How many units of land would you hire if you needed to pay $200 rent per unit? Think about it. How much is that land worth to you? The answer lies in the MRP schedule, which is the firm's demand schedule for land.

OK, time's up. You'd hire just one unit of land because only that first unit is worth $200. Sorry if you missed that one, but don't despair. I'll give you another chance.

Let's do some marginal analysis.

TABLE 5	Hypothetical MRP Schedule				
(1) Units of Land	(2) Output	(3) Marginal Physical Product	(4) Price	(5) Total Revenue Product	(6) Marginal Revenue Product
1	18	——	$12	——	——
2	34	——	12	——	——
3	48	——	12	——	——
4	59	——	12	——	——
5	68	——	12	——	——
6	74	——	12	——	——
7	77	——	12	——	——
8	78	——	12	——	——

TABLE 6	Hypothetical MRP Schedule of the Perfect Competitor				
(1) Units of Land	(2) Output	(3) Marginal Physical Product	(4) Price	(5) Total Revenue Product	(6) Marginal Revenue Product
1	18	18	$12	$216	$216
2	34	16	12	408	192
3	48	14	12	576	168
4	59	11	12	708	132
5	68	9	12	816	108
6	74	6	12	888	72
7	77	3	12	924	36
8	78	1	12	936	12

How many units of land would you hire if the rent were $150? Go back to the MRP schedule. What do you say? Three units? Did you say three units? If you did, then you may proceed to the next plateau.

Careful now. How many units of land would you hire if its price were $90? Assume the land is indivisible. That means you can't subdivide it. OK, what's your answer? Four units? Five units? Sorry, only one guess to a customer. The answer is: four units. Why not five? Because the fifth unit of land is worth only $80 according to your own MRP schedule. Would you shell out $90 for something worth only $80 to you? I hope you wouldn't.

Let's work out one more MRP schedule. Fill in Table 5, and then check your work with the figures in Table 6.

One last question: Is the firm whose MRP schedule is shown in Table 6 a perfect competitor or an imperfect competitor? The envelope, please. The answer is: The firm is a perfect competitor. How do we know? We know because the firm can sell its entire output at the same price—$12.

How many workers would you hire if the wage rate were $72? And how much would your firm's wage bill be? You would hire six workers and your firm's wage bill would be $432. Next set of questions: How many workers would you hire if the wage rate were $144 and what would your firm's wage bill come to? You would hire three workers and your wage bill would be $432.

TABLE 7 Hypothetical MRP Schedule

(1) Units of Land	(2) Output	(3) Marginal Physical Product	(4) Price	(5) Total Revenue Product	(6) Marginal Revenue Product
1	18	18	$12	——	——
2	34	16	11	——	——
3	48	14	10	——	——
4	59	11	9	——	——
5	68	9	8	——	——
6	74	6	7	——	——
7	77	3	6	——	——
8	78	1	5	——	——

TABLE 8 Hypothetical MRP Schedule of the Imperfect Competitor

(1) Units of Land	(2) Output	(3) Marginal Physical Product	(4) Price	(5) Total Revenue Product	(6) Marginal Revenue Product
1	18	18	$12	$216	$216
2	34	16	11	374	158
3	48	14	10	480	106
4	59	11	9	531	51
5	68	9	8	544	13
6	74	6	7	518	−26
7	77	3	6	462	−56
8	78	1	5	390	−72

The MRP of the Imperfect Competitor

How do we distinguish between the perfect competitor and the imperfect competitor? Suppose we compare the demand curve of the perfect competitor with those of the monopolist, the monopolistic competitor, and the oligopolist. While the perfect competitor has a horizontal demand curve, the demand curves of the others slope downward to the right. A horizontal demand curve reflects the fact that the firm can sell its entire output at a constant price. A downwardly sloping demand curve means the firm must continually lower its price to sell more and more output.

We're concerned here with how a downwardly sloping demand curve for the final product affects the demand for resources. In Table 7 we have the same outputs and marginal physical products as in Table 6, but instead of a constant price, it lowers as output increases. This reflects the downwardly sloping demand curve of the imperfect competitor.

Fill in the columns for total revenue product and MRP in Table 7, and then check your work with the data in Table 8.

Does your Table 7 match my Table 8? If it does, go on to the next paragraph. If it doesn't, then please read the box, "Finding the Imperfect Competitor's MRP."

How many workers would the firm hire if the wage rate were $150? How much would the wage bill come to? At a wage rate of $150, two workers would be hired, so the firm's wage bill would be $300.

How do we distinguish between the perfect competitor and the imperfect competitor?

Finding the Imperfect Competitor's MRP

How much was your MRP for two units of labor in Table 7? Was it $176? And for the third unit of labor, was your MRP $140? What you did, then, was try to find MRP by multiplying marginal physical product by price, and that simply does not work for the imperfect competitor.

What *does* work in finding the MRP of the second unit of labor is subtracting the total revenue product of the first unit of labor from the total revenue product of the second unit of labor. Go back to Table 7 and do that. Did you get $158? Good. Now find the MRP of the third unit of labor. Subtract the total revenue product of the second unit of labor from the total revenue product of the third unit of labor. I'll bet you got $106.

For practice, fill in Table A.

Table A

Units of Labor	Output	Marginal Physical Product	Price	Total Revenue Product	Marginal Revenue Product
1	10		8		
2	19		7		
3	27		6		

How did you do? I hope your Table A is identical to Table B.

Table B

Units of Labor	Output	Marginal Physical Product	Price	Total Revenue Product	Marginal Revenue Product
1	10	10	8	80	80
2	19	9	7	133	53
3	27	8	6	162	29

If the wage rate were $51, how many workers would be hired? How much would the firm's wage bill be? At a $51 wage rate, four workers would be hired, and the firm would pay $204 in wages.

If we take a numerical example from Tables 6 and 8, this will become clear. Using Table 6 of the perfect competitor, one unit of labor produces 18 units of output, which is sold at $12, yielding total revenue product of $216. Two workers produce 34 units of output sold at $12 each for a total revenue product of $408.

The imperfect competitor (Table 8) has somewhat different data. The first worker produces 18 units sold at $12 each for a total revenue product of $216; but two workers producing 34 units sold at just $11 produce a total revenue product of only $374.

Why do two workers under perfect competition produce a product sold for $408 while the same two workers under imperfect competition produce a product sold for only $374? The answer is that the perfect competitor can sell as much as she wants to sell at a constant price, while the imperfect competitor must lower her price to sell additional units of output.

The MRP schedule is derived from the total revenue product schedule. It follows that because the total revenue product of the imperfect competitor rises more slowly than that of the perfect competitor, the imperfect competitor's MRP schedule will decline more rapidly.

Changes in Resource Demand

Changes in Resource Demand versus Changes in Quantity of Resource Demanded

At the beginning of Chapter 17 in *Economics* and Chapter 5 in *Microeconomics,* I put on a dog and pony show to help you distinguish between changes in demand and changes in the quantity demanded. Our analysis of MRP parallels our earlier analysis of demand for a final product. Now, however, we're talking about a firm's demand for a resource. In other words, *the MRP schedule is a firm's demand schedule for a resource.* As the price of that resource declines, the firm demands larger quantities.

The Four Reasons for Changes in Resource Demand

Four things cause shifts in the MRP schedule: (1) changes in the demand for the final product, (2) productivity changes, (3) changes in the prices of other resources, and (4) changes in the quantities of other resources.

Changes in the Demand for the Final Product   This is by far the most important influence on the demand for a factor of production. A firm that had no sales would have no demand for land, labor, capital, or entrepreneurial ability. Looking at things more optimistically, let's suppose the demand for the final product shown in Table 4 were to rise so much that its price was driven from $10 to $20. What would happen to the firm's MRP schedule?

The most important influence on resource demand is a change in the demand for the final product.

Would the MRP schedule in Table 4 be raised or lowered (i.e., will the firm's demand for land be raised or lowered)? There's only one way to find out. Turn back to Table 4, change price from $10 to $20, and recalculate the MRP schedule. Once you've done the necessary calculations, check your work with that in Table 9. Obviously, MRP doubled.

Productivity Changes   Productivity is output per unit of input. If output per unit of input is doubled, what will happen to productivity? Check it out, using the data in Table 6. Double the marginal physical product and multiply each figure by price.

What happened to your MRP? It doubled at each price, right?

Now we'll ask what raises productivity. Nearly all of any increase comes from two sources: better capital and better trained and educated labor. The computerization of the American industrial and service sectors has been the main factor responsible for the growth of productivity increases of the last decade. Not only have we introduced more and better computer systems, but many members of our labor force, particularly workers in office jobs, have acquired the skills to use them.

What raises productivity?

Changes in the Prices of Other Resources   There are four factors of production. Sometimes one factor may be used as a substitute for another. When land is scarce, as it is in Bangladesh, labor is substituted for land. Each acre of land is cultivated much more intensively than it would be in the United States. When a new machine replaces several workers, we are substituting capital for labor.

TABLE 9	Hypothetical MRP Schedule				
(1) Units of Land	(2) Output	(3) Marginal Physical Product	(4) Price	(5) Total Revenue Product	(6) Marginal Revenue Product
1	20	20	$20	$ 400	$400
2	38	18	20	760	360
3	53	15	20	1,060	300
4	65	12	20	1,300	240
5	73	8	20	1,460	160
6	78	5	20	1,560	100
7	80	2	20	1,600	40
8	80	0	20	1,600	0
9	79	−1	20	1,580	−20

Substitute Factors   If the price of a factor of production, say labor, goes up, business firms tend to substitute capital or land for some of their now more expensive workers. This is the substitution effect. Similarly, a decline in the wage rate will lead to a substitution of labor for capital or land. We're assuming, of course, that the price of capital or land hasn't changed (or if it has, it hasn't fallen as much as the wage rate).

The substitution effect

There's also an output effect, which works in the opposite direction. When the price of any resource rises, this raises the cost of production, which in turn lowers the supply of the final product. When supply falls, price rises, consequently reducing output. In other words, according to the output effect, if the cost of a factor of production rises, output will decline, thereby reducing the employment of all factors of production. Conversely, a decline in the cost of a factor will raise output, thereby raising the use of all factors of production.

The output effect

In sum:

1. *The substitution effect: If the price of a resource rises, other resources will be substituted for it.* If the price of a resource is lowered, it will be substituted for other resources.

2. *The output effect: If the price of a resource rises, output of the final product will decline,* thereby lowering the employment of all resources. If the price of a resource falls, output of the final product will rise, thereby increasing the employment of all resources.

What we have, then, are contradictory effects. When the price of a resource rises, for example, the substitution effect dictates that more of the other resources will be used, thus increasing their employment. But the output effect pushes their employment down.

The two effects are contradictory.

Which effect is stronger? Take the case of the introduction of computers in offices. The substitution effect pushed down the employment of labor, but the output effect pushed it way up. White-collar employment has risen sharply since the introduction of computers, so the output effect has clearly outweighed the substitution effect.

Which effect is stronger?

Now you *know* I'm going to present a case where the substitution effect outweighs the output effect. Output rose with the mechanization of agriculture in the South during the late 1940s, but more than three-quarters of the agricultural labor force in the deep South was forced off the land. Here the substitution effect (of capital for labor) swamped the output effect.

Sometimes, then, the substitution effect is stronger than the output effect, while at other times the opposite holds true. Thus, if you are asked whether automation raises or lowers the employment of labor, you will sound well informed when you explain that it will raise employment if the output effect is stronger and lower it if the substitution effect dominates.

Complementary Factors   Although resources are usually substitutable at least to some degree, they also usually work well together. In fact, you need at least some labor to produce virtually every good or service, and labor productivity may be greatly enhanced by land, capital, and entrepreneurial ability.

Complementary factors of production

We say that two factors are complements in production if an increase in the use of one requires an increase in the use of the other. If a bicycle messenger service purchased 100 new bicycles, it would need to hire 100 messengers to ride them; or if 100 new messengers were hired, the firm would need to purchase 100 bicycles.

To carry our example further, suppose the price of bicycles rose considerably. What would happen to the firm's demand for bicycles (or capital)?

You said it would go down, right? What would happen to the firm's demand for riders (labor)? It, too, would go down.

What if, instead, the wage rate for bicycle riders rose sharply? What would happen to the firm's demand for bicycle riders and for bicycles? It would fall.

Now we can generalize. When the price of a resource rises, the demand for a complementary resource will fall; when the price of a resource falls, the demand for a complementary resource rises.

Changes in the Quantities of Other Resources If we go back to one of the eternal questions of economics—Why are workers in one country more productive than those in another country?—the answer is that they have more land, capital, and entrepreneurial ability with which to work.

As already noted, the farmer in Bangladesh has a lot less land with which to work than the American farmer has, and the Chinese construction worker has a lot less capital backing him than his American counterpart does. It would follow that an increase in land would greatly raise the productivity of the farmer in Bangladesh, while the Chinese construction worker's productivity would soar if he were given heavy construction equipment.

We can conclude, then, that an addition of complementary resources would raise the MRP of any given resource, while a decrease in complementary resources would have the opposite effect.

Why are workers in one country more productive than those in another country?

Optimum Resource Mix for the Firm

So far, we have been deciding how much of a resource should be hired by a firm. We hire more and more labor until the MRP of the last worker hired is equal to the going wage rate. Similarly, we hire land until the MRP of the last unit of land hired is equal to the going rent. Finally, more and more capital is hired until the last unit of capital hired is equal to the interest rate.

We can generalize by saying that the firm will use increasing amounts of a resource until the MRP of that resource is equal to its price. We'd hire workers until the MRP of labor equals the price of labor (or the wage rate). Suppose we divide both sides of the equation by the price of labor.

$$(1)\ \text{MRP of labor} = \text{Price of labor}$$

$$(2)\ \frac{\text{MRP of labor}}{\text{Price of labor}} = \frac{\text{Price of labor}}{\text{Price of labor}}$$

This may be simplified to:

$$(3)\ \frac{\text{MRP of labor}}{\text{Price of labor}} = 1$$

Remember, anything divided by itself equals one.
Now let's do the same thing with land.

$$(1)\ \text{MRP of land} = \text{Price of land}$$

$$(2)\ \frac{\text{MRP of land}}{\text{Price of land}} = \frac{\text{Price of land}}{\text{Price of land}}$$

$$(3)\ \frac{\text{MRP of land}}{\text{Price of land}} = 1$$

And with capital:

$$(1)\ \text{MRP of capital} = \text{Price of capital}$$

$$(2)\ \frac{\text{MRP of capital}}{\text{Price of capital}} = \frac{\text{Price of capital}}{\text{Price of capital}}$$

$$(3)\ \frac{\text{MRP of capital}}{\text{Price of capital}} = 1$$

Next, we may combine the three equations into one.

$$\frac{\text{MRP of labor}}{\text{Price of labor}} = \frac{\text{MRP of land}}{\text{Price of land}} = \frac{\text{MRP of capital}}{\text{Price of capital}} = 1$$

$$\frac{\text{MRP of labor}}{\text{Price of labor}} = 1$$

$$\frac{\text{MRP of land}}{\text{Price of land}} = 1$$

$$\frac{\text{MRP of capital}}{\text{Price of capital}} = 1$$

$$\frac{\text{MRP of labor}}{\text{Price of labor}} = 1$$

$$\frac{\text{MRP of land}}{\text{Price of land}} = 1$$

TABLE 10	Hypothetical MRP Schedules for a Firm				
Units of Land	MRP of Land	Units of Capital	MRP of Capital	Units of Labor	MRP of Labor
1	$12	1	$15	1	$30
2	10	2	13	2	26
3	8	3	10	3	21
4	6	4	7	4	15
5	4	5	3	5	8
6	2	6	0	6	1
Rent = $8		Interest = $3		Wage rate = $15	

$$\frac{\text{MRP of capital}}{\text{Price of capital}} = 1$$

A firm will keep hiring more and more of a resource up to the point at which the MRP is equal to its price.

After all, things equal to the same thing (in this case, 1) are equal to each other.

The reason I dragged you through all of this (besides showing off my algebra) is to reinforce the conclusion we reached a few minutes ago: *A firm will keep hiring more and more of a resource up to the point at which its MRP is equal to its price.* This great truth enables us to do another set of problems. You could have slept through everything up to this point and still get this problem set right.

Given the data in Table 10, how many units of land, capital, and labor would you hire? It's easy. Reread the italicized statement in the previous paragraph.

The answers? Do we have the envelope? Ah yes. We would hire three units of land, five units of capital, and four units of labor.

Next we're going to take up each of the four resources in turn, beginning with labor in the next two chapters. The questions we will answer are why the wage rates are what they are, and why rent, interest, and profit are what *they* are.

Current Issue: Washing Machines and Women's Liberation

I can remember my mother scrubbing clothes on a washboard and hanging them on a clothesline which stretched from our living room window to a telephone pole about 20 feet away. It was a really big deal when our landlord installed a washing machine in our basement. On the downside, we lived in an apartment house with 47 other families.

Washing machines had come down enough in price during the 1950s that almost every home had one. At the same time, laundromats sprang up, it seemed, on every other block.

Perhaps the washing machine played as much of a role in liberating housewives from housework as the women's liberation movement did in the 1970s.

Vacuum cleaners, dishwashers, microwave ovens, blenders, toasters, and other household appliances also made housework much easier. And, in the wake of the women's liberation movement, husbands began to pitch in with housework and child care.

Of course we know what came next—most of these women eventually went out and got jobs. Instead of spending long hours washing clothes by hand and hanging them outside to dry, women now had more free time. Most of them went out to work.

From an economic prospective, as the price of a capital good (the washer/dryer) was significantly reduced, tens of millions of housewives substituted capital for labor. Now let's look at the substitution and output effects. The lower price of capital lowered the number of hours women spent doing housework. So the substitution of capital for labor lowered the employment of housewives. But as women left their homes to take paying jobs, their employment rose. So the output effect of the declining price of capital was an increase in the employment of former housewives.

Which was greater—the substitution effect or the output effect? I would say that the output effect outweighed the substitution effect. In other words, the decline in the employment of housewives was smaller than the increase in the paid employment of the former housewives.

Questions for Further Thought and Discussion

1. If automatic dishwashers and human dishwashers can be substituted for one another, and if the wage rate for dishwashers rises, what happens to the demand for automatic dishwashers according to (a) the substitution effect and (b) the output effect?

2. As output rises, which MRP curve declines more quickly—the MRP of the perfect competitor or the MRP of the imperfect competitor? Explain your answer.

3. How is the demand for a resource affected by (a) changes in the demand for the final product and (b) productivity changes?

4. Using the substitution and output effects, explain how a decline in the price of resource A might cause an increase in the demand for substitute resource B.

Workbook for Chapter 26

Name _____   Date _____

Multiple-Choice Questions

Circle the letter that corresponds to the best answer.

1. Derived demand is the demand for _____.
   a) final goods and services
   b) resources
   c) final goods as well as services and resources
   d) neither final goods and services nor resources

2. When the demand for wheat rises, the demand for farm labor _____.
   a) rises
   b) falls
   c) may rise or fall

3. The demand for resources is based on _____.
   a) only the demand for the final product
   b) only the productivity of the resource
   c) both the demand for the final product and the productivity of the resource
   d) neither the demand for the final product nor the productivity of the resource

4. Which statement is true?
   a) Resources and final products are both measured by units of input.
   b) Resources and final products are both measured by units of output.
   c) Resources are measured by units of input, and final demand is measured by units of output.
   d) Resources are measured by units of output, and final products are measured by units of input.

5. Which statement is true?
   a) Productivity is output per unit of input.
   b) Productivity is input per unit of output.
   c) Productivity is neither of the above.

6. Relative to the Chinese economy, the U.S. economy is _____.
   a) more capital intensive
   b) more labor intensive
   c) more labor intensive and more capital intensive
   d) less labor intensive and less capital intensive

7. The added output for which one additional input of labor is responsible is its _____.
   a) marginal revenue product
   b) marginal physical product
   c) average revenue product
   d) average physical product

8. The firm's demand schedule for a resource is its _____ schedule.
   a) MPP   c) total revenue
   b) MRP   d) output

9. The firm will hire workers until the wage rate and the _____ of the last worker hired are equal.
   a) marginal physical product
   b) MRP
   c) output

10. A firm will operate at that point where _____ is equal to one.
    a) the marginal physical product of capital/price of capital
    b) the MRP of capital/price of capital
    c) the price of capital/marginal physical product of capital
    d) the price of capital/MRP of capital

11. A firm will keep hiring more and more of a resource up to the point at which its MRP is equal to _____.
    a) one
    b) its marginal physical product
    c) its price
    d) its output

12. If the MRP of the last worker hired is lower than the wage rate, the firm has _____.
    a) hired too many workers
    b) hired too few workers
    c) hired the right number of workers

13. If the wage rate is higher than the MRP of the last worker hired, _____.
    a) the firm might be able to profitably hire at least one more worker
    b) the firm has already hired too many workers
    c) there is no way of knowing whether the firm has too few or too many workers

14. The most important influence on a firm's demand for a factor of production is _____.
    a) the quantities of other resources
    b) the prices of other resources
    c) its productivity
    d) the demand for the final product

15. If the price that a perfect competitor receives for her final product doubles, the firm's MRP schedule will _____.
    a) rise   c) double at each price
    b) fall   d) stay about the same

16. The most effective way to increase the productivity of labor would be to _____.
    a) increase capital
    b) increase labor
    c) lower capital
    d) shift workers from white-collar work to blue-collar work

17. Capital and labor are _____ factors of production.
    a) substitute
    b) complementary
    c) both complementary and substitute
    d) neither complementary nor substitute

18. Automation will raise the level of employment if the _____.
    a) output effect is equal to the substitution effect
    b) output effect is greater than the substitution effect
    c) substitution effect is greater than the output effect

19. A firm will try to be in each of these situations except _____.
    a) MRP of capital = Price of capital
    b) MRP of land/Price of land = 1
    c) 1 − Price of labor = MRP of labor
    d) MRP of land/Price of land = MRP of labor/Price of labor

20. The decline in washing machine prices in the 1950s led to an increase in the employment of women because the _____.
    a) output effect outweighed the substitution effect
    b) substitution effect outweighed the output effect
    c) substitution and output effects offset each other

Fill-In Questions

1. A firm will use increasing amounts of a resource until the _____ of that resource is equal to its _____.

2. If Melissa produces twice as much per hour as Adam, we would say that she is _____ as productive as he is.

3. Our economy is relatively _____ intensive, while the Chinese economy is relatively _____ intensive.

4. If farmland became five times as expensive, farmers would use much more _____ and _____ per acre.

5. When the productivity of a resource rises, its _____ and its _____ also rise.

6. When the price of a substitute resource declines, the price of a resource will _____.

7. The MRP of the fourth unit of output = the _____ less the _____.

8. The producer's surplus of rented land is the difference between how much this land is

_____ and how much _____.

9. A firm will keep hiring more and more of a resource up to the point at which its _____ is equal to _____.

10. A firm will keep leasing additional units of land until the MRP of that land is equal to the _____.

11. An increase in the productivity of labor will _____ the MRP of labor.

12. If the price of labor goes up and a firm replaces some workers with machines, this is the _____ effect; when the price of a resource declines and the level of production consequently rises, this is the _____ effect.

13. If labor and capital are complementary resources and the price of labor goes up, then the employment of capital _____.

Problems

1. (a) Fill in Table 1. (b) Is the firm a perfect or an imperfect competitor? (c) If the wage rate were $60, how many workers would be hired? How much would the total wage bill come to? (d) If the wage rate were $35, how many workers would be hired? How much would the total wage bill come to?

TABLE 1

(1) Units of Labor	(2) Output	(3) Marginal Physical Product	(4) Price	(5) Total Revenue Product	(6) Marginal Revenue Product
1	15	____	$6	____	____
2	28	____	6	____	____
3	40	____	6	____	____
4	50	____	6	____	____
5	57	____	6	____	____
6	62	____	6	____	____
7	64	____	6	____	____
8	65	____	6	____	____

2. (a) Fill in Table 2. (b) Is the firm a perfect or an imperfect competitor? (c) If the wage rate were $250, how many workers would be hired? How much would the total wage bill come to? (d) If the wage rate were $99, how many workers would be hired? How much would the total wage bill come to?

TABLE 2

(1) Units of Labor	(2) Output	(3) Marginal Physical Product	(4) Price	(5) Total Revenue Product	(6) Marginal Revenue Product
1	22	____	$20	____	____
2	43	____	19	____	____
3	63	____	18	____	____
4	81	____	17	____	____
5	96	____	16	____	____
6	109	____	15	____	____
7	119	____	14	____	____
8	127	____	13	____	____

3. Given the data in Table 3, how many units of land, labor, and capital would you hire?

Units of Land	MRP of Land	Units of Capital	MRP of Capital	Units of Labor	MRP of Labor
1	$20	1	$35	1	$31
2	17	2	33	2	24
3	13	3	27	3	16
4	8	4	20	4	9
5	2	5	12	5	5
6	1	6	4	6	2
Rent = $8		Interest = $27		Wage rate = $24	

TABLE 3

4. A perfect competitor charges a price of $5. The first worker he would hire would have a marginal physical product of 20, the second worker he would hire would have a marginal physical product of 18, the third worker would have a marginal physical product of 16, and the fourth worker would have a marginal physical product of 14. (a) How many workers would he hire if the wage rate were $90? How much would his wage bill be? (b) How many workers would he hire if the wage rate were $70? How much would his wage bill come to?

Chapter 27

Labor Unions

Until the late 1930s the standard workweek was six days. As in the Book of Genesis, the Sabbath was the one day of rest. When labor unions secured a 40-hour, 5-day workweek, it quickly became the new standard not just for the unionized workforce, but for nearly everyone else as well. In 1938 the Fair Labor Standards Act required that employers pay time and a half for nearly everyone who put in more than 40 hours. Rather than pay this premium, many employers held the workweek to 40 hours and hired more employees to take up the slack. Today just one in eight American workers is a union member, but without labor unions, we might all still be working a six-day week.

America needs a raise.
—John Sweeney,
President, AFL–CIO

CHAPTER OBJECTIVES

These are the high points of this chapter:

- A short history of the labor movement.
- Labor legislation.
- The economic power of unions and employers.

- The economic power of monopsonies.
- Collective bargaining.
- The strike.

A Short History of the American Labor Movement

The Early Years

Labor unions are a traditional American institution, with their own national holiday, replete with parades, speeches, and picnics. This, of course, was not always so. Until the 1940s most Americans had unfavorable opinions of unions. In the popular mind, they were subversive organizations set up to obtain exorbitant wage increases and possibly overthrow the American economic system. Union leaders were regarded as racketeers, communists, or political bosses. And some were guilty as charged.

Labor unions were considered subversive until the 1940s.

Although the trade union movement in the United States is some two centuries old, most labor historians consider the modern era to have begun with the founding of the original American Federation of Labor in 1886 or with its predecessor, the Knights of Labor, which rose to prominence in the mid-1880s. Within the ranks of these organizations there was an almost continual struggle between those who sought specific

The AF of L rang in the modern era of unions in 1886.

gains—better wages, hours, and working conditions—and those who advocated more far-reaching reforms—a universal eight-hour day, elimination of the wage system, and the establishment of producers' cooperatives to replace private enterprise.

By the late 1880s the American Federation of Labor, or the AF of L (AFL) as it became known, had become the predominant labor organization. Samuel Gompers, who served as its president until his death in 1924, stressed the importance of "bread-and-butter unionism." Why the AF of L succeeded where the Knights had failed is explained largely by their opposing philosophies as well as by the changing conditions of the American economy.

The emergence of the large corporation, which replaced the small workshop, meant the wage relationship was here to stay. Forget about small producers' cooperatives and start worrying about securing enough bargaining strength to obtain better wages, hours, and working conditions. An individual worker has little bargaining power against a huge corporation, but thousands of workers, banded together in craft unions—the ironworkers, cigar makers, carpenters—did have a certain amount of leverage. They could, if they didn't get what they wanted, withhold their labor. In other words, they could go out on strike.

This might not sound all that radical, but during the first three decades of the 20th century most Americans saw unions as subversive, foreign, and, in some cases, downright evil. Employers fought them tooth and nail. Union members were blacklisted, those suspected of having union sympathies were fired, court orders were obtained to prohibit strikes as well as milder forms of union activity, and sometimes private detectives, labor goons, and sympathetic local police were used to put down strikes violently.

Key Labor Legislation

National Labor Relations Act (Wagner Act, 1935) The Wagner Act and the Taft-Hartley Act are by far the two most important pieces of labor legislation. The Wagner Act, named for New York Senator Robert Wagner, committed the federal government to promote collective bargaining and to support union organizing.

The Wagner Act prohibited employers from engaging in such "unfair labor practices" as (1) coercion or interference with employees who are organizing or bargaining; (2) refusal to bargain in good faith with a union legally representing employees; and (3) in general, penalizing employees for union activity.

The act set up a three-member (now a five-member) board to protect workers in organizing unions and to administer representation elections (that is, to determine which union will represent the workers of a company). If 30 percent of the employees in an entire company, or just one unit of that company, decide to be represented by a union, these people petition the National Labor Relations Board to conduct an election. If the union gets a majority of votes, it then represents *all* the employees of that company or unit, even those who are not members of the union.

This law put the force of the federal government behind collective bargaining, at the same time lending unions a certain legitimacy. It established unions as an American institution. In addition, the Wagner Act provided the necessary machinery to ensure that large corporations would allow unions to organize and would bargain in good faith.

During World War II strikes were considered unpatriotic; but 1946 set a record for strikes—a record that still stands. The late 1940s were a time of inflation and prosperity, and labor used the strike weapon to get what it considered its fair share of the economic pie. Partially in response to these disturbances, the Republicans captured control of Congress in 1946 for the first time in 14 years. They felt they had a mandate not only to redress the imbalance between the power of labor and the power of management, but as many observers noted, "to put labor in its place."

Taft-Hartley Act (1947) Just as the Wagner Act protected employee rights, the Taft-Hartley Act protected employer rights. Here are its three main provisions: (1) it allows the president to call an 80-day "cooling-off" period; (2) it allows the states to ban the union shop; and (3) it severely limits the closed shop.

Margin notes:

Bread-and-butter unionism

The wage relationship was here to stay.

Wagner Act

Prohibition of unfair labor practices

The Wagner Act put the force of the government behind collective bargaining.

Taft-Hartley Act

The Closed Shop, Union Shop, Open Shop, and "Right-to-Work" Laws

(1) Closed shop An employer may hire only union members. The Taft-Hartley Act outlawed this arrangement, but sometimes union hiring halls operate as de facto closed shops. If an employer, generally a construction firm, hires only those sent by the union, we have a closed shop, even though it is nominally a union shop.

(2) Union shop Under a union shop contract, all employees must join the union, usually within 30 days after they are hired. This arrangement effectively increases union membership because many workers would not have joined unless they were forced to. A variation of the union shop is the agency shop, in which you don't have to join the union, but you must pay dues.

(3) Open shop No one is forced to join the union, although it does represent all the workers in contract negotiations. Union members often resent nonmembers who are "getting a free ride," because they don't have to pay dues.

(4) Right-to-work laws Section 14b of the Taft-Hartley Act permitted the states to pass laws prohibiting the union shop. Some 20 states have done this, which means in those states you can work in a shop that is organized without having to join the union. Organized labor has struggled in vain since 1947 to get this controversial section repealed because these right-to-work laws have been responsible for lower union membership in the states that passed them.

Strikes that "imperil the national health or safety" may be halted by court order at the request of the president, who determines which strikes imperil Americans' health and safety. If a settlement is not reached during the 80 days allowed, the union may resume the strike.

The most controversial part of the law is Section 14b. This section allows the states to enact "right-to-work" laws, which prohibit union shop contracts. (About 20 states—mainly in the South—have laws prohibiting contracts that require union membership as a condition of employment.)

Section 14b: right-to-work laws

The act severely limits the extent of the closed shop (closed to nonunion members). However, unions have sometimes gotten around this prohibition by calling a closed shop a union shop (see the nearby box).

Closed shop

Taft-Hartley also prohibits jurisdictional disputes and secondary boycotts. A jurisdictional dispute occurs when two unions, each vying to organize a company, picket that company, which has no dispute with either union. A secondary boycott is directed against a company that isn't party to a strike, such as a trade supplier or a customer or a retail outlet.

Jurisdictional disputes and secondary boycotts are prohibited.

The 80-day cooling-off period puts the union at a strategic disadvantage. For 80 days the company can stockpile inventory, making it easier for it to weather a strike and perhaps less likely to make concessions. However, by committing itself to ensuring labor peace, not to mention to protecting the nation's health and safety, the administration is more likely to put pressure on both parties to settle their dispute.

80-day cooling-off period

Craft Unions versus Industrial Unions

As you can see from Figure 1, union membership rose spectacularly from the mid-1930s to the mid-1940s. The major impetus was the Wagner Act, which legitimized unions and facilitated their organizing workers in the nation's basic industries of auto, steel, and rubber. During this time a split developed within the AFL, leading to the formation of the Congress of Industrial Organizations (CIO) in 1935. The split was caused by a dispute over whether to organize along craft lines, as the AFL had been doing for 50 years, or along industry lines, as advocated by the leaders of the CIO.

Union membership rose spectacularly in the mid-1930s.

Craft unions are organized along the lines of particular occupations, such as air traffic controllers, plumbers, operating engineers, airline pilots, or teachers. In general these are relatively well-paid jobs requiring years of training.

Craft unions

Industrial unions, such as the United Steel Workers, the United Auto Workers, and the United Mine Workers, are organized along industry lines, without regard to craft.

Industrial unions

Figure 1

Union Membership, 1900–2004
The total number of union members reached its peak in the late 1970s (see panel A), declining substantially since then. Union membership as a percentage of the civilian labor force (see panel B) reached a peak in the late 1950s and has declined steadily since the mid-1970s. The best decades for the labor movement were the 1930s, 1940s, and 1950s.
Source: Bureau of Labor Statistics.

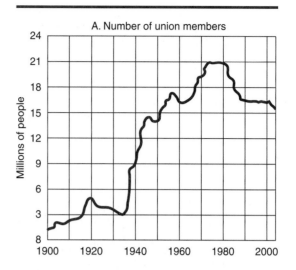

A. Number of union members

B. Union membership as a percentage of the civilian labor force

Lumped together in one union are skilled and unskilled workers doing varied types of work. What bonds them is that they all work in the same industry.

In some industries, particularly those with unskilled or semiskilled mass-production workers, it makes more sense to organize along industrial rather than craft lines. Unlike plumbers or airline pilots, the people who put together cars can be trained in a couple of hours—and replaced just as quickly. They simply don't have a craft that sets them apart from their co-workers.

The conflict within the AFL over whether to organize along craft or industrial lines led to the great schism of the organization in 1935. Most of the AFL leadership, who headed the craft and building trades unions, believed that machinists, for example, whether employed in autos, steel, or any other industry, should be organized into a machinists' union. But the leaders of the breakaway Congress of Industrial Organizations believed all the workers in an industry should be organized into an industrywide union regardless of craft.

In the mid- to late 1930s there was a tremendous spurt of labor organizing by the CIO in steel, autos, rubber, oil, and other areas of heavy industry. The AFL also began organizing along industrial lines during this period. As we can see in Figure 1, these were the golden days of union organizing.

AFL–CIO merger

The Taft-Hartley Act unintentionally sparked efforts to reunite the AFL and the CIO. The main obstacle to the merger was no longer the philosophical one of whether organization should be carried out along craft or industrial lines. That issue had been settled by the late 1930s when the AFL began to organize its own industrial unions.

In 1955 the two groups merged to form the AFL–CIO.

In 2004, when 12.5 percent of all working Americans were union members, the five states with the lowest percentage of union members were in the South—North Carolina (2.7); South Carolina (3.0); Arkansas (4.8); Mississippi (4.8); and Texas (5.0). No surprise there. The most highly unionized states were New York (25.3); Michigan (21.6); New Jersey (19.8); Washington (19.3); and Minnesota (17.5). Two factors were largely responsible for this vast differential in the unionization rates of these two groups of states. The states with very low unionization rates are all "right-to-work" states, which makes union organizing very difficult. And the states with very high unionization rates all have heavy concentrations of manufacturing industries, which have generally been relatively easy for unions to organize.[1]

Union Organizing Since the 1950s

The South continues to be the least unionized section of the country. Long the target of AFL–CIO organizers, this region has remained a tough nut to crack. Right-to-work laws, strong local conservatism, and antiunion feeling, as well as the economic power of the local firms, have kept labor organizing at a low ebb.

Union membership peaked decades ago (see Figure 1). Today just 12.5 percent of the labor force is unionized. Millions of workers have shifted from manufacturing to service industries, and it is much harder to organize computer programmers, insurance adjusters, and financial analysts than it is to organize factory workers.

Wal-Mart is the nation's largest employer. It is the nation's 500-pound economic gorilla, setting off shockwaves by just walking into a room. For example, Wal-Mart's plan to open 40 supercenters in California by 2008 was largely responsible for a strike and lockout in 2003 at the state's three largest unionized supermarket chains—Ralphs, Vons, and Albertsons. The chains had demanded that their workers accept a two-year wage freeze for current workers, a lower pay scale for new hires, and greater employee contributions for health coverage. All this so the three chains could compete with Wal-Mart, whose employees' pay and benefits was about $10 to $14 an hour less than those at unionized supermarkets. The strike lasted from October 2003 to February 2004 and ended with some cuts in benefits, and a two-tier wage system.

Wal-Mart has 1.3 million employees in the United States, but not one is a member of a union. The United Food and Commercial Workers did manage to organize butchers in a Texas Wal-Mart, but two weeks later the company closed down its meat-cutting departments nationwide. A store in Quebec where employees were unionized was also closed.

Why has Wal-Mart been such a tough nut for unions to crack? Aside from management's fierce opposition, there are two other important factors: Wal-Mart has a large part-time, transient workforce and many Wal-Mart employees work in Southern states where unionism isn't welcome.

In early 2005 the United Food and Commercial Workers suspended its strategy of seeking to unionize Wal-Mart store by store. "When you're dealing with a company that's so big and ruthless, you can't even get enough leverage going store by store," said Paul Blank, the union's Wal-Mart campaign director. "Even when you win an organizing drive, you lose because the company will simply shut down a store."[2]

The United Auto Workers, whose workforce at the Big Three (General Motors, Ford, and DaimlerChrysler) has shrunk to just 220,000 from over 650,000 in 1979, is caught in a bind. It has been unable to organize in any of the foreign-owned plants (owned by Honda, Toyota, Nissan, and other companies), located mainly in the South. In 2005, these plants employed 57,000 workers. Until now, to make unionization less attractive, the foreign-owned factories have boosted wages very close to the UAW's $25 an hour. But as they gain market share, the pressure to match Big Three wages will lessen. Former UAW president Douglas Fraser, now a labor studies professor at Wayne State University in Detroit, has observed, "Sooner or later… the Big Three are going to say, 'We're becoming noncompetitive, and unless you organize the transplants, we're going to have to modify the proposals we make to you.'"[3]

---

[1] If you're interested in politics, it is striking that the 10 most heavily unionized states are all so-called "blue states," which tend to vote Democratic, while the 10 least unionized states are all so-called "red states," which tend to vote Republican.

[2] Steven Greenhouse, "Opponents of Wal-Mart to Coordinate Efforts," *The New York Times,* April 3, 2005, p. 20.

[3] See *BusinessWeek,* June 10, 2002, p. 78.

Which is the biggest labor union today? As you can see in Table 1, it's the National Education Association, with 2.7 million members.

There has been a precipitous decline in private sector union membership over the last three decades (see Figure 2). In 1973 24.2 percent of all workers in the private sector were union members, but just 7.8 percent were members in 2005. These losses were partially offset by the unionization of the public sector. In 2005 36.4 percent of the public sector was unionized. Union membership as a percentage of the labor force has been falling since the mid-1950s (see Figure 1B), but the decline in big craft and industrial unions has been even faster. Their decline was partially offset by the rapid unionization of government employees during the 1970s and 1980s. Which unions in Table 1 have large numbers of government employees? They are the National Education Association

TABLE 1	Membership of Top 10 Labor Unions, 2004
Union	Membership
National Education Association	2,700,000
Service Employees International Union	1,600,000
International Brotherhood of Teamsters	1,400,000
United Food and Commercial Workers	1,400,000
American Federation of State, County and Municipal Employees	1,400,000
American Federation of Teachers	1,300,000
United Steel Workers	1,200,000
Laborers' International Union	800,000
International Brotherhood of Electrical Workers	728,000
United Automobile and Aerospace Workers	710,000
Communications Workers of America	700,000

Source: The World Almanac, 2006.

F*igure* 2

Private Sector Union Membership as a Percentage of Total Private Sector Employment, 1973–2005
In 1973 nearly one of every four people working in the private sector was a union member. By 2005 fewer than one in thirteen was a union member.
Source: Bureau of Labor Statistics.

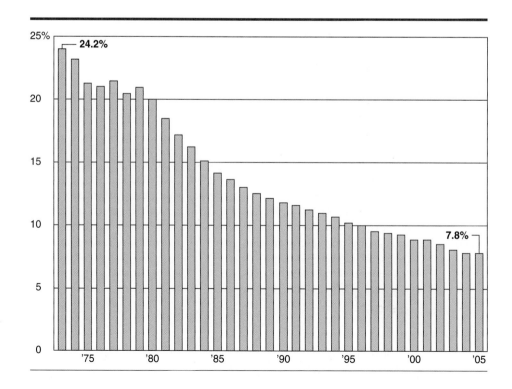

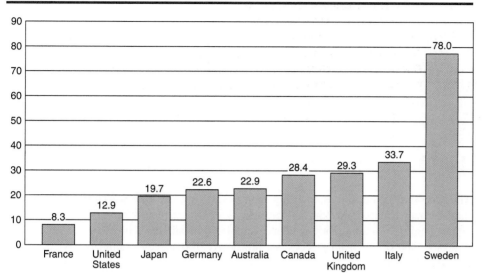

F*igure* 3

Union Membership as a
Percentage of Labor Force,
Selected Industrial Countries,
2003

Source: Jelle Visser, "Union Membership
Statistics in 24 Countries," *Monthly
Labor Review,* January 2006.

(number 1); the Service Employees International Union (number 2) (a substantial minority of members are government employees); the American Federation of State, County, and Municipal Employees (tied for third place); and the American Federation of Teachers (number 6).

The Formation of Change to Win

Upset with declining union membership, five large unions withdrew from the AFL–CIO in 2005, taking with them 40 percent of the federation's members. The Teamsters, the Service Employees' International Union, the United Food and Commercial Workers, the Laborers' International Union, and Unite Here! (which represents hotel, restaurant, textile, and apparel workers)—formed the Change to Win coalition. They were joined by the United Farm Workers, which left the AFL–CIO a few months later, and the Carpenters and Joiners, which had pulled out of the AFL–CIO in 2001.

The new 5.4 million-member group hopes to stanch labor's decline by mounting a national recruiting drive involving entire industries. It has targeted the 50 million workers whose jobs cannot be sent overseas or be replaced by machines. Many of these jobs pay poverty-level wages and include janitors, dishwashers, hotel maids, cashiers, nursing home aides, and security guards. Possible targets for unionization drives include Home Depot, Federal Express, Wal-Mart, as well as the large hotel chains. Change to Win Chairwoman Anna Burger declared that "Organizing is our core principle. It is our North Star."

America is one of the *least* unionized industrial nations in the world. Among the nations shown in Figure 3, which has data for the year 2003, the United States and France had, by far, the lowest unionization rates.

Jobs: Exportable and Nonexportable

There is work that must be done in the United States, and there is work that can be done abroad. If we import a good or service, then obviously it can be produced in another country. Since the mid-20th century, four main groups of unionized workers have lost their jobs to foreigners—those in the auto, steel, textile, and apparel industries. Clearly, we can import cars, steel, textiles, and clothing.

One thing we can't import is trucking deliveries. And that service is dominated by the International Brotherhood of Teamsters. Why do these folks earn well over $20 an hour, while millions of other Americans work just as hard for only $8 or $9 an hour?

*Had the employers of the past
generation dealt fairly with men,
there would have been no trade
unions.*

—Stanley Baldwin,
former Prime Minister,
Great Britain

How much someone is paid comes down to the supply of labor and the demand for that labor. But when that labor must be used locally, then that supply is limited to those currently residing in the United States.

Fifty years ago our largest unions were industrial and craft unions, most of whose members worked in manufacturing. Now, as you can see from glancing at Table 1, a majority of our union members are service workers. And more to the point, their jobs are relatively safe from foreign competition.

The Economic Power of Labor Unions

Labor is the capital of our working man.

—Grover Cleveland, U.S. President

Many people accuse unions of being monopolies. Indeed, they were prosecuted under the Sherman Antitrust Act during the first two decades of this century. In a sense, of course, unions *are* monopolies. For example, the painters', plumbers', carpenters', longshoremen's, and teamsters' trades are nearly 100 percent unionized. Aren't these monopolies?

We define a monopoly as the seller of a good or service for which there are no close substitutes. Of course, labor is not really a good or service but rather a factor that helps produce a good or service. But if we brush aside that technicality, then for all intents and purposes unions *are* sometimes monopolies.

Unions have two ways of asserting power: inclusion and exclusion.

Unions have two basic ways of exerting power. They can take in as members virtually everyone who works in a particular craft or industry. This is the *method of inclusion,* and it could give the union a monopoly. Examples are the United Steel Workers, the United Auto and Aerospace Workers, and the Teamsters.

A second way of exerting power, which is quite common in the building trades, is the *principle of exclusion.* You don't take in just anyone. There are tests, you might need experience, and believe it or not, it probably wouldn't hurt to know someone—preferably a close relative like a father or an uncle—who happens to be an influential member of the union. By keeping people out, you keep down the supply of carpenters, plumbers, bricklayers, and electricians, and amazingly, wages go all the way up.

Let's see what the principles of inclusion and exclusion look like graphically. In Figure 4A we have the inclusive union, generally a large industrial union such as the United Steel Workers. The union tries to obtain a high standard wage from U.S. Steel (now part of USX), Nucor, Republic, and the other companies. But at a high wage rate, the companies will hire fewer workers than they would have hired at lower wages.

We get the same results from the exclusive union (see Figure 4B). This time, however, the union has restricted the supply of workers by allowing only certain people into its ranks. It's clear, then, that both exclusion and inclusion will lead to higher wages.

Are unions too powerful? Public opinion is divided on this issue, but before we even attempt to answer this question, we should look at the other side of the coin. Are large corporations too powerful?

The Economic Power of Large Employers

The case of monopsony

We've seen that workers, who were once powerless to bargain individually with huge corporate employers, have formed unions that have become quite powerful. Let's consider an extreme case of corporate power, that of monopsony. The seller of a product for which there are no close substitutes is a monopolist. *Monopsony is the market situation in which there is only a single buyer for a product.* The most common kind of monopsony is a labor market where there is only a single employer. At one time or another General Electric in Schenectady, New York; textile producer J. P. Stevens in several towns in the South; and the military bases in various towns around the country have completely dominated the local job markets. Sometimes 60 to 80 percent of the jobs in these areas

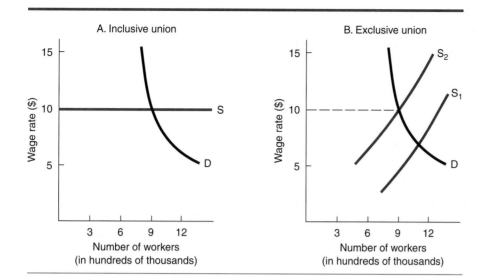

Figure 4
Inclusive and Exclusive Unions
For both inclusive unions
(see panel A), like the large
industrial unions, and exclusive
unions (see panel B), more typically
craft unions, the wage rate is set by
supply and demand.

have been provided by a single employer. Technically, a monopsonist is a single buyer, but these towns came pretty close. Bentonville, Arkansas, home of Wal-Mart, has a population of 19,730. Wal-Mart headquarters has 20,000 employees.

Winston-Salem, North Carolina, home of R. J. Reynolds, was a typical company town. Because the company paid double or triple the local average manufacturing wage, they were able to support restaurants, dry cleaners, day care and other service industries. Dean Foust and Brian Grow described the company town atmosphere in *BusinessWeek:*

> Reynolds could be like a stern father—for years it banned long hair and frowned on divorce—but that didn't bother locals who earned as much as $60,000 a year at the company's factory in nearby Tobaccoville. "I've gotten a lot of checks over the years from customers that they'd stamped with the words 'Tobacco Pays My Bills,'" says Penny Terry, who runs a furniture store near the plant.[4]

But in response to declining demand for cigarettes, and rising competition from discount cigarette makers using cheaper foreign tobacco, R. J. Reynolds began laying off workers. By 2004 it was down to just 3,500 employees in Winston-Salem, from 14,000 in 1983.

In this chapter we are concerned with the monopsonist as the dominant employer in a locality, but a monopsonist, in more general terms, faces the entire supply curve of anything being sold—labor, other resources, or any good or service. Perhaps the prime example today exists in Japan's Toyota City, with its rings of auto supplier firms radiating outward from the Toyota Motor Company headquarters. This city of 350,000 is a prime example of a company town, where nearly everyone is employed, directly or indirectly, by the same company.

The monopsonist faces the entire supply curve of labor. Because that curve sweeps upward to the right (that is, to induce more people to work more, you have to pay them a higher wage rate), the monopsonist who wants to hire more workers will have to offer a higher wage rate. The best-known monopsonists these days are professional baseball, football, and basketball leagues (see the box, "Professional Sports as Monopsonies").

The monopsonist faces the entire supply curve of labor.

When a union that controls the supply of labor is opposed by an employer that controls the demand for labor, we have a bilateral monopoly. Using that term loosely, we may call several labor markets bilateral monopolies: auto workers, professional baseball players, teachers in most large school districts, and aerospace workers. Like the very

---

[4]Dean Foust and Brian Grow, "Blues for a Company Town," *BusinessWeek,* October 6, 2003, p. 56.

Professional Sports as Monopsonies

If you happen to be a professional athlete, you probably don't have many prospective employers to whom you can sell your services. Take baseball. If you're a really good prospect, the chances are you'll be drafted by one of the major-league teams, and if you're *really* good, you'll work your way up to the big leagues. But then you'll have to play for the team that drafted you for another five years before you may become a free agent and sell your services to other teams willing to bid on them.

Professional football had virtually no free agency until 1993. Until then if you were one of the better players in the National Football League, you were virtually tied to your team for your entire career, unless you were traded to another team. Every 8 or 10 years a rival league would spring up and a bidding war would ensue, driving up salaries. In the 1960s there was the American Football League, which later merged with the National Football

League. In the 1970s we had the World Football League, and in the 1980s the United States Football League. These two leagues folded, but not before they pushed up salary levels in the National Football League.

The National Basketball Association, which has dominated professional basketball since the 1940s, eventually merged with the newer American Basketball Association, but not until a costly bidding war had raised salaries into the millions.

Today the professional baseball, football, and basketball leagues have pure monopsony power. So, too, does professional hockey, which endured labor stoppages before the play-offs in 1992 and for the entire 1994–95 and 2004–05 seasons. Although professional athletes are handsomely paid, and although they do enjoy some degree of free-agent power, their salaries would be even higher if there were more bidders for their services.

competitive oligopolists we talked about a few chapters back, a union dealing with a monopsony employer knows that any move it makes will invite a countermove by the firm. And vice versa. At the bargaining table, who ends up with what depends largely on the relative power on both sides.

Collective Bargaining

The main arena

The strike and the ability to take a strike are the ultimate weapons.

Collective bargaining is the main arena of the power struggle between labor and management. In general, labor tries to secure substantial increases in wages, fringe benefits, and perhaps better working conditions. Management, of course, offers considerably less than labor wants. And so they bargain. But backing up their bargaining power are their two ultimate weapons: for labor, it is the strike; for management, it is the ability to take a strike.

Strikes, Lockouts, and Givebacks

The lockout

Some observers say the lockout is management's ultimate weapon. That's like saying that if labor's ultimate weapon is to punch management in the nose, management can beat labor to the punch, so to speak, by punching *itself* in the nose. If a strike hurts the company by cutting off production, so does a lockout. But in 2002 when the West Coast longshoremen staged a work slowdown, the port operators felt they had no choice but to enforce a lockout (see the box, "Lockout on the Docks").

No, the ultimate weapon of management is the ability to take a strike. To carry my analogy further, a good fighter must be able to take a punch. Perhaps in other fields the term *glass jaw* or *canvas back* might be laudatory, but not in boxing—and not in collective bargaining. If the union knows management cannot withstand a strike, it will certainly push much harder for a favorable settlement.

Which firms and industries can best withstand a strike?

The ability to take a strike, of course, varies from firm to firm and from industry to industry. Generally, manufacturing fares better than services because the manufacturer can build up inventories in anticipation of a strike. On the rare occasions when the Taft-Hartley Act is invoked by the president, such a company can add even more to its

Lockout on the Docks

In the fall of 2002, 10,500 members of the International Longshore and Warehouse Union were locked out of their jobs at 29 West Coast ports after engaging in a month-long work slowdown. After 11 days, President George W. Bush invoked the 80-day cooling off period of the Taft-Hartley Act (for the first time in 24 years), the ports were reopened, and less than two months later, both sides resolved their dispute and signed a six-year contract.

During the lockout, the economy was losing about $1 billion a day, and would have been losing considerably more if the lockout had lasted longer. Automobile assembly lines, dependent on just-in-time deliveries, had begun shutting down, and retailers were worried about having the inventory needed to stock their shelves for the Christmas shopping season.

The crux of the dispute was over the introduction of information technology such as bar-codes, which would greatly improve efficiency, but lead to the loss of 400 clerical jobs. In the agreement, in exchange for the loss of these jobs, the union extracted a guarantee of lifetime employment for all the 1,600 current clerks. In addition, the longshoremen, who earned an average of $100,000 a year, received an 11 percent pay increase over the life of the contract.

stockpiles during the 80-day halt of the strike. As a strike wears on, orders can be filled from this large inventory. Also, delivery times can be stretched out from the normal two months to three or four months. When the strike is over, workers can be put on overtime and extra workers temporarily hired to help build up the depleted inventories and fill any backlog of orders.

Firms in service industries are less able to take a strike than those in manufacturing because they do not have an inventory to help them cushion the effects of lost production. An airline, an insurance company, a bank, a computer firm, or a real estate company cannot make up lost sales because their competitors will have picked up the slack.

A diversified firm, particularly a large conglomerate, can ride out a strike more easily than can the firm that produces a single good or service. A strike will affect only one or two divisions; the others will keep operating. Similarly, a large firm has a better chance of surviving a strike than a small firm does because it has greater financial resources. Finally, a multinational corporation might simply shift operations to another country in the event of a strike.

All this brilliant analysis notwithstanding, one can occasionally draw exactly the opposite conclusion about negotiating strength varying with the ability to take a strike. It's like the rhetorical question "Would you hit a person wearing glasses?" Then, of course, you put on a pair of glasses.

What does this have to do with the ability to take a strike? I'm glad you asked. If you worked for a company that might go under, would *you* call for a strike? You'd probably win the strike and be out of a job. That's why the United Auto Workers did not dare call a strike in the 1970s and early 1980s, although they could have easily defeated Chrysler. To carry this a bit further, if a company like Chrysler is financially weak, you won't ask for much of a wage increase. In fact, during the 1981–82 recession, some unions actually negotiated not only no wage increases but even wage reductions. Saving jobs, especially during the economic doldrums of the early 1990s, has often led to wage reductions.

Productivity increases are a key issue because they provide the basis for pay increases. If workers produce more, they have a good argument for increased pay; and if more is produced, the company can afford to pay more. Unfortunately, productivity—output per labor hour—is not often measured accurately. A union might argue that productivity is rising 4 percent a year, and management might just as reasonably counter that the figure is only 2 percent.

The United Steelworkers have taken a very cooperative approach towards collective bargaining, helping to restructure the ailing U.S. steel industry. In 2003, it helped create a plan to revitalize Goodyear Tire & Rubber Co., the nation's largest tire maker, which had lost $1.5 billion the previous year, and a large slice of its market share to rivals selling cheap tires made in low-wage countries.

Industrial relations are like sexual relations. It's better between two consenting parties.
            —Vic Feather,
    British trade-union leader

COLAs

Productivity increases

The union appeared to have just two options—either allow Goodyear to replace some of its 14 U.S. plants with ones in Asia, or to call a strike that might force the company into bankruptcy. But the United Steelworkers came up with a third choice—slash labor costs by $1.15 billion over three years and cut 3,000 jobs in exchange for Goodyear's promise to keep—and invest in—12 of its 14 U.S. factories and to limit imports from its factories in Brazil and Asia. In addition to the job cuts, USW members won't get a raise for three years. But this may have been a small price for the thousands of workers who will be able to keep their $22 an hour jobs.

Pattern-setting wage increases

Finally, there's the issue of pattern-setting wage increases. For example, after the uniform services (police, fire, and sanitation) negotiations are completed in New York, the city then begins negotiations with the other municipal unions. The bargaining teams for those unions do not want to go back to their members with less than the other guys got. It's as simple as that. During periods of rapid inflation, with the added pressure of keeping up with the rising cost of living, the unions sometimes view the pattern-setting settlements as minimums that must be exceeded. This tends to create still newer pattern setters, which themselves become goals to be surpassed.

The Collective Bargaining Agreement

Collective bargaining negotiations will end with either an agreement or a strike. The collective bargaining agreement is a contract running from a page or two up to several hundred pages. The first key provision is wages and hours. The second is job security and seniority. Other areas often covered include grievance procedures, working conditions, and the role of the union in the day-to-day running of the firm. Also spelled out in the contract are health benefits, the number of paid holidays, paid sick leave and personal leave days, and vacation days.

Grievance procedure

The focal point of negotiations is generally the wage increase.

The focal point of the negotiations is generally the amount by which wage rates will be increased. In fact, progress reports on the negotiations generally refer to the latest wage offer. Everything else gets lumped together as "other issues."

Job security and seniority

Job security and seniority are also important contract provisions. Generally, the last people hired are the first to be laid off. Seniority is often the most important criterion for promotion as well. This has tended to pit older, more experienced workers against younger workers, but a union negotiating team will almost always regard seniority as sacrosanct, especially because older workers tend to dominate most unions.

Company officials typically dislike union wage scales and seniority provisions because they require everyone to be paid at the same rate regardless of individual productivity differences. Furthermore, officials are legally bound to lay off the least senior workers during bad economic times—times when it would make more sense to lay off the least efficient workers. Union officials counter that it would be arbitrary and unfair to use any criterion other than seniority as the basis for wage rates, promotion, and order of layoffs.

As a general rule, remuneration by fixed salaries does not in any class of functionaries produce the maximum of zeal.
—John Stuart Mill,
Principles of Political Economy

Another important provision in many contracts is the grievance procedure, which is spelled out step-by-step. For example, an assembly line worker whose supervisor yelled at her might first have to go to her shop steward, who then talks to the supervisor. If the grievance is not settled at that level, it might go to the chief steward and the head of the department. Beyond that, the contract may specify two or three still higher levels. However, most grievances are settled at the steward–supervisor level.

The Strike

Show me a country in which there are no strikes and I'll show you that country in which there is no liberty.
—Samuel Gompers

Very few strikes have disrupted the U.S. economy. Since the passage of the Taft-Hartley Act in 1947, only two have caused major economic disruption: the 1959 steel strike and the United Auto Workers' strike against General Motors in 1970.

Figure 5 provides a historical record of work-time lost to strikes. Since the late 1980s, we have never lost as much as one-tenth of one percent of worktime because of strikes.

Very few strikes have disrupted our economy.

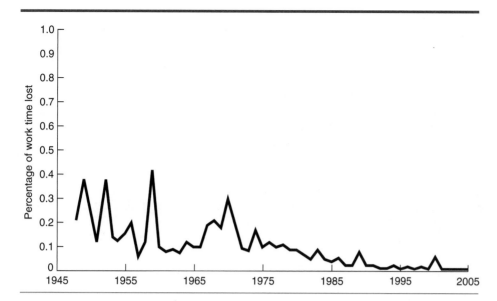

F*igure* **5**
Work Time Lost because of
Strikes, 1945–2005
From 1946 through 1970, strikes
often resulted in very substantial
losses of labor hours. Since 1970,
there has been a marked decline in
hours lost, and since the mid-1970s,
we have never had a year in which
those losses amounted to even one-
tenth of one percent of total work
time.
Source: U.S. Department of Labor,
Monthly Labor Review, various issues.

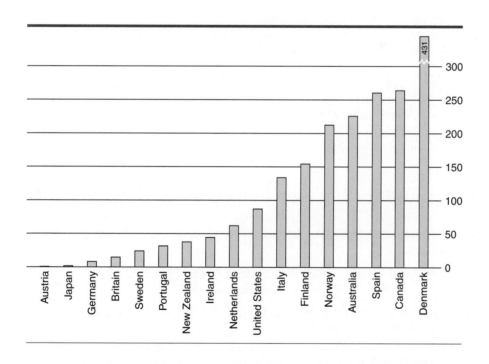

F*igure* **6**
Working Days Lost per 1,000
Employees, Annual Average,
1994–2003
Source: The Economist, April 30, 2005.

The American economy, despite some acrimonious collective bargaining, rarely experiences major strikes. This conclusion would be reaffirmed by glancing at Figure 6. Denmark, Canada, Spain, Australia, and Norway each lost at least twice as many working days per thousand workers as the U.S.

Averting Strikes: Mediation and Arbitration

Collective bargaining is the basic way of averting strikes. The two sides sit down together and, after some tough bargaining, hammer out an agreement that each can live with.

But what if they can't reach an agreement? Or what if they can't even agree to sit down together in the same room? In those cases, a mediator or an arbitrator may be called in, either by the parties themselves or by the federal government.

A mediator is literally a go-between, who tries to speed up the process of negotiations, getting each side to give a little more and take a little less. Often he or she sits down with each side separately and then, when an agreement seems possible, gets both sides together for what is, the mediator hopes, the final bargaining session.

The mediator does not have the power to impose a settlement but can play a valuable role as an expediter. The job of an arbitrator is to impose settlements. This takes the decision out of the hands of labor and management, making arbitration a situation both sides usually want to avoid. Under compulsory arbitration, a labor contract or law actually stipulates that if the two parties cannot reach an agreement, an arbitrator will make the decision.

Current Issue: Will You Ever Be a Member of a Labor Union?

Fifty years ago most families had at least one union member. People were very reluctant to cross picket lines. And powerful unions like the Teamsters and the Longshoremen could shut down much of the economy by going out on strike.

Unless you end up working in the public sector, the chances are very slight that you will ever join a union. From kindergarten through the high school, it's very likely that your teachers were union members. And the chances are, the professors at your college are also unionized. So if you end up teaching, then there's probably a union card in your future.

If you happen to have a family tree handy, what would you learn by researching who in your family was ever a union member? I suspect that as you moved from your great grandparents' generation to your grandparents', and then to that of your parents and their siblings, you'd find fewer and fewer union members. Unless, of course, many of your family members have been government employees.

Questions for Further Thought and Discussion

1. Which key provisions of the Taft-Hartley Act persuaded union leaders that the law was antilabor?
2. What are the basic provisions of a collective bargaining agreement?
3. Explain the differences between mediation and arbitration.
4. Explain how a monopsonist operates in the labor market, and illustrate your explanation with an example.
5. On average, do unionized workers earn higher wages than comparable nonunion workers? Why?
6. How do you account for the declining membership in labor unions?
7. Was President George W. Bush right in invoking the Taft-Hartley Act to end the 2002 lockout of the longshoremen?

Workbook for Chapter 27

Name _____   Date _____

Multiple-Choice Questions

Circle the letter that corresponds to the best answer.

1. Unions have _____.
   a) increased wages
   b) decreased wages
   c) had no effect on wages

2. Which statement is true about labor unions in the United States?
   a) They have always been very popular.
   b) They did not gain widespread acceptance until the 1940s.
   c) They have never gained widespread acceptance.
   d) None of these statements is true.

3. Which is the most accurate statement?
   a) Collective bargaining is almost always between the two parties of a bilateral monopoly.
   b) Monopsonies are illegal under the Taft-Hartley Act.
   c) The United States has a lower percentage of its work force unionized than most other industrial nations.
   d) Most physicians are now members of labor unions.

4. The American Federation of Labor became the nation's predominant labor organization in _____.
   a) the early 19th century
   b) the 1880s
   c) the early 20th century
   d) the 1940s

5. The AFL has always been basically interested in _____.
   a) better wages, hours, and working conditions
   b) the formation of small producers' cooperatives
   c) the creation of true socialism
   d) none of the above

6. The act that supported union organizing was the _____.
   a) National Labor Relations Act
   b) Taft-Hartley Act
   c) Landrum-Griffin Act
   d) Sherman Antitrust Act

7. Employers' rights were protected in the _____.
   a) National Labor Relations Act
   b) Taft-Hartley Act
   c) Clayton Act
   d) Sherman Antitrust Act

8. Jurisdictional disputes and secondary boycotts are prohibited under the _____ Act.
   a) National Labor Relations   c) Clayton
   b) Taft-Hartley   d) Sherman Antitrust

9. Limits on takeovers of locals by national unions and a listing of the financial responsibilities of union officials were provisions of the _____ Act.
   a) National Labor Relations   c) Clayton
   b) Taft-Hartley   d) Sherman Antitrust

10. Under a(n) _____ shop, an employer may hire only union members.
   a) closed   c) open
   b) union

11. Right-to-work laws promote the formation of _____.
   a) closed shops   c) open shops
   b) union shops

12. In 1935 the _____.
   a) AFL was organizing along industry lines and the CIO was organizing along craft lines
   b) AFL was organizing along craft lines and the CIO was organizing along industry lines
   c) AFL and the CIO were both organizing along craft lines
   d) AFL and the CIO were both organizing along industry lines

13. The AFL and CIO split up in _____ and got back together in _____.
    a) 1915, 1935
    b) 1935, 1955
    c) 1955, 1975
    d) 1975, 1985

14. The only prolabor name among the following is _____.
    a) Sherman
    b) Clayton
    c) Taft-Hartley
    d) Wagner

15. Which statement is true?
    a) No union is a monopoly.
    b) Some unions are monopolies.
    c) All unions are monopolies.

16. Which statement is true with respect to the two basic ways unions have of exerting power?
    a) Only inclusion leads to higher wages.
    b) Only exclusion leads to higher wages.
    c) Both inclusion and exclusion lead to higher wages.
    d) Neither inclusion nor exclusion leads to higher wages.

17. A monopsony is _____.
    a) the only seller of a product for which there are no close substitutes
    b) the only buyer of a product for which there are no close substitutes
    c) both the seller and the buyer of a product for which there are no close substitutes
    d) neither the seller nor the buyer of a product for which there are no close substitutes

18. Each of the following companies except _____ was once a monopsony.
    a) General Electric
    b) J. P. Stevens
    c) R. J. Reynolds
    d) AT&T

19. The ultimate weapon that management can use against unions is _____.
    a) collective bargaining
    b) the strike
    c) the ability to take (or withstand) a strike
    d) the lockout

20. The firm with the least ability to withstand a strike would be a _____.
    a) manufacturing firm
    b) service firm
    c) diversified firm

21. A collective bargaining negotiation is _____.
    a) solely a test of power
    b) solely a presentation and discussion of real issues
    c) both a test of power and a presentation and discussion of real issues
    d) neither a test of power nor a presentation and discussion of real issues

22. Pattern-setting wage increases tend to be viewed as _____.
    a) minimums by unions engaged in subsequent bargaining
    b) maximums by unions engaged in subsequent bargaining
    c) irrelevant by unions engaged in subsequent bargaining

23. Collective bargaining negotiations _____ end with a strike.
    a) always
    b) usually
    c) occasionally
    d) never

24. The two key areas covered by provisions of collective bargaining agreements are _____.
    a) wages and hours, and job security and seniority
    b) wages and hours, and working conditions
    c) job security and seniority, and working conditions

25. The job of a(n) _____ is to impose a settlement.
    a) arbitrator
    b) mediator
    c) collective bargaining team leader

26. Most strikes _____.
    a) cause widespread economic disruption
    b) cause little economic disruption
    c) cause no economic disruption

27. Which group of workers would be the easiest for a union to organize?

a) Employees at a Wal-Mart store

b) Employees of a county government

c) Employees at a Honda plant in Ohio

d) Employees at a textile mill in North Carolina

28. You would most likely be a union member if you _____.

a) were a teacher

b) lived in the South

c) worked for Wal-Mart

d) were a corporate executive

29. Which is the most accurate statement?

a) Within 10 years there will be no manufacturing jobs in the United States.

b) In general, it is harder to export service jobs than manufacturing jobs.

c) A higher percentage of private employees than government employees are unionized.

d) The employees of Wal-Mart are among the highest paid retail workers in the United States.

30. Which is the most accurate statement?

a) In recent years the United States has experienced relative labor peace.

b) The last few years have been excellent ones for American labor unions.

c) Labor union membership today is at an all-time low.

d) Most nations have lost less time to strikes (per thousand workers) than the United States.

31. Which statement is true?

a) In good economic times, employers demand more givebacks from labor unions than in bad economic times.

b) We have not had a major strike in over ten years.

c) The United States is one of the most heavily unionized nations in the world.

d) There are at least five unions with at least one million members.

32. You would most likely be a union member if you lived in _____.

a) the United States

d) Germany

b) Japan

e) Sweden

c) Canada

Fill-In Questions

1. The two most important pieces of labor legislation were the _____ Act and the _____ Act.

2. The apparatus for conducting union representation elections was set up under the _____ _____ Act.

3. The _____ Act put the force of the federal government behind collective bargaining.

4. Jurisdictional disputes and secondary boycotts are prohibited under the _____ Act.

5. Under the _____ shop, an employer may hire only union members.

6. Under the _____ shop, no one is forced to join the union.

7. Industrial unions are organized along _____ lines, while craft unions are organized along _____ lines.

8. The biggest spurt in union membership occurred during the decade of the _____.

9. The conflict within the AFL over whether to organize on a craft basis or an industrial basis led to _____ _____.

10. Unions have two basic ways of exerting power. They are to (1) _____ and (2) _____.

11. A monopsony is _____
    _____.

12. _____ is the main arena of the
    power struggle between labor and management.

13. The ultimate weapon for labor is _____,
    while the ultimate weapon for management is
    _____.

14. At collective bargaining sessions, management
    operates under two main constraints:
    (1) _____
    and (2) _____.

15. Collective bargaining negotiations will end with
    either _____ or _____.

660

Chapter 28

Labor Markets and Wage Rates

In the United States, as well as in most other countries, there is a wide disparity in income. People like Giorgio Armani, Tom Clancy, Stephen King, Tom Hanks, Britney Spears, Alex Rodriguez, David Letterman, Jay Leno, and the presidents of major corporations, as well as heart surgeons and even the writers of best-selling economics textbooks, make millions of dollars a year.

Two thousand five was a very good year for movie-maker George Lucas (*Star Wars*), who pulled in $290 million. Oprah Winfrey ($225 million), Mel Gibson ($185 million), Tiger Woods ($87 million), and Steven Spielberg ($80 million) ranked 1–5 on *Forbes Magazine's* 100 Top Celebrities List. Shaquille O'Neal was paid $33 million (plus perhaps as much in endorsements) to play basketball, and some four dozen other basketball players earned more than $10 million. But the typical American wage-earner was paid between $25,000 and $35,000.

Why do people earn such widely varying incomes? There are several reasons for this disparity, but the bottom line remains the same. You guessed it: supply and demand.

CHAPTER OBJECTIVES

In this chapter you'll learn about:

- The supply of labor.
- The demand for labor.
- High wage rates and economic rent.
- Employment discrimination.

- Real wages and productivity.
- The minimum wage.
- The living wage.

The Supply of Labor

Noncompeting Groups

There are various classes, or strata, of labor. There is skilled labor, which includes carpenters, plumbers, machinists, computer programmers, printers, schoolteachers, and airline pilots. There is semiskilled labor, such as assembly-line workers, file clerks, short-order cooks, receptionists, and supermarket checkers. Finally, there is unskilled labor, which includes freight handlers, dishwashers, porters, janitors, and gas station attendants.

Skilled, semiskilled, and unskilled labor

In a sense, there are thousands of noncompeting groups. But that doesn't mean there's no overlap or that people with one skill do not compete for jobs with those who have other skills. In fact, an employer is often faced with the decision to hire either a skilled worker for high pay or a lower-paid trainee. One might say that in the long run we are all potential competitors for the same jobs.

If the opportunities arise in certain fields—professional sports, engineering, accounting, computer programming, medicine—people will go through the necessary training and compete for jobs. If there are large numbers of relatively high-paying jobs, people currently in those fields will eventually be joined by huge numbers of competitors.

We are all competitors in the same employment pool.

In still another sense, we are all competitors in the same employment pool. Certain skills are partially substitutable for other skills. One 100-word-per-minute typist is a perfect substitute for another 100-word-per-minute typist; but an electrician who can type 20 words per minute is only a partial substitute. Similarly, a plumber's assistant is a partial substitute for a plumber, and a file clerk is an even more partial substitute for a plumber's assistant.

In the long run most of us can learn to do many different jobs. In some cases it takes just a few hours, but it takes many years to learn other skills. In the short run, however, we are all partial substitutes for one another. The question is, how partial?

There *are* noncompeting groups, but these distinctions tend to blur in the long run. To the degree that there is a good deal of labor mobility—the ability to change occupations and/or geographic locations—there is less demarcation among the nation's various occupational groups.

The Theory of the Dual Labor Market

Primary and secondary labor markets

Obviously, we are not all in the same labor market, primarily because we are separated by skill, ability, and training. A more radical theory than that of noncompeting groups places the entire labor force into two broad categories: the primary and secondary labor markets.

The primary market has most of the good jobs, which not only pay well but offer good opportunities for advancement. Examples of such jobs include the skilled crafts, management, the professions, and virtually all the other jobs requiring college degrees. (See the box, "Are You in the Primary Market or in the Secondary Market?")

Are You in the Primary Market or in the Secondary Market?

Thirty years ago, you could graduate from high school, get married, have kids, and have a decent life in a blue-collar town.

—Gary Bauer, president of the Family Research Council (quoted in *BusinessWeek,* March 13, 1995, p. 74)

Average Annual Earnings by Amount of Education, 2005

Some high school	$18,734
High school diploma	27,915
College degree	51,206
Advanced degree	74,602

Source: U.S. Census Bureau.

As you can see from the table, a person's average earnings rises with her level of education. Someone with an advanced degree earns, on average, about four times what a high school dropout earns. And the income of a college graduate is almost double that of a high school graduate.

Does this mean that a college degree will almost double your earnings? Increasingly, the answer is no.

A diploma remains a *necessary* condition for a person to move from the secondary to the primary labor market. But that diploma is no longer a *sufficient* condition. You not only need a college degree, but you also need to be educated (the two are not necessarily synonymous)—and maybe a little lucky or well-connected. However, if you *don't* have a college degree, your chances of ever getting a job in the primary market are nil—unless, of course, your parents own the company.

A College Degree Is the Ticket out of Poverty

If you grow up in a poor family, but manage to get a college degree, it's very unlikely that you'll still be poor. But that door to the middle class is closing. In 1979 students from the richest 25 percent of American homes were four times as likely to attend college as those from the poorest 25 percent; by 1994 they were ten times as likely. Why? The main reason is that since 1979 the cost of going to college has gone up twice as fast as the rate of inflation.

To make matters still worse, Pell Grants, which help the children of the poor and working class to attend college, and covered 84 percent of the cost of attending a four-year public college in 1979, now cover just one-third the cost. The only way that most low-income students can afford college is to work long hours at part-time jobs, while attending a 2-year, rather than a 4-year school.

At an elite university, you are 25 times more likely to run into a rich student than a poor one. As educator Terry Hartle has put it, "Smart poor kids go to college at the same rate as stupid rich kids."

Let's look at the record. *BusinessWeek* published these findings:

A mere 4.5 percent of those from the bottom quartile of income brackets get a degree by age 24, according to an analysis of Census Bureau data by Thomas G. Mortenson, who publishes an education research newsletter in Oskaloosa, Iowa. About 12 percent of students in the next quartile get a BA, while 25 percent of those in the third quartile do. In the top quarter, meanwhile, 51 percent of students finish college. *

*Aaron Bernstein, "A British Solution to America's College Tuition Problem," *BusinessWeek*, February 9, 2004, p. 72.

The secondary market consists of all the jobs that are left over. The pay is low, and there is little chance for advancement. Often the jobs are temporary, and the people who hold them are called "disposable workers." These jobs include work in laundries, hospitals, fast-food chains, and clothing factories or spraying pesticides, stripping hotel beds, shampooing carpets, and scrubbing toilets. These positions are often filled by minority group members, women, and immigrants.

In *Nickel and Dimed,* Barbara Ehrenreich describes her experiences working in the secondary job market as a waitress, a hotel maid, a cleaning woman, a nursing home aide, and a Wal-Mart sales clerk. Here is her description of her downtime at her waitress job:

> Managers can sit—for hours at a time if they want—but it's their job to see that no one else ever does, even when there's nothing to do, and this is why, for servers, slow times can be as exhausting as rushes. You start dragging out each little chore because if the manager on duty catches you in an idle moment he will give you something far nastier to do. So I wipe, I clean, I consolidate catsup bottles and recheck the cheesecake supply, even tour the tables to make sure the customer evaluation forms are all standing perkily in their places—wondering all the time how many calories I burn in these strictly theatrical exercises. In desperation, I even take the desserts out of their glass display case and freshen them up with whipped cream and bright new maraschino cherries; anything to look busy. When, on a particularly dead afternoon, Stu finds me glancing at a *USA Today* a customer has left behind, he assigns me to vacuum the entire floor with the broken vacuum cleaner, which has a handle only two feet long, and the only way to do that without incurring orthopedic damage is to proceed from spot to spot on your knees.[1]

Barbara Ehrenreich (Sigrid Estrada)

The dual labor market theory is a class theory of employment. The rich stay rich, and the poor stay poor. The college degree seems to be a dividing line, a line that is seldom crossed by those from poorer economic backgrounds (see the box, "A College Degree Is the Ticket out of Poverty").

One problem with this theory is that it doesn't account for the huge middle level of occupations—nursing, teaching, social work, and noncollege-graduate positions in

The rich stay rich, and the poor stay poor.

---

[1]Barbara Ehrenreich, *Nickel and Dimed* (New York: Henry Holt, 2001), pp. 22–23.

insurance, banking, and retailing. But the theory *does* support the contention that there are noncompeting groups in the labor market. The only question is, how many?

The Backward-Bending Labor Supply Curve

When we talk about the supply of labor, I ask my students whether they would be willing to do clerical work for $5.15 an hour. Nobody would. How about $10 an hour? A lot of hands go up. And at $100 an hour, everyone volunteers.

The substitution effect

This demonstrates the *substitution effect.* As the wage rate rises, people are willing to substitute more work for leisure time because leisure time is becoming more expensive. Imagine if an hour of leisure time cost you $100! Suppose the wage rate were increased to $1,000 an hour. Now an hour of leisure time would cost you $1,000! That's a lot of money to give up for just one hour of watching TV, playing bingo, or hanging around the shopping mall.

Something else is happening as your wage rate keeps getting higher. You're making all this money. You're rich! You're making $1,000 an hour. But if you keep working more and more hours, when are you going to be able to spend your money? When are you going to have time to see your family and friends? And when are you going to have time to sleep?

At some point, as your wage rate continues to rise, you will say to yourself, "I want more leisure time for myself, if only so that I'll be able to spend some of my money." Now you're willing to give up some income in exchange for more leisure time. We call this the *income effect*.

The income effect

How many hours would you work picking up money?

Let's see how the substitution and income effects work for *you*. How would you like a job picking pennies up off the floor? You get to keep all the pennies you pick up. What's the catch? There *is* no catch. Just tell me how many hours per week you'd be willing to work.

Of course some people would not stoop so low as to take a job picking up pennies. How about nickels? Dimes? Quarters? Half-dollars? How about dollar bills? All right, I'll even let you pick up five-dollar bills. What I want to know is how many hours per week you would be willing to work picking up each of these denominations of coins and bills.

Write down your answers. Then compare them to mine in Table 1. Of course, there *is* no "right" answer. Everyone has his or her own schedule of hours of willingness to work.

Most people would work more hours to pick up nickels than they would to pick up pennies. And more hours to pick up dimes than to pick up nickels. That's the substitution effect at work: They're substituting more work for leisure time. But at some point their hours reach a maximum. In this example, people would work 65 hours to pick up dollar bills. Beyond that point, the income effect will outweigh the substitution effect, as they give up some income in exchange for more leisure time.

Turning to Figure 1, we see that as the wage rate rises from very low levels to higher and higher levels, people substitute extra work for leisure time. That's the substitution effect. And it happens up to point J. Beyond point J the curve begins to move upward to the left as the wage rate continues to rise. That's the income effect.

TABLE 1	Hypothetical Work Schedule Picking Up Money
Type of Money	Hours per Week
Pennies	35
Nickels	50
Dimes	58
Quarters	61
Half-dollars	63
Dollar bills	65
Five-dollar bills	62

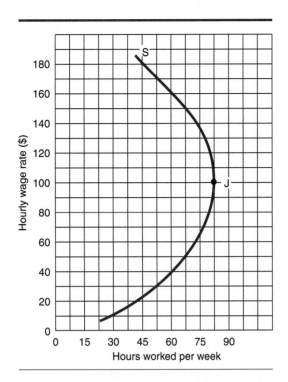

Figure 1
Hypothetical Labor Supply
Curve
A person will be willing to work an
increasing amount of hours per
week as the hour wage rate goes
up. But at some point (point J) he
will begin to cut back on his hours
as the wage rate continues to rise.
Up to point J he is substituting
extra work for leisure time. Beyond
point J the curve bends backward as
the income effect outweighs the
substitution effect and this person is
willing to trade away some money
for more leisure time.

To summarize: The substitution effect means that you trade away leisure time for more money, and the income effect means that you trade away some money for more leisure time. At wage rates below point J on the curve, the substitution effect outweighs the income effect. At point J the two effects just offset each other. Above J the income effect outweighs the substitution effect.

We call curve S in Figure 1 the labor supply curve. Perhaps the typical individual will work a maximum of 80 hours a week.

Do you recall that the chapter "Demand in the Factor Market" introduced a different substitution effect? For example, if the price of labor went up, business firms would tend to substitute capital or land for some of their now more expensive workers. So *that* substitution effect described substituting one resource for another. In *this* chapter the substitution effect that describes how, as wage rates rise, people are willing to substitute more work for leisure time. Economists are usually good at giving the same concept two or three different names. In the case of the substitution effect, however, we've given the same name to two different concepts.

The Demand for Labor

The Marginal Revenue Product Schedule

You may have noticed that I have been trying to impress on you the idea that the wage rate is determined by two factors, supply and demand. We just covered supply. Demand is the firm's MRP schedule for labor.[2] In the more general sense, the demand for a particular type of labor is the sum of all the firms' MRP schedules.

Like nearly all demand curves we've encountered, the general demand curve for labor, shown in Figure 2, slopes downward to the right. It conforms to *the law of demand,* a concept first introduced in Chapter 3: *When the price of a good is lowered, more of it is demanded; when it is raised, less is demanded.* Because every firm's MRP curve

Demand for labor is represented by the MRP schedule.

---

[2]We covered MRP two chapters back in "Demand in the Factor Market."

Figure 2

Hypothetical General Demand
Curve for Labor
This is the sum of every firm's
MRP curve. As the wage rate is
lowered, increasing quantities of
labor are demanded.

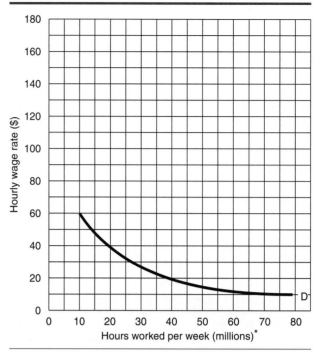

*We have gone from average hours worked per week to millions of hours
worked per week to reflect the total labor market with millions of people selling
their labor.

slopes downward to the right (as the wage rate, or price of labor, declines), it follows that the general demand curve for labor, which is the sum of these curves, also slopes downward to the right.

We may ask what determines the demand for labor or, more specifically, the MRP schedule of each firm. Remember that the demand for each factor of production—land, labor, capital—is a derived demand. It is derived from the demand for the final product.

Firms hire labor because that labor produces a final product, which is then sold. Not all labor is identical. Some people are more productive because they are better trained, more skilled, or have more natural ability.

Obviously, workers who are more productive will be more in demand and better paid than less productive workers. The more highly skilled machinist and the better basketball player will usually earn more than their less productive colleagues. Some people become more productive because of education and training, some because of work experience, and, of course, some are just born with greater natural ability.

Specialized skills

Closely related to worker productivity are specialized skills possessed by some workers, which also influence the demand for labor. Generally, the highly skilled worker or the highly trained specialist will earn higher wages than the person with less developed skills. Specialists in medicine and dentistry, in law, and in engineering are usually among the best paid practitioners of their professions. This is especially true when their skills are in relatively high demand in relation to their supply.

Finally, some workers are in demand because of the natural abilities they possess. Obvious examples abound in show business and professional athletics. A little later we'll consider the special cases of David Letterman and Willie Mays.

Nonhomogeneous Jobs

Still another factor accounting for different wage rates is worker preference with respect to working hours and conditions. Those willing to work longer hours, night shifts, and weekends will usually earn higher wages than will those who work the standard Monday-to-Friday, nine-to-five workweek; those who work under unsafe conditions earn higher wages as well. Pay differentials are institutionalized, for example, for window washers who work above the 20th floor.

Harder, more unpleasant, or less convenient work is usually somewhat better paid than the more conventional occupations. Night workers and those who work overtime get pay differentials. The out-of-town salesman is better paid than his home territory counterpart, while the sandhog who builds tunnels is given much shorter hours and higher pay than most other construction workers.

Pay differentials adjust for harder, more unpleasant, less convenient work.

More than a century ago John Stuart Mill took a diametrically opposite view of how well people were paid to do undesirable work:

> The really exhausting and the really repulsive labours, instead of being better paid than others, are almost invariably paid the worst of all… The hardships and the earnings, instead of being directly proportional, as in any just arrangements of society they would be, are generally in an inverse ratio to one another.[3]

Do you happen to know the year in which Martin Luther King, Jr., was assassinated? It was 1968. And in which city? Memphis. What was King doing in Memphis? He was leading a strike of sanitation workers. The Memphis sanitation workers were predominantly black, and they were paid little more than minimum wage. Because there was so much employment discrimination against blacks, especially in the South, many black men were forced into doing this undesirable work at very low wages.

How do we get people to pick up our garbage?

But the situation was different in New York City. Not only were sanitation workers relatively well paid, but few were black or Hispanic. In fact, for years public school teachers complained that garbage men were paid more than *they* were. So New York got its garbage picked up by paying white men very well to do it; Memphis got *its* garbage picked up by not allowing black or Hispanic men to do more desirable types of work.

How does our society get its dirty work done? By paying people enough to make it worth their while? Or by calling on oppressed minorities to work as migrant farm laborers, bedpan orderlies, janitors, dishwashers, and launderers? This disturbing question may be argued persuasively from either side.

The Effects of Employment Discrimination on Wages

The civil rights movement of the 1960s and the women's liberation movement of the 1970s had a profound impact on the nation's workplace. As late as the 1960s, the job ads of newspapers were divided into two sections—male and female. Employment agencies had not-so-secret numerical codes. For instance an employer with a job opening for a secretary might call to ask for a 1, which meant WASP (White Anglo-Saxon Protestant). It was understood, of course, that this was a woman's job. "Send me a 4" meant that an African American was needed for some menial job.

People from many different groups were discriminated against, but the two largest targets were women and African Americans. And if you happened to be an African American woman, then, of course, you had two strikes against you before you even came to bat.

Employment Discrimination against Women

In Chapter 2 we saw how employment discrimination leads to a misallocation of our economy's resources. Over 47 percent of our labor force are women, so let's try to get some idea of how much employment discrimination affects their wages.

---

[3]John Stuart Mill, *Principles of Political Economy,* ed. H. Ashley, p. 388.

Back in 1964, about a decade before the women's liberation movement, women made, on average, 59 percent of what men made. By 2005 they made 77 percent. Clearly there's been substantial progress. Professions that had been largely closed to women—medicine, law, corporate management, and public administration—are now almost gender blind. But the number of women who are Fortune 500 CEOs is still just seven—Mary Sammons (Rite Aid); Annie Mulcahy (Xerox); Pat Russo (Lucent); Andrea Jung (Avon); Marce Fuller (Mirant); Ellen Scott (Pathmark); and Marion Sandler (Golden West Financial). Until many more women reach the upper levels of corporate management, it is apparent that a glass ceiling is still in place.

Perhaps the best measure of the absence of employment discrimination is the degree to which there is equal pay for equal work. How does the pay of women stack up against that of their male counterparts in various jobs? Not all that well according to the numbers in Figure 3.

You'll see that for each of the eleven jobs listed, women earn less than their male colleagues. Please look at the listings vertically, first starting at the top and reading down. Now read them again, this time starting at the bottom.

Did you notice a pattern? Please take a minute to summarize your observation right here. You can probably do it in just a couple of sentences.

Here's *my* observation: Only in the lower paying jobs do both sexes earn roughly the same. The further up the pay scale and the higher the education, the wider the earnings gap. The top five or six professions listed—bookkeeper, cashier, administrative assistant, registered nurse, secretary, and, possibly, psychologist—are what may be termed "women's jobs," because most of these jobs are held by women. Traditionally women's jobs have paid more poorly than other jobs. Interestingly, even in *these* jobs, women are paid somewhat less than men. But when we get into jobs traditionally closed to women—judge and lawyer, financial manager, and physician and surgeon—the pay differential between women and men becomes much more pronounced.

The field of work with the highest proportion of female workers is kindergarten and preschool teaching. Women hold 98 percent of these particular jobs, but a man in this job typically earns $5,000 more than a woman.

Figure 3

Unequal Pay for Equal Work

Source: Betsy Morris, "How Corporate America Is Betraying Women," *Fortune,* January 10, 2005.

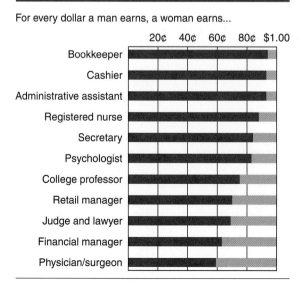

Are there any jobs in which women earn more than men? Yes—financial analysts, speech pathologist, radiation therapist, library worker, and biological technician. Female sales engineers make 43 percent more than their male counterparts, while female statisticians earn 35 percent more. But these jobs are rare exceptions to the rule: Men earn more than women doing the same work.

In recent years women have filed numerous sex discrimination suits. Although sexual harassment suits have gotten the most attention, the suits against employment discrimination have yielded the best financial results:

- Boeing agreed to pay $73 million to settle a class-action suit brought by female employees who asserted that they were paid less than men and not promoted as quickly.

- Morgan Stanley agreed to a $100-million-plus settlement to a class-action that made similar allegations.

- Nine hundred women who filed a sex discrimination suit against Merrill Lynch were paid over $100 million.

- UBS, Europe's largest bank, was ordered by a federal jury in New York to pay Laura Zubulake $29 million for mistreating her for being a woman, and then firing her after she complained to the Equal Employment Opportunity Commission.

In the mother of all class-action sex discrimination suits, Wal-Mart is being sued on behalf of 1.6 million current and past women employees. Women make up more than 72 percent of the company's hourly workers, but hold only about one-third of the store manager jobs. In addition, women earn substantially less than men in similar jobs. For example, women store managers made an average of $89,280 a year, $16,400 less than men.

While working as an assistant Sam's Club manager in Riverside, California, Stephanie Odle said she was surprised to discover that a male assistant manager at the store was making $60,000 a year, $23,000 more than she was earning.

"I was outraged," Ms. Odle said. "When I went to the district manager, he first goes, 'Stephanie, that assistant manager has a family and two children to support.' I told him, 'I'm a single mother and I have a 6-month-old child to support.'"[4]

Women are only 10 percent of the regional vice presidents, 10 percent of the district managers, and 14 percent of the store managers. And yet 89.5 percent of the cashiers and 79 percent of the department heads are women. Is there a glass ceiling at Wal-Mart? Perhaps when the lawsuit is settled, we'll have a definitive answer.

Employment Discrimination against African Americans

Like women, African Americans have made spectacular employment advances in recent decades. An interesting project would be to watch tapes of TV shows from the 1950s and compare them to current programming. Back in Chapter 2, we discussed the racial employment barriers that had been in place for centuries.

Despite their fantastic employment gains, African American men earn just 76 percent of what white men earn, while African American women earn only 65 percent. Incidentally Hispanic Americans fare even worse. Compared to white men's earnings, Hispanic men earn 60 percent and Hispanic women earn 55 percent.

In 1999 Franklin Raines became the first African American to head a major American corporation when he was named the CEO of the mortgage-financing giant, Fannie Mae. He was soon joined by four others—Barry Rand (Avis); Kenneth Chenault (American Express); Stanley O'Neal (Merrill Lynch); and Richard Parsons (AOL Time Warner). In 2006 Ron Williams became the CEO of Aetna. But still more spectacular were the appointments by President George W. Bush of Colin Powell as his first secretary of state, and of Powell's successor, Condolezza Rice.

---

[4]Steven Greenhouse, "Wal-Mart Sex Discrimination Suit Is Granted Class-Action Status," *The New York Times,* June 23, 2004, p. C8.

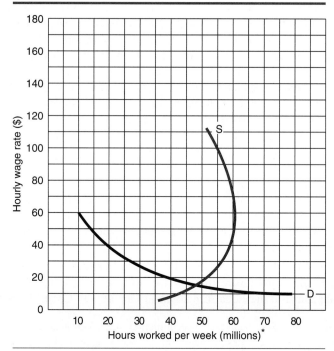

Figure 4
Hypothetical General Demand and Supply for Labor
The wage rate is set by the intersection of the general demand and supply curves for labor. In this case the wage rate is about $15 an hour.

*We have gone from average hours worked per week to millions of hours worked per week to reflect the total labor market with millions of people selling their labor.

Conclusion

May we conclude that employment discrimination fully explains the wage differentials that we have just noted? What about work experience, educational attainment, and, in the case of most women, the impact on career advancement of taking years off for child rearing?

It goes well beyond the scope of this book, not to mention the competence of the author, to discuss the degree to which sex discrimination accounts for the differences in the earnings of women and men. That said, I strongly suspect that sexual discrimination is alive and well in the American workplace.

The Wage Rate: Supply and Demand

Here's what we've all been waiting for. It's all there in Figure 4.

Much of this course is based on a simple law: the law of supply and demand. When quantity demanded is equal to quantity supplied, we've got our price. In this case the price of labor, or the wage rate, is about $15 an hour. But remember, this is only a *hypothetical* wage rate. How much is the *actual* wage rate? A lot lower? In many cases, yes. It all depends on the type of work you do and on the demand and supply schedules in each of hundreds, or even thousands, of job markets.

High Wage Rates and Economic Rent

In the early 1950s, when the Giants still played baseball at New York's Polo Grounds, Willie Mays joined the team as a young rookie and quickly established himself as the most exciting player in the game. Like most ballplayers of his generation, Mays came from an economically deprived background and was eventually earning unheard-of sums of money.

I don't think it's what I'm worth. It's what the market holds, what the organizations are willing to pay a player. The popularity I have, whether it's positive or controversial, people want to come out and see Jose Canseco play.

—Jose Canseco, outfielder for the Oakland A's who signed a five-year, $23.5 million contract in 1990. He retired in 2002 and in 2005 admitted that he regularly took steroids.

Lou Gehrig, the star first baseman on the great 1920s and 1930s Yankee teams, and Willie Mays, who began his long career as the New York Giants centerfielder in 1951, had an interest in common—besides being elected to the baseball Hall of Fame. Both loved playing ball so much that in their spare time, they played stickball in the street with the neighborhood kids. On the off-chance that you're not familiar with stickball, all you need is a broom handle and a rubber (Spaldeen) ball, and you can play it on a side street where there isn't too much traffic.

Professional baseball, football, basketball, hockey, tennis, and other sports give a few thousand people a chance to make a living playing kids' games. Although they negotiate for huge salaries, many, like Willie Mays, would have been willing to play for a lot less. Maybe it's a chance to prolong one's childhood for a few more years. Perhaps that's what gave Roger Kahn the idea for the title of his story of the 1953 Brooklyn Dodgers, *The Boys of Summer.*

Whenever a person gets paid more than the minimum she would be willing to accept, we call the excess over the minimum *economic rent*. For example, I might be willing to accept just $20,000 to be an economics professor. As I am now collecting a salary of $950,000, my economic rent is $930,000.

In January 1998 the ABC, CBS, and Fox networks agreed to collectively pay $17.6 billion for the rights to broadcast National Football League games for the next eight years. Question: What effect did this deal have on the players' salaries and on their economic rent? Obviously it raised both salaries and economic rent.

How much does David Letterman make? Although Mr. Letterman asked me not to disclose his exact earnings, it is estimated at $40 million a year. I will try to put aside my personal misgivings about a mere show business personality earning even more than I do.

We come back again to supply and demand. There may be thousands of would-be comics occasionally getting a gig here and there, but there are perhaps half a dozen really good ones. Thus, we have a graph like that in Figure 5, in which the wage rate comes to $30 million.

It all comes back to supply and demand.

Now David Letterman probably could scrape by on $10 million a year if he really had to. If that were his secret bottom line—if he was really willing to work for that paltry sum—his economic rent would be some $30 million.

Is David Letterman overpaid? The question boils down to supply and demand. Good stand-up comedians, great athletes, cosmetic surgeons, and authors capable of writing best-sellers are all in relatively short supply. If supply is relatively low in relation to demand, the resulting wage rate will be high.

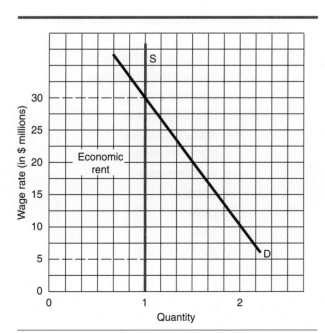

Figure 5

Determination of Economic Rent by Supply and Demand
How much of David Letterman's earnings are economic rent? If his earnings of $30 million are set by supply and demand, then his economic rent would depend on the minimum wage he would be willing to accept. For instance, if that were $5 million, then his economic rent would be $25 million.

Winner-Take-All Markets

Why do the chief executive officers of large American corporations earn on average about 500 times the salary of the average production worker? Is Yahoo CEO Terry Semel worth the $231 million he took home in 2005? Did Barry Diller, CEO of IAC/Interactive, earn every penny of the $156 million he was paid? The heads of America's 500 biggest companies received an aggregate 54 percent pay raise in 2005. Thirteen made over $50 million.

Robert Frank and Philip Cook note that top corporate executives in the United States, unlike their foreign counterparts, are relatively free to move from firm to firm, going to the highest bidder, in what the authors call "winner-take-all markets." These are mar-

kets in which a handful of top performers walk away with the lion's share of total rewards. This payoff structure has always been common in entertainment and professional sports, but in recent years it has permeated many other fields—law, journalism, consulting, investment banking, corporate management, design, fashion, even the hallowed halls of academe.* The star system is distorting American society by diverting talented young people into competition that most will lose.

---

*Robert Frank, "Talent and the Winner-Take-All Society," *The American Prospect,* Spring 1994, p. 95. See also, Robert Frank and Philip Cook, *The Winner-Take-All Society* (New York: Free Press, 1995).

These explanations as to why a tiny fraction of our population makes so much more than the rest of us, cloaked in such terms as *marginal revenue product* and *economic rent,* may still leave us wondering if these folks are *really* worth such huge incomes. For another view, see the box, "Winner-Take-All Markets."

Real Wages versus Money Wages

American wages versus wages in other industrial countries

How do American wages stack up against those of other industrial countries? Until the late 1970s or early 1980s this country paid higher wages than any other nation. But as you can see in Figure 6, a few countries have overtaken us.

If you were offered a job today at a salary of, say, $100,000, you probably would be inclined to take it. But what if you were locked into that salary for life? Isn't it

Figure 6

Hourly Wage and Fringe Benefits in Manufacturing, Selected Countries, 2004
Back in the 1970s and 1980s, U.S. workers led the world in wages and fringe benefits, but today, we are no longer number one. Denmark, Germany, Britain, and France have recently passed us. In addition, workers in relatively poorer countries, especially in the newly industrial countries in Western Asia, have largely closed the wage gap.
Source: Bureau of Labor Statistics; *The Economist,* December 17, 2005, p. 94.

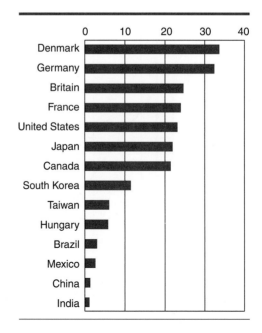

conceivable that by the time you reach middle age, $100,000 won't buy all that much? With the cost of living quadrupling since 1970, who knows what will happen to prices over the next 20 or 30 years? By real wages, economists mean what you can actually buy with your wages. If the rate of inflation were 10 percent a year, you'd need a 10 percent pay raise each year just to maintain your standard of living. And a person who earned $100,000 in 1970 would need about $400,000 today to continue living the same lifestyle.

What are real wages?

Suppose your wage rate rises from $5 an hour in 1993 to $8.40 an hour in 1999. Meanwhile, the consumer price index (CPI) rises from 100 in 1993 (the base year) to 120 in 1999 (the current year). How much is your real hourly wage in 1999, and by what percentage has it increased since 1993?

Solution:

$$\text{Real wages (current year)} = \frac{\text{Money wages (current year)}}{\text{CPI (current year)}} \times 100$$

$$= \frac{\$8.40}{120} \times 100$$

$$= \$.07 \times 100$$

$$= \$7.00$$

We found, then, that your real wage rate is $7 an hour in 1999. You'll notice that when I substituted numbers into the formula, I placed $8.40 over 1. I did this because I wanted to cross multiply. When you set up future problems, always put your money wages over 1.

For the second part of the problem we want to find the percentage increase in real wages from 1993 to 1999. We just found real wages of $7 for 1999. How much were real wages in 1993? There's only one choice—$5, which was given. Because 1993 was the base year, we're comparing what an hour's wages bought you in 1993 to what an hour's wages buy you in 1999.

So what is the percentage change when we go from $5 to $7?

Solution:

$$\text{Percentage change} = \frac{\text{Change}}{\text{Original number}}$$

$$= \frac{\$2}{\$5}$$

$$= .04$$

$$= 40\%$$

When we convert a decimal to a percentage, we move the decimal point two places to the right and add a percentage sign: .4 = .40 = .40.% = 40%.

If calculating percentage changes is not your strong suit, then please read the box titled "Calculating Percentage Changes," which you'll find about halfway through Chapter 9 in *Economics* and *Macroeconomics*.

Here's the next problem. Mr. Zitnik, who was earning $20,000 in 1994, received several promotions and is earning $32,500 in 1997. Over this same period the CPI rose to 125. Assume that 1994 was the base year. How much are Mr. Zitnik's real wages in 1997, and by what percentage did they change since 1994? Work out your solution to both parts of the problem right here, and then check your work.

Solution:

$$\text{Real wages (1997)} = \frac{\text{Money wages (1997)}}{\text{CPI (1997)}} \times 100$$

$$= \frac{\$32,500}{125} \times 100$$

$$= \$260 \times 100$$

$$= \$26,000$$

$$\text{Percentage change} = \frac{\text{Change}}{\text{Original number}}$$

$$= \frac{\$6,000}{\$20,000}$$

$$= .30$$

$$= 30\%$$

Are you getting the hang of this? We'll try one more, but I'll warn you in advance, it's a little tricky. All set? All right, then, here it comes: Ms. Klopman has been working at the same job since 1989, the base year. She was making $400 a week at that time, and now, in 1999, she is earning $540 a week. If the CPI rose to 180 in 1999, how much are Ms. Klopman's real wages in 1999, and by what percentage did they change? (Be careful how you answer this.)

Solution:

$$= \frac{\$540}{180} \times 100$$

$$= \$3 \times 100$$

$$= \$300$$

Between 1989 and 1999 Ms. Klopman's money wages rose from $400 to $540, but they rose more slowly than the CPI rose. Her *real* wages fell from $400 to just $300, a decline of 25 percent.

What has happened to real wages in the United States since the 1970s? Have they gone up or down? Most people's real wages went down. You'll see that immediately when you look at Figure 7. This graph shows what's happened to real wages and money wages since 1973. Money wages rose steadily while real wages remain stuck below $9 (in 1982–1984 dollars).

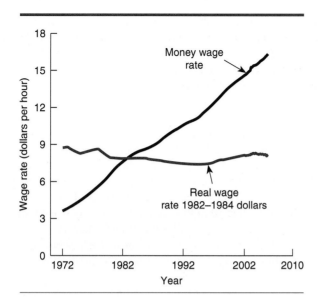

F*igure* 7
Real Wage Rate and Money
Wage Rate, 1972–2005
Since 1973 money wages have
quintupled, but real wages are
actually lower today than they
were in 1973.
*Source: Economic Report of the
President,* 2006; www.bls.gov.

Let's take a closer look at Figure 7. Basically real average hourly earnings fell between 1973 and 1993, hitting a low in the mid-1990s about 17 percent below their 1973 peak. Since then, real wages rose again, but in early 2006 were still 9 percent less than in 1973. *Think* about it. Never before in our history have real wages fallen over such an extended period of time. And yet, even though this period was marked by five recessions, real per capita GDP actually doubled. We need to ask two questions: (1) Why did real wages fall? And (2) How did families manage to keep up their standard of living?

Real wages cannot grow unless productivity grows. But productivity growth slowed from the late 1970s through the mid-1990s from an annual average of well over 2 percent to barely 1 percent. Meanwhile factories were closing left and right as our relatively high-paying manufacturing jobs went to Mexico, Japan, Southeast Asia, and China. In 1973, two out of seven Americans worked in manufacturing, but by 1996, just one in seven did.

So where did people find jobs? They found them in the relatively lower paying service sector, which, incidentally, was less likely than manufacturing to be unionized. Today, with 1.3 million employees, Wal-Mart is the largest employer in America. In 2005 it paid its sales clerks an average hour wage of less than $10, and not one employee was a union member.

As you can observe in Figure 2 of the previous chapter, the unionization rate of private sector employment fell by more than two-thirds between 1973 and 2005. Unionized workers generally earn at least 20 percent more than their nonunionized counterparts.

Another factor holding down real wages has been rapidly increasing health care premiums, which are paid by the employers of over 60 percent of the labor force. In effect, then, the money that would have otherwise gone towards pay increases was eaten up by rising health care costs.

Finally we have the effects of globalization, which has depressed American wages in two ways. As we've already noted, millions of high-paying manufacturing jobs have migrated to low-wage countries. But perhaps even more important, tens of millions of American workers are, directly or indirectly, competing with much lower paid workers in China, India, Mexico, and other low-wage countries. Even doctors and lawyers are learning that since the advent of high-speed worldwide communications, much of their work can be performed abroad. Everyone in the labor force should be asking herself or himself, Will my employer soon find a way to give my job to someone in another country who will do it for one-fifth my salary?

As the forces of globalization proceed, the wages in all the richer countries may be depressed by what has been termed, "the race to the bottom." As a growing number of workers in these countries find themselves competing with much lower paid workers in the less developed countries, will their real wages decline? Has this process already taken hold? Look again at the real wage rate line in Figure 7. It would appear that the race to the bottom has already begun.

Now let's answer our second question: How did families manage to keep up their standard of living? Mainly by having formerly stay-at-home moms going out and getting jobs to help support their families. Elizabeth Warren and Amelia Warren Tyagi believe that most two-income families are actually worse off today than their one-income counterparts were in the 1970s. They observe that "Today, after an average two-income family makes its house payments, car payments, insurance payments, and childcare payments, they have less money left over, even though they have a second, full-time earner in the workplace."[5]

That's the middle class. They're managing, but barely. The people *really* hurting are the working poor. In 2005 some 30 million Americans, nearly one out of every four workers, made less than $9 an hour, which placed them and their families below the poverty line, a concept we'll define in the chapter after next. Beth Schulman's *The Betrayal of Work* describes who the working poor are and the jobs they perform:

> They are nursing home workers and home health-care workers who care for our mothers and fathers, yet make so little income that many qualify for food stamps. They are poultry processing workers who bone and package the chicken we eat for our dinner, yet are not allowed to leave the line to go to the bathroom. They are retail store workers who help us in department stores, grocery stores and convenience stores, but can't get enough hours or benefits to support themselves without working at least two jobs. They are hotel workers who ensure that the rooms we sleep in on our business trips and family vacations are clean, but who have no sick days or funeral leave or vacation time. They are janitorial workers who empty our wastebaskets after dark but who have no childcare. They are catfish workers who process the fish we enjoy, but must work with injured wrists from continuous motion on the line. They are 1-800 call-center workers who answer our requests and take our orders while under constant management surveillance. And they are childcare workers who educate and care for our children while their own live in poverty.[6]

Our opulent lifestyle is subsidized by the low-wage work performed by tens of millions of Americans, not to mention tens of millions of foreign workers earning even less. Barbara Ehrenreich and Beth Schulman believe these workers should be better paid, even though this would raise prices. What do *you* think?

The Minimum Wage and the Living Wage

The Minimum Wage Rate: 1938 to the Present

The Fair Labor Standards Act

In 1938 Congress passed the Fair Labor Standards Act calling for a 25-cent-an-hour minimum wage (raised to 30 cents in 1939), a standard workweek of 44 hours (reduced to 40 hours in 1940), and the payment of time and a half for overtime. You know, of course, that 25 cents bought a lot more in 1938 than it does today.

Since then the minimum wage has been raised periodically, but these raises have not kept pace with inflation. In 1991 it reached $4.25, and $5.15 in 1997 (See Figure 8). Most Americans earn a lot more than the minimum wage, but about 10 million workers who were earning under $5.15 received increases. In addition, as a ripple effect, several million others who were earning $5.15 or slightly more also got pay raises.

Beth Schulman (The New Press)

We have thousands and thousands of people working on full-time jobs, with part-time incomes.

—Martin Luther King, Jr.

---

[5]Elizabeth Warren and Amelia Warren Tyagi, *The Two-Income Trap* (New York: Basic Books, 2003), pp. 51–52.

[6]Beth Schulman, *The Betrayal of Work* (New York: The New Press, 2003), pp. 5–6.

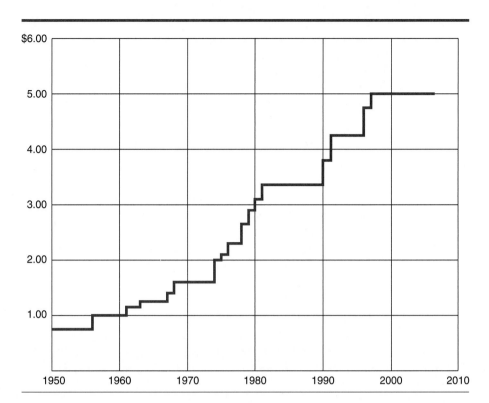

Figure 8
U.S. Minimum Hourly Wage,
1950–2006

The minimum wage has not been
raised since 1997.
Source: U.S. Bureau of Labor Statistics,
Employment and Earnings, January 2005.
www.bls.gov/cps.home.htm

Since the minimum wage rate was last raised in 1997, there has been some inflation. So $5.15 today buys substantially less than it did back in 1997. By doing the
math in the accompanying box "The Real Minimum Wage," we find that if one hour's
wages bought $5.15 worth of goods and services in 1997, by 2005 it bought just $4.23
worth of goods and services. The minimum wage should have risen to $6.27 in 2005
just to have kept pace with inflation. In other words, if we were to have maintained
the real minimum wage between 1997 and 2005, the nominal minimum wage should
have risen from $5.15 to $6.27.

There have been repeated efforts by the Democratic minority in Congress to raise
the minimum wage beyond $5.15, but as of mid-2006, they have not been successful.
Raising the minimum wage, it is sometimes argued, would hurt many small businesses,
which could not easily afford to pay their workers more money. If it were raised to, say,
$6.50, would there be layoffs and would some small companies be driven out of busi-
ness? The answer is *yes*. But how *many*?

Should There Be a Minimum Wage Rate?

According to many conservative economists, the minimum wage law hurts the very
people it is supposed to help—young workers, the unskilled, and those whose productivity is low. These economists use marginal revenue product analysis (which we covered
a couple of chapters back) to support their claim that the basic effect of the minimum
wage is to cause millions of marginal workers to be unemployed. And they point to the
high teenage unemployment rate as their proof.

Figure 9 shows a hypothetical MRP curve for unskilled labor (that is, the demand for
unskilled labor) and a hypothetical labor supply curve. It is obvious that at $5.15 an hour,
the current minimum wage, there is a surplus of unskilled labor. By allowing the wage
rate to fall to the equilibrium level, we can help 4 million more people find work.

Many younger workers are familiar with the catch–22 of job interviews: "Come
back when you have some experience." Where are you supposed to get that experience
before you land your first job? The conservative economists would help younger workers

Conservatives: The minimum
wage law hurts the very people
it is supposed to help.

*To fix the minimum of wages is
to exclude from labour many
workmen who would otherwise
have been employed; it is to
aggravate the distress you wish
to relieve.*

—Jeremy Bentham,
A Manual of Political Economy

ADVANCED WORK

The Real Minimum Wage

The minimum wage has been stuck at $5.15 since 1997. The consumer price index rose from 160.5 in 1997 to 195.3 in 2005. Can you figure out by what percentage the real hourly wage declined? Give it your best shot and then see if your answer agrees with mine.

We found that the real minimum wage had declined from $5.15 in 1997 to just $4.24 in 2005. Next question: By how much would the minimum wage need to be raised just to enable it to catch up with the inflation of the last eight years? Again, do the math and then check your work.

Solution:

Real minimum wage in 2005 = Minimum wage in 1997 × $\frac{\text{CPI in 1997}}{\text{CPI in 2005}}$

Real minimum wage in 2005 = $5.15 × $\frac{160.5}{195.3}$

= $4.23

Solution:

Nominal minimum wage in 2005 = Minimum wage in 1997 × $\frac{\text{CPI in 2005}}{\text{CPI in 1997}}$

= $5.15 × $\frac{195.3}{160.5}$

= $6.27

Figure 9

Hypothetical Demand and Supply Schedules for Unskilled Labor
According to hypothetical schedules, equilibrium wage rate is $4.00. At minimum wage rate of $5.15, there is a surplus of about 2 million workers. These are people who would be willing to work for $5.15 but can't find jobs.

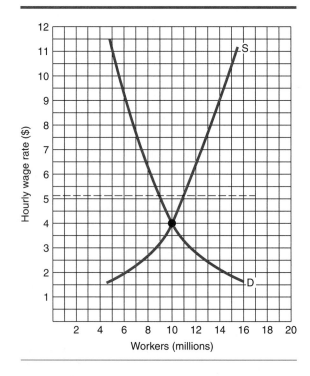

get that experience by suspending the minimum wage. Once they acquired the requisite experience, they would be able to get jobs that pay at least the minimum wage.

This raises another issue. My students—many of whom staff the fast-food emporiums of America—claim they do the same work as older workers. Were the minimum wage lowered for teenagers, this would just be an excuse to pay them even less. In fact, the whole attack on the minimum wage is suspect on the same grounds.

Who in America can live on $5.15 an hour? And who is worth *less* than $5.15 an hour? Wasn't the idea of minimum wage legislation to help abolish sweatshop wage levels? Would those who would abolish the minimum wage have us return to those conditions?

Who earns the minimum wage? In 2006 nearly 3 million Americans did. They included hamburger flippers, gas station attendants, garment workers, salesclerks, and janitors. About two-thirds were adults, while most of the rest were teenage members of low-income families for whom the wages were an important source of income.

As of March 2006 18 states and the District of Columbia had minimum hourly wage rates of more than $5.15. Washington state paid the highest, $7.63, and adjusts that minimum for inflation each year. Oregon's minimum was $7.50, followed by Connecticut at $7.40 (scheduled to rise to $7.65 on 1/1/07). Washington, D.C., has a minimum that is set automatically $1 above the federal minimum.

To "help" teenagers, President Reagan proposed lowering their minimum wage to $2.50 an hour.

The Living Wage

The living wage is a minimum hourly wage rate that must be paid to employees of major contractors doing business with over 100 municipalities. But nationwide, only about 150,000 workers are covered; about one-third are in New York City. In a few cities, like Santa Fe, New Mexico, the living wage must also be paid to city employees. In most cases, the stipulated hourly rate is between $7.50 and $10.00. Other major cities with living wage laws include Boston, Cincinnati, Los Angeles, Baltimore, Chicago, Minneapolis, Denver, and San Francisco.

A study of 36 cities by David Neumark of Michigan State University found that while such laws did tend to reduce employment somewhat among low-wage workers, they also resulted in a moderate decline in urban poverty. Although more localities will soon be passing living wage laws, it is quite unlikely that they will cover even 1 percent of the U.S. labor force.

In the chapter before this, we saw how labor unions, largely by restricting the supply of labor, have raised the wages of their members. And in this chapter, we saw how the federal minimum wage as well as local living wage laws have placed a floor under wages. These are two instances of interference with the functioning of the market forces of supply and demand. But at best, about 20 percent of our labor force is affected by unions, the minimum wage, or the living wage. So our bottom line remains the same: The wage rate is determined mainly by supply and demand.

Current Issue: The Education Gap

Societies are almost always divided between the "haves" and the "have-nots." Generally the haves have much more money, a much higher standard of living, and much greater social standing than the have-nots.

That has always been the case in our country, even back in colonial times. But today, increasingly, the great divide between the haves and the have-nots is a college degree. A college degree provides entrée to the primary job market. And, as it happens, college graduates, on average, earn almost twice as much as high school graduates. And people with professional degrees—for example, MBAs, CPAs, lawyers—earn almost 50 percent more than what a college graduate earns.

So it makes sense for children to study hard and get good grades from elementary school through college and graduate school. But then one must consider the odds of getting a college degree, which seem to be determined largely by family background. If your family has an income of over $90,000, your chances of getting a college degree by the age of 24 are 1 in 2. A child in a family earning $35,000 to $61,000 has a 1 in 10 chance. But if your family earns less than $35,000, you've got just a 1 in 17 chance of getting a college degree by the time you're 24.

You might think, then, that poor students can't afford college. But surprisingly, with so much financial aid now available, lack of money is no longer a major deterrent. Nor are stringent entrance requirements. Perhaps one third of the nation's colleges will take anyone with a high school diploma, or an 18-year-old birth certificate.

New York Times columnist David Brooks believes that cultural differences between educated, relatively rich parents and less educated, relatively poor parents, largely determine whether or not their children will go to college. Just as elementary, middle, and high schools often have tracking systems for the college bound, and for the educationally left-behinds, there is a parallel tracking system among families. Brooks summed it all up in these two sentences: "Educated parents not only pass down economic resources to their children, they pass down expectations, habits, knowledge and cognitive abilities. Pretty soon you end up with a hereditary meritocratic class that reinforces itself generation after generation."[7]

Do you agree that there is, then, an educational tracking system, not just within schools, but within families? And do you believe that our society can be dichotomized between those with college degrees and those without? If you do, then you're clearly hoping to end up a "have" rather than a "have-not."

Questions for Further Thought and Discussion

1. Are you in the primary labor market or the secondary labor market? Use your answer to show how these markets differ.
2. Explain why the backward-bending labor supply curve has this shape.
3. Should there be a minimum wage rate for teenagers? Present both sides of the issue.
4. What is economic rent? Make up an example that illustrates this concept.
5. What is the most important factor underlying the long-run increase in average real wage rates in the United States?

---

[7]David Brooks, "The Education Gap," *The New York Times*, September 25, 2005, Section 4, p. 11.

Workbook for Chapter 28

Name _____ Date _____

Multiple-Choice Questions

Circle the letter that corresponds to the best answer.

1. According to the backward-bending supply curve, as the hourly wage rate increases from 0 to $10,000 the number of hours worked per week by the average person will _____.
   a) be constant
   b) decrease, then increase
   c) increase, then decrease
   d) increase steadily
   e) decrease steadily

2. The demand for labor in a particular market is _____.
   a) the sum of all the individual labor supply curves
   b) the sum of all the firms' MRP curves
   c) the sum of all the individual labor supply curves and all the firms' MRP curves
   d) none of these

3. Which statement is true?
   a) Differences in wage rates are explained entirely by differences in productivity.
   b) Differences in wage rates are explained entirely by differences in education and training.
   c) Differences in wage rates are explained entirely by whom you know (rather than what you know).
   d) None of these statements is true.

4. The possibility of earning economic rent is great if _____.
   a) the supply of a factor is very high relative to demand
   b) the demand for a factor is very high relative to supply
   c) both demand for a factor and supply of a factor are high
   d) both demand for a factor and supply of a factor are low

5. If Tiffany Kuehn is earning $200,000 a year today and she were to earn $400,000 a year 10 years from today, her _____.
   a) real wages and money wages will both have increased
   b) real wages and money wages will both have decreased
   c) real wages will have increased
   d) money wages will have increased

6. Which job would pay the highest real wages over the last 20 years? One that paid _____.
   a) twice the minimum wage rate
   b) a fixed wage of $10 an hour
   c) a starting hourly wage of $10 with raises adjusted to the Consumer Price Index
   d) exactly the real average hourly wage rate in 1982 dollars

7. Conservative economists believe the minimum wage law _____.
   a) helps all workers equally
   b) hurts all workers equally
   c) hurts teenagers more than other workers
   d) helps teenagers more than other workers

8. Which statement is the most accurate?
   a) The federal minimum wage rate is indexed to the rate of inflation: Each year it's raised equal to the rate of inflation during the previous year.
   b) Over 10 million Americans are covered by a living wage law.
   c) There is considerable disagreement as to whether the federal minimum wage helps the unskilled workers more than it hurts them.
   d) Very few people's wage rates are actually determined by supply and demand.

9. If the minimum wage were eliminated, the employment of marginal workers would _____.
   a) rise a lot
   b) rise a little
   c) stay exactly the same
   d) fall a little
   e) fall a lot
   f) fall by an indeterminate amount
   g) rise by an indeterminate amount

10. The living wage set by municipalities tends to be _____.
   a) higher than the federal minimum wage
   b) lower than the federal minimum wage
   c) about the same as the federal minimum wage

11. When the minimum wage is abolished, the wage rate for marginal workers will _____.
   a) fall and employment will fall
   b) fall and employment will rise
   c) rise and employment will rise
   d) rise and employment will fall

12. Which statement is true?
   a) Over time the distinctions among noncompeting groups tend to blur.
   b) Over time the distinctions among noncompeting groups tend to become sharper.
   c) Over time there is no tendency for the distinctions among noncompeting groups to change.

13. Which statement is true?
   a) The primary job market has most of the good jobs.
   b) The secondary job market has most of the good jobs.
   c) Neither the primary nor the secondary job market has the best jobs.
   d) None of these statements is true.

14. According to the theory of the backward-bending labor supply curve, _____.
   a) first the substitution effect sets in, then the income effect
   b) first the income effect sets in, then the substitution effect
   c) the substitution effect and the income effect set in at the same time
   d) there is neither a substitution effect nor an income effect

15. Which statement is true about incomes in the United States?
   a) Almost everyone earns about the same income.
   b) Almost everyone is either very rich or very poor.
   c) There is a wide disparity in income.
   d) None of these statements is true.

16. Which statement(s) is/are true?
   Statement I: A college diploma is still a necessary condition for a person moving from the secondary to the primary labor market, but that diploma is no longer a sufficient condition.
   Statement II: Professional basketball (especially the National Basketball Association) is an example of a winner-take-all market.
   a) Statement I is true and statement II is false.
   b) Statement II is true and statement I is false.
   c) Both statements are true.
   d) Both statements are false.

17. On average
   a) people with professional degrees earn about twice as much as high school dropouts.
   b) college graduates earn about four times as much as high school graduates.
   c) high school dropouts earn less than $20,000 a year.
   d) people with college degrees earn about $100,000 a year.

18. Which statement is true?

    a) The minimum wage has kept up with the rate of inflation.

    b) Average real hourly earnings are much higher today than they were in 1973.

    c) A college degree is definitely not a ticket out of poverty since so many college graduates are poor.

    d) Over half of the college students whose parents' incomes are in the top quartile finish college.

19. Which statement is true?

    a) The average hourly wage in the United States is $5.15 an hour.

    b) If the minimum wage rate were lowered, more unskilled workers would find jobs.

    c) The hourly wage rate in the United States is higher than that in any other country.

    d) Many cities have laws requiring most private employers to pay a "living wage."

20. Compared with 1973 the nominal hourly wage rate is _____ and the real hourly wage rate is _____.

    a) higher, higher   c) higher, lower

    b) lower, lower   d) lower, higher

21. Which statement about production workers is true?

    a) They earn more in the U.S. than anywhere else in the world.

    b) They earn more in the U.S. than almost anywhere else in the world.

    c) They earn about the same in the U.S. as in most other countries.

    d) They earn less in the U.S. than in most other countries.

22. Beth Schulman makes the point that workers in nursing homes, retail stores, hotels, and child care are

    a) well paid considering that their work is not very important.

    b) lucky they have jobs at all.

    c) doing important work, but not being paid enough money.

    d) not well paid, but generally well regarded by their employers.

23. _____ a minimum wage rate higher than the federal minimum wage rate.

    a) All states have   c) About 18 states have

    b) Most states have   d) No state has

24. Which statement is true?

    a) The federal minimum wage has ensured that virtually everyone employed full-time earns enough to support a family above the poverty line.

    b) The federal minimum hourly wage rate is currently $5.15.

    c) The federal minimum wage rate is raised each year to keep up with the rate of inflation.

    d) The federal minimum wage was last raised in 2003.

25. Which is the most accurate statement?

    a) The fall in real wages between 1973 and 1993 was the longest in our history.

    b) Although real wages fell between 1973 and 1993, by 2005 they were the highest they have ever been.

    c) Real wages fell in the 1970s and 1980s, and money wages fell even more.

    d) The period between 1973 and 1993 was a period of rising real wages.

26. Which statement is true?

    a) Only 10 percent of the Fortune 500 corporations are headed by either women or African American men.

    b) In most occupations, women earn about the same as men.

    c) The wage gap between women and men has closed somewhat over the last 40 years.

    d) Each of these statements is true.

    e) None of these statements is true.

27. Which is the most accurate statement?

    a) Employment discrimination has been almost entirely wiped out over the last few decades.

    b) The glass ceiling no longer exists.

    c) Nearly everyone agrees that Wal-Mart is an equal opportunity employer.

    d) Women have won huge settlements in sex discrimination suits against their employers.

28. A woman is most likely to earn as much as a man in the same occupation if she is a _____.
   a) cashier
   b) lawyer
   c) college professor
   d) physician

29. Which one of these groups has the lowest earnings?
   a) Hispanic women
   b) Hispanic men
   c) African American women
   d) African American men

30. Which job would pay the highest real wages over the last 20 years? One that paid _____.
   a) twice the minimum wage rate
   b) a fixed wage of $10 an hour
   c) a starting hourly wage of $10 with raises adjusted to the Consumer Price Index
   d) exactly the real aevearage hourly wage rate in 1982 dollars

Fill-In Questions

1. The dual labor market consists of a _____ market and a _____ market.

2. The substitution effect (on the backward-bending labor supply curve) takes place when _____ _____.
   The income effect takes place when _____ _____.

3. At very low wage rates the _____ effect outweighs the _____ effect; at very high wage rates the _____ effect outweighs the _____ effect.

4. The wage rate is always determined by two factors: _____ and _____.

5. Economic rent is _____.

6. By real wages, economists mean what you can _____.

7. If we abolished the minimum wage law, employment of low-wage workers would _____.

8. If the minimum wage were eliminated, wages would definitely _____ for some marginal workers, and the employment of marginal workers would definitely _____.

9. If the minimum wage were abolished, there would be a substantial increase in the employment of marginal workers only if the MRP for marginal labor was very _____ and the supply of marginal labor was very _____.

Problems

1. Ms. Spielvogel was paid $400 a week in 1987, the base year. By 1995 she was earning $900 a week. If the consumer price index was at 180 in 1995, how much were Ms. Spielvogel's real wages that year, and by what percentage had they changed?

2. Karryn Bilski made $2,400,000 in 2001, the base year. By 2004 she was earning $3,600,000. If the CPI rose to 120 by 2004, how much were her real wages that year, and by what percentage had they changed?

Refer to Figure 1 to answer Problems 3 and 4.

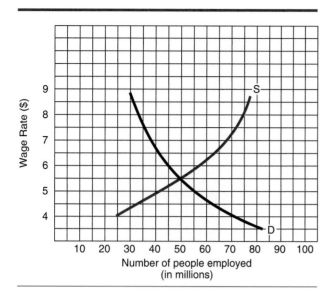

Figure 1

3. An increase in the minimum wage to $6 would cause
_____ million people to lose their jobs.

4. An increase in the minimum wage to $7 would cause
_____ million people to lose their jobs.

5. Mr. Dostievsky earned $40,000 in 1999, the base
   year. By 2006 he was earning $80,000. If the
   consumer price index was at 160 in 2006, how much
   would Mr. Dostievsky's real wages be that year, and
   by what percentage would they have changed?

Chapter 29

Rent, Interest, and Profit

W e're ready to tackle the payments to the remaining three factors of production—land, capital, and entrepreneurial ability. As you might have expected, rent and interest are determined by supply and demand. Profits, however, are determined somewhat differently.

CHAPTER OBJECTIVES

We'll take up each of these topics in turn:

- What is land?
- Economic rent.
- Are prices high because rents are high, or are rents high because prices are high?
- What is capital?

- How is the interest rate determined?
- The net productivity of capital.
- The capitalization of assets.
- The present value of future income.
- How are profits determined?
- Theories of profit.

Rent

What is Land?

Land is a resource or a factor of production. The owner of land is paid rent for allowing its use in the production process. The amount of rent paid for a piece of land is based on the supply of that land and the demand for that land.

This raises four questions: (1) Exactly what *is* land? (2) How does one piece of land differ from another? (3) How is the supply of land derived? (4) How is the demand for land derived?

Exactly What Is Land?   Land is land. An acre of land in Lake Forest, Illinois, an affluent Chicago suburb, is a suitable site for building a home. A half acre in downtown Los Angeles could be used for an office building, and 160 acres in Kansas might do well for growing wheat. How land is used depends on its location, its fertility, and whether it possesses any valuable minerals.

Sometimes we confuse land with what is built on it. A plot of land with apartment houses, stores, or office buildings will bring a lot more rent than a plot that lies vacant. But, strictly speaking (in economic terms), we pay rent on the land itself. We'll call the payments on buildings and other capital goods a form of interest, which we'll cover in the next part of this chapter.

Sometimes we confuse land with what is built on it.

How Does One Piece of Land Differ from Another?   As I just noted, a plot of land may have a few alternative uses. If it is used at all, it will be used by the highest bidder—the one willing to pay the most for it. For example, real estate developers bought up hundreds of dairy farms in central New Jersey over the last two decades. The developers made these farmers offers they could not refuse. In effect, then, the land was worth more as housing sites than as farms.

The basic way in which one piece of land differs from another is location. Only four plots of land can be located at the four corners of one of the most expensive pieces of real estate in the world, Fifth Avenue and 57th Street in Manhattan. Land that is just off this intersection is nearly as expensive. Land near airports, near highway interchanges, in shopping malls, or in the downtown sections of cities is more expensive than less desirably located land.

How Is the Supply of Land Derived?   The supply of land is virtually fixed. Aside from the efforts of the Dutch to reclaim small parcels of land from the North Sea, and relatively minor dredging and draining projects around the world, about one-quarter of the earth's surface is land. Until we're ready for interplanetary travel, everything we've got to work with is on the earth's surface. To go one step further, at any given location there's a fixed amount of land.

Of course, we can make more efficient use of that land. In cities, for example, we build straight up so that thousands of people can work on just one acre. Unfortunately, we've been unable to duplicate this feat in the suburbs because of the extensive acreage we've found it necessary to devote to parking lots.

There is a finite amount of land.

Any way we slice it, we have a finite amount of land. In economics we say the supply of land is fixed. We represent the supply of land as a vertical line, such as the one in Figure 1. We're lumping all land together in that graph, but technically there are tens of thousands of different supplies of land because each location differs from every other location.

How Is the Demand for Land Derived?   The demand for land, like the demand for labor and capital, is derived from a firm's MRP curve. The land will go to the highest bidder; the demand curve in Figure 1 represents the MRP schedule of the firm willing to pay the most for the land.

The demand for land is derived from a firm's MRP curve.

*F*igure 1

Determination of Rent
The demand for rent is the MRP schedule of the highest bidder for a specific plot of land. The supply of that land is fixed, so its supply curve is perfectly inelastic. The rent, like the price of anything else, is set by supply and demand.

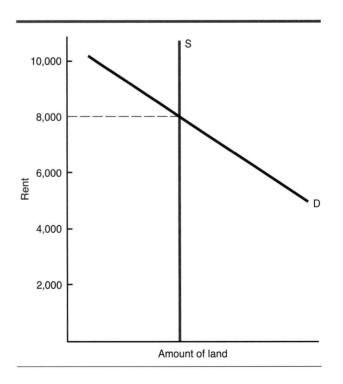

Why does the demand curve for land slope downward to the right? You may remember that a firm's MRP curve declines with output because its marginal physical product declines with output (due to diminishing returns). In addition, if the firm is an imperfect competitor, it must lower its price to increase sales, thereby further depressing MRP as output expands.

How Is Rent Determined?

You do not have to be a great economist to answer the question of how rent is determined. It is determined by the law of supply and demand. In Figure 1, we find that rent is $8,000.

Just to make sure you've got this straight, if the demand for land were D_1 in Figure 2, how much would the rent be?

Did you say $120,000? Good! If demand for land rose to D_2, how much would rent be?

Was your answer $160,000? All right, then. Did you notice that when the demand for land rises, the rent goes up as well? This is exactly what you'd expect under the law of supply and demand.

There is one peculiarity, though. You've noticed that the supply of land is fixed, or perfectly inelastic. Because supply doesn't change, changes in price are brought about by changes in demand.

We can use this information to analyze rents charged on three different plots of land. Suppose plot 1 is 100 miles from the nearest city and is not in demand for any use. How much rent does it bring?

It brings nothing because no one wants to use it. It's what we call marginal land. Suppose someone sets up a store on this land with the permission of the landlord but pays no rent. Very few people shop in this store because it's in the middle of nowhere. If the store owner's capital costs are $10,000, the cost of his labor is $20,000, and his sales are $30,000, he will make zero economic profits.

Now we'll move on to plot 2, just 30 miles from the center of town. This store also has capital costs of $10,000 and labor costs of $20,000, but its sales are $45,000. Guess how much rent this store owner will pay?

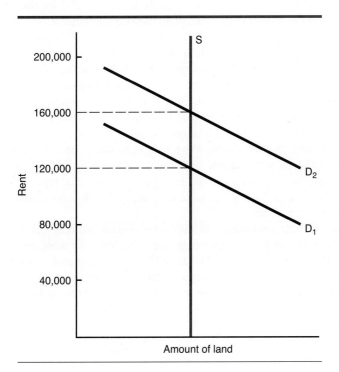

Figure 2

Increase in Demand for Land
Since the supply of land is perfectly inelastic, an increase in demand is reflected entirely in an increase in price (and not an increase in the quantity of land).

She will pay $15,000. You see, business is so good at this location that if the rent were anything less than $15,000, the guy who built his store on the marginal (or free) land in the boondocks would have bid $15,000. The location of the land closer to town, where so many more potential customers pass by, makes plot 2 worth $15,000 to at least one firm.

Finally, we have plot 3, right in the center of town where people pass by in droves. How much rent will someone pay for this plot? It will bring much more than $15,000. If the costs of capital are $10,000, the costs of labor $20,000, and sales $100,000, how much will this land rent for?

It will rent for $70,000. If it were renting for less, someone would come along and offer the landlord $70,000. The owner of the store on plot 1 certainly would; and so would the owner of the store on plot 2.

Now I'd like you to try this one on for size. Suppose costs remain the same, but sales on plot 1 rise to $40,000. Will the owner of plot 1 pay any rent? How much? He will pay $10,000 in rent.

If sales on plot 2 rise to $55,000, how much rent will it bring? It will bring $25,000.

If sales on plot 3 rise to $110,000, how much rent will it bring? It will bring $80,000.

To summarize, location is the basic differentiating factor in the rents of various plots of land, and the demand for each piece of land determines how much rent is paid.

Economic Rent

Payment in excess of what people would be willing to accept is economic rent.

Should landlords be paid anything at all?

Henry George, American economist

What Henry George overlooked

In the last chapter, I introduced the concept of economic rent, the amount of money certain people are paid beyond what they would be willing to work for. For example, baseball players who love the sport, like the legendary Willie Mays, are willing to play for a lot less than they're paid, and perhaps David Letterman would actually accept a measly $5 million a year instead of whatever it is that he earns. The surplus is called economic rent.

Economic rent, then, is the payment above the minimum necessary to attract this resource to the market. Rent paid to landlords (exclusive of any payment for buildings and property improvements) is, by definition, economic rent.

We may ask whether landlords should indeed be paid any rent at all for their land. After all, the land was always there; it certainly wasn't created by the landlords. (See the box, "Who Created the Land?") Whether they expropriated it, inherited it, or even purchased it, the land really belongs to society. More than 120 years ago a man named Henry George even started a single-tax movement whose objective was to finance government solely by taxing land rent. George reasoned that the land did not really belong to the landlords and the payment of rent did not increase production (because the land is there for the taking), so why not tax away this unearned surplus?

In his best-selling book, *Progress and Poverty* (1879), George observed that as the frontier closed and the nation's population continued to rise very rapidly, the demand for land was growing. But the supply was fixed, or, as you've seen in Figure 2, perfectly inelastic. The landlords were reaping huge returns for merely holding land.

Although this tax proposal has been criticized on several counts,[1] it does have considerable merit. A tax on land would raise revenue, and such a tax would fall largely on unproductive resource owners.

But Henry George overlooked an important attribute of rent: As the price for the use of land, it serves as a guidance mechanism, directing the most productive (that is, highest-paying) enterprises to the most desirable (that is, expensive) land. Because the most desirable locations bring the highest rents, they are inevitably occupied by the highest bidders. If we taxed away these rents, we might conceivably have some effect on

---

[1]It would raise only a small fraction of needed government revenue; landlords sometimes improve the land; and rent on land is not the only kind of income that is unearned.

Who Created the Land?

Do you remember the very first words of the Bible? "In the beginning God created the heaven and the earth" (Genesis 1:1). This raises an interesting question. Why do landlords get to charge rent on this land? If you have ever posed this question, let's look at Leviticus (25:23): "The land shall not be sold for ever: for the land is mine; for ye are strangers and sojourners with me."

Pierre-Joseph Proudhon carried this reasoning to its logical conclusion: "Who is entitled to the rent of land? The producer of the land without doubt. Who made the land? God. Then, proprietor, retire!" Just to sum things up, Proudhon asked himself this question: What is property? His answer? "Property is theft!"

A very strong current in economic thought denies the landlord's claim to rent. However, the problem we have had since being banished from the Garden of Eden is that we need to deal with scarcity, and rent is an excellent means of efficiently allocating the use of scarce land.

Pierre-Joseph Proudhon, French journalist (Brown Brothers)

the allocation of land. For instance, if I owned a plot of land in midtown San Francisco and all my rent were taxed away, I might just as soon rent it to a candy store as to a fancy boutique.

Are Prices High because Rents Are High, or Are Rents High because Prices Are High?

How many times have you gone into a store in a high-rent district and been overwhelmed by the prices? Didn't you say to yourself, "Their prices are high because the owner has to pay such a high rent"? Fair enough. A store situated in an expensive area has to charge high prices to make enough money to pay its greedy landlord.

We're going to digress for a couple of minutes and a couple of centuries because this same question came up in early 19th-century England. David Ricardo, the great economist, set the record straight: "Corn is not high because a rent is paid, but a rent is paid because corn is high."[2]

The price of corn (and wheat) was high because there was a great demand for it caused by the Napoleonic Wars. Because the supply of farmland in England was entirely under cultivation (and therefore fixed), a rise in the demand for corn raised the demand (or the MRP) for farmland, thereby driving up rents.

Now, back to the present. You've seen that stores in expensive neighborhoods charge high prices and pay high rents. But *why* do they pay high rents? Because they outbid all the other prospective tenants. Why did they bid so high? Because they wanted the desirable location. Stores located in busy shopping areas pay much higher rents than do stores in less busy areas. Why? Because their locations are so desirable that their rents are bid up.

David Ricardo, English economist (The Granger Collection, New York)

Do certain stores charge high prices because they have to pay high rents?

---

[2]David Ricardo, *The Principles of Political Economy and Taxation,* ed. L. Reynolds and W. Fellner (Burr Ridge, IL: Richard D. Irwin, 1963), p. 34.

691

Now we'll look at the same question from the other side. Suppose a store happens to pay a low rent—say a mom-and-pop grocery not far from where you live. How do its prices compare with supermarket prices? They're higher, right? But you'd expect them to be lower, if low rents lead to low prices.

High rents don't cause high prices.

Here's the final word. High rents don't cause high prices. Desirable locations attract many prospective renters, who bid up rents because they believe they will get a lot of business. In other words, following Ricardo's analysis, rents are high because the demand for the final product—and consequently the derived demand—is high.

Interest

What Is Capital?

Capital consists of office buildings, factories, stores, machinery and equipment, computer systems, and other synthetic goods used in the production process. When we invest, we are spending money on new capital. When we build an office park, a shopping mall, or an assembly line, or when we purchase new office equipment, we are engaged in investment.

Economists feel good when they can think in terms of stocks and flows. The stock of capital increases by means of a flow of investment. Suppose you have half a glass of water; that's your capital stock. You can fill up that glass by letting tap water flow into it; that's your investment flow. When you've filled your glass, you have doubled your capital stock.

To use a machine example, say you have a capital stock of four machines. You buy two more. That's your investment for the year. Now you have a capital stock of six machines.

How Is the Interest Rate Determined?

The law of supply and demand

You guessed it! The interest rate is determined by the law of supply and demand. Figure 3 shows this.

The demand for capital is the firm's MRP schedule for capital. As we've seen, MRP curves always slope downward to the right.

Figure 3

Determination of the Interest Rate

The interest rate is determined by the demand for loanable funds and the supply of loanable funds.

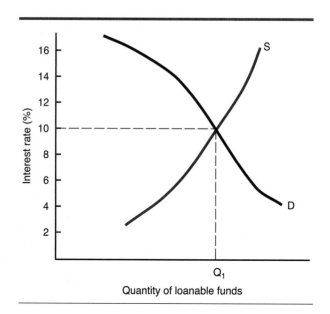

ADVANCED WORK

Usury in Ancient Times

Mosaic laws in the book of Deuteronomy strictly forbid not only usury (lending money at exorbitant interest rates), but even the taking of any interest. In those days loans were made mainly for charitable purposes, so the prohibition made a great deal of sense.

Aristotle considered the charging of interest to be the most unnatural method of accumulating wealth:

*The most hated sort, and with the greatest reason, is usury, which makes a gain out of money itself, and not from the natural objects of it. For money was intended to be used in exchange, but not to increase at interest ... Of all modes of getting wealth this is the most unnatural.** *

These same views continued to be reflected in the rules of the Church, which prevailed until the end of the Middle Ages. With the rise of commerce, however, the basic purpose of most loans changed, and the prohibitions against taking interest were dropped. But what constitutes a "fair" rate of interest on consumer loans continues to be debated to this day.

Unlike Christians and Jews, Muslims to this day follow the stricture of the Koran, that one neither gives nor receives interest. However, banks in Islamic countries do have ways of getting around this inconvenience. Suppose you wanted to buy a Toyota Camry. Your bank would buy it from the dealer, for $18,000, and you buy your car from

Aristotle, Greek philosopher (The Granger Collection, New York)

your bank for $21,000, paid out in monthly installments over three years.†

Islamic banking avoids using the term "interest," but the mark-up—in this case, $3,000—that is paid to the bank certainly looks and smells a lot like interest.

---

*Aristotle, *Politics*, ii, p. 1258.
†See Jerry Useem, "Banking on Allah," *Fortune*, June 10, 2002, p. 155.

The supply of loanable funds, however, unlike the supply of land (which is perfectly inelastic), slopes upward to the right. You may remember that the backward-bending labor supply curve of the previous chapter slopes upward to the right, until, at extremely high wage rates, it bends backward.

Why does the supply of loanable funds or savings slope upward to the right? Because the amount of money people save is somewhat responsive to interest rates. The higher the interest paid, the more people will save.

Interest Rates and Consumer Loans

Do high interest rates deter borrowing for consumer loans? Obviously they do. And do the banks charge too much on credit card loans? They *do*? Then maybe a legal ceiling should be placed on the interest that may be charged on these and other loans.

Although there is no federal law on the books, many states have what are called usury laws, which place legal ceilings on the interest rates that may be charged on certain types of loans. (See the box, "Usury in Ancient Times.") Usury is defined as charging "an unconscionable or exorbitant rate of interest." Usury laws are intended to curb this greedy practice. But, as the old saying goes, the road to hell is paved with good intentions.

Usury laws, however popular with the public, drive many economists wild. Why? There are two reasons. First, these laws may hurt the very people they are intended to help by creating a shortage of loanable funds. This is illustrated in Figure 4, which we'll look at in a minute.

Do banks charge too much interest on credit card loans?

Usury laws place limits on how much interest may be charged.

Figure 4

Interest Rate Ceiling
An interest rate ceiling is set at
16 percent, well below the
equilibrium level of 24 percent.
How much is the resulting shortage
of loanable funds? Since, at 16
percent, $550 billion in loanable
funds is demanded but only $200
billion is supplied, the shortage is
$350 billion. What would be the
best way to eliminate that shortage
of loanable funds? Answer:
Eliminate the 16 percent interest
rate ceiling and allow the interest
rate to rise to its equilibrium level
of 24 percent.

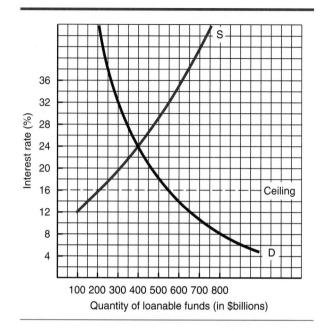

A second reason why economists love to hate usury laws is that these laws blatantly interfere with the price mechanism, more familiarly known as the law of supply and demand. Prices signal the buyers and sellers in the market. When prices are low buyers try to buy more, and when they're high sellers offer more of their goods or services for sale. Because the interest rate is the price of money, a high price signals sellers to provide more loanable funds, while discouraging borrowers from borrowing. A high enough interest rate would completely eliminate the shortage of loanable funds.

Let's look at Figure 4 to see how the price mechanism would work. First, if there *were* a legal ceiling on interest rates of 16 percent, there would be a shortage of how much? It looks to me like $350 billion ($550 billion demanded − $200 billion supplied). And how much is the equilibrium interest rate? That's right—it's 24 percent. So if we eliminated the interest ceiling, the interest rate would quickly rise to 24 percent, and the shortage would be eliminated.

You may recall our discussion of price ceilings and price floors in the chapter titled "Supply and Demand." Usury laws are price ceilings because they prevent the interest rates from rising to their equilibrium levels. In other words, usury laws place an upper limit on interest rates. Consequently, there are a lot more borrowers in the market than lenders, which creates a shortage of loanable funds.

So how exactly do usury laws hurt borrowers? They hurt the borrowers with relatively poor credit ratings. For example, if the interest rate were fixed at 16 percent, lenders would be willing to lend out only about $200 billion, all of which would go to people they considered the most creditworthy borrowers. The rest of us would be completely left out. Some of us would go to consumer finance companies (for example, Household Finance, Seaboard Finance, and Beneficial Finance); these might not be covered by usury laws and could therefore charge higher interest rates. Or we might go to loan sharks who often charge a straight 10 percent interest—that's 10 percent a week! So the next time you think you're paying an arm and a leg in interest on a bank credit card, consider the alternative.

While I'm still up on my soapbox, I'd like to make the connection between usury laws and other legal obstacles to the price mechanism. Farm price supports, or price floors, are one such obstacle. In the last chapter we discussed the minimum wage law, another price floor. Wage and price controls were mentioned a few times in the earlier chapters of *Economics* and *Macroeconomics*. Still another legal interference with the law of supply and demand is rent control, which puts a ceiling on how much rent landlords may charge for apartments.

Usury laws are price ceilings.

Economists dislike the laws that set up these obstacles because they interfere with the price mechanism and often end up harming the very people they were intended to help. That said, a case can be made for each one of these laws. And while in general most economists would prefer not to tamper with the forces of supply and demand, many of us are prepared to make certain exceptions. My own predilection is for minimum wage laws, which I believe do a lot more good than harm. Another exception I'd make is to place a cap on so-called "payday loans" (see Current Issue, "Subprime, Fringe, and Payday Lending" at end of this chapter). The issue comes down to making judgment calls. But those judgment calls are yours—not mine.

Price ceilings and price floors interfere with the price mechanism.

The Present Value of Future Income

Economists are fond of saying that a dollar today is worth more than a dollar you will have in the future. Why? Inflation?

While it's true that most of us have never known anything *but* inflation in our lifetimes, a dollar today would be worth more than a future dollar even if there were no inflation. If no inflation were expected in the future, lenders would charge borrowers what we call the real rate of interest.[3]

A dollar today is worth more than a dollar you will have in the future.

Let's say you have a dollar today and no inflation is expected over the next year. If you can get 5 percent interest by loaning out your dollar, that means one year from now you will have $1.05. On the other side of the coin, so to speak, the person who borrows the dollar from you today is willing to pay you $1.05 in one year. Why, then, is a dollar today worth more than a future dollar? Because it can be lent out to earn interest.

Waiting necessarily commands a price.
—Gustav Cassel,
The Nature and Necessity of Interest

Next question. If a dollar today is worth more than a future dollar, how *much* more is it worth? If the interest rate were 8 percent, how much would $100 today be worth in terms of dollars you will have one year from now?

The correct answer is $108. Naturally, we have a formula to figure these problems out.

The present value of a dollar received one year from now is $1/(1 + r)$, when r is the interest rate. Substitute .08 for r (remember 8 percent is equivalent to the decimal .08) in the formula, and see what you get.

Present value of a dollar received n years from now =
$$\frac{1}{(1 + r)^n}$$

Did you get 92.59 cents? (The actual answer is 92.592592592, with the three numbers repeating themselves ad infinitum.) So a dollar one year from now would be worth only 92.59 cents today.

What if the interest rate were 5 percent? How much would a dollar received one year from now be worth today?

Solution: $\dfrac{1}{1 + r} = \dfrac{1}{1.05} = 95.24$ cents

We'll do one more—when the interest rate is 12 percent.

Solution: $\dfrac{1}{1 + r} = \dfrac{1}{1.12} = 89.29$ cents

---

[3]During times of inflation, the expected inflation rate is factored into the interest rates charged to borrowers. You may recall this from the section headed "Anticipated and Unanticipated Inflation" in Chapter 10 of *Economics* and *Macroeconomics*.

We can say, then, that when the interest rate rises, the present value of future dollars will decline; when the interest rate falls, the present value of dollars held in the future will rise.

We can use a general formula for the present value of dollars held any number of years into the future:

$$\text{Present value of a dollar received } n \text{ years from now} = \frac{1}{(1 + r)^n}$$

Remember that time is money.
—Benjamin Franklin

If you're uncomfortable with algebra, don't worry. Once you plug in the numbers for r and n, it's no longer algebra, but just arithmetic.

The letter n is an exponent. It tells us to multiply what's inside the parentheses by itself n times. If the numbers inside the parentheses are $(1 + .12)$ and n is 3, what should we do? We should multiply $1.12 \times 1.12 \times 1.12$.

Now we'll work out a couple of problems using the formula. If the interest rate is 6 percent and you will be paid a dollar in two years, what is the present value of that dollar? Work it out to the nearest cent right here:

Solution: $\dfrac{1}{(1 + r)^n} = \dfrac{1}{(1.06)^2} = \dfrac{1}{(1.06) \times (1.06)} = \dfrac{1}{1.1236} = 89 \text{ cents}$

Let's recap, and then we'll work out one more problem. The higher the interest rate, the lower the present value. And the longer you must wait for your money, the less it is worth to you today. Another way of looking at these relationships is to see what a rising interest rate and a rising waiting period do to the denominator of the formula. Clearly they raise it, which lowers the present value of the asset.

What is the present value of $1,000 that will be paid to you in three years if the interest rate is 5 percent? Work it out to the nearest cent.

Solution: $\begin{aligned} \text{Percent value} &= \$1,000 \times \frac{1}{(1 + r)^n} \\[6pt] &= \$1,000 \times \frac{1}{(1.05)^3} \\[6pt] &= \$1,000 \times \frac{1}{(1.05)(1.05)(1.05)} \\[6pt] &= \$1,000 \times \frac{1}{1.157625} \\[6pt] &= \$1,000 \times .863838 \\[6pt] &= \$863.84 \end{aligned}$

Now that I've put you through all those moves computing present value, I'm going to show you a shortcut. You may be able to find a table like the one in the box, "How Much Is $100 Received in the Future Worth to You Today?" Or if you have a really good pocket calculator, you should be able to find present value a lot faster. But if n is only 1 or 2, then I'm sure you can work out most problems with our handy formula in just a minute or two.

How Much Is $100 Received in the Future Worth to You Today?

This may not be a question people commonly ask you, but it is an interesting one, at least to economists. First, you may give a general answer: less than $100. But how *much* less than $100? That depends on two factors—when you will receive that $100 and what the interest rate is. The table here gives us a lot of answers.

So, what is the present value of $100 received four years from now if the interest rate is 12 percent? It's $63.55. And how much is the present value of $100 received in 15 years if the interest rate is 6 percent? It's $41.73.

Are you ready for a couple of generalizations? All right, then, here they come. First, as the interest rate rises, the present value declines. Second, as your years of waiting for your money increase, the present value declines. To generalize, the present value of a future dollar payment is inversely related to both the interest rate and how long you have to wait for your money.

Suppose you've just won $10,000,000. Exactly how much is that $10,000,000 actually worth? I hate to tell you, but it's worth a lot less than $10,000,000. You'll still take it? OK, then, let's get some idea of how much you actually won.

First you'll have to pay federal income tax, and very likely, state income tax as well. Let's say that the government takes a 40 percent slice, leaving you with $6 million. Still not too shabby.

Now comes the fun part—figuring out the present value of the $6 million. You'll probably get paid in annual installments, say over 20 years. That would come to $300,000 a year. Suppose that you receive your first installment one year after you win. Its present value would depend on the going rate of interest. The higher that is, the lower the present value of your payments.

If the interest rate were 4 percent can you figure out the present value of your first year's payment?

It would be $288,450 (Using the table, multiply $300,000 by 0.9615.) How much is the present value of 20th payment?

That comes to just $136,920 ($300,000 × 0.4564). What if the interest rate were 12 percent? See if you can find the present value of the first payment and then the 20th payment.

Solution: The first payment comes to $267,870.

The 20th payment comes to $31,110.

So it turns out that how much money you actually won, at least in terms of present value, depends largely on the going rate of interest. The higher the interest rate, the lower the present value.

Years in the Future	2 Percent	4 Percent	6 Percent	8 Percent	12 Percent
1	98.04	96.15	94.34	92.59	89.29
2	96.12	92.46	89.00	85.73	79.72
3	94.23	88.90	83.96	79.38	71.18
4	92.39	85.48	79.21	73.50	63.55
5	90.57	82.19	74.73	68.06	56.74
6	88.80	79.03	70.50	63.02	50.66
7	87.06	75.99	66.51	58.35	45.23
8	85.35	73.07	62.74	54.03	40.39
9	83.68	70.26	59.19	50.02	36.06
10	82.03	67.56	55.84	46.32	32.20
15	74.30	55.53	41.73	31.52	18.27
20	67.30	45.64	31.18	21.45	10.37

Profits

Profits, the last topic of this chapter, does not lend itself to any mathematical formulas or computations. Indeed, except for some problems at the end of this chapter, you have seen the last of the mathematical computations you will be asked to perform in this book. The entire study of profits, unlike that of rent and interest, is hotly debated by economists, politicians, and social critics. Let's begin by looking at how profits are determined and how large they are, and then I'll outline a few theories of profits.

How Are Profits Determined?

Profits are considered a residual left after payment of rent, interest, and wages.

Until now I've been saying that the law of supply and demand determines the price of just about everything. Now I'm going to have to change my tune. Economists treat profits as a residual left to the entrepreneur after rent, interest, and wages have been paid. One could argue that because these three resource payments are determined by supply and demand, then what's left over, profits, are indirectly determined by supply and demand.

What do *you* think? Does that sound plausible? Should we just leave it at that? Profits are indirectly determined by supply and demand?

Considering that this section goes on for another few pages, apparently *I'm* not too thrilled with leaving it at that. After all, if profits are the catalytic agent, the prime motivating factor, the ultimate reward for the entrepreneur, surely we can do better than to treat them as a mere residual. True, the business firm must pay rent, interest, and wages, and it may keep any remaining profits, but surely profits are a little more exciting than that, if I may be so bold.

How Large Are Profits?

What do we know about profits so far? At the beginning of Chapter 4, we talked about their role as an economic incentive under capitalism. The lure of profits is what gets business firms to produce the huge array of goods and services that provide the industrial countries of the world with such high standards of living.

We also know that economists derive profits somewhat differently from the way accountants derive them. Both subtract explicit costs (out-of-pocket or dollar costs, such as wages and salaries, cost of materials, fuel, electricity, rent, insurance, and advertising) from sales. But economists also subtract implicit costs (opportunity costs of additional resources used, such as the wages the owner of the firm and family members could have earned working elsewhere, and interest on money tied up in the firm that could have been earned by investing it elsewhere). Subtracting both explicit and implicit costs from sales means that economic profits are somewhat lower than accounting profits.

Large corporations have no implicit costs, but the majority of the nation's 4 million corporations are very small businesses with substantial implicit costs.

In 2002 corporate profits before taxes were $1,352 billion, and proprietors' income was $939 billion. Profits, then, were a total of $2,291 billion of a national income of $10,904 billion paid to all the factors of production, or 21 percent.

Theories of Profit

Capitalism without bankruptcy is like Christianity without hell.

—Frank Borman,
Astronaut and business executive

Economic profit is the payment for entrepreneurial ability—whatever *that* is. The entrepreneur is rewarded for recognizing a profit opportunity and taking advantage of it. There are four somewhat overlapping theories of how the entrepreneur earns a profit: (1) as a risk taker; (2) as an innovator; (3) as a monopolist; and (4) as an exploiter of labor. We'll take up each in turn.

To win you have to risk loss.

—Jean-Claude Killy,
Professional skier

The Entrepreneur as a Risk Taker   Have you ever played the lottery? Did you ever hit the number? The $5 or $10 that most lottery players spend each week is a very risky "investment." Why do it? Because the payoff is so high. And if you don't play, then you can't even *dream* of winning.

The only way to get people to make risky investments is to offer high rates of return. In general, the riskier the investment, the higher the average rate of return. I mean, would *you* play the lottery if your chance of winning were one in a million and the payoff were 10 percent of your investment? Or 100 percent? Or even 1,000 percent?

Not too many folks are drilling for oil in the United States these days, but at one time you could hardly move without running into an oil well in wide stretches of Texas, Oklahoma, and a few other Southwestern states. Wildcatters may do all kinds of geological surveys and probability studies, or they may just trust dumb luck. Either way, you're taking one big risk when you start drilling down 5,000 feet or more. You're spending tens of thousands of dollars and you're either going to hit a gusher or you're going to come up dry. But as they say, nothing ventured, nothing gained.

According to Frank Knight's classic *Risk, Uncertainty, and Profit,* all economic profit is linked with uncertainty. Think of the telephone, the television, the automobile, and the airplane. Who knew for certain that they would work technologically and catch on commercially? Think of the wildcat oil-well drillers. These people took risks and made huge fortunes, but a lot of other people took risks and failed. As many rich Texans have long been fond of saying, money is just a way of keeping score.

Frank Knight saw profit as the reward for risk bearing. And those profits, while relatively uncertain and unstable, are also much higher than the normal profits earned by the owners of mainstream business enterprises.

The Entrepreneur as an Innovator   We need to distinguish between invention and innovation. An invention is a new idea, a new product, or a new way of producing things. An innovation is the act of putting the invention to practical use. Sometimes the inventor comes up with something commercially feasible, but for one reason or another—usually a shortage of capital—does not market it. The Wright brothers, for example, never made a penny from commercial air flight, although Alexander Graham Bell, of all people, tried to steal their ideas.

Jay Sorensen is an inventor, an innovator, and an entrepreneur. The story in the accompanying box describes how he got his inspiration and how he followed through. As Thomas Edison put it, invention is 2 percent inspiration and 98 percent perspiration.

Joseph Schumpeter, one of the foremost business cycle theorists, stressed the preeminence of innovation as the basis for economic advance.

> Whenever a new production function has been set up successfully and the trade beholds the new thing done and its major problems solved, it becomes much easier for other people to do the same thing and even to improve upon it. In fact, they are driven to copying it if they can, and some people will do so forthwith. It should be observed that it becomes easier to do the same thing, but also to do similar things in similar lines—either subsidiary or competitive ones—while certain innovations, such as the steam engine, directly affect a wide variety of industries.... Innovations do not remain isolated events, and are not evenly distributed in time, but ... on the contrary they tend to cluster, to come about in bunches, simply because some, and then most, firms follow in the wake of successful innovation.[4]

Schumpeter went on to say that "risk bearing is no part of the entrepreneurial function."[5] That's done by the capitalist who puts up the money. If the entrepreneur himself puts up the money, then he bears the risk of losing it as a capitalist, not as an entrepreneur. Finally, Schumpeter notes that in a purely competitive economy, profit "is the premium put upon successful innovation in capitalist society and is temporary by nature: it will vanish in the subsequent process of competition and adaption."[6]

Frank Knight, American economist (The University of Chicago)

Distinction between invention and innovation

Schumpeter's theory of innovation

Joseph Schumpeter, American economist (Harvard University Archives)

---

[4]Joseph A. Schumpeter, *Business Cycles* (New York: McGraw-Hill, 1964), p. 75.

[5]Ibid., p. 79.

[6]Ibid., pp. 79–80.

Jay Sorensen, Inventor, Innovator, and Entrepreneur

Jay Sorensen's inspiration came when he was sitting in a coffee house and managed to spill coffee on his lap. Here's what happened next (as described in a CNN/Money online article).*

"It got me thinking that there had to be a better way," said Sorensen, who began to notice that other coffee-house patrons were holding steaming cups between their thumb and forefingers to avoid burning their hands.

Sorensen's solution? A cardboard sleeve that would fit around the coffee cups.

He developed the idea, then offered it to Starbucks. The then-nascent chain wanted exclusive rights and it was "dragging its feet" about the product. So Sorensen went out on his own, putting his last finances on the line to found his company, Java Jacket.

"At that point I had about six months of living expenses," he said.

Sorensen borrowed $3,000 from his parents to hire a patent attorney, and he ended up piling up credit card debt to have 100,000 coffee cup jackets made from waffled, recycled cardboard.

"I had to pay for the order up front," he recalls. *"It seemed like a ton at the time."*

The day he picked up the prototypes in his pickup truck, Sorensen returned to the cafe where he had originally spilled the coffee on his lap. He had no appointment but was told he could see the owner if he was willing to wait a bit.

While he waited, he read about a coffee trade show to be held a week later. He had no money to attend. A few minutes later he was introduced to the cafe owner, who immediately bought some jackets.

"He was kind enough to ask, 'Do you need a check now?' I said, 'Sure, that'd be nice,'" laughs Sorensen. *He promptly used the money to attend the trade show, where he got orders from 150 cafes. His wife, Colleen—now company CEO—followed up with hand-written notes and a sample sleeve to the other 3,500 trade-show attendees.*

The efforts paid off big time. Today, the family-owned company sells between 20 million and 25 million sleeves a month, including neighborhood cafes to national chains.

*Leslie Haggin Geary, CNN/Money Staff Writer, "From Rags to Riches," Money.cnn.com/2003/05/21.

If we distinguish, then, between the capitalist and the entrepreneur, the reward for entrepreneurship would be profits due to innovation. The capitalist's return would be interest, not profits. The capitalist's interest rate would depend on the risk.

Distinction between capitalist and entrepreneur

So far we've depicted the entrepreneur as a risk taker and an innovator. No more Mr. Nice Guy. From here on, we'll see the entrepreneur cast in the role of economic villain.

The Entrepreneur as a Monopolist   Do the monopolist and the oligopolist, for that matter, make a profit? They sure do! In the previous chapters devoted to these kinds of firms, we concluded that they were able to make profits because of a shortage of competition. If this shortage of competitors is due to hard work, foresight, and innovation, one could hardly complain about the evils of big business.

Natural scarcities versus contrived scarcities

Still, we need to make a distinction between "natural scarcities" and "contrived scarcities." A firm that develops a technology before anyone else (as IBM and Xerox both did) or one that possesses a unique location (as does the owner of land at a busy intersection) is the beneficiary of a natural scarcity and consequently earns monopoly profits.

Then there are the other guys, who have created or are able to take advantage of a contrived scarcity. The controllers of patents and those who own or have cornered the market on a vital resource (DeBeers diamonds, the National Football League) will almost always restrict output so they can earn monopoly profits. These are the economic bad guys because they are holding output below the levels at which the public wishes to purchase. (See the box, "Which Theory of Profits Do We Apply?")

Marxist exploitation theory

The Entrepreneur as an Exploiter of Labor   Karl Marx based his theory of profits on the supposition that the capitalist exploits the worker. To illustrate this relationship, we'll take a simple numerical example. Suppose a worker needs to work 12 hours a day

Which Theory of Profits Do We Apply?

Can you imagine what would happen if a pharmaceutical company came up with a drug that really *did* promote substantial hair growth? Its marketers would probably use the advertising slogan "Gone today, hair tomorrow." Or what if the company discovered a drug that reversed the aging process. Or how about a company that produced a drug that really did allow us to lose weight while eating as much as we wanted?

Now try to imagine what would happen to the profits of a company that discovered a miracle drug that grew hair, reversed the aging process, *and* helped us lose weight.

Which theory of profits do we apply to this example? Innovation? Certainly this company is an innovator. Monopoly? Until its patent runs out, the firm has a monopoly. Is the firm being rewarded for being a risk taker? I think we can argue that it took the risk of spending millions on research that might pay off big—but might not pay off at all.

So we can't neatly pigeonhole this entrepreneurial profit in any of these three categories. But if you *had* to pick one, which one would you pick? Which one would I pick? I'd have to go with profit as a reward for innovation. But it's not an easy call.

---

to have enough money to buy food. But suppose he could produce this food in just six hours working for the capitalist. The reason he can produce so much food is because he uses the capitalist's machinery.

The worker produces enough food for two people in 12 hours. The capitalist gives him just enough wages to buy one day's food and keeps the other day's food for himself. Thus, a capitalist's role is to exploit his employees. Not bad work if you can get it.

Marx calls the expropriation of the proceeds of six hours of labor time "surplus value." The capitalist uses this to buy more capital. Then he will be able to exploit even more workers.

Surplus value

Capital, then, comes from the surplus value that has been stolen from the worker, and that surplus value represents the capitalist's profit.

Conclusion

What does all of this add up to? Which theory of profits is correct? Well, you know my style by now. I ask you what you think, I let you sweat for a while, and then, finally, I reveal the truth to you. I'll give you some time to go back over each of the four theories of profit. Imagine we're playing a couple of minutes of music while the clock is ticking away. OK—time's up! What's your answer?

Whichever answer you chose is right because there is a lot of truth in each of the four theories—even the Marxist theory. After all, more than 1 billion Chinese can't all be completely wrong! Furthermore, it's undeniable that monopolists *do* make profits. And surely there are plenty of profits earned by innovators and risk takers.

What we may conclude, then, is that everybody's right. And we may conclude that nobody has a monopoly on the truth.

Current Issue: Subprime,[7] Fringe, and Payday Lending

The poorer you are, the harder it is to borrow money. And because poor people are not great credit risks, they are forced to pay high, and sometimes exorbitant, interest rates. Late night TV is flooded with ads that always seem to say, "Bad credit? No problem." You can get a "subprime loan." The only problem is that you'll have to pay between

---

[7]Large creditworthy corporate borrowers pay the prime interest rate, which may be 2 or 3 percentage points below mortgage rates. But subprime borrowers, who have less than splendid credit ratings, may pay 6 or 8 times prime rate. The prime interest rate is discussed in Chapter 13 of *Economics* and *Macroeconomics*.

15 and 30 percent interest as well as additional high fees. Since 1995 the subprime lending business has more than quadrupled to well over $300 billion a year, and has attracted some of the nation's largest banks, including Citibank and Wells Fargo.

H & R Block, Jackson Hewlitt, and many other tax preparation firms issue tax refund anticipation loans, mainly to the working poor. The loans typically are issued for flat fees, often $78 or $88, which usually equate to annual interest rates of more than 100 percent, and sometimes as much as 1,500 percent.

But if you're *really* poor, your only credit option may be "fringe lending." So-called payday stores, often operating out of pawnshops and liquor stores, charge interest rates as high as 400 percent. Basically you're getting a loan until payday, but since you're strapped for cash in the first place, chances are you won't be able to pay off your loan without taking out still another one. Once you're hooked, you'll be paying sky-high interest rates, and falling deeper in debt.

Surrounding nearly all of our nation's hundreds of military bases you'll find a multitude of payday lenders like *Moneyback, Checkmate,* or even those with official-sounding names like *Military Financial Network.* All are quite happy to extend military personnel and their families instant no-questions-asked loans to tide them over until payday. What could be *bad*?

Say you wanted to borrow $500 until payday, less than two weeks from now. No problem. Just write out a check for $575, which we promise not to cash until payday, and you'll walk out of here with $500 cash. That comes to an annual interest rate of over 390 percent, and that's just for starters. If you were short $500 two weeks before *this* payday, and you're starting out the *next* pay period $575 behind...well, you can see where this is going. A month from now you'll be back for a bigger loan, and before long you'll owe thousands of dollars in interest on that original $500 loan you never really got out from under.

At least a quarter of all military families do business with high-cost instant lenders. Many have become trapped in a spiral of borrowing that not only ruins their finances, but distracts them from their duties, and even destroys their careers.

U.S. Navy Petty Officer Second Class Jason Withrow, 24 years old, married, and struggling to make ends meet on an annual salary of about $20,000, is a typical payday lender. His plight is described by Laura Bruce, a writer for *Bankrate.com.*

> An ad in the base newspaper for one of the many payday lenders located near the base got Withrow thinking that an advance on his next paycheck might be his salvation. He took out a $300 loan and agreed to pay back $390 when he got his next check, less than two weeks later. Withrow paid off that first loan but needed more and immediately took out a second loan, and a third.
>
> "I kept it up for a couple months, then I went to another payday lender and got a check for $500. That was pretty tight. I was bouncing between the two for a while, then they both had to be paid at the same time. I couldn't do it so I went to a third lender," Withrow says.
>
> In six months Withrow had borrowed approximately $1,700. Combined, he owed the three payday lenders a crushing $7,000 in interest. He had no option but to go to his command and fess up.
>
> "I was afraid I would lose my career. If you're in debt, they can kick you out of the Navy."
>
> Withrow's commanders didn't give him the boot; instead they referred him to the base's Fleet and Family Support Center where civilian Larry Johnson, a financial educator, arranged an interest-free loan to get the payday lenders off the young sailor's back, and secured from Withrow a promise that he would never go back.
>
> Paydays lenders populate the fringes of military bases across the country. Like steel to a magnet, payday lenders are drawn to the military person's steady paycheck and the knowledge that if the borrower gets in trouble, the military might pay the loan.[8]

[8]Laura Bruce, "Payday Lenders: Uphill Battle for the Military," www.bankrate.com/cweb/news/sav/20040202al. asp.

Payday lending, which is legal in 37 states, operates in the other 13 under various guises, such as catalog retailers or Internet cafes. But like the 50 states, Congress has been unwilling to seriously clamp down on these outfits.

Questions for Further Thought and Discussion

1. Are prices high because rents are high, or are rents high because prices are high? Use an example to illustrate your answer.

2. What are usury laws? Why do economists hate them?

3. Explain why a dollar today is worth more than a dollar you will have in the future.

4. Why is the supply of loanable funds upward sloping? Why is the demand for loanable funds downward sloping?

5. Outline the main theories of profits. Which one(s) do you subscribe to?

6. Many states have usury laws, which place a ceiling on interest rates. Why do most economists dislike these laws?

Workbook for Chapter 29

Name _____ Date _____

Multiple-Choice Questions

Circle the letter that corresponds to the best answer.

1. Which statement is true?
   a) All land has the same economic value.
   b) The most important factor affecting rent is location.
   c) The economic value of a plot of land is determined exclusively by the raw materials it contains.
   d) None of these statements is true.

2. The supply of land _____.
   a) is fixed
   b) varies from time to time
   c) rises with demand
   d) is higher in urban areas than in rural areas

3. Land is most efficiently used in _____.
   a) cities   c) rural areas
   b) suburban areas

4. The rent on a particular piece of land is based on _____.
   a) the supply of land
   b) the buildings located on that land
   c) the MRP schedule of the highest bidder
   d) the MRP schedule of the lowest bidder

5. When the demand for a plot of land rises, _____.
   a) its supply will fall   c) its price will fall
   b) its supply will rise   d) its price will rise

6. The supply of land is _____.
   a) perfectly elastic   c) relatively elastic
   b) perfectly inelastic   d) variable in elasticity

7. Rent on marginal land is _____.
   a) very high   c) zero
   b) above zero   d) negative

8. Each of the following is a valid criticism of Henry George's ideas except that _____.
   a) a tax on land would raise only a small fraction of needed government revenue
   b) landlords sometimes improve the land
   c) like rent, other kinds of income are unearned
   d) a tax on land would result in a decrease in the supply of land

9. Which statement is true?
   a) Prices are high because rents are high.
   b) Rents are high because prices are high.
   c) David Ricardo believed high rents would drive English farmers out of business.
   d) None of these statements is true.

10. As interest rates rise _____.
    a) more borrowing will be undertaken
    b) less borrowing will be undertaken
    c) there is no change in the level of borrowing

11. In the Middle Ages the taking of interest was forbidden to _____.
    a) both Jews and Christians, but not Muslims
    b) both Christians and Muslims, but not Jews
    c) both Jews and Muslims, but not Christians
    d) Jews, Christians, and Muslims

12. A clothing store on fashionable Rodeo Drive charges more for the same clothes than another store in less fashionable Compton. Why does the first store charge more?
    a) They have to pay a higher rent.
    b) They know their customers can afford to pay more.
    c) They advertise more.
    d) Because they can.

13. If there were no inflation, a dollar today would be worth _____.
    a) exactly the same as a dollar received in the future
    b) more than a dollar received in the future
    c) less than a dollar received in the future

14. Which statement is true?

    a) Profits are determined by supply and demand.

    b) Profits are solely a reward for risk taking and innovation.

    c) Profits are derived solely from the exploitation of workers.

    d) None of these statements is true.

15. Which statement is true?

    a) Profits are about one-quarter of GDP.

    b) Profits are about 1 percent of GDP.

    c) Accounting profits are larger than economic profits.

    d) None of these statements is true.

16. Which economist believes all profits are linked with uncertainty and risk?

    a) Frank Knight   c) Karl Marx

    b) Joseph Schumpeter   d) John Maynard Keynes

17. "Innovations do not remain isolated events, and are not evenly distributed in time, but ... on the contrary they tend to cluster, to come about in bunches, simply because some, and then most, firms follow in the wake of successful innovation." Who made this statement?

    a) Frank Knight   c) Karl Marx

    b) Joseph Schumpeter   d) John Maynard Keynes

Use Figure 1 to answer questions 18 through 20.

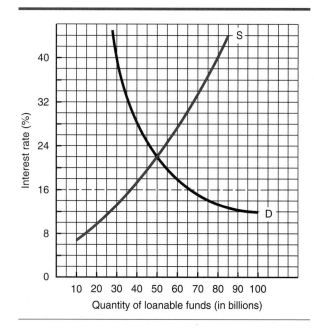

Figure 1

18. The horizontal dotted line is _____.

    a) a price ceiling

    b) a price floor

    c) either a price ceiling or a price floor

    d) neither a price ceiling nor a price floor

19. If there were no usury law, the interest rate would be _____ percent.

    a) 16   d) 22

    b) 18   e) 24

    c) 20

20. With the usury law in effect there is a _____ of _____ billion.

    a) shortage, $28   c) shortage, $56

    b) surplus, $28   d) surplus, $56

21. The present value of a dollar declines as _____.

    a) the interest rate declines and the number of years you wait for your money declines

    b) the interest rate rises and the number of years you wait for your money rises

    c) the interest rate declines and the number of years you wait for your money rises

    d) the interest rate rises and the number of years you wait for your money declines

22. Which statement is true?

    a) Only the owners of labor can earn an economic rent.

    b) Only the owners of land can earn an economic rent.

    c) Both the owners of land and labor can earn an economic rent.

    d) Neither the owners of land nor the owners of labor can earn an economic rent.

23. Which statement is true?

    a) At different times in history Jews, Christians, and Moslems were forbidden to charge interest.

    b) Jews have never been forbidden to charge interest.

    c) Christians have never been forbidden to charge interest.

    d) Moslems have never been forbidden to charge interest.

24. For a usury law to be effective, it must set the interest rate ceiling _____.
    a) above the equilibrium rate of interest
    b) below the equilibrium rate of interest
    c) at exactly the equilibrium rate of interest

25. Which of the following is the most accurate statement about payday lenders?
    a) Virtually all of them operate illegally.
    b) Nearly all military families owe them money.
    c) They charge extremely high interest rates.
    d) They are very useful to low-income families, because they force the families to save.

26. If you took out a payday loan, you could expect to pay an annual interest rate of _____.
    a) less than 5 percent
    b) between 5 and 10 percent
    c) between 10 and 30 percent
    d) between 30 and 100 percent
    e) over 100 percent

27. Surrounding most military bases in the United States you will find _____.
    a) banks
    b) payday lenders
    c) credit unions
    d) savings and loan associations

28. The practice of usury _____.
    a) is illegal in the United States
    b) is legal in some states and illegal in others
    c) is legal only if borrowers are in the military service
    d) was approved of by most major religions until just a few centuries ago

29. These lenders avoid using the term "interest," but their borrowers still do pay a charge for borrowing money. This would be considered _____ lending.
    a) Islamic
    b) payday
    c) fringe
    d) subprime

30. Why do Starbucks customers at busy downtown locations in major cities pay more for a cup of coffee than they would at less busy locations?
    a) Starbucks coffee is better than that of any other company.
    b) They are willing to pay more for the convenience of Starbucks' location.
    c) Starbucks must pay more rent than stores located in less expensive neighborhoods.
    d) The lines are always shorter at Starbucks because of their higher prices.

Fill-In Questions

1. The amount of rent paid for a piece of land is based on the _____ and the _____.

2. In economic terms, we pay rent only on _____ _____.

3. Plots of land are differentiated mainly with respect to _____.

4. The amount of land in the world is virtually _____.

5. In a demand and supply graph for land, supply is represented by a(n) _____ line.

6. The main thing Henry George advocated was a _____.

7. An important attribute of rent overlooked by Henry George was its role as a _____, directing the most productive enterprises to the _____.

8. Rent is high because _____.

9. We can add to our stock of _____ by means of a flow of _____.

10. The interest rate is determined by the law of _____ and _____.

11. If the interest rate were 7 percent, $100 today would be worth _____ in dollars you will have one year from now.

707

12. If interest rates fall, the present value of future dollars will _____.

13. Economists treat profits as a _____ left to the entrepreneur after _____, _____, and _____ have been paid.

Problems

1. If the interest rate is 10 percent and a dollar will be paid to you in three years, what is the present value of that dollar (to the nearest 10th of a cent)?

2. What is the present value of $10,000 that will be paid to you in four years if the interest rate is 8 percent? Work it out to the nearest cent.

3. If the interest rate is 12 percent and a dollar will be paid to you in four years, what is the present value of that dollar (to the nearest cent)?

4. Which has a higher present value? (a) $100 in 10 years when the interest rate is 2 percent or (b) $100 in 3 years when the interest rate is 8 percent?

5. Which would you rather have? (a) $1,000 in 6 years if the interest rate is 4 percent or (b) $1,000 in 3 years if the interest rate is 8 percent?

6. Which is worth more? (a) $100 today or (b) $300 in 15 years if the interest rate is 8 percent?

7. Which is worth more? (a) $500 today or (b) $1,000 in 9 years if the interest rate is 8 percent?

Income Distribution and Poverty

The economic history of the United States has been one of tremendous growth, a rising standard of living, and a home in the suburbs for most American families. But income has not been distributed evenly, and tens of millions of Americans have been left far behind. Indeed, poverty amid plenty has been one of the basic failures of our society.

Fifth Avenue is the eastern border of New York's Central Park. More than a dozen billionaires have Fifth Avenue addresses, living in duplexes and triplexes with great views of the park. Many homeless people also have Fifth Avenue addresses, but they live in cardboard boxes just inside the park.

Visit any welfare office and you'll see dozens of very poor children waiting with their mothers for a worker to see them about their cases. But these children are rich compared to the children you'll find picking through garbage in the outlying areas of most large South American cities. Go out at night and you'll find children sleeping on the sidewalks.

This chapter is divided into two parts: income distribution and poverty. If income were distributed evenly, every American would have an income of $35,000 a year—that's every man, woman, and child—and there would be no poverty. In fact, if income were distributed evenly, there would be virtually nothing to write about income distribution and poverty.

The forces of a capitalist society, if left unchecked, tend to make the rich richer and the poor poorer.

—Jawaharlal Nehru

CHAPTER OBJECTIVES

When you have finished this chapter, you will know the answers to these questions:

- How unequal is income distribution in the United States?
- What determines how income is distributed?
- How does the distribution of income differ from the distribution of wealth?
- How is poverty defined?

- Who are the poor?
- What are the main government transfer payments to help the poor?
- What are the causes of poverty?
- What are the solutions?
- Has welfare reform been successful?

Income Distribution in the United States

The Poor, the Middle Class, and the Rich

How unequal is income distribution in the United States? To answer this question, we must first answer three subsidiary questions: How unequal are the incomes of (1) the poor and the rich? (2) blacks and whites? and (3) males and females? There are no big

I've been rich and I've been poor; rich is better.

—Sophie Tucker

surprises here. The rich make more money than the poor; whites make more than blacks; and men make more money than women. The question is, How much more?

Do you know what a quintile is? I'll bet no one ever asked you *that* before. A quinquennial is an event that occurs every five years; a quintuplet is one of five babies born at the same time. A *quintile* is one-fifth, just like a quarter is one-fourth. We'll use this term to measure income distribution.

The poor are in the lowest quintile, the middle class in the next three quintiles, and the rich in the upper quintile. Is it accurate to say that 20 percent of our population is poor, 60 percent is middle class, and 20 percent is rich? Maybe not. But because social scientists can't agree about where to draw the dividing lines between the poor and the middle class and between the middle class and the rich, this arbitrary arrangement is as good as any other. And besides, we get to deal with nice round numbers—20, 60, and 20.

When all U.S. households are divided by income into quintiles, the middle 20 percent of households earns roughly between $35,000 and $55,000. Table 1 shows us how much the households in each quintile earned in 2004.

Now we're going to analyze a Lorenz curve, named for M. O. Lorenz, who drew the first one in 1905. Let's begin by looking at the axes of Figure 1. On the horizontal axis we have the percentage of households, beginning with the poor (0 percent to 20 percent), running through the middle class (20 percent to 80 percent), and ending with the rich (80 percent to 100 percent). The vertical axis shows the cumulative share of income earned by these households.

Figure 1 has just two lines. The straight line that runs diagonally from the lower left to the upper right is the line of perfect equality. You'll notice that the poorest 20 percent of the households receive exactly 20 percent of the income, and that 40 percent of the

Margin notes:

Who is rich, who is middle class, and who is poor?

The Lorenz curve

TABLE 1	U.S. Household Income, by Quintile, 2004	
		Upper Income Limit
Lowest quintile		$18,500
Second quintile		34,738
Third quintile		55,325
Fourth quintile		88,029
Top quintile		

Source: www.census.gov/hhes/income/histinc/holar.html.

F*igure* 1

Hypothetical Lorenz Curve
The line of perfect income equality shows that any given percent of households receives that same percent of income. For example, the lowest 20 percent of all households would receive 20 percent of the income. Every household would receive the same income: There would be no rich or poor. The Lorenz curve shows the actual income distribution. In this particular example, the poorest 20 percent of all households receive about 5 percent of all income, while the richest fifth receives 60 percent.

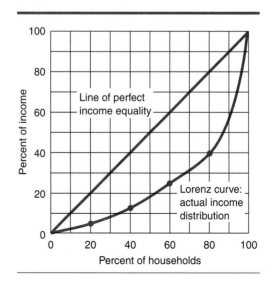

Finding the Percentage of Income Share of the Quintiles in Figure 1

The lowest quintile receives 5 percent of all income. Right? How much does the second quintile get? It gets 7.5 percent. Where did we get that number? What is the percentage share of income earned by the lowest 40 percent of households? It looks like 12.5 percent—right? Now if the bottom quintile earns 5 percent, and the lowest two quintiles earn a total of 12.5 percent, how much do households in the second-lowest quintile earn? They earn 7.5 percent (12.5 percent − 5 percent).

Next question: How much is the cumulative percentage share of income of the lower 60 percent of households? It comes to 25 percent. So how much is the third quintile's income share? It's 12.5 percent (25 percent − 12.5 percent). In other words, we take the lower 60 percent of households' share (25 percent) and subtract from it the combined share of the lower two quintiles (12.5 percent).

The lower 80 percent receives 40 percent of income. From that, we subtract the income share of the lower 60 percent (25 percent), which leaves the fourth quintile with a 15 percent income share. One more quintile to go—the highest quintile. If 100 percent of all households receive 100 percent of all income and the lowest 80 percent of all households receive a total of 40 percent, what's left for the top quintile? You got it—60 percent.

households receive exactly 40 percent of the income. In other words, every household in the country makes exactly the same amount of money.

The curve to the right of the straight diagonal line is the Lorenz curve, which tells us how income is actually distributed. What percent of income does the poorest 20 percent of all households receive? And how much does the next poorest 20 percent receive? Put your answers here:

Lowest fifth:

Second fifth:

Third fifth:

Fourth fifth:

Highest fifth:

The lowest fifth receives just 5 percent of all income; the second fifth receives 7.5 percent; the third fifth receives 12.5 percent; the fourth fifth receives 15 percent; and the highest fifth receives 60 percent. (If you don't know how I got these numbers, please read the box, "Finding the Percentage of Income Share of the Quintiles in Figure 1.")

What do you think of *that* income distribution? Not very equal, is it? You'll notice the Lorenz curve is pretty far to the right of the diagonal line. That diagonal is the line of perfect equality, so the farther the Lorenz curve is from it, the less equal the distribution of income becomes.

Do you know what I forgot to do? I forgot to define the Lorenz curve. Do *you* want to take a stab at a definition? Here's mine: *A Lorenz curve shows the cumulative share of income earned by each quintile of households.*

Definition of the Lorenz curve

How does our own income distribution look? It's plotted for you in Figure 2. Once again, figure out the distribution of income, and write your answers here:

Lowest fifth:

Second fifth:

Third fifth:

Figure 2

Lorenz Curve of Income
Distribution of the United
States, 2004
Would you say that the United
States has an equal distribution of
income? No? I would agree. OK,
what percentage of all income is
received by those in the poorest
20 percent of all households, and
what percentage of all income is
received by those in the richest
20 percent of all households?
The poorest 20 percent received
3.4 percent of all income; the
richest 20 percent received
50 percent of all income.
Source: U.S. Bureau of the Census,
Current Population Reports, Series P-60;
www.census.gov/hhes/www/income/
histinc/ho2ar.html.

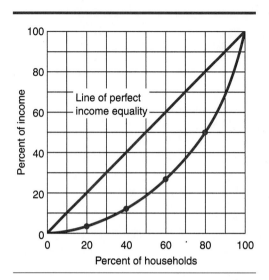

TABLE 2	Percentages of Total Income before Taxes Received by Each Fifth of American Families, 1968 and 2004

Income Rank	1968	2004
Lowest fifth	5.6%	3.4%
Second fifth	12.4	8.7
Third fifth	17.7	14.7
Fourth fifth	23.7	23.2
Highest fifth	40.5	50.0

Source: U.S. Bureau of the Census, *Current Population Reports,* Series P-60;
www.census.gov/hhes/income/histinc/incfamdet.html.

Fourth fifth:

Highest fifth:

Check your answers against those in the right-hand column of Table 2. Your figures don't have to match mine exactly because we're both making our own observations from the graph.

It doesn't take a rocket scientist to figure out that income distribution was more uneven early in the 21st century than it was in the late 1960s. We know that changes in our tax laws have been a major factor. Income tax rates and taxes on capital gains were cut, especially for the rich, while payroll tax rates were raised, taking a large bite out of the incomes of the working poor, the working class, and the lower middle class. Indeed, about 75 percent of all Americans pay more today in payroll taxes than they do in personal income tax.

The rich also reaped huge capital gains in the 1980s and 1990s, largely from increases in stock prices, real estate, and investments in their own businesses. During this same period the average hourly wage rate fell by more than 10 percent. Meanwhile the relatively high-paying manufacturing sector has been shedding hundreds of thousands of jobs almost every year, while employment in the relatively low-paying service sector has been rising rapidly.

Has income become more
equally distributed since 1968?

Now, let's compare the distribution of income in 2004 with that in 1968. Has income become *more* evenly distributed or *less* evenly distributed? A society in which the poorest fifth of the population gets just 3.4 percent of the income and the richest fifth gets half has a very uneven distribution of income. Since 1968, the top fifth's share of income rose from 40.5 percent to 50 percent, whereas the share of the lower three-fifths declined from 35.7 percent to 26.8 percent. In short, then, the rich are getting richer and the poor are getting poorer.

When it is said that our income is unevenly distributed, we need to ask: relative to what standard? Obviously it is unevenly distributed relative to the line of perfect income equality in Figure 2. It is less evenly distributed relative to its distribution in the late 1960s.

How well off is the typical American family? Probably the best way to measure that is by finding the median, or middle income, of all families. For instance if we had just seven families, with the following incomes—$10,000; $14,000; $23,000; $26,000; $31,000; $46,000; and $872,000—find the median income.

The median income would be $26,000. Economists often use median income, rather than average income, because it is not distorted by extreme values, like the family income of $872,000. If we calculated the average income of this group, it would come to $146,000. Clearly the income of the family earning $872,000 pulled up the average. And yet, six of the seven families earned considerably less than the $146,000 average.

Imagine if we could list all American household incomes in ascending order. How much would the median income be? By glancing at the left bar in Figure 3 you'll find the answer for our median income in 2004. How much was it?

It came to exactly $44,389. Of course some folks did better than others. Asian-American families did the best, with a median income of $57,518; black families did the worst, earning a median income of just $30,134.

Now let's see how our overall median income fared over time. The record since 1967 is presented in Figure 4.

You'll notice from the title of Figure 4 that we're looking at "Real Median Household Income," which is measured in 2004 dollars (in other words, dollars of constant purchasing power). So the typical family earned just under $35,000 in 1967, and a little over $44,000 in 2004.

We know, of course, that over this period, the quality of goods and services improved substantially, and many new ones became available. So the typical American family is much better off than it was back in 1967.

If you glance again at Figure 4, you'll notice the shaded areas designating periods of recession. It's no surprise that during each of the recessions over the last 35 years, real median household income declined. But take a look at the period from 2000 through 2004. Real median income declined during each of those years. A decline is fully understandable during a recession year, and perhaps even one year later as the economy recovers. But such a prolonged decline is highly unusual, and unless it's reversed, more and more American families will feel the pain.

The global divide between the rich and the poor is much more apparent in the area of consumption spending. The richest 20 percent of humanity consumes 86 percent of

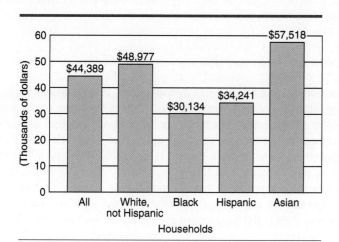

Figure 3

Median Household Income, by Selected Characteristics, 2004

The median household income in 2004 was $44,389. Half of all households earned less than $44,389 and half earned more than $44,389. Median household income for white and Asian households was higher than the overall median; it was lower for black and Hispanic households than the overall median.

Source: U.S. Bureau of the Census, http://www.census/gov.

F*igure* **4**

Real Median Household
Income: 1967 to 2004, in 2004
Dollars
Median household income—the
level at which half of all
households earn more money and
half earn less reached its all-time
peak of $46,128 (in 2004 dollars)
in 1999. It has fallen each year
since then.

Note: The data points are placed at the
midpoints of the respective years.
Median household income data are not
available before 1967.

Source: U.S. Census Bureau, Current
Population Survey, 1968 to 2005 Annual
Social and Economic Supplements.

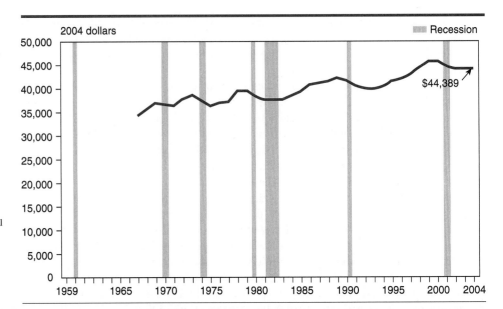

all goods and services, while the poorest fifth consumes just 1.3 percent. In other words, when we look at the consumption rate of all the people on this planet, someone in the richest fifth consumes about 66 times as much as someone in the poorest fifth.

Distribution of Wealth in the United States

The rich are different from you and me.

—F. Scott Fitzgerald

Yes, they are different. They have more money.

—Ernest Hemingway

There is inherited wealth in this country and also inherited poverty.

—President John F. Kennedy

Who made *Forbes* magazine's top 10 list of American billionaires? It's shown in Table 3. It should come as no surprise that Bill Gates heads the list, and most of the other names should also be familiar.

Let's make sure we're clear on the difference between wealth and income. Your income this year includes your annual wages or salary, as well as any interest, dividends, profits, rent, and government transfer payments you received (for example, Social Security benefits, unemployment insurance benefits). Wealth includes housing and other real estate, checking and savings accounts, certificates of deposit, stocks and bonds, and other valuable assets. One reason for the greater concentration of wealth in the hands of the rich is the slashing of federal income tax rates paid by the very rich. In 1981 the top tax bracket was 70 percent; today it is 35 percent. But the main reason why the distribution of wealth in America is becoming less equal is because the distribution of income is becoming less equal. In summary, the rich are getting richer and the poor are getting poorer.

Distribution of Income: Equity and Efficiency

First we'll consider what a fair and just distribution of income would be, and then we'll talk about how income distribution affects the efficient operation of our economy.

Is it fair that some people earn hundreds of millions of dollars a year while others don't make enough to put food on the table and a roof over their heads? Shouldn't we be a more egalitarian society, where no one is superrich or dirt poor? Or should we go even further and ensure that we all earn approximately the same income?

There is widespread agreement that it's good for the rich to give some of their money to the poor. After all, the tens of millions of Americans who give to charity each year can't all be wrong. And if the government uses some of our tax dollars to help the truly needy, that too is something that most of us could support.

| TABLE 3 | The Forbes 2004 Top 10 List of American Billionaires* | |

Name and Rank	Main Source of Income	Net Worth (in $ billions)
1. William H. Gates, III	Microsoft (cofounder)	$51
2. Warren E. Buffett	Stock market	40
3. Paul G. Allen	Microsoft (cofounder)	23
4. Michael Dell	Dell (founder)	18
5. Lawrence J. Ellison	Oracle (founder)	17
6. Christy Walton	Daughter of Wal-Mart founder	16
7. Jim C. Walton	Son of Wal-Mart founder	16
8. S. Robson Walton	Son of Wal-Mart founder	16
9. Alice L. Walton	Daughter of Wal-Mart founder	16
10. Helen R. Walton	Widow of Wal-Mart founder	15

*Two things stand out when we look at this list of the world's richest people. First, five of them inherited their money from Sam Walton, who founded Wal-Mart. And second, four others, William Gates, Paul Allen, Lawrence Ellison, and Michael Dell founded computer companies. So if you want to be really wealthy, either found a computer software company, or pick very rich parents. Donald Trump did not make the top 10. He's number 83 with a fortune estimated at $2.7 billion.
Source: www.forbes.com/richlist 2004. http://webcenters.netscape.compuserve.com/pf/package.jsp?name=pf/pm/forbes 400_05.

OK, so would it be such a bad thing for a rich guy to fork over a buck or two to a poor guy? After all, that money would mean a whole lot more to the poor guy, while the rich guy would hardly miss it. But what if we carry this redistribution scheme to its logical conclusion? Let's have everyone who's earning more than the average income give his surplus to those earning less. When we've finished, we'll all have exactly the same income. I have just stated the utilitarian case for equality.

What do *you* think? Is this fair? What about the people who worked hard for their money, putting in hours of overtime, holding down two jobs, and never seeing their families or friends? And what about the lazy bums who don't even bother looking for a job because they know they'll have exactly the same income as the working stiffs?

So much for a fair and just distribution of income. How does income distribution affect our economic efficiency? Well, for starters, what would an equal distribution of income do to work incentives? Would *you* work hard if you'd end up with exactly the same income as a lot of people who just sat at home and waited for their checks? Two of the things that make our economy go are the carrot and the stick. The carrot is all the money you can make by working hard. And the stick is that if you don't work, you don't eat.

Another incentive that would suffer is the incentive to save. Considering that the interest you'd get from your savings would be divided among everyone, why bother to save at all? Why invest, for that matter? Why bother to engage in any productive activities whatsoever, when we'll all end up with the same income no matter what we do?

Of course, if we were to pursue this reasoning to its logical conclusion, we would end up with very little output (because only a few workaholics would still be producing) and therefore very little real income.

So what should we do? Neither extreme seems desirable. Complete income equality would rob us of our productive incentives. And substantial income inequality would mean a great deal of human suffering, because many of the poor would not be able to afford even the basic necessities of life.

Whatever the means of income redistribution, the ends are always the same—to take from the rich and give to the poor. Robin Hood may not have won favor with the Sheriff of Nottingham or with the rich people he robbed, but most folks agree that the rich—*and* the middle class—should give some of their money to the poor. The only question is, How much?

Poverty is an anomaly to rich people; it is very difficult to make out why people who want dinner do not ring the bell.
—Walter Bagehot

Short of genius, a rich man cannot imagine poverty.
—Charles Péguy

How does income distribution affect our economic efficiency?

What Determines Income Distribution?

About two-thirds of all personal income is earned in wages and salaries, so we'll concentrate on the factors causing these incomes to vary so widely. And then we'll take a look at property income, which accounts for a little less than one-quarter of all personal income. Finally, we'll look at government transfer payments, which account for the rest.

Differences in Wages and Salaries   Medical doctors are among the highest paid workers in the United States. Is that because of all those years of training? Of course all that training doesn't hurt, but the main reason they earn so much is that doctors are in short supply relative to the demand for their services. But I've overlooked the intelligence and ability of the person who becomes a doctor. These factors also greatly influence how much doctors earn. One might ask why, then, PhDs in history, philosophy, or even economics don't earn what doctors do. Once again, we're back to supply and demand. All your professors are still waiting for that long-predicted PhD shortage to materialize, so college teaching salaries will finally start going up.

The main reasons the college graduate earns so much more than the grade school dropout are that the college graduate is probably smarter, richer, and more motivated; has better connections; and comes from a home with a more supportive learning environment. In other words, the personal characteristics of the two people, rather than their respective educations, determine their earning power. This is not to say that education does not affect earning power at all or that many poor people, given the opportunity, could not do well in school and go on to brilliant careers selling junk bonds or even writing economics textbooks.

The 1960s and 1970s were decades of great social upheaval. The women's liberation movement and the civil rights movement sought to place women, blacks, and other minorities squarely in the socioeconomic mainstream. Although these movements and the public- and private-sector hiring programs they engendered have had a major impact in promoting equal economic opportunity, employment discrimination persists.

Through the 1960s women working full time were stuck earning around 60 percent of what men earned. In 1973 the median wage for women was just 63 percent of that for men. By 2004 it had risen to 77 percent.

Property Income   As you might have suspected, most property income goes to the rich. These payments are in the form of rent, interest, dividends, and profits (which include capital gains). The two largest sources of wealth, exclusive of inheritance, have been the fortunes made in the stock market and the starting up of new companies (see Table 3).

Property income may also be derived from ownership of stocks, bonds, bank deposits, and other assets. Because the poor and the working class hold little property, little (if any) of their income comes from this source. The Tax Policy Center has determined that families with incomes of less than $50,000 derived just 3 percent of their income from capital gains and dividends; families with incomes in excess of $10 million received 61.4 percent of their incomes from those sources.

Income from Government Transfer Payments   In addition to wages, salaries, and property income, some people receive government transfer payments. For retirees, Social Security benefits may be their main means of support. For most people collecting unemployment benefits, these checks are usually their sole means of support. And public assistance recipients all depend on these benefits plus food stamps for most or all of their income.

As you observe in Figure 5, Social Security, Medicare, and Medicaid are the big three of federal income transfer programs. Although the poor benefit from all three, only Medicaid spending is "means tested."

Why do some people earn more than others?

Why does a college graduate earn more than a grade school dropout?

Some people's money is merited. And other people's money is inherited.

—Ogden Nash

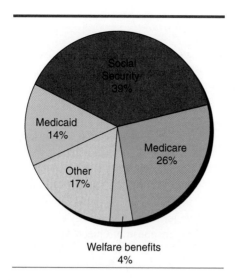

Poverty in America

"I still have the audacity to believe that people everywhere can have three meals a day."

–The Reverend Martin Luther King, Jr.–

The poor will never cease out of the land.
—Moses, *Deuteronomy,* 15:11

Poverty Defined

There are two basic ways to define poverty—as a relative concept and as an absolute concept. By defining the poor as the lowest income quintile (that is, the lowest 20 percent) in the nation, we're saying that this group of people is poor relative to the rest of the population.

The relative concept of poverty

There are a couple of problems with this definition. First, suppose everyone's standard of living quadrupled from one year to the next. We'd *still* be calling those in the lowest quintile poor, even though most of the "poor" would be living better this year than the entire middle class lived last year. Although Jesus *did* say, "Ye have the poor always with you" (Matthew 26:11), *these* poor people would be driving late-model cars, living in nice houses, and eating in fancy restaurants three or four nights a week.

Viewed over time, poverty is clearly a relative concept. Nearly 90 percent of Americans living in 1900 would fall below the poverty line as it is defined today.

A second difficulty with the concept of relative poverty is that the lowest income quintile in the United States and other relatively rich countries is infinitely better off than the average citizens of the world's poorest nations. In Bangladesh, Ethiopia, Mali, and Zambia, most people struggle to survive on maybe $200 or $300 a year. Even our homeless population fares considerably better than that.

What about the absolute concept of poverty? Well, there's one basic problem here, too. Who gets to determine the dividing line between poor and not poor, and how is that determination reached? The best approach is to set up a minimum basic standard of living and figure out how much it costs to maintain that standard from year to year. So far, so good. Who gets to set up this basic living standard, and what goods and services should go into it?

The absolute concept of poverty

Just how bad is the problem of poverty in the rest of the world? One-third of the world's people have no access to electricity and nearly two-thirds have never made a phone call (see box, "The Price of Safe Drinking Water"). Almost half of the world lives on less than $2 a day. There is general agreement that the world's greatest concentration of poverty is in sub-Saharan Africa. According to Cornell's International Labour Organization more than three-quarters of the population in 14 countries lives on less than $2 a day—Nigeria, Mali, Madagascar, Zambia, India, Burkina Faso, Niger, Pakistan, Gambia, Central African Republic, Nepal, Mozambique, Bangladesh, and Ethiopia.

The Price of Safe Drinking Water

Americans, on average, drink over 25 gallons of bottled water a year. And globally, bottled water is now a $50-billion industry. At the other end of the economic spectrum, more than one billion of the world's poor people lack reliable access to safe drinking water. Writing in *The New York Times,* Tom Standage noted that "The World Health Organization estimates that at any given time, around half the people in the developing world are suffering from diseases associated with inadequate water or sanitation, which kill around a million people a year."*

So while the world's relatively affluent folks think nothing of shelling out a dollar for a bottle of water—rather than drink perfectly adequate tap water—over one billion people don't have any safe drinking water at all. What would it take to provide them with clean water? The International Water Management Institute estimates that clean water could be provided to everyone on earth for an outlay of $1.7 billion a year beyond current spending on water projects. But despite the best efforts of rock star Bono and hundreds of other advocates, the world's rich countries have not given sufficient help.

Perhaps $1.7 billion seems like a lot of money, so let's break that down to nickels. Worldwide we buy 50 billion bottles of water. How much money would we raise if we paid a nickel deposit on each bottle of water we purchased? Go ahead and do the math.

We would raise $2.5 billion. Wouldn't *you* be willing to pay a nickel each time you bought a bottle of water for such a worthy cause? Still, you may remember the response of Queen Marie Antoinette during the days just before the French Revolution when told that the people had no bread. "Let them eat cake!" she declared. And so, when we're told that over one billion poor people don't have safe drinking water, we say, "Let them drink *bottled* water!"

---

*Tom Standage, "Bad to the Last Drop," *The New York Times,* August 1, 2005. See online at www.globalpolicy.org/socecon/inequal/2005/0801badtolastdrop.

A better measure of economic well-being for the poor would be their level of consumer spending. In the Labor Department's latest Consumer Expenditures Survey (2003), the average reported income for the bottom quintile of households was just $8,201, but reported consumption outlays were $18,492. How do we explain how the poor can spend more than twice their incomes? Clearly, most poor people don't report their entire incomes. And then, too, they are going deeper into debt each year. Whatever the full explanation, the poor are obviously better off than the official poverty level would indicate.

The most widely used poverty standard in the United States is the official poverty line calculated each year by the U.S. Department of Agriculture. The department bases its estimate on the assumption that poor families spend about one-third of their incomes on food. Each year it calculates the minimum food budget for a family of four for one week, multiplies that figure by 52 for the family's annual food budget, and then triples that figure to get the official poverty line. In 2004 that line was set at $19,157 for a family of four.[1]

The official poverty line

Can a family of four live on $19,157? It all depends on what you mean by living. Is it enough to put food on the table, clothes on your back, and a roof over your head? In some parts of the country, the answer is yes. In the more expensive cities such as New York, Boston, and San Francisco, as well as in many suburban communities, especially in the Northeast, $19,157 won't provide even the bare necessities, largely because of relatively high rents.

Once the poverty line has been established, we can find the poverty rate by dividing the number of poor people by the total population of the country. So the poverty rate is the percentage of Americans who are poor. In 2004 our poverty rate was 12.7, which means that 12.7 percent of Americans were poor.

---

[1]When this method of calculating poverty was devised in the early 1960s, food accounted for 24 percent of the average family budget (not 33 percent); today food accounts for just 10 percent.

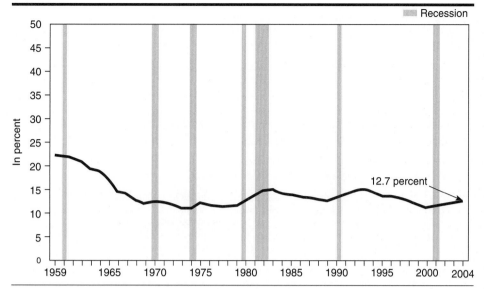

Figure 6
U.S. Poverty Rate: Percentage
of Individuals Below the
Poverty Line, 1959–2004
The poverty rate was cut in half
between 1960 and 1973, largely
because of President Lyndon
Johnson's war on poverty, much of
which was continued and even
expanded under President Richard
Nixon. It remained above 12
percent from 1980, began falling
steadily since 1993, and finally got
below 12 percent in 1999. However,
it began rising again in 2001,
reaching 12.7 in 2004.

Note: The data points are placed at the
midpoints of the respective years.

Source: U.S. Census Bureau, Current
Population Survey, 1960 to 2005 Annual
Social and Economic Supplements. U.S.
Census Bureau, Current Population
Reports, PV 60–229 Income, Poverty,
and Health Insurance Coverage in the
United States: 2004, issued August 2005.

The Census Bureau has been tracking the poverty rate since 1959. As you can observe in Figure 6, there was a sharp decline throughout the 1960s and early 1970s. In 1973 the rate bottomed out at about half the 1960 rate. The main causes of the decline were the prosperity of the 1960s and the War on Poverty conducted by the administration of President Lyndon Johnson. The federal government spent tens of billions of dollars on education, job training, and the creation of government jobs for millions of poor people.

You'll notice the shaded parts of Figure 6, which indicate periods of recession. Usually the poverty rate rises during recessions and falls again once we've recovered. But it has been rising since 2000 even though our last recession ended in November 2001.

Some conservative critics point out that the poverty rate would be substantially lower if we counted the value of noncash, or in-kind, benefits given to the poor by the government. These include Medicaid, housing subsidies, low-rent public housing, food stamps, and school lunches. If these in-kind benefits were counted, the poverty rate would have been 9.7 percent in 2004 rather than the reported 12.7 percent.

The poverty rate would be substantially lower if we counted the value of in-kind benefits.

Who Are the Poor?

Who *are* the poor? Old people? Traditionally, people older than 65 have had a much higher poverty rate than the general population, but the advent of Medicare, higher Social Security benefits, and supplementary Social Security benefits over the last three decades has reduced the poverty rate for older Americans to well below the overall rate. The proportion of retirees living in poverty has fallen from 35 percent in 1960 to just 9.8 percent in 2004.

Are most poor people black? No, most poor people are white. It *is* true that almost one out of four blacks is poor, but only 13 percent of our population is black. Figure 7 shows the relative poverty rates for white, black, Hispanic, and Asian Americans. The poverty rates for both blacks and Hispanics is more than double the poverty rate for non-Hispanic whites.

Most poor people are white.

If you happen to be a member of a female-headed household with children, your chances of being poor are about one out of two. And if that household happens to be black or Hispanic, then you stand an even better chance. To a large degree, then, your chances of being rich or poor in the United States have a lot to do with how skillfully you have chosen your ancestors.

So who *are* the poor? About three-quarters are single mothers and their children. People living in the rural South and in the Appalachian region have relatively high poverty

God must love the poor—he made so many of them.

—Abraham Lincoln

*F*igure 7

Poverty Rates by Race, 2004
The poverty rates of blacks and
Hispanics are both more than
double that for whites.
Source: U.S. Bureau of the Census.

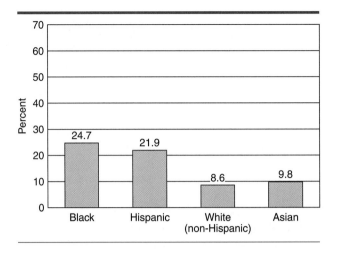

rates. In 2004 the states with the highest poverty rates were New Mexico and Mississippi
with 17.3 percent, while New Hampshire had the lowest—just 5.6 percent, and Maryland,
with 7.2 percent, had the second lowest. Migrant farm workers, native Americans, and
recent immigrants are also much more likely than the general population to be poor.

How much would a person need to earn to bring her family up to the poverty line
of $19,157 for a family of four? Assuming she worked 40 hours a week, 52 weeks a
year, she would need to earn $9.21 an hour. Let's do the math.

First, multiply 40 × 52 to get the number of hours per year she would work.
40 × 52 = 2,080 hours. Next, let's figure out how much she would need to make an
hour in order to earn the $19,157. We need to divide $19,157 by 2,080. So it would take
an hourly wage of $9.21 just to keep a family of four at the poverty line.

Millions of Americans work at or close to the minimum wage ($5.15 an hour) in fast-
food restaurants, laundries, and hospitals, on farms, and even in illegal sweatshops around
the country. A person earning $5.15 an hour for 40 hours a week earns an annual income
of just $10,712 (before taxes), which would clearly leave a family of four—or three, for
that matter—with an income of about half the level at the poverty line.

The working poor   All the people employed at or just above the minimum wage could be considered
the working poor. Most of them receive little or no government benefits yet somehow
manage to make ends meet from paycheck to paycheck. But even if they don't get one
cent from the government, they are still part of our poverty problem.

Among the working poor are hundreds of thousands of Wal-Mart employees. According to a February 2004 report by the Democratic staff of the House Education and Workforce Committee, for a 200-employee Wal-Mart store, the government is spending $108,000
a year for children's health care; $125,000 in tax credits and deductions for low-income
families; and $42,000 a year in housing, or about $2,100 per Wal-Mart employee.

The long-term unemployed   Finally, there are the chronically (long-term) unemployed and the discouraged workers.
Although the U.S. unemployment rate has been relatively low since the mid-1990s, this
measure does not take into account the millions of Americans who have been out of work
for years. The official unemployment statistics count only those who have actively sought
employment; people who have given up looking for jobs are not included. And at the very
bottom of the economic barrel are the homeless (see the box, "The Homeless").

Hurricane Katrina put a vivid face on poverty. Nearly all of the thousands of New
Orleanians stranded in the Superdome and the city's convention center were poor and black.
After days of unconscionable delay, many were finally taken by bus to another improvised
shelter—the Houston Astrodome. The president's mother, Barbara Bush, upon visiting the
evacuees remarked, "So many of the people in the arenas here, you know, were underprivi-
leged anyway. So this is working very well for them." If this were a step up for the evacuees,
then, perhaps a flood that destroyed their homes and nearly all their earthly possessions had
done them a great favor. To extend that logic, perhaps the federal government should flood out
every poor neighborhood and house the displaced in football stadiums around the country.

The Homeless

The law, in its majestic equality, forbids the rich as well as the poor to sleep under bridges, to beg in the streets, and to steal bread.

–Anatole France–

We've created a lot of $6-an-hour jobs and not much $6-an-hour housing.

–John Donahue–
Chicago Coalition for the Homeless

There have always been homeless people in America—the hobo jungles of the Depression era, the skid rows (or skid roads, as they are known in the West), and, of course, the isolated shopping-bag ladies and other folks who lived out on the street, in doorways, or in train stations. But now there are literally millions of them. In a nation of some 300 million people, between 2 and 3 million are homeless.

A convergence of four trends has multiplied the number of homeless people who congregate in all our large cities. Since World War II the number of entry-level factory jobs almost disappeared from every large city. Meanwhile, the availability of cheap housing (basically furnished rooms) has also declined as the cities' more dilapidated neighborhoods were demolished to make way for urban renewal projects.

A third trend has been gentrification, which has pushed rents through the roof, so to speak, in New York, San Francisco, Boston, Chicago, and most other major cities. Finally, the deinstitutionalization of the mentally ill over the last two and a half decades (without the promised halfway houses to treat and shelter them) has further added to the homeless population.

Which city has the largest homeless population? New York and Los Angeles have long headed the list with official counts of over 50,000 each. But since August 2005, New Orleans has clearly become number one. Of course New Orleans' homeless population no longer resides in that city, but is scattered across the nation.

The U.S. Department of Health and Human Services estimates that one-third of the homeless are mentally ill and that half of the homeless are alcoholics or drug addicts. The Veteran's Administration estimates that nearly 200,000 veterans of various wars are homeless on any given night, many as a result of substance abuse. Interestingly, about one-quarter of the homeless work full time, according to the U.S. Conference of Mayors. The problem for them is being trapped between jobs that pay too little and housing that costs too much.

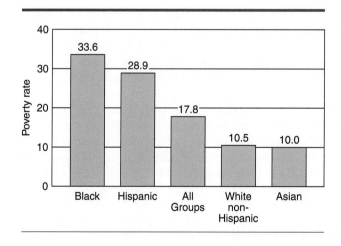

Figure 8

Children under 18 below Poverty Level by Race and Hispanic Origin, 2004

The child poverty rate is more than three times as high for black children than for white and Asian children. More than 1 in 3 black children lives in poverty.

Source: Bureau of Labor Statistics and Bureau of the Census, *CPS Annual Demographic Survey, March Supplement,* March 2005; http://pubdb3.census.gov/macro/032005/pov/new01_100.htm.

Child Poverty

Perhaps the most striking thing about poverty in America is how it affects children. Particularly hard hit by poverty are black children and Hispanic children (see Figure 8). "Children are our future" may be a cliché, but they are nevertheless a future that we neglect at our peril.

The child poverty rate fell from its most recent peak of 22.7 percent in 1993 to 17.8 percent in 2004. Among black children the poverty rate is 33.6 percent and among Hispanic children it is 28.9 percent (see Figure 8).

Figure 9

Child Poverty Rates in Selected Countries: Children Living in Households with Income less than 50 Percent of the National Median Income, 2004

Of the countries shown here, the United States has the second highest rate of child poverty. Note that this measure is somewhat different from defining the childhood poverty rate as the percentage of children in families living below the official poverty line shown in Figure 8.

Source: Unicef; *The Economist,* March 5, 2005, p. 104.

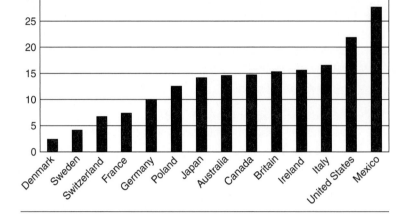

It is said that a society may be judged by how it treats its children. In 2004 17.8 percent of American children lived in poverty. It is astounding that a nation as rich as ours can permit this to happen.

You can see from Figure 9 that the relative poverty rate of American children is extremely high. We cannot conclude that poor American children are worse off than poor Italian or British children or Canadian children. But we certainly *can* say that the standard of living of poor American children is extremely low compared to middle-class and rich American children.

Perhaps the most troubling statistic is that 52.9 percent of all American children under six in a family headed by a female lived in poverty in 2004. Using this information, Katherine Boo draws an interesting conclusion: " ... for children a two-parent household is the most effective anti-poverty program we know. Three out of four white children are born to such households. Only one in three black children is."[2]

Large-scale, high-rise, low-income public housing projects have been especially good breeding grounds for this culture of poverty. In these neighborhoods at least three-quarters of the families are on welfare, most of the girls get pregnant before they are 18, and there is a great degree of drug dependency and an extremely high rate of violent crime. The gangs are the real authority in the ghetto, according to Nicholas Lemann. The gang "forces kids through physical terror, to give up school and work and become professional criminals."[3] To some degree this phenomenon has evolved in poor Hispanic and non-Hispanic white neighborhoods as well.

There is a very strong correlation between crime and poverty. The poor are much more likely to commit crimes and to be the victims of crimes than the general population. Since the early 1990s both crime and poverty have been on the decline. In a provocative, best-selling book, Steven Levitt and Stephen Dubner argue that the widespread availability of abortions—especially to poor women—is largely responsible for these trends (see the box, "Abortion, Crime, and Poverty").

A decent provision for the poor is a true test of civilization.

—Samuel Johnson

The Main Government Transfer Programs

Until the 1930s, the poor depended on help from friends and family, an failing that, from private charities. But when millions of otherwise respectable middle class and working class Americans were thrown out of work during the Great Depression, they demanded that the federal government provide them with some means of support, whether jobs,

---

[2]Katherine Boo, "The Black Gender Gap," *The Atlantic Monthly,* January/February 2003, p. 107.

[3]Nicholas Lemann, "The Origins of the Underclass," *The Atlantic Monthly,* June 1986, p. 39.

Abortion, Crime, and Poverty

As you well know, abortion is perhaps the most contentious political issue of the last three and a half decades. Being "pro-life" or "pro-choice" requires making a value judgment, something we don't do in economics. Still, we can ask, as do the authors of the controversial *Freakonomics,* what effect does the widespread availability of abortions have on crime and poverty?*

In 1973 the U.S. Supreme Court decided in *Roe v. Wade* that women are constitutionally guaranteed the right to have abortions. Between 1973 and 1980 the annual number of abortions performed in the United States rose from 750,000 to 1.6 million. Steven Levitt and Stephen Dubner ask the provocative question: Had these children been born, how would their lives have turned out?

> *What sort of woman was most likely to take advantage of Roe v. Wade? Very often she was unmarried or in her teens or poor, and sometimes all three. What sort of future might her child have had? One study has shown that the typical child who went unborn in the earliest years of legalized abortion would have been 50 percent more likely than average to live in poverty; he would have also been 60 percent more likely to grow up with just one parent. These two factors—childhood poverty and a single-parent household—are among the strongest predictors that a child will have a criminal future. Growing up in a single-parent home roughly doubles a child's propensity to commit crime. So does having a teenage mother. Another study has shown that low maternal education is the single most powerful factor leading to criminality.*
>
> *In other words, the very factors that drove millions of American women to have abortions also seemed to predict that their children, had they been born, would have led unhappy and possibly criminal lives.*

> …

> *In the early 1990s, just as the first generation of children born after Roe v. Wade was hitting its late teen years—the years during which young men enter their criminal prime—the rate of crime began to fall. What this generation was missing, of course, were the children who stood the greatest chance of becoming criminals. And the crime rate continued to fall as an entire generation came of age minus the children whose mothers had not wanted to bring a child into the world. Legalized abortion led to less unwantedness; unwantedness leads to high crime; legalized abortion, therefore, led to less crime.†*

Levitt and Dubner argue that more abortions in the 1970s led to a marked drop in the crime rate in the 1990s. In addition, fewer unwanted births also led to a steep drop in the poverty rate from 1993 through 2000 (see Figure 5).

We know that teenage boys—especially those from one-parent households—are certainly responsible for much of our violent crime, so it is very plausible that since fewer of these boys were born since the mid-1970s, there would be a large drop in violent crime in the 1990s.

Did the higher abortion rate also lead to a lower poverty rate? Or could the declining poverty rate since 1993 be explained entirely by the rapid rate of economic growth and the creation of some 20 million new jobs? Your guess is as good as mine.

---

*Steven D. Levitt and Stephen J. Dubner, *Freakonomics* (New York: William Morrow, 2005).

†Ibid., pp. 138–9.

welfare payments, or any other programs that would keep the wolf from the door. Today, of course, the government continues to provide most of help given to the poor, but private charities also continue to help as well.

The poor are not invisible. The people lined up outside food pantries or inside check cashing stores are usually living below the poverty line or pretty close to it. But you might be surprised to learn that some of them are in military families. Their economic situation is described in the box, "Support Our Troops."

The Social Security Act of 1935 set up three major programs: Social Security, unemployment insurance, and public assistance. Taxes paid by workers and their employers financed the first two programs. Public assistance, which was intended to help families experiencing temporary economic distress, was the only means-tested program. To obtain public assistance (or relief, as it was then called), you needed to demonstrate that your income or means of support was insufficient to cover your basic needs.

The Social Security Act of 1935

Support Our Troops

Walk through any parking lot and count the "Support Our Troops" bumper stickers. That's also the implicit message of the American flag lapel pins worn by our president, vice president, and most members of Congress. After all, it's the least we can do for those risking their lives to defend our country.

From the American Revolution on, civilians have willingly sacrificed to support our troops. And our political leaders have unfailingly raised taxes to pay for these wars. Now, for the first time in our history, civilians have not been asked to make any sacrifice whatsoever. Indeed, President George W. Bush and the Republican congressional majorities have managed to push through two major tax cuts, with the promise of more to come.

Today perhaps 200,000 veterans are homeless, and the average waiting time to get medical treatment from the Veteran's Administration is six months. Apparently we've somehow forgotten the sacrifices these people made. In the words of General Douglas McArthur, "Old soldiers never die. They just fade away."

We noted in the last chapter how our military bases are surrounded by payday lenders, only too happy to extend our service men and women and their spouses short term loans at exorbitant interest rates. But these companies are just symptoms of an underlying problem, not the cause. The problem is that we don't pay our troops enough to keep their heads above water. Hundreds of thousands of military families live from paycheck to paycheck, leaving them at the mercy of these predatory lenders.

In a book describing hunger in America, Loretta Schwartz-Nobel wrote a chapter entitled, "From Front Lines to Food Lines." Here's how she explains why so many military families run into financial problems:

Advocates for the military families consistently point out that the acute problem comes when an enlisted man marries and has children. That is partly because there is no additional food allowance for the family of an enlisted man, and also because housing allowances are never enough to cover the costs of housing, food and all the other added expenses of families. In fact, they usually aren't even enough to cope with housing expenses alone. As a result, families who are living in areas with high rents often end up moving forty or fifty miles away from their duty stations to areas where housing is less expensive and more available. But even that has a downside,

because it means that now they have to maintain both a car and costly insurance.

If they live in military housing, the government pays for their utilities, but if they live off base, the utilities are often a large additional expense. Unfortunately, many bases have very little housing and extremely long waiting lists. *

Most of those joining the military are hoping for a step up on the economic ladder. How well paid *are* the members of our armed forces? In 2005 a private first class with less than two year's active service earned $1,456.20 a month before taxes ($17,474.40 on an annual basis). That leaves a family of four well below the 2004 poverty line of $19,157.

Here's an excerpt from an article entitled, "Thousands of US Military Families Live in Poverty," by Brian Mann.

Ms. Levesque runs a food pantry in Watertown, New York, a short drive from the Fort Drum Army base. She says Army families make up 20 percent of the people who come in, looking for free meals and supplies. "The military kind of has a 'we take care of our own' motto, which you realize that they kind of don't," she said. "And there are a lot of people who fall through the cracks and need the assistance who aren't getting it."

Ms. Levesque speaks from experience, as a social service worker, but also as the wife of a soldier. Her husband, an army specialist, brings home roughly $1,300 a month after taxes—not enough to pay for rent, food, utilities and other necessities. "I have always worked two jobs," said Amy Levesque. "And my husband, he's in the military plus he has a nighttime job. Luckily we don't have any children. With children, it would be very difficult."†

Supporting our troops takes a lot more than just displaying a bumper sticker or wearing a lapel pin. If our nation truly believes that message, then we need to spend enough to provide our troops with the income support they need and deserve.

---

*Loretta Schwartz-Nobel, *Growing Up Empty: The Hunger Epidemic in America* (New York: HarperCollins, 2002), pp. 99–100.

†*Source:* www.globalpolicy.org/socecon/inequal/2003/0115military.htm.

Can you name our biggest antipoverty program? The one that lifts more people out of poverty than any other government program?

Would you believe the answer is Social Security? OK, I know, Social Security is not an antipoverty program. But that's just being picky. The fact is, if it were not for Social Security, one out of every two Americans over 65 would be living below the poverty line. And for two-thirds of the elderly, Social Security supplies much of their income. So we can say that while Social Security is not a poverty program per se, it certainly has that effect. (See Current Issue: "Will Social Security Be There for You?" at the end of this chapter.)

Two major programs, Medicare and Medicaid, were added in the mid-1960s under President Johnson's Great Society program. Medicare, which is really a supplement to Social Security, provides retirees and their families with free or very low-cost medical care. Free medical care is provided to the poor under Medicaid.

Medicare and Medicaid

Today one out of every ten Americans receives food stamps, which represents just 40 percent of those who are eligible. The food stamp program, which also began in the 1960s, enabled the very poor as well as the working poor to buy enough food. Like Medicare and Medicaid, it has expanded tremendously since the late 1960s.

Still another very important form of aid to the working poor is the earned income tax credit, which is written into our Internal Revenue Code. Those eligible, instead of *paying* income tax actually receive what amounts to a refund check from the Internal Revenue Service. The purpose of the earned income tax credit is to encourage the poor to work by supplementing their earnings. Up to a certain income—$11,000 in 2005 for a couple with two children—the more you earned, the larger your refund check. If you earned between $11,000 and $16,400, you received a check for $4,400. But for every additional $1,000 of earned income, your check was reduced by about $210. Families earning above $37,263 received no earned income tax credit. About 19 million Americans receive the credit, with about 5 million gaining enough to rise above the poverty line (see the box, "Helping the Poor Get Money Back from the IRS"). The earned income tax credit is popular with liberals because it provides a substantial amount of income to the poor, and it is also popular with conservatives because only families with a working member are eligible. Today it is, by far, the biggest single federal policy targeting the

Helping the Poor Get Money Back from the IRS

In a column in *Newsweek,* Bob Burke tells how he organized a program to help poor families get substantial tax refunds.

One day I had an idea. I knew the federal government had tax credits to ease the burden on working-poor families, but the process for claiming these credits was simply too complicated for most to get the assistance they had coming. I came up with a plan: I would gather a group of business professionals to offer free tax-preparation services. We'd meet at the school on Saturday mornings and get the word out in the community that we were there to help.

...

After about an hour, these volunteers usually had the pleasant task of informing a hardworking,

low-income family that they would receive thousands of dollars back from the Internal Revenue Service. All that without a commercial tax-preparation service's taking out a big chunk.

I vividly remember when a single mother of two, who hadn't earned enough in three years to file a return, burst into tears when I told her that the IRS had withheld too much from her paychecks and owed her $10,000. She said she would use the money to fix the leaky roof on her house. Others were equally emotional, making plans to pay overdue bills, buy clothes and school supplies for their children or even move to a safer neighborhood.

Source: Bob Burke, "Helping the Needy Crack the Tax Code," *Newsweek,* April 26, 2004, p. 15.

poor. In addition, about a dozen states have also introduced their own EITC programs that supplement the federal credit.

Have these programs worked? Yes, they have. Each has accomplished what it was set up to do. But there are three major problems: (1) their costs have gone through the roof; (2) they have fostered a permanent dependency on government support among millions of poor families; and (3) they have not ended poverty.

Public assistance has been the greatest disappointment. Intended to provide "temporary relief," public assistance instead engendered a permanent dependence in millions of families.

One misconception about welfare mothers is that they keep having more and more children so that they can collect bigger checks. Indeed, many states no longer increase the size of a welfare grant if more children are born into a family. But 72 percent of all welfare families have only one or two children.

The welfare culture

A welfare culture evolved over decades, giving rise to second-, third-, and fourth-generation welfare families. Typically, teenage girls become pregnant, keep their babies, go on welfare, do not marry, and have no hope of becoming self-supporting. In a sense, the young mothers are provided with surrogate husbands in the form of public assistance checks. Eventually their children grow up, become teenage parents themselves, and continue the welfare pattern through another generation.

The number of people receiving public assistance remained remarkably steady—at about 11 million—from 1975 through 1992. But the welfare rolls shot up from 11 million in mid-1993 to a peak of 14.4 million in March 1994 (see Figure 10 near the end of this chapter). The main reason for this increase was the recession of 1990–91. By early 1994, the benefits of the subsequent economic expansion finally began to reach people at the bottom of the economic ladder, and the welfare rolls began to decline. Another important factor was that many states have restricted eligibility for welfare. And then, too, the passage of the Welfare Reform Act—which we'll discuss near the end of the chapter—was perhaps the main reason why so many mothers found work and left welfare.

The words of one welfare mother are especially poignant: "I'm sorry I got myself into this and my children into this. And I don't know how to get them out of it. If I don't get them away from here, they're going to end up dead, in jail, or like me."[4]

Theories of the Causes of Poverty

Any theory of poverty must take into account our entire socioeconomic system, how it is set up, how it is run, and who gets what. Poor people live on the margin or even beyond the system. They are basically superfluous and rarely have much impact on the system. They are an unfortunate presence, by-products that have been discarded but are grudgingly tolerated by society's "productive" members.

At least a dozen theories of poverty have attracted support, and each has at least *some* apparent validity. But because there are so many different poverty groups, no single theory can have universal applicability. We'll begin by briefly outlining a few theories, and then we'll look at the two with the largest number of adherents: the conservative and liberal theories.

The Poor Are Lazy   This theory was popular through most of the 19th century and right up to the time of the Great Depression. God's chosen people, who were destined to go to heaven, worked hard all their lives and were rewarded by attaining great earthly riches. And the poor? Well, you can figure out for yourself where they were headed. This theory went down the tubes when the Great Depression hit and millions of relatively

---

[4]See Celia W. Dugger, "On the Edge of Survival: Single Mothers on Welfare," *The New York Times,* July 6, 1992, p. B6.

affluent Americans were thrown out of work, lost their life savings, and had to ask the government for handouts.

The Heritage of Slavery   Because blacks were brought here in chains and held back for three centuries by slavery and a feudal sharecropping system in the South, the current poverty of many blacks can be explained by centuries of oppression. Not only were blacks systematically excluded from all but the most menial jobs, but they were denied the educational opportunities open to almost all other Americans. Mortgage loans, restaurant meals, hotel and motel lodging, union membership, and apartment rentals were routinely denied. In effect, then, blacks were systematically excluded from the nation's economic mainstream until the 1960s. Is it any wonder, ask adherents of this theory, that after so many years of oppression both during and after slavery, many blacks still find themselves mired in poverty?

Employment Discrimination   Employment discrimination has been especially strong in holding down the incomes of women, blacks, Hispanics, and other minorities. The fact that women working full-time have generally earned about three-quarters of what their male counterparts have earned clearly points toward discrimination. Similar figures for blacks and Hispanics arouse the same suspicion.

Full-time working women have earned 60 percent of what full-time working men earned.

But other factors have also contributed to these wage differentials—education, training, and experience, and, in the case of many women, the years taken off work to raise children. Social scientists generally believe that about half of these wage differentials result from employment discrimination and the other half from other factors. As more employment opportunities become available to women and to minorities, we may see a narrowing of wage differentials. Meanwhile, employment discrimination has obviously been playing a major role in the poverty of women, blacks, Hispanics, and other minorities.

Black Male Joblessness   Back in 1970, about 33 percent of all black families were headed by women. By the mid-1990s, the number had jumped to over 60 percent. The growing perception of a permanent welfare population of single black mothers and their children has raised the question of where are the young black males who got them pregnant? In college? Playing major-league ball? Probably not.

While more than four-fifths of all white males aged 20 to 44 are employed, only about half of their black counterparts have jobs. What are the rest of them doing? Some are officially unemployed, and some are "discouraged workers" who have stopped looking for work. And where are the rest of these guys? Some may be working in the underground economy—in either the legal or illegal sector. And others have just slipped through the cracks.

Only half of all black males aged 16 to 64 are employed.

William A. Darity, Jr., and Samuel L. Myers, Jr., argue that "black men are being excluded from the emerging economic order; they are socially unwanted, superfluous, and marginal." Consequently there is a shrinking pool of marriageable black men. This growing marginality has led to drug abuse, violent crime, incarceration, and a high death rate, further depleting the ranks of marriageable young black men. Cutting welfare benefits, Darity and Myers observe, will do nothing to lower the number of black female-headed households, because the underlying problem is finding meaningful employment for millions of black men.[5]

The absence of eligible males does explain why there are so many single young black women, but it doesn't explain why these women are having so many children. Some conservatives, most notably Charles Murray,[6] believe that they allow themselves to get pregnant because they want to get on welfare. However, substantial research indicates

[5]William A. Darity, Jr., and Samuel L. Myers, Jr., "Family Structure and the Marginalization of Black Men: Policy Implications," presented at the American Economic Association Meetings, Washington, DC, January 1995.

[6]Charles Murray, *Losing Ground: American Social Policy, 1950–1980* (New York: Basic Books, 1984).

that although public assistance is the main source of support once these girls give birth, peer pressure, the wish to go through the rite of passage into womanhood, and the desire for something to love are the real motivating factors.[7]

Let's pause here for a minute to catch our breath. We've been talking for a while about the causes of what is mainly black poverty. Keep in mind that most poor people are white. But when we distinguish between short-term poverty and a permanent underclass, we are talking mainly about a problem that has affected blacks, who constitute about 60 percent of the long-term poor.

Poverty Breeds Poverty Poverty itself generally breeds poverty. Before birth an infant may suffer from poor prenatal care or even acquire an addiction to drugs, particularly crack. During childhood inadequate nutrition and a lack of medical and dental care also take their tolls. An unsafe—or even violent—environment, emotional deprivation, and a broken home also militate against a good childhood. This situation makes it extremely difficult to do well in school, so the easiest course is to give up.

Inadequate Human Capital Human capital is defined as the acquired skills of an individual—education, training, and work habits. People who grew up poor usually had poor home learning environments, attended poor schools, dropped out before graduation, acquired little useful work experience, did not develop good work habits, and have poorly developed communication skills. In sum, they are virtually unemployable in today's economy.

The Conservative View versus the Liberal View

Now we're ready for the Super Bowl of poverty theory debate—the conservatives versus the liberals. Representing the conservative view will be Charles Murray, whose book *Losing Ground* depicts overly generous public assistance programs as perpetuating a dependent underclass. William Julius Wilson is perhaps the most prominent of Murray's liberal critics, so he'll represent their view.[8]

The conservatives and liberals agree on ends but disagree on means.

Did the Great Society program help alleviate poverty?

The conservatives and the liberals agree completely on ends—getting the long-term poor off welfare and into self-supporting employment—but they disagree completely on the appropriate means. Basically, the liberals favor the carrot approach, while the conservatives advocate the stick.

During the Great Depression, President Franklin Roosevelt's New Deal program attempted to lift one-third of all Americans out of poverty. Poverty wasn't rediscovered until the 1960s,[9] and the response was President Lyndon Johnson's Great Society program. Did this program and its extension through the 1970s actually help alleviate poverty? Here's Murray's response:

> In 1968, as Lyndon Johnson left office, 13 percent of Americans were poor, using the official definition. Over the next 12 years, our expenditures on social welfare quadrupled. And, in 1980, the percentage of poor Americans was—13 percent.[10]

Murray draws this conclusion: By showering so much money on the poor, the government robbed them of their incentive to work. Using the archetypal couple, Harold and Phyllis, showed how in 1960 Harold would have gone out and gotten a minimum-wage

Charles Murray, American economist (1993 Susan Muniak)

[7]P. Cutright, "Illegitimacy and Income Supplements," *Studies in Public Welfare,* paper no. 12, prepared for the use of the Subcommittee on Fiscal Policy of the Joint Economic Committee. Congress of the United States (Washington, DC: Government Printing Office, 1973); C. R. Winegarden, "The Fertility of AFDC Women: An Economic Analysis," *Journal of Economics and Business* 26 (1974), pp. 159–66; William Julius Wilson, *When Work Disappears* (New York: Knopf, 1996), pp. 107–9.

[8]Wilson would probably reject any label, but his views are supported by nearly all liberals.

[9]Interest was sparked by Michael Harrington's book, *The Other America* (New York: MacMillan, 1962).

[10]Murray, *Losing Ground,* p. 8.

job to support Phyllis and their newborn baby. But 10 years later the couple would be better off receiving public assistance and food stamps, living together without getting married, and having Harold work periodically. Why work steadily at an unpleasant, dead-end job, asks Murray, when you can fall back on welfare, food stamps, unemployment insurance, and other government benefit programs?

All of this sounds perfectly logical. But Murray's logic was shot full of holes by his critics. We'll start with welfare spending. Although payments *did* increase from 1968 to 1980, when we adjust them for inflation these payments actually decreased between 1972 and 1980. William Julius Wilson really lowers the boom:

> The evidence does not sustain Murray's contentions. First, countries with far more generous social welfare programs than the United States—Germany, Denmark, France, Sweden, and Great Britain—all have sharply lower rates of teenage births and teenage crime.
>   Second, if welfare benefits figured in the decision to have a baby, more babies would be born in states with relatively high levels of welfare payments. But careful state-by-state comparisons show no evidence that [public assistance] influences childbearing decisions; sex and childbearing among teenagers do not seem to be a product of careful economic analysis.[11]

Another problem with Murray's analysis is that the unemployment rate doubled between 1968 and 1980, yet the poverty rate remained constant. Why? Because of all the social programs that were in place—unemployment insurance, public assistance, food stamps, and Medicaid, among others. Although there was substantial economic growth throughout most of the 1970s, this growth was insufficient to absorb all of the housewives and baby boomers who had entered the labor market.

Murray blamed the antipoverty programs for increasing poverty. Liberals would say he really had it backward: These programs prevented a bad situation from getting worse. During a time of rising unemployment, particularly among black males, it was actually a triumph of social policy to keep the poverty rate from rising.

All of this said, Murray's thesis should not be dismissed out of hand. There *are* plenty of people out there who choose welfare as the easy way out. Even more to the point, a culture of poverty *has* developed during the last four decades. Had he said that the largesse of the federal government had induced a sizable minority of the poor to succumb to the joys of living on the dole, he would have had a valid point. Murray simply overstated his case.

Decades ago, when I was a case worker for the New York City Welfare Department, I saw hundreds of thick case folders documenting the lives of second-, third-, and fourth-generation welfare families, consisting of scores of people, virtually all of whom had spent most or all of their lives dependent on public assistance. Had Murray confined his theory to this group, he would have had the support of the large majority of those working directly with the welfare population. Again, there *is* no valid general theory of the causes of welfare dependency.

In his landmark work *The Truly Disadvantaged,* Wilson begins by describing the black ghettos as they were more than 40 years ago. Sure there was crime, but it was still safe to walk the streets at night. And sure there was joblessness, but nothing like what there has been these last 30 years. Then he goes on to describe other social problems:

Forty years ago the ghettos were a lot kinder and gentler places to live.

> There were single-parent families, but they were a small minority of all black families and tended to be incorporated within extended family networks and to be headed not by unwed teenagers and young adult women but by middle-aged women who usually were widowed, separated, or divorced. There were welfare recipients, but only a very small percentage of the families could be said to be welfare-dependent. In short,

[11]William Julius Wilson, Introduction to Lisbeth B. Schorr and Daniel Schorr, *Within Our Reach* (New York: Doubleday, 1989), p. xxv.

William Julius Wilson, American sociologist (Harvard University Archives)

The outward migration of middle- and working-class blacks had a significant impact on those left behind.

unlike the present period, inner-city communities prior to 1960 exhibited the features of social organization—including a sense of community, positive neighborhood identification, and explicit norms and sanctions against aberrant behavior.[12]

So what happened? What happened was the civil rights revolution led by Martin Luther King, Jr., in the early 1960s and the subsequent legislation that lowered racial housing and employment barriers. Until then the big-city ghettos had been socioeconomically integrated. But this quickly changed by the late 60s as millions of blacks, who had been penned up in the ghettos, were finally able to move out. They moved into the houses and apartments that had been vacated by the whites who had fled to the suburbs.

How did this outward migration affect those who were left behind?

The exodus of middle- and working-class families from many ghetto neighborhoods removes an important "social buffer" that could deflect the full impact of the kind of prolonged and increasing joblessness that plagued inner-city neighborhoods in the 1970s and early 1980s.... Even if the truly disadvantaged segments of an inner-city area experience a significant increase in long-term joblessness, the basic institutions in that area (churches, schools, stores, recreational facilities, etc.) would remain viable if much of the base of their support comes from the more economically stable and secure families. Moreover, the very presence of these families during such periods provides mainstream role models that help keep alive the perception that education is meaningful, that steady employment is a viable alternative to welfare, and that family stability is the norm, not the exception.[13]

This isolation makes it harder to find a job; few ghetto dwellers are tied into the job network. And because few relatives or neighbors have steady work, tardiness and absenteeism are not considered aberrant behavior. Consequently, those who do find jobs seldom hold them very long.

Lack of jobs is the key.

So the key is jobs—or rather the lack of them:

The black delay in marriage and the lower rate of remarriage, each associated with high percentages of out-of-wedlock births in female-headed households, can be directly tied to the employment status of black males. Indeed, black women, especially young black women, are confronting a shrinking pool of "marriageable" (that is, economically stable) men.[14]

The migration of black middle- and working-class families from the ghettos removed the key social constraint against crime. And the erection of huge, high-rise, low-income public housing projects further destroyed the remaining sense of community. Place together a large number of female-headed families with a large number of teenage children (who commit more crime than any other population group) and you've got the recipe for not only high crime rates but almost complete social breakdown.

Wilson's thesis is a direct repudiation of Murray's, which blames public assistance and other social programs for the emergence of the permanent black underclass. Wilson finds no evidence to support that contention. Instead, he blames a whole range of social and economic forces, including past employment discrimination.

Solutions

The best way to help poor people is to not be one of them.

—Reverend Ike,
New York City preacher

All poor people have one thing in common: They don't have nearly enough money. Or, in the words of the great wit Finley Peter Dunne, "One of the strangest things about life is that the poor, who need the money the most, are the very ones that never have it."

---

[12]William Julius Wilson, *The Truly Disadvantaged* (Chicago: University of Chicago Press, 1987), p. 3.

[13]Ibid., p. 56.

[14]Ibid., p. 145.

The basic liberal solution—in addition to combating employment discrimination—is to provide the poor with better education and training, and with millions of government jobs. The conservatives have placed their faith in providing the poor with jobs mainly in the private sector. But the basic strain running through conservative thought about welfare recipients may be summed up in just three little words: Cut 'em off. A solution with widespread support, workfare, combines the liberal carrot of training and jobs with the conservative stick of cutting off the benefits of those who refuse to seek training or work.

The Conservative Solutions To end the poor's dependency on government largesse, Charles Murray would simply pull the plug on the life-support system:

> [Scrap] the entire welfare and income-support structure for working-aged persons, including [public assistance], medicaid, food stamps, unemployment insurance, workers' compensation, subsidized housing, disability insurance, and the rest. It would leave the working-aged person with no recourse whatsoever except the job market, family members, friends, and public or private locally funded services.[15]

The Liberal Solutions While the conservatives claim the government has done too much for the poor, the liberals believe much too little has been done. Barbara Ehrenreich, for example, points out that an increasing number of jobs do not pay enough to subsist on.[16] The solution? Government jobs.

Government jobs doing what? Jobs rebuilding the nation's crumbling highways and bridges, and staffing hospitals, schools, libraries, and day care centers. Jobs rebuilding dilapidated inner-city housing and cleaning up toxic waste dumps. In the 1930s, the Works Progress Administration (WPA) of the New Deal employed millions of Americans building highways, airports, bridges, parks, and school buildings. Much of this infrastructure is badly in need of repair. In addition we need millions of people to staff day care centers, libraries, and after-school programs. Why not create a labor-intensive, minimum-wage public service jobs program of last resort for today's low-skilled and jobless workers?[17]

Jobs, jobs, jobs

But some liberals acknowledge that even a massive jobs program won't get *all* of the poor off the dole. Remember that nearly all people receiving public assistance are women with young children.

Our country will need to go beyond providing jobs if we are to succeed in greatly reducing poverty. The lives of those in the permanent underclass are filled with hopelessness and despair. The lack of jobs put most of these families into this predicament, but it will take more than jobs, three or four generations later, to get them out of it.

Dr. David Rogers, president of the Robert Wood Johnson Foundation, remarked that "human misery is generally the result of, or accompanied by, a great untidy basketful of intertwined and interconnected circumstances and happenings"[18] that all need attention if a problem is to be solved. This point was amplified by Lisbeth and Daniel Schorr in their landmark work *Within Our Reach*:

More is needed than providing jobs.

> The mother who cannot respond appropriately to a child's evolving needs while simultaneously coping with unemployment, an abusive husband or boyfriend, an apartment without hot water, insufficient money for food, and her own memories of past neglect—even a mother who is stressed to the breaking point can be helped by a neighborhood agency that provides day care, counseling, and the support that convinces her that she is not helpless and alone.[19]

[15]Murray, *Losing Ground,* pp. 227–28.

[16]Barbara Ehrenreich, *Nickel and Dimed* (New York: Henry Holt, 2001); Beth Schulman, *The Betrayal of Work* (New York: The New Press, 2003).

[17]See William Julius Wilson, *When Work Disappears* (New York: Knopf, 1996), pp. 225–38; and Sheldon Danziger and Peter Gottschalk, *America Unequal* (Cambridge, MA: Harvard University Press, 1995), p. 174.

[18]Robert Wood Johnson Foundation, *Annual Report,* 1984.

[19]Lisbeth B. Schorr and Daniel Schorr, *Within Our Reach* (New York: Doubleday, 1989), p. 151.

Figure 10

Recipients of Temporary Assistance for Needy Families, 1985–2005

After climbing from 1989 through 1993, the welfare rolls declined every year. The decline was especially sharp between 1994 and 1999.

Source: Statistical Abstract of the United States, 2006; U.S. Department of Health & Human Services, www.acf.dhhs.gov/programs/ofa/caseload/2005/4qrtrecipients.htm.

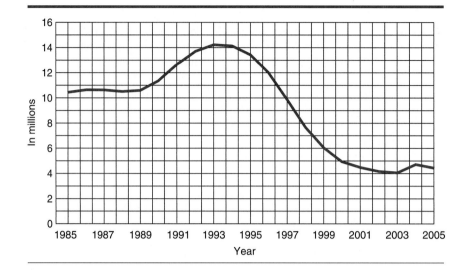

Workfare is now the law of the land.

Welfare Reform: The Personal Responsibility and Work Opportunity Reconciliation Act of 1996

This was the most significant piece of welfare legislation since the Social Security Act of 1935. These are its main provisions:

- The federal guarantee of cash assistance for poor children is ended.
- The head of every welfare family would have to work within two years or the family would lose benefits.
- After receiving welfare for two months adults must find jobs or perform community service.
- Lifetime welfare benefits would be limited to five years. (Hardship exemptions would be available to 20 percent of families.)
- Each state receives a lump sum to run its own welfare and work programs.
- Up to 20 percent of those on public assistance—the ones who are least employable—will be allowed to remain on the rolls beyond the time limit.

The trouble with being poor is that it takes up all your time.

—Willem de Kooning

For the first time since 1935 the federal government no longer guaranteed support to all of America's children. Critics have pointed out that the law requires some 4 million mothers, nearly all with little education and poor job skills, to somehow go out and find jobs that will support their families. And most significantly, the law creates no new jobs, pays for no training programs, and makes no provision for additional free or low-cost day care facilities.

Around the time that Congress had passed and President Clinton had signed the Welfare Reform Act there were dire predictions that when families were thrown off public assistance, we would see children starving in the streets. But a study by Kathryn Edin and Laura Lein found that virtually all poor single mothers—whether working or receiving public assistance—were supplementing their income with money from a support network of relatives, boyfriends, or the absent fathers of their children.[20]

Has welfare reform been successful? The answer is yes—and no. In March 1994, the welfare rolls stood at a peak of 14.4 million recipients. (See Figure 10.) The rolls, which began falling in 1994, continued to fall steadily through the next 9 years. (See the box, "Going the Extra Mile.") The welfare rolls reached a low of 4 million in 2003.

In the wake of the 2001 recession and the subsequent "jobless" recovery, which dragged on through 2003, one would have expected the public assistance rolls to not just

---

[20]Kathryn Edin and Laura Lein, *Making Ends Meet* (Ithaca, NY: Cornell University Press, 1997).

Going the Extra Mile

President Ronald Reagan used to refer to "Welfare Queens"—women who lived high off the hog on their welfare checks and made no effort to support themselves or their children. While there are indeed still some "Welfare Queens," most of the women on welfare are either working, very actively looking for work, or are being trained for some form of work. In order to work, poor single mothers not only have to find jobs, find transportation to those jobs, but they have to arrange child care as well. This is what six Greenwood Mississippi women must go through every working day:

Six Leflore County mothers are picked up in vans at 3 a.m. for a ride to jobs in faraway chicken

processing plants where they earn about $6 an hour, or $12,000 a year. With stops to deliver children to sitters, the trip takes three or four hours.

The women still collect a welfare check because the pay does not lift them above the poverty line, and the state pays for their child care and the van, and gives them $5 a day for lunch and a $3,000 bonus for working for two years. *

---

*Peter T. Kilborn, "Recession Is Stretching the Limit on Welfare Benefits," *The New York Times*, December 9, 2001.

---

stop falling, but to begin rising again. After all, we *have* seen an uptick in the poverty rate for four consecutive years, so why didn't the welfare rolls follow suit?

Writing in *The New York Times,* Robert Pear identifies four reasons why welfare rolls continued falling:

1. People work harder to find jobs before seeking public assistance.
2. Welfare recipients have learned job skills and a work ethic.
3. States provide child care and other noncash help, so they can keep jobs after leaving welfare.
4. New rules and requirements may intimidate poor people from seeking welfare.[21]

Essentially people who might otherwise qualify for welfare are making do, not just by holding low-paying jobs, but relying more on family and friends. And then, too, from 2001 to 2005, the number of households receiving food stamps rose by 35 percent. In sum, the welfare rolls have been reduced by two-thirds since 1994, but the large majority of former recipients remain poor.

The current mantra is "work first," the policy of putting people to work without detours through training and education. So far, the state strategies appear to be paying off, since recipients have fled the welfare rolls in record numbers. But there have been serious problems. The wages earned by former welfare mothers average less than $7 an hour, and 75 percent of them also lacked medical benefits. About one-third of those who left the rolls were back on welfare within a year.

Current Issue: Will Social Security Be There for You?

When you attain the age of 65, will you be able to collect Social Security benefits? After all, you will have paid Social Security taxes your entire working life. And ditto for Medicare taxes. There's no question that you're entitled. But will you be able to *collect?*

---

[21]Robert Pear, "Despite Sluggish Economy, Welfare Rolls Actually Fell," *The New York Times,* March 22, 2004, p. A 21.

My own guess is that there will be a watered down version of both programs. You'll receive *some* benefits, but not at nearly the level that your grandparents received.

Right now we are paying about $150 billion more in Social Security taxes than we're spending on Social Security benefits. That surplus is deposited in the Social Security trust fund, which consists of trillions of dollars of U.S. government securities. But what's also happening is that the government, which has been running humongous budget deficits, is using the Social Security surpluses each year to offset part of the deficits. Each year, then, the U.S. Treasury spends the surplus and places its i.o.u.'s into the Social Security trust fund.

In 2011 the baby boomers (born between 1946 and 1964) will begin retiring, and by 2017, the annual Social Security surplus will disappear. But don't worry, because we can just draw down the trust fund until it runs out of money around 2040. The only problem is that the trust fund consists of U.S. treasury bills, bonds, notes, and certificates. The trust fund administrators aren't going to send people these U.S. government securities every month instead of checks. No problem, they can just go out and sell them to the public. But they'd soon be selling hundreds of billions of U.S. government securities on top of financing our huge—and probably growing—federal budget deficit.

Long before the Social Security trust fund runs out of money around 2040, this massive government borrowing will very likely push up interest rates to record levels and possibly precipitate a financial crisis. That's if no strong measures are taken to raise Social Security taxes and lower benefits.

OK, that's the good news. The bad news is Medicare, which is even more seriously underfunded than Social Security. By 2018, Medicare spending will surpass Social Security spending. Remember all those retiring baby boomers? Medicare is a lot more complex than Social Security, but I promise that you'll soon be hearing a lot more about an impending Medicare crisis. These are topics usually not covered in much depth in economics texts, but remember that you read it here first.

Questions for Further Thought and Discussion

1. What's the difference between the distribution of income and the distribution of wealth? Describe the distribution of income and the distribution of wealth in the United States.

2. Discuss the basic determinants of income distribution.

3. Who are the poor in the United States? A few population groups have very high incidences of poverty. Explain why people in each of these groups tend to be poor.

4. There are several theories of the causes of poverty. Why can't a single theory explain all the poverty in the United States?

5. Compare and contrast the conservative and liberal views of poverty.

6. What has happened to the welfare rolls since the mid-1990s? What are the causes of this trend?

Workbook for Chapter 30

Name _____   Date _____

Multiple-Choice Questions

Circle the letter that corresponds to the best answer.

1. Most social scientists define the poor as being the lowest _____ percent of our income recipients.
   a) 10
   b) 20
   c) 3
   d) 40
   e) 50

2. Which is the most accurate statement?
   a) Although there are several theories of poverty, it is possible to formulate just one theory which completely explains 99 percent of all poverty in the United States.
   b) There are at least a dozen theories of poverty, and each has at least some apparent validity.
   c) Poverty can be explained largely by employment discrimination.
   d) Poverty is no longer a major socioeconomic problem in the United States.

3. The Darity-Myers thesis is an attempt to explain _____.
   a) black poverty
   b) the poverty of the elderly
   c) worldwide poverty
   d) the permanent underclass

4. An equal distribution of income would _____.
   a) hurt both the work incentive and the incentive to save
   b) hurt neither the work incentive nor the incentive to save
   c) hurt the work incentive but not the incentive to save
   d) hurt the incentive to save but not the work incentive

5. Doctors earn more than people in other professions basically because _____.
   a) they need to be compensated for all those years they spent in school
   b) they are in short supply relative to the demand for their services
   c) it costs a lot more to be a doctor—office expenses, support staff, and malpractice insurance—than it does to be in almost any other profession
   d) doctors put in longer hours than most other people

6. To keep a family of four at the poverty line a person working a 40-hour week would need to earn over _____ an hour.
   a) $5
   b) $7
   c) $9
   d) $11
   e) $13

7. Compared to their levels in 1999, the poverty line has _____ and the minimum hourly wage has _____.
   a) gone up, gone up
   b) stayed the same, stayed the same
   c) gone up, stayed the same
   d) stayed the same, gone up

8. Women working full-time earn about _____ percent of what is earned by their male counterparts.
   a) 33
   b) 50
   c) 75
   d) 100

9. Each of the following is a major source of great wealth except _____.
   a) earning large salaries
   b) starting up new companies
   c) real estate
   d) inheritance

10. Which is not aimed solely at the poor?

   a) Food stamps

   b) Public assistance

   c) Social Security

   d) Medicaid

11. Which statement is true?

   a) Very few poor people hold jobs.

   b) The main reason for poverty is that some people refuse to work.

   c) A person holding a minimum wage job could raise her family out of poverty.

   d) There are millions of people whose jobs don't pay enough to support their families.

12. Which statement is false?

   a) About three-fourths of the poor are single mothers and their children.

   b) About half of the poor are elderly.

   c) People living in the South are more likely to be poor than those living in the rest of the country.

   d) None of these statements is false.

13. About _____ million Americans are homeless.

   a) 2 to 3

   b) 6 to 8

   c) 12 to 15

   d) 20 to 25

   e) 40 to 50

14. Which statement is true?

   a) Most poor people are black.

   b) Most black people are poor.

   c) People over age 65 have a higher poverty rate than the overall rate for Americans.

   d) None of these statements is true.

15. Darity and Myers predict that _____.

   a) welfare reform will lead to a sharp decline in the number of black families living below the poverty line

   b) cutting welfare benefits will increase the ranks of marriageable young black men

   c) the underlying cause of poverty is too much government intervention

   d) there will be an increasing number of black families headed by females

16. "The exodus of middle- and working-class families from many ghetto neighborhoods removes an important 'social buffer'" was said by _____.

   a) Nicholas Lemann

   b) Charles Murray

   c) Barbara Ehrenreich

   d) William Julius Wilson

17. Which statement is true?

   a) Virtually none of the homeless have jobs.

   b) Many of the homeless are mentally ill.

   c) The homeless are concentrated in a few large cities.

   d) None of these statements is true.

18. More than one out of every _____ children lives in poverty.

   a) two

   b) six

   c) eight

   d) eleven

19. Social scientists believe _____ the differential between what women and men earn can be explained by employment discrimination.

   a) almost all of

   b) about half of

   c) only a small part of

20. Which statement is false?

   a) Poverty breeds poverty.

   b) Poor people have low human capital.

   c) The liberals and conservatives disagree on how to get people off the welfare rolls and into self-supporting jobs.

   d) None of these statements is false.

21. It would not be reasonable to say that poor people are _____.

   a) grudgingly tolerated by society's "productive" members

   b) largely superfluous to our socioeconomic system

   c) basically self-supporting

   d) poor for a variety of reasons

22. Which one of the following statements is false?

 a) The poor pay higher prices to buy groceries, furniture, and appliances.

 b) Low-income families can pay over $500 more for the same car bought by a higher-income household.

 c) The poor pay higher interest rates than people with higher incomes.

 d) Very few poor people can claim the earned income tax credit.

23. The earned income tax credit is _____.

 a) a form of welfare

 b) a refund check paid to the working poor by the Internal Revenue Service

 c) a very minor form of government aid to the poor

 d) opposed by both liberals and conservatives

24. The superrich get most of their income from _____.

 a) rent, interest, and profits

 b) wages

 c) illegal transactions

 d) none of the above

25. The richest fifth of all American families receives _____ percent of our total income.

 a) almost 35   c) more than 60

 b) 50   d) more than 75

26. The top quintile of U.S. households receives about _____ of total income.

 a) one quarter   d) two thirds

 b) one third   e) three quarters

 c) one half

27. Between 1968 and 2004, the percentage share of total income grew for the _____.

 a) lowest two quintiles

 b) the middle three quintiles

 c) the highest quintile

 d) the highest quintile and the lowest quintile

28. Between 1968 and 2004, our income distribution has _____.

 a) became more equal

 b) stayed about the same

 c) became less equal

29. Real median family income in the U.S. has _____.

 a) grown each year since 2000

 b) declined each year since 2000

 c) doubled since the late 1960s

 d) become lower today than it was in 1975

30. Which of the following statements is the most accurate?

 a) The welfare rolls today are much lower than they were in 1996.

 b) About 1 in 8 Americans lives below the poverty line.

 c) Without Social Security benefits, at least 75 percent of all senior citizens would be poor.

 d) The Welfare Reform Act of 1996 has cut the poverty rate by almost 60 percent.

31. Which statement is true?

 a) All of the 10 richest Americans inherited their fortunes.

 b) In order to make the top ten list of American billionaires, you need a fortune of at least $15 billion.

 c) The two richest families in the United States today are the Rockefellers and the Fords.

 d) Most of the 10 richest Americans own large manufacturing companies.

32. Which is the most accurate statement?

 a) Although there are poor children in the U.S., our child poverty problem is not nearly as bad as that of most other rich countries.

 b) The reason so many people in poor countries still don't have safe drinking water is that it would cost at least $50 billion a year to provide it.

 c) Poor people in the U.S. spend more than double their reported incomes.

 d) Although some war veterans are poor, virtually none is homeless because of the efforts of the Veteran's Administration to find them housing.

33. Which statement is true?

   a) If we redistributed income every year so that everyone would get the same amount, this would hurt the efficiency of our economy.

   b) Virtually everyone agrees that we should redistribute most of the income received by the rich to the poor.

   c) The poor get a great deal more satisfaction from each additional dollar of income than the rich.

   d) There is no relationship between the distribution of income and economic incentives.

34. The largest government program aimed exclusively at helping the poor is _____.

   a) the earned income tax credit

   b) public assistance

   c) food stamps

   d) Social Security

35. Which is the most accurate statement?

   a) The 1973 *Roe v. Wade* decision ultimately had some affect on the crime and poverty rates.

   b) Unwanted pregnancies have no economic outcome.

   c) There is no relationship between the rates of crime and poverty.

   d) Virtually all Americans support the *Roe v. Wade* decision because it has led to fewer births of unwanted children.

36. What is the most likely conclusion to be drawn from *Freakonomics* by Levitt and Dubner?

   a) Abortion is immoral and must be made illegal.

   b) Abortion averts the births of a relatively high number of children who would have grown up to commit crimes.

   c) A high abortion rate causes a high poverty rate.

   d) Immediately after the Supreme Court's *Roe v. Wade* decision, the crime and poverty rates declined.

37. Which statement is true?

   a) Over 90 percent of the families receiving public assistance are headed by people who are employed.

   b) Nearly 90 percent of those in the workforce earn at least $10 an hour.

   c) The welfare rolls are much lower today than they were in 1994.

   d) If every adult on welfare were willing to work, we could cut the number of welfare families by over 75 percent.

38. Between 2000 and 2004 the poverty rate _____.

   a) rose for four consecutive years

   b) fell for four consecutive years

   c) rose for two years and then fell for two years

   d) fell for two years and then rose for two years

39. What would be the most effective way of raising people out of poverty?

   a) Cut off welfare payments to every family with at least one adult member between the ages of 18 and 64.

   b) Raise the minimum hourly wage.

   c) Eliminate the earned income tax credit.

   d) Have the government put welfare recipients to work at minimum wage jobs.

40. Which one of the following statements is the most accurate?

   a) Our nation provides cradle-to-grave security for our military personnel and their families.

   b) Because of the relative high pay and benefits provided by the military, very few military families run into financial problems.

   c) No military family lives below the poverty line.

   d) Some military families depend on food pantries.

41. Within the city of New Orleans, most of the victims of Hurricane Katrina were _____.

   a) rich and white

   b) rich and black

   c) poor and white

   d) poor and black

42. Which is the most accurate statement?

   a) Because of the efforts of the Veterans Administration, only a handful of veterans are homeless.

   b) Most military families have to get by on food stamps and help from food pantries and soup kitchens.

   c) Military pay is high enough to keep virtually all military families well above the official poverty line.

   d) Although nearly all of our leading politicians wear American flag lapel pins, they do not provide enough economic support to our troops, so many military families are in severe financial difficulty.

43. Who made this statement? "I still have the audacity to believe that people everywhere can have three meals a day."

   a) Charles Murray

   b) William Julius Wilson

   c) Barbara Bush (mother of President George W. Bush)

   d) Martin Luther King, Jr.

   e) Lisbeth B. Schorr

Fill-In Questions

1. The richest 1 percent of our population owns over _____ percent of our wealth.

2. The two biggest benefit programs aimed solely at the poor are _____ and _____.

3. About one out of every _____ black Americans is poor.

4. About _____ percent of all poor people are black.

5. The basic problem with the absolute concept of poverty is finding the _____.

6. The poverty line is set by the _____.

Problems

Use Figure 1 to answer problems 1 through 4.

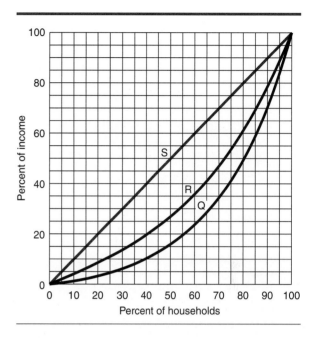

Figure 1

1. How much is the percentage of income received by the lowest quintile on line R?

2. How much is the percentage of income earned by the highest quintile on Lorenz curve Q?

3. How much is the percentage of income received by the highest quintile on line R?

4. How much is the percentage of income received by the middle three quintiles on line S?

Chapter 31

International Trade

More and more of our imports come from overseas.
—President George W. Bush

Huge container ships steam into Seattle every day loaded with shoes, clothing, textiles, furniture, TVs, and cameras that were made in Asia. On their return trip these same ships leave half empty, bearing chemicals, meat, grain, as well as hay and scrap paper. These cargoes vividly illustrate our relationship with our Asian trading partners: We buy what they make, but they don't buy that much of what we make.

Trillions of dollars' worth of business in international trade is conducted every year. Certain trading nations—Japan, the United Kingdom, Singapore, the Netherlands, Korea, and Taiwan among them—draw their economic lifeblood from foreign trade, while others, such as the United States, France, Germany, Russia, and China, are relatively self-sufficient. Yet even the United States has become increasingly dependent on imported TVs, apparel, textiles, steel, compact cars, oil, and other goods.

How this trade is conducted is the subject of this chapter; how it is financed is the subject of the next. The thread that runs through international trade and finance is specialization and exchange. If all the nations of the world were self-sufficient, there would be no international trade and little need for international finance. But if that were to happen, the world would have a much lower standard of living.

CHAPTER OBJECTIVES

These are the international trade topics you'll learn about:

- Specialization and trade.
- Domestic exchange equations.
- Absolute advantage and comparative advantage.
- Tariffs or quotas?
- The arguments for protection.

- The causes of our trade imbalance.
- What we can do to restore our balance of trade.
- Our trade deficits with Japan and China.
- U.S. trade policy: A historical view.

America is being flooded with imports, and millions of workers are being thrown out of work. Americans are buying not just foreign-made cameras and DVD players, but also foreign-made steel, textiles, apparel, personal computers, cars, and toys. But why worry? After all, the world is now a global village, and we all buy from and sell to each other. Why should we buy something from an American firm when we can get a better deal from a foreign firm?

International trade is really good for everyone. As consumers, we are able to purchase a whole array of goods and services that would not have otherwise been available—at least, not at such low prices. Hence, we can thank international trade for much of our high standard of living. As producers, we are able to sell a great deal of our output abroad, thereby increasing our employment and profits. So far, so good. The only trouble is that during the last two decades or so, we have been buying a lot more from foreigners than they have been buying from us.

So what do we *do*? Do we throw up protective tariff barriers to keep out lower-priced foreign imports? Or, like the old Avis rent-a-car commercials, do we just try harder? After a brief history of U.S. trade, in Part II of the chapter we'll consider the theory of international trade, why such trade is so wonderful, and why we should not do anything to impede its flow. In Part III we'll take a closer look at the practice of international trade and try to zero in on the causes of our trade imbalance and what we can do to redress it. And then, in Part IV, we'll look at why we've been running huge trade deficits with Japan and China.

Part I: A Brief History of U.S. Trade

The United States did not always run large trade deficits. Indeed, we ran surpluses for virtually the entire first three-quarters of the 20th century. Let's look at that record, and at U.S. government trade policy over the years.

U.S. Trade before 1975

We ran trade surpluses before 1975 and deficits after 1975.

Why 1975? Because that's the last year we ran a trade surplus. Until 1971 the United States had run a surplus nearly every year of the 20th century.

Until the early 1900s we were primarily an agricultural nation, exporting cotton and grain to Europe in exchange for manufactured goods. These included not just consumer goods—shoes, clothing, books, and furniture—but also a great deal of machinery and equipment for our growing industrial sector. We ran relatively small trade deficits through most of the 19th century.

But once we had become a powerful industrial nation, by the turn of the 20th century, we had not only less need of European manufactures but we were now exporting our own manufactured goods. With the outbreak of World War I in 1914, we added armaments to our growing list of exports, as our trade surpluses mounted. In the 1920s we inundated the world with Model T Fords, as well as a host of other American vehicles, along with radios, phonographs, toasters, waffle irons, and other consumer appliances.

The Great Depression of the 1930s depressed not only worldwide production of goods and services but their export as well. Our trade surpluses increased in the 1940s, with the advent of World War II, when, once again, we shipped huge quantities of food and armaments to England, the Soviet Union, China, and our other allies. It took 15 years for the world's other leading industrial powers to recover from the devastation of the war, during which time we supplied the world from our cornucopia of manufacturing and agricultural products. During this period, and well into the 1960s, we continued running substantial trade surpluses.

U.S. Trade since 1975

We faced increasing trade competition in the 1960s.

By the early 1960s Japan and the industrial nations of Western Europe had rebuilt their factories and stemmed the flood of American imports. Later in that decade these nations, especially Japan, were exporting cars, TVs, cameras, and other consumer goods to the United States and going head-to-head with American manufacturers throughout the world. By the late 1970s our trade deficits were mounting (see Figure 1). Although these deficits rose and fell over the years, by 1984 they crossed the $100 billion mark.

Our positive balance of trade in services has been overwhelmed by our huge and growing negative balance of trade in goods. Since 1991 our overall trade balance has declined sharply, reaching $726 billion in 2005.

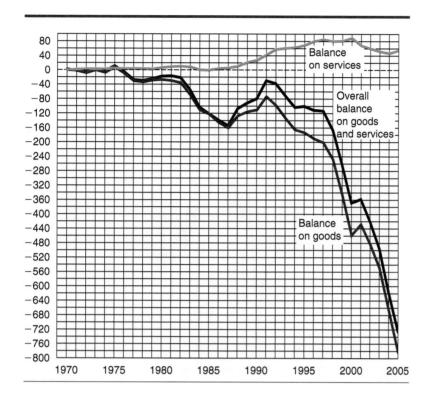

Figure 1

U.S. Balance of Trade in Goods and Services, and Overall Balance, 1970–2005 (in billions of dollars)

Since the late 1980s we have been running a large and growing surplus on services. Our balance on goods, which has been negative since the mid-1970s, has grown much worse since 1991.

Sources: Economic Report of the President, 1985–2006; Survey of Current Business, May 2006.

TABLE 1	U.S. Balance of Trade, 2005 (in billions of dollars)	
Goods		
Imports		−$1,675
Exports		+ 893
Balance of goods		− 782
Services		
Imports		−$322
Exports		+ 379
Balance of services		+ 57
Balance of trade*		−$726

*Numbers do not add up exactly because of rounding.

In the late 1990s, our trade deficit really took off. Some of the contributing factors were the high U.S. dollar (which made our exports more expensive and our imports cheaper), our rapid economic growth, which expanded our demand for foreign goods and services, and our insatiable appetite for foreign consumer goods.

Table 1 provides a snapshot view of our imports, exports, and balance of trade in 2005. In that year our trade deficit set a national and world record. As you can see, we imported $726 billion more in goods than we exported. Services continued to be the one bright spot of our trade balance, since we exported $57 billion more than we imported.

U.S. Government Trade Policy

We can get a snapshot view of this policy over the last two centuries by glancing at Figure 2. The relatively high tariffs through most of the 19th century and during the Great Depression reflected the political climate of those times.

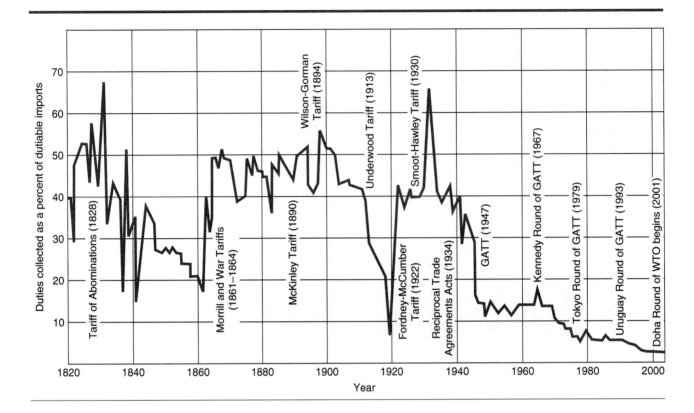

Figure 2

U.S. Tariffs, 1820–2005

Although tariffs fluctuated widely from the 1820s through the early 1930s, there has been a strong downward trend. Today tariffs average less than 5 percent of the price of our imported durable goods.
Source: U.S. Department of Commerce.

A century of high protective tariffs

Back in Chapter 1 we talked about the high protective tariff being a cause of the Civil War. How did that come to be? Initially the tariff was purely a revenue-raising device, but after the War of 1812 war-born industries found it impossible to meet British competition, and the tariff took on a protective tinge. In 1816 the first protective tariff was adopted, followed in 1828 by the "Tariff of Abominations." But to whom was this tariff so abominable? To the South, which was primarily an agrarian economy, exporting cotton and importing manufactured goods. Of course the industrial Northern manufacturers wanted the South to buy their own goods rather than import them from Europe. However the South, allied with the Western states joining the union, was able to induce Congress to progressively lower tariffs until the Civil War. Note that, in 1861, when the 11 states of the Confederacy withdrew from the union, tariffs went right back up once more. Business-oriented Republican administrations kept them high until the Underwood Tariff of 1913, which, incidentally, was passed by a Southern-dominated Democratic Congress.

Again, during the Great Depression, virtually every industrial power, beset with massive unemployment, raised its tariffs to keep out foreign goods. Of course, since everyone was doing this, world trade dwindled to a fraction of what it had been in the 1920s. While certain jobs were protected, others, mainly in the export sector, were lost. Economists believe that these high tariffs, especially the Smoot-Hawley Tariff of 1930, made the depression a lot worse than it might have otherwise been.

A downward trend in tariffs since 1947

The GATT (General Agreement on Trade and Tariffs) treaty of 1947 began a downward trend in tariffs all around the world, leading to the formation of the World Trade Organization, which was set up to further facilitate world trade. GATT and the World Trade Organization were discussed in Chapter 8 of *Economics* and *Macroeconomics*.

Economists are virtually unanimous in their support of free trade, and increasingly, so are our presidents. Our last three presidents, Ronald Reagan (1981–89), George Bush (1989–93), and Bill Clinton (1993–2001), were all ardent supporters of free trade as is President George W. Bush. However, many Americans, especially labor union members and environmentalists, prefer what they call "fair trade."[1]

Almost everyone seems to support free trade.

Part II: The Theory of International Trade

Since 1992 our trade deficit has ballooned from just $30 billion to $726 billion in 2005. What can we do to reverse this trend? Should we restrict this profusion of imports, or should we listen to the reasoning of the economics profession, which is nearly unanimous in arguing for free trade?

If we will not buy, we cannot sell.
—President William McKinley

Specialization and Trade

The basis for international trade is specialization. Different nations specialize in the production of those goods and services for which their resources are best suited. An individual who attempts to be entirely self-sufficient would have to make her own nails, grow her own food, spin her own cloth, sew her own clothes, make her own tools, ad infinitum. It is much easier and a lot cheaper to work at one particular job or specialty and use one's earnings to buy those nails, food, clothes, and so on.

Specialization is the basis for international trade.

What makes sense individually also makes sense internationally. Thus, just as it pays for individuals to specialize and trade, it pays for nations to do so. And that's exactly what we do: On a national basis we specialize and trade. But it would be impossible to do this unless there were a big enough market in which to buy and sell the goods and services we produce. Of course, the United States has long been the world's largest national market.

It pays for nations to specialize, just as it pays for individuals.

Adam Smith recognized the advantages of foreign trade more than two centuries ago when he wrote:

> If a foreign country can supply us with a commodity cheaper than we ourselves can make it, better buy it of them with some part of the produce of our own industry, employed in a way in which we have some advantage. The general industry of the country ... will not thereby be diminished ... but only left to find out the way in which it can be employed with the greatest advantage.[2]

Smith's argument provides the basis for international trade. Country A specializes in making the products that it can make most cheaply. Country B does the same. When they trade, each country will be better off than they would have been if they didn't specialize and trade.

Comparative Advantage

Back in Chapter 2 we introduced production possibility curves, which showed how much a country could produce if its output were limited to just two goods. Now we'll look at the production possibilities frontiers of Peru and Pakistan (see Figure 3).

Notice that the production possibilities frontiers of Peru and Pakistan are straight lines, rather than the curves we had in Chapter 2. To keep things simple, let's assume that the resources used to produce corn are equally suitable for producing cameras.

---

[1]This topic as well as NAFTA, WTO, and the European Union are discussed in Chapter 8 of *Economics* and *Macroeconomics*.

[2]Adam Smith, *The Wealth of Nations*, vol. 1, ed. Edwin Cannan (London: University Paperbacks by Methuen, 1961), pp. 478–79.

Figure 3

Production Possibilities Curves
Peru, operating at full capacity, can produce 80 bushels of corn or 40 cameras. Pakistan, operating at full capacity, can produce 40 bushels of corn or 80 cameras.

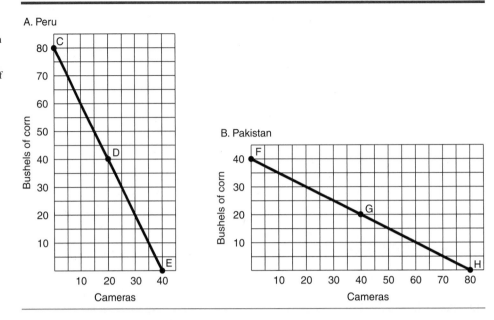

That enables us to have straight-line production possibility frontiers, which will help us demonstrate the law of comparative advantage.

Peru can produce two bushels of corn for every camera it makes. And Pakistan can produce one bushel of corn for every two cameras it makes. Are you ready for the million dollar question? OK, here's the question: Should Pakistan and Peru trade with each other?

What's your answer? If you said "yes," then you're right! That's because both nations are better off by trading than by not trading. Pakistan gains by trading cameras to Peru for corn; Peru gains by trading corn to Pakistan for cameras. So both nations gain by trading.

Let's go back to the concept of opportunity cost. What is Pakistan's opportunity cost of producing two cameras? In other words, to produce two cameras, what does Pakistan give up?

The answer is one bushel of corn. Now what is the opportunity cost of growing two bushels of corn for Peru?

Peru's opportunity cost is one camera. Now we're ready for the law of comparative advantage. *The law of comparative advantage states that total output is greatest when each product is made by the country that has the lowest opportunity cost.* If the relative opportunity costs of producing goods (what must be given up in one good in order to get another good) differ between two countries, there are potential gains from trade.

Please glance back at Figure 3. You'll notice that Peru produces at point D (40 bushels of corn and 20 cameras). Pakistan is at point G (20 bushels of corn and 40 cameras). Table 2 restates points D and G.

We know that Pakistan can gain by trading cameras for corn, while Peru can gain by trading corn for cameras. So let's have Pakistan specialize in the production of cameras,

TABLE 2	Production and Consumption of Corn and Cameras before Specialization and Trade	
	Pakistan	Peru
Bushels of corn	20	40
Cameras	40	20

TABLE 3	Production of Corn and Cameras after Specialization	
	Pakistan	Peru
Bushels of corn	0	80
Cameras	80	0

TABLE 4	Consumption of Corn and Cameras after Trade	
	Pakistan	Peru
Bushels of corn	40	40
Cameras	40	40

placing it at point H of Figure 3. Meanwhile Peru, which now specializes in growing corn, will produce at point C of Figure 3. Table 3 restates points C and H.

Now Peru and Pakistan can trade. Let's assume the terms of trade are one camera for one bushel of corn. Pakistan will send Peru 40 cameras in exchange for 40 bushels of corn. This brings us to Table 4.

It should be pretty obvious that both countries gained by specializing and trading. Just compare the numbers in Table 2 with those in Table 4. Pakistan gained 20 bushels of corn and Peru gained 20 cameras.

Let's work out another comparative advantage example. If France used all its resources, it could turn out 10 cars or 20 flat screen TVs, while Spain, using all its resources could turn out 5 cars or 15 TVs.

Which country has a comparative advantage in building cars, and which country has a comparative advantage in building TVs? Write your answers here:

_____ has a comparative advantage building cars.
_____ has a comparative advantage building TVs.

Solution: The opportunity cost to France of producing one car would be two TVs. The opportunity cost to Spain of producing one car would be three TVs. So France has a comparative advantage building cars and Spain has a comparative advantage building TVs.

Suppose the terms of trade were five TVs for two cars. Why would it pay for France to trade two cars in exchange for five TVs?

Solution: If France produced both cars and TVs, for every five TVs it made, it would be making two and a half less cars. But if France traded with Spain, she could produce just two cars and get five TVs in exchange.

Next question: Why would it pay for Spain to trade five TVs for two cars?

Solution: If Spain produced both cars and TVs, for every two cars she made, Spain would be making six less TVs. But if Spain traded with France, she could produce just five TVs and get two cars in exchange. If you'd like a little more practice, see the box, "How Comparative Advantage Leads to Gains from Specialization and Trade."

You probably never heard of the renowned facelift surgeon Dr. Khorsheed, but he is a legend in his own country, not just for his splendid work, but because of the great illustration he provides of the law of comparative advantage (see the box, "To Facelift or to File: *That* Is the Question").

HELP

Just glance at Figure A and answer this question: Which country should specialize in producing telescopes and which country should specialize in producing microscopes?

Solution: If Canada used all its resources, it could produce either 60 telescopes or 30 microscopes. The opportunity cost of producing one microscope would be two telescopes. If Belgium used all its resources it could produce either 30 telescopes or 90 microscopes. The opportunity cost of producing one telescope would be three microscopes.

Clearly, then, Canada should specialize in making telescopes and Belgium should specialize in making microscopes.

If one microscope could be traded for one telescope, let's see how Canada would gain by trading its telescopes for Belgium's microscopes.

If Canada didn't specialize and trade, the opportunity cost for every microscope it produced would be not producing two telescopes. But it can now trade one telescope and receive in return one microscope. It's better to give up one telescope in exchange for one microscope than to give up two telescopes for one microscope (by producing both rather than specializing and trading).

Now let's see how Belgium gains from trading its microscopes for Canada's telescopes. If Belgium didn't trade, the opportunity cost of producing one telescope would be three microscopes. But if Belgium specialized in making microscopes, it would give up just one microscope in exchange for one telescope.

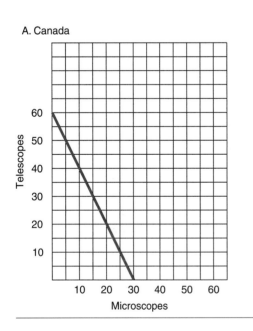

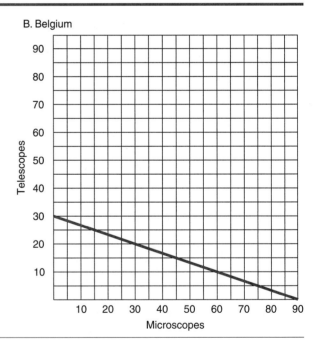

Figure A

Production Possibilities Curves

Operating at full capacity, Canada can produce 60 telescopes and 30 microscopes. Operating at full capacity, Belgium can produce 30 telescopes and 90 microscopes.

Fereydoon Khorsheed is known in his country as the Michaelangelo of facelifts. He can do two a day at $3,000 a pop. The only problem is that he has to spend half the day doing paperwork, leaving him time to perform just one operation. So he hires Ashok Desai for $200 a day to deal with insurance companies, to do billing, filing, scheduling, and to keep the books. Now he is free to spend his entire working time doing facelifts, and his earnings double to $6,000 a day.

A perfectionist, Dr. Khorsheed soon discovers that it takes Mr. Desai a full day to do what he, Dr. Khorsheed, did in just half a day.

Question: Who has an absolute advantage in doing paperwork and who has an absolute advantage in doing facelifts?

Answer: Dr. Khorsheed has an absolute advantage in both endeavors. Mr. Desai can't do facelifts at all, and Dr. Khorsheed is twice as fast at paperwork.

Next question: Should Dr. Khorsheed fire Mr. Desai and do the paperwork himself?

Answer: Clearly not. He now earns $6,000 doing facelifts, pays Mr. Desai $200, leaving a net income of $5,800. If Dr. Khorsheed did paperwork for half the day, he'd have time for only one facelift and earn just $3,000.

So while Dr. Khorsheed is both a better facelifter and a better paperworker, it pays for him to specialize in facelifting, in which he has a comparative advantage, and leave the paperwork to Mr. Desai.

Absolute Advantage versus Comparative Advantage

One of the things economists are fond of saying is that you can't compare apples and oranges. Here's a corollary: You can't compare absolute advantage and comparative advantage. The words may not exactly trip off your tongue, but still they ring true. Let's see why.

First, what *is* absolute advantage? It means that one country is better than another at producing some good or service (that is, it can produce it more cheaply). For example, the United States enjoys an absolute advantage over Japan in building commercial aircraft. But the Japanese enjoy an absolute advantage over the United States in making cameras. They can turn out cameras at a lower cost than we can, while we can build planes at a lower cost than the Japanese can.

So absolute advantage is a comparison of the cost of production in two different countries. What about comparative advantage? Let me quote myself: "The law of comparative advantage states that total output is greatest when each product is made by the country that has the lowest opportunity cost."

So we can say that as long as the relative opportunity costs of producing goods differ among nations, there are potential gains from trade even if one country has an absolute advantage in producing everything. Therefore *absolute* advantage is not necessary for trade to take place, but *comparative* advantage is.

"The Gains from Trade" box summarizes most of what we've covered over the last 8 or 10 pages. I guarantee that when you have worked your way through this discussion, you will become a great advocate of free trade.

The Arguments for Protection

"America's gargantuan trade deficit is a weight around American workers' necks that is pulling them into a cycle of debt, bankruptcy and low-wage service jobs."

–Richard Trumka–
AFL–CIO secretary-treasurer

As America continues to hemorrhage manufacturing jobs, there is a growing outcry for protection against the flood of foreign imports. But American consumers are virtually addicted to Japanese cars; South Korean TVs, Chinese microwave ovens, and hundreds of

The Gains from Trade

Let's look at the gains from trade, this time from a somewhat different prospective. By just glancing at Table A, you should easily be able to answer these questions:

1. Which country has an absolute advantage in producing shoes and which country has an absolute advantage in producing soybeans?

2. Which country has a comparative advantage in producing shoes and which country has a comparative advantage in producing soybeans?

Did you write down your answers? Please do that now. OK, let's see if we got the same answers:

1. The United States has an absolute advantage in producing both shoes and soybeans.

2. The United States has a comparative advantage in producing soybeans, while China enjoys a comparative advantage in producing shoes.

So it will pay for the United States to trade soybeans for Chinese shoes. And, of course, it will pay for the Chinese to trade their shoes for our soybeans.

I'd like to take credit for this example, but it actually appeared in the Federal Reserve Bank of Dallas's 2003 annual report. As we'll see, trade expands the economic pies of both China and the United States, leaving the consumers of both nations much better off than before they traded. That, indeed, is the reason why economists love free trade.

Table B shows China and the U.S. before and after trade. Before trade, China produced 500 pairs of shoes and the United States produced 300 pairs. After trade, China produced all the shoes—all 2,000 pairs. So total shoe production after trade rose from 800 pairs to 2,000 pairs.

Now let's see what happened to soybean production, which is shown in Table B. Before trade, the U.S. produced 4,000 bushels, while China produced 3,000. After trade the U.S. produced 10,000 bushels, while China did not produce any soybeans. So total output of soybeans rose from 7,000 before trade to 10,000 after trade.

Because trade enabled the U.S. to specialize in soybean production, and China to specialize in shoe production, the total output of both goods rose very substantially.

At the bottom of Table B, we have consumption of shoes and soybeans in both countries. Trade enabled China to increase its consumption of shoes from 500 pairs

Table A Hypothetical Labor Force and Output, U.S. and China

	CHINA	UNITED STATES
Labor Force	500	100
Output per Worker		
Shoes (pairs)	4	5
Soybeans (bushels)	8	100

Table B Hypothetical Employment, Production, and Consumption, U.S. and China

	CHINA		UNITED STATES	
Employment	No Trade	Free Trade	No Trade	Free Trade
Shoes	125	500	60	0
Soybeans	375	0	40	100
Production				
Shoes	500	2,000	300	0
Soybeans	3,000	0	4,000	10,000
Consumption				
Shoes	500	1,500	300	500
Soybeans	3,000	5,000	4,000	5,000

to 1,500 pairs. In the U.S., shoe consumption rose from 300 pairs to 500. Similarly, soybean consumption rose from 3,000 bushels to 5,000 in China, while in the U.S. it rose from 4,000 to 5,000.

Let's sum up. China enjoyed a comparative advantage in producing shoes, while the U.S. had a comparative advantage in producing soybeans. By specializing in the good each nation produced most efficiently, and then trading for the other good, both nations were much better off.

---

*Table A and Table B are reproduced from the 2003 Annual Report of the Federal Reserve Bank of Dallas, p. 16.

other manufactured goods from all over the world. How do we justify taxing or excluding so many things that so many Americans want to buy?

Four main arguments have been made for protection. Each seems plausible and strikes a responsive chord in the minds of the American public. But under closer examination, all four are essentially pleas by special interest groups for protection against more efficient competitors.

Four main arguments for protection

(1) The National Security Argument

Originally this argument may have been advanced by American watchmakers, who warned the country not to become dependent on Swiss watchmakers because in the event of war Americans would not be able to make the timing devices for explosives without Swiss expertise. Yet during one long, drawn-out war, World War II, the United States was able to develop synthetics, notably rubber, to replace the supplies of raw materials that were cut off. And the Germans were able to convert coal into oil. It would appear, then, that the Swiss watch argument may have been somewhat overstated.

Does our dependence on foreign suppliers make us vulnerable in time of war?

If our country were involved in a limited war, it is conceivable that our oil supplies from the Mideast might be cut off (although no American president would stand by passively while this happened), but we could probably replace these imports by producing more oil ourselves and by drawing on our strategic oil reserve. When Iraqi forces invaded Kuwait in 1990 President George Bush was able to put together an international coalition that quickly defeated Iraq. And if there were a third world war we would certainly not have to worry about a cutoff of needed war material because the war would last only a few minutes.

If the national security argument is applied only to limited or local wars rather than to worldwide wars, it is possible that we do need to maintain certain defense-related industries. A justification that the United States should make its own aircraft, ordnance (bombs and artillery shells), and nuclear submarines might well be valid on a national security basis. But these industries have done extremely well in international markets and are hardly in need of protection.

(2) The Infant Industry Argument

In the late 18th century American manufacturers clamored for protection against "unfair" British competition. British manufacturers were "dumping" their products on our shores. By pricing their goods below cost, the British would drive infant American manufacturers out of business. Once their American competition was out of the way, the British companies would jack up their prices.

Are American industries still infant industries?

Whatever validity this reasoning once had has long since vanished. American manufactured products are no longer produced by infant industries being swamped by foreign giants. About the best that can be said is that some of our infant industries never matured, while others went well beyond the point of maturity and actually attained senility. Perhaps a senile industry argument might be more applicable to such stalwarts as steel, textiles, clothing, and automobiles.

(3) The Low-Wage Argument

The reasoning here is best summed up by this question: How can American workers compete with foreigners who are paid sweatshop wages (see box)? Certain goods and services are very labor intensive (that is, labor constitutes most or nearly all of the resource costs). Clothing manufacturing, domestic work, rice cultivation, most kinds of assembly-line work, and repetitive clerical work are examples. There is no reason for American firms to compete with foreign firms to provide these goods and services.

How can the United States compete against countries that pay sweatshop wages?

Why *are* certain workers paid higher wage rates than others? Why *are* some countries high-wage countries, while others are low-wage countries? In general, high-wage workers produce more than low-wage workers. The main reason workers in high-wage countries produce more is that they have more capital with which to work than do workers in low-wage countries.

Why are some countries high-wage countries, while others are low-wage countries?

And so labor was paid more in the United States than almost anywhere else in the world during the three decades following World War II because we had more capital

Sweatshop Labor

Sweatshop employees put in very long hours under very poor working conditions for very low pay. Most of the clothing and footwear we import is produced by sweatshops. Reebok, Nike, Liz Claiborne, the Gap, J.C. Penney, Sears-Kmart, Wal-Mart, Disney, and Target are some of the leading sellers of goods made in sweatshops in Asia and Latin America.

In El Salvador alone, 200 factories make clothing for the American market. In 1995, conditions were so bad in her factory, a contractor for the Gap, Abigail Martinez, helped lead a strike that got the Gap's attention. This is a *New York Times* then-and-now account:

Six years ago, Abigail Martinez earned 55 cents an hour sewing cotton tops and khaki pants. Back then, she says, workers were made to spend 18-hour days in an unventilated factory with undrinkable water. Employees who displeased the bosses were denied bathroom breaks or occasionally made to sweep outside all morning in the broiling sun.

Today, she and other workers have coffee breaks and lunch on an outdoor terrace cafeteria. Bathrooms are unlocked, the factory is breezy and clean, and employees can complain to a board of independent monitors if they feel abused.

The changes are a result of efforts by Gap, the big clothing chain, to improve working conditions at this independent factory, one of many that supply its clothes.

Yet Ms. Martinez today earns 60 cents an hour, only 5 cents more than six years ago.

But consider the alternative. If Abigail Martinez quits, will she get a better job? And if wages in El Salvador were to rise, the Gap and other foreign clothing firms would move to another low-wage country.

In 2003 *BusinessWeek* reported that a dozen companies belonging to the Fair Labor Association (www.fairlabor.org) made public labor audits of the overseas factories that produce their products. Among their findings were that workers were forced to do overtime and work seven straight days, there were arbitrary firings, very limited drinking water, widespread sexual harassment, dirty toilets, no sick leave, and no pay stubs.

Sources: Leslie Kaufman and David Gonzalez, "Labor Standards Clash with Global Reality," *New York Times,* April 24, 2001, p. A1; Aaron Bernstein, "Sweatshops: Finally, Airing the Dirty Linen," *BusinessWeek,* June 23, 2003, p. 100.

(plant and equipment) per worker than any other country. But as other countries succeeded in rebuilding and adding to their capital, our advantage disappeared.

The low-wage countries of Asia, Africa, and Latin America have a competitive advantage. So do the high-capital countries of Japan, the United States, Canada, and the European Union. Why not combine the best of both worlds—low wages and high capital?

That's just what multinational corporations have done around the world. Just across the Rio Grande in northern Mexico, thousands of factories churn out everything from cars and refrigerators to water beds and garage-door openers; they then ship most of these goods back into the United States. The factories are called *maquiladoras,* from the Mexican word for handwork. The workers are seldom paid much more than $1 an hour, less than a quarter of the U.S. minimum wage of $5.15.

The question, then, is how to deal with low-wage competition. The answer is to deal with it the way we always have. We have always imported labor-intensive goods—sugar, handmade rugs, wood carvings, even Chinese back scratchers—because they were cheap. By specializing in the production of goods and services in which we excel, we can use the proceeds to buy the goods and services produced by people who are forced to work for low wages.

(4) The Employment Argument   Hasn't the flood of imports thrown millions of Americans out of work? There is no denying that hundreds of thousands of workers in each of the industries with stiff foreign competition—autos, steel, textiles, clothing, consumer electronics, and petroleum—have lost their jobs due to this competition. If we had restricted our imports of these goods by means of tariffs or quotas, most of these jobs could have been saved.

But the governments of our foreign competitors would have reciprocated by restricting our exports. Furthermore, a nation pays for its imports by selling its exports. By curbing our imports, we will be depriving other nations of the earnings they need to buy our exports. In sum, if we restrict our imports, our exports will go down as well.

If we restrict our imports, our exports will decline.

The jobs we save in steel, autos, textiles, clothing, consumer electronics, and petroleum will be lost in our traditional export industries—machinery, office equipment, aircraft, chemicals, computer software, and agricultural products. From an economic standpoint, this would involve a considerable loss because we would be shifting production from our relatively efficient export industries to our relatively inefficient import industries. Is that any way to run an economy?

Nevertheless, you may ask about the human cost. What happens to the workers who are thrown out of work by foreign competition? Should their employers help them or should the government? And what can be done to help them? Ideally, these displaced workers should be retrained and possibly relocated to work in our relatively efficient industries. Those who cannot be retrained or cannot move should be given some form of work, if only to keep them off the welfare rolls.

What about the workers who lose their jobs because of imports?

Who should help these displaced workers adjust? In a sense, their employers are responsible because these people were loyal and productive employees for perhaps 20 or 30 years. Often, however, the companies that should bear most of the responsibility for helping their employees are hardly in a position to do so. After all, they wouldn't be laying off workers if business were good to begin with.

That leaves the party of last resort: the federal government. What does the federal government do for workers who are displaced by foreign competition? Not very much. These workers receive extended unemployment benefits, are eligible for job retraining, and may receive some moving expenses. But the bottom line is that a middle-aged worker who loses her $20-an-hour job will probably not find another one that pays close to that, and government programs will not begin to compensate for this loss (see box, "Does the United States Win from Globalization?").

Does the United States Win from Globalization?

No one has ever disputed that globalization has made some people winners and others losers. As consumers, of course, we're all winners, but how many of us have already lost our jobs or will lose them over the next few years?

So far most of the work sent abroad has been labor-intensive and lower skilled, so the job losses were limited to blue-collar factory workers. As long as we're specializing in high skilled work, and have plenty of it, the job losses are confined to our most poorly educated and low skilled workers.

But now we are seeing more and more offshoring of so-called white-collar jobs, which are performed by nearly half our workforce. Today that brainpower can zip around the world at low cost, and a global labor market for skilled workers seems to be emerging for the first time—and has the potential to upset traditional notions of national specialization.

What if blue- and white-collar employees alike are thrown into the global labor pool? Tens of millions of workers could end up losing more than they gain in lower prices.

Let's take a closer look at globalization's job losers. Just 30 percent of laid-off workers earn the same or more after three years. In fact only 68 percent even hold a job at that point, while the rest are unemployed, retired, or just not in the labor force. On average, those reemployed earn 10 percent less than they did on their old jobs.

You might not even need to lose your job to be adversely affected by globalization. What if you found yourself competing against much lower-paid foreign professionals, like many of today's radiologists, programmers, and software writers? Or what if you found yourself in a profession being crowded by thousands of laid-off Americans? All you would need would be a simple supply and demand graph to show you that your wage rate would be going down.

Ten years ago economists were virtually unanimous in extolling the advantages of globalization. But now, a growing minority is not so sure. While there's no holding back the tide of globalization, one can wonder if there isn't more we could do to ensure that all of our economic boats rise with the tide.

Tariffs or Quotas

Although economists are loathe to be in such a situation, suppose it came down to choosing between the two main forms of protection: tariffs and import quotas. Which would be better? Or, more accurately, which is the lesser of two evils?

A tariff is a tax on imports. Throughout most of U.S. history until World War I, the tariff was our main source of federal revenue. The United States, which has lower tariffs than most other countries, charges less than 5 percent of the value of most imports.

A quota is a limit on the import of certain goods. Sometimes this is a legal limit (as in the case of steel, apparel, textiles and sugar), and sometimes it is a "voluntary" limit (as was the case with cars from Japan). In the early and mid-1980s the Japanese limited their export of cars to the United States to fewer than 2.5 million a year, but only because of the threat of more stringent legal limits in the form of higher tariffs.

We have long maintained textile import quotas, which, in recent years, have been especially effective in keeping out low-priced Chinese textiles. Although the quotas on Chinese textiles were ostensibly removed on New Year's day of 2005, American textile producers were able to get nearly half reinstated later in the year. In addition we persuaded the Chinese to voluntarily adhere to quotas.

Both tariffs and quotas raise the price that consumers in the importing country must pay. However, there are three important differences in the effects of tariffs and quotas.

First, the federal government receives the proceeds of a tariff. Under import quotas there *are* no tax revenues.

Second, a tariff affects all foreign sellers equally, but import quotas are directed against particular sellers on an arbitrary basis. For example, in 1986 various Japanese car manufacturers had widely varying quotas, but the import of South Korean Hyundais was unrestricted.

A third difference involves relative efficiency. Efficient foreign producers will be able to pay a uniform tariff that less efficient producers will not be able to meet. But arbitrary import quotas may allow relatively inefficient foreign producers to send us their goods while keeping out those of their more efficient competitors. This comes down to somewhat higher prices for the American consumer because less efficient producers will charge higher prices than more efficient producers.

Figure 4 illustrates the effects of a tariff. A $50 tariff on cameras raises the price of a camera from $200 to about $245. And it causes the quantity purchased to fall from 2.25 million to 2.1 million.

F*igure* 4

A Tariff Lowers Supply
This $50 tariff lowers supply from S_1 to S_2. Price rises from $200 to about $245, and quantity purchased falls from 2.25 million to 2.1 million. We move from equilibrium point E_1 to E_2. The tariff of $50 is the vertical distance between S_1 and S_2.

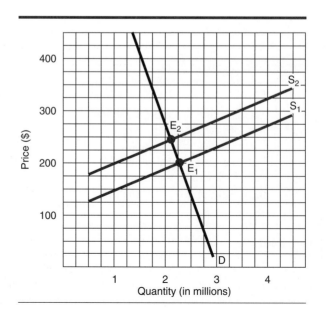

Petition of the Candlemakers to Shut Out the Sun

The case of protection against "unfair" competition was extended to its absurd conclusion by Frédéric Bastiat, a mid-19th-century French economist who wrote an imagined petition to the Chamber of Deputies. Parts of that petition follow.

*We are suffering from the intolerable competition of a foreign rival, placed, it would seem, in a condition so far superior to ours for the production of light, that he absolutely inundates our national market with it at a price fabulously reduced. The moment he shows himself, our trade leaves us—all consumers apply to him, and a branch of native industry, having countless ramifications, is all at once rendered completely stagnant. This rival . . . is no other than the Sun. What we pray for is, that it may please you to pass a law ordering the shutting up of all windows, skylights, dormerwindows, outside and inside shutters, curtains, blinds, bull's eyes; in a word, of all openings, holes, chinks, clefts, and fissures, by or through which the light of the sun has been in use to enter houses . . . ***

Frédéric Bastiat,
19th-century French economist.
(Courtesy Roger-Viollet)

*Frédéric Bastiat, *Economic Sophisms* (Edinburgh: Oliver and Boyd, Tweeddale Court, 1873), pp. 49–53.

Incidentally, a tariff, like any other excise tax, causes a decrease in supply—that is, a smaller quantity is supplied at every possible price. The effect of taxes on supply was discussed at length near the end of the elasticities of demand and supply chapter in *Economics* and *Microeconomics*.

To summarize, tariffs are better than quotas, but free trade is best. In the long run, the American consumer must pay for trade restrictions in the form of higher prices.

Tariffs are better than quotas, but free trade is best.

Conclusion

The case for free trade is one of the cornerstones of economics. (See the box, "Petition of the Candlemakers to Shut Out the Sun.") Economics is all about the efficient allocation of scarce resources, so there is no reason why this efficient allocation should not be applied beyond national boundaries. A baseball team that has more pitchers than it knows what to do with but needs a good-hitting shortstop will trade that extra pitcher or two for the shortstop. It will trade with a team that has an extra shortstop but needs more pitching. This trade will help both teams.

International trade helps every country; we all have higher living standards because of it. To the degree that we can remove the tariffs, import quotas, and other impediments to free trade, we will all be better off.

It has been estimated that lower-priced imports kept the rate of inflation one or two points below what it would otherwise have been since the mid-1980s. This is still another important reason for not restricting imports.

Imports pressure American companies to become more efficient. It is obvious, for example, that Toyota, Nissan, Honda, and the other Japanese automakers drove Detroit to make far better cars with far fewer workers than it used to. Indeed, our annual productivity gains of 10 percent would have been inconceivable without the spur of Japanese competition. Our chemical, steel, pharmaceutical, computer, textile, apparel, commercial

No nation was ever ruined by trade.

—Benjamin Franklin

aircraft, machine tool, paper copier, and semiconductor industries have all been spurred to much higher levels of efficiency by their foreign competitors.

None of this is to deny that there are problems. The millions of workers who have lost their jobs due to foreign competition cannot be expected to cheerfully make personal sacrifices in the interest of the greater national economic well-being. In the long run we may all be better off if there is worldwide free trade, but, as John Maynard Keynes once noted, "In the long run we are all dead."

While the economics profession is nearly unanimous in advocating free trade, there is nearly complete disagreement over what to do about our huge trade deficit. If we do nothing, as fervent free traders advocate, can we count on our trade imbalance to eventually correct itself? Or will foreigners—especially the Japanese and Chinese—continue to outsell us? These are just two of the questions I'll try to answer in the third part of this chapter.

The economics profession nearly unanimously backs free trade.

Part III: The Practice of International Trade

What Are the Causes of Our Trade Imbalance?

Here are the top seven reasons for our huge and growing trade imbalance.

We are consuming more than we are producing, borrowing more than we are saving, and spending more than we are earning.

—Murray Weidenbaum

(1) We Have Become a Nation of Consumption Junkies   The United States is the world's greatest consumption superpower. Today we are borrowing about $2 billion a day from foreigners to finance our consumption habit. Most Americans believe that somehow we're entitled to all these goods and services, even if we need to borrow to pay for them.

(2) Our Low Saving Rate   Americans are notoriously poor savers. Indeed in 2005 we managed to spend 100.5 percent of our disposable personal income. If you're not saving, it's hard to invest. Luckily foreign savers have been picking up the slack by lending us hundreds of billions of dollars a year. But this windfall will not continue indefinitely.

(3) Huge Oil Imports   Because we are so dependent on gasoline for transportation, we import two-thirds of our oil. And yet, we pay just a fraction of what the citizens of other industrial nations pay for gasoline. As our domestic production of oil continues to decline, our dependency on oil imports will keep growing. In 2005 the cost of our oil imports, driven by tight global supplies, reached a record high of $252 billion.

(4) High Defense Spending   The United States spends about as much on defense as the rest of the world put together. Stretching our armed forces around the globe comes at an extremely high price.

Our schools are turning out students who cannot read or write.

(5) Our Failing Educational System   The American educational system, once second to none, is now second to practically everyone's. The illiterate high school graduate is no longer the rare exception, and about one-third of all college freshmen need remedial work in the three Rs—reading, writing, and arithmetic. Nearly every college—even the Ivy League schools—has special classes for students unprepared to do college work. In test after test, Americans rank at or near the bottom of the industrial countries.

Half our high school math and science teachers are unqualified to teach those subjects. In Florida and in Massachusetts, thousands of teachers failed exams testing them on the very subject matter they had been hired to teach. No wonder that our educational system turns out one million functional illiterates every year—not exactly job candidates for today's high-tech economy.

Most of the science, math, and computer graduate students receiving PhDs in our universities are foreigners, more and more of whom are returning home, mainly to China,

India, and other Asian countries. As our manufacturing base erodes, we are losing our cutting-edge intellectual superiority in product design, software engineering, and other vital fields. Today, most patent applications are made by foreigners, and in the not too distant future, the term "Made in America" may become an anachronism.

(6) The Role of Multinationals   Before the 1960s the vast low-wage workforces of the world's poorer nations were no threat to the workers in the high-wage economies like the United States. Our workers were many times more productive than those in the poorer nations because they had so much more capital to work with.

All of this began to change in the 1960s as multinational corporations began to move their manufacturing operations offshore to take advantage of this low-wage labor pool. By providing these workers with sufficient plant and equipment, the multinationals were able to increase their productivity to the level of American assembly-line workers.

More capital, higher productivity, and higher wages

The term *hollow corporation* gained currency in the last two decades as more and more companies put their names on imported goods. These companies' sole function is to sell such goods as the Dodge Colt or the Panasonic TV, both of which are made in Japan. Yet our import business is not dominated by firms that market goods for foreign producers, but rather by our own multinational corporations that have shifted most of their production overseas. Joel Kurtzman describes their operations:

The hollow corporation

> These multinationals have transformed themselves from producers of goods to importers and marketers of goods made overseas by their foreign divisions and affiliates. Because so many of our imports come to us in the form of trade between the different divisions of American multinationals, the balance-of-payments deficit has become structurally integrated into our economy.[3]

(7) Relative Growth Rate   So far we've talked about all our deficiencies contributing to our balance of trade deficit. But even our virtues seem to contribute to that deficit. Since 1995 we have had one of the highest rates of economic growth in the industrialized world. Countries with high economic growth rates import more goods and services than they would have if they had low growth rates.

Can these problems be solved? It would be easy enough to come up with a list of solutions. But most would be very difficult to implement because they would be very strongly opposed. Let's look at proposed solutions to two problems—our huge oil imports and our failing educational system.

Because gasoline is so heavily taxed in most other countries, Americans pay just a fraction of what most other people pay. Consequently we tend to drive gas guzzling SUVs, and we still manage to complain about the high price of gas. But few politicians would dare to face the ire of voters by proposing even a 25 cents a gallon tax hike, let alone an increase of $3 or $4.

An attempt to correct some of the problems of our failing educational system was made by President George W. Bush when he got Congress to pass the "Leave No Child Behind" law, which mandated testing of children at different grade levels to ensure that all children would meet certain national educational standards. Though this legislation was passed with widespread bipartisan support, its implementation has proven very controversial, and widespread opposition has arisen from state and local educational establishments.

While we're on the subject, what do you think of *this* educational reform? Every teacher must pass an 8th grade reading test and every math teacher must pass a test covering the math that she or he teaches. Whenever this idea is proposed, you can't imagine the opposition it generates from teachers' unions and other interest groups.

Still another reason for our huge and growing trade imbalance is that since the 1960s we've lost a good part of our manufacturing base as American companies shipped

---

[3]Joel Kurtzman, *The Decline and Crash of the American Economy* (New York: W. W. Norton, 1988), p. 131.

The Chemical Industry in Decline

Through the late 1990s, the United States led the world in making chemicals, with the largest market, the latest technology, and the best know-how. And U.S. plants had a natural advantage thanks to an abundant supply of cheap natural gas, a building block for plastics, fertilizers, and even pharmaceuticals. Today none of that is true. U.S. natural gas prices are the highest in the world, while the bigger, faster growing markets are overseas. And new facilities in the developing world are as sophisticated and productive as those in the United States.

Some 120 chemical plants are being built around the world with price tags of $1 billion or more. Only one of those plants will be in the United States, but 50 are being built in China. The reason: It's becoming much too costly to produce chemicals in the United States.

As chemical production facilities close across the United States—Dow Chemical has closed over 25 percent of its plants since the new millennium—the next casualty will be the engineers and scientists doing workaday research. In 2004, Du Pont opened a lab in Shanghai that will grow into a basic research center with 200 scientists within three years.

Our balance of trade in chemicals had long been one of our economic mainstays. As recently as 1997 we had a $20 billion surplus. But just six years later that surplus became a $10 billion deficit.

Our $500 billion chemical industry will not disappear overnight, but its demise is emblematic of the decline and fall of the entire American manufacturing sector. And with respect to our trade deficit, our chemical industry, instead of holding down the deficit, is becoming a major contributor.

production and jobs abroad. Cars, steel, consumer electronics, computers, textiles, and clothing were once among our leading exports, but millions of jobs in those industries have disappeared. Still, for decades, our chemical industry seemed largely immune from foreign competition. No more. Although that industry will certainly not disappear any time soon, it may be fighting a losing battle against foreign competitors who can undersell us (see the box, "The Chemical Industry in Decline").

Part IV: Our Trade Deficit with Japan and China

For most of the 1980s and 1990s, Japan was our fiercest trade competitor. In addition, year after year we ran huge trade deficits with that country. In the long run, however, our largest trade deficits are with China, which overtook Japan in 2000. (See Figure 5.)

Many goods once made elsewhere in Asia—in Japan, Taiwan, Singapore, South Korea—are now produced in foreign-owned factories that have been moved to China. So our growing deficit with China is partially offset by declining deficits with other Asian nations.

Japanese Trading Practices

The American economy has long been, by far, the largest in the world. But in the years after World War II, as the only major nation with an undamaged economy, we produced half the world's manufactured goods. Our economy had been built on the dual foundations of mass production and mass consumption. Basically we mass produced consumer goods, which were then sold to the vast American market.

The Japanese economic infrastructure had been largely destroyed by our relentless bombings during the war. And even if the Japanese had somehow been able to produce low-cost consumer goods, their market was not only much smaller than the American market, but much, much poorer. So the Japanese government and business leaders developed a strategy to rebuild their economy. They would flood the rich American market with very cheap, low-end consumer goods, and then move up the economic

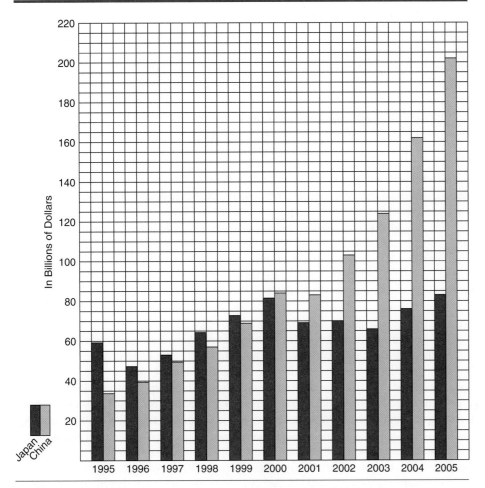

Figure 5

U.S. Trade Deficit with Japan and China, 1995–2005
Our deficit with China grew steadily since 1990 and has surpassed our deficit with Japan.
Sources: Economic Report of the President, 1996–2006; *Survey of Current Business,* May 2006.

feeding chain, eventually producing black and white TVs, color TVs, motorcycles, and cars.

The Japanese would compete first on the basis of low price, and later on the basis of product quality. That was the conclusion reached by the MIT Commission on Industrial Productivity: "Mass production was the driving force behind American postwar prosperity, but it is often no longer an appropriate model for managers and workers in the changed circumstances of today."[4] The commission uses the Japanese automobile industry as an example of how product quality can be raised:

> The Japanese have succeeded by providing different products for each segment of the market. To do so efficiently and profitably, they have developed technologies, product development methods, and patterns of workplace organization that allow them to reduce the volume of production and increase the speed with which new products are brought to market.[5]

What it all comes down to is that the Japanese compete not just on the basis of price but on the basis of product quality. They have taken our system of mass production one step further, turning out a wide range of customized variations, while we continue to concentrate on single standardized products.

The Japanese compete on the basis of price and quality.

[4]Michael L. Dertouzos, Richard K. Lester, and Robert M. Solow, *Made in America: Regaining the Productive Edge* (Cambridge, MA: MIT Press, 1989), p. 46.
[5]Ibid., p. 48.

Our Trade Deficit with China

When we began trading with China in the mid-1970s, after President Richard Nixon's historic trip to open relations with that nation, American exporters had great hopes that the world's most populous nation would eventually become the world's largest consumer market. Three decades later, toys, athletic shoes, clothing, textiles, and other relatively low-price manufactured goods are flooding into the United States, along with an increasing stream of higher-priced goods such as tools, auto parts, electronic gear, microwave ovens, and personal computers. Although U.S. exports to China are growing rapidly, our exports are only about one-sixth of our imports.

Why are we importing so much from China? Mainly because U.S. retailers are seeking the cheapest goods available and finding them in China. Wal-Mart Stores imported over $18 billion worth of goods in 2005, and Target, Sears-Kmart, Toys 'R' Us, and other giant retailers also found that the price was right in China.

One of the big trade issues between China and the United States is that thousands of Chinese factories, many controlled by top officers of the Chinese army, have been making unauthorized, or knock-off, copies of American movies, CDs, and most important, computer software. Days after the premier of the latest *Terminator* film in the U.S., pirate copies were on sale throughout China. More than 90 percent of the movies, music, and software are illegal copies sold at a fraction of the original price.

It's bad enough that the Chinese are pirating American goods and services and selling them in their own country. But now they're taking their piracy a step further. In 2005, the U.S. Patent and Trademark Office said that 66 percent of the counterfeit goods seized at American borders now come from China, up from just 16 percent five years ago. Indeed Chinese-made fakes are so good that bogus Duracell batteries, Oral-B toothbrushes, and pretend Prestobarba disposable razors are sold all over the world. And the U.S. Chamber of Commerce says that Chinese piracy and counterfeiting have cost American industry over $200 billion a year.

Our $202 billion trade deficit with China in 2005 was the highest deficit ever recorded with any country and 25 percent above the previous record, which was set with China in 2004. The Bush administration has been trying to dissuade Congress from enacting a retaliatory tariff on Chinese goods, and China bashing has become a favored election-year tactic. But closer inspection reveals that our trade deficit with China is grossly overstated.

Most often "made in China" is actually made elsewhere—by multinational companies in Japan, South Korea, Taiwan, and the United States, that are using China as the final assembly station in their vast global production networks. Indeed, about 60 percent of this country's exports are controlled by foreign companies. A Barbie doll may cost $20, but China gets only about 35 cents of that.

Back in 1990, when Japan was the United States' dominant trading partner in the Pacific, Asia accounted for 38 percent of American imports. By 2005, even as the Asian share of American imports slipped to 36 percent, China replaced Japan as our dominant trading partner. During this period some production and a great deal of assembly work shifted from Japan, Taiwan, Singapore, and other Asian nations to China.

While China had a trade surplus of over $200 billion with the United States, it ran a trade deficit of $137 billion with the rest of Asia in 2005. What were the Chinese importing? Much of their imports were components of television sets, cars, refrigerators, microwave ovens, and other consumer electronics. When these products were assembled and shipped out as final products, China's exports appeared to be much greater than they actually were. Consequently its trade surplus with the United States was greatly exaggerated.

Since the beginning of the new millennium we have lost some three million manufacturing jobs. Some of these losses may be attributed to China, but probably other nations and certainly the huge multinational corporations—many of which are based in the United States—should bear much more of the blame. And it is the American consumer who has benefited the most from the flood of low-cost goods that were assembled, if not made, in China.

Trading with China and Japan: More Differences than Similarities

There is one striking similarity between the Japanese and Chinese development models. Both were pulled by the engine provided by the huge American market. After World War II, the only consumers who had the money to buy Japanese exports were the Americans. So the Japanese economic recovery plan was, essentially, a no-brainer. Close the much smaller Japanese home market to American producers, while selling the bulk of their manufactures to the rich Americans.

When the Chinese launched their industrial development plan in the early 1980s, they followed a similar strategy—create an export platform on the East China coast to sell cheap manufactured goods to the rich Americans, and, to a lesser degree, to the rich consumers of Western Europe and Japan. The Chinese, unlike the Japanese before them, had a relatively open economy. Foreign manufacturers were more than welcome to set up shop in China.

Was the Chinese market closed to foreigners? *What* market? Few Chinese consumers had the money to buy relatively expensive imported goods. But as Chinese economic development really began to take off, and relatively cheap Chinese manufactured products flooded the world, the American consumer could no longer finance this expansion. No problem. The Chinese government simply lent Americans much of the money we needed each year to finance our huge and growing trade deficit.

During the Japanese industrial revival of the 1950s and 1960s, their manufacturers went head-to-head with ours. In the production of black and white TVs, and later, color TVs, the Japanese built on our technology, undersold American manufacturers in the vast American market, while the Japanese market remained closed to American TVs. As a result, American TV manufacturers were driven out of business.

But our relationship with the Chinese has been very different. Since the early 1980s they have been sending us toys, clothing, shoes, watches, and other low-end consumer products that are no longer produced in this country.

Our trading position with Japan is very much like a colony and a colonial power. Our trading relationship with the Chinese is very different. We send airplanes, computers, movies, compact disks, cars, cigarettes, power-generating equipment, and computer software in exchanges for toys, clothing, shoes, and low-end consumer electronics. Much of what they're sending to us used to come from Japan back in the 1950s. "Made in Japan" has been replaced by "Made in China."

Our huge trade deficit with China will probably continue to grow, but even more importantly, its entire nature is rapidly evolving. We have long assumed this division of labor: The Chinese would focus on lower-skill sectors, while the United States would dominate the knowledge-intensive industries. But as Harvard economist Richard B. Freeman observed, "What is stunning about China is that for the first time we have a huge, poor country that can compete both with very low wages and in high tech. Combine the two, and America has a problem."

So far the hardest hit industries have been those that were destined to migrate to low-cost nations anyway. But now China is moving into more advanced industries where America remains competitive, adding state-of-the-art capacity in motor vehicles, specialty steel, petrochemicals, and microchips. In other words, the United States has been losing its lead in the knowledge economy, while China evolves from our sweatshop to our competitor.

Japanese gains in the production of semiconductors, machine tools, steel, autos, TVs, and VCRs led directly to the loss of millions of well-paying American jobs. Although Chinese products may compete on a broader scale with American goods in the future, Chinese exports so far have generally not translated into major job losses in the United

States. China's leading exports are products that have not been produced in large quantity by American factories for more than a decade.

The Chinese, like the Japanese before them, have insisted on licensing agreements and large-scale transfer of technology as the price for agreeing to imports. These agreements, of course, lead to the eventual elimination of imports from the United States. However, the Chinese have taken this process one step further. Sometimes, instead of entering into licensing agreements, Chinese factories simply manufacture pirated versions, or knock-offs, of American videos, CDs, computer software, and designer apparel.

From the mid-1980s through the mid-1990s we engaged in a good deal of Japan-bashing, blaming that country for our growing trade deficit. To a large degree our complaints were justified. Not only were our manufacturing jobs migrating to Japan, but the Japanese market was largely closed to American exports.

In recent years we have shifted much of the blame to China, with whom we now run our largest trade deficit (see Figure 5). But the nature of our trade deficit with China today is not, in any sense, like our deficit with Japan two decades ago. Japan was competing in businesses that were at the heart of the American economy. But our imports from China—clothing, toys, shoes, textiles, TVs, and consumer electronics—are mainly merchandise we stopped making here decades ago. Furthermore, China is remarkably open to trade. Between 1995 and 2005, our exports to China almost quadrupled. In coming years, this rapid growth will continue as the Chinese consumer market continues its rapid expansion.

My own prediction is that by the end of this decade, not only will we be running much larger trade deficits with China, but we will be importing more than a million very low-priced Chinese cars each year. By then China bashing may have been elevated from an art form to the national sport.

In 2005 we ran a $202 billion trade deficit with China and one of $83 billion with Japan. Our oil import bill came to $252. Together these three items accounted for nearly three-quarters of our trade deficit.

Final Word

Two major issues have been raised in this chapter. First, that there are clear advantages to free trade. And second, that the United States, which has been a strong free trade advocate, has been running large and growing trade deficits. Let's take one more look at both issues.

Free Trade in Word and Deed

Going back to the early 1980s, every president has strongly advocated the principle of free trade and has helped reduce tariffs and other trade barriers throughout the world. Robert Zoellick, the chief trade negotiator during the first term of President George W. Bush, pushed various proposals within the World Trade Organization to lower tariffs and export subsidies, as well as to remove all barriers to the free flow of goods and services across national borders. European Union members, most notably France, have refused to lower subsidies.

Members of the European Union called our free trade advocacy hypocritical when in March 2002, President Bush raised tariffs on imported steel. In fact they brought a case against the United States before the World Trade Court. In December 2003, President Bush rescinded the tariffs.

A second deviation from our free trade policy is our huge agricultural subsidies—averaging about $19 billion a year. The world's poorer nations, where up to 90 percent of the labor force is engaged in agriculture, have demanded that the United States, the European Union, and other rich nations abolish these subsidies, which, clearly, make it impossible for the poorer nations to sell their agricultural goods on the world market (see the box, "Farm Subsidies and the Poorer Nations").

On balance, the United States has long been a free trading nation. Chief Trade Representative Robert Zeollick was very active in negotiating free trade agreements

Farm Subsidies and the Poorer Nations

The world richest countries provide over $300 billion in subsidies to their farmers. These subsidies enable farmers from the United States, the European Union, Canada, and Australia to export much of their output at artificially low prices. The farmers of the world's poorer nations cannot match these low prices, so they are largely shut out of world agricultural markets. Consequently these nations cannot export their agricultural surpluses and get foreign exchange.

Mexico is the world's birthplace of corn. But after the signing of the North American Free Trade Agreement (NAFTA) in 1994, American farmers flooded the Mexican market with low-priced corn. Since then, the price of Mexican corn fell more than 70 percent, severely reducing the incomes of the 15 million Mexicans who depend on corn for their livelihood.

Of the $19 billion a year that American taxpayers shell out in farm subsidies, more than $10 billion goes to corn farmers. This allows them to sell their corn at prices far below what it cost them to produce it. In effect, then, the American taxpayer has subsidized the shipment of cheap corn to Mexico, where it has pushed the poorest farmers out of business.

Japan's subsidies are 59 percent of the value of production, while those of the European Union are 34 percent of production and in the United States they are 21 percent. Will these nations agree to lower or eliminate these subsidies? Probably not in *our* lifetime. It would be political suicide. Imagine what would happen to all those senators and representatives from the farm states, not to mention all those presidential electoral votes.

with Singapore, Chile, South Africa, and other countries. Our $19 billion in agricultural subsidies are just 6 percent of the annual subsidies provided to farmers in the world's richest countries. Still, had President Bush not imposed steel tariffs in 2002, our free trade credentials would be a lot more impressive.

Reducing Our Trade Deficit

To reduce our overall trade deficit we need to make a combination of four things happen. First, we need to maintain our high rate of productivity growth and keep improving the quality of American goods and services. Second, we need to lower our dependence on oil imports, perhaps by raising the tax on gasoline. Third, we must reduce our rapidly rising deficit with China. And finally, we need to face up to the fact that we are a nation of consumption junkies. In sum, we consume much more than we produce, and have done so by running up a multitrillion dollar tab.

No man is an island, entire of itself.

—John Donne

Perhaps our best hope to reduce our trade deficit lies with the rapidly expanding Internet, which makes it much easier to provide services of all types—banking, education, consulting, retailing, and even gambling—through websites that are globally accessible. Since the United States has long had a positive trade balance in services, there is good reason to expect the Internet to continue pushing up our export of services.

Current Issue: Buy American?

Our nation has long been committed to free trade, but a growing number of Americans believe that we need to curb our imports, largely to keep jobs from being off-shored as well as to preserve our economic independence. As recently as 1965 merchandise imports were just 1.6 percent of GDP; today they are 13 percent. In the face of these ongoing trends, are we as a nation becoming more inclined to "buy American"?

For much of the time since World War II, Japanese consumers willingly paid more for domestically produced goods than they would have for foreign imports. They did this not just to help Japanese manufacturers through their long recovery from the devastation caused by American bombing during the war, but also in the sometimes misguided belief that somehow Japanese products better met their needs. This practice was best exemplified by the widely accepted claim that Japanese-made skis were better suited than imported skis for the unique Japanese snow.

But the American consumer has never been very susceptible to calls for patriotic buying. Even during the era of bad national feeling toward the French for opposing our 2003 invasion of Iraq, about the best we could do to punish the French was to refer to french fries as "freedom fries." Take *that,* you ingrates! And after all we did for you during World War II! More significantly, during 2003 our imports from France actually went up.

Perhaps a better case for economic nationalism could be made against Saudi Arabia. We now import two thirds of our oil, and that country has long been one of our largest suppliers. Although 15 of the 19 plane hijackers on 9/11 were Saudis, we never considered curbing oil imports from that country, let alone going to war.

Today there's a good deal of China bashing for running $200 billion trade surpluses with us, flooding our stores with low-cost TVs, DVD players, microwave ovens, toys, and textiles. But all that bad feeling toward the Chinese has not hurt business at Wal-Mart, which sells more Chinese exports than any other company in the world. Back in the early 1970s, when we began running large trade deficits with Japan, our leading Japan basher was Treasury Secretary John Connally, who declared that as far as he was concerned, the Japanese could sit in their Toyotas on the docks of Yokohoma, watching their Sony TVs. Still, through the next two decades, our trade deficit with Japan continued to mount.

The bottom line is that Americans are consumers first, while paying just lip service to economic nationalism. No nation of economic nationalists would run up our long string of record-setting trade deficits. So pass the freedom fries and, in the words of the old Beach Boys song, "I better turn on the lights, so we can ride my Honda tonight."

Questions for Further Thought and Discussion

1. Explain what comparative advantage is. Make up an example to illustrate this concept.

2. What is wrong with having tariffs and quotas? Which is the lesser of the two evils, and why?

3. Explain why globalization is good for the United States. What are the drawbacks of globalization for our economy?

4. What would you suggest we do to reduce our trade deficit?

5. We run huge trade imbalances with two countries. Explain the cause of the imbalances.

6. Should we be worried about our trade deficit? Explain why or why not.

7. What is the economist's case for free trade?

8. Can you think of any valid reason for tariff protection? Try to make a case for it.

Workbook for Chapter 31

Name _____   Date _____

Multiple-Choice Questions

Circle the letter that corresponds to the best answer.

1. Our balance of trade _____.
   a) has always been positive
   b) turned negative in the mid-1970s
   c) turned negative in the mid-1980s
   d) has always been negative

2. Which makes the most sense economically?
   a) Individual self-sufficiency
   b) National self-sufficiency
   c) National specialization
   d) None of these

3. Which statement do you agree with?
   a) There are several problems causing our huge trade deficit; there are no easy solutions to these problems.
   b) We could quickly eliminate our trade deficit by raising tariffs.
   c) The main reason we have a large trade deficit is that foreigners refuse to buy American goods and services.
   d) The main reason for our large trade deficit is our relatively low rate of economic growth.

4. The Chinese economic expansion since the early 1980s and the Japanese economic expansion from the late 1940s through the 1980s were _____.
   a) virtually identical
   b) both dependent on the American market
   c) based in the economic principles of Karl Marx
   d) based on closing their domestic markets to American goods and services

5. Which statement is false?
   a) No nation will engage in trade with another nation unless it will gain by that trade.
   b) The terms of trade will fall somewhere between the domestic exchange equations of the two trading nations.
   c) Most economists advocate free trade.
   d) None of these statements is false.

6. Our largest trade deficit is with _____.
   a) Japan   d) Mexico
   b) Canada   e) Germany
   c) China

7. Which one of the following does NOT contribute to our huge trade deficit?
   a) Our failing educational system
   b) Our high defense spending
   c) Our high saving rate
   d) Our huge oil imports

8. The least applicable argument for protecting American industry from foreign competition would be the _____ argument.
   a) national security   c) low-wage
   b) infant industry   d) employment

9. Imports would be lowered by _____.
   a) tariffs only
   b) import quotas only
   c) both tariffs and import quotas
   d) neither tariffs nor import quotas

10. Of these three choices—tariffs, quotas, and free trade—economists like _____ the most and _____ the least.
    a) tariffs, quotas   d) free trade, quotas
    b) tariffs, free trade   e) quotas, free trade
    c) free trade, tariffs   f) quotas, tariffs

11. Our biggest trade deficit was more than _____ billion.
    a) $100
    b) $200
    c) $300
    d) $400
    e) $500

12. Which country regularly counterfeits American goods and services, a practice which costs American industry over $200 billion a year?
    a) Mexico
    b) Canada
    c) China
    d) Japan

13. Which would be the most accurate statement with respect to our chemical industry?
    a) It is on the decline and now contributes to our balance of trade deficit.
    b) It is large and growing.
    c) It generally provides a trade surplus of about $20 billion a year.
    d) It will almost completely disappear by the year 2010.

14. Each of the following would reduce our trade deficit except _____.
    a) increasing saving
    b) cutting defense spending
    c) increasing investment
    d) raising interest rates

15. Our trade deficit with China in 2005 was _____.
    a) under $100 billion
    b) between $100 billion and $150 billion
    c) between $150 billion and $200 billion
    d) over $200 billion

16. Statement 1: Our trade deficit with China is larger than our trade deficit with Japan.
    Statement 2: Americans pay lower taxes on gasoline than do the citizens of most of the nations in Western Europe.
    a) Statement 1 is true, and statement 2 is false.
    b) Statement 2 is true, and statement 1 is false.
    c) Both statements are true.
    d) Both statements are false.

17. Of the following, our imports of _____ contribute most to our trade deficit.
    a) oil
    b) clothing
    c) textiles
    d) consumer electronics

18. Which of the following would best describe our trading relationship with China five years from now?
    a) Our trade deficit will be higher and we will be importing a higher proportion of "low-skill" products.
    b) Our trade deficit will be higher and we will be importing a higher proportion of "high-skill" products.
    c) Our trade deficit will be lower and we will be importing a higher proportion of "low-skill" products.
    d) Our trade deficit will be lower and we will be importing a higher proportion of "high-skill" products.

19. Which statement is the most accurate?
    a) Globalization has made some people winners and others losers.
    b) Globalization has been good for everyone involved.
    c) Globalization has been bad for everyone involved.
    d) Virtually all economists believe that globalization has almost no downside.

20. Which statement is true about how globalization has affected American workers?
    a) The only jobs that have been lost or will be lost are blue-collar factory jobs.
    b) Most workers who have lost their jobs because of globalization have ended up in better paying jobs.
    c) Until now a relatively high proportion of Americans perform high-skill, well paying jobs, while a relatively high proportion of Chinese perform low-skill, poorly paying jobs.
    d) Globalization cannot be considered a threat to the livelihoods of highly-skilled, well paid American workers.

21. Which is the most accurate statement?

   a) The United States can be described as a purely free trading nation.

   b) The United States is one of the most protectionist nations in the world.

   c) The rich nations provide hundreds of billions of dollars in agricultural subsidies to the poorer nations.

   d) The United States provides smaller agricultural subsidies than does Japan and the European Union.

22. Which statement is true?

   a) Comparative advantage is not necessary for trade to take place, but absolute advantage is.

   b) Absolute advantage is not necessary for trade to take place, but comparative advantage is.

   c) Both absolute and comparative advantage are necessary for trade to take place.

   d) Neither absolute nor comparative advantage are necessary for trade to take place.

23. Which statement is true?

   a) There are basically no arguments that can be made on behalf of trade protection.

   b) The arguments for trade protection are more valid than the arguments for free trade.

   c) The United States has had a record of fully supporting free trade since the early 20th century.

   d) Much of what we import has been produced by "sweatshop labor."

24. In order for trade between two countries to take place, _____.

   a) absolute advantage is necessary

   b) comparative advantage is necessary

   c) both absolute and comparative advantage are necessary

   d) neither absolute nor comparative advantage is necessary

25. Which of the following is the most accurate statement?

   a) Americans are very willing to buy domestically produced goods, even if they are more expensive than imported goods.

   b) We import more foreign goods than we did 40 years ago, but merchandise imports are still about the same percentage of our GDP.

   c) In the decades following World War II, the Japanese consumer has strongly favored domestically manufactured goods over imports.

   d) France paid a high economic price when many Americans switched from french fries to freedom fries.

Fill-In Questions

1. The basis for international trade is _____.

Use Figure 1 to answer questions 2 and 3.

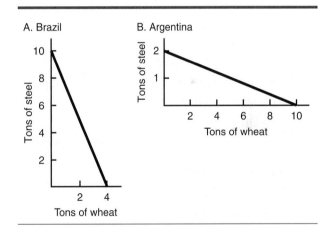

Figure 1

2. Brazil is better at producing _____ than at producing _____.
   Argentina is better at producing _____ than at producing _____.

3. If 1 ton of steel could be traded for 1 ton of wheat, Brazil would trade its _____ for Argentina's _____.

4. _____ is the country with which we have the largest trade imbalance.

5. It would greatly reduce our trade deficit the most if we could curb our import of _____.

6. Our trade deficit in 2005 was $ _____.

7. If our trade deficit with China and Japan were 0, our total trade deficit would be reduced by about _____ percent.

8. The law of comparative advantage states that total output is greatest when each product is made by the country that has the _____.

9. A tariff is a tax on _____;
a quota is a limit on _____.

10. _____ was the last year in which we ran a trade surplus.

Problems

Assume Bolivia and Chile use the same amount of resources to produce tin and copper. Figure 2 represents their production possibilities curves. Use it to answer problems 1 through 4.

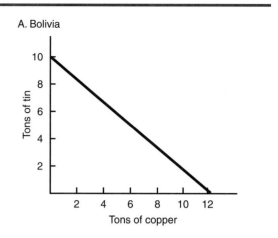

A. Bolivia

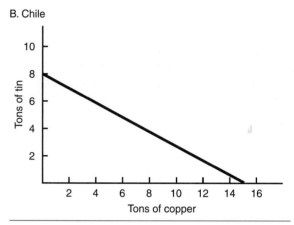

B. Chile

Figure 2

1. Bolivia has a comparative advantage in the production of which metal?

2. Chile has a comparative advantage in the production of which metal?

3. Bolivia will trade _____ for _____.

4. Chile will trade _____ for _____.

Chapter 32

International Finance

The United States is the world's largest economy and the world's largest trading nation. We import more and export more than any other nation. We also run the world's largest negative trade balance—$726 billion in 2005.

How do we finance all this trading, and how do we finance our negative balance in trade? International trade is just one part of international finance. The other part encompasses foreign investment, capital inflows and outflows, exchange rates, and other international transactions, as well as the finance of international trade.

One consequence of our mounting trade deficits is that foreigners are buying up American assets. How much of America is foreign owned today, and will most of this country one day be owned by foreigners? Will foreigners soon have enough financial leverage to influence—or even dictate—our economic and foreign policies? Stay tuned, and by the end of the chapter you will learn the answers to these important questions.

CHAPTER OBJECTIVES

These are the international finance topics you'll learn about:

- Financing international trade.
- The balance of payments.
- Exchange rate systems.
- Globalization of the U.S. dollar.
- Current account deficit.

The Mechanics of International Finance

Think of international trade and finance as an extension of our nation's economic activities beyond our borders. Instead of buying microchips from a firm in California, we buy them from a firm in Japan. Instead of selling Cadillacs in Miami, we sell them in Rio de Janeiro. And rather than building a factory in Chicago, we build one in China.

Financing International Trade

When an American importer buys $2 million of wine from a French merchant, how does she pay? In dollars? In euros? In gold? Gold is used only by governments, and then only on very rare occasions, to settle international transactions. Dollars, although sometimes acceptable as an international currency, are not as useful as euros to the French wine merchant. After all, the merchant will have to pay his employees and suppliers in euros.

TABLE 1	U.S. Balance of Payments, 2005 (in $ billions)*
Current Account	(billions of dollars)
Exports of goods and services	+1,272
Imports of goods and services	−1,997
Net investment income	−2
Net transfers	−79
Current account balance	−805
Capital Account	
Foreign investment in the U.S.	+1,293
U.S. investment abroad	−492
Statistical discrepancy	+4
Capiatal account balance	+805

*Numbers may not add up due to rounding.
Source: Survey of Current Business, May 2003; Economic Indicators, May 2006.

There's no problem exchanging dollars for euros in either the United States or France. Many banks in New York have plenty of euros on hand, and virtually every bank in the country can get euros (as well as other foreign currencies) within a day or two. In Paris and every other French city, dollars are readily available from banks and storefront foreign exchange dealers. On any given day—actually, at any given minute—there is a market exchange rate of euros for dollars; all you need to do is find the right teller and you can exchange your dollars for euros or euros for dollars within minutes.

Financing international trade is part of the economic flow of money and credit that crosses international boundaries every day. For the rest of this chapter we'll see where these funds are going and, in particular, how the United States is involved. We'll begin with the U.S. balance of payments, which provides an accounting of our country's international financial transactions.

The Balance of Payments

Often our balance of payments is confused with our balance of trade. Actually, the balance of trade is a major part of the balance of payments. *The entire flow of U.S. dollars and foreign currencies into and out of the country constitutes the balance of payments,* while the trade balance is just the difference between our imports and our exports.

The balance of payments has two parts: the current account and the capital account.

The balance of payments consists of two parts. First is *the current account, which summarizes all the goods and services produced during the current year that we buy from or sell to foreigners.* The second part is the capital account, which records the long-term transactions that we conduct with foreigners. The total of the current and capital accounts will always be zero; that is, our balance of payments never has a deficit or a surplus. When we look at these accounts in more detail, the picture should become clearer.

Table 1 shows the U.S. balance of payments in 2005. The great villain of the piece is our huge trade deficit. Next we have income from investments. From the turn of the century to the early 1980s the United States had a substantial net investment income because Americans invested much more abroad than foreigners invested in the United States. Because of our huge trade deficits in recent years, however, foreigners have been left holding trillions of dollars, most of which they have invested in the United States. The return on this investment has been growing rapidly. In fact, in 2005, for the first time since the early years of this century, the flow of income from investments—interest, profits, dividends, and rent—turned negative. Why? Because foreigners have invested a lot more in the United States than Americans have invested abroad. Finally, we have net transfers, which include foreign aid, military spending abroad, remittances to relatives living abroad, and pensions paid to Americans living abroad.

I think that our net unilateral transfers abroad are a lot larger than $79 billion listed in Table 1. According to the Inter-American Development Bank, the amount of money sent to Latin America in 2004 was more than $32 billion. (See the box, "Sending Money Home.") This was sent mainly by recent immigrants to their families in Mexico, the Caribbean, and to Central and South America. Probably immigrants from elsewhere send home at least as much. These remittances are just a part of our net unilateral transfers abroad (which include another $37 billion in U.S. government grants and pensions), so I would estimate this total to be about $100 billion. But who am I to argue with official U.S. government statistics.

Our balance on the current account is a clear indicator of how we're doing. A negative balance on the current account of $805 billion means that we went $805 billion deeper into debt with foreigners.

When we add up the numbers that go into our current account, it is easy to see why this figure is negative and why our current account deficit has been growing in recent years. (See Figure 1.) But what international finance takes away with one hand, it pays back with the other. Thus, by definition, our current account deficit is balanced by our capital account surplus.

Our current account deficit is balanced by our capital account surplus.

Although our balance of payments every year, by definition, is zero, foreigners are buying up more and more of our country. So it is tempting to refer to our current account deficit as our balance of payments deficit (I've slipped a few times myself). Please remember that our huge current account deficit is offset by our capital account surplus.

The way it works is that we buy much more from foreigners than they buy from us. In effect, they lend or give us the money to make up the difference between our imports and our exports. It would not be an exaggeration to say that we borrow so much from foreigners to finance our current account deficits that we sell them pieces of the American rock, so to speak. Those pieces consist mainly of corporate stock and real estate, but they also lend us hundreds of billions of dollars each year in the form of purchases of corporate and government bonds and other debt instruments.

Sending Money Home

My maternal grandmother, the oldest of eight children, grew up in a small town in Russia, not far from the Black Sea. While still a teenager she was sent to America where she would work in a garment factory, saving up money to send for her younger siblings, one-by-one. Together, they earned enough within a few years to bring the entire family to America. This was a familiar family saga in the decades before the restrictive immigration laws were passed in the 1920s, intended to restrict the influx of "undesirables" from Eastern and Southern Europe.

Today recent immigrants cannot easily send for their families, but they do provide them with substantial support by regularly wiring them money. If you'll glance at Table 1, you'll notice that $79 billion in net transfers was sent abroad in 2005. About three-quarters of those funds were remittances sent by recent immigrants to their families back home.

Here's the deal: We hire immigrants to harvest our crops, tend our lawns, take care of our children, staff our restaurants, clean our offices and homes, and pay them minimum, or even sub-minimum wages, often off the books. They live as cheaply as possible, scrimping and saving so they can send money home to their parents and children, often providing the sole means of support for their families. To sum up: These folks perform low-wage work that most Americans won't do themselves, and then send home a large part of their wages.

The $60 billion that these immigrants send abroad accounts for about 7 or 8 percent of our current account deficit. So in addition to our $726 billion trade deficit, we can take on another $60 billion of goods and services that foreigners provide to us without getting any goods and services in return.

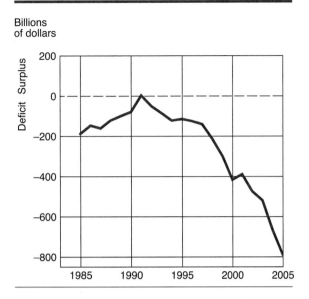

Billions of dollars

Figure 1

Current Account Surpluses and Deficits, 1985–2005
Since 1991 our current account deficits have grown steadily,
reaching $790 billion in 2005.
Source: Economic Report of the President, 2006.

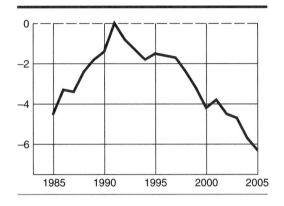

Figure 2

U.S. Current Account Deficit or Surplus as a Percentage of
GDP, 1985–2005
In 1991 we ran a tiny surplus—$3 billion—on our current account. But
in subsequent years we ran mounting deficits. By 2005 our current
account deficit was 6.3 percent of GDP.
Source: Economic Report of the President, 2006.

Now that foreigners own more investment assets in the United States than Americans own abroad, they are receiving more interest, rent, dividends, and profits than we are. In the early 1980s, when we held more assets abroad than foreigners held in the United States, Americans earned a net investment income of over $30 billion a year. This net inflow fell sharply over the next decade as foreigners bought up more and more American stocks, bonds, and real estate, and purchased American corporations or built their own factories, office buildings, and retail outlets. In 2005 there was a net outflow of $2 billion in investment income.

In future years, we can expect this net outflow of investment income to continue growing. Unless we can reduce our deficit in the trade of goods and services, our current account deficit will keep growing, and foreigners will have little choice but to keep sending most of those dollars back here to buy up more and more of our assets.

As you can see from Figure 2, our current account deficit as a percentage of GDP has been rising very rapidly since the early 1990s. By 2005 we were borrowing 6.3 percent of our GDP from foreigners. Alan Greenspan, who served as Federal Reserve chairman from 1987 to January 2006, and his successor, Ben Bernanke, have termed this trend of rising current account deficits as "unsustainable." But just weeks after he took office, Bernanke stated that it may be ten years before the deficit can be substantially reduced.

Figure 3 shows how our current account deficit as a percentage of GDP compared with that of other relatively rich countries in 2004. Most of these countries had current account surpluses. But the United States, along with Australia and Spain, ran relatively large deficits as a percentage of GDP.

Exchange Rate Systems

The basis for international finance is the exchange of well over 100 national currencies. Until the 1930s the world's currencies were based on gold. Since then a relatively free-floating exchange rate system has evolved. Under this system exchange rates are determined largely by the forces of supply and demand. In other words, how many yen, yuan, euros, or pounds you can get for your dollars is determined largely by the impersonal forces of the market.

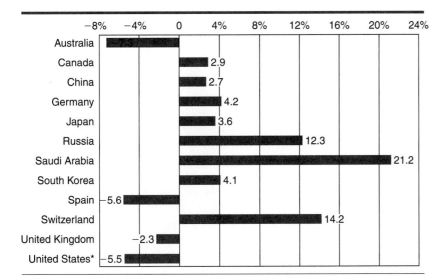

F*igure* 3

Current Account Deficit or Surplus as Percentage of GDP, Selected Countries, 2004[*]

Among these countries, the United States is running one of the largest current account deficits relative to its GDP.

[*]In 2005 it rose to 6.3%

Source: The World Bank, World Development Report 2006.

An exchange rate is the price of a country's currency in terms of another currency. If you received 100 Japanese yen for $1, then you could say that a yen is worth one cent. And if a British pound were exchanged for $2, then you could say that a dollar is worth half a pound. In February 2006, you needed about 84 euros (the euro is the official currency of Germany, France, Italy, and nine other European countries) to get $100. So a euro was worth about $1.19.

There are three fairly distinct periods in the recent history of exchange rates. First, we'll examine the period before 1934, when most of the world was on the gold standard. Second, we'll look at the period from 1934 to 1973, when international finance was based on fixed exchange rates. Finally, we shall review the period from 1973 to the present, when we have had relatively freely floating exchange rates.

Three distinct periods

The Gold Standard

There has been some talk in recent years about a return to the gold standard, but it's not going to happen. Exactly what *is* the gold standard, what are its advantages, and what are its disadvantages? Funny you should ask.

Exactly what is the gold standard?

A nation is on the gold standard when it defines its currency in terms of gold. Until 1933 the U.S. dollar was worth 1/23 of an ounce of gold. In other words, you could buy an ounce of gold from the Treasury for $23 or sell this department an ounce for $23. Paper money was fully convertible into gold. If you gave the Treasury $23, you would get one ounce of gold—no ifs, ands, or buts. In 1933, just before we went off the gold standard (along with the rest of the world), we raised the price of gold to $35 an ounce, which meant a dollar was worth 1/35 of an ounce of gold.

To be on the gold standard, a nation must maintain a fixed ratio between its gold stock and its money supply. That way, when the gold stock rises, so does the money supply. Should gold leave the country, the money supply declines.

That brings us to the third and last requirement of the gold standard: There must be no barriers to the free flow of gold into and out of the country.

When we put all these things together, we have the gold standard. The nation's money supply, which is based on gold, is tied to the money supply of every other nation on the gold standard. It is the closest the world has ever come to an international currency. This system worked quite well until World War I, when most of the belligerents temporarily went off the gold standard because many of their citizens were hoarding gold and trying to ship it off to neutral nations.

How the gold standard works

Ideally, here is how the gold standard works. When Country A exports as much as it imports from Country B, no gold is transferred. But when Country A imports more than it exports, it has to ship the difference, in gold, to the trading partners with whom it has trade deficits.

Suppose the United States had to ship 1 million ounces of gold to other countries. This would lower our gold stock and, consequently, our money supply. When our money supply declined, so would our price level. This would make our goods cheaper relative to foreign goods. Our imports would decline and our exports would rise because foreigners would find American imports cheaper than their own goods.

A self-correcting mechanism

What we had, then, was a self-correcting mechanism. A negative balance of trade caused an outflow of gold, a lower money supply, lower prices, and ultimately, fewer imports and more exports. Thus, under the gold standard, negative trade balances eliminated themselves.

After World War I the nations that had left the gold standard returned to the fold, but some nations' currencies were overvalued (relative to their price in gold) while others' currencies were undervalued. Adjustments were difficult because the nations whose currency was overvalued would have faced a gold drain and, consequently, lower prices and lower wages. But wages and prices are rarely downwardly flexible.

An alternative was to devalue—that is, lower the price of money in relation to gold. For example, a 10 percent devaluation would mean that instead of getting 10 British pounds for an ounce of gold, you now get 11. As the Great Depression spread, one nation after another devalued, and within a few years virtually everyone was off the gold standard.

Evaluation of the gold standard

Let's step back for a moment and evaluate the gold standard. It *did* work for a long time, automatically eliminating trade surpluses and deficits. And it *did* stimulate international trade by removing the uncertainty of fluctuating exchange rates.

But the gold standard has a downside. First, it will work only when the gold supply increases as quickly as the world's need for money. By the early 20th century this was no longer the case. Second, it will work only if participating nations are willing to accept the periodic inflation and unemployment that accompany the elimination of trade imbalances. In today's world political leaders must pay far more attention to their domestic constituencies than to their trading partners. Finally, strict adherence to the gold standard would render monetary policy utterly ineffective. If gold were flowing into the United States, the Federal Reserve would be powerless to slow the rate of monetary growth and the ensuing inflation. And if there were an outflow of gold, the Federal Reserve would be unable to slow the decline in the money supply and thereby prevent the advent of a recession.

With the breakdown of the gold standard in the 1930s, protectionism returned as one nation after another raised tariff barriers higher and higher. Devaluation followed devaluation until the entire structure of international trade and finance was near complete collapse. Then came World War II—and with it, a great revival of economic activity. While the war was still raging, the Bretton Woods conference was called to set up a system of international finance that would lend some stability to how exchange rates were set.

The Gold Exchange Standard, 1934–73

Fixed exchange rates

The Bretton Woods (New Hampshire) conference set up the International Monetary Fund (IMF) to supervise a system of fixed exchange rates, all of which were based on the U.S. dollar, which was based on gold. The dollar was defined as being worth 1/35 of an ounce of gold, so gold was $35 an ounce, and dollars were convertible into gold at that price.

Other currencies were convertible into dollars at fixed prices, so these currencies were indirectly convertible into gold. But this was short of a gold standard because the money supplies of these nations were not tied to gold and no longer would trade deficits or surpluses automatically eliminate themselves. If a nation ran consistent trade deficits, it could devaluate its currency relative to the dollar. A devaluation of 10 percent or less could be done without the IMF's permission (larger cuts required permission).

The new system functioned well for 25 years after World War II. The United States ran almost continual balance-of-payment deficits during the 1950s and 1960s, which eventually led to an international financial crisis in 1971. But until that year these deficits contributed to international liquidity. This is because U.S. dollars as well as gold were held as reserves for international payments by virtually every country in the world but the United States.

Why were U.S. dollars acceptable to other nations? First, the United States held the largest stock of gold in the world and stood ready to sell that gold at $35 an ounce to the central banks of all nations. Second, the American economy was by far the largest and strongest in the world.

Why were U.S. dollars so acceptable?

By the late 1960s, as our gold stock dwindled and as foreign governments found themselves with increasing stocks of dollars, these nations began to ask some embarrassing questions. If the United States continued to run balance-of-payments deficits, would we be able to redeem the dollars they were holding for gold at $35 an ounce? Would the United States be forced to devaluate the dollar, thus making other countries' dollar holdings less valuable?

The Freely Floating Exchange Rate System, 1973 to the Present

To return to 1971, when our payments deficits finally forced us to abandon the gold exchange standard—and forced the rest of the world off as well—the IMF needed to set up a new system fast, and that system was, in computer terminology, a default system.

We were back to the old system that economists fondly refer to as the law of supply and demand. How does it apply to foreign exchange? The same way it applies to everything else.

We were back to the law of supply and demand.

Figure 4 shows hypothetical supply and demand curves for British pounds. Inferring from these curves, you can get 1.5 dollars for a pound.

Who sets this exchange rate? Basically, the forces of supply and demand do. The question then is, Where does the supply and demand for pounds come from?

The demand curve for pounds represents the desire of Americans to exchange their dollars for pounds. Why do they want pounds? To buy British goods and services, stocks, bonds, real estate, and other assets.

Likewise, the supply curve of pounds represents the desire of British citizens to purchase American goods, services, and financial assets.

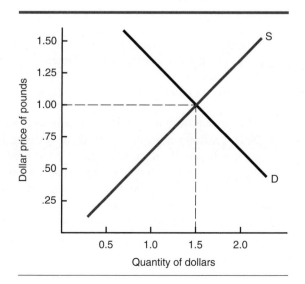

Figure 4

Hypothetical Demand for and Supply of British pounds
How is the exchange rate set between dollars and pounds? It is set by the forces of demand and supply.

Now we get to the beauty of the law of supply and demand. The point at which the two curves cross tells us the exchange rate of pounds and dollars. In Figure 2 we have a rate of 1.5 dollars for 1 pound.

With freely floating exchange rates, currencies will sometimes *depreciate* in value relative to other currencies. If the pound, for instance, depreciates with respect to the dollar it may fall from one pound equals 1.5 euros to one pound equals 1.4 euros. *Depreciation of a currency occurs when one currency becomes cheaper in terms of another currency.* Similarly, a currency can *appreciate* in value relative to another currency. Before appreciation 125 yen equaled one euro, but after the yen appreciated 120 yen equaled one euro. *Appreciation of a currency occurs when one currency becomes more expensive in terms of another currency.* Whenever one currency depreciates, another currency must appreciate.

We don't have completely
free-floating exchange rates.

If we had completely free-floating exchange rates (that is, no government interference), the market forces of supply and demand would set the exchange rates. To a large degree, this is what happens; but governments do intervene, although usually for just a limited time. In other words, government intervention may temporarily influence exchange rates, but exchange rates are set by the forces of supply and demand in the long run.

China is the big exception to the freely floating exchange rate system. For many years the Chinese government tied its currency to the dollar at the rate of 8.28 yuan to the dollar. By the new millennium it was clear that the yuan was undervalued and that if it was allowed to float freely, fewer yuan would be exchanged for each dollar. Finally in the summer of 2005 the Chinese government depreciated the yuan by 2 percent, pegging it at 8.11 yuan to the dollar. But the yuan was clearly still greatly undervalued; if allowed to float freely it probably would exchange at 5 or 5.5 to the dollar.

How have the Chinese managed to manipulate the exchange rate of the yuan against the dollar? Because they have been running huge trade surpluses with the United States, the Chinese government would use their surplus dollars to buy dollar-denominated securities, largely U.S. government bonds. By maintaining an undervalued yuan, they were able to make Chinese exports more attractive to American consumers by keeping down their prices.

Presumably the Chinese monetary authorities will allow the yuan to very slowly drift upward in value against the dollar. (By early May 2006 the yuan had risen from 8.11 to the dollar to 8.01 to the dollar.) So it does not appear that future appreciations of the yuan will substantially reduce our trade deficit with China. Indeed, it rose by 25 percent to a record $202 billion in 2005. As *The Economist* observed:

> America's trade deficit is due mainly to excessive spending and inadequate saving, not to unfair Chinese competition. If China has contributed to America's deficit it is not through its undervalued exchange rate, but by holding down bond yields and so fuelling excessive household borrowing and spending. From this point of view, global monetary policy is now made in Beijing, not Washington.[1]

Three factors influence the exchange rates between countries. The most important factor is the relative price levels of the two countries. If American goods are relatively cheap compared to German goods, there will be a relatively low demand for euros and a relatively high supply of euros. In other words, everyone—Germans and Americans—wants dollars to buy American goods.

A second factor is the relative growth rates of the American and German economies. Whichever is growing faster generates a greater demand for imports. If the American economy is growing faster, it will raise the demand for euros (to be used to buy imported goods from Germany) while decreasing the supply of euros (the Germans will hold more euros and fewer dollars because they are not buying many American goods).

The third and final factor is the relative level of interest rates in the two countries. If the interest rates are higher in Germany than they are in the United States, American

---

[1]*The Economist*, July 30, 2005, p. 11.

investors will want to take advantage of the higher rates by buying German securities. They will sell their dollars for euros, driving up the price of euros. In effect, then, the demand for euros will rise and their supply will decline.

Figure 5 shows five important exchange rates. If the weighted-average exchange value of the U.S. dollar in Panel A confuses you, then help is on the way. You'll find it in the box, "Interpreting the Top Line in Figure 5."

Let's see how the dollar stacks up against the currencies of our leading trading partners as of February 15, 2006. Figure 6 tells us how many euros, pounds, yen, and other foreign currencies we could have gotten for a dollar.

Suppose you bought a Volkswagen Beetle for 11,500 euros. How much would that come to in dollars and cents?

Solution: First, note that, since the exchange rate in Figure 6 is 0.84 euros for a dollar, the number of dollars you need to pay is less than the number of euros. To find the answer, divide the 11,500 euros by the exchange rate of 0.84.

$$\frac{11,500}{0.84} = \$13,690$$

How Well Do Freely Floating (Flexible) Exchange Rates Work?

Until 1973 most countries had fixed exchange rates because they feared flexible rates would fluctuate wildly. Has that happened since 1973? While there certainly have been some ups and downs, most notably with the dollar, we can still say so far, so good.

So far, so good.

The Euro

On January 1, 1999, most of Western Europe introduced a single currency, the euro. (See Panel C, Figure 5.) The European Monetary Union has 12 members—Austria, Belgium, Finland, France, Germany, Greece, Ireland, Italy, Luxembourg, Netherlands, Portugal, and Spain. Flying into Spain from Finland now involves no more hassle than the hop from Chicago to New York. No need to show a passport and—thanks to the euro—no need for the traveler to change money or grapple with baffling prices.

Imagine if the United States were divided into 50 states, each with its own currency. Think how hard it would be to do business. Not only would exchange rates change, literally from minute to minute, but, since business payments are often made 30 or 60 days after delivery, you might end up paying 5 or 10 percent more—or less—than the contractual price. This added element of uncertainty would make it much harder to do business. So, what the members of the euro area are doing, then, is attempting to move toward a unified market with a single currency, just like the one we've long enjoyed in the United States.

As the dollar has fallen in value, the euro has been replacing it as an international currency. While the dollar is still the currency of choice throughout the world, if the dollar continues to decline, the euro, and perhaps the Chinese yuan, will become more important players on the international financial stage.

The Yen and the Yuan

As we noted in the previous chapter, our two biggest trade deficits are with China and Japan. And, as it happens, the Chinese and Japanese monetary authorities have kept the value of their currencies low against the dollar. Indeed the Chinese yuan has been pegged at 8.28 from 1984 until mid-2005 when it was lowered slightly to 8.11. It was estimated that in the spring of 2006 the yuan was artificially undervalued by about 40 percent against the dollar. This made Chinese goods and services cheaper to American consumers and American goods and services more expensive to

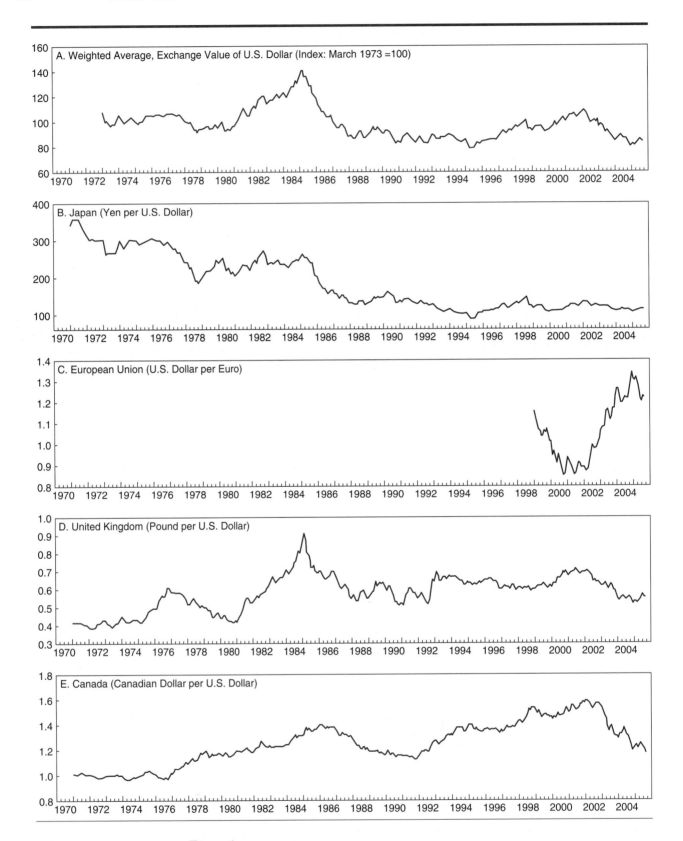

Figure 5

International Exchange Rates, 1972–2005

The value of the U.S. dollar in relation to the yen, the pound, and other currencies has fluctuated rather widely over the last 35 years. To a large degree the dollar has appreciated and depreciated relative to all other major currencies, moving up in value in the early 1980s, down in the later 1980s, up in the late 1990s, and down again in the new millennium.

Source: Business Cycle Indicators, December 2005.

Interpreting the Top Line in Figure 5

The graph line in Panel A of Figure 5 shows how the U.S. dollar has fluctuated against other major currencies since 1972. When the line rises, that means the dollar has risen in value against a weighted average of 10 major foreign currencies. What does this mean in plain English?

First, a weighted average of currencies is similar to your grade point average. If you're really curious about how weighted averages are constructed, look at the box "Construction of the Consumer Price Index" in Chapter 10 in *Economics* and *Macroeconomics*.

Figure 5 charts an index of the dollar's relationship to other major currencies, with a base of March 1973. Let's say that in March 1973 a dollar traded for 50 francs. We set that base year at 100. Suppose the index rose to 200 a few years later. Then you might be able to get 100 francs for your dollar.*

The index did rise from 95 in 1980 to just over 140 in 1985; so the dollar rose by about 60 percent. What did this mean to American consumers? It meant that on the average they could get about 60 percent more foreign currency for their dollars than they could have just five years before.

Suppose a Honda Accord cost 1,000,000 yen in 1985. If 250 yen exchanged for one dollar, the car cost an American $4,000 (1,000,000/250). By 1988 you could get only 125 yen for your dollar. If that new Accord still cost 1,000,000 yen, how many dollars did you need to buy it? Don't wait for me to tell you. I'd like you to work out the answer here:

Here's the solution: 1,000,000/125 = $8,000.

When the dollar rises in value, foreign goods become cheaper; at the same time American goods become more expensive to foreigners. What do you think this does to our trade balance? That's right—it makes it worse. Since the late 1980s the index has generally fluctuated within a range of 80 to 100.

---

*This is, of course, an oversimplification, because the dollar will not have risen by 100 percent against every currency during this period. It will have risen by more than 100 percent against some and by less than 100 percent against others.

$1 Will Buy

2.14	Brazilian reals
0.57	British pounds
1.16	Canadian dollars
8.05	Chinese yuan
0.84	euros
44.2	Indian rupees
117.9	Japanese yen
10.5	Mexican pesos
28.2	Russian rubles
973.5	South Korean won
1.31	Swiss francs

Figure 6

Exchange Rates: Foreign Currency per American Dollar, February 15, 2006
How many Mexican pesos would you get for a dollar? You would get 10.5 pesos. Can you figure out how many dollars (actually how many cents) would you get for a peso? You would get about 9½ cents, or $0.095. Exchange rates fluctuate from minute to minute, and they are usually calibrated to hundredths, or even thousandths of a cent.
Source: The New York Times, February 16, 2006, p. C12.

Chinese consumers. Japan, too, extremely concerned about falling exports, has kept the yen artificially low against the dollar, making its exports to the U.S. cheaper and American imports more expensive.

Japan has long been one of our major trading partners, so the exchange rate between the yen and the dollar is very closely watched. What would happen to the number of yen you could get for a dollar if the supply of dollars rose and the demand for dollars fell?

Figure 7

Hypothetical Supply of and Demand for Dollars Relative to Yen

If the supply of dollars outside the United States were to go up from S_1 to S_2 while the demand for dollars went down from D_1 to D_2 what would happen to the price of the dollar relative to yen? It would go down, in this case from 100 yen to 80 yen.

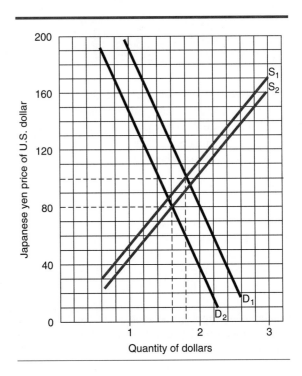

You should be able to figure that out very easily. In Figure 7, we show the question in graphic form, and as we can see, in this particular case, the dollar fell from 100 yen to 80 yen.

The chances are you've never heard of the hamburger standard or the Big Mac index, but you're about to. Begun by *The Economist* as a tongue-in-cheek effort to see if the dollar was undervalued or overvalued, the hamburger standard has actually taken on a life of its own (see the box, "The Hamburger Standard").

Running Up a Tab in the Global Economy

What should be pretty clear by now is that, as a nation, we have been living well beyond our means for more than 25 years—and that the party can't last forever. The United States quickly shifted from being the world's largest creditor nation to the largest debtor. What happened?

From Largest Creditor to Largest Debtor

During the second half of the 19th century the United States borrowed heavily from Great Britain and other European nations to finance the building of railroads and the construction of much of our plant and equipment. Our country was a classic debtor nation, importing manufactured goods, exporting agricultural products, and borrowing capital in order to industrialize.

On the eve of World War I with the process of industrialization largely completed, we finally became a creditor nation. In 1914 foreigners owed us more than we owed them. The assets Americans held in foreign countries—factories, real estate, office buildings, corporate stock and bonds, and government bonds—were greater than the assets foreigners held in the United States. Our creditor status rose substantially during the war as we loaned the Allies billions of dollars. We became the world's leading creditor nation, a position we held until 1982.

How did we lose this position and fall into debt, quickly becoming the world's largest debtor? How could the largest, most productive economy in the world—a nation with low unemployment and stable prices—manage to run up such a huge tab?

During World War I the United States became the world's leading creditor nation.

The Hamburger Standard

Suppose you were addicted to Big Macs, so no matter where you were in the world, you would rush to MacDonald's for dinner. If you did this in the United States on January 9, 2006, a Big Mac would have cost you, on average, $3.15. If you had been in China, after you changed your dollars into yuan, that same Big Mac would have cost you just $1.30 (see graph). But in Switzerland, after changing your dollars into Swiss francs, you would have had to shell out $4.93.

The Big Mac index was created by *The Economist* to determine whether or not the dollar was overvalued or undervalued. If it were overvalued with respect to another currency, then you would be getting a bargain when you exchanged your dollars for that currency. You'd certainly have gotten a bargain in China when you exchanged your dollars for yuan and bought that Big Mac for the equivalent of just $1.30. That same hamburger would have cost you $3.15 in the United States. Indeed, we could say that the yuan was undervalued with respect to the dollar. By the same logic, you would not have gotten your money's worth in Switzerland, paying the equivalent of $4.93 for your Big Mac. We could say that the Swiss franc was overvalued with respect to the dollar.

See if you can figure out by what percent the Swiss franc is *over*valued relative to the dollar. Be sure to write down your answer.

Solution: It's overvalued by 57 percent. Here's the math: You're overpaying by $1.78 ($4.93 − $3.15).
$$\frac{\$1.78}{\$3.15} = 0.57 = 57\%$$

One last question. By what percent is the Chinese yuan *under*valued relative to the dollar?

Solution: It's undervalued by 59 percent.
You're underpaying by $1.85. $\frac{\$1.85}{\$3.15} = 0.59 = 59\%$

Published two or three times a year by *The Economist,* The Big Mac index is intended as a light-hearted guide to whether currencies are at their "correct level."

. . . in the long run, exchange rates should move toward rates that would equalise the prices of an identical basket of goods and services in any two countries. To put it simply: a dollar should buy the same everywhere. Our basket is a MacDonald's Big Mac, produced locally to roughly the same recipe in 118 countries. *

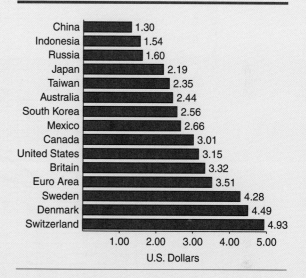

The Hamburger Standard: The Price of a Big Mac in Selected Countries
Source: The Economist, January 14, 2006, p. 102.

*"Economic focus/McCurrencies," *The Economist,* June 11, 2005, p. 70.

The main reason for this turnaround was our large and growing trade deficits. As a nation we are living for today and not worrying about what will happen tomorrow. To say that, as a people, Americans are world-class consumers would not be an exaggeration. "Born to shop" and "shop till you drop" are apt descriptions of tens of millions of American consumers.

You can see the trend in foreign assets in the United States and U.S. assets abroad by looking at Figure 8. In 1985 we became a net debtor nation, and since that year, foreign investment in the United States has far outstripped our investment abroad. These trends

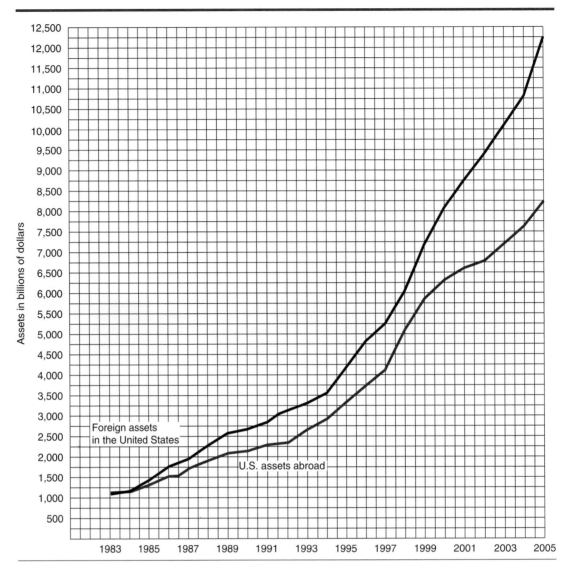

F*igure* **8**

U.S. Assets Abroad and Foreign Assets in the United States, 1983–2005
In the mid-1980s we went from being a creditor nation to a debtor nation. Almost each
year since 1985 the gap between foreign assets in the United States and U.S. assets
abroad has kept growing.
Sources: Economic Report of the President, 1992 and 1995; *Survey of Current Business,* May 2006.

will continue into the foreseeable future as foreigners continue accumulating dollars and
using them to buy up our assets.

Until 2005, American investors were earning more interest, dividends, and profits on
their investments abroad than were foreigner investors on their investments in the United
States. How could that be? William Cline provides a succinct explanation:

> The large and liquid U.S. asset market, with its legal guarantees and (despite Enron)
> transparency, make the United States the natural place for foreign investors to place the
> lower-risk spectrum of their portfolios. Conversely, U.S. investors will tend to seek foreign
> assets to obtain the higher-risk, higher-return spectrum of their portfolios.[2]

_____

[2]William R. Cline, *The United States as a Debtor Nation* (Washington, DC: Institute for International
Economics, 2005).

Dark Matter: America's Invisible Wealth

If the United States is the world's largest debtor nation, how come we have been earning substantially more on our foreign assets than we pay out to service the assets foreigners hold in our country? Two economists, Ricardo Hausmann and Frederico Sturzenegger, have suggested that perhaps the United States is not a net debtor at all, but still a net creditor. And that America may have more foreign wealth than we can see.

The Economist summarized their theory:

The two authors have borrowed a name for this invisible wealth: dark matter. In theoretical physics, dark matter is the stuff in the universe that we can identify only by its gravitational pull. For the Harvard economists, dark matter is foreign wealth, the existence of which we can infer from the income it provides.*

Even if Hausmann and Sturzenegger are right—and theirs is certainly a minority viewpoint—our net investment income from foreign assets had disappeared by 2005. William Cline, an economist who seconds their analysis, has projected that by 2010 the United States will clearly be a debtor nation. In that year our net foreign assets would amount to −$3.8 trillion and we will have a net investment income of −$190 billion.[†] So if indeed the dark matter theory was valid, that dark matter will have disappeared well before the end of this decade.

---

*The Economist, January 21, 2006, p. 74. See also, "U.S. and Global Imbalances: Can Dark Matter Prevent a Big Bang?" at www.utdt.edu/fsturzen/Publications.htm and www.rgemonitor.com/blog/setser/113810.

[†] See William Cline, *The United States as a Debtor Nation*, (Washington, D.C.: Institute for International Economics, 2005).

If we add up all the assets that foreigners own in the United States and subtract the assets that Americans own abroad, we would get the U.S. stock of net foreign assets. You can see in Figure 8 that it began to grow very rapidly at around the beginning of the 21st century. But is it possible that our standing as the world's greatest debtor nation is somewhat exaggerated? This view is discussed in the box, "Dark Matter: America's Invisible Wealth."

Something's gotta give. Most likely the dollar's decline, which began in 2002, will continue. This will make our exports cheaper, so foreigners will buy more from us. Similarly, the lower-valued dollar will make imported goods and services more expensive, so we'll import less. As the dollar falls—note that I said "as" and not "if"—our exports will rise, our imports will fall, and so our trade deficit will shrink.

But a declining dollar, as Paul Krugman notes, makes foreign investment in dollar-denominated assets much less attractive, thereby slowing the inflow of foreign investment:

Right now foreign investors are willing to hold 10-year U.S. government bonds, even though they pay only a slightly higher interest rate than their European counterparts. Those investors seem to believe, in other words, that today's strong dollar will persist for another 10 years. But the size of our trade deficit makes that unlikely. So foreign investors, and therefore the value of the dollar, are arguably doing a Wile E. Coyote—one of these days they will look down, realize that they have already walked over the edge of the cliff, and plunge.[3]

Well over $1 trillion of our currency remains abroad where it circulates as a medium of exchange. The Federal Reserve estimates that over two-thirds of all the U.S. currency being printed is eventually used as unofficial legal tender in China, Russia, Mexico, Romania, Bolivia, the Philippines, Tajikistan, Vietnam, and dozens of other countries. Lithuania, Argentina, and Brazil have formally pegged their currencies to the dollar, while many others have done so informally. In effect, then, much of the world is unofficially on the dollar standard.

---

[3] Paul Krugman, "Deficit Attention Disorder," *New York Times*, March 26, 2000, section 4, p. 17.

The Role of Drug Money

There are no hard figures or even reliable estimates on the amount of money sent abroad to pay for cocaine and heroin imports. But considering that the United States is clearly the world's leading drug importer, it is reasonable to say that more than $30 billion a year is sent abroad to drug growers and traffickers. The transfer of funds is done by cash or electronically through the worldwide banking network and is not easy to trace.

How does this affect our balance-of-payments deficit? It doesn't, except that we often run "statistical discrepancies" of some $30 billion to $60 billion. Now where could all that money be coming from? And where could it be going?

Some of it is coming back into the United States to purchase legitimate businesses, some to buy luxury condominiums along South Florida's "Gold Coast," and some may even be going to buy up part of the national debt. The point is, however reprehensible the drug dealers are, the economic effect of their transactions is similar to the effects of any other imports. The bottom line is that Americans are buying today's pleasures with tomorrow's income.

Laura D'Andrea Tyson, Dean of the London School of Economics (Courtesy of Haas School of Business, University of California-Berkeley)

The U.S. Treasury depends on the foreign saver to finance the deficit.

We are living for today and not worrying about tomorrow.

The U.S. dollar is actually the official currency of more than two dozen countries, the largest of which are Ecuador, El Salvador, Guatemala, and Panama. And several others, including Mexico and Argentina, have been considering dollarization.

Laura D'Andrea Tyson, Dean of the London Business School, explains how the de facto dollar standard works:

In a dollar-standard world, global growth fuels the demand for liquid dollar assets, and the United States can provide these assets, whether in the form of currency, government securities, or private securities, with no well-defined time frame for net repayment. As a result, the United States seems to enjoy a virtually unlimited line of credit denominated in its own currency with the rest of the world. This credit finances America's large and growing current-account deficit. The United States benefits from this arrangement because it can consume much more than it produces. But the rest of the world also benefits both because it gets the dollar holdings it requires and because the United States uses the credit to import goods and services and serve as the world's growth engine.[4]

As long as we can maintain a low inflation rate and currency stability, the world may continue to accept our dollars in exchange for a multitude of goods and services. We're certainly getting a great deal. We get to buy hundreds of billions of dollars' worth of stuff each year and pay for it just by printing money.

The foreign saver has a strong voice in setting the interest rates—not just for U.S. government securities but indirectly for other interest rates as well. As our dependence on funds from abroad grows, we are abdicating not just our role as the world's leading economic power but our economic sovereignty. As time goes by, decisions affecting the American economy will be made not in New York and Washington but in Tokyo, London, Beijing, Frankfurt, and other financial capitals outside the United States.

As a nation we are living for today and not worrying about what will happen tomorrow. "America has thrown itself a party and billed the tab to the future," says Harvard economist Benjamin Friedman.[5] But all parties must end sometime, and someone is going to be left with a mess to clean up. (See the box, "The Role of Drug Money," for a discussion of another aspect of our living for today.)

---

[4]Laura D'Andrea Tyson, "In the Dollar We (and All Other Nations) Trust," *BusinessWeek,* October 28, 2002, p. 26. Dr. Tyson was Chair of the President's Council of Economic Advisors, 1993–95.

[5]Benjamin M. Friedman, *Day of Reckoning* (New York: Random House, 1988), p. 4.

Living beyond Our Means

The root cause of our problems has been that we as a nation have been consuming more than we have been producing, spending more than we have been earning, or, in short, living for today without providing for tomorrow. In the 19th century, when this country also ran up a large international debt, we were financing capital expansion. This investment in the future enabled us to vastly expand our production and quickly pay off our debt.

Today we are following a radically different course. We are not borrowing from abroad to finance capital expansion but rather to pay for a massive spending spree. What are we buying? We're buying consumer electronics, cars, designer clothes, and oil.

America has become a nation of consumption junkies. This is not, in itself, such a terrible thing if we supported our habit. But we can't. So we ask foreigners to indulge us. And so far they have—at a price. We've been giving them IOUs in the form of U.S. dollars, and more and more, foreigners have been cashing them in for pieces of America. It seems as though everyone—the British, the Japanese, the Dutch, the Canadians, the Chinese, the Germans—owns a piece of the rock.

Since the early 1980s we've seen a massive recycling of dollars. As our trade deficits rose, the dollars we sent abroad were lent back to us as foreigners took advantage of our relatively high interest rates to purchase Treasury securities and corporate bonds. But they have increasingly been using their dollar stash to buy up pieces of America in the form of real estate and corporate stock. One might say foreigners are now not just America's creditors but its owners as well. *The Economist* summed up our current account dilemma:

> Just as an individual cannot pile on credit-card debt forever, so a country cannot increase the burden of its foreign debt indefinitely. Eventually, interest on the accumulated debt would use all the economy's resources, leaving nothing for domestic spending.[6]

We are a nation of consumption junkies.

We are selling off the rock—piece by piece.

A Codependent Relationship

China, and to a lesser degree, Japan and a few other East Asian countries, are locked into a codependent relationship with the United States. As long as we keep buying from them, even though we're running huge bilateral trade deficits, they continue to finance those deficits by lending us money. Indeed, China and Japan alone not only finance over half our trade deficit, but over half our federal budget deficit as well.

This is a great deal for us, because we get to consume much more than we produce. Why are these nations so nice to us? Because the huge American market enables them to expand production and job creation beyond what their own populations can consume. In addition, these Asian nations are so eager to keep their goods inexpensive, that they are willing to buy hundreds of billions of dollars in U.S. Treasury securities each year to prevent the dollar from depreciating too quickly.

Had the central banks of China, Japan, and America's other major Asian trading partners not made these purchases, the market forces of supply and demand would have driven the dollar well below its current level. A lower dollar would have made our imports more expensive and our exports cheaper, helping to reduce our trade deficit. But our codependent relationships with these nations precluded that from happening.

The Economist summarized the consequences of our codependent relationships with our Asian trading partners:

> The Asian central banks are masking market signals; America's current-account deficit reflects insufficient saving by households and an excessive budget deficit. Normally, investors would demand higher bond yields to compensate them for the increased risk, thereby giving the government a warning as well as an incentive to borrow less. But Asia's

---

[6]"The Price of Profligacy," *The Economist*, September 20, 2003, p. 7.

buying of Treasury bonds, with little regard for risk and return is keeping yields artificially low, which makes pruning the budget seem less urgent. At the same time low interest rates prolong America's unhealthy consumer spending and borrowing binge.[7]

The United States borrows $2 billion a day from foreigners, largely to finance our trade deficit, but much of this money is also used to finance the federal budget deficit as well. The Japanese and Chinese governments are the largest holders of U.S. government securities. Together they are keeping us financially afloat.

This arrangement has operated smoothly as we began running larger and larger trade and budget deficits, with the salutary effect of holding down our interest rates. Presumably it will continue into the foreseeable future because we, the Chinese, and the Japanese have too much to lose by upsetting the financial apple cart. But the time may come, perhaps five or ten years down the road, when our foreign creditors strongly disagree with some policy of the American government.

I won't even speculate as to what might set off such a conflict, but increasingly, we will have to take into account the opinions of our creditors. Most alarming, each year, we are digging ourselves into a deeper and deeper financial hole.

Why We Need to Worry about the Current Account Deficit

Ours is the world's largest economy, our rate of productivity growth is quite high, and we are on the cutting edge of the latest technology. So why worry about our current account deficit?

Countries that use American dollars for their currency as well as countries that hold U.S. government securities as assets have somewhat limited needs and will reach a point when they don't need any more dollars or U.S. Treasury debt. And as we continue selling off our nation's assets and debt to foreigners, they will reach the limit of how much they are willing to hold.

When that happens, foreigners will demand fewer dollars, the dollar will depreciate in value, foreigners holding American assets will suffer tremendous losses, and Americans will find that they have to pay a lot more for imported goods. Our living standard will fall, and we'll probably have a really bad recession or even a depression.

Today we still have a choice. We can bring our current account deficit under control or we can pay the consequences a few years from now. My guess is that we'll let things keep drifting until it's too late. In the meanwhile, keep your eye on the current account deficit.

Current Issue: Editorial: American Exceptionality

Toward the end of the main section of daily newspapers, you'll find the editorial page. Here's where the editors get a chance to say what they *really* think. This may surprise readers, who find plenty of opinions expressed in news articles. But economics textbook authors are held to a higher standard. We are expected to present both sides of most controversial economics issues. So while our personal viewpoints may well show through, we really do make a strong effort to be, in the words of Fox News, "fair and balanced."

In this last section of the last chapter, I'd like to shift gears, going from neutral to fast forward. Let me tell you what I *really* think about the American economy and where it's headed.

---

[7]"A Fair Exchange?" in *The Economist*, October 2, 2004, p. 16.

For a century we've been the world's largest economy, and for most of this time we have enjoyed the highest standard of living in history. There has long been a strong belief in American exceptionalism, perhaps best expressed by this line from our hymn, *America the Beautiful,* "God shed his grace on thee."

Since the implosion of the Soviet Union in 1991, we are the world's only superpower. Indeed we spend as much on armaments as the rest of the world combined. There are some who see parallels between our recent military record and those of the Roman, the Spanish, and British empires. In fact, one can easily make the case that our empire is not only in decline, but may soon begin to fall apart.

There are many people, both in this country and abroad, who believe that, like the Romans, the Spanish, and the British before them, the Americans have built a huge empire to serve its economic interests. And like the *Pax Britannica* that lasted a century from the end of the Napoleonic Wars in 1815 to the beginning of World War I in 1914, we too have used our military might to impose what has been termed a "New World Order." And what would be the coin of our realm? You *guessed* it! The U.S. dollar! Bill Bonner and Addison Wiggin describe the economic workings of this American empire, and how it differs from its predecessors.

> America provides a *pax dollarium* for nearly the entire world. But the United States does not take direct tribute from its vassal states and dependent territories for providing this service. Instead, it borrows from them. Living standards rise in the United States. But they are rising on borrowed money, not on stolen money. The big difference is that America's vassal states can stop lending at any time. If they care to, they can even dump their current loans on the open market destroying the U.S. dollar and forcing interest rates so high that a recession—or depression—is practically guaranteed. What is worse, the longer the present system continues, the worse off Americans are.[8]

Let's look at the facts:

- We are running unsustainably large federal budget deficits.
- Our huge current account deficit, fueled by our trade deficit, is spiraling out of control.
- Our defense spending is growing at an unsustainable pace, while our military is stretched to the breaking point.
- We are living well beyond our means, depending on the kindness of foreigners.
- We have lost most of our manufacturing base and are now losing our innovative edge as well.
- Americans have one of the lowest savings rate of all nations.
- American students have among the lowest scores on international tests.
- We import two-thirds of our oil.

Considered individually, none of these facts is too alarming, but what conclusions do you reach when you look at the entire package? What trends do you see? Do you think our nation can sustain this course indefinitely?

By nature economists are usually pessimists. That's why economics has long been called "the dismal science." So here we have the United States at the top of its economic game, the unchallenged leader of the world, and I'm suggesting that our game is almost up, that we've been building up to a great fall.

One of the endearing characteristics of economics is that different people can look at the same set of facts and reach diametrically opposed conclusions. I've concluded that we are headed for an economic collapse—a collapse that will certainly come sometime

---

[8]Bill Bonner and Addison Wiggin, *Empire of Debt* (Hoboken, NJ: John Wiley and Sons, 2005), p. 40.

in the next two or three decades. But you might have looked at these same facts and concluded that the best is yet to come. Hopefully we'll both live long enough to see which one of us is right.

Questions for Further Thought and Discussion

1. What is meant by our balance of payments? Explain what current account and capital account are.

2. What is the gold standard? How does it work?

3. Why does the dollar fluctuate with other currencies?

4. How did the United States go from being the world's largest creditor nation to the world's largest debtor?

5. Foreigners are buying up hundreds of billions of dollars in American assets. In what ways should this be a matter of concern to Americans?

6. Can there be a deficit on Current Account and a deficit on Capital Account at the same time? Explain.

7. For several months before your vacation trip to Germany you find that the exchange rate for the dollar has increased relative to the euro. Are you pleased or saddened? Explain.

8. If the dollar depreciates relative to the Japanese yen, will the Sony DVD player you wanted become more or less expensive? What effect will this have on the number of Sony DVD players that Americans buy?

9. Explain why a currency depreciation leads to an improvement in a nation's balance of trade.

10. What is a foreign exchange rate? Provide a few examples.

11. How is the exchange rate determined in a freely floating rate system?

12. Who demands Japanese yen? Who supplies yen?

Workbook for Chapter 32

Name _____   Date _____

Multiple-Choice Questions

Circle the letter that corresponds to the best answer.

1. Which statement is true?
   a) The dollar rose from 1980 to 1985 and then declined.
   b) The dollar declined from 1980 to 1985 and then rose.
   c) The dollar has been rising since 1980.
   d) The dollar has been falling since 1980.

2. We became a debtor nation in _____.
   a) 1975   c) 1985
   b) 1980   d) 1990

3. In 2005 our net foreign debt was about $ _____ trillion.
   a) one   c) three
   b) two   d) four

4. Which statement is true?
   a) In the 1980s we did not receive many dollars in investment funds from foreigners.
   b) In the 1980s foreign investment funds were attracted by our high interest rates.
   c) Our military spending has helped reduce our current account deficit.
   d) None of these statements is true.

5. During the 1980s, _____.
   a) both American investment abroad and foreign investment in the United States increased
   b) both American investment abroad and foreign investment in the United States decreased
   c) American investment abroad increased and foreign investment in the United States decreased
   d) American investment abroad decreased and foreign investment in the United States increased

6. The world's leading debtor nation is _____.
   a) Argentina   c) Mexico
   b) Brazil   d) the United States

7. Which statement is true?
   a) Foreigners own most of the assets in the United States.
   b) We own more assets in foreign countries than foreigners own in the United States.
   c) Foreigners are driving up interest rates in the United States.
   d) None of these statements is true.

8. Which one of the following statement is the most accurate?
   a) As a percentage of GDP, the United States has the highest current account surplus of any nation.
   b) As a percentage of GDP, the United States has the highest current account deficit of any nation.
   c) As a percentage of GDP, our current account deficit is roughly the same as it was 10 years ago.
   d) Our current account deficit is rising at an unsustainable pace.

9. An American importer of Italian shoes would pay in _____.
   a) dollars   c) euros
   b) gold   d) lira

10. The total of our current and capital accounts _____.
    a) will always be zero
    b) will always be negative
    c) will always be positive
    d) may be positive or negative

11. In recent years we bought _____ from foreigners than they bought from us, and we invested _____ in foreign countries than foreigners invested in the United States.
    a) more, more   c) less, more
    b) less, less   d) more, less

12. Today international finance is based on _____.
    a) the gold standard
    b) mainly a relatively free-floating exchange rate system
    c) fixed rates of exchange

13. The international gold standard worked well until _____.
    a) World War I
    b) 1940
    c) 1968
    d) 1975

14. If we were on an international gold standard, _____.
    a) inflations would be eliminated
    b) recessions would be eliminated
    c) trade deficits and surpluses would be eliminated
    d) no nation would ever have to devaluate its currency

15. Which of the following is false?
    a) The gold standard will work only when the gold supply increases as quickly as the world's need for money.
    b) The gold standard will work only if all nations agree to devaluate their currencies simultaneously.
    c) The gold standard will work only if participating nations are willing to accept periodic inflation.
    d) The gold standard will work only if participating nations are willing to accept periodic unemployment.

16. The gold exchange standard was in effect from _____.
    a) 1900 to 1934
    b) 1934 to 1973
    c) 1955 to 1980
    d) 1973 to the present

17. The United States began to consistently run on the balance of payments current account deficits since _____.
    a) 1961
    b) 1971
    c) 1981
    d) 1991
    e) 2001

18. Today currency exchange rates are set by _____.
    a) the International Monetary Fund
    b) the U.S. Treasury
    c) bilateral agreements between trading nations
    d) supply and demand.

19. The most important influence on the exchange rate between two countries is _____.
    a) the relative price levels of the two countries
    b) the relative growth rates of the two countries
    c) the relative level of interest rates in both countries
    d) the relative wage rates of both countries

20. Devaluation would tend to _____.
    a) make the devaluating country's goods cheaper
    b) make the devaluating country's goods more expensive
    c) have no effect on the value of the devaluating country's goods

21. Which is the most accurate statement?
    a) Since the euro was introduced it has lost almost half its value.
    b) The euro has facilitated trade among the members of the euro zone.
    c) The euro is now the world's most important reserve currency.
    d) The euro circulates as currency in most of the countries of the world.

22. The main reason why we are the world's largest debtor nation is _____.
    a) our military spending
    b) our trade deficit
    c) inflation
    d) high taxes

23. Which is the most accurate statement?
    a) Since our current account deficit is matched by our capital account surplus, we have no problem with respect to our international transactions.
    b) Foreigners invest all the dollars they receive from our capital account deficit to buy American assets.
    c) Our current account deficits are declining and should disappear before the year 2012.
    d) A declining dollar makes foreign investment in dollar-denominated assets much less attractive to foreigners.

24. Which of these is the most accurate statement?
    a) There is no basis for the claim that the United States is living beyond its means.
    b) Our current account deficit is not a serious problem.
    c) Our current account deficit is a major economic problem.
    d) Since 2002 the dollar has been rising against most major currencies.

25. If you were going to spend time in Italy, France, and Germany, you would be paying for things with _____.
    a) lira, francs, and marks
    b) dollars
    c) euros
    d) gold

26. Which is the most accurate statement?
    a) Our balance on the current account is negative.
    b) Since our balance of payments is always zero, there is little to worry about.
    c) The income Americans receive from their foreign investments is much greater than the income foreigners receive for their American investments.
    d) Because our imports are much greater than our exports, the federal government is forced to make up the difference.

27. Suppose the world was on the gold standard. If Peru ran persistent trade deficits, _____.
    a) Peru would be able to continue doing so with no consequences
    b) Peru's money stock would decline, its prices would fall, and its trade deficit disappear
    c) Peru would soon suffer from inflation
    d) Peru would raise tariffs and prohibit the shipment of gold from the country

28. Suppose that in the year 2008 we run a trade deficit of $900 billion. Our current account deficit would be about _____ billion.
    a) $600
    b) $800
    c) $900
    d) $1,000
    e) $1,200

29. The most accurate statement would be:
    a) The current account deficit is high, but falling.
    b) The current account deficit will bankrupt us by 2010.
    c) If our trade deficit begins falling, the current account deficit will fall.
    d) Our trade deficit is much higher than our current account deficit.

30. According to the "Big Mac Index," _____.
    a) the U.S. dollar is too highly valued relative to virtually all other currencies
    b) the U.S. dollar is valued too low relative to virtually all other currencies
    c) you will be able to buy a Big Mac much more cheaply in China or Russia than in the United States
    d) you will have to pay much more for a Big Mac in China or Russia than you would in the United States

31. Which is the most accurate statement? In early 2006 there was strong evidence that the _____.
    a) yuan and yen were overvalued against the dollar
    b) yuan and yen were undervalued against the dollar
    c) yuan was undervalued against the yen
    d) yen was undervalued against the yuan

32. Running mounting current account deficits is analogous to _____.
    a) running up debt on a credit card
    b) taking money out of one pocket and putting it in another
    c) owing money to ourselves
    d) borrowing money that never has to be repaid

Fill-In Questions

1. The entire flow of U.S. dollars and foreign currencies into and out of the country constitutes our _____.

2. Most all the dollars that foreigners have earned from trading with the United States have been _____ in the form of _____.

3. The basis for international finance is the exchange of _____.

4. A nation is on the gold standard when it _____ _____.

5. To be on the gold standard, a nation must maintain a fixed ratio between its gold stock and _____ _____.

6. Under the gold standard, if country J imports more than it exports, it has to ship _____ _____ to the trading partners with whom it has trade deficits. This will depress country J's _____, and its price level will _____.

7. Under the gold standard, if country K's price level declines, its imports will _____ and its exports will _____.

8. Today exchange rates are set by _____ and _____.

9. If Tim Matray wanted to buy wine from a French merchant, he would pay her with _____.

10. The main difference between our being a debtor nation in the 19th century and our being a debtor nation since the early 1980s was that in the 19th century we ran up a debt by buying _____ goods; since the early 1980s we have run up a debt buying _____ goods.

Problems

Use the exchange rates listed in Figure 6 of the chapter to find how much it would cost in U.S. dollars and cents to make the purchases listed in problems 1–4.

1. A Toyota Corolla priced at 1.4 million yen.

2. A carton of Canadian paper priced at $9.00 Canadian.

3. A British book priced at 12 pounds.

4. A German camera priced at 250 euros.

Use the exchange rates listed in Figure 6 to find how much it would cost in the currency specified to make the purchases listed in problems 5–8.

5. A DVD priced at $10 is sold in Toronto.

6. Windows 2007 priced at $100 is sold in China.

7. A Cadillac priced at $20,000 is sold in London.

8. A bottle of Viagra priced at $20 is sold in Berlin.

9. A country had exports of $100 billion, imports of $90 billion, net transfers from abroad of −$10 billion, and −$5 billion of net income from foreign investments. What is the country's current account balance?

10. Brazil ran a current account deficit of $55 billion. What is its balance on the capital account?

11. If you could buy a market basket of goods and services in the United States for $1,000 and those same goods and services cost you $1,200 after you converted your dollars into euros, (a) is the euro undervalued or overvalued relative to the dollar? (b) by what percent?

12. If you could buy a market basket of goods and services in the United States for $10,000 and those same goods and services cost you $7,000 in Russia after you converted your dollars into rubles, (a) is the ruble undervalued or overvalued relative to the dollar? (b) by what percent?

Glossary

a

Ability-to-Pay Principle   The amount of taxes that people pay should be based on their ability to pay (that is, their incomes).

Absolute Advantage   The ability of a country to produce a good at a lower cost than its trading partners.

Accelerator Principle   If sales or consumption is rising at a constant rate, gross investment will stay the same; if sales rise at a decreasing rate, both gross investment and GDP will fall.

Accounting Profit   Sales minus explicit cost. Implicit costs are not considered.

Aggregate Demand   The sum of all expenditures for goods and services.

Aggregate Demand Curve   Curve showing planned purchase rates for all goods and services in the economy at various price levels.

Aggregate Supply   The nation's total output of goods and services.

Aggregate Supply Curve   Curve showing the level of real GDP produced at different price levels during a time period, *ceteris paribus*.

Allocative Efficiency   Occurs when no resources are wasted; it is not possible to make any person better off without making someone else worse off.

Anticipated Inflation   The rate of inflation that we believe will occur; when it does, we are in a situation of fully anticipated inflation.

Antitrust Laws   These laws, including the Sherman and Clayton acts, attempted to enforce competition and to control the corporate merger movement.

Appreciation   An increase in the value of a currency in terms of other currencies.

Arbitration   An arbitrator imposes a settlement on labor and management if they cannot reach a collective bargaining agreement.

Asset Demand   Holding money as a store of value instead of other assets such as stocks, bonds, savings accounts, certificates of deposit, or gold.

Automatic Stabilizers   Programs such as unemployment insurance benefits and taxes that are already on the books to help alleviate recessions and hold down the rate of inflation.

Autonomous Consumption   The minimum amount that people will spend on the necessities of life.

Average Fixed Cost   Fixed cost divided by output.

Average Propensity to Consume   The percentage of disposable income that is spent; consumption divided by disposable income.

Average Propensity to Save   The percentage of disposable income that is saved; saving divided by disposable income.

Average Tax Rate   The percentage of taxable income that is paid in taxes; taxes paid divided by taxable income.

Average Total Cost (ATC)   Total cost divided by output.

Average Variable Cost (AVC)   Variable cost divided by output.

b

Backward-Bending Labor Supply Curve   As the wage rate rises, more and more people are willing to work longer and longer hours up to a point. They will then substitute more leisure time for higher earnings.

Balanced Budget   When federal tax receipts equal federal government spending.

Balance of Payments   The entire flow of U.S. dollars and foreign currencies into and out of the country.

Balance of Trade   The difference between the value of our imports and our exports.

Balance on Capital Account   A category that itemizes changes in foreign asset holdings in one nation and that nation's asset holdings abroad.

Balance on Current Account   A category that itemizes a nation's imports and exports of goods and services, income receipts and payments on investment, and unilateral transfers.

Bank   A commercial bank or thrift institution that offers checkable deposits.

Bank Run   Attempts by many depositors to withdraw their money out of fear that that bank was failing, or that all banks were failing.

Barrier to Entry   Anything that prevents the entry of new firms into an industry.

Barter   The exchange of one good or service for another good or service; a trade.

Base Year   The year with which other years are compared when an index is constructed: for example, a price index.

Benefits-Received Principle   The amount of taxes people pay should be based on the benefits they receive from the government.

Bonds   (See Government Bonds or Corporate Bonds.)

Boom   Period of prolonged economic expansion.

Break-Even Point   The low point on the firm's average total cost curve. If the price is below this point, the firm will go out of business in the long run.

Budget Deficit   When federal tax receipts are less than federal government spending.

Budget Surplus   When federal tax receipts are greater than federal government spending.

Business Cycle   Increases and decreases in the level of business activity that occur at irregular intervals and last for varying lengths of time.

C

CPI   (See Consumer Price Index.)

Capital   All means of production (mainly plant and equipment) created by people.

Capital Account   The section of a nation's international balance of payments statement in which the foreign purchases of that nation's assets and that nation's purchases of assets abroad are recorded.

Capitalism   An economic system in which most economic decisions are made by private owners and most of the means of production are privately owned.

Capital/Output Ratio   The ratio of capital stock to GDP.

Cartel   A group of firms behaving like a monopoly.

Central Bank   A bank whose chief function is the control of the nation's money supply.

Certificate of Deposit (CD)   A time deposit (almost always of $500 or more) with a fixed maturity date offered by banks and other financial institutions.

Change in Demand   A change in the quantity demanded of a good or service at at least one price that is caused by factors other than a change in the price of that good or service.

Change in Supply   A change in the quantity supplied of a good or service at at least one price that is caused by factors other than a change in the price of that good or service.

Checkable-Deposit   Any deposit in a commercial bank or thrift institution against which a check may be written.

Circular Flow Model   Goods and services flow from business firms to households in exchange for consumer expenditures, while resources flow from households to business firms in exchange for resource payments.

Classical Economics   Laissez-faire economics. Our economy, if left free from government interference, tends toward full employment. The prevalent school of economics from about 1800 to 1930.

Closed Shop   An employer may hire only union members; outlawed under the Taft-Hartley Act.

Collective Bargaining   Negotiations between union and management to obtain agreements on wages, working conditions, and other issues.

Collusion   The practice of firms to negotiate price and/or market share decisions that limit competition in a market.

Commercial Bank   A firm that engages in the business of banking, accepting deposits, offering checking accounts, and making loans.

Communism   An economic system characterized by collective ownership of most resources and central planning.

Comparative Advantage   Total output is greatest when each product is made by the country that has the lowest opportunity cost.

Competition   Rivalry among business firms for resources and customers.

Complementary Goods   Goods and services that are used together; when the price of one falls, the demand for the other rises (and conversely).

Concentration Ratio   The percentage share of industry sales by the four leading firms.

Conglomerate Merger   Merger between two companies in unrelated industries.

Constant-Cost Industry   An industry whose total output can be increased without an increase in long-run-per-unit costs; an industry whose long-run supply curve is flat.

Constant Dollars   Dollars expressed in terms of real purchasing power, using a particular year as the base of comparison, in contrast to current dollars.

Constant Returns to Scale   Cost per unit of production are the same for any output.

Consumer Price Index   The most important measure of inflation. This tells us the percentage rise in the price level since the base year, which is set at 100; represented by CPI.

Consumer Surplus   The difference between what you pay for some good or service and what you would have been willing to pay.

Consumption   The expenditure by individuals on durable goods, nondurable goods, and services; represented by C.

Consumption Function   As income rises, consumption rises, but not as quickly.

Contraction   The downturn of the business cycle, when real GDP is declining.

Corporate Bonds   This is a debt of the corporation. Bondholders have loaned money to the company and are its creditors.

Corporate Stock   Share in a corporation. The stockholders own the corporation.

Corporation   A business firm that is a legal person. Its chief advantage is that each owner's liability is limited to the amount of money he or she invested in the company.

Cost-of-Living Adjustments (COLAs)   Clauses in contracts that allow for increases in wages, Social Security benefits, and other payments to take account of changes in the cost of living.

Cost-Push Inflation   Rising costs of doing business push up prices.

Craft Unions   Labor unions composed of workers who engage in a particular trade or have a particular skill.

Credit Unions   Financial institution cooperatives made up of depositors with a common affiliation.

Creeping Inflation   A relatively low rate of inflation, such as the rate of less than 4 percent in the United States in recent years.

Crowding-In Effect   An increase in private sector spending stimulated by federal budget deficits financed by U.S. Treasury borrowing.

Crowding-Out Effect   Large federal budget deficits are financed by Treasury borrowing, which then crowds private borrowers out of financial markets and drives up interest rates.

Crude Quantity Theory of Money   The belief that changes in the money supply are directly proportional to changes in the price level.

Currency   Coins and paper money that serve as a medium of exchange.

Current Account   The section of a nation's international balance of payments that records its exports and imports of goods and services, its net investment income, and its net transfers.

Cyclical Unemployment   When people are out of work because the economy is operating below the full-employment level. It rises sharply during recessions.

d

Decreasing Cost Industry   An industry in which an increase in output leads to a reduction in the long-run average cost, such that the long-run industry supply curve slopes downward.

Deficit   (See Budget Deficit.)

Deflation   A decline in the price level for at least two years.

Deflationary Gap   Occurs when equilibrium GDP is less than full-employment GDP.

Demand   A schedule of quantities of a good or service that people will buy at different prices; represented by D.

Demand Curve   A graphical representation of the demand schedule showing the inverse relationship between price and quantity demanded.

Demand Deposit   A deposit in a commercial bank or other financial intermediary against which checks may be written.

Demand, Law of   When the price of a good is lowered, more of it is demanded; when the price is raised, less is demanded.

Demand-Pull Inflation   Inflation caused primarily by an increase in aggregate demand: too many dollars chasing too few goods.

Demand Schedule   A schedule of quantities of a good or service that people are willing to buy at different prices.

Depository Institutions Deregulation and Monetary Control Act of 1980   This made all depository institutions subject to the Federal Reserve's legal reserve requirements and allowed all depository institutions to issue checking deposits.

Depreciation   A fall in the price of a nation's currency relative to foreign currencies.

Depression   A deep and prolonged business downturn; the last one occurred in the 1930s.

Deregulation   The process of converting a regulated firm or industry into an unregulated firm or industry.

Derived Demand   Demand for resources derived from demand for the final product.

Devaluation   Government policy that lowers the nation's exchange rate so that its currency is worth less than it had been relative to foreign currencies.

Diminishing Marginal Utility   Declining utility, or satisfaction, derived from each additional unit consumed of a particular good or service.

Diminishing Returns, Law of   If units of a resource are added to a fixed proportion of other resources, marginal output will eventually decline.

Direct Tax   Tax on a particular person. Most important are federal personal income tax and payroll (Social Security) tax.

Discounting   The method by which the present value of a future sum or a future stream of sums is obtained.

Discount Rate   The interest rate charged by the Federal Reserve to depository institutions.

Discouraged Workers   People without jobs who have given up looking for work.

Discretionary Fiscal Policy   Changes in government spending and taxes to promote full employment, price stability, and economic growth.

Diseconomies of Scale   An increase in average total cost as output rises.

Disequilibrium   When aggregate demand does not equal aggregate supply.

Disinflation   Occurs when the rate of inflation declines.

Disposable Income   Aftertax income. Term applies to individuals and to the nation.

Dissaving   When consumption is greater than disposable income; negative saving.

Dividends   The part of corporate profits paid to its shareholders.

Division of Labor   The provision of specialized jobs.

Durable Goods   Things that last at least a year or two.

e

E-commerce   Buying and selling on the Internet.

Economic Cost   Explicit costs plus implicit costs.

Economic Goods   Goods that are scarce, for which the quantity demanded exceeds the quantity supplied at a zero price.

Economic Growth   An outward shift of the production possibilities frontier brought about by an increase in available resources and/or a technological improvement.

Economic Problem   When we have limited resources available to fulfill society's relatively limitless wants.

Economic Profit   Sales minus explicit costs and implicit costs.

Economic Rent   The excess payment to a resource above what it is necessary to pay to secure its use.

Economics   The efficient allocation of the scarce means of production toward the satisfaction of human wants.

Economies of Scale   Reductions in average total cost as output rises.

Efficiency   Conditions under which maximum output is produced with a given level of inputs.

Elasticity of Demand   Measures the change in quantity demanded in response to a change in price.

Entrepreneurial Ability   Ability to recognize a business opportunity and successfully set up a business firm to take advantage of it.

Equation of Exchange   Shows the relationship among four variables: M (the money supply), V (velocity of circulation), P (the price level), and Q (the quantity of goods and services produced). $MV = PQ$.

Equilibrium   When aggregate demand equals aggregate supply.

Equilibrium Point   Point at which quantity demanded equals quantity supplied; where demand and supply curves cross.

Equilibrium Price   The price at which quantity demand is equal to quantity supplied.

Equilibrium Quantity   The quantity bought and sold at the equilibrium price.

Euro   The common currency in most of Western Europe.

European Union (EU)   An organization of European nations that has reduced trade barriers among themselves.

Excess Reserves   The difference between actual reserves and required reserves.

Exchange   The process of trading one thing for another.

Exchange Rates   The price of foreign currency; for example, how many dollars we must give up in exchange for marks, yen, and pounds.

Excise Tax   A sales tax levied on a particular good or service; for example, gasoline and cigarette taxes.

Expected Rate of Profit   Expected profits divided by money invested.

Expenditures Approach   A way of computing GDP by adding up the dollar value at current market prices of all final goods and services.

Explicit Costs   Dollar costs incurred by business firms, such as wages, rent, and interest.

Exports   Goods and services produced in a nation and sold to customers in other nations.

Externality   A consequence of an economic activity, such as pollution, that affects third parties.

f

FDIC   (See Federal Deposit Insurance Corporation.)

Factors of Production   The resources of land, labor, capital, and entrepreneurial ability.

Featherbedding   Any labor practice that forces employers to use more workers than they would otherwise employ; a make-work program.

Federal Deposit Insurance Corporation   Insures bank deposits up to $100,000.

Federal Funds Rate   The interest rate banks and other depository institutions charge one another on overnight loans made out of their excess reserves.

Federal Open Market Committee (FOMC)   The principal decision-making body of the Federal Reserve, conducting open market operations.

Federal Reserve Note   Paper money issued by the Federal Reserve.

Federal Reserve System   Central bank of the United States, whose main job is to control our rate of monetary growth.

Fiat Money   Paper money that is not backed by or convertible into any good; it is money because the government says it is money.

Financial Intermediaries   Firms that accept deposits from savers and use those deposits to make loans to borrowers.

Firm   A business that employs resources to produce a good or service for profit and owns and operate one or more plants.

Fiscal Policy   Manipulation of the federal budget to attain price stability, relatively full employment, and a satisfactory rate of economic growth.

Fiscal Year   Budget year. U.S. federal budget fiscal year begins on October 1.

Fixed Costs   These stay the same no matter how much output changes.

Fixed Exchange Rate   A rate determined by government and then maintained by buying and selling quantities of its own currency on the foreign exchange market.

Floating Exchange Rate   An exchange rate determined by the demand for and the supply of a nation's currency.

Foreign Exchange Market   A market in which currencies of different nations are bought and sold.

Foreign Exchange Rate   The price of one currency in terms of another.

Fractional Reserve Banking   A system in which depository institutions held reserves that are less than the amount of total deposits.

Free Trade   The absence of artificial (government) barriers to trade among individuals and firms in different nations.

Frictional Unemployment   Refers to people who are between jobs or just entering or reentering the labor market.

Fringe Benefits   Nonwage compensation, mainly medical insurance, that workers receive from employers.

Full Employment   When a society's resources are all being used with maximum efficiency.

Full-Employment GDP   That level of spending (or aggregate demand) that will result in full employment.

g

GATT (General Agreement on Tariffs and Trade)   An agreement to negotiate reductions in tariffs and other trade barriers.

GDP   (See Gross Domestic Product.)

GDP deflator   A price index used to measure price changes in the items that go into GDP.

GDP gap   The amount of production by which potential GDP exceeds actual GDP.

Gold Standard   A historical system of fixed exchange rates in which nations defined their currency in terms of gold, maintained a fixed relationship between their stock of gold and their money supplies, and allowed gold to be freely exported and imported.

Government Bonds   Long-term debt of the federal government.

Government Expenditures   Federal, state, and local government outlays for goods and services, including transfer payments.

Government Failure   Misallocation of resources in the public sector.

Government Purchases   All goods and services bought by the federal, state, and local governments.

Gross Domestic Product (GDP)   The nation's expenditure on all the goods and services produced in the country during the year at market prices; represented by GDP.

Gross Investment   A company's total investment in plant, equipment, and inventory. Also, a nation's plant, equipment, inventory, and residential housing investment.

h

Herfindahl-Hirschman Index   A measure of concentration calculated as the sum of the squares of the market share of each firm in an industry.

Horizontal Merger   Conventional merger between two firms in the same industry.

Household   An economic unit of one or more persons living under one roof.

Hyperinflation   Runaway inflation; in the United States, double-digit inflation.

i

Imperfect Competition   All market structures except perfect competition; includes monopoly, oligopoly, and monopolistic competition.

Implicit Costs   The firm's opportunity costs of using resources owned or provided by the owner.

Imports   Goods and services bought by people in one country that are produced in other countries.

Income   A flow of money to households.

Income Approach   Method of finding GDP by adding all the incomes earned in the production of final goods and services.

Income Effect   A person's willingness to give up some income in exchange for more leisure time.

Incomes Policy   Wage controls, price controls, and tax incentives used to try to control inflation.

Increasing Costs, Law of   As the output of a good expands, the opportunity cost of producing additional units of this good increases.

Increasing Returns   An increase in firm's output by a larger percentage than the percentage increase in its inputs.

Increasing Returns to Scale   A situation in which a firm's minimum long-run average total cost decreases as the level of output rises.

Indirect Tax   Tax on a thing rather than on a particular person; for example, sales tax.

Induced Consumption   Spending induced by changes in the level of income.

Industrial Union   A union representing all the workers in a single industry, regardless of each worker's skill or craft.

Inelastic Demand   A demand relationship in which a given percentage change in price results in a smaller percentage change in quantity sold.

Inelastic Supply   A supply relationship in which a given percentage change in price results in a smaller percentage change in quantity supplied.

Inferior Goods   Goods for which demands decrease when people's incomes rise.

Inflation   A general rise in the price level.

Inflationary Gap   Occurs when equilibrium GDP is greater than full-employment GDP.

Innovation   An idea that eventually takes the form of new, applied technology or a new production process.

Interest   The cost of borrowed funds.

Interest Rate   Interest paid divided by amount borrowed.

Interlocking Directorates   When one person serves on the boards of at least two competing firms.

Intermediate Goods   Goods used to produce other goods.

Inventory Investment   Changes in the stocks of finished goods and raw materials that firms keep in reserve to meet orders.

Investment   The purchase or construction of any new plant, equipment, or residential housing, or the accumulation of inventory; represented by I.

j

Jurisdictional Dispute   A dispute involving two or more unions over which should represent the workers in a particular shop or plant.

k

Keynesian Economics   As formulated by John Maynard Keynes, this school believed the private economy was inherently unstable and that government intervention was necessary to prevent recessions from becoming depressions.

Kinked Demand Curve   The demand curve for a noncollusive oligopolist, which is based on the assumption that rivals will follow a price decrease and will ignore a price increase.

l

Labor   The work and time for which employees are paid.

Labor Force   The total number of employed and unemployed people.

Labor Union   Worker organization that seeks to secure economic benefits for its members.

Laffer Curve   Shows that at very high tax rates, very few people will work and pay taxes; therefore government revenue will rise as tax rates are lowered.

Laissez-Faire   The philosophy that the private economy should function without any government interference.

Land   Natural resources used to produce goods and services.

Law of Demand   An increase in a product's price will reduce the quantity of it demanded, and conversely for a decrease in price.

Law of Diminishing (Marginal) Returns   The observation that, after some point, successive equal-sized increases of a resource, added to fixed factors of other resources, will result in smaller increases in output.

Law of Increasing Costs   As the output of one good expands, the opportunity cost of producing additional units of this good increases.

Law of Supply   An increase in the price of a product will increase the quantity of it supplied; and conversely for a decrease in price.

Legal Reserves   Reserves that depository institutions are allowed by law to claim as reserves; vault cash and deposits held at Federal Reserve district banks.

Legal Tender   Coins and paper money officially declared to be acceptable for the settlement of financial debts.

Less Developed Countries (LDCs)   Economies in Asia, Africa, and Latin America with relatively low per capita incomes.

Leveraged Buyouts   A primarily debt-financed purchase of a controlling interest of a corporation's stock.

Limited Liability   The liability of the owners of a corporation is limited to the value of the shares in the firm that they own.

Liquidity   Money or things that can be quickly and easily converted into money with little or no loss of value.

Liquidity Preference   The demand for money.

Liquidity Trap   At very low interest rates, said John Maynard Keynes, people will neither lend out their money nor put it in the bank, but will simply hold it.

Loanable Funds   The supply of money that savers have made available to borrowers.

Long Run   When all costs become variable costs and firms can enter or leave the industry.

Lorenz Curve   Data plotted to show the percentage of income enjoyed by each percentage of households, ranked according to their income.

m

M   The money supply—currency, checking deposits, and check-like deposits (identical to M1).

M1   Currency, checking deposits, and checklike deposits.

M2   M1 plus savings deposits, small-denomination time deposits, and money market mutual funds.

M3   M2 plus large-denomination time deposits.

Macroeconomics   The part of economics concerned with the economy as a whole, dealing with huge aggregates like national output, employment, the money supply, bank deposits, and government spending.

Malthusian Theory of Population   Population tends to grow in a geometric progression (1, 2, 4, 8, 16), while food production tends to grow in an arithmetic progression (1, 2, 3, 4, 5).

Marginal Cost (MC)   The cost of producing one additional unit of output.

Marginal Physical Product (MPP)   The additional output produced by one more unit of input.

Marginal Propensity to Consume (MPC)   Change in consumption divided by change in income.

Marginal Propensity to Save (MPS)   Change in saving divided by change in income.

Marginal Revenue (MR)   The revenue derived from selling one additional unit of output.

Marginal Revenue Product (MRP)   The demand for a resource, based on that resource's marginal output and the price at which it is sold.

Marginal Tax Rate   Additional taxes paid divided by taxable income.

Marginal Utility   The additional utility derived from consuming one more unit of some good or service.

Margin Requirement   The maximum percentage of the cost of a stock purchase that can be borrowed from a bank, stockbroker, or any other financial institution, with stock offered as collateral; this percentage is set by the Federal Reserve.

Market   Any place where buyers and sellers exchange goods and services.

Market Failure   A less than efficient allocation of resources.

Market Period   A period during which sellers are unable to change quantity offered for sale in response to a change in price.

Maximum Profit Point   A firm will always produce at this point; marginal cost equals marginal revenue.

MC = MR Rule   For a firm to maximize its profits, marginal cost must equal marginal revenue.

Measure of Economic Welfare   A measure developed by James Tobin and William Nordhaus that modifies GDP by excluding "economic bads" and "regrettable necessities" and adding household, unreported, and illegal production.

Mediation   A third party acts as a go-between for labor and management during collective bargaining.

Medium of Exchange   Items sellers generally accept and buyers generally use to pay for a good or service; the primary job of money.

Merchandise Trade Balance   The difference between the value of merchandise exports and the value of merchandise imports.

Microeconomics   The part of economics concerned with individual units such as firms and households and with individual markets, particular prices, and specific goods and services.

Minimum Wage   An hourly wage floor set by government that firms must pay their workers.

Mixed Economy   An economy in which production and distribution is done partly by the private sector and partly by the government.

Monetarism   A school of economics that places paramount importance on money as the key determinant of the level of prices, income, and employment.

Monetary Policy   Control of the rate of monetary growth by the Board of Governors of the Federal Reserve.

Monetary Rule   The money supply may grow at a specified annual percentage rate, generally about 3–4 percent.

Money   Main job is to be a medium of exchange; also serves as a standard of value and a store of value.

Money Supply   Currency, checking deposits, and checklike deposits (M or M1).

Monopolistic Competition   An industry that has many firms producing a differentiated product.

Monopoly   An industry in which one firm produces all the output. The good or service produced has no close substitutes.

Monopsony   A market in which a single buyer has no rivals.

Multinational Corporation   A corporation doing business in more than one country; often it owns production facilities in at least one country and sells in many countries.

Multiplier   Any change in spending (C, I, or G) will set off a chain reaction leading to a multiplied change in GDP. Equation is $1/(1 - MPC)$.

n

NNP   (See Net National Product.)

National Debt   (See Public Debt.)

National Income   Net domestic product minus indirect business taxes.

Natural Monopoly   An industry in which a single firm can provide cheaper service than could several competing firms.

Negative Income Tax   Cash payments by the government to the poor—an income tax in reverse. The cash payments decrease as income levels increase.

Net Exports   One country's exports to other countries minus its imports from other countries.

Net Investment   Gross investment minus depreciation.

Net National Product   Gross domestic product minus depreciation.

Net Productivity of Capital   The expected annual profit rate.

Net Worth   The difference between assets and liabilities.

Nominal GDP   The value of the final goods and services produced in a given year valued at that year's prices.

Nominal Interest Rate   The real interest rate plus the inflation rate.

Noncompeting Groups   Various strata of labor that do not compete for jobs; for example, doctors and secretaries, skilled and unskilled workers.

Nondurable Goods   Goods that are expected to last or be used for less than one year.

Normal Good   A good whose demand varies directly with income; nearly all goods are normal goods.

Normal Profits   The return to the businessowners for the opportunity cost of their implicit inputs.

North American Free Trade Agreement (NAFTA)   A free trade area consisting of the United States, Canada, and Mexico.

O

Oligopoly   An industry with just a few firms.

Oligopsony   A market in which there are only a few buyers.

Open Economy   An economy linked to the rest of the world through international trade.

Open-Market Operations   The purchase or sale of Treasury securities by the Federal Reserve; main monetary policy weapon.

Open Shop   When no one is forced to join a union even though the union represents all the workers in contract negotiations.

Opportunity Cost   The forgone value of what you give up when you make a choice.

Output Effect   When the price of any resource rises, the cost of production rises, which, in turn, lowers the supply of the final product. When supply falls, price rises, consequently reducing output.

P

P   The price level, or the average price of all goods and services produced during the current year.

Paradox of Thrift   If everyone tries to save more, they will all end up saving less.

Partnership   A business firm owned by two or more people.

Payroll Tax   (See Social Security Tax.)

Per Capita Real GDP   Real GDP divided by population.

Perfect Competition   An industry with so many firms that no one firm has any influence over price, and firms produce an identical product.

Perfectly Elastic Demand Curve   A perfectly horizontal demand curve; the firm can sell as much as it wishes at that price.

Perfectly Elastic Supply Curve   A perfectly horizontal supply curve; the slightest decrease in price causes the quantity supplied to fall to zero.

Perfectly Inelastic Demand Curve   A perfectly vertical demand curve; no matter what the price is, the quantity demanded remains the same.

Perfectly Inelastic Supply Curve   A perfectly vertical supply curve; quantity supplied remains constant no matter what happens to price.

Permanent Income Hypothesis   Formulated by Milton Friedman, it states that the strongest influence on consumption is one's estimated lifetime income.

Personal Income   Income received by household, including both earned income and transfer payments.

Phillips Curve   Curve showing inverse relationship between the unemployment rate and the rate of inflation.

Plant   A store, factory, office, or other physical establishment that performs one or more functions in the production, fabrication, and sales of goods and services.

Poverty   A situation in which the basic needs of an individual or family exceed the means to satisfy them.

Poverty Rate   The percentage of the population with incomes below the official poverty line established by the federal government.

Present Value   The value today of the stream of expected future annual income that a property generates.

Price   The amount of money needed to buy a particular good, service, or resource.

Price Ceiling   Government-imposed maximum legal price.

Price Discrimination   Occurs when a seller charges two or more prices for the same good or service.

Price Floor   Government-imposed minimum price (used almost exclusively to keep agricultural commodity prices up).

Price Index   An index number that shows how the weighted average price of a market basket of goods changes through time.

Price Leadership   One firm, often the dominant firm in an oligopolistic industry, raises or lowers price, and the other firms quickly match the new price.

Price Level   A measure of prices in a given month or year in relation to prices in a base year.

Price System   Mechanism that allocates resources, goods, and services based on supply and demand.

Prime Rate   Rate of interest that banks charge their most creditworthy customers.

Product Differentiation   The distinction between or among goods and services made in the minds of buyers.

Production   Any good or service for which people are willing to pay.

Production Function   A technological relationship expressing the maximum quantity of a good attainable from different combinations of factor inputs.

Production Possibilities Curve   The potential total output combinations of any two goods for an economy.

Production Possibilities Frontier   A curve representing a hypothetical model of a two-product economy operating at full employment.

Productivity   Output per unit of input; efficiency with which resources are used.

Profit   The difference between total revenue and total cost.

Progressive Tax   Places greater burden on those with best ability to pay and little or no burden on the poor (for example, federal personal income tax).

Proportional Tax   A tax whose burden falls equally among the rich, the middle class, and the poor.

Proprietorship   An unincorporated business firm owned by just one person.

Protective Tariff   A tariff designed to shield domestic producers of a good or service from the competition of foreign producers.

Public Debt   The amount of federal securities outstanding, which represents what the federal government owes (the accumulation of federal deficits minus surpluses over the last two centuries).

Public Goods   Goods or services produced by the government; they can be jointly consumed by many individuals simultaneously at no additional cost and with no reduction in quality or quantity.

q

Q   Output, or number of goods and services produced during the current year.

Quantity Theory of Money   Crude version: Changes in the money supply cause proportional changes in the price level. Sophisticated version: If we are well below full employment, an increase in M will lead to an increase in output. If we are close to full employment, an increase in M will lead mainly to an increase in P.

Quotas   Numerical limits imposed on the quantity of a specific good that may be imported.

r

Rational Expectations Theory   This is based on three assumptions: (1) that individuals and business firms learn through experience to anticipate the consequences of changes in monetary and fiscal policy; (2) that they act immediately to protect their economic interests; and (3) that all resource and product markets are purely competitive.

Real Balance Effect   The influence a change in household purchasing power has on the quantity of real GDP that consumers are willing to buy.

Real GDP   GDP corrected for inflation; actual production.

Real Income   Income adjusted for price changes.

Real Interest Rate   Nominal interest rate minus inflation rate.

Real Wages   Nominal wages corrected for inflation.

Recession   A decline in real GDP for two consecutive quarters.

Recovery   Phase of business cycle during which real GDP increases from trough level to level of previous peak.

Regressive Tax   Falls more heavily on the poor than on the rich; for example, Social Security tax.

Rent   (See Economic Rent.)

Rent Control   Government-set price ceiling on rent.

Required Reserve Ratio   Percentage of deposits that must be held as vault cash and reserve deposits by all depository institutions.

Required Reserves   Minimum vault cash or reserves; held at the Federal Reserve District Bank.

Reserves   Vault cash and deposits of banks held by Federal Reserve district banks.

Resources   Land, labor, capital, and entrepreneurial ability used to produce goods and services.

Retained Earnings   Earnings that a corporation keeps for investment in plant and equipment or for other purposes, rather than distributed to shareholders.

Right-to-Work Laws   Under the Taft-Hartley Act, states are permitted to pass these laws, which prohibit the union shop. (Union membership cannot be made a condition of securing employment.)

Rule of Reason   Mere size is no offense. Market conduct rather than market share should determine whether antitrust laws have been violated.

s

Saving   Disposable income not spent for consumer goods; equal to disposable income minus personal consumption expenditures.

Saving Function   As income rises, saving rises, but not as quickly.

Say's Law   Supply creates its own demand.

Scarcity   The inability of an economy to generate enough goods and services to satisfy all human wants.

Seasonal Unemployment   Unemployment resulting from the seasonal pattern of work in certain industries, with workers regularly laid off during the slow season and rehired during the busy season.

Secondary Boycott   A boycott of products or a company that sells the products of a company that is being struck.

Sherman Act   The federal antitrust law enacted in 1890 that prohibited monopolization and conspiracies to restrain trade.

Shortage   The amount by which the quantity demanded of a product exceeds the quantity supplied at a particular (below-equilibrium) price.

Short Run   The length of time it takes all fixed costs to become variable costs.

Shut Down   Cessation of a firm's operations as output falls to zero.

Shut-Down Point   The low point on the firm's average variable cost curve. If price is below the shut-down point, the firm will shut down in the short run.

Socialism   An economic system in which the government owns most of the productive resources except labor; it usually involves the redistribution of income.

Social Security Tax   A tax paid equally by employee and employer, based on employee's wages. Most proceeds are used to pay Social Security retirement and Medicare benefits.

Sole Proprietorship   An unincorporated business firm owned by one person.

Specialization   Division of productive activities so that no one is self-sufficient.

Stagflation   A period of either recession or stagnation accompanied by inflation.

Stock   (See Corporate Stock.)

Strike   When a collective bargaining agreement cannot be reached, a union calls for a work stoppage to last until an agreement is reached.

Structural Unemployment   When people are out of work for a couple of years or longer.

Substitute Goods   Products or services that can be used in place of each other. When the price of one falls, the demand for the other falls, and conversely with an increase of price.

Substitution Effect   If the price of a resource, say labor, goes up, business firms tend to substitute capital or land for some of their now-expensive workers. Also, the substitution of more hours of work for leisure time as the wage rate rises.

Supply (s)   A schedule of quantities that people will sell at different prices.

Supply, Law of   When the price of a good is lowered, less of it is supplied; when the price is raised, more is supplied.

Supply-Side Economics   Main tenets: economic role of federal government is too large; high tax rates and government regulations hurt the incentives of individuals and business firms to produce goods and services.

Surplus   The amount by which the quantity supplied of a product exceeds the quantity demanded at a specific (above-equilibrium) price.

Surplus Value   A Marxian term: the amount by which the value of a worker's daily output exceeds the worker's daily wage.

t

Tariff   A tax on imported goods.

Terms of Trade   The ratio of exchange between an imported good and an exported good.

Time Deposit   A deposit in a financial institution that requires notice of withdrawal or must be left for some fixed period of time.

Total Cost   The sum of fixed and variable costs.

Total Revenue   The price of a good or service multiplied by the number of units sold.

Transactions Demand for Money   The demand for money by individuals and business firms to pay for day-to-day expenses.

Transfer Payment   Payment by one branch of government to another or to an individual. Largest transfer payment is Social Security.

Transmission Mechanism   The series of changes brought about by a change in monetary policy that ultimately changes the level of GDP.

u

Unanticipated Inflation   A rate of inflation that is either higher or lower than expected.

Underemployment   Failure to use our resources efficiently. A situation in which workers are employed in positions requiring less skill and education than they have or other resources are employed in their most productive use.

Underground Economy   Unreported or illegal production of goods and services that is not counted in GDP.

Unemployment   The total number of people over 16 who are ready, willing, and able to work, who have been unsuccessfully seeking employment.

Unemployment Rate   Number of unemployed divided by the labor force.

Union Shop   All employees must join the union, usually within 30 days after they are hired.

Utility   The satisfaction you derive from a good or service that you purchase. How much utility you derive is measured by how much you would be willing to pay.

v

Variable Costs   These vary with output. When output rises, variable costs rise; when output declines, variable costs fall.

Velocity (V)   The number of times per year each dollar in the money supply is spent.

Vertical Merger   The joining of two firms engaged in different parts of an industrial process, or the joining of a manufacturer and a retailer.

w

Wage   The price paid for the use or services of labor per unit of time.

Wage and Price Controls   Rules established by the government that either place a ceiling on wages and prices or limit their rate of increase.

Wealth   Anything that has value because it produces income or could produce income.

Workfare   A plan that requires welfare recipients to accept jobs or to enter training programs.

World Trade Organization (WTO)   The successor organization to GATT, which handles all trade disputes among member nations.

Index

a

A&P markets, 572–573, 610
ABC network, 615, 671
Abortion, 723
Absolute advantage, 749
Absolute concept of poverty, 717
Accounting profit, 507, 508
Accounting scandals, 616–627
Actual reserves, 333
Adams, Franklin Pierce, 237
Adaptive expectations hypothesis, 369
Adelphi Communications, 618
Adidas, 182
Adizes, Ichak, 557
Administered prices, 592
Advertising
    for brand loyalty, 444
    deceptive, 468
    and elasticity of demand, 443–444
    false, 444
    in Federal Trade Commission Act, 611
    monopolistic competition, 570–571
    purpose, 443–444
Aetna, 669
Affluent society, 24
AFL-CIO merger, 646
Africa
    AIDS epidemic, 402
    poorest countries, 401, 717
African Americans
    characteristics of ghettos, 729–730
    child poverty, 721
    employment discrimination, 27–28, 669, 727
    female-headed households, 731
    income, 713
    male joblessness, 727–728
    migration from ghetto, 722, 729
    poverty rate, 720
    slavery theory of poverty, 726–727
Aggregate demand
    in classical economics, 255–256
    exceeds aggregate supply, 266
    in Keynesian economics, 263
    in Keynesian policies, 267
    leading to inflation, 262
    and long-run aggregate supply, 257
    role in Keynesian economics, 360
    and taxes, 275
Aggregate expenditures model, 263–265
    consumption and saving functions, 264
    disposable income, 264

finding equilibrium GDP, 265
    investment sector, 264–265
Aggregate supply
    classical vs. Keynesian, 261
    exceeds aggregate demand, 267
    in Keynesian economics, 263
    in supply-side economics, 365
Aggregate supply curve
    long-run, 257–258
    ranges of, 262
    short-run, 258–259
Agricultural subsidies, 762, 763
Agriculture; *see also* Farm policy
    basic cash crops, 4
    in China, 74
    collective farms, 90
    Dust Bowl of 1930s, 8
    early 20th century, 6
    and GATT, 180
    Green Revolution, 402n
    household production, 205
    in late 20th century, 15–16
    in Malthusian theory, 402
    in 19th century, 2–4
    as perfect competition, 519
    Southern states, 3–4
    in Soviet Union, 73
AIDS epidemic, 402
AIG, 123, 618
Airbus Industrie, 613
Air fares, 616
Airline Deregulation Act of 1978, 616
Air pollution, 80–81
Alaska, 91
Alazar, Roberto, 371
Albertson's supermarkets, 443, 647
Aley, James, 552
Allen, Paul, 24, 715
Allis-Chalmers, 586–587
Alm, Richard, 236
Aluminum Company of America, 553
    antitrust case, 611–612
Amazon.com, 17, 25, 130, 160, 516, 611
American Airlines, 613
American Bankers Association, 317
American Basketball Association, 652
American Cancer Society, 416
American Communist Party, 589
American Economic Review, 416
American exceptionality, 786–788
American Express, 305, 323, 669
American Federation of Labor
    founding of, 643–644

merger with CIO, 646
    split in, 645–646
American Federation of State, County, and Municipal Employees, 648, 649
American Federation of Teachers, 648, 649
American Football League, 549, 652
American Jobs Creation Act of 2004, 163
American Motors, 584
American Sugar Refining Company, 608
American Tobacco Company, 549, 609
American Tobacco Trust, 607
    breakup of, 609
America Online, 25, 615, 619
America the Beautiful, 787
Ameritech, 619
Amoco, 609, 619
Amtrak, 163, 556
Anticipated inflation, 236–237
Antitrust
    Alcoa case, 611–612
    AT&T case, 612
    breakup of trusts, 549n, 609
    Clayton Act, 610
    and collusion, 589
    effectiveness, 617
    in Europe, 613–614
    Federal Trade Commission Act, 610–611
    in global marketplace, 618–619
    historical perspective, 607
    and labor unions, 650
    Microsoft case, 612–613
    modern era, 611–614
    partial breakdown of rule of reason, 611–612
    political background, 608
    relevant market argument, 612
    rule of reason, 609–610
    Sherman Act, 608–610
    60 percent rule, 612
    Standard Oil case, 609
AOL Time Warner, 612, 614, 669
Appleby twine binder, 4
Apple Computer, 25, 570
Arab oil embargo, 56, 584, 625
Arbitration, 655–656
Archer Daniels Midland, 588
ARCO, 609
Aristotle, 82, 303, 693
Armani, Giorgio, 661
Armco, 587
Army Corps of Engineers, 83
Arnaz, Desi, 27

Arnett, Ramona E. F., 507
Arnold, Benedict, 139
Arnott, Richard, 57
Arthur Andersen, 616, 617
Ashley, H., 667n
Ashley, William J., 153n
Asian Americans
    child poverty, 721
    income, 713
    poverty rate, 720
Assembly line, 6
AT&T, 607, 619
    antitrust case, 612
    breakup of, 616
AT&T Broadband, 619
Atchison, Topeka, and Santa Fe, 81
Atlanta Federal Reserve District Bank,
    342
Atlantic Monthly, 79
Atlantic Richfield, 609
Audi, 583
Australia, benefit of farm subsidies,
    763
Automated teller machines, 315, 320
Automatic stabilizers, 282–285, 286
    corporate profits tax, 284–285
    credit availability, 284
    made more effective, 286
    origin and purpose, 282
    payroll tax, 283–284
    personal income tax, 283–284
    personal saving, 284
    to prevent recessions, 282
    transfer payments, 285
    unemployment compensation, 284
Automobile industry
    bureaucracy in, 491
    concentration ratios, 583
    development of, 6
    in Japan, 759
    loss of monopoly in U.S., 553
    as oligopoly, 584
    post-World War I, 7
    post-World War II, 11–12
    unionized, 647
Autonomous consumption, 104–107
Average cost, 479–491
    and diseconomies of scale, 490–491
    and economies of scale, 489–490
    fixed costs, 480
    graphing, 482–486
    and law of diminishing returns,
        487–488
    summary on, 491–492
    total cost, 481
    U-shaped cost curves, 485–486
    variable costs, 480
Average fixed cost, 480
    contrasted with fixed cost, 483
    graphing, 482–485
Average propensity to consume, 99, 100,
    105
    versus propensity to save, 97–98
Average propensity to save, 98–100

Average tax rate, 151, 152
Average total cost, 481
    of cartels, 584
    declining for drugs, 489
    graphing, 482–485
    in marginal analysis, 509–514
    in perfect competition, 521–523,
        525
    and plant size, 497–498
    and stay-in-business decision, 495,
        496
Average total cost curve
    and economies of scale, 489
    in loss calculation, 512–513
    monopolistic competition, 566–567
    of monopoly, 543
    monopoly vs. perfect competition,
        544–545
    of oligopoly, 581
    perfect competition, 521–527, 601
Average variable cost, 480
    graphing, 482–485
    in loss calculation, 512–513
    and stay-in-business decision, 495,
        496
Average workweek/workyear, 390–391
Avis, 669
Avon Products, 668
AZT drug, 441

b

Baby-boom generation, 1, 12
    and changes in demand, 416
    and future of Social Security, 734
    retirement, 403
Backstreet Boys, 206
Back to the Future, 2
Bagehot, Walter, 715
Balanced budget, 288, 290
Balance of payments
    capital account, 770–772
    current account, 770–772
    current account deficit, 771–772, 773,
        786
    definition, 770
    in international finance, 770–772
    net transfers, 771
    of U.S. in 2005, 770
    at zero, 771
Balance of payments deficits, 770–772
    role of drug money, 784
Balance of trade
    with Canada and Mexico, 178
    causes of imbalance, 756–758
    with gold standard, 774
    negative, 173
    positive, 173
    of U.S. 1970–2005, 742–743
    of U.S. in 2005, 175
Baltimore & Ohio, 81
Banca d'Italia, 332
Banco Boliviano Americano, 241n

Bank America, 619
Bank charters, 320–321
Banking Act of 1999, 348–349
Bank of America, 305, 316, 318, 319,
    320, 338
Bank of Canada, 332
Bank of England, 329, 332
Bank of France, 329
Bank of Japan, 310, 332
Bank One Corporation, 619
Bank panics, 321, 329–330
Bankrate.com, 702
Bank regulation
    ATM wars, 320
    bank charters, 320–321
    Banking Act of 1999, 348–349
    branch vs. unit banking, 310–320
    Check Clearing Act of 2004, 337
    deregulation act of 1980, 347–348
    Federal Deposit Insurance
        Corporation, 321
    interstate banking, 321
    savings and loan debacle, 321–322
    Wal-Mart bank proposal, 322–323
Banks and banking
    ATM use, 320
    birth of modern banking, 313
    borrowing excess reserves, 343
    branch vs. unit banking, 319–320
    business loans, 130
    charters, 320–321
    check clearing, 336–338
    commercial banks, 314–315
    consolidation, 315
    credit unions, 315
    demand deposits, 303–304
    deposit expansion, 335–336
    Depository Institutions Deregulation
        and Monetary Control Act of
        1980, 347–348
    electronic funds transfer, 304, 337
    failures in Great Depression, 8,
        321
    fewer institutions since 1980, 348
    financial intermediaries, 317–318
    first law of banking, 347
    foreign banks in U.S., 315
    under Glass-Steagall Act, 348
    history of, 311–313
    Industrial Loan Company, 323
    interstate, 321
    investment banks, 348n
    Islamic, 693
    largest banks, 315, 316
    legal reserve requirement,
        332–334
    lending by, 315–316
    limits to deposit creation, 319
    main aims of, 335
    modern, 313–318
    money creation, 318–319
    money destruction, 319
    in mortgage market, 317–318
    mutual savings banks, 315

number of bank branches, 320
overdraft privileges, 323
primary and secondary reserves, 334–335
prime rate, 312, 589
reserve requirement changes, 344
reserves, 314
savings and loan associations, 315
welfare banks, 317
Barclays, 316
Barnes & Noble, 548, 611
Barnum, P. T., 302
Barrett, Craig R., 392
Barriers to entry
control of essential resources, 549
economies of being established, 551–552
economies of scale, 549–550
lacking in perfect competition, 518
legal
government franchises, 551
licensing, 550
overcoming, 553
patents, 550–551
limits to, 553
lowered by Internet, 530n
required scale for innovation, 551
and success in collusion, 589
Barter, 205–206
versus money, 302–303
Baseball Hall of Fame, 671
Base year, 230, 234
BASF AG, 588
Bastiat, Frédéric, 78, 147, 755
Bates, Katherine Lee, 17
Bauer, Gary, 662
Baumol, William, 398
Baumol's Disease, 398, 404
Bayer AG, 553
Bayer aspirin, 443
Beach Boys, 764
Becker, Gary, 209n, 440
Behavioral economists, 371
Belgium, comparative advantage, 748
Bell, Alexander Graham, 25, 699
Bell, Frederick W., 416
Bell Atlantic, 619
Bell Laboratories, 612
BellSouth, 555, 619
Bell telephone companies, 555, 616
Benedict Arnold companies, 139
Beneficial Finance, 318, 694
Benefits of production, 209
Bentham, Jeremy, 458, 677
Bernanke, Ben, 331, 772
Berner, Richard, 399
Berners-Lee, Tim, 25
Bernstein, Aaron, 663, 752
Bethlehem Steel, 587
Betrayal of Work (Schulman), 676
Bhatia, Sabeer, 394
Bierce, Ambrose, 122
Big Mac index, 781

Bigness
and antitrust policy, 609
benefits, 558
and corporate hierarchy, 556
disadvantages, 556
economic case against, 558
rule of reason doctrine, 610
and size of Wal-Mart, 558, 559–560
trend toward, 617–619
Bilateral monopoly, 651–652
Billings, Josh, 109
Bill paying, 304
by the poor, 317
Birthrate, 12
Birthrate in less developed countries, 401
Black male joblessness, 727–728
Blackout of 2003, 468
Blank, Paul, 647
Blowin' in the Wind, 182
Blue laws, 27
Blue states, 647n
BMW, 583
Board of Governors of Federal Reserve
changing reserve requirements, 344
description, 330–331
on FOMC, 340, 341
independence, 332
membership, 380
Boeing Company, 613, 669
Bolivia, 241
Bondholders, 215
Bond prices, 340
Bonds, 215
Bonner, Bill, 787
Bono, 718
Boo, Katherine, 722
Borman, Frank, 698
Borrowing, crowding-out effect, 291
Boston and Maine Railroad, 81
Bottled water, 718
Bowie, David, 614
Boys of Summer (Kahn), 671
Bradford, William, 74
Brain drain, 394
Branch banking, 319–320
Brand loyalty, 444
Branson, Richard, 490
Bread-and-butter unionism, 644
Break-even point, 495–496, 513, 515–516, 529
graphing, 511, 512
in perfect competition, 516–517
and plant size, 497
Bretton Woods system, 774–775
Bridge to nowhere, 91
Bristol-Myers Squibb, 443
British Empire, 18
British Petroleum, 124, 609, 619
British pound, 775, 778
Brokaw, Tom, 4
Brooklyn Dodgers, 27, 28, 671
Brooklyn Jewish Hospital, 518
Brooks, David, 680
Bruce, Laura, 702

Buchanan, James, 292
Budget
balanced, 288, 290
preparation chronology, 147
as stabilization tool, 163
Budget deficits, 18
and balanced budgets, 290
and Bush fiscal policy, 295
crowding-in effect, 291–292
crowding-out effect, 290–292
definition, 288
disadvantages, 289–290
in early Depression, 8
in fighting inflation, 378
in fighting recession, 378
fiscal years 1970 to 2003, 289
foreign financing of, 138, 290, 293–294, 785–786
history of, 288–290
in Keynesian economics, 360
Keynesian-monetarist debate, 290–292
as limit on policy, 381
national comparisons, 290
perpetuity of, 295–296
reduced in 1990s, 17
since terrorist attack, 389
of states, 161
Budget surplus
definition, 288
history of, 288–290
Monetarist view, 364
national comparisons, 290
Buffett, Warren, 24, 715
Bureaucracy, 490–491, 557
Bureau of Engraving, 330n
Bureau of Labor Statistics, 108, 223, 225, 230, 234–235
Burger, Anna, 649
Burger King, 74, 444, 570, 590
Burke, Bob, 725
Bush, Barbara, 720
Bush, George H. W., 12, 15, 287, 288, 295, 745, 751
Bush, George W., 16, 29, 83, 84, 147, 150, 159, 178, 242, 243, 286, 287, 291, 292, 295, 331, 370–371, 372, 394, 452, 616, 653, 669, 724, 741, 745, 757, 762–763
Bush administration (2nd), 12, 146, 161, 289, 760
Business cycle, 217–223
automatic stabilizers and, 282–285, 286
in behavioral economics, 371
conventional three-phase cycle, 219–220
definition, 217–218
endogenous theories, 220–221
exogenous theories, 221
external demand shock theory, 221
forecasting, 221–223
hypothetical, 220, 285
innovation theory, 220
inventory cycle theory, 221

Business cycle—*Cont.*
  leading economic indicators, 222
  Monetarist view, 362–363
  monetary theory, 221
  overinvestment theory, 221
  peak, 218
  psychological theory, 220–221
  recovery, 219
  trough, 218
  turning points, 218–219
  underconsumption theory, 221
  war theory, 221
Business Cycle Data Committee,
    218–219
Business loans, 130
Business sector; *see also* Market structure
  business population, 126, 127
  in circular flow model, 76–77
  computerization, 519
  corporations
    advantages, 122
    capitalization and control,
        125–126
    corporate income tax, 123
    definition, 122
    disadvantages, 124
    double taxation, 122n
    formation of, 124
    low personal income tax, 122
    in Middle East, 126–127
    share of total sales, 127
    small, 123
    stocks and bonds, 125
    ten largest in sales, 123, 134
    widely held, 125
  harm from inflation, 236
  hybrid business forms, 124
  limited liability company, 124
  limited partnerships, 124
  partnerships, 122
  proprietorships, 121–122
  saving by, 389
  small business, 571
Business-to-business e-commerce, 395
BusinessWeek, 113, 180, 343, 519, 571,
    617, 651, 663, 752
Buy America campaign, 763–764

C

Cadillac, 6
Cadillac Seville, 541
CAFTA; *see* Central American–
    Dominican Republic Free Trade
    Agreement
California marijuana production, 206
Camel cigarettes, 444
Canada
  benefit of farm subsidies, 763
  comparative advantage, 748
  and NAFTA, 177–178
Canadian dollar, 778
Cannan, Edwin, 745n

Canon, 553
Canseco, Jose, 670
Capacity utilization rate, 27, 133, 347
Capital
  building capital, 132
  and economic growth, 37
  as economic resource, 24–25
  economic role, 84–85
  for less developed countries, 403
  nature of, 692
  origin of, 85–86
  source of, 85
  and standard of living, 86
Capital account, 770–772
Capital formation, 113, 138
Capital gains, 712
Capital gains tax, 113
  rate lowered in 2003, 159
Capital goods vs. consumer goods,
    85
Capital-intensive production, 626
Capitalism, 75, 86–87
Capitalistic democracies, 87
Capitalization, 125–126
Capital spending, 129, 390
Capital stock, 512–513, 692
Carlyle, Thomas, 425
Carnegie, Andrew, 5, 25, 607
Carpenters and Joiners Union, 649
Cartels, 584–586
  trusts as, 608
Carter, Jimmy, 14, 15, 242, 615, 616
Carvel's ice cream, 552
Cashless society, 337
Cassel, Gustav, 695
CBS network, 671
Census Bureau, 79, 229
Centers for Disease Control, 158
Central American–Dominican Republic
    Free Trade Agreement, 179
Central planning, 71–72
Change to Win coalition, 649
Charter school movement, 393
Check clearing, 336–338
Check Clearing Act of 2004, 337
Checking accounts/deposits, 303–304
  legal reserve requirements, 333
  overdraft privileges, 323
Checkmate, 702
Checks, 303
Chemical industry decline, 758
Chenault, Kenneth, 669
Chevron, 609
ChevronTexaco, 123, 609
Chicago Board of Trade, 80
Chicago Coalition for the Homeless,
    721
Chicago Cubs, 548
Chicago Tribune, 163
Chief executive officers
  compensation, 557, 672
  women, 668
Child income tax credit, 159
Child labor, 27

Child poverty
  and crime, 722, 723
  locus of, 722
  national comparisons, 722
  by race, 721
China
  and American consumer spending,
      114–115
  codependent relationship with U.S.,
      785–786
  collective farms, 74
  currency policy, 776
  economic transformation, 89–90
  licensing agreements, 762
  multinational corporations in, 760
  pirated products, 760
  purchase of U.S. securities, 349
  technology transfer to, 762
  trade deficit in Asia, 760
  U.S. trade deficit with, 760–762
  U.S. trade with, 761–762
China-bashing, 764
Chinese Exclusion Act, 394n
Chinese yuan, 776, 777–780
Choices, 458
Christiana Securities, 610
Chrysler Corporation, 491, 584, 653
Churchill, Winston, 88, 113
Ciba-Geigy, 611
Cigarette industry cartel, 588
Cigarettes
  price level and demand, 440
  tax on, 157, 158, 440
$C+I+G+X_n$ line, 176, 190
Cinemax, 490
Circular flow diagram, 76–77, 192
Cisco Systems, 29, 130
Citibank, 318, 319, 338, 346, 349
Citicorp, 619
Cities
  effect of suburbanization, 14
  gentrification, 721
Citigroup, 123, 315, 316, 349
Civil Aeronautics Board, 616
Civilian Conservation Corps, 286
Civil rights movement, 667, 716, 730
Civil War
  economic conflicts leading to, 3
  and tariff policy, 744
Clancy, Tom, 661
Clary, John, 392
Classical economic system, 251–263
  equilibrium
    aggregate demand curve, 255–256
    foreign purchases effect, 256
    interest rate effect, 256
    long-run aggregate supply curve,
        257–258
    real balance effect, 256
    short-run aggregate supply curve,
        258–259
  flexible wages and prices, 359
  interest rate mechanism, 359
  Keynesian critique, 260–263

versus Keynesian policies, 267
quantity theory of money, 359
recessions, 358
role of government, 359–360
saving, 359
Say's law, 251–253, 358
supply and demand, 253–254
wages and prices in, 253–254, 260
Class theory of employment, 663
Clayton Antitrust Act, 610
Clean Air Act Amendments, 80
Clean Air Act of 1972, 80
Clearing House Interbank Payments
    System, 337
Cleveland, Grover, 650
Cline, William R., 782, 783
Clinton, Bill, 12, 180, 242, 243, 287,
    288, 295, 732, 745
Clinton administration, 614
Closed shop, 645
CNN/Money, 700
Coca-Cola Company, 467, 551, 552,
    553, 575
Coke, 549
Colbert, Jean-Baptiste, 151
Coleman, John S., 150
Collective bargaining, 652–656
    agreements, 654
    cost-of-living adjustments, 237, 653
    grievance procedures, 654
    health issues in, 396–397
    job security and seniority, 654
    mediation and arbitration, 655–656
    pattern-setting wage increases, 654
    and productivity increases, 653
    and strikes, 654–655
    strikes, lockouts, and givebacks,
        652–654
    wage and hour issues, 654
    in Wagner Act, 644
Collective farms, 90
Collective ownership failure, 74
College costs, 508
College graduates
    earnings potential, 663, 716
    and family background, 679–680
    national comparisons, 392–393
College parking, 60
College textbook publishers, 557, 570
    cutthroat competition, 593
Collusion
    covert, 586–587
    in Japan, 588
    likelihood of success, 589
    open, 586
    price leadership, 587–589
Columbia Pictures, 614
Comcast, 619
Command-and-control regulations, 80
Commercial banks, 314–315
    deregulation of, 348
Common stock, 125
Communications, 490
Communication Workers of America, 648

Communism
    Chinese transformation of, 89–90
    collapse of, 89
    end of, 1
    nature of, 87–88
Communist Manifesto
    (Marx & Engels), 87
Company town, 651
Comparative advantage
    versus absolute advantage, 749
    Canada vs. Belgium, 748
    gains from trade, 748
    law of, 749
    and opportunity cost, 746–748
Compensation
    of CEOs, 672
    CEOs vs. employees, 557
Competition; *see also* Market structure
    in Clayton Act, 610
    cutthroat, 589–592, 593
    definition, 74–75
    degrees of, 592
    imperfect, 542–544
    in international trade, 742
    perfect, 516–531
    perfect vs. imperfect, 602–603,
        631–632
    trend toward bigness, 617–619
Complementary factors of production,
    633–634
Computerization, 17, 400, 519
Computer literacy, 395
Computer software industry, 29, 489
Concentration ratios
    measure of oligopoly, 582–583
    in selected industries, 582
    shortcomings, 583
Conference Board, 222
Confucius, 24
Conglomerate mergers, 615
Congressional Budget Office, 147
Congress of Industrial Organizations
    founding of, 645
    merger with AFL, 646
    organizing efforts, 646
Connally, John, 764
ConocoPhillips, 123
Conservatives
    on minimum wage, 677–678
    on solutions to poverty, 731
    on unemployment rate, 228
    view of poverty, 728–730
    view of unemployment, 225
Conspicuous consumption, 110
Consumer behavior, 459–469
    consumer surplus, 464–467
    in postwar Japan, 5
    and price gougers, 468
    and product differentiation, 569
    and utility
        calculating utility, 462
        definition, 460
        formula, 463
        limitations of applications, 464

        marginal utility, 460–461, 468–469
        maximizing utility, 461–463
        total utility, 461
        water–diamond paradox, 463
Consumer expectations, 110
Consumer Expenditures Survey, 718
Consumer finance companies, 318
Consumer goods
    versus capital goods, 85
    spending on, 390
Consumer loans, 693–695
Consumer price index
    annual percentage change 1945 to
        2005, 230
    calculating changes in, 230–231
    construction of, 234–236
    definition, 230
    hypothetical annual rate, 233
    measure of cost of living, 236
    from 1915 to 2002, 238
    and real minimum wage, 678
    and wage rates, 673–674
Consumers
    American, 114–115
    cost of tariffs and quotas, 754
    feedback from, 557
    generational changes, 111–112
    in Keynesian economics, 263
    living beyond their means, 785
    patriotic buying, 763–764
    and perfect competition, 529
    with perfect knowledge, 530
    stock of durable goods, 110
    stock of liquid assets, 109–110
Consumer spending
    benefits to importers, 114–115
    and disposable income, 96–97
    kinds of purchases, 107–108
    and poverty, 718
    promoted by government, 113
    versus saving, 111–113
Consumer surplus, 464–467
    calculating, 465–466
    definition, 464
    demand schedules, 466
    finding, 467
    and marginal utility, 465
    and price discrimination, 574
Consumption
    autonomous, 104–107
    average propensity to consume,
        97–98, 99, 100
    categories of, 107–108
    determinants of
        conspicuous consumption, 110
        consumer expectations, 110–111
        credit availability, 109
        disposable income, 108–111
        permanent income hypothesis, 111
        stock of durable goods, 110
        stock of liquid assets, 109–110
    and disposable income, 97–98, 99
    effect of excise taxes, 157–158
    graphing, 105

Consumption—*Cont.*
  induced, 106–107
  versus investment, 132
  marginal propensity to consume, 100
  national comparisons, 100
  and paradox of thrift, 283
  and saving function, 104
  tastes and preferences, 416
Consumption function, 96–97
  and autonomous consumption, 106
  and investment, 136–137
  in Keynesian economics, 264
Consumption junkies, 756, 785
Continental Airlines, 613
Continental Baking Company, 38
Continental Oil, 609
Contractionary monetary policy, 346
Contrived scarcity, 700
Control in corporations, 125–126
Cook, Philip, 672
Coolidge, Calvin, 7, 226, 252
Cooling-off period, 645, 653
Copyright infringement, 206
Corporate concentration, 607
Corporate hierarchy, 557
Corporate income tax, 123, 124
  as automatic stabilizer, 284–285
  as direct tax, 153
Corporate misconduct, 616–618
Corporate saving, 114
Corporate welfare, 163
Corporations
  advantages, 122–123
  bureaucracy in, 557
  capitalization and control, 125–126
  corporate income tax, 123
  definition, 122
  disadvantages, 123
  double taxation, 122n
  and early unionism, 644
  economic power of, 650–652
  formation of, 124
  hierarchy of authority, 491
  hollow, 757
  internal fund-raising, 130
  low personal income tax, 122
  in Middle East, 126–127
  percentage of firms and sales, 127
  profits in 2002, 698
  small, 123
  stocks and bonds, 125
  top ten in sales, 123, 124
  widely held, 125
Corvette, 569
Cost(s)
  average
    fixed costs, 480
    graphing, 482–486
    law of diminishing returns, 487–488
    operate decision, 492–494
    and production function, 487–488
    shut-down decision, 492–494
    summary on, 491–492

  total cost, 481
  U-shaped cost curves, 485–486
  variable costs, 480
break-even point, 495–496, 511, 512, 513, 515
of bureaucracy, 490–491
concept of margin, 477
diminishing marginal output, 487–488
diseconomies of scale, 32–33, 490–491
of economic activity, 210
economies of scale, 32–33, 489–490
for entertainment, 490
explicit, 508, 698
external, 78–79
fixed costs, 476
  average, 480
  contrasted with average fixed cost, 483
  graphing, 477, 482–486
  spreading, 489
going-out-of-business decision, 494–497
implicit, 507, 508, 698
law of increasing costs, 32–33
long run, 479
marginal cost, 476–478, 627
in natural monopoly, 554
and negative returns, 487–488
Parkinson's law, 491
plant size, 497–498
and prices, 241
private, 78
of production, 208–209, 420
and proportional return to scale, 491
and quantity discounts, 489
and sales ad total revenue, 475
short run, 479
shut-down point, 495–496, 511, 512, 513, 515
stay-in-business decision, 494–497
sunk costs, 476
total cost, 476
  average, 481
  graphing, 477, 482–486
  variable costs, 476
    average, 480
    graphing, 477, 482–486
of weddings, 498n
Costco, 590
Cost curves
  graphing, 482–486
  in loss calculation, 512–513
  of monopoly, 542–544
  U-shaped, 485–486
Cost of living, decline in, 236
Cost-of-living adjustments, 237
Cost-push inflation, 239–240
Cost schedule, competitive oligopolist, 591
Cotton gin, 4
Council of Economic Advisors, 180
Counterfeit products, 760
Countryside Credit, 317

Covert collusion, 586–587
Cox, W. Michael, 236
Craft unions, 645
Credit Agricol, 316
Credit availability
  as automatic stabilizer, 284
  and demand for money, 309
  determinant of consumption, 109
Credit cards, 284, 304
  compared to money, 305
Credit crunch, 12, 58, 346
Creditors, effect of inflation, 236
Credit rationing, 346
Credit unions, 304, 315
Creeping inflation, 241
Crime
  corporate misconduct, 616–617, 618
  drug money, 784
  illegal products, 206
  and poverty, 393, 722, 723
Crisonino, Ginny, 494
Crowding-in effect, 290–292
Crowding-out effect, 290–292, 347n
  Monetarist view, 364
Cultural Revolution, 90
Culture of poverty, 722, 728
Currency
  in circulation, 304–306
  elastic, 330
  issuance of, 331
Currency appreciation, 776
Currency depreciation, 776
Currency devaluation, 774–775
Current account, 770–772, 785
Current account deficit, 786
  national comparisons, 773
  of United States, 771–772
Current account surplus, 772
Customer service departments, 571
Customization, 570
Cutright, P., 728n
Cutthroat competition, 589–592, 593
Cyberspace, 411
Cyclical unemployment, 228

d

DaimlerChrysler, 124, 584, 647
Dango, 587, 588
Darity, William A., Jr., 727
Das Kapital (Marx), 84, 85, 132
Daughters of the American Revolution, 393
Day, Sherrie, 443
Dayan, Moshe, 291
DeBeers Diamond Company, 541, 549, 700
Debit cards, 304, 305, 320
Debtors, effect of inflation, 236
Deceptive advertising, 468
Decision lag, 379, 380, 381
Deere, John, 4

Defense spending, 147
  effect on productivity, 400
  impact on productivity, 398
  by less developed countries, 403
  and trade deficits, 756
Deflation, 231–233, 360
Deflationary gap, 276–277
  and multiplier, 281–282
  in rational expectations theory, 368
Deinstitutionalization, 721
De Kooning, Willem, 732
Dell, Michael, 715
Dell Computer, 130, 570, 715
Del Monte Corporation, 402n
Delta Air Lines, 613
Demand; *see also* Elasticity of demand;
    Labor demand; Supply and
    demand
  causes of changes in
    changes in tastes/preferences, 416
    income changes, 415
    population changes, 416
    price changes, 415–416
    price expectations, 416
    problems, 412–414
  changes in, 411–414
    decrease, 412
    increase, 411–412
  and consumer surplus, 466
  definition, 47–48, 409, 413
  derived, 625–626
  final, 625
  for final product, 633
  individual and market, 410–411
  inelastic, 436–437
  for land, 688–689
  law of demand, 409–410, 422,
    665–666
  long-run response to increase in,
    448–449
  and marginal utility, 460–461
  and prices, 47–48
  shifts in, 51–55
  short-run response to increase in,
    448
  unit-elastic, 441
Demand-based price discrimination, 574
Demand curve, 48
  graphing, 421–423, 506
  imperfect competition, 631–632
  inelastic, 446
  kinked, 589–590
  for labor, 665–666
  for land, 689
  in monopolistic competition, 566
  for monopoly, 542–544
  monopoly vs. monopolistic
    competition, 569
  in perfect competition, 519–527
    long run, 522–527
    short run, 520–522
  perfectly elastic, 436–437
  perfectly inelastic, 437
  relative elasticity, 437–438

  shifts in, 51–55
  straight line, 438, 439
Demand deposits, 303–304
Demand for money, 306–310
  and credit availability, 309
  effect on interest rates, 310–311
  and income, 308
  and inflation, 308
  and interest rates, 308–309
  Keynesian motives, 307
  and liquidity trap, 310
  precautionary motive, 307, 309
  and price level, 307–308
  speculative motive, 307, 309
  and supply of money, 311
  total, 310
  transactions motive, 307, 308–309
Demand-pull inflation, 238–239, 262
Demand schedule
  competitive oligopolist, 591
  for money, 309–310
Democracy, 86
Democratic Party, 278, 610, 647n, 677
Deng Xiaoping, 90
Denison, Edward S., 387
Denziger, Sheldon, 731n
Department of Agriculture, 55, 718
Department of Commerce, 207
Department of Health and Human
    Services, 721
Department of Homeland Security,
    145, 161
Department of Justice, 577, 584, 612,
    614, 617
Department of Labor, 227, 230, 387–388
  Consumer Expenditures Survey, 718
Deposit creation limits, 319
Deposit expansion, 335–336
Deposit expansion multiplier, 335–336
  modifications of, 337
Depository Institutions Deregulation and
    Monetary Control Act of 1980,
    314, 347–348
Depreciation, 131–132
  and Gross Domestic Product, 192–193
  negative, 194n
Depreciation allowance, 130, 389
Depression, 220, 262
Deregulation, 615–616
  of banking, 314, 348
  record since 1970s, 616
  and start of new economy, 17
Derived demand
  and changes in final demand, 625–626
  definition, 625
  for land, 688–689
Dertouzos, Michael L., 759n
Desai, Ashok, 749
Deuteronomy, 693, 717
Deutsche Bundesbank, 332
Developing nations, 86
DeVito, Harriet, 519
Digital publishing houses, 570
Diller, Barry, 672

Diminishing marginal output, 487–488
Diminishing marginal utility, 460, 463
Diminishing returns, 32, 33, 487–488
Direct taxes, 153
Dirksen, Everett M., 288
Disasters, 468
Discounting, 343
Discount rate, 342–344
Discount stores, 234
Discouraged workers, 223, 225, 720
Discovery card, 323
Diseconomies of scale, 32–33, 490–491
  and plant size, 497–498
Disequilibrium
  aggregate demand exceeds aggregate
    supply, 267
  aggregate supply exceeds aggregate
    demand, 267
  and attainment of equilibrium, 267
Disinflation, 233
Displaced workers, 753
Disposable income
  autonomous vs. induced consumption,
    104–107
  and average propensity to consume,
    98–100
  and consumption function, 96–97, 103
  determinant of consumption, 109
  in Great Depression, 360
  and investment, 136–137, 138
  in Keynesian economics, 264–265
  and marginal propensity to consume,
    100
  and marginal propensity to save, 101
  saving as percentage of, 97
  and saving function, 104
Disposable workers, 663
Distribution system, 72
Dividends, taxation of, 159
Division of labor, 6
Dodge Colt, 757
Dole Foods, 402n
Dollar Tree, 519
Domhoff, G. William, 557
Donahue, John, 721
Donne, John, 763
Dot-com crash, 18
Double taxation, 122n
Dow Chemical, 758
Downsizing, 229
Drug money, 784
Drugs, average total cost, 489
Drugs (illegal), 393
Dual labor market, 662–664
Dubner, Stephen L., 530n, 722, 723
Dugger, Celia W., 726n
Dumont television, 209
Dunne, Finley Peter, 730
DuPont Corporation, 5, 609, 610, 758
  antitrust case, 612
Durable goods, 107–109, 110
Dust Bowl of 1930s, 8
Dylan, Bob, 28, 182
Dynergy, 618

e

Earned income tax credit, 725–726
Earnings, 111
    differences, 716
    and education, 662, 663
eBay, 17, 25, 337, 411, 519, 530n
Ebbers, Bernard, 618
E-commerce, 234, 395
Economic behaviorists, 371
Economic expansion, 219–220
Economic fluctuations
    automatic stabilizers and, 282–285,
        286
    business cycle forecasting,
        221–223
    business cycles, 217–220
    business cycle theories, 220–221
    inflation, 229–242
    and misery index, 242
    unemployment, 223–229
Economic growth
    and capital spending, 390
    collapse in Great Depression, 7–10
    components, 35–37
    and deregulation, 615–616
    and exchange rates, 776
    factors affecting rate of
        declining school quality, 391–393
        environmental protection, 398
        immigration restrictions, 393–394
        investment rate, 389–390
        labor force changes, 390–393
        military spending, 398
        permanent underclass, 393
        saving rate, 388–389
        special interest groups, 499
        terrorist attack, 398–399
        workweek/workyear, 390–391
    and future health care costs, 403–404
    growth in 20th century, 386
    and health care costs, 396–398
    in Industrial Revolution, 385–386
    from innovation, 699
    in less developed countries, 401–403
    Malthusian theory, 401, 402
    mass consumption, 6, 7
    mass production, 6, 7
    Monetarist view, 362–363
    new economy of 1990s, 16–17
    in 19th century, 2–6
    in Reagan years, 15
    record of productivity growth,
        387–394
    shift to service economy, 396–398
    and stagflation, 14–15
    summary on, 399–401
    and technological change, 394–396
    and trade imbalance, 757–758
    in 20th century, 6–17
    in USSR, 89
    Western vs. Middle East, 126–127
    during World War II and after,
        10–14

Economic nationalism, 763–764
Economic policy; *see also* Fiscal policy;
        Monetary policy
    budget deficits as limit on, 381
    fighting inflation, 378
    fighting inflationary recessions,
        378–379
    fighting recessions, 377–378
    fiscal and monetary lags, 379–381
    goals of, 239, 380
    Keynesian prescriptions, 267–268
    limits of, 381
    major disagreements on, 370
    policy dilemmas, 378
    in rational expectations theory,
        368–370
    unmet goals, 276
Economic problem, 24, 26
Economic profit, 507, 508, 698
    in perfect competition, 530
    zero, 526–527
Economic regulation, 164
Economic rent, 670–672, 690–691
Economic Report of the President,
        177, 400
Economic resources, 24–25, 76
Economics; *see also* Economic theory
    of bigness, 558
    central fact of, 24–26
    circular flow model, 76–77
    definition, 24, 62, 514
    as dismal science, 402
    production and distribution, 72
Economic stimulus, 286–287, 290–292
Economic theory
    behavioral economists, 371
    capital, 84–86
    capitalism, 86–87
    Chinese transformation, 89–90
    circular flow model, 76–77
    classical economics, 251–259,
        358–360
    Communism, 87–88
    competition, 74–75
    equation of exchange, 355–356
    equity and efficiency, 75–76
    fall of Communism, 89
    fascism, 88
    interest rate mechanism, 359
    invisible hand, 73–74
    Keynesian critique of classical
        theories, 260–263
    Keynesian economics, 15, 263–266,
        360–361
    Monetarist school, 361–365
    new classical economics, 367
    political pressures, 91
    presidents and, 372
    price mechanism, 74
    quantity theory of money, 357–358
    rational expectations theory, 367–370
    socialism, 88–89
    supply-side economics, 15, 365–367
    trust, 75

    in 21st century
        behavioral economics, 371
        supply-side revival, 370–371
        Weidenbaum's view, 371
Economies of scale, 32–33
    in banking, 315
    in communications, 490
    and costs, 489–490
    versus diseconomies of scale,
        490–491
    in entertainment, 490
    and limits of monopoly power, 553
    in monopoly, 549–550
    in natural monopoly, 553–556
    and plant size, 497–498
    quantity discounts, 489
Economist, 349, 616, 776, 781,
        783, 785
Economists
    criticisms of monopolistic
        competition, 575
    on free trade, 755
    Keynes on, 355
    opposition to usury laws, 693–695
    Shaw on, 355
Economy/Economies
    automatic stabilizers for, 286
    efficient, 35
    government role, 77–78, 145–146,
        162–165
    private vs. public sector, 71
    production and distribution, 72
    reliance on consumers, 114–115
    self-sufficiency in, 173
    specialization and exchange in,
        172–173
    stabilization policies, 163–164
    trillion-dollar, 203
    underground, 206–207
Edgar Thomson steel works, 5
Edin, Kathryn, 732
Edison, Thomas A., 25, 302, 699
Education
    and earnings, 662, 663
    expenditures, 148, 160
    foreign students in U.S., 175
    inadequate human capital, 728
    and labor market, 679–680
Educational system
    charter school movement, 393
    decline in quality, 391–393
    in Europe, 392
    and functional illiteracy, 228
    as government failure, 83
    Leave No Child Behind law, 757
    school vouchers, 393
    talent search, 392
    and technological advance, 395
    and trade imbalance, 756–757
Education gap, 679–680
Efficiency, 75–76, 514–516
    and income distribution, 714–715
    and monopolistic competition,
        575–576

in perfect competition, 516–517, 529–530
productive, 345
and profit maximization, 515–516
of tariffs and quotas, 754
in types of competition, 603
Ehrenreich, Barbara, 663, 676, 731n
80-day cooling-off period, 645, 653
Einstein, Albert, 82
Eisenhower, Dwight D., 13, 233
Elastic currency, 330
Elasticities
formula, 434
meaning of, 435–440
monopoly vs. monopolistic competition, 569
perfect, 436–437
relative, 437–438, 442
unit, 438, 439
Elasticity of demand
and advertising, 443–444
and availability of substitutes, 442
for cigarettes, 440
definition, 433
determinants of degree of, 440–443
for food, 453
formula, 434
for gasoline, 441
and income, 442
meaning of, 435–440
measuring, 433–435
necessities vs. luxuries, 442
for oil, 439, 452
and product use, 442–443
in short- or long-run, 448–449
and tax incidence, 449–452
and time, 442
and total revenue, 445–446
Elasticity of supply, 433
meaning of, 446–447
and tax incidence, 449–452
over time
long run, 448–449
market period, 447–448
short run, 448
Electric power production, 7
Electric utilities
as natural monopoly, 554
regulation of, 555
Electronic funds transfer, 304, 337
Eli Lilly and Company, 553
Ellison, Lawrence J., 24, 715
EMI Group, 614
Emission rights trading, 80
Employment
advances by minorities and women, 29
class theory, 663
effect on expansionary fiscal policy, 363–364
hours of work, 207–208
of illegal immigrants, 207

job creation in World War II, 10–11
and monopsony, 650–652
outsourcing/offshoring, 175–176
by sector 1940–2004, 72
since 1990, 1–12
in U.S. in 2003, 223–224
working poor, 720
Employment argument, 752–753
Employment discrimination, 27–28
against African Americans, 669
effect on wages, 667–670
persistence of, 716
theory of poverty, 727
against women, 667–669
Employment pool, 662
Endogenous theories of business cycle, 220–221
Engels, Friedrich, 87
Enron, 616, 617, 618
Entertainment, 490
Entrepreneur(s)
Chinese in U.S., 394
exploiter of labor, 700–701
innovator, 699–700
monopolist, 700
motivation of, 73
profit as reward for, 698
risk taker, 698–699
in United States economy, 25
Entrepreneurial ability, 25
as economic resource, 24
Entrepreneurial innovation, 17
Environmental issues, 398
Environmental pollution, 80–81
Environmental Working Group, 16n
Equal Employment Opportunity Commission, 669
Equal pay for equal work, 668
Equation of exchange, 355–356, 359
Equilibrium
in classical economics, 263
aggregate demand curve, 255–256
foreign purchases effect, 256
interest rate effect, 256
long-run aggregate supply curve, 257–258
real-balance effect, 256
short-run aggregate supply curve, 258–259
effect of changes in demand, 52
effect of changes in supply, 54
effect of price controls, 55–59
in Keynesian economics, 260–261, 262, 266–267
and market clearing, 425
supply and demand, 424–426
shortages, 50–51, 425
surpluses, 50–51, 425
Equilibrium GDP, 255
in aggregate expenditures model, 263, 265
definition, 276
and deflationary gap, 276–277
determinants, 255

and inflationary gap, 277–278
and multiplier, 281
and spending level, 276
Equilibrium interest rate, 694
Equilibrium price
and change in supply or demand, 51–55
in classical economics, 253–254
definition, 50
finding, 426–427
and price floors, 55
and shortages or surpluses, 50
supply and demand analysis, 424–427
Equilibrium quantity
and change in supply or demand, 51–55
in classical economics, 253
finding, 426–427
supply and demand analysis, 424–427
Equipment; see Plant and equipment
Equity, 75–76
and income distribution, 714–715
Ernst & Young, 614
Esar, Evan, 575
Essay in the Principle of Population (Malthus), 402
ESSO, 609
Established firms, 551–552
Estate tax, 159
phaseout, 452
Euro, 777, 778
Europe
flat tax in, 153n
unemployment rate, 227
European Central Bank, 332
European Commission, 577
Microsoft case, 613
European Common Market, 176
European Monetary Union, 332, 777
European Union, 176
antitrust in, 613–614
benefit of farm subsidies, 763
euro, 777
farm policy, 16
farm subsidies, 180
as free trade zone, 178
membership map, 179
on U.S. steel tariffs, 762
Excess reserves, 333, 337, 343
Exchange
and international trade, 172–173
money as medium of, 302
Exchange rate systems, 174–175, 772–780
basis of international finance, 772
Big Mac index, 781
Bretton Woods system, 774–775
currency appreciation, 776
currency depreciation, 776
currency devaluation, 774–775
definition, 773
dollar standard, 783–784
and economic growth, 776

Exchange rate systems—*Cont.*
   euro, 777
   fixed exchange rates, 774–775
   floating rates, 775–777
   gold exchange standard, 774–775
   gold standard, 773–774
   and interest rates, 776–777
   international rates 1972–2005, 778
   in international trade, 770
   and price levels, 776
   and U.S. dollar, 779
   weighted average of currencies, 779
   yen and yuan, 777–780
Excise tax, 157–159
   as indirect tax, 153
Excite!, 17
Exclusive dealings, 610
Exogenous theories of business cycles, 221
Expansionary fiscal policy, 363
Expansionary monetary policy, 363
   and union contracts, 370
Expedia, 411
Expenditures approach to GDP, 191–192, 196
Explicit costs, 508, 698
Export-import sector; *see* International trade
Exports
   to Canada and Mexico, 178
   effect of import restrictions, 753
   effect of price level, 256
   of United States, 173–175
Export subsidies, 180
External benefits, 78–79
External costs, 78–79
External demand shock theory, 221
Externalities, 78–79
Exxon, 558, 609, 614, 619
ExxonMobil, 80, 123, 124, 609

f

Face rate, 339
Factors of production; *see also* Labor *entries*
   capital, 692
   changes in quantity of resource demanded, 632–633
   changes in resources demanded, 632–633
   complementary, 634
   definition, 625
   derived demand for, 625–626
   determinants of amounts, 627
   final demand and change in derived demand, 625–626
   land, 687
   marginal revenue product, 626–632
      of imperfect competition, 631–632
      and productivity, 628
   margin concept, 627

optimum mix for firms, 635–636
output effect, 634, 636–637
price of substitute resources, 626
and production function, 487–488
productivity, 626
reasons for changes in resource demand
   change in demand for final product, 633
   changes in price of other resources, 633–634
   changes in quantities of other resources, 635
   productivity changes, 633
substitution effect, 634, 636–637
Factor suitability, 33
Fair Labor Association, 752
Fair Labor Standards Act, 643, 676
Fairlie, Henry, 72
Fallacy of composition, 283
False advertising, 444
Family planning, 401–403
Fannie Mae, 669
Farm policy
   in European Union, 16
   as government failure, 82
   and price floors, 55–56
   price supports, 16
Farm subsidies, 762, 763
Farm Subsidy Database, 16n
Fascism, 88
Fastow, Andrew, 618
Feather, Vic, 653
Feather, William, 288
Federal budget; *see* Budget *entries*
Federal Deposit Insurance Corporation, 8, 306, 314, 321
   origin and functions, 321
Federal Emergency Management Agency, 83
Federal Express, 37, 395, 649
Federal funds, 334
Federal funds market, 342
Federal funds rate, 334
   changes in, 342–344
   increased 2004–2006, 348
   from 1954 to 2006, 343
Federal Housing Administration, 11, 13
Federal Open Market Committee, 340–342
   and Fed funds rate, 344
   membership, 340
Federal Reserve Act of 1913, 330, 342
Federal Reserve Bank of Dallas, 489
Federal Reserve Bank of San Francisco, 338, 345
Federal Reserve District Banks, 330
   issuance of currency, 331
   lenders of last resort, 332
   primary reserves, 334–335
Federal Reserve System, 221, 239, 241, 291, 304, 306, 319, 329–347
   Banking Act of 1999, 348–349
   bank regulation, 320–321, 347–349

Board of Governors, 9, 10, 330–332
chairman, 331
check clearing, 336–337, 338
control of interest rates, 311
credit crunch, 12
and decline of monetarism, 364–365
deposit expansion, 335–337
deposit expansion multiplier, 335–336, 337
economic stimulation policy, 10
effectiveness of policies, 346–347
electronic funds transfer, 337
and fiscal policy, 349
independence of, 332
inflation control, 12
and interest rates, 349
legal reserve requirements, 332–334
lender of last resort, 332, 343
main jobs, 330
map of districts, 332
Monetarist view, 362–363
monetary policy tools
   changes in reserve requirements, 344
   discount rate, 342–344
   Federal Open Market Committee, 340–342
   Fed funds rate, 342–344
   margin requirements, 345
   open market operations, 339–340
origin of, 320–330
primary reserves, 334–335
repeal of Glass-Steagall, 348–349
secondary reserves, 335
Federal Trade Commission, 439, 552, 572, 613
Federal Trade Commission Act, 610–611
Feedback from consumers, 557
Feige, Edgar L., 207
Fellner, W., 691n
Female-headed households, 719–720, 722, 731
Final demand, 625–626
Final product, demand for, 633
Finance companies, 694
Financial intermediaries, 317–318
   nonbank, 318
   shrinking number of, 348
Financial investment, 128, 130–131
Financial transactions, and Gross Domestic Product, 197
Firms; *see also* Bigness; Cartels; Corporations; Monopolistic competition; Monopoly
   advantage of being established, 551–552
   break-even point, 495–496, 529
   bureaucracy in, 490–491
   case study, 494
   company size, 438
   concentration ratios, 583
   corporate hierarchy, 556
   demand curve, 520

economic power of large employers, 650–652

economies of being established, 551–552

going-out-of-business decision, 494–497

oligopolistic, 581

optimum resource mix, 635–636

in perfect competition, 517–518

plant size, 497–498

reasons for investing, 135

shut-down decision, 492–494

shut-down point, 495–496

stay-in-business decision, 494–497

total loss calculation, 512–513

withstanding strikes, 653

First Bank of the United States, 329n

First National City Bank, 320

Fiscal policy, 275–292

automatic stabilizers, 282–285

and balanced budget, 290

characteristics, 275

crowding-in effect, 290–292

crowding-out effect, 290–292

deficit dilemma, 288–290, 295–296

deflationary gap, 276–277

discretionary

effective automatic stabilizers, 285–288

government spending changes, 287

public works, 286

tax rate changes, 286–287

in fighting inflation, 378

in fighting recession, 377

goals, 275–276, 380

inflationary gap, 277–278

Keynesian-monetarist debate, 290–292

Keynesian origin, 275

lags in, 379–380

meshed with monetary policy, 349

Monetarist view, 363–364

and multiplier, 278–282

and national debt, 292–295

politics of, 287

responsibility for, 287–288

state and local dilemma, 160–161

unmet goals, 276

Fiscal year, 146

Fisher, Irving, 237

Fitzgerald, F. Scott, 714

Fixed costs

average fixed cost, 479

contrasted with average fixed cost, 483

definition, 476

of electric utilities, 554n

graphing, 482–486

of Internet, 490

in short run, 479

in shutting down, 492–493

spreading, 489

Fixed exchange rates, 774–775

Flat-tax proposal, 153n

Floating exchange rates, 775–777

Flow-of-income approach to GDP, 192–195, 196

national income, 193–195

national product, 192–193

Food and Drug Administration, 618

Food prices, 453

Food stamp program, 14, 146, 725

Food supply, in Malthusian theory, 402

Forbes, 444

100 top celebrities list, 661

top ten billionaires, 714, 715

Forbes, Steve, 153n, 444

Ford, Gerald, 242

Ford, Henry, 5, 6, 25, 76, 268, 529, 552, 625

Ford Motor Company, 25, 74, 123, 124, 396, 404, 491, 518, 584, 617, 647

Forecasting

in adaptive expectations hypothesis, 369

business cycles, 221–223

in rational expectations theory, 368–370

Foreign aid, 149

to less developed countries, 403

Foreign banks, 315

Foreign investment, 138

in United States, 131

Foreign investors, 770–772, 781–784, 785–786

Foreign ownership of debt, 294

Foreign purchases effect, 256

Foreign savers, 290

Forster, Julie, 552

Fortune, 28, 83

Four tigers of Asia, 403

Foust, Dean, 651

Fox network, 671

France, Anatole, 721

France, and Iraq War, 290

Franchises, government, 551

Frank, Robert H., 490, 672

Franklin, Benjamin, 18, 113, 153, 228, 283, 311, 696, 755

Fraser, Douglas, 647

Freakonomics (Levitt & Dubner), 530, 723

Freeman, Richard B., 761

Free-market economy, 62

Free Markets Inc., 519

Free trade

agreements, 762–763

case for, 755–756

deviations from, 762

support for, 745

Free trade zones

CAFTA, 178

European Union, 178

Mercosur, 178

NAFTA, 176–178

Freund, William, 222

Frictional unemployment, 226–227, 257

Friedman, Benjamin M., 784

Friedman, Milton, 111, 238, 239, 362

Friedman, Thomas, 25, 87, 224, 395

Fringe lending, 701–702

Full employment, 26–29

in classical economics, 255, 263

definition, 228, 276

and demand-pull inflation, 239

Keynesian view, 361

in long run, 257

and underemployment, 29

Full-employment equilibrium, 258, 260–261

Full-employment GDP, 258–259

definition, 276

and deflationary gap, 276–277

and inflationary gap, 277–278

and multiplier, 281–282

and unemployment rate, 276

Fuller, Marce, 668

Full production, 26–29

Fumento, Michael, 444

Functional illiteracy, 228

Future value, 695–697

g

Gains from specialization, 748

Gains from trade, 748, 750

Galambos, Louis, 607

Galbraith, John Kenneth, 24, 74, 110, 222

Gale, William, 289

Gap Inc., 752

Garson, Barbara, 334

Gary, Elbert, 587

Gasbuddy.com, 530n

Gas lines, 56

Gasoline prices, 411, 441

Gasoline tax, 80–81, 157, 158

national comparisons, 158

Gas prices, 62–63, 584

Gates, William H., III, 24, 25, 491, 714, 715

GATT; *see* General Agreement on Tariffs and Trade

GDP deflator, 198–199, 200

Geary, Leslie Haggin, 700

Gehrig, Lou, 671

Gender discrimination

in employment, 667–669

and pay differentials, 668

General Accounting Office, 440

General Agreement on Tariffs and Trade, 177, 178–180, 182, 744

General Electric, 123, 124, 323, 586–587, 610, 615, 650

General Motors, 6, 10, 74, 80, 123, 124, 128, 130, 241, 396, 404, 491, 497, 584, 610, 617, 647

General Theory of Employment, Interest, and Money (Keynes), 135, 260n, 360

Gentlemen's Agreement, 394n

Gentrification, 721

George, Henry, 690
Germany, hyperinflation in, 241
Ghettos, 722, 729
GI Bill of Rights, 12–13
Gibson, Mel, 661
Gillespie, Donna B., 440
Gillette Company, 619
Glass-Steagall Act repeal, 348–349
GlaxoSmithKline, 553
Glaxo Wellcome, 619
Gleason, Jackie, 303
Global competition, 400
Global Crossing, 616, 618
Global economy/Globalization, 17, 400
    effect on real wages, 675–676
    and plant location, 27
    and productivity, 395–396
    protests against, 180–181
    reservations about, 181–182
    uncertain benefits of, 753
    U.S. as debtor nation, 780–784
    United States in, 173–174
Godfather (Puzzo), 339
Going-out-of-business decision,
    494–497
Goldberg, Rube, 88
Golden West Financial, 316, 319,
    668
Gold exchange standard, 774–775
Goldman, Bea, 552
Goldsmiths, 312–314
Gold standard
    definition, 773
    evaluation of, 774
    operation of, 774
    self-correcting, 774
Gompers, Samuel, 644, 654
Gonzalez, David, 752
Goods and services
    in circular flow model, 76–77
    consumer categories, 107–109
    elasticity of demand, 433, 441
    final demand, 625–626
    in GDP, 189–190
    inferior goods, 415
    intermediate, 195–197
    luxuries, 442
    necessities, 442
    normal goods, 415
    private, 81–82
    production of, 72
    public, 81–82, 163
    related, 415–416
    substitutes, 442
Goodwin, Doris Kearns, 11
Goodyear Tire & Rubber Company,
    653–654
Google Inc., 17, 25, 530n
Gorbachev, Mikhail, 87, 88
Gordon, John Steele, 5
Gordon, Robert J., 287
Gorney, Jay, 18n
Gottschalk, Peter, 731n
Government bond houses, 339, 342

Government failure
    budget deficits, 83
    farm price supports, 82
    Hurricane Katrina response, 83
    versus market success, 83–84
    price controls, 55–59
    public education, 83
    tax code, 82
    war on poverty, 82
Government franchises, 551
Government intervention
    pollution control, 80–81
    price ceilings/floors, 55–59
Government jobs, 731
Government ownership, 556
Government purchases, versus transfer
    payments, 149–150
Government regulation, 78
    versus deregulation, 615–616
    economic, 164
    of natural monopoly, 555–556
    for pollution control, 80–81
    in supply-side economics, 365
Government saving, 114
Government sector
    basic economic influences, 145–146
    in circular flow model, 77
    in classical economics, 359–360
    and consumer spending, 113
    economic role, 162–165
        Adam Smith's view, 164–165
        economic regulation, 164
        income redistribution, 163
        in 19th century, 608
        public goods and services, 163
        stabilization policies, 163–164
    farm price supports, 16
    federal revenue sources, 155–159
    federal spending, 146–148
    federal system, 77
    fiscal year, 146
    graphing C+I+G line, 150
    growth of economic role, 145–146
    and income distribution, 75–76
    and legal barriers to entry, 550–551
    obligations in state/local government,
        162
    policy dilemma, 378–379
    and postwar housing demand, 11
    protection of property rights, 62
    public goods and services, 81–82
    purchases and transfer payments,
        149–150
    in rational expectations theory, 368,
        369
    Reagan's view of, 15
    response to market failure, 79
    revenue sources, 146
    role in Keynesian economics, 360–361
    saving by, 388–389
    state/local fiscal dilemma, 160–161
    state and local spending, 148–149
    taxation, 150–162
Government securities outstanding, 339

Government spending
    crowding-out effect, 290–292
    defense spending, 147
    deficit dilemma, 288–290
    and discretionary fiscal policy, 287
    on education, 148
    to end Depression, 9
    to end recession/depression, 267–268
    federal level, 146–148
    foreign aid, 149
    highway program, 11–12
    interest on debt, 147
    in Keynesian economics, 360–361
    Keynesian-Monetarist debate, 363–364
    main transfer programs, 723–726
    measuring, 150
    on Medicare/Medicaid, 146, 147–148
    on police protection, 148
    required, 147
    revenue sources, 146
    Social Security, 147–148
    state and local, 148–149
    in supply-side economics, 365
    transfer payments, 146, 149–150
    unfunded mandates, 161
Grapes of Wrath (Steinbeck), 8
Graphs
    average costs, 482–486
    break-even point, 511, 512
    C+I+G+X_n line, 176, 190
    colluding oligopolist, 587
    consumption function, 102–103
    consumption/investment, 138
    cost-push inflation, 240
    cutthroat oligopolist, 591
    deflationary gap, 277
    demand and marginal revenue, 506
    demand curve, 48, 52, 421–423
    demand-pull inflation, 240
    elasticity of demand, 436–440
    exchange rates, 778
    horizontal axis, 422
    inflationary gap, 276
    loanable funds, 60–61
    Lorenz curve, 710, 712
    monopolistic competition, 566–568
    monopoly, 542-544
    perfect competition, 521–527
    price ceilings/floors, 58–59
    production possibilities curve, 30–31,
        34, 36–38
    reading, 101–102, 546
    saving function, 104
    sector employment, 72
    shut-down point, 511, 512
    supply curve, 53, 54, 423–424
    taxation, 154
    taxation and supply, 451
    total profits and losses, 527
    vertical axis, 422
Great Depression, 34, 145, 164, 201,
    726–727
    bank failures, 8
    and classical economics, 260

deflation in, 231
Dust Bowl, 8
ended by World War II, 10
high tariffs during, 744
impact on trade, 742
investment during, 129
Keynesian response, 260–263, 360
New Deal, 8–9, 268, 728
and origin of fiscal policy, 275
public works projects, 286
saving rate in, 97
severity of, 7
start of, 7–8
unemployment rate, 228
Great Leap Forward, China, 90
Great Northern Railroad, 81
Great Society programs, 146, 150, 725, 728
Greenhouse, Steven, 647–648, 669n
Green Revolution, 402n
Greenspan, Alan, 329, 331, 332, 345, 390, 772
Grievance procedures, 654
Gross, Jane, 84
Gross Domestic Product; *see also* Full-employment GDP; Per capita real GDP; Real GDP
    alternate definition, 190
    budget deficit/surplus percentage, 289–290
    calculating percentage change, 198
    C+I+G+X$_n$ line, 176
    circular flow diagram, 192
    common mistakes
        multiple counting, 195–197
        treatment of transfer payments, 196
    components in 2005, 191
    and consumption and saving, 264
    and costs of economic activity, 210
    current account percentage of, 772, 773
    defense spending in, 398
    definition, 95, 189
    equation, 190
    foreign aid as percentage of, 149
    and Gross National Product, 193
    versus Gross Progress Index, 209–210
    growth in 20th century, 386
    health care costs in, 396, 398
    household sector, 95–96
    international comparisons, 202
    makeup of, 209
    measuring
        expenditures approach, 191–192, 196
        flow-of-income approach, 192–194, 196
    and multiplier, 279–282
    national product and income, 193
    and net domestic product, 194
    and net national product, 131
    nominal vs. real, 197–202
    ratio of saving to, 114
    review of approaches to, 196
    and Say's law, 252–253

shortcomings
        excluded production, 205–207
        human costs and benefits, 208–209
        treatment of leisure, 207–208
    tax receipts percentage of, 161, 162
    transfer payment percentage of, 150
    U.S. exports/imports percentage, 173–174
    in U.S. 1930 to 2005, 200
    with or without automatic stabilizers, 285
Gross investment, 131–132, 193
    in 2005, 138
    components 1993–2005, 139
Grossman, Michael, 440
Gross national product, 193
Gross Progress Index, 209–210
Gross saving, 114, 388–389
Grow, Brian, 651
GTE, 619
Gurney, Edward J., 82

h

Hailey, Arthur, 311
Hallmark Cards, 551
Hamermesh, Daniel S., 441, 574, 590
Hand, Learned, 612
H&R Block, 702
Hanks, Tom, 661
Harburg, Yip, 18n
Harding, Veronica, 318
Harding, Warren G., 26
Harford, Tim, 182, 442n, 576
Hariman, Edward, 607
Harrington, Michael, 24, 728n
Hartle, Terry, 663
Hausmann, Ricardo, 783
Hawley, Frederick Barnard, 699
Health care costs, 400
    effect on productivity, 396–398
    effect on real wages, 675
    national comparisons, 396
    percent of Gross Domestic Product, 396
    persistent increase in, 403–404
    price discrimination in, 573
    reasons for excess, 397
    single payer system, 404
HealthSouth, 618
Heating oil market, 452
Heller, Walter, 366, 370
Helmsley, Leona, 159
Hemingway, Ernest, 714
Henderson, Leon, 241
Herfindahl-Hirshman Index, 583
Heritage of slavery theory, 727
Herold, Don, 97, 233
Hicks, John, 558
High-tech bubble, 288
Highway program, 11–12
Hispanics
    child poverty, 721

employment discrimination, 27–28, 727
income, 713
poverty rate, 720
wage rates, 669
Hitler, Adolf, 88, 241
Hoffman-La Roche, 588
Hollow corporation, 757
Holmes, Oliver Wendell, 164
Home Box Office, 490
Home Depot, 83, 649
Home equity loans, 130, 284
Homeless, 721
Honda Motors, 131, 553, 584, 617, 647, 755, 764
Hoover, Herbert, 7, 8, 194, 260, 294, 360
Hoovervilles, 8
Horizontal axis, 422
Horizontal mergers, 614
Hotmail, 394
Houghton-Mifflin, 557
Hours of work, 207–208
    40-hour week, 643
    income effect, 664–665
    national comparisons, 390, 391
    substitution effect, 664–665
House Education and Workforce Committee, 720
Household Finance, 318, 694
Household International, 317–318
Household production, 205–206
Household sector
    autonomous consumption, 104–107
    average propensity to consume, 97–98, 99–100
    average propensity to save, 98–100
    in circular flow model, 76–77
    consumer spending, 107–108, 114–115
    consumption function, 96–97, 102–103
    determinants of consumption level, 108–111
        conspicuous consumption, 110
        consumer expectations, 110–111
        credit availability, 109
        disposable income, 109
        stock of liquid assets, 109–110
        store of durable goods, 110
    expenditure categories 2005, 108
    graphing
        consumption function, 102–103
        saving function, 104
    GDP percentage, 85–96
    harm from inflation, 236–237
    income distribution, 709–716
    income growth 1968–2004, 712–714
    income tax payments, 159
    induced consumption, 106–107
    marginal propensity to consume, 100
    marginal propensity to save, 101
    median income, 713–714
    mortgage markets, 317–318
    past vs. present conditions, 111–112

Household sector—*Cont.*
  permanent income hypothesis, 111
  saving function, 104
  saving rate, 97
  spending vs. saving, 112–113
  total income before taxes, 712
  total saving, 113–114
  two-income families, 112, 676
Housing
  effect of rent control, 57
  Levittown solution, 13
  past vs. present, 111
  post-World War II demand, 11
  residential construction, 128, 130
Housing market, 427
Housing prices, 130
Howell, James, 236
HSBC Group, 315, 316
Hubbard, Frank McKinney, 234
Hudson automobile, 446
Human capital, inadequate, 728
Humphrey, George, 109
Hungary, hyperinflation in, 241
Hurricane Charley, 468
Hurricane Katrina, 83–84, 209–210, 243,
    468n, 559, 720
Hybrid business forms, 124
Hyperinflation, 241
Hypothetical business cycle, 220, 285
Hyundai, 754

i

IAC/Interactive, 672
IBM, 110, 123, 130, 541, 553, 556, 558,
    700
Ike, Reverend, 730
Illegal immigrants, 206–207, 225–226
Illegal production, 206
Illiteracy rate, 228
ImClone, 618
Immigrants
  in high-tech jobs, 394
  illegal, 206–207, 225–226
  long working hours, 207–208
  money sent home, 771
Immigration, 416
  Chinese Exclusion Act, 394n
  Gentlemen's Agreement, 394n
  restrictions, 393–394, 400
Immigration and Naturalization Service,
    400
Impact lag, 379, 380, 381
Imperfect competition, 542–544
  marginal revenue product, 631–632
  versus prefect competition, 602–603
Implicit costs, 507, 508, 698
Imports
  and Buy America campaign, 763–764
  from Canada and Mexico, 178
  and capacity utilization rate, 133
  from China, 760
  effect of price level, 256

effect on concentration ratios, 584
effects of restricting, 752–753
effects of U.S. recession on, 221
flood of, 741
quotas or tariffs on, 754–755
of United States, 173–175
Income; *see also* Disposable income;
    Wages
  in classical economics, 252–253
  compared to wealth, 714
  consumption function, 96–97
  and demand for money, 308
  disposition of, 76
  and education, 663, 716
  effect of changes in, 415
  median income, 713–714
  permanent income hypothesis, 111
  present value analysis, 695
  and price, 442
  from property, 716
  quintiles, 710–712
  saving function, 104
  from transfer payments, 716
  from wages and salaries, 716
Income disparity, 661
Income distribution, 75–76
  determinants
      property income, 716
      transfer payments, 716
      wage and salary differences, 716
  distribution of wealth, 714, 715
  equity and efficiency, 714
  family income growth 1968–2004,
      712–714
  global divide, 713–714
  Lorenz curve, 710–712
  the middle class, 709–714
  national income, 195
  the poor, 709–714
  by quintiles, 710–712
  the rich, 709–714
  utilitarian view, 715
Income effect, 664–665
Income equality, 713, 715
Income redistribution, 163, 714–715
  and utility, 464
Income tax
  corporate, 123
  personal, 122
  rate cuts, 712
  Reagan era cuts, 15
Income tax surcharge, 286
Incorporate Yourself (McQuown), 122
Increasing returns, 488
Index of leading economic indicators, 222
Indirect taxes, 153
Individual demand, 410–411
Individual supply, 417–418
Induced consumption, 106–107
Industrial capitalists, 5–6
Industrial competition, oligopolistic,
    581–593
Industrialization
  and capital, 86

early auto industry, 6
mass production, 5
post-Civil War, 5–6
post-World War I, 7
pre-Civil War, 3
Industrialized nations, 401
Industrial Loan Company, 323
Industrial Revolution, 385–386
Industrial unions, 645–646
Industry concentration ratios,
    582–583
Industry standards, 552
Inefficiency in monopolistic competition,
    575–576
Inelastic demand, 436–437
  definition, 436
  for luxuries, 442
  and price discrimination, 574
  and total revenue, 445–446
Inelastic supply, 446, 447
Infant industry argument, 751
Inferior goods, 415
Inflation, 12, 229–242
  aggregate demand leading to, 262
  anticipated, 236–237
  and consumer price index, 234–236
  conventional fiscal policy, 368
  creeping inflation, 241
  current value of dollar, 237–238
  defining, 229–231
  versus deflation, 231–233
  and demand for money, 308
  and disinflation, 233
  double-digit, 378
  excess reserves during, 337
  expectations of, 370
  Fed effectiveness against, 346–347
  and Federal Open Market Committee,
      342
  and hyperinflation, 241
  and interest rates, 237, 695n
  in late 1970s, 364–365
  in Monetarist view, 362–364
  and money supply, 221
  post-World War II, 233–234
  in present value analysis, 695–697
  as psychological process, 240
  and real interest rate, 237
  in recession of 1973, 14–15
  rising tax receipts, 283
  tax bracket adjustments, 156n
  and tax increases, 286
  theories of causes
      cost-push inflation, 239–240
      demand-pull inflation, 238–239,
          262
      profit-push inflation, 239
      supply-side shocks, 239–240
      wage-price spiral, 239
  unanticipated, 236–237
  unconventional fiscal policy, 368
  in U.S. in 1960s–70s, 362–363
  in U.S. in 1970s, 74
  winners and losers, 236–237

Inflationary gap, 277–278
    and multiplier, 281–282
    in rational expectations theory, 368
Inflationary psychology, 240
Inflationary recessions, 378–379
Inflation rate
    below 3 percent, 234
    GDP deflator, 200
    misery index, 242
    and wage rates, 229
Information technology, 395
    and economic growth, 37
Ingram Book Group, 611
Inheritance law, Islamic, 127
Initial public offerings, 130
Inland Steel, 587
Innovation, 551
Innovation theory of business cycle, 220
Innovator, 699–700
Inputs, 626
Insurance companies, 318
Intel Science Talent Search, 392
Inter-American Development Board, 771
Interest, 76
    ancient opposition to, 693
    on national debt, 147, 295–296
    and nature of capital, 692
    and usury, 693
Interest rate effect, 256
Interest rate mechanism, 359, 361
Interest rates
    in classical economics, 253–254
    and consumer loans, 693–695
    control of, 311, 349
    and demand for money, 308–309
    determinant of investment, 134
    determination of, 60–61, 310–311,
        692–693
    effect of deficits, 289
    and exchange rates, 776–777
    and expansionary monetary policy, 363
    and expected rate of profit, 135
    and foreign investment, 131
    and foreign investors, 784
    and inflation, 237, 695n
    and investment, 380
    in Japan, 310
    and liquidity trap, 310
    on mortgages, 130
    nominal, 237
    present value analysis, 695–697
    prime rate, 312, 589, 701n
    real, 237
    during recessions, 129
    and savings and loan debacle,
        321–322
    subprime lending, 701–702
    Treasury securities, 339–340
    and usury laws, 57–58, 693–695
    variety of, 60, 311
Interlocking directorates, 610
Interlocking stockholding, 610
Intermediate goods, 195–197
Internal Revenue Code, 124, 725

Internal Revenue Service, 82, 123, 124,
    152, 725
International Brotherhood of Electrical
    Workers, 648
International finance, 769–788
    balance of payments
        capital account, 770–772
        current account, 770–772
        net transfers, 771
        of U.S. in 2005, 770
    basis for, 772
    Bretton Woods system, 774–775
    co-dependent relationships, 785–786
    current account deficit, 771–772,
        773, 786
    dollar standard, 783–784
    exchange rate systems, 772–780
        Big Mac index, 781
        currency appreciation, 776
        currency depreciation, 776
        currency devaluation, 774–775
        definition, 773
        euro, 777
        fixed exchange rates, 774–775
        floating rates, 775–777
        gold exchange standard, 774–775
        gold standard, 773–774
        supply and demand analysis,
            775–776
        yen and yuan, 777–780
    foreign investors in U.S., 770–772,
        781–784, 785
    mechanics of
        balance of payments, 770–772
        financing trade, 769–770
    role of drug money, 784
    and U.S. consumption, 785
    U.S. largest debtor nation, 780
International GDP comparisons, 202
International Labor Organization, 717
International Longshoremen's Union,
    399, 653, 656
International Monetary Fund, 180, 181,
    774–775
    protests against, 180
International Nickel company, 549
International Planned Parenthood
    Federation, 403
International Thompson, 557, 593
International trade, 741–764; *see also*
    Trade *entries*
    Adam Smith's view, 172
    balance of payments, 770–772, 773
    balance of U.S. trade 1970–2005, 743
    basis for, 171–172
    benefits, 742
    causes of imbalances
        consumption junkies, 756
        failing educational system,
            756–757
        huge oil imports, 756
        low saving rate, 756
        multinational corporations, 757
        relative growth rate, 757–758

    and exchange rates, 174–175
    exports/imports of U.S., 173–176
    financing, 769–770
    with floating exchange rates, 775–777
    free trade
        case for, 755–756
        deviations from, 762
        support for, 745
    free trade agreements, 762–763
    free trade zones, 177–178
    gains from trade, 748, 750
    globalization, 753
    with gold exchange standard, 774–775
    with gold standard, 774
    graphing $C+I+G+X_n$ line, 176
    and Gross Domestic Product, 174
    history of U.S. trade
        government policy, 743–745
        high protective tariffs, 744
        before 1975, 742
        since 1975, 742–743
        post-World War II tariffs, 74–745
    increasing competition in, 742
    most favored nation principle, 180
    outsourcing/offshoring and, 175–176
    patriotic buying, 763–764
    production possibilities curve,
        745–748
    specialization and exchange in,
        172–173
    and sweatshop labor, 182, 752
    theory
        absolute advantage, 749
        comparative advantage, 745–749
        conclusions, 755–756
        protectionist arguments, 749–753
        specialization, 745
        tariffs or quotas, 745–755
    trade deficits
        with China, 760–762
        with Japan, 758–762
        means of reducing, 763
    U.S., Canada, and Mexico, 177–178
    world trade agreements, 176–177,
        178–182
International Waste Management
    Institute, 718
Internet, 25
    fixed costs, 490
    and perfect knowledge, 519
    procurement marketplace, 411
    and productivity, 395
    and trade deficit reduction, 763
Internet retailing, 530n
Internet Tax Freedom Act, 160
Interstate banking, 321
Interstate Commerce Act of 1887, 609n
Interstate Commerce Commission, 616
Interstate highway network, 163
Inventions, 25, 699
    farm machinery, 4
Inventive-based regulations, 80–81
Inventory cycle theory, 221
Inventory investment, 128, 129

Investment, 126–139
    and balance of payments, 770
    building capital, 132
    and capital, 692
    in classical economics, 253
    components 1993–2005, 139
    and consumption function, 136–137,
        138
    definition, 128
    determining level of
        capacity utilization rate, 133
        expected rate of profit, 134–135
        interest rates, 134
        reasons for investing, 135
        sales outlook, 132–133
    financial vs. real, 128
    foreign investment in U.S., 131
    graphing C+I line, 136–137, 138
    gross investment 2005, 138
    gross vs. net, 131–132, 193
    in inventory, 128–129
    in Keynesian economics, 260,
        264–265, 360
    measuring level of, 137
    in plant and equipment, 129, 132
    portion of GDP, 137
    and price level, 256
    real vs. financial, 130–131
    during recessions, 129
    in residential construction, 130
    risky, 699
    saving and, 130–131
    in supply-side economics, 365
    trends, 399
    in United States 1991–2001, 137
Investment banks, 348n
Investment bank scandals, 618
Investment flow, 692
Investment income, net ouflow, 772
Investment rate
    effect on productivity, 389–390
    and interest rates, 380
Investment tax credit, 286
Invisible hand, 73–74
Iranian Revolution, 56, 584
Iraq
    invasion of Kuwait, 12, 751
    U.S. war in, 26, 290
Irrational exuberance, 345
Islamic banking, 693
Islamic Middle East, 126–127
iUniverse, 570

j

J. C. Penney, 752
J. P. Morgan Chase, 315, 316, 319,
    619
J. P. Stevens Company, 650
Jackson Hewitt, 702
Jaguar, 583
Japan
    automakers, 584, 759
    banks in, 315

codependent relationship with U.S.,
    785–786
collusion in, 588
deflation in, 232–233
exports to United States, 7
farm subsidies, 763
interest rates, 310
investment in U.S., 131
Keynesian policies, 268
patriotic buying, 763–764
price and quality competition, 759
purchase of U.S. securities, 349
television makers, 761
Toyota City, 651
trading practices, 758–759
unemployment rate, 227
U.S. trade deficit with, 758–762
U.S. trade with, 761–762
after World War II, 5
Japanese yen, 779–780
Java Jacket, 700
Jefferson, Thomas, 109
Jeter, Derek, 409
Jevons, William Stanley, 463
Job creation, 1
    since 2001, 243
    in World War II, 10–11
Job exodus, 17
Jobless recovery, 37–38
Jobs
    exportable or nonexportable, 649–650
    lost in manufacturing, 760–761
    lost to foreign competition, 753
    and monopsony, 650–652
    nonhomogeneous, 666–667
    outsourcing/offshoring, 175–176
    primary labor market, 662–664
    protectionist argument, 752–753
    rated by skill, 661
    secondary labor market, 662–664
    solution to poverty, 731
    sweatshop labor, 182
    unpleasant, 667
    women's, 668–669
Jobs, Steven, 25
Job security, 654
Job seniority, 654
Johnson, Larry, 702
Johnson, Lyndon B., 14, 82, 147, 150,
    242n, 286, 718, 725, 728
Johnson, Samuel, 722
Johnson & Johnson, 443
John Wiley & Sons, 494, 557
Joint stock companies, 126
Jolie, Angelina, 409
Josephson, Matthew, 608
Jung, Andrea, 668
Junk bonds, 322
Jurisdictional disputes, 645

k

Kahn, Roger, 671
Kahneman, Daniel, 371

Kaiser-Fraiser, 446
Kaufman, Leslie, 752
KaZaA, 206
Keely, Chris, 323
Kellogg's, 552
Kemp-Roth tax cut, 159, 286, 365, 370
Kennedy, John F., 13–14, 227n, 714
Kennedy, Robert F., 227
Kennedy administration, 286
Kerry, John, 139
Keynes, John Maynard, 9, 24, 96, 135,
    260, 262, 263, 264, 276, 307, 310,
    355, 360, 372
    origin of fiscal policy, 275
    response to Great Depression,
        260–263
    and Say's law in 21st century,
        268–269
Keynesian economic system
    aggregate demand, 360
    aggregate demand curves, 261
    aggregate expenditures model,
        263–265
        consumption/saving functions, 264
        finding equilibrium GDP, 265
        investment sector, 264–265
    aggregate supply curves, 262
    consumption function, 96–97
    critique of classical economics,
        260–263
    debate with Monetarists on fiscal
        policy, 290–292, 363–364
    disequilibrium/equilibrium
        aggregate demand exceeds
            aggregate supply, 266
        aggregate supply exceeds
            aggregate demand, 267
        attaining equilibrium, 267
    government spending, 360–361
    investment, 360
    long-run aggregate supply curve, 261
    modified aggregate supply curve, 261
    policy prescriptions, 267–268
    presidents and, 372
    quantity theory of money, 371
    reasons for holding money, 307,
        309–310
    recessions, 360–361
    rejection of Say's law, 263
    versus supply-side economics, 15
    validity of, 361
Khorsheed, Fereydoon, 749
Khosla, Vinod, 394
Khrushchev, Nikita, 86
Kilborn, Peter T., 733
Killy, Jean-Claude, 698
King, Martin Luther, Jr., 492, 667, 676,
    717, 722, 730
King, Stephen, 661
Kinked demand curve, 589–590
Kleenex, 553, 556
Klein, Joel, 611
Kmart, 443
Knight, Frank, 699
Knights of Labor, 643–644

Kopczuk, Wojciech, 452
Koran, 126–127, 693
Korean War, 13, 233
Kosher food, 443
KPMG, 618
KPMG Peat Marwick, 614
Kraft Foods, 552
Kroc, Ray, 589
Krugman, Paul, 783
Kuran, Timur, 126–127
Kurtz, David L., 226
Kurtzman, Joel, 757
Kuwait, 12, 751

l

Labor
   and economic growth, 37
   as economic resource, 24
   entrepreneur as exploiter of, 700–701
   job migration, 385
   misallocation of, 366
   in sweatshops, 751, 752
Labor demand
   graph of, 666
   marginal revenue product schedule,
      665–666
   and minimum wage, 677–678
   nonhomogeneous jobs, 666–667
   and pay differentials, 667
   for specialized skills, 666
Labor demand curve, 665–666
Laborers' Union International, 649
Labor force
   composition of, 223–224
   expansion of, 229
   illegal immigrants in, 225–226
   job changes, 227
   productivity in U.S., 385
   young adults in, 226
Labor force changes
   average workweek/workyear,
      390–391
   declining education, 391–393
   declining quality, 399–400
   immigration restrictions, 393–394
   permanent underclass, 393
   rising quantity, 399
Labor-intensive production, 626
Labor legislation
   Fair Labor Standards Act, 643, 676
   minimum wage law, 676–679
   National Labor Relations Act, 644
   Taft-Hartley Act, 644–645
Labor market
   bilateral monopoly, 651–652
   in classical economics, 254
   disposable workers, 663
   dual, 662–664
   education gap, 679–680
   high-tech vs. bad schools, 392
   imperfectly competitive, 370
   and monopsony, 650–652
   rated by skill, 661–662

Labor supply
   backward-bending labor supply curve,
      664–665
   versus control of demand, 651–652
   employment pool, 662
   hours of work, 664–665
   income effect, 664–665
   and minimum wage, 677–678
   noncompeting groups, 661–664
   primary market, 662–664
   secondary labor market, 662–664
   semiskilled labor, 661
   skilled labor, 661
   substitution effect, 634, 636–637,
      664–665
   unskilled labor, 661
Labor supply curve, 651
   backward-bending, 664–665
Labor unions, 643–656; *see also*
      Collective bargaining
   and auto industry, 647
   bread-and-butter unionism, 644
   catch-up wage increases, 240
   closed shop, 645
   contract rigidity, 370
   cooling-off period, 645
   cost-of-living adjustments, 237
   economic power, 650
   and economic power of employers,
      650–652
   exportable/nonexportable jobs,
      649–650
   history of
      AFL-CIO merger, 646–647
      Change to Win program, 649
      craft vs. industrial unions,
         645–647
      early years, 643–644
      organizing since 1950s, 647–649
   jurisdictional disputes, 645
   key legislation, 644–645
   Longshoremen's lockout, 653
   membership
      future of, 656
      increase in 1930s, 645
      national comparisons, 649
      private sector decline, 648
      private sector unions, 648
      state comparisons, 646–647
      top ten unions, 648
      in U.S. 1900–2004, 646
   method of inclusion, 650, 651
   as monopoly, 650
   open shop, 645
   principle of exclusion, 640, 651
   representation elections, 644
   right-to-work laws, 645
   secondary boycotts, 645
   unfair labor practices, 644
   union shop, 645
   wage-price spiral, 239
   and Wal-Mart, 559, 647
Laboy, Wilfredo, 391
Laffer, Arthur, 366
Laffer curve, 366–367

Lags
   in economic policy, 379
   in fiscal policy, 379–380
   in monetary policy, 380–381
Laissez-faire economics, 260
Land
   availability of, 3
   characteristics, 687
   derivation of demand, 688–689
   derivation of supply, 688
   determination of rent, 688, 689–690,
      691–692
   differences in, 688
   as economic resource, 24
   as factor of production, 687
   marginal, 689
   origin of, 691
   rent as price for use, 690–691
Langeswiesche, William, 79
Last Angry Man, 574
Lavin, Philip, 210
Law of demand, 409–410, 422,
      665–666
Law of diminishing marginal utility, 460,
      463
Law of diminishing returns, 32, 33,
      487–488
Law of increasing costs, 32–33
Law of supply, 424
Lay, Kenneth, 616
Laziness theory of poverty, 726–727
Leacock, Stephen, 443
Leading economic indicators, 222
Leave No Child Behind law, 757
Legal barriers to entry
   kinds of, 550–551
   overcoming, 553
Legal reserve requirements, 332–334
Legal system, 77
Legal tender, 304
Lein, Laura, 732
Leisure time, 207–208
Leisure vs. work, 664–665
Leland, Henry, 6
Lemann, Nicholas, 722
Lender of last resort, 330, 332, 343
Lending
   by banks, 315–316
   consumer loans, 693–695
   first law of banking, 347
   fringe, 701–702
   by goldsmiths, 313–314
   impact of usury laws, 694
   payday, 701–702
   subprime, 317–318, 701–702
   tax refund anticipation loans, 702
Leno, Jay, 409, 661
Leonard, Devin, 84n
Leontief, Wassily, 260
Less developed countries, 385
   economic growth in, 401–403
   effect of farm subsidies, 762, 763
   family planning, 401–403
   military spending, 403
   poorest nations, 401, 717

Less developed countries—*Cont.*
  population growth, 401
  sources of capital, 403
  sweatshop labor, 751, 752
Lester, Richard K., 759n
Letterman, David, 661, 666, 671, 690
Levesque, Amy, 724
Levinson, Marc, 381
Levi-Strauss & Company, 182
Levitt, Steven D., 530n
Levitt, William, 13
Levittown, U.S.A., 13
Lewes, Jessica, 83–84
Lewy, Henry, 123
Lewy, Jonas, 123
Lewy, Nadja, 123
Liberals
  on solutions to poverty, 731
  on unemployment rate, 228
  view of unemployment, 225
  views on poverty, 728–730
Licensing, 550
Licensing agreements, 762
Life Magazine, 17
Liggett & Myers, 609
Limited liability, 122
Limited liability company, 124
Limited partnerships, 124
Lincoln, Abraham, 3, 304, 719
Lincoln Continental, 541
Liquid assets, 109–110
Liquidity, 335
Liquidity preference curve, 310
Liquidity trap, 310
Litigation
  covert collusion case, 586–587
  on price-fixing, 588
  sex discrimination suits, 669
  against Wal-Mart, 559
Living wage, 679
Liz Claiborne, 182, 189, 752
Loanable funds
  in classical economics, 254
  shortage of, 58
  supply and demand of, 60–61
  and usury laws, 693–694
Local government
  fiscal dilemma, 160–161
  revenue sources
    property tax, 160
    sales tax, 160
  spending by, 148–149
  unfunded federal mandates, 161
Local monopoly, 542
Lockouts, 652, 653
Lohr, Steve, 25
Long Island College Hospital, 519
Long run, 448–449
  cost in, 479
  monopolistic competition, 567–568, 602
  monopoly in, 548, 602
  operate vs. shut down, 513

perfect competition, 601
  plant size in, 497–498
Long-run aggregate supply curve, 257–258
  Keynesian, 261
Long-run supply curve, 512–513, 515
Long-term interest rate, 348
Long-term unemployed, 720
Lorenz, M. O., 710
Lorenz curve, 710–712
Losing Ground (Murray), 728
Losses
  alternative calculation, 527–528
  minimization, 507–514
  by monopolistic competition, 602
  by monopoly, 545, 548
  in perfect competition, 520–528
Lott, Stephen D., 722, 723
Lowe, Janet, 614
Lowrey, Christopher, 95
Low-wage argument, 751–752
Lucas, George, 661
Lucas, Robert, 368
Luce, Henry, 17, 18
Lucent Technologies, 668
Lugar, Richard, 16
Luxuries, 442

m

M1 definition of money, 304–306
M2 definition of money, 304–306
M3 definition of money, 304–306
MacArthur, Douglas, 724
Madigan, Kathleen, 343
Mafia, 586
Malthus, Thomas Robert, 401, 402
Malthusian population theory, 401, 402
Management
  ability to withstand strikes, 652–653
  lockouts by, 652
  women in, 668
Manifest destiny, 1
Mann, Brian, 724
Mannesmann, 619
Manufacturing
  capacity utilization rate, 133
  chemical industry decline, 758
  declining importance of, 617
  inventory investment, 128–129
  investment in plant and equipment, 129
  job exodus from U.S., 17
  job losses, 752–753, 760–761
  outsourcing jobs, 175
  protectionist arguments, 749–753
  quantity discounts, 489
  sweatshop labor, 751, 752
Mao Tse-tung, 86, 89–90
Maquiladoras, 752
Marathon Oil, 609
Margin, concept of, 477, 627

Marginal analysis, 629–630
  calculating total loss, 512–513
  monopoly output and profit, 545–548
  of output for profit maximization, 507–514
Marginal cost, 496, 627
  definition, 476–478
  graphing, 482–485
  in marginal analysis, 509–514
  for monopoly, 542–544
Marginal cost curve
  in loss calculation, 512–513
  in monopolistic competition, 566, 567
  in oligopoly, 592
Marginal efficiency of capital/investment, 134, 264, 360
Marginal output, 32, 627
Marginal physical product, 627
  and productivity, 628
Marginal product, 488
Marginal propensity to consume, 100, 105, 279–280, 477
Marginal propensity to save, 101, 477
Marginal revenue, 477, 505–506
  concept of margin, 627
  definition, 628
  in marginal analysis, 509–514
  in monopolistic competition, 566
  and productivity, 628
Marginal revenue curve
  graphing, 506
  in loss calculation, 512–513
  of monopoly, 543–545
  in oligopoly, 592
  in perfect competition, 522
Marginal revenue product
  calculating, 628–631
  of capital, 692–693
  changes in resource demand
    and changes in demand for final product, 633
    and changes in price of other resources, 633–634
    and changes in quantities of other resources, 634
    versus changes in quantity demanded, 632–633
    and productivity changes, 633
  concept of margin, 477, 627
  imperfect competition, 631–632
  labor demand schedule, 665–666
  of land, 688–689
  marginal analysis, 629–630
  and minimum wage, 677
  optimum resource mix, 634–635
  schedule, 627–628, 630–631
Marginal tax rate, 151–153, 477
  cuts in, 159, 371
  Laffer curve, 366–367
  nine leading wealthy nations, 157
  and productive market exchanges, 366
  in U.S. 1954 to 2006, 156
  work-leisure decision, 365

Marginal utility, 468–469
  calculating, 462
  and consumer surplus, 465
  definition, 460–461
  water–diamond paradox, 463
  at zero, 463
Margin requirements, 345
Marie Antoinette, 453, 718
Marine Midland Bank, 315
Market(s)
  definition, 411
  limits on monopoly power, 553
  winner-take-all, 672
Market basket of goods and services, 235
Market clearing, 425
Market demand, 410–411
  and cartels, 585
Market failure
  curbing pollution, 80–81
  definition, 78
  externalities, 78–79
  lack of public goods and services,
    81–82
Market period, 447–448
Market power, of cartels, 585–586
Market price
  determination of, 520
  versus equilibrium price, 50, 254
  in perfect competition, 525
Market share
  Herfindahl-Hirshman Index, 583
  and monopoly, 612
Market-sharing agreements, 586–587
Market structure
  imperfect competition, 542–544
  monopolistic competition, 565–577,
    602
  monopoly, 541–560, 602
  and monopsony, 650–652
  oligopoly, 581–593, 602
  perfect competition, 501, 516–531
  perfect vs. imperfect competition,
    602–603
Market supply, 417–418
Marks & Spencer, 442
Marling, Karal Ann, 576
Marshall, Alfred, 410, 425, 464
Marshall, John, 157
Marsh brothers' harvesting machine, 4
Martinez, Abigail, 752
Marx, Karl, 1, 84, 85, 87, 132, 700–701
Massachusetts Institute of Technology
    Commission on Industrial
    Productivity, 759
Mass consumption, 5, 6, 7
Mass production, 5, 6, 7
  in Japan, 759
MasterCard, 284, 305, 320, 323
Matsushita, 552, 614
Mattel, Inc., 551
Maximizing utility, 461–462
Mays, Willie, 666, 670–671, 690
Mazda, 553
MCA, 614

McCormick, Cyrus, 4, 5
McDonald's, 444, 570, 576, 590, 781
McDonnell Douglas, 613
McGeehan, Patrick, 318n
McGraw-Hill Companies, 557, 593
MCI Communications, 612
McKinley, William, 745
McKinsey & Robbins, 175–176
McKinsey Global Institute, 385
McLuhan, Marshall, 308
McMillan, John, 62, 90, 588
MC=MR, 508–509, 512–514, 544
McQuown, Judith, 122
Means of production, 24, 25, 35, 84; *see
    also* Factors of production
Means-tested programs, 716, 723
Meany, George, 220, 370
Mechanical cotton picker, 16
Mechanical reaper, 4
Median income, 713–714
MediaOne Group, 619
Mediation, 655–656
Medicaid, 14, 150, 197, 397, 716–717, 725
  spending on, 146, 147–148
Medicare, 14, 150, 197, 397, 716–717,
    718, 725
  negative cash flows, 295–296
  spending on, 146, 147–148
  underfunded, 166, 734
Medicare drug prescription program, 4
Medicare taxes, 157
Medium of exchange, 302
Mellon, Andrew W., 294
Mellon National Bank, 320
Mercosur, 178
Mergers and acquisitions, 607, 614–619
  blocked
    by European Union, 613–614
    by Federal Trade Commission, 611
  conglomerate mergers, 615
  corporate concentration, 607
  corporate misconduct, 616–617, 619
  and deregulation, 615–616
  effectiveness of antitrust, 617
  historical perspective, 607
  horizontal mergers, 614
  largest in U.S., 619
  largest worldwide, 619
  trend toward bigness, 617–619
  vertical mergers, 614–615
Merrill Lynch, 113, 669
Method of inclusion, 650
Metropolitan Opera, 549
Metropolitan Transit Authority of Boston,
    556
Mexico
  and farm subsidies, 763
  maquiladoras, 752
  and North American Free Trade
    Agreement, 177–178
Meyer, F. V., 23
Microsoft Corporation, 25, 29, 74, 370,
    489, 549, 552, 558, 602, 715
  antitrust case, 612–613

Middle class, 676, 709–714
Middle East, 126–127
Military Financial Network, 702
Mill, John Stuart, 153, 236, 357, 654, 667
Minimum wage, 56, 392
  arguments for and against, 677–679
  real, 678
  in U.S. 1938 to present, 676–677
  and working poor, 720
Minimum wage law, 694, 695
Minorities
  employment advances, 29
  employment discrimination, 27–28
Mirant, 668
Misery index, 242
Mitsubishi, 553
Mitsubishi Tokyo, 316
Mixed economy
  capital, 84–86
  capitalism
    compared to Communism, 87–88
    compared to fascism, 88
    compared to socialism, 88–89
    nature of, 86–87
  circular flow model, 76–77
  competition, 74–75
  equity and efficiency, 75–76
  external costs/benefits, 78–79
  and fall of Communism, 89
  government failure, 82–84
  government role, 77–78
  invisible hand, 73–74
  and market failure, 78–82
  and political pressures, 91
  price mechanism, 74
  private vs. public sector, 71
  production decisions, 71–73
  profit motive, 73
  public goods and services and, 81–82
  transformation of China, 89–90
  trust element, 75
Mizucho Financial, 316
Mobil Oil, 80, 609, 614, 619
Monetarist school
  basic propositions
    depressed interest rates, 363
    flaws in expansionary fiscal policy,
      363–364
    flaws in expansionary monetary
      policy, 363
    money supply increase, 362
    temporary reduction in
      unemployment, 363
    temporary rise in output/
      employment, 363–364
  cause of recessions, 362
  crowding-out effect, 364
  debate with Keynesians on fiscal
    policy, 290–292, 363–364
  decline of, 364–365
  monetary rule, 364
  quantity theory of money, 362
  rate of monetary growth, 361–362
Monetary Control Act of 1980, 334

Monetary multiplier, 342
Monetary policy
    definition, 329
    effectiveness, 346–347
    in fighting inflation, 378
    in fighting recession, 378
    goals of, 380
    Greenspan's role, 332
    of International Monetary Fund, 181
    lags in, 380–381
    meshed with fiscal policy, 349
    Monetarist view, 363
    shift under Volcker, 364–365
    stop-and-go, 362
    tools of
        changing reserve requirements,
            344
        discount rate, 342–344
        Federal funds rate, 342–344
        Federal Open Market Committee,
            340–342
        to fight inflation, 346
        to fight recession, 346–347
        margin requirements, 345
        open market operations, 339–340
Monetary rule, 364
Monetary theory of business cycle, 221
Money; *see also* Demand for money
    versus barter, 302–303
    in circular flow model, 76–77
    compared to credit cards, 305
    creation of, 318–319
    debit cards and, 304
    destruction of, 319
    functions, 301–302
        medium of exchange, 302
        standard of value, 302
        store of value, 302
    and liquidity trap, 310
    and multiplier, 279
    origin of dollar, 304
    and price level, 256
    quantity theory, 357–358, 359,
        361
    reasons for holding, 307
    velocity of, 356
Moneyback, 702
Money balances, 308
Money Makes the World Go Around
    (Garson), 334
Money market mutual funds, 306, 318
Money supply
    annual percentage change 1960–2005,
        307
    components, 303–304
    contracting, 340
    decreased to fight inflation, 342
    and demand for money, 311
    in demand-pull inflation, 239–240
    in fighting inflation, 378
    in fighting recession, 378
    with gold standard, 773
    growing, 306
    increased to fight recession, 341

M1 definition, 304–306
M2 definition, 304–306
M3 definition, 304–306
    means of increasing, 344
    in Monetarist school, 362–365
    and monetary policy, 329
    monetary rule, 364
    not increased by new money, 345
    in rational expectations theory, 368
    and recession, 221
Money wages, 672–676
Monopolist, entrepreneur as, 700
Monopolistic competition, 565–577
    average total cost curve, 566–567
    compared to monopoly, 569
    customization, 570
    definition, 565, 602
    demand curve, 566
    inefficiency issue, 575–576
    in long run, 567–568, 602
    marginal revenue curve, 566
    number of sellers, 603
    output and profit, 566–567
    price and output, 603
    price discrimination, 572–575
    product differentiation, 568–570
    product type, 603
    profit and efficiency, 603
    selling status, 576–577
    in short run, 565–567, 602
    total profit, 566–567
    typical competitor, 570–572
Monopoly, 541–560; *see also* Natural
    monopoly
    barriers to entry
        control of resources, 549
        economies of being established,
            551–552
        economies of scale, 549–550
        legal barriers, 550–551
        limits to power, 553
        required scale for innovation, 551
    bigness issue, 556–558
    bilateral, 651–652
    calculating profit, 544–545
    cartels as, 584–585
    in Clayton Act, 610
    and community opposition, 559–560
    company size, 548
    compared to monopolistic
        competition, 569
    compared to oligopoly, 581
    conclusions on, 558
    corporate hierarchy, 557
    definition, 541–542, 602
    finding price and output, 545
    graphing, 541–544
    Herfindahl-Hirshman Index, 583
    justifications for, 553
    labor unions as, 650
    local vs. national, 542
    losing money, 545, 548
    and market share, 612
    number of sellers, 603

price and output, 603
product type, 603
profit and efficiency, 603
review of economic analysis,
    545–548
in Sherman Act, 609
in short or long run, 548, 602
Monopoly game, 541, 551
Monopsony, 650–652
Monty Python and the Holy Grail, 367
Morgan, J. P., 607, 608
Morgan Stanley, 387, 669
Morris, Betsy, 668
Mortenson, Thomas G., 663
Mortgage interest rates, 11, 130
Mortgage markets, 317–318
Mosaic law, 693
Most favored nation principle, 180
Most Happy Fella, 308
Mulcahy, Annie, 668
Multilith-Addressograph, 553
Multinational corporations, 617–618
    and balance of trade, 757
    in China, 760
    in low-wage countries, 752
Multiple counting in GDP, 195–197
Multiplier
    applications, 280–282
    deposit expansion, 335–336, 337
    finding, 282
    and fiscal policy, 278–282
    formula, 279
    monetary, 342
    and paradox of thrift, 283
Muni, Paul, 574
Murphy, Eddie, 409
Murphy, Kevin, 440
Murray, Charles, 727, 728–729, 731
Mutual savings banks, 315
Myers, Samuel L., Jr., 727

n

NAFTA; *see* North American Free Trade
    Agreement
Namath, Joe, 549
Nash, Ogden, 716
Nash automobile, 446
National Basketball Association, 652
National Bureau of Economic Research,
    218
National City Bank, 316
National debt
    definition, 292
    and future generations, 294
    held by foreigners, 294
    holders of, 292
    interest on, 147, 295–296
    paying off, 294–295
    projected increase, 295–296
    size of, 292–293
    during wartime, 294
National Education Association, 648

National Football League, 27, 549, 553, 652, 671, 700

National Foundation for American Policy, 392

National Gardening Association, 205

National income, 193–194
distribution of, 195

National Labor Relations Act, 644

National Labor Relations Board, 644

Nationally chartered banks, 320–321

National product, 192–193

National railroad network, 4–5

National security argument, 751

National vs. local monopoly, 542

Nations Bank, 619

Natural monopoly
benefits of, 558
definition and examples, 553–554
policy alternatives
government ownership, 556
government regulation, 555–556
reasons for, 554–555

Natural scarcity, 700

Natural unemployment rate, 229

Nazario, Sonia L., 241n

NBC network, 615

Necessities, 442

Negative balance of trade, 173

Negative depreciation, 194n

Negative returns, 487–488

Negro League Baseball Museum, 28

Nehru, Jawaharlal, 709

Net domestic product, 131, 192–193, 194

Net exports, 176

Net interest, 194

Net investment, 131–132, 193

Net investment income, 770, 783

Netscape Communications, 612

Net transfers, 771

Neumark, David, 679

New classical economics, 367

New Deal, 7, 8–9, 268, 361, 728

New economy, 16–17

New Jersey Institute of Technology, 175

New Jersey Transit System, 556

Newly industrializing nations, 401

Newsweek, 725

New York, New Haven, and Hartford
Railroad, 81

New York Central, 81

New York City
blackout of 2003, 468
rent control, 57

New York City Welfare Department, 729

New Yorker, 397

New York Federal Reserve District Bank, 338, 340

New York Giants, 670–671

New York Jets, 549

New York State Power Authority, 556

New York State Public Service
Commission, 555

New York Times, 16, 25, 84, 318, 468, 680, 718, 733, 752

New York trash cartel, 586

New York Yankees, 671

Nicaragua, 241

Nickel and Dimed (Ehrenreich), 663

Nike, Inc., 182, 752

Nissan Motors, 131, 553, 584, 647, 755

Nixon, Richard M., 74, 234, 241, 372, 760

Nobel prizes, 392

No Child Left Behind Act, 161

Nominal GDP vs. real GDP, 197–202

Nominal interest rate, 237

Nonbank financial intermediaries, 318

Noncompeting groups, 661–664

Nondurable goods, 107–109

Nonexcludable goods and services, 82

Nonhomogeneous jobs, 666–667

Nonrivalrous goods and services, 82

Normal goods, 415

Norris, Floyd, 294

North American Free Trade Agreement, 176, 177–178, 763

North American Uniform Cap
Corporation, 123

Norway, socialism in, 89

NOW accounts, 304, 348

Nucor Steel, 241, 650

Numbers, 95–96

O

Odle, Stephanie, 669

Office Depot, 610

Office of Budget and Management, 147

Offshoring, 175–176
of jobs, 243

Of Plymouth Plantation (Bradford), 74

Ohmae, Kenichi, 381

Oil price increases, 12, 14–15, 221, 234, 239, 420

Oil prices, 452

Oil shortages, 56

Oil supply, 585–586

Oklahoma, 529

Okun, Arthur, 242n

Olds, Henry, 6

Oligopoly, 581–593
administered prices, 592
automobile industry, 584
college textbook market, 593
compared to monopoly, 581
competitive position
cartels, 584–586
without competition, 589–592, 593
conclusions on, 592
covert collusion, 586–587
open collusion, 586
price leadership, 587–589
definition, 581, 602
kinked demand curve, 598–590
measures of
concentration ratios, 582–583

Herfindahl-Hirshman Index, 583–584
number of firms, 581
number of sellers, 603
product differentiation, 581
product type, 603
profit and efficiency, 603

Oliner, Stephen, 395

O'Neal, Shaquille, 409, 661, 669

OPEC; *see* Organization of Petroleum
Exporting Countries

Open collusion, 586

Open market operations, 344
Federal Open Market Committee, 340–342
nature of, 339–340

Open shop, 645

Operate decision, 492–494

Oppel, Richard A., 318n

Opportunity cost, 26
of attending college, 508
in comparative advantage, 746–748
of holding money, 309
as implicit cost, 507
and law of increasing costs, 32–33
for production possibilities curve, 34
of tax cuts, 161

Oracle Corporation, 29, 715

Organization of Petroleum Exporting
Countries, 12, 14, 221, 234, 239, 398
as cartel, 585–586
membership, 585

Organized crime, 322

O'Rourke, P. J., 157

Orszag, Peter, 289

Other America (Harrington), 24, 728n

Otis, James, 618

O'Toole, John, 443

Output
collapse in Great Depression, 8
effect on expansionary fiscal policy, 363–364
and efficiency, 515–516, 517
law of diminishing returns, 487–488
and law of increasing costs, 32–33
long-run, 257–258
and marginal cost, 476–478
of monopoly, 542–545
monopoly vs. perfect competition, 544–545
percentage growth 1870–2005, 11
in perfect competition, 529
productive efficiency, 35
in productivity growth, 387
for profit maximization, 507–514
real GDP as measure of, 200
short-run, 258–259
in types of competition, 603
of U.S. in World War II, 10
and variable costs, 476
where MC=MR, 508–509, 512–514, 544
during World War II, 10–11

Output effect, 634, 636–637

Outsourcing, 175–176
Overdifferentiation, 575
Overdraft privileges, 323
Overinvestment theory of business cycle, 221

P

P. Lorillard, 609
Pace, Eric, 13
Packard automobile, 446
Paige, Satchell, 28
Panasonic, 610, 757
Panic of 1907, 329–330
Papa John's International, 444
Paper money, 313
Paradox of thrift, 283
Paramount Pictures, 615
Parker Brothers, 551
Parkinson, C. Northcote, 491
Parkinson's law, 491
Parsons, Richard, 669
Partnerships
    characteristics, 122
    in Islamic law, 126
    percentage of firms and sales, 127
Patents, 550–551
Pathmark, 443, 668
Patriotic buying, 763–764
Pattern-setting wage increases, 654
Patterson, James T., 13
Pauley, William, H., III, 618
Paul VI, Pope, 416
Payday lending, 701–702
Pay differentials, 667
    gender-based, 668
    and poverty, 727
    and race, 669
Pay Pal, 337
Payroll tax, 157, 712
    as automatic stabilizer, 283–284
    burden of, 449
    incidence of, 155
Peak, 218, 219
Pear, Robert, 733
Pearson, 557, 593
Peck, Gregory, 574
Péguy, Charles, 715
Pell Grants, 663
Penn State University, 551
Pennsylvania Railroad, 81
Pension funds, 318
Pepsi, 549
PepsiCo, 551, 552
Per capita real GDP
    calculating, 204
    comparisons over time, 203–204
    definition, 202–203
    and Industrial Revolution, 386
    international comparisons, 204–205
    in poorest countries, 401
Percentage change calculation, 198–202
Perdue, Frank, 8

Perfect competition
    average total cost, 521–523, 525
    characteristics, 516–517
    compared to imperfect competition, 631–632
    compared to monopolistic competition, 568
    defining, 516–518
    definition, 601
    demand curve, 519–527
        long run, 522–527
        short run, 520–522, 523
    efficiency, price, and profit, 529–530
    versus imperfect competition, 602–603
    in long run, 601
    versus monopoly output, 544–545
    number of sellers, 603
    perfect knowledge, 518–519, 530
    perfect mobility, 518
    price taker, 518, 528–529
    product type, 603
    profit and efficiency, 603
    profit and output, 603
    profit and loss calculation, 527–528
Perfect elasticity, 436–437
Perfect knowledge, 518–519, 530n
Perfectly elastic demand, and tax burden, 540
Perfectly inelastic demand, and tax burden, 540
Perfect mobility, 518
Perfrect price discrimination, 573, 574
Perkins, Frances, 29
Permanent income hypothesis, 111
Permanent underclass, 393, 400
Perot, Ross, 292
Persian Gulf War, 12
Personal income tax, 122, 155–156
    as automatic stabilizer, 283–284
    burden of, 449
    deductions, 156
    as direct tax, 153
    progressive tax, 153, 156
    of states, 160
    top marginal rate 1954 to 2006, 156
Personal saving, 114, 388–389
    as automatic stabilizer, 284
Peter, Laurence J., 222, 346
"Petition of the Candlemakers" (Bastiat), 755
Petty, William, 156, 159
Pfizer, Inc., 553, 619
Pharmacia, 619
Pharmaceutical industry price-fixing, 577
Philco, 209
Phillips, A. W., 242
Phillips Van Heusen, 182
Pigou, A. C., 205
Pirated products, 206, 760
Pitney-Bowes, 553
Pitofsky, Robert, 611
Pitts thresher, 4
Pizza Hut, 444, 576

Pizzo, Stephen P., 322
Plant, 497
Plant and equipment
    capacity utilization rate, 133
    depreciation, 192–193
    depreciation allowance, 130
    investment in, 128, 129
Plant size, 497
Plato, 153
Plot Against America (Roth), 208
PNC Bank, 323
Pohl, Karl Otto, 229
Police protection, 148
Policy dilemma, 378–379
Politics
    democracy, 86
    dictatorship, 87
    of fiscal policy, 287
    pork barrel, 91
Pollution, 78–79
    acceptable level of, 81
Pollution control
    command-and-control regulations, 80
    emissions rights trading, 80
    incentive-based regulations, 80–81
Polytechnic University of New York, 175
Poor, the, 709–714
    characteristics, 719–723
    exploited by rich countries, 181
    impact of farm subsidies, 180
    poorest nations, 717
    safety net for, 285
    welfare banks, 317
Population
    demand and changes in, 416
    on farms, 16
    in Malthusian theory, 401, 402
    shifts to suburbs, 14
Population Council, 403
Population growth
    in less developed countries, 401
    in U.S. 1789–2006, 3
Pork barrel politics, 91
Porsche, 583
Port, Otis, 392
Positive balance of trade, 173
Poverty, 24
    abortion and crime, 723
    absolute, 717
    characteristics, 719–721
    child poverty, 721–723
    conservative vs. liberal views, 728–730
    and consumer spending, 718
    culture of, 722
    definition, 717–719
    discouraged workers, 720
    extent of, 75
    homeless, 721
    long-term unemployed, 720
    main transfer programs, 723–726
    military families, 724
    permanent underclass, 393, 400
    the poor in U.S., 709–714
    relative, 717

solutions, 730–733
sweatshops as symptom of, 182
theories of
    black male joblessness, 727–728
    employment discrimination, 727
    heritage of slavery, 727
    inadequate human capital, 728
    laziness, 726–727
    poverty breeds poverty, 728
welfare reform, 730–733
working poor, 676, 720
world's poorest countries, 401
Poverty line, 718–719, 720
Poverty rate
child poverty, 721–722
in United States, 718–721
Powell, Colin, 669
Precautionary motive for holding money,
    307, 309, 310
Preferences, changes in, 416
Preferred stock, 125
Present value of future income, 695–697
Presidential election of 2000, 161
Price(s)
administered, 592
of bottled water, 718
and changes in demand, 411–414
in classical economics, 253–254
complementary factors of production,
    633–634
and consumer surplus, 464–467
and costs, 241
decline in Great Depression, 8
and demand, 47–48
downward flexibility, 359
effect of cartels, 585–586
effect of Internet, 530
and elasticity of demand, 433–440
and elasticity of supply, 446–449
and equilibrium price, 50
of factors of production, 633–634
and GDP deflator, 201
and income, 442
Keynesian vew, 260
in law of demand, 409–410
in marginal analysis, 507–514
in market demand, 411
and mass production, 5
of monopolists, 544–545
oligopolist decisions, 590–592
of other goods, 422
output effect, 634, 636–637
in perfect competition, 516–517, 520,
    522–527, 529–530
of related goods and services, 415–416
in relation to rent, 691–692
rent as, 689–690
of substitute resources, 626
substitution effect, 633–634, 636–637
and supply, 48–49
and supply and demand, 425
and supply changes, 417–421
and total revenue, 445–446
in types of competition, 603

Price ceilings, 55–59, 63
and price mechanism, 695
usury laws as, 694
Price.com, 519
Price controls
imposed by Nixon, 74, 234, 241
during World War II, 10
Price-Costco, 234
Price discrimination
air fares, 572–573
in Clayton Act, 610
definition, 572
demand-based, 574
examples, 572–573
health care, 573
and inelastic demand, 574
in monopolistic competition, 572–575
movie theaters, 575
new vs. old customers, 574
perfect, 573, 574
separate groups of buyers, 572, 573
Price elasticity of demand, 433, 441, 444
Price expectations
changes in, 416
future changes, 421, 427
Price-fixing
litigation, 586–587, 588
by trusts, 608
Price floors, 55–59
minimum wage, 676–679
and price mechanism, 694–695
Price gougers, 468
Price leadership, 587–589
and prime rate, 589
Price level
in adaptive expectations hypothesis,
    369
in aggregate demand curve, 255–256
and deflation, 231–233
and demand for money, 307–308
and disinflation, 233
and exchange rates, 776
foreign purchases effect, 256
and GDP, 200–202
and inflation, 229–231
and interest rate effect, 256
and interest rates, 256
and investment, 256
in Keynesian model, 263
and money balances, 308
percentage changes in, 231, 232
post-World War II, 233–234
and real balance effect, 256
during recession, 378
in U.S. 1915–2005, 238
Price makers, 518, 528–529
Price mechanism, 51
and competition, 74–75
definition, 74
and land use, 690–691
missing in Communism, 88
obstacles to, 694–695
rationing function, 61–62
and usury laws, 694

Price shock theory, 221
Price stability, 163, 240
Price supports, 16, 399, 694
as government failure, 82
Price takers, 518, 528–529
Primary labor market, 662–664
Primary reserves, 334–335
Prime rate, 701n
and price leadership, 589
in U.S. 1978 to 2006, 312
Principle of exclusion, 650
Prison population, 225, 229
Private cost, 78
Private goods, 81–82
Procter & Gamble, 497, 619
Product(s)
counterfeit, 760
customization, 570
differences in, 572
identical, 518
identical vs. differentiated, 565
overdifferentiated, 575
purpose of advertising, 443–444
in types of competition, 603
use and demand for, 442
Product differentiation
benefit of, 575–576
customization, 570
versus identical products, 565
monopolistic competition, 568–570,
    602
in oligopoly, 581
versus overdifferentiation, 575
Production
capital-intensive, 626
definition, 207
excluded from Gross Domestic
    Product
    household production, 206
    illegal production, 206
    underground economy, 206–207
human costs and benefits, 208–209
labor-intensive, 626
in Say's law, 251–253
Production costs
for cars, 550
changes in, 420
and output effect, 634
Production decisions
under Communism, 87
in mixed economy, 71–73
Production function, 487–488
Production possibilities curve,
    30–35
Canada vs. Belgium, 748
and economic growth, 35–37
finding opportunity cost, 34
for international trade, 745–748
and investment rate, 389–390
law of increasing costs, 32–33
productive efficiency, 35
in two-product economy, 30–35
during World War II, 36
Production possibilities frontier, 27, 29

Productive capacity
    long run, 448–449
    short run, 448
Productive efficiency, 345
Productive market exchanges, 366
Productivity
    of American agriculture, 15–16
    annual percentage change 1970–2005,
        387
    country differences, 635
    definition, 387, 626
    and globalization, 395–396
    of immigrants, 394
    and information technology, 395
    and Internet, 395
    and marginal physical product, 628
    mass production, 5
    and real wage, 675
    reasons for increase in, 633
    resource demand and changes in, 633
    tied to wage increases, 653
Productivity growth
    annual changes 1970–2005, 386, 387,
        388
    annual rate 1970–2005, 387, 388
    factors affecting
        environmental issues, 398
        globalization, 395–396
        health care costs, 396–398,
            403–404
        information technology, 395
        labor force changes, 390–394
        military spending, 398
        special interest groups, 399
        summary on, 399–401
        terrorist attack, 398–399
    and investment rate, 389–390
    in less developed countries, 401–403
    main sources of, 387
    and Malthusian population theory,
        401, 402
    national comparisons, 391
    record of, 387–394
    and saving rate, 388–389
    slowdown in 1970s, 400
    from technological advance, 394–396
Product quality, Japan, 759
Professional sports
    as monopsonists, 652
    wage rates, 670–671
Profit
    accounting, 507, 508
    alternative calculation, 527–528
    of corporations in 2002, 698
    determination of, 698
    economic, 507, 508
    expected rate of, 134–135
    and marginal revenue, 505–506
    of monopoly, 544–545
    need for, 516
    in perfect competition, 520–527,
        529–530
    under price discrimination, 573
    size of, 698

    as surplus value, 701
    theories of
        application of labor, 701
        entrepreneur as exploiter of labor,
            700–701
        entrepreneur as innovator,
            699–700
        entrepreneur as monopolist, 700
        entrepreneur as risk taker, 698–699
        reward for entrepreneurship, 698
    and total revenue, 505–506
    in types of competition, 603
Profit expectations, 264
Profit maximization, 507–514
    and efficiency, 515–516
    profit per unit, 524
    total profit, 524
Profit motive, 73
Profit per unit, 524
Profit-push inflation, 239
Progress and Poverty (George), 690
Progressive taxes, 153, 154
    state income tax, 160
Property as theft, 691
Property income, 716
Property rights, 62
Property tax, 160
Proportional returns to scale, 491
Proportional taxes, 153, 154
Proprietorships
    characteristics, 121–122
    percentage of firms and sales, 127
Prosperity, 219–220
Protectionism
    arguments for, 749–753
        employment argument, 752–753
        infant industry argument, 751
        low-wage argument, 751–752
        national security argument, 751
    Bastiat's response to, 755
    tariffs or quotas, 754–755
Protective tariffs, 608, 743–755; *see also*
    Tariffs
Proudhon, Pierre-Joseph, 86, 691
Psychological theory of business cycle,
    220–221
Psychology, inflationary, 240
Public assistance, 723, 726
Public debt; *see* National debt
Public education system, 83
Public goods and services, 81–82, 163
Public housing projects, 722
Public utilities, 551, 554
Public works
    in discretionary fiscal policy, 286
    in Great Depression, 286
    in Japan, 268
    solution to poverty, 731
Public Works Administration, 286
Publish on demand, 570
Puff Daddy, 206
Purchasing power, 164
    and price level, 256
Purchasing power parity, 781

q

Quantity demanded, 50, 409; *see also*
    Elasticity of demand
    of resources, 632–633
    in supply and demand analysis,
        424–425
Quantity discounts, 489, 491
Quantity supplied, 50; *see also* Elasticity
    of supply
    versus change in supply, 420
    and price, 417
    in supply and demand analysis,
        424–425
Quantity theory of money
    in classical economics, 359
    crude version, 357
    equation of exchange, 355–356
    in Keynesian economics, 361
    Monetarist school, 362
    sophisticated version, 357–358
Quesnay, François, 24
Quintiles
    finding percentage of income, 711
    global divide, 713–714
    household income, 710
    income before taxes, 712
    income distribution, 710–712
Quotas, 754–755
Quotesmith.com, 530
QWERTY keyboard, 552
Qwest Communications, 555, 618, 619

r

R. J. Reynolds Company, 588, 651
Racism
    in employment, 669
    employment discrimination, 27–28
    in housing developments, 13
    and pay differentials, 669
Railroads, 4–5, 81
    and Standard Oil, 608
Raines, Franklin, 669
Ralph's supermarkets, 647
Ralston Purina, 402n
Rand, Barry, 669
Rational expectations theory, 367–370
    versus adaptive expectations, 369
    assumptions, 368–369
    criticisms of, 370
    real Gross Domestic Product, 368
    role of government, 368, 369
Rationing function of prices, 61–62
RCA Corporation, 209
Reagan, Ronald W., 13, 15, 112, 145,
    150, 160, 242, 365, 370, 371,
    372, 379, 615, 616, 679, 733,
    745
Reagan administration, 366, 614
Real balance effect, 256
Real GDP; *see also* Per capita real GDP
    and aggregate demand, 255, 259

and aggregate supply, 257, 258, 262
annual percentage change 1970–2005, 387
in business cycle, 219
equilibrium full-employment level of, 258
versus nominal GDP, 197–202
at peak of business activity, 218
in rational expectations theory, 368
in U.S. 1958–2002, 218
Real investment, 128, 130–131
Real minimum wage, 678
Real rate of interest, 237
Real wage, 672–676
Recession
in classical economics, 267, 358–360
conventional fiscal policy, 377
corporate income tax during, 284–285
decline in median income, 713
decline in taxes, 283–284
definition, 218
versus depression, 220
excess reserves during, 337
Fed effectiveness against, 346–347
and Federal Open Market Committee, 341
fiscal policy in, 278
GDP in 1981–82, 201
investment spending during, 129
jobless recovery and, 37
in Keynesian economics, 262, 264, 267–268, 360–361
Monetarist view, 362
and paradox of thrift, 283
policy dilemma, 378
post-World War II, 218–219
price level during, 378
in rational expectations theory, 368, 369
saving decline during, 284
tax cuts during, 286–287
of 2001, 288
unconventional fiscal policy, 378
unemployment compensation, 284
in U.S. 1937–38, 9–10
in U.S. 1973–79, 14–15
in U.S. 1981–82, 15, 260
in U.S. 1982 to 2003, 218
in U.S. 1990, 15
in U.S. 2001, 243, 372
in U.S. since 1945, 12
Recognition lag, 379, 380, 381
Recovery, 219
Rediscounting, 343
Red states, 647n
Reebok International, 752
Reed, Orville, 87
Regional differences, 3–4
and poverty, 719–720
and tariff policies, 744
in union membership, 646–647
Regressive taxes, 153–155
excise tax, 158
sales tax, 160
Reingold, Jennifer, 519

Relative concept of poverty, 717
Relative elasticity, 437–438
Relevant market argument, 612
Remington Sewing Machine Company, 552
Rent
determination of, 688, 689–690, 691–692
economic rent, 670–672, 690–691
and gentrification, 721
and nature of land, 687–689
as price for use of land, 690–691
prices vs. rent, 691–692
Rent control, 57, 694
Replica Books, 570
Republican Party, 3, 278, 608, 644, 647n
Republic National, 315
Republic Steel, 587, 650
Required reserves, 314
Reserve ratio, 337, 344
of goldsmiths, 313–314
Reserve requirements, 332–334
changing, 344
Reserves, 314
actual vs. excess, 333
primary and secondary, 334–335
Residential construction, 128, 130
Resource allocation, 75
in economics, 24
and market failure, 78
in Soviet Union, 87
by supply and demand, 47
Resource demand
optimum mix for firm, 634–635
reasons for changes in, 632–634
Resources
economic, 24–25, 76
factors of production, 625
monopoly control of, 549
scarcity of, 23–24
substitute, 626
underemployment, 29
Resource utilization
with full employment, 26–29
land use, 688
and law of diminishing returns, 487–488
opportunity cost of, 26
and production possibilities curve, 30–35
for productive efficiency, 35
scarcity problem, 24–26
underemployment of, 29
Restraint of trade issue, 610
Retained earnings, 130, 389
Revco, 611
Reynolds, L., 691n
Reynolds, Lloyd G., 86n
Ricardo, David, 251–252, 302, 691
Rice, Condoleezza, 669
Rich, the, 709–714
and corporate welfare, 163
payment of taxes, 159
Rickey, Branch, 27

Riegle-Neal Interstate Banking and Branching Efficiency Act, 321
Rigas, John, 618
Rigas, Timothy, 618
Right-to-work laws, 645, 647
Risk, Uncertainty, and Profit (Knight), 699
Risk taker, 698–699
Rite Aid, 491, 611, 668
Roach, Stephen S., 387
Roadrunner, 574
Roaring Twenties, 7
Roberts, Julia, 409
Robert Wood Johnson Foundation, 731
Robinson, Jackie, 27, 28
Rochester Electric Company, 555
Rockefeller, John D., 5, 7, 25, 607, 608, 614
Rodriguez, Alex, 409, 661
Roe v. Wade, 723
Rogers, Bob, 218
Rogers, David, 731
Rogers, Will, 146, 153
Rolling Stones, 614
Rolls-Royce, 583
Roosevelt, Franklin D., 8–10, 29, 145, 268, 360, 361, 393, 607, 611, 614, 728
Roosevelt, Theodore, 607, 609
Rosenberg, Tina, 181
Ross, Steven J., 699
Roth, Philip, 208
Royal Bank of Scotland, 316
Royal Dutch/Shell, 124, 619
Rule of reason doctrine, 609–610
partial breakdown of, 611–612
Russell, Robert R., 9
Russo, Pat, 668
Rust Belt, 228
Rutgers University, 551
Ruth, Babe, 194

S

Saab, 583
Safety net, 285
Safeway, 489
Salary differences, 716
Sales outlook, 121–133
Sales tax, 160
excise tax, 157–159
as indirect tax, 153
Sammons, Mary, 668
Sam's Club, 590, 669
Samsung Electronics, 209
Sanderson, William, Jr., 444
Sandler, Marion, 668
Sandoz, 611
Sanitation workers, 667
Santayana, George, 2
Saudi Arabia, 764
Savin, 553

Saving
    as automatic stabilizer, 284
    and capital formation, 113
    in classical economics, 252–253, 359
    components of, 113–114
    versus consumer spending, 111–113
    effect of deficits on, 290
    graphing, 105
    gross saving rate, 388–389
    investment of, 130–131
    in Keynesian economics, 260
    marginal propensity to save, 101
    and paradox of thrift, 283
    as percentage of disposable income,
        97, 98
    ration to GDP, 114
    in supply-side economics, 365
Saving function, 104
    in Keynesian economics, 264
Saving rate
    and budget deficits, 399
    decline, 97
    effect on productivity, 388–389
    reasons for decline, 113
    and trade deficits, 756
Savings and loan associations, 315
    bailout, 322
    debacle, 321–322
Savings deposits, 306
Say, Jean Baptiste, 163, 251
Say's law, 251–253, 258, 358
    Keynesian rejection of, 263
    and Keynes in 21st century, 268–269
SBC, 555, 619
Scania, 613
Scarcity, 35
    central fact of economics, 23
    natural vs. contrived, 700
    and need to economize, 24
Scherer, F. M., 588n
Schering-Plough, 588
Schlosstein, Steven, 557
Schmeltzer, John, 163n
School vouchers, 393
Schorr, Daniel, 729n, 731
Schorr, Lisbeth B., 729n, 731
Schulman, Beth, 676, 731n
Schumpeter, Joseph, 220, 699
Schwartz, Anna Jacobson, 362
Schwartz-Nobel, Loretta, 724
S corporations, 124
Scott, Ellen, 668
Screen Actors Guild, 615
Seaboard Finance, 694
Seaboard Railroad, 81
Sears-Kmart, 752, 760
Seasonal unemployment, 228
Seattle antiglobalization protests, 180
Secondary boycotts, 645
Secondary labor market, 662–664
Secondary reserves, 335
Second Bank of the United States, 329n
Securities and Exchange Commission, 8
Security Pacific Corporation, 345

Semel, Terry, 672
Semiskilled labor, 662
Seniority, 654
Service Employees International Union,
    648, 649
Services, 107–109
    bartering, 205–206
    outsourcing, 175–176
Service sector, 398
Sesame Street, 441
7-Eleven Stores, 571
Sex discrimination suits, 669
Share draft accounts, 304
Sharp, 553
Shaw, George Bernard, 27, 355
Shelf space, 552
Shell Oil, 128
Sherman, John, 609
Sherman Antitrust Act, 650
    and breakup of trusts, 609
    and horizontal mergers, 614
    partial breakdown of rule of reason,
        611–612
    passage of, 608–609
    provisions, 608–609
    rule of reason doctrine, 609–610
Shiller, Robert J., 74
Shipbreaking, 79
ShopRite, 443
Shortages, 50–51
    and equilibrium price, 425
    from price ceilings, 56–57
Short run, 448
    cost in, 479
    elasticity of supply, 448
    monopolistic competition, 565–567,
        602
    monopoly in, 548, 602
    operate or shut down, 492–494,
        513
    plant size in, 497–498
Short-run aggregate supply curve,
    258–259
Short-run supply curve, 512–513, 515
Short-term interest rate, 348
Showtime, 490
Shut-down decision, 492–494
Shut-down point, 495–496, 513, 515
    graphing, 511, 512
Sichel, Daniel, 395
Silicon Valley, 17, 394
Single-tax movement, 690–691
60 percent rule, 612
Skilled labor, 661–662
    specialized, 666
Slavery, 3
Slavery theory of poverty, 727
Slemrod, Joel, 82, 452
Slotting fees, 552
Small business, 571
Small corporations, 123
Smith, Adam, 24, 73, 109, 164–165, 172,
    260, 358, 458, 490, 497, 745
SmithKline Beecham, 619

Smoot-Hawley Tariff of 1930, 744
Socialism
    nature of, 88–89
    Norwegian version, 89
    Swedish version, 89
Social Security, 8, 197, 718
    future of, 165–166, 733–734
    negative cash flows, 295–296
    as poverty program, 725
Social Security Act of 1935, 723, 732
Social Security Administration, 304
Social Security benefits, 716–717, 734
    and consumer price index, 235–236
    indexed for inflation, 237
Social Security taxes, 157, 734
    as direct tax, 155–156
    incidence of, 155
    regressivity, 152–155
Social Security Trust Fund, 293, 734
SOCONY-Mobil-Vacuum, 609
Sohio, 609
Solow, Robert M., 209n, 395, 759n
Solzhenitsyn, Aleksandr, 223
Sony Corporation, 552, 570, 610, 614
Sorensen, Colleen, 700
Sorensen, Jay, 699, 700
Southern agriculture, 3–4
Southern Pacific, 81
Southern Railroad, 81
South Pacific, 529
South Street Seaport Museum, 95
Soviet Union
    agriculture in, 73
    Communism in, 87–88
    distribution system, 72
    means of production, 84
    post-World War II, 10
    production decisions, 71–72
    transition in, 87
Spears, Britney, 206, 661
Special interest groups, 399
Specialization
    and absolute advantage, 749
    and comparative advantage,
        745–749
    and international trade, 172–173
    and trade, 745
Specialized skills, 666
Speculative motive for holding money,
    307, 309, 310
Spielberg, Steven, 661
Sprint, 555, 612
Stabilization policies, 163–164
Stagflation, 14–15, 234
Stah, Max Lowes, 241
Stalin, Joseph, 85, 89
Standage, Tom, 718
Standard of living
    and capital, 85
    and Industrial Revolution, 386
    and international trade, 742
    and per capita real GDP, 203–205
    and wage rates, 676
Standard of value, 302, 303

Standard Oil Company, 25, 549, 614
Standard Oil of California, 609
Standard Oil of Indiana, 609
Standard Oil of New Jersey, 609
Standard Oil of New York, 609
Standard Oil of Ohio, 609
Standard Oil Trust, 5, 607
　breakup of, 609, 611
　and railroads, 608
Standard-setting, 552
Stanley Steamer, 552
Staples, 234, 610
Starbucks Corporation, 576, 700
State-chartered banks, 320–321
Stated rate, 339
State government
　fiscal dilemma, 160–161
　revenue sources
　　personal income tax, 160
　　sales tax, 160
　spending by, 148–149
　unfunded federal mandates, 161
Status, 576–577
Stay-in-business decision, 494–497
Steel industry, 5
　price leadership, 587
　tariffs, 762
Steinbeck, John, 8
Steinberg, Bruce, 113
Stepanek, Marcia, 519
Stevens Institute of Technology, 175
Stevenson, Robert Louis, 252, 304
Stewart, Martha, 618
Stiglitz, Joseph, 182
Stock, 122, 130, 215
Stockholders, 215
Stock market
　boom and bust in 1990s, 371
　crash of 1929, 7, 345, 348
　margin requirements, 345
Stored-value cards, 304
Store of value, 302
Strikes
　ability to withstand, 652–653
　averting, 655–656
　California supermarkets, 647
　General Motors strike in 1970, 654
　national comparisons, 655
　post–World War II, 644
　professional hockey, 652
　sanitation workers, 667
　steel strike of 1959, 654
　in Taft-Hartley Act, 645
　time lost 1945–2005, 655
Structural unemployment, 227–228,
　257
Studebaker, 446
Stumpf, Koleman S., 440
Sturzenegger, Frederico, 783
Subprime lending, 317–318, 701–702
Subsidies
　for agriculture, 16, 180, 762, 763
　export, 180
Substitute factors of production, 633–634

Substitute resources, 626
Substitutes
　availability of, 442
　lacking for monopoly, 541
Substitution effect, 636–637
　on labor supply, 664–665
Suburbanization
　consequences of, 14
　Levittown, 13
　post–World War II, 11–12
Suburban sprawl, 111
Sun Belt, 3, 228
Sunk costs, 476
Sun Microsystems, 394
SunTrust Bank, 316, 342
Suppliers, change in number of, 421
Supply
　causes of changes in
　　future price expectations, 421
　　number of suppliers, 421
　　prices of other goods, 421
　　production costs, 420
　　taxation, 421
　　technological advance, 420
　changes in, 418–420
　definition, 48, 417, 420, 513
　effect of tariffs, 754–755
　individual and market, 417–418
　of land, 688
　law of supply, 424
　and prices, 48–49
　quantity supplied vs. changes in, 420
　shifts in, 51–55
Supply and demand, 47–63
　applications, 60–62
　in classical economics, 253–254
　　aggregate demand curve, 255–256
　　equilibrium price and money, 253
　　long-run aggregate supply curve,
　　　257–258
　　prices and wages, 253–254
　　saving and investment, 253
　　short-run aggregate supply curve,
　　　258–259
　equilibrium
　　shortages, 50–51
　　surpluses, 50–51
　equilibrium point, 424–426
　in perfect competition, 518
　in Say's law, 251–253
　shifts in, 51–55
　in specific market, 49
Supply and demand analysis
　college parking, 61
　equilibrium price, 424–427
　equilibrium quantity, 424–425
　farm products, 4
　floating exchange rates, 775–777
　gas prices, 62–63
　housing market, 427
　interest rates, 60–61, 692–693
　labor demand, 665–667
　labor supply, 661–665
　price ceilings/floors, 55–59

price of fish, 416
　rationing function of prices, 61–62
　of rent, 689–692
　wage rates, 649–650, 661–667,
　　670–676
Supply curve
　graphing, 423–424
　for labor, 664–665
　long run, 512–513, 515
　perfectly elastic, 447
　perfectly inelastic, 447
　shifts in, 51–55
　short run, 512–513, 515
Supply-side economics, 15
　basic premise, 371
　elimination of productive market
　　exchanges, 366
　emergence in 1980s, 365
　Laffer curve, 366–367
　presidents and, 372
　revival in 21st century, 370–371
　saving and investment effects, 365
　work effect, 365
Supply-side shocks, 239–240
Supra Telecom, 555
Surowiecki, James, 397
Surplus capital, 85
Surpluses, 50–51
　and equilibrium price, 425
　from price floors, 55–56
Surplus value, 701
Sweatshop labor, 182, 751, 752
Sweden, socialism in, 89
Sweeney, John J., 112, 643
Swift meat packing, 5
Syrus, Publilius, 460

t

Taco Bell, 576
Taft, William Howard, 607, 609
Taft-Hartley Act, 645, 646, 652–653,
　654
Talk America, 555
Target Stores, 74, 323, 489, 752, 760
Tariff of Abominations, 744
Tariffs, 754–755
　and Civil War, 3, 744
　in Great Depression, 744
　in 19th century, 608
　post–World War II, 744–745
　in steel, 762
Tastes, changes in, 416
Taxation, 150–162
　and aggregate demand, 275
　as automatic stabilizer, 283–284
　average tax rate, 151
　burden of, 449–452
　and change in supply, 421
　cigarette tax, 158, 440
　corporate income tax, 123
　direct taxes, 153
　double taxation, 122n

Taxation—*Cont.*
    earned income tax credit, 725–726
    federal revenue sources
        corporate income tax, 157
        estate tax, 159
        excise taxes, 157–159
        payroll tax, 157
        personal income tax, 155–157
    flat-tax proposal, 153
    gasoline tax, 80–81, 158
    as government failure, 82
    and income distribution, 712
    indirect taxes, 153
    marginal tax rate, 151–152
    national comparisons, 160–162
    and national income, 193–194
    and opportunity cost, 162
    as percentage of Gross Domestic
        Product, 161, 162
    personal income tax, 122
    progressive taxes, 153, 154
    proportional taxes, 153, 154
    recent legislation
        Internet Tax Freedom Act, 160
        Kemp-Roth tax cut of 1981, 159
        tax cut of 2001, 159
        tax cut of 2003, 159
        Tax Reform Act of 1986, 159
    regressive taxes, 153–155
    single-tax movement, 690–691
    for social programs, 88
    state and local fiscal dilemma,
        160–161
    state and local revenue sources
        personal income tax, 160
        property tax, 160
        regressivity of taxes, 160
        sales tax, 160
    in supply-side economics, 365
    tariffs, 754
Tax cuts
    as economic stimulus, 290–292
    of 1981, 159, 286, 365, 370
    of 1986, 159
    opportunity cost, 161
    in Reagan era, 15
    of 2001, 159, 286, 288, 372
    of 2003, 159, 286, 288
Tax incidence, 449–452
    payroll tax, 155
    Social Security taxes, 155
Tax Policy Center, 716
Tax rates
    average, 151, 152
    corporate, 157n
    cuts in, 712, 714
    in discretionary fiscal policy, 286–287
    marginal, 151–153, 156, 157, 159,
        366–367, 477
    and productive market exchanges, 366
    rate of 15 percent, 152
Tax Reform Act of 1986, 159, 365
Tax refund anticipation loans, 702
Tax refund of 2001, 287

Tax refunds, 725
Teamsters Union, 648, 649, 650, 656
Technological advance
    in agriculture, 4
    and change in supply, 421
    early 20th century, 6
    and economic growth, 394–396
    and inflation rate, 234
    originating in U.S., 25
    in Silicon Valley, 17
Technology
    best available, 29
    for economic growth, 35–37
Technology transfer, 762
Teenage mothers, 726
Tele-Communications, 619
Telecommunications Act of 1996, 555
Telephone companies, 555
Telephone service, 554–555
Television makers, 761
Television sets, 209
Temporary Assistance for Needy
      Families, 732
Temporary-help industry, 229
Tennessee Valley Authority, 556
Term life insurance, 530
Terrorist attack of 2001, 12, 18
    effect on budget deficits, 389
    impact on productivity, 398–399
Textile import quotas, 754
Thatcher, Margaret, 464
Theory of the Leisure Class (Veblen), 110
Three-phase business cycle, 210–220
Thurow, Lester, 394
TIAA-CREF, 318
Tight money, 332, 346, 379
Time deposits, 306
Time Inc., 614–615
Times Mirror Company, 80
Time Warner, 614, 615, 619
Time Warner Home Box Office, 490
To Kill a Mockingbird, 574
Total Corporation, 124
Total cost, 507
    average total cost, 481
    definition, 476
    and efficiency, 514
    graphing, 482–486
    in shutting down, 492–493
Total loss, 512–513
    calculating, 512–513
    graphing, 527
Total profit, 507
    graphing, 527
    in marginal analysis, 509–514
    maximizing, 524
    monopolistic competition, 566–568
    of monopoly, 544
    of natural monopoly, 555
Total revenue, 505–506
    and break-even point, 495
    definition, 445
    and elasticity of demand, 445, 446
    and inelastic demand, 445–446

    in marginal analysis, 509–514
    and shut-down decision, 492–493
    and shut-down point, 495
Total utility
    calculating, 462
    definition, 461
Toyota Camry, 569
Toyota City, 651
Toyota Motor Company, 124, 131
Toyota Motors, 518, 553, 583, 584, 617,
      647, 755, 764
Toys "R" Us, 234, 760
Trade barriers; *see also* Protectionism
    negative effect, 752–753
    quotas, 754–755
    reduced by GATT, 180
    tariffs, 754–755
Trade deficits, 18, 390
    and capital and current accounts, 770
    causes of
        consumption junkies, 756
        failing educational system,
            756–757
        high defense spending, 756
        huge oil imports, 756
        low saving rate, 756
        multinational corporations, 757
        relative growth rate, 757–758
    with China, 776
    with China and Japan, 785–786
    and gold exchange standard, 774–775
    means of reducing, 763
    origin of, 742–743
    and protectionist arguments, 749–752
    and recycling dollars, 785
    and U.S. dollar position, 781–782
Trade policy; *see also* Protectionism;
      Quotas; Tariffs
    downward trend in tariffs, 744–745
    high protective tariffs, 743–744
    Smoot-Hawley Tariff, 744
    Tariff of Abominations, 744
Trade surplus, 742
Transactions motive for holding money,
      307, 309–310
Transcontinental railroad, 608
Transfer payments
    as economic stabilizer, 285
    versus government purchases,
        149–150
    and Gross Domestic Product, 197
    income from, 716–717
    increase since 1970, 146
    main programs, 723–726
    percentage of Gross Domestic
        Product, 150
    problems from, 726
    welfare culture, 726
Transit Act of 2005, 91
Traub, James, 149
Travelers Group, 619
Treaster, Joseph B., 468n
Treasure Island (Stevenson), 304
Treasury Department, 163, 304

Treasury securities, 335
    total value of, 339
Trillion-dollar economies, 203
Trough, 218, 219
Trucking industry deregulation, 616
Truly Disadvantaged (Wilson), 729–730
Truman, Harry, 83, 607, 611
Truman administration, 614
Trumka, Richard, 749
Trump, Donald, 715
Trust, 75
Trustbusters, 607
Trusts, 608
    breakup of, 609
Tucker, Sophie, 709
Twain, Mark, 315
Two-income families, 676
Two-Income Trap (Warren & Tyagi), 112
Two-product economy, 30–35
Tyagi, Amelia Warren, 112, 676
Tyco International, 618
Tying contracts, 610
Typewriter keyboard, 552
Tyson, Laura D'Andrea, 295, 784

u

UBS, 669
Unanticipated inflation, 236–237
Underconsumption theory of business
    cycle, 221
Undercover Economist (Harford), 182
Underemployment, 29, 37–38
Underground economy, 206–207
Unemployment, 163, 223–229
    black male joblessness, 727–728
    discouraged workers, 223, 720
    displaced workers, 753
    and expansionary monetary policy,
        363
    from foreign competition, 753
    jobless recovery, 37–38
    long-term unemployed, 720
    problem of, 223
    public works programs for, 286
    Robert Kennedy on, 227
    types of
        cyclical, 228
        frictional, 226–227
        seasonal, 228
        structural, 227–228
Unemployment compensation, 223
    as automatic stabilizer, 284
    extension of, 286
Unemployment insurance, 723
Unemployment rate
    accuracy of, 225–226
    African Americans, 224, 225
    computing, 223–224
    data sources, 223
    in depressions, 220
    and full employment, 27, 29,
        257

in Great Depression, 8, 228
illegal immigrants, 225–226
liberal vs. conservative views, 225
misery index, 242
national comparisons, 227
natural, 229
prison population, 225
in recession of 1937–38, 10
in recession of 1981–82, 15
of selected groups of workers, 224
and social programs, 728
in U.S. 1948 to 2005, 226
and Welfare Reform Act of 1996, 225
during World War II, 10
young adults, 226
Unfair labor practices, 644
Unfunded federal mandates, 161
Union shop, 645
Unit banking, 319–320
United Automobile and Aerospace
    Workers, 648, 650
United Auto Workers, 399, 645, 647, 653
United Farm Workers, 649
United Food and Commercial Workers
    Union, 647, 648, 649
United Mine Workers, 645
United Nations, 403
United States
    foreign college students, 175
    health care spending, 396
    leading drug importer, 784
    national debt 1980–2006, 293
    nation of immigrants, 393–394
    as only superpower, 787
    origin of technology, 25
    permanent underclass, 393
    population growth, 3
    regional differences, 3–4
United States Chamber of Commerce, 760
United States Conference of Mayors,
    721
United States Congress, 287
United States Constitution, 160
United States dollar
    and American empire, 787
    in Big Mac index, 781
    and Chinese currency policy, 776
    and Chinese yuan, 776, 777–780
    and current account deficit, 786
    current value, 237–238
    decline in, 783
    versus euro, 777
    exchange rates for, 779
    foreign legal tender, 783, 784
    on gold exchange standard, 774–775
    held by foreigners, 770
    and Japanese yen, 779–780
    origin of, 304
    recycling, 785
    weighted average value, 777, 778
United States economy, 1–18; *see also*
    Mixed economy
    American exceptionality, 786–788
    assets held abroad, 781–782

balance of payments in 2005, 770
balance of trade 1970–2005, 742–743
balance of trade in 2005, 175
balance of trade with Canada/Mexico,
    178
benefit of farm subsidies, 763
causes of trade imbalance, 756–758
components of GDP 2005, 191
consumer spending, 107–108,
    111–112, 114–115
creditor nation, 780, 783
current account deficit, 772
current problems, 2
current status, 1–2
entrepreneurs in, 25
exports and imports, 173–175
foreign decision making on, 784
foreign investment in, 131
future prospects, 786–788
on gold exchange standard, 774–775
government role, 145–146, 162–165
GDP 1930 to 2005, 200
gross saving rate 1947–2007, 389
growth of, 709
history of trade
    government policy, 743–745
    high tariffs, 744
    before 1975, 742
    post-World War II policies,
        744–745
    since 1975, 742–743
income distribution, 709–716
in Industrial Revolution, 385–386
internationalization of, 381
in international trade, 172
investment 1991–2001, 137
job exodus, 17
labor union history, 643–649
largest debtor nation, 780–784
national income 2005, 193–194
nation of consumption junkies, 785
negative trade balance, 769
net investment income, 783
in 19th century
    agricultural development, 2–4
    agricultural technology, 4
    conflicts leading to Civil War, 3
    industrial capitalists, 5–6
    mass production/consumption, 5, 6
    national rail network, 4–5
and NAFTA, 177–178
output growth 1870–2005, 11
per capita real GDP 1776–2005, 204
persistence of inflation, 230
place in history, 17–18
potential for deflation, 233
poverty, 717–733
production decisions, 71–72
productive efficiency, 35
productivity growth, 387–394
real GDP 1958–2002, 218
recessions of 19th century, 358
recessions since World War II,
    218–219

United States economy—*Cont.*
  sector employment 1940–2004, 72
  sectors of, 385
  self-sufficiency era, 173
  since 1976, 268–269
  tax cut incentives, 159
  ten largest banks, 316
  trade deficits
    with China, 776
    with China and Japan, 758–762,
      785–786
    origin of, 742–743
  trade with Canada and Mexico,
    177–178
  trade with Japan and China, 761–762
  in 20th century, 6–17
    automobile industry, 6
    Eisenhower years, 13
    GI Bill of Rights, 12–13
    Great Depression, 7–10
    industrial economy, 6–7
    Kennedy-Johnson era, 13–14
    Levittown, 13
    New Deal, 9
    new economy of 1990s, 16–17
    peacetime prosperity, 11–13
    post-World War II recessions, 12
    Reagan era, 15
    Roaring Twenties, 7
    stagflation decade, 14–15
    state of agriculture, 15–16
    suburbanization, 14
    supply-side economics, 15
    World War II, 10–11
  union membership 1900–2004, 646
  worker productivity, 385
United States Football League, 652
United States Patent and Trademark
  Office, 760
United States Steel, 25, 587, 609, 650
  antitrust case, 610, 611
United States Supreme Court
  antitrust rulings, 549n, 609, 610,
    611–612
  breakup of Standard Oil, 609
  membership changes, 611
  partial breakdown of rule of reason,
    611–612
  Roe v. Wade, 723
  rule of reason doctrine, 609–610
  60 percent rule, 612
United States Trade Representative, 762
United Steel Workers, 645, 648, 650,
  653–654
Unite Here!, 649
Unit elastic, 436, 438, 439, 441
Unit of output, 626
Unlimited liability, 122
Unskilled labor, 661–662, 677–678
U.S. Bancorp, 316
Useem, Jerry, 693
Usefulness, 459
U-shaped cost curves, 485–486
U.S. Shoe Machinery Company, 551

Usury, 693
Usury laws, 57–58, 693–695
U.S. West, 619
Utilitarianism, 715
Utility, 459–464
  calculating, 462
  and consumer surplus, 464–467
  definition, 460
  formula, 463
  and free goods and services, 463
  law of diminishing marginal utility,
    460
  limitations of application, 464
  marginal utility, 460–461, 468–469
  maximizing utility, 461–463
  and price gougers, 468
  total utility, 461
  utility schedules, 460, 461
  vesus usefulness, 459
  water–diamond paradox, 463

𝒱

Vanderbilt, William, 608
Variable costs
  average variable cost, 479
  definition, 476
  graphing, 482–486
  in long run, 479
  in shutting down, 492–493
  and stay-in-business decision, 495, 496
Varker, Bonnie, 498n
VCR formats, 552
Veblen, Thorstein, 110
Velocity of money, 356
Verizon Communications, 130, 555
Vertical axis, 422
Vertical mergers, 614–615
Veterans Administration, 11, 721, 724
Viacom, 615
Viagra, 553, 602
Victoria's Secret, 574
Vietnam War, 14, 233
Virgin Group, 490
Visa, 284, 305, 320, 323
Visser, Jelle, 649
Vodafone AirTouch, 619
Volcker, Paul, 364–365
Volkswagen, 177, 518, 583, 584, 777
Volvo, 613
Vons supermarkets, 647

𝒲

W. W. Norton, 557
Wachovia, 316
Wage and price controls, 694
  imposed by Nixon, 234, 241
  during World War II, 10
Wage-price spiral, 239
Wage rates
  of CEOs, 672

and consumer price index, 673–674
decline in 1980s–1990s, 712
and economic rent, 670–672
and employment discrimination
    African Americans, 669
    women, 667–668
equal pay for equal work, 668
income effect, 664–665
and inflation rates, 229
national comparisons, 672
and productivity increases, 653
and standard of living, 676
substitution effect, 664–665
supply and demand analysis, 661–667,
    670–676
Wages
  catch-up increases, 240
  in classical economics, 252, 253–254
  in collective bargaining, 654
  differences in, 716
  downward flexibility, 359
  in early unionism, 644
  and education, 662, 663
  and income disparity, 661
  Keynesian view, 260
  and labor supply, 664–665
  living wage issue, 679
  minimum wage, 392, 676–679
  pattern-setting agreements, 654
  pay differentials, 667, 727
  protectionist argument, 751–752
  real vs. money, 672–676
  for sweatshop labor, 752
  two-income households, 112
  as variable cost, 476
  at Wal-Mart, 559
Wagner, Robert, 644
Wagner Act, 644, 645
Waksal, Saul, 618
Wall Street Journal, 95, 241, 323
Wal-Mart Bank proposal, 322–323
Wal-Mart Stores, 25, 74, 123, 124, 175,
    234, 395, 443, 489, 552, 555,
    558–559, 647, 649, 650, 663, 669,
    675, 715, 720, 752, 760, 764
  response to Hurricane Katrina, 83–84
Walt Disney Company, 614, 752
Walton, Alice L., 715
Walton, Christy, 715
Walton, Helen R., 715
Walton, Jim C., 715
Walton, S. Robson, 715
Walton, Sam, 24, 25, 715
War, and national debt, 294
Warner Communications, 615
Warner-Lambert, 619
War on Poverty, 718
  as government failure, 82
Warren, Elizabeth, 112, 676
War theory of business cycle, 221
Washing machines, 636–637
Washington, George, 3, 289, 304
Washington Mutual, 316
Water and sanitation, 718

Water–diamond paradox, 463
Wealth
    compared to income, 714
    distribution of, 714
    held by richest 20 percent, 713–714
    and property income, 716
    top ten billionaires, 715
Wealth of Nations (Smith), 164–165, 358, 490
Weaver, Warren, 29
Weidenbaum, Murray, 112, 371, 756
Weighted average of currencies, 779
Welfare
    conservative vs. liberal views, 731
    and culture of poverty, 722
    main programs, 723–726
    means-tested programs, 716, 723
Welfare banks, 317
Welfare culture, 726
Welfare queens, 733
Welfare Reform Act of 1996, 82, 225, 726, 732–733
Wells, H. G., 443
Wells Fargo, 316, 319, 320
Wendy's, 518, 576
Western Electric, 612
Westinghouse, 586–587
Wheeler-Lea Amendment, 611
White Castle, 518
Whitney, Eli, 4
Wicksteed, Philip H., 252, 286
Wiggin, Addison, 787
Williams, Ron, 669
Wilson, Earl, 109
Wilson, Harold, 239
Wilson, William Julius, 728–731
Wilson, Woodrow, 610
Winegarden, C. R., 728n
Winfrey, Oprah, 409, 661

Winner-take-all markets, 672
Within Our Reach (Schorr & Schorr), 731
Withrow, Jason, 702
Women
    as CEOs, 668
    employment advances, 29
    employment discrimination, 27–28, 667–669, 727
    in labor force, 229
    sex discrimination suits, 669
    working full time, 727
Women's liberation movement, 636–637, 667, 716
Woods, Tiger, 661
Work, cost and benefits of, 208–209
Work effect, 365
Worker insecurity, 229
Working poor, 676, 720
Work-leisure decision, 365, 664–665
Work Opportunity Reconciliation Act of 1996, 732–733
Works Progress Administration, 286, 731
Workweek/workyear, 643
    national comparisons, 390, 391
    in United States, 390–391
World Bank, 180, 181
    protests against, 180
WorldCom, 616, 618
World Football League, 652
World Health Organization, 718
World trade agreements, 176–177
    GATT, 178–180
    World Trade Organization, 180–182
World Trade Court, 762
World Trade Organization, 177, 744, 762
    description of, 180–182
    Dispute Settlement Body, 180
    and International Monetary Fund, 182
    most favored nation principle, 180

    protests against, 180–181
    and World Bank, 182
World War I, 7, 173
    halt to gold standard, 773
World War II, 145, 173
    economy during, 10–11
    end of Great Depression, 10, 268
    and postwar prosperity, 11–13
    production possibilities curve during, 36
    recessions since, 218–219
World Wide Web, 25
Wright brothers, 6, 699

x

Xerox Corporation, 541, 553, 556, 558, 618, 668, 700

y

Yahoo!, 17, 25, 530n, 672
Yen, 779–780
Young, Don, 91
Young adult unemployment, 226
Yuan, 776, 777–779

z

Zappa, Frank, 87
Zero economic profit, 565–566
Zero excess reserves, 334
Zero profits, 522–527
Zhao Ziyang, 90
Zoellick, Robert, 762–763
Z-tel, 555
Zubulake, Laura, 669

LABOR FORCE PARTICIPATION[1] RATE, SELECTED YEARS, 1950–2005

Year	Males	Females
1950	85.3	33.3
1955	84.5	35.4
1960	83.3	37.7
1965	80.7	39.3
1970	79.7	43.3
1975	77.9	46.3
1980	77.4	51.5
1985	76.3	54.5
1990	76.4	57.5
1995	75.0	58.9
2000	74.8	59.9
2005	73.3	59.3

[1]Civilian labor force as percent of civilian noninstitutional population.

UNEMPLOYMENT RATE, SELECTED YEARS, 1975–2005

Year	White	Black	Hispanic
1950	—	—	—
1955	—	—	—
1960	—	—	—
1965	—	—	—
1970	—	—	—
1975	7.8	14.8	12.2
1980	6.3	14.3	10.1
1985	6.2	15.1	10.5
1990	4.8	11.4	8.2
1995	4.9	10.4	9.3
2000	3.5	7.6	5.7
2005	4.4	10.0	6.0

AVERAGE HOURLY EARNINGS, PRIVATE EMPLOYEES, 1964–2005

Year	Current Dollars	1982 Dollars
1964	$2.53	$7.86
1965	2.63	8.04
1966	2.73	8.13
1967	2.85	8.21
1968	3.02	8.37
1969	3.22	8.45
1970	3.40	8.46
1971	3.63	8.64
1972	3.90	8.99
1973	4.14	8.98
1974	4.43	8.65
1975	4.73	8.48
1976	5.06	8.58
1977	5.44	8.66
1978	5.87	8.67
1979	6.33	8.40
1980	6.84	7.99
1981	7.43	7.88
1982	7.86	7.86
1983	8.19	7.95
1984	8.48	7.95
1985	8.73	7.91
1986	8.92	7.96
1987	9.13	7.86
1988	9.43	7.81
1989	9.80	7.75

Year	Current Dollars	1982 Dollars
1990	10.19	7.66
1991	10.50	7.58
1992	10.75	7.55
1993	11.03	7.52
1994	11.32	7.53
1995	11.64	7.53
1996	12.03	7.57
1997	12.49	7.68
1998	13.00	7.89
1999	13.47	8.00
2000	14.00	8.03
2001	14.53	8.11
2002	14.95	8.24
2003	15.35	8.27
2004	15.68	8.24
2005	16.09	8.17